*A Reader's Guide
to the Short Stories of*

HENRY JAMES

A
Reference
Publication
in
Literature

Everett Emerson
Editor

A *Reader's Guide* to the Short Stories of
HENRY JAMES

Christina E. Albers

G.K. Hall & Co.
An Imprint of Simon & Schuster Macmillan
New York

Prentice Hall International
London Mexico City New Delhi Singapore Sydney Toronto

G.K. Hall & Co.
An Imprint of Simon & Schuster Macmillan
1633 Broadway
New York, NY 10019

Library of Congress Catalog Card Number: 97-6444

Printed in the United States of America

Library of Congress Cataloging-in-Publication Data

Albers, Christina E.
    A reader's guide to the short stories of Henry James / Christina
E. Albers.
        p.   cm. — (A reference publication in literature)
    Includes bibliographical references and index.
    ISBN 0-8161-9099-2
    1. James Henry, 1843-1916—Criticism and interpretation.
    2. Short story. I. Title. II. Series.
PS2124.A38 1997
814'.4—dc21   97-6444
                                                                          CIP

This paper meets the requirements of ANSI/NISO Z39.48-1992 (Permanence of Paper).

To my parents,
Henry and Wilma Albers,
and
to my husband,
Michael Kuczynski

Contents

The Author

Christina Albers received her M.A. and Ph.D. from the University of North Carolina at Chapel Hill and her B.A. from Harvard, all in English and American Language and Literature. She has taught at Chapel Hill, North Carolina State, and Tulane University. Her publications include essays on Henry James and the contemporary Southern writer Berry Morgan, and she has presented papers on Henry James, Edith Wharton, and Willa Cather. Currently, she is the director of the First Presbyterian Child Development Program in New Orleans.

Introduction

In a 1913 letter James spoke of his tales as "little tarts," in contrast to the hearty "beef and potatoes" of his novels, and critics tended, early on, to adopt his hierarchy. James wrote a large number of "little tarts," however, 112, so that taken together they constitute several sides of beef, and have by now generated amounts of criticism that far outweigh in number of words the original works. The task of this volume is to provide an introduction to the tales and some kind of coherence to the criticism. Each tale is treated in its own chapter of four parts. The first part, "Publication History," traces the history of the tale's published appearances; the second, "Circumstances of Composition, Sources, and Influences," looks before the tale's publication to consider the circumstances that surrounded its writing, as well as the sources and influences on its construction—from life and literature, as well as from other disciplines and artistic forms. The third, "Relation to Other Works," looks at the relations between the tale and other of James's works, including not only the other tales, but also the novels, plays, and nonfiction. The fourth, and generally the largest, section, "Interpretation and Criticism," considers different possible approaches to each tale and surveys the history of its interpretation. Each chapter concludes with its own works-cited section of primary and secondary sources.

I use the term "tale" as it is an elastic one that can be applied to all of James's short fictions. In fact, the terminology for the tales has been a subject of debate. The "short story," as James remarks in the preface to *The Lesson of the Master*, was defined by magazines of his time under a "hard-and-fast-rule" as a fiction "'from six to eight thousand words,'" while he preferred "on the dimensional ground" the nouvelle, or as he praised it, "the beautiful and blest *nouvelle*" (*Criticism* 2, 1227–28). Some critics have followed the guidelines James cites in his preface, defining the "short story" and the "nouvelle," or novella, based on length. Wegelin, for example, while noting James's "informal" terminology, calls any piece of fiction over 8,000 words a nouvelle (1984, 343). Springer stretches the limits of the short story by placing the length of the typical novella between 15,000 and 50,000 words (8). As James recalled in his preface, it was the editor of *The Yellow Book*, Henry Harland, who in 1894 offered James an outlet for his longer tales. Of the three works James published in *The Yellow Book*, however, Matthiessen and Murdock see "The

Death of the Lion" at 13,400 words and "The Next Time" at 15,100 words remaining as short stories, judging that only "The Coxon Fund," at 20,000 words, "passed over into the class of the nouvelle" (N 149–50). Fadiman similarly places the limit of the short story at 20,000 words, giving James a sum of eighty short stories (xix). To Timms, however, the prefatory comments on its genesis establish "The Death of the Lion" "unproblematically" as a nouvelle (98). Hoffman also disagrees with the use of length as the primary criterion, and so takes exception to Fadiman's inclusion of "The Beast in the Jungle" in his collection as a short story (102–4). Edel, too, scorns classifying James's works by length. Asserting that by "modern" standards any work above 50,000 words would be a short novel, he maintains that *The Turn of the Screw* should nevertheless be read as a tale, despite its 53,000 words (Gale's count assigns it only 39,600) (CT 1, 9). His categories still fit within word limits, although liberal ones. All works 53,000 words or below are "tales"; all those between 53,000 and 100,000 words are "short novels."

Not everyone puts an emphasis on the distinction between forms. Beach wrote early that it is "but a step, and that a matter of length" from tale to nouvelle (3). Later, Putt, charging that James was not good at "forms," declared, "Over the whole span of James's writing career there is indeed little difference, whether in texture or general effect, between tales and his full-dress novels" (23). While the traditional view is perhaps that of Segal, who sees James's "genius" as "for the more leisured forms," the nouvelle and the novel, it is by no means universal (168). Gale contends, for example, that it is James's long novels and his "so laboriously compressed short stories" (under 25,000 words) that "deserve the closest study" (245).

In his discussion of the nouvelle in the preface to *The Author of Beltraffio*, James contrasts it not with the short story per se, but with the "anecdote." The "anecdote," he writes, works from the "outer edge" of its "situation" inward, while the nouvelle works "from its centre outward" (*Criticism* 2, 1238). In the preface to *The Reverberator*, he tells us, the "anecdote" is always a story of "something that has oddly happened to someone," a description that could be applied even to such a lengthy work as "A Passionate Pilgrim" (25,800 words) (*Criticism* 2, 1193). Although, as Cowdery remarks, James's theorizing seems "not prospective but retrospective," there is in it a sense that the nouvelle is, in her words, "categorically more significant than the anecdote" (28, 32). Lest the term "anecdote" sound too dismissive, one should recall that "The Middle Years" (7,500 words) was among the tales James saw having to "masquerade as little anecdotes" (*Criticism* 2, 1240). James did not, however, provide labels for all his works. The histories of *The Golden Bowl* and *The Spoils of Poynton*, both begun as short stories, meanwhile, illustrate James's propensity to move from genre to genre as his topic unfolds and his tales lengthen. Often, however, as he indicates in the preface to *The Lesson of the Master*, he only needed the "rigour" of the magazine length limits "a little relaxed" (*Criticism* 2, 1228). His average tale, Edel observes, is between 10,000 and 20,000 words (CT 1, 9). Using Gale's word estimates in table I to *The Caught Image*, as I have throughout, there are thirty tales between 5,000 and 9,000 words, and thirty-five between 10,000 and 14,000, but only twenty between 15,000 and 19,000, nineteen between 20,000 and 29,000, and seven between 30,000 and 39,000 words.

I speak at length of such distinctions here, partly because such general concerns do not fit easily within the structure of this book, but more particularly because in some cases I have used such classifications as part of the decision to include or exclude a work from consideration. When I began this project I was, quite wisely, counseled to select only a representative number of stories to discuss. Instead, I set to amassing bibliography on all 112 tales, until I realized it would indeed be too much to treat in one book. I still wanted, however, to produce a work that treated more than a representative part. The distinction between nouvelle and tale seemed a logical way to arrive at a workable number. I began by ruling out the longest tales of 29,000 words or more, a stopping point that had the merit of fitting with at least one critic's categories, those of Voss, who places the lower boundary of the "modern" short novel at 30,000 words (127). This limit eliminated ten works: *Madame de Mauves* (1874), *An International Episode* (1878), *The Siege of London* (1883), *Lady Barbarina* (1884), *A London Life* (1888), *The Aspern Papers* (1888), *The Turn of the Screw* and *In the Cage* (1898), *Covering End* (1898), and *The Papers* (1903). There are also seven omissions below that limit, primarily late tales. *Daisy Miller* (1878), *The Pupil* (1891), and *The Beast in the Jungle* (1903) each seemed to me to have acquired sufficient independent reputation, study, and survey to make their inclusion here not only unwieldy but unnecessary. More shakily, perhaps, I omitted *Julia Bride* (1908), despite its mere 13,000 words, on the grounds of its publication as an independent volume and its conception by James as a "pendant" to *Daisy Miller*. Like Matthiessen and Murdock I kept the similarly sized "The Next Time" and "The Death of the Lion," while casting off *The Coxon Fund*. Two final tales, *The Birthplace* (1903) and *The Bench of Desolation* (1909), I also omitted as they seem regarded most commonly as nouvelles. In truth, if I had had more time and space, I would have been happy to include the last four mentioned. Still included are several longer tales. Some of these, such as "The Author of Beltraffio" and "The Lesson of the Master," have been talked of as nouvelles, but have not attained the independent status of such a work as *Daisy Miller*, and remain essential to a consideration of the tales as a whole. Some are early or minor works, whose claim to nouvelle status seems reduced to word length alone, such as "Guest's Confession" (1872, 21,700 words) or "The Modern Warning" (1888, 24,100 words). Their seeming inadequacy as nouvelles may bolster the view that the definition is a qualitative as well as a quantifiable one.

Even such a minor work as "The Modern Warning," however, exists in two versions, while James often reprinted—and revised—more significant or popular works several times. Only sixteen tales—all written by 1876—were abandoned by James after their magazine appearance without being reproduced in any collection. Only four tales—"The Tree of Knowledge" (1900), "The Abasement of the Northmores" (1900), "The Third Person" (1900), and "The Altar of the Dead" (1895)—failed of magazine publication before appearing in a collection, and of those, three appeared in the New York Edition. At each reappearance James revised his work, sometimes lightly, sometimes, as in the case of early tales reprinted in the New York Edition, quite heavily. The question of James's revisions has been a persistent and a contentious one, particularly in regard to the authority of the New York Edition, which contains sixty-six of James's tales. In preparing this book, I looked at each version of each tale that I could—including the manuscript of "The Impressions of a Cousin," at the Pierpont Morgan Library, of "Crawford's Consistency," at the National Institute of Arts and Letters, and the typed manuscript of "The Jolly Corner" at the Houghton—and have commented on a few occasions on changes. For the most part, however, I have confined myself to discussing textual issues when they have become a subject of critical debate as in the case of "Four Meetings" and "A Passionate Pilgrim."

For my own text, I have chosen Edel's twelve-volume *Collected Tales of Henry James*, which offers the first book version of each tale (except, of course, in the case of tales that were never collected by James). While traditionally the New York Edition has been the privileged text, not only does it omit several stories treated here, it also presents all its tales very much as late James. In the case of early or even middle tales, as Putt writes, the New York Edition revisions "blur the freshness and occasional naïveté of the original version" (61). An additional weakness of the revisions can be seen in the way some critics read their increased elaborateness as irony, and some as emphasis. The "ideal solution," according to Aziz, who has written persuasively of the need to recognize the multiple texts in which the tales exist, is a variorum edition (271). He has begun such a work with three volumes of James's tales, which take as their copy text the original magazine versions with the later variants presented separately. Aziz's edition is also noteworthy for offering the original text of five early tales that first appeared in book form in James's 1885 *Stories Revived*. In Edel's edition, these five—"A Landscape Painter" (1866), "A Day of Days" (1866), "Poor Richard" (1867), "A Most Extraordinary Case" (1868), and "Master Eustace" (1871)—are represented by their 1885 versions. Designed for British audiences unfamiliar with his early work, James called the volume "revived" not "revised" as "a fair general description of what I have done to them" (1993, 96–97). Nevertheless, as Ruhm points out, Edel's choice of the later versions, separated in some cases by nearly twenty years from the originals, provides the reader with a book text too distant from its first appearance for a "developmental account." Ruhm, too, wished for a variorum edition. As Aziz's edition, however, is complete only up to 1879, and as it is still not as widely available, I have stayed with Edel's for all the tales.

There are a few other omissions from this book apart from the nouvelles. I have left out consideration both of the fragment "Hugh Merrow," first published in 1987, and the chapter James contributed to the 1908 composite novel *The Whole Family*—"The Married Son." Neither has produced extensive critical commentary. I have also had to restrict the type of criticism I could include, enforcing a cutoff date of 1989, with the exception of primary material such as collections of letters. Similarly, I have not included criticism in languages other than English, although, since much of it is significant, I have recorded any foreign language sources following the works-cited section for each tale. The large number of dissertations on James, however, made them too many even to cite. Several have since appeared as articles or books, but for those that have not, one should consult the appropriate bibliographies. Articles revised into books are discussed, in most cases, only in their book form. Commentary on the tales in anthologies and textbooks is included, but not comprehensively, as such sources proved difficult to locate. Citations to the standard primary sources, such as the notebooks and the tales themselves, as well as the Edel biography, are given parenthetically within the text, signaled by abbreviations, a list of which follows this introduction. While this book aims to be as representative and accurate as possible, it is of course impossible as well as undesirable to reproduce critical arguments fully. It is intended to serve as an independent introduction to the tales, but not as a replacement for a reading of the sources themselves. In the case of connections between stories, I found I could not even mention all those offered by such critics as Granville Jones and Richard Gage. Finally, while I began with the aim of making each chapter self-contained, I soon realized that that would make the book both tediously repetitious and too long. Thus, discussions that treat more than one tale may appear in only one chapter. While I have flagged some of the more significant overlaps with bracketed references to the relevant chapter, readers should be sure to check the index for the particular story they are researching. No doubt there are some inadvertent omissions as well. I hope they are few.

The reason for so much omission is quite simply the huge amount of criticism that has been accorded James. Not surprisingly, the quality of the criticism is uneven, and I have tried, without simply catering to my own taste, to grant the most space to the most significant analyses. On many occasions, critics pay little—too little—attention to the observations of those who wrote before them. In cases where I have found discoveries announced as new more than once, I have sought to restore credit to the initial discoverer. I hope, too, that such a book as this may help to lessen the number of such duplications in future. An earlier volume in the series by Lea Newman saved my beginning a needless article on Melville's "Bartleby." Ezra Pound declared that part of James's work "can perhaps only be criticised as 'etc.'" since he is "strewn over about forty [volumes]—part of which must go into desuetude, have perhaps done so already" (31, 39). There are, however, despite the continuing references to tales as "neglected" or "minor," few indeed that suffer from a genuine lack of critical attention. Even those tales that could benefit from an increased readership are not necessarily bereft of criticism. Many of the major tales are in dire need of a respite to allow some fresh ideas to germinate.

In putting together his first collection of short stories in 1873, James saw it as a "volume . . . of tales on the theme of American adventurers in Europe" (*Letters* 1, 357). Two years later, when *A Passionate Pilgrim* appeared, all but one of the six tales indeed concerned Americans in Europe. James would continue to name his collections after a particular tale for over twenty years with the exception of the 1884 *Tales of Three Cities*, and, if one will, the 1885 *Stories Revived. Terminations* in 1895 was the first of six collections in which James grouped his stories together under thematic headings. The unity of these volumes has received a fair amount of comment. While a contemporary reviewer found "the Jamesian vocabulary" unclear so that the meaning of the title *The Soft Side* "eluded" him, Ziff locates in the tales a clear focus on passion (*Nation* 71, 430; Ziff 61). Krook points to an "overlapping of themes, situations and ideas" in *The Better Sort* (326). Gage looks closely at the relation among all the thematic collections, including volumes of the New York Edition. It is *The Finer Grain*, however, that has received the bulk of such analysis, perhaps because James himself linked the tales in his brief preface, perhaps because the volume follows the New York Edition, whose groupings have been subjected to frequent analysis. Tintner indeed argues that *The Finer Grain* "present[s] in microcosm" what James "had exhaustively attempted in his Collected Edition but which had brought him neither money nor critical esteem" (1975, 357). Macnaughton goes so far as to see James in the volume "consciously trying to create a quasi-novelistic short-story cycle" anticipating *Dubliners* (126).

From *A Passionate Pilgrim* to *The Finer Grain*, James was, like Joyce later, deeply concerned with the problem of narration and point of view. In the preface to *The Spoils of Poynton*, he lamented the loss of "intensity" in *A London Life* brought about by his departing from the viewpoint of his center of consciousness, Laura Wing, for one scene. "The real fun," he wrote, "would have been in not, by an exceptional collapse of other ingenuity, making my attack on the spectator's consciousness a call as immediate as a postman's knock" (*Criticism* 2, 1154). While early critics of James generally granted themselves the luxury of taking James's narrators at their word, later critics sought to show themselves as ingenious as the master. The turning point came with Edmund Wilson's "The Ambiguity of Henry James," following which critics have seized on each possible shortcoming in James's narrators to challenge their reliability.

When the Jamesian narrator stumbles, is it James or his character? A similar dilemma was one of the highlights of the 1992 London theater season when, during a production of *Hamlet*, the actor playing Polonius appeared to lose his way in a speech. So convincing was his confusion that audiences were uncertain whether it was the actor or the character who was fumbling for words. When they realized it was the character, the actor's accomplishment was considered a tour de force of naturalness. With James, however, part of the problem is in deciding what James considered a stumble, a decision made more difficult by changes in sensibilities over the years since James wrote. People sometimes make the dangerous assumption that James objects to what they do. One critic of "Glasses," for example, assumes that the narrator is not reliable because he is anti-Semitic, but the comments in the tale about Jews very closely echo comments James made in private letters. In looking at "The Liar," another locus of such discussion, the question is in part one of whether James could have sympathized with such an egotistical artist. In "The Beldonald Holbein," Tintner appears to find James sympathizing with the narrator's treatment of Mrs. Brash as a painting, an object, while many other critics are horrified (1989, 224).

Why did James choose such an approach to narration? Wegelin, dismissing the whole debate as "hackneyed," contends that James merely sought an "essentially realistic" form of narration to mirror the oblique way in which people actually experience events (1973, 484). Edith Wharton, however, in speaking of the Assinghams of *The Golden Bowl*, objected to the way they were "forced" into their roles "for the sole purpose of acting as spies and eavesdroppers." To her, James's attempt to avoid the Victorian author's habit of "chatting with his readers" was "perhaps even more unsettling to the reader's confidence than the old-fashioned intrusion of the author among his puppets" (91–92). Beach, too, less censoriously, explains the use of such agents as stemming from James's desire to avoid what he called the "mere muffled majesty of irresponsible 'authorship.'" Beach adds that, naturally, the observer was "not represented as an intrusive person with no more legitimate interest in the story than our universal human curiosity. That would be to make him too disagreeable for the purpose; or it would be too obviously a device for plausibility. His relation to the other characters must always be a natural one" (68–70). To subsequent critics, such an instinct may be natural, but it is less impartial. According to Powers, it was "one of James's great artistic achievements" to put at the center of a work the "phenomenon" that "a witness's report may tell us more about the witness than about the event he is reporting" (141). Even so, Vaid insists that "not to take James's narrators, in the absence of clear internal evidence, as reliable personae would therefore force us into perverse readings of almost all his first-person tales." To Vaid it is not the "personal involvement" of the narrators that is the "pretense." He sees the narrators as genuinely detached such that "Wherever they precipitate the catastrophe, an irony is produced because their intentions are almost always unquestionable" (252).

If some of the more elaborate exposés of the first-person narrators do seem far-fetched, their vulnerability to such attacks continues. Quite simply, the amount of attention it takes to record a story seems to require in most people's judgment an equal concern or involvement. In *The Sacred Fount* James has Obert, artist and member of the Royal Academy, declare that searching other people's secrets is "made not only quite inoffensive . . . but positively honourable, by being confined to psychologic evidence . . . resting on psychologic signs alone, it's a high application of intelligence. What's ignoble is the detective and the keyhole" (65–66). Many, however, have taken exception to James's—or Obert's—definition of "honourable." F. R. Leavis charged that James had lost his "moral touch" in his later works, questioning his evident demand of sympathy for less than sympathetic characters (159–60).

For some, the disjunction in sympathy is due to the snobbishness they sense in James. A contemporary reviewer of *The Finer Grain*, for example, saw James as writing "chiefly for that surrendered leisure class who have nothing to do but fill themselves mentally and emotionally" (*Independent*). To others it is due to James's devotion to art itself. Frank O'Connor charges James with being one of the "literary men who seem to me to have loved literature too well; who cared more for its form than its content and adopted toward it the fetishistic attitude of impoverished old maids inheriting ancestral mansions." Writes O'Connor, "Ordinary human love was something that none of them could describe because literature was their own true love" (224–25). James himself recognized the tension between art and love, indeed between art and life. His famous statement on the subject, that "It is art that *makes* life, makes interest, makes importance," appears in the context of his 1915 debate with H. G. Wells to serve mainly as a distinction between James's kind of novel, artful in its crafted form, and Wells's, artless in its attempt to mirror formless life. However, there is much elsewhere in James, both work and life, that makes it reasonable this phrase has been adopted as indicating a general belief. Still, earlier in the 1900s he would write his friend Jocelyn Persse praising his "Art of Life which beats any Art of mine hollow" (*Life* 5, 186). Not long before, in 1900, he wrote to Morton Fullerton of the "*essential loneliness*" of his life, "deeper" even than his art (*Life* 4, 350).

In a cartoon of the author, Beerbohm depicted James staring bemusedly at the shoes of lovers at a hotel. James himself in his works produced many such pictures of a person studying a phenomenon beyond his reach. In *The*

Princess Casamassima, Hyacinth must "look at the good things of life only through the glass of the pastry-cook's window." James saw himself similarly, writing in his autobiography of himself as a child regarding his peers: "They were so *other*—that was what I felt; and to *be* other, other almost anyhow, seemed as good as the probable taste of the bright compound wistfully watched in the confectioner's window; unattainable, impossible, of course, but as to which just this impossibility and just that privation kept those active proceedings in which jealousy seeks relief quite out of the question" (101). Yeats speaks in comparable terms of Keats in his poem "Ego Dominuus Tuus" (1917), where one speaker declares, "No one denies to Keats love of the world; / Remember his deliberate happiness." The second speaker answers,

> "His art is happy, but who knows his mind?
> I see a schoolboy when I think of him,
> With face and nose pressed to a sweet-shop window,
> For certainly he sank into his grave
> His senses and his heart unsatisfied."

In both Keats and James, there is an intensity of consciousness combined with a sense of exclusion or isolation.

In James, the combination produced the virtue of renunciation, the value of which has been much debated. In his tales, a diminished life is often not only the lot of the artist, but a part of the general human condition. It represents, at times, however, not so much a complete renouncing of life as a turn to a vicarious life. In his autobiography James recalled how during the Civil War his brother Wilky was wounded at the battle of Fort Sumter. The son of a family friend, Cabot Russell, had been declared missing at the same battle, and his father had gone in search of his son. Unable to find him, James records, "The stricken father . . . had with an admirable charity brought Wilky back to a waiting home instead, and merged the parental ache in the next nearest devotion he could find." Renunciation, then, can serve a positive good. Even as a negative virtue, it is not without its appeal in a time when people increasingly believe themselves entitled to have it all, with the definition of "all" constantly expanding.

I have assembled my sources from several others to which I owe great thanks. For information on the stories themselves, I drew primarily and heavily on the bibliography by Leon Edel and Dan H. Laurence (Oxford: Claredon, 1982). For critical works on James, the G. K. Hall reference guides were particularly helpful: for 1866–1916 by Linda J. Taylor; 1917–1959, Kristin McColgan; 1960–1974, Dorothy Scura; and 1975–1987, Judith H. Funston. Extremely useful also were the annual surveys of Jamesian criticism in *American Literary Scholarship*. Among other works I consulted were the

MLA annual bibliography; Lewis Leary's *Articles on American Literature, 1900–1950* and *1951–1967* (Durham, NC: Duke University Press, 1954, 1970); John Budd's *Henry James, A Bibliography of Criticism 1975–1981* (Westport, CT: Greenwood, 1983); Beatrice Ricks's *Henry James: A Bibliography of Secondary Works* (Metuchen NJ: Scarecrow, 1975); Nicola Bradbury's *An Annotated Critical Bibliography of Henry James* (Brighton, Sussex: Harvester, 1987); Warren S. Walker's *Twentieth-Century Short Story Explication* (Hamden, CT: Shoestring, 1977); Robert Spiller's essay on James in *Eight American Authors*, added to by Robert Gale (New York: Norton, 1971); and the earlier Eunice Hamilton's "Biographical and Critical Studies of Henry James, 1941–48," added to by Viola Dunbar (*American Literature* 20 [1949]: 424–35 and 22 [1950]: 56–61); as well as Maurice Beebe and William Stafford's Checklist "Criticism of Henry James" (*Modern Fiction Studies* 12 [1966]).

Twenty-five years ago my mother leant me a copy of *The Portrait of a Lady*. Although I did not make it past the first appearance of Mme Merle at the time, it was the start of a long appreciation of James. Since then I have been indebted to several others who have shared their knowledge of James, including my teachers at Harvard, Alan Heimert and Craig Werner, and at Chapel Hill, Richard Rust and the late Robert Bain. My former colleagues at Tulane offered much encouragement, and I owe particular thanks to Marvin Morillo. I did my research at several libraries, the Howard Tilton Memorial Library at Tulane, the Bodleian Library at Oxford, the Widener Memorial and Houghton Libraries at Harvard, and the Falmouth Public Library, and I appreciate the help of the staff at each. The editor of this series, Everett Emerson, has, throughout the six years I took on this project, been a most loyal supporter and friend, offering attentive comments with astonishing promptness no matter how long the wait between chapters. The errors that remain are, of course, my own.

My deepest debt is to my family. My parents have provided immeasurable encouragement as well as much measurable support ranging from typing to babysitting. My husband has not only babysat and cooked, sustained and inspired, but even read the entire manuscript. The babysat themselves, Sarah Anne and Henry Edward, despite their occasional impatience at being born into a family of critics, remain to me the truest proof that it is life that makes art, makes interest, makes importance.

Works Cited

Anon. Review of *The Finer Grain*. 1910. *The Independent* 69 (November 17): 1091.

Aziz, Maqbool. 1968. "'Four Meetings': A Caveat for James Critics." *Essays in Criticism* 18 (July): 258–74.

Beach, Joseph Warren. [1918] 1954. *The Method of Henry James*. Philadelphia: Albert Saifer.

Cowdery, Lauren Tozek. 1986. *The Nouvelle of Henry James in Theory and Practice.* Studies in Modern Literature 47. Ann Arbor: UMI Research Press.

Fadiman, Clifton. 1945. *The Short Stories of Henry James*. New York: Modern Library.

Gage, Richard P. 1988. *Order and Design: Henry James' Titled Story Sequences*. New York: Peter Lang.

Gale, Robert L. [1954] 1964. *The Caught Image: Figurative Language in the Fiction of Henry James*. Chapel Hill: University of North Carolina Press.

Hoffman, Charles G. 1957. *The Short Novels of Henry James*. New York: Bookman.

James, Henry. 1993. *The Correspondence of Henry James and the House of Macmillan 1877–1914*. Ed. Rayburn S. Moore. Baton Rouge: Louisiana State University Press.

James, Henry. 1901. *The Sacred Fount*. New York: Scribner's.

Jones, Granville H. 1975. *Henry James's Psychology of Experience: Innocence, Responsibility, and Renunciation in the Fiction of Henry James*. The Hague: Mouton.

Krook, Dorothea. [1962] 1967. *The Ordeal of Consciousness in Henry James*. New York: Cambridge University Press.

Leavis, F. R. [1948] 1964. *The Great Tradition: George Eliot, Henry James, Joseph Conrad*. New York: New York University Press.

Macnaughton, William R. 1987. *Henry James: The Later Novels*. Boston: Twayne.

O'Connor, Frank. 1956. *The Mirror in the Roadway: A Study in the Modern Novel*. New York: Knopf.

Pound, Ezra. 1918. "A Shake Down." *The Little Review* 5 (August): 9–39.

Powers, Lyall H. 1970. *Henry James: An Introduction and Interpretation*. New York: Holt, Rinehart.

Putt, S. Gorley. 1966. *Henry James: A Reader's Guide*. Ithaca, NY: Cornell University Press.

Ruhm, Herbert, ed. 1961. *"Lady Barberina" and Other Tales: "Benvolio," "Glasses," and Three Essays*. The Universal Library. New York: Vanguard.

Segal, Ora. 1969. *The Lucid Reflector: The Observor in Henry James' Fiction*. New Haven: Yale University Press.

Springer, Mary Doyle. 1975. *Forms of the Modern Novella*. Chicago: University of Chicago Press.

Timms, David. 1989. "Contrasts in Form: Hemingway's *Old Man and the Sea* and Faulkner's 'The Bear.' In *Modern American Novella*. Ed. Robert A. Lee, 97–112. London: Vision; New York: St. Martin's.

Tintner, Adeline R. 1989. *The Pop World of Henry James: From Fairy Tales to Science Fiction*. Ann Arbor: UMI Research Press.

———. 1975. "The Metamorphoses of Edith Wharton in Henry James's *The Finer Grain*." *Twentieth-Century Literature* 21: 355–79.

Vaid, Krishna B. 1964. *Techniques in the Tales of Henry James*. Cambridge, MA: Harvard University Press.

Voss, Arthur. 1973. *The American Short Story: A Critical Survey*. Norman: University of Oklahoma Press.

Wegelin, Christof, ed. 1984. *Tales of Henry James*. New York: Norton.

———. 1973. "Henry James and the Treasure of Consciousness." *Die Neueren Sprachen* 72: 484–91.

Wharton, Edith. 1925. *The Writing of Fiction*. New York: Scribner's.

Ziff, Larzer. 1966. *The American 1890's: Life and Times of a Lost Generation*. New York: Viking.

Abbreviations

CT	James, Henry. 1964. *The Collected Tales of Henry James*. Ed. Leon Edel. 12 vols. Philadelphia and New York: Lippincott.
Aziz	James, Henry. 1973. *The Tales of Henry James*. Ed. Maqbool Aziz. 3 vols. Oxford: Clarendon.
Criticism 1	James, Henry. 1982. *Literary Criticism. Essays on Literature, American Writers, English Writers*. Ed. Leon Edel and Mark Wilson. New York: The Library of America.
Criticism 2	James, Henry. 1982. *Literary Criticism. French Writers, Other European Writers, The Prefaces to the New York Edition*. Ed. Leon Edel and Mark Wilson. New York: The Library of America.
Letters	James, Henry. 1984. *Letters*. Ed. Leon Edel. 4 vols. Cambridge, MA: Belknap Press of Harvard University Press.
Autobio-graphy	James, Henry. [1913–17] 1956. *Autobiography: A Small Boy and Others; Notes of a Son and Brother; The Middle Years*. Ed. Frederick W. Dupee. Princeton: Princeton University Press.
CN	James, Henry. 1987. *The Complete Notebooks of Henry James*. Ed. Leon Edel and Lyall H. Powers. New York: Oxford University Press.
N	James, Henry. 1947. *The Notebooks of Henry James*. Ed. F. O. Matthiessen and Kenneth B. Murdock. Chicago: The University of Chicago Press.
Life 1	Edel, Leon. 1953. *Henry James: The Untried Years: 1843–1870*. New York: Avon.
Life 2	Edel, Leon. 1962. *Henry James: The Conquest of London: 1870–1881*. New York: Avon.
Life 3	Edel, Leon. 1962. *Henry James: The Middle Years: 1882–1895*. New York: Avon.
Life 4	Edel, Leon. 1969. *Henry James: The Treacherous Years: 1895–1901*. New York: Avon.
Life 5	Edel, Leon. 1972. *Henry James: The Master: 1901–1916*. New York: Avon.
Life	Edel, Leon. 1985. *Henry James: A Life*. New York: Harper & Row.

The Abasement of the Northmores

Publication History

Unable to place it in any magazine, James first published "The Abasement of the Northmores" in his 1900 volume *The Soft Side*. He also included it in the New York Edition.

Circumstances of Composition, Sources, and Influences

James recorded the "tiny fantasy" behind the story in an entry in his notebook on November 12, 1899, at Lamb House. The story projected there of the two widows and their letters is, as Matthiessen and Murdock point out, basically the same as in the completed story (N 297). James, however, still wondered if he could improve the ending. Having pictured Mrs. Hope "*avenged!*" by the failure of Northmore's letters and then going on to publish her husband's letters to her, he wrote:

> *Those* SHE has kept! (*rather!!*) but delicacy, etc., the *qu'en dira-t-on?* has prevailed. Now it goes. She doesn't care. She wants to score. She publishes—and does.—*Or is there anything ELSE in it?—in connection with the letters she eventually publishes* ????—???—??? (CN188)

Edel speculates that James may have been remembering the private printing of his late sister's diary (1974, xxvi).

Gale notes that the phrase "turned her face to the wall" used of the despondent Mrs. Hope also appears in two other works of the same period, "The Beldonald Holbein" and *The Wings of the Dove* (1963, 100 n.12). Tintner, who repeats the linking, points to the source of the allusion in the story of Hezekiah, who, like Mrs. Hope, despaired of life and then recovered (1989, 74).

Relation to Other Works

Many critics have followed James's lead in the preface to the New York Edition by pointing to the tale's link with "The Tree of Knowledge" in their mutual brevity and rejection (*Criticism* 2, 1240; Jefferson 4; McCarthy 100;

Cowdery 29). Austin Wright also connects the two (along with Cather's "Flavia and Her Artists") in contrast to "Paste" because the protagonists in both are surprised not by having their views refuted but confirmed, seen here in Mrs. Northmore's witnessing of the failure of Lord Northmore's letters (196).

Wright also contrasts the tale with the later "Fordham Castle," where the original loneliness of the protagonist, unlike Mrs. Hope's, is never eased (59 n.35). In addition, in noting the scarcity of early stories treating "career-ambition," Wright lists as two of the few exceptions "The Abasement of the Northmores," where the wife is concerned with her husband's career, and the more unusual reverse, "Flickerbridge," where the man is concerned with his fiancée's (31 n.5).

Several critics have linked the tale with other Jamesian examinations of the role of the creative person in society. McElderry links it with "The Real Right Thing" among the tales of writers in its discussion of biography (122). Edgar links the tale with "The Lesson of the Master" as a comparison of "wordly success" and "undeserved failure"; Putt emphasizes the latter in a comparison with "Broken Wings" (Edgar 169; Putt 291). Looking at the other side of the contrast, Austin Wright includes it in a list of James's stories where characters seek after "Society with a capital S" (51). As such, Jones compares Northmore to Lord Mellifont, and Ezra Pound judges the tale an even more effective treatment of the "vacuity of the public man" than "The Private Life" (Jones 237; Pound 35). Using a similar contrast of public and private, Edel also finds it fits with James's earlier stories of writers. Such a shifting makes sense given that Edel characterizes the tales of the early 1900s as increasingly representing revenge rather than renunciation (CT 11, 7–9). Putt finds it shares with several of the artist tales the same source—"brooding about the caprices of posthumous fame"—and he notes *The Aspern Papers* as showing James's ambiguous feelings toward the publication of private papers (234–35). Edel also makes the connection with *The Aspern Papers*, and with "Sir Dominick Ferrand," as sharing the subject of old letters, but takes as the moral the description of the letters—"if many were pages too intimate to publish, most of the others were too rare to suppress"— and applies it to his own treatment of James's surviving letters (1974, xxv–vi). Bell finds a resemblance between Mrs. Hope and the sister of "John Delavoy" as well as the granddaughter in an Edith Wharton story, "The Angel at the Grave," in their difficult role as caretaker of the reputation of a dead writer (230–31). One might also note Wharton's 1900 novella *The Touchstone*, whose protagonist remarks of the selling of some letters, "It was my self I sold" (153).

Andreas and Wagenknecht both compare Mrs. Hope and Christopher Newman of *The American*, Andreas writing that remarkably even "after a lifetime of acidulous envy," Mrs. Hope rises, like Newman, to an "unexpected insight into the vanity of revenge" (Andreas 55–56; Wagenknecht 127). Looking at her husband, Gale notes a similarity between the "easy power" attributed to him and that attributed to Roderick Hudson and speculates that they may also have shared similar flaws (1963, 100 n.11).

A similarity in theme and mood can also be found in James's description of the origin of "The Altar of the Dead," as James recalls the rejection of a memorial article by a friend of a friend with the editorial comment "I really don't see why I should publish an article about Mrs. X *because*—and because *only*, so far as I can make out—she's dead," and his feeling that her death was "the most beautiful of reasons." This recognition prompted the "general black truth that London was a terrible place to die in" due to "the awful doom of general dishumanisation." One can see in James's statement that "the very tradition of sensibility . . . has here and there to be rescued, to be saved by independent, intelligent zeal; which type of effort however, to avail, has to fly in the face of the conditions," an anticipation of Mrs. Hope's struggle to memorialize her husband. Even in life, James sees society relying on the "coarser [flowers]—which form together the rank and showy bloom of 'success,' of multiplied contact and multiplied motion; the bloom of a myriad many-coloured 'relations'—amid which the precious plant that is rare at the best becomes rare indeed," the basic contrast of the triumphant Northmore and the defeated Hope (*Criticism* 2, 1248–49).

Interpretation and Criticism

In noting James's extreme compression of the story's possibilities, Edgar praises Mrs. Hope's distinction as a writer's wife and laments James's failure to show "a fuller measure" of the "generous comradeship" she provided her husband (169). Anderson, too, speaks praisingly of the Hopes, seeing James using in the story his father's distinction between the "identity" we receive from the world and the "individuality" we create—a contrast seen in several other stories, particularly "The Real Thing." According to Anderson, of the two men whom he describes as "collaborators," Lord Northmore had only "identity" while Hope possessed the "individuality associated with creative power" (142–43).

After discussing the story's germ, Matthiessen and Murdock, followed by Wagenknecht, note that Mrs. Hope has two possibilities for further revenge. The first, publishing Northmore's letters to her, she rejects out of pity for his widow. The second, publishing Hope's to her, she decides to accept only posthumously (N 297). Wagenknecht, unlike Matthiessen and Murdock, considers her choice new in the story, the "*anything ELSE*" James sought to add to his idea (127).

Gale takes a different direction building on the "*anything ELSE*" of the notebook by following on the precedent begun with Wilson's reading of *The Turn of the Screw*, and questions Mrs. Hope as a reliable reflector of events, seeing her as "prejudiced and bereaved to the point of dementia" (1963, 98). The weakest part of Gale's argument is his assumption that the events of the story make no sense without questioning Mrs. Hope's reliability. As early as 1874, before he had any reason for a personal quarrel with fame, James had written that "optimists and pessimists agree . . . imbeciles [are very apt] to be in great places, people of sense in small" (*Criticism* 2, 998). The extremity of Mrs. Hope's grief does not necessarily prove its cause illusory, anymore than Hamlet's putative madness or thwarted ambition proves false his inclusion of "the spurns / That patient merit of the unworthy take" in his catalogue of life's ills.

Gale questions further the motives of the Hopes, wondering at the same time why Hope might have secretly wished the exposure of the man to whom he sacrificed his career and whether Mrs. Hope's eventual forgiveness of the Northmores is sincere. Contrary to Andreas, who feels that the magnanimous Mrs. Hope delays publication to avoid "invidious comparison," Gale finds in her desire for early death at the end a selfish, and perhaps naïve, desire to show up her rivals through the publication of her husband's letters (Andreas 56; Gale 1963, 101–2). The story appears to support Mrs. Hope, who seems to have so little expectation of early publication that she makes no omissions in the volume: "By the time they should be published——! She shook her head, both knowingly and resignedly, as to criticism so remote" (CT 11, 132). As Gage points out, she has only—as her name indicates—"hope" (45).

In a more clear-cut example of error, Edel has stated that Mrs. Hope, in keeping with James's "doctrine about letters: the ultimate assertion of privacy," leaves an instruction in her will for the sole printed volume of her husband's letters to be destroyed (1974, xxvi). But while she has had the type broken up, Mrs. Hope leaves "a definite provision for the issue, after her death, of such a volume" (CT 11, 132).

Elsewhere, Gale would record the water imagery associated with the Hopes and the doglike humbling of the Northmores (1964, 19, 28, 69). Apart from a seconding by Stein, his earlier thesis has attracted no significant following (Stein 114). Austin Wright considers Mrs. Hope's decision not to publish Northmore's letters to her more a result of her "discovery"—his already sufficient exposure—than a "choice" or "change of attitude," but he does not question the validity of her view, includes her in a list of Jamesian renouncers, and praises her solidarity with her husband in the face of society's indifference (46, 74, 115, 196). Putt offers a similar reading of her decision about Northmore's letters, calls the tale a "self-pitying parable," and seems to mock Mrs. Hope's waiting for "merciful and justifying death to right all wrongs." Nevertheless, he neither questions her character explicitly nor implies that James meant to (235).

Similarly, Wagenknecht rejects Gale's "ingeniously argued" hypothesis. Wagenknecht does find the story's only "serious weakness" its failure to demonstrate *how* Northmore achieved success through his use of Hope, but concludes, "There can be no question . . . that this is what James intended the reader to believe" (126, 249 n.9). Ziff locates Hope's superiority in his possession of passion (62).

Vaid seems to imply James is "cramped" in the "omniscient-narrator anecdotes" such as this (192, 276 n.1). Wright notes the use of "directly presented flashbacks" (312 n.1), one way James may have sought to contain his material within the limits he prescribed for it. Although Edgar calls the story "admirably written" given the conditions James imposed on himself (169), it may be that this struggle for brevity, rather than any intentional ambiguity on James's part is again the culprit for any confusion of readings.

Works Cited

Primary Works

James, Henry. 1900. "The Abasement of the Northmores." *The Soft Side*. London: Methuen; New York: Macmillan, 150–71.

———. 1909. "The Abasement of the Northmores." *The Novels and Tales of Henry James*. New York Edition. Vol. 16, 191–222. New York: Scribner's.

Secondary Works

Anderson, Quentin. 1957. *The American Henry James*. New Brunswick, NJ: Rutgers University Press.

Andreas, Osborn. 1948. *Henry James and the Expanding Horizon: A Study of the Meaning and Basic Themes of James's Fiction*. Seattle: University of Washington Press.

Bell, Millicent. 1965. *Edith Wharton and Henry James: The Story of Their Friendship*. New York: Braziller.

Cowdery, Lauren Tozek. *The Nouvelle of Henry James in Theory and Practice*. Studies in Modern Literature 47. Ann Arbor: UMI Research Press.

Edel, Leon. 1974. Introduction. *Henry James: Selected Letters*. Cambridge, MA: Belknap Press of Harvard University Press.

Edgar, Pelham. [1927] 1964. *Henry James, Man and Author*. New York: Russell & Russell.

Gage, Richard P. 1988. *Order and Design: Henry James' Titled Story Sequences*. New York: Peter Lang.

Gale, Robert L. [1954] 1964. *The Caught Image: Figurative Language in the Fiction of Henry James*. Chapel Hill: University of North Carolina Press.

————. 1963. "The Abasement of Mrs. Warren Hope." *PMLA* 78 (March): 98–102.

Jefferson, D. W. 1964. *Henry James and the Modern Reader*. New York: St. Martin's.

Jones, Granville H. 1975. *Henry James's Psychology of Experience: Innocence, Responsibility, and Renunciation in the Fiction of Henry James*. The Hague: Mouton.

McCarthy, Harold T. 1958. *Henry James: The Creative Process*. New York and London: Thomas Yoseloff.

McElderry, Bruce R., Jr. 1965. *Henry James*. New York: Twayne.

Pound, Ezra. 1918. "A Shake Down." *The Little Review* 5 (August): 9–39.

Putt, S. Gorley. 1966. *Henry James: A Reader's Guide*. Ithaca, NY: Cornell University Press.

Stein, Allen F. 1984. *After the Vows Were Spoken: Marriage in American Literary Realism*. Columbus: Ohio State University Press.

Tintner, Adeline R. 1989. *The Pop World of Henry James: From Fairy Tales to Science Fiction*. Ann Arbor: UMI Research Press. Revised from "Hezekiah and *The Wings of the Dove*: The Origin of "She Turned her Face to the Wall." *NMAL: Notes on Modern American Literature* 3: Item 22.

Vaid, Krishna B. 1964. *Technique in the Tales of Henry James*. Cambridge, MA: Harvard University Press.

Wagenknecht, Edward. 1984. *The Tales of Henry James*. New York: Frederick Ungar.

Wharton, Edith. 1900. *The Touchstone*. New York: Scribner's.

Wright, Austin McGiffert. 1961. *The American Short Story in the Twenties*. Chicago: University of Chicago Press.

Ziff, Larzer. 1966. *The American 1890's: Life and Times of a Lost Generation*. New York: Viking.

Adina

Publication History

"Adina" appeared in *Scribner's Monthly* from May to June in 1874. James evidently did not care much for the "nature" of *Scribner's* as the first sight of an issue with his tale made him "cross myself with gratitude" that he had decided not to place his first novel with the magazine (*Letters* 1, 452). James never reprinted the tale in his lifetime. After his death it was first collected in Mordell's 1919 edition of *Travelling Companions*. Left out of Lubbock's edition of the *Novels and Stories* in the early 1920s, it appeared more luridly in 1931 as "The Mad Lovers and the Emperor's Topaz" from Little Blue Books of Girard, Kansas, who also reprinted "At Isella" and "Professor Fargo."

Circumstances of Composition, Sources, and Influences

Wright argues that the tale was written during James's 1874 stay in Italy at the time he was also starting *Roderick Hudson* (203) while Edel places its writing during an earlier trip to Rome the previous year (*Life* 2, 102). James's father read the proof for the tale in March of 1874 while James was still in Italy (W. James 226). In Slabey's reading, the tale is not strictly autobiographical, but indicative of James's views at the time (91). Kelley points to a more specific source: the depiction of a shepherd in James's *Transatlantic Sketches* who "had thrown himself down under one of the trees in the very attitude of Meliboeus" looking like a figure of Arcady, "a symbol of old-world meanings to new world eyes" anticipating the figure of Angelo (143).

Charles Anderson connects "Adina" and Hawthorne's *The Marble Faun* and its characters, who are also "obsessed" with Rome, and Donatello in particular, who symbolizes "the mysterious power of the past over the present" in that city (13; also Gardaphe 121). Looking at European sources, Maves finds Angelo resembling Stendhal's Fabrice (42) while Fabris points to the story's roots in Mérimée (cited in Tilby 166).

Among the story's sources in legend, Horrell discovers in the name "Adina" an anagram for Diana, and finds the story recreating parts of the Diana and Endymion myth (208–9). Hovanec calls attention to the reference to Peter Schlemihl, a character from Jewish German legend, and to "a pair of ravishers in a German ballad" (51–52; also Stone 140, Gale 114). Putt compares Angelo to an "avenging Pied Piper" or a more contemporary Italian from E. M. Forster (79).

Tintner points to two famous intaglios, the "Grand Camée de France" and the "Gemma Augustea," which James may have used as a model for his topaz here (41) belonging to the great emperor Tiberius. Critics have focused on different aspects of Tiberius's legend: Edel noting the connection with the Gospel of Luke; Nathalia Wright commenting on his reputation as the "sensual emperor"; and Quentin Anderson on his stinginess (*Life* 2, 103; Wright 224; Anderson 154).

Relation to Other Works

"The Last of the Valerii" had a mysterious statue; Adina has an imperial intaglio. Both bring their possessors into a dangerous proximity to the Italian past. Both relics are returned in the end to ground or water, although Edel notes that the reburying of the past here does not restore the love its uncovering forfeits (*Life* 2, 104). Accordingly, the two tales have been frequently paired, a pairing that has generally ranked "Adina" second. Kelley gives as the cause for the tale's inferiority its use of Mérimée as a model, providing insufficient challenge as James had already aimed at and bested the French writer in "The Last of the Valerii" (156–57). Quentin Anderson designates the link as the concern with the effect of Italy's past on the present, naming as the source in each case Hawthorne's *The Marble Faun*, as does Kraft, who is almost alone in deeming the theme of "limited value" (Anderson 38; Kraft 77; also C. Anderson 13; Slabey 91; Holder 270). Edel sees the European past endangering American innocence in particular, a representation that he sees also reflecting James's sense of potential danger in his own American past, to both of which, Edel argues, art can serve as the safe middleground (*Life* 2, 102–5). One might point out, however, that both the topaz and the statue are art. Churchill also notes the threat Europe poses to Americans in both, adding "Benvolio," in which the poet's art suffers from his rejection of the Countess (or Europe) for Scholastica (or America), as James's qualifying statement that Americans needed some part of Europe for wholeness (159). Edel finds James more comfortable, although still not entirely so, with the "visitable past" depicted in the late *The Sense of the Past* than in the confrontation in these two tales with the far removed classical past (*Life* 4, 330–31).

In Wegelin's view, the reliance on stereotypes of Italy in both keep them from being fully effective in their depiction either of individuals or the clashes of culture (27). Similarly, Charles Anderson thinks both "overly romantic" as well as unimaginative in both story and character (13). Gardaphe contrasts the simplistic romantic antithesis of Italy and America in such early works as

"Adina" and even *Daisy Miller* with the modern complex attitude to Italy seen later in "The Author of Beltraffio," which, Gardaphe suggests, may have led James to redraw such early Italianate characters as Christina Light and Gloriani (121–22, 127). Wagenknecht, however, stresses the differences between the two early tales, judging "Adina" "entirely human and realistic," lacking both the scope and the supernatural romance of "The Last of the Valerii" (178). Edel, on the other hand, contrasts the supernatural evil of Europe as exemplified in both tales with the human evil of Europe exemplified in the Baron of *Madame de Mauves* (*Life* 2, 120). Maves finds both stories sharing with "The Madonna of the Future" the detached narrator, the beautiful Italian, and the work of art at the center (39–40).

The protagonist of the tale has generally been put in even more dubious company. Quentin Anderson locates in Scrope the same lack of "a kind of piety marked by fear" as the narrator of *The Aspern Papers*, in contrast to Brooke of "Travelling Companions," whose openness to the power of the past allows him to change (153–55). Wright places Scrope as a collector in the dubious company of Gilbert Osmond among other "sensitive but immoral" characters (223–24). Jones contrasts Scrope and Max of "The Light Man," seeing Scrope both as less "consciously" and more casually cruel (98–99).

Scrope's foil Angelo is, on the other hand, Wright notes, like the rest of James's Italians, aristocrat or peasant, "intellectually simple" with an "air of duplicity" that is really more "an inscrutable neutrality" (237). Wright also notes that like Roderick Hudson and Ned Rosier after him, Angelo goes to the Colosseum in his moment of "mental anguish" (227).

Interpretation and Criticism

"Adina" has rather more claim to neglect than the usual James tale. Still, Edel detects an allusion to "Adina" in Constance Fenimore Woolson's reference to an intaglio ring in a letter of 1883 to James, so the memory of the tale remained with some that far (*Letters* 3, 553, 558 n.12; *Life* 3, 93). When Mordell included it in his 1919 *Travelling Companions*, an otherwise unimpressed critic found James here "already an artist, already a man who knows that love is a mystery, already able to make us believe in the unaccountable" (*New Republic*). Subsequent critics who have taken up the tale have been less impressed, and have focused less on the mystery of love it presents than its misuse.

The tale's protagonist is generally taken as one of James's villains, who sins against love, against Italy, and against his own potential as a human being. Putt notes that Scrope loses by his "poor response" to Europe—the topaz and Angelo (79). Wright designates Scrope's first error —"denying his own sensitivity"—as bringing on his subsequent "intemperate behavior" (224). In Quentin Anderson's argument, Scrope's failure to respond to Europe is due to the same unreflective possessiveness that causes his failure with Adina and that makes him unworthy of either. Pointing out that his name is an anagram of corpse, Anderson dismisses him as "morally dead" (154–56). While the narrator pleads that Scrope's youth makes Scrope's "vices innocent," Jones argues that Scrope is innocent only in the sense that he is so consumed by egotism that he does not see the harm he is doing (98–99).

According to Maves, Scrope is a "new type" in James in being not simply indifferent to Italian romance, but hostile to it, its victimizer rather than its victim. Maves points to the narrator's remark on how the beauty of Italy makes Scrope aware of his own ugliness, and prompts him as he looks at Angelo "to regale himself, once for all, with the sense of an advantage wrested, if not by fair means, then by foul, from some sentient form of irritating Italian felicity" (CT 3, 221). Quentin Anderson has commented on the jealousy behind Scrope's theft of the jewel from Angelo (154), and in a reading reminiscent at times of *Billy Budd* with its beautiful sailor and loathsome Claggart, Maves similarly points to the narrator's explanation—"you must remember how very ugly the poor fellow was"—as the secret of his antipathy, which leads him to the impulsive cheating of Angelo. In Maves's reading, Italy makes Scrope's ugliness moral as well (40–41, 49, 71). Mackenzie goes even further, picturing a Scrope who recognizes in Angelo another self and therefore a threat to his identity. To save himself exposure as a nonentity, he steals the jewel to "displace" Angelo, thus beginning a "revenge cycle." Scrope, in his view, believes that by possessing the symbol of European power, he makes that power his own, and unlike the contentedly appreciative narrator, is desperate to do so. But his desire to keep his knowledge secret cannot last, and so he chooses in the end to renounce an act that, according to Mackenzie, still cannot place Scrope in any other than his original "false position" as American outsider (5–8).

The misery Scrope brings on himself has been assigned to various sources, but rarely to Angelo. Tanner, while noting Scrope "virtually robs" Angelo, finds it the past that has "poisoned his life." Similarly, Putt writes that one is "intended to feel that the revenge is exacted by the topaz itself rather than by its simple owner," noting that Angelo is hardly terrifying in his vulnerability to malaria (79). Such readings seem to imitate Scrope's major error—the confusion of people and objects, however conveniently symbolic. Jones, more aptly, judges Scrope's throwing away the topaz "as if *it* were to blame" as an indication that he has learned nothing from his experience (98–99).

Unlike Scrope, Angelo eventually learns to discriminate between the jewel and the woman. Originally, in wooing Adina, he seems to have been motivated simply by the desire to get something from Scrope in return for the topaz. But as Jones argues, Scrope's act causes a transformation in Angelo, taking him from a "boyish ignorance" or innocence to a knowledge of evil (98–99), a knowledge, one might say, he then employs in eloping with Adina. Maves, however, emphasizes James's use of the word "ignorance" instead of "innocence," speculating that it indicates Angelo is now mature but not corrupt. He, too, however, marks a transformation, the first among James's Italians, in Angelo's ability in the end to recognize, as he tells the narrator, that Adina is "better than the topaz" (42).

Such perspicacity is a good sign for Adina, but her fate is still vague at the end of the story. Her farewell note reads: "Good-bye to everything! Think me crazy if you will. I could never explain. Only forget me and believe that I am happy, happy, happy!" (CT 3, 253). Whether she is indeed happy has not much concerned critics. Wagenknecht, for example, indicates that one would condemn Angelo if he had sought a violent revenge against Scrope, but "since he merely woos Adina at the garden window," one sees Scrope as getting his just deserts, an explanation that leaves out the question of Adina's (178). Admittedly, Adina could have rejected Angelo's suit. Then again, Isabel Archer could have rejected Osmond's, but it is still counted against him and Madame Merle that they connived in it. Certainly the fact that Adina is moving not only into a way of life foreign to her, but also less affluent, was no doubt significant to James, although it also adds to the romance of her gesture. Maves draws attention to the narrator's uncertainty over what "sort of a future" Adina was destined for, but finds what he calls their "natural desire" unshadowed by the curse of the topaz, pointing to the narrator's pride in "having assisted . . . at this episode": "As mere *action*, it seemed to me really superb, and in judging of human nature I often weighed it mentally against the perpetual spectacle of strong impulses frittered in weakness and perverted by prudence. There has been no prudence here, certainly, but there has been ardent, full-blown, positive passion." Such passion, as Maves notes, is indicative of the standards peculiar to Italy, valuing not proper behavior but "splendor" (44). More briefly, Nathalia Wright exhibits quite a positive assessment of the ending by listing Adina as one of the many James characters whose love affairs in Italy turn out successfully (221).

Mackenzie, on the other hand, sees Adina acting a "self-sacrificial" part in her choice, her marriage resembling "a conspiratorial liaison," but does not make clear what would qualify it to be the "authentic relationship" he states it fails to be (7–8). Kelley sees Adina, whom she finds an unsatisfactory heroine, fascinated by the romance associated with Angelo, and so becoming pagan by following him, rather than converting him to the present (156–57). Putt also sees Adina adopting Angelo's ways in a symbolic interpretation that has Angelo taking the representative modern woman into his "own private Golden Age" (79). Edel takes a different tack, saying of her that she "triumphs over ancient evil" (CT 3, 9). Quentin Anderson provides perhaps the most intriguing reading in arguing that the passive Adina appears to have walked into a marriage little different than the one she might have had with Scrope (155 n.45).

Part of the difficulty in unraveling the riddle of Adina's fate is a problem Maves points to, the lack of knowledge on the part of the narrator of the motives behind the actions he describes (40). Kelley argues that the narrator "does what he can" to make the story ring true, but faults James for failing to provide him with the fully realized characters that would make it do so, the Europeans here remaining "fantastic," the Americans "grotesque" (157). Admitting that, it seems that in this tale James wants his Americans, assuredly Scrope, to be grotesque, and wants his Europeans fantastic. In "The Last of the Valerii" he had subordinated the grotesque to a minor non-American role, and concentrated on the clash between the moral American woman and the European fantastic male, and achieved a certain success. Here, he introduces another element, the American grotesque, to the combination, and it seems simply too much for him to resolve, so that the elements remain individually of interest but fail ultimately to cohere.

Works Cited

Primary Works

James, Henry. 1874. "Adina." *Scribner's Monthly* 8 (May–June): 33–43, 181–91.

———. 1919. "Adina." *Travelling Companions*. Foreword by Albert Mordell. New York: Boni and Liveright.

———. 1931. "The Mad Lovers and the Emperor's Topaz." Little Blue Book 1675. Girard, KS: Haldeman-Julius.

Secondary Works

Anderson, Charles R. 1977. *Person, Place and Thing in Henry James's Novels*. Durham, NC: Duke University Press.

Anderson, Quentin. 1957. *The American Henry James*. New Brunswick, NJ: Rutgers University Press.

Anon. 1919. Review of *Travelling Companions*. *New Republic* 19 (30 July): 422.

Churchill, Kenneth. 1980. *Italy and English Literature, 1764–1930*. New York: Barnes & Noble.

Gardaphe, Fred L. 1989. "The Echoes of *Beltraffio:* Reading Italy in Henry James's 'The Author of *Beltraffio.*'" *RLA: Romance Languages Annual* 1: 121–27.

Holder, Alan. 1966. *Three Voyagers in Search of Europe: Henry James, Ezra Pound, and T. S. Eliot*. Philadelphia: University of Pennsylvania Press.

Horrell, Joyce Tayloe. 1970. "A 'Shade of a Special Sense': Henry James and the Art of Naming." *American Literature* 42: 203–20.

Hovanec, Evelyn. 1979. *Henry James and Germany. Costerus* n.s. 19.

James, William. 1992. *The Correspondence of William James.* Vol. 1: *William and Henry: 1861–1884.* Ed. Ignas K. Skrupskelis and Elizabeth M. Berkeley. Charlottesville: University Press of Virginia.

Jones, Granville H. 1975. *Henry James's Psychology of Experience, Innocence, Responsibility, and Renunciation in the Fiction of Henry James.* The Hague: Mouton.

Kelley, Cornelia Pulsifer. [1930] 1965. *The Early Development of Henry James.* Urbana: University of Illinois Press.

Kraft, James. 1969. *The Early Tales of Henry James.* Carbondale: Southern Illinois University Press.

Mackenzie, Manfred. 1976. *Communities of Honor and Love in Henry James.* Cambridge, MA: Harvard University Press.

Maves, Carl. 1973. *Sensuous Pessimism: Italy in the Works of Henry James.* Bloomington: Indiana University Press.

Putt, S. Gorley. 1966. *Henry James: A Reader's Guide.* Ithaca, NY: Cornell University Press.

Slabey, Robert M. 1958. "Henry James and 'The Most Impressive Convention in All History.'" *American Literature* 30 (March): 89–102.

Stone, Edward. 1964. *The Battle of the Books: Some Aspects of Henry James.* Athens: Ohio University Press.

Tanner, Tony. 1963. "James's Little Tarts." *The Spectator* 210 (4 January): 19.

Tilby, Michael. 1980. "Henry James and Mérimée: A Note of Caution." *Romance Notes* 21: 165–68.

Tintner, Adeline R. 1986. *The Museum World of Henry James.* Ann Arbor: UMI Research Press.

Wagenknecht, Edward. 1984. *The Tales of Henry James.* New York: Frederick Ungar.

Wegelin, Christof. 1958. *The Image of Europe in Henry James.* Dallas: Southern Methodist University Press.

Wright, Nathalia. 1965. *American Novelists in Europe, The Discoverers: Allston to James.* Philadelphia: University of Pennsylvania Press.

Foreign Language
Fabris, Alberta. 1969. *Henry James e la Francia*. Rome: Edizioni di storia e letteratura.

The Altar of the Dead

Publication History

"The Altar of the Dead" first appeared in James's 1895 collection, *Terminations*, and subsequent to that as the title story of volume 17 in the New York Edition.

Circumstances of Composition, Sources, and Influences

James had the idea for "The Altar of the Dead," as he recorded, "from ever so far back." In the preface he also recalls two incidents that crystallized his sense of the "free intelligence . . . waylaid or arrested . . . by some imagined appeal of the lost Dead." In the first, he met a former acquaintance, a police magistrate, whom he had formerly been in the habit of meeting at the house of a hospitable couple, now dead. On recalling "the dear So-and-So's" to the magistrate, however, he was rebuked, "Why, they're Dead, sir—dead these many years." In the second, James was struck by an editor's rejection of a friend's proposal of a commemorative essay on another friend. The editor saw no reason to publish anything about the woman "*because*—and because *only*, so far as I can make out—she's dead" (*Criticism* 2, 1246–48). In the story, one may recall that even Acton Hague is the victim of a brief obituary, his career "compressed by the newspaper into a dozen lines" (CT 9, 237). The need for a better way of remembering is clear.

In the first notebook entry, in September 1894, James already has his title, although the altar was solely in the mind. As that did not provide "adequate action," he turned to a physical one. His protagonist, driven by his sense of the modern treatment of the dead—"unhonoured, neglected, shoved out of sight"—and spurred by the recent death of his mother or "some dear friend," wanders into a church and so begins his ritual. The climax was to stem from the man's sense that his altar was not complete until his own taper was lighted on it. In September the action was to be in London; in early October James switched it to the suburbs (CN 98–99). On October 24, 1894, James wrote that he had started the tale, but broken off, "quite losing conceit of my subject," and thinking the "little fancy" might not sustain a tale. He ends by saying that for such "a little thing" the idea will probably do, that working more will "bring it out," and reminding himself that "I have always put things through" (CN 99–100). Given the publication date, he evidently did soldier ahead, although at a little over 13,000 words the work is not particularly short, even for James. Matthiessen and Murdock comment on the discrepancy between James's doubts here and his evident high valuation of the story later. As they also point out, however, most of the story's plot was added after the notebook entry, so that it may be that the addition of the woman, with Stransom's change from a "relatively abstract symbol" to a complex personality who feels resentment as well as grief, were what gave James his later confidence (N 166–67; also Wagenknecht 1984, 89–90). Seeing the initial problem as one of length, Thorp also finds that the new character "deepened . . . and complicated the action," turning the tale into a nouvelle (x).

In the preface James denied being able to trace his inspiration to any "definite moment" or "particular shock" (*Criticism* 2, 1247). Edel, however, not only traces the tale to James's talks with Paul Bourget, while visiting him at Oxford, of the "Oxford dead," but more specifically to his shock at the apparent suicide of his friend Constance Fenimore Woolson in January 1894. As Edel observes, when he first recorded his idea, James was living in Oxford at No. 15 Beaumont Street, where Woolson had once lived. Edel argues that James felt betrayed, his peace destroyed by her self-destruction, which "somehow violated the altar of his art, his private altar." On the basis of the tale, Edel argues that between the two writers there had been "a strange matching of personalities, and strange distortions in their mutual vision of one another." James thought he had in Fenimore a "disinterested devotion" consistent with his own freedom, but was disillusioned by her making "claims." Finally, her death created an "intolerable" mystery, which kept James from taking "possession" of her memory, as he had done with others of his dead, including his cousin Minny Temple and others of his family (*Life* 3, 381–86; *Life* 4, 147; *Life* 5, 137; CT 9, 10; 1970, 354–56).

Edel sees James's relationship with Woolson reflected in three other notebook entries. One is a germ recorded the next year in which the peace of an elderly man who enjoys simple activities such as "a quiet walk, a quiet read" is disturbed by the return of his estranged wife. Once she succeeds in ousting him, she enjoys "the same quiet little joy that he did" (*Life* 4, 147; CN 139–41). In the second, from November 1894, a writer discovers that a woman friend of his has anonymously been "slating" his books in magazine reviews. In the third, also of 1894, James pondered "the contrasted opposition of the 2 forms of pride": that which "can harden and stiffen the heart," and that which "suffers" (*Life* 3, 384–85; CN 107–8). While none of these entries became tales, Edel sees Woolson's death as lying behind "The Altar of the Dead" as well as other completed tales, including "The Figure in the Carpet," "The Beast in the Jungle," and "The Friends of the Friends" (*Life* 5, 137).

Matthiessen quotes from the tale's preface to caution that despite James's "attested predilection for poor sensitive gentlemen," one should not identify

James with his characters (1947, 244–45). Nevertheless, autobiographical connections have been common. Krook indeed calls it one of James's "semi-autobiographical" tales (352). Stransom's manner of worship—"solitary visits to churches and cathedrals"—was also James's own, according to Edel (*Life* 1, 111). In Walter Wright's formulation, the tale is not autobiographical in the usual sense, but "an enquiry by its author into the inner recesses of his own thought and feeling" (212). Troy calls it "something like a testament of belief" (270). More censoriously, Dupee objects that James is "too much his own hero" in the "overwrought" tale (154). Jones, on the other hand, finds it "difficult to identify Henry James permanently with so desperate and blocked a man as George Stransom" (278).

Applying the tale's central metaphor to James's life, Fox calls James's three autobiographical volumes "his own candles" in tribute to the past (82). Gerlach finds in Stransom's inability to be satisfied with a single candle, his desire for the perfect arrangement, a parallel to James's approach to the short story, which he felt should depict not just "a single incident" but a "foreshortened representation of a large and complex action" (84). In a letter to the *Times* after James's death, Edmund Gosse spoke of the belief that the church near James's home into which "he often silently slipped," All Saints, was thought to be the site of "The Altar of the Dead." Now, however, he wrote, the tale would be identified with Old Chelsea Church, site of his funeral (Hyde 286; *Life* 5, 562).

Geismar and Tanner both find the tale indicative of James's "weary" or "dark" mood during a "difficult period" (Geismar 131; Tanner 81–82). Hartsock, however, objects to such gloomy readings, pointing ahead instead to the affirmation of James's 1914 letter to Henry Adams, that one can still "cultivate" interest and choose life (378). Other critics, however, look even farther back for parallels. McElderry associates the mood of the piece with James's reading of William's letter at their father's grave in 1882, and observes that "the memory of the dead" was, for James, having no conventional religion, "a kind of immortality deeply influential on the living" (116). Similarly, Hartsock connects the tale to James's 1905 visit to the family graves, seeing his experiencing at the cemetery an epiphany similar to that of Stransom's final vision, "a full and felt acceptance of death and life" (375). In his autobiography James spoke of the Civil War dead and of the survivors' "wanting, never ceasing to want, to 'do' something for them"—a mood akin to Stransom's, and Matthiessen comments on how James's experience as a civilian during that war may have contributed to his intense awareness of the interconnection of the living and the dead (1947, 246–47).

Dupee locates in the tale much of James's "own cult of Minny Temple and of old pieties in general" (155). Even Stransom's wish that his friends might die so that he could establish with them "a connection more charming" Edel sees as reflecting James's "difficulty" in relating to the living, compared to his imaginative ease with the dead (*Life* 3, 386). Similarly, Przybylowicz compares James, particularly in his relationship to Minny, to Stransom in that each "perceives people as more attractive in their spiritual than in their fleshly form." Like his heroes, she writes, James was "uncomfortable when confronted with the physical and sexual aspects of life" (229–30). According to Bronfen, Stransom takes over Mary Antrim in the same way James did Minny (111–13). Cautioning that "James is not Stransom," Krupnick puts a slight remove between James's attitude toward death—his "strange joy" at his mother's death or his quick transformation of Minny from life to art—and Stransom's, which parodies it. Unlike Stransom, he argues, James remained as committed to actuality as to the ideal (39).

Thinking of the "more charming" connection one can enjoy with the dead, Stransom continues the thought by appending that, "in regard to those from whom one was separated by the long curves of the globe such a connection could only be an improvement: it brought them instantly within reach" (CT 9, 243). James had of course a good number of family and friends across an ocean, but it was his friend Stevenson whose removal in 1888 to the South Seas had caused James to exclaim to him, "You are too far away—you are too absent—too invisible, inaudible, inconceivable," his voice coming "from too far away, from the other side of the globe" (*Letters* 3, 239). Having left England for his health, Stevenson would be dead in December 1894.

After a year of ingratiating himself with "bland ecclesiastics," Stransom is able to rent a chapel of a suburban church for his own devotions (CT 9, 240). Remarks Graham Greene of the transaction, "Surely no one so near in spirit, at any rate in this one particular, to the Catholic Church was ever so ignorant of its rules" (35). Brooks, too, doubts the likelihood of one man being allowed to take over an altar in any real Catholic church (132–33). Hartsock, however, argues that such doubters would be enlightened by a reading of Joyce and J. F. Powers (372).

The mood and imagery of the tale have engendered many comparisons. Elton sees "its unencumbered impulse toward beauty" as akin to Maeterlink's (368). Both Putt and Hartsock see its attitude to the past and to mutability recalling that of Proust (Putt 394; Hartsock 373). Spender and Troy, on the other hand, see its response to the influence of the dead as creating a link with James Joyce's "The Dead," and, for Spender, also with the criticism of T. S. Eliot (Spender 50, 113). Additionally, Troy compares its sympathy for the dead to that of Baudelaire (271). Other analogies to the French include Krupnick's comparison of James's making something out of nothing in the tale—even as contemporary American architecture built around a central "empty space"—to Flaubert's wanting to write a novel about "nothing" and Mallarmé's wanting to write a book entitled "Sumptuous Allegories of Nothingness" (38, 41). Attributing to Stransom a "hyperattenuated symbolist consciousness," Auchard notes echoes of Baudelaire, Verlaine, and

Huysmans (34, 40–41). Tintner also points to the Symbolists, particularly the artist Fernand Khnopff, as influences, observing that Beethoven and Schubert, both mentioned in the tale, were favorite composers of the Symbolists (1986, 136).

More particular comparisons include Gerlach's indebting of the story's unified drive to its conclusion to Poe, with the conclusion itself—with its "all-consuming blaze of candles" and Stransom held by his "sisterly woman"—"tonally" similar, minus the gothicism, to the conclusion of "The Fall of the House of Usher," whose hero also destroys himself through "an obsession with death" (83). Auchard constructs a connection with Pater's description of "La Gioconda," seeing the "vampirish" Stransom taking "plunges," as the text informs us, "into depths quieter than the deep sea-caves," even as Pater's Mona Lisa is like a "vampire" and "a diver in deep seas." While Pater sought a "hard, gemlike flame" inspired by life, however, Auchard sees Stransom seeking a "brightness vast and intense," which he opposes to life (41). A more sedate comparison may reside in the characterization of the woman's neighborhood as "pairs of shabby little houses, semi-detached but indissolubly united . . . like married couples on bad terms" (CT 9, 251). Victorian author Emily Eden's two novels of married life were *The Semi-Attached Couple* and *The Semi-Detached House*.

Blackmur ranks the tale in beauty with such classic elegies as "Lycidas," "In Memoriam," and "Adonais," although its focus is not on an individual but on "all the dead" ([1942] 1983, 55). Likewise, Pearce places the tale in the tradition of the pastoral elegy, although, not being told in the first person, it lacks the singer's voice (836). Burleson finds in the tale's nine sections a symmetry of imagery and subjects that creates an image of "The Altar" not unlike that in Herbert's shaped poem "The Altar." A different echo of the Renaissance is offered by Wright, who sees Stransom's obsession with the phrase "just one more" and his final illness as similar to Lear's madness in "sorting out irrelevancies" on the way to true vision (217).

In what Wright calls an "epic touch," James compares Stransom and the woman talking of their dead as "they" to "a pair of pagans of old alluding decently to the domesticated gods" (215; CT 9, 248). Warminski casts the woman as a "disarticulating Echo to Stransom's Narcissus," responding, for example, to his final "one more, one more" with "no more, no more" (284). Stransom's need to forgive Hague, Edel suggests, recalls Christ's sermon in Matthew 5:23–24: "Therefore if thou bring thy gift to the altar, and there rememberest that thy brother hath ought against thee; Leave there thy gift before the altar, and go thy way; first be reconciled to thy brother, and then come and offer thy gift" (*Life* 3, 382). Mary Antrim, in Frame's reading, appears at the altar like Dante's Beatrice to show Stransom the way to salvation (254).

The tale was filmed in 1978 by Truffaut as *La Chambre Verte*. Round has pointed out how Truffaut blends the tale with "The Beast in the Jungle" to produce a story of "death conceived of as selfishness, the refusal ever to let go of what once belonged to one; the refusal to accept love and friendship unless the lover or friend is safely dead." Branch notes a third, smaller source in "The Friends of the Friends," as Truffaut attributes a vision of a dead loved one to both hero and heroine. Tintner emphasizes the way in which Truffaut, despite a basic sympathy with Stransom's affection for the dead, "rational-ize[s]" his obsession by placing it in the context of World War I, and by mak-ing him a writer of obituaries (1980, 80). Branch sees some of the same changes as attempts to compensate for the necessary loss of "interiority" in moving from short story to film (186–87). Edel, however, considers the film a "touchstone" for transferring James into other media, praising Truffaut for having captured "the ritualism of grief" (1989, 108–9).

Relation to Other Works

James's brother William questioned James's choice of title for his 1895 collec-tion, asking "why" *Terminations* (370)? Most critics, however, have found the title logical enough, and to Gage "The Altar of the Dead" is a fitting con-clusion to the collection in its addition of love and forgiveness to the subject of death (20–21, 284). As Gerlach points out, James's use of the death of his protagonist as a conclusion was typical of his approach in many stories, if not his novels (82, 89). Buitenhuis links the tale particularly with "Crapy Cornelia" in its "commemoration" of the dead and its emphasis on the relationships between those who remember the same dead (224–25). In Hoffman's view, Stransom's "illusion of the past" allows him to accept the present, even as the writer Dencombe comes to accept the present by giving up the "delusion of a future" (54). Mrs. Gracedew's "piety toward the past" in *Covering End*, Wagenknecht suggests, has "some affinity" with Stransom's (1984, 180).

James recorded the idea for another tale of death, *The Wings of the Dove*, in 1894, although he did not complete the novel until the next century. According to Segal, the theme of forgiveness is the strongest link between the two works, while Samuels finds the overwhelming air of death the more pertinent connection (Segal 191; Samuels 74). In between the two works, as Macnaughton points out, James created several characters whose focus is on the dead, including the characters of "Maud-Evelyn" and Mr. Longdon of *The Awkward Age* (85).

Stevenson finds a "trace" of the turning from life to death in "The Birthplace," which, in Dupee's estimate, is the better work due to its humor and its greater inclusion of "the world" (Stevenson 72–73; Dupee 155). Cowdery links both tales with *The Aspern Papers*, which also depicts a char-acter who "broods over talismans" of the dead (31). Juliana's offering of her talismans—the letters—for the sake of Tina is, however, Hartsock contends, a reflection of the valuing of love over death also affirmed in "The Altar of the Dead" (377). Krupnick, alternatively, sees in both tales a "pattern of loss and restitution" (40–41). The presence of Acton Hague, "come back from beyond the grave, as it were" to take the woman from Stransom, according to Goetz, creates a triangle similar to that between the dead Aspern, the narrator, and Tina (163).

James evidently classed the tale with what he called the "quasi-supernatural" and included it, as Edel observes, with the ghost tales in the New York Edition. It is, however, in Edel's judgment, more "morbid" than "gruesome" (1970, 353; CT 9, 10). As a "non-apparitional" work, Edel omitted it from his 1963 edition of James's *Ghostly Tales*. Auchincloss similarly rejects it as a ghost story, remarking that there are in the tale no "actual" ghosts or anyone who thinks he has seen them (93). Vaid calls it the least "ghostly" of James's "ghostly tales" (223). To Banta, however, the couples in both "The Altar of the Dead" and "The Beast in the Jungle" "seek meaning in terms of inner lives so hidden from the daylight view and yet so powerful in their shaping influences" that their stories become "variations on the 'occult'" (1972, 52). Auchard also includes both tales with "Maud-Evelyn" and "The Jolly Corner" as works that share an obsession with "the sickly and the ghostly" (34). More specifically, Banta objects to the too rapid change from Stransom's enlightenment to his death, seeing the same weakness in the ghostly "Sir Edmund Orme" (1972, 152). The theme and "psychological atmosphere," according to Hoffman, anticipate the supernatural *The Sense of the Past*, even as the tale's style, scenic method, symbols, and imagery anticipate such later works as *The Spoils of Poynton* and particularly *The Turn of the Screw* (54–55).

The tone of the tale is perhaps more religious than ghostly. According to Gale's calculations, the later works of James, and those included in the New York Edition, generally contain more religious imagery, other examples being "The Birthplace" and "The Velvet Glove" (164–65). In Slabey's view, James had moved from a solely aesthetic appreciation of Catholicism to a sense of the consolation and continuity provided by its ritual, and by little else in modern society. He links Stransom with Isabel, Maggie, and Milly as people whose stories represent "religious experience outside a creed" (92, 101). The appreciation of Catholicism here, Cargill places in contrast with the "Protestant horror" at it in *The American* (52, 59 n.37). Still, Auchard finds the "monastic, quasi-Catholic fascination" "suggested mildly" in "The Madonna of the Future" and *Roderick Hudson* (40). One might also recall the kneeling Italian woman accompanied by a more hesitant companion and envied by the protagonist in the early "Travelling Companions" (CT 2, 208). Stransom's similar envy of the woman's religious grief Putt compares to that of Strether visiting Notre Dame (393). Still, in Sicker's view, Strether's fate is preferable to Stransom's, in that he is separated by distance, not death, from the image he worships, one "gilded by a European splendor" (125–26).

To Krupnick, Stransom's creation of the altar is as removed from reality as the theories of the narrators of *The Sacred Fount* or *The Turn of the Screw* (42). Ward sees the tale as treating the tension between the impulse to impose a set form on life and the ability to accept its disorder, a theme present also in *The Sacred Fount* and *The Golden Bowl*. In Ward's view, while the tension is "unresolved" in *The Sacred Fount*, both Maggie and Stransom learn to give up an artificial order for a "living" one (220–21).

The Jamesian character perhaps best known for learning Maggie's lesson "too late" is John Marcher. As Matthiessen and Murdock note, James placed "The Beast in the Jungle" as a companion piece to "The Altar of the Dead" in his collected edition, although they judge it different in being about what "might have been" rather than the dead (N 312). In Tate's view, both tales are close to allegory in their paucity of "naturalistic detail" (10). Vaid responds that rather than dismissing the tales as allegories one might better "revise" the definition of allegory, joining with the two tales both "The Great Good Place" and "The Jolly Corner" (232). Still, Krupnick includes both tales in a list of later works "organized about an absence" along with *The Sacred Fount*, *The Turn of the Screw*, and *The Ambassadors* (37).

To Edel, the main similarity between the two tales is the "poor sensitive gentlemen" who serve as protagonists (CT 9, 10; also Sicker 99; Fussell 446; Goetz 151). The experience of both men, Allen argues, demonstrates that "intelligence and sensibility" can work against their possessor when used to rationalize the avoidance of experience (121). In linking the two heroes with Pemberton of *The Pupil* and Dencombe of "The Middle Years" as seeking "to substitute less intimate for more intimate kinds of love," Dupee sees Marcher as trying to make May assume the maternal role that the woman here takes on in the final scene (157). Blackmur also speaks of *The Pupil*, "The Beast in the Jungle," and "The Altar of the Dead" as tales where love is accompanied by, even "engorge[d]" by, "destructiveness and retribution" ([1952] 1983, 225–26). Putting together a different trio, Thorberg sees the subject of "The Beast in the Jungle," "The Altar of the Dead," and "The Jolly Corner" as "obsession." However, while Brydon and Marcher are "magnified" by their obsessions, in Thorberg's view, Stransom's concerns with the dead and revenge represent a "limitation" that makes the tale unfortunately morbid (186–87). If a bad sign for a character, Auchincloss judges a protagonist's possession of a "dominant trait" or "quirk" a hallmark of some of James's best short stories, including his tales of Stransom, Marcher, and Dencombe (28–29). Ward gives a practical rationale for the isolation of Marcher and Stransom as well as the narrator of *The Aspern Papers* by citing the usefulness to James of such restrictions for keeping his nouvelles within acceptable limits. He notes also, however, the similar test each faces in the acceptance or rejection of a relationship, a test he sees only Stransom successfully facing (1967, 23). Goetz places "The Altar of the Dead" and "The Private Life" as "transitional" tales between the writer tales and the later, more ghostly "The Beast in the Jungle" and "The Jolly Corner." Even as the disciples in the writer tales "The Lesson of the Master" or "The Figure in the Carpet" face a "greater consciousness," Stransom, in Goetz's formulation, is dominated by what the text calls the "sovereign presence" of Mary Antrim, Marcher confronts May and his "fate," and Brydon his alter ego. Their sense of living "in ignorance while true authority, mastery of knowledge resides elsewhere," Goetz sees reflected also in James's autobiography. The religious imagery of "The Altar of the Dead" and such other tales as *The Aspern Papers* he attributes to James's increasing reverence toward the "other consciousness" (158–64).

Sharp emphasizes the role of the women characters, classifying the woman in "The Altar of Dead" with Alice and May as Jamesian confidantes whose "presence" is "integral" to the story. In all three tales, she writes, the "committed woman is morally superior to the selfish man," showing James's "ideal of woman" becoming exalted almost into the "realm of romantic fancy." The selfishness of the men, however, she notes, is typical of James's confiders after 1890—women as well—for example, in *The Spoils of Poynton* and *The Golden Bowl* (3, 48, 261–62). In Allen's view, the "passive and patient" quality of the love the woman and May offer makes it easier for the men to avoid experience (121). All four characters, Przybylowicz argues, live unhealthily in the past and so miss love (102). Much earlier, Stephen Spender placed both Stransom and the woman with Marcher, Rowland Mallet, and such Jamesian confidantes as Mrs. Tristram of *The American*, Maria Gostrey, and Fanny Assingham as "studies" for Strether in their passive lives (28).

A critic at the *North American Review*, in reviewing *The Finer Grain*, found "The Bench of Desolation" mildly reminiscent of "The Altar of the Dead" as a "study in a long fidelity and continuity of purpose." Dodd, Stransom, and Marcher, according to Bender, are all defined according to one primary symbol, an obsession that is at the same time both "perversely egotistic" and beyond the control of characters who are "not altogether responsible for themselves," but "helplessly drawn toward fulfilling their fates" (256–57). In the cases of Strether and Dodd, but less so Marcher, Perosa stresses the force of circumstances in limiting their lives (142).

The woman with her "obscure destiny" provides a link, according to Zabel, not only with "The Bench of Desolation," but also "Brooksmith" and *The Princess Casamassima* as examples of James's treating the lower class with "searching compassion" (12). Auchard calls her "a more forceful version" of Mary Garland in Roderick Hudson (41). Stransom meanwhile, Wright argues, resembles Lyon of "The Liar" in his false belief that he fully understands a woman he believes to be simple, although unlike Lyon he is at least "kind and tender" (216). To Edel, however, the man and woman are engaged in a "struggle . . . between mirror-images of power," like that of Isabel and Osmond (Life 3, 383).

Interpretation and Criticism

The tale has generated extreme judgments. Hartsock traces much of the controversy and sees the balance weighing slightly toward the negative, remarking that "hostile critics . . . often look upon it as a test-case." To like the tale is an indication of membership in the Jamesian "cult" (372). Similarly, Wagenknecht speaks of its critics dividing into "the sheep and the goats" (1984, 85). Taking sides with the sheep, James's sister-in-law, Alice, found it, according to her husband, William, "*splendid*" (W. James 369). Other early readers praised it: the *North American Review* called it "that absolutely perfect story." Even those who did not remember it quite right admired it: Ella Hepworth Dixon was shocked at the gossiping of the author of "that exquisite story, *An Altar of Friendship*" (Page 28). Even James himself was evidently pleased, telling Bailey Saunders it was the work with which he was "least dissatisfied" (Hyde 287). West proclaimed the story a masterpiece, with "so perfect a beauty that one can read every separate paragraph every day of one's life for the music of the sentences and the loveliness of the presented images, which takes ritual from the trembling hands of the coped old men and exhibits it as something that those who love the natural frame of things and hate superstition need not fear to accept" (100–1). To Beerbohm, the "dear masterpiece" was the best expression of James's "reverence for noble things and horror of things ignoble" (26).

Still, it was "The Altar of the Dead" that H. G. Wells spoke of in his famous attack on James in *Boon*. He describes a work by James "like a church lit but without a congregation to distract you, with every light and line focused on the high altar. And on the altar, very reverently placed, intensely there, is a dead kitten, an egg-shell, a bit of string . . . Like his 'Altar of the Dead,' with nothing to the dead at all" (*Life* 5, 534). Others would join the attack. Objecting to the treatment of the story as a masterpiece, F. R. Leavis proclaimed the tale "a piece of sentimentality so maudlin and rank that an admirer of James, one would have thought, would rather not be reminded of its existence" (234). Geismar returned in his generation to attack the status of the tale, which he considered James could have used "as the germ of another satiric fable on literary vogues" (132). The extremes of criticism can even be found within individual critics. Brooks, for example, includes the tale both with "The Great Good Place," "Maud-Evelyn," and "The Beast in the Jungle" as a tale of "autumnal beauty" and with the "oppressive" late tales, which irritate the reader because they "do not follow the lines of life" (132–33, 151–53).

The main problem for most is the main theme, what James in his note-book calls the man's "noble and beautiful religion . . . the worship of the Dead," which fills the need for "something, not of this world, to cherish, to be pious to, to make the object of a donation" (CN 98). Such, as has been seen, was a feeling James shared. In his reconstruction of James's writing of the tale, Frame remarks that James could not have generated a conflict about the rightness of Stransom's "rite" as he was "obviously not embarrassed by the morbidity of the original conceit" (253–54). Some critics have simply commented on how such a conceit is "very peculiarly" Jamesian, with, as the *Athenaeum* put it, "a half-perverse air of subtlety and remoteness that sets Mr. James . . . entirely apart from the heartier and more robust forms of human motive and desire" (769). Others, like Edgar, while granting James's artistic prerogative, and even his awareness of Stransom's establishment of the altar as "an act which lifts his hero out of all relation with our rough breathing world," still find the narrow focus rather extreme and artificial. Edgar questions further the reality of the central character, declaring himself "stubbornly dubious" as to his ability to have been a friend to so many (103–5). Geismar reads the sympathy for the dead in the tale as a screen for James's sense of his own neglect as a writer; other critics such as Briggs and Fussell have seen it as genuine morbidity, assigning to Stransom an inability to face the present, a "spiritual ill-health" (Geismar 132; Briggs 150–51; Fussell 446; see also Auchard 39, 42; Q. D. Leavis 223). In Nalbantian's defini-tion, Stransom is a consummate Decadent to whom even his own life is sim-ply "a postponement of his own death: a digression" (53). Such criticism might be deflected if Stransom's devotion to the dead were not so thorough, but as James wrote in his preface, "the cultivation" in Stransom's "cultivated habit" is "really the point." He later ties that "cultivation" to the "*cultivation*" in the unwelcoming air of London of the "finer flowers—creatures of cultiva-tion as the finer flowers essentially are" (*Criticism* 2, 1246, 1248). Stransom's habit may be too deliberate for modern critics, but if it were less so, it would be insufficient for James's intention.

In their judgments of Stransom, critics tend to cite one passage over and over: "There were hours at which he almost caught himself wishing that cer-tain of his friends would now die, that he might establish with them in this manner a connection more charming than, as it happened, it was possible to enjoy with them in life" (CT 9, 242). To some such a wish is evidence of Stransom's selfishness (Round 166; Honig 91). To others it is a bad sign of Stransom's distance from life (Hartsock 377; Ward 220–21; Lebowitz 206). Krupnick uses the passage to argue that James is aware of the "perversity" of Stransom's preference for the dead, showing Stransom as "an aesthetic dandy" (38; see also Warminski 282). More neutrally, Auchard sees in the pas-sage a "monastic, quasi-Catholic fascination" (40). Blackmur, however, can quote the passage sympathetically, and both Todorov and Wright portray

Stransom's wish as a "natural consequence" of his devotion to the dead, the "order and harmony" they represent. As Todorov observes, after imagining the deaths of his friends, Stransom goes on to envisage his own death (Blackmur [1942] 1983, 55; Todorov 166, 188). Wright, however, stresses that James's "matter of fact" recording of Stransom's wish indicates that James, while "always sympathetic" to the "humanly selfish" Stransom does not always approve of him (214). It may be that Stransom's betrayal by his most "intimate" friend may have impressed on him the fear that friends live only to betray one, as indeed the woman does. Still, for Tintner, the passage is a "parodic extension" of Stransom's obsession "in a wryly humorous improvisation" (1980, 79). A pertinent sidelight might be the similarity of Stransom's wish to that of Miss Birdseye in *The Bostonians*, whose "best hours had been spent in fancying that she was helping some Southern slave to escape. It would have been a nice question whether, in her heart of hearts, for the sake of this excitement, she did not sometimes wish the black back in bondage" (26).

James himself, as Hartsock observes, anticipated the charge of morbidness, writing that "to be caught in any rueful glance at them [the dead] was to be branded at once as 'morbid.'" In the preface, too, James speaks of Stransom's "exasperated piety" as a result of his living "amid the densest and most materialised aggregation of men upon earth, the society most wedded by all its conditions to the immediate and the finite" (*Criticism* 2, 1247, 1249). Hartsock and McCarthy both present the tale as a "rebuke" to such a society (Hartsock 374; McCarthy 133–34). Stransom, writes Vaid, represents the "few" who remember their dead, men such as Creston, "the many" who don't (216). Troy also, despite picturing the tale as "fluttering on the edge of a morbid emotionalism," reads it as a response to a society marked by "pathetic isolation" by a man who believed "we exist only by virtue of the existence of others, living and dead, with whom we have ever had relations." To provide some "continuity in human experience," James created a ritual in the tale with an emphasis on the dead as a "metaphor for the whole tradition of civilized humanity," the necessary "continuum between past and present." James's altar, writes Troy, is the "body of humanity stretched out in imagination in time and space." It is an interpretation that—minus the "tragic" emphasis—Anderson praises (Anderson 10–11).

Other critics have stressed that Stransom's attentiveness to the dead does not cut him off from the living. Fadiman, in an estimate seconded by Vaid, sees the tale as "far removed from the ghostly or the morbid" in its effective tribute to the dead based on a recognition of the value of life (Fadiman 358; Vaid 223; see also Wagenknecht 94; Branch 185). In his preface, James writes, "The sense of the state of the dead is but part of the sense of the state of the living; and, congruously with that, life is cheated to almost the same degree of the finest homage (precisely this our possible friendships and intimacies) that we fain would render it" (*Criticism* 2, 1249). Such a sense of the interdependence of

the living and the dead has been a part of most of the affirmative readings of
the tale (e.g., Banta 1964, 180 n.23; Hoffman 54; Tanner 81–82). It leads
Blackmur to call Stransom's altar "one of the most beautiful as it is one of the
most needful that man has ever raised in the desert of his need" ([1942]
1983, 55–56). Even as the *Athenaeum* had noted the "natural accidents" leading Stransom to his worship of the dead, Putt finds the story capturing the
"perfectly normal experience of the elderly" in its recognition of man's vulnerability to change and death (*Athenaeum* 769; Putt 392–94). His defense
has, however, been judged limited by Hartsock and by Warminski, who finds
Putt making the story into "an old folks' tale" as if that were not equally as
legitimate as a young folks' one (Hartsock 375; Warminski 265).

Putt, in fact, notes a complex of qualities in the tale and in Stransom, as do
several other critics. While Markow-Totevy sees in the tale James's desire "to
prove that death can also be made the means of life," he also discerns in the
tale a "denial of death" and "the continual presence of nothingness" (119). To
Jones, Stransom is the ultimate Jamesian renouncer, who gives up the living
for the dead out of "his own fear of being lost and forgotten." Still, he speaks
of Stransom as having thereby "a more earnest and more satisfying life in the
imagination than most people have in the actual world," and as saving not
only his own "innocence" but that of his dead friends (276–78). Tintner,
while admitting it "hard to view Stransom as anything but a compensated
psychotic," also reminds herself that James, too, believed the afterlife was
dependent on the "consciousness of the remembering person" and that
Stransom builds rather than destroys relationships by his memorials (1980,
78–79). In Sicker's view, the tale only escapes morbidity by what he sees as its
implicit criticism of "dead-image worship at the expense of life" (99–100).

While casting Stransom's devotion to the dead as "an affirmative 'act of
life,'" Hartsock at the same time offers a rebuttal to Dupee's complaint that
while Stransom is initially "in the thick of things" due to his wealth and public
office, he gradually withdraws until the "social entity" "has shrunk to almost
nothing" (Dupee 154–55). She finds a solid, if not detailed, role in the story
for the "social entity" (373–74). Indeed, McElderry cautions those who find
the tale morbid because of the isolation of the two worshipers that the story
shows only a part of their lives (116–17). Looking at the text, one can see that
Stransom throughout keeps up his public role—seemingly a significant one,
as is evident by the newspapers' chronicling of his falling out with Hague,
who himself dies a colonial governor and K. C. B. Until the end, when he has
survived his friends, Stransom has other ties; even toward the end he still
works, and travels abroad. The woman is a writer who publishes in the magazines. Stransom's visits to the altar, on the other hand, while they constitute
the matter of the tale, are often spaced over a period of weeks or even
months. It takes him "months and months" to learn the woman's name,
"years and years to learn her address" (CT 9, 251). Such a stretch of years also

serves to set apart their friendship from the hurried relationships James decried in his preface. As Hartsock points out, the tale speaks of Stransom's "loaded life," and Stransom himself views his public duties as "re-invigorated, not impoverished" by his worship of the dead, giving it "fruitful consequences" (374).

To Hartsock, Stransom's—and James's—attitude is "unusual" only in that it is one confined to those of large imagination (375). Earlier critics also emphasized Stransom's similarity to the artist. The similarity is not necessarily a good thing in Honig's reading, which declares that Stransom achieves "esthetic consistency rather than that possibly greater thing, an act of human forgiveness." From the start, he argues, Stransom's "cult" has a "double nature," being both "esthetic discipline" and "human charity." His being like James a man who "had never, never forgotten" confers on him a "painful talent" that could have been expressed in art, but instead takes the form of the altar. His "substitute 'work of art'" demands, in turn, an audience—the woman. But the addition of an audience emphasizes the failure of the other purpose of his cult as Stransom is "unwittingly false" to her in what his art excludes. Even if Stransom is valuing his art over his audience, his sense of failure at the revelation of her relationship to Hague stems directly from his identification of his worship with her, and, Honig argues, is further damaged by a very human jealousy. Her reappearance is thus a "vindication of Stransom's artistic integrity." There is, however, Honig contends, an element of ambiguity in that by dying, Stransom triumphs again, knowing that the woman will now serve his dead, not Hague (91–95).

Wright also presents Stransom as a man who "sees life in images and, like a novelist, creates concrete symbols to give intensity and singleness to his visions" (212). So, too, Vaid sees Stransom's decision to make a physical shrine representing "the union, in his mind, of his aesthetic and religious cravings." His character, Vaid writes, illustrates James's habit of making later heroes if not actual artists, men of "highly refined imagination and sensibility." He takes deliberate exception, however, to Honig's sense of the ending. According to Vaid, the conflict over Hague shows Stransom's religion to be "incomplete" until he includes his enemy. At first, Vaid observes, Stransom "takes refuge . . . in an aesthetic objection" that to add a candle would disrupt the symmetry of the altar; he then recognizes that one more candle is needed for its order, so that the "demand of the spirit and of aesthetics" is the same. He returns to "surrender," giving up his egotism to complete "aesthetically" and "symbolically" the altar (217–22, 227 n.5). Ward similarly portrays Stransom as an artist figure who undergoes a process of humanization, coming to realize that a candle for Hague would perfect—not upset—his altar's symmetry. Beginning, according to Ward, by seeking to "compensate" himself for the injuries of life through the "art" of his altar, Stransom makes life "increasingly repellent" to himself, so that his art "cancels out life." His forgiving and inclusion of Hague, however, changes him, Ward asserts, from a man "who would possess and control the dead to one who loves and forgives them" (220–21).

Artistry is again negative in Krupnick's reading. As the tale states, Stransom had "done almost all things but one: he had never forgotten" (CT 9, 231). In contrast to Hartsock, Krupnick challenges the statement, writing that "it might have been more accurate to say: 'He had *not* done many things in the world.'" The parallel "proud affirmation" that Stransom had "never forgotten," Krupnick charges, is an "affirmation rooted in and organized about an absence." The tale, too, is "ordered about a central blankness," like most of James's fictions, its theme "the loss of the earthly and restitution in art." Stransom, he argues, lives at a distance from life, particularly troubled by the presence of women, whom he transforms into "muses or anima-figures." With his fellow worshiper he organizes his life about the "gap" created by Acton Hague. Stransom approaches this "human dilemma" like "a problem in aesthetic composition," "fussing" about the symmetry of the altar, or in the words of the text, "handling the empty shells and playing with the silence" (CT 9, 267). The problem is solved only by the "*dea ex machina*" of Mary Antrim. Even so, Krupnick offers a more positive reading of the conclusion than Honig, with Stransom realizing that his egotism has "kept him from an act of life." The artifice of the altar reveals also, Krupnick contends, the artifice of the tale, and affirms the "priority" of life to both kinds of art.

Superimposed, some would say, on such themes is what Putt calls the "silly tit-for-tat sub-plot" of Stransom's relationship with the woman (393). Others see it as integral. According to Frye, the story fails by the standards of realism, becomes a "tissue of improbable coincidence, inadequate motivation, and inconclusive resolution," but when regarded as a modern "ironic myth"—the "story of how the god of one person is the *pharmakos* [scapegoat] of another"—becomes "simple and logical" (42–43). Vaid also assigns the tale to a genre, the parable, which makes the coincidence if not equally significant, allowable (217). To McElderry, the coincidence with the "slow, deliberate development" of plot gives the tale "special depth" (117). James softened the coincidence, however, according to Gerlach, by deliberately incorporating the "surprise"—the woman's dedication of the candles to Hague—in the middle, so that the story emphasizes not the coincidence itself, but its "working out" (75). Ward still finds the plot device somewhat contrived, even while accepting the suitedness of action to idea, the woman's role fitting the message of forgiveness and acceptance (53–54). Stransom's relationship with the woman, records Sharp, is the "means" by which James "externalized" the tale's subject—Stransom's inner life (51). More fully, Frame imagines how James set out to "dramatize" a situation whose "appeal for him lay, not in the action that might develop from the situation, but in the situation itself." In his first notebook entry, Frame remarks, James "clearly . . .

had no idea of what to *do*" with his idea, and so failed at his first attempt to write the tale. The problem was that James lacked what he called an "adequate action"—a plot or "objective correlative" to turn the "private symbol" of the altar into a communicable idea. James, Frame conjectures, turned then to the traditional solution of "some sort of conflict." Frame looks past the woman to see the source of conflict as Stransom's hatred of Hague, the woman serving simply as his representative in the tale. This schema, Frame argues, allowed James to keep his original idea that the altar would be complete with the death of the founder, but also to create a "profound public meaning" in Stransom's forgiveness of Hague, by "embedding his original image in an action" (251–56).

Tanner separates the tale's theme of "remembrance" from the "actual narrative action" of Stransom's relationship with the woman (81). Many, however, praise the action as constituting a central, if second, theme. Fadiman values the woman's contribution, calling the tale a "love story" ending in a *Liebestod* (358–60; also Gage 21). Blackmur writes approvingly of how Stransom's "service of the altar" becomes "the service of each other" ([1942] 1983, 56). In Hartsock's reading, the second theme of love is an integral part of the first theme of death. The woman, she writes, is with Kate Creston one for whom Stransom "might be unfaithful to the memory of Mary Antrim." Together they find love—"genuine community fulfilling mutual need"—but deny it in their disagreement over Hague. Being separated from the woman and his dead teaches Stransom to choose "love and life" over "death and memory." This final lesson, Hartsock contends, even brings into question the "hasty earlier judgment" of Creston's remarriage (376–78). Pearce notes the irony of Stransom's discovery of a living woman at the same time he discovers a form to honor the "long-dead ideal woman," Mary, but argues that the living woman "produces a more passionate shaping and ordering of his tribute to the dead" (841).

In his reading of the "curious drama" of Stransom and the woman, Edel emphasizes the hostile, characterizing their relationship as the "power-struggle" of two people who share the same obsession and want final rights to its shaping. The woman, writes Edel, is "contrite at the last moment; but she may well be. For, finally, he has yielded, and she has her triumph. *She* has been unyielding" (CT 9, 11; *Life* 3, 383). So, of course, has Stransom, and both have come ready to yield to the other. Przybylowicz also sees in their relationship a "battle for power" (102). Sharp, too, stresses their conflict, but to a different effect. She acknowledges that Stransom, while more interested in himself than in the woman, is later able to recognize his alienation from her as too great a "privation," in the words of the text, not just for "the privation he bore," but also "the privation he inflicted." Still, if Strether fails in the "exploitation" of the woman, it is only because Hague got there first: his own selfishness is no "different in its motivation." The terminology remains that of combat; the woman makes an "effective antagonist" and Stransom becomes the only Jamesian confider "humiliated by a confidante who loves his enemy" (47–51).

Two other readings emphasize Stransom's possessiveness. Wright portrays Stransom as someone initially very like James, believing that "one lives the more intensely as he projects himself imaginatively into the minds of others, either the living or the dead." A tension becomes evident, however, in his strong reaction against the new Mrs. Creston. The death of Hague further interrupts the "lyric" of his imaginative memory. At first, Stransom looks at the woman simply as "confirmation of the validity of his religion," but then he begins to wonder about her as an individual, wanting to make her "disloyal" to her own dead for the sake of his. On his first visit to her home, we are told, he feels "at last in real possession of her." Stransom, of course, is at that point quickly disillusioned, but Wright sees the "daring shift in the perspective" in the last paragraph when we "enter the woman's mind," putting both Stransom and the reader in true "possession." Still, in all, Wright views Stransom's transformation from his original egotism a "great positive adventure" (211–19). To Bronfen, Stransom wants not simply to possess the past but "the dead." The nameless woman she sees as relatively powerless in the face of the absent dead named woman, Mary Antrim. She sees death resolving both Stransom's "ambivalent position" between the two, and his jealousy of Acton. His death allows him a new closer relationship with the nameless woman as he becomes her Muse (114–15).

Fadiman divides the plot even further, separating the subplot involving Acton Hague from the one involving the woman, and judging it inferior (358–60). Oppositely, Samuels finds the theme of Stransom's learning to forgive more admirable, but lost in the story's worship of the dead (74). To Gage, however, the story's themes of forgiveness, love, and death are braided close together (19–21). Certainly, the themes of Stransom's relationships with the woman and with Hague are. At the time of their quarrel, Stransom recognizes, "Acton Hague was between them, that was the essence of the matter; and he was never so much between them as when they were face to face" (CT 9, 263). Stephen Spender goes so far as to describe the tale's situation as "two people, typical Jamesian spectators, whose eyes are turned always to death, because the hero of the drama which they were watching has died before them" (28). Rebecca West presents Stransom's forgiving of Hague as a natural progression from his memorializing tendency, so that the candles he has already lit bring him to light the last one (100). Even those who point out his selfishness in his relationship with the woman tend to see his failure to acknowledge Hague as Stransom's fatal flaw. Her discovery of his failure produces, as Sharp and Vaid have observed, the only "scene" in the story (Sharp 49; Vaid 219). Appropriately enough, he learns from the woman herself, who has had to learn how to forgive (e.g., Hoffman 54; Wagenknecht

89). Hartsock objects, however, to Troy's implication that his forgiving Hague means he must "vaguely love the dead," stating that the problem here is "concrete," and that James disliked such "Whitman-like 'merging'" (377). Todorov also stresses the theme of forgiveness, seeing Stransom's failure to forgive Hague as giving the dead man control over the living. Still, Todorov sees the tale as affirming "the power of death, the presence of absence," with forgiveness serving to clear "the last barrier on the road to death" (165–67). In a second essay, Todorov accords less joyousness to Stransom's death, emphasizing instead the significance of the "presence" of the woman and their "relation" (188).

Todorov observes that at first, given the choice between Stransom and Hague, the woman chooses Hague (167). Such critics as Wright and Jones point out that the woman as well as Stransom is in ways selfish and needs to learn to forgive. Still, like most readers, they see her as morally superior (Wright 218; Jones 277). To Auchard, her superiority is evidenced by her "wordlessness." While both she and Stransom forgive Hague, the text records, "His forgiveness was silence, but hers was mere unuttered sound"—what Auchard calls "her more vibrant quietness" (41). Warminski offers a reading that also attests to the woman's superiority, but subordinates it to a context of recent controversies in literary criticism. In his view the story is a "text *about* the possibility of making a passage from text to history." The story announces the "death of the reader, the death of reading" or at least of a "certain kind." Its "entire itinerary," writes Warminski, is in the punning variations the title offers on "altar" and "alter" (the dead in the tale are "the *Others*"), on prepositions and their possessors that break down "the imposing, monumental figure of the altar." At first a "closed tropological system" with Stransom as its "total author and total reader," the altar is upset by his difference with the woman, her refusal, in the words of the text to "return to the old symbols" (CT 9, 263–64). As the "second reader," Warminski contends, she has disrupted the text by "a linguistic intention that is utterly outside the grasp of a self or a subject." The story itself is really two stories—and two economies—one in which "time, history, memory, narrative" redeem and one in which they do not. The tale is marked by zeugma, as Stransom and the woman worship "side by side"—"radically disjunct while indissolubly bound together." She is a "performative" or "grammatical" reader; Stransom a metaphorician. Stransom talks of "intentions," she speaks of a "spell." Even their conception of "zero" is different. In each of their many contrasts, Warminski portrays Stransom as inferior: his altar is the "product of a symbolic, metaphorical imagination," hers of an imagination "fetishistic, metonmyical, indeed allegorical." Further, in Warminski's view, by dedicating all the candles to Hague, the woman is dedicating the altar to Stransom's death *"as though he were already dead."* When Stransom tries "to re-aestheticize and re-historicize" the altar by aestheticizing her, he only "repeat[s]" Hague's mistreatment of her. By refusing to take her as "other," by seeing her only as a "a *man's* other," he leaves her out of the altar. In conclusion, Warminski asserts, just as her return to the "old symbols" is impossible, so is a return from "deconstruction" to "history." Such a return would be a "cover-up"—a "new and empty formalism." Unfortunately, however, for Warminski's reading, he omits the woman's final act, which is not to walk away from the altar but to return to it, telling Stransom, "the sense of our difference left me" (CT 9, 271).

The woman attributes her change of heart to "a miracle, the sweetest of miracles." Throughout, as Gale observes, the tale is marked by a religious imagery that creates an "almost allegorical tone and an occasional Biblical idiom" (53). The use of such Christian symbolism, in Frame's argument, gave James the necessary "enlargement" for his *donnée*. Hague's exclusion became the darkness of damnation, the altar the light of salvation (255–57). To Vaid, its "rich and refulgent images"—religious and secular—are its "mortar," and give it "the shape almost of an emblem and the tone almost of an incantation" (223). Many others, including Gerlach and Gale, have paid tribute to the sustaining effect of the tale's imagery, including, Gale notes, rare examples of Jamesian synesthesia, and what Edel repeatedly calls the tale's grand "organ tones" (Gerlach 88–89; Gale 178; Edel 1970, 353; *Life* 3, 282; CT 9, 10–11; also Hoffman 53; Troy 270). While critics stress the inspecificity of the tale (e.g., Vaid 217), it is solidly anchored in the "great grey suburb" of its church. The details are few, but they allow one to put together a picture of the woman's bleak life, and contrastingly, Stransom's life of public office, servants, and musical evenings at St. James. As both Vaid and Frame indicate, James also constructed his story carefully in a series of parallel and contrasting scenes (Vaid 216–19; Frame 258).

The story's mixture of vagueness and specificity is also reflected in people's analysis of the precise relationship between Stransom's worship of the dead and of conventional religion. In 1912 Gretton objected to Stransom's "purchasing the altar as a private preserve" and discerned in the tale an atmosphere more that of a parlor than a church. The religion of the tale he faulted as bereft of "community"—a flaw he suggested may have stemmed from James's Puritan heritage, with its emphasis on the individual conscience (508–10). Many years later, Graham Greene also saw James as inadequately informed. While sympathizing with James's desire of "something more living" to commemorate the dead than Anglican "marble monuments," he found the tale ultimately "ridiculous as well as beautiful, and it is ridiculous because James never understood that his desire to help the dead was not a personal passion, that it did not require secret subjective rites" (35). At the start of the tale, Stransom's cult of the dead is explicitly not that of conventional religion, "It was in the quiet sense of having saved his souls that his deep strange instinct rejoiced. This was no dim theological rescue, no boon of a contingent world; they were saved better than faith or works could save them, saved for the warm world they had shrunk from dying to, for actuality, for continuity, for the certainty of human remembrance" (CT 9, 267). The lack of a belief in a life after death is starkly illustrated when Stransom proclaims after the woman's defection, that in the case of his death, "What . . . would the Others matter to him, since they only mattered to the living?" (CT 9, 268). Still, at its conclusion the religious imagery of the tale is marked. Mary Antrim appears "from the glory of heaven"; Stransom says to the returning woman "God sent you!" and "God sent me too, I think" (CT 9, 270). Even so, most critics continue to find that for Stransom—who is, Troy declares, the "only one" of James's characters "to come face to face with the problem of religion"—the issues of religion remain "wholly without any theological cast" (270–72; also Edel CT 9, 11). Both Hoffman and Kaul depict a man in need not of God, but of symbol and ritual (Hoffman 54; Kaul 219; also Hartsock 375). Such, writes Gill, was to James a sufficient way of "assuaging the sense of loss and isolation" (23). Wagenknecht, however, deems James's lack of religion exaggerated, finding here a "deep and abiding sense of the sacred" (1948, 130; 1983, 259).

Other muddles remain. In the proper manner for Jamesian critics, they remain divided over whether Stransom is dead or alive at the end of the tale. On Stransom's face, we are told is the "whiteness of death" (CT 9, 271). Some, for instance, Gerlach, believe Stransom to be dead, while Krupnick is brave enough to specify a "fatal heart attack" (Gerlach 84; Krupnick 42). Others, such as Branch, see Stransom as fainting in a "foreshadowing of his impending death" (185). Vaid observes that *if* Stransom does die it is a fitting reward for his forgiveness of Hague (222). Hartsock, however, asserts that Stransom is not dead at the end of the tale, which concludes with "the marriage of minds of the two now re-committed to life" (376). There is also disagreement over the dedication of the last candle on the altar. Both Honig and Sharp see a misunderstanding at the heart of the final exchange, such that the woman mistakenly concedes to what she believes is Stransom's dying request that the "one more" be for himself (Honig 94–95; Sharp 50). Jones emphasizes the regret in its being "too late" for a living Stransom to give the last candle to Hague (277). The conflicting renunciations produce, according to Vaid, a candle for Hague, which, without additional conflict, can equally recognize Stransom (217–22, 227 n.5). To Frame, the meaning of the last "one more" is "unmistakable," the candle is to commemorate both men (255–56)

Krupnick in 1976 stated that "The Altar of the Dead" was "ignored and deserves to be resurrected" (37). Certainly, it has not been ignored, and despite the occasional bashing it has received, it also continues to be one of the most highly praised of James's stories. Wagenknecht, for example, has been consistent in his praise, calling it in 1948 one of James's two best tales and in 1984 his "most beautiful" (1948, 129; 1984, 85). The world it portrays, however, is far from beautiful. Even if one takes the most affirmative reading of the work's conclusion, and sees its two characters understanding each other, forgiven and forgiving, at the end, one is still left with a man with the "whiteness of death" and a woman "in great dread of what might still happen"—whether to him or to herself (CT 9, 271). The tale depicts the beauty of death, but also shows the difficulty of life. A talented, sensitive, beautiful woman is used and impoverished. An equally sensitive man—rich and well connected—is bereaved and betrayed. When the two finally admit each other to their private lives, they immediately clash. Certainly any triumph here will be hard won and rarefied. Remembering the forgotten Kate, however, Stransom thinks of how "the closed eyes of dead women could still live. . . . They had looks that remained, as great poets had quoted lines" (CT 9, 237). Gender roles aside, the story is about survival, the survival of remembrance. As such, the comfort it offers is limited. Discouraged with his first attempt at writing the tale, James wrote:

> *Plus je vais*, the more intensely it comes home to me that solidity of subject, importance, emotional capacity of subject, is the only thing on which, henceforth, it is of the slightest use for me to expend myself. Everything else breaks down, collapses, turns thin, turns poor, turns wretched—betrays one miserably. Only the fine, the large, the human, the natural, the fundamental, the passionate things. (CN 99)

The same in fiction as in life. James needed a living relationship to give life to his story of the dead. Stransom and the woman needed to pay tribute to the dead to live. "Finer flowers" do still bloom to carry on the "tradition of sensibility" through their "independent, intelligent zeal" (*Criticism* 2, 1249).

Works Cited

Primary Works

James, Henry. 1895. "The Altar of the Dead." *Terminations*. London: Heinemann; New York: Harper, 185–242.

———. 1909. "The Altar of the Dead." *The Novels and Tales of Henry James*. New York Edition. Vol. 17, 1–58. New York: Scribner's.

———. 1916. "The Altar of the Dead." *The Uniform Tales of Henry James*. London: Martin Secker.

———. 1969. *Henry James: Letters to A. C. Benson and Auguste Monod*. Ed. E. F. Benson. New York: Haskell House.

———. [1886] 1996. *The Bostonians*. Harmondsworth: Penguin.

Secondary Works

Allen, Elizabeth. 1984. *A Woman's Place in the Novels of Henry James*. New York: St. Martin's.

Anderson, Quentin. 1957. *The American Henry James*. New Brunswick, NJ: Rutgers University Press.

Anon. 1895. Review of *Terminations*. *Athenaeum* 35/29 (15 June): 769–70.

Anon. 1911. Review of *The Finer Grain*. *North American Review* (February): 302.

Auchard, John. 1986. *Silence in Henry James: The Heritage of Symbolism and Decadence*. University Park: Pennsylvania State University Press.

Auchincloss, Louis. 1975. *Reading Henry James*. Minneapolis: University of Minnesota Press.

Banta, Martha. 1972. *Henry James and the Occult: The Great Extension*. Bloomington: Indiana University Press.

———. 1964. "Henry James and 'The Others.'" *New England Quarterly* 37 (June):171–84.

Beerbohm, Max. 1930. "Jacobean and Shavian." In *Around Theatres*. New York: Knopf, 260–65, 323–26. Reprint. 1963. *Henry James: A Collection of Critical Essays*. Ed. Leon Edel, 18–26. Englewood Cliffs, NJ: Prentice-Hall.

Bender, Bert. 1976. "Henry James's Late Lyric Meditations upon the Mysteries of Fate and Self-Sacrifice." *Genre* 9, no. 3 (Fall): 247–62.

Blackmur, R. P. [1952] 1983. "*The Golden Bowl*." In *Studies in Henry James*. Ed. Veronica A. Makowsky, 221–42. New York: New Directions. Reprinted from *The Golden Bowl*. New York: Grove.

———. [1942] 1983. "*The Sacred Fount*." In *Studies in Henry James*. Ed. Veronica A. Makowsky, 45–68. New York: New Directions. Reprinted from *Kenyon Review* 4: 328–52.

Branch, Beverly. 1987. "François Truffaut and Henry James." In *Transformations: From Literature to Film*. Ed. Douglas Radcliff-Umstead, 184–89. Kent, OH: Kent State University Press.

Briggs, Julia. 1977. *Night Visitors: The Rise and Fall of the English Ghost Story*. London: Faber.

Bronfen, Elisabeth. "Dialogue with the Dead: The Deceased Beloved as Muse." *New Comparison* 6: 101–18.

Brooks, Van Wyck. 1925. *The Pilgrimage of Henry James*. New York: Dutton. Reprint. New York: Octagon, 1972.

Buitenhuis, Peter. 1970. *The Grasping Imagination: The American Writings of Henry James*. Toronto: University of Toronto Press.

Burleson, Donald R. 1986. "Symmetry in Henry James's 'Altar of the Dead.'" *Studies in Weird Fiction* 1, no. 1 (Summer): 29–32.

Cargill, Oscar. 1961. *The Novels of Henry James*. New York: Macmillan.

Cowdery, Lauren Tozek. 1986. *The Novelle of Henry James in Theory and Practice. Studies in Modern Literature* 47. Ann Arbor: UMI Research Press.

Dupee, F. W. [1951] 1956. *Henry James*. Garden City, NY: Doubleday Anchor.

Edel, Leon. 1989. "Henry James and the Performing Arts." *Henry James Review* 10: 105–11.

————, ed. 1970. *Henry James: Stories of the Supernatural*. New York: Taplinger.

————, ed. [1949] 1963. *The Ghostly Tales of Henry James*. New Brunswick, NJ: Rutgers University Press. Reprinted in part in Robert W. Stallman and Arthur Waldhon, eds., *American Literature: Readings and Critiques*, 637–38. New York: Putnam, 1961.

Edgar, Pelham. [1927] 1964. *Henry James, Man and Author*. New York: Russell & Russell.

Elton, Oliver. 1903. "The Novels of Mr. Henry James." *Quarterly Review* 198 (October): 358–79.

Fadiman, Clifton, ed. 1948. *The Short Stories of Henry James*. New York: Modern Library.

Fox, Hugh. 1968. *Henry James, A Critical Introduction*. Conesville, IA: John Westburg.

Frame, J. Douglas. 1973. "The Practice of Creativity: Henry James' Approach." *The English Quarterly* 6: 249–62.

Frye, Northrop. 1957. *Anatomy of Criticism: Four Essays*. Princeton: Princeton University Press.

Fussell, Edwin. 1958. "Henry James and 'The Common Doom.'" *American Quarterly* 10: 438–53.

Gage, Richard P. 1988. *Order and Design: Henry James' Titled Story Sequences*. New York: Peter Lang.

Gale, Robert L. [1954] 1964. *The Caught Image: Figurative Language in the Fiction of Henry James*. Chapel Hill: University of North Carolina Press.

Geismar, Maxwell. 1963. *Henry James and the Jacobites*. Boston: Houghton Mifflin.

Gerlach, John. 1985. *Toward the End: Closure and Structure in American Short Stories*. University: University of Alabama Press.

Gill, Richard. 1972. *Happy Rural Seat: The English Country House and the Literary Imagination*. New Haven: Yale University Press.

Goetz, William R. 1986. *Henry James and the Darkest Abyss of Romance*. Baton Rouge: Louisiana State University Press.

Greene, Graham. 1952. "Henry James: The Religious Aspect." In *The Lost Childhood and Other Essays*, 31–39. New York: Viking.

Gretton, M. Sterge. 1912. "Mr. Henry James and his Prefaces." *Contemporary* 101 (January): 69–78. Reprinted in *Henry James: The Critical Heritage*. Ed. Roger Gard, 503–12. London: Routledge & Kegan Paul.

Hartsock, Mildred E. 1974. "Dizzying Summit: James's 'The Altar of the Dead.'" *Studies in Short Fiction* 11 (Fall): 371–78.

Hoffman, Charles George. 1957. *The Short Novels of Henry James*. New York: Bookman.

Honig, Edwin. 1949. "The Merciful Fraud in Three Stories of Henry James." *The Tiger's Eye*, no. 9 (October): 83–96.

Hyde, H. Montgomery. 1969. *Henry James at Home*. New York: Farrar, Straus.

James, William. 1983. *The Correspondence of William James*. Vol. 2: *William and Henry: 1885–1896*. Ed. Ignas K. Skrupskelis and Elizabeth M. Berkeley. Charlottesville: University Press of Virginia.

Jones, Granville H. 1975. *Henry James's Psychology of Experience, Innocence, Responsibility, and Renunciation in the Fiction of Henry James*. The Hague: Mouton.

Kaul, R. K. 1989. "Henry James as an Art Critic." In Amritjit Singh and K. Ayyappa Paniker, eds., *The Magic Circle of Henry James: Essays in Honour of Darshan Singh Maini*, 210–23. New York: Envoy.

Krook, Dorothea. [1962] 1967. *The Ordeal of Consciousness in Henry James*. New York: Cambridge University Press.

Krupnik, Mark L. 1976. "Playing with the Silence: Henry James' Poetics of Loss." *Forum* (University of Houston) 13, no. 3: 37–42.

Leavis, F. R. 1947. "The Appreciation of Henry James." *Scrutiny* 14 (Spring): 229–37.

Leavis, Q. D. "Henry James: The Stories." *Scrutiny* 14 (Spring): 223–29. Reprinted in *Collected Essays*. Vol. 2: *The American Novel* and *Reflections of the European Novel*, ed. G. Singh, 177–84. Cambridge: Cambridge University Press.

Lebowitz, Naomi. 1965. *The Imagination of Loving: Henry James's Legacy to the Novel*. Detroit: Wayne State University Press.

McCarthy, Harold T. 1958. *Henry James: The Creative Process*. New York: Thomas Yoseloff.

McElderry, Bruce R., Jr. 1965. *Henry James*. New York: Twayne.

Macnaughton, William R. 1987. *Henry James: The Later Novels*. Boston: Twayne Publishers.

Markow-Totevy, Georges. 1969. *Henry James*. Trans. John Griffiths. London: Merlin.

Matthiessen, F. O. 1947. *The James Family: Including Selections from the Writings of Henry James, Sr., William, Henry, and Alice James*. New York: Knopf.

Nalbantian, Suzanne. 1983. *Seeds of Decadence in the Late Nineteenth-Century Novel: A Crisis in Values*. New York: St. Martin's.

Page, Norman, ed. 1984. *Henry James: Interviews and Recollections*. New York: St. Martin's.

Pearce, Howard. 1975. "Henry James's Pastoral Fallacy." *PMLA* 90: 834–47.

Perosa, Sergio. 1980. *Henry James and the Experimental Novel*. New York: New York University Press.

Przybylowicz, Donna. 1986. *Desire and Repression: The Dialectic of Self and Other in the Late Works of Henry James*. University: University of Alabama Press.

Putt, S. Gorley. 1966. *Henry James: A Reader's Guide*. Ithaca, NY: Cornell University Press.

Round, Richard. 1978. "Turning Points: Ruiz and Truffaut." *Sight & Sound*, no. 3 (Summer): 163–66.

Samuels, Charles Thomas. 1971. *The Ambiguity of Henry James*. Urbana: University of Illinois Press.

Segal, Ora. 1969. *The Lucid Reflector: The Observer in Henry James' Fiction*. New Haven: Yale University Press.

Sharp, Sister M. Corona. 1963. *The Confidante in Henry James: Evolution and Moral Value of a Fictive Character*. Notre Dame, IN: Notre Dame University Press.

Sicker, Philip. 1980. *Love and the Quest for Identity in the Fiction of Henry James*. Princeton: Princeton University Press.

Slabey, Robert M. 1958. "Henry James and 'The Most Impressive Convention in All History." *American Literature* 30 (March): 89–102.

Spender, Stephen. 1953. *The Destructive Element*. Philadelphia: Albert Saifer.

Stevenson, Elizabeth. [1949] 1981. *The Crooked Corridor: A Study of Henry James*. New York: Octagon.

Tanner, Tony. 1985. *Henry James: The Writer and His Work*. Amherst: University of Massachusetts Press.

Tate, Allen. 1950. "Three Commentaries: Poe, James, Joyce." *Sewanee Review* 58: 1–15. Reprint. 1950. In *The House of Fiction*. Ed. Caroline Gordon and Allen Tate. New York: Scribner's, 1972. In *Critics on Henry James*. Ed. J. Don Vann, 75–78. Coral Gables: University of Miami Press.

Thorberg, Raymond. 1967. "Terror Made Relevant: James's Ghost Stories." *Dalhousie Review* 47 (Summer): 185–91.

Thorp, Willard, ed. 1962. *The Turn of the Screw and Other Short Novels*. New York: New American Library, Signet Classic.

Tintner, Adeline R. 1986. *The Museum World of Henry James*. Ann Arbor: UMI Research Press.

———. 1980. "Truffaut's La Chambre verte: Homage to Henry James." *Literature/Film Quarterly* 8:78–83.

Todorov, Tzvetan. 1977. *The Poetics of Prose*. Trans. Richard Howard. Ithaca, NY: Cornell University Press.

Troy, William. [1943] 1945. "The Altar of Henry James." In *The Question of Henry James*. Ed. F. W. Dupee, 267–72. New York: Henry Holt. Reprinted from *New Republic* 108 (15 February): 228–30.

Vaid, Krishna B. 1964. *Technique in the Tales of Henry James*. Cambridge, MA: Harvard University Press.

Wagenknecht, Edward. 1984. *The Tales of Henry James*. New York: Frederick Ungar.

———. 1983. *The Novels of Henry James*. New York: Frederick Ungar.

———. 1948. "Our Contemporary Henry James." *College English* 10: 123–32.

Ward, Joseph A. 1967. *The Search for Form: Studies in the Structure of James's Fiction*. Chapel Hill: University of North Carolina Press.

Warminski, Andrzej. 1988. "Reading over Endless Histories: Henry James's *Altar of the Dead*." *Yale French Studies* 74: 261–84.

West, Rebecca. [pseud].1916. *Henry James*. London: Nisbet.

Wright, Walter F. 1962. *The Madness of Art: A Study of Henry James*. Lincoln: University of Nebraska Press.

Zabel, Morton Dauwen. 1958. Introduction. *Henry James: In the Cage and Other Tales*. Garden City, NY: Doubleday. Reprinted in *American Literature: Readings and Critiques*. Ed. Robert W. Stallman and Arthur Waldhon, 638. New York: Putnam, 1961.

Foreign Language
Poulet, Georges. 1961. *Les Métamorphoses du cercle*. Paris: Plon.

At Isella

Publication History

"At Isella" appeared in the August 1871 issue of *Galaxy,* "horribly printed," as James wrote his friend Grace Norton (Adams 10). John Adams has compiled the twenty-five typographical errors that so offended James. James never reprinted the tale, although it was posthumously printed, errors intact, by Mordell in *Travelling Companions.* One of the omissions from Lubbock's edition of James's *Novels and Stories*, it was next issued as "The Runaway Wife" by Little Blue Books of Girard, Kansas, in 1931.

Circumstances of Composition, Sources, and Influences

Given that James himself stayed at Isella where he saw Italy for the first time "before me warm and living and palpable," it is natural that critics have noted the autobiographical parallels (*Letters* 1, 128). Opinions of them range from Levy's view that the narrator is "transparently James himself" to Slabey's view that the character is only "revealing" of James's ideas (Levy 22; Slabey 91; also Delbaere-Garant 31). Adams, in particular, describes the story as "deeply personal" and cites James's letter to his brother describing his trip across the Alpine Simplon Pass from Switzerland to Italy—the same route the narrator follows—when he "communed with immensity and sniffed Italy from afar" (10). James himself described the tale as "the fruit of a vague desire to reproduce a remembered impression and mood of mine" (*Letters* 1, 258).

Kelley describes how James draws on Mérimée in this tale and other contemporary tales of travel in selecting an "incident" that shows the character of the country visited with the change that in Mérimée the incident is primary, while James subordinates it to description (112). One might also point out the example of Howells, who used travel writing as a bridge into fiction. As James wrote, "At the time, I wanted something to happen; I have improved on vulgar experience by supposing that something *did*," although he adds it is "not much" (*Letters* 1, 259).

While James spoke of the Italian woman to Grace Norton as a "gross fit," the narrator more romantically describes her as "the heroine of all my stories," and the numerous allusions he invokes in connection with her and her environment have attracted much attention (*Letters* 1, 259). As Delbaere-Garant points out, the dinner itself puts the narrator in mind of the French stage (31). Kenton draws attention to the fitting nature of the dinner time discussion of Dumas (12). The tone is generally theatrical. The heroine reminds the narrator of Andromeda, Lucrezia Borgia, Bianca Capello, and the heroines of Stendhal. Kelley agrees with the narrator, calling the woman "in truth, a heroine from Stendhal," noting that unlike a George Sand heroine, she does not allow her reason to interfere with her passion (116). Wagenknecht, on the other hand, finds the numerous associations "faintly absurd," casting doubt on the likelihood that such a woman would confide so fully in a new acquaintance (178).

Relation to Other Works.

The most frequent comparisons are with its near contemporaries that also feature Americans traveling in Europe. Levy remarks on the link with "A Passionate Pilgrim," which Stone is unusual in finding inferior to the Italian story (Levy 22; Stone 189). Kraft and Kelly link "At Isella" with both "A Passionate Pilgrim" and "Travelling Companions," according to what Kraft calls their "preoccupation" with foreign travel (Kraft 37; Kelley 112). Quentin Anderson links the two Italian tales with "Adina" in their portrayal of the "dangerous incompleteness" of the Americans' pursuit of the "picturesque" abroad (150). Kelley adds a distinction, seeing James as depicting in "Travelling Companions" the Italy travelers usually see of art and religion, and in "At Isella" the inside Italy "of romance, of passion, of life." She notes, however, that both sides are necessary for an accurate view (115–16).

Looking ahead, Levy locates in the story "the opening of the Jamesian subject," the innocently eager American on his self-proclaimed "pilgrimage" to Europe admitted to its rich life as represented in a woman, in a manner prefiguring Strether's encounter of Madame de Vionnet, and so encountering the same issues of evil and innocence (22–23). Wegelin notes the Italian woman as an early example of the Jamesian heroine's clash with the "established order" seen throughout his career up to such late works as *The Outcry* of 1911 (58). Maves sees the enthusiasm for Italy repeated in Theobald of "The Madonna of the Future," Roderick Hudson, and the narrator of *The Aspern Papers*. The romance of Italy associated here with life Maves sees shifting to an association with death in *The Wings of the Dove* (91, 111).

Walter Wright finds it the first of several traditional romances James wrote depicting love's escape from tyrannous control, later examples including "Gabrielle de Bergerac," "Adina," and "The Sweetheart of M. Briseux" (126). (See also "Travelling Companions.")

Interpretation and Criticism

Readings of the story generally focus first on James's lengthy opening description. Buitenhuis, for example, calls "At Isella" and "Travelling Companions" "merely extensive travelogues" (46). Still, critics also pay tribute to the general euphoria of the tale. Putt comments on the "*joie de vivre*" exhibited in the story's "eloquent mock-hyperbole," typical of the early James (41). McElderry sees the narrator as identifying himself "with romantic Europe" and notes the pleasure evident in James's descriptions (1965, 31; 1949, 289). So too Kelley, who judges that the European setting gave James's writing a valuable new "spontaneity" (112). While Churchill sees no change, Kelley finds that the narrator "*feels* Italy, even on its threshold, in a far intenser way than his predecessors," indeed he even "meets it" in the form of the woman (Churchill 158; Kelley 116).

Lanzinger finds the narrator disillusioned in his experience of an Italy that would force a woman into a marriage she does not want (139–40). Nathalia Wright, while she notes that the encounter with the woman "causes him to revise some of his preconceptions" of Italy, still keeps the focus on the "association of romantic love with Italy." In her reading, it is present not only in his experience of helping the woman escape her marriage, but in his being on route to meet *his* fiancée, whom he expects to marry in Rome (221). Andreas sees the incident as indicating James's loyalty to individual fulfillment over strict morality (69). Peterson finds the narrator learning less, and notes that the Italian characters are pleased to fall in with the narrator's romantic preconceptions of their country (144 n.27). Maves, similarly, sees the narrator's encounter with romance resulting from the narrator's insistence on seeing in Italy romance and drama, so that his experience comfirms rather than revises any of his preconceptions. Maves judges the story like its narrator overly theatrical and almost comic in its naive devotion to romance (19–24). Donald Stone notes the rather ironic contrast, typical of James's early stories, between the American "hungry for experience and art" and the European, who, already having both, longs for "simplicity and nature" (189). In that sense, both the narrator and the Signorina find in their encounter what they are looking for.

Works Cited

Primary Works
James, Henry. 1871. "At Isella." *Galaxy* (August): 248–55.

———. 1919. "At Isella." *Travelling Companions*. Foreword by Albert Mordell. New York: Boni and Liveright.

―――. 1931. "The Runaway Wife." Little Blue Book 1673. Girard, KS: Haldeman-Julius.

Secondary Works

Adams, John R. 1943. "At Isella: Some Horrible Printing Corrected." *Mark Twain Quarterly* 5 (Spring): 10, 23.

Anderson, Quentin. 1957. *The American Henry James*. New Brunswick, NJ: Rutgers University Press.

Andreas, Osborn. 1948. *Henry James and the Expanding Horizon: A Study of the Meaning and Basic Themes of James's Fiction*. Seattle: University of Washington Press.

Buitenhuis, Peter. 1970. *The Grasping Imagination: The American Writings of Henry James*. Toronto: University of Toronto Press.

Churchill, Kenneth. 1980. *Italy and English Literature, 1764–1930*. Totowa, NJ: Barnes & Noble.

Delbaere-Garant, Jeanne. 1970. *Henry James: The Vision of France*. Paris: Société d'Editions Les Belles Lettres.

Edel, Leon. 1960. *Henry James*. University of Minnesota Pamphlets on American Writers 4. Minneapolis: University of Minnesota Press.

Kelley, Cornelia Pulsifer. [1930] 1965. *The Early Development of Henry James*. Urbana: University of Illinois Press.

Kenton, Edna, ed. 1950. *Eight Uncollected Tales of Henry James*. New Brunswick, NJ: Rutgers University Press.

Kraft, James. 1969. *The Early Tales of Henry James*. Carbondale: Southern Illinois University Press.

Lanzinger, Klaus. 1989. *Jason's Voyage: The Search for the Old World in American Literature: A Study of Melville, Hawthorne, Henry James, and Thomas Wolfe*. New York: Peter Lang.

Levy, Leo B. 1957. *Versions of Melodrama: A Study of the Fiction and Drama of Henry James, 1865–1897*. Berkeley: University of California Press.

McElderry, Bruce R., Jr. 1965. *Henry James*. New York: Twayne.

―――. 1949. "The Uncollected Stories of Henry James." *American Literature* 21 (November): 279–91.

Maves, Carl. 1973. *Sensuous Pessimism: Italy in the Works of Henry James*. Bloomington: Indiana University Press.

Peterson, Dale E. 1975. *The Clement Vision: Poetic Realism in Turgenev and James*. Port Washington, NY: Kennikat.

Putt, S. Gorley. 1966. *Henry James: A Reader's Guide*. Ithaca, NY: Cornell University Press.

Slabey, Robert M. 1958. "Henry James and the Most Impressive Convention in All History." *American Literature* 30 (March): 89–102.

Stone, Donald David. 1972. *Novelists in a Changing World: Meredith, James, and the Transformation of English Fiction in the 1880's*. Cambridge, MA: Harvard University Press.

Wagenknecht, Edward. 1984. *The Tales of Henry James*. New York: Frederick Ungar.

Wegelin, Christof. 1958. *The Image of Europe in Henry James*. Dallas: Southern Methodist University Press.

Wright, Nathalia. 1965. *American Novelists in Italy, The Discoverers: Allston to James*. Philadelphia: University of Pennsylvania Press.

Wright, Walter F. 1962. *The Madness of Art: A Study of Henry James*. Lincoln: University of Nebraska Press.

The Author of Beltraffio

Publication History

"The Author of Beltraffio" was the first of five stories James published in Macmillan's new *English Illustrated Magazine*, where it appeared in the June–July issues of 1884. The next year it appeared both in America as the title story of a collection of mostly recent tales, as well as in England as the newest of the *Stories Revived*. James featured it again as the lead story in volume 16 of the New York Edition.

Circumstances of Composition, Sources, and Influences

In April 1883, James wrote the publisher James R. Osgood, recounting two possible plots for stories he had discussed with Richard Gilder, editor of the *Century*. One was for "The Impressions of a Cousin," the other "an episode in the lives of a group of contemporary 'aesthetes.'" James continued:

> [It] briefly, is the history of an American aesthete (or possibly an English one), who conceives a violent admiration for a French aesthete (a contemporary novelist), and goes to Paris to make his acquaintance; where he finds that his Frenchman is so much more thoroughgoing a speci-

men of the day than himself, that he is appalled and returns to
Philistinism. Or else (I haven't settled it) he is to discover that the
Frenchman who is so Swinburnian in his writings, is a regular quiet
bourgeois in his life; which operates upon the aesthete as a terrible disillusionment. I may add that there will be a woman in the case. The idea
of the thing is to show a contrast between the modern aesthete, who
poses for artistic feelings, but is very hollow, and the real artist—who is
immensely different. (*Letters* 2, 414)

The plot has not been connected with "The Author of Beltraffio," but it has
many of its elements, the visit of the young admirer, the international contrast, the clash between aestheticism and Philistinism on one hand and true
art on the other, the quiet life of Ambient, the "woman in the case."

Within a year, however, James had a new element to add, Edmund Gosse's
description of the "extreme and somewhat hysterical aestheticism" of the
writer J. A. Symonds and his wife's disapproval of his "immoral, pagan, hyper-
aesthetic" books. In his notebook James projected the wife's disapproval as
the cause for the extreme form of her husband's aestheticism and chose the
effect on a child to examine the force of the contrast. He first imagined a
debate over the future of the child but then turned to the idea of the child's
dying a "victim" of the "heavy pressures" of his parents' disagreement
(Symonds had a sickly daughter). The mother's realization that the father
does not believe he will meet the child after death is the final stimulus to her
allowing him to die. Not wanting to show the child's death, James settled on
a narrator who "guesses" the secret. Despite judging it "very probably too
gruesome," James continued with the tale, "for the general idea is full of
interest and very typical of certain modern situations" (CN 25–26).

In his preface James recounts the discussion with a friend "of an eminent
author, these several years dead." The friend told him of "some of the embarrassments" of the author's life and of his "character," concluding, "Add to
them all, moreover, that his wife objects intensely to what he writes. She
can't bear it (as you can for that matter rather easily conceive) and that naturally creates a tension —!" "*There,*" recalled James, "had come the air-blown
grain which, lodged in a handful of kindly earth, was to produce the story of
Mark Ambient." All that was left for James to do was "Dramatise it, dramatise
it!" (*Criticism* 2, 1241).

The friend who provided him with the germ, Gosse, would later write
James to praise the tale. James, although pleased, responded that he was
confused by his statement that he had "divined the innermost cause" of
Symonds's "discomfort." Declaring himself "devoured with curiosity as to this
further revelation" that Gosse had spotted on page 571, James signed himself
"the perhaps-already-too-indiscreet—H.J." The contents of Gosse's answer, if
any, are not known (*Selected Letters* 32). Edel proposes as the indicated passage one in which the narrator writes, "I saw that in his books he had only

said half of his thought, and what he had kept back—from motives that I deplored when I learnt them later—was the richer part. It was his fortune to shock a great many people, but there was not a grain of bravado in his pages" (*Life* 4, 126).

Others saw Symonds in Ambient, as James was aware (Hyde 49). In February 1885, defending himself against charges of having satirized Elizabeth Peabody in *The Bostonians*, James added that "The Author of Beltraffio" was generally held to be "a living and scandalous portrait of J. A. Symonds and his wife, whom I have never seen" (*Letters* 3, 71). The "whom" may be intended to refer merely to Symonds's wife. Nevertheless, James's assertions that he did not know Symonds or "the innermost cause" of Symonds's "discomfort" have been challenged by modern critics. The issue is significant as the chief cause of Symonds's marital problems was most probably his homosexuality, a characteristic known to a small group of sympathizers including Gosse.

There is little direct evidence of James's awareness: it was seven years later that Gosse loaned James a copy of Symonds's *A Problem in Modern Ethics* (1891) on homosexuality. Calling Symonds "the Gladstone of the affair," James found the work "remarkable," even gallant, but regrettably lacking in humor (Moore 90). In 1969 Edel accepted the chronology that James learned of Symonds's homosexuality only after writing the tale, but later charged that his defense was disingenuous, asserting that James had met Symonds once in 1877 and had learned much of him from Gosse (*Life* 4, 125–27; *Letters* 3, 72; *Letters* 3, 29–31; CN 25 n.1). Moore states that Gosse had "suggested something" of Symonds's homosexuality, but offers no evidence apart from Edel (32). Wagenknecht also argues that James probably knew of Symonds's homosexuality, although he does not think James used the information in his depiction of Ambient (28–29). After James had learned of Symonds's homosexuality, he was not entirely comfortable with it, at least in public. Offered the opportunity to write a biographical essay on Symonds after his death in 1893, James declined, indicating that he found a "whole side" of Symonds "strangely morbid and hysterical," and that to write of him "without dealing with it, or at least looking at it, would be an affectation; and yet to deal with it either ironically or explicity would be a Problem—a problem beyond me" (*Life* 4, 127–28).

Tintner considers the possibility that James was aware of Symonds's homosexuality and made it part of the tale, casting the "other great man, the one in America" who gives the narrator his letter of introduction to Ambient as Whitman, indicating that the narrator as a friend of Whitman's is also probably homosexual (1987, 139). Discussing Whitman in the context of the literary history of homosexuality, Moon places Dolcino as an "abject boy" in the tradition of "male-purity" discourse that began in America in the nineteenth century (259). Conley also sees a "homerotic center" to the tale, but one less indebted to Symonds. Citing Perrot's reading, he notes that James in his reading of Vasari and Jean-Paul Richter's *Literary Works of Leonardo da Vinci*, would have learned of Leonardo's "preferred apprentice" Boltraffio. Leonardo thus becomes Ambient, and the beloved Boltraffio becomes Dolcino (220–21).

James was unaware of Symonds's sexuality, according to Putt, who charges that the omission of such a "credible" motive for the wife's hatred falsifies the basic situation (218). Tintner in part concurs, but also reminds us that in the notebook Symonds's "hysterical aestheticism" was considered "sufficient reason" for her dislike (1989, 138–40). Similarly, Bass speaks of the Symonds sources as simply an indication of James's "uneasy but real" relationship with aestheticism (114 n.6). James's correspondence with Symonds focused on Italy. James sent Symonds, whose most noted work was *Renaissance in Italy*, his own 1882 essay "Venice." Symonds wrote back praising the work and James wrote his thanks, in return, in February 1884, just a month before recording the germ of the tale. Gardaphe points to James's long stay in Italy in 1881, and his publication of *Portraits of Places,* which includes descriptions of Tuscany, the scene of Ambient's *Beltraffio*, in order to read the "certain modern situations" James is attempting to describe here as the influence of a foreign country on the artist (124–25).

The reference in the preface to the "eminent author, these several years dead" was also taken, before the publication of the notebooks, to refer to Robert Louis Stevenson (N 58–59; Matthiessen 1944, "Portrait," 2). Indeed, ironically or perhaps significantly, this may be due to an essay on James by his original informant. In the essay, Gosse discusses on the same page James's friendship with Stevenson, and James's method of transforming a raw idea into a story. Giving an example of the latter, he writes, "After thirty-five years I may confess that this extraordinarily vivid story was woven around a dark incident in the private life of an eminent author known to us both, which I, having told Henry James in a moment of levity, was presently horrified and even sensibly alarmed to see thus pinnacled in the broad light of day" (30). The close association is taken by Richardson as Gosse's identification of Ambient with Stevenson (xl). Hellman also cites the Gosse essay to link the two authors, similar in their appearance and aesthetics. In particular, he sees Stevenson's wife's demand that he burn the manuscript of a book about an "immoral" woman translated into the death of the child (340–43).

Symonds and Stevenson are not the only authors who have been discussed as sources for the aesthetic Ambient. "Pre-Raphaelite but not quite Yellow Book," he is, in Geismar's view, "almost a fusion" of several writers including Stevenson, Wilde, Swinburne, and Pater (57). Matheson and Kermode have also noted in the tale's aestheticism what Kermode calls a "dangerously Paterian air" (Matheson 223; Kermode 14). Matthiessen, too, sees Ambient as closest to Pater, and argues that James was hampered in writing the tale because of his uncertainty at the time as to how much of the "aesthetic gospel" he himself believed, the "excesses" of which are satirized in the sister. He, however, like Horne, notes the similarity between Ambient's rejection of the "smoothed . . . down and tucked . . . in" to James's demand for literature to reproduce the "impression of life itself" (Horne 41; Matthiessen 1944, "Portrait," 2–3). Neff points to a dramatist Mark Ambient, born 1860, as a possible source for the name, not the character, of James's writer (14).

Ambient's "foreign air" and velvet coat are to Rebecca West signs of a suspect affectation— one might recall that the sham sculptor in "The Tree of Knowledge" dressed similarly. Despite her initial surprise at James's attention to the aesthetes descended from Leigh Hunt and Ruskin and "given the middle-class touch by Oscar Wilde," she recalls also the significance of the value they accorded the written word in an England not very interested in beauty (78–82). Even so, Pound objects that the portrayal of Ambient is unrealistic in that English novelists then paid no attention to foreign literature (23). The problem of the "morality of art" here, Roditi asserts, is "much the same" in Wilde's *Pen, Pencil, and Poison* (54). To Knox, Mrs. Ambient resembles Wilde's Salome in the exaggerated depiction of her deadliness (225). Winner, however, places Ambient with the Pre-Raphaelites, the first generation of British aestheticism, not with the second generation of Wilde (46, 180 n.10; also Wagenknecht 28).

Grover looks to the continent to show James in sympathy with much of the "L'Art pour l'Art" movement, tracing the tale's image of the golden vessel to Gautier, and calling Flaubertian both Ambient's exclamation against the "hatred of art . . . of literature!" and his theory that "The greatest morality . . . lies in the perfect rendering of the fullest possible human experience" (137–39). Similarly, Tremper finds Ambient in appearance a composite of the writers in Flaubert's circle whom James had met in 1884, including Zola and Daudet. His philosophy she sees reflecting the addition of James's own aestheticism to their more "narrow" version (12–13, 16). Pickering, too, pictures James as a supporter at the time of the realism of the French naturalists, whose revolt against convention, Geismar comments, makes that of Ambient and his real-life counterparts appear "rather subdued" (Pickering 178; Geismar 57).

Donald Stone places the tale in the context of critical attacks on James that made him defensive about his artistic views. An 1882 essay by Howells had helped to identify James with the "new" school of fiction that Besant castigated in his 1884 essay on "Fiction as One of the Fine Arts." James would write "The Art of Fiction" in response to Besant, and Stone sees James practicing some of his arguments here, both the lament against the "hatred of art" and the effort of art to catch life's "peculiar trick" (241; also Tremper 13; Gardaphe 122). Mottram finds some of the story's ideas in a different essay, by James's father, "Socialism and Civilization" (167).

Pickering also links the tale to "The Art of Fiction." In his interpretation James wrote "The Author of Beltraffio" as his first response to Besant, who had argued for a "conscious moral purpose" in art, giving Besant's view to Beatrice, and his own to Ambient. Dolcino symbolizes the novel itself, which the Philistine British would rather see dead than impure. The aestheticism of Symonds is represented, according to Pickering, not by Ambient, but by the American narrator. At the same time he sees the narrator's visit to Ambient as based on James's meeting with the equally dedicated and "energetic" artist William Morris, with Ambient's sister Gwendolen based on Morris's wife. Jane Morris, Pickering points out, caused James to wonder if she were "an original or a copy," even as the narrator concludes that Gwendolen is "the inevitable imitation" of her "original" brother. Ambient's wife, on the other hand, is a Reynolds, an exhibition of whose paintings James had recently attended with John Singer Sargent. Beatrice, Besant, and Reynolds are thus set off as defenders of formalism and morality against Ambient, James, and the Pre-Raphaelites, "champions of realism," to form the story's basic contrast. McCarthy, on the other hand, who also links Gwendolen and Jane Morris, sees her character as satiric (157; also Berland 32 n.41). In Horne's phrase, she is a "pseudo-Raphaelite" (137). Wirth-Nesher even suggests an echo of the actress Nell Gwynn in her character (125)

Other critics have associated Ambient's views on art with those of James. Geismar and Walter Anderson both note in the two authors the same "passion for form," Anderson adding resemblances in their lack of popularity and their contempt for critics and the public (Geismar 59; Anderson 1981–82, 620; 1982, 528). Edgar, however, noting Ambient's dissatisfaction with his "smoothed . . . down" works, finds it opposite to James's shaping of facts from germ to story as discussed in the prefaces to *The Spoils of Poynton* and *The Aspern Papers* (173). Citing the same passage, Swan points to James's late work as showing an even greater formalism, one that Swan contends was justified as necessary to James's vision (9). One of the reasons for the conflicting views of Ambient and James may be that both are, at the time of the tale, in a moment of transition from one kind of work to another. Walter Anderson argues for an even greater complexity by maintaining that the seeming improbability of such a melodramatic plot in a work that avows a devotion to "the purest distillation of the actual" may be explained by the way Mrs. Ambient's "moral revulsion" at her husband's subject matter indicates James's own uneasiness with the "shocking" subjects hidden beneath his own elegant style (1982, 528–29).

Similarities have also been noted between James and the narrator, particularly in his response to England. The narrator sees everything in England "*as* if they were reproductions of something that existed primarily in art or literature. It was not the picture, the poem, the fictive page, that seemed to me a copy; these things were the originals, and the life of happy and distinguished people was fashioned in their image" (CT 5, 307). Early on, Kelley described James as seeing Europe first in just this way, and it is one of the passages in James that has taken on a life of its own (111). Buitenhuis, for example, places it alongside James's description in his autobiography of England's fitting "with a romantic rightness that had the force of a revelation" the vision of England that he had derived from its pictures and prose (45). Others have also seen the passage as speaking for James, including Asthana and Przybylowicz, who both note in it James's habit of giving the superior place to art over life (Asthana 95; Przybylowicz 50; also Putt 61). Donald Stone finds the attitude connecting the narrator's view more to those of Whistler and Wilde, who found life interesting only as it reflected art (240). Pound also questions the narrator's tone, asking whether admirers of art at that time did "gush up to this extent" (23).

The description of the Philistines' hatred of art Pound finds more accurate, comparing literature at the time to science ". . . in the days of Galileo and the Inquisition" (25). In the tale, attitudes to art are often illustrated by painters. Gale notes the preponderance of images of painting over fiction in the work (124). Mrs. Ambient is compared to a Gainsborough, a Reynolds, a Romney, and a Lawrence, painters Segal notes whom James considered "deeply English," but not Wagenknecht remarks, Philistine, as her behavior suggests. He notes, too, the "distinguished literary tradition" behind her view that art should have a "purpose" (Segal 116 n.13; Wagenknecht 29). In a manner similar to Pickering, Tintner sees the tale as containing two opposing portraits: that of Mrs. Ambient, a general type, but perhaps most closely akin to Reynolds's portrait of the Countess of Pembroke and her son; and Miss Ambient, a "composite Rossetti" most reminiscent of Jane Morris. She notes as well allusions to specific Pre-Raphaelite landscapes and a general criticism of their attempt to render all life artistic. Both the classic beauty of the old English school, and the Pre-Raphaelite "preoccupation" with art, are in this story, according to Tintner, shown to be misleading (1986, 51–55).

Mrs. Ambient's given name is itself rich in associations. Beatrice inspired the poet in Dante, killed an abusive father in Shelley, unwittingly poisoned a lover in Hawthorne. Its Italianate associations fit well with Ambient's Italianate art, but not, in Segal's view, with Beatrice's character (121). Gardaphe similarly finds the allusion to Dante ironic, as Mrs. Ambient is anything but an inspiration to her husband and insistently English in a way that complicates the tale's view of Italy. It is Miss Ambient with her affected Italian allusions of dress and manner who most suggests Italy, he argues, and he remarks that Beatrice is the only character to use her English given name, Gwendolen, perhaps as a way of calling her back to reality (125–26). Edel and Shine both compare Mrs. Ambient to Medea, who killed her children to spite their father, Edel finding her reflecting James's "deepest fear of women" in her ability to kill all a man creates, in art and life (Life 3, 143; Life 2, 346; CT 5, 11; Shine 74). Mrs. Ambient also resembles, according to Tintner, a Botticelli madonna that Pater called "peevish looking," and of whom James wrote in 1874, "Such a melancholy mother as this of Botticelli would have strangled her baby in its cradle to rescue it from the future." She detects further associations with the Italian Renaissance and Pater in Beatrice's name, noting that Botticelli illustrated Dante; in the Renaissance artist Boltraffio whose *Virgin and Child* was in the National Gallery; and in the invocation of Dürer's *Melancholia*, which Pater compared to the Mona Lisa. She sees all these allusions contributing to the tale of an unfortunate encounter of a mother who would kill her child to save it and an art-struck narrator who, believing her and her child to be works of art and so inherently sympathetic to the aesthetic view of life, creates a disaster (1987, 150–55). Curtsinger also casts Mrs. Ambient as a Boltraffio madonna, but one in Milan who wears a black ribbon even as Beatrice does (62–63).

Shortly after referring to Scott's *Quentin Durward*, the narrator calls Ambient's house a "palace of art," an allusion to Tennyson noted by Kermode (448 n.9). Ross notes that Ambient talks of Browning and Balzac, both early enthusiasms of James (26). Tintner considers both, with their interest in aberrant psychology, part of the "decadent" atmosphere of the tale (1987, 266–67). Bewley, however, places the tale in the context of Hawthorne's concerns with the morality of the author which he finds far more anxious than James's. Still, he sees Dolcino in more danger than the victims of the artistic Ethan Brand (222–23).

A possible influence proposed by Edward Stone is the novel *Mose Evans* by William Mumford Baker, serialized in the *Atlantic Monthly* in 1874. Including allusions to Medea and Beatrice as well as a blundering narrator, it tells of a woman who from religious zeal so hated the books her husband read that she raised her jealously-guarded child as an illiterate (43–52).

A possible allegorical reading is suggested by Gardaphe that makes the narrator the snake who enters the Ambient's garden paradise and leads Mrs. Ambient to taste the knowledge that kills. His reading emphasizes the allusion in Ambient's first name to the gospel writer Mark, noted for his realism, a realism, Gardaphe contends, that Ambient is still working toward (123–25). As he regards his progress, Ambient reworks the classic line ars longa vita breva in his complaint that "life is really too short for art" (CT 5, 333).

Looking ahead, Goodman points to parallels between the victimized children in "The Author of Beltraffio," *The Pupil,* and D. H. Lawrence's stories "The Rocking-Horse Winner" and "England, My England." She pairs particularly this tale and "England, My England," noting the "Edenic" English setting, the artistic men, their upper-class wives, and the golden children who contribute to the marital battle, and suffer accordingly. Matheson finds the characters here larger than life, and Ambient in particular following Shaw's definition of the "man of genius" "manifesting the Life Force in its enlightening process," while Mrs. Ambient represents the contrasting "moral attitude" (224). Tintner sees the tale as providing the basis for Philip Roth's *The Ghost Writer*, with its story of a young writer eagerly setting off to visit his hero at his secluded country home only to become involved in a distressing domestic incident (1981).

Relation to Other Works

In the phrasing of Edel, "The Author of Beltraffio" is James's first foray into the "fantastic-gruesome" (CT 5, 11). The victim of the journey, Dolcino, has a good amount of company among other Jamesian children. In her discussion of "sacrificed" children, Shine also includes Verena of *The Bostonians*, Hyacinth of *The Princess Casamassima*, Effie of *The Other House*, Nanda of *The Awkward Age*, the children in "My Friend Bingham" and "A Problem," and the heroine of *In the Cage*, all in contrast to the cherished Principino of *The Golden Bowl* (29–30, 75, 110; see also Knights 28). Such interest in the deaths of children Putt objects to as "sadistic" (215). Rahv finds in the story's depiction of childhood innocence being used as "the precipitant of the corrupt and sinister" a kinship between Dolcino, Pansy in *The Portrait of a Lady*, Maisie, Morgan of *The Pupil*, and Miles and Flora of *The Turn of the Screw* (416). Edel observes that it is the boys who die, Dolcino, Miles, Morgan, and Owen Wingrave, unlike Flora and Maisie (*Life* 4, 207). Jones sees Pansy like Morgan and Dolcino appearing "too pure to live," but notes that, unlike them, her case is not settled at the end (28). Edel links not only the children, but the deadly women who sacrifice them, in *The Pupil*, *The Other House*, and *The Turn of the Screw* and here (*Life* 3, 144; CT 5, 11; also Jones 16). Segal points particularly to the kinship between the wife and the governess in the "moral pressure" they exert upon the children in their care (114–15). Gardaphe sees both women obsessed with protecting the children from "sexual knowledge" (122 n.2). Both in *The Other House* and here, Fryer observes, the child is the victim of the parents' struggle (188). Cargill, however, rejects Edel's comparison of Rose's motivation to Beatrice's (Edel 1949, 679; Cargill 217 n.28).

Morgan, Miles, and Dolcino are grouped together most frequently. In Moon's judgment, the deaths of all three have "homophobic" overtones (258–59). Unlike the passive Dolcino, Morgan, Mottram argues, at least offers some resistance to his fate (173). Swan sees both *The Turn of the Screw* and

"The Author of Beltraffio" treating "an unspecified evil and the corruption of a child," but argues that the tale unlike the novella lacks pity in its tragedy (12). Geismar similarly objects to what he sees as the sacrifice of the two boys in the name of James's childhood problems (58–59, 436). Taking a more detached approach, Vaid finds James expertly meeting the challenge of the death scenes of all three, such that death arrives "inevitably, not arbitrarily," leaving the reader "profoundly moved" (164).

Quentin Anderson discusses Dolcino and Maisie together as "vessel[s]" for the repository of their parents' disputes and attitudes (145–46). The two, Jones observes, share not only duelling parents but a precocious charm, although he notes that while Dolcino is "possessed," Maisie is "exposed" (5–7). Tyler compares Dolcino to Maisie and Miles as exemplifying James's "sophisticated view of innocence in children," which held that their innocence could coexist with startling knowledge of adult sexuality. Both Miles and Dolcino, however, are undone by the "inferior" morality of their guardians (235–36). In contrast, Curtsinger poeticizes Dolcino's death, seeing him as dying into his father's work, even as in "The Madonna of the Future" Serafina's baby dies "into the painting" while his mother holds him (2, 64).

Beatrice herself, according to Krook, belongs with the other Jamesian English who suffer "bewilderment . . . in the presence of ideas," including such characters as Julia Dallow and Lady Agnes of *The Tragic Muse*, Lord Lambeth of *An International Episode*, and Lord Mark of *The Golden Bowl* (235; also Leavis 161). Segal also locates a subordinate "English theme" in the tale, comparing the wife to Julia and Lady Barbarina in her philistinism (115–16). Ward, however, finds her like two Americans, Mrs. Newsome and Olive Chancellor, in her exercise of the "tyranny of self-righteousness" (14). Delbaere-Garant compares Beatrice to a different American, Madame de Mauves, another deadly Puritan with a pagan spouse (252). In "The Art of Fiction," James reflected on the Protestant belief that art has "some vaguely injurious effect," a belief, Walter Wright observes, that Beatrice shares (85–86). Similarly, Asthana associates the preference Ambient attributes to his wife for a blinkered reality in her novels to James's critique in "The Art of Fiction" of novels written for Mrs. Grundy (101–2).

More sympathetically, Bowden compares Beatrice and Isabel Archer. The lesson of *The Portrait of a Lady*, he asserts, is "the importance of human morality to taste," and Beatrice, like Isabel, comes to see "the deadening evil of a life devoted to the esthetic and nothing more" (59–60). Lawson, more problematically, argues for a similarity on the basis of the errors each woman makes and calls for an equally critical treatment of both. While both, as he states, marry men unsympathetic to their views, it is hard to equate Isabel's return to Osmond, which he maintains critics generally commend, with Beatrice's allowing her child to die.

The split between the Ambients, in Berland's analysis, follows the Arnoldian polarities of Hebraism and Hellenism seen also in such contrasted characters as Christopher Newman and the minister Babcock, and Mrs. Newsome and Mme de Vionnet (31–32). James, however, according to Walter Wright, took his Hellenism with "an Hebraic bent" (132).

The Hellenic Ambient is actually, as Nathalia Wright points out, in the words of the tale "impregnated—even to morbidity—with the spirit of Italy." Accordingly, she sees him as one of many James characters, Roderick Hudson in particular, weakened by exposure to Italy (223). Gardaphe compares Ambient to another foreigner under the influence of Italy, the more "insidious" Osmond (127). To Reilly, Ambient fits in a list of Jamesian villains including Madame Merle, Mrs. Gereth of *The Spoils of Poynton*, and the narrator of *The Aspern Papers* (17). Ambient's death, according to Ward, like that of Paraday and Milly Theale, demonstrates James's interest in the "moral evil" of "unwarranted human intervention" (7). On a lighter note, Segal finds "delightful intellectual amusement" in the critical discussion of pretend masterpieces by such as Ambient, Limbert, Dencombe, St. George, and Overt (108).

The tale has naturally been classified with James's other artist tales, an approach Edel objects to on the grounds that its subject is more marriage than literature (CT 5, 11; *Life* 3, 143). Other critics have also taken notice of the different emphasis, without changing the categorization. Distinguishing it from tales such as "The Figure in the Carpet" and "The Middle Years" that portray Jamesian authors solely in their roles as artists, Rahv sees in "The Author of Beltraffio" a particular type of artist, "the English gentleman-aesthete of the late Victorian age," in a wider role (415–16). Similarly, Wagenknecht notes that the story treats not art itself but the "domestic crisis" in an artist's life (28). Gardaphe links the two sides, saying it can be read as treating the relationship between writer and critic, and the danger of intruding on the private life of the writer, and suggests a comparison with James's "The Private Life" (123). In Jacobson's view also, Ambient has two sides, but both are part of his identity as an aesthete, and neither are flattering—manipulator and poseur. In the first role, Ambient is superseded by his wife; in the second he is imitated by his sister. She points to Gabriel Nash in *The Tragic Muse* as a character who plays both roles simultaneously (76).

Given such readings, it is not surprising that a common link is with "The Lesson of the Master," which also discusses the artist's balancing of public and private life. In both, Horne contends, it is the wife who upsets the balance (36). The two are also sometimes linked disparagingly as inferior examples of the Jamesian artist tale. While Walter Anderson sees Ambient's contempt for the public, similar to that of John Marcher, reflecting James's own, the artist figure in both stories, in Goetz's judgment, has "little in common" with James (Anderson 1982, 528; Goetz 150). Edgar finds both "The Author of Beltraffio" and "The Lesson of the Master" less "intimate" in what they say about James as author than "The Middle Years," "The Figure in the Carpet," "The Next Time," and "The Death of the Lion" (161–68; also Kraft 70). According to Matthiessen, in the two earlier artist tales, James was not yet "writing from the heart" (1944 "Portrait," 3). Similarly, while Bass sees "The Author of Beltraffio" as linked with the three artist tales James wrote for *The Yellow Book*, he also argues that the two earlier tales served to dispose of "matters irrelevant to the artist": in "The Author of Beltraffio" aestheticism, in "The Lesson of the Master" "personal passion" (113). Without such qualifications, Donald Stone looks at both tales as two sides of the same problem. In his view, "The Lesson of the Master" shows the danger of sacrificing art to life in its ambivalent master; "The Author of Beltraffio" shows the equal danger of sacrificing life to art in the equally ambivalent Ambient (178). Along the same lines, Wirth-Nesher argues that the young disciples in both at first see art as a separate realm their admired artists inhabit, and instead enter their lives to learn "painful lesson[s]" on the interdependence of art and life. In "The Author of Beltraffio," however, the disciple sacrifices the artist's family to his mistaken belief, while in "The Lesson of the Master" the disciple's happiness is sacrificed to the master's (120–21).

Knox sees a further link between the two tales in their "blending" of narrator and hero, a phenomenon she observes also in "The Death of the Lion" (214). More modestly, Vaid observes that the narrator in each is "an earnest disciple of the hero" (72). Although Sharp classes the narrator with the "peripheral observers" of "Pandora," "'Europe,'" and "The Tree of Knowledge," most critics consider his role a significant one (xxii). Quentin Anderson is sympathetic to it, seeing the narrator as "an artist who has not yet achieved his form and tries to borrow it from the world," even as the young James is seen doing in *The Middle Years* or Isabel Archer would do if James could allow artistry to a woman (195). Horne points out how the American visitor comes under the spell of Ambient in a way similar to the narrator of "The Madonna of the Future," and observes that like the young disciple in "The Middle Years," he must learn that all he can do for his literary master in his troubles is to "like" him (37, 41). Pearce compares the narrator as a "'light' pastoralist" to Felix of *The Europeans* and the frame narrator of *The Turn of the Screw* (843). In Bass's estimate, however, the narrator here, like the young devotees in *The Yellow Book* tales "must be absolved of the charge 'aesthete,'" a sin of which he is particularly guilty so that he, like the other young men, serves as a scapegoat "carrying off some of the 'evil' that would otherwise burden the artist." The narrator in "The Death of the Lion" has a more balanced perspective, he adds, despite his greater contribution to the author's tragedy. Indeed, Bass considers the loss of Paraday's manuscript "a more meaningly fearsome truth" than the death of Dolcino. All four devotées, he concludes, "do considerable harm" in their efforts to help (115–16, 120). Matheson, too, sees the narrators in both "The Death of the

Lion" and "The Author of Beltraffio" as the unwitting cause of death (223). In inducing Mrs. Ambient to read her husband's manuscript, Segal argues, the narrator exhibits the experimental coldness of Lyon in "The Liar" (123).

Donald Stone links the narrator's "flawed sensibility" with that of the narrator of *The Aspern Papers* (251). Arguing for a different, more extended link between the two tales, Tyler contends that the narrator's upholding of the originality of "the picture, the poem, the fictive page" is included in the "apocryphal significance" of letters and documents, usually concerning love or marriage, in James, including the letters in *The Aspern Papers*, "The Abasement of the Northmores," *The Wings of the Dove*, and *The Ivory Tower* (235–36). Holder sees similar responses in "A Passionate Pilgrim," where the narrator responds to the English scenery "as children greet the loved pictures in a story-book lost and mourned and found again," and in *The Portrait of a Lady*, where Isabel Archer sees Gardencourt as "a picture made real" (281). To Knox, the relationship between master and disciple is but part of a larger theme of "secrets and mysteries," present in several James stories toward the end of the century, including "The Figure in the Carpet." In each James, Knox argues, worked to "conceal rather than reveal tantalizing mysteries" as if he aimed "to arouse his reader's curiosity only in order to frustrate it" (211).

"The Author of Beltraffio," unlike the earlier "Benvolio," is, according to McCarthy, a successful allegory, its "image and idea" fused (121). Similarly, in Matheson's view, its plot, like that of "The Figure in the Carpet," is symbolic rather than realistic (224). Even so, Reiman finds its subtlety in sharp contrast to the spelling out of the morals of "Greville Fane," "The Tree of Knowledge," or even "The Beast in the Jungle" (509). Stewart, too, sees the "violence" of the idea showing the "continued urgency" for James of the conflict between art and life, evident in his work since *Roderick Hudson*, and shortly to go through a "phase of some morbidity" (98). Ambient's criticism of his own work as "smoothed . . . down and rounded . . . off" was applied by Matthiessen to what he judged the overly "balanced" conclusion of *The Golden Bowl* as achieved by Maggie (1944, *Major* 101). Less censoriously, Pearce sees the "ambivalent symbol" of Ambient's "golden vessel" as anticipating the novel's central image (841).

Interpretation and Criticism

In 1974, when director Tony Scott and script writer Robin Chapman filmed "The Author of Beltraffio," they allowed themselves the liberty of following the narrator's imagination to picture Dolcino's death, with his mother watching and reading the father's work (Andrews 215–16). The story does not make it so easy for its readers, and one of the key questions of interpretation has been in picturing the tone of that death scene and, even more significantly, the responsibility for it.

Originally the choice was between assigning greater blame to father or mother. The relationship between the two is marked by conflict, with the son at its center. Their roles in the conflict have frequently been read metaphorically or allegorically. Shine calls Dolcino Ambient's "most beautiful and meaningful creation." The child, "emblematic of beauty, purity, and innocence," is placed, however, "in a vortex of forces" hostile to such qualities and which, in destroying the child, destroys "the creative capability of the artist" as well (73–75). Powers contends that in letting Dolcino die, the wife is killing one product of her husband's "creative energy" out of disappoval of another (15–16). Similarly, Delbaere-Garant sees Dolcino as representing art, destroyed by the debate between two views of it (252). Calling the scheme "simple and virtually allegorical," Kermode observes how the use of husband and wife to represent two schools of thought intensifies the dispute. The conflict of the "life of art" with the "life of evangelical conscience" issues in the loss of life itself (12–13). Geismar, however, not only finds the conflict between the husband and wife a "rather pedagogical and propagandistic" defense of art, but also objects to the death of Dolcino as coming out of James's convictions more than the situation of his parents. When first read, it seems convincing, but, he charges, it falls apart when one thinks it over because its motives are too detached from reality (57–60). Walter Wright escapes such categories by calling the work a fairy tale, its characters "both real and symbolic" (86).

Reading the tale as a "fable about innocence," Jones focuses on the child, caught between his mother and father. An advocate of views Ambient has moved away from, the narrator meddles inappropriately in the conflict. When the narrator praises Dolcino as "a perfect work of art," for example, his father responds, "Oh don't call him that. . . . You'll make his little future very difficult." The narrator is seeking, Jones argues, to help Dolcino harmonize his two halves: "his mother's devotion to goodness, his father's devotion to beauty." Instead, as a result of the child's death and his role in it he too must "qualify his faith in art," worrying not about its "effect" as before, but like Mark about its "viability." Noting the many ways of reading Dolcino's death— art killed by puritanism, nature by society, life by fear, a child by overpowering parental love—Jones finds the final irony the fact that his mother does indeed save his innocence from corruption (3–5).

Perhaps the most strikingly allegorical reading is that of Curtsinger, who casts Dolcino as the "divine gift" needing to be wrought into the work of art. Dolcino, in his analysis, must leave behind the ideal garden of the imagination represented by Ambient's home for the world of "things as they are" in his novels. The narrator represents the "outermost" part of the artist, "intricately akin" to Ambient. Beatrice is the "reluctant muse," the madonna who must hand over her son to death for the sake of art. Mark is vaguely aware of this and so frightened. Dismissing other readings for following the notebooks or preface, Curtsinger points out that the mother is not "doing nothing" while her son dies, as the notebook contemplated, but reading Ambient's manuscript and so feeding him—the imagination—into the work. Thus Beatrice is not Medea but Mary, and although Curtsinger never says it quite outright, Ambient is God. Ambient's sister, Curtsinger writes, simply fails to understand the sanctity of the mystery. In the end, however, Curtsinger himself acknowledges the uncertain value of such a mystery (61–68). Certainly it calls for even a sterner allegory than the conflict between art and morality, for in this reading Beatrice lets her child die not to protect him but to enrich art. However intriguing symbolically, it is also hard to accept how Dolcino's death benefits Ambient's work. He had already written masterpieces before without the need for blood sacrifice, and barely manages to finish a book after.

Others tend to be more down to earth in their analysis of the Ambients' marital troubles. McElderry calls the tale "a study in the incompatibility of an author and his wife" (80). According to Shine, the child here figures as an "instrument of adult hostility." Using the child, Beatrice pays back her husband for the freedom of imagination and feeling from which she envyingly recoils; Mark in turn plays on the child's affection to antagonize his wife; Gwendolen, who sees the child's fate with what the narrator calls a "terrible lucidity," stays silent as a form of revenge on her brother "whose brilliance robbed her of her identity" (73). Andreas, while taking the author's side, presents his wife's rather strikingly. She not only sees his sifting of life as "a gratuitously corrosive act," but, writes Andreas, "has a child . . . whose world is being pulled down around his ears by writers such as his father" (108).

In the view of Quentin Anderson, Ambient is James's "most delightful instance of the worldly or greedy man turned artist." Ambient errs by putting things—not consciousness—first, and is, in Anderson's estimate, "comically frank" about his failure, admitting, "Perhaps I care too much for beauty." In the words of the tale he "reproduce[s]" beauty or in Anderson's reading, "appropriate[s]" it rather than representing it. His wife is equally "demonic," as righteous as he is greedy. Both qualities, Anderson writes, are "modes of appropriation." Thus, despite Ambient's sense of his responsibility as a parent, their struggle over Dolcino can end only with "the destruction of the representative of their social selves." The narrator, for his part, calls Dolcino "an orphan or a changeling," and Anderson cites Henry James Sr.'s picture of man and wife as intended to be "utterly disunited in themselves, and united only in their offspring." Here Dolcino is simply the representative of his parents' love or hate. The "supreme spiritual greed" of the parents is seen in their attempt to "appropriate their child." Even as Beatrice wears Dolcino's portrait, the two turn the child into a "dead image" by the end, and die soon after, having "condemned themselves to death through spiritual pride" (143–44, 146).

To Tyler, however, there is "no doubt" that James is on the side not only of Dolcino, but his father. Ambient, he writes, is "happy and distinguished" as the narrator writes those whose lives resemble fiction are (235–36; also Horne 39). McElderry even finds part of Ambient's charm his "quiet forbearance" toward his wife (80). Stevenson points to flaws. The name Mark Ambient, she writes, contains "the two counter but necessary qualities of a writer," but Ambient himself suffers from a a "tragic loss of communication," which is a signal problem for an artist (70, 95). Matthiessen objects more to James's characterization than the character, stating that Ambient is an unconvincing pagan given his "correct English gentleman" behavior (1944 "Portrait," 2). Horne dissents from Matthiessen's view on a strictly factual ground, arguing that Ambient may have something of the aesthetic in him, but is not a proponent of "art for art's sake" as he bases his art on reality (38). In the notebook the author was to be "perfectly decent in life," and in the tale he is first seen chatting amiably with the vicar, although he does later admit to disliking him. Indeed, several critics have found his character deeply ambivalent. Donald Stone notes that his espousing of seemingly contradictory viewpoints might be excused as an attempt to combine all viewpoints. The even sharper aestheticism of the narrator, however, Stone finds, calls Ambient's into doubt (240). Grover also detects an ambiguity in the character, and refuses to separate the Ambient who produced the "aesthetic war-cry" of *Beltraffio* and the realist who declares, "I want to be truer than I have ever been." In his reading, both Ambient and James stand for an art that is at the same time truthful and beautifully formed. Such ambiguity, he reasons, is vindicated in the tale, while Mrs. Ambient's "moral" and "unambiguous" approach is shown to be false. Young Dolcino should indeed not read his father's work as a child, writes Grover, but then novels are not to be written to a child's understanding (137–39). Tintner pictures the Ambient who wants to be "truer than I have ever been" at a point of transition, worried that he has unduly shortchanged life for art and wanting to amend. Such questioning of his art is not a weakness, in her view, but a sign that he is a true artist, unlike his sister and the early narrator (1986, 53–54).

In the notebook entry it is clear that the wife's sense of the artist's "extreme and somewhat hysterical" aestheticism is at least correct. But James already places some of the blame on the wife, so that Ambient's love of beauty is "aggravated, made extravagant and perverse, by the sense of his wife's disapproval." Most significantly, it is Beatrice who is blamed for the death of the child. Thus, contemporary critics, while objecting to the immorality of the tale, were generally more shocked by the mother (e.g., *Literary World*). The *Independent* called Beatrice "as near to being a monomaniac as a sane . person can be." While labeling the husband "morally rotten," the *Critic* was still aghast at the wife's decision to let the child die rather than be exposed to his rottenness in print. The *Nation* took a different stance. First seeming to cast doubt on the wife who objects to her husband's work for "what she is pleased to consider moral reasons," the *Nation* argues that the idea of purity in literature for "English-speaking people" was an idea so strongly rooted that to change it would require "a change of race-characteristics," and while noting it "difficult to imagine a more unpleasant relation" than that of the wedded Ambients, opined that most readers would have more sympathy for the wife than the author.

Later critics have continued to view the wife as a type, and an unsympathetic one. Rahv calls her the "guardian-spirit of British respectability," and Edgar a "moral fanatic" (Rahv 416; Edgar 168). To most, there is little difference between the two. Horne acknowledges the naturalness of her concern for her child, but censures her insufficient appreciation of her "clever" husband and her inability to face reality seen in her desire for art with a "'purpose'" (39–41). Markow-Totevy writes sympathetically of how Ambient has to persevere in the face of his wife's "prudish" objections, her "hatred of art" (96–97). His wife believes, Todorov asserts, that the husband is responsible for their boy's sickness, and so brings about his death herself in her attempt to prove his responsiblity (184). A further irony in her role, according to Bock, is that in the end Beatrice's grief produces in her a need for the complex fiction she once feared, and the fear of which led her to the act that caused her grief (259 n.3). In Berland's view, James is "perhaps *too* harsh in his suggestion that the demand for explicit morality in art—a Philistine morality—can accompany a cruel immorality in life" (32). One has then opposites—the moral aesthete, the immoral prude.

Others see a more balanced situation. For Bewley, while it is Beatrice's conventional view, rather than her husband's aesthetic that kills, James balances the two approaches by showing Ambient as also "vulnerable," the flaws in his aesthetic made visible in his sister (221–23). Similarly, while Segal puts James "clearly" on the writer's side, she sees him presenting a fair case for the wife by giving her the more tragic role, by associating Ambient with the somewhat scandalous nineties aesthetes, and by picturing the sister as an unattractive sham (116–18). Tintner even substantiates some of the mother's fears, by seeing in Dolcino's "flirtatious" behavior toward the narrator proof of the corrupting influence the mother feared (1987, 267). Similarly, Kermode notes the possibility that Dolcino's "more than mortal bloom" may be a genuine sign of corruption (13).

Still, despite the twists and turns of later criticism, most critics continue to hold the wife responsible for Dolcino's death (e.g., Knights 28). Segal states that the story leaves no question in judging the wife's action (115). To Fryer, Beatrice is one of James's fatal women who "draws her strength from her power over her husband" (183). Wagenknecht, more moderately, sees Mrs.

Ambient as neither monster nor martyr, and notes that she, too, dies as the result of her action. Still, he sees it, whatever the legitimacy of its motivation, as an example of the wrongful use of people (30). Particularly indicting the wife, Gill sees as a significant subtheme in the tale "the poignant contrast between the great house and the smallness of its occupants." The naïve narrator expects to see life in England in terms of its literature, and so sees the house as a "palace of art," refusing to be dissuaded even when told of Mrs. Ambient's hatred of art. The final reversal of his mistaken belief Gill finds in the child's death in "the charming house" itself (73–74).

In the debate over the competing virtues of wife and husband, the narrator was originally left on the sidelines. Beach, for example, classes him as the typical "objective observer" marked by literary interests and a "friendly sympathy" (69). Edel praises his "calm suavity," its effect of "benign aloofness," as helping to "soften the horror" of the subject (*Life* 3, 143–44; CT 5, 11). Even such a late critic as Goetz places the story with the other artist tales where, he declares, the disciple narrator is "never—at least ostensibly—telling his own story" and so remains objective (158). Segal gives him something more of a role, seeing a difference here between the "experiencing" and "narrating" observer—which she notes is unusual in James—so that the narrator is more restrained and more critical of his own actions. According to Segal, James chose an American outsider for narrator because his ignorance contributes to the contrasts of the tale: he is surprised by the true natures of both Ambients and comes to realize Mark Ambient's "happy combination" of gentleman and genius really a "sad compromise." His ignorance even contributes some humor to the tale, his conversations with Beatrice making a "delightful international comedy of errors." Most significantly, Segal writes that James could not "resist the temptation" of involving his narrator in the action in a way that goes beyond the functional. The narrator's desire to "convert" Mrs. Ambient not only reflects his character, she writes, but betrays a certain callousness also evident in his concluding understatements about the Ambients' loss (119–24).

Objections to the form of narration began gradually. Rebecca West took exception to the implausibility that Beatrice would tell her problems so promiscuously, a result, she says, of James's choice of "so small a peephole" for presenting his story (79). Similarly, without blaming the narration, Stevenson asserts that Ambient reveals more of his sense of his marriage than is proper to the narrator (103). Harris points out how James's typical lack of specificity, his leaving it up to the reader to imagine what Ambient's beliefs are, naturally turns the interest toward the point-of-view character—a kind of sleight-of-hand (87).

Toward the start the narrator, speaking of his habit of looking at English landscapes as copies of works of art, comments that he will not tell whether his approach has changed since then, "especially as the discerning reader will be able to judge for himself' (CT 5, 307). The reason it should have changed in the view of many critics is that he is a significant part of the tragedy of the tale. Tintner, for one, takes the narrator's comment as an indication that he has been cured of his "confusion between life and art" and will not try again to impose artistry upon life (1986, 50–55). Gargano, too, commenting on the competing looks of mother and child—Dolcino's "plea" for the narrator's interference and Mrs. Ambient's "great cold stare, meant apparently as an admonition to me to mind my business"—sees the narrator in the end wishing he had chosen Mrs. Ambient's "mute counsel" (304). Similarly, Kermode points to the narrator's sense that he may have caused the tragedy, that Mrs. Ambient may have been right that "art may after all prey upon life"(13–14). Still, the amount of blame assigned him varies. McElderry simply states that he "feels involved" (80). Cornwell is among those who picture him as well intentioned, but misguided (146–47). Wagenknecht excuses his "youthful enthusiasm," which contributed to the tragedy, but not his seeking to enforce it on others (30).

Reiman was the first to launch a full-scale assault on the narrator's motives and methods. From the beginning, Reiman writes, the narrator clings to an aesthetic sensibility Ambient himself has moved beyond—even if he does pose again in response to the narrator's flattery. In Reiman's view, the narrator's tendency to see characters and landscapes in terms of art leads him to attempt the "logical, artistic resolution" of the conflict between Ambient and his wife. While the wife and husband are equally guilty of their attempts to "mold" Dolcino, Reiman sees the narrator, abetted by the sister, as creating the final crisis, a guilt he reveals without realizing it. James's view of aestheticism, Reiman holds, is "irrelevant." Ambient is, however, the "proximate cause" of Dolcino's death, the Frankenstein who created the monster who destroyed his family. Donald Stone, too, blames the narrator, noting particularly not only the narrator's foolishness in giving Ambient's novel to his wife, but also the questionable "aesthetic *frisson*" he experiences at seeing the dead Dolcino (240). Pearce's analysis closely resembles Reiman's and Stone's in its indictment of the narrator who, he charges, denies the reality of the Ambient home by trying to transform it into a kind of pastoral *locus amoenus* stemming from his reading of *Beltraffio*. Despite his confession, the narrator, in Pearce's view, fails to learn his lesson, enshrining the dead Ambient in a perfect world he had left behind (840–41).

Offering a modification of Reiman's reading, Scoggins cautions against an automatic discrediting of the narrator. Instead he increases the guilt of Ambient, who creates the "ambience" of events. The narrator, in contrast, he sees as acting more spontaneously than deliberately. Scoggins still assigns him a pivotal role, noting that as a disciple of the author he presents an example to the already anxious mother of the effects of his works. As such, he upsets by his enthusiasm the tenuous balance between the conflicting claims of art and life that husband and wife had so far been able to maintain. Spontaneity is no excuse for Shine, who sees the narrator as "unconsciously envious" of Ambient, a fatal meddler who should have been able to read Mrs. Ambient's character and refrained from interference. Rather than accept responsibility, Shine observes, he ironically pins his act on an imaginary plea from the child who represents the only purity in the story. As such, she writes, he is destroyed by the adults that surround him as a sign of what they have lost (72–75).

The narrator, in Wirth-Nesher's analysis, is the main source of the decadence in the tale. In her view, James was still critical of the French school to which the narrator is a new convert full of "exaggerated zeal" and a "desire to proselytize." Thinking himself very clever, he is really full of "preconceived notions," particularly a desire to categorize everything symmetrically so that Gwendolen, for example, will be the opposite of Beatrice. The story, however, she observes, destroys such symmetry. The aesthetic Gwendolen still believes "one must be good" and sends for the doctor, while the moral Beatrice lets her child die. Because in Wirth-Nesher's view Beatrice wants "perfection" but distrusts art, she looks for it in life, in the "form" of the "perfect innocence of childhood." As a result "her displaced aesthetic drive corrupts far more than we imagine Ambient's books can." Even more ironically, by letting her child die rather than read his father's books, Beatrice shows her faith in the power of art. The narrator's attempt to convert Beatrice, according to Wirth-Nesher, is "motivated by guilt" stemming from a lingering American sense of a "dichotomy" between art and morality. To convert Beatrice would be to disprove the morality that still claims him. This "deeper motive," writes Wirth-Nesher, is hidden by his "moral imperialism," his sense of superiority as a man to a seemingly "frigid" woman whom he can seduce into art. In Wirth-Nesher's reading, the narrator never recognizes his mistake, as evident in his "slightly ruffled" and "slyly" triumphant tone at the end (118–120).

In place of the narrator, some critics have turned the spotlight on Ambient's sister. Originally, the sister's role was seen as discrediting Ambient's more "sympathetic" aestheticism (e.g., N 59; Hyde 49; Bass 114). McElderry saw her character useful in giving "credibility" to the situation by her acceptance of it (80). Quentin Anderson, however, saw her opposing the Ambients' misuse of Dolcino "in a somewhat mechanical fashion" (196 n.10). Putt dismissed her as a character without a role (215–18). Assigning her a rather dubious one, Freier takes Reiman's view that Gwendolen enjoys the tragedy a step further, arguing that there is no hard evidence of Beatrice's guilt, and that it is simply a product of the sister's jaundiced imagination, believed too quickly by a flattered narrator.

Macnaughton, however, rallies to Gwendolen's side, arguing that she is the "moral heroine" of the tale, casting the narrator again as the villain, and both wife and husband as "morally guilty" parties. He sees in the tale James's own uncertainty as to whether the artist is entitled to write freely about all of life or whether fiction is "potentially deleterious." At first the tale seems to favor the former view. But Ambient's quiet life, he argues, indicates an awareness that in life if not in art, compromises are necessary. Out of their compromise, husband and wife have created "a delicate, beautiful child." The snake is in the form of the "inevitable imitation" which, he contends, is not Miss Ambient but the narrator, who, seeing them all as potentially perfect, wants them to be reconciled to make a perfect pattern. Trying to make life like art, he goads Mrs. Ambient and encourages Mark's "showing off." The narrator's reaction to his mistake shows a mixture of emotions, but finally he stays with the "mythologizing" of Dolcino's death. The most important problem caused by the narrator's bias, according to Macnaughton, is his inability to see beyond Miss Ambient's affectations. In his view, Miss Ambient has tried not to interfere with the marriage, to smooth over its difficulties, and has recognized throughout that "one must be good." (153–56). Pearce also has some praise for the sister's "deep and complex" awareness of life's tragedy. The narrator rejects her, he writes, simply because her "dark romantic vein" does not fit his aesthetic pastoralism (841–42). Wagenknecht takes a moderate approach, noting the sister's "absurdities" but absolving her of evil intent (30–31).

Stein sees as the central theme of the tale the egotism that leads each character to attempt to impose his will on reality, making Dolcino and others "dehumanized figures" in a "personal vision." Like Macnaughton, he sees the conflict at the start as dormant but dangerous. Although both husband and wife really value the other, they still can't give up their own view of things. As Ambient says of his wife, "Damn her point of view" (CT 5, 324). With the arrival of the narrator, each character wants to make "the Ambient marriage" fit their "private fiction." Unlike the narrator, Ambient has moved beyond a devotion to symmetry, but he still holds to an ideal of "aesthetic integrity," which seeks "an impression of life itself" by refraining from any interference with life in an approach that Stein calls "life for art's sake." Thus, although he anticipates trouble for his son, he makes no effort to save him, taking the position of the detached author, becoming both character and observer in his own story. Beatrice, for her part, is committed to a "drama of personal salvation for herself and her son." Ambient has broken their truce by inviting the narrator, encouraging him, and confiding in him, including him as a character in the Ambient story. Indeed, Stein writes, Ambient then, following his aesthetic theory, allows the narrator a free hand in bringing about events. The narrator, thinking he has "seized Mark Ambient's point of view," is, however, still following the rule of symmetry (CT 5, 323). Both he and Ambient are more interested in acting parts than in saving Dolcino, although Ambient, in Stein's view, is not a "blatant villain" who wants his son to die. Nor can he, unlike the narrator, ever bring himself to write of Dolcino's death, even as Beatrice repents of her desire to shape life (89–97, 101)

In Knox's view the tale seems to want to keep its mystery hidden, and she suggests an autobiographical reading to explain why. To her, James makes Ambient a self-portrait—"albeit a self-caricature, a parody"—and the narrator, in turn, sees himself in Ambient, so that in the tale James "visits, observes and admires himself." Even Dolcino, in her reading, is a "self-caricature" as his angelic nature recalls James's childhood nickname, "Angel." She notes further the mystery of the subject matter of *Beltraffio*, the many negative comments about women, and the mannered decoration of the prose, which she judges like the beautiful Dolcino effeminate, to produce a reading in which an insecure James indirectly reveals his homosexuality. The "real love situation," argues Knox, is Ambient's love for Dolcino, who serves as a "catamite." The narrator's giving of Ambient's works to Beatrice is implicitly a request that she accept her husband's homosexuality and "relinquish her own claims as a wife in favor of the boy's." Moon also emphasizes the issue of sexuality in the tale, seeing "homophobic implications" in the tale's symbolism whereby Dolcino dies as "a 'punishment' for and/or a required 'sacrifice' to his father's homosexuality—or, more precisely, the homosexuality of his author-father's writing" (259).

Conley also offers a reading in which Dolcino becomes the focus of conflicting loves—homosexual and maternal. He sees Beatrice's "morbidly protective love" for her child standing in the way of "the two males' homosexual desire for the child and for each other." The hallmark of his reading, however, is his detailed analysis not just of words, but of "multiple configurations of letters." He takes the tale as standing at the beginning of modernism with its interest in "perception and motion" as well as its "foreboding view" of art itself. In a reading that makes the tale seem almost Joycean, Conley depicts the process by which the narrator "unwittingly murders (or cannibalizes) the fragile symbolic systems of the welcoming country," leaving in their place "a greater, more permanent work of art—the enduring monument of a conquest." The narrator thus becomes the "'author' of 'Beltraffio.'" The victory is, however, a "devastatingly narcissistic triumph" requiring Dolcino's murder, and thus the tale ends "on an implicitly negative tone" that warns the reader against literature as a danger to life. Conley provides many glosses on names, including the "mismated" Ambient, and Mrs. Ambient, who misses her husband's mark as Miss Ambient misses the point of his art. He rings changes on the letters "I" and "O" that lead into the tale from the last letters of the title, are echoed in the Roman numerals of the three sections, and recur at their conclusion. The "I" is the individual gaze, the "O" "the well, whole, hole or O" upon which it gazes. Their significance permutates as the tale traces the narrator's increasingly "obsessive ambition of totalizing his mentor," of becoming

Mark Ambient. Not surprisingly, the end result of such a reading is to "dismantle the stability of perception."

Gardaphe also emphasizes "signs," and the tale's place in James's movement into modernism, placing those signs in an international context. In his reading, the narrator's untrustworthiness and his guilt seem a given, his inability to read the tale's "Italian signs" being of greatest import. Dolcino's Italian name shows that Italian influence "defines" him. Therefore, in his death James is "killing off the sweetness that Italy used to signify in his earlier days." While Gardaphe pictures Dolcino as dying of diphtheria, literally suffocated by his mother's attempts to shield him, he also suggests that Dolcino may have contracted the disease from Italy or the "diseased mental ambience." He seems, indeed, to take an equally dim view of Ambient's effect, noting that the narrator sees in Gwendolen "evidence of Mark's ability to corrupt decent people through his art." Because Gwendolen imitates Mark, just as he imitates Italy, she becomes, in Gardaphe's estimate, the "strongest echo" of Italy in the tale and so represents "all the poor imitation that comes from cultural exchange." While Gardaphe suggests a translation of "beltraffio" as "Bel traffico" or "beautiful traffic" and thus exchange of "intercultural influences," his interpretation seems to fit more with Knox's suggestions of "beautiful intrigue" or "beautiful betrayal," with a "trafficone" being a busybody or meddler like the narrator (Knox 227 n.1).

Several contemporary reviewers of the collection that headlined "The Author of Beltraffio" found the intrigue overwhelming the beauty. They objected to what was seen as James's turn toward the French decadent, or in the *Nation*'s word, to "weirdness," the *Critic* begging James to return to his "former delightful self" (*Critic* 207). The *Literary World* quotes the humorous description of the sister, but finds in the rest of the tale that James's "talent goes far afield, and he succeeds only in being disagreeable," the last word echoed as well by the *Independent*. The *Critic* was even less enthusiastic, calling it "a painful and repulsive story" and likening the art of the volume as a whole to "touching the lips of a corpse with carmine." James himself was relatively proud of the tale, although seeing himself, like Ambient, on the way to better things. After the first installment, he wrote Gosse thanking him for his praise: "Of course it is tragic—almost (I fear) repulsively so. But the *2d* part is better written than the 1*st*, & I agree with you in thinking the thing is more solid than many of my things. I feel it to be more *packed*—more complete. But I shall do much better yet!" (*Selected Letters* 31). For modern critics, the repulsion is part of the attraction, and the tale continues to be the subject of much critical attention despite frequently mixed reviews (e.g., Putt 215–18; Horne 36–37).

Tolstoy and his wife were once surprised by a visitor who out of his enthusiasm over the author's "The Kreutzer Sonata" had castrated himself. The artist lives at the intersection of art and life, and the encounters there show the depth and the danger of the connection as James attempted to illustrate in his tale of the author of *Beltraffio*, living in a world and among characters he did not author.

Works Cited

Primary Works

James, Henry. 1884. "The Author of Beltraffio." *The English Illustrated Magazine* 1 (June–July): 563–73, 628–39.

———. 1885. "The Author of Beltraffio." *The Author of Beltraffio*. Boston: James R. Osgood, 7–78.

———. 1885. "The Author of Beltraffio." *Stories Revived*. Vol. 1, 1–70. London: Macmillan.

———. 1909. "The Author of Beltraffio." *The Novels and Tales of Henry James*. Vol. 16, 1–17. New York Edition. New York: Scribner's.

———. 1988. *Selected Letters of Henry James to Edmund Gosse, 1882–1915: A Literary Friendship*. Ed. Rayburn S. Moore. Baton Rouge: Louisiana State University Press.

Secondary Works

Anderson, Quentin. 1957. *The American Henry James*. New Brunswick, NJ: Rutgers University Press.

Anderson, Walter E. 1982. "The Visiting Mind: Henry James's Poetics of Seeing." *The Psychoanalytic Review* 69 (Winter): 513–32.

———. 1981–82. "Henry James versus American Culture." *Dalhousie Review* 61 (Winter): 618–30.

Andreas, Osborn. 1948. *Henry James and the Expanding Horizon: A Study of the Meaning and Basic Themes of James's Fiction*. Seattle: University of Washington Press.

Andrews, Nigel. 1974. "Henry James on Location." *Sight & Sound* 43: 215–16.

Anon. 1885. Review of *The Author of Beltraffio*. *Independent* 37 (9 April): 459.

Anon. 1885. Review of *The Author of Beltraffio*. *The Critic* 6 (2 May): 206–7.

Anon. 1885. Review of *The Author of Beltraffio*. *The Nation* 40, no. 1028 (12 March): 226.

Anon. 1885. Review of *The Author of Beltraffio*. *Literary World* 16 (21 March): 102.

Asthana, Rama Kant. 1980. *Henry James: A Study in the Aesthetic of the Novel*. New Delhi: Associated Publishing House.

Bass, Eben. 1964. "Lemon-Colored Volumes and Henry James." *Studies in Short Fiction* 1 (Winter): 113–22.

Beach, Joseph Warren. [1918] 1954. *The Method of Henry James*. Philadelphia: Albert Saifer.

Berland, Alwyn. 1981. *Culture and Conduct in the Novels of Henry James*. Cambridge: Cambridge University Press.

Bewley, Marius. 1959. *The Eccentric Design: Form in the Classic American Novel*. New York: Columbia University Press.

Bock, Darilyn. 1979. "From Reflective Narrators to James: The Coloring Medium of the Mind." *Modern Philology* 76 (February): 259–72.

Bowden, Edwin T. [1956] 1960. *The Themes of Henry James: A System of Observation Through the Visual Arts*. Yale Studies in English 132. New Haven: Yale University Press.

Buitenhuis, Peter. 1970. *The Grasping Imagination: The American Writings of Henry James*. Toronto: University of Toronto Press.

Cargill, Oscar. 1961. *The Novels of Henry James*. New York: Macmillan.

Conley, Tom. 1989. "Wells of Perception: Movement and Letter of 'The Author of Beltraffio.'" In *Perspectives on Perception: Philosophy, Art, and Literature*. Ed. Mary Ann Caws, 205–22. New York: Peter Lang.

Cornwell, Ethel F. 1962. *The 'Still Point': Theme and Variations in the Writing of T. S. Eliot, Coleridge, Yeats, Henry James, Virginia Woolf, and D. H. Lawrence*. New Brunswick, NJ: Rutgers University Press.

Curtsinger, E. C. 1986. *The Muse of Henry James*. Mansfield, TX: Latitudes Press.

Delbaere-Garant, Jeanne. 1970. *Henry James: The Vision of France*. Paris: Société d'Editions Les Belles Lettres.

Edel, Leon, ed. 1949. *The Complete Plays of Henry James*. Philadelphia: Lippincott.

Edgar, Pelham. [1927] 1964. *Henry James, Man and Author*. New York: Russell & Russell.

Freier, Mary P. 1987. "The Story of 'The Author of Beltraffio.'" *Studies in Short Fiction* 24 (Summer): 308–9.

Fryer, Judith. 1976. *The Faces of Eve: Women in the Nineteenth-Century American Novel*. New York: Oxford University Press.

Gale, Robert L. [1954] 1964. *The Caught Image: Figurative Language in the Fiction of Henry James*. Chapel Hill: University of North Carolina Press.

Gardaphe, Fred L. 1989. "The Echoes of *Beltraffio*: Reading Italy in Henry James's 'The Author of Beltraffio.'" *RLA: Romance Languages Annual* 1: 121–27.

Gargano, James W. 1979. "The 'Look' as a Major Event in James's Short Fiction." *Arizona Quarterly* 35, no. 4 (Winter): 303–20.

Geismar, Maxwell. 1963. *Henry James and the Jacobites*. Boston: Houghton Mifflin.

Gill, Richard. 1972. *Happy Rural Seat: The English Country House and the Literary Imagination*. New Haven: Yale University Press.

Goetz, William R. 1986. *Henry James and the Darkest Abyss of Romance*. Baton Rouge: Louisiana State University Press.

Goodman, Charlotte. 1979–80. "Henry James, D. H. Lawrence, and the Victimized Child." *Modern Language Studies* 10, no. 1: 43–51.

Gosse, Edmund. 1922. "Henry James." *Aspects and Impressions*. New York: Scribner's.

Grover, Philip. 1973. *Henry James and the French Novel: A Study in Inspiration*. London: Paul Elek.

Harris, Wendell V. 1979. *British Short Fiction in the Nineteenth Century: A Literary and Bibliographic Guide*. Detroit: Wayne State University Press.

Hellman, George S. 1926. "Stevenson and Henry James, The Rare Friendship between Two Famous Stylists." *Century* n.s. 89 (January): 336–45.

Holder, Alan. 1966. *Three Voyagers in Search of Europe: A Study of Henry James, Ezra Pound, and T. S. Eliot*. Philadelphia: University of Pennsylvania Press.

Horne, Helen. 1960. *Basic Ideals of James's Aesthetics as Expressed in the Short Stories Concerning Artists and Writers*. Marburg: Erich Mauersberger.

Hyde, H. Montgomery. 1969. *Henry James at Home*. New York: Farrar, Straus.

Jacobson, Marcia. 1983. *Henry James and the Mass Market*. University: University of Alabama Press.

Jones, Granville H. 1975. *Henry James's Psychology of Experience: Innocence, Responsibility, and Renunciation in the Fiction of Henry James*. The Hague: Mouton.

Kelley, Cornelia Pulsifer. [1930] 1965. *The Early Development of Henry James*. Urbana: University of Illinois Press.

Kermode, Frank, ed. 1986. *The Figure in the Carpet and Other Stories*. London: Penguin.

Knights, Lionel Charles. 1976. "Henry James and Human Liberty." *Explorations* 3. Pittsburgh: University of Pittsburgh Press, 24–37.

Knox, Melissa. 1986. "'Beltraffio': Henry James' Secrecy." *American Imago* 43, no. 3 (Fall): 211–27.

Kraft, James. 1969. *The Early Tales of Henry James*. Carbondale: Southern Illinois University Press.

Krook, Dorothea. [1962] 1967. *The Ordeal of Consciousness in Henry James*. New York: Cambridge University Press.

Lawson, Don S. 1986. "Isabel Archer, Beatrice Ambient, and the 'Very Straight Path': Henry James' Heroines Who Make the Wrong Choice." *Tennessee Philological Bulletin* 23 (July): 76–77.

Leavis, Q. D. 1985. "The fox is the novelist's idea: Henry James and the house beautiful." *Collected Essays*. Vol. 2. Ed. G. Singh, 158–76. Cambridge: Cambridge University Press.

McCarthy, Harold T. 1958. *Henry James: The Creative Process*. New York: Thomas Yoseloff.

McElderry, Bruce R., Jr. 1965. *Henry James*. New York: Twayne.

Macnaughton, W. R. 1974. "The First-Person Narrators of Henry James." *Studies in American Fiction* 2 (August): 145–64.

Markow-Totevy, Georges. 1969. *Henry James*. Trans. John Griffiths. London: Merlin.

Matheson, Gwen. 1968. "Portraits of the Artist and the Lady in the Shorter Fictions of Henry James." *Dalhousie Review* 48: 222–30.

Matthiessen, F. O. 1944. "Introduction: Henry James' Portrait of the Artist." *Henry James: Stories of Writers and Artists*. Norfolk, CT: New Directions. Reprinted as "Henry James's Portrait of the Artist." *Partisan Review* 11 (1944): 71–87.

———. 1944. *Henry James the Major Phase*. New York: Oxford University Press.

Moon, Michael. 1989. "Disseminating Whitman." *South Atlantic Quarterly* 88: 247–65.

Mottram, Eric. 1985. "'The Infected Air' and 'The Guilt of Interference': Henry James's Short Stories." In *The Nineteenth-Century American Short Story*. Ed. A. Robert Lee, 164–90. London: Vision; Totowa, NJ: Barnes & Noble.

Neff, John C. 1938. "Henry James the Reporter." *New Mexico Quarterly* 8 (February): 9–14.

Pearce, Howard. 1975. "Henry James's Pastoral Fallacy." *PMLA* 90: 834–47.

Pickering, Samuel F. 1973. "The Sources of 'The Author of Beltraffio.'" *Arizona Quarterly* 29 (Summer): 177–90.

Pound, Ezra. 1918. "A Shake Down." *The Little Review* 5 (August): 9–39.

Powers, Lyall H. 1969. *The Merrill Guide to Henry James*. Columbus, OH: Charles E. Merrill.

Przybylowicz, Donna. 1986. *Desire and Repression: The Dialectic of Self and Other in the Late Works of Henry James*. University: University of Alabama Press.

Putt, S. Gorley. 1966. *Henry James: A Reader's Guide*. Ithaca, NY: Cornell University Press.

Rahv, Philip, ed. 1944. *The Great Short Novels of Henry James*. New York: Dial.

Reilly, Robert. 1967. "Henry James and the Morality of Fiction." *American Literature* 39 (March): 1–30.

Reiman, Donald H. 1962. "The Inevitable Imitation:The Narrator in 'The Author of Beltraffio'" *Texas Studies in Literature and Language* 3 (Winter): 503–9.

Roditi, Edouard. 1949. "Oscar Wilde and Henry James." *University of Kansas City Review* 15: 52–56.

Richardson, Lyon N., ed. 1941. *Henry James: Representative Selections, with Introduction, Bibliography, and Notes.* New York: American Writer Series. Reprint. Urbana: Illinois University Press, 1966.

Ross, M. L. 1974. "Henry James's 'Half-Man': The Legacy of Browning in 'The Madonna of the Future.'" *Browning Institute Studies* 2: 25–42.

Scoggins, James. 1963. "'The Author of Beltraffio': A Reapportionment of Guilt." *Texas Studies in Literature and Language* 5 (Summer): 265–70.

Segal, Ora. 1969. *The Lucid Reflector: The Observer in Henry James's Fiction.* New Haven: Yale University Press.

Sharp, Sister M. Corona. 1963. *The Confidante in Henry James: Evolution and Moral Value of a Fictive Character.* Notre Dame, IN: University of Notre Dame Press.

Shine, Muriel G. 1969. *The Fictional Children of Henry James.* Chapel Hill: University of North Carolina Press.

Stein, Allen F. 1984. *After the Vows Were Spoken: Marriage in American Literary Realism.* Columbus: Ohio State University Press.

Stevenson, Elizabeth. [1949] 1981. *The Crooked Corridor: A Study of Henry James.* New York: Octagon.

Stewart, J. I. M. 1963. "Henry James." In *Eight Modern Writers. Oxford History of English Literature.* Vol. 12, 71–121. New York: Oxford University Press.

Stone, Donald David. 1972. *Novelists in a Changing World: Meredith, James, and the Transformation of English Fiction in the 1880's.* Cambridge, MA: Harvard University Press.

Stone, Edward. 1969. *A Certain Morbidness: A View of American Literature.* London: Feffer & Simons; Carbondale: Southern Illinois University Press.

Swan, Michael, ed. 1948. *Ten Short Stories of Henry James.* London: John Lehmann.

Tintner, Adeline R. 1989. *The Pop World of Henry James: From Fairy Tales to Science Fiction.* Ann Arbor: UMI Research Press

———. 1987. *The Book World of Henry James: Appropriating the Classics.* Ann Arbor: UMI Research Press. Revised in part from "Another Germ for the 'Author of Beltraffio': James, Pater and Botticelli's Madonnas." *The Journal of Pre-Raphaelite Studies* 1, no. 1 (1980): 14–20.

———. 1986. *The Museum World of Henry James.* Ann Arbor: UMI Research Press.

———. 1981. "Henry James as Roth's Ghost Writer." *Midstream* 27, no. 3: 48–51.

Todorov, Tzvetan. 1977. *The Poetics of Prose*. Trans. Richard Howard. Ithaca, NY: Cornell University Press.

Tremper, Ellen. 1981. "Henry James's 'The Story in It': A Successful Aesthetic Adventure." *Henry James Review* 3, no. 1 (Fall): 11–16.

Tyler, Parker. 1964. *Every Artist His Own Scandal: A Study of Real and Fictive Heroes*. New York: Horizon.

Vaid, Krishna B. 1964. *Technique in the Tales of Henry James*. Cambridge, MA: Harvard University Press.

Wagenknecht, Edward. 1984. *The Tales of Henry James*. New York: Frederick Ungar.

Ward, J. A. 1961. *The Imagination of Disaster: Evil in the Fiction of Henry James*. Lincoln: University of Nebraska Press.

West, Rebecca [pseud.]. 1916. *Henry James*. London: Nisbet.

Winner, Viola Hopkins. 1970. *Henry James and the Visual Arts*. Charlottesville: University Press of Virginia. Revised in part from "The Artist and the Man in 'The Author of Beltraffio.'" *PMLA* 83 (March 1968): 102–8.

Wirth-Nesher, Hana. 1984. "The Thematics of Interpretation: James's Artist Tales." *Henry James Review* 5: 117–27.

Wright, Nathalia. 1965. *American Novelists in Italy, The Discoverers: Allston to James*. Philadelphia: University of Pennsylvania Press.

Wright, Walter F. 1962. *The Madness of Art: A Study of Henry James*. Lincoln: University of Nebraska Press.

Foreign Language

Gioli, Giovanna Mochi. 1971. "*The Turn of the Screw nella sue opposizioni strutturali.*" *Studi Americani*, no. 17: 75–92.

Murakami, Fujio. 1960. "The Question of the Aesthete in Henry James: 'The Author of Beltraffio.'" *Jimbun Kenkyu* 11 (June): 101–14. [Japanese]

Perrot, Jean. 1982. *Henry James: une écriture énigmatique*. Paris: Aubier.

The Beldonald Holbein

Publication History

"The Beldonald Holbein" appeared first in the October 1901 issue of *Harper's New Monthly Magazine*, illustrated by Lucius Hitchcock. In 1903 James included it in *The Better Sort* and later chose it for the New York Edition as well.

Circumstances of Composition, Sources, and Influences

In his New York Edition preface, James backed off from describing its genesis, saying "*that* story—by which I mean the story *of* it—would take us much too far" (*Criticism* 2, 1286). It would take one indeed to Rome where the germ for "The Beldonald Holbein" came to him in May 1899 at the house of Maud Howe near St. Peter's—a "flowered terrace on high roof of Palazzo Rusticucci, with *such* a view." She told him of the visit of her mother, Julia Ward Howe, the year before, who had created a sensation among the artists there at the age of seventy-eight for her beauty like a proper Holbein. Immediately James seized the "AWFULLY good little subject," reduced the woman's age to seventy-five, and added the idea of a foil (CN 183).

Tintner finds James drawing on "A Burne-Jones Head," an 1894 story by Clara Sherwood Rollins that tells of a woman, in this case a young one, finding by virtue of her resemblance to a painting a brief social success, ended by the jealousy of another woman. In Rollins's work, however, the "painting" is able to become a real person again (1989, 217–24). There is a similarity nevertheless in the limited worlds in which each succeeds. The Holbein, the narrator relates, debuts before "the world—I speak of course mainly of the art world," while the Burne-Jones is "exhibited to the world—that is, to Mrs. Tilbury's world" her "indolent dilettante Bohemian New York circle" (1989, 218, 224).

Even so, James himself might have been grateful for such a success. While he first wrote admiringly "*Revanche*—at 75!," in the story he reduces his heroine's age further to match his own, fifty-seven (CN 183). Tintner argues differently, that James reduces the woman's age to match that of his Holbein model, the portrait of *Lady Butts*, which his friend Isabella Gardner had recently purchased. She spots an additional allusion to another of Gardner's purchases, the *Rape of Europa*, in Lady Beldonald's resemblance to a Titian, but finds the inspiration for Mrs. Brash to be Gardner herself (1986, 201–5). Gale puts the contrast between Titian and Holbein as one between smoothness and "carefulness" (123). Thorberg, similarly, sees James using Titian here to represent mere coloring, while Holbein stands for a deeper reality (83). The artist narrator, Tinter argues, is based on Sargent and Paul Outreau on his friend Paul Helleu (1986, 94–95).

Wharton's 1928 "After Holbein" provides a far different view of old age at home in America, its punning title seeking perhaps a connection for a story depicting the encounter of an elderly woman who, like Lady Beldonald, believes in her own lasting beauty, but, unlike her, has thereby lost all touch with reality, and who like Mrs. Brash, has a last triumph, but one of mistaken perception, through an elderly man who has mistaken the night of an invitation and becomes a part of her macabre reenactment of the festivities of her prime.

Relation to Other Works

This tale treats both the world of the successful artist and the fashionable London that provides the artist his success. Perhaps for this reason, McElderry sees the series of artist tales it begins as less serious than earlier tales such as "The Middle Years" or "The Madonna of the Future" (145). Tintner notes an association with two other tales of London society and its artists, "The Special Type" and "The Tone of Time," remarking how in each tale the portraits become "substitutes" for people (1986, 99). Krook comments on the explicit recognition of the denizens of "our superior sophisticated world" both here and in "The Tone of Time," and finds Lady Beldonald as hard-hearted a London "*mondaine*" as Mrs. Cavenham of "The Special Type," Mrs. Brissenden, and Charlotte Stant (326–27). Looking instead at the victims, Gage links Mrs. Brash with Alice of "The Special Type." Gage also draws parallels with the previous tale in *The Better Sort*, "Broken Wings," whose country house Mundham is recalled in the worldly Mrs. Munden, while the focus changes from the artists' pride to Lady Beldonald's vanity (64–65, 76–77).

There are several links to "The Real Thing" including the narrator's threatening promise to make Lady Beldonald's portrait "the real thing" (CT 11, 306; also Horne 120). The artist narrators in both are at first not interested in age, but while the artist friend Outreau corrects the narrator's vision as does Jack Hawley in "The Real Thing," here it is in favor of the older model. Thorberg notes a resemblance between Mrs. Brash and the "plastic" Miss Churm of "The Real Thing" and between the fixed Lady Beldonald and the Monarchs (84). Winner, on the other hand, finds Mrs. Brash more like the Monarchs, pointing to the artist's view that although she would be a good subject for one or two paintings, she would not make a good model (109). Like the Monarchs she is simply what she is. Jones notes the resemblance between the empty Monarchs and Lady Beldonald, but also points out how Mrs. Brash, unlike the Monarchs, has the wisdom to realize that as the "real thing," she is a poor model (243–45).

Looking at the narrator, Krook notes a resemblance with the narrators of "The Special Type," "Mora Montravers," "The Velvet Glove," and *The Sacred Fount* in their need to rationalize their intense interest in the doings of others (329). Jones compares the narrator in his moral responsibility to Mrs. Brash to Frank Granger in "Flickerbridge" and the narrator of "The Real Thing" (244). Bowden sees him fulfilling that responsibility, praising the narrator's attitude in a comparison with Ralph Touchett of *The Portrait of a Lady*. Both men, he argues, while referring to women in terms of art works, do so in appreciation not only of a physical likeness but "the beauty of character" that is greater than art alone (64).

Looking at the *ficelle* Mrs. Munden, Sharp classifies her with Mrs. Penniman of *Washington Square,* Mrs. Beever of *The Other House,* Mrs. Brookenham of *The Awkward Age*, and Mrs. Brissenden of *The Sacred Fount* as one of the few women in James who serve as a friend to the protagonist without fitting the definition of "confidante" (247). Beach assigns her greater significance, and classes her with such characters as Maria Gostrey, Mrs. Assingham, and Mrs. Wix ([1918] 1954, 70–71).

Looking at the two contrasted women, Edel speaks of the story as another study of "Two Faces" (Life 4, 325; CT 11, 8; also Gage 67–68). While Przybylowicz sees Mrs. Brash as caught in the past like the "old things" of Poynton or the "living remnants" in The Aspern Papers (156), Winner finds a contrast between the artful preservation of Lady Beldonald and the genuine beauty of Mrs. Brash like that between the formality of Poynton and the "humanized" grace of Ricks (152–53). Similarly, Tintner notes of Mrs. Brash that she is a "natural masterpiece" as Milly Theale's resemblance to the Bronzino is natural (1986, 99). Jones compares the renunciatory deaths of Mrs. Brash and Milly (243–44). At the same time, Jones sees Mrs. Brash as a living work of art sacrificed to life as in "The Author of Beltraffio," Flickerbridge," and "The Velvet Glove." What she needed to forestall her fate, Jones adds, was a sophisticated but sensitive champion like Mrs. Alsager of "Nona Vincent" (245). In her humbleness, however, Gage suggests a parallel with "The Story in It," which also makes an argument for the humble subject as best for art (189).

Gage sees Lady Beldonald in her "plate-glass case" protecting herself from experience like John Marcher, and adds a resemblance to Beadel-Muffet, the missing celebrity of *The Papers* who has a "glass case all to himself" (90, 96). While Mrs. Brash does not need Europe to provide her with experience, Lady Beldonald, Thorberg argues, would have evolved into a type of Sarah Pocock of *The Ambassadors* if she had not come abroad (82). Wagenknecht draws a parallel between the exposé portrait proposed for Lady Beldonald at the tale's conclusion and the one of Colonel Capadose in "The Liar" (135).

Interpretation and Criticism

Contemplating the newly designated Holbein, Mrs. Brash, the narrator declares, "Time and life were artists who beat us all" (CT 11, 297). Still, the story he tells of the Holbein's reception in the artistic world of London, at least that "bounded on the north by Ibsen and on the south by Sargent" (CT 11, 302), has engendered sharp controversies over which indeed is the victor in this tale, life or art, and what is the nature of the victory. Thorberg, for example, finds the story going counter to the usual Jamesian line in showing life's superiority. Putt, however, writes that, as usual in James, art here "expose[s] and shatter[s]" life (236). Austin Wright allows art a more partial superiority in noting that Mrs. Brash's beauty is only appreciated by artists, and Thorberg admits, too, the story's reliance on the "special perceptivity" of the artist (Wright 106; Thorberg 79).

In his New York Edition preface, James examined the tale in a different light, speaking of the idea as "but a stray spark of the old 'international' flame" (*Criticism* 2, 1280). Appropriately therefore, Jefferson characterizes the story as an American tall tale in a British setting, a combination he finds producing a certain strain (163). The strain reproduces the international tensions of the tale, for it is the American Mrs. Brash who strains the boundaries of British society here. Most critics, however, who speak of the tale as international combine the theme with the aesthetic. Matthiessen and Murdock, for example, see the situation as relying on "an international contrast in aesthetic standards" (N 291). Wegelin senses the introduction of an "unquiet air of irony" about the international theme in the tale, in the fact that "unenlightened" America has produced a beauty that the "'aesthetic' perceptive 'European' 'air'"—as James spoke of it—cannot (52–53). Switching the emphasis, Horne states that James's concern is less with a contrast between two countries as between two views of art—that of the artist and the layman (120).

In its contrast of art and life or artist and layman, the story focuses on the contrast between two women, Lady Beldonald and Mrs. Brash, as presented through the viewpoint of the male narrator with the additional comments of one woman, Mrs. Munden, and one man, Paul Outreau. Unlike the women, both men are artists, and the character of the narrator has become the center of most critics' evaluation of the tale and the characters. The illustrations by

Hitchcock make the narrator appear, as Bogardus objects, rather "silly," an undistinguished bohemian with an upturned moustache. He is shown in one illustration, however, as producing what appears a competent portrait (78). In Beach's early view the narrator is not only competent, but Jamesian, and he sees James describing himself in the narrator's statement, "It's not my fault if I am so put together as often to find more life in situations obscure and subject to interpretation than in the gross rattle of the foreground" ([1918] 1954, 151; CT 11, 295–96; also Delbaere-Garant 220). Thus Beach sees the main objective of the tale as simply for the trio of narrator, author, and reader, to give evidence of their "superior good taste" through their ability to appreciate the Holbein (1921, 104). Kappeler, however, discerns in the narrator an artistic egotism not shared by James (99).

As is the tendency with Jamesian narrators, the one here has come under question, both by those who see him as reflecting James's own viewpoint, and those who do not. Although Blackall places him "on the periphery" of his tale (155), even Beach noted that his interest as an observer is sharpened by having "a little grudge of his own to gratify" ([1918] 1954, 69). Martineau is far more condemnatory, calling him little better than a murderer, arguing that with Mrs. Munden as his accomplice, he takes delight in a situation that produces at first discomfiture and then death for its object. The narrator, she notes, is not even the first one to recognize Mrs. Brash as a Holbein (Outreau is), yet still uses her to create for himself the social success his own paintings have not yet brought him. Even while the narrator criticizes Lady Beldonald for her social ambitions, which Martineau finds the "dramatic focus" of the tale, his, he argues, are no loftier. In Martineau's view, James is fully aware of his narrator's faults and presents them ironically "by allowing him to underplay the humane significance of events and to overplay their social significance" (22-25). One objection to Martineau's reading is that in the story the narrator appears to be already comfortably established in society. Such an established position need not, however, be an end to ambition or even malicious maneuvering. Like Martineau, Gage sees the narrator as deliberately harmful in his championing of Mrs. Brash while insulting Lady Beldonald, and sees his motivation throughout an egotistical desire to reinforce his sense of his own superiority. Even Mrs. Brash, whose side he apparently took, Gage argues, he "dehumanizes" at the end into a painting. In comparison, Gage judges Lady Beldonald's vanity and social ambition a minor fault (64–67).

In Walter Wright's reading, the narrator, who wishes to seem "calmly intellectual," also misses the significance of his narrative, but not from any maliciousness. To Wright, the story of Mrs. Brash serves simply as the frame for the more technically complicated problem, the portrait of Lady Beldonald. Her treatment of Mrs. Brash, Wright argues, provides the "glass case" needed to show her as she truly is, a fact even the narrator who is still pondering at the end how to capture her, does not recognize (135-36).

The discrediting of the narrator, however, is not yet universally accepted. Tintner, for example, takes straight the narrator's anger at Lady Beldonald and his intended "revenge" on her for Mrs. Brash's death through a portrait and speaks of the tale as showing the power of the portraitist to "blast society with the image he creates" (1989, 223; 1986, 95). Taking the story as the narrator presents it produces an aesthetic interpretation such as that of Horne, who argues that the narrator in the tale comes to recognize that art is not meant to be simply "decorative," that a painter must have a subject with character, not just surface (120).

Absolving the narrator can also switch—or perhaps return—the focus of the tale to the two women. Austin Wright reads the tale as the saga of Lady Beldonald's "comeuppance" delivered in the form of Mrs. Brash's success, a lesson she fails to accept, however, as illustrated by her failure to recognize Mrs. Brash's beauty, her firing of her, and her continued devotion to her own beauty seen in her hiring of a new companion (189–90). In Jones's reading, the tale is "one of James's most successful parables about art and life," its focus being the "single incisive, believable symbol, Mrs. Louisa Brash." Lady Beldonald, he argues, only comes to life to squelch the threat of Mrs. Brash, although both women have no conception of why the narrator and his friends are so taken with Mrs. Brash. Jones attributes her death not so much to despair as to a sense of completion, of sufficient triumph that can go no further. While keeping the women at the center, Jones also looks at the narrator, arguing that he recognizes the moral implications of flattering Mrs. Brash, the possible danger to her. But as he indicates, it is not the narrator, but Mrs. Brash who acts on this, refusing his offer to pose. The narrator, Jones argues, "feel[s]" but does not "know" she ought not to be painted, feeling guilty instead at having failed to capture her in paint, and so failing art as he has failed life. His only possible consolation, exposing Lady Beldonald in portraiture, Jones implies, will prove inadequate (242–45). The narrator at one point confesses that he was unsure "to the end . . . [Mrs. Brash] quite made it all out," an opinion Kappeler finds undercutting both his earlier justification of his promoting of her as providing her with "a deep draught of the very pride of life" and his tragic reading of her death. If she was never aware of her great triumph, its ending, Kappeler reasons, could not have killed her (99–101).

While many critics have questioned the narrator, most have accepted his charge that the preservation of Lady Beldonald's beauty rests on her avoidance of experience and emotion (e.g., Andreas 136). Thorberg's reading, which accepts the narrator as sincere, begins with his charge to contrast the genuine beauty of life visible in Mrs Brash with the professional, but ultimately unsatisfying veneer of Lady Beldonald. While noting Lady Beldonald's one moment of vision, Thorberg finds it insufficent to transform her. Certainly

Lady Beldonald's name, with its evocation of the poisonous belladonna, is against her. The woman is not, however, without friends. Macnaughton and Martin replace Lady Beldonald as villain with the narrator's "despicable friend" Mrs. Munden to expose the narrator whom they argue James treats with almost complete irony. They question Mrs. Munden's report about Lady Beldonald, hypothesizing that she is mistaken about her use of her companions as foils, and that she wants the narrator to paint Lady Beldonald only in order to expose her. Seeking to refurbish her reputation, they take her protestation of love for Brash as sincere, her reaction to her fame as more perplexed than jealous, and her "banishment" of Mrs. Brash as likely a result of Brash's own exhaustion. In their argument, the narrator accepts Mrs. Munden's jealous view of Lady Beldonald without evaluating it in return for her accepting his view of Mrs. Brash. The narrator, as a result, loses their sympathy. They particularly object to Thorberg's argument that he comes to recognize the superiority of life to art, stating that from start to finish the narrator sees Mrs. Brash only as a painting. In their view, the narrator is losing his original sensitivity as he becomes enured to society, and so patronizes Mrs. Brash, and fails to recognize how the American connection he looks down on has contributed to her distinction. While their placing of the narrator in a transitional state could explain some of the differing interpretations, there is little in the text to indicate that his position is in fact changing.

The narrator certainly has something of a cruel streak as is seen in his often-quoted description of Lady Beldonald, who remains "*naturally* new, as if she took out every night her large, lovely, varnished eyes and put them in water" and his seeing her, as he openly tells her, "with a long pin straight through your body" (CT 11, 293; see Gale 79, 220). His treatment of Mrs. Brash also raises the question of what relation there is, if any between aesthetic knowledge and compassion. When Mrs. Brash first looks at him "as if I had been trying on her some possibly heartless London trick" (CT 11, 296), she is reading both the potential of London and the narrator correctly. He is a part of the society and hence a part of the cruelty he would satirize and James does, and his reflection often stops with social categories. He is, as Macnaughton and Martin observe, capable of speaking of people as things, of Mrs. Brash as "a treasure to dispose of" or a "poor old picture . . . its face to the wall" (CT 11, 298, 306).

Whatever his faults, the narrator does at least have his moment of vision (perhaps as Lady Beldonald has hers) when he is bested, even if he cannot sustain it. He does at least initially concede defeat to the superior artistry of "Time and life." It is also likely that some of the mixture in his character, and the consequent confusion, stems from a similar mixture in James, who also deplored the cruelty of London and relished the details of its gossip, and who was subject to divided loyalties between his art and the life that inspired it.

Works Cited

Primary Works

James, Henry. 1901. "The Beldonald Holbein." *Harper's New Monthly Magazine* 103 (October): 807–21.

———. 1903. "The Beldonald Holbein." *The Better Sort*. New York: Scribner's, 24–49.

———. 1909. "The Beldonald Holbein." *The Novels and Tales of Henry James*. New York Edition. Vol. 18, 373–406. New York: Scribner's.

Secondary Works

Andreas, Osborn. 1948. *Henry James and the Expanding Horizon: A Study of the Meaning and Basic Themes of James's Fiction*. Seattle: University of Washington Press.

Beach, Joseph Warren. [1918] 1954. *The Method of Henry James*. Philadelphia: Albert Saifer.

———. 1921. "Henry James." *The Cambridge History of American Literature* 3. Ed. William Peterfield Trent, et al., 96–106. New York: Putnam's.

Blackall, Jean Frantz. 1965. *Jamesian Ambiguity and* The Sacred Fount. Ithaca, NY: Cornell University Press.

Bogardus, Ralph F. 1984. *Pictures and Texts: Henry James, A. L. Coburn and New Ways of Seeing in Literary Culture*. Ann Arbor: UMI Research Press.

Bowden, Edwin T. [1956] 1960. *The Themes of Henry James: A System of Observation Through the Visual Arts*. Yale Studies in English 132. New Haven: Yale University Press.

Delbaere-Garant, Jeanne. 1970. *Henry James: The Vision of France*. Paris: Société d'Editions Les Belles Lettres.

Gage, Richard P. 1988. *Order and Design: Henry James' Titled Story Sequences*. New York: Peter Lang.

Gale, Robert L. [1954] 1964. *The Caught Image: Figurative Language in the Fiction of Henry James*. Chapel Hill: University of North Carolina Press.

Horne, Helen. 1960. *Basic Ideals of James's Aesthetics as Expressed in the Short Stories Concerning Artists and Writers*. Marburg: Erich Mauersberger.

Jefferson, D. W. 1964. *Henry James and the Modern Reader*. New York: St. Martin's.

Jones, Granville H. 1975. *Henry James's Psychology of Experience: Innocence, Responsibility, and Renunciation in the Fiction of Henry James*. The Hague: Mouton.

Kappeler, Susanne. 1980. *Writing and Reading in Henry James*. New York: Columbia University Press.

Krook, Dorothea. [1962] 1967. *The Ordeal of Consciousness in Henry James*. New York: Cambridge University Press.

McElderry, Bruce R., Jr. 1965. *Henry James*. New York: Twayne.

Macnaughton, W. R., and W. R. Martin. 1976. "'The Beldonald Holbein': Another Jamesian Trap for the Unwary." *English Studies in Canada* 2: 299–305.

Martineau, Barbara. 1972. "Portraits are Murdered in the Short Fiction of Henry James." *Journal of Narrative Technique* 2: 16–25.

Przybylowicz, Donna. 1986. *Desire and Repression: The Dialectic of Self and Other in the Late Works of Henry James*. University: University of Alabama Press.

Putt, S. Gorley. 1966. *Henry James: A Reader's Guide*. Ithaca, NY: Cornell University Press.

Sharp, Sister M. Corona. 1963. *The Confidante in Henry James: Evolution and Moral Value of a Fictive Character*. Notre Dame, IN: Notre Dame University Press.

Thorberg, Raymond. 1968. "Henry James and the Real Thing: 'The Beldonald Holbein.'" *Southern Humanities Review* 3 (Winter): 78–85.

Tintner, Adeline R. 1989. *The Pop World of Henry James: From Fairy Tales to Science Fiction*. Ann Arbor: UMI Research Press. Revised from "James's 'The Beldonald Holbein' and Rollins' 'A Burne-Jones Head': A Surprising Parallel." *Colby Library Quarterly* 14 (1978): 183–90.

———. 1986. *The Museum World of Henry James*. Ann Arbor: UMI Research Press. Revised from "The Real-life Holbein in James's Fiction." *AB Bookman's Weekly* (8 January): 278–87.

Wagenknecht, Edward. 1984. *The Tales of Henry James*. New York: Frederick Ungar.

Wegelin, Christof. 1958. *The Image of Europe in Henry James*. Dallas, TX: Southern Methodist University Press.

Winner, Viola Hopkins. 1970. *Henry James and the Visual Arts*. Charlottesville: University Press of Virginia.

Wright, Austin McGiffert. 1961. *The American Short Story in the Twenties*. Chicago: University of Chicago Press.

Wright, Walter F. 1962. *The Madness of Art: A Study of Henry James*. Lincoln: University of Nebraska Press.

Benvolio

Publication History

"Benvolio" was the last of eleven tales that James published in the magazine *Galaxy*, where it appeared in the August 1875 issue. Four years later James included it in the British collection *The Madonna of the Future*, and four years after that in the Collective Edition of 1883. He did not publish it again in his lifetime. It next appeared in the 1920 collection *Master Eustace*, and then in Lubbock's edition of James's *Novels and Stories*.

Circumstances of Composition, Sources, and Influences

In September of 1874, James returned from Europe determined, he later said, to remain in the States "and be a good American citizen." He took up residence in New York City and supported himself by writing reviews. At the end of a year, however, James evidently abandoned his determination and returned to Europe (*Life* 2, 188–90).

"Benvolio" was the only story James published during his American interlude, and despite Kraft's caution against "reading too much of James's life" into the tale (81), it has frequently been read as an autobiographical reflection on the intersections of nationality, identity, and artistry, as treating indeed the "dilemma of the American artist" (Daugherty 95). To Mordell Benvolio is a "bit of self-portraiture," and Donald Stone calls his story "the most philosophical—and autobiographical" of the period (Mordell 2; Stone 192). Six years later, in *The Portrait of a Lady*, Ralph Touchett declares that one can't "give up one's country any more than one gives up one's grandmother. They're both antecedents to choice—elements of one's composition that are not to be eliminated." In this tale James appears to be asking whether one can indeed give up one's country, and if so, what the consequences would be. The camouflage of the fairy tale, Ruhm argues, is James's way of "distancing himself" from material otherwise too close to home (124).

Taking the tale's allegory as a cover for James's view on the position of the American artist, critics generally cast the Countess as Europe, or more specifically Italy, and Scholastica as America, or more specifically New England (e.g., Long 33–35). And according to most readings, James hangs on to both ancestries, while refusing to be confined to either. Although in his introduction to the tale Edel, for example, speaks of James's decision to "set sail to live with the Countess" (CT 3, 10), in his biography he stresses that James, while moving to Europe, chose not to eliminate any part of himself, but rather without much anguish to add on to himself as does Benvolio, to become cosmopolitan (*Life* 2, 192–93). Stone, who argues that Benvolio chooses America, sees him as failing thereby, and James so implying that he has himself succeeded by refusing to settle (192). Kelley reads the two poles of the story as Romance and Realism, to which James was alternately drawn— hoping to reconcile them both, afraid to give up either, particularly afraid that he might become dull by jettisoning romance (233–34). Many years later, in discussing the opposition of romance and reality in the preface to *The American*, James spoke of "the law of some rich passion in him for extremes," a passage Tintner cites as evidence of James's continuing appreciation of the contrast (1987, 57).

When not cast as countries, the Countess and Scholastica are usually seen as two approaches to literature or life. Edel and McElderry see the Professor and Scholastica as representing the philosophical life of James's father, or, Edel added later, his brother (*Life* 2, 191; *Life* 175; McElderry 34). Tanner remarks that James preferred "flirting with the Countess" (1963). In Edel's formulation, Benvolio functions with the Countess as the creative writer, while with Scholastica he becomes the critic. Here again, according to Edel, James never abandoned either role (*Life* 2, 192). Stressing Benvolio's gregarious side, Beebe sees James defending his own active social life and at the same time his right to give it up if he chose (203). Stressing the author's solitary side, Rogers reads the story's conclusion as illustrating how James's artist character—like himself—"throws over all other women to marry his muse" (101). Putt sees Benvolio's and James's satisfaction in their aloofness from society as adopted by necessity, but with "good grace" (90). Linking the two, Benvolio, as Long points out, becomes the noted playwright James would later strive to be (33). Edel remarks that James later read his play of *The American* to the imperious Isabella Gardner even as Benvolio read his plays to a Countess (*Life* 3, 41). The drama, in Ruhm's analysis, represents the bridge between the world of art and society in its demanding of the artist not only his private creation, but also his public involvement. He notes, however, that Benvolio is little concerned with the public reception of his play, spending the night of his second premiere with Scholastica (123). Edel finds the same "ambivalence and withdrawal" of the tale in yet another literary form, the "ritual" of James's notebooks (CN xii–xiii).

Allegory was, of course, a favorite form for Hawthorne, and McCarthy finds the allegory here suffering from the same intellectual abstractness James accused Hawthorne of in his 1879 biography (121). Beach finds the tale particularly Hawthornesque in its lack of dialogue, its use of "functions"—

Countess, Professor—for names, and its vague setting (186). More specifically, Anderson sees the story as a reversal of "Rappaccini's Daughter," in which the old scholar and his daughter, who here represents the muse, become "wholly benign." The reversal, according to Anderson, shows James's dissenting from Hawthorne's fear of the "impersonality of intelligence," showing that while the poet is limited if he does not go into society and "multiply . . . relations," society cannot even exist without the poet's imagination that creates it (38–39; also *Life* 2, 190). Long, on the other hand, sees something fatal in Scholastica's effect on Benvolio's art. The story for Long becomes James's demonstration that America could not sustain him as a writer, as it had Hawthorne (34–35, 169).

Despite the heavy critical emphasis on autobiographical interpretation, the characters have also been given literary sources. The sources for the Countess are, naturally enough, most often European. Kelley compares the Countess to a character from George Sand (233). Beebe and Tintner have linked her to Balzac's Fedora in *Le Peau de chagrin,* of whom it is said that "she is Society" (Beebe 202; Tintner 1987, 53). Beebe offers a source for Benvolio in the character of Shubin in Turgenev's *On the Eve,* who also suffers from alternating moods, and sees his behavior in turn providing a precedent for Shaw's poet, Eugene Marchbanks, in *Candida* (202–3). Wagenknecht notes a general reflection of George Eliot's *Romola* (179). Delbaere-Garant remarks a negative source, pointing out that James criticized the French naturalists for confining their art to Scholastica and neglecting its public, Countess side (218).

Benvolio's name also has literary echoes. Edel argues that the name comes from *Romeo and Juliet,* where Benvolio is the one who seeks to keep peace between the Montagues and Capulets, as the artist here plays peacemaker between his two selves (Life 2, 174). Melchiori counters that the name is more likely a play on Malvolio in *Twelfth Night,* noting the allusion to Illyria, the setting of that play, as support (9; also Tintner 1987, 53). Vaid, in turn, finds the allusion to Illyria contributing to the "romantic atmosphere" (274 n.14).

Benvolio at one point writes a "little poem in the style of Milton's *Penseroso,*" which is his "happiest performance" (CT 3, 375). Hence, Tintner traces the "polarities" of the tale as stemming from the paired poems *L'Allegro* and *Il Penseroso,* which show the "refreshing" balance possible between attention to society and scholarship. She points at the same time to Eastman Johnson's painting of *Milton Dictating Paradise Lost to His Daughters* as contributing to James's depiction of the professor's study, as well as his character and his relationship to his daughter. Through the two characters, Tintner argues, James blends together the poet and his "legend" (1986, 66–67, 152; 1987, 51–57).

Just before Benvolio first observes Scholastica, he buys a painting of Perseus and Andromeda that is particularly remarkable because of its "hidden radiance . . . which showed brightest when the room was half darkened" (CT 3, 366). Tintner finds that the painting approximates one by Carracci, also finding resemblances to a painting of "Roger and Angelica" by Ingres. The most important feature of the painting, shared by its two sources, she argues, is Perseus's riding of Pegasus, which represents the romantic imagination freed from the Gorgon of reality. Also significant, she notes, is the more poignant resemblance between Andromeda and Scholastica, who share an additional kinship with Milton's Melancholia (1987, 54–57).

Relation to Other Works

Several critics, including Edel, who finds both characters reflections of James's own personality, have remarked on how Benvolio's split personality anticipates that of his fellow writer Clare Vawdrey in "The Private Life." Edel notes, however, that unlike the later Vawdrey, whose two halves work together to allow him to do his work, the two halves of Benvolio are at war with each other (CN xii; 1970, 211; also Vaid 148). He finds several ambivalent heroes earlier in James as well, in *Daisy Miller,* and in "Longstaff's Marriage" and "Four Meetings," Benvolio's companion tales in its volume of the 1883 collected edition (*Life* 3, 69).

Jones notes some of the allegorical elements in James's presentation of the conflict of life and art recurring in the more complex full-length *Roderick Hudson*, with Christina Light paralleling the Countess, and Mary Garland, Scholastica (65). Wright observes that Benvolio without Scholastica "cannot fully benefit" from Italy, putting him in the company of such James characters as Roderick Hudson who fail there through a disarrangement of art and love (223). Donald Stone also links Benvolio and *Roderick Hudson*, seeing the same theme—the artist caught between private duty and public pleasure—in both (192). Long remarks on how one story depicts an artist's death in America, the other in Europe (36). Matthiessen finds the allegory in both works, as in "The Romance of Certain Old Clothes," stemming from Hawthorne (71). Tanner sees the contrasting Scholastica and Countess a prevision of the contrasting women in another later international novel, Mrs. Newsome and Mme de Vionnet in *The Ambassadors* ([1966] 1987, 110).

"The Lesson of the Master," according to Beebe, shows what might have become of Benvolio had he married the Countess (208). Tintner also compares the two stories, seeing James contrasting two approaches to life in each with a comic touch, and providing each with a "kind of do-it-yourself ending"

(1989, 145, 155). Kraft distinguishes two kinds of the tension between life and art present here in later James works. In *Roderick Hudson* and "The Lesson of the Master" the artists seek to create an art apart from ordinary life, and such characters as Ralph Touchett and Milly Theale, whose "life is their art," struggle for that life (82). Vaid sees the uncut pages of Benvolio's manuscript at the Countess's anticipating the unread work of Neil Paraday at Mrs. Wimbush's (274 n.17).

The Countess has also been likened to the Princess Casamassima, Anderson citing Benvolio's speech to her, "If a man were a revolutionist, you would reconcile him to society," as anticipating the theme in the novel (39 n.; also Maves 56). Edel finds Hyacinth, like Roderick and Benvolio before him, a man torn between two worlds (*Life* 3, 183). One might add also Mrs. Gracedew of *Covering End* as an example of a beautiful, persuasive woman who more successfully reconciles a man to society. Edel adds *The Tragic Muse* as a demonstration of the same split between art and society, particularly in the character of Peter Sherringham, who had "two men in him, quite separate" (*Life* 3, 255–56, 261).

Judging it an equivocal fairy tale, Tintner calls "Benvolio" James's farewell to the genre until "Mrs. Temperly" (1989, 30). Edward Stone emphasizes James's continued interest in the form throughout his career, citing *The Turn of the Screw* as another example (139–40).

Interpretation and Criticism

The form of the tale is a mixed one, and has received many labels over the years. The tale begins after the manner of a fairy tale, "once upon a time." But James has his narrator immediately caution, "This is not a fairy-tale." Still, Benvolio himself was "in some respects as pretty as any fairy prince," and the narrator slips at times in the story, and beginning his conclusion with regrets that he said it was not a fairy tale, he ends with an apology, "But excuse me; I am writing as if it *were* a fairy-tale!" (CT 3, 351, 401). As many critics have responded, it *is* one (e.g., Long 33). Vaid points out that the relaxed omniscient narration—Springer refers to it as "conspicuous"— and its apologies are typical of the oral narration of such a tale (Springer 140; Vaid 146–47). Benvolio is different perhaps from the typical fairy-tale hero because he is a poet, and his "magic ring," as the narrator tells us, is simply his "poetic imagination" (CT 4, 352).

Such a difference has led to different, more serious, labels. Vaid and Putt, for example, both speak of the tale as a parable (Vaid 145). In Putt's view the "poetic imagination" Benvolio possesses was, for James, "very largely the matter of seeing things from both sides" (91), and focusing their readings on the tale's intense duality, most critics categorize it as an allegory. As Edel notes,

James generally disliked allegory, saying it ruined "two good things—a story and a moral, a meaning and a form" (*Life* 2, 190). In preference to allegory, Springer offers the term "apologue"—an "inductive kind of fable" with fuller characterization. She notes that James himself used the term to speak of "Flickerbridge," and cites Paul Bourget to explain that the apologue does not argue points, but "shake[s] up" ideas in a more interesting, less dogmatic way (127, 143–44). One need not change terms, however, to see the tale as an allegory with a difference—as Tintner terms it, a "playful allegory"—that, as Vaid writes, never turns wooden (Tintner 57; Vaid 151–52). Perhaps its fusion with the fairy tale is what saves it from such a fate.

Benvolio himself is characterized as "a tissue of absolute contradictions": "It was as if the souls of two very different men had been thrown together in the same mold and they had agreed. . . . to run the machine in alternation." Benvolio's two souls are embodied outwardly in the tale's many contrasts, including the contrast between his two rooms, the one like a "monastic cell," the other opening onto the town, and between his two loves, the Countess and Scholastica (CT 4, 354). Springer observes that the contrast between the two women is "prepared for" by Benvolio's own divided character (145). Putt goes even further, dismissing their role as simply a further elaboration of the already clear contrast established by the two rooms. He emphasizes instead Benvolio's "love of direct impressions and the sensuous appreciation even of his somewhat artificial austerities," which owe their loyalty to neither woman (90).

Nevertheless, the two women have occupied a fair amount of the critics' attention. The first, the Countess, as Vaid acknowledges, represents the world, but not necessarily, he cautions, "at its best" (148). Springer, on the other hand, stresses how Benvolio's compliments make the Countess, in the narrator's words, not only "happier, but . . . better," indicating that the poet can improve the world, even a shallow one (152–53). Mull notes a similarity between the Countess and Benvolio in their privileges, drawing attention to the significance of money in the description of Benvolio having "the voice as it were of a man whose fortune has been made for him, and who assumes, a trifle egotistically, that the rest of the world is equally at leisure to share with him the sweets of life, to pluck the wayside flowers, and chase the butterflies afield" (15).

Scholastica, in Springer's estimate, is never the equal of the Countess, merely an alternative. Nevertheless, she finds Scholastica's ability to advise Benvolio that "a poet ought to run all risks. . . . But he ought to escape them all!" an indication that her character is more than allegorical (155–56, 188–89). Vaid also rates her highly, speaking of her as the "muse in isolation from the world" with whom Benvolio has a "greater intellectual affinity." He notes that James is careful to portray her through the poet's view, while he leaves the picture of the Countess to the narrator. Scholastica, in his view, really loves Benvolio and appreciates him as a poet, unlike the Countess (148–50).

Scholastica has two kinsmen who also play allegorical roles. Vaid notes that the presence of the father opposes the world not simply to the muse, but more narrowly to "the dusky world of fact," and Springer argues that the latter is the purer contrast of world and cell (Vaid 149). But if the transcendental father lives in the garden, its actual owner, Long points out, is the business-minded brother, whom Springer takes as representing the "sacrifice of libido" in the "exclusively scholarly life" (Long 33–35; Springer 155–56).

If the general emphasis is on Benvolio the artist, some critics have pointed out that the conflicts he faces hold true for everyone, Long calling the tale an "allegory of general human duality" (34). Andreas finds the conflict between the superiority of the social and scholarly life for the artist less significant than the basic conflict between vocation and love (86). Kraft observes that the conflict here between "the desire to live fully, but also to articulate and define life in some effective way" exists for any sensitive person. For James, however, he argues that the only workable solution is to deny the "limitations of any position," making the "artist and the internationalist" the most likely to achieve it (82–83).

Critics have differed over whether Benvolio achieves such a solution, and whether at the end he is forced to make a choice. Kelley, Long, Tanner, and Daugherty all argue that Benvolio chooses Scholastica, which, the narrator indicates makes his poetry dull (Kelley 233; Long 33–35; Tanner 1963; Daugherty 95). The conclusion also tells us, however, that before bringing Scholastica back Benvolio was not writing anything at all. Thus, Vaid argues, Benvolio has failed to achieve the necessary balance between "the world and the muse" (148–52).

The concluding paragraph, however, is hedged by the narrator's apology that he is writing as if the story were a fairy tale. The story proper appears to end with Benvolio's farewell to the Countess as he tells her that he cared for her "only by contrast," preferring for his one "constancy" his own "poetic brow" (CT 4, 401). Several critics have, accordingly, emphasized Benvolio's constancy through contrasts. As Beebe writes, Benvolio "makes use of everything without succumbing to anything" (203). Both McElderry and Edel state that Benvolio does not choose absolutely, that he lives harmoniously content with both approaches to life as he lives them, unhampered by doubt (McElderry 34; *Life* 2, 193–94). Such an alternation, Springer argues, is necessary for the poetic imagination; choosing between the two, while appropriate to a fairy tale, would be untenable for the real poet (141–43).

The tale is sui generis in the James canon. Its uniqueness has brought forth varied responses. Donald Stone is unimpressed by what he sees as the "trivial treatment" of a significant theme (192). Vaid, however, finds it sufficiently serious, maintaining that it merits greater attention due to its "immense biographical and thematic significance as well as intrinsic narrative charm and excellence of execution" (145). The tale is, as Edel calls it, a *"jeu d'esprit"* (*Life* 2, 190). It is also, as Schelling has it, "delightful" (171) and, as Springer calls it, "charming" (139). Kelley acknowledges its origins in James's "amus[ing] himself by dashing off a whimsical little story" without finding they take away from its message (233). Just as the story celebrates opposites, its decorative playful surface and underlying profundity peacefully coexist and nurture each other.

Works Cited

Primary Works
James, Henry. 1875. "Benvolio." *Galaxy* 20 (August): 209–35.

———. 1879. "Benvolio." *The Madonna of the Future and Other Tales*. London: Macmillan.

———. 1883. "Benvolio." *Collective Edition*. Vol. 13. London: Macmillan.

———. 1920. "Benvolio." *Master Eustace*. Preface by Albert Mordell. New York: Thomas Seltzer, 203–80.

———. 1921–23. "Benvolio." *The Novels and Stories of Henry James*. Vol. 24. Ed. Percy Lubbock. London: Macmillan.

Secondary Works
Anderson, Quentin. 1957. *The American Henry James*. New Brunswick, NJ: Rutgers University Press.

Andreas, Osborn. 1948. *Henry James and the Expanding Horizon: A Study of the Meaning and Basic Themes of James's Fiction*. Seattle: University of Washington Press.

Beach, Joseph Warren. [1918] 1954. *The Method of Henry James*. Philadelphia: Albert Saifer.

Beebe, Maurice L. 1964. *Ivory Towers and Sacred Founts: The Artist as Hero*. New York: New York University Press.

Daugherty, Sarah B. 1981. *The Literary Criticism of Henry James*. Athens: Ohio University Press.

Delbaere-Garant, Jeanne. 1970. *Henry James: The Vision of France*. Paris: Société d'Editions Les Belles Lettres.

Jones, Granville H. 1975. *Henry James's Psychology of Experience: Innocence, Responsibility, and Renunciation in the Fiction of Henry James*. The Hague: Mouton.

Kelley, Cornelia Pulsifer. [1930] 1965. *The Early Development of Henry James*. Urbana: University of Illinois Press.

Kraft, James. 1969. *The Early Tales of Henry James*. Carbondale: Southern Illinois University Press.

Long, Robert Emmet. 1979. *The Great Succession: Henry James and the Legacy of Hawthorne*. Pittsburgh: University of Pittsburgh Press.

McCarthy, Harold T. 1958. *Henry James: The Creative Process*. New York: Thomas Yoseloff.

McElderry, Bruce R., Jr. 1965. *Henry James*. New York: Twayne.

Matthiessen, F. O. 1944. *Henry James: The Major Phase*. New York: Oxford University Press.

Maves, Carl. 1973. *Sensuous Pessimism: Italy in the Work of Henry James*. Bloomington: Indiana University Press.

Melchiori, Giorgio. 1965. "Locksley Hall Revisited: Tennyson and Henry James." *Review of English Literature* 6 (October): 9–25. Reprinted in Barbara Melchiori and Giorgio Melchiori. *Il Gusto di Henry James*. Turin: Guilio Einaudi editore, 1974.

Mull, Donald. 1973. *Henry James's "Sublime Economy": Money as Symbolic Center in the Fiction*. Middletown, CT: Wesleyan University Press.

Putt, S. Gorley. 1966. *Henry James: A Reader's Guide*. Ithaca, NY: Cornell University Press. Revised from "'Benvolio': Everyone was a little someone else.'" *Scholars of the Heart: Essays in Criticism*. London: Faber, 141–235.

Rogers, Robert. 1970. *A Psychoanalytic Study of the Double in Literature*. Detroit: Wayne State University Press.

Ruhm, Herbert, ed. 1961. *"Lady Barbarina" and Other Tales: "Benvolio," "Glasses," and Three Essays*. The Universal Library. New York: Grosset & Dunlap.

Schelling, Felix E. 1922. "Some Forgotten Tales of Henry James." *Appraisements and Asperities: As to Some Contemporary Writers*. Philadelphia: Lippincott, 169–74.

Springer, Mary Doyle. 1978. *A Rhetoric of Literary Character: Some Women of Henry James*. Chicago: University of Chicago Press. Reprinted in part in "Henry James," comp. Dennis Lane and Rita Stein. In *A Library of Literary Criticism: Modern British Literature* 5, 2d supplement, 249–54. New York: Frederick Ungar.

Stone, Donald David. 1972. *Novelists in a Changing World: Meredith, James, and the Transformation of English Fiction in the 1880's*. Cambridge, MA: Harvard University Press.

Stone, Edward. 1964. *The Battle and the Books: Some Aspects of Henry James*. Athens: Ohio University Press.

Tanner, Tony. 1987. "The Watcher from the Balcony: *The Ambassadors*." In *Henry James*. Ed. Harold Bloom. New York: Chelsea House. Reprinted from *Critical Inquiry* 8, no. 1 (Spring 1966): 105–23.

———. 1963. "James's Little Tarts." *The Spectator* 210 (4 January): 19.

Tintner, Adeline R. 1989. *The Pop World of Henry James: From Fairy Tales to Science Fiction*. Ann Arbor: UMI Research Press.

———. 1987. *The Book World of Henry James: Appropriating the Classics*. Ann Arbor: UMI Research Press. Revised from "The Countess and Scholastica: Henry James's 'L'Allegro' and 'Il Penseroso.'" *Studies in Short Fiction* 11 (Summer 1974): 267–76.

———. 1986. *The Museum World of Henry James*. Ann Arbor: UMI Research Press.

Vaid, Krishna B. 1964. *Technique in the Tales of Henry James*. Cambridge, MA: Harvard University Press.

Wagenknecht, Edward. 1984. *The Tales of Henry James*. New York: Frederick Ungar.

Wright, Nathalia. 1965. *American Novelists in Italy, The Discoverers: Allston to James*. Philadelphia: University of Pennsylvania Press.

Broken Wings

Publication History

"Broken Wings" was the only story James published in *Century* magazine, where it appeared in the 1900 Christmas issue with an illustration by Maurice Greiffenhagen and a title decoration by F. C. Gordon. James then included it in both the 1903 collection *The Better Sort* and the New York Edition.

Circumstances of Composition, Sources, and Influences

James mailed this story to his agent, Pinker, on September 17, 1899, writing the day before to Kipling with, in his words, "a crabbed hand—a plume from a broken or at least weary—wing" (*Letters* 4, 120). In the New York Edition preface James admits himself unable to recall the "buried germ" that led to the writing of "Broken Wings," but continues:

> when had I been, as a fellow scribbler, closed to the general admonition
> of such adventures as poor Mrs. Harvey's . . . to such predicaments as
> Stuart Straith's. . . . The appeal of mature purveyors obliged, in the very

interest of their presumed, their marketable, freshness, to dissimulate the grim realities of shrunken "custom," the felt chill of a lower professional temperature—any old note-book would show *that* laid away as a tragic "value" not much less tenderly than some small plucked flower of association left between the leaves for pressing. (*Criticism* 2, 1241–42)

He notes, further, that the "admonition" to "Dramatise, dramatise, dramatise!" had remained difficult until he hit upon the idea of using a "*pair* of situations," in which the encounter of the two artists would provide sufficient drama for a tale (*Criticism* 2, 1242). This gave him the "double-case technique" he also used in "The Abasement of the Northmores" and "Fordham Castle" for foreshortening (Segal 112 n.8).

His notebooks do contain an entry on February 16, 1899, that provides the basic situation of the two artists, their mutual misunderstanding brought about by failure and pride and their final reunion, an entry Matthiessen and Murdock argue James had by his side while writing the preface (CN 179; N xi). Wagenknecht sees in it a reflection of James's return to fiction after his failure on the stage in 1895 and locates the same sentiment in his 1914 letter to Henry Adams, in which he proclaims himself "that queer monster, the artist, an obstinate finality, an inexhaustible sensibility" and writes "it all takes doing—and I do. I believe I shall do yet again—it is still an act of life" (127–29). Apart from Putt, who suspects James's motives in criticizing society, critics have generally reacted approvingly to the tale's reflection of James's experiences as a writer (236).

Taking a psychoanalytic approach to the tale, Edel pictures James as writing the story just before the arrival at Lamb House of his brother William in October as a fantasized reconciliation based on his own sense of failure and William's failed health (*Life* 4, 326, 338).

Taking the tale as another form of biography, Tintner names Mrs. Oliphant, whose husband was a painter, as a model for Mrs. Harvey, noting that both were hard-working novelists who outlived their fashionableness, Mrs. Oliphant becoming a contributor of a "letter" to *Blackwood's* even as Mrs. Harvey writes for the *Blackport Banner* (1989, 188–93). Earlier Ned Limbert wrote for the *Blackport Beacon*, and like Limbert Mrs. Harvey is far more of a serious artist than James considered Mrs. Oliphant to be.

Tintner also compares the tale with Edith Wharton's tale "Copy," which depicts the reencounter of two mature artists who earlier loved each other. In Wharton's tale there is no rekindling of love, but a renunciation of the intent to exploit it by burning rather than publishing their love letters to each other (1986, "Wharton," 4).

Tintner offers Mentmore Towers the modern Renaissance palace of the Roseberys as a model for Mundham (1986, *Museum*, 210).

Relation to Other Works

Ranging for similarities among the thematically linked stories of *The Better Sort*, Gage draws comparisons between the bitter Straith and the artist of "The Beldonald Holbein," between the pride of both Straith and Mrs. Harvey and the vanity of Lady Beldonald, and between their failure and renunciation and that of Frank Granger in "Flickerbridge." Perhaps most tellingly, he contrasts the reunion after ten years time of Straith and Harvey and that of John Marcher and May Bartram in "The Beast in the Jungle," finding them more comparable to the successfully united pair of *The Papers*, to which one might add the different reencounter of the artist Lyon and his former love in the earlier "The Liar" (64–65, 74, 84, 89, 109). Ward links the protagonists not only with Marcher but also Fleda Vetch, Stransom of "The Altar of the Dead," and Isabel Archer among others in their pride, less "dynamic" than Isabel's, but less hardened than Marcher's, leaving them "essentially moral" characters (89–90). Similarly, by its subject of "false pride" and second chances, Jones links it with "The Bench of Desolation" and "The Jolly Corner" (249). Blackall sees connections also with *The Sacred Fount*, another argument against the "wasting of life," although unlike it and "The Beast in the Jungle," "Broken Wings" also depicts the putting off of the "masks" of pride that puts an end to such waste (168–72).

The story takes its place among James's artist tales in its mourning of the way society punishes and impoverishes the serious artist (e.g., Dietrichson 128–30; Krook 350). As Straith says of himself and Mrs. Harvey, "We can't afford the opulent"—they take not only one's money, but one's imagination. And so the focus of criticism has often been on the new "antipathy" to country house life Edel sees also in *The Sacred Fount* (*Life* 4, 339). Holder links the tale with "The Death of the Lion" in showing the failure of the aristocracy to fulfill their role as patrons of the arts, while Walter Wright finds them, though well intentioned, similar to the hostile countess in "The Middle Years" (Holder 294–95; Wright 80). Jefferson finds the same animal imagery linking the "great gilded cages" of Mundham, the circus of Mrs. Wimbush's house in "The Death of the Lion," and the Roman circus of Burbeck in "The Two Faces" (51–52). Powers, who reads the name of the country house Mundham as indicating the opposition between "*ars et mundus*," more optimistically sees the artists' failure as protecting them from Paraday's fate (102). Gill sees them rather than the aristocrats making the crucial decison to "retreat" from country house life "in self-protection" (80). There are echoes of the Monarchs of "The Real Thing," who exhibit both the upper-class lack of imagination and the artists' poignant "appeal" as "mature purveyors" still attempting to keep up appearances despite reverses. The title of the play Straith helped design, "The New Girl," indicates, as Tintner notes, how they have been left behind, even as the success of Churm and Oronte strands the Monarchs (1989, 191).

Interpretation and Criticism

Most critics focus on the sympathy apparent in James's preface for his two artists, evident particularly in the story's "poignant" conclusion (Krook 350; also Horne 105). Even Putt praises the suffering artists as genuine, "too real" for James's geometrical plot (236). Matheson remarks several resolutions, between Woman and Art, the male artist and the female, fiction and the pictorial arts, all sustained by the respectful portrait of a woman as a serious artist, although she warns such resolutions do not augur any reconciliation with society. She also feels it necessary to qualify James's unusual inclusiveness further, opining that Mrs. Harvey "in some ways hardly seems female" and appears uninterested in motherhood (228–29). Horne corrects Andreas's argument that the two marry only because they no longer expect any "strenuous artistic career" by quoting the story's concluding line—"And now to work!" (Andreas 94; Horne 104).

Some critics have focused less on the theme of society vs. art, and more on the universal—or personal—issue of pride. Jones in particular disagrees with Putt's blaming of society, stating that to extricate themselves from their predicament, Straith and Harvey do not need artistic or social success, but an honest recognition of failure and its value in human relationship (250–51). In the tale the pair "turned for relief from pain to a perversity of pride" and in his notebook James had speculated about what would be "the situation that BREAKS DOWN THEIR MUTUAL PRIDE" (CT 11, 233; CN 179). It is that—the "final abandonment of pride"—that produces the "relief" described in the preface as the story's "drama" (CT 11, 236; *Criticism* 2, 1242). The story, Ward notes, forgives its protagonists their pride (89). As Gage observes, Straith and Harvey gain "virtue and happiness" by renouncing not only society but also their renunciation of each other (63). Thus James produced one of his few tales that can accurately be classified as a romantic comedy, as Austin Wright has done (386). Since, as Putt notes, it is the pair's failure, whatever its causes, that brings them together, it makes sense that they accept their defeat, in McElderry's phrase, "good-naturedly" (Putt 236; McElderry 122). If theirs is a fall, it is a fortunate one.

Works Cited

Primary Works
James, Henry. 1900. "Broken Wings." *Century Magazine* 61 (December): 194–203.

———. 1903. "Broken Wings." *The Better Sort*. London: Methuen; New York: Scribner's, 1–23.

———. 1909. "Broken Wings." *The Novels and Tales of Henry James*. New York Edition. Vol. 16, 135–64. New York: Scribner's.

Secondary Works

Andreas, Osborn. 1948. *Henry James and the Expanding Horizon: A Study of the Meaning and Basic Themes of James's Fiction*. Seattle: University of Washington Press.

Blackall, Jean Frantz. 1965. *Jamesian Ambiguity and* The Sacred Fount. Ithaca, NY: Cornell University Press.

Dietrichson, Jan W. 1969. *The Image of Money in the American Novel of the Gilded Age*. Oslo: Universitetsforlaget; New York: Humanities.

Gage, Richard P. 1988. *Order and Design: Henry James' Titled Story Sequences*. New York: Peter Lang.

Geismar, Maxwell. 1963. *Henry James and the Jacobites*. Boston: Houghton Mifflin.

Gill, Richard. 1972. *Happy Rural Seat: The English Country House and the Literary Imagination*. New Haven: Yale University Press.

Holder, Alan. 1966. *Three Voyagers in Search of Europe: A Study of Henry James, Ezra Pound, and T. S. Eliot*. Philadelphia: University of Pennsylvania Press.

Horne, Helen. 1960. *Basic Ideals of James's Aesthetics as Expressed in the Short Stories Concerning Artists and Writers*. Marburg: Erich Mauersberger.

Jefferson, D. W. [1960] 1971. *Henry James*. New York: Capricorn.

Jones, Granville H. 1975. *Henry James's Psychology of Experience: Innocence, Responsibility, and Renunciation in the Fiction of Henry James*. The Hague: Mouton.

Krook, Dorothea. [1962] 1967. *The Ordeal of Consciousness in Henry James*. New York: Cambridge University Press.

McElderry, Bruce R., Jr. 1965. *Henry James*. New York: Twayne.

Matheson, Gwen. 1968. "Portraits of the Artist and the Lady in the Shorter Fictions of Henry James." *Dalhousie Review* 48: 222–30.

Powers, Lyall H. 1970. *Henry James: An Introduction and Interpretation*. New York: Holt, Rinehart.

Putt, S. Gorley. 1966. *Henry James: A Reader's Guide*. Ithaca, NY: Cornell University Press.

Segal, Ora. 1969. *The Lucid Reflector: The Observer in Henry James' Fiction*. New Haven: Yale University Press.

Tintner, Adeline R. 1989. *The Pop World of Henry James: From Fairy Tales to Science Fiction*. Ann Arbor: UMI Research Press. Revised from "'Broken Wings': Henry James' Tribute to a Victorian Novelist," *AB Bookman's Weekly* 75, no. 16 (22 April 1985): 2016–28.

———. 1986. *The Museum World of Henry James*. Ann Arbor: UMI Research Press.

————. 1986. "Wharton and James: Some Literary Give and Take." *Edith Wharton Newsletter* 3, no. 1 (Spring): 3–5, 8.

Wagenknecht, Edward. 1984. *The Tales of Henry James*. New York: Frederick Ungar.

Ward, J. A. 1961. *The Imagination of Disaster: Evil in the Fiction of Henry James*. Lincoln: University of Nebraska Press.

Wright, Austin McGiffert. 1961. *The American Short Story in the Twenties*. Chicago: University of Chicago Press.

Wright, Walter F. 1962. *The Madness of Art: A Study of Henry James*. Lincoln: University of Nebraska Press.

Brooksmith

Publication History

"Brooksmith" was published in May of 1891, appearing in the United States in *Harper's Weekly*, where it was illustrated by Charles Howard Johnson, and in England in *Black and White*, where it was illustrated by John H. Bacon. James included it the next year in his collection *The Lesson of the Master*. He also included it in the New York Edition.

Circumstances of Composition, Sources, and Influences

"Brooksmith" began with James's hearing of the response of a maid to the death of her mistress, Mrs. Duncan Stewart, who three years later would be James's model for the "genial, clever, worldly, old-fashioned, half comforting, half shocking" Lady Davenant in *A London Life* (CN 38). According to her daughter, the maid told her, "You continue to see good society, to live with clever, cultivated people: but I fall again into my own class, I shall never see such company—hear such talk—again" (CN 28–29). James recorded the incident on June 19, 1884, but did not make use of it for some years. In his preface, he recounts the episode, explaining that he substituted a butler for the maid because a butler would have more opportunity to hear "rare table-talk" than the "more effaced tirewoman," and so accordingly replaced the intended "modified" portrait of Mrs. Stewart with a man (*Criticism* 2, 1282–83).

In November of 1890 James was intending to send "Brooksmith," being typed at the time, to Horace E. Scudder at the *Atlantic*, although he wrote him that he was nervous about doing so since they had just refused to print *The Pupil*, of which he was so confident (*Letters* 3, 307). By March of 1891 he had decided that Scudder had no right to reject work by an author of his reputation and had sent "Brooksmith" to *Black and White* (*Letters* 3, 338–39).

In a notebook entry in 1892 James projected the possibility of another tale treating the situation of an underappreciated servant, considering the "idea of a servant suspected of doing the mean things—the base things people in London take for granted servants do—reading of letters, diaries, peeping, spying, etc" while being quite innocent (CN 65–66).

Gerlach notes how the story's beginning with the death of its central character is typical of James, but how in his notebook entry the story's conclusion remains "a pious hope"; as James put it, "Represent this . . . with denouement if possible" (76, 88).

While Vaid compares the form of the tale to a sketch by Lamb or Stevenson (49), Harris compares the technique of the beginning of the story to Kipling and notes that "Brooksmith" appeared the same year as James's introduction to Kipling's *Soldiers Three*, in which he sees James praising qualities similar to those of his tale, the stories of common people told by a "narrator, who never arranges or glosses or falsifies" (103–4). One might also find a resemblance between the final situation of Brooksmith still "changing plates" for the gods despite his service on earth and that of Kipling's Gunga Din (1890) ". . . squattin' on the coals/Givin' drink to poor damned souls." The servitude of both is depicted as infinite, despite the fact that they both appear superior to those who tell their stories, as Kipling's narrator acknowledges, declaring, "You're a better man than I am, Gunga Din." In treating the relationship between servant and master, the tale has, as Fadiman indicates, a long literary history, including the relationship between Don Quixote and Sancho Panza (292).

When the friends of the late Offord meet, the narrator imagines them thinking of each other "Yes, you too have been in Arcadia" (CT 8, 13). Pearce interprets the allusion with an emphasis on the fellowship in "song"—conversation here—of Arcady—Offord's garden-like salon—which is broken by the intrusion of death. In the tale, he argues, art is opposed to reality, and to deny the power of death, the narrator "poetise[s]" the facts of Brooksmith's end in the manner of "Lycidas" or Spenser's November eclogue (838–40). Tintner places Offord's Arcadia in the "golden age" of eighteenth-century France, comparing it to Candide's garden (1986, 113–13, 116). Logically, therefore, she sees the relationship between Brooksmith and Mr. Offord (who is likened to "the dying Voltaire") as based on that between Voltaire and his devoted secretaries (1987, 214–16). One might note a further connection in that Candide comes to the conclusion that one must cultivate one's garden only after a trial of the world, which proves that that is the most one can hope for. The world here proves similarly inhospitable to Brooksmith, who no longer has even a garden to return to.

Wagenknecht finds him as "pitiful" as Bartleby (62).

Relation to Other Works.

"Brooksmith" takes its part as the short story in a trilogy of James's works treating lower-class characters, including the novella *In the Cage* and the novel *The Princess Casamassima*. Frantz draws a tighter connection between "Brooksmith" and *In the Cage*, arguing that for the novella James returned to the female center originally considered for "Brooksmith" since the telegraph office provided for her the larger context necessary. He pictures the intelligence and imagination of Brooksmith and the telegraphist as tantalized but ultimately thwarted by their limited exposure to a "better" society (225-26). Indeed, both are fundamentally eavesdroppers on a society they never fully enter. Jones notes how Brooksmith, like Hyacinth Robinson, becomes "more cultivated than his social station can accommodate" (201). Krook finds, however, that in all three works the lower-class characters are made so "refined," and seen so wholly in their relations to the upper class, who indeed control what we see of them, even as our view of the models in "The Real Thing" is dependent on the artist narrator, that they make an ineffective case for James's interest in the lower class (4–5 n.1). Similarly, Edward Stone finds them owing more to James's imagination than to his experience (6–7). (See also "The Patagonia.")

Gage points to further connections with "The Real Thing" in the shared presentation of artistic lower-class people in contrast with ineffective members of the upper class, although he distinguishes Brooksmith from Churm and Oronte in his greater sensitivity and their greater success. Gage also contrasts Pandora, the self-made American girl, with Brooksmith, also self-made, but destroyed by a less receptive society (183, 185, 188). Similarly, Edel classes four tales, "Brooksmith," "The Real Thing," "The Private Life," and "Greville Fane" as illustrating "social conditioning"—although one evidently based on inherent qualities of the individual. In the first tale, Brooksmith, having evolved into an artist, is unable to become again a butler; in the second, the Monarchs, stolidly real, are incapable of such artistic evolution (CT 8, 8–9).

Geismar disparagingly classifies Brooksmith and Hyacinth among James's "little gentlemen" with Morris Gedge, Merton Densher, and Fleda Vetch (256–57). Jones similarly, but more praisingly, links him not only with Gedge but also the suffering sensitives of "The Real Thing" (200), while Austin Wright links him with the hero of "Flickerbridge" in his hatred of vulgarity (105).

The tale is one of opportunity granted and then denied. Accordingly, Walter Wright compares Brooksmith to Mrs. Brash of "The Beldonald Holbein" in his short experience of the joys of an accepting, cultured circle followed by an "exile from bliss" (139). Vaid finds Brooksmith's speech to the narrator reflecting some of the intensity and significance of the signature speech of another exile, Lambert Strether (53). Donald Stone sees the tale as reflecting James's current view of the artist just as "Benvolio" had earlier, but stressing the boundaries rather than the opportunities the author encounters (252–53). In a more positive view, Haddick focuses on the early scenes to link the tale with *The Pupil* in depicting the "possibility of happy masculine life together" (20). One could place in contrast Pearce's observation that the "ultimate image" of Brooksmith's fallen world is "female and proletarian," or in the words of the tale "vague prying beery females" (839). Looking at the end of the relationship, Gage finds "implied homosexual overtones" in Brooksmith's grief (185).

Interpretation and Criticism

In working on "The Real Thing," James recalled the "very tight squeeze" required to keep "Brooksmith" to its short length, under 7,000 words (CN 56). The "technical economy and sharpness of emphasis" James's effort produced has won him praise from critics including Matthiessen and Murdock, and McElderry, with Harris deeming it "one of the most successful" of James's truly short short stories (N 64; McElderry 113; Harris 103). Indeed, the tale is, for James, so economical it has been spoken of as bordering on a sketch, with Vaid analyzing the three-part structure—the establishment of the tone of Offord's salon, its decline, and Brooksmith's subsequent fate—that provides the sketch's frame (49–54).

The form of narration makes a significant contribution to the tale's technical excellence and economy. Ward includes this tale among those in which James chose a "relative outsider" as his "reflector" and that prohibited him any self-analysis in order to keep him from taking over the interest from the actual subject (57). Vaid notes how James through the "careful modulation" of the narrator's voice creates the character of Brooksmith, and locates the success of the tale in the narrator's "control over his voice," which keeps the tale from being sentimental (49, 54). O'Faolian writes for the dissent, finding that James by "indulging a constitutional, if not professorial loquacity" and by failing to establish a time frame to match the "frame of place," makes a "natural" subject for a short story longer than it need have been (170). James himself pointed to Brooksmith, not the narrator as the "intense *perceiver*" in the tale (*Criticism* 2, 1096).

At the start James referred to the tale as *The Servant* (*Letters* 3, 307). Naturally enough, Brooksmith's profession or properly his class has been a focal issue. As one of James's few tales to center on a servant, it has become a locus for discussion of James's view of the lower class. Both Ezra Pound and McElderry have praised the way James indicates Brooksmith's character through distinctive, appropriate dialogue (Pound 17; McElderry 161). Earlier, however, Q. D. Leavis dismissed the portrait as simply "a whimsical expression of James's social ideal" (223). She has been followed by Vaid and Berland, both of whom judge Brooksmith too "spoiled," as the last line of the story terms him, for his place in life, making Brooksmith not a representative but a "special case" (Berland 2). The result, in Vaid's regard, is less a critique of the class system than James's "romanticized" version of the myth of the British butler fitting his particular "aesthetic and social refinements" (53–55).

Representative perhaps of a difference between American and English attitudes, Garnett dismisses Fadiman's observation that the tale's "scaffolding" depends on "a class-stratified society" to be "silly, as all civilised human societies are, and always have been, class-stratified" (ix). Nevertheless, other critics have taken issue with the assumptions of such societies as portrayed in the tale, finding the "whimsical" or "romanticized" treatment of Brooksmith, the man at the bottom of the scaffold, unacceptable. Geismar, in particular, has little use for the "peculiar . . . impossible notoriety" given by critics to the tale, for the protected world of "luxury, leisure and literature" in Offord's salon. Like Vaid, he finds James's tale more an expression of James's own preferences than an imaginative projection into what an actual servant might experience. He draws scornful attention, too, to the conclusion of the "tragicomedy" with its implication that even heaven is divided accorded to class (110–12).

Other critics have shifted the discussion by reading the story less as the tale of a servant than of an artist, Horne commenting that the fate of a butler alone would be "of minor concern to James" (55). Dow points to the way Brooksmith's name indicates he is the "smith" or artist who has the necessary "art to direct through a smiling land, between suggestive shores, a sinuous stream of talk." Matthiessen and Murdock locate the tale's real significance in its presentation of a common James topic—"the dilemma of the highly sensitive intelligence" who suffers for lack of a proper "environment" (N 65). Even more generally, Andreas sees the tale as an examination of the stability of personal identity, illustrating how Brooksmith loses his identity when his environment is destroyed (124–25). Fadiman and Walter Wright both analyze Brooksmith as an artist, Fadiman noting the absence of the self-pity usual in James's artist tales (Wright 79, 139; Fadiman 291–92). Vaid objects to such readings as "farfetched" (53), but they have continued. Tintner sees the tale as "a story about 'art'" and Brooksmith as an artist whose material is social life as gathered in Offord's salon (1987, 215). Rawlings also sees the tale as a treatment of the situation of an artist, but indicates that it is never quite clear "how far the narrator's imagination extends." It is the narrator, he cautions, who judges Brooksmith's leaving his last position as a "great and romantic fact," who speaks of "the mercenary prose of butlerhood" in contrast to "the struggle for the poetry." As a result, not only is Brooksmith the artist of Offord's salon, the "prime minister" to his "sovereign," but the narrator is a writer who takes Brooksmith as his subject and "skillfully constructs a work of art" through his "creative interpretation" of his life. His view of the narrator, however, is largely sympathetic: he notes that the narrator has also lost something with the ending of the salon and that Brooksmith's "ghost" stays with him (xii–xiii).

Others have abstracted themes of passing time and mutability from Brooksmith's particular case. Jones, for example, finds the poignancy of the tale accented by the absence of youth, the pressing nature of time (200–1). The themes of art and death merge in Pearce's and Tintner's Arcadian readings, and soon produce complications. Tintner notes that following Offord's demise, Brooksmith cannot accept "the notion of death," while the narrator can (1986, 116). But surely that has something to do with the fact that, as the story's germ indicates, the death of Offord has far less effect on the narrator than on Brooksmith. Looking at the way the narrator accepts Brooksmith's own death, Pearce writes that the narrator takes upon himself the task of song that Brooksmith is forced to surrender, and notes the narrator "refuses to interpret as defeat—possibly intentionally *mis*interprets—the sordid details of Brooksmith's disappearance" (840). The narrator's mistake illustrates the problem of trying to fit a person into a poetic schema. It can, in part, deny that person's reality, and in this case, may be a way of avoiding a sense of one's own culpability. Lycidas and Adonais died at sea far from their poet elegists, but Brooksmith dies in the waters of the narrator's own London.

The fact remains that Brooksmith is a butler, and one may ask whether treating him as an artist is a way of obscuring his poor treatment as one or a way of ennobling his behavior as one. This question returns us to the actions and attitude of the narrator. Many critics have accepted his upper-class explanations of why Brooksmith was doomed. Vaid asserts that Offord's limited means keep the small legacy from being a reproach against the former master (52). Similarly, Jones accepts the narrator's rationale that it would "offend" Brooksmith if one of Offord's friends offered him "an inferior post with them" (201).

Admittedly, if Brooksmith is a victim of upper-class manners, he is not a protesting one. Both Walter Wright and Horne attribute his death to his dependence on society, Horne going so far as to call him a parasite who "receives from society much more than he gives" (Wright 391; Horne 53). Still she judges the tale a genuine tragedy because it refuses to assign blame either to Brooksmith or to society, so that his fate becomes inevitable given the initial situation and the world as it is (55). Apart from his one speech of protest at his master's approaching death, Brooksmith accepts his role. Both Vaid and Jones praise this acceptance, Vaid finding Brooksmith's concern for the salon habitués "touching," and Jones writing that Brooksmith "in his justifiable pride finally disappears rather than be a burden on those he knew in his glorious past" (Vaid 51). To Jones, Brooksmith is "the victim of his own impeccable taste" (201). Edgar remarks that "The poor man was at the best of times never vociferously alive—the quiet dignity of his office forbade this" (101).

Wagenknecht, however, finds the legacy left Brooksmith "pitifully inadequate" (62), and it certainly seems a charge against the circle depicted here that together they cannot find a way to sustain a person who so sustained them. Brooksmith's death has unfortunate echoes of suttee or Sardanapulus, the sense that his death tidies things up or provides a proper tribute after Offord's death. Austin Wright classes the story's plot as one of repeated choices in constantly changing circumstances with a double protagonist (387, 391). The narrator, like Brooksmith, has multiple opportunities to act or even to speak that he lets pass out of a sense of propriety, of not offending. The primary virtues the narrator seems to practice are those of not calling attention to the unpleasant, and the only virtues allowed to Brooksmith are uncomplaining service and self-sacrifice.

Putt, in a nicely balanced analysis, notes both the inadequate legacy and the "false delicacy" of the narrator as James presents a society in which a servant is the one left holding on to the "old order." The sensitive narrator, he argues, is necessary to balance Brooksmith's "own imputed sensibility," but the tale itself is "violently ironical" in its treatment of the upper class (280–81).

The story would certainly be easier to sympathize with today if one could believe that James wrote the tale as a protest of the position of the servant class. But such a stance is not clearly established, and as is evident from above, many critics have read it without finding any need to search for it. Wagenknecht remarks on the "charm" the piece maintains despite its "depressing" story, a fact he attributes to "the humanity and understanding by which it is informed" (62). It is hard, however, to shake the feeling after reading the story that what Brooksmith needed was something more concrete than "humanity and understanding" and that an upper class that prides itself on such qualities and can accomplish nothing more than it does in this story, while still enjoying the benefits of its position, has little to offer.

Works Cited

Primary Works

James, Henry. 1891. "Brooksmith." *Harper's Weekly* 35 (2 May): 321–33. *Black and White* 1 (2 May): 417–20, 422.

———. 1892. "Brooksmith." *The Lesson of the Master*. New York and London: Macmillan, 180–201.

———. 1909. "Brooksmith." *The Novels and Tales of Henry James*. New York Edition. Vol. 18, 347–72. New York: Scribner's.

Secondary Works

Andreas, Osborn. 1948. *Henry James and the Expanding Horizon: A Study of the Meaning and Basic Themes of James's Fiction*. Seattle: University of Washington Press.

Berland, Alwyn. 1981. *Culture and Conduct in the Novels of Henry James*. Cambridge, MA: Cambridge University Press.

Dow, Eddy. 1969. "James's 'Brooksmith'—paragraphs 4 & 5." *Explicator* 27 (January): Item 35.

Edgar, Pelham. [1927] 1964. *Henry James, Man and Author*. New York: Russell & Russell.

Fadiman, Clifton, ed. 1948. *The Short Stories of Henry James*. New York: Modern Library.

Frantz, Jean H. 1959. "A Probable Source for a James 'Nouvelle.'" *Modern Language Notes* 74 (March): 225–26.

Gage, Richard P. 1988. *Order and Design: Henry James' Titled Story Sequences*. New York: Peter Lang.

Garnett, David, ed. 1946. *Fourteen Stories by Henry James*. London: Rupert Hart-Davis.

Geismar, Maxwell. 1963. *Henry James and the Jacobites*. Boston: Houghton Mifflin.

Gerlach, John. 1985. *Toward the End: Closure and Structure in American Short Stories*. University: University of Alabama Press.

Haddick, Vern. 1976. "Colors in the Carpet." *Gay Literature* 5: 19–21.

Harris, Wendell V. 1979. *British Short Fiction in the Nineteenth Century: A Literary and Bibliographic Guide*. Detroit: Wayne State University Press.

Horne, Helen. 1960. *Basic Ideals of James's Aesthetics as Expressed in the Short Stories Concerning Artists and Writers*. Marburg: Erich Mauersberger.

Jones, Granville H. 1975. *Henry James's Psychology of Experience: Innocence, Responsibility, and Renunciation in the Fiction of Henry James*. The Hague: Mouton.

Krook, Dorothea. [1962] 1967. *The Ordeal of Consciousness in Henry James*. New York: Cambridge University Press.

Leavis, Q. D. 1947. "Henry James: The Stories." *Scrutiny* 14 (Spring): 223–29. Reprinted in *Collected Essays*. Vol. 2: *The American Novel and Reflections of the European Novel*, ed. G. Singh, 177–84. Cambridge: Cambridge University Press.

McElderry, Bruce R., Jr. 1965. *Henry James*. New York: Twayne.

O'Faolian, Sean. 1948. *The Short Story*. London: Collins.

Pearce, Howard. 1975. "Henry James's Pastoral Fallacy." *PMLA* 90: 834–47.

Pound, Ezra. 1918. "A Shake Down." *The Little Review* 5 (August): 9–39.

Putt, S. Gorley. 1966. *Henry James: A Reader's Guide*. Ithaca, NY: Cornell University Press.

Rawlings, Peter. 1984. Introduction. *Henry James's Shorter Masterpieces*. Vol. 1. Sussex: Harvester; Totowa, NJ: Barnes & Noble.

Stone, Donald David. 1972. *Novelists in a Changing World: Meredith, James, and the Transformation of English Fiction in the 1880's*. Cambridge, MA: Harvard University Press.

Stone, Edward. 1964. *The Battle and the Books: Some Aspects of Henry James*. Athens: Ohio University Press.

Tintner, Adeline R. 1987. *The Book World of Henry James: Appropriating the Classics*. Ann Arbor: UMI Research Press.

———. 1986. *The Museum World of Henry James*. Ann Arbor: UMI Research Press. Revised in part from "High Melancholy and Sweet: James and the Arcadian Tradition." *Colby Library Quarterly* 12 (September 1976): 109–21.

Vaid, Krishna B. 1964. *Technique in the Tales of Henry James*. Cambridge, MA: Harvard University Press.

Wagenknecht, Edward. 1984. *The Tales of Henry James*. New York: Frederick Ungar.

Ward, Joseph A. 1967. *The Search for Form: Studies in the Structure of James's Fiction*. Chapel Hill: University of North Carolina Press.

Wright, Austin McGiffert. 1961. *The American Short Story in the Twenties*. Chicago: University of Chicago Press.

Wright, Walter F. 1962. *The Madness of Art: A Study of Henry James*. Lincoln: University of Nebraska Press.

A Bundle of Letters

Publication History

"A Bundle of Letters" was published first on December 18, 1879, in the *Parisian*, an Anglo-French journal published by a friend of James, the Englishman Theodore E. Child, who had requested a tale of him (N12; *Life* 2, 342). By publishing abroad, James made himself vulnerable to being pirated in America, and on January 24, 1880, his story appeared in a small pamphlet in Boston "very chastely 'gotten up'" as even James acknowledged, with wrappers lined to look like the writing paper of the letters. James, still enjoying the popularity of *Daisy Miller*, regretted mainly the loss of a possible five or six hundred dollars he expected to get from its publication by *Harper's* (*Letters* 1, 271). Stern takes issue with Edel, who identifies the pirate as Frank Loring, a friend of the family, identifying the man instead as A. K. Loring, who, in a manner that would have suited the indignant James, went bankrupt the next year. The story was nevertheless pirated again on February 23, 1880, in the Seaside Library published by George Munro in combination with "Sweet Nelly, My Heart's Delight" by Walter Besant.

According to Margolis, James learned through this experience the popularity of the theme of the American girl, as his story moved from Loring's twenty-five-cent volume to the more accessible Seaside Library's ten-cent version (36). If so, he proved he had learned his lesson well by including it himself in the London edition of *The Diary of a Man of Fifty* in April 1880, with a London edition of *Washington Square* in 1881 (as suggested by his publisher at Macmillan), and with *Daisy Miller* in March 1883 in a Franklin Square Library edition. It also had a place in the Collective Edition of 1883 and even appeared in translation in a Russian periodical in 1882, Kenton suspects through the influence of James's friend Turgenev (Edel and Laurence 47–49; *Correspondence* 52, 59; Kenton 535). James continued to be fond of the story, including it also in the New York Edition.

Circumstances of Composition, Sources, and Influences

In December of 1879 James was in Paris, planning to move on shortly to Italy, when a blizzard left him snowbound in his hotel. He later recalled in its New York Edition preface how, during the enforced seclusion, he produced the

tale in one sitting (*Criticism* 2, 1221; also *Life* 2, 395). Its writing was, however, only part of a period of great productivity. In 1881 in some notebook rem-
iniscenses he includes its writing along with the completion of *Hawthorne*
and *Confidence* and the start of *Washington Square* as one of the compensa-
tions for his inability to travel much in France on that visit (CN 219).

The sources for the tale may well go further back. In 1867 William had
been the first James brother to travel solo in Europe, and he wrote Henry
from his hotel in France of the usefulness of his experience for an aspiring
writer:

> There are 70 or 80 people in this etablissement, no one of whom I have
> as yet particularly cottoned up to. It's incredible how even so slight a bar-
> rier as the difference of language with most of them, and still more as the
> absence of local and personal associations, range of gibes and other com-
> mon ground to stand on, counts against one's scraping acquaintance. It's
> disgusting and humiliating. There is a lovely maiden of *etwa* 19 sits in
> sight of me at the table with whom I am falling deeply in love. She has
> never looked at me yet, and I really believe I should be quite incapable of
> conversing with her even were I "introduced," from a sense of the above
> difficulties and because one doesn't know what subjects or allusions may
> be possible with a jeune fille. I suppose my life for the past year would
> have furnished you, as the great American nouvelliste, a good many
> "motives" and subjects of observation—especially so in this place. I wish I
> could pass them over to you—such as they are you'd profit by them
> more than I and gather in a great many more. (*Autobiography* 503)

No doubt by 1879 William had had the hour's "interview" with Henry he
wished for in this letter and had shared even more of his experience, much of
which seems similar to the setting and sensibility of "A Bundle of Letters," so
that this epistolary story may have had in part an epistolary source.

By 1879 Henry had his own experiences of Europe to draw on. When
Evelyn Vane writes that "Lady Battledown makes all her governesses take the
same name" (CT 4, 453), James is, as Edel records, making use of his new
insight into the English upper-class "code" for servants, which he conveyed
also in letters home to his sister Alice (*Life* 2, 38–49; *Letters* 2, 224, 226 n.1).
Putt finds such an example of "European vileness" nicely balancing the criticism of America in the tale (125). According to Beach, both Henry and Alice
looked down on such vileness, and he sees James putting their reaction to it
in the character of Miranda (lvii).

Another epistolary source has been offered by Zabel, who connects the
story to the description of the French scene in James's Parisian letters for the
Tribune (ix–x). James had considered writing a story made out of letters earlier in the year, recording in January the germ for a story that was to consist
of an exchange of letters between a "highly conscientious" mother and her

daughter, showing their misunderstanding of each other on the subject of the girl's romance (CN 11).

As literary sources for the use of letters, Lerner offers Turgenev's "A Correspondence" where the author also plays editor, although only for two correspondents (40; also Long 41). Peterson objects to Lerner's connection, arguing that Gustave Droz's "Un Paquet de Lettres" is a more probable source (142).

Bishop notes the significance of Miranda's name, recalling Shakespeare's Miranda, who also encountered a "brave new world" and who gave, rather than took, language lessons (102 n.13). Melchiori points out how James places a Prosper in the cast of characters to complement her (9).

The Bostonian Louis Leverett has had his roots traced in two directions. The first is literary, with Tintner noting the source for his name and some of his character in Balzac's Louis Lambert, even as she traces the pension format to *Le Père Goriot* (256–57). In Beach's view, Leverett's thinking is indebted in its worship of the "hard gem-like flame" to Pater's philosophy that James had "assimilated" but not adopted, modified by the "strenuous tone" of "The Psalm of Life" (lviii–lix). McCarthy sees Leverett as a caricature of dilettantish aesthetes who understand little of the writers they cite. He comments on Leverett's rather vague attributions to Arnold, Swinburne, or Pater, and finds James depicting him playing with terms he knows little about. To Leverett, McCarthy argues, "to live" is simply an openness to sensation, while to James such openness was the first step to a serious examination of all facets of life (47–48).

Even as McCarthy notes the difference between James's thinking and Leverett's, others have seen James examining his own philosophy and personality through the fictional character. Kraft finds Leverett the closest of the characters to James himself, but points to an essential difference in Leverett's resting in lifeless observation (114–16). In Donald Stone's view, James is not simply parodying himself in Leverett, but also how readers such as his brother William conceived of him. He notes that James in the story actually achieves what Leverett hopes to—the comparison and contrast of "national types"—but cannot adequately accomplish because of his limited point of view (100–1). Beach records how often Leverett follows his French phrases with "as they say here" (lviii). The habit may seem affected, but it is remarked also by Long in James's 1879 *Hawthorne* (6) and may be another bit of conscious or unconscious self-parody.

Staub also has literary debts. According to Beach, his letter shows a familiarity with Matthew Arnold's "Friendship's Garland," a rather surprising source (lviii). Staub declares that America is "unprecedented and unique in the history of mankind; the arrival of a nation at an ultimate stage of evolution without having passed through the mediate one; the passage of the fruit, in other words, from crudity to rottenness, without the interposition of a period of useful (and ornamental) ripeness. With the Americans indeed the crudity and the rottenness are identical and simultaneous" (CT 4, 463). A similar remark, that "America is the only nation in history which miraculously has gone directly from barbarism to degeneration without the usual interval of civilization," is attributed to Georges Clemenceau.

Relation to Other Works.

The first of two tales James wrote through the medium of letters, the tale's technique has naturally drawn attention to itself. Powers sees it as anticipating *What Maisie Knew* in its "reflexive characterization," which interests the reader as much in what the letter-writer's descriptions tell us about what they "know" as about what there is to know. The technique, he adds, is seen throughout James, in such works as "The Liar," "The Beast in the Jungle," *The Turn of the Screw*, *In the Cage*, *The Sacred Fount*, and *The Ambassadors* (1969, 23). Quentin Anderson distinguishes the tale from "The Real Thing," arguing that while its comedy stems from "the fact that people make radically different assumptions about one another," it does not, like "The Real Thing," draw on the fact that readers also make such assumptions, and therefore resists attempting to educate the reader beyond generalizations ([1950] 1957, viii). Powers, however, argues that James expects his readers to pay attention to the unreliable competing narrations in a manner anticipating the mutiple reflectors of *The Awkward Age*, although in the later works he notes the characters themselves allow more for the unreliability of speech than do the characters here. In his view, the tale is evidence of James's interest in narration turning from action to character (1970, 140–41). Meanwhile, according to Gerlach, James did not follow up on the experimental form because it did not allow him to show the more significant development of character over time seen in more typical works such as "Four Meetings" (82). Fadiman also contrasts the two works, noting the "pathos" in the earlier tale and the comedy in this one (79).

Louis Leverett declares, "The great thing is to *live*, you know, to feel, to be conscious of one's possibilities; not to pass through life mechanically and insensibly, even as a letter through the post office" (CT 4, 439), and the resemblance of his remark to Lewis Lambert Strether's injunction to "Live all you can; it's a mistake not to" has been duly noted (e.g., Beach lix; Putt 125). Arguing that the Howells anecdote that prompted *The Ambassadors* may have reminded James of the earlier tale, Cargill extends the connection, discerning in Miranda hints of Maria Gostrey, and in Leverett's feeling "wooly" after his experiences with the judgmental Johnsons a suggestion of the later

Woolett (304). While Powers stresses the transformation from comic to serious in early to late (1970, 88–89), Anderson and Bishop approach the two texts the other way round, using the earlier "burlesque" version, to which Anderson adds Greville Fane's enjoining her son "to live, because that gave you material," to undercut the authority of Strether's advice (Anderson 1957, 212; Bishop 20).

The aesthetic Leverett has other soulmates. While Putt sees in him the hunger for art of *Roderick Hudson*, Kraft emphasizes his eagerness to "plunge" into life seen also in Eugene Pickering and Longmore of *Madame de Mauves* (Putt 125; Kraft 114–15). Funston footnotes the latter remark, by noting that a leverett is a young hare and that the knowledge of life Leverett seeks is sexual. Jefferson, however, who considers Leverett the "rawest" of such American aesthetes as Florimond Daintry, Felix Young, and Little Bilham, also points out that part of the humor of their types is "how intense they can be without ever doing anything" (1964, 66–68, 123; also Buitenhuis 134). Stone notes a transition from the comic treatment of aesthetes such as Leverett and Daintry to the illustration of the harm they can cause through such characters as Dr. Sloper, Osmond, and Ralph Touchett to the dispensation of responsibility accorded Hyacinth Robinson and Miriam Rooth (43, 332–33). Kraft is kinder, seeing Leverett as "not really intolerant or unpleasant," but rather a "lighter" Ralph Touchett (111–12).

Leverett describes Miranda going everywhere, "skirting the edge of obscene abysses without suspecting them; pushing through brambles without tearing her robe" (CT 4, 443). Putt finds her in this regard resembling Daisy Miller (125). The phrasing also anticipates the behavior not only of Lucretia in "A New England Winter" who also "skirts abysses," but also Isabel Archer, who discovers that some of her husband's "traditions made her push back her skirts." Fowler in turn points out that Miranda's fearlessness is a result of the conditions observed by Miss Sturdy, in "The Point of View," in America where "life's arranged" for the young and the innocent. She supports Leverett's characterization of Miranda as "sexless" finding it an attribute of the Jamesian American girl from Daisy Miller to Milly Theale (36, 44–45). Allen sees both Miranda and Violet Ray here with Lizzie Acton in *The Europeans* and Daisy Miller as "less refined" examples of the classic American girl in James (42, 212 n.10). Kraft compares their British counterpart, the docile Evelyn Vane, to Lord Warburton's sisters in *The Portrait of a Lady* (112). (See particularly "The Point of View" and "The Pension Beaurepas.")

Interpretation and Criticism

Edgar struck the main critical note early on, calling it and "The Pension Beaurepas" "impressions of manners rather than stories," full of "amusing strokes of characterisation" (29). Remarking that the story is truly a "bundle," Gerlach analyzes its distinctive structure, showing how James created a "sense of completeness and closure" through its many varied, often opposed, viewpoints and the positioning of Miranda as a "more significant" character, who is given both the first and last words. According to Gerlach, however, its completeness is only formal, there being no significant change in the lives of the characters (80–82).

While Gerlach finds that the failure of the structure to encompass any change makes the tale as a whole thin, Bishop finds the structure designed to challenge the very idea of "authoritative textuality" (Gerlach 80–82; Bishop 21). Most other critics, however, have concentrated less on what is absent that what is present, in particular the internationally-flavored humor. Fadiman, for example, praises the tale for its humorous capturing of Americans' hunger for the foreign, its gentle satire of types both American and European. In the opposition as usual, Geismar finds the tale, which he calls a "rather pleasant sketch," unworthy of Fadiman's praise (36n). Jefferson, however, finds the work's spoofing of various cultural types demonstrating James could have been the "Peacock of his generation" (1964, 68). McElderry, too, praises the successful "mimicry" which leaves out the usual Jamesian manner to capture character (77).

The European characters are clearly caricature, and Delbaere-Garant objects both to the stereotypical lightness of the French characters and their obsession with pretty women and to what she calls the "exaggeratedly heavy" portrayal of the German (290–91). In 1918 Beach, however, found the "quaintest of Teutonic philosophical method" in Staub's letter, making it the "most screamingly funny" of the bundle (lvii). Other critics such as Kraft have found the heaviness appropriate not exaggerated, and the portrait "frightening" rather than comic (112). Several have placed their analyses in historical context. Pound finds Staub's prediction of the "general pervasiveness" of "the deep-lunged children of the fatherland!" a frighteningly accurate prediction of World War I and cites as relevant Flaubert's remark on the Franco-German War of 1870, "If they had read my *Education Sentimental*, this sort of thing wouldn't have happened" (8). The earlier war, in its turn, may well lay behind James's sense of the German national character. Writing within a few years of World War II, Fadiman stresses the sinister note in the "ridiculous" Dr. Staub, and Rahv finds the character "truly amazing" in its encapsulation of "the entire tradition of Prussian militarism," which revels in theories of the inferiority of others while lacking the ability to understand the others it so dismisses (Fadiman 78–81; Rahv 270).

Among the Americans, Leverett has attracted little unqualified admiration. Jefferson, however, notes that Leverett at least has a "style," one with a certain American verboseness (1964, 67–68). As Delbaere-Garant points out, James is careful to show the "false note" Leverett strikes as an American attempting to assume a new identity, an attempt that keeps him from seeing things accurately (291). In a balanced view, Beach notes that both Leverett and his compatriot Miranda exhibit traits that "with a slight change of emphasis" James admired. It is the ignorance of their assumptions that makes their eagerness for culture absurd. At the same time Beach sees James criticizing through Leverett—who shares with him a fondness of French phrases, an admiration for Balzac, and a criticism of American meagreness—certain aspects of his own character (lvii–lviii).

While Leverett is all form and pretense, his compatriot, Miranda lacks any form or presentation, yet has attracted a similarly mixed press. She has her definite detractors, including Jefferson, who finds her "demanding," and a "rather farcical New England maiden" (1964, 79; [1960] 1971, 46). Even they, however, often come around to find her the best of a bad bunch. Jones, for example, piles on the adjectives to picture Miranda as "stupid, shallow, vulgar, tasteless, fresh, wide-eyed, and utterly unaware," but later notes that Miranda, while still a caricature and far from the equal of such later sensitive spirits as Isabel Archer, is at least "thoroughly alive" and thereby the best of the characters in this assemblage (59, 73). Similarly, Andreas finds Miranda's viewpoint the "least provincial" in the story, if "slightly priggish," and notes that she is the only one of the correspondents who does not enjoy excluding others—an omission he notes James would applaud (141–42). Rahv sees James treating her with an appropriate amount of humor, but praises her bravery (270). Kraft, however, while he acknowledges her striving to be the most honest, still considers her to have "so much to learn . . . that she will never transcend the limitations of her background" (111). Wagenknecht is the most positive in his praise, stating that Miranda is "the one from whom we hear the most and most wish to hear. Miranda is naive, ignorant if you like, but she is a sincere, basically sensible girl, with plenty of spunk, who does in Paris exactly what she had done in Bangor and finds that she has done exactly right" (21).

In the most elaborate analysis, Bishop reads the letters as illustrating the process of "learning the language" and so gaining power, a use of language seen particularly in Verdier and Staub. He focuses his analysis of language on Miranda, pointing out how Miranda first makes sense of things, such as Violet's haughtiness, by comparisons with books. He judges her acquisitive, on the grounds that she desires "profit" in her relationship with Platt, steals the idea of living in a French pension by eavesdropping, and lists all the furniture in her room. He sees her evolving further, learning to lie through her tutoring by Verdier. Transforming Verdier's desire for Miranda into Miranda's own "censored" desire, Bishop posits that Miranda loses her virginity to Verdier within the "hole in the text" between her third and last letters, and then backtracks by an appeal to the story's mocking of "author-ity," which could establish the event's certainty, at the same time that he states he needs no proof because in James "it is sufficient that the possibility exists" (13–25).

In reading the story, however, it is clear that Verdier is a louse, who, as McElderry early noted, thoroughly misreads Miranda's innocent independence and is unlikely and undeserving of any reward (77). Although Bishop offers some support for his reading in tracing the tale to the notebook entry on the "complicated relationship" between mother and daughter (CN 11), the connection seems slight. Perhaps one can consider Bishop a seventh correspondent, contributing his own mixture of insights and misconceptions.

Indeed, throughout the story, as Kraft notes, James presents the characters "passing judgments on themselves as they arrogantly and insensitively judge one another" through the perspective of their individual and national vanity. Such a technique, Kraft argues, makes clear the necessity of a multifaceted view of the world. Still, he ends by judging the tale "too clever to be serious" (111–12). It is a somewhat odd opposition, and others have been higher in their praise, Rahv finding the tale "one of the most brilliant stories of national differences in any language," showing James's abilities to treat America and Europe not just as "static contraries" but in conflict and combination (269–70). It is this bundling together of many different tones and types that gives the tale its distinction and ultimate success.

Works Cited

Primary Works

James, Henry. 1879. "A Bundle of Letters." *The Parisian*, no. 38 (18 December): 7–9.

———. 1880. *A Bundle of Letters*. Boston: Loring.

———. 1880. "A Bundle of Letters." *Sweet Nelly, My Heart's Delight by Walter Besant and James Rice and A Bundle of Letters by Henry James, Jr. Seaside Library* 34, no. 702 (23 February): 20–26.

———. 1880. "A Bundle of Letters." *The Diary of a Man of Fifty and A Bundle of Letters*. New York: Harper, 69–135.

———. 1881. "A Bundle of Letters." *Washington Square*. London: Macmillan.

———. 1883. "A Bundle of Letters." Collective Edition. Vol. 14. London: Macmillan.

——— 1883. "A Bundle of Letters." *Daisy Miller*. Franklin Square Library 303. New York: Harper.

———. 1908. "A Bundle of Letters." *The Novels and Tales of Henry James*. New York Edition. Vol. 14, 477–533. New York: Scribner's.

———. 1993. *The Correspondence of Henry James and the House of Macmillan, 1877–1914*. Ed. Rayburn S. Moore. Baton Rouge: Louisiana State University Press.

Secondary Works

Allen, Elizabeth. 1984. *A Woman's Place in the Novels of Henry James*. New York: St. Martin's.

Anderson, Quentin. 1957. *The American Henry James*. New Brunswick, NJ: Rutgers University Press.

————, ed. [1950]. 1957. *Henry James: Selected Short Stories*. New York: Rinehart.

Andreas, Osborn. 1948. *Henry James and the Expanding Horizon: A Study of the Meaning and Basic Themes of James's Fiction*. Seattle: University of Washington Press.

Beach, Joseph Warren. [1918] 1954. *The Method of Henry James*. Philadelphia: Albert Saifer.

Bishop, George. 1988. *When the Master Relents: The Neglected Short Fictions of Henry James*. Ann Arbor: UMI Research Press. Revised from "Addressing 'A Bundle of Letters': Henry James and the Hazard of Authority." *Henry James Review* 8 (1987): 321–34.

Buitenhuis, Peter. 1970. *The Grasping Imagination: The American Writings of Henry James*. Toronto: University of Toronto Press.

Cargill, Oscar. 1961. *The Novels of Henry James*. New York: Macmillan.

Delbaere-Garant, Jeanne. 1970. *Henry James: The Vision of France*. Paris: Société d' Editions Les Belles Lettres.

Edel, Leon, and Dan H. Laurence. [1957] 1982. *A Bibliography of Henry James*. 3d ed. Oxford: Clarendon Press.

Edgar, Pelham. [1927] 1964. *Henry James, Man and Author*. New York: Russell & Russell.

Fadiman, Clifton, ed. 1948. *The Short Stories of Henry James*. New York: Modern Library.

Fowler, Virginia. 1984. *Henry James's American Girl: The Embroidery on the Canvas*. Madison: University of Wisconsin Press.

Funston, Judith E. 1989. "Letter." *Henry James Review* 10: 220.

Geismar, Maxwell. 1963. *Henry James and the Jacobites*. Boston: Houghton Mifflin.

Gerlach, John. 1985. *Toward the End: Closure and Structure in American Short Stories*. University: University of Alabama Press.

Jefferson, D. W. 1964. *Henry James and the Modern Reader*. New York: St. Martin's.

————. [1960] 1971. *Henry James*. New York: Capricorn.

Jones, Granville H. 1975. *Henry James's Psychology of Experience: Innocence, Responsibility, and Renunciation in the Fiction of Henry James*. The Hague: Mouton.

Kenton, Edna. 1934. "Some Bibliographical Notes on Henry James." *Hound & Horn* 7 (April–May): 535–40.

Kraft, James. 1969. *The Early Tales of Henry James*. Carbondale: Southern Illinois University Press.

Lerner, Daniel. 1941. "The Influence of Turgenev on Henry James." *Slavonic Review* 20 (December): 28–54.

Long, Robert Emmet. 1979. *The Great Succession: Henry James and the Legacy of Hawthorne*. Pittsburgh: University of Pittsburgh Press.

McCarthy, Harold T. 1958. *Henry James: The Creative Process*. New York: Thomas Yoseloff.

McElderry, Bruce R., Jr. 1965. *Henry James*. New York: Twayne.

Margolis, Anne. 1985. *Henry James and the Problem of Audience: An International Act*. Ann Arbor: UMI Research Press.

Melchiori, Giorgio. 1965. "Locksley Hall Revisited: Tennyson and Henry James." *Review of English Literature* 6 (October): 9–25. Reprinted in Barbara Melchiori and Giorgio Melchiori. *Il Gusto di Henry James*. Turin: Guilio Einaudi editore, 1974.

Peterson, Dale E. 1975. *The Clement Vision: Poetic Realism in Turgenev and James*. Port Washington, NY: Kennikat.

Pound, Ezra. 1918. "Brief Note." *The Little Review* 5 (August): 6–9.

Powers, Lyall H. 1970. *Henry James: An Introduction and Interpretation*. New York: Holt, Rinehart.

————. 1969. *The Merrill Guide to Henry James*. Columbus, OH: Charles E. Merrill.

Putt, S. Gorley. 1966. *Henry James: A Reader's Guide*. Ithaca, NY: Cornell University Press.

Rahv, Philip. 1947. *Discovery of Europe: The Story of American Experience in the Old World*. Boston: Houghton Mifflin.

Stern, Madeline B. 1980. "A Lesson for the Master: Henry James and A. K. Loring." *Henry James Review* 2: 87–90.

Stone, Donald David. 1972. *Novelists in a Changing World: Meredith, James, and the Transformation of English Fiction in the 1880's*. Cambridge, MA: Harvard University Press.

Tintner, Adeline R. 1987. *The Book World of Henry James: Appropriating the Classics*. Ann Arbor: UMI Research Press.

Wagenknecht, Edward. 1984. *The Tales of Henry James*. New York: Frederick Ungar.

Zabel, Morton Dauwen, ed. 1961. *Henry James: Fifteen Short Stories*. New York: Bantam Books.

Foreign Language
Onishi, Akio. 1963. "Trilogy of International Theme." *Bungaku Ronshu* (Kansai University) 12 (January): 1–45. [Japanese]

The Chaperon

Publication History

"The Chaperon" appeared in the *Atlantic Monthly* from November to December 1891. Two years later James collected it in *The Real Thing*. He also included it in the New York Edition.

Circumstances of Composition, Sources, and Influences

The story began, as James recalled in his preface, in "a ramshackle inn on the Irish Coast"—the Marine Hotel in Kingstown, Ireland—and its writing on a table "of an equilibrium so vague that I wonder to-day how any object constructed on it should stand so firm." For him, its writing was enveloped in the "strange sad charm of the tearful Irish light." The writing was done in July of 1891, but as James recalls, the idea had come two or three years earlier in London in the mention of a compromised woman returning to society under the guidance of her daughter (*Criticism* 2, 1154). In his notebook that July James attributed his knowledge of "the situation of Mrs. M and one of her daughters" to a Mrs. Earle, also a writer, and while beginning it mentions he may have made an earlier notebook entry on the subject which, if he did, is no longer extant. James projects a girl, not interested in society for herself, plunging into it to do for her mother the services a mother would normally do for her daughter, to be "*her* chaperon and protectress." The whole was to be a "vivid London picture." James had the first part done in a week, and followed his initial ideas fairly closely, although he altered his original ending in which the mother retains a "grievance" because her daughter cannot persuade her husband to accept her. The last words of the tale were to be her saying, "No, mamma, I'm afraid I can't do that too" (CN 58–59).

Being in the midst of his "attack on the theatre," James not surprisingly speaks of making the tale "purely dramatic," of setting the stage, and arranging the second half in a "series of *scènes de comédie*" (CN 59). Following such an approach, it seems logical that the playwright Arthur Wing Pinero, responding to James's praise of his *The Second Mrs. Tanqueray*, would find "the germ of a fine comedy for the theatre" in the tale. Accordingly, James made some notes for a play, but he never finished it (CN 247–52; *Life* 3, 294). James returned to the idea in 1907 at the time when he was also rewriting two other works, *Covering End* and *The Other House*, into dramatic form and there is a "Rough Statement" remaining of his effort (*Life* 5, 369; see CN 439–65). In McElderry's opinion the material indicates that "The Chaperon" might have been a better "social comedy" than any of the complete plays (98–99).

Shine makes a connection between Rose and the "'scenic' trio" of women James projects for a story in a notebook entry dated October 5, 1899. He writes there of three types of American girl, one kept from seeing Europe by a protective mother, and two seeing it all before marriage "either to show it herself to her husband, or because she will, *after*, with the shelved and effaced state of so many, precisely, *by* marriage, have no chance." According to Shine, James never wrote the story, because he had already treated the theme several times by then, including the year before in "The Chaperon" (100–01). It is hard to figure out precisely how Rose fits into the trio, especially as she is not American, although she does travel before marriage and she is unprotected.

The tale describes, as Jones notes, "The History of a Young Lady's Entrance into the World," a genre stemming from the courtesy book (xiv–xv). He mentions as analogues Fanny Burney's *Evelina*, whose subtitle provides his terminology, as well as Austen's *Mansfield Park* and James's own *A London Life*, *What Maisie Knew*, and *The Awkward Age*. Jacobson points to Rose's more modern reading of "the new American books" to "see how girls got on by themselves" as an allusion to a popular theme of the time (23–24). Rawlings adds that James had written some of the books himself and also notes how James carries over the metaphor of reading into Rose's evaluation of others as she "reads" them (xv).

Tintner compares James's description of the piazza of Milan Cathedral as "builded light" to Monet's Cathedral series of 1892 (1986, 108).

Relation to Other Works

In his preface James classed "The Chaperon" with *A London Life* and *The Spoils of Poynton* as essentially "'stories about women,' very young women, who, affected with a certain high lucidity, thereby become characters; in consequence of which their doings, their sufferings or whatever, take on, I assume, an importance." To all three women, Rose, Laura Wing, and Fleda Vetch, he attributed "acuteness and intensity, reflexion and passion . . . above all a contributive and participant view of her situation" (*Criticism* 2, 1147–48). He held in fact "The Chaperon" superior to *A London Life* in its stricter adherence to the viewpoint of its heroine (*Criticism* 2, 1154–55). Horrell also links Rose and Laura, noting how they "rise above conventional society" and are paired with men with appropriately birdlike names, Jay and Wendover (208). Perhaps it is in being more earthbound that Rose is, in contrast with the winged Laura, able to bloom. Putt sees the difference in the daughter's joining in her mother's exile from society, contrasted with the sister's flight from such a possibility (281). Gale finds Rose's flowery name putting her in good company with Daisy Miller, Lily Gunton, and Violet Grey of "Nona Vincent" (56).

Several critics have focused on the reversal of roles between parent and child in the tale. Rawlings finds a similar reversal in *The Pupil* and *What Maisie Knew* (xv). Shine finds both "The Chaperon" and "Pandora" unsuccessful in their treatment of such a reversal because their comic approach does not fit with James's actual disapproval of usurping children, witnessed, she feels, in his ambivalence toward both Pandora and Rose. Shine points out that Rose goes Pandora one better, establishing her mother in society, not simply herself (51–52). Her superiority is further indicated, as Edgar remarks, in her jeopardizing a secure position for the sake of her mother, while Pandora works to keep her parents from interfering with her desire for social position (102).

In her control of her family, Edel compares Rose not only to Pandora, but also Adela Chart of "The Marriages," but with a difference (CT 8, 9). As McElderry indicates, Rose, unlike Adela in regard to her father, has the "insight" to understand her mother's situation and the "courage" to support her (112). In Jones's analysis it is Rose's practicality that makes her the only worker in the cause of family who "saves more than she loses" in contrast to such as Laura, Adela, Agatha of "The Patagonia," and even Guy Domville. Jones contrasts her astute awareness of the task she is undertaking with Daisy Miller's ignorance, although, he remarks, such social awareness does not always produce success, as is witnessed in the case of Julia Bride. Unlike the others, Jones argues, but similarly to the narrator of *In the Cage*, she is able to achieve a state of "worldly contentment" (117, 119, 121, 158).

The London society portrayed in "The Chaperon" and "The Marriages," ready to forgive the strayed in return for their entertainment value, is according to Edel, the same as in *A London Life* and *The Siege of London* (CT 8, 9). Indeed, Wagenknecht comments that the tone here is even more "disillusioned" than in the last example (63). Similarly, Andreas and Voss connect the tale with "Mrs. Medwin" in its exposure of society's loose standards, the way in which a pariah can become a social attraction (Andreas 133–35; Voss 151). Tintner, more positively, links the tale with "Nona Vincent" and "The Real Thing" and "Brooksmith" in its treatment of social arts (1987, 215).

Interpretation and Criticism

As the comparisons indicate, there are two sides to this tale, that of the family and that of the city, and Rose is placed squarely between them. James acknowledged both moods in sketching out his play version, as he sought to intensify both the sense of the daughter's struggle and to increase the satire of the mother's situation (CN 248).

Rose herself has come under varying interpretations. In projecting the play version, James recalled Rose "reversing with courage and compassion, the usual relation" with her mother and records her willingness to sacrifice her lover (CN 248). The *Athenaeum* in 1893, on the other hand, found her "a little hard and unsympathetic" (601–2). As Rose prepares to take on her task, we are told, "Of her mother intrinsically she thought very little now, and if her eyes were fixed on a special achievement it was much more for the sake of that achievement and to satisfy a latent energy than because her heart was wrung by this sufferer. Her heart had not been wrung at all, though she had quite held it out for the experience. Her purpose was a pious game, but it was still essentially a game" (CT 8, 78). Clair takes this statement as an indication that the irony of the tale is not meant to be directed simply against the reversal of roles, but against Rose herself. Her motives, he argues, are "less than altruistic" and include not simply her mother's restoration but her own freedom from her mother's "taint" and her independence, and that of her siblings, from her grandmother (107). Similarly, Putt takes the passage as indicating Rose's lack of sympathy for her mother, at the same time as her taking her job as a "game" shows her "still essentially . . . the child of her parents." The result is a protest against Victorian hypocrisy, a picture of London society where no one has moral authority, where the satire can turn against anyone (281–83). Rawlings, in a reading that seems more likely at least in regards to Rose, takes the mention of the "game" as an indication that Rose recognizes the small value of London society, but at the same time is "unwilling to resist the challenge it presents" (xiv). There is certainly, as the narrator acknowledges, a satisfaction for Rose in "the idea of triumph" possible in her attempt (CT 8, 78), but that does not necessarily disqualify her heroism. It is significant that her major objection to Jay's reaction to her taking on her mother is his failure to understand "that a daughter should be merciful" (CT 8, 88).

Clearly, the society in which Rose seeks to triumph is far from exemplary. Horrell points out the way the names Mangler and Maresfield evoke society's "cruelty and stupidity" (208). Clair notes the shabby treatment Rose and her mother receive when first accepted back by society, as people engage them "for a fixed hour, like the American imitator and the Patagonian contralto" (108; CT 8, 116). Andreas sees the tale as undercutting the idea of elite society by showing up the "adventitious character" of its standards for admission (133–34). As Jefferson remarks, there is a seeming paradox: the mother's desire for social acceptance is a "weakness," but her daughter's helping her toward it is seen as a valid exercise, the value of society being a given in James (119–20). Back in the 1870's James himself made the significant declaration that ". . . a position in society is a legitimate object of ambition" (*Life* 223).

The mother, however, is no James. The *Athenaeum* reviewer particularly enjoyed the epigrams at Mrs. Donovan's expense, such as the description of her as "poor, but honest—so scrupulously honest that she was perpetually returning visits she had never received" (601–2). In 1907 in his "rough sketch" James would recall with equal satisfaction the "figure" he had used to depict her, waiting with "'her things on'" for a carriage to a "happy place to which she has not the faintest chance of going" (CN 463). Jones contrasts Rose's innocence "a kind of dogged concentration on her duty" with her mother's lack of awareness (117). Wagenknecht argues that James recognized both the limitations of the mother and of her ambition, and so eliminated the unhappy ending to remove the focus from her (64). She thus, in his view, is unworthy of a tragic ending, even as in the notebook James projected the mother "flimsy and trivial, in spite of all her pathos and her troubles" (CN 59). In the tale, however, he acknowledges that those very troubles may have contributed to her triviality, remarking on her discussing of dressmakers only one day after her reunion with her daughter, "Of course, poor thing, it was to be remembered that in her circumstances there were not many things she *could* talk about" (CT 8, 79). Putt does her the credit of speaking of her abandoned husband as the "kind of husband from whom any high-spirited wife might well have absconded," although he goes on to find her little better (281).

"A sword in one hand and a Bible in the other" with "a Court Guide concealed somewhere about his person," Rose's suitor Captain Jay obviously thinks of himself as someone of moral authority (CT 8, 85). Nevertheless, in projecting the play version James argued the "sufficiently unheroic . . . doesn't *do*—as he is—for the hero." Intending to keep Jay simply for the "comedy interest," he planned a new, sensitive hero (CN 249). In his later sketch, he recalls Jay as "rather priggish and precautionary, but really decent and sincere" and introduces no new hero, but allows Rose to bring out his "finer humanity" (CN 441, 461). Readers have had similarly mixed feelings. Perhaps because of the transformation the Captain is portrayed as undergoing, the *Athenaeum* judged him downright contradictory (601–2). Wagenknecht questions his appeal for Rose, seeing her marrying him "perhaps out of gratitude" (64). His role in the reestablishment of Mrs. Tramore has also been analyzed. Rawlings argues that it is possible Jay deliberately managed things so that he could marry Rose, making Rose "the outwitter . . . outwitted" and judges it therefore appropriate that the story ends with "a circular dialogue" as Rose and Jay attempt to give each other the credit for Mrs. Tramore's success (xv). Clair also emphasizes the role of Jay in reestablishing the mother, but sees it as managed by Rose, who uses him to produce a threesome that will attract attention. In his reading Jay's questions in the final dialogue are like Jay himself "eminently *naïve*." Nevertheless, he deems the marriage a happy one, as Jay is as gallant as he is unaware (107–9). There is, indeed, an air of happy triumph at the end of this tale that it seems a mistake to dismiss as ironic or ambiguous or even seriously shadowed.

The tale has generally received high marks, deserved ones, from its readers. Putt praises it as James at top form, master of his style and his subject (282). More modestly, the *Athenaeum* called it "amusing," while Anderson speaks of it as a "pretty inversion of the commonplace" (601–2; Anderson 41). Matthiessen and Murdock see the story's strength—its elevation from "mere anecdote"—in its keeping to Rose's point of view, noting that James changed the notebook ending with its emphasis on the mother to one that focuses still on Rose (N108; also Wagenknecht 64). Reviewing the tale for the New York Edition, James was also pleased, as he judged himself to have stayed loyal to the "principle of composition" staying within the "light of the intense little personal consciousness" he had assigned to his tale. He viewed the tale as straddling the line between "anecdote" and "picture"—"picture aiming at those richly summarised and foreshortened effects—the opposite pole again from expansion inorganic and thin—that refer their terms of production, for which the magician has ever to don his best cap and gown, to the inner compartment of our box of tricks," producing even in the slight tale something of "the true grave close consistency in which parts hang together even as the interweavings of a tapestry" (*Criticism* 2, 1155). The story has indeed the air of something whole, both in its panoramic picture of a faulty London society, and in its close focus on the individual consciousness confronting it and wringing from it a rare nonrenunciatory victory.

Works Cited

Primary Works

James, Henry. 1891. "The Chaperon." *Atlantic Monthly* 68 (November–December): 659–70, 721–35.

———. 1893. "The Chaperon." *The Real Thing*. New York and London: Macmillan, 181–245.

————. 1908. "The Chaperon." *The Novels and Tales of Henry James*. New York Edition. Vol. 10, 435–500. New York: Scribner's.

Secondary Works

Anderson, Quentin. 1957. *The American Henry James*. New Brunswick, NJ: Rutgers University Press.

Andreas, Osborn. 1948. *Henry James and the Expanding Horizon: A Study of the Meaning and Basic Themes of James's Fiction*. Seattle: University of Washington Press.

Anon. 1893. Review of *The Real Thing*. *Athenaeum*, no. 3420 (13 May): 601–2.

Clair, John A. 1965. *The Ironic Dimension in the Fiction of Henry James*. Pittsburgh: Duquesne University Press.

Edgar, Pelham. [1927] 1964. *Henry James, Man and Author*. New York: Russell & Russell.

Gale, Robert L. [1954] 1964. *The Caught Image: Figurative Language in the Fiction of Henry James*. Chapel Hill: University of North Carolina Press.

Horrell, Joyce Tayloe. 1970. "A 'Shade of a Special Sense': Henry James and the Art of Naming." *American Literature* 42: 203–20.

Jacobson, Marcia. 1983. *Henry James and the Mass Market*. University: University of Alabama Press.

Jefferson, D. W. [1960] 1971. *Henry James*. New York: Capricorn.

Jones, Granville H. 1975. *Henry James's Psychology of Experience: Innocence, Responsibility, and Renunciation in the Fiction of Henry James*. The Hague: Mouton.

McElderry, Bruce R., Jr. 1965. *Henry James*. New York: Twayne.

Putt, S. Gorley. 1966. *Henry James: A Reader's Guide*. Ithaca, NY: Cornell University Press.

Rawlings, Peter, ed. 1984. *Henry James's Shorter Masterpieces*. Vol. 1. Totowa, NJ: Barnes & Noble.

Shine, Muriel G. 1969. *The Fictional Children of Henry James*. Chapel Hill: University of North Carolina Press.

Tintner, Adeline R. 1987. *The Book World of Henry James: Appropriating the Classics*. Ann Arbor: UMI Research Press.

————. 1986. *The Museum World of Henry James*. Ann Arbor: UMI Research Press.

Voss, Arthur. 1973. *The American Short Story: A Critical Survey*. Norman: University of Oklahoma Press.

Wagenknecht, Edward. 1984. *The Tales of Henry James*. New York: Frederick Ungar.

Collaboration

Publication History

"Collaboration" appeared in the September 1892 issue of *The English Illustrated Magazine*. The next year, James included it, like "Owen Wingrave," in both the English *The Private Life* and the American *The Wheel of Time*.

Circumstances of Composition, Sources, and Influences

Tintner locates in the collaboration of James's friends Wolcott Balestier and Rudyard Kipling, an American from the West and an Englishman from the East, on a novel, *The Naulahka* (1891), the main source of the international collaboration here. She adds that James was probably further prompted toward his theme the next year by reading the manuscript of Paul Bourget's *Cosmopolis*. Disagreeing with Bourget's view that cosmopolitanism led to decadence, James proffers one that shows it working toward greater civilization, as he felt Balestier, who died in December of 1891, would have (1983, 141–42). Balestier died in Dresden and James went there to help his mother and sisters with the funeral arrangements. His mixed impressions of Germany—the service gave him "a higher idea of German civilization," but the military was "bull-necked" and the general populace "ugly and mighty"—and his attendance at an opera there may also have contributed to the tale (*Letters* 3, 364–67).

James's earlier awareness of a belligerent Germany is evidenced in the publication of his early playlet "Still Waters" on April 12, 1871, in *Balloon Post* no. 2 at the French Fair in Boston, "in aid of the destitute people of France" during the Franco-Prussian War.

Writing in 1893, Payne finds it making a case for "art for art's sake," an idea suffering at the time from the "extravagance of its later devotees" (344). Tintner has drawn attention to several appropriately international sources. Among them she finds Heidenmauer's initials an allusion to Heinrich Heine, another German who loved France, and Felix Vendemer, an allusion to Balzac. The narrator's playing "a mere mocking Mephistopheles" draws in Milton and particularly the opera *Faust*, which combines the music of a

Frenchman, Gounod, with the poetry of a German, Goethe. She notes the irony of Brindes's pen name of Claude Lorrain, who left France for Italy in pursuit of his art just as the two men do here (1989, 75; 1983, 142–43). In the discussion of "le roman russe" she finds an acknowledgment of James's own appropriation of the work of Turgenev (1987, 236–37). James may also have drawn on his "overdose" of Wagner during musical evenings at Paul Zhukovski's in Paris in 1876 (Edel *Life* 2, 229, 405; Blackall 120). According to Edel, a few years later James became disillusioned with Zhukovski, in part because of his excessive worship of Wagner and in part perhaps because of his recognition of his friend's homosexuality (*Life* 253).

Bishop argues that Vendemer and Heidenmauer's exile draws on a February 5, 1892, notebook entry concerning Paul Bourget and his wife, who had to live away from Paris because "Paris wouldn't *tolerate* a united pair." Bishop also considers the reference to "poor Lady M. H.," who broke an engagement and ended a "dreary old maid," a model for Paule de Brindes (84). A slight problem with this is that Paule is not left "pining for her lost love" as Bishop puts it, but playing the music of Heidenmauer, the narrator informing us that she always loved Vendemer less than he loved her (CT 8, 430).

Vendemer, as Gale notes, thinks of his fiancée as resembling Jeanne d'Arc (CT 8, 415; 89 n.12).

Edel connects the tale as well with James's evident consideration that spring of the possibility of collaborating on a play with Constance Fenimore Woolson. Edel speculates that for the usually solitary James, collaborating on a play might have been the sole kind of collaboration he could offer Woolson (*Life* 3, 318–19).

Relation to Other Works

The tale immediately previous to this one, "Sir Dominick Ferrand," also describes an artistic collaboration—in popular song rather than grand opera—that leads in that case to marriage.

In 1894 the *Atlantic* found the tale effective primarily because it reinforced the impression of the recent "The Lesson of the Master," noting however that the "bitter" irony of sacrifice in the first is "merely suggested" here in the hint that Paule transfers her affections at the end (568). Tanner also links it with "The Lesson of the Master" in its preaching the need to renounce both "public rewards" and "domestic consolation" for the sake of art (80). Vendemer's declaration that women have "a moral hatred of art" also links him, as Jones remarks, to Henry St. George as well as the author of *Beltraffio* (147). A similar renunciation might be located in Nick Dormer's situation at the end of *The Tragic Muse*. Edel leaves out the concern with art in order to link the tale with "Lord Beaupré" on the grounds that the men in each tale would find their lives "greatly simplified" without women (CT 8, 10). Like most critics, Edel does not call much attention to the fact that Heidenmauer is cut off by a brother just as Vendemer is by a fiancée.

Levy links the story with "Owen Wingrave" in its criticism of patriotism (249). Andreas offers "The Modern Warning" as another Jamesian argument for tolerance between different nations (132–33). Rowe notes in the duel between Valentin and Kapp in *The American* echoes of the Franco-Prussian War, which takes center place here (91, 97 n.16). Edel finds Heidenmauer as a sympathetic German unusual in James, noting the more typical satire of "A Bundle of Letters" and "Pandora," while Walter Wright adds a contrast with the caricatures of "Fordham Castle" and *Covering End* (*Life* 1, 155; Wright 75). Jones finds the view of art bringing together disparate peoples similar to that Hyacinth Robinson evolves in *The Princess Casamassima* (146).

Interpretation and Criticism

The topic of nationalism here is usually remarked on as an unusual one for James (e.g., Stevenson 28). Levy finds its treatment an expresssion of James's "liberal internationalism," his opposition to "imperialism and militarism" (249). Payne notes that it is an international tale, but "Franco-German" instead of James's more usual Anglo-American (344). The switch would seem necessary to the *Athenaeum* which, in praising the treatment of its topic, remarked that it "would seem almost impossible to an Englishman" but rings "very true" in its French setting (61). Jones sees the two men's work together as providing a symbolic healing of the rift between France and Germany (146). If the American narrator is a cosmopolite, his compatriot Bonus, who represents what seems a rather harmless, if provincial American boosterism, may be there to indicate James's uneasiness about its danger if America ever adopted the warlike attitudes of the European states. When America did, in the Spanish-American War of 1898, James saw in the event a "deep embarrassment of thought—of imagination," and declared that he "hated . . . almost loathed" the war (*Life* 4, 238).

In the tale, such patriotism is put into conflict with art, McElderry calling the tale a "satirical comment on the idea that art has no country," and McCarthy an illustration that art must be "the common property of the human race" (McElderry 121; McCarthy 159). Winner considers the tale in the context of James's interest in expatriation and notes how the central story of Vendemer and Heidenmauer serves to illustrate the narrator's injunction to Bonus not to subordinate art to national prejudice or even pride (117-18). The conflict gives rise to much talk, praised by a contemporary reviewer for its "terseness and 'actuality'" (*Athenaeum*), but disparaged by Wagenknecht who finds it overly theoretical and unengaging (135, 179). Aswell calls these grand themes into question, seeing James beginning with such abstractions, but crowding his tale so that they become eventually unconvincing. Focusing on the narrator whom he finds "smug," Aswell notes how he engineers the collaboration between Félix and Herman, and how he ends his tale before there are any results to present as the triumph of art (181–83). Bishop, although he finds the narrator's role in the collaboration negligible, also argues that his "ironic" stance calls into question the story's claims for art. In addition, Bishop sees the artists' stand against the divisions of nationalism undercut by their own standing together in their own, much smaller, group (77–84). Such privileging, however, was unlikely to make James nervous. As Blackall puts it, the story "embodies the idea that art embraces a community of men in a more profound and significant way than national patriotism may do" (119).

However the themes work out, the focus remains, as Stevenson indicates, on their effect on character (28). Aswell locates double entendres in the narrator's references to the two artists' "unholy union" and "unnatural alliance," but argues that it is unclear whether they represent James's or the narrator's interpretation of their relationship (182–83). Edel finds the admiration of the two artists for each other's work at least in part a cover for their love of each other and desire of a life together without women. The reading, then, is a reversal of Edel's own biographical interpretation in which James offered an artistic collaboration as a substitute for an emotional collaboration he did not wish (*Life* 3, 318–19). Elsewhere Edel argues that the implication is more homosocial than sexual, James illustrating "a fundamental emotional incompatibility" between men and women greater than the gulf between the German and French (CT 8, 10). Haddick finds it a "productive gay alliance," but there is little in the story that indicates what he describes as Vendemer's fascination with Heidenmauer's "person" (20). In any case, such readings need to take into account the narrator's seeming contradiction of such an interpretation, when he writes at the end, "The strange course taken by Vendemer (I mean his renunciation of his engagement) must moreover be judged in the light of the fact that he was really in love" (CT 8, 430).

Putt's reading, Vendemer does not very much mind giving up his engagement, but he judges the significance of that fact mainly in its rendering his character more complex, less a mere mouthpiece for his (or James's) artistic viewpoints. As a result, Putt argues, the treatment of the artistic theme is more successful (223–24). Tanner finds James sincere in the story's avowal of the power of art, but also finds the story reflecting James's fear of the effects of involvement with women (80). Norrman, on the other hand, sees Vendemer as feeling his loss more deeply and objects to the hoops James puts his characters through here, disparaging the "morality of compensation" the story articulates as a "chiastic see-saw" that demands a sacrifice (such as a fiancée or funding) in return for a reward (artistic success), noting that at the same time neither James nor his characters seem certain the system works (161). Jones is most austere, finding that Vendemer is "better off" unmarried as he can now properly devote himself to art, a greater good (146–47).

Whatever James's intentions, they are hard to pin down in this tale full of Wagenerian vagueness and half hints. Certainly, the rhetoric is high flown; the narrator speaks of his studio as "a chamber of justice, a temple of reconciliation" and Art as a protective Catholic Church who "guarantees paradise to the faithful" while Vendemer calls it "the search for the Holy Grail" (CT 8, 408, 425). Gale observes how art with its "power for international good" seems a religion for James (165–66). It would again in "The Great Good Place" a few years later. Part of the problem for contemporary readers may be in reading of a Frenchman and German working together at the turn of the century "for civilization . . . for human happiness," in being asked "Don't we live fast after all, and doesn't the old order change?," and promised in conclusion "more illustrations" of "mighty" Art's triumph over the nations (CT 8, 430–31). We have the dubious benefit of knowing how the next century would shortly bring a relighting of the same national hatreds in a war that James would write of as "the wreck of our belief that through the long years we had seen civilization grow and the worst become impossible" (*Letters* 4, 713). Somehow, there is in this story a sense that such a belief is foolish without a corresponding sense that, even so, it is the best that one can achieve and so must work for.

Works Cited

Primary Works

James, Henry. 1892. "Collaboration." *The English Illustrated Magazine* 9 (September): 911–21

———. 1893. "Collaboration." *The Private Life*. London: Osgood, Mcilvaine.

———. 1893. "Collaboration." *The Wheel of Time*. New York: Harper.

Secondary Works

Andreas, Osborn. 1948. *Henry James and the Expanding Horizon: A Study of the Meaning and Basic Themes of James's Fiction*. Seattle: University of Washington Press.

Anon. 1893. Review of *The Private Life*. *Athenaeum* 102 (8 July): 60–61.

Anon. 1894. Review of *Wheel of Time*. *Atlantic* 73 (April): 568.

Aswell, E. Duncan. 1966. "James's Treatment of Artistic Collaboration." *Criticism* 8: 180–95.

Bishop, George. 1988. *When the Master Relents: The Neglected Short Fictions of Henry James*. Ann Arbor: UMI Research Press.

Blackall, Jean Frantz. 1965. *Jamesian Ambiguity and* The Sacred Fount. Ithaca, NY: Cornell University Press.

Gale, Robert L. [1954] 1964. *The Caught Image: Figurative Language in the Fiction of Henry James.* Chapel Hill: University of North Carolina Press.

Haddick, Vern. 1976. "Colors in the Carpet." *Gay Literature* 5: 19–21.

Jones, Granville H. 1975. *Henry James's Psychology of Experience: Innocence, Responsibility, and Renunciation in the Fiction of Henry James.* The Hague: Mouton.

Levy, Leo B. 1958. "Henry James and the Jews: A Critical Study." *Commentary* 26 (September): 243–49.

McCarthy, Harold T. 1958. *Henry James: The Creative Process.* New York: Thomas Yoseloff.

McElderry, Bruce R., Jr. 1965. *Henry James.* New York: Twayne.

Norrman, Ralf. 1982. *The Insecure World of Henry James's Fiction: Intensity and Ambiguity.* New York: St. Martin's.

Payne, William Morton. 1893. Review of *The Wheel of Time. Dial* 15 (1 December): 344.

Putt, S. Gorley. 1966. *Henry James: A Reader's Guide.* Ithaca, NY: Cornell University Press.

Rowe, John Carlos. 1987. "The Politics of Innocence in Henry James's *The American.*" In *New Essays on The American.* Ed. Martha Banta, 69–97. Cambridge: Cambridge University Press.

Stevenson, Elizabeth. [1949] 1981. *The Crooked Corridor: A Study of Henry James.* New York: Octagon.

Tanner, Tony. 1985. *Henry James: The Writer and His Work.* Amherst: University of Massachusetts Press.

Tintner, Adeline R. 1989. *The Pop World of Henry James: From Fairy Tales to Science Fiction.* Ann Arbor: UMI Research Press.

———. 1987. *The Book World of Henry James: Appropriating the Classics.* Ann Arbor: UMI Research Press.

———. 1983. "Rudyard Kipling and Wolcott Balestier's Literary Collaboration: A Possible Source for James's 'Collaboration.'" *Henry James Review* 4, no. 2: 140–43.

Wagenknecht, Edward. 1984. *The Tales of Henry James.* New York: Frederick Ungar.

Winner, Viola Hopkins. 1970. *Henry James and the Visual Arts.* Charlottesville: University Press of Virginia.

Wright, Walter F. 1962. *The Madness of Art: A Study of Henry James.* Lincoln: University of Nebraska Press.

Crapy Cornelia

Publication History

Appearing in October 1909, "Crapy Cornelia" was the final story James published in *Harper's Magazine*, where he had first appeared thirty years before, in the 1879 "Diary of a Man of Fifty." In his listed income for 1909 James recorded the receipt on June 17 of his payment for "Crapy Cornelia," £923.6 with the commision for his agent James B. Pinker taken out (CN 601). The next year James included the tale in the collection *The Finer Grain*. After his death, it appeared in Lubbock's edition of the collected novels and stories.

Circumstances of Composition, Sources, and Influences

"Crapy Cornelia" is one of three late tales for which there is no notebook entry (N ix n.1). According to James's secretary, Theodora Bosanquet, it began with the request for a story of 5,000 words from *Harper's*: in her account, "each promising idea was cultivated in the optimistic belief that it would produce a flower too frail and small to demand any exhaustive treatment." Nevertheless, despite writing by hand and dictating only "rigidly restricted" interpolations, each tale had turned out too long, so that Bosanquet records it was "almost literally true" that the contents of *The Finer Grain* consisted of the tales rejected as overlength. As both "The Velvet Glove" and "A Round of Visits" are no longer than "Crapy Cornelia," presumably it was "The Bench of Desolation" and "Mora Montravers" that were rejected as too long for *Harper's*. Even so, at 10,000 words "Crapy Cornelia" was twice as long as intended, which may be why Bosanquet erroneously records James's annoyance at the tale taking two numbers (248–49). The emphasis on length may also explain why James referred to the story to Pinker as "the small abomination" (*Letters* 4, 505).

Both Bewley and Putt have commented on the fact that in describing the New York of the Gilded Age here, James is treading on the territory of Edith Wharton, Bewley commenting on the superiority of her knowledge of New York to James's (Bewley 1959, 242; Putt 1977, 180). Edel, however, goes further in linking the character of Mrs. Worthingham to Edith Wharton in her polished, pastoral yet modern wealth (*Letters* 4, xxviii–xxix; *Life* 690). Tintner takes the connection still further, arguing that James made Mrs. Worthingham out of some of the characteristics of Wharton he "found difficult to accept unless transformed into burlesque terms," including her wealth, modernity, and "too-good taste." Accordingly, James uses some of the same images to describe Mrs. Worthingham that he used for Wharton, images of brightness and the dance (1975, 368–71). She locates what is perhaps even a deeper divide between the two writers in James's exclamation in a 1907 letter, after a visit with Wharton, "I can't *ever* again attempt, for more than the fleeting hour, to lead other people's [lives]"—a recognition she argues is the moral of the tale. The "immensity of life" visible from the homes of a Worthingham or a Wharton was, according to Tintner, what "the aging novelist wished to contract" (1971, 494–95). Even as Tintner sees Mrs. Worthingham's home as modeled on Wharton's Park Avenue residence, she finds the location of Cornelia's apartment near Riverside Avenue significant in its proximity to a Civil War monument, a sign of the past (1976, 420–24). Cornelia herself, the opposite of Wharton, she associates with Wharton's dear sister-in-law Mary Cadwalader Jones, whose house provided a more comfortable atmosphere for James on his recent New York visit. Meanwhile, she sees the contrast between the two fictional women as also reflecting the contrast between the cousins Lily Bart and Gerty Farish in *The House of Mirth* (1975, 370–71). In drawing a parallel between Mrs. Worthingham and Wharton, one should, however, also note that James had said of Wharton: "You may find her difficult, but you will never find her stupid, and you will never find her mean"—qualities that set her apart from Mrs. Worthingham (Bell 190).

James himself provided a source for the character of White-Mason in a 1909 letter to his friend Etta Reubell. From Lamb House he wrote, "Dearest Etta Reubell—my very old friend indeed! Your letter charms and touches me, and I rejoice you were moved to write. You have understood 'Crapy Cornelia'—and people so very often seem not to understand—and that alone gives me pleasure." He continued, observing that "life becomes more and more [ghostly]" and concluding, "But with you the shepherdess of the flock it will be all right. You are not Cornelia, but I am much White-Mason, and I shall again sit by your fire" (*Letters* 4, 139–40). Critics have generally accepted the identification. Putt, for example, remarking on the shared "weariness," dislike of new money, and fondness for the "tone of time," comments that White-Mason's "consciousness is so completely his author's own that its presentation might have come straight from the autobiographical volumes" (1966, 302–4; also Edgar 72; Wagenknecht 167).

Looking at classical mythology, Tintner sees "Crapy Cornelia" emphasizing the idea of *"lares penates"* or "household gods." She points to the quotation from Virgil speaking of the "pictures, precious goods" left floating after the shipwreck in the first book of the *Aeneid*. It is, according to Gale, the longest classical quotation in James (115 n.27). The *"tabulaeque"* in this case, Tintner argues, are *carte-de visite* photographs, and with them, Cornelia and White-Mason set to the task taken on by the defeated Trojans, to reassemble a ruined past (1989 *Pop*, 141–43; 1986, 192–94). To Tintner, the river near Cornelia's apartment and White-Mason's visit to Central Park also create "Virgillian overtones" suggestive of a trip to the underworld. Those who remember the past, she argues, create "an underworld of memory" in the midst of the modern city. The pastoral tones of Central Park Tintner associates with Shakespeare's *The Tempest* and Sonnet XXX (1976, 416, 423–24). Martin and Ober note another classical allusion in the name Cornelia, the name of the mother of the Gracchi, a representative of "the best in the ancient Roman tradition" (63). Finally, in a look at the world of fairy tales, Tintner speaks of Cornelia as an "aged Cinderella" (1989 *Pop*, 138).

There is just a scrap of an allusion to Tennyson, noted by Gale, in White-Mason's vision of "the form of the 'glimmering square' of the poet" (112).

Tintner also proposes a more up-to-date influence, that of the new cinematograph, particularly the film of the Corbett-Fitzsimmons fight James viewed in 1898 (1986, 187–92). Without arguing for any influence, Putt senses a Proustian nostalgia in the tale for which Cornelia's photographs serve as the *madeleine* (1966, 304). Smith argues that T. S. Eliot's "The Love Song of J. Alfred Prufrock," with its inconclusive encounter between a man and woman and its speaker's climatic recognition that he is old, is indebted to both "The Beast in the Jungle" and "Crapy Cornelia" (15; also Holder 13). Tintner traces the name of the hero's mother Cornelia in Louis Auchincloss's highly Jamesian *The Book Class* back to this tale (1989 "Tradition," 332).

Relation to Other Works

In Matthiessen's judgment, the "least considerable" of the late New York tales, "Crapy Cornelia" has still given rise to many comparisons with its fellow New York stories (xxii). The contrast between America's quieter past and its overactive modernity, Wegelin finds repeated in *Julia Bride* (162). According to Buitenhuis, however, the story is the lightest of the late American tales, indeed the only "comic" one (201). Still, while Geismar notes the treatment of society as "lighter" than in "A Round of Visits" in particular, Krook sees a harsher judgment (Geismar 365; Krook 337–40). The satire in all three tales Auchincloss labels "crude," arguing that James had "insufficiently digested" New York. He reserves his highest praise for the nonfiction *The American Scene*, although he acknowledges the unfinished novel *The Ivory Tower* as being superior to the tales (46, 49). The hero of that novel, Fielder, as Jones notes, like White-Mason and Spencer Brydon, feels threatened both by the "mutiplied vulgarities" of the American present, and like White-Mason and John Marcher, by the prospect of emotional commitment. In response, Jones notes that like Brydon, White-Mason turns to the past for peace, with a greater justification than Brydon in his positive memories (91, 257, 260, 287). Both men in the end, according to Ward, accept "the comfort of a human relation," although he sees White-Mason's case treated in a lighter, comic manner (166). Looking back at *The Europeans*, Bewley finds its evocation of a pastoral America much more effective by virtue of the complementary European perspective (1959, 243–44). In that work, New England had, like old New York here, the virtue of gracefully hiding its wealth, and at times the old New York here seems more like New England.

The topic of New York serves, in Putt's view, to make the character of White-Mason more vivid than Traffle of "Mora Montravers" or Taker of "Fordham Castle," not because his character is superior, but because his interest in "life *outside* himself" expresses James's vigor in an acuteness of observation comparable to that of Lambert Strether (1966, 301–2). Still, the tale is told, according to Beach, with the same subjective narration of such other late tales as "The Beast in the Jungle" and "The Bench of Desolation" (70). Like the hero of the latter tale, Gage notes, White-Mason, too, evades realities, sitting on his own bench in Central Park as he harps on the past (251, 261, 264). Other seated spectators in James are noted by Tanner in "Mora Montravers" and at the conclusion of *A Little Tour in France*, where the spectator is James himself (1987, 122–23).

On his bench, White-Mason thinks not only of the city, but of the women in it. Looking at *The Finer Grain* as a whole, Edel sees its female characters as being of such a "coarser grain," that James felt no compunction in off-handedly insulting them, as he does in calling Mrs. Worthingham "as ignorant as a fish" (CT 12, 9). Buitenhuis also notes their coarseness, adding earlier examples including Mrs. Luna of *The Bostonians* and Mrs. Beck of "Guest's Confessions," but taking a lighter approach to their vulgarity (221). One might add the British widow Mrs. Churchley of "The Marriages." To Krook, however, Mrs. Worthingham is a diminished version of the more interesting worldly type of Charlotte Stant or Mrs. Brissenden (339). In Przybylowicz's reading she suffers from what James saw as the "moral taint" of the *nouveau riche*, a taint shared variously by Daisy Miller, Milly Theale, and Adam Verver—all of whom, like Mrs. Worthingham, have no past worth speaking of (137). Tanner sees the harshly unflattering portraits here and in "A Round of Visits" and "Miss Gunton of Poughkeepsie" as showing James's revision of his sense of the "bright young" American woman of his early works, after his return to the States (1985, 124). Perhaps as a result, Mrs. Worthingham, according to Wagenknecht, resembles the nemesis of the chief example of those "bright young" women, and is, like Mme. Merle, best defined by her setting, her possessions (168). The portrait of Cornelia, on the other hand, according to Edgar, is more ladylike than even Isabel Archer (72–73). The contrast between the two women, meanwhile, each representing a nearly opposite approach to life, recalls that between the Countess and Scholastica in "Benvolio."

Faced with the prospect of marrying Mrs. Worthingham, White-Mason savors the sensation of "*vertige de l'âbime*," which Purdy glosses as the "lure of self-destruction," or in Jamesian slang, the thrill of "dishing" oneself, as Julia Bride does (CT 12, 354; 1970, 428). For Julia, however, "dishing" oneself meant being kept from marrying, while in White-Mason's case, it is marriage itself, at least to Mrs. Worthingham. As Gage observes, while Monteith eagerly seeks someone to receive his message, the equally egotistic White-Mason keeps his message, his proposal, closely buttoned up (246–47). Segal compares his relief at being left single to that of the fearful lovers in James's early works, and Buitenhuis sees him in particular as a "white" or older version of Ferdinand Mason of "A Most Extraordinary Case," while also resembling Roger Lawrence in *Watch and Ward*, whose proposal to the worldy Mrs. Keith was rejected (Segal 222; Buitenhuis 65, 221). His reluctance to commit similarly prompted Geismar to compare him to Pendrel of *The Sense of the Past* (434). Keeping Cornelia safely as a confidante, White-Mason behaves, according to Sharp, like Strether, Marcher, or the earlier Rowland Mallet of *Roderick Hudson* (62). Even though, as Buitenhuis observes, Cornelia like Maria Gostrey "almost proposes," White-Mason like Strether won't marry (223). The relationship between both pairs, according to Przybylowicz, fits the "patient-analyst paradigm" also found in "The Beast in the Jungle" and "The Jolly Corner"(139). White-Mason's ambivalence toward Mrs. Worthingham, Putt argues, reflects Strether's feelings toward Mrs. Newsome (1966, 302–3).

Taking as a key the symbolic pattern of the burdened man's rebirth from "The Great Good Place," Shroeder links "Crapy Cornelia," "The Beast in the Jungle," and "The Jolly Corner" as stories in which the men are freed of their burdens through the agency of motherly women. In "Crapy Cornelia," Shroeder contends, White-Mason seeks and gains escape from the burden of "modern vulgarity" through Cornelia who, like the maternal Alice Staverton, stands for the "mystical virtues of the past" and so appeals to the "regressive" White-Mason. (See also "Impressions of a Cousin.")

Interpretation and Criticism

Arnold Bennett called the tale "an exceedingly brilliant exercise in the art of making stone-soup," which is perhaps why he referred to it as "Crafty Cornelia" (265). In Krook's view, the prime ingredient in the soup is the subject of modernity (339). Approaching the same subject from the other side, Beach observes how in this tale the phrase the "tone of time," normally reserved by James for Europe, is used to describe old New York (170 n. 4).

Appreciating both, Putt praises particularly James's possession here of the "external correlatives . . . the distancing and discriminations of an essayist in fiction" (1966, 301).

The contrast between old and new in the story is given its own "external correlatives" in the tale through patterns of imagery. Tintner views the tale as underlaid by an "architectural structure," contrasts between types of interior decoration and between the "glaring" light of new New York and the "shaded world of the daguerreotype and of the old New York" (1976, 418, 422–23). Such visual contrasts born out also in the "repetitive counterpointing" of the harsh bright image of Mrs. Worthingham and the soothing dim one of Cornelia, in Matthiessen's view, help to offset "any impression of overstuffed heaviness" from James's late style (xxii–iii). Cornelia herself first appears as an "incongruous object," which resolves into sight "after the manner of images in the cinematograph" (CT 12, 343). Cornelia goes on, however, according to Tintner, to be identified with the old-time photograph and Mrs. Worthingham with the "glaring" new cinematograph (1986, 187–96).

The tale's style has also received much attention. Menikoff examines the manner in which James uses punctuation in the tale to underline point of view, bringing the reader in to the story through White-Mason's perspective, and providing suspense at the introduction of Cornelia (31–35). The *Times Literary Supplement*, in its review, commented on the structure of James's sentences: "Those sentences positively splitting at the seams with significance, sentences which even at their worst seem like a drawer pulled gradually open till it suddenly spills at our feet countless odds and ends 'bristling' with innuendo. As the mind thinks, so Mr. James narrates." Such is the manner in particular of White-Mason's talk with Cornelia, and although Wagenknecht objects to their frank talk as more appropriate to Mrs. Worthingham's set, McElderry praises the sprightly dialogue for keeping the story from becoming "conventionally sentimental" (Wagenknecht 170; McElderry 144). Both Purdy and Martin and Ober provide readings of the syle, particularly of the final conversations, that praise its subtlety. In the absence of action, Purdy notes, the tale becomes an "impressionistic representation" of White-Mason's reactions. Purdy traces patterns of imagery including that of light, which becomes associated with vulgarity, and music, which becomes associated with the crucial "tone of time." He points as well to recurrent words, particularly the "counterpoint of association" surrounding the word "know." For Mrs. Worthingham to be "in the know" shows a lack of taste. But, Purdy argues, as Cornelia and White-Mason work through its meanings in their final, highly artful conversation he leads her to his higher level of "knowing" and they establish themselves as the "real 'knowers'" (1970). Martin and Ober also concentrate on Cornelia and White-Mason's conversation and James's use of imagery. They note how James speaks of their talk first as a dance and later as a fire in order to portray the oblique approaches and hesitations that allow Cornelia to achieve her insights. Portraying Cornelia as the leader in the dance, they argue further that the conversation between the two illustrates the ideal relationship for James between author and reader. Among other patterns of imagery they record the dark of "crapy" Cornelia, which fruitfully balances the lightness of White-Mason's name, while the "glare" Mrs. Worthingham creates simply drives him to "goggles." Criticizing H. G. Wells and Edel for their failure to appreciate what Edel once called the "excess of style and decoration" in the late tales, Martin and Ober counter that the "hoverings" of James's sentences are necessary to allow their "final dash towards truth."

The two women of the tale, marked by their different colors, represent the two sides to the story. As Przybylowicz comments, they embody the dichotomies of the tale—Europe and America, appearance and reality, self and other—and so represent White-Mason's alternate selves (139). While Wagenknecht judges the "two women and two ways of life" as "masterfully contrasted," in Bewley's estimate, the cynical depiction of what is wrong with modern New York in Mrs. Worthingham is far superior to the "sentimentalized" depiction of the virtues of old New York in Cornelia, a reading of Cornelia to which Buitenhuis takes exception (Wagenknecht 169; Bewley 1959, 242–44; Buitenhuis 224).

Reading the women according to such a schema, Ward early on praised White-Mason for rejecting the superficial appearance of Mrs. Worthingham for the reality of Cornelia (165–66). Putt, however, while noting that White-Mason's rejection of a marriage for "aesthetic" reasons is highly moral in the Jamesian universe, contends that because he is rejecting a woman, not a concept, his behavior seems unacceptably cold (1966, 302). Przybylowicz, while recognizing in White-Mason's rejection of Mrs. Worthingham James's rejection of America, also sees White-Mason as an emotional lightweight. She observes, too, that his egotism may well prevent him from recognizing the possibility that Mrs. Worthingham is not much impressed with him, either (136, 138–39). Even among those who treat Mrs. Worthingham more as a person than as a symbol, reactions vary. Wagenknecht questions whether White-Mason would ever have seriously considered her as a wife, while Andreas sees White-Mason realizing from his reencounter with Cornelia that Mrs. Worthingham would "always be a stranger to him," and as such a poor choice for a spouse (Wagenknecht 169–70; Andreas 94). Similarly, Tintner argues that White-Mason simply comes to recognize that Mrs. Worthingham is the "wrong medium" for him, and so turns to the more restful Cornelia (1986, 187–96). Jefferson, however, objects to the "irritating implications" of White-Mason's abandonment of his proposal (139–40).

Most critics' irritation becomes more profound at White-Mason's next step. For some, it is his choice of Cornelia, or at least what he means it as. Buitenhuis, for example, questions not so much his turning from the showy and superficial Mrs. Worthingham, but his turning at forty-eight from the very idea of a wife to the safety of a mother figure (221–25). Critics, in discussing Cornelia, tend to accept White-Mason's typing of her as irretrievably old. Auchincloss, for example, calls her a "faded old maid" (46). White-Mason does indeed turn from a younger woman to an older woman, as Buitenhuis observes, but that does not mean she is older than he. When White-Mason indicates he is nearly as old as she is, she corrects him quickly, stating that he is "exactly a year and ten months older" (CT 12, 363). Certainly Cornelia's room indicates she is much at home in the past. But while McCarthy indicates that Cornelia has never really left the past (116), she is first seen at the home of the very modern Mrs. Worthingham, and she does not seem to regard herself as beyond change. McElderry argues that Cornelia "subtly" persuades White-Mason not to marry Mrs. Worthingham (144), and she certainly suggests quite directly that White-Mason could marry her. It is White-Mason who casts himself and Cornelia as "conscious, ironic, pathetic survivors of a dead and buried society," and thinks to himself that they should "*make* together, make over and recreate, our lost world," a plan that requires no marriage vows (CT 12, 353, 357).

Accordingly, most critics object more to White-Mason's treatment of Cornelia than his choice of her. In reclaiming the past through Cornelia without any commitment to her, White-Mason according to Gage is yet "another Jamesian renouncer who does not really want what he renounces" (256). Sharp dismisses White-Mason as distinctly "less capable" than previous Jamesian heroes, but still sees him following the pattern of the "confiding male" who makes use of the accomplished Cornelia—someone who "understands yet is superior to her environment"—as a confidante, while keeping her "at a safe distance" (60–62). Przybylowicz, too, criticizes White-Mason's egotistic exploitation of Cornelia, but also argues that Cornelia in turn "lives vicariously" through his affairs, as is seen in her memory of Mary Cardew (138–39).

Others are more sympathetic to White-Mason and his discovery of peace. In the reading of Martin and Ober, White-Mason's declaration that he does not wish to marry Cornelia exemplifies "the achievement, without bitterness or rancour, of a truth." They see their private relationship—signified in the exchange of photographs of Mary Cardew—as satisfying, free from the need for an "explicit, publicly-stated and, as it were, material tie" (65, 68). With less emphasis on Cornelia, Vaid sympathetically points to the "restful note on which the tale ends" (234). Similarly, Jones cites a notebook entry in which an old man wards off a threat to his peace, which ends with the remark, "One watches and sympathizes, one is amused and touched, one likes to think the old party is safe for the rest of time" (CN 139–40). Such, Jones remarks, appears to be James's attitude to many of his elderly adventurers who find a haven in the end. Looking more explicitly at White-Mason's avoidance of marriage, Jones—in response to Putt's labeling of him as "maimed"—argues that James was more likely to have seem him as a "decent, desperate, fortunate man." To marry Cornelia, Jones writes, would destroy White-Mason's image of "his own innocent youth." Jones judges theirs an "achieved and respectable renunciation" similar to the "instinctual renunciation" advocated by the late, pessimistic Freud, although theirs is based on a rejection rather than a subordination of reality. This difference, Jones argues, explains why James's renouncers are so happy with themselves, and critics so unhappy with them. Still, despite its elements of "narcissism and retreat," he sees in such renunciation "high morality and self-preservation" (258, 276).

While acknowledging that such a conclusion was comedic to James, Geismar questions both its avoidance of emotional challenges, and the taking of refuge in "old age . . . old money and old real estate" (364–66). Earlier, Bewley had maintained that James was "fully conscious" of the problems of the upper class and of his own temptation to excuse them. Still, Bewley argues, in his "formulation" of its problems, James may have permitted his protagonist to solve his problems too easily in allowing him to "overcome the grandiose temptation of luxurious irresponsibility in the present by submitting to an equally pernicious sentimentalization of the past" (1952, 76n).

One passage is key. It is, according to Edel "one of the rare instances" when James took on "the stance and tone of a prophet" (CT 12, 7). In general, critics have fallen in line with James's confession to Etta Reubell that he was White-Mason, and have taken this passage as particularly revealing (e.g., Geismar 365; Gage 250; Putt 1985, 10). Presenting what Edel calls James's vision of the future in America, the passage is also his vision of its past (*Life* 4, 501). Mulling over his visit with Mrs. Worthingham, White-Mason thinks to himself:

> This was clearly going to be the music of the future—that if people were but rich enough and furnished enough and fed enough, exercised and sanitated and manicured and generally advised and advertised and made 'knowing' enough, *avertis* enough, as the term appeared to be nowadays in Paris, all they had to do for civility was to take the amused ironic view of those who might be less initiated. In *his* times, when he was young or even when he was only but a little less middle-aged, the best manners had been the best kindness, and the best kindness had mostly been some art of not insisting on one's luxurious differences, of concealing rather, for common humanity, if not for common decency, a part at least of the intensity or the ferocity with which one might be 'in the know.'
> (CT 12, 348)

As a credo, what does James's speech tell us? According to Putt, in this disquisition on the "best manners" and the "best kindness" James's "moral and aesthetic nerves are twitching as one." He cites further White-Mason's self-defense: "You can have means and not be blatant. . . . Even though not of the truly bloated I've at least means to be quiet. Every one among us—I mean among the moneyed—isn't a monster on exhibition" (1977, 180–81).

It would seem then to boil down to a matter of taste, and it is not hard to sympathize with James's revulsion at the ostentatiousness of the new wealth or to recognize in James's critique of it the "still amazingly energetic social critic" Putt praises James for being (1966, 302). Kimbel sees this tale as treating "the disparity between social pretensions and moral truths," James's emphases including "the vulgarity of new money" and "the protective cloak of social privilege" (39). His depiction of the old wealth, however, in the two passages seems to pride itself mainly on a kind of dissembling that requires wealth to sustain it. In other words, there is no issue here of virtue without "means." As Buitenhuis notes, the virtuous here have the "manners of an aristocracy, or at least an *elite* in a democratic society" (224). More harshly, Przybylowicz speaks of White-Mason's and Cornelia's "reactionary and snobbish class attitude" (137). Indeed, even at its first publication, the reviewer for the *North American Review* found the tale "one of James's studies in sordidness and smallness," stating that James had "a touch" of the characteristic of Lydgate in *Middlemarch*, "the quality that believes that for some reason elegance and fineness really do reside in the best of furniture and the most modern of hangings." With the exception of the word "modern," the criticism seems valid with regard to this tale.

Reactions to the tale have been varied. Early on Bewley judged it "interesting but uneven" (1952, 76n). Putt, too, has also picked the story apart in his evaluation. Calling it a "beautifully controlled tale," Putt has praised the "moral intelligence" of its author while criticizing the "emotional cowardice" of its protagonist, while also arguing that there was no real need to flesh out the story's essential social criticism with its "few half-dead figures" (1966, 301–2, 304). Wagenknecht, while refusing to decide whether or not it fits into the category of a "major" work, judges it "certainly a tale of considerable art" (169). Less hesitantly, Purdy judges it a "masterwork of the major phase," a "final climax" to James's late style (139). Certainly, the fluidity of the style, its easy transition from caricature to nostalgia, from colloquialism to lyricism, its painting of character through a simple gesture, and its recollection of an era in an image, is striking and a delight in itself. In the story it tells, however, one comes up hard against how closely interwoven are the qualities in James most attractive and most disturbing—the valuing of simplicity and peace, the snobbishness, the almost unconscious reliance on a certain standard of wealth, the smug acceptance of one person's sacrifice to another. White-Mason may settle down into his chair by Cornelia's fire finally free of his perpetual scowl, but the brow of the reader is likely to remain furrowed. White-Mason makes a problematic modern Diogenes. Indeed, the contrast between him and Cornelia seems another version of that between the old and new wealth. White-Mason flaunts his virtue even as Mrs. Worthingham flaunts her riches. His posturing may not be as offensive as her material ostentation, but, especially given the deep flaws in his character, it has a certain bad taste to it all the same.

Works Cited

Primary Works

James, Henry. 1909. "Crapy Cornelia." *Harper's Magazine* 119 (October): 690–704.

———. 1910. "Crapy Cornelia." *The Finer Grain*. New York: Scribner's; London: Methuen, 187–233.

———. 1921–23. "Crapy Cornelia." *The Novels and Stories of Henry James*. Vol. 28. Ed. Percy Lubbock. London: Macmillan.

———. 1920. *The Letters of Henry James*. Vol. 2. Ed. Percy Lubbock. New York: Scribner's.

Secondary Works

Andreas, Osborn. 1948. *Henry James and the Expanding Horizon: A Study of the Meaning and Basic Themes of James's Fiction*. Seattle: University of Washington Press.

Anon. 1911. Review of *The Finer Grain*. *The North American Review* 193 (February): 302.

Anon. 1910. Review of *The Finer Grain*. *The Times Literary Supplement* (13 October): 377.

Auchincloss, Louis. 1975. "Henry James's Literary Use of His American Tour (1904)." *South Atlantic Quarterly* 74, no. 1 (Winter): 45–52.

Beach, Joseph Warren. [1918] 1954. *The Method of Henry James*. Philadelphia: Albert Saifer.

Bell, Millicent. 1965. *Edith Wharton and Henry James: The Story of Their Friendship*. New York: George Braziller.

Bennett, Arnold. 1917. "Henry James." *Books and Persons, Being Comments of a Past Epoch, 1908–1911*. New York: George H. Doran, 263–66.

Bewley, Marius. 1959. *The Eccentric Design: Form in the Classic American Novel*. New York: Columbia University Press. Revised from "Henry James and 'Life.'" *Hudson Review* 11 (1958): 183–84.

———. 1952. *The Complex Fate: Hawthorne, Henry James, and Some Other American Writers*. London: Chatto & Windus.

Bosanquet, Theodora. 1924. *Henry James at Work*. London: Hogarth.

Buitenhuis, Peter. 1970. *The Grasping Imagination: The American Writings of Henry James*. Toronto: University of Toronto Press.

Edgar, Pelham. [1927] 1964. *Henry James, Man and Author*. New York: Russell & Russell.

Gage, Richard P. 1988. *Order and Design: Henry James' Titled Story Sequences*. New York: Peter Lang.

Gale, Robert L. [1954] 1964. *The Caught Image: Figurative Language in the Fiction of Henry James*. Chapel Hill: University of North Carolina Press.

Geismar, Maxwell. 1963. *Henry James and the Jacobites*. Boston: Houghton Mifflin.

Holder, Alan. 1966. *Three Voyagers in Search of Europe: A Study of Henry James, Ezra Pound, and T. S. Eliot*. Philadelphia: University of Pennsylvania Press.

Jefferson, D.W. 1964. *Henry James and the Modern Reader*. New York: St. Martin's.

Jones, Granville H. 1975. *Henry James's Psychology of Experience: Innocence, Responsibility, and Renunciation in the Fiction of Henry James*. The Hague: Mouton.

Kimbel, Ellen. 1984. "The American Short Story: 1900–1920." In *The American Short Story: 1900–1945*. Ed. Philip Stevick, 33–69. Boston: Twayne.

Krook, Dorothea. [1962] 1967. *The Ordeal of Consciousness in Henry James*. New York: Cambridge University Press.

McCarthy, Harold T. 1958. *Henry James: The Creative Process*. New York: Thomas Yoseloff.

McElderry, Bruce R., Jr. 1965. *Henry James*. New York: Twayne.

Martin, W. R., and Warren U. Ober. 1980. "'Crapy Cornelia': James's Self-Vindication?" *Ariel: A Review of International English Literature* 2, no. 4: 57–68.

Matthiessen, F. O., ed. 1947. *The American Novels and Stories of Henry James*. New York: Knopf.

Menikoff, Barry. 1970. "Punctuation and Point of View in the Late Style of Henry James." *Style* 4: 29–47.

Przybylowicz, Donna. 1986. *Desire and Repression: The Dialectic of Self and Other in the Late Works of Henry James*. University: University of Alabama Press.

Purdy, Strother B. 1970. "Henry James's Abysses: A Semantic Note." *English Studies* 51 (October): 424–33.

———. 1967. "Language as Art: The Ways of Knowing in Henry James's 'Crapy Cornelia.'" *Style* 1 (Spring): 139–49.

Putt, S. Gorley, ed. 1985. *An International Episode and Other Stories*. Harmondsworth: Penguin.

———. 1977. "Henry James, Radical Gentleman." *Massachusetts Review* (Spring): 179–86.

———. 1966. *Henry James: A Reader's Guide*. Ithaca, NY: Cornell University Press.

Segal, Ora. 1969. *The Lucid Reflector: The Observer in Henry James' Fiction*. New Haven: Yale University Press.

Sharp, Sister M. Corona. 1963. *The Confidante in Henry James: Evolution and Moral Value of a Fictive Character*. Notre Dame, IN: Notre Dame University Press.

Shroeder, John W. 1951. "The Mothers of Henry James." *American Literature* 22 (January): 424–31.

Smith, Grover. 1965 [1974]. *T. S. Eliot's Poetry and Plays*. Chicago: University of Chicago Press.

Tanner, Tony. 1987. "The Watcher from the Balcony: *The Ambassadors*." In *Henry James*. Ed Harold Bloom. New York: Chelsea House. Reprinted from *Critical Inquiry* 8, no. 1 (Spring 1966): 105–23.

———. 1985. *Henry James: The Writer and His Work*. Amherst: University of Massachusetts Press.

Tintner, Adeline R. 1989. *The Pop World of Henry James: From Fairy Tales to Science Fiction*. Ann Arbor: UMI Research Press.

———. 1989. "The Jamesian Tradition in *The Book Class*: Louis Auchincloss's *A Small Boy and Others*." In *The Magic Circle of Henry James: Essays in Honour of Darshan Singh Maini*. Ed. Singh, Amritjit and K. Ayyappa Paniker, 326–41. New York: Envoy.

———. 1986. *The Museum World of Henry James*. Ann Arbor: UMI Research Press.

———. 1976. "Landmarks of 'The Terrible Town': The New York Scene in Henry James' Last Stories." *Prospects* 2: 399–435.

———. 1975. "The Metamorphoses of Edith Wharton in Henry James's *The Finer Grain*." *Twentieth-Century Literature* 21: 355–79.

———. 1971–72. "James's Mock Epic: 'The Velvet Glove,' Edith Wharton, and Other Late Tales." *Modern Fiction Studies* 17 (Winter): 483–99.

Vaid, Krishna B. 1964. *Technique in the Tales of Henry James*. Cambridge, MA: Harvard University Press.

Wagenknecht, Edward. 1984. *The Tales of Henry James*. New York: Frederick Ungar.

Ward, J. A. 1961. *The Imagination of Disaster: Evil in the Fiction of Henry James*. Lincoln: University of Nebraska Press.

Wegelin, Christof. 1958. *The Image of Europe in Henry James*. Dallas: Southern Methodist University Press.

Crawford's Consistency

Publication History

In August 1876 "Crawford's Consistency" was the first of James's stories to appear in *Scribner's Monthly*. The tale was not in print again until Edna Kenton's 1950 *Eight Uncollected Tales*. A manuscript of the story, signed Henry James Jr., 29 Rue de Luxembourg Paris, located at the American Academy and Institute of Arts and Letters, is one of his few story manuscripts to survive.

Circumstances of Composition, Sources, and Influences

In 1873 James's father sent him a letter relating "a regular Tourgéneff subject," the marital history of a friend from Albany, Matthew Henry Webster (*Autobiography* 402). In a letter to his mother from Rome, James relayed thanks to his father for the story, which he had since recorded in his notebook "with religious care." He cautioned, however, that its "first class theme" would "require much thinking out" (*Letters* 1, 357). Evidently it did. A letter dated April 11, 1876, from James in Paris to his father tells of sending off "two short tales," one based on his father's idea that he "had had . . . in mind" for the past three years, the other "The Ghostly Rental" (*Letters* 2, 39, 40 n.4). The second letter disproves Kelley's conjecture, based on the ground of its poor quality, that the tale was written in 1873, but not produced until the request from *Scribner's* (129–30). Edel speculates that James interrupted work on *The American* to write the two tales in order to earn some quick money (he was paid $300) following a charge of "extravagance" made by his mother back in January (*Life* 2, 246–47).

In his *Notes of a Son and Brother*, James quotes his father's letter about Mr. Webster, although, as Kenton points out, he dates the letter 1870 and neglects to name the story where he made use of it (6). The main events in the story remain the same, although James postpones his hero's loss of fortune so that it disrupts his marriage, rather than canceling his engagement, and makes its cause magnanimous rather than reckless.

Gale points to two brief allusions in the tale, one to Sheridan's *The School for Scandal* and one to Martin Luther (130, 163).

Relation to Other Works

Kelley sees the story—with its young woman who turns away her fiancé at her family's bequest and the fiancé who proves superior to it all—as the germ for *The American*, adding that the French setting makes the concept, unconvincing in New York, a reasonable one (238–39; also *Life* 2, 255). Fox sees Crawford as a less wise version of a different American in Paris, Lambert Strether (12).

Kenton compares the way Crawford first recognizes his future wife as a "type" to Baxter's recognition of his future wife, Marian, in "The Story of a Masterpiece," and at the same time finds a shared "equanimity" between Crawford and Marian, showing that James's interest in the type antedated his father's story. She also finds Crawford as "actor" related to John Marcher and argues that James "rejected" the earlier tale because its treatment was not worthy of the subject (6–7, 15–16). Putt puts a very low value on Crawford's consistency in staying in a bad marriage, comparing it to Isabel Archer's faithfulness to her misguided marriage vows, while Stein finds in Crawford's fate the culmination of James's fear of marriage evident also in *Madame de Mauves* and "The Last of the Valerii" (Putt 268; Stein 83–84). Edel's description of the way the wife "reverses roles" with Crawford fits the story into the "sacred fount" theme (*Life* 2, 256).

Putt sees in the wife some of Millicent Henning's "robustness" while Kraft categorizes her as a "typical" lower class person in contrast to the "exceptional" Brooksmith and the heroine of *In the Cage* (Putt 268; Kraft 87). Walter Wright sees her behavior as "sensational and cheaply dramatic" in a manner typical of the early tales (87–88).

Interpretation and Criticism

Estimates of the story have never been high. Edel calls the tale one of James's "shameless potboilers," while remarking that it has "a competence pleasing to the magazines" (CT 4, 7). It is hard to imagine, however, what a reader of potboilers would make of the tale. Kelley blames the tale's crudity on James's inability to write convincingly of America, and calls the characters "puppets" (129). Crawford's character, in particular, has proved a stumbling block. James forces his first-person narrator to construct Crawford's character from the outside, just as his father had to construct Webster's. The narrator's comment on Crawford's marriage, for example,—"What he did—what he was—in solitude, heaven only knows; nothing, I am happy to say, ever revealed it to me"— echoes James's father's more interested ignorance—"her he pretended to take to his bosom in private, with what a shudder one can imagine" (CT 4, 39; *Autobiography* 409). Indeed the narrator readily admits, "I had never got behind him, as it were; I had never walked all round him" (CT 4, 15). While such first-person narration, Kenton agrees, is typical of the early tales, the result, as Stone puts it, is a "peculiarly ambiguous hero"—either a remarkable idealist or masochist, a split Wagenknecht sees as representing the "inscrutable" nature of human nature and its capacity for "both incredible folly and incredible self-control" (Stone 190; Wagenknecht 180–81). Jones offers a way around an explanation, stating that Crawford is a motiveless hero in a "naturalistic" drama beyond his control (101).

The only explanation the narrator offers—Crawford's admirable "equanimity"—is retained, as Kenton notes, from James's father and has failed to satisfy most readers (CT 4, 48). Of those who explain further, Kenton emphasizes the physician narrator's sense of Crawford as an actor deeply attached "to the part he had undertaken to play" and unwilling to "raise a corner of the mask"—a characterization suggested by the mention of the stage actor Edwin Forrest in James Sr.'s letter (6, 16). Mackenzie sees Crawford's rebound as an attempt to hold together his identity after his rejection by the Ingrams. He deals with the "shock" of his injury by denying its "implicit humiliation," hiding it under the veil of "consistency." His wife becomes the victim thereby, and he makes it up to her by allowing her to abuse him (1974, 354–55; 1976, 92). Stein nominates contempt as the motive behind Crawford's "parody" marriage: contempt for his former fiancée, her family, the society that shares their mercenary concept of marriage, and even for himself and his own sexuality (81–83). Only Kraft seems to find any virtue in Crawford's behavior, arguing that Crawford's insistence on *being* a gentleman instead of simply appearing one makes him superior to his society. Kraft also asserts that Crawford's marriage to his "Matilda Jane" is no more grotesque than one to the vacuous Miss Ingram would be (86–87).

As Tanner notes, both women are "rather chilling." Putt is intrigued by the "hysterically vindictive" depiction of the two women, but objects to the implication that Crawford's "real escape" was his original jilting. However, although Putt and Jones see James as maliciously inventing the two women's ghastly ends, the fiancée's smallpox at least was not invented by James, but taken from life (Putt 267–68; Jones 100). Edel sees the two representing the two types of women in James: "the young and the unattainable or the cruel and the destructive" (*Life* 2, 256).

In writing to his father in 1876, James described the story's "pretensions" as "small," confiding that he had intended to make it longer but "decided it was too lugubrious to be spun out," adding that his father will now probably think it "brutally curt" (*Letters* 2, 39). It seems a fair assessment.

Works Cited

Primary Works
James, Henry. 1878. "Crawford's Consistency." *Scribner's Monthly* 12 (September): 569–84.

Secondary Works
Fox, Hugh. 1968. *Henry James, A Critical Introduction*. Conesville, IA: John Westburg.

Gale, Robert L. [1954] 1964. *The Caught Image: Figurative Language in the Fiction of Henry James*. Chapel Hill: University of North Carolina Press.

Jones, Granville H. 1975. *Henry James's Psychology of Experience: Innocence, Responsibility, and Renunciation in the Fiction of Henry James*. The Hague: Mouton.

Kelley, Cornelia Pulsifer. [1930] 1965. *The Early Development of Henry James*. Urbana: University of Illinois Press.

Kenton, Edna, ed. 1950. *Eight Uncollected Tales of Henry James*. New Brunswick, NJ: Rutgers University Press.

Kraft, James. 1969. *The Early Tales of Henry James*. Carbondale: Southern Illinois University Press.

Mackenzie, Manfred. 1976. *Communities of Honor and Love in Henry James*. Cambridge, MA: Harvard University Press.

———. 1974. "A Theory of Henry James's Psychology." *Yale Review* 63 (Spring): 347–71.

Putt, S. Gorley. 1966. *Henry James: A Reader's Guide*. Ithaca, NY: Cornell University Press.

Stein, Allen F. 1984. *After the Vows Were Spoken: Marriage in American Literary Realism*. Columbus: Ohio State University Press.

Stone, Donald David. 1972. *Novelists in a Changing World: Meredith, James, and the Transformation of English Fiction in the 1880's*. Cambridge, MA: Harvard University Press.

Tanner, Tony. 1963. "James's Little Tarts." *The Spectator* 210 (4 January): 19.

Wagenknecht, Edward. 1984. *The Tales of Henry James*. New York: Frederick Ungar.

Wright, Walter F. 1962. *The Madness of Art: A Study of Henry James*. Lincoln: University of Nebraska Press.

A Day of Days

Publication History

"A Day of Days," the first of James's stories to appear in New York's new magazine *The Galaxy*, debuted on June 15, 1866. James later included it in his 1885 *Stories Revived*. It was first published after his death in the 1920 collection *A Landscape Painter* and next in Lubbock's edition of James's novels and stories.

Circumstances of Composition, Sources, and Influences

The first mention of "A Day of Days" is in a letter dated May 21, 1866, to the editor of the *Galaxy*, C. W. Church, in which James indicates he has added five pages at Church's request, having decided "on reflection" that Church was right. He also offers, "if it is not too late," a new title: "Tom Ludlow's Letters" (LeClair 412 n.31). Evidently it was too late, or else Church did not like the new name. According to Aziz, James's dealings with the editors of the *Galaxy* were never easy, beginning with their inability to include "A Day of Days" in their inaugural issue in May, perhaps due to the dispute James alludes to in his letter (1, xxxv). Martin and Ober suggest that the missing five pages occur between "half an hour more" and "well, I have very little time" to provide a look inside Adela's mind in order to prepare for her invitation to Ludlow, making her seem less forward and therefore more sympathetic. If so, James kept the five pages in 1885, and similarly revised "looked him full in the eyes" to the more demure "without meeting his eyes" (CT 1, 106).

Edel finds James's "predilection for separating his people, instead of bringing them together" similar to that of the Russian authors of the day (CT 1, 21). While he adds that James had not yet read the Russians, Tedford has made a case for James's reading Turgenev in the 1850's (41). Buitenhuis observes "incidentally" that the hero's name, Ludlow, is from Hawthorne's "Prophetic Pictures" (39). Tintner argues that Gustave Moreau's 1864 painting of *Oedipus and the Sphinx* may have served as inspiration for the encounter between Adela and Ludlow, particularly Adela's questioning of Ludlow, while also noting echoes of Bluebeard in Adela's restless curiosity (1986, 22; 1989, 24–25). Gale, however, objects to the invocation of

Bluebeard as "weak" (118–19). Aziz suggests that the story is a version of Tennyson's "The Lady of Shalott" (xlix–l).

Relation to Other Works

Kelley links the tale with "A Landscape Painter," seeing in both stories a new emphasis on character, with "A Day of Days" reversing the poor girl-rich man configuration of the former story (55, 57). Habegger sees James protecting his heroine from a misalliance, as he did in such other early tales as "Poor Richard" (249). Stevenson characterizes all three as "sound but pallid" productions, written before Europe had provided James with the passion necessary for better work (46, 114). Vaid, on the other hand, judges such "anecdotic" tales as this, "A Tragedy of Error," or "The Romance of Certain Old Clothes" to be more successful than most of his early tales (134).

Habegger judges Adela to be James's first portrait of a lady, while Kraft considers her to be a similar but less complex type than Isabel (Habegger 172). Krook develops the view of Isabel as an "*ur*-Isabel"—"engaging" yet "introspective" and capable of renunciation, the subject of "good-humored" irony on the part of the author. Focusing on his concern for "facts," Kraft finds Ludlow a precursor of Caspar Goodwood, Christopher Newman, and Lambert Strether; in the view of Krook he is a combination of Newman with Basil Ransom (Kraft 12–14; Krook 82–84). Levy sees Ludlow as practicing the same avoidance of experience as John Marcher and Spencer Brydon (32–33).

Interpretation and Criticism

In 1885 James thought enough of the tale while "digging up, refurbishing, and reprinting" tales for *Stories Revived* to send it to his old friend Grace Norton. However, when she wrote him praising it, he responded, "It is very good of you to care for that product at all; I don't myself, really. I think you overestimate it; I hope that sounds neither vainglorious nor conceited! It was a very young thing . . ." (Letters 3, 76). The story's "odd incident" as Putt has called it, eliminates plot to focus on character, examining a chance relationship between a man and a woman, and the criticism has followed suit (36). Jefferson finds Adela the "most manifestly American" of the very early heroines and notes the "slightly humorous, unromantic way" James describes Adela's "great dexterity" in "outflanking" suitors (72–73). Kelley, echoed by LeClair, finds the abundant analysis not enough to make the unnatural encounter of upper-class heroine and lower-class hero convincing, particularly doubting the young man's ability to interest Adela so quickly (57–58). Buitenhuis also finds the reasons for her interest inadequately given, and the portrayal of Ludlow unconvincing. He locates the problem in James's lack of familiarity with contemporary American society, which causes him to import inappropriate ideas about class from British literature (25–26). Wagenknecht, on the other hand, finds the analysis of character convincing even if the conversation conveying it is often implausible (181). All three criticize in particular either the execution or effect of the hero's extended self-analysis: "I'm no man of genius. There's something I miss . . . I'm vulgar . . . the vulgar son of vulgar people" (CT 1, 158–60).

McElderry finds the story "deliberately contrived to disappoint the sentimental expectations of readers," an approach that leaves the story little more than a "sketch" (1965, 26; 1949, 288). Indeed, the heroine begins the day in a "romantic mood . . . prepared to be interested" but the hero ends it by leaving it a "very pretty little romance as it is" (CT 1, 150, 162). Buitenhuis finds the hero's indifference to the heroine and his fleeing of her seemingly attractive offer as an impediment to his course typical of James (25–26; also Andreas 86). Kraft assigns the blame for the separation to Adela's cautiousness, not Ludlow's, but it is to Ludlow that James gives the final decision: "She's a different sort from any I have met, and just to have seen her like this—that is enough for me!" (13; CT 1, 164). Delbaere-Garant attributes the ending to James's distrust of women, which makes Ludlow's escape a lucky one (228). For his part, Wagenknecht sees "moods and impulses" rather than temperaments the main factor (181). Jones, who finds Adela in the country regaining her innocence after her more worldy city life, appears to be alone in his affirmative reading, which has both characters, but particularly Adela, benefiting from their brief romance and their unselfish renouncing of it. He concurs wih Tom that what they experience together is "enough" (156–57). For whatever reasons, James evidently agreed, seeing it best that their relationship should stay like the tale (according to Wagenknecht) "slight but rather charming" (181).

Works Cited

Primary Works
James, Henry. 1866. "A Day of Days." *The Galaxy* 1 (15 June): 298–312.

———. 1885. "A Day of Days." *Stories Revived*. Vol. 1, 246–80. London: Macmillan.

———. 1920. "A Day of Days." *A Landscape Painter*. Preface by Albert Mordell. New York: Scott and Seltzer.

———. 1921–23. "A Day of Days." *The Novels and Stories of Henry James*. Ed. Percy Lubbock. London: Macmillan.

Secondary Works
Andreas, Osborn. 1948. *Henry James and the Expanding Horizon: A Study of the Meaning and Basic Themes of James's Fiction*. Seattle: University of Washington Press.

Buitenhuis, Peter. 1970. *The Grasping Imagination: The American Writings of Henry James*. Toronto: University of Toronto Press.

Delbaere-Garant, Jeanne. 1970. *Henry James: The Vision of France*. Paris: Société d'Editions Les Belles Lettres.

Gale, Robert. [1954] 1964. *The Caught Image: Figurative Language in the Fiction of Henry James*. Chapel Hill: University of North Carolina Press.

Habegger, Alfred. 1989. *Henry James and the "Woman Business."* Cambridge: Cambridge University Press.

Jefferson, D. W. 1964. *Henry James and the Modern Reader*. New York: St. Martin's.

Jones, Granville H. 1975. *Henry James's Psychology of Experience: Innocence, Responsibility, and Renunciation in the Fiction of Henry James*. The Hague: Mouton.

Kelley, Cornelia Pulsifer. [1930] 1965. *The Early Development of Henry James*. Urbana: University of Illinois Press.

Kraft, James. 1969. *The Early Tales of Henry James*. Carbondale: Southern Illinois University Press.

Krook, Dorothea. 1982. "Prefigurings of Isabel Archer." *Hebrew University Studies in Literature*: 80–98.

LeClair, Robert C. 1955. *Young Henry James, 1843–1870*. New York: Bookman.

Levy, Leo B. 1957. *Versions of Melodrama: A Study of the Fiction and Drama of Henry James, 1865–1897*. Berkeley: University of California Press.

McElderry, Bruce R., Jr. 1965. *Henry James*. New York: Twayne.

———. 1949. "The Uncollected Stories of Henry James." *American Literature* 21: 279–91.

Martin, W. R., and Warren U. Ober. 1988. "'5 M. S. Pages': Henry James's Addition to 'A Day of Days.'" *Studies in Short Fiction* 25: 153–55.

Putt, S. Gorley. 1966. *Henry James: A Reader's Guide*. Ithaca, NY: Cornell University Press.

Stevenson, Elizabeth. [1949] 1981. *The Crooked Corridor: A Study of Henry James*. New York: Octagon.

Tedford, Barbara Wilkie. 1979. "Of Libraries and Salmon-Colored Volumes: James's Reading of Tugenev through 1873." *Resources for American Literary Study* 9: 39–49.

Tintner, Adeline R. 1989. *The Pop World of Henry James: From Fairy Tales to Science Fiction*. Ann Arbor: UMI Research Press.

———. 1986. *The Museum World of Henry James*. Ann Arbor: UMI Research Press.

Vaid, Krishna B. 1964. *Technique in the Tales of Henry James*. Cambridge, MA: Harvard University Press.

Wagenknecht, Edward. 1984. *The Tales of Henry James*. New York: Frederick Ungar.

De Grey: A Romance

Publication History

"De Grey: A Romance" was published in July 1868 in the *Atlantic*. Never reprinted by James, it did not appear again until Mordell's 1919 *Travelling Companions*. Not included by Lubbock in his edition of *The Novels and Stories*, it was, however, published in 1931 under the title "Queer People and a Burning Passion" by Little Blue Books, which also reprinted "Adina" and "Professor Fargo."

Circumstances of Composition, Sources, and Influences

One critical approach takes the tale as a reflection of James's subconscious. Thus, in Edel's view, the tale illustrates James's fear that women rob men of their strength, an anxiety Edel attributes to what he judges the unequal relationship of James's parents, the father weak, the mother strong (*Life* 1, 54-55). Feinstein's view is even more strongly accented. In his reading, the father—under the "suspicion of insanity"—is James Sr.; Paul is William away in Europe at the time; and Margaret is Henry. Feinstein discovers a "sibling bond" between Paul and Margaret on the grounds of their shared "maternal protector" and sees James representing through Margaret's acute sympathy with Paul and her "brave" attempt at rescue, the intensity of James's tie to his brother and his worry over what cost that tie might exact (230–31). There is certainly the idea of such an exchange of strength in James's letter on the occasion of Minny Temple's death, which both critics cite, as James describes her lapsing into death as he returned to health (Edel 1970, 28; also Beebe 207–8; Zablotny 210).

Hawthorne is the main literary influence nominated for the story. Buitenhuis points to a specific connection with "Rappaccini's Daughter," in which Beatrice unwillingly poisons the man she loves even as Margaret exerts a "noxious influence" on Paul through, as he puts it, "the poisoned garden of her will" (43). The family curse is also Hawthornesque, as Buitenhuis notes, and later critics have named *The House of the Seven Gables* as its specific source (Buitenhuis 42; Briggs 118; Kerr 135; Brodhead 126). To Fox, however, the reversal of the curse is "almost amusing," and he cites James's description of its "execrable, infernal comedy" as a sign that James did not share Hawthorne's fatalism (7). Long also finds a divergence from the source, placing the Gothic in the tale at odds with the final Hawthornesque ambiguity (18). Although filmmaker Chabrol states that "The ambiguities . . . are so heavily underlined that they stop being ambiguous," Buitenhuis argues that they make the tale more effective than the earlier "The Romance of Certain Old Clothes" (Dawson 13; Buitenhuis 43). Kraft, however, judges both adaptations poor, arguing James had not yet learned how to make a Hawthornesque tale "psychologically unusual" (20). Brodhead reads the tale as a composite, put together by James as he sought to master Hawthorne's themes, particularly the tension between supernatural predictions and human attempts to shape one's own future, seen also in Hawthorne's "The Prophetic Pictures" and "The Threefold Destiny," and the theme of "sexual ambivalence," seen in "Rappaccini's Daughter." Along the way, Margaret, according to Brodhead, evolves from a simple Priscilla to a complex Beatrice. James, however, he contends, deletes the irony from Hawthorne's tale by endorsing the hero's condemnation of the heroine (126–28).

The tale also has debts to Poe, although Tytell calls most attention to what James did not take from his sources, noting the lack both of the symbolic foreshadowing of Hawthorne and the atmospheric setting of Poe (1). Zablotny, on the other hand, points to elements from both authors. While she sees James abandoning Poe's fantasy for a Hawthornesque realism in shifting the central attraction between Mrs. De Grey and Paul to Margaret and Paul, she finds him still following Poe's "Ligeia" in the depiction of Margaret's immense will, the draining of one life for another (209). Similarly, Buitenhuis credits the contribution of Poe's psychological Gothic to the story (43).

The foreign elements amid the American setting have been widely remarked on. Kelley finds the tale reeking of the influence of George Sand—its hero even dies in the same manner as her father had—and judges that for once her romantic approach fit James's topic (87–88; also LeClair 405). Adams points to a source in Balzac's *La Peau de chagrin*, in which a man is similarly destroyed by a curse that threatens his life if he loves. In both works, Adams observes, the heroine considers suicide to save the hero, but survives only to hold his dead body at the end (462; also Kraft 20). Edel more generally notes the influence of French romance in the story's melodramatic elements and in its resident priest. Edel also points to James's recent reviews of two continental Catholic works, and along with Tytell notes the resemblance of Father Herbert to the character of the love-stricken priest in Howells's 1875 *A Foregone Conclusion* (Edel 1970, 26–27; Tytell 1).

Wagenknecht, meanwhile, finds Father Herbert's counseling of star-crossed lovers redolent of *Romeo and Juliet* (1984, 182). Kerr likens Margaret's shriek heard three miles away by Paul to the call that brings Jane Eyre back to Rochester (135). Torgovnick meanwhile locates in "De Grey" what she terms a "quasi-epilogue" or short "after-history" that, unlike the traditional Victorian epilogue, reopens rather than settles the issues raised by the work. Putt tries to draw on the Alcestis myth as justification of "dying *for* someone as well as merely *of* someone" (36). But as Kenton points out, although Mordell in his edition printed that "While she was living for him, he was dying for her," James did indeed write that he was "dying of her" (5).

Akiyama compares the tale to a Japanese work *Kaidan Botan Dōrō* by Sanyūtei Enchō, which also treats the survival of the instinct of revenge after death (157–58).

In 1973 Claude Chabrol filmed hour-length versions of "De Grey" and "The Bench of Desolation" for French television. "De Grey" was adapted by Roger Grenier, Catherine Jourdan played Margaret, and Yves Lefebvre of the Comédie Francaise was Father Herbert (Dawson).

Relation to Other Works

The tale's main significance in the James canon is probably as the terminus ad quo of the "vampire" or "sacred fount" theme (e.g., Gale 37; Beebe 207–8; Putt 34, 259). The connection with *The Sacred Fount* was first mentioned by Kelley in a footnote (88 n.37) and was later commented on by Kenton (5). It was Edel who turned the footnote into a major critical concern, evolving the concept of the "Vampire Theme" in which mutual love inevitably saps the strength of either the woman or the man (1970, 26–27; *Life* 1, 54–55). Edel pointed to the early "Longstaff's Marriage" as an additional example, while Banta discovered the presence of human or non-supernatural vampirism also in "Poor Richard," "The Last of the Valerii," "Professor Fargo," and "The Romance of Certain Old Clothes," and indeed throughout James's fiction, judging such heroines as Isabel Archer, Milly Theale, and Maggie Verver as vampiric even if not acknowledged as such by James (82, 85). Wagenknecht, for his part, agrees with the placement of the motif in "De Grey," "Osborne's Revenge," and "Longstaff's Marriage" but disqualifies *The Sacred Fount* itself (1983, 174). Segal adds that while the theme is the center of interest in the tales, it is subordinated in the later novel to the interest in the narrator-observer (147). More generally, Tanner speaks of the tale's melodramatic treatment of the more subtle, later theme of the terror beneath civilized relationships (12).

At their first meeting, when Paul asks Margaret to tell him her adventures, she replies, "My adventures? . . . I have never had any." Paul responds, "Good! . . . that in itself is an adventure" (CT 1, 408). Putt cites the exchange as a foreshadowing of "The Beast in the Jungle" (34). Kenton finds in the same remarks the theme of "The Story in It" (5).

Edel places Father Herbert in the context of James's interest in formal religion, particularly Catholicism and its concept of renunciation, seen also in *Guy Domville* and *The American*, as well as "The Ghostly Rental," "The Altar of the Dead," and "The Great Good Place" (1970, 26–27). The link between the two interests is provided by Herbert's final revelation of his surviving love for the young Italian girl who died of the love of De Grey's father.

Looking at Margaret's attempt to save Paul, Jones discerns an analogy with Rowland's attempt to save Roderick Hudson from his fate (73–74). The heroine of "The Last of the Valerii" is luckier as she manages to save the life and most of the affection of her husband. In the comic "The Third Person," two women manage a completely successful exorcism.

Tytell compares Mrs. De Grey's taking on Margaret to Mrs. Touchett's patronage of Isabel (1). Dawson, who argues that events here bear little relation to character, contrasts their unmotivated development with the "unswerving will power" of the woman in "The Bench of Desolation" who creates her own destiny (12). (See particularly "The Romance of Certain Old Clothes" and "Longstaff's Marriage.")

Interpretation and Criticism

In "De Grey" the setting is allegedly American, but as many critics have noted, little else about it is (e.g., McCarthy 105; McElderry 1949, 289). In their view, Claude Chabrol would have had little to apologize for in filming his version of the tale in Paris. Among what she judges as the many inappropriately French elements, Kelley points particularly to the "religious parasite," Father Herbert (87). Providing an explanation for the "strong old-world flavor," as Kraft terms it, Buitenhuis argues that James by now had already switched his focus to Europe, and so failed to take seriously the Americanness of his historical romance (Kraft 20; Buitenhuis 44).

The tale is highly melodramatic, and its melodrama has not been well received. Edgar finds it "the weakest and most wildly romantic" of the early tales (15). Stephen Spender, who seemingly bases his interpretation on a reading of the equally disapproving Beach, dismisses "De Grey" as an example of James's early "extremely violent and melodramatic" work that ought to have been "the outpouring of an adolescent" (Spender 427; Beach 184–85). The melodrama starts late, and Tytell finds little preparation for the gothic events that begin when Margaret revokes the curse, and the "romantic retreat from articulation" that breaks the conclusion from the realism of the rest of the story. LeClair similarly judges the final death and madness extravagant and out of control (405). Kraft also objects to the melodrama, finding the tale hurt by its "unintentionally humorous or mock-sophisticated tone" revealing a lack of the confidence necessary to be serious (21). Kelley, on the other hand, while acknowledging it as a bit much at times, claims for the work a certain force and form, arguing that the device of the curse keeps the story moving steadily on without being clogged by James's usually excessive analysis of character (87–88). LeClair maintains that the historical background given the curse helps make it believable (405), while Brodhead speaks of the same chronicling as a "delightful burst of extravagance" and Chabrol as a "gag" (Brodhead 126; Dawson 13). Edel meanwhile adds to its misogynism by mistakenly stating that the curse requires that the doomed beloved produce an heir before dying (CT 1, 20).

As James's second supernatural tale, "De Grey" has been classified by Todorov as "fantastic" because its events admit of either a supernatural or a more realistic explanation (179–80). The ambiguity may be due to the split in interest Beach observes between the establishment of a ghostly atmosphere and the psychology it is meant to represent (184). Translating the supernatural into the psychological, one is left still with a nearly occult influence of individuals on each other. In her application of the "vampire" theme to the tale, Zablotny casts Mrs. De Grey as the original vampire, noting the gossip that she "lives in the dark" and that she grows younger in her son's absence, and seeing the latter as an attempt to attract Paul home again. But Mrs. De Grey then turns to her protege Margaret to do her work for her, and Zablotny cites the description of the "passionate vitality" and "determined, devoted will" that Margaret develops under her care as well as her "paroxysm of sobs" at the older woman's feet as signs of her demonic possession. Under Mrs. De Grey's tutelage, Zablotny argues, Margaret becomes infatuated with the absent Paul. The ending image of her holding the dead Paul, Zablotny sees as "a demon parody of the Pietà," as the now mad Margaret stands in for the mother who has drained her child of life. Still, while Zablotny finds the idea of the vampire "deeply rooted" in James's thinking, she finds the working out of it in this story "flimsy and contrived" (207–10).

Even in such an occult reading, it is clearly the characters who are the main motivators, and Buitenhuis attributes the tale's relative success to its characters, who contain in themselves the force attributed to the supernatural, so that their behavior makes sense and provides sufficient horror, even without it (43). Similarly, Wagenknecht, while dismissing both the curse and the overly dramatic conclusion it brings about, argues that "if these things could happen to anybody, the reader is made to feel, it must be to just such tense, passionate people as we meet here" (1984, 182).

Of the tense and passionate characters, the passive Paul has attracted little comment, perhaps because his situation and character pales in comparison to that of the stronger, more complex Margaret, even as his quick death seems simple in comparison to Margaret's succumbing to madness. In the words of the story, she "blindly, senselessly, remorselessly drained the life from his being" (CT 1, 425). Accordingly, many critics seem to blame Margaret, as indeed Buitenhuis argues James did, for the results of her struggle against the curse. Akiyama, however, sees her more positively as showing her upbringing "in a liberal society" in revoking the "mythology of an old, doomed race" (156–57). The text does provide one important criticism of Margaret's decision, writing of her choice to keep the knowledge of the curse from Paul, "Deluded fool that she was, for a day, for an hour, to have concealed her sorrow from her lover! . . . . What neither might endure alone, they might have surely endured together" (CT 1, 425). This criticism, however, in a way undercuts rather than reinforces the vampiric reading because it argues that a couple in love can triumph over fate if only they work in coordination. Working alone makes Margaret's victory over the curse ironic. As Jones notes, her success is her failure (74).

The tale has both a mother and a father. The mother, Mrs. De Grey, has received most attention from Zablotny. Dietrichson emphasizes the power the mother's wealth has to restore Margaret (75), which would seem to add another ingredient to the exchange of health. Similarly, Dawson notes the fine balance Mrs. De Grey strikes between egotism and philanthropy by taking Margaret in (12). Walter Wright pays attention to Mrs. De Grey's lack of a moral "history," as James terms it, and notes that the history brought to her by her suffering is so disordered it has "little philosophical value" (137).

Father Herbert, who seems at first to be on the sidelines of the story, has drawn a fair amount of attention. LeClair praises the characterization for practical reasons, stating that he helps make the supernatural credible (405). Torgovnick gives him greater significance, arguing that in the "quasi epilogue" to the tale James does the same. Father Herbert's final comment on "survivors," with its revelation of his love for the elder De Grey's dead love, she argues, turns him into a significant "active participant" and moves the interest of the story to what happened before it even began (186). Observing Herbert's love for the dead Italian girl, Chabrol argues for an attachment to Mrs. De Grey as well, in order to extrapolate that Herbert "regularly" loved the same women as De Grey and thus "was even in love with the man himself!" (Dawson 13).

In 1919 a reviewer was already able to look on such turmoil as curiously antique and remote: "pleasant like a fashion-plate many years old, all faded colors and quaint inabilities to draw the human figure, and such an odd fashion-plate! in which the figures are so placed as to tell the artless story of a fatal and hereditary curse" (*New Republic*). Even in the year of its writing, brother William appreciated the story's suspense and "richness of coloring" but found little "human" interest in the tale (52). What interest it does have centers on those who, Herbert asserts, suffer the most, the survivors, and particularly the one character who faced the curse head on and sought to defy it, and was defeated nevertheless, not ground in the very mill of the conventional, as was Isabel Archer, but in the mill of melodrama.

Works Cited

Primary Works

James, Henry. 1868. "De Grey: A Romance." *Atlantic Monthly* 22 (July): 57–78.

———. 1919. "De Grey: A Romance." *Travelling Companions*. Foreword by Albert Mordell. New York: Boni and Liveright.

———. 1931. "Queer People and a Burning Passion." Little Blue Book no. 1671. Girard, KS: Haldeman-Julius.

Secondary Works

Adams, Percy G. 1961. "Young Henry James and the Lesson of his Master Balzac." *Revue de Littérature Comparée* 35 (July–September): 458–67.

Akiyama, Masayuki. 1987–1988. "Sanyūtei Enchū, Ch'ū Yu, and Henry James: Stories of the Supernatural." *Tamkang Review* 18 (Autumn–Summer): 151–59.

Anon. 1919. Review of *Travelling Companions*. *New Republic* 19 (30 July): 109.

Banta, Martha. 1972. *Henry James and the Occult: The Great Extension*. Bloomington: Indiana University Press.

Beach, Joseph Warren. [1918] 1954. *The Method of Henry James*. New Haven: Yale University Press.

Beebe, Maurice L. 1964. *Ivory Towers and Sacred Founts: The Artist as Hero*. New York: New York University Press.

Briggs, Julia. 1977. *Night Visitors: The Rise and Fall of the English Ghost Story*. London: Faber.

Brodhead, Richard H. 1986. *The School of Hawthorne*. New York: Oxford University Press.

Buitenhuis, Peter. 1970. *The Grasping Imagination: The American Writings of Henry James*. Toronto: University of Toronto Press.

Dawson, Jan. 1973–1974. "The Continental Divide." *Sight & Sound* 43 (Winter): 12–15.

Dietrichson, Jan W. 1969. *The Image of Money in the American Novel of the Gilded Age*. Oslo: Universitetsforlaget; New York: Humanities.

Edel, Leon, ed. 1970. *Henry James: Stories of the Supernatural*. New York: Taplinger. Revised in part from *The Ghostly Tales of Henry James*. New York: The Universal Library, Grosset & Dunlap, [1949] 1963.

Edgar, Pelham. [1927] 1964. *Henry James, Man and Author*. New York: Russell & Russell.

Feinstein, Howard M. 1984. *Becoming William James*. Ithaca, NY: Cornell University Press. Reprinted in part from "A Singular Life: Twinship in the Psychology of William and Henry James." In *Blood Brothers: Siblings as Writers*. Ed. Norman Kiell, 301–28. New York: International University Press, 1983.

Fox, Hugh. 1968. *Henry James, A Critical Introduction*. Conesville, IA: John Westburg.

Gale, Robert L. [1954] 1964. *The Caught Image: Figurative Language in the Fiction of Henry James*. Chapel Hill: University of North Carolina Press.

James, William. 1992. *The Correspondence of William James*. Vol.1: *William and Henry: 1861–1884*. Ed. Ignas K. Skrupskelis and Elizabeth M. Berkeley. Charlottesville: University Press of Virginia.

Jones, Granville H. 1975. *Henry James's Psychology of Experience: Innocence, Responsibility, and Renunciation in the Fiction of Henry James*. The Hague: Mouton.

Kelley, Cornelia Pulsifer. [1930] 1965. *The Early Development of Henry James*. Urbana: University of Illinois Press.

Kenton, Edna, ed. 1950. *Eight Uncollected Tales of Henry James*. New Brunswick, NJ: Rutgers University Press.

Kerr, Howard. 1983. "James's Last Early Supernatural Tales: Hawthorne Demagnetized, Poe Depoetized." In *The Haunted Dusk: American Supernatural Fiction, 1820–1920*. Ed. Howard Kerr, John W. Crowley, and Charles L. Crow, 135–48. Athens: University of Georgia Press.

Kraft, James. 1969. *The Early Tales of Henry James*. Carbondale: Southern Illinois University Press.

LeClair, Robert Charles. 1955. *Young Henry James, 1843–1870*. New York: Bookman.

Long, Robert Emmet. 1979. *The Great Succession: Henry James and the Legacy of Hawthorne*. Pittsburgh: University of Pittsburgh Press.

McCarthy, Harold T. 1958. *Henry James: The Creative Process*. New York: Thomas Yoseloff.

McElderry, Bruce R., Jr. 1949. "The Uncollected Stories of Henry James." *American Literature* 21 (November): 279–91.

Putt, S. Gorley. 1966. *Henry James: A Reader's Guide*. Ithaca, NY: Cornell University Press.

Segal, Ora. 1969. *The Lucid Reflector: The Observer in Henry James' Fiction*. New Haven: Yale University Press.

Spender, Stephen. 1934. "The School of Experience in the Early Novels." *Hound & Horn* 7 (April–May): 417–33. Reprinted in *The Destructive Element*, 23–46. Philadelphia: Albert Saifer, 1953.

Tanner, Tony. 1985. *Henry James: The Writer and His Work*. Amherst: University of Massachusetts Press.

Todorov, Tzvetan. 1977. *The Poetics of Prose*. Trans. Richard Howard. Ithaca, NY: Cornell University Press.

Torgovnick, Marianna. 1978. "James's Sense of an Ending: The Role Played in Its Development by the Popular Conventional Epilogue." *Studies in the Novel* 10: 183–98.

Tytell, John. 1969. "Henry James and the Romance." *Markham Review* 1, no. 5 (May): 1–2.

Wagenknecht, Edward. 1984. *The Tales of Henry James*. New York: Frederick Ungar.

———. 1983. *The Novels of Henry James*. New York: Frederick Ungar.

Wright, Walter F. 1962. *The Madness of Art: A Study of Henry James*. Lincoln: University of Nebraska Press.

Zablotny, Elaine. 1979. "Henry James and the Demonic Vampire and Madonna." *Psychocultural Review* 3, nos. 3–4 (Summer–Fall): 203–24.

The Death of the Lion

Publication History

"The Death of the Lion" appeared as the lead tale in the new *Yellow Book* in April 1894 at the invitation of its editor, Henry Harland. It was collected the next year in *Terminations*. James also included the tale in both the New York Edition and the 1914 *Uniform Tales*.

Circumstances of Composition, Sources, and Influences

At his home in London James began a notebook entry on February 3, 1894, on "the idea of the great (the distinguished, the celebrated) artist" in a day of celebrity hunters. Bit by bit he pieced together the features of his tale, "The Lion": the death of the artist, his coming late to fame, the admiring observer, his attempts to save the lion, the country house and its hostess, the last project. A few days later he returned to add the first lines of what was now "The Death of the Lion," starting, "I had simply what is called a change of heart" (CN 86–87).

A second notebook entry also lies behind both this tale and "The Next Time," according to Jacobson. It describes a man who breaks with the girl who is his literary confidante for a showy marriage: "The woman he marries has taken him away; but he has died, as it were, in her hands" (N 144). In this, Jacobson sees shades of Paraday's surrender to Mrs. Wimbush and the narrator's marriage to his admirer (97–98).

James began his preface by recounting how during "old Kensington days" Henry Harland had come to visit him to request a story for his new quarterly, "joyously christened even before reaching the cradle," *The Yellow Book.* While appreciative of its "note of bright young defiance," and "amused" and "charmed" on the spot by the project, or at least its projector, James was nevertheless relieved that the accompanying Aubrey Beardsley—later dropped by Harland as too *outré*—would not be the illustrator of his own "comparatively so incurious text." James was pleased most at "the golden truth that my composition might absolutely assume, might shamelessly parade in, its own organic form" and so "conform . . . to its true intelligible nature." There would be none of the usual need for the "short story" to struggle any further ". . . under the rude prescription of brevity at any cost, with the opposition so offered to its really becoming a story." Here it might even take the form of the "ideal, the beautiful and blest *nouvelle*" (*Criticism* 2, 1225–27). Indeed, to Isle, the primary reason James continued publishing with the aesthetic journal was its lack of limits on length (22).

In the opinion of Ford Madox Ford, *The Yellow Book* marks a turning point in the English art world in its move away from its previous amateurish cast (78–79, 145–46). But while Harland greatly admired James, calling him "the only master of considered prose we've got," James's feelings toward the journal were rather less enthusiastic (Mix 170). In May he wrote to his brother William and sister-in-law, Alice, "I haven't sent you 'The Yellow Book'—on purpose. . . . I say on purpose because although my little tale which ushers it in . . . appears to have had, for a thing of mine, an unusual success, I hate too much the horrid aspect and company of the whole publication. And yet I am again to be intimately—conspicuously—associated with the second number. It is for gold and to oblige the worshipful Harland. . . . Wait and read the two tales in a volume . . ." (*Letters* 3, 483). In writing to Gosse in April 1894, he relayed to him Harland's news that the magazine was going into a second edition, "the only way—almost—that I have managed to attain even a fraction of an out-of-printedness" (*Selected Letters* 110). Perhaps that was another reason that James, despite his misgivings about the aesthetes, went on, as Swan observes, to publish his next tale in the same journal.

To other critics, there is less need of explanation. Beach sees James's appreciation of "art for art's sake" as a link with *The Yellow Book* (30–31). Similarly, to both Beebe and Lee, the tale fits well there given its attack on society and exaltation of the artist (Beebe 223; Lee 51). Nicholas calls it an "appropriate fantasy" (143). Auchard also remarks on how James's work "accommodated itself to the adventure of their *fin-de-siècle* refinement" (32–33). Both Ziff and Pearson, for their part, see the daring of *The Yellow Book* as exaggerated, Ziff noting the many "safe names" including James's (Ziff 133; Pearson 205). At the time, however, Theodore Roosevelt found the publication "the last state of degradation" (Monteiro 5). The magazine became particularly notorious when the newspapers—at Oscar Wilde's arrest—featured headlines reading "YELLOW BOOK UNDER HIS ARM," although the yellow book was a French novel. James's anxiety about *The Yellow Book*, in Rawlings's analysis, is responsible for some of the tale's humor, as he satirized the "modern" trends it might represent including "the larger latitude" and the associated confusion of "the genders and the pronouns" (xxii–xxiii). Beaver, indeed, sees the humor directed particularly at Wilde (53).

Other reflections of James's experience can be seen in the tale. Bell sees James depicting the "cruel, or at least callous, aspects" of the hospitality he had received at country homes, noting that he would come to sense something of this in Edith Wharton's Parisian salon (91–92, 137). One may sense some of the same susceptibility to the demands of society in Percy Lubbock's description of James as a lavish host with a "standard of hospitality . . . so high . . . as to make him at times impatient of the consequences it entailed." Lubbock continues of James, "He could take nothing lightly, and the burden of sociability roused him to much eloquent lamentation. Yet he soon missed it in solitude, and he was easily tempted by any congenial call; he was not less generous as a guest than as a host, and in a circle which was not exactly that of society or of the arts or of the professions, but mingled of all three, he enjoyed himself and gave enjoyment." Lubbock, however, concludes his characterization of James by emphasizing his "remarkably strong" constitution, and the fact that "Nothing . . . was ever allowed to interrupt the industrious regularity of his work." Likewise, Jefferson distinguishes James not only from Paraday, but also such sensitive writers as Dencombe and Limbert, on the grounds of a superior strength and resiliency ([1960] 1971, 67). Also distinguishing James's situation from Paraday's, Matthiessen points out that James gained fame early and then lost it, the reverse of Paraday's career (1944, 4; also Wallace 164). Appropriately perhaps, William Dean Howells saw the tale, along with the earlier "The Lesson of the Master," as an example of James's finest work that could still reach a "larger public" than ever before (Matthiessen 1947, 509). Pointing out that this was the first tale James wrote after the suicide of Constance Fenimore Woolson, Edel attributes the tale's "savage wit" in part to James's distress at the event (*Life* 3, 373).

The narrator describes the lion's project as "Loose, liberal, confident, it might have passed for a great gossiping, eloquent letter—the overflow into talk of an artist's amorous plan . . . in summarised splendour a mine of gold, a precious independent work" (CT 9, 82). Edel cites the description as an indication of the "kind of confidentiality" James sought in his notebooks (CN xi). Both Putt and Kermode comment on its resemblance to James's own scenarios (Putt 227; Kermode 451 n.1). When H. G. Wells wrote asking to see one, James admitted, "I always do draw up a preliminary *private* outpouring. But this latter voluminous effusion is, ever, so extremely familiar, confidential and intimate— in the form of an interminable garrulous letter addressed to my own fond fancy—that, though I always, for easy reference, have it carefully typed, it isn't a thing I would willingly expose to any eye but my own" (CN xxii).

The experience of other lions may also have contributed to the tale. Kirkby locates a passage in W. P. Frith's memoirs (1887–88) describing Thomas Moore as "a lion thoroughly lionised . . . . nearly smothered" by a group of admiring women, as possible inspiration for the tale (39–40). In January 1894 the serialization of *Trilby* by James's good friend George Du Maurier began. While Du Maurier had a secure reputation as a cartoonist for *Punch*, the phenomenal success of the novel, whose instalments continued through July, was unlike anything he had encountered before. Edel records James's reaction to his friend's befuddlement by his sudden fame—already known, like Paraday, to the cognoscenti (*Life* 4, 173–74). Hetherington compares to Paraday's the disgust of Melville's Pierre at the personal inquiries that follow fame (266–67). Hoag, however, sees the narrator misguided in seeking for Paraday the experience of such as Melville or Dickinson to whom fame came posthumously (168).

Grover points to the Goncourts' *Charles Demailly*, which also shows the destruction brought by newspaper publicity to the true artist, and Balzac's *Illusion perdues*, which reveals a similar dislike for journalism. Grover, however, notes that James's attitude toward journalism is less bitter and more ironic, and that in James the responsibility for Paraday's death is shared by the social world. Still, according to Grover, James was becoming more and more convinced that Flaubert was right that the public hated literature (150–51). Paraday resembles Flaubert, according to Mack, in his monklike country retreat from which he makes his venture into the capital. But despite his similar advocacy of "*la religion de la beaute*," Mack notes Flaubert's greater endurance (22–23). Without drawing a direct parallel, Delbaere-Garant discusses a counterexample, Mérimée's abandonment of his art "to become a man of the world," which decision, she writes, "could only fill James with a mixture of awe and admiration" (129–30).

Mix suggests Mary Chavelita Dunne, who wrote as George Egerton, and had a work in the first volume of *The Yellow Book*, as a possible model for Guy Walsingham (171–73). Kermode comments that such women writers using male names were more common than the reverse exemplified by Dora Forbes, and cites Pearl Craigie, who wrote under the name John Oliver Hobbes, as a contemporary example (22).

Vaid suggests that James was recalling Mrs. Leo Hunter of Dickens's *The Pickwick Papers* in the character of Mrs. Wimbush (270 n.9). Bass and Nicholas refer to the names in the tale as Dickensian and Wallace judges the minor characters themselves "Dickensian caricature[s]," but Hoag finds the names of Lady Augusta Minch and Lord Dorimont more reminiscent of Congreve and Etherege (Bass 115; Nicholas 143; Wallace 165; Hoag 166–67).

Among the other autographs in the book Fanny carries for her friend are Washington, Schiller, and Hannah More, all safely dead, an interesting collection of types of fame.

Springer puts Fanny in a tradition of the "positive good" in satire, including also the Portuguese sea captain in *Gulliver's Travels*, the "young Samaritan" in James Joyce's "Grace," the "girl in green" in Jacques Tati's *Playtime*, and even the "positive proposals" in *A Modest Proposal* (1975, 91–97). Roselli has discovered a parody by Max Beerbohm that offers a new conclusion in which Fanny continues her high-minded avoidance of Paraday by vowing never to look at the lost scenario should it be found, as "to look would be to undo all that I did for him." Grossman finds the same basic situation in James's artist tales—including also "The Next Time" and "The Figure in the Carpet"—of a bustling society indifferent to the artists in its midst, repeated in the Hollywood of George S. Kaufman's plays. Hoag offers a comparison with Gulley Jimson of Joyce Carey's *The Horse's Mouth* (172).

Relation to Other Works

Noting that James kept the three tales together in volume 15 of the New York Edition, Bass discusses the tale in connection with James's two other pieces for *The Yellow Book*. To all three—"The Death of the Lion," "The Coxon Fund," and "The Next Time"—he assigns the august themes of "the public's antagonism to art and the artist's devotion to art." Still, he finds their manner "lighter"—more comic—and therefore more successful than James's other artist tales (114–15). Similarly, Wagenknecht, while pointing to the several elements shared with "The Middle Years," emphasizes how the satirical tone here makes the tale in comparison "a light piece," although more "elaborate" than "The Next Time" (77–78, 82). Rebecca West, however, judges all the tales of writers, with the exception of "The Coxon Fund," "sad stories" (92–93). To Horne this tale is comic only in treatment, unlike "The Next Time," which is comic by virtue of its situation (74). Both tales are comic, according to Austin Wright, due to their emphasis on the exposure of the stupidity of the public as witnessed by the narrator (191). Grover classes the two with "The Figure in the Carpet" as "ironic and satiric" works about the "non-artistic" who pretend to admire the artist (148)

The artist in this case, Paraday, Mackenzie classes with his fellow writer Dencombe of "The Middle Years," Ralph Touchett, and the heroines of "The Visits" and "The Patagonia" as late examples of "extraordinary cases," who weakly allow their consciousness of "shame or self-deprecation" to kill them (36–37). Both Dencombe and Paraday, Matheson asserts, are destroyed by a woman (226). Jefferson objects that James's "supersubtle fry" such as Paraday, Limbert, Ambient, and Vereker are unnaturally removed from British and American literary tradition and that James acknowledges only their vulgar opposites (such as Guy and Dora here) rather than the many genuine artists of his day. Seeing their origin in James's anger at his poor popular reception, Jefferson contends that his artists are so close to "the archetypal aesthete and decadent" that they ironically serve to perpetuate public misunderstanding (1964, 120–22; [1960] 1971, 67). Baxter, however, classifies the "too secular" Paraday with St. George as illustrating a different failing from the "too sanctified" Theobald of "The Madonna of the Future" (230). Paraday, at least, Charney observes, has eliminated the problem of the model and his great lost work did at least exist (72–74). Remaining in the story's imagery, according to Powers, is a depiction of artistic endeavor as religious enterprise similar to that in "The Madonna of the Future," and found also in "Broken Wings," "The Next Time," and "The Coxon Fund" (1970, 101, 107). Such religious imagery, Nicholas adds, is also evident in "The Real Right Thing" (146). Matheson sees a different linking, between literature and the "esoteric," here and in *The Aspern Papers* (227).

While "The Private Life" to Blackmur illustrates a writer's need for privacy, "The Death of the Lion" in his view is "a plea for the protection of that privacy" given the power of public exposure to kill genius (84). Indeed, Vaid judges the tale in relation to "The Private Life" as "a powerful refutation of any complacent notion about the 'private life' of a genius and its invulnerability" (72). Powers sees the need to protect the artist's life from social demands demonstrated also in "Broken Wings," "The Figure in the Carpet," "The Real Right Thing," and *The Tragic Muse* (1970, 101–02). The idea that an artist's true presence is in his work anticipates "The Figure in the Carpet," according to Nicholas (145). The narrator in *The Aspern Papers*, according to Donald Stone, still needs to learn that lesson (251). In their treatment of the artist and society, however, Poole judges that "The Death of the Lion," "The Private Life," *The Aspern Papers*, and even "The Middle Years" are "only by ironic indirection concerned with the acts of writing and reading." Instead, they "represent the parodies and substitutes and alternatives that seek to pass for such an intimate and demanding intercourse" (x–xi).

In his notebook entry James asked "whether any one . . . does know, really, when it comes to the point, the first word of the work the hero's reputation for having produced which is the very basis of their agitation" (CN 86). In "John Delavoy," the public would not consider the source of the author's fame, because of the alleged immorality of his work; here the public—seemingly quite at home with the "larger latitude"—is simply too busy to read. In both tales, journalism is a prime target, and Delbaere-Garant associates the attack on journalism with that in *The Reverberator* (307 n.5). Another target, the country-house "world," Lee observes is similarly scorned by Gabriel Nash in *The Tragic Muse* (55). Nevertheless, Austin Wright sees the actual relation between artist and society in such artist tales as this one, "The Lesson of the Master," and "The Next Time," despite the animadversions they lodge against society, as amicable. He also points out, however, that the artists are used primarily for entertainment, as in "The Lesson of the Master" and in "The Coxon Fund," even as another group of outsiders, the Americans, are used in "Mrs. Medwin" (40 n.8, 50, 52–53, 145). Holder compares Prince Amerigo as outsider to artists such as Paraday, and Nettels links Paraday with May Bartram and Madame de Cintré as sacrificial victims to others' egotism (Holder 120; Nettels 413). Similarly, Leyburn classes Wimbush with Mona in *The Spoils of Poynton* and Mrs. Lowder of *The Wings of the Dove* as destructive fools (81). To Hoag, the threat of marriage to the artist in "The Lesson of the Master" becomes the threat of the world here (171). Even Bass, who observes that Saltram in "The Coxon Fund" seems in "genuine need of a patroness," still finds the moral of both tales that to "touch" genius kills it, in contrast to "The Next Time," which depicts an "incorruptible" genius (116, 119).

As in "The Middle Years" a young man sets out to save a great author for his next work, and fails. Horne, who observes that Dencombe dies before the sudden transformation of fame Paraday experiences, sees the narrator becoming like the sympathetic Dr. Hugh, although he begins more like the narrator in "The Figure in the Carpet" (75). To Mottram the narrator never leaves that category, remaining like the critics of "The Figure in the Carpet" among those who prey on the writer (177–78). In Segal's estimate a comparison with the narrator of "The Figure in the Carpet" is not all bad. She refers to both narrators as well as the narrator of "The Next Time" as chosen by James to be tellers as subtle as their artist subjects, who could, when necessary, speak for James himself, a choice recorded in the preface to "The Next Time" (110–11). (See particularly "The Author of Beltraffio.")

The role of Fanny, the silent partner in the narrator's admiration, has also come under scrutiny. As an American entering England like a "stranger in fairyland," she is compared by Sharp to Granger of "Flickerbridge" (36). Horne classes her with Marian of "The Lesson of the Master" and Maud of "The Next Time" as a woman appreciative of the arts (75). Powers compares her to the Corvicks of "The Figure in the Carpet" in forbearing from bothering an artist (1961, 226). Sharp observes that she is one of the youngest of the Jamesian confidantes, and like Cecilia in *Roderick Hudson* in that her confidences concern not her confider, but a third person. In Sharp's view, although her character is a "concession to popular taste," in contrast to the serene older women in "Flickerbridge" and "Nona Vincent," she lodges no criticism of what she calls the "stock 'happy ending,'" noting that for Fanny, as for Henrietta Stackpole, "all's well that ends well" (28, 36, 40). To Hoag, however, Fanny is a "pain in the behind," an undistinguished precursor of the undistinguished Fanny Assingham, her relationship to the narrator at the end sustained by a devotion to a dead Paraday "comically suggestive" of "Maud-Evelyn" or "The Altar of the Dead" (169–70). Matheson, on the other hand, emphasizes the way a common literary interest provides the bond as in "The Figure in the Carpet" and "Broken Wings" (227). Charney, too, sees in the union of Fanny and the narrator the intermingling of life and work advocated in "The Figure in the Carpet" (74). Hartsock, however, finds the love of the narrator for Fanny "unconvincing," like that of Rowland Mallet for Mary Garland, and argues that the relationship between the two men in each work—the narrator and Paraday, and Roderick and Rowland—though non-sexual, is the real "emotional core" (308). More pejoratively, Geismar finds in the relationship between master and disciple here and elsewhere "oedipal and perhaps homosexual components" (130–31). Bass simply notes the love interest between Fanny and the narrator as a "minor point" that will become a significant second theme in "The Coxon Fund" (116). Taking Fanny as a positive good, Wallace detects an ambiguity in the way the narrator "protects" Paraday from her, even as St. George "protects" Overt from Marian, questioning whether Paraday might have been better off for knowing Fanny (167). Without the irony, Kappeler also sees a similarity in the narrator's "sacrifice" and Overt's (79).

Interpretation and Criticism

When Paraday wakes up and finds himself famous, ambushed on the way to posterity, he becomes the focus of a series of concentric circles of people who all claim some interest in him and his fame: the narrator, the world of journalism, the world of society. His entire story is marked throughout, as Vaid observes, by "bestial imagery," its "controlling image," as Tintner writes, the circus, with Paraday as the resident captive lion (Vaid 73; Tintner 161). If such imagery can be blamed on the narrator, the names still stand as indications of what Horrell sees as the pervasive sense of phoniness in the tale (213). Indeed, Edward Stone, who judges the tale "too-angry," gives the names as evidence (115). A key example is the two authors of the "third sex"—the "success-sex" as Blackmur dubs it—whom James referred to in the notebook as A. B. and B. A. (Blackmur 85; CN 87). Norrman argues that James found the confusion of gender in Guy and Dora appealing because it allowed him to practice a favorite technique, that of "pronominal ambiguity" or unclear pronoun references. He considers the intent humorous, but also indicative of a "relativism" stemming from James's "insecurity and uncertainty" (144). Horrell sees their names as indications of their "literary fraud," and Ziff classes them with the "literary grotesqueries of the day" (Horrell 213; Ziff 60). Hartsock comments on the narrator's "distaste for the demeaning of sex" implicit in their "literary transvestism" (308 n.26, 311).

Other examples of parodic names abound, and have been frequently listed. Mr. Pinhorn's name has been glossed by Edward Stone as being painful as a "pin," by Bass as a "tinhorn," and by Springer as a "pinheaded tinhorn" (Stone 115; Bass 115; Springer 1975, 86). It aptly combines, as Horrell observes, "the smallness of his mind with the loudness of his editorial mouth" (213). Vaid, Hoag, and Springer all see what Vaid calls Mr. Morrow's "ominous" name as pointing to the future, either for Paraday or literature, while Horrell sees it reflecting Morrow's concern with "the next deadline" (Vaid 75; Hoag 213; Springer 1975, 86; Horrell 213). To Stone, Wimbush is a "bush" of "whims," to Springer an "ambush for the lion" (Stone 115; Springer 1975, 86). Both Horrell and Hoag note the time limit applied to her whims in her name "Weeks" (Horrell 214; Hoag 168). Wimbush's house is similarly "rather heavily" named in Hoag's judgment, and its name Prestidge has been frequently commented on, Blackmur observing that prestige is "a surface quality obtained . . . by slight of hand" (Hoag 168; Blackmur 85; also Horrell 214; Leavis 226; Springer 1975, 86). Most of the other names in the tale appear to be parodic labels: Lord Crouchley, Mrs. Bounder, Mr. Rumble (see Springer 1975, 86; Horrel 213).

Even Paraday's name seems to limit him, as Springer observes, by fitting in with the other satiric "species" (1975, 86). Edward Stone glosses the name to read, People "kneel" to Paraday for only "a day" (115). Hoag adds that Neil comes from the Gaelic for "champion," and that "para" may mean "one virtuously outside his own times" or "parry" "a defensive battle with the day." He also deems its resemblance to "parody" significant (168). Similarly, Springer reads Neil Paraday as "nothing ('nil') but a 'parody' of what a true lion should be" (1975, 86). Knox asks if the name "Paraday" is meant as an indication that James is "*parading* himself" (214). Horrell contends not only that Neil Paraday "becomes a paragon for a day" as people kneel to him "in a ceremony that parodies genuine acclaim," but that his name accumulates meaning from the tale's religious imagery, making in the end a "real ceremony—an act of devotion to a great writer, not a curiosity" (214).

To Ford Madox Ford the tale is James's attempt to find a place "or at least a corner" in England that would value the artist (78–79, 145–46). In the tale, the search is a difficult one as the society, in Edgar's phrase, is both "unintelligently refined" and possessed of a "predatory curiosity," showing, according to Brooks, James's late belief that the English were philistines (Edgar 164; Brooks 147–48). In Markow-Totevy's view the subject here is "intellectual superficiality" (48). Gage, too, emphasizes the stupidity of Paraday's non-readers as they bring about the "double death" of Paraday, of the man and of his work (16). Geismar particularly enjoys the satire of the country-house types (131). For Kappeler, the relationship between society and artist is harmed by the temptation of each "to dabble in the sphere of the other," although society is helped by its "instinct for self-preservation." Still, Kappeler writes, the artist needs society as subject matter, audience, and financial support, creating the need for a "mediating class" of critics who fight "a paradoxical battle" for writers, as they seek both to promote their work and protect their privacy (85).

Another "mediating class" is present in the tale, that of the journalists. To Powers, Morrow is a particularly pernicious representative of personal journalism and literary ignorance (1970, 101). Vaid takes a different approach to praise the "brilliantly comic" encounter with Morrow and the "funny and concentrated account" of how the narrator got his assignment. The latter, Vaid writes, constitutes a "complete anecdote" in itself, presenting an effective "satirical picture" of the newspapers (73, 75). To Geismar, however, James's attack on the newspapers is overdone, stemming from his discontent at having failed to gain fame (129–31).

In the presence of such publicity, Vaid notes the narrator's typical "warning" that the story is meant as a private record (73). Poole comments on the "ironies of the traffic between the private and public aspects of writing" in the tale, observing that an author has generally the "advantages of a kind of ghostly or spectral existence" in his work. In the tale, however, the living Paraday is "both dangerous and vulnerable" so that the narrator "perversely urges" him, "You must be as dead as you can." Because reading is a private act, it is an easy subject of deception, and so, Poole writes, involves issues of "trust" on the part of both the reader and writer (x). In Seltzer's reading, the narrator sees a "radical incompatibility" between the "professional and artistic interests" of a writer. Calling attention to the way the narrator acknowledges that his "essentially private" notes may become public, Seltzer contends that the narrator sees the circulation "in person" of Paraday and his manuscript as ideal. The story then, according to Seltzer, through the loss of both manuscript and author in the process, demonstrates the need for a more public market system (164–65). Perhaps, but, James might add, need it be the market of Morrow and Pinhorn?

According to Matheson, James contrasts the "impersonal . . . masculine attitude" of Paraday with the "personal," presumably female, attitude of "the herd" (227). Stewart, too, calls attention to the role of women in Paraday's "artistic shipwreck," in particular Paraday's "absentee wife" (99). While Horne finds the mentions of the absent wife unintegrated into the story, Kappeler contends that Paraday appropriately divorced his wife "in order to live with his art alone" (Horne 79). In Kappeler's view Fanny is equally a threat to Paraday's relationship with the muse, one the narrator "effectively staves off" by marrying her himself, thereby being "destined to become (only) a literary critic or editor" (79). As the narrator remarks, her name sounds "ominous" (CT 9, 102). The name of "Hurter" is, however, in the judgment of Springer and Horrell ironic, as she is the "most harmless" character in the tale (Springer 1975, 86; Horrell 214). Fanny illustrates the "proper" attitude toward a writer in contrast to such as Mrs. Wimbush (Beattie 98; Bass 116, Springer 1978, 190–91). Her restrained role, as Kermode observes, is "surprising" for a woman in James's artist tales (22–23). Vaid sees Fanny presented with less seriousness, but with "affectionate irony" as the narrator's success in keeping Fanny from Paraday "ironically contrasts" with his failure to restrain Mrs. Wimbush. The narrator's love for Fanny, however, he judges "just an incidental cog in James's 'machinery of entertainment'" (76–77). Sharp, who sees James as taking a benignly "comic" attitude toward Fanny, assigns her a somewhat more important part in the machinery, seeing James bringing in a "confidante" to fill in for the fading Paraday. The letters to the sympathetic Fanny, Sharp records, provide a "pleasant variety" to the "narrative method," and their "more acrid" present tense makes the scene at Prestidge more immediate for the reader (33–34). Beattie assigns the theme of marriage she introduces an even more significant role (98).

In the notebook entry, James wrote of the narrator that the "*consciousness of the moral*" rests only in him. He refers to him as "the narrator, the friend, the lover, the knower, the protector" (CN 87). According to Edgar, James added the journalist as a witness to ensure that the reader would take Paraday's genius as genuine (164). In Blackmur's view, the narrator is marked primarily by "a strong sense of allegiance to the great" (84). Vaid refers to him as a "poor honest scribe" unable to stop the process of Paraday's collapse (72). But while Ward classifies the narrator here as a "relative outsider" prohibited from any self-analysis that would take the focus from the actual subject, Booth sees the addition of an involved narrator to the subject of the artist as a sign of a shift in the direction of the story (Ward 1967, 57; Booth 344 n.8).

Others have since seen the narrator's motives, or character, as more dubious. Bass holds him responsible for Paraday's fate because he wrote the first article on him, after which the other papers "take up the scent" (116). His statement about Paraday, that he had "taken to the man still more than I had ever taken to the books," in Powers's judgment "qualifies [him] for membership" in the group that destroys Paraday (1961, 226). Goetz criticizes the narrator for treating Paraday as if he were dead even before he is (162). Putt, however, finds the application for pity for Paraday in the tale "uncertain," in part because Paraday with his servant and "modest mahogany" does not seem all that "poor" an artist. In the end, however, he pins the blame on the narrator, writing that it is "the eternal Jamesian narrator who makes all the fuss, and not Paraday himself." While Paraday is "no humbug, the narrator *is*"

(228). Reading the story as a "tale about subordination," Smith observes how Paraday's fame is subordinated to his art, the narrator's work to Paraday, the heroine's curiosity to the concern for art. The theme is reflected, Smith argues, in the tale's predominant use of complex sentences, but he also argues that the subordination of the narrator who manages to marry through serving Paraday is "more apparent than real," which may explain why James later turned to different sentence types (164). To Sharp, part of the tale's "comic effect" is the way the narrator tells how he keeps Fanny from Paraday. However, although he benefits from his behavior, she attributes to him no conscious intent or ill will (33–35).

Nicholas takes further exception to what he sees as the "comically unreliable" narrator's "exaggerated sympathy." The narrator, he argues, distorts "the perfectly reasonable insistence" that one must know an artist's work to know him until it becomes a "foolish insistence that interest in the man and interest in his work are mutually exclusive." This "comic over-reaction" reaches its high point in his relationship with Fanny, whose original "personal" interest in Paraday included an interest in his "talent." The narrator, however, treats her as a danger, acting not out of a love for literature, Nicholas charges, but for her. As a result, Fanny becomes, in Nicholas's reading, even more extreme in her avoidance of Paraday. The irony, according to Nicholas, is intensified by the "suggestion that Paraday may have been killed by the absence of any genuinely personal interest in him and his work" such as Fanny could have offered. Nicholas also mentions the implication that the narrator by the end has lost his own "personal, selfless interest" in the man.

Others trace more of a change in the narrator, originally as Kermode calls him, "something of a hack" (22). At first, in his words, "unregenerate" (CT 9, 78), the narrator depicts himself as undergoing a conversion. Drawing on the religious imagery, Mack produces a reading that sees the narrator transformed from prosecutor Saul into apostle Paul in the cause of the "monastic" Paraday. His interpretation includes a defense of the romantic subplot. With a face "like an angel," Fanny fits with the narrator's new aesthetic faith. His reading, however, makes only Paraday a saint, as he acknowledges both the narrator's enjoyment of discomfiting others and his profiting by his relationship with Paraday to win Fanny, although he sees no "base motive" in the writing of the story itself, an appropriate "witness" to Paraday's "martyrdom." Rawlings adds an additional twist, seeing the narrator undergoing not just one, but two changes of heart, first switching his sympathies to Paraday, but then vying with Mrs. Wimbush over Paraday and coming to hope for a success of his own (xxiii).

Paraday himself was early subjected to such scrutiny, Brooks writing that "It is intolerable to be asked to regard as 'great' the lion who is so afraid of his hostess" (132–33). In the view of some he is a victim, of "too much adulation for the wrong reasons and in the wrong way," according to Canby, of unnatural meddling, according to Ward (Canby 235; Ward 1961, 7). Fame, wrote Milton, is the "last infirmity of a noble mind," and many critics have found it hard to account for Paraday's infirmity, even as he dies of it. To Ziff, the lesson of the tale is that an artist should "resist the idolizing, which, in effect, ignores what he stands for" (60). According to such a reading, Paraday can only serve as a negative example. Stewart comments that James "seems to take for granted an abject obedience to society's call," but Stevenson sees vanity behind Paraday's susceptibility and finds it ironic for the Jamesian artist "who is anything and everything in his own mind" to be "attempting anxiously to be something or other in the social world" (Stewart 99; Stevenson 69). The lack of clarity about Paraday's motives is, in Jefferson's view, a problem. To be stronger, he reasons, the tale should make clear Paraday's flaw in wanting both recognition and solitude (1964, 120). Gill, on the other hand, finds it natural that an artist should enjoy "what the country house offers his senses and imagination" although he finds it equally clear that in the later James the life there is ultimately "alien" to the artist's "needs and values" (79). Kappeler assigns to Paraday "a slight perversity, a trace of masochism" (84). The passage she cites, however, also provides something of a rationale for his behavior, attributing Paraday's behavior to his artistic imagination, "he pays for his imagination, which puts him . . . in the place of others and makes him feel, even against himself, their feelings, their appetites, their motives. It's indeed inveterately against himself that he makes his imagination act" (CT 9, 109–10).

Others simply see Paraday as weak, dying in the words of Markov-Totevy "exhausted and resigned to his fate" (100; also Matheson 227). Once a lion, Blackmur writes, ". . . Paraday soon *wants* to become ill again; he knew what was happening to him, but he could not help surrendering to it" (84; also Rawlings xxii). In Andreas's view, Paraday, having led such a quiet life, is simply unable to handle the new demands on him (31). According to Delbaere-Garant, he loses the balance between art and life, and his sudden fame marks "the beginning of his decline as an artist," although one might argue that it more accurately marks his silencing (129, 218). Horne sees Blackmur relying "perhaps a bit too much on an intuitive understanding of Paraday's subconscious." She similarly dismisses Brooks's and Stevenson's readings, arguing that Paraday showed he did not wish to become a lion by fleeing Morrow. Her explanation that he did not flee Mrs. Wimbush "out of a feeling of responsibility to his public" sounds a little less convincing (79–80). While seeing a "process of artistic disintegration" that begins with Paraday's loss of privacy, Vaid also urges moderation, maintaining that "Paraday's own lack of resistance . . . is neither stressed nor suggested with undue irony, the whole point being his utter helplessness in the circumstances . . ." (72, 77). Jones tries to give a more positive reading of Paraday's behavior, citing the narrator that Paraday made the "great renouncement" of his art to his social duties, only to die "disillusioned," the victim of "the duty of fame" (200).

In his preface, James had asserted that the "maximum sense" of the tale depended on the "importance" of Paraday, adding, "It was *amusing* to make these people 'great,' so far as one could do so without making them intrinsically false" (*Criticism* 2, 1231). To Hoag, Paraday is worse than weak, and those who have expressed their doubts about Paraday have not gone far enough. Like Lynd, who doubts the value of the lost manuscript, he questions whether Paraday's achievement is "fact, real, or fancied" (Lynd 117). Although he admits that there is much of James in Paraday, and that the character is "never very carefully or concretely realized," he draws on the mention of "irony" in the preface to contend that Paraday "may be an honest, if complex *man* but not a great *novelist*." Hoag includes both the narrator and Fanny in his expose, arguing that the narrator, although reasonably intelligent, is a "venal, if not shocking, fraud," while Fanny is such a "fool" that the narrator's affection for her further undercuts his trustworthiness. He sees a "tension" between the narrator and Paraday dominating the tale, and questions whether the narrator is really seeking to protect Paraday or just competing with Morrow, and notes as a further irony his failure to do either. The role of the narrator, particularly his romance with Fanny, "undercuts and distracts" from Paraday, but does not, Hoag maintains, let Paraday off the hook. Of Paraday he writes, "He is James's flawed man pulled again in two directions, or more, and none of them certainly rewarding." Indeed, writes Hoag, "The strongest suggestion . . . is the absurdity of all the alternatives, and the best testimony of Paraday's intelligence is his comic perception of this." It is an assessment that Wagenknecht, while offering sympathy for those who find Paraday "spineless," refuses to accept (78, 232 n.3).

To Nicholas, one of the marks against Paraday is that he allows himself to be compared with the false artists Dora Forbes and Guy Walsingham (170). Certainly their role in the tale, apart from comedy, is largely one of contrast to Paraday (e.g., Vaid 79). Like Morrow, such success-seeking writers "betray" the public on whose behalf they claim to act, writes McCarthy (150). Anderson states that the reader will not find any "usable generalizations about the artist" in the tale (vi). But while their dramatization may keep James's ideas about art in the tale, in Horne's view, admirably hidden "well below the surface," they also provide some general guidelines (79). At the heart of the tale, argues Stokes, is the narrator's comment that "the best interviewer's the best reader," a statement he takes as ambiguous, a possible indication of the "mystification" of his work (158). Walter Wright reads the line without irony as bearing out the previous statement that "the artist's life's his work, and this is the place to observe him," a statement McWhirter sees James supporting "wholeheartedly" (Wright 134; McWhirter 18). Nicholas, however, views the narrator's conception of Paraday's "emergence as a public figure in terms of his disappearance as a person" as a satire not only of journalism, but also "a curiously prophetic attack on those post–Eliotic critics who, like Fanny Hurter, avoid the author at all costs because of their veneration for his work, i.e. his absence" (146). Todorov takes the issues of absence and presence more seriously, seeing in the tale the problem of "art and life" represented in the "relation between an author's life and his work." He cites particularly the narrator's claim, "Let whoever would represent the interest in his presence. . . . I should represent the interest in his work—in other words in his absence" (CT 9, 95). Noting that "psychological criticism" takes the author as the "absolute and absent cause" of the work's "presence—though unimportant in itself," Todorov argues that James "reverses this relation: the author's life is merely appearance, contingency, accident; it is an unessential presence." In seeking the work, indeed, the tale shows, the "second knowledge" of the man can destroy both man and work (169). Writing that the artist and his work are "fairly interchangeable" in this tale, so that the death of the author and the loss of the work come down to nearly the same thing, Charney sees the typical triangle of artist-work-model replaced here by one of artist-work-reader. She offers a positive reading of the tale's conclusion, however, noting that while both life and art continue without Paraday, in James "someone is always listening" (72–74).

One of the reasons Hoag puts forward as calling for a reevaluation of Paraday's greatness, is that to accept him as great "we must sacrifice the comedy of the story or question the callousness of the tone" (171). The question of the tale's tone has indeed been an issue throughout its critical history. Much of the story is comic. Poole points to the "outrageous comedy" in the fact that Paraday's "readers" "do not need actually to *read* a single word to make some sort of profit out of an author and his works" (x). Kermode comments on the contribution of James's typical doubles to the farcical atmosphere (22). Although Canby finds James's "protests" here "a little on the defensive" then "wrathful" at the end, Matthiessen argues that the comic handling of the subject shows how James avoided looking "grimly" at his problems (Canby 235; Matthiessen 4, 1944). To Bass, while "the narrative view is taut with resentment, its futility remains comic." Even the loss of the manuscript, although significant, remains comic, he contends, because "no one can directly be blamed" (115–16).

The main problem in reading the tale as straight comedy is, of course, Paraday's death, which Geismar describes as "too heavy a blow" for the preceding social comedy (131; also Rawlings xxi–ii). Vaid, too, finds the death of Paraday the "only overdone touch," and he charges further that his ignorance of the loss of the fragment "could have been easily spared, for it is incongruous with the tone of the rest of the tale" (79). Hoag takes a different approach, arguing that to take the death scene seriously makes it "high-brow *kitsch*." Further, he writes, it is not necessarily unpleasant to be Paraday "if you can die laughing" (171). But while Paraday is said at first to "fill his lungs with the queer comedy of his fate," that comedy kills him, and Paraday is not shown laughing on his deathbed, but talking of his work. Edel judges the tale one of James's "bitterest—and most amusing" literary tales (*Life* 3, 373). Hoag's response to Edel is that the tale becomes "less bitter and more comic" if one discounts Paraday as a true artist, making the tone one of "open, purgative amusement" (165, 171). But to do that is to excise one of the tale's moods, rather than to account for it.

Early on, as Vaid observes, the "effect of exaggeration" as in most of the artist tales produces a "comedy bordering on fantasy or, if you like, fantasy bordering on comedy." Although Vaid praises the way James keeps the many elements of his tale from being "held down" by their seriousness, he also acknowledges their seriousness, charting the way the tone changes at the end to one "informed with righteous indignation." In Vaid's estimate the change is "appropriate" as it is intended "to portray sarcastically forces that are not merely ridiculous but also monstrous" (72, 78–79). Sharp, too, without assigning any blame, remarks on the "shade" cast on the comedy by Paraday's death, remarking at the same time on how the narrator's "new life of romance" grows from Paraday's "decline" (29, 34). In Horne's analysis, the tale is also a combination, a tragedy turned comic by its treatment, but with a lingering tension between the two modes. Unlike Sharp, she includes all three central characters in the tragedy, while viewing the minor characters as parts of a farce. Even so, she sees the irony working against the comedy by its bitter depiction of a society killing the celebrity it has created (74–75, 78). Grover judges the tone less hostile, "ironic and lightly satirical," but still finds "the significance of the tale is serious indeed: the comedy is high comedy and the outcome is tragic in terms of Paraday's life and work" (151). Markow-Totevy, too, calls the work both "tragic and comic" (99). The combination makes for an uneven, or rather a complex tone, and one might follow Horne to argue that the genre of the story depends on who you are. For Paraday it is a tragedy, for Hurter and the narrator a classic comedy, for the other characters a farce or satire.

Two critics, Wallace and Springer, turn to a broader definition of satire to account for the tale's mingling of modes. Noting the "tragic movement of the plot," Wallace still finds the story "highly comic" since it keeps its focus not on Paraday, but on the society about him, which includes "a whole gaggle of comic caricatures." They include the "comic doubles of the narrator," Morrow and Mrs. Wimbush, and the "comic doubles of Paraday," Walsingham and Forbes, whose reversed sexes provide a "running joke." The narrator himself, in his "unconscious participation in the humorous society which he himself ridicules," in the "discrepancy" between his motives and his "achievements" provides a "comic irony" of his own. Paraday, however, Wallace argues, is "never comic," serving instead as "the moral norm of the satire" (164–68).

In Wallace's schema, a classic note of "comic continuity" is provided by the way Paraday's works will "live on" in the narrator and Fanny, whose union Matheson also depicts as a "brighter note" in a bleak tale (Wallace 178; Matheson 227). In her reading of the tale as satire, Springer gives Fanny an even larger role, casting her rather than Paraday as the moral norm. The initial subject, she records, is "a single minor crime of middle-class society, the 'lionizing' of noted authors." James takes a realistic approach to his subject, following "the structure of the relatively plotted story," because such a plot with the death of the artist as its logical end best fits his satire, as he recognized in his "bloodthirsty" notebook entry. Thus, while Paraday is a "fine and fragile" character, James uses several devices to keep the reader at a "satiric remove" from him, including the minimizing of his dialogue, the secondary love plot, and the filtering effect of the narrator who is concerned primarily with what is "next for *him*." The story is not about the lion but about "lionization." Paraday cannot be too sympathetic as his being so would jeopardize the satire, since lionizing is dependent in part on "the lion's own vanity and blindness." He is instead "a mere device." Only Fanny, in Springer's estimate, is "a serious departure from the order of satire," although "integral" to it. She is there to absent herself from the satiric *cena* at Prestidge, "to *be* good, distinct from characters who are there to be agents of satire" (83–87, 90, 95–97).

With less attention to genre, Teddy Roosevelt wrote upon reading "The Death of the Lion" that James's "polished, pointless, uninteresting stories about the upper social classes of England make one blush to think that he was once an American" (Monteiro 5). Brooks, of course, was also unsympathetic with James's adoption of England, and he included this tale in his general criticism of the late James as "ventriloquist" not "actor" (133–34). More representative assessments, however, come from Vaid and Dupee, who class this story among James's greatest tales, Vaid for its "sustained irony," Dupee for its accommodation of both "cleverness and pathos" (Vaid 79; Dupee 152). Even Nicholas, who assigns it a more limited range, calls it a "masterpiece" (143). Some of the greatness of the tale, however, is undoubtedly the variety of its elements. A few years earlier in "The Solution," James had portrayed the serious consequences of a single practical joke; here most everything is a joke, but there is still a seriousness present not only in the consequences, but in the core. There are passages that are laugh-out-loud funny, others that are poignant, others that leave one at a loss to point out their predominant tone—all of which produce a mingling of "bliss and bane" that is remarkably like the life James sought to capture.

Works Cited

Primary Works

James, Henry. 1894. "The Death of the Lion." *The Yellow Book* 1 (April): 7–52.

———. 1895. "The Death of the Lion." *Terminations*. London: Heinemann; New York: Harper, 1–58.

———. 1909. "The Death of the Lion." *The Novels and Tales of Henry James*. New York Edition. Vol. 15, 97–154. New York: Scribner's.

———. 1915. "The Death of the Lion." *The Uniform Tales of Henry James*. London: Martin Secker.

———. 1988. *Selected Letters of Henry James to Edmund Gosse, 1882–1915: A Literary Friendship*. Ed. Rayburn S. Moore. Baton Rouge: Louisiana State University Press.

Secondary Works

Anderson, Quentin, ed. [1950] 1957. Intro. *Henry James: Selected Short Stories*. New York: Rinehart.

Andreas, Osborn. 1948. *Henry James and the Expanding Horizon: A Study of the Meaning and Basic Themes of James's Fiction*. Seattle: University of Washington Press.

Auchard, John. 1986. *Silence in Henry James: The Heritage of Symbolism and Decadence*. University Park: Pennsylvania State University Press.

Bass, Eben. 1964. "Lemon-Colored Volumes and Henry James." *Studies in Short Fiction* 1 (Winter): 113–22.

Baxter, Annette K. 1955. "Independence vs. Isolation: Hawthorne and James on the Problem of the Artist." *Nineteenth-Century Fiction* 10: 225–31.

Beach, Joseph Warren. [1918] 1954. *The Method of Henry James*. Philadelphia: Albert Saifer.

Beattie, Munro. 1967. "The Many Marriages of Henry James." In *Patterns of Commitment in American Literature*. Ed. Marston La France, 93–112. Toronto: University of Toronto Press.

Beaver, Harold. 1983. "'The Real Thing' and Unreal Things: Conflicts of Art and Society in Henry James." *Fabula* (Villeneuve d'Ascq) 1 (March): 53–69.

Beebe, Maurice L. 1964. *Ivory Towers and Sacred Founts*. New York: New York University Press.

Bell, Millicent. 1965. *Edith Wharton and Henry James: The Story of Their Friendship*. New York: George Braziller.

Blackmur, R. P. [1945] 1983. "In the Country of the Blue." In *Studies in Henry James*. Ed. Veronica A. Makowsky, 69–90. New York: New Directions. Reprinted from *Kenyon Review* 5 (Autumn): 595–617. Also reprinted in *The Question of Henry*

James, ed. F. W. Dupee, 191–211, New York: Henry Holt, 1945, and *Critiques and Essays on Modern Fiction*, 303–18. New York: Ronald, 1945, 1952.

Booth, Wayne C. [1961] 1983. *The Rhetoric of Fiction*. Chicago: University of Chicago Press.

Brooks, Van Wyck. 1925. *The Pilgrimage of Henry James*. New York: Dutton. Reprint. New York: Octagon, 1972.

Canby, Henry Seidel. 1951. *Turn West, Turn East: Mark Twain and Henry James*. Boston: Houghton Mifflin.

Charney, Hanna. 1978. "Variations by James on a Theme by Balzac." *New York Literary Forum* 2: 69–75.

Delbaere-Garant, Jeanne. 1970. *Henry James: The Vision of France*. Paris: Société d'Editions Les Belles Lettres.

Dupee, F. W. [1951] 1956. *Henry James*. Garden City, NY: Doubleday Anchor.

Edgar, Pelham. [1927] 1964. *Henry James, Man and Author*. New York: Russell & Russell.

Ford, Madox Ford. 1913. *Henry James: A Critical Study*. London: Martin Secker.

Gage, Richard P. 1988. *Order and Design: Henry James' Titled Story Sequences*. New York: Peter Lang.

Geismar, Maxwell. 1963. *Henry James and the Jacobites*. Boston: Houghton Mifflin.

Gill, Richard. 1972. *Happy Rural Seat: The English Country House and the Literary Imagination*. New Haven: Yale University Press.

Goetz, William R. 1986. *Henry James and the Darkest Abyss of Romance*. Baton Rouge: Louisiana State University Press.

Grossman, James. 1945. "The Face in the Mountain." *Nation* 16 (8 September): 230–32.

Grover, Philip. 1973. *Henry James and the French Novel: A Study in Inspiration*. London: Paul Elek.

Hartsock, Mildred E. 1968. "Henry James and the Cities of the Plain." *Modern Language Quarterly* 29 (September): 297–311.

Hetherington, Hugh W. 1961. *Melville's Reviewers, British and American, 1846–1891*. Chapel Hill, NC: University of North Carolina Press.

Hoag, Gerald. 1975. "The Death of the Paper Lion." *Studies in Short Fiction* 12: 163–72.

Holder, Alan. 1966. *Three Voyagers in Search of Europe: A Study of Henry James, Ezra Pound, and T. S. Eliot*. Philadelphia: University of Pennsylvania Press.

Horne, Helen. 1960. *Basic Ideals of James's Aesthetics as Expressed in the Short Stories Concerning Artists and Writers*. Marburg: Erich Mauersberger.

Horrell, Joyce Tayloe. 1970. "A 'Shade of a Special Sense': Henry James and the Art of Naming." *American Literature* 42: 203–20.

Isle, Walter Whitfield. 1968. *Experiments in Form: Henry James's Novels: 1896–1901*. Cambridge, MA: Harvard University Press.

Jacobson, Marcia. 1983. *Henry James and the Mass Market*. University: University of Alabama Press.

Jefferson, D. W. 1964. *Henry James and the Modern Reader*. New York: St. Martin's.

————. [1960] 1971. *Henry James*. New York: Capricorn.

Jones, Granville H. 1975. *Henry James's Psychology of Experience: Innocence, Responsibility, and Renunciation in the Fiction of Henry James*. The Hague: Mouton.

Kappeler, Susanne. 1980. *Writing and Reading in Henry James*. New York: Columbia University Press.

Kermode, Frank, ed. 1986. *The Figure in the Carpet and Other Stories*. London: Penguin.

Kirby, David K. 1973. "A Possible Source for James's 'The Death of the Lion.'" *Colby Library Quarterly* 10 (March): 39–40.

Knox, Melissa. 1986. "'Beltraffio'": Henry James' Secrecy." *American Imago* 43, no. 3 (Fall): 211–27.

Leavis, Q. D. 1947. "Henry James: The Stories." *Scrutiny* 14 (Spring): 223–29. Reprinted in *Collected Essays*. Vol. 2: *The American Novel and Reflections of the European Novel*, ed. G. Singh, 177–84. Cambridge: Cambridge University Press.

Lee, Brian. 1978. *The Novels of Henry James: A Study of Culture and Consciousness*. New York: St. Martin's.

Leyburn, Ellen Douglass. 1968. *Strange Alloy: The Relation of Comedy to Tragedy in the Fiction of Henry James*. Chapel Hill: University of North Carolina Press.

Lubbock, Percy. 1912. "Henry James." *Dictionary of National Biography. Second Supplement, 1901–1911*. Vol. 1. Ed. Sidney Lee. London: Oxford University Press.

Lynd, Robert. 1952. "Literary Life." *Books and Writers*. Foreword by Robert Church. New York: Macmillan.

McCarthy, Harold T. 1958. *Henry James: The Creative Process*. New York: Thomas Yoseloff.

Mack, Stanley Thomas. 1976. "The Narrator in James's 'The Death of the Lion': A Religious Conversion of Sorts." *Thoth: Syracuse University Graduate Studies in English* 16, no. 1: 19–25.

Mackenzie, Manfred. 1976. *Communities of Honor and Love in Henry James*. Cambridge, MA: Harvard University Press.

McWhirter, David. 1989. *Desire and Love in Henry James: A Study of the Late Novels*. Cambridge: Cambridge University Press.

Markow-Totevy, Georges. 1969. *Henry James*. Trans. John Griffiths. London: Merlin.

Matheson, Gwen. 1968. "Portraits of the Artist and the Lady in the Shorter Fictions of Henry James." *Dalhousie Review* 48: 222–30.

Matthiessen, F. O. 1947. *The James Family: Including Selections from the Writings of Henry James, Sr., William, Henry, and Alice James*. New York: Knopf.

———. 1944. "Introduction: Henry James' Portrait of the Artist." *Henry James: Stories of Writers and Artists*. Norfolk, CT: New Directions. Also reprinted as "Henry James's Portrait of the Artist." *Partisan Review* 11 (1944): 71–87.

Mix, Katherine Lyon. 1960. *A Study in Yellow: "The Yellow Book" and its Contributors*. Lawrence: University of Kansas Press.

Monteiro, George. 1965. *Henry James and John Hay: The Record of a Friendship*. Providence, RI: Brown University Press.

Mottram, Eric. 1985. "'The Infected Air' and 'The Guilt of Interference': Henry James's Short Stories." In *The Nineteenth-Century American Short Story*. Ed. A. Robert Lee, 164–90. London: Vision; Totowa, NJ: Barnes & Noble.

Nettels, Elsa. 1974. "The Scapegoats and Martyrs of Henry James." *Colby Library Quarterly* 10 (June): 413–27.

Nicholas, Charles A. 1972. "A Second Glance at Henry James's 'The Death of the Lion.'" *Studies in Short Fiction* 9 (Spring): 143–46.

Norrman, Ralf. 1982. *The Insecure World of Henry James's Fiction: Intensity and Ambiguity*. New York: St. Martin's.

Pearson, Hesketh. *Oscar Wilde: His Life and Wit*. New York: Harper.

Poole, Adrian, ed. 1983. Introduction. *Aspern Papers and Other Stories*. Oxford: Oxford University Press.

Powers, Lyall H. 1970. *Henry James: An Introduction and Interpretation*. New York: Holt, Rinehart.

———. 1961. "A Reperusal of James's 'The Figure in the Carpet.'" *American Literature* 33 (May): 224–28.

Putt, S. Gorley. 1966. *Henry James: A Reader's Guide*. Ithaca, NY: Cornell University Press.

Rawlings, Peter, ed. 1984. *Henry James's Shorter Masterpieces*. Vol. 1. Sussex: Harvester; Totowa, NJ: Barnes & Noble.

Roselli, Daniel N. 1971. "Max Beerbohm's Unpublished Parody of Henry James." *Review of English Studies* n.s. 22: 61–63.

Segal, Ora. 1969. *The Lucid Reflector: The Observer in Henry James' Fiction*. New Haven: Yale University Press.

Seltzer, Mark. 1984. *Henry James and the Art of Power*. Ithaca, NY: Cornell University Press.

Sharp, Sister M. Corona. 1963. *The Confidante in Henry James: Evolution and Moral Value of a Fictive Character*. Notre Dame, IN: Notre Dame University Press.

Smith, William F., Jr. 1973. "Sentence Structure in the Tales of Henry James." *Style* 7 (Spring): 157–72.

Springer, Mary Doyle. 1978. *A Rhetoric of Literary Character: Some Women of Henry James*. Chicago: University of Chicago Press.

———. 1975. *Forms of the Modern Novella*. Chicago: University of Chicago Press.

Stevenson, Elizabeth. [1949] 1981. *The Crooked Corridor: A Study of Henry James*. New York: Octagon.

Stewart, J. I. M. 1963. "Henry James." In *Eight Modern Writers. Oxford History of English Literature*. Vol. 12, 71–121. New York: Oxford University Press.

Stokes, John. 1989. *In the Nineties*. Chicago: University of Chicago Press.

Stone, Donald David. 1972. *Novelists in a Changing World: Meredith, James, and the Transformation of English Fiction in the 1880's*. Cambridge, MA: Harvard University Press.

Stone, Edward. 1964. *The Battle and the Books: Some Aspects of Henry James*. Athens: Ohio University Press.

Swan, Michael, ed. 1948. *Lesson of the Master and Other Stories by Henry James*. London: John Lehmann.

Tintner, Adeline R. 1986. *The Museum World of Henry James*. Ann Arbor: UMI Research Press.

Todorov, Tzvetan. 1977. *The Poetics of Prose*. Trans. Richard Howard. Ithaca, NY: Cornell University Press.

Vaid, Krishna B. 1964. *Technique in the Tales of Henry James*. Cambridge, MA: Harvard University Press.

Wagenknecht, Edward. 1984. *The Tales of Henry James*. New York: Frederick Ungar.

Wallace, Ronald. 1975. *Henry James and the Comic Form*. Ann Arbor: University of Michigan Press.

Ward, Joseph A. 1967. *The Search for Form: Studies in the Structure of James's Fiction*. Chapel Hill: University of North Carolina Press.

———. 1961. *The Imagination of Disaster: Evil in the Fiction of Henry James*. Lincoln: University of Nebraska Press.

West, Rebecca. [pseud]. 1916. *Henry James*. London: Nisbet.

Wright, Austin McGiffert. 1961. *The American Short Story in the Twenties*. Chicago: University of Chicago Press.

Wright, Walter F. 1962. *The Madness of Art: A Study of Henry James*. Lincoln: University of Nebraska Press.

Ziff, Larzer. 1966. *The American 1890's: Life and Times of a Lost Generation*. New York: Viking.

The Diary of a Man of Fifty

Publication History

"The Diary of a Man of Fifty" appeared first in the United States in the July 1879 issue of *Harper's New Monthly Magazine* and in England in *Macmillan's Magazine*, James being very careful to ensure that the publication was simulataneous so that he not jeopardize copyright in either country, as he mistakenly did later that year with "The Bundle of Letters" (*Correspondence* 28–30). That same year James included it in *The Madonna of the Future* and the next year in a collection with "A Bundle of Letters." He published it for the last time in the 1883 Collective Edition.

Circumstances of Composition, Sources, and Influences

On December 12, 1878, in his notebook, James considered the possibility of "A man of a certain age" who "sees a certain situation of his own youth reproduced before his eyes and hesitates between his curiosity to see at what issue it arrives in this particular case and the prompting to interfere, in the light of his own experience, for the benefit of the actors." At this stage, as he crafted his situation of the man encountering the daughter of a former and "dangerous" love, James seems to find the wise choice is to interfere and ends his entry with the warning, not its debunking. On January 17 he reported the story as finished without further comment (CN 8–9).

Kelley finds the heroine reminiscent of those of George Sand and Maves of Stendhal's Duchessa San Severino in *Chartreuse de Parme* (Kelly 246 n.4; Maves 64). Otherwise most critics have focused on what Garnett first called the tale's charming "flavour of Turgenev" (x). Buitenhuis further specified the flavor as Turgenev's similarly titled "Diary of a Superfluous Man," seeing James as turning at the time from the influence of Hawthorne to Turgenev in his interest in the "determining power of character" (106). Peterson elaborates, noting that both tales chronicle retrospectively the youthful romance of a cynical older man who examines both himself and the "alternative self" his narrative contains, with the difference that in James the narrator takes the burden of his failure on himself (56–59). An additional Turgenev parallel may be found in the novella *Spring Torrents* of 1870, whose narrative of young love is also framed by the meditations of a man now in his fifties. Turgenev's fifty-three-year-old protagonist looks back thirty years to 1840; James's fifty-two-year-old one twenty-seven years to 1847. In Turgenev's tale, there is also a daughter but no Stanmer, and the woman the narrator once loved is alive, if happily married. The narrator, now successful but dissatisfied, makes his own leap of faith at the novel's conclusion by moving from St. Petersburg to New York where she now lives. Wagenknecht speculates that James's story may have, in turn, been behind the narrative frame of Edward Sheldon's play *Romance* (182).

Grover sees the tale as a rewriting of Dumas's *Le Demi-Monde* in its consideration of a woman whose reputation is challenged, seeing James to have created a more complex work in his objection to Dumas's strict policing of social categories (590–93). Tintner pictures the story as a response to another French author, Octave Feuillet, its title echoing his *Le Journal d'une femme*, and its main characters—the woman who flirts to hide her true feelings and the man who recognizes that only when it is too late—resembling those of his *La Petite Comtesse* (1974, 222, 226–29). She, like Gale earlier, also cites the painter Andrea del Sarto's jealousy of a fickle wife as a source (Tintner 1986, 30–32; Gale 157).

Relation to Other Works

Nathalia Wright includes Stanmer among the many James characters who experience "successful" romances in Italy. The narrator's "esthetic-erotic failure," on the other hand, can be traced to his "denial of the values of 'old' Italy," seen also in the characters of Winterbourne and the narrator of *The Aspern Papers*. She acknowledges that his tendency to focus more on Italian violence than romance may be "partly encouraged" by the Countess's address—the Via Ghilbellina (221, 225; also Maves 66). Edel locates in the tale a reflection of Roderick Hudson's "original bafflement" with Christina, but finds in the overturning of the man's fears an anticipation of *The Sacred Fount* (*Life* 2, 358). Kraft links the narrator with Winterbourne, Longmore of *Madame de Mauves*, and the narrator of "Four Meetings," who also suffer from a small-mindedness that keeps them on the "outside" of life, remarking that in James it is usually the men who demonstrate cowardice while the women show character (110). Maves locates in the story the first use of the theme of "too late" of "The Beast in the Jungle" noting that Marcher and May also met in Italy, and that the sense of loss here is connected with the unattainable Italy of the imagination as well as the women who lived there (64, 160 n.25; see also Sharp xxix). Tintner also connects the two tales, adding *Confidence* as a work that treats the same theme but with a happy ending, and noting that while James provides Stanmer a happy ending, it is the narrator's unhappy one that sets the tone (1974, 227). Putt finds the man's discovery—"If I marred her happiness, I certainly didn't make my own. And I might have made it—eh? That's a charming discovery for a man of my age!"—to be the same as Strether's in *The Ambassadors* (269). The analogy the narrator attempts within the story may find its best analogy in "The Lesson of the Master" where one generation again advises the next to avoid the dangers of women and marriage.

Maves finds the first-person retrospective designed to fit the mood of nostalgic romance as in such other Italian tales as "The Madonna of the Future," "Adina," and "The Solution," as well as the 1878 essay "Italy Revisited" (63–64, 95). Stone compares the narrator to Rowland Mallet, noting the significance in such a character being mistaken, as was the case for the first time in *Confidence* (200). Maves attributes to the Countess Christina's "moodiness," while Walter Wright finds James's portrait of a complex, ambiguous woman improved from "The Story of a Masterpiece" (Maves 65; Wright 156–57).

Interpretation and Criticism

While McElderry calls attention to the "nostalgic description" of Italy in the tale, Kelley considers the story as perhaps reflecting James's reasons for leaving Florence. Both consider the tale "otherwise unimportant," Kelley as a temporary step backward to romanticism (McElderry 77; Kelley 245–46, 273 n.7). Kraft not only finds the subject matter "unrealistic," but deems the diary form unhelpful (103). O'Faolian, on the other hand, finds the technique of the diary making the story a "magnificent exception" to James's tendency to "sprawl" (171). Other estimates have also been generally positive, as—judging from the number of reprintings—was James's early judgment of the tale. Even Edel, although he classes the tale with James's "commercial" efforts, considers it "suavely-written" (CT 4, 10). Q. D. Leavis singles out the "mathematical elegance" of the parallel stories as representative of one of James's key "method[s] of artistic procedure," one that allows for the dramatic tension that makes "a work of art instead of a narrative" (226). Putt agrees with Leavis, and finds the story's success in its use of "direct self-fantasy," unconstrained by an "irritatingly symmetrical" pattern. He praises the narrator for coming to his remorseful conclusion through reason not sentimentality, although as Maves points out it was an excess of reason that caused his failure (Putt 269; Maves 65).

Kraft notes that the story leaves open the question whether the narrator would have been happier married to the Countess, but makes clear the narrator's fault in never venturing to find out (110). Segal points to the high value assigned to flirtatiousness in James (222 n.8). Peterson discusses the "self-serving protectiveness" motivating the ambivalently minded narrator's unsuccessful attempt to turn Stanmer into his double, while pointing out that the story leaves open the possibility that Stanmer's happier case may be equally risky to generalize from. While Winner notes that the shared admiration of Stanmer and the narrator for Italian Pre-Raphaelite art usually indicates in James "cultivation or an aesthetic temperament," Peterson emphasizes the contribution that Anglo-Saxon prurient suspiciousness of Italian culture makes to the narrator's failure (Winner 80; see also Maves 65). He therefore considers it particularly appropriate that the statues of Pomona and Hermes wordlessly undercut his arguments to Stanmer (Peterson 54–56; also Zablotny 217–18).

Like Putt, Sharp finds the narrator a representative of James, a rather sad self-portrait for a successful writer of forty-six (xxix; also Tanner). Edel focuses on the story's revelation of James's "uncertainty and anxiety" about young women, motivating in part James's decision not to marry (*Life* 2, 358). In Zablotny's interpretation, the narrator remains trapped in "infantile fantasy," responding to the Countess as a mother figure—a "devouring vampire mother" at that. Zablotny considers the tale significant, however, as the first departure from James's depiction of women as dangers to be avoided (216–21). Instead, the tale sounds what Matthiessen and Murdock call a "familiar kind of Jamesian regret" (N 9). As Levy argues, James varies his usual depiction of the fear of evil, such that here it becomes "the fear of life itself" (31). Since the story clearly criticizes the narrator, James's identification with such a character reveals James's sense of his own limitations more than it does those of women. After his marriage Stanmer writes to the narrator, "Things that involve a risk are like the Christian faith; they must be seen from the inside" (CT 4, 423). The explicit religious metaphor is striking for James and reminds us that James himself never lay claim to such an inside view. The story gives us in addition to its tale of two men and two women James's look at the consequences for a writer, here the first-person diarist, concerned as James was with the portrayal of the relations of men and women, of having always to portray them from the outside.

Works Cited

Primary Works
James, Henry. 1879. "The Diary of a Man of Fifty." *Harper's New Monthly Magazine* 59 (July): 282–97; *Macmillan's Magazine* 40 (July): 205–23.

————. 1879. "The Diary of a Man of Fifty." *The Madonna of the Future and Other Tales*. London: Macmillan.

————. 1880. "The Diary of a Man of Fifty." *The Diary of a Man of Fifty and A Bundle of Letters*. New York: Harper, 9–68.

————. 1883. "The Diary of a Man of Fifty." *Collective Edition*. Vol. 14. London: Macmillan.

————. 1993. *The Correspondence of Henry James and the House of Macmillan, 1877–1914*. Ed. Rayburn S. Moore. Baton Rouge: Louisiana State University Press.

Secondary Works

Buitenhuis, Peter. 1970. *The Grasping Imagination: The American Writings of Henry James*. Toronto: University of Toronto Press.

Gale, Robert L. [1954] 1964. *The Caught Image: Figurative Language in the Fiction of Henry James*. Chapel Hill: University of North Carolina Press.

Garnett, David, ed. 1946. *Fourteen Stories by Henry James*. London: Rupert Hart-Davis.

Grover, P. R. 1973. "Henry James and the Theme of the Adventuress." *Revue de Littérature Comparée* 47 (October–December): 586–96.

Kelley, Cornelia Pulsifer. [1930] 1965. *The Early Development of Henry James*. Urbana: University of Illinois Press.

Kraft, James. 1969. *The Early Tales of Henry James*. Carbondale: Southern Illinois University Press.

Leavis, Q. D. 1947. "Henry James: The Stories." *Scrutiny* 14 (Spring): 223–29. Reprinted in *Collected Essays*. Vol. 2: *The American Novel and Reflections of the European Novel*, ed. G. Singh, 177–84. Cambridge: Cambridge University Press.

Levy, Leo B. 1957. *Versions of Melodrama: A Study of the Fiction and Drama of Henry James, 1865–1897*. Berkeley: University of California Press.

McElderry, Bruce R., Jr. 1965. *Henry James*. New York: Twayne.

Maves, Carl. 1973. *Sensuous Pessimism: Italy in the Works of Henry James*. Bloomington: Indiana University Press.

O'Faolian, Sean. 1948. *The Short Story*. London: Collins.

Peterson, Dale E. 1975. *The Clement Vision: Poetic Realism in Turgenev and James*. Port Washington, NY: Kennikat.

Putt, S. Gorley. 1966. *Henry James: A Reader's Guide*. Ithaca, NY: Cornell University Press.

Segal, Ora. 1969. *The Lucid Reflector: The Observer in Henry James' Fiction*. New Haven: Yale University Press.

Sharp, Sister M. Corona. 1963. *The Confidante in Henry James: Evolution and Moral Value of a Fictive Character*. Notre Dame, IN: Notre Dame University Press.

Stone, Donald David. 1972. *Novelists in a Changing World: Meredith, James, and the Transformation of English Fiction in the 1880's*. Cambridge, MA: Harvard University Press.

Tanner, Tony. 1963. "James's Little Tarts." *The Spectator* 210 (4 January): 19.

Tintner, Adeline R. 1986. *The Museum World of Henry James.* Ann Arbor: UMI Research Press.

———. 1974. "Octave Feuillet: *La petite comtesse,* and Henry James." *Revue de Littérature Comparée* 48: 218–32.

Wagenknecht, Edward. 1984. *The Tales of Henry James.* New York: Frederick Ungar.

Winner, Viola Hopkins. 1970. *Henry James and the Visual Arts.* Charlottesville: University Press of Virginia.

Wright, Nathalia. 1965. *American Novelists in Italy, The Discoverers: Allston to James.* Philadelphia: University of Pennsylvania Press.

Wright, Walter F. 1962. *The Madness of Art: A Study of Henry James.* Lincoln: University of Nebraska Press.

Zablotny, Elaine. 1979. "Henry James and the Demonic Vampire and Madonna." *Psychocultural Review* 3, nos. 3–4 (Summer–Fall): 203–24.

Eugene Pickering

Publication History

"Eugene Pickering" appeared first in the *Atlantic Monthly* from October to November 1874. At the time, James was becoming increasingly noticed by the magazines and, while he had originally promised the tale to *Scribner's,* he gave it instead to the *Atlantic* when Howells wrote to James worried about his possible defection (*Life* 2, 159–60). A translation by Lucien Biart appeared in January 1876 in the *Revue des Deux Mondes* and was included the same year in a collection, *Une Femme Philosophe: Le Premier Amour d'Eugène Pickering,* a copy of which Constance Fenimore Woolson was still able to purchase in Bamberg in 1884 (*Letters* 3, 541, 547 n.7). James himself included the story the next year in the collection *A Passionate Pilgrim* and in 1879 in *The Madonna of the Future.* He reprinted it for the last time in the Collective Edition of 1883.

Circumstances of Composition, Sources, and Influences

On January 9, 1874, James wrote William Dean Howells from Florence in part to announce the sending under separate cover of a tale, which he stated was "unusually happy in subject" and pronounced "quite brilliant" by his brother (*Letters* 1, 424). Despite sending it in two parts he begged Howells in May, "*do*, oh do, if possible put him through in a single number," a wish not granted (*Letters* 1, 445).

Kelley places the genesis of the tale at Homburg, where James spent the summer of 1873 and where he wrote *Madame de Mauves* (160). He sets his tale in an earlier, more prosperous Homburg than the one he visited after the Franco-Prussian War had ended for a time its gambling splendor, leaving his inn "dejected and forlorn" (*Criticism* 2, 1206). McElderry notes that it is one of the few times James used Germany in his fiction, and Tintner praises the use of the resort's local color (McElderry 33; Tintner 1987, 28).

Madame Blumenthal is, as Marks has noted, an arch romantic (67–68). To Eugene, listening to her "adventures" is like "hearing the opening tumult of one of Beethoven's symphonies," an allusion Gale sees as indicating his naïveté (CT 3, 334; 138). The narrator compares her to both Bettina von Arnim and Rachel (CT 3, 301). Most pertinently, the minor character Niedermeyer describes her first novel as being "in the George Sand manner, but really out-Heroding Herod" (CT 3, 327). Marks sees her as deliberately imitating George Sand (69), but the initial resemblance, an early unfortunate marriage, would appear to have been beyond her control. Her relationship with Eugene and with the Major seem to draw partly on two of Sand's love affairs James had read of. Anastasia is seven years older than Eugene, even as George Sand was six years older than Alfred de Musset when they embarked for Italy, a tumultuous affair the end of which was to leave Musset weeping for four months upon his return to Paris (*Criticism* 2, 605–7). Her relationship with the Major, however, recalls Sand's affair with Prosper Mérimée. The Major objects to his beloved's writing: "He didn't believe in women knowing how to write at all, and it irritated him to see this inky goddess scribbling away under his nose for the press; irritated him the more that . . . he was in love with her . . ." (CT 3, 329). Similarly, James twice related the incident of Mérimée's "lively irritation" at George Sand one morning as she set to work before Mérimée had woken. James, however, is on the side of the woman who, he states, "rose early because she was pressed to write" even as Madame Blumenthal tells the Major that she "write[s] from an inner need" (*Criticism* 2, 703, 740; CT 3, 329). It is unlikely, however, that James intended to attribute to Madame Blumenthal the same genius.

Donald Stone finds the main situation—"a weak young man caught between a strong, possessive woman and an inexperienced girl"—stemming from Turgenev (190). Peterson specifies *Spring Torrents* as the Turgenev work, while altering the pattern. He sees Anastasia as combining the experienced temptress and innocent idealist in Turgenev's tale, while Pickering's fiancée remains outside the picture. Peterson judges James's work less gloomy than the Russian's, but like it simultaneously "antiromantic" and nostalgic for the lost theories of romance abandoned for a more "natural" way of life (49–53). Long proposes Irina in *Smoke* as the closest to James's "sincere attitudinizer" and notes that the setting also associates the tale with Turgenev (41).

Adams locates a source for Eugene's excessively sheltered and schooled upbringing in that of Félix in Balzac's *Le Lys dans la vallée*, which leads him, too, to fall in love with the first woman he meets (464–65). One might also point to Balzac's heroine Eugénie Grandet, who has the feminized version of Eugene's name and lives quietly. A similar situation is to be found in George Meredith's *Ordeal of Richard Feveral*. Marks points to how Richard's father, Sir Austin, looked to "a Golden Age . . . when fathers accepted their solemn responsibility and studied human nature with a scientific eye," and so ruined his son's life (65; also Wagenknecht 183).

Tintner finds a parallel for the major in Major Stultz of *The Initials* by Baroness Tautphoeus, a work read by James as a young boy, which is almost a double source, since, like this tale, it alludes to Weber's *Der Freischütz* (1989, 158). Marks takes the singing of the prayer from *Der Freischütz* as providing an alternative to the sound of gaming, and a parallel to Miss Vernor, who is compared to an "angular seraph in a medieval carving." The religious associations with Miss Vernor are carried further, according to Marks, through the recovering Eugene's admiration for a "meek-faced virgin of Hans Memling" (66–67, 70).

Tintner locates in the tale—which she calls James's only burlesque—a conflation of Shakespeare's *Romeo and Juliet*, with its young lovers and delayed letter, and *Antony and Cleopatra*, with the narrator playing Enobarbus, Madame Blumenthal a self-styled Cleopatra, and Eugene as Antony replaced by the major. Unlike the originals, all ends happily. Although, as Tintner notes, Antony and Cleopatra drop out before the conclusion, the story does not at that point lose all of the "world" encompassing breadth she locates in their romance. Homburg may be "trivial," but Eugene must still travel a long way to be united with his Juliet (1987, 23–28, 368 n.32). As a variation on the Romeo and Juliet theme, the story anticipates Rostand's *Romantics*, in which the matchmaking fathers seek to unite their children by forbidding their marriage.

Jones finds Madame Blumethal renouncing Eugene for his own good, while keeping that knowledge from him, like the heroine of Dumas's *La Dame aux camélias* (23).

Relation to Other Works

The tale is most frequently compared with its near contemporary *Madame de Mauves* (e.g., Kelley 165). Howells originally linked the two as "romantic subjects which we find less real than the author's romantic inspirations" (71). Cary links the two in terms of quality, finding Eugene like Longmore one of the few early characters "as successfully executed as it is ingeniously conceived," while Voss finds him only a sketch of the romantic deceived by Europe, better portrayed in *Madame de Mauves* (Cary 43–44; Voss 130–31). On a lesser note, Tintner notes that both works allude to Milton and Memling (1986, 32, 152). Peterson finds in both James returning to the international theme, a return Beach finds highly beneficial to "Eugene Pickering," but which Putt sees as detracting from the interest in individual character (Peterson 41; Beach 185; Putt 91).

Kelley notes that in *Roderick Hudson* the hero's experiences in Germany resemble Eugene's, and she sees James here as filling in the European education he attributes to his American heroes in "De Grey" and "Master Eustace" (165–66, 184). Kraft elaborates, comparing the German woman to Christina Light, and describing Pickering as a mixture of Roderick Hudson's energies and Longmore's fears (79–80). Roderick's struggle between art and life has often been noted, and Putt finds their split personalities the link between Benvolio and Eugene Pickering, as well as the later Hyacinth Robinson (91). Jones compares Eugene as a dominated child to Nora in *Watch and Ward*, Maisie of *What Maisie Knew*, and Pansy Osmond, whose father also selfishly shapes his child according to his narrow preconceptions (1, 25, 34). But Eugene escapes his childhood, and Moore contrasts both Eugene and Benvolio to Clifford Wentworth in *The Europeans* in their greater ability to profit from the tutelage of an older European woman (8–9). While Europe may have been too much for Roderick, the problem for Clifford may have been having to stay in Massachusetts for his education. As Buitenhuis notes, in both "Benvolio" and this tale James returns to a European setting after his previous American and realistic tale, "Professor Fargo," in order to treat a romance (74). In the end, however, Eugene sails to Smyrna for his cloistered fiancée, even as Benvolio sails to the Antipodes to reclaim his Scholastica.

McElderry finds Eugene's realization that "life is learning to know one's self" anticipating in a small way the discoveries of *The Ambassadors* (33). In discussing "unuttered utterances," Norrman links the letter here with that from Milly at the end of *The Golden Bowl*. The fact that Eugene is wrong, despite his certainty, about the message of the unopened letter casts doubt, in Norrman's view, on the accuracy of Kate and Merton's beliefs about the later unopened letter (129).

Interpretation and Criticism

Eugene declares, "Pleasure and pain are empty words to me; what I long for is knowledge,—some other knowledge than comes to us in formal, colorless, impersonal precept" (CT 5, 81). To the narrator, Eugene's "passionate consciousness" of his situation it itself "a very ardent life" (CT 3, 315). Madame Blumenthal's Cleopatra asks, "What, after all, is life but sensation, and sensation but deception?" (CT 3, 320). Naturally enough, the tale is often read as a referendum on the benefits and types of experience. Peterson reads the tale as posing the debate between "plunging" in or renouncing. Pickering, he argues, achieves the transformation from innocence to experience without a "fall." The narrator, according to Peterson, represents an equally legitimate approach, and Walter Wright finds its anticipation of later James the main significance of the tale (Peterson 51–52, 144 n.27; Wright 126–27).

The name of James's hero proclaims that he was well born. James also provided his young hero with a highly unusual upbringing, which from the start has been a focus of criticism, mostly negative. Early on, Howells objected to the excessive amount of "machinery" James used to produce Eugene's unsophistication, which could have equally and more plausibly been produced by "common conditions" in America (71–72). Fox provides some rationale by considering Eugene's early "poodle-dog" life as intended to represent America (16). Jones, on the other hand, remarks on the irony of Madame Blumenthal's taking his innocence as typically American when it is in fact highly idiosyncratic (23). Marks subordinates the issue of national identity to that of personal identity. Pickering's father may be right that independence is a "delusion," but takes too much power onto himself in treating Eugene as his own construction (66).

However representatively American Eugene may be, he encounters the Old World in the shape of Madame Blumenthal, who has herself been the source of critical disagreement. William James spoke of the tale as the "story about the ingenuous youth in Baden & the Coquette" and "the Coquette" has her firm detractors, among them Andreas, who depicts her as having "fleeced" Eugene, provoking him so as to use his reactions in her writing, and so receiving her due reward, "moral solitude" (James 226–27; Andreas 45; also Wagenknecht 183; Marks 68). Among her defenders, Peterson gives as the narrator's primary flaw his slander of Mme. Blumenthal (144 n.27). Jones attempts a reading which provides some insight to her thinking and also partly clears the narrator of Peterson's charge of slander. In Jones's reading, Eugene has fallen not among thieves, but those who respect his innocence. The narrator watches Eugene protectively but without interfering until he sees the dangerous depth of his infatuation with Madame Blumenthal. Though he, too, is impressed with her, he nevertheless appeals to her to let him go (with shades of Lambert Strether and Mme Vionnet) and she, being kindly, does so in a manner that keeps him from feeling an object of charity. In sum, they have steered him from his childhood cloister to a happy existence in the wider world (22–23). Jones perhaps does not fully credit the narrator's lingering doubts about Madame Blumenthal. Nor does the explanation entirely capture all of Madame Blumenthal's complexity, her frustration at her lot, her rapacity in her search both for experience and advantageous alliances. Early on, Howells complained that what he saw as the "tortuous workings" of her thinking responsible for her "self-contradictory behavior" toward Eugene, were unsatisfactorily indicated (72), and she remains something of an undigested fact in the tale.

Eugene is not without responsibility for his plight. Kelley finds Eugene's education harming the plausibility of events by making Eugene less rather than more likely to be taken in by Madame Blumenthal (167). But that the books he had read had been no substitute for the experience he had been deprived of is evident in how easily he is enraptured by Anastasia. At the same time, his unusual origins make him picturesque to her. As the narrator tells him afterwards, he used her "intellectually" just as she used him—it was "diamond cut diamond" (CT 3, 346). Edel notes the contrast between her European sophistication and his "deadly serious American-adolescent view" of Europe, and it is just this contrast that makes them susceptible to each other (CT 3, 9–10).

Despite the emotional turmoil he has endured, Eugene breaks at this point from the Romantic pattern, as Wagenknecht indicates, by not becoming a suicide from disappointed love (183). Instead, the exit, for whatever reasons, of Madame Blumenthal brings him to what Andreas terms "moral manhood" (45). It brings Eugene to face first himself and then his spurned fiancée, Miss Vernor of Smyrna. The locale strikes Putt and Wagenknecht as eccentric and brings in an unfortunate rhyme, as Tintner points out (Putt 93; Wagenknecht 183; Tintner 1987, 27). But that does not necessarily undo the force of the tale's resolution, which as Kraft moderately states is "not depressing" (79). After all, Miss Vernor's name and place of residence come from her father just as did Eugene's unfortunate beginnings, and she like him has declared independence from them. While Kelley judges both the fiancée and the letter incidental to the story, she admits they allow for an "interesting ending" (167–68). It is not only "interesting" but significant as it reinforces James's lesson that it is possible to overcome the conditions other people have set to one's life, and provides a reward for two people who have done so. Eugene is not Isabel returning to the prison of Rome and Osmond, but setting off for the possible beginning of a shared freedom. Indeed, though the story does not stress it, Miss Vernor's own first name is Isabel.

As Marks notes, while Pickering appears to be returning to his father's view of things, he does so now not out of duty but with open eyes (70). Marks charts his transformation from the "soundless" childhood his father crafted for him, through the music of romanticism, the risks of love and gambling, the intoxication of exuberant speech to a more mature control of language, a control that comes from within. Eugene's father was wrong to believe in complete determination; Eugene wrong to believe in complete freedom. His experience proves, however, as Marks notes, a fortunate fall (64–71). He follows in the end the advice of the narrator: "Honest love is the most convenient concentration of experience!" (CT 3, 312).

The tale's readers have generally pointed to the elaborate parallel plot as its weakness—Putt refers to it as "absurd rigamarole" (Putt 92; also McElderry 33; Beach 185). But another strain of criticism focuses on what Howells in 1875 called the story's "spirit, wit, and strength" (71). Pound picks it as the best of James's early tales (22). Kelley praises the capturing of Eugene's awkward freshness, his surprised reactions to new experiences, the naturalness of his talk, even his "big" speeches (166, 168). Kraft, too, finds the tale full of "sensitive perceptions" and "great charm and lightness" (80). It is that freshness and spirit, mirroring Eugene's surprised reactions to a new world and a determination to get the most of it, that form the story's lasting charm.

Works Cited

Primary Works

James, Henry. 1874. "Eugene Pickering." *Atlantic Monthly* 34 (October–November): 397–410, 513–26.

———. 1875. "Eugene Pickering." *A Passionate Pilgrim*. Boston: James R. Osgood, 179–259.

———. 1879. "Eugene Pickering."*The Madonna of the Future and Other Tales*. London: Macmillan.

———. 1883. "Eugene Pickering." *Collective Edition*. Vol. 14. London: Macmillan.

Secondary Works

Adams, Percy G. 1961. "Young Henry James and the Lesson of His Master Balzac." *Revue de Littérature Comparée* 35 (July–September): 458–67.

Andreas, Osborn. 1948. *Henry James and the Expanding Horizon: A Study of the Meaning and Basic Themes of James's Fiction*. Seattle: University of Washington Press.

Beach, Joseph Warren. [1918] 1954. *The Method of Henry James*. Philadelphia: Albert Saifer.

Buitenhuis, Peter. 1970. *The Grasping Imagination: The American Writings of Henry James*. Toronto: University of Toronto Press.

Cary, Elisabeth Luther. 1905. *The Novels of Henry James: A Study*. New York: Putnam's.

Fox, Hugh. 1968. *Henry James, A Critical Introduction.* Conesville, IA: John Westburg.

Gale, Robert L. [1954] 1964. *The Caught Image: Figurative Language in the Fiction of Henry James.* Chapel Hill: University of North Carolina Press.

Howells, William Dean. 1961. Review of *The Passionate Pilgrim and Other Tales.* Reprinted in *Discovery of a Genius: William Dean Howells and Henry James,* ed. Albert Mordell. New York: Twayne.

James, William. 1992. *The Correspondence of William James.* Vol. 1: *William and Henry: 1861–1884.* Ed. Ignas K. Skrupskelis and Elizabeth M. Berkeley. Charlottesville: University Press of Virginia.

Jones, Granville H. 1975. *Henry James's Psychology of Experience: Innocence, Responsibility, and Renunciation in the Fiction of Henry James.* The Hague: Mouton.

Kelley, Cornelia Pulsifer. [1930] 1965. *The Early Development of Henry James.* Urbana: University of Illinois Press.

Kraft, James. 1969. *The Early Tales of Henry James.* Carbondale: Southern Illinois University Press.

Long, Robert Emmet. 1979. *The Great Succession: Henry James and the Legacy of Hawthorne.* Pittsburgh: University of Pittsburgh Press.

McElderry, Bruce R., Jr. 1965. *Henry James.* New York: Twayne.

Marks, Patricia. 1979. "Culture and Rhetoric in Henry James's 'Poor Richard' and 'Eugene Pickering.'" *South Atlantic Bulletin* 44, no. 1: 61–72.

Moore, Susan. 1982. *The Drama of Discrimination in Henry James.* St. Lucia: University of Queensland Press.

Norrman, Ralf. 1982. *The Insecure World of Henry James's Fiction: Intensity and Ambiguity.* New York: St. Martin's.

Peterson, Dale E. 1975. *The Clement Vision: Poetic Realism in Turgenev and James.* Port Washington, NY: Kennikat.

Pound, Ezra. 1918. "Brief Note." *The Little Review* 5 (August): 6–9.

Putt, S. Gorley. 1966. *Henry James: A Reader's Guide.* Ithaca, NY: Cornell University Press. Revised in part from "'Benvolio': Everyone was a little someone else.'" In *Scholars of the Heart: Essays in Criticism,* 141–235. London: Faber, 1962.

Stone, Donald David. 1972. *Novelists in a Changing World: Meredith, James, and the Transformation of English Fiction in the 1880's.* Cambridge, MA: Harvard University Press.

Tintner, Adeline R. 1989. *The Pop World of Henry James: From Fairy Tales to Science Fiction.* Ann Arbor: UMI Research Press.

————.1987. *The Book World of Henry James: Appropriating the Classics.* Ann Arbor:

UMI Research Press. Revised from "'Eugene Pickering': Henry James' Shakespearian Burlesque." *AB Bookman's Weekly* 69, no. 13 (29 March 1982): 2430, 2432, 2434, 2436, 2438, 2440, 2442.

———. 1986. *The Museum World of Henry James*. Ann Arbor: UMI Research Press.

Voss, Arthur. 1973. *The American Short Story: A Critical Survey*. Norman: University of Oklahoma Press.

Wagenknecht, Edward. 1984. *The Tales of Henry James*. New York: Frederick Ungar.

Wright, Walter F. 1962. *The Madness of Art: A Study of Henry James*. Lincoln: University of Nebraska Press.

Europe

Publication History

"Europe" was first published as "'Europe'" in *Scribner's* in June 1899, and formed a part the next year of *The Soft Side*. James also included it—without the quotation marks—in the New York Edition. According to Anesko, the tale was originally intended for volume 14, the "international" volume, with such tales as "Pandora" and *Lady Barbarina*, but space considerations placed it in volume 16 (379).

Circumstances of Composition, Sources, and Influences

"Europe" began in 1895 with James's being "greatly struck" in hearing from Lady Playfair of "the prolongation—and the effects of it—of her aunt, old Mrs. Palfrey, of Cambridge, Mass.," the widow of historian John Gorham Palfrey. James pictures the "long, blank patience" in which Mrs. Palfrey's daughters spend their elderly lives and contemplates as a conclusion the mother's dying at the shock of learning that a daughter has died of old age (CN 117; Matthiessen xxi). In a list compiled on May 7, 1898 James spoke of the tale as *Les Vieux* or *The Waiters* (CN 169). In his preface he recalls a visit to Mrs. Palfrey, "an ancient lady whose talk, whose allusions and relics and spoils and mementoes and credentials, so to call them, bore upon a triumphant sojourn in Europe, long years before" (*Criticism* 2, 1243). This telling gives an additional theme to his tale—Europe itself (N 190–91).

Edel and Powers point as a source to an earlier notebook entry from July 27, 1890, also on the theme of Europe, that James made while at Vallombrosa. It pictures a young American who "surrounds himself with a European 'atmosphere'" through books, and who, even when offered a change to "see the realities" stays at home "held by the spell of knowing it all *that* way" (CN 55).

In the tale, Cambridge became Brookbridge. In planning for the New York Edition, James asked photographer Alvin Langdon Coburn for "an American view . . . that ought to be at Cambridge, Mass., if at all remotely findable" (*Letters* 4, 430). Both Higgins and Bogardus note the irony of such a lovely photograph serving as the introduction to such a "grim" story (674). Bogardus sees its representation of New England fences that "genteely try to keep out life" a contrast to the central symbol of the tale, Europe and its freedom (192). Still, just as the picture shows houses dappled with sunlight and shaded by leaves, the narrator originally notes the "almost pastoral sweetness" of the setting. Hudspeth notes the ironic evocation of fertility in the elms "like gigantic wheat-sheaves" (391). In *The American Scene*, James referred to the cover of the trees as "the mantle of charity" over stark New England villages. There James has the New England elms boast of their achievement and challenge the visitor to "come back in winter." To which James replies, " . . . you wouldn't, however, go back in winter on any account whatever . . ." (39–40). The narrator in "Europe" never visits in winter, but the tale shows nevertheless the bare emotional winter of the village residents that James sees lying beneath the beauty of the elms, or in Hudspeth's formulation, the interior norm of neurosis beneath the normative exterior view.

James himself sometimes spoke of Europe in quotation marks. In a late letter to his brother, for example, he speaks of America becoming to him "almost as romantic to me as 'Europe,' in dreams or in my earlier time . . . used to be" (cited Matthiessen xxii).

Austin Wright sees the tale as anticipating modern tales of the 1920s both in its "caustic" depiction of the "incomplete" "comeuppance" of Mrs. Rimmle and its treatment of "loneliness" (60, 209). More specifically, Buitenhuis compares the effect of the concluding picture of the aged Maria and her mother to the understated Gothic horror of Faulkner's "A Rose for Emily" (176). Powers, in turn, compares the "blood" Jane tastes in Europe to the blood that spills on Lucy Honeychurch's postcards in Florence in an earlier modern work, Forster's *A Room with a View*, both indicative of an encounter with "life" (77).

To Jefferson, the tale's setting in the past, "the American time," gives it the air of a legend, a Greek play of the demise of an honorable house (158). Edward Stone points to a resemblance between the extraordinary preservation of the protagonist in *The Picture of Dorian Gray* and that of the women here (1964, 152). In the three daughters' longing for Europe there is also a kinship with Chekov's *Three Sisters* and their desire for Moscow, such as Edel identifies in "Four Meetings" (CT 4, 10).

Relations to Other Works

The tale with its three daughters caught in New England and longing for Europe has been most frequently compared with the early "Four Meetings," in which Caroline Spencer yearned for Europe (e.g., CT 10, 11; McElderry 111). Ward sees in both a woman "of imagination and intelligence" frustrated in her growth by her inability to get to Europe, and notes the "irony" that in each case it is the woman's "generosity" that prevents her going, a goodness that also hampers Catherine Sloper (32–33). Similarly, Magalener and Volpe indicate that generally in James innocent but intelligent Americans can become "rich and magnificent people" by going to Europe (206). Although both tales consist of a series of meetings, Buitenhuis deems the tale superior through its greater unity of impression, provided by the narrator, and its subtler villainy (173–76). Vaid distinguishes "Europe" from both "Four Meetings" and "A Passionate Pilgrim," judging it more complex, with four equally important characters (43). Matthiessen, observing that James forbears following his heroine abroad here as he did in showing Caroline's brief hours at LeHavre, argues that the tale represents no advance in the treatment of America and that James himself saw the tale's significance in its form, not its content (xxi). He bases his argument, however, partly on James's omission of the tale from the "American" volume of the New York Edition, which appears to have been a matter of space not design. Walter Wright cites in relation to both tales an 1874 essay, "Florentine Notes," which pictures a young American reading of carnival "by a remote New England fireside," who "determines, with a heartbeat, to go and see it all—twenty years hence" (56).

Nathalia Wright classifies Jane with Gertrude Whittaker of "Poor Richard" as a spinster finding a larger world in Europe (222), a theme also seen in "The Beldonald Holbein." Buitenhuis finds the theme again in *The Ambassadors*, another common comparison (177). Bewley, for example, finds Jane's deprivation and sudden release in Strether, and before that in Roderick Hudson (235). Magalener and Volpe place it generally with the turn of the century tales of "the wasted life," such as "The Beast in the Jungle" and *The Ambassadors* (205). Strether, however, went to a very modern Europe, and one can discover some of the same danger of hanging on to the Europe of the past one sees here in the early tales "The Last of the Valerii" and "Adina," where it also interferes with human relationships.

Looking at the mother, Leyburn links the extreme satire she calls forth with that given the "Countess" in "Four Meetings" and Abel Gaw in *The Ivory*

Tower (87). Walter Wright finds Mrs. Rimmle feeding on her daughters following the pattern of *The Sacred Fount* (96). Q. D. Leavis ranks the tale as a whole with James's "painful triumphs in morbid psychology," such as *The Turn of the Screw* and *The Bostonians* (224).

Interpretation and Criticism

The tale tends to produce strong reactions, Bogardus being one of the mildest readers in speaking of it as "charming though disquieting" (192). Less affected, the *London Speaker* dismissed the tale's effects as "entirely factitious," its significances "strained" (626). More commonly, it is seen as James's black comedy, a tale that in Fadiman's formula combines humor and horror (383). Bewley finds the tale's events "grotesque, or perhaps a little monstrous" and the story itself a "very tragic and macabre comedy" (235, 237). Wagenknecht, too, noting James's pride in what he called his "obscure, or at least . . . muffled, tragedy," notes that it is a black comedy as well (118). Most of both qualities stem from the central figure, the near mythic Mrs. Rimmle. Leyburn notes how the "dreadful comedy of Mrs. Rimmle" simply intensifies the tragic situation of her daughters (86). Taking a somewhat different approach, such critics as Walter Wright and Edward Stone have attributed the story's mixed modes to a combination of realism and romanticism, Stone comparing it to a fairy tale in which the mythically old mother both enslaves and protects her children (Wright 95–96; Stone 1964, 151–52). Either view puts Mrs. Rimmle in the position of power. The position of the daughters is succinctly put by Vaid: they are "caught between the two elemental forces of life and death, between Europe and Mrs. Rimmle" (43).

Mrs. Rimmle draws strength from two sources. The first is her place as head of a New England family in a time of lingering Puritanism. The tale speaks of "puritanism refined and reclaimed," and Hudspeth, finding no effective response to Mrs. Rimmle possible, gives as the moral of the tale that the American Puritan tradition is incapable of redemption (395). To Buitenhuis, the tale illustrates the "quintessence of the New England idea of duty and conscience," virtues that here turn "deadly" (177; also Fadiman 383). As Buitenhuis emphasizes, the narrator is a New Yorker, so Brookbridge is "another world" to him (174), making him an ineffective judge of what is typically Puritan. The "second New England voice" of the narrator's sister-in-law, however, according to Hudspeth, shows by her acceptance of the behavior of the Rimmles that it is not exceptional but exemplary (390). Others, including Jefferson, have seen the tale less as exhibiting the typical operation of Puritanism than its "extreme possibilities" (156). Walter Wright sees the white-washed Puritanism the narrator at first admires yielding to its "demonic perversion" (95–96). Geismar further questions the tale's praised insight into the Puritan mind, thinking that James simply attributes to it his own sense of the bleakness of New England and concomitant desire to escape to the Old World (196–97).

It is the power of that Old World that is Mrs. Rimmle's second source of strength. James describes in his preface the irony of the mother feeding them on "the social cake" of Europe and never allowing them to experience it themselves (*Criticism* 2, 1244). Instead, Europe here, according to Putt, is what is denied rather than enjoyed, at the same time that the tale reinforces James's view that the true meaning of Europe is "freedom" (83). Fadiman points out how the mother will not deny the experience of Europe "in form" but "in fact" (384), an approach that may well be crueller. The Europe here is a Europe of imagination or memory only. As Wegelin observes, the story, despite its title, is more about Americans than Europe, the original quotation marks indicating that the only "Europe" it discusses is in "the minds of its characters," specifically the mother's, whose absurd view that Europe is only a source of "food for conversation" is contrasted with the genuine "fulfilment" Jane finally attains there (52). Similarly, Powers locates the main irony in the contrast between Mrs. Rimmle's mistaken belief that America represents "real life" with the truth that keeping her daughters in America denies them the real life they could gain in Europe (77). Both Bewley and Buitenhuis call the tale "intensely American" precisely because it is about the desire for Europe (Bewley 230; Buitenhuis 173).

While denying it to her daughters, Mrs. Rimmle takes on herself the timelessness of Europe. James observes in his preface that, in the years of the story, Europe changes, the sisters change, and only the mother remains the same (*Criticism* 2, 1244). The narrator recalls her strange attitude to time: "Mrs. Rimmle spoke of her return as of something of the year before last, but the future of her daughters was, somehow, by a different law, to be on the scale of great vistas, of endless aftertastes. I think that, without my being quite ready to say it, even this first impression of her was somewhat upsetting; there was a large placid perversity, a grim secrecy of intention, in her estimate of the ages" (CT 10, 431). Critics have picked up on the implication that her misestimates—of time, of Europe, even of her daughters' ages—are not entirely unconscious. As Jefferson remarks, the mother seems to be "secretly enjoying her position" (157–58).

The woman who wields such control over her family becomes almost superhuman or, as Wagenknecht calls her, "larger than life" (118). Buitenhuis asserts that the mother's hold is indicated by imagery rather than openly discussed, symbolism that Vaid judges the tale's chief strength (Buitenhuis 176; Vaid 49). The imagery itself, however, is far from subtle, with dramatic comparisons to a vulture, a witch, a "sovereign of indistinguishable sex," and in the end "the immemorial mummy" (CT 10, 445, 448). It also, as Hudspeth records, becomes more and more damning as the story progresses (392–93), such that Mrs. Rimmle gradually assumes, in Vaid's view, a "mythical aspect," as a "symbol of death" (49). Bewley notes the irony of this, the transformation of the mother as a life symbol into one of "life-in-death" (237). Not only is she virtually dead, but she is, in Andreas's image, like a vampire feeding on her own (37)—a reversal of the traditional image of the pelican mother who feeds her children her own flesh. Walter Wright compares her to a witch who lives off her magical power over her daughters. Yet, even as he marks the horrifying triumph of evil in the story, he cannot resist saying of Mrs. Rimmle that she is "indeed wonderful" (95–96).

Critics have come to different estimates of Mrs. Rimmle's success in keeping her amazing control. Vaid finds her terrifying fierceness the final impression of the story, only somewhat alleviated by Jane's escape (49). Often the focus is on Mrs. Rimmle's last statement, that the dead Becky is in Europe. Vaid sees it as an indication that Mrs. Rimmle has come to a "malevolently fantastic identification" of Europe and death (48). According to Buitenhuis, however, because her strength stems from her ability to deny her daughters' experience, she has lost when Jane escapes, and so can allow Becky a posthumous triumph by saying she's gone to Europe, because she herself has already won "that battle" (176). Fadiman characterizes the statement as more defensive: Mrs. Rimmle is seeking to deny any responsibility for having in effect killed her daughter (384). Austin Wright also casts it as a denial, a deliberate confusion of the fates of Jane and Becky, to hide the fact that she has actually lost her daughters (190). Leyburn grants her a larger triumph and reads the last line as a realistic touch, James letting the victimizer have the last word (87).

The daughters so victimized have also commanded their share of attention. Indeed, Vaid argues that the "disagreeable" task of portraying the mother is necessary primarily in order to show the daughters' situation (43). Gage sees the desire of the daughters for European experience simultaneously a desire to flee their identities, as confined by Brookbridge, and to come into contact with a deeper one, as represented by Europe. It seems unlikely that even such martyrs as they are, however, would wish, as Gage suggests, for the trip as a way of bringing them closer to their mother, to whom they are already suffocatingly tied. As Andreas comments, even the unrebellious Maria is "conscious of her martyrdom" (37). Gage is more on the mark in pointing to the shared identity of Europe and New England they wish to explore, however much their romantic views may cloud it (36). Bewley differentiates more between the three, seeing the sisters as representing a spectrum of "maladjustments to life, symbolized by Europe," with Rebecca and Maria the best representations of the story's tragedy. He notes that Rebecca, the "most attractive" sister, dies while Maria replaces her mother as Brookbridge's "symbol of life-in-death" (237–38). More positively, Vaid comments on how the experience of Europe, even by proxy, brings out Becky "metaphorically and literally" as she is seen outside the Rimmle house for the first time after Jane's trip to Europe (47). Similarly Hudspeth traces how James contrasts Becky's generosity toward Jane with the grasping nature of her mother, even as they become nearly identical in their great age, and sees her as receiving some compensation in the understanding of the narrator (394).

The one who escapes, Jane, has received various appraisals. One school sees her behavior as that of a pathetic old maid making a "deranged and drunken grab at life" (Stone 1964, 151–52; Stone 1969, 11–12; Bewley 237). Wegelin and Hudspeth, however, picture Jane enjoying a new, vital life abroad (Wegelin 52; Hudspeth 393). Their view seems more in keeping with the narrator's picture of her as "a well-preserved woman" enjoying "a sort of rich, ripe *seconde jeunesse* by the Arno" (CT 10, 448).

James boasted of the tale's brevity in the New York Edition preface, of its transformation through the "innumerable repeated chemical reductions and condensations" that make the short story "like the hard, shining sonnet, one of the most indestructible" literary forms (*Criticism* 2, 1244–45). The review-er for *The London Speaker* was not impressed, unfavorably likening the story to an "anatomical study by an old master" (626). Otherwise, most critics have concurred, praising the tale's concentration and richness (e.g., Vaid 44–45). Ford Madox Ford enthusiastically named it as "that most wonderful of all sto-ries" (81). In a more focused analysis, Hudspeth finds James's concision par-ticularly appropriate for conveying the contrast between the outer and inner life of New England as seen in the Rimmles. He notes how the narrator, who speaks for the larger experience of Europe, originally finds the family simply comic, but then comes to recognize the tension beneath their surface calm. All the big events, Hudspeth observes, occur in between the narrator's visits, a fact that underlines that such events are "hidden," muffled beneath layers of Puritan pretense.

Han also examines the form of the tale, citing James's statement on organ-ic unity that "in proportion as it lives it will be found . . . that in each of the parts there is something of each of the other parts." He finds "Europe," which he recommends as a good introduction to James for students, a per-fect example. In his reading, the story's first line spoken by Mrs. Rimmle—"Our feeling is, you know, that Becky *should* go"—sets up a series of possibilities that, increasingly complicated by variations on the phrase throughout the story, are never fully resolved until the last line—"To Europe"—completes the thought of the first in a manner impossible to have anticipated. Oddly, he does not mention the title, which prepares for the first line and anticipates the last.

Much of the credit for the tale's brevity goes, as Vaid has demonstrated, to the use of the narrator and as *ficelle* his sister-in-law (45–46). Macnaughton assigns the sister-in-law a larger role than other critics, seeing the narrator ignoring her statements that could alter his preconceptions either of the mother's enormity or Jane's achievement (157, 178 n.15). There is little in the tale to support this, however, and in general the narrator has escaped the questioning often given James's narrators, although Buitenhuis points out how the narrator's "complacent superiority . . . is given a delicate rebuke" in Jane's quoting of Byron and speaks of his "cat-like curiosity" to see the end of the situation (175–76). Most likely, critics recognize that he would stand little chance in defying the formidable Mrs. Rimmle. Instead, his role is usually seen formally, Buitenhuis finding his "retrospective consciousness" providing the tale's unity (174). Hudspeth notes, too, the way the presence of the narrator protects against a sentimental reaction to the sisters' plight (391).

The story is unusual for James in that it seems to show renunciation as absurd. The goodness of the daughters simply feeds the selfishness of the mother. When the sister-in-law objects to the narrator's lamenting that the sisters are so "infernally good" because it is "what keeps them up," he replies that it's "what keeps *her* up too" (CT 10, 435). And so it does. Mrs. Rimmle is a cruel idol who will accept all the sacrifices given her, and in the fate of the daughters, the tale seems to indicate such an idol is not worth the sacrifice.

Works Cited

Primary Works

James, Henry. 1899. "'Europe.'" *Scribner's Magazine* 25 (June): 753–62.

———. "'Europe.'" *The Soft Side*. London: Methuen; New York: Macmillan, 30–51.

———. 1909. "Europe." *The Novels and Tales of Henry James*. Vol. 16, 339–69. New York Edition. New York: Scribner's.

———. 1968. *The American Scene*. Introduction and notes by Leon Edel. Bloomington: Indiana University Press.

Secondary Works

Andreas, Osborn. 1948. *Henry James and the Expanding Horizon: A Study of the Meaning and Basic Themes of James's Fiction*. Seattle: University of Washington Press.

Anesko, Michael. 1986. *"Friction with the Market": Henry James and the Profession of Authorship*. New York: Oxford University Press.

Anon. 1900. Review of *The Soft Side*. *The London Speaker*. As reprinted in *Current Literature* 29 (November): 626–27.

Bewley, Marius. 1959. *The Eccentric Design: Form in the Classic American Novel*. New York: Columbia University Press. Revised from "Henry James and 'Life.'" *Hudson Review* 11 (1958): 183–84.

Bogardus, Ralph F. 1984. *Pictures and Texts: Henry James, A. L. Coburn and New Ways of Seeing in Literary Culture*. Ann Arbor: UMI Research Press.

Buitenhuis, Peter. 1970. *The Grasping Imagination: The American Writings of Henry James*. Toronto: University of Toronto Press.

Fadiman, Clifton, ed. 1948. *The Short Stories of Henry James*. New York: Modern Library.

Ford, Ford Madox. 1913. *Henry James: A Critical Study*. London: Martin Secker.

Gage, Richard P. 1988. *Order and Design: Henry James' Titled Story Sequences*. New York: Peter Lang.

Geismar, Maxwell. 1963. *Henry James and the Jacobites*. Boston: Houghton Mifflin.

Han, Pierre. 1970. "Organic Unity in 'Europe.'" *South Atlantic Bulletin* 35, no. 3: 40–41.

Higgins, Charles. "Photographic Aperture: Coburn's Frontispieces to James's New York Edition." *American Literature* 53: 661–75.

Hudspeth, Robert N. 1975. "A Hard, Shining Sonnet: The Art of Short Fiction in James's 'Europe.'" *Studies in Short Fiction* 12: 387–95.

Jefferson, D. W. 1964. *Henry James and the Modern Reader*. New York: St. Martin's.

Leavis, Q. D. 1947. "Henry James: The Stories." *Scrutiny* 14 (Spring): 223–29. Reprinted in *Collected Essays*. Vol. 2: *The American Novel and Reflections of the European Novel*, ed. G. Singh, 177–84. Cambridge: Cambridge University Press.

Leyburn, Ellen Douglass. 1968. *Strange Alloy: The Relation of Comedy to Tragedy in the Fiction of Henry James*. Chapel Hill: University of North Carolina Press.

McElderry, Bruce R., Jr. 1965. *Henry James*. New York: Twayne.

Macnaughton, W. R. 1975. "The Narrator in Henry James's *The Sacred Fount*." In *Literature and Ideas in America: Essays in Memory of Harry Hayden Clark*. Ed. Robert Falk, 155–81. Athens: Ohio University Press.

Magalaner, Marvin, and Edmund L. Volpe, eds. 1961. "Henry James." *Twelve Short Stories*. New York: Macmillan, 205–9.

Matthiessen, F. O., ed. 1947. *The American Novels and Stories of Henry James*. New York: Knopf.

Powers, Lyall H. 1970. *Henry James: An Introduction and Interpretation*. New York: Holt, Rinehart.

Putt, S. Gorley. 1966. *Henry James: A Reader's Guide*. Ithaca, NY: Cornell University Press.

Stone, Edward. 1969. *A Certain Morbidness: A View of American Literature*. London: Feffer & Simons; Carbondale: Southern Illinois University Press.

———. 1964. *The Battle and the Books: Some Aspects of Henry James*. Athens: Ohio University Press.

Vaid, Krishna B. 1964. *Technique in the Tales of Henry James*. Cambridge, MA: Harvard University Press.

Wagenknecht, Edward. 1984. *The Tales of Henry James*. New York: Frederick Ungar.

Ward. J. A. 1961. *The Imagination of Disaster: Evil in the Fiction of Henry James*. Lincoln: University of Nebraska Press.

Wegelin, Christof. 1958. *The Image of Europe in Henry James*. Dallas: Southern Methodist University Press.

Wright, Austin McGiffert. 1961. *The American Short Story in the Twenties*. Chicago: University Press of Chicago.

Wright, Nathalia. 1965. *American Novelists in Italy, The Discoverers: Allston to James*. Philadelphia: University of Pennsylvania Press.

Wright, Walter F. 1962. *The Madness of Art: A Study of Henry James*. Lincoln: University of Nebraska Press.

The Figure in the Carpet

Publication History

"The Figure in the Carpet" appeared in January–February 1896, the first issues of *Cosmopolis*, the first of two stories James published in the short-lived journal, whose editor, F. Ortmanns, had requested a tale from him in November 1895 (CN 143). *Cosmopolis* was, in Gohdes's estimate, "perhaps the most ambitious magazine of the century." Calling itself an "international review," it was published by T. Fisher Unwin and run primarily from Britain and the Continent, but it also had a New York agent (57, 62). It may have been too ambitious: James would recall its slowness paying him as late as 1910 (*Letters* 4, 544). "The Figure in the Carpet" appeared again that year in the collection *Embarrassments*. Later James included it in both the New York Edition and the *Uniform Tales*.

Circumstances of Composition, Sources, and Influences

While at Torquay on October 24, 1895, James recorded the "little subject" in the idea of an author whose works "contain a very beautiful and valuable, very interesting and remunerative *secret*, or latent intention, for those who read them with a right intelligence—who see *into* them, as it were—bring to the perusal of them a certain perceptive sense." The novels have "art and style and skill" but more particularly "this interior thought—this special *beauty* (that is mainly the just word) that pervades and controls and animates them." Most of the rest of the extensive first entry is devoted to working out the sequence of knowledge sought, shared or withheld that makes up the action of the story. The narrator, at this point, is a critic who sticks to a "vulgar explanation" while his friends search, but eventually succumbs to his unsatisfiable curiosity (CN 136–39). Earlier, as Lock notes, James had recorded the names of Vereker and Corvick, in lists of possible character names (159).

In early November back in London James decided to write up the tale for *Cosmopolis*, sketching out the incidents in more detail, and later in the month recording that he had written three-fourths of the tale, keeping a sharp eye on length. Aiming for 11,000 words, he brought it in at nearly 14,000 (CN 143–44).

As usual, James has been identified with his fictional author. In 1904 Claude Bragdon indicated that if the tale had been written after his most recent novels, it could have been taken as a "hint at his own predicament," a statement that indicates, perhaps surprisingly, that it would not have been necessary earlier (146). Similarly, van Cromphout sees Vereker's "predicament" as James's, James's art being so intricate, so subtle, so new that it "could not possibly be appreciated by the elegant but superficial impressionistic criticism of the last decades of his life," a fact James recognized, and which van Cromphout sees rectified by the more modern "rigorously analytic" criticism (140). Still, according to Segal, Vereker, like James, "ultimately reconciles himself" to being misunderstood (109). Swan, however, distinguishes between the two writers, saying James's "meaning is there to be seen." Vereker's meaning "dies with him" (1948, 10). The prefaces to the New York Edition are, according to Edel, James's remedy for the critical incomprehension of his aims, and the edition itself is constructed according to a "ruling theory" (*Life* 1, 262; *Life* 626–27). Cowdery juxtaposes the figure of Vereker with the James of the prefaces—an eager "enthusiast" but also a "punster forced finally to explain the answers to his riddles" (34).

Kanzer takes a psychoanalytic approach to Vereker's resemblance to James. He agrees with Vereker that every writer has a "figure," and argues that their figure is a varying treatment "of a single theme which attracts him and is rooted in an infantile fixation that he seeks to master repetitively in his phantasies." For both James and Vereker, he states, the figure was "joy," what James called "felt life." James himself, he continues, gained such joy through his work, which was to him "more real than life itself." The plot of "The Figure in the Carpet" he sees rehearsing the "child's traditional search for sexual information" and repression of it. Vereker takes the role of the father, and the critics represent Henry, William, and Alice, who seek their father's favor through "erudition." While Kanzer asserts that James had in general worked out a satisfactory mastery of life through art, he argues that at the time of this tale, given his unsuccessful playwriting, his satisfaction in art was "gravely threatened." In such tales as "The Figure in the Carpet" and "The Middle Years," then, one sees "strongly regressive" doubts and "a desire for more direct libidinal gratifications" taking the form even of "suicidal phantasies" in all the deaths of writers. The solution, however, for James at the time, according to Kanzer, was precisely these "eroticized" deaths, which, combined with the "passionate adoration of the few" in the tales created a "cult" in which he could, by "bringing his readers to life and dying exhibitionistically before them," achieve satisfaction. Eventually, through fiction, Kanzer concludes, James discovered and accepted "the figure in his own life."

Walter E. Anderson also offers a psychological reading that seems to imply that James's "poetics of seeing"—in different terms his "almost unqualifed quest for esoteric sexual knowledge"—is the figure (529–30). Quentin Anderson compares Vereker's "organ of life" or "heart" both with the concept James took from his father that a man is a "house of life" and with James's own sense of the "house of fiction" (168–70).

Edel notes the anticipation of the title and something of the concept of the tale in an 1880 story "Miss Grief" by Constance Fenimore Woolson written shortly before she met James, in which an author trying to edit out a character from the play of a woman writer friend discovers that "to take him out was like taking out one especial figure in a carpet: that is impossible unless you unravel the whole." Edel sees the tale reflecting both James's discouragement at the critical misunderstanding of his work and his fear that he had misunderstood Woolson's "secret" (*Life* 2, 416; *Life* 4,147, 150; also Boren 1982, 465).

The phrase "the figure in the carpet" was a common one with James, as was, Finch notes, the image of the pearls on a string, which Chambers finds "rather banal" (Finch 99; Chambers 160). Gale comments that James appears to have valued pearls even over diamonds, associating them with works of art (188). In "The Middle Years," Dencombe describes the work he will still do as having "strings of pearls . . . between the columns of the temple" (CT 9, 70). (See also "Glasses.") Rawlings points to the image of the figure in James's commentary on Balzac: "the figured tapestry, all over-scored with objects in fine perspective, which symbolizes to me (if we may have a symbol) the last word of the achieved fable. Such a tapestry, with its wealth of expression of its subject, with its myriad ordered stitches, its harmonies of tone and felicities of taste, is a work, above all, of closeness" (xv). In his essay on *The Tempest*, James refers to "the figured tapestry, the long arras that hides him," an odd invoking of Polonius that suggests the writer hiding behind his work (*Criticism* 1, 1220). He used the term of more than literature. In 1904 he wrote of New England with its "scattered wild apples . . . like figures in the carpet" (*Life* 593). In a letter to Wharton in 1907, he speaks of her "Dear old Aubusson carpet—what a more and more complex minuet it will see danced, with the rich Oriental note of Rosa [Fitz-James] flashing through (doubtless more closely still) & binding & linking the figures!" (*Letters* 4, 462). In 1892 James himself was called by Henry Adams "only a figure in the same old wallpaper" (*Life* 4, 57).

In January 1892 Charlotte Perkins Gilman's "The Yellow Wallpaper" centered on "one of those sprawling, flamboyant patterns committing every artistic sin" and the struggle of the woman, a first-person narrator as here, who watches it to focus on "a strange, provoking, formless sort of figure" behind it. In the process, as she watches the figure become a woman wanting to get out, she projects herself into the entrapped figure and ends in near madness. A more comic mingling of pattern and person is in Mark Twain's "Story of the Old Ram" from *Roughing It* (1872). In it a man falls into the machinery at a carpet factory. At the funeral they attach a sign to his remains—the carpet—designating it "sacred to the memory of fourteen yards of three-ply carpet containing all that was mortal" of William Wheeler (257).

While Chambers compares Vereker to Poe's Dupin, Krupnick sees James's heroes more like Hawthorne's, both in their curiosity and their "mixed desire and dread" of the "dark lady" heroines, attributes that stem in turn from the two authors' "mingling of prurient curiosity and puritan restraint" (Chambers 161). At the same time, while the "self-parodic" picture of the author makes Krupnick think of Joyce and Mann, he finds James's "skepticism" different from the modern version in Mann or Conrad. Instead, its roots are in the "fanatical urge to demystification" of nineteenth-century American Romanticism seen also in the deflating of appearance offered in Poe's *Arthur Gordon Pym*, *Moby-Dick*, and *The Red Badge of Courage* (169, 174, 176).

In his 1866 review of "The Novels of George Eliot," James states that "the critic's first duty in the presence of an author's collective works is to seek out some key . . . some indication of his ruling theory," a comment Edel takes as an indication of an early interest in the idea of the "figure" (*Life* 1, 262). Citing the same review, Donald Stone sees the idea as one James later abandoned and then satirized in this tale (182). If so, the essay on Eliot was an appropriate place for the misfired summons as it is her character Casaubon who seeks in vain a Key to All Mythologies, a resemblance noted by Lock (161). Within the tale, the narrator compares Gwendolen to "the grim gamblers at Monte Carlo," and Lainoff uses the analogy to compare her to another grim gambler, Gwendolen of *Daniel Deronda* (1962). Salmon also sees a parallel, although she finds the key point that both heroines change (803 n.16). Gossman compares the "beauteous and highflown" Gwendolen "in her heroics about the narrator's possible insult to 'the Dead'" to "Jinny-Gwinny" Dubedat in Shaw's *The Doctor's Dilemma* (22).

The narrator asks Vereker if the key might be something in the style, "Perhaps it's a preference for the letter P!" he "profanely asks" (CT 9, 284). Although much has been made by some critics of his choice of the letter P, the narrator's recitation of "Papa, potatoes, prunes" comes straight from the genteel Mrs. General in Dickens's *Little Dorrit*, who advocates "Papa, potatoes, poultry, prunes, and prism" as "very good words for the lips."

Corvick searching for the figure seems to the narrator like "the maniacs who embrace some bedlamitical theory of the cryptic character of Shakespeare," but Corvick tells the narrator that "if we had Shakespeare's own word for his being cryptic he would immediately have accepted it. . . . we had nothing but the word of Mr Snooks" (CT 9, 291–92). Of the two Oscar Wilde stories—"The Model Millionaire" and "The Portrait of W. H."—in which Roditi detects "aesthetic ambiguities" similar to James, the second chronicles a quest for the identity of the dedicatee of Shakespeare's sonnets. Roditi judges Wilde's story superior in its detailed examination of the poet's work, in contrast to the skimpy description accorded the works of Vereker, which, he argues, leaves the reader with little interest in the search for their meaning (1949, 55; [1947] 1986, 73–75).

Powers connects what he sees as the tale's selection of style as the signal mark of a writer's work with the doctrines of Flaubert (1969, 16). Chambers compares the tale to Flaubert's "Un cœur simple," although there it was society that frustrated and art that consoled, and here it seems the opposite (178). Lock discerns in Balzac's "Facino Cane" a similar opposition of "depth and surface" in the search of a superior "narrator-seer" for the answer to a riddle, although he argues that James is parodying the theme of special, hidden knowledge (170–71).

If the figure is only a pretense on the part of Vereker, writes Wirth-Nesher, the tale becomes a "literary version" of "The Emperor's New Clothes," but with the emperor aware of his nakedness (124). Lock speaks of Corvick and Gwendolen as "a modern version of Paolo and Francesca," who "succumb to the desire of the text" (161).

In the original magazine version of the tale, Vereker said to the narrator, "I do it in my way . . . You don't do it in yours." In the New York Edition it became "I do it in my way . . . Go *you* and don't do it in yours." Matthiessen, however, in his edition omits the "don't" (289). At any rate, the revised version of the injunction recalls the concluding "Go thou and do likewise" from the parable of the good Samaritan, a parable that enjoins a compassion little evident in the tale.

The critics in the tale, according to Quentin Anderson, belong in Dante's limbo "where without hope one lives in desire" (149). Corvick, in Kanzer's view, resembles Oedipus as he faces the riddle of sexual "knowledge" (342–43). Gwendolen herself quotes Virgil when she receives the telegram from Corvick announcing that he has found the figure, telling the narrator, *"Vera incessu patuit dea!"* The line refers to Aeneas's recognition of his mother, Venus. Powers argues, however, against interpreting the allusion as identifying the figure with "a message about love," asserting that James identified Venus with art and noting that Aeneas recognizes Venus by the *"style* of her movement," which Kermode translates as "gait" (1970, 103; Kermode 453 n.3). Weber cites Aeneas's reproachful response to Venus, "Why do you mock your son so often and so cruelly—with these lying apparitions? Why can't I ever join you, hand to hand, to hear, to answer you with honest words," which he notes expresses the desire of both the narrator and Corvick, and the desire of Iser's reader, who seeks a linking with the text (213).

Corvick's book on Vereker "was to have been a supreme literary portrait, a kind of critical Vandyke or Velasquez" (CT 9, 307). Deeming Corvick "arrogant," Gale declares that in James, Vandykes are generally associated with "clever but unpleasant persons," for example Madame de Bellegarde of *The American* (124–25). Chambers, however, sees the metaphor making his book, "in intention, a work of art" (179 n.6).

Tintner picks up on Deane's looking at the narrator "like a dim phrenological bust" to connect the search for the figure and phrenology, noting that Vereker spoke of the figure as the "organ of life," and that while in phrenology bumps stand for different "organs," there is no all-inclusive organ of life. As a result, the narrator like a pseudo-scientist is missing the true meaning while staring at meaningless small clues (1989, 165–66).

Blackmur compares the tale to Kafka "manqué, the exasperation of the mystery without the presence of the mystery, or a troubled conscience without any evidence of guilt" (82). More positively, Gossman compares the "organ of life" mentioned in the tale to Robert Frost's "felt thought" and Coleridge's "truth carried alive into the heart" (21). Powers sees the issues of "identity and self-reliance" in the tale figuring also in James Baldwin's *Another Country* (1984, 655).

Edward Stone calls attention to the appearance of the names Vereker and Deane in James Thurber's 1932 parody "Something to Say," which he argues draws mainly on "The Coxon Fund," and Thurber's more sustained 1949 parody entitled "A Final Note on Chanda Bell" (174–75, 178–80). In the latter, the narrator—named Thurber—is a critic who is the authority on the obscure writer Bell, a woman who believes "only the uncomfortable are capable of pure attention" and who taunts him, "You have found the figure . . . but have you found the carpet?" The narrator wonders if she has drawn him "into the glittering web of a monstrous deceit, in order to destroy, by proxy and in effigy, the entire critical profession." After her death, the narrator continues to search for the proof of whether he is "an egregious ass or a uniquely perceptive individual."

Even as the figure became a recurrent phrase for James, it has become a household term for critics. The tale, as Matthiessen puts it, has "yielded a symbol" (1944, *Major* 42). The phrase has been used to discuss many writers, even Lenin and Tolstoy, and Edel sees the tale as saying that every serious writer has a discernible "figure in the carpet" to his works if the critic will pay the proper attention (Macherey 127; CT 9, 8). More particularly, Matthiessen ties the phrase to the new textual criticism of his time, which he sees as stemming from James and points to T. S. Eliot's use of the term in his introduction to Wilson Knight's book on Shakespeare. In that introduction, Eliot had spoken of James as well as George Eliot as novelists in whose works, like Shakespeare's, was discernible what Eliot called a "pattern of the carpet" (xiii). Gossman sees it applying not only to Knight's criticism but that of Robert Heilman as well as the fiction of C. P. Snow (21). Ironically, André Gide, whose use of the term Matthiessen cites, declared James had no such "figure" in his work (1944, "Portrait" 7; Gide 2, 409, 3,111; Lee 6 n.6).

Relation to Other Works

Commenting on the imagistic titles of such late James works as *The Wings of the Dove*, *The Golden Bowl*, *The Sacred Fount*, "The Beast in the Jungle," and "The Figure in the Carpet," Markow-Totevy sees the titles representing the greater symbolism of the works themselves. In them, the characters struggle with the problems of life "surrounded by the hidden, dense universe of portents, symbolic connexions and forebodings" (134). The struggles here are depicted through the eyes of a nameless first-person narrator, and Salmon observes that each time James used such a figure, as also in *The Sacred Fount* and *The Turn of the Screw*, he produced "a highly controversial work" (794). Rimmon, however, distinguishes this tale from the other two, arguing that in this story it is not the narrator's veracity which is ambiguous, but the existence of the figure, that is the veracity of Vereker and Corvick. The narrator is but "one of the testing figures," although in all three works the solution of the riddle is frustrated by a "gap" (1977, 102; 1973, 197).

Many critics have remarked the resemblance to *The Sacred Fount*, which contains, as Edel notes, the same kind of search and frustration (*Life* 4, 150). Stevenson puts the two works in the same category as the ghost stories, seeing the answer to the "symbolic puzzle" here "coincident with the unanswerableness of life" (138). The narrators in both, Levy observes, suffer from a "terrible psychic impotence" and are examples of "James's obsessed demons . . . who frantically pry and fumble at a door which will admit them to some charmed circle." He marks an additional suggestion of *The Sacred Fount* in Gwedolen's "increasing bloom" after remarriage (461–63). Segal contrasts the two searches, pointing out that the narrator in *The Sacred Fount* has already deduced his "figure in the carpet" and is looking simply for further proof, and that he is dealing with people, not books. Indeed, she compares the narrator in *The Sacred Fount* to Corvick, not the narrator here because he not only wants to solve the problem, but also wants to solve it the "right" way. Both searches, however, are directed outward and so remain unresolved, in contrast to the "inner-directed" search in "The Beast in the Jungle," which comes to a resolution (147, 153, 212). In addition to the first two, Levy points to several other untrustworthy narrators in James characterized by a "brisk impertinence of tone," a sense of superiority, and "sporadic maliciousness" in their prying—in *The Aspern Papers*, *The Turn of the Screw*, and "The Patagonia" (462). Blackall adds the narrator of "The Private Life" to the list of obsessed searchers, and observes that in "The Figure in the Carpet," *The Aspern Papers*, and *The Sacred Fount*, the curiosity of the narrator, once simply "functional," becomes "an obsession which is psychologically interesting" (162–65).

In both "The Figure in the Carpet" and *The Turn of the Screw*, Vaid observes, the narrator plays a "dual role" as storyteller and participant (90–91). The two tales are further linked, writes Kappeler, by "complexity of plot and obsession with an impenetrable secret" (172). The unspeakable horror James wished his readers to imagine, as Horne indicates, becomes the unnamed figure here (89 n.2). Perhaps for those reasons, as Hutchinson remarks, both stories are read in two opposed ways: apparitionist—what is the figure?—and nonapparitionist —*is* there a figure? (62–63). The narrator here, like the governess, and like John Marcher, Irwin contends, chases an abstraction that may or may not exist, encouraging the reader to follow, a result "very much akin to inventing your own ghost" (21-23).

Gwendolen says of the triumphant Corvick that the figure "simply sprung out at him like a tigress out of the jungle" (CT 9, 297). The similarity of the image to that in "The Beast in the Jungle" has been frequently noted (e.g., Tyler 37). Others point to thematic similarities as well. Lainoff argues that with Corvick's death, he, like May and Milly Theale, "bears to his grave a secret of existence the loss of which leaves his survivors the poorer." The critics, he continues, are like Marcher "ungiving" (1961, 40, 45). Levy focuses just on the narrator as a man who, like Marcher, cannot see what is before him— Marcher his fate, the narrator the figure (463). In both tales, according to Krupnick, James shows "how a man's posture toward experience can become his destiny." Both Marcher and the narrator are "narcissistic," keeping themselves at a distance from life. They give themselves over only to the "compulsion to know" and so experience "yearning and dread" at their fate. The fate of each meanwhile is connected to a woman, and frustrated by her death and the loss of her "precious life-giving knowledge" (174–75).

Such compulsion and such narcissism are also generally attributed to the narrator in *The Aspern Papers*, and many have remarked on the resemblance, particularly on the willingness of both men to contemplate marriage for the sake of gaining a literary secret (e.g., *Life* 4, 149; Lainoff 1961, 41; Labrie 161; Levy 461; Geismar 138; Rimmon 1973, 202; Cox 501–2; Kermode 27). Rimmon points out that both narrators attribute to the women at the time a new "brightness" or "bloom" as if to rationalize or make palatable their consideration (1977, 108–9). Nevertheless, as Wirth-Nesher observes, it is their very subordination of life to literature that "severs literature from its source in passion and in life," which hampers their search (124). Krupnick takes the narrator's "vexed relation" to Gwendolen as the most important "element" in the tale, and sees him and the narrator in *The Aspern Papers* as "parasites of the literary life" who "cannot love," who remain baffled by the concept of male power, and so "misunderstand the meaning of art" (171, 175, 178). While the two narrators are like others of the middle period in *The Turn of the Screw* and "The Lesson of the Master" "agent-narrators" rather than simply "witness-narrators," their searches being the theme of the story, Segal writes, they are still "unappeased" at the end (74, 91). Jones names John Berridge of "The Velvet Glove" as another frustrated searcher (234–35). Bell considers such frustration the natural result of "interpretative compulsion," and sees James demonstrating in *The Aspern Papers* and "The Beast in the Jungle" that such a belief in a "secret design and significance" to life or to a life's work is necessarily illusory (44–45). Quentin Anderson sees a similar warning in the "portrait theme" of *The Aspern Papers* and "The Figure in the Carpet" where the wanting of form in place of life shows a "spiritual greed," a greedy "curiosity" he finds also among the journalists of *The Reverberator* and "Flickerbridge" (148).

Such curiosity is, however, perhaps natural, given, as Swan observes "how often" James "refuses to enlighten us about certain things we are most anxious to know," including "what is evil" in the works of the author of *Beltraffio*, what Miles did at school, and what the "figure in the carpet" is (1948, 14). Similarly, McWhirter adds his endorsement to Todorov, finding most of James's works built on "the unveiling of *some* hidden truth," whether a hidden liason such as Osmond and Merle's, the bad behavior of the Bellegardes, or the "figure in the carpet" of this text (153). Walter Wright traces the Jamesian fascination with "guessing" and the errors it produces back to "A Bundle of Letters" and forward to *The Awkward Age*, *The Golden Bowl*, and *In the Cage* (128). *In the Cage* is, according to Chambers, another example of a Jamesian work where the central reflector is "excluded" from the sexual world as is "The Lesson of the Master" (169–70). Kanzer earlier saw the hidden knowledge in James as primarily a sexual knowledge, and asserts that James shows in his work his envy of women's greater access to it—the masculine is "creative" while the feminine is "experiencing"—by his criticism of women writers in "Greville Fane," "The Next Time," and "The Death of the Lion." The same concern, argues Kanzer, lies behind James's depiction in

"The Madonna of the Future" of an artist ruined by his need to idealize women, and in "The Story in It" the need for the sheltered Maud—whom he calls a writer—to write works of "substitute experiences in living and loving." To such as Maud, however, writes Kanzer, James gave his sympathy (346–47).

In *The American*, James described Tom Tristram in Paris as if standing before a painting "vaguely looking at it, but much too near to see anything but the grain of the canvas," a failure in perception Recchia compares to that of the narrator here (362). Strether of *The Ambassadors*, on the other hand, according to Krupnick, "does come through." He is still, however, "isolated from relationship" and confined to seeing, giving to the work a "lingering sense of pain and loss" in its depiction of man's "awe before the great world" (179–80). Horne compares the narrator to Mrs. Bridgenorth in "The Tone of Time" and the Princess Casamassima as a striver for a goal undone by his own efforts, his inappropriate methods (87). Krook sees Maggie's words to her husband to "*Find out . . . Find out for yourself,*" recalling both Vereker's injunction to the narrator and the thrust of the tale as a whole (315).

Both "The Figure in the Carpet" and *The Portrait of a Lady*, writes Johnson, are "told with the unveiling of a hidden truth in mind." Johnson refers to James's comment that it might be better that "the exposure of Mme Merle should never be complete" because "the *whole* of anything is never told," to see in both works the "theme of the resistance of character to interpretation." In *The Portrait of a Lady*, mystery becomes "a form of sanctity," a way of protecting a character. In both works, knowledge is difficult to gain, and once attained, unnamable. At the same time, Johnson sees Ralph's relationship to Isabel as a "muted form" of the narrator's obsession with Gwendolen (230–45). Labrie offers a comparison between the narrator and Osmond, each man a "critic/consumer" who focuses on art, in contrast to the "artist/producer" Vereker who also values life (163).

Others have focused on the relationships with the other artist tales. Rawlings compares Corvick's possible "communion with an author and his intention" with that seen in "Nona Vincent" and "The Middle Years," noting the dependence of "creative writing" on "creative reading" (xv–xvi). Voss, however, looks at Dr. Hugh's initial missing of Dencombe's point as an indication that even sincere admirers may initially fail to give the kind of reading James felt a true artist deserved, an achievement both Dr. Hugh and some of the readers here attain ultimately (139). Segal points to the similarity with "The Lesson of the Master" in the "perfectly ambiguous situation" (151). Labrie sees the wedded Corvicks becoming like St. George "too immersed in life to produce" (166). Both Vereker and St. George, according to Wirth-Nesher, are "temperamental and self-contradictory," and both tales pose problems of interpretation focused on questions of intention that serve as a "metaphor of all human interaction" (123–26). The *Athenaeum* linked the tale with "The Next Time"—as well as with Flaubert—in its protest against the "crass ignorance and carelessness of the public," their "dislike and even distrust" of high art even when armed with critical "jargon" (158). In both Edel sees James expressing his bitterness at the misunderstanding of his own work (*Life* 3, 374).

"The Next Time," "The Figure in the Carpet," and "The Death of the Lion" are all, according to Wallace, "structured around a central extended 'joke'" and express their "positive theme[s]" through negative statements. Unlike the narrator in "The Death of the Lion," however, the narrator in "The Figure in the Carpet" does not renounce his intentions of self-advancement (162, 174, 178). Segal comments on how the narrators of such literary tales are "fully conscious of their narrative role, in which they frankly delight" (111). Labrie focuses on the similarity between Gwendolen and George Corvick and the narrator and Fanny in "The Death of the Lion." Both the figure and the lost manuscript, he says, "become submerged in the general intensity of the love between the characters." The literary prizes seem increasingly unreal and valueless, even to the reader, in the "warm atmosphere" such love creates (165). George and Gwendolen adopt the attitude of Fanny, Powers notes, leaving the writer alone while concentrating on his works, satisfying the need for the "personal" in their marriage. The narrator, on the other hand, while he avoids a concentration on Vereker the man is inadequate in the "limp curiosity" he accords his work. The tale as a whole, however, Powers asserts, focuses on the "world" harassing the artist, rather than the artist himself (1961; 1969, 16; 1970, 102–3).

Other critics make more general connections between the tale and James's artistic theory. Beach argues that James may well have put in his tales ideas "modesty and pride forbade him to let us have straight from himself" (145). Similarly, Cowie finds James's theory of literature partly deducible from his works "The Figure and the Carpet" and *The Sacred Fount* in particular (857 n.115). Matthiessen argues that we can arrive at James's "philosophy of life" only by "apprehending the pattern of his work as a whole" as "suggested" in this tale (1947, 245). More particularly, Labrie compares Vereker's view of art with that in James's "The Art of Fiction," citing James's statement that "a Novel is in its broadest definition a personal, a direct impression of life" and that "form . . . is to be appreciated after the fact "as similar to Vereker's view on the close connection of art and life (162). Matthiessen links James's "plea for discrimination" with that in his lecture on Balzac, condemning the literary world's "production untouched by criticism, unguided, unlighted, uninstructed, unashamed" (1947, 553). Horne distinguishes perception, which she calls the subject of the story, from mere understanding, and notes the correspondence between "the organ of life" Vereker speaks of and the "felt life" James sought in literature (89).

While Swan declared in 1957 that no one yet had expressed the "awful thought" that James, too, had a secret that he took with him, many have in fact followed up on what Beach calls the great "temptation" to suppose that James was hinting through Vereker at his own secret (Swan 27; Beach 145–47). Irwin, indeed, speaks of the attempt to apply the tale to James as its more "practical" side (22). Matthiessen cautions that while the injunction to look at the whole, not the part, is a valid one, still the "essential design," can also be found in a single masterpiece, for example, *The Wings of the Dove* (1944, *Major*, 42–43). Berland sees the quest as a good one in as much as it has produced a good amount of critical attention, but bad in as much as it has led critics to believe that James can be reduced to "a single overriding formula" (8–9).

One way of reading the figure is to tie it to James's form or style rather than his subject matter (e.g., Markow-Totevy 99). To Sherman it is "beauty" the transformation of "chaos into order" that James valued above all else in his work (75–76). Brooks suggests the figure is the "difficulty" of James's art, its architecture, and its indirect presentation—what James called the "secrets of the kitchen" (128–30). Earlier, Beach, while noting James's characters' capacity for renunciation, also looked at the manner of presentation, the use of "subjective accompaniment" rather than a straight telling as James's "figure" (Beach 153–54; also Gordon 115–16). While Cornwell sees the "figure" as a kind of Coleridgean "organic unity" within each work, Tintner emphasizes its varying shape from work to work (Cornwell 130; Tintner 1976, 123). Powers cites Beach in seeing the figure as "the *art*" of James's work, although he argues that the figure itself is not the point, what the tale is calling for is careful "attention" to the work or carpet (1961; 1969, 16; also 1970, 102–3).

While noting that James left more of an indication of his literary views than did Vereker, Edgar focuses on Vereker's reference to the "organ of life" in his work as implying James's emphasis on "life and character" in literature rather than style alone (115–17). Similarly, Stephen Spender began in 1935 by entertaining the idea that the figure is the careful geometry of James's plots, but then dismissed that as "too crude and obvious and elaborate," and turned to the phrase "the organ of life" as referring instead to the "method of indirect presentation," writing that through his very artificiality James placed "personality and character . . . on the surface" of his works in a manner more musical than literary (51–53). In 1988 Spender saw the figure as contained in the belief that "art makes life." The artist creates characters of a "super-reality" who are themselves "figures in a pattern"—the "architecture" of the work. More than that, Spender says, James's works are like parables, not strictly allegories, but somehow "symbolic" such that their "felt life" stands out in an "unfeeling" world (Leeming 1988, 133–35). Also focusing on the "organ of life," Edel combined it with the statement that "art makes life," to produce as James's figure the idea that art—Vereker's "order, form, and texture of a work"—is the organ of life (*Life* 4, 148). To Canby, the "organ of life" is the heart, the "inner core of passion" revealed by the "unwrapping" of situation in literature (235–36). More loosely, Boren associates the figure with the human voice that conveys "the throb of life" (1989, 6). The idea that life may be "missed" is to Allott James's "figure" (322).

Among the other nominees for the figure are James's "interest in the clarification of the ethical structure of his work"—from Vivas; James's refashioning of past literature as *his* literature—from Edel; and the theme of "enslavement"—from Schneider (Vivas 582; *Life* 167; Schneider 4–7). Leeming nominates Dencombe's speech on the "madness of art," the narrator's belief that he has been tested and had his glory, as the closest direct statement of the "figure," a principle he sees borne out also in the stories of Strether, Maggie, and Milly (1988, 135). Kaye also focuses on late works, pointing to a figure in *The Awkward Age*, *The Sacred Fount*, and *The Ambassadors*. Baumgaertel draws on the criticism of T. S. Eliot in a comparison of James to the metaphysical poets to argue that his combination of philosophy and reality is the source of a pattern that is "essentially spiritual" and focuses on the boundary points between disparate worlds including Europe and America, the here and now and the hereafter. Tyler offers in place of what he judges the usual suggestion of James's ambiguity his theme of the "morality of love, courtship, and marriage," in particular "sexual passion as a ritual mystery" (227, 234). Beattie similarly names marriage as the figure, while Haddick sees "half-concealed, half-revealed" in James's work "the record of a gay life experience" (Beattie 96–98; Haddick 19; also Knox 221). As early as 1904, Bragdon spoke of a pattern "of which the eye can make nothing intelligible until, looked at by chance, askance, or from a certain point of view, . . . [it] all at once reveals itself," but then concluded that there is no figure, no overriding philosophy or system in James's work apart from "the pattern of his wonderful mind" (146, 150).

Interpretation and Criticism

The story is marked by patterns, and so is the voluminous criticism of it, the reading of which will send the critic on a search as long and nearly as tortured as that of the tale's hapless narrator. "The Figure in the Carpet" is for Jamesians the equivalent of the Enigma Variations, joining the ranks of the unspecified in James—the "obscure object" of *The Ambassadors*, the illness of Milly Theale, the crimes of Quint and Jessell. Vereker's "figure" may well take its place in the lead. For all of the extraordinary actions of the critics in the tale, and efforts out of it, no universal confirmation has ensued, either to the figure's identity or its existence. The critical history begins with discussion of the figure, then a questioning of it, with the doubts and affirmations focusing on varying characters, with an increasing emphasis on issues of "life" in general, and then on sexuality in particular, as connected with the figure.

Then comes the infusion of new types of theory —formalism and structural-ism, reader response and deconstruction—with a continued attention to the sexual element.

In his notebook entry, speaking of the critics in the tale, James had eager-ly noted the "lovely chance for fine irony on the subject of that fraternity" and then proceeded to make his narrator one of the obtuse critics (CN 137). With a different tone he speaks of the tale in the preface as a "significant fable" and decries "our so marked collective mistrust of anything like close or analytical appreciation" (*Criticism* 2, 1232, 1234). In his own critical writings, James was capable of expressing quite a high view of literary criticism. In "The Lesson of Balzac," for example, he declared "criticism is the only gate of appreciation, just as appreciation is, in regard to a work of art, the only gate of enjoyment" (*Life* 5, 281). The need for critics may also be located in the passage Kermode cites from "The Art of Fiction": the novelist's "manner is his secret, not nec-essarily a jealous one. He cannot disclose it as a general thing if he would; he would be at a loss to teach it to others." Here, however, the critics seem equally at a loss, and so the tale becomes in part "an elaborate skit on inef-fectual criticism" (25–26). While Armstrong sees in the narrator's disillusion-ment an indication that James recognized that too much concentration on the analysis of literature could ruin the "pleasures of immersion" in it, the reading of the tale either as a rebuke to "superficial criticism" or a plea for attentive criticism is a more standard one (Armstrong 63; e.g., Markow-Totevy 99; Andreas 149–50; Salmon 791, 803 n.10; Voss 139). Bell, on the other hand, reads its "fable for critics" as arguing against the hope of "finding in the work of art what they think the artist finds in life—a total suppression of unmeaning" with each element adding to the central pattern of signifi-cance, and sees James in the tale questioning even his own life's work (44–45).

To Canby, the readers in the tale are "rather absurd hangers-on of great-ness" (235–36). According to Stevenson, the tale is James's most "effective and teasing" presentation of the "break" between author and reader (70–71). Looking at the break, Scholes sees James as portraying the tasks of the critic and the creative writer as "totally separate." The writer's task in his work's interpretation is done with the writing of the work. It is, then, the critic's task to see the figure and help the larger audience to see it in turn (162). Tintner takes a different stand, seeing the tale as an example of James's belief in the cooperative work of the reader and writer (1976, 123). In Austin Wright's reading, the reader tends to identify with the narrator, who, however, as a stand-in for the unappreciative world, has little insight to offer. As a result, the reader must reach to the level of Vereker and James to get the "joke" of the tale or else be content to laugh at himself from below (192). McElderry is less certain of the direction of the humor, concluding that "James may be laughing at critics, or pretentious authors, or both" (122).

At one point in the tale, the narrator declares, "Literature was a game of skill, and skill meant courage, and courage meant honour, and honour meant passion, meant life" (CT 9, 296). Despite its source, the claim has often been taken as an expression of James's sincere belief, Wegelin particularly emphasizing the interrelationship depicted in it between art and life (Wegelin 76, 181 n.15; also e.g., Matthiessen 1944 "Portrait" 6; Segal 137 n.23). To Matthiessen and Murdock, the quote illustrates James's "favorite game" (N 223). Such gameplaying, however, is not to every critic's taste. Finding such high aims rather out of place in the tale, Geismar points to the qualifying introductory phrase, "For the few persons, abnormal or not, with whom my anecdote is concerned." In his critique, the tale with its abundant satire is more of an argument against "close analytical appreciation" than for it (137–39).

The term "the figure in the carpet" is used first by the narrator, and then accepted by Vereker, who adds to it the image of the pearls on a string. According to Horne, the fact that the figure is never named is not a weakness, but a way of allowing the story to be meaningful to each reader (89). The figure and Vereker's work are at times confused, as Irwin points out, in calling attention to the narrator's remark that they are "the same thing" (20). While the existence of Vereker's writing, however, has never been questioned, the existence of the figure often has.

The questioning of the figure began with Blackmur's suggestion in 1943 that "we know what the puzzle is precisely to the extent we realize it is insoluble, like the breath of life." Observing that "the secret of perception in readers comes very near the secret of creation in artists," he sees James assigning high aims to the story in the preface, but finds the story itself saying only "there is a figure in the carpet if you can imagine it for yourself; it is not there to discover" (81–82). Subsequent critics have taken issue with Blackmur's reading, Horne seeing it undercut by Corvick's success, Levy seeing its subjective emphasis as going counter to James's philosophy, and Vaid seeing Blackmur as speaking largely out of "impatience" with the complex tone of the tale (Horne 92; Levy 485; Vaid 87–88).

To say there is no figure, to Swan, means to say that James is making fun of those who search for it—"but if so that in itself is a 'figure.'" Swan prefers a view of the tale as an allegory of the "quest" in reading. Otherwise it becomes "an unending series of Japanese boxes!" (1948, 10; 1957, 27). To Matthiessen and Murdock, however, the "highly complicated plot" does cause the tale to resemble "a series of ingenuously mystifying Russian boxes" (N 223). According to Zabel, James believed a "life in art . . . pledges its votary to a secret that eludes his powers of communication." In this tale not only is "secrecy" the "central clue," but it presents an "ultimate case of the 'caged consciousness' caught not only in a human riddle but in an aesthetic one—a virtual paradigm of James's notion of the creative mystery" (19–20).

In his influential reading, Todorov put secrecy at the heart of almost all of James's work, designating as his recurrent figure *"the quest for an absolute and absent cause."* In "The Figure in the Carpet," he argues, such a quest puts into motion "the whole present machinery of the narrative." He calls it a "metaliterary" story "devoted to the constructive principle of the tale." Although, he notes, one may seem at the same place at the end of the tale as in the beginning, there has actually been "the entire narrative," and since the "secret" is the "secret," we have learned Vereker's "in the only way possible." To name the figure would be to destroy it (145–46, 175).

Bayley agrees with Todorov, seeing the late James as concentrating more on process than "possibilities and effects." In this tale, Bayley discerns "a kind of parody of his own processes, playing with the reader, or the critic, in the rather elephantine manner which the play of art had come to assume for James" (49). Auchincloss, too, without citing Todorov, argues that there "probably" is no secret as "James was fond of unanswerable riddles" (Leeming 1989, 67). James E. Miller, however, sees Todorov leaving only a skeleton—a rearranged one at that—of James's complex intention and unduly emphasizing technique over theme (309–10). Kermode objects to what he sees as Todorov's—and also Rimmon's—failure to take account of the tale's "wicked" humor, while Williams criticizes Todorov for seeking a "ready-made code or meaning" (Kermode 26–27; Williams 110).

Zgorzelski offers a counterreading to Todorov, contending that the secret is not the quest itself. The narrator is incompetent, and asks the wrong questions to find the figure, but Corvick does succeed. When Todorov says the reader is as "ignorant" at the end as at the beginning, Zgorzelski contends, he is putting himself in the place of the unreliable narrator. The "true theme," however, is not the "figure" but the "character of the searcher" and his attitude to literature. The tale is "autothematic" in that it speaks against treating literature as the "vehicle" of a "message." Corvick, for example, finds the message, according to Zgorzelski, only when he ceases being a critic. He notes, too, the "equivalence" established between the attitudes of readers and of lovers. Both should be "interested in the object alone." What is important in both relations is not absence but "the presence of the process which is significant as contact." The story becomes "autotelic" only in the reactions of its critics, which demonstrate the "inadequacy" of critical methods. Rather than congratulating himself on his own ignorance in the manner of a deconstructionist, Zgorzelski concludes by stating that he would be "happy to believe" he had overcome such "inadequacy."

The comedy that Kermode found Todorov inadequately acknowledged has been emphasized by others (e.g., Finch 98). Wallace reads the tale primarily as comedy, in response to what he sees as an undue critical seriousness. "The Figure in the Carpet" is a "satiric attack" on the public, and the narrator represents, despite his profession, "practically a direct personification" of the humorous society." James "multiplies the comedy by multiplying the characters," providing the narrator with a "comic double" in the equally obtuse Lady Jane, who, like him, cannot distinguish between an author and his writing. Corvick is a different and a better case, and Wallace considers his discovery of the figure as genuine. He is helped, as Vereker thought he might be, by his love for Gwendolen, and Wallace suggests that his attachment to her may keep him from repeating the mistake of the narrator in an undue focus on the author. The narrator's flaws, on the other hand, are the same in literature and in life, and he becomes "almost inhuman" in the end, turning Deane into his own "comic double" (173–78).

What comedy has been noted in the tale has generally been turned against the narrator. But as is typical of a James tale, nearly every character has come under close scrutiny and received at least one pan. Vereker may seem above it all. Even his name—as many critics have noted—suggests both truth, *veritas*, and the triumphant cry "eureka" (e.g., Tyler 233; Tintner 1986,166; Halter 35). However, a contemporary reviewer for the *Athenaeum* remarked that while James vented most of his displeasure at readers, he was at the same time "smiling a little very gently at the occasional attitudes of himself and his brother artists" (158). Subsequent critics have focused their complaints on Vereker's vaunted "figure." One is "tempted," writes Edgar, "to say that an artist of Vereker's competence had no business to leave his intention so obscure" (167–68). Similarly, Lynd finds it "difficult . . . to believe in the existence of a brilliant novelist who is a favourite of the critics, not one of whom can see the point of what he writes, however, though he has done all in his power to assist them" even if one reads the tale as James's defense "both to an indifferent public and to an equally depressing claque of yes-men and yes-women" (114–16). Edward Stone objects that if the figure is indiscernible it is "not an idea," and that if it is not an idea, only "a device or trick," it is not worth searching for (179). Wagenknecht also indicates exasperation, writing that "since art *is* communication, a writer who fails to be understood not only by the stupid and uncomprehending but even by his most intelligent and earnest devotees has failed as an artist and succeeded only as a solipsist or mental masturbator." Corvick and Gwendolen in turn simply continue Vereker's "cat-and-mouse game" (92).

In the more elaborate reading of Westbrook, Vereker is not simply an incompetent novelist, but a duplicitous one. In presenting his novelist as the victim of critics in his preface, James, according to Westbrook, was reversing his tale, in which the critics are the "victims of a pretentious novelist." The critics here may be "dupes," but the novelist is a "fraud." Indeed, Vereker's only saving grace is that he "belatedly regrets his boastful loose talk" and tries to warn off the narrator. But he has already set the search in motion, and Corvick will pretend to have found the figure in order to win Gwendolen. James, he argues, "stooped" to the "device" of Vereker's death only to emphasize the "irony" of the deceit, reinforced by the "fantasy" of the events following Corvick's death. The ending is a "belly laugh" as Deane and the narrator renew the vain search (137–40). Finch also suggests that Vereker is simply making up the story of the figure (100).

Feidelson, too, portrays Vereker as a flawed novelist, although not a deceitful one, in a reading that sees such flaws as part of the natural state of the artist. Vereker is the "godlike creator" in contrast to the earthbound critic, and the tale considers the "problematic meeting-point between artistic creation and imaginative comprehension." Vereker rejects such disjunctions of criticism as form versus feeling, maintaining that his figure does not "*refer* to life; it is an 'organ of life.'" Equally "governed by a paradoxical principle beyond their control," the critics cannot understand him, as his conception of "life" is different from what they know. The skeptical narrator, in Feidelson's view, is the worst, while Corvick is the best, able to come to the understanding of the figure as "a vital apprehension." His meeting with Vereker, then, "symbolizes complete realization of a theoretical possibility which is assumed throughout the story: a common imaginative life in which the Master's transcendent life-as-consciousness and the critic's consciousness, immanent in life, would merge into one." Even so, Corvick's death, Feidelson suggests, keeps him from an unavoidable disappointment in trying to articulate his discovery, and whatever he found has "certainly evaporated" in Gwendolen's possession. He refrains, however, from seeing the story as a "cautionary tale," arguing for it as a more profound if "ironic legend of an aspiration that contains its own fatality" (49–55).

Wirth-Nesher also has little good to say about Hugh Vereker, seeing his name rather than asserting the truth, passing the buck—"you verify." She notes the suggestion of harm to the critic in Vereker's images of cage, hook, and mousetrap, which the narrator passes over to look for a "buried treasure." If there is not a figure, she writes "then Vereker, like James, is pulling the strings here" and his action "smacks a little of the charlatan." She points to a shift in intention from notebook and tale to the preface, seeing the notebook and tale as harder on the author and the critics while in the preface James emphasized the plight of the misunderstood author. While he writes in the preface of a "small group of well-meaning persons," no one she asserts, not even Vereker, is well meaning in the tale, which takes place "not [in] a world of shared perceptions, but a world of tightly guarded secrets that may not exist at all, that may be a hoax." Still, she ends by placing the greatest blame on the narrator who misses out on "life itself" in searching for the figure, and so offering in his search the negative figure of the tale (123–26).

Goetz, like Feidelson, absolves Vereker of conscious deceit. Rather he sees Vereker suffering from the same "authorial fallibility" that turned James's tale of a "*sure*" secret to a "problematic" one of accidents and guesses. Corvick, according to Goetz, serves at first as a "double" to the ineffectual narrator, but becomes more and more like Vereker as he comes closer to his secret, ending as his "mirror image." Yet Corvick's attempted "mediation" between author and reader fails ultimately, even as all such attempts at literary mastery "must inevitably misfire" (166–72).

Gwendolen Erme in general has received much less praise than Vereker, brought to task for her intensity in literature and her willingness to be consoled in life. While Beattie objects to her "atrocious name," J. Hillis Miller, who describes Vereker as "strongly masculine, even male chauvinist," seems to imitate his stance in speaking of Gwendolen as being "passed from man to man among the critics" (Beattie 95; Miller 116). In one reading at least she is the outright villain, tied to one of the tale's many deaths.

The rapid succession of deaths is one of the most striking elements of the tale. Buckler and Sklare set students to explaining their role (415). In the notebook, Lock indicates, James seemed mainly interested in "when" not "*why*" they would die (159). Many critics see the deaths as simply of technical significance, in Krook's phrase "neatly contrived 'tactical' deaths" (305; also Matheson 228). Kermode sees death as another "running joke," along with sex, in the tale (27). Rawlings suggests that they contribute to the "general air of infinite instability" in the tale (xxiii). Geismar, however, sees a certain "mental sadism" or "intellectual voyeurism" in the contortions the plot puts its characters through, and Rimmon, while taking the deaths mainly as necessities of plot, pauses to note that their "cold rendering" fits with the narrator's "spiritual impotence" (Geismar 137–39; Rimmon 1973, 203–4).

Gwendolen's mother is the first to die, shortly after Corvick has discovered the secret, and after Gwendolen, intending to marry Corvick, has told the narrator that her mother will have "to swallow the dose." In Foster's telling, Gwendolen, "eager . . . to hurry her mother underground," says her "mother *must* agree to a prompt death," quite an extraordinary request (43). As the narrator recalls it, "I read some singular things into Gwendolen's words and some still more extraordinary things into her silences" (CT 9, 303). Sweeney reads these "things" as an indication that Gwendolen murdered her mother in order to make possible her marriage to Corvick and so her knowledge of the figure. He notes further that in a story of two marriages, two births, and five deaths there is little attention paid to the human drama, one of the few exceptions being the narrator's initial sympathy for Gwendolen after Corvick's death. Sweeney argues that whether the figure is real or not, the search for it is distorted by the false belief that "knowing life is knowing Vereker and that knowing Vereker is the discovery of the figure." While it may be acceptable to treat literature as a "game of skill," it is, he argues, the wrong approach to life.

Most of the blame for such coldness is generally bestowed on the narrator, who has, in Beach's phrase, a "little axe of his own to grind" (69). As Beattie and Segal observe, his role is somewhere between that of an observer and a participant (Beattie 95; Segal 74; also Cox 501). He is, according to most, exemplary in neither capacity. In Jones's reading, the narrator fails because he is motivated simply by a "desire to *know*" the secret, "tell it, and be done with it," unlike Corvick and Erme, who approach the quest from a sympathy with Vereker and his work (234–35). Gage observes that the narrator's continued ignorance constitutes the "embarrassment" of the collection's title (22).

The narrator is often his own worst enemy. Although he sees him as possessed of genuine "capabilities," Recchia finds him wasting them through "wrong-headed critical methods" (359). The positive quality most readily granted the narrator is wit. He describes Gwendolen, for example, as "one of those persons whom you want . . . to shake, but who have learnt Hungarian by themselves" (CT 9, 290–91). His claim to wit, however, is often disqualified on the grounds that it is simply part of his function as a narrator. But he has received some approval. Krook, while commenting on his insensitivity, stops to point out that he is insensitive only in terms of Jamesian supersensitiveness (307). Finch praises his interest in analysis in the face of the public's lack of interest in reading (101). Horne emphasizes Vereker's compliments to his intelligence (84). Gossman even judges him a "rather engaging young man" (24). He does not, however, always receive fair treatment from critics. Many, for example, such as Lainoff and Gossman, draw attention to his grudging nursing of his brother (Lainoff 1961, 43; Gossman 23). But the fact remains that he does spend crucial months abroad tending him back to health. Sometimes the narrator undercuts his own good qualities. Going to visit Gwendolen after Corvick's death he wonders "if some day she would accept me," but all he can bring himself to say aloud is to insult Corvick's discovery (CT 9, 307). At times, too, the narrator at least has the insight to recognize his own embitterment. Writing of his irritation at Gwendolen and Corvick's collaboration, he adds, "That statement looks unamiable, and what probably happened was that I felt humiliated at seeing other persons derive a daily joy from an experiment which had brought me only chagrin" (CT 9, 291).

The narrator's failure is typically contrasted with the comparative achievements of the other characters. Rawlings, for example, notes that the narrator fails to pick up on Vereker's warning against separating "element[s] of form" from "element[s] of feeling," and so missing the indication of an organic unity in his art. Corvick, on the other hand probably saw the figure, even if he could not communicate it. To grasp it, Rawlings suggests, Corvick followed "a process of germination . . . analogous to that of the author's," an approach that, unlike the narrator's, emphasizes harmony (xii–xv).

Gossman refuses to pin the blame solely on the narrator, although she does give him the lion's share. She sees James's "operative irony" as the chief element in the tale, according to which each character in part is the object of satire and in part "illuminates some aspect of the ideal for artist and critic." In her reading, however, Vereker is "too benevolent" to fool the narrator, and Corvick receives the "mildest satire." Indeed, Gossman argues, in a tale in which the reader never gets to see the central figure, the ability "to share James's irony at the narrator's expense" is the reward. Gwendolen shows her virtue in "living" on the secret, in a story in which Gossman sees the interaction of life and literature emphasizing the necessity of humanity in both.

Buckler and Sklare ask their readers to differentiate between the "mystery" raised in the story and "the main question raised *by* the story" (415). To do so, it seems, one needs to break away from the viewpoint of the narrator. The name "Corvick" sounds something like a linking of the victory of the heart and the critic, and the second theme often linked with literature in the tale is love. In his reading, Quentin Anderson classed the other critics with the narrator as failures doomed by their inability to love. Writing that James found curiosity "despicable," he sees the critics seeking to "appropriate the artist's form, quite detached from the life that informs it." Even Corvick, who thinks he has found the figure, has only found an "image" of his own "greedy self" and so—as his wife will later—dies an "emblematic" death. The tale does not say what the figure is because it wants instead to focus on the artist as "celebrant" who "loves the image as it reflects life" (148–49). In response, Rimmon points out that Anderson's reading does not account for Vereker's death or the narrator's survival (1973, 203 n.46).

Anderson's reading has continued to have influence. While Nalbantian sees the figure as Vereker's "Decadent" rather than realistic style and so argues that those who see it die because it is "antithetical to life," others emphasize its links to life (129). Horne and Edgar, for example, argue the narrator fails by responding to Vereker's mention of the "organ of life" with the abstractness of "some idea about life," and by seeking the secret through the effort of others (Edgar 117). According to Horne, Corvick, who has always had, in his own words, a "sense of something or other" in Vereker's work, succeeds, because he turns to life for the answer. When he dies, Gwendolen takes the place of Vereker as the frustrating master who "lives" her truth. Those who gain the secret, in Horne's reading, are distinguished by their perception, rather than abstract understanding, their experience rather than their cleverness (85–89). As Isle takes the metaphor, the figure and the carpet, or the form and its "human subject," are "inseparable" and each must be perceived accurately "in its relationship to the other" (22).

In 1961, Lainoff set out to "enlarge" upon Anderson. His reading agrees with Anderson's on the selfishness of the narrator's life marked by a "continued hesitancy to assume the responsibilities of love and friendship," and an appreciation of literature based on the possibilities it offers of self-advancement, only partially redeemed by a personal liking for Vereker himself. Ironically, according to Lainoff, had the narrator been willing to sacrifice life for literature, he might have gained the secret. Lainoff accordingly dissents from Anderson's reading of Corvick, arguing that he is the "critical hero" of the story, willing to give up his job and his book contract to visit Vereker. Nor does he see Corvick's death as the sign of a decline. It is rather an "immolation." Gwendolen, however, while having being given the secret as witness the "greater dimensions of her life and art" shows through her second marriage and her third novel her less sure mastery of it. The secret then begins in Vereker's "subtle knowledge of life" and becomes visible not in itself but in the "enlarged behavior" of those who discover it.

To Vaid, however, Corvick is no hero. While affirming the existence of a figure, he argues that none of the critics in the tale is able to solve its riddle. As the "ironic center of revelation," the narrator soon gives up his search to try to get the secret out of others, his "critical motivation" being reduced to "a journalist's hunger for news." His sources of information, however, are little better. While Gale detects a mistake in the narrator's image of Corvick's game of chess with his ghostly opponent who "would take up a chessman and hold it poised a while over one of the little squares, and then would put it back in its place with a long sigh of disappointment" on the grounds that one is never supposed to touch a piece without moving it, Vaid objects to the image as a whole as an inappropriate metaphor for criticism (Gale 216–17; also Wirth-Nesher 125). Corvick, he suggests, continues the search for the sake of Gwendolen, and may even fabricate his discovery to win her. If Corvick had genuinely found the secret, in Vaid's view, the "entire meaning of the tale is eclipsed" as it would inappropriately shift the responsibility for the narrator's failure from his own critical shortcomings to the series of deaths. Perhaps, concludes Vaid, the tale could have been more "explicit." Maintaining that the theme of the tale is criticism not literature, however, he considers blaming Vereker the worst mistake possible as it shifts the focus from its proper place, the failure of the critics (80–89).

In a reading that at times anticipates Iser, Levy also offers a corrective to Anderson. He agrees that the key is the failure to love, but argues, like Lainoff, that Corvick and Erme escape such failure. He sees Corvick recognizing the figure, not because of his voyage to India, but because of "some undisclosed heightening of intimacy and understanding" between himself and Gwendolen, a connection even the narrator vaguely recognizes. The knowledge is "some sort of elixir of life," and it is significant that Gwendolen dies in childbirth, an "act of love." Even Deane, according to Levy, is in on the subject, but out of pity humors the narrator in his continued quest. The tale as a whole then, "a sort of parable of what we now know as the 'intentional fallacy,'" shows that "understanding of form and total intention must be a human and humane action, an act of life." The product of the artist is also dependent on the experience of the reader, his own "exquisite scheme" such that reading becomes a "collaborative act" although not one of "total subjectivity," gaining importance from "a community of shared values." The burden remains on the individual reader, however, as fiction "tests" his humanity.

Recchia not only believes there is a figure and Corvick the hero who sees it, but also contends that Vereker tells the narrator his secret directly. The narrator simply fails to realize it, remaining fixed on some idea of "deeper meaning," even as, Recchia charges, subsequent critics have. While praising Lainoff, he argues that "life" is not the "product" of the secret, but the "secret itself." The "organ of life" is the secret, the "*quality* of his work's being alive, not just a particular sense of life or an idea about life." The ideas are the pearls, but when linked by the string, they take on a new life. As a result, the "surface" of fiction, or in James's words, the "look of things," takes on great significance. Corvick is able to achieve the necessary "mental distance" to allow him to see the work in this way. Looking at Corvick's death so shortly after his achievement, Recchia first acknowledges Kanzer's reading, agreeing that his death may be meant as "symbolic punishment" for intending to profit from his insight. However, he also considers that it may just be "one of those improbable occurrences that demonstrate how precarious is the existence of any state of knowledge or any state of happiness." His death, at any rate, switches the focus to the narrator and also to Gwendolen, who shows a "second hand" incomplete knowledge of the secret in her work, and may, Recchia speculates, marry Deane simply because he is so little of a threat. Through the different characters, he concludes, James hoped to lead his readers, by their very identification with the narrator, to see that they should strive like Corvick to "gain sufficient 'altitude' from our immediate experience to look down and see ourselves, next to the narrator, wandering through the trees in search of the forest."

Boland uses the themes and figures of Eastern philosophy as a key to her reading, citing the Hindu belief that "all life is fashioned upon a unifying element." She presents the narrator as so shut up in his selfishness that he is unable to grasp the secret, while Corvick by his journey to the complex world of India, and Gwendolen by her marriage and children see the life in Vereker's work, his system being perhaps simply "an approximation so close to life that it allows all levels of interpretation." To show the flexibility of the figure, she quotes from James's "Art of Fiction," "The thing of profit is to *have* your experience—to recognize and understand it, and for this almost anything will do; there being surely no absolute ideal about it beyond getting from it all it has to give."

Like Boland, Krook emphasizes the role of the reader's experience, setting herself the question of why readers take James's ambiguous texts in such different ways. She posits that each such text "*logically* implies two Readers, one for each possible reading of the text," and sees James putting both as "concrete Reader figures *in* the story." Still, she contends, it is the previous experience of the individual reader that will determine whether he sees a figure in the carpet. She cites as evidence James's comments on *The Turn of the Screw*, that "there is in such a case no eligible *absolute* of the wrong; it remains relative to fifty other elements, *a matter of appreciation, speculation, imagination—these things moreover quite exactly in the light of the spectator's, the critic's, the reader's experience.*" Thus, concludes Krook, a superior experience will produce a superior reading, or in the words of Blake, "As a man is, so he sees." Because "The Figure in the Carpet" is about reading, she judges it a particularly good example. Corvick in the tale is the "Sensitive or Perceptive Critic"; the narrator the "Insensitive or Imperceptive critic" and the reader must choose between the two on the basis of their experience, "mainly literary." To explain why, if he believes there is no figure, the narrator would keep looking for it, she has recourse to James's interest in the "subtler psychological aberrations of the human mind" such as its "suggestibility." At the same time, his "obsession" could serve as his "punishment" for being a bad critic and thus offer James some "harmless revenge." In conclusion, however, she contends that since one cannot study Vereker, one is invited to turn instead to the very similar James, the two critics in the tale becoming then readers of James, and the message of the tale being that the reader should direct his close study to the original author. The reason for all the deaths in the tale is "to ensure that each individual Reader shall be compelled to do the job for himself."

While Edward Stone, who finds the tale absurd, states that all the characters "put aside all other concerns in life," it is really only the narrator who does so (178–79). At one point the narrator asks in exasperation, "Was the figure in the carpet traceable or discernible only for husbands and wives—for lovers supremely united?" (CT 9, 306). Earlier, Vereker had informed him that marriage might "help" in the search. To Krook, the clue is "quite the most baffling" although perhaps a "symbol or metaphor for something in art" (304, 308). Others have pointed to the association in the tale of love and literature, without finding any clear significance in it (e.g., Rawlings xiii–iv; Matheson 228; Stewart 99). Rimmon simply attributes the contingency of Corvick's marriage and his revelation of the secret to "cultural conventions" (201 n.43). Beattie, however, emphasizes the theme of marriage and literature, and Lebowitz stresses the "direct interdependence" between the figure and genuine marriage (Beattie 97; Lebowitz 17). Similarly, Powers sees the story indicating that those who are capable of love are more capable of recognizing this truth, and observes that it is their combination of love and "artistic temperament" that give Gwendolen and George success in matters moral, artistic, and emotional (1970, 102–3; 1984, 655). Commenting on the "odd sexuality of the language," Kermode emphasizes first the narrator's confusion, his belief that "the secret of the bridal chamber can only be Vereker's secret" so that his his quest becomes "a sort of prurience, a kind of perversion, a vulgar ignorance at best." He goes on to see the figure as "a triumph of patience, a quality pervading the life of the subject, like marriage" (26–28).

The figure must be taken "on faith," according to Tyler, who first turned the focus to the "equally grand effect its discovery by the critic has on his own sexual destiny." He points to the way Corvick's finding of the figure is portrayed as a "feat . . . of knightly prowess" chosen by his lady. Turning to the charge that James did not do justice to the "sexual passion," Tyler rejoins that James did, but that he turned it to "a moral passion." Here, for example, Corvick's love for Gwendolen increases his perceptiveness, and Gwendolen herself, despite her early greediness, is transformed so that she accepts the figure as "her life." It serves as the "intellectual or spiritual progeny" of her union with Corvick. Tyler points to the puns in the tale as support for his reading. The pun in "Vera incessu patuit dea" on "dear," which the narrator picks up on, links "dear Gwendolyn, dear truth, dear goddess" and all are connected to the "figure." He also sees a suggestion of pregnancy in Corvick's calling the figure "immense" and of the Annunciation in Gwendolyn's answer "Angel." Corvick's name, however, not only puns on "heart," but also suggests he is, like St. George whose name he shares, the "victor *over* the body" or "corps." Thus Tyler sees James again "converting the sexual passion as such into the civilized status of *moral* passion" (228–36).

Kanzer also emphasizes the sexual element in the "figure." He divides the secret into two incarnations, one being the passion of the writer expressed through art, the other "the direct physical pleasure that can be 'lived upon' but does not produce art." The first is the "greater" reality of a James or Vereker, but the second is the one Gwendolen "lives" on, and following her, Deane, even if he does not know it. But the story, according to Kanzer, also suggests that those who gain the full secret will be punished by death, as is Corvick. The ignorance of the narrator, then, is safer.

Looking at the "intimacy between life and art" in the tale, Labrie sees the narrator as doomed by his inability to acknowledge it, his belief that art should look "only towards itself for its norms." Vereker, however, recognizes the relationship and so has greater hope for Corvick in his love for Gwendolen. The narrator can only ask if the secret is reserved for "husbands and wives" without seeing why. Gwendolen and Corvick's love, however, both "joyfully assimilated the figure in the carpet and transcended it" and allows Gwendolen to "live" on the secret even after her husband's death. Their greater success in life also "ironically" makes them more successful in art than the obsessed narrator. It is significant, however, in Labrie's view, that neither Corvick, who is "too immersed in life to produce," or the narrator, who is "too removed," is able to show his insight. Only Vereker, he concludes, has the "necessary balance" and he is given a "slight role" because of James's stated belief that "any presentation of the artist *in triumph* must be flat" (161–67).

Krupnick objects to readings that emphasize the "art" in the secret, contending that Vereker states that the "secret quality inheres in the formal elements of art; he does not say the formal elements *are* the secret." James's concentration on artifice, he argues instead, "barely conceals a despair about meaning." He sees the tale evolving from a "spoof on critics" into a more profound confession by the author himself of his "personal frustration and an attempt by art to overcome it." Because of the choice of the narrator-critic as point of view, the relationship between critic and author becomes more important than the character of the author by himself. While, he argues, James's identification with Vereker is "obvious," he sees Vereker as only James's "public mask" while James's "emotional involvement" with the narrator is more significant. The narrator faces a secret, torn up by "unsatisfied curiosity" in one of James's "epistemological dramas." James was like the narrator a "kind of coerced spectator" who could say with him, "All my life had taken refuge in my eyes." In the tale, then, James demonstrates his recognition that the artistic imagination is never entirely free from "the infantile instinctual vicissitudes which determine for life the objects of the artist's attention." The continual putting-off of the moment of revelation in the tale, he argues, may be due to the fact that James is "himself in the dark. The Jamesian magic is the other side of the Jamesian doubt."

This ignorance becomes linked again in Krupnick with a sexual reading. As he notes the turn of the narrator's interest from Vereker to Corvick and Gwendolen, Krupnick observes, "It is very easy to forget at times that the narrator's quest is specifically for a literary secret." In his reading, Gwendolen serves mainly as a barrier between the narrator and Corvick and Vereker, even as Corvick is "only a screen" for Vereker. However, with her death, he sees the narrator as losing also his "masculine will." The "organ of life," then, for James becomes again the phallus, with "aesthetic response" as the narrator's manner of expressing his sexuality, one which is "autoerotic but inspired by fascination with Vereker, and which is never gratified." His "way of loving" is his curiosity and "the secret never divulged is the tie that binds him to Vereker in the most sublimated of homosexual loves." The narrator's pain and isolation at the end, then, are versions of James's own.

Earlier, Putt had called the tale "inbred, almost auto-erotic," and the same year as Krupnick Tintner supplied a more comic reading of the motif in the tale (232). Tintner begins with the tale's mention of "phrenology" and combines it with Vereker's "organ of life" and the narrator's mention of the letter P to name as Vereker's secret "the joy of having a penis" particularly for self-pleasure. She asserts this truth in the face of what she rather endearingly sees as "the reluctance of modern criticism to come to terms with it" and suggests that James could have expected such friends as Gosse or A. C. Benson to get the joke. Admitting, however, that it is "absurd" to imagine Vereker writing twenty books on the topic, she suggests as James's final message that "the intent of a writer could be as private as the most private sexual act" (1982, 50–53)."

In a reading that recalls Wallace, Kappeler sees the narrator as going wrong not so much in seeking an "object" as in checking with the writer. According to her theory, marriage is helpful to the critic largely because it wards against incestuous "intimacy" between writer and reader who ought to be in contact only through the text. The writer, in turn, should be married only to his muse, which may be why Corvick put off marriage to Gwendolen, and why Gwendolen's best work was either before or between her marriages. Gwendolen, she suggests, may even have chosen Deane over the narrator because of Deane's "ignorance of the incestuous content of her first marriage." The secret itself, she conjectures, can only be "shown," not "told," for it is, in the words of the text, "the very flower of the performance" (75–79, 190).

Lock applies contemporary theory to his reading of the tale's mingled textuality and sexuality, arguing that the tale makes no sense unless "tackled as an exercise in production and interpretation." To him the "force and pattern" of the text are "made up out of desire and figure." Throughout, he argues, the search for the figure is spoken of in "terms of desire," although he does not agree with Pontalis's literalistic reading of the tale as "a sequence of successful or unsuccessful homosexual or heterosexual acts." Instead, the secret is in the text, and it is its force that operates like "the dynamic unconscious repressed." Character is subordinated to its "machine" as seen in the convenient death of Gwendolen's mother or the poorly timed illness of the narrator's brother. Thus "The Figure in the Carpet" is not *about* anything: it is what it unfolds and it is what unfolds it." Both Vereker's text and the narrator's become forces that control and can even kill. Still, Lock detects in the story also an important element of "play." While other critics have fastened on the letter "P," Lock points particularly to the many key "V" words, such as Vereker, Virgil, Vishnu, Vandyke, and Velasquez to see a suggestion of the vulva. There is, however, really no such "buried treasure" in the text. Vereker himself, in his role as "a figure in the text" figures simply as "surface" and it is Corvick's recognition of this fact that gives him success. Nevertheless, although a game and a continual process, reading, Lock insists, is "not a futile or meaningless or frivolous pastime" but "an active quest for pattern and meaning . . . which is inseparable from living." There remains, however, the image of the veil that separates reader and text and the implication that the lowering of the veil brings death. The suggestion of "fate" in the "ker" of Vereker's name finally brings together truth and death as does the text, making of reading a dangerous, but still necessary game.

Looking at Vereker and the narrator's first encounter at dinner at Bridge, Johnson notes that the narrator "had caught Vereker's glance" (CT 9, 278). From that point on he sees Vereker as author first encouraging then warning off the narrator from knowledge of his "secret." Pointing to James's 1866 essay on Eliot in which he proclaimed that "in every novel the work is divided between the writer and the reader," Johnson cites further James's statement in it that "the writer makes the reader very much as he makes his characters. . . . When he makes him well, that is, makes him interested, then the reader does quite half the labor." Such an invitation to read, however, to Johnson, is also a lure into the same trap as the narrator, caught by curiosity. The writer with his own "compulsion to tell" seduces, then betrays the reader. The switch to the issue of sexual knowledge in the latter half of the tale, Johnson takes as a maneuver on the part of Vereker to throw the narrator further off the track. He sees little genuine "sexual jealousy" in the narrator as he follows the relationship between Corvick and Erme, but the same desire to know its secret. His "consolation" is in his "imagination and the power to write." This "consolation," however, in Johnson's view, calls into question the narrator's seeming ignorance. He proposes a view of the narrator at the end as knowing Vereker's secret "whether he knows it or not." Thus, like Vereker, he attempts to hide the secret of Vereker's fiction behind the screen of the story of Corvick and Erme, having forgotten and forgiven his betrayal. In the end, the story illustrates "the resistance of character to interpretation" in a way that also connects "ways of knowing and the problems of composing" and provides lessons for alert readers.

Earlier, in a more strictly theoretical reading, Rimmon analyzed what she sees as the story's "mutually exclusive 'finalized' hypotheses," primarily that there is a figure and that there is not. The ambiguity here, she argues, is "prospective" with a "permanent central gap" from the start. To create the ambiguity, James used two different techniques, "ancillary gaps," such as the lack of any quotation or description of Vereker's work, and "retardatory devices," such as the numerous deaths in the tale that evade the giving of the secret and so create suspicion. She notes additional contradictions in the text, such as whether Corvick and Gwen are engaged. Such contradictions, according to Rimmon, suggest that there may be no figure, although one might point out that there was an engagement, or at least a marriage. Again, it is impossible to determine whether Corvick actually discovers the figure. Throughout it is unclear whether characters are covering their ignorance or expressing their knowledge. Is Deane, for example, pretending ignorance in order to honor the dead and humor the narrator? Or is he really unaware of the secret? The "figures" for the "figure" itself suggest "entrapment" and, concludes Rimmon, what gets caught is not the secret but the reader. But Rimmon also points to an opposed image in the way we are told the secret springs at Corvick "like a tigress out of the jungle." Because the tigress is in her "natural element" unlike the caged bird, the caught fish or mouse, Rimmon suggests there may be an implication that the figure must be "organic." She offers no answer, simply concluding that since the tale is "metaliterary" its uncertainty "duplicates itself in the inevitable interplay with the implied reader" (1977, 95–115).

In a separate reading, Rimmon applied some of Barthes's terminology to the analysis of the tale's patterns of delay or "*leurres*." She designates the "hermeneutic code" or "voice of truth" as predominant in the story of an "enigma." She points to the way Vereker refuses to give the narrator a "personal, extra-textual clue," seeing it as consistent with the "intuitive, imaginative, inventive" approach of a writer in contrast to the critic's "analytical, interpretative, elucidatory" mode. Corvick, however, resembles the writer in his desire not "to be told too much." The text's "incertitude" as to whether the search is noble or foolish is, she writes, characteristic of the "*texte scriptible*," but because she sees only two choices possible in the resolution of the incertitude, she sees the text's ambiguity as limiting its plurality, placing it as a "*texte limite*" somewhere between the text "*lisible*" and "*scriptible*." In conclusion, she suggests that a theory, such as Barthes's, that seems to produce for illustration mainly "limit-texts" is perhaps "a limited text of its own kind" (1973).

Salmon responds to Rimmon's reading not only as a "serious misreading of that tale but also a false view of James's poetic." She acknowledges that the text yields "contradictory hypotheses," but maintains that within "characters and readers" such "logical contradictions may coexist." While Rimmon rejects such a form of "paradox" as requiring an appeal to a "higher" level, Salmon argues that it can be "simply an experience of simultaneity which abrogates, while it lasts, our ordinary framework of chronology." One can also, according to Salmon, test Rimmon's "assertion of the difference between ambiguity in life and art" by taking marriage as a "metaphor for reading." James, she writes, "blurs the distinctions between persons and objects of art" in a way that draws into question Rimmon's distinction between "mimetic and nonmimetic modes." Corvick, unlike the narrator, does not draw firm lines between art and life or form and content. He wants "communion, not communication: the experience rather than the paraphrase" and thus sets out "to relive the creative process as a critic." The narrator, on the other hand, blames exterior circumstances for his failure. She contends that "nobody who dies was about to reveal anything" and so the series of deaths is thematically insignificant. The narrator simply cannot provide the proper structure to his own story even as he cannot find the figure. Once one has acknowledged his unreliability, Salmon contends, Rimmon's "problem of implausibility disappears."

While Corvick provides the clearest contrast with the narrator initially, Salmon sees Gwendolen as undergoing a transformation from greediness to openness that underlines the narrator's failure to change. Her second novel, as the narrator acknowledges, is a "a carpet with a figure of its own." She marries Deane for "something else" than literature, and shows her art in her life instead. "A truly 'married' person," she argues, "is Vereker's metaphor for one who can truly 'read,' because sexual union provides an apt analogy for the interaction of text and reader." Gwendolen's death, like that of Corvick is not a failure but "the hallmark of their enlightenment." It is only the ignorant who remain alive. In such a reading, she argues, ambiguity is not an "end" but a "means" to a "defamiliarization" that focuses the reader on the experience so that he can reenact the search for the figure in a "marriage" of reader and text. The apparent ambiguity ends in "simultaneous perception: the figure exists for those capable of seeing it."

In J. Hillis Miller's deconstructionist reading, Rimmon, while correct in her objection to "monological" readings, is "too rational," failing to do justice to the "*mise en abyme*" of the work. He argues that the tale's ambiguities are not simply "alternative possibilities" but "intertwined with one another in a system of unreadability, each possibility generating the others in an unstilled oscillation." In his view, the tale is "James's most explicit allegorical narrative" of "catachresis." "Unreadability," he continues, is different from Iser's conception of "reader response" as it is "an effect the words of the work impose on the reader." While a reader looks for some "logos" or "single meaning" in a work, "unreadability is the generation by the text itself of a desire for the possession of the *logos*, while at the same time the text itself frustrates this desire." "The Figure in the Carpet" "dramatizes" this experience or at least "presents figures for it" including the series of relationships between the characters. Vereker's own analogies for the figure are prime examples of catachresis, even while they offer images of entrapment and death. Like other critics, he notes the association of the secret with sexual knowledge, but argues that as there is no way of telling what is revealed through such knowledge, the story remains a "*mise en abyme* of analogies," not the least important of which is the analogy between the frustrated activity of decipherment performed on Vereker's work by the narrator and that performed on James's own figure in the carpet by the reader (1971).

The exchange that followed between Rimmon and J. Hillis Miller focuses more on theory than the tale. Rimmon first reasserts her belief that ambiguity is an element of some texts, not all, as is Miller's unreadability, and then sets out to document Miller's use of many of the terms associated with an ambiguous reading of the tale, and finally contends that Miller's deconstructive stance leads to her structuralist stance and vice versa in a continuing cycle. She points out, too, that in giving the subject of the tale as "unreadability," Miller is offering the kind of "unified" reading he deplores, "paradoxically," in her view, making the tale "more readable" than in her reading of the tale as ambiguous (1980–81).

In response, Miller discredits Rimmon's structuralism by labeling it a "science." He, on the other hand, sought "to 'express' the 'experience' . . . of the failure of an attempt at mastery" and thus failed as do the characters of "The Figure in the Carpet" and James himself. He further rejects her use of genre distinctions between ambiguous and nonambiguous texts, classing all texts together as unreadable, and argues that her own scientific argument, like all such in literary criticism, is necessarily "invaded" by the "'alogical' in the literary texts it seeks to reduce," and concludes rather magisterially by "welcome[ing] her as a guest" in the house of deconstruction (1981).

Earlier Iser read the story as marking the imminent demise of one kind of criticism, represented by the narrator, and the birth of another, represented by Vereker and Corvick. The narrator is a "Philistine," a "parasitic" critic who thinks it his task to "extract" meaning from a text in a way that leaves it "an empty shell." But Vereker rejects the narrator's review of his novel, and James's readers gradually recognize the narrator as the roadblock in their own approach to Vereker and so turn to reading "against the grain," even against their "own prejudices" derived from traditional criticism. The reader can then see the "signals" of Vereker's images of the "figure in the carpet" and the "string of pearls." The text provides a pattern with "empty space[s]" to fill, and meaning becomes "imagistic in character" without the "frame of reference to the world outside the narrator needs." To James, Iser argues, "appearances are no longer the veil concealing the substance of a meaning" but the means of creating something new. Such a new way of reading demands a merging of text and reader in place of the old "division between subject and object." Unlike the narrator, Corvick succeeds at this new kind of reading as an "effect to be experienced," and as a result his life is changed even if he cannot "explain or convey the meaning." The effect may be "exaggerated," but it is, to Iser, clear evidence of the superiority of an imagistic reading over an explanatory one (35–42).

While finding strong affinities between the tale and Iser's "heuristic model of the reading process," Williams objects to Iser's reading of the tale itself as "restrictive and inadequate." Still Williams disagrees with J. Hillis Miller as well, stating that Vereker's images are "generally positive" as they "direct the critic firmly back towards a close engagement with the text." The concluding images in particular—the foot in the shoe and the pearls on the string—show a "mutually supportive" relationship between reader and text. Vereker says that the figure "chooses every word . . . dots every i . . . places every comma," indicating, says Williams, that "[the] secret is not only within the text; it shadows forth the ways in which the structures of the text may become available to, and be activated by, the constructive reader." Such a process he finds similar to Iser's concept of the "implied reader." The reader fills in the text guided by its structure to create a "plausible interpretation," which can then be checked within the "community of interested readers" allowing for "repeated" and "enriching" readings.

"The Figure in the Carpet" is, of course, as Williams observes, "not only a kind of fictionalized parable of the reading process" but "a text available for interpretation." Williams contends that Iser does not pay adequate attention to the unreliability of the narrator, who, along with his colleagues, falls victim to a "sort of intellectual short-circuit" by trying to force a linking between art and life that should evolve naturally. While Iser praised Corvick, Williams sees his judgment, too, called into question by his devotion to the exaggerated Gwendolen. He sees Corvick, even after finding the secret, as unable to maintain his achievement, beginning to enjoy possessing it, rather than communicating it, a fault Williams attributes also to Vereker. But the irony with which the characters are portrayed also suggests to Williams James's "operative irony," creating "inverse image[s]" of ideal readers. With Corvick's death, he sees James seeming "to undermine the entire structure of his tale . . . in the sheer contingency of ordinary experience." But, Williams counters, this negation is itself "negated" as the story ends with the narrator's revenge on Deane, his winning through losing. If such a reading seems to support Miller's deconstruction, however, he contends that the ending there is only the end of a "single temporal cycle." The text can be reread and reinterpreted. While such readings may produce different conclusions, Williams sees the chief significance of the tale and of fiction in the way such reading allows the reader to absorb "the meaning into his own existence" so that it can "enrich the modulations of the reader's own consciousness."

Foster also begins in response to Iser, but adds a touch of allegory following de Man. Picturing Iser breaking away from the chasing of the narrator's "phantom" to join Corvick, and Vereker, and yes, James, in laughing at his search, Foster is still not satisfied with his reading of the "figure," arguing that to substitute the concept "image" for "figure" adds little. Foster instead turns to looking at the story itself as a "version of a Vereker figure" that the narrator has reproduced without realizing it. In the tale, mastery is prohibited, but the narrator's failure can produce success. He notes how in their parallel searches Gwendolen and George gain a new "form for passion." Still, Foster sees Corvick, worried that Gwendolen might be "seduced" by Vereker, seeking to master the figure himself. She marries him for the secret, and after her death stands as its possessor and thus the "sole master of the critic's desire." In this series of events, Foster descries not a "definition of the figure but a pattern of effects that arise from the desire to know about the figure." In each case it has been used "to evoke a response from someone who stands in a relation of rivalry or opposition" to the searcher. Looking back at the first interview with Vereker, Foster sees a pun on the word "eye" in the indication that the figure "dots every i." Combining the pun with the image of the "mousetrap," Foster arrives at an allegory that combines the literary and the sexual themes. In it, Vereker deliberately leads the narrator on although he cannot even offer him his own self, since it is "not really his to bestow" because "it is nothing but the figure manifested in every word he writes." The writer has no "expressible self," only an "I" with which it can tempt the critic. At the same time, the reader's "attempt at knowledge produces a sense of longing and obligation for which no direct satisfaction exists." It is hardly a pleasant state of affairs. Desiring "transcendence," but bound by the "conventions" of the literary world, each critic wants to "appropriate" whom they write about, even Lady Jane, in an attempt to "supplant" "the priority of another's text." Vereker himself plays on this "resentment" as it helps to perpetuate his work. The allegory implies a constant "repetition" of what has gone before in continued retellings that seek to explain the previous failed telling, but still remain "indeterminate" as there is no point at which "reality and allegory meet." The "I" is the "anterior" text or "figure" that the narrator perpetuates, passing it on to Deane so that Deane in his search becomes "an imitation of himself, an allegory of his own 'I.'" Thus, like Vereker, he gains power, by transforming "his reader's narratives into allegories of himself" even though that self never existed "except as a prior narrative." Hence, his joy is "bitter" and the figure continually elusive even in its passing on.

The desire for knowledge is marked here, and Weber has observed that the relationship between master and disciple in the tale makes a Lacanian reading appropriate (214 n.11). Halter offered one, tracing the desire for knowledge in the text, while beginning with J. Hillis Miller's concept of "aporias." In his view, Vereker's images of the "word," the dotted i and the comma, imply that "the essence is at one and the same time something *behind* or *in* the work and something that is identical with, and inseparable from, the *whole* text." But he wishes to move beyond Rimmon and Miller's conclusion of inconclusiveness. If Rimmon says that the story is an "attempt to fill in the missing information," Halter very aptly points out that it is the narrator who does so, the reader doing so only indirectly. The tale itself makes use of "indirectness" through its choice of a reflector barred from "direct access to the riddle." But, says Halter, his problem is added to, since he is "as much mystified by the people and the events as by Vereker's novels themselves." He locates the same "surface-depth opposition" in both the narrator's consideration of Vereker and of his friends showing that "ultimately, there is no difference between interpreting a text and interpreting another human being." The reader, however, is "better off" than the narrator in both forms of interpretation, and can see the way James contrasts the narrator with Corvick from the start. Noting again the linking of sexual and literary knowledge, Halter finds Corvick and Gwendolen happy even when searching because of their relation to one another. Still, Gwendolen is interested in Corvick largely because she believes he can learn the secret.

Citing Lacan's belief that "love is based on the Knowledge located in the Other" and the desire to gain that knowledge, Halter sees that desire central to the text. He explains Gwendolen's refusal to pass on the secret, by arguing that the attempt to gain truth is "inherently aggressive." She is not only "wooed" by the narrator, but "cornered," an aggressiveness seen also in the tale's metaphors. Corvick appears the ideal reader, but dies, and Halter suggests that his death, while not necessarily the "passive suicide" suggested by Pontalis, may well be an indication that he "overestimated" his abilities, his sure hold of the secret. His uncertainty, however, is natural in the world of late James where "there *is* nothing but appearances whose interpretations remain doubtful." The "gap" between self and other, ignorance and knowledge is "never closed" and the story "paradigmatically enacts this perennial act of decipherment." It is thus "unreadable" only if one expects "'the great last word' that will make all others superfluous." As a representation of the unending "act of reading," however, it has much to say in its illustration of the perpetual need to interpret. As Halter quotes the narrator on Corvick in conclusion, "He called it letters, he called it life—it was all one thing" (CT 9, 190).

Weber takes issue with Iser, who, he suggests, is like the narrator in offering his own "discursive meaning" even if it is one that argues against discursive meanings. At the same time, he argues, his imagistic reading is dependent on the authority of Vereker and James and thus dependent on an erroneous idea of the text as the "legitimate property of an author, that is, of a self-consciousness that 'possesses' the object that its intentionality produces." The figure itself is far from benign in Weber's reading where Virgil's *incessu* suggests not only a vision, but an invasion, as evidenced in all the deaths. Nor does Weber accept Iser's reading of Corvick, finding him, like the narrator, Philistine in his desire to "get *at*" Vereker and produce the "great last word" on him, and like Vereker, and indeed Iser, in giving conflicting messages that one must speak for oneself and yet speak for the author. Vereker, too, has a sinister aspect, his images for the "figure" suggesting traps, but ones that as in "The Beast in the Jungle" are "*sprung* precisely by *never springing*." According to Weber, the critic can never accept the "authorial intention" without which his naming of the figure can never be authorized. One is left then, in Weber's reading, with the image, if one may say so, of Vereker's and the narrator's encounter in an "impossible place," namely the narrator's bedroom, which represents "*the spectacle of a certain desire*" to which the narrator "submits himself." Vereker, standing on the "rug" becomes not the figure "in" the carpet, but a "*body*, the vulnerable object and subject of desire." Weber notes other sexual allusions by linking the suggested letter P with the "organ of life" to designate the phallus "the transcendental signifier of narcissistic desire" as perhaps "the privileged figure of the 'game' being played out here." Vereker leaves, however, counseling the narrator to give up, and the narrator himself survives by "*not* doing" anything. Even the story he writes "names no hidden secret, except perhaps the all too blatant one of an 'unappeased desire'" (201–12).

Szegedy-Maszák emphasizes the role played by "convention" in the attempted readings within and without the text. James, he asserts, believed in culture as "a system of institutionalized conventions which a community considers valid." Within such a system signs can create meaning. The narrator, however, cannot "decode" Vereker's works because they represent a new convention he has not learned. He fails because he lacks the experience that would create its own "sign system"—subjective but not "individual" because of the importance James attached to convention. It is even difficult for the reader to interpret the tale as a whole because one cannot tell which convention to use as a key. The tale, Szegedy-Masák asserts, undermines the code of the parable, whose "mood" is "imperative" even as the mood here is "interrogative." While one can gain the meaning of parables from others, as the narrator can do here, the tale here is "anti-parable, a metafictional text." It speaks of "wrong and right approaches to art" at a time when the conventions of art were themselves in transition. James, according to Szegedy-Maszák, kept to his faith in convention as "outwardly gratuitous" but "inwardly unarbitrary." Thus, there is "courage" and "honour" and "passion" at issue, and our uncertainty is the price of "our greater freedom" (234–40, 244).

Looking for a book of Vereker's, the narrator says he would have gladly "spent half the night with him" (CT 9, 285). To Chambers, his wish shows the "Jamesian identification of text with author" and creates an "image of reading as interpersonal intimacy that is central to the text." However, in his analysis not only does the narrator fail at such a reading, the only people in the story who read at all are part of a "closed world" of professionals who are all themselves writers. Critics are portrayed as speaking not to the public, but to each other in a "network of rivalries and ambitions," as they seek to "master" texts in order to advance their own careers. There is a way out of this "anti-model" in what Chambers judges the "evolution of the narrator" from such a critic to a man who gains a new awareness and "ironic distance" from his failure at the game. Chambers does not attribute to the narrator any release from his obsession, but he does see him through his encounter with Vereker becoming in the writing of the story itself a transmitter of Vereker's "art of elusive textuality." The audience for such a text, contends Chambers, is outside the literati, among ordinary people who can see the "game" as simply "an aspect, albeit ludic and marginal, of 'life.'" Vereker himself enjoys the game, talking to the narrator in figurative and "inconsistent" language that, Chambers suggests, "mimes" his written work. It is not simply, Chambers counters Iser, that the narrator asks poor questions; Vereker enjoys having the "upper hand" in the relationship between author and critic, knowing the impossibility of "saying, a 'secret' that does not exist in discursive form—or that is identical with the discursive form in which it is referred to." Indeed, he writes, Vereker's superiority seems one of "successful deployment of discoursive strategies" rather than possession of the secret. Later, Gwendolen takes the place of Vereker as "the text for whose mastery" the critics fight, and the rivalry becomes a more explicitly sexual one. Although Chambers sees Gwen as a "worthy successor" to Vereker in her literariness and her independence, he also argues that because she is a woman, and because she is obsessed with a "secret" belonging to someone else, there is necessarily a greater distinction between her art and life. Thus, when Corvick discovers the secret, she "yields without hesitation to his presumed mastery" seen in the title of her novel *Overmastered*. Corvick himself, however, it turns out has not truly mastered the secret, only the critical audience. It is in his marriage with Gwendolen that he gets the "true prize: the appeasement of desire." This union also, however, represents to Chambers a "necessary 'drift'" between Vereker as literary text and Corvick as critical, because Corvick does not "consummate" the union with Vereker. The "drift," however, simply seems to be an understandable difference between literary and sexual consummation. Corvick does, after all, confirm his discovery with Vereker at Rapallo. The narrator, as Chambers points out, never gains as much since such a union is a reward for critical success, not a means to it. Instead, at the end, he repeats the tale again, by telling the story of the figure to Deane as Vereker did to him as a way of "repairing a social gaffe." There is a distinction, though, between the narrator in his story, and the narrator, as he tells his story, speaking of his "getting of wisdom," which has allowed him to gain an ironic, comic vision of the melodramatic world to which he introduces Deane. Such irony, Chambers opines, is the "form of satisfaction most readily available to the impotent." Since the narrator, unlike Vereker, is ignorant of the heart of his story, his relation of it is a "*mise en abyme* of the act of narration." The reader, too, although not necessarily in the critical community, becomes like the narrator a "coerced spectator," a victim like him of "unappeased desire."

Chambers then turns his attention to the critical readers of the story, finding it "surprising" that so many follow the narrator in his obsession with the secret. Although he sees later structuralist, poststructuralist, and particularly deconstructionist readings as moving away from this practice somewhat, he still sees them "defining the critical issues in terms of the narrator's quest." "Descendants of Drayton Deane," they "jostle" one another for the "crown" of critical certainty, even when they deny the existence of such certainty.

To Bales, Iser's reading of "The Figure in the Carpet" is "quite bizarre" as well as "polemical" in its attack on previous criticism in the advancement of his own. The very statement that "meaning is imagistic" Bales sees as a "referential meaning" of the sort Iser wishes to do away with. In response, he notes many possible versions of the encounter with Vereker. In what he calls

James's version,Vereker "knows that he has created something new and uniquely his" and "the critic wants to appropriate the work, fails, and is bothered by the failure." In what he calls Iser's version the author is challenging the reader to use his "common sense" to find the "figure in the carpet" that gives his work importance. In what he calls, without authorization, Stanley Fish's version, Vereker and James "have attributed to them whatever meaning or significance a particular 'interpretative community' chooses" and while the members can freely come and go, the author is captive to their choice. Counter to such a reading, however, he points to the narrator's inability to change. Nor does he judge Corvick as able to change as Iser does, stressing instead the extreme difficulty of his struggle to read Vereker properly. Bales then turns to the issue of writer's and reader's intentions as necessary to reading, taking Szegedy-Maszák's reading together with Culler's poststructuralism as support. He dissents from Szegedy-Maszák's argument that the narrator cannot read Vereker because he does not know the necessary convention by asserting "that the narrator did read Vereker's novel and, in his own opinion, read it well," although one could point to more evidence in the text challenging the validity of his reading than Bales cites. The readers are seen to fail in this text, writes Bales, only as judged by the intention of the author, who is put here in "extraordinarily close communication" with the reader. Usually such intentions must be inferred. Bales, however, has no problem with such inferences, arguing that they are necessary to critical reading, even when they are mistaken. He cites Culler's characterization of intention as something that is not "prior" to a text but an "important organizing structure identified" within it. In "The Figure in the Carpet," however, Bales contends there is no "explicit line of argumentation," rather "an *absent* 'line of argumentation' that must be inferred from the dramatized conflict." Thus, he rather open-mindedly concludes that both such psychological readings as Iser and Szegedy-Maszák and such deconstructionist readings as Culler can be helpful in confronting a text.

Bishop speaks of "The Figure in the Carpet" as an "acknowledged" "masterwork"—"a text to be beaten." While noting the possibility of multiple readings, he provides something of a reading of his own by looking at the names, particularly the similarity between "Vereker" and "Corvick." "Erme," he observes, provides the missing vowels to make Corvick Vereker, so that Corvick and Erme together make "a kind of sloppy anagram" for Vereker, with the leftover being "'me,' the signal of the unnamed narrator's cleverness and egotistic obsession." As a result, he sees Vereker's secret as residing not in his work, but "in a kind of cancellation through approximation" in the marriage of Corvick and Erme that will "write 'the name of the author,'" and so end the search. Like Corvick, however, he seems to have trouble keeping the horse and the cart in proper order. Looking over the accumulated mass of analyses, it is hard not to agree with Bishop that the tale has assumed some of its current status because of the way it "allows" for critical commentary and fits the aims of modern critical movements. Although he notes the parodying of the critic, he still finds "grounded" in the text "our right and our need to exist." He goes on, however, to declare that "the critical act, as the perpetuation of interpretation, has its own value *previous* to the text it operates upon" [my emphasis]. Thus, the definition of the Master is "unnecessary" "perhaps even undesirable" as long as it allows for continued criticism. While Bishop is no doubt not alone in such a view, it seems a sad one, a view of criticism as busywork that keeps academics employed and tenured, but that has no truth to offer and no desire to find one. Certainly, one value of literature is that it gives people issues to discuss, but to imply that its only value is to keep critics fed seems overly reductionist (5–9).

James wrote his friend Gosse that his tale was a "simple (but I won't affectedly say artless) little tale" (Tintner 1982, 53). His brother William, after reading the first installment, found that the story began well, but in reading through the collection *Embarrassments*, however, found that the tale was not one of his favorites. As he wrote Henry, "I wish I could say hurrah with a whole heart, but this recent manner of yours of using such an excessively small bit of *matter*, and that so fanciful, to show a great deal of art by, seems to me to be full of peril, if you get deeper into it" (396, 410–11). One of the problems of the tale for critics has indeed been the seeming disproportion between what one learns of the central secret and the manner—or series of events and characters—that overwhelms it. Many critics have found illuminating ways to tie the two together, and certainly the manner is well done: Lock praises its "autonomous formal narrative design"; Zabel calls it "one of the most sheerly ingenious" of Jamesian fables (Lock 159; Zabel 20). Stewart, however, dismisses it as James's "closest approach to the mere *chic* of its melancholy decade" (99). Others continue to complain. In Putt's view, the story, while "beautifully done," would have been best left undone (231–33). To Wagenknecht, it is the "least satisfying" of the artist tales of the same period (90).

Unless one accepts one of the proffered solutions, part of the problem continues to be the resistant riddle at the center. Iser writes that "it is absurd to imagine something with which one is already confronted" and so sees no outside reference in the tale (41). Others, including Bishop, Todorov, and J. Hillis Miller, continue the tendency in Jamesian criticism that wants to focus only on the indefinable. Such may indeed be a tendency in the work of James himself, at least the later James. Still, Lainoff can state with good cause that James believed "good art and the appreciation of art should be as concretely rich as life itself" (1961, 43). It is the narrator who turns the Iserian "blanks" into permanent absences. Along with other critics, Williams cites the issue of Gwendolen and Corvick's engagement as an example of an unresolvable mystery (117). But the fact that the narrator does not know what precisely happened does not mean that such events are beyond explaining—if one could see into Corvick or Gwendolen as one can into the narrator, one would have the answer. Engagements are assumed, formed, broken off, and patched together all the time, but the couple does not always fill friends in on the details of the process. The problem with the narrator is that he thinks it is his business. Certainly, however, it is harder to imagine the meeting at Rapallo with Corvick and Vereker discussing their shared secret than to fill in a possible scenario for an engagement. Secrets are usually specific, and it is not easy to think of one that would provide the necessary rapture.

At the same time, a large part of the appeal to academics is James's subject and its style. As Geismar observes, "literary critics like stories about literary critics" (138). It is a rather natural feeling and if Lynd speaks of the tale as a "first-rate magazine story for the intellectuals" and Blackmur as "a tea-time and tepid whiskey fable," its limitations need not be held against critics (Lynd 114–16; Blackmur 81–82). Lately, however, critics tend to project the narrator's unreliability not on criticism but on literature. As Krook says of such critics, "I can always see what Henry James's story is doing for their theories, but I can't always see so clearly what their theories are doing for James's story" (300). We began by writing of a story, and end by writing of a text, but the literature in the tale survives—it's the critic that goes mad. In his analysis, Chambers points out that at the time of the tale criticism was emerging as a profession apart from journalistic reviewing. The critic was no longer a "mere parasite" but "part of the literary garden." In the tale, however, he sees criticism as serving as a conduit not between the author and the common man but between one critic and another (153). This hardly seems helpful, anymore than the blanket rewriting of the tale as "unreadable." Certainly James strove toward communication, however flighty Vereker or his followers may be. To believe literature should not be doctrinaire does not deprive it of all significance, nor should it transfer all rights to speak to the critic. Chambers is one of the many critics to cite Vereker's statement that the "critic just *isn't* a plain man: if he were, pray, what would he be doing in his neighbour's garden?" (CT 9, 282-83). In the face of so much contemporary criticism it may seem naive to say so, but surely, if the critic is in someone else's garden, the least he can do, if he is not going to leave, is to help the garden grow.

Works Cited

Primary Works
James, Henry. 1896. "The Figure in the Carpet." *Cosmopolis* 1 (January–February): 41–59, 373–92.

———. 1896. "The Figure in the Carpet." *Embarrassments*. London: Heinemann; New York: Macmillan, 3–82.

————. 1908. "The Figure in the Carpet." *The Novels and Tales of Henry James*. New York Edition. Vol. 15, 217–77. *The Lesson of the Master*. New York: Scribner's.

————. 1916. "The Figure in the Carpet." *The Uniform Tales of Henry James*. London: Martin Secker.

————. 1969. *Henry James: Letters to A. C. Benson and Auguste Monod*. Ed. E. F. Benson. New York: Haskell House.

Secondary Works

Anon. 1896. Review of *Embarrassments*. *Athenaeum* 3588 (1 August): 158.

Allott, Miriam. 1953. "Symbol and Image in the Later Work of Henry James." *Essays in Criticism* (Oxford) 3 (July): 321–36.

Anderson, Quentin. 1957. *The American Henry James*. New Brunswick, NJ: Rutgers University Press. Reprinted from "Henry James and the New Jerusalem." *Kenyon Review* 8 (Autumn 1946): 515–66.

Anderson, Walter E. 1982. "The Visiting Mind: Henry James's Poetics of Seeing." *The Psychoanalytic Review* 69 (Winter): 513–32.

Andreas, Osborn. 1948. *Henry James and the Expanding Horizon: A Study of the Meaning and Basic Themes of James's Fiction*. Seattle: University of Washington Press.

Armstrong, Paul B. 1989. *The Phenomenology of Henry James*. Chapel Hill: University of North Carolina Press.

Bales, Kent. 1986. "Intention and Readers' Responses." *Neohelicon* 13, no. 1: 177–94.

Baumgaertel, Gerhard. 1959. "The Concept of the Pattern in the Carpet: Conclusions from T. S. Eliot." *Revue des Langues Vivantes* (Brussels) 25 (July–August): 300–6.

Bayley, John. 1988. *The Short Story: Henry James to Elizabeth Bowen*. Brighton: Harvester.

Beach, Joseph Warren. [1918] 1954. *The Method of Henry James*. Philadelphia: Albert Saifer. Also reprinted as "The Figure in the Carpet," in *The Question of Henry James*, ed. F. W. Dupee, 92–104. New York: Henry Holt, 1945.

Beattie, Munro. 1967. "The Many Marriages of Henry James." In *Patterns of Commitment in American Literature*. Ed. Marston La France, 93–112. Toronto: University of Toronto Press.

Bell, Millicent. 1984. "Henry James, Meaning and Unmeaning." *Raritan* 4: 29–46.

Berland, Alwyn. 1981. *Culture and Conduct in the Novels of Henry James*. Cambridge: Cambridge University Press.

Bishop, George. 1988. *When the Master Relents: The Neglected Short Fictions of Henry James*. Ann Arbor: UMI Research Press.

Blackall, Jean Frantz. 1965. *Jamesian Ambiguity and* The Sacred Fount. Ithaca, NY: Cornell University Press.

Blackmur, Richard P. [1943] 1983. "In the Country of the Blue." In *Studies in Henry James*. Ed. Veronica A. Makowsky, 69–90. New York: New Directions. Reprinted from *Kenyon Review* 5 (Autumn): 595–617. Reprinted in *The Question of Henry James*, ed. F. W. Dupee, 191–211, New York: Henry Holt, 1945; *Critiques and Essays on Modern Fiction*, ed. John W. Aldridge, 303–18, Ronald Press, 1952.

Boland, Dorothy M. 1977. "Henry James's 'The Figure in the Carpet': A Fabric of the East." *Papers in Language & Literature* 13: 424–29.

Boren, Lynda S. 1989. *Eurydice Reclaimed: Language, Gender, and Voice in Henry James*. Ann Arbor: UMI Research Press.

———. 1982. "'Dear Constance,' 'Dear Henry': The Woolson/James Affair—Fact, Fiction, or Fine Art." *Amerikastudien* 27: 457–66.

Bragdon, Claude. 1904. "The Figure in Mr. James's Carpet." *Critic* 44 (Fall): 146–50.

Brooks, Van Wyck. [1925] 1972. *The Pilgrimage of Henry James*. New York: Dutton. Reprint. New York: Octagon.

Buckler, William, and Arnold B. Sklare. 1960. *Stories from Six Authors*. New York: McGraw-Hill.

Canby, Henry Seidel. 1951. *Turn West, Turn East: Mark Twain and Henry James*. Boston: Houghton Mifflin.

Chambers, Ross. 1984. "Not for the Vulgar? The Question of Readership in 'The Figure in the Carpet.'" In *Story and Situation: Narrative Seduction and the Power of Fiction*. Theory and History of Literature 12, 151–80. Minneapolis: University of Minnesota Press.

Clemens, Samuel. [1972] 1989. "The Story of the Old Ram." In *Anthology of American Literature*. 4th ed. Vol. 2. Ed. George McMichael, et al., 254–57. New York: Macmillan.

Cornwell, Ethel F. 1962. *The 'Still Point': Theme and Variations in the Writing of T. S. Eliot, Coleridge, Yeats, Henry James, Virginia Woolf, and D. H. Lawrence*. New Brunswick, NJ: Rutgers University Press.

Cowdery, Lauren Tozek. 1986. *The Nouvelle of Henry James in Theory and Practice*. Studies in Modern Literature 47. Ann Arbor: UMI Research Press.

Cowie, Alexander. 1948. *The Rise of the American Novel*. New York: American Book Company.

Cox, C. B. 1988. "James and the Triumph of Consciousness." *Sewanee Review* 96 (Summer): 497–506.

Edgar, Pelham. [1927] 1964. *Henry James, Man and Author*. New York: Russell & Russell.

Eliot, T. S. [1930] 1949. "Introduction." *The Wheel of Fire: Interpretations of Shakespearian Tragedy*, by G. Wilson Knight. London: Methuen, xiii–xx.

Feidelson, Charles, Jr. 1970. "Art as Problem in 'The Figure in the Carpet' and 'The Madonna of the Future.'" In *Twentieth Century Interpretations of "The Turn of the Screw" and Other Tales.* Ed. Jane P. Tompkins, 47–55. Englewood Cliffs, NJ: Prentice-Hall.

Finch, G.A. 1968. "A Retreading of James's Carpet." *Twentieth Century Literature* 14 (July): 98–101.

Foster, Dennis A. 1987. *Confession and Complicity in Narrative.* New York: Cambridge University Press.

Gage, Richard P. 1988. *Order and Design: Henry James' Titled Story Sequences.* New York: Peter Lang.

Gale, Robert L. [1954] 1964. *The Caught Image: Figurative Language in the Fiction of Henry James.* Chapel Hill: University of North Carolina Press.

Geismar, Maxwell. 1963. *Henry James and the Jacobites.* Boston: Houghton Mifflin.

Gide, André. 1948. *Journal, 1889–1939.* Trans. and ann. Justin O'Brien. New York: Knopf.

Gilman, Charlotte Perkins. [1892] 1989. "The Yellow Wallpaper." In *Anthology of American Literature.* 4th ed. Vol. 2. Ed. George McMichael, et al., 639–49. New York: Macmillan.

Goetz, William R. 1986. *Henry James and the Darkest Abyss of Romance.* Baton Rouge: Louisiana State University Press.

Gohdes, Clarence. 1944. *American Literature in Nineteenth-Century England.* Carbondale: Southern Illinois University Press.

Gordon, Caroline. 1958. *How to Read a Novel.* New York: Viking.

Gossman, Ann. 1962. "Operative Irony in 'The Figure in the Carpet.'" *Descant* 6 (Spring): 20–25.

Haddick, Vern. 1976. "Colors in the Carpet." *Gay Literature* 5: 19–21.

Halter, Peter. 1984. "Is Henry James's 'The Figure in the Carpet' 'Unreadable'?" In *Continental Approaches to Narrative.* Ed Anthony Mortimer, 25–37. Tübingen: Gunter Narr.

Horne, Helen. 1960. *Basic Ideals of James's Aesthetics as Expressed in the Short Stories Concerning Artists and Writers.* Marburg: Erich Mauersberger.

Hutchinson, Peter. 1983. *Games Authors Play.* London and New York: Methuen.

Irwin, Michael. 1989. "Henry James and the Vague *Nouvelle.*" In *The Modern American Novella.* Ed. Robert A. Lee, 13–29. London: Vision; New York: St. Martin's.

Iser, Wolfgang. [1978] 1987. "Partial Act-Total Interpretation: Henry James, 'The Figure in the Carpet,' In Place of an Introduction." In *Henry James's "Daisy Miller," "Turn of the Screw" and Other Tales.* Ed. Harold Bloom, 35–42. New York: Chelsea House. Reprinted from *The Act of Reading: A Theory of Aesthetic Response,* 3–10. Baltimore and London: Johns Hopkins University Press.

Isle, Walter Whitfield. 1968. *Experiments in Form: Henry James's Novels: 1896–1901.* Cambridge, MA: Harvard University Press.

James, William. 1983. *The Correspondence of William James.* Vol. 2: *William and Henry: 1885–1896.* Ed. Ignas K. Skrupskelis and Elizabeth M. Berkeley. Charlottesville: University Press of Virginia.

Johnson, Warren. 1988. "Parable, Secrecy, and the Form of Fiction: The Example of 'The Figure in the Carpet' and *The Portrait of a Lady.*" *Journal of English and German Philology* 87 (April): 230–50.

Jones, Granville H. 1975. *Henry James's Psychology of Experience: Innocence, Responsibility, and Renunciation in the Fiction of Henry James.* The Hague: Mouton.

Kanzer, Mark. 1960. "The Figure in the Carpet." *American Imago* 17 (Winter): 339–48.

Kappeler, Susanne. 1980. *Writing and Reading in Henry James.* New York: Columbia University Press.

Kaye, Julian B. 1963. "*The Awkward Age, The Sacred Fount,* and I: Another Figure in the Carpet." *Nineteenth-Century Fiction* 17 (March): 339–53.

Kermode, Frank, ed. 1986. *The Figure in the Carpet and Other Stories.* London: Penguin.

Knox, Melissa. 1986. "'Beltraffio'": Henry James' Secrecy." *American Imago* 43, no. 3 (Fall): 211–27.

Krook, Dorothea. 1988. "As a Man Is, So He Sees: The Reader in Henry James." *Neophilogus* 72 (April): 300–15.

Krupnick, Mark L. 1972. "Henry James' Curiosity." *Modern Occasions* 2: 168–80.

Labrie, Ernest Ross. 1969. "Sirens of Life and Art in Henry James." *Lakehead University Review* (Port Arthur, Ont.) 2: 150–69.

Lainoff, Seymour. 1962. "James and Eliot: The Two Gwendolens." *Victorian Newsletter,* no. 21 (Spring): 23–34.

———. 1961. "Henry James' 'The Figure in the Carpet': What is Critical Responsiveness?" in *Twentieth Century Interpretations of "The Turn of the Screw" and Other Tales.* Ed. Jane P. Tompkins, 40–44. Englewood Cliffs, NJ: Prentice-Hall. Reprinted from *Boston University Studies in English* 5 (Summer): 122–28 .

Lebowitz, Naomi. 1965. *The Imagination of Loving: Henry James's Legacy to the Novel.* Detroit: Wayne State University Press.

Lee, Brian. 1978. *The Novels of Henry James: A Study of Culture and Consciousness.* New York: St. Martin's.

Leeming, David Adams. 1989. "A Conversation with Louis Auchincloss on Henry James." *Henry James Review* 10: 60–67.

————. 1988. "A Conversation with Stephen Spender on Henry James." *Henry James Review* 9: 128–35.

Levy, Leo B. 1962. "A Reading of 'The Figure in the Carpet.'" *American Literature* 33 (January): 457–65 .

Lock, Peter W. 1981. "'The Figure in the Carpet': The Text as Riddle and Force." *Nineteenth-Century Fiction* 36: 157–75.

Lynd, Robert. [1948] 1952. "The Literary Life." In *Books and Writers*. New York: Macmillan, 113–17.

McElderry, Bruce R., Jr. 1965. *Henry James*. New York: Twayne.

Macherey, Pierre. 1978. *A Theory of Literary Production*. Trans. Geoffrey Wall. London: Routledge & Kegan Paul.

McWhirter, David. 1989. *Desire and Love in Henry James: A Study of the Late Novels*. Cambridge: Cambridge University Press.

Markow-Totevy, Georges. 1969. *Henry James*. Trans. John Griffiths. London: Merlin.

Matheson, Gwen. 1968. "Portraits of the Artist and the Lady in the Shorter Fictions of Henry James." *Dalhousie Review* 48: 222–30.

Matthiessen, F. O. 1947. *The James Family: Including Selections from the Writings of Henry James, Sr., William, Henry, and Alice James*. New York: Knopf.

————. 1944. "Introduction: Henry James' Portrait of the Artist." *Henry James: Stories of Writers and Artists*. Norfolk, CT: New Directions. Also reprinted as "Henry James's Portrait of the Artist." *Partisan Review* 11 (1944): 71–87.

————. 1944. *Henry James: The Major Phase*. New York: Oxford University Press.

Miller, James E. 1983. "Henry James and the Language of Literature and Criticism." *Revue des Littérature Comparée* 57: 303–13.

Miller, J. Hillis. 1981. "A Guest in the House: Reply to Shlomith Rimmon-Kenan's Reply." *Poetics Today* 2, no. 1b (Winter): 189–91.

————. 1971. "The Figure in the Carpet." *Poetics Today* 1:107–18. Reprinted in *Henry James's "Daisy Miller," "The Turn of the Screw" and Other Tales*. Ed. Harold Bloom, 61–74. New York: Chelsea House, 1987.

Nalbantian, Suzanne. 1983. *Seeds of Decadence in the Late Nineteenth-Century Novel: A Crisis in Values*. New York: St. Martin's.

Powers, Lyall H. 1984. "Henry James and James Baldwin: The Complex Figure." *Modern Fiction Studies* 30: 651–67.

————. 1970. *Henry James: An Introduction and Interpretation*. New York: Barnes & Noble.

————. 1969. *The Merrill Guide to Henry James*. Columbus, OH: Charles E. Merrill.

————. 1961. "A Reperusal of James's 'The Figure in the Carpet.'" *American Literature* 33 (May): 224–28.

Putt, S. Gorley. 1966. *Henry James: A Reader's Guide*. Ithaca, NY: Cornell University Press.

Rawlings, Peter, ed. 1984. Introduction. *Henry James's Shorter Masterpieces*. Vol. 2. Sussex: Harvester; Totowa, NJ: Barnes & Noble.

Recchia, Edward. 1973. "James's 'The Figure in the Carpet': The Quality of Fictional Experience." *Studies in Short Fiction* 10 (Fall): 357–65.

Rimmon-Kenan, Shlomith. 1980–81. "Deconstructive Reflections on Deconstruction: In Reply to Hillis Miller." *Poetics Today* 2: 185–88.

———. 1977. *The Concept of Ambiguity: The Example of Henry James*. Chicago: University of Chicago Press.

———.1973. "Barthes' 'Hermeneutic Code' and Henry James's Literary Detective: Plot-Composition in 'The Figure in the Carpet.'" *Hebrew University Studies in Literature* 1: 183–207.

Roditi, Edouard. [1947] 1986. *Oscar Wilde*. New York: New Directions.

———. 1948. "Oscar Wilde and Henry James." *University of Kansas City Review* 15: 52–56.

Salmon, Rachel. 1980. "A Marriage of Opposites: Henry James's 'The Figure in the Carpet' and the Problem of Ambiguity." *English Literary History* 47: 788–803.

Schneider, Daniel J. 1978. *The Crystal Cage: Adventure of the Imagination in the Fiction of Henry James*. Lawrence: Regents Press of Kansas.

Scholes, Robert. 1967. *The Fabulators*. New York: Oxford University Press.

Segal, Ora. 1969. *The Lucid Reflector: The Observer in Henry James' Fiction*. New Haven: Yale University Press.

Sherman, Stuart P. [1917] 1945. "The Aesthetic Idealism of Henry James." In F. W. Dupee, ed., *The Question of Henry James: A Collection of Critical Essays*, 70–91. New York: Henry Holt.

Spender, Stephen. 1935. *The Destructive Element*. Philadelphia: Albert Saifer.

Stevenson, Elizabeth. [1949] 1981. *The Crooked Corridor: A Study of Henry James*. New York: Octagon.

Stewart, John Innes Mackintosh. 1963. "Henry James." In *Eight Modern Writers. Oxford History of English Literature*. Vol. 12, 71–121. New York: Oxford University Press.

Stone, Donald David. 1972. *Novelists in a Changing World: Meredith, James, and the Transformation of English Fiction in the 1880's*. Cambridge, MA: Harvard University Press.

Stone, Edward. 1964. *The Battle and the Books: Some Aspects of Henry James*. Athens: Ohio University Press.

Swan, Michael. 1957. *Henry James*. London: Longmans, Green.

————, ed. 1948. "Introduction." *Ten Short Stories of Henry James*. London: John Lehmann.

Sweeney, Gerard. 1983. "The Deadly Figure in James's Carpet." *Modern Language Studies* 13: 79–85.

Szegedy-Maszák, Mihály. 1984. "Henry James, European or American?" In *The Origins and Originality of American Culture*. Ed. Tibor Frank, 233–45. Budapest: Akadémia Kiadó.

Thurber, James. 1953. "A Final Note on Chanda Bell." *Thurber Country*, 151–63. New York: Simon & Schuster.

Tintner, Adeline R. 1989. *The Pop World of Henry James: From Fairy Tales to Science Fiction*. Ann Arbor: UMI Research Press.

————. 1986. *The Museum World of Henry James*. Ann Arbor: UMI Research Press.

————. 1982. "Hiding Behind James: Roth's *Zuckerman Bound*." *Midstream* 28, no. 4 (April): 49–53.

————. 1976. "A Portrait of the Novelist as a Young Man: The Letters of Henry James." *Studies in the Novel* 8 (Spring): 121–28.

Todorov, Tzvetan. 1977. *The Poetics of Prose*. Trans. Richard Howard. Ithaca, NY: Cornell University Press.

Tyler, Parker. 1964. *Every Artist His Own Scandal: A Study of Real and Fictive Heroes*. New York: Horizon Press. Reprinted from "The Child as 'The Figure in the Carpet.'" *Chicago Review* 11 (Winter 1958): 31–42 .

Vaid, Krishna B. 1964. *Technique in the Tales of Henry James*. Cambridge, MA: Harvard University Press.

Van Cromphout, G. 1968. "Artist and Society in Henry James." *English Studies* 49 (April): 132–40.

Vivas, Eliseo. 1943. "Henry and William (Two Notes)." *The Kenyon Review* 5: 580–94.

Voss, Arthur. 1973. *The American Short Story: A Critical Survey*. Norman: University of Oklahoma Press.

Wagenknecht, Edward. 1984. *The Tales of Henry James*. New York: Frederick Ungar.

Wallace, Ronald. 1975. *Henry James and the Comic Form*. Ann Arbor: University of Michigan Press.

Weber, Samuel. 1986. "Caught in the Act of Reading." In *Demarcating the Disciplines: Philosophy, Literature, Art*. Glyph Textual Studies 1, 181–214. Minneapolis: University of Minnesota Press.

Wegelin, Christof. 1958. *The Image of Europe in Henry James*. Dallas: Southern Methodist University Press.

Westbrook, Perry D. 1953. "The Supersubtle Fry." *Nineteenth-Century Fiction* 8 (September): 134–40.

Williams, M. A. 1984. "Reading 'The Figure in the Carpet': Henry James and Wolfgang Iser." *English Studies in Africa* 27: 107–21.

Wirth-Nesher, Hana. 1984. "The Thematics of Interpretation: James's Artist Tales." *Henry James Review* 5: 117–27.

Wright, Austin McGiffert. 1961. *The American Short Story in the Twenties*. Chicago: University of Chicago Press.

Wright, Walter F. 1962. *The Madness of Art: A Study of Henry James*. Lincoln: University of Nebraska Press.

Zabel, Morton Dauwen, ed. 1958. *Henry James: In the Cage and Other Tales*. Garden City, NY: Doubleday.

Zgorzelski, Andrzej. 1984. "The Quest for the Indecipherable: Todorov's Non-Existent Mystery of the 'Figure in the Carpet.'" In *Litterae et Lingua: In Honorem Premislavi Mroczkowski*. Ed. Jan Nowakowski, 171–77. Wroctaw: Pol. Akad. Nauk.

Foreign Language
Canavaggia, Marie. 1957. "Traduction et Presentation de "L'image dans le tapis." Paris: Editions Pierre Horay.

Cestre, Charles. 1945. *La Littérature Américaine*. Paris: Librairie Armand Colin.

Cixous, Hélène. 1970. "L'écriture comme placement: Henry James." *Poétique* 1: 51–63.

Hofmann, Gert. 1957. *Interpretationsprobleme Bei Henry James*. Diss. Freiburg.

Onishi, Akio. 1965. "Henry James: 'The Figure in the Carpet.'" *Eigo Eibungaku Ronshu* (Kansai University) 9 (February): 53–70. [Japanese]

Pontalis, J. B. 1968. "La Lecteur et son auteur." In *Après Freud*. Paris: Gallimard.

Flickerbridge

Publication History

"Flickerbridge" appeared first in *Scribner's Magazine* in February 1902, a date that James complained to William Dean Howells was nearly two years after its acceptance (*Letters* 4, 223). James included the story the next year in *The Better Sort*, and later in his New York Edition.

Circumstances of Composition, Sources, and Influences

In February 1899 James read a tale by Sarah Orne Jewett, identified by Matthiessen and Murdock as "A Lost Lover" (N 288). An hour after finishing it, James recorded as a germ for the tale Jewett's description of a girl visiting a "new-found old-fashioned" relation: "Her repression and rare words of approval, had a great fascination for a girl who had just been used to people who chattered and were upon most intimate terms with you directly, and could forget you with equal ease." James put a young man recovering from influenza, as James was himself at the time, in the same situation. To his protagonist, the woman's manner is a "cool bath" in a world of "chatter," including that of his fiancée. In the original plan, the fiancée does come to visit, transforming the cousin into a "show old woman," and interpreting the man's "regret" as jealousy. The man "retreats, *flees*, leaving *her* in chattering and raving possession" (CN 181–82). James kept the basic situation, while transferring the cousin from the man to the woman, making—as Matthiessen and Murdock point out—her visit more likely, even as he avoids it by having the man leave first (N 288). In his preface, however, James found the story quite "cover[ed] its tracks, and could find no source for the tale apart from its "stray spark of the old 'international' flame" (*Criticism* 2, 1280, 1283–84).

Granger tells Miss Wenham, "You're the Sleeping Beauty in the wood," adding later, "That's just your beauty—your 'sleeping' beauty" (CT 11, 340, 344), and Tintner has offered Burne-Jone's *Briar Rose Series* as the specific source for the recurring images of the tale. Burne-Jones left his princess and palace asleep in protest against the modern world's excessive business, and so, Tintner argues, Granger says of Flickerbridge, "Its only safety, of a truth, was to be left still to sleep." Applying more of a psychological than a sociological interpretation to the tale, she maintains that James changes the fairy tale's representation of the postponement of heterosexuality into a "repudiation of heterosexuality," seen in Granger's rejection not only of the wide-awake Addie but even the still sleeping Miss Wenham (1986, 147–50; 1989, 10, 17–24, 45). Unrue casts Miss Wenham, in James's description of her "almost Gothic grotesqueness," as a metaphorical folk figure who represents Granger's journey from ignorance to knowledge (298-99). Combining the folk images, Sharp sees her as a "gnome-like" fairy godmother, similar to Susan Stringham (36). Wagenknecht, on the other hand, suggests that Miss Wenham's grotesque appearance may have come from the Maupassant tale "Miss Harriet," to which James alludes directly in his story (138; also Tinter 1986, 147).

James had recorded the name of Miss Wenham's peacefully sleepy world in his notebook on May 7, 1898 (CN 170). Its isolation is a classic attribute of the English countryside seen in such works as Gray's "Elegy on a Country Churchyard," its changelessness in Keats's "Ode on a Grecian Urn." The quirky nature of its main inhabitant is reminiscent of Gaskell's *Cranford*, which James had discussed in a letter to Grace Norton on Christmas 1898 (*Letters* 4, 93). Shady Hill, the home of Grace's father, Charles Eliot Norton, has a similarly peaceful sound, and was located in one of New England's many "bridge" towns, Stockbridge. Shulman, however, sees the town's name as parodic (49).

The threatened disturber of the peace, Addie, may have owed something to James's dismay at an early example of journalistic invasion of privacy that had already led him to write *The Reverberator*. When Mary Marcy McClellan wrote a letter about her visits in Venice to the New York *World* in 1886, her hosts—and James—took it as a violation of hospitality. In a letter James complained, "Good heavens, what a superfluous product is the smart, forward, over-encouraged, thinking-she-can-write-and-that-her-writing-has-any-business-to-exist American girl! Basta!" (*Life* 3, 230).

Relation to Other Works

Several critics have compared the tale with "A Passionate Pilgrim," "Flickerbridge," being in Edgar's view "a matured version" of the earlier tale (62; e.g., Jones 218). Putt elaborates, judging the later tale more masterful, particularly in the way Miss Wenham is made to embody her setting as the thinner Miss Searle failed to, at the same time that she is an authentic English spinster of the same type as Ambient's sister in "The Author of Beltraffio" and Lady Aurora Langrish in *The Princess Casamassima* (247). Segal also classes Miss Wenham and Miss Searle together with Lord Warburton's sisters in *The Portrait of a Lady*, noting the "simplicity" of each (10). Jones and Edward Stone both compare Granger's approach to Miss Wenham to Searle's approach to Miss Searle, his Sleeping Beauty (Jones 218; Stone 141). "Flickerbridge," in Putt's view, is ultimately a more complex if still loving judgment of "old" England than "A Passionate Pilgrim," preceding the full "disillusionment" of *The Sense of the Past* (65–67). Perosa, on the other hand, links "Flickerbridge" with *The Sense of the Past* in the heroes' "deep feeling of identification" with the past, contrasting with the women's focus on the present and America (135).

Both Searle and Granger are, Putt argues, along with Ralph Pendrel of *The Sense of the Past* and Mrs. Gracedew of *Covering End*, examples of a Jamesian type, the "unexpected American visitor" (247). In their visits, according to McCarthy, Granger, Searle, and Mrs. Gracedew bring a strong admiration for the old country (116). Gill also makes a connection with *Covering End*, seeing them representing—a bit too obviously—James's ideal of the English country house (81–82). Appropriately, therefore, Zabel connects the tale with the essays in the 1905 *English Hours* (x). Sharp finds the "mellow" tone akin to that of *The Ambassadors* (38). Similarly, Jones compares Frank's view of Flickerbridge's perfection to Strether's and James's view of Mme de Vionnet or the critic's at Dedborough in *The Outcry* (240, 273). Walter Wright praises the vividness of the depiction of Flickerbridge (121). Austin Wright, however, sees James suggesting but not specifying its beauty in the same manner as he treats the evil in *The Turn of the Screw*, out of a desire to emphasize Granger's choice rather than the setting (356–57).

However it is depicted, Flickerbridge is surrounded by a far different world. Howard finds throughout *The Better Sort* the depiction of an age in which "everyone and everything are *sold*," pointing in particular to this tale, "Broken Wings," "The Birthplace," and *The Papers*, where not only imagination, but those possessing it, are treated as a commodity, and where those who hold out against such materialism are "the real better sort" (56–57). Gage contrasts Granger's unwillingness to cooperate with modern forces in the publicizing of Flickerbridge with Gedge's compromise with similar forces in "The Birthplace." Such resolution is not easy. As Gage notes, while in "Mrs. Medwin" the individual pursued society, here society pursues the individual (104, 106, 113 n.35). The prime weapon is the newspaper, and both Perosa and Wagenknecht note that the tale's concern with publicity is shared with *The Reverberator* (Perosa 135; Wagenknecht 138–39). Zabel adds *The Bostonians* and *The Portrait of a Lady* (xxvi), and Addie does seem a debased version of Henrietta Stackpole, who also wanted to put her hosts in print. Another victim of the pursuit of society is "The Beldonald Holbein," and Sharp, Gage, and Wagenknecht all draw parallels between Mrs. Brash and Miss Wenham (Sharp 288 n.5; Gage 82; Wagenknecht 138–40). Jones contrasts Granger's sympathetic approach to the selfish one of the narrator in *The Aspern Papers* (218).

In such a world, Flickerbridge represents a retreat, one as Tintner argues that is necessarily temporary, just as in "The Great Good Place" (1986, 147; also Wagenknecht 138). In both tales, Gill observes, retreat is specifically associated with the English country home (92, 229). Gage finds Miss Wenham's isolation less extreme and less harmful than that of Maud Blessingbourne in "The Story in It" (191). Sharp compares her isolation to that of Tina Bordereau in her consequent "puzzlement" about the outside world (37–38).

Emphasizing Granger's role, Tintner came to see the retreat here more as one from women than from the world. She lists all of James's subsequent works, both novels and tales, with the exception of *The Papers*, as illustrating the same lack of male passion for the female (1989, 22–23). Earlier, Wilson classed Granger with such other "sensitive" Jamesian men as Longueville of *Confidence* and Marcher (122). Gage compares him to both the renunciative painter Straith in "Broken Wings" and the renunciative Shirley Sutton, who, in "The Two Faces," gives up his lady out of an unwillingness to witness her exploitation of others (84).

Interpretation and Criticism

A contemporary review of *The Better Sort* found that while at first the tale's idea seems "impossibly exaggerated in importance," it gradually becomes "moving and significative." The idea rests in Granger's declaration that "we live in an age of prodigious machinery, and all organised to a single end. That end is publicity—a publicity as ferocious as the appetite of a cannibal" (*Bookman*). James himself was to become increasingly aware of its appetite, and, as Matthiessen and Murdock observe, James's denunciation of modern publicity is even more highly wrought in the preface (N 288). There, James finds the "deadly epidemic of publicity" even more to be feared than "the Black Death" (*Criticism* 2, 1284). Many years later, Stowell would still find its consideration of publicity making "Flickerbridge" an "extremely modern" tale (32).

It is an American in this story who threatens old England with unwanted publicity, and Shulman sees the tale as a series of "ingenious inversions" with Europe now innocent and sympathetic, America knowing and threatening (50). Wegelin sees the emphasis here not on Europe itself but "American images of Europe." By making the intrusive Addie Miss Wenham's relation, Wegelin argues, James creates "a twist to the old theme of the American claimant," indicating that the English line taken to America becomes vulgarized. What he considers most important in the story, however, is the contrast between the two different kinds of "admiration, vulgar and delicate" of the two Americans and the "surprised unconsciousness" of Miss Wenham, who cannot quite fathom the cause for Granger's concern (52, 180 n.26).

Miss Wenham is, as Jones remarks, the center of the tale (221). It is she who possesses what James saw as his subject, the "rarity, precious rarity" so endangered by modern times (*Criticism* 2, 1284). She represents the past as well, without, as Sharp remarks, even realizing it (37). The two Americans in their responses to her thus represent different responses to the past. James's own sympathies were often with the past, and Sharp finds in the tale a concentration of James's "sense of the past, his moral sense, and his sense of beauty" (37). Unrue observes how Granger, whose name suggests a "rural innocence," a way of life represented by Miss Wenham, gradually comes to recognize her superiority to Addie's destructive analysis (298–99).

In the notebooks, Granger was to be a barrister or journalist, but James transformed him into an artist. Kappeler remarks on his instinctive making of pictures of all he sees (106). As Sharp points out, Granger is more an artist in his perception than in his work, but like other critics, she has noted that his artistic perceptions evolve during the course of the story (37; also Gage 82). To Tintner he is a "weary Impressionist" who is restored by a Pre-Raphaelite "vision" of the Middle Ages (1986, 108). To Stowell he is a "second rate" painter who evolves from a strictly representational to an almost impressionistic approach that acknowledges the fluid nature of relations. Such change, Stowell argues, is the central theme of this story of "phenomenological relations" (31–32).

Granger seeks, however, to avoid change by leaving Flickerbridge, an effort many critics judge futile. Tintner, pointing out that it is the same forces that caused Granger's exhaustion that also threaten Flickerbridge, foresees Granger as having brought about the place's ruin (1986, 147). Gage, too, depicts Granger as having "unwittingly cast" the seed of modernism (83). Stowell adds that neither Granger nor Miss Wenham is willing to acknowledge that *their* relationship has brought about change (33). Jones is less censorious, if no more optimistic, arguing that Granger's retreat is not cowardly but a "pragmatic and idealistic withdrawal," a refusal "to participate in the dissolution of the ideal." In his view, the tale argues for renunciation as the "true art of life" and memory as the only force that can preserve what passes (220, 287). Edgar notes that while Granger's running away inevitably conveys weakness, there really was no alternative if Granger was to retain his "memory unsullied and unimpaired" (63). Similarly, Kappeler writes that Granger leaves so as to save "his precious private glimpse" of Flickerbridge, not Flickerbridge itself (108–09).

In leaving, Granger sacrifices a friendship and an engagement. Sharp characterizes the friendship as one of the "outstanding friendships" in James, even if it is more one of appreciation than true communication (36–37), and Shulman sees the true sacrifice for Granger as the loss of his elderly friend, not his young fiancée (52). Tintner links both sacrifices, pointing up the significance of the shared name between "the old Addie" and "the young Addie," and finds in them James's "official signing off of women" (1989, 15, 20, 45). Such is necessary for the artist in the Jamesian world, according to Kappeler, a world where fraternization with model or muse is death to the art (109–10).

Others focus more on the rejection of the young Addie, beginning with Wilson, who used the story as an occasion to observe that in James "the men are always deciding *not* to marry the women" and found it very difficult to sympathize with Granger, despite what he felt is James's unambiguous approval of him (122–23). Similarly, Przybylowicz accuses Granger of retreat into the past out of a fear of life and sexuality and even ambition, arguing that Miss Wenham's life is "static" and "isolated" in contrast to "dynamic, independent, and aggressive" Addie. She remarks, too, that Addie is a "successful artist" (one feels James might have taken issue with her terms) while Granger is unproductive (157). Matthiessen and Murdock had earlier noted that Addie has "much more energy" than Granger (N 287). James makes Addie's energy clear in his notebook sketch of her: "*She* chatters, she raves. She writes— she's clever—(she masculine?) she's conscious and appreciative of everything" (CN 182). Addie's "New England emphasis," as the tale calls it, is no longer quaint, but rather the Puritan work ethic run rampant (CT 11, 329). As Walter Wright asserts, Addie has the wit to recognize the uniqueness of Flickerbridge but not its vulnerability. She may, however, be dangerous precisely because she is, as Wright asserts, "a clever, interesting young woman" and "not a caricature" (78).

When Granger breaks off with Addie, he is, as Austin Wright comments, rejecting not just her but the society she represents to him (191). In contrast to Przybylowicz's censure, Andreas rather commonsensically remarks that Granger's experience in Flickerbridge has made him realize his and Addie's incompatibility. While Granger's perceptions have expanded, hers remain limited to a "sense of the picturesque" (100). Perhaps thinking along the same lines, Gage calls Granger's renunciation "specious" on the grounds that he no longer wishes to marry a journalist (190). There is no indication that Addie might learn from Flickerbridge, rather than destroy it. As Sharp recognizes, Granger is partly selfish in wanting to keep Flickerbridge to himself, but she also contends that his (and James's) decision to keep Addie out preserves not only his but also the reader's pleasure (38–39). To Wagenknecht, however, Frank's giving up of Addie on the grounds of something he *thinks* she *might* do is rather strained. He judges it, however, along with the idea that Miss Wenham might become a sudden popular success, quite Jamesian, observing by the way that James "is by no means wholly a realistic writer" (140).

Looking at the entire tale, Wagenknecht, Geismar, and Putt all find it flawed by what Putt calls its "frankly . . . incredible" theme (Wagenknecht

140; Geismar 255n; Putt 65). Vaid, however, praises it as one of James's "few excellent anecdotes," and Edgar places the tale for "perfection of surface" among the august company of "The Beast in the Jungle," "The Altar of the Dead," "The Great Good Place," and "The Middle Years" (Vaid 7; Edgar 206). The tale is, as Shulman terms it, a bittersweet comedy (52), and its strength is in its capturing of that mood. The bittersweet air comes from its central subject, which Putt finds rises above the tale's flaws, the capturing of the English past and present (65). As Gale observes, in the story Granger at least gets to make his decisions in a garden (41 n.3).

Works Cited

Primary Works

James, Henry. 1902. "Flickerbridge." *Scribner's Magazine* 31 (February): 170–80.

———. 1903. "Flickerbridge." *The Better Sort*. London: Methuen; New York: Scribner's, 143–67.

———. 1908. "Flickerbridge." In *The Novels and Tales of Henry James*. New York Edition. Vol. 18, 437–69. New York: Scribner's.

Secondary Works

Andreas, Osborn. 1948. *Henry James and the Expanding Horizon: A Study of the Meaning and Basic Themes of James's Fiction*. Seattle: University of Washington Press.

Anon. 1903. Review of *The Better Sort*. *Bookman* 24 (April): 30.

Edgar, Pelham. [1927] 1964. *Henry James, Man and Author*. New York: Russell & Russell.

Gage, Richard P. 1988. *Order and Design: Henry James' Titled Story Sequences*. New York: Peter Lang.

Geismar, Maxwell. 1963. *Henry James and the Jacobites*. Boston: Houghton Mifflin.

Gill, Richard. 1972. *Happy Rural Seat: The English Country House and the Literary Imagination*. New Haven: Yale University Press.

Howard, David. "Henry James and 'The Papers.'" In *Henry James: Fiction as History*. Ed. Ian F. A. Bell, 49–64. London: Vision; Totowa, NJ: Barnes & Noble.

Jones, Granville H. 1975. *Henry James's Psychology of Experience: Innocence, Responsibility, and Renunciation in the Fiction of Henry James*. The Hague: Mouton.

Kappeler, Susanne. 1980. *Writing and Reading in Henry James*. New York: Columbia University Press.

McCarthy, Harold T. 1958. *Henry James: The Creative Process*. New York: Thomas Yoseloff.

Perosa, Sergio. 1983. *Henry James and the Experimental Novel*. New York: New York University Press.

Przybylowicz, Donna. 1986. *Desire and Repression: The Dialectic of Self and Other in the Late Works of Henry James*. University: University of Alabama Press.

Putt, S. Gorley. 1966. *Henry James: A Reader's Guide*. Ithaca, NY: Cornell University Press. Revised in part from "The Passionate Pilgrim: An Aspect of Henry James." *The Wind and the Rain* 4 (1948): 230–32.

Segal, Ora. 1969. *The Lucid Reflector: The Observer in Henry James' Fiction*. New Haven: Yale University Press.

Sharp, Sister M. Corona. 1963. *The Confidante in Henry James: Evolution and Moral Value of a Fictive Character*. Notre Dame, IN: Notre Dame University Press.

Shulman, Robert. 1968. "Henry James and the Modern Comedy of Knowledge." *Criticism* 10 (Winter): 41–53.

Stone, Edward. 1964. *The Battle and the Books: Some Aspects of Henry James*. Athens: Ohio University Press.

Stowell, H. Peter. 1984. "Impressionism in James's Late Stories." *Revue de Littérature Comparée* 58 (January–March): 27–36.

Tintner, Adeline R. 1989. *The Pop World of Henry James: From Fairy Tales to Science Fiction*. Ann Arbor: UMI Research Press.

———. 1986. *The Museum World of Henry James*. Ann Arbor: UMI Research Press. Revised from "Henry James and the Sleeping Beauty: A Victorian Fantasy of a Fairy-Tale Theme." *Topic* 37 (Fall 1983): 10–22.

Unrue, Darlene. 1976. "Henry James and the Grotesque." *The Arizona Quarterly* 32: 293–300.

Vaid, Krishna B. 1964. *Technique in the Tales of Henry James*. Cambridge, MA: Harvard University Press.

Wagenknecht, Edward. 1984. *The Tales of Henry James*. New York: Frederick Ungar.

Wegelin, Christof. 1958. *The Image of Europe in Henry James*. Dallas: Southern Methodist University Press.

Wilson, Edmund. 1960. "The Ambiguity of Henry James." In *A Casebook on Henry James's "The Turn of the Screw."* Ed. Gerald Willen, 115–59. New York: Thomas Y. Crowell.

Wright, Austin McGiffert. 1961. *The American Short Story in the Twenties*. Chicago: University of Chicago Press.

Wright, Walter F. 1962. *The Madness of Art: A Study of Henry James*. Lincoln: University of Nebraska Press.

Zabel, Morton Dauwen, ed. 1961. *Fifteen Short Stories by Henry James*. New York: Bantam.

Fordham Castle

Publication History

"Fordham Castle" appeared first in the 1904 Christmas issue of *Harper's Magazine*, and was also included by James in the New York Edition.

Circumstances of Composition, Sources, and Influences

"Fordham Castle" spent several years in the notebooks before emerging as a tale. James first made a notation of one half of its theme, "the immense typical theme of the *manless* American woman, in Europe" and the "total suppression of the husband" in 1891, proposing to treat it through two women and their husbands (CN 65). Seven years later, inspired by Gaillard T. Lapsley's comments on two American girls at an embassy tea, he tried out the idea of "the American phenomenon of the social suppression of the parents," picturing a socially ambitious son and daughter passing off their "compromising" mother as dead, with the mother "submissively and bewilderedly— *devotedly*, above all" consenting (CN 170). Returning to the idea several months later back at Lamb House, James was striving above all things for brevity, and so decided to adopt the point of view of the mother, although he bracketed the scene of the mother in her European pension with scenes of the two children, now both daughters, all presented through a first-person narrator (CN 175–76). In Rome in May 1899, James put the two ideas together as "The Mother and Husband (American) Meeting thing" (CN 184). Again in October he recalled the "2 American appendages"—the "shunted mother" and "relegated husband"—who pass for dead to help a daughter and a spouse through "some social squeeze." As he sees it now, "the little affair *is* their talk"—as they learn from each other how they are spoken of (CN 185). He had to remind himself one more time, a year later, "*Don't give up*— DON'T give up the American girls and their suppressed mother" (CN 194).

Dyson points as another line of development to two entries, the first from January 1894, the second from February 5, 1895, which Edel and Powers take as the germ of "The Jolly Corner." In them, James imagines the "living death" of a man who gives up his artistic aspirations, and the woman to whom he has confided them, for a showy political career and wife. He becomes the "spectator of his own tragedy," his first love coming to represent his "Dead

Self," which still "lives a little" in her. In Dyson's reading, Sue is the wife bringing death, and Mrs. Magaw the woman offering new life (Dyson 43–44; CN 82–84, 112–13)

In the first notebook entry, James mentioned as the epitome of the manless woman Mrs. L of New York, whom Edel and Powers speculate was Florence Bayard, a friend of Sarah Butler Wister (CN 65).

Mrs. Magaw's hair makes Taker think of an "old-fashioned 'work'" with "weeping willows and mortuary urns" (CT 12, 128). The comparison to a "mourning picture" strikes Tintner as a sign of James's renewed nostalgia for an old-fashioned America, at a time when he was considering a revisit there (181–82). Mrs. Magaw's hairstyle, as Gale points out, is described similarly to that of Mrs. Ruck in "The Pension Beaurepas," but according to Putt, there is "a world of emotional distance" between the picture evoked here and that of the similar memorial to Miss Pynsent's parents in *The Princess Casamassima* (Gale 53–54; Putt 299).

Vaid compares the tale to Hawthorne's "Wakefield," where the husband through absence from his wife becomes "the Outcast of the Universe" (201). Ezra Pound compares the tale to Maupassant's *Toine* as treating a similar "case" (35). The names, as Vanderbilt notes, are distinctly Dickensian (62).

In this late tale, James seems to have looked ahead to the future of Americans abroad—literary ones at least. Jefferson compares Mrs. Taker to Wharton's Undine Spragg, while the characters impress Wilson as coming out of Sinclair Lewis (Jefferson 158; Wilson 142). Vanderbilt finds Jay Gatsby, once James Gatz, seeking, like Sue Taker, a new life with the help of a new name (65). Putt sees the tale "perilously near the brink of the world of raw cannibalism" in Tennessee Williams's "Desire and the Black Masseur" (299).

Relation to Other Works

In his preface James speaks of trying to redeem "too unbroken an eternity of mere international young ladies" by his treatment of an older generation (*Criticism* 2, 1277). Appropriately, therefore, Wagenknecht finds the "sympathetic" tone similar to that accorded the older couple in "Broken Wings". Pandora, Wagenknecht adds, is another, but kinder, version of the social climbing daughter who casts off her family (143). Sicker compares Taker to another of James's young ladies, Julia Bride, seeing both as trapped and isolated "faceless characters" (170–71). Similarly, Edel places "Fordham Castle" with "Julia Bride" and "The Jolly Corner" as "sketches of Americans in a world of obscure or lost identities" (CT 12, 8–9).

Taker's renunciation is, Austin Wright contends, like the renunciation of the daughters in "Europe," motivated by a proper sense of obligation, but taken such severe advantage of that the reader is brought to question its wisdom (117–18). Przybylowicz compares Taker to another renouncer, Marcher in "The Beast in the Jungle," with its theme of "the unlived life." For both men, she asserts, the past is meaningless because they will not seek to determine their futures, a failure which makes their present lives equally empty (90–92).

Vaid compares the offstage Mrs. Taker to the offstage Mrs. Newsome of *The Ambassadors* (198).

Interpretation and Criticism

On his arrival in New York in 1904, James was met at the dock by an "amiable representative of the house of Harper," and was therefore able to relay to his agent as he read proof for the tale that "it has been intimated to me (rather funnily!) that 'the whole house' are particularly pleased with it!" (*Letters* 4, 321–23). In 1898 James had spoken of his idea as containing "pathos and drollery" (N 268). Later critics tended to see little comedy in the tale (e.g., Tilton xii). Instead, the emphasis has been on what Wagenknecht calls the tale's "astringency" (143). As Tintner recognizes, the comedy here is a very particular kind, "a kind of early black humor—half burlesque and half tragedy," marked by a constant reference to death (181).

The story's plot, such as it is, revolves around names. Indeed, Horrell declares the basis of the "entire story" here to be "the relationship between a name and social success" (210). Andreas charts Taker's evolution through his change of names, seeing him undergoing a reflective change of identity as he becomes Addard, following his wife's mercenary one. He wishes, Andreas asserts, to maintain the intermediate identity of Addard, averse to becoming Mr. Sherrington Reeves following his wife, and not allowed by her to remain Abel F. Taker (128–29). The names throughout seem ironic. Mrs. Taker does not want to keep the name that so aptly fits her, wanting to "take" from him even the name he gave her. The name he takes in the meantime, Addard, evokes the poisonous "adder," even as his real first name, Abel, marks him as a victim.

The playing with names, however, brings in more serious issues of identity. Deprived of all "external signs of identity," according to Matthiessen and Murdock, Taker and Mrs. Magaw enter into a form of "death in life" (N 294). Living indefinitely in a spot meant for vacationing, the two seem suspended in a void. At times they even seem, Mackenzie observes, to be their own survivors, although he adds that they have never really lived at all (43). They certainly do little now, and the story was the occasion for Pound to observe that James's "people are so much more, or so much more often, 'sitters' than 'actors'" (35).

Taker is, perhaps, even for James, a remarkably subdued hero. Edel calls him a "whimsical-pathetic" character, while Putt, with less tolerance, objects to his "abjectly masochistic" behavior (CT 12, 9; Putt 299). Similarly Jefferson, while viewing Mrs. Taker as the *"terminus ad quem"* of the ruthless Midwesterner "making good," argues that because he and Mrs. Magaw accept their roles so easily, it is inappropriate to read the tale as a moral indictment of their victimizers. Jefferson finds the strength of the story to be its capturing of Abel's viewpoint. For Taker, Jefferson writes, playing dead is "merely the culmination, the last of many marital humiliations" (158–62). Vaid, on the other hand, absolves Abel of morbidity, seeing his speaking of himself as dead as a "desperate protest against a loss of identity," even if a weak one (198). Similarly, Przybylowicz traces the manner in which, robbed of his past and thus of his specific identity, Taker responds to his loss as "a kind of mortality" and so reinterprets the world around him, seeing death everywhere. Citing Taker's admission that he "is nothing" without his wife, Przybylowicz sees him left suspended in a "purgatory of anonymity" because he is unable to act against the "external forces" his wife represents (91–92, 101).

Taker does manage to muster the energy to fall in love with Mrs. Magaw— "after a fashion," as Matthiessen and Murdock put it (N 294). Taker's "incipient love," however, while according to Vaid consistent with the tale's "romantic" and "comic-fantastic" nature, also, Vaid argues, contributes to the pathos of Taker's eventual extinction (197–98). As Sicker notes, Taker uses his friendship with Mrs. Magaw to try out the possibility of his new identity, telling her, "You're conversing with C. P. Addard. *He* may be alive—but even this I don't know yet . . . I'm trying him, Mrs. Magaw, on you" (170–71). Jones also emphasizes Taker's brief achievement of an independence and purpose of sorts through his alliance with Mrs. Magaw, but finds its "dreamlike state of isolation and timeless *nothing*" interrupted by the "*something*" of Mrs. Magaw's recall to the world, and so serving in the end mainly to render his second death the more devastating (205–6; also Przybylowicz 91). When Mrs. Magaw leaves, Taker comes to a final recognition: "Why certainly I'm dead" (CT 11, 149). The last statement has been much quoted, and represents as Jefferson puts it a "different tone" in Taker's acceptance (158–62; also Mackenzie 43).

Dyson, in his reading, emphasizes the difference in experience between the two "dead" characters, Taker and Mrs. Magaw, even as he records James's emphasizing in his notebook the "mutuality of experience" in the capitalized phrase "EACH OTHER" as the two learn to "pass for" "Death and 'Separation.'" All four characters, he argues, undergo some kind of death, but experience "varying afterlives." Taker is willing to accept his new identity, but—Dyson contends— needs to enter into a "living relationship" to be truly alive. Mrs. Magaw, on the other hand, is unwilling to accept the reality behind the metaphor, declaring that she "won't help to bury" Taker, and so, ironically, does, completing the extinction begun by Sue. Thus, for Taker, despite his greater consciousness, "The metaphor is the reality; the separation *is* the death."

Taking his clue from James's reference to the tale in his preface as "complicated music at short order," Vanderbilt uses a musical schema as the context for a quite different reading. In Vanderbilt's analysis, the four characters ring changes on three motifs: the "celebration of those who actively affront their destiny"; "a vital sense of being"; "a capacity for giving." Poor Taker represents only the negative "inversions" of the tale's motifs. He is, in Vanderbilt's estimate, "perhaps the most pathetic" of James's "passive males"—a "virtual leech" with a selfishness indicated in his name that makes him unworthy even of pity. Denying Taker the seriousness accorded him and his situation by Dyson and others, Vanderbilt makes him the butt of the story's satire, not its profound seer.

At the same time, Vanderbilt offers rationales for the behavior of the "possibly admirable" women who seem to fail him. According to his schema, Mrs. Magaw is at least giving, Mattie energetic with a "worthy hunger" for social success, and Sue resourceful in her ambition as well as helpful to young Mattie. Additionally, Vanderbilt declares, Mrs. Magaw's rejection of Taker's appeal can be taken as an understandable rejection of an unwanted sexual advance, and Sue's rejection of Taker as a sincere if somewhat ruthless attempt to redeem the mistake of an early marriage, and to choose a new, more appropriate destiny.

In his preface, James declared the story still a "scrap." Since then, critics have varied in their estimates. A chronic objection is to the obvious parallelism of Mrs. Magaw's and Taker's cases, which Putt finds absurd and which O'Connor argues "diminishes [the theme] by robbing the characters of their uniqueness," and threatens the tale's realism (Putt 299; O'Connor 233–34). Vaid, however, while spelling out several of the resemblances, judges them not only understandable in a story tinged with the fantastic, but also outnumbered by the differences between the two characters, arguing that the contrast between Taker's ironic manner and Mrs. Magaw's simplicity provides the tale with its humor (194–96).

Matthiessen and Murdock echo James's verdict in the preface that he had missed the "larger connexion" in the tale (N 294; *Criticism* 2, 1277). Dyson, however, counters that James only meant to deprecate the lack of the "downtown" element in the tale, not render an "absolute value-judgement" (41 n.2). Both he and Vanderbilt argue that the tale deserves reconsideration (Vanderbilt 66). The story, indeed, is not without admirers. Pound early on saw it as "excellently, perhaps flawlessly done" (35). Jefferson argues that Taker's point of view is the chief strength in the tale (158–62). While Vaid maintains that the point of view is more omniscient than limited, he lists other strengths, judging the tale a successful treatment of several themes: "the effect on a sensitive character of a loss of identity," the "American Eve" who casts off her Adam as she seeks a "European Eden," and the one initially indicated by James, "the American phenomenon of the social suppression of the parents" (198–200). Voss, however, judges it not one of James's best, either as an example of the international theme or as a treatment of the theme of death in life (137–38). Edgar and Putt are among the most negative, Edgar calling it "a clumsily contrived *jeu d'esprit*, over-valued by its author" (64). Putt objects primarily to the characters' "almost subhuman lack of integrity," locating the tale's only vitality in its "marginal expressions of loathing" for its "tasteless frauds" (298–99). Indeed, while one need not go so far as Putt, it is primarily one's capacity to regard such helpless characters as Taker as either profound or amusing which will determine one's regard for the tale.

Works Cited

Primary Works

James, Henry. 1904. "Fordham Castle." *Harper's Magazine* 110 (December): 147–58.

———. 1909. "Fordam Castle." *The Novels and Tales of Henry James*. New York Edition. Vol. 16, 393–426. New York: Scribner's.

Secondary Works

Andreas, Osborn. 1948. *Henry James and the Expanding Horizon: A Study of the Meaning and Basic Themes of James's Fiction*. Seattle: University of Washington Press.

Dyson, John Peter. 1979. "Death and Separation in 'Fordham Castle.'" *Studies in Short Fiction* 16: 41–47.

Edgar, Pelham. [1927] 1964. *Henry James, Man and Author*. New York: Russell & Russell.

Gale, Robert L. [1954] 1964. *The Caught Image: Figurative Language in the Fiction of Henry James*. Chapel Hill: University of North Carolina Press.

Horrell, Joyce Tayloe. 1970. "A 'Shade of a Special Sense': Henry James and the Art of Naming." *American Literature* 42: 203–20.

Jefferson, D. W. 1964. *Henry James and the Modern Reader*. New York: St. Martin's.

Jones, Granville H. 1975. *Henry James's Psychology of Experience: Innocence, Responsibility, and Renunciation in the Fiction of Henry James*. The Hague: Mouton.

Mackenzie, Manfred. 1976. *Communities of Honor and Love in Henry James*. Cambridge, MA: Harvard University Press.

O'Connor, Frank. 1956. *The Mirror in the Roadway: A Study of the Modern Novel.* New York: Knopf.

Pound, Ezra. 1918. "A Shake Down." *The Little Review* 5 (August): 9–39.

Przybylowicz, Donna. 1986. *Desire and Repression: The Dialectic of Self and Other in the Late Works of Henry James.* University: University of Alabama Press.

Putt, S. Gorley. 1966. *Henry James: A Reader's Guide.* Ithaca, NY: Cornell University Press.

Sicker, Philip. 1980. *Love and the Quest for Identity in the Fiction of Henry James.* Princeton: Princeton University Press.

Tilton, Eleanor M., ed. *Henry James: "The Marriages" and Other Stories.* A Signet Classic. New York: New American Library.

Tintner, Adeline R. 1986. *The Museum World of Henry James.* Ann Arbor: UMI Research Press.

Vaid, Krishna B. 1964. *Technique in the Tales of Henry James.* Cambridge, MA: Harvard University Press.

Vanderbilt, Kermit. 1980. "Complicated Music at Short Order in 'Fordham Castle.'" *Henry James Review* 2: 61–66.

Voss, Arthur. 1973. *The American Short Story: A Critical Survey.* Norman: University of Oklahoma Press.

Wilson, Edmund. 1960. "The Ambiguity of Henry James." In *A Casebook on Henry James's "The Turn of the Screw."* Ed. Gerald Willen, 115–59. New York: Thomas Y. Crowell.

Wagenknecht, Edward. 1984. *The Tales of Henry James.* New York: Frederick Ungar.

Wright, Austin McGiffert. 1961. *The American Short Story in the Twenties.* Chicago: University of Chicago Press.

Four Meetings

Publication History

"Four Meetings" appeared first in the November 1877 issue of *Scribner's Monthly*. James reprinted it several times: first in 1879 in the British edition of *Daisy Miller*. In 1879 a translation, "Les Quatre Recontres," also appeared in *Revue des Deux Mondes* (Hill 18). James included the story in the 1883 Collective Edition, and proposed including it that same year with *The Siege of London* and *Lady Barbarina* (CN 20 n.3). In 1885 he reprinted it in *The Author of Beltraffio*. All of this may have been the reason he informed a bibliographer in 1905 that he had no recollection of where he had collected the tale (*Letters* 4, 360). Finally, heavily revised, it appeared in the New York Edition.

Circumstances of Composition, Sources, and Influences

James and his family arrived at Le Havre on their 1859 journey to Europe, an event LeClair sees as providing material for the description of Le Havre here along with their stay in Boulogne (253, 298; also *Life* 1, 145). In Kelley's view, James's later visit in 1876 is more significant (259). According to Kraft, Caroline's failure to recognize that Le Havre is "not a great thing" is a sign of her faulty vision (100; also Vaid 39). It was Italy, however, to which both Caroline and James attached most importance, as Nathalia Wright points out (217). Appropriately, therefore, Tintner notes the many allusions to Byron in the tale, while arguing that Caroline, who knows Europe only from books, is unable to distinguish the truly Byronic from the false and so is taken in by inferior versions of it in her cousin and the countess (1987, 97). Veeder remarks that the narrator is right that Europe had become "dis-Byronized" (133). For the New York Edition James, however, wanted an "American view" as the frontispiece (*Letters* 4, 430).

The "native American passion," according to the tale, is "the passion for the picturesque." James, Jefferson argues, would be willing to accept the fact that he, too, suffered from the "disease" as he called it in the revised version, as long as his greater "sophistication" was also credited (62). Tintner, on the other hand, brings James a little more to Caroline's level, by pointing out that the photographs of the opening scene recall James's early reliance on photographs for his views of Europe (1986, 240).

On a manuscript of the tale James originally headed his story "Three Meetings," but then corrected it to "Four Meetings" (Aziz). In a letter of March 1879 James mistakenly thanked a critic for her praise of *Daisy Miller* and "Three Meetings." Commenting on the latter slip, Edel locates its significance in the existence of a Turgenev tale by that title (*Letters* 2, 219, 223 n.1). One of the early critics of James's story, Mrs. F. H. Hill, hit upon the resemblance when, commenting on its translation into French, she remarked on the way it suited the "French mind" and observed: "It might be a wonderfully clever translation of a French story, by Charles de Bernard; or even, to pay Mr. James a higher compliment, it might be an English rendering from Turgenieff" (18). More specifically, Lerner observes, both tales feature a detached male narrator who watches, without being able to help, a young woman in trouble (39–40). Peterson also judges both tales to be closely allied in structure and theme on the grounds of their pairing of unwitting narrator and victimized provincial (60–64). Seamon faults the narrator in each for confusing "propriety" with "timidity" (156–57 n.6). Picking up on the French influence, Rebecca West ascribed the tale's "detachment" to James's study of French writers (37). Similarly, Kelley deems the work generally "original," but argues that James's exposure to French ideas of narration and form may have contributed to its excellence (260–61).

The original magazine version already had four meetings, but was divided only into three parts. Perhaps to distinguish it further from Turgenev's tale, James in the first book edition changed the original three sections to four by dividing the central French section in half (Gooder xxx). Nevertheless, James's brother William, reading the tale for the first time in 1892 in a Tauchnitz edition, collapsed the two meetings in Le Havre, writing James in high indignation that they had "*estropie*'d" the tale, "which surely can't have ended in the original in that place—'unsatisfactory' as your endings are accused of being! If this is so, it is an outrage and they ought to know it. It ends after the *third* meeting, at Grimwinter with the french woman in possession." Evidently William took the final "presentiment" as implying more to come. There is no record of what Henry thought of his brother's misreading (229).

Originally, Caroline lived in Grimwinter, a name that James softened in the revision to North Verona (51). While Griffin comments on the "incongruity" of the new name, Vanderbilt sees it evoking the idea of the passionate Juliet, entombed alive (Griffin 48, Vanderbilt 747, 751). The entombed Caroline is compared by Fadiman to Sinclair Lewis's Carol Kennicott, who also hungered for culture among those who did not (37).

The narrator, according to Martin, has an unpleasant sense of seeing some of himself in the Countess, a mirroring technique he locates in such different works as Milton's *Samson Agonistes*, Austen's *Emma*, and Conrad's *Lord Jim*, as well as James's own "The Beast in the Jungle" (498–99).

Relation to Other Works

Fadiman finds the tale the first of James's to "display mastery," although less subtle than the depiction of the encounter of Europe and America in *The American* later that same year, or especially the much later *The Ambassadors* and *The Golden Bowl* (38). In comparison with "A Bundle of Letters," Gerlach argues that the structure of "Four Meetings" with its "clearly linear time" is more typical of James. It fits, too, according to Gerlach, with James's frequent practice of beginning his stories with the death of the central character (82, 88).

The pattern of "bringing Europe to America" in the tale, Thorp notes, is repeated in next year's *The Europeans*, both works, according to Putt, showing the "seamy side" of such an encounter (Thorp xiii; Putt 119). The Countess serves as a cheapened version of the Baroness. American virtue, however, can be constraining, and Walter Wright likens Caroline to Gertrude Wentworth as an uneasy Puritan (85). Observing that the ending for Gertrude is happier, Long casts Caroline's failure as a "frosty" corrective to the "openness" advocated in *The Europeans* (27, 63).

Several connections have also been drawn to two other international works in which, more typically, Americans go to Europe, *Madame de Mauves* and *Daisy Miller*. Ward compares the tale to *Madame de Mauves* in order to illustrate the difference between the short story and the expansive *nouvelle*, and finds Caroline evidencing no development over the course of the meetings (21–22). Her character as "unrepentant romantic," however, Granville Jones compares to Mme de Mauves as well as Graham Fielder of *The Ivory Tower* (114). The renunciations of both Caroline and Mme de Mauves, Morgan judges, unlike that of Christopher Newman, are "sterile and unattractive" (83–84). Kaplan pictures Caroline as "strangely victorious" in her renunciation in the manner of Milly Theale, one of the "superior victims" who, like Isabel and Strether, share her hunger for experience (255).

Looking at the male observers, Ward finds the narrator a neutral technical device to present Caroline's picture in contrast to the involved Longmore's presentation of Mme de Mauves (21–22). Kraft classes the two observers with Winterbourne as overly timid males (110). Peterson, on the other hand, contrasts Winterbourne with Caroline, Winterbourne being excessively hesitant toward America, and Caroline insufficiently wary toward Europe (64). Comparing the two heroines, McElderry uses the vast difference between Daisy and Caroline as proof of James's versatility (161). Tartella also points to the contrast, seeing Caroline as one of the frailest of

James's "frail vessels," without the lively stubbornness of Daisy or the strength and intelligence of Isabel, and more naïve even than Catherine Sloper (28).

On the grounds of class and hunger for Europe, one can also place Caroline with the original "passionate pilgrims" Clement Searle and Theobald. Ezra Pound, however, draws a distinction between what he sees as the narratorial "detachment" in "The Four Meetings" and the "commiseration" in "A Passionate Pilgrim" (38–39). Segal characterizes "Four Meetings" as treating a "Europe of the spirit" just as "A Passionate Pilgrim" depicted an "England of the spirit" (2). Vaid likens the tale to both "A Passionate Pilgrim" and "The Madonna of the Future" in its depiction of the "American disease," but also distinguishes it from the previous two stories as being more concerned with the creation of individual character, while they focused more on theme as James was still busy resolving his own split national loyalties (40–41). Concentrating on the second tale, Long calls Caroline's story a version of Theobald's failure of perception in the face of things European (27, 63).

Other comparisons also focus on the international. Bewley judges Caroline "two dimensional" in comparison to such other hungerers for Europe as Roderick Hudson (233–34). Kuhlman, on the other hand, takes Caroline as the Jamesian archetype of the "victim of the starved imagination." She discerns as the source for both her sacrifice and her cousin's greed the hunger for experience, noting that the same hunger also produces the egoism of Marcher and Osmond and the sensitivity of Isabel and Strether. In particular she relates the satisfaction Caroline takes in her sacrifice to Milly Theale's giving away of her dream. Her reaching out from her bleakness to the narrator as witness Kuhlman and Kaplan parallel to Tina's appeal in *The Aspern Papers*, although, Kuhlman argues, for Caroline the bleakness—being American—is greater, and her treatment more sympathetic (Kuhlman 254–55; Kaplan 255). Tintner finds Caroline losing to Europe because of an inadequate sense of history, in comparison to Bessie Alden of *An International Episode* whose greater knowledge allows her a triumph (1987, 171). Powers looks ahead to Strether in *The Ambassadors*, who will, like Miss Spencer, visit Europe only to "miss" it (1970, 89). Seamon emphasizes the failure of the narrator rather than Caroline in comparing him to Marcher, who also lives in the "alienating exile of his fantasy" (160). More generally, Davis considers the international contrast here "more emphatic" than in later works (183).

Among the few noninternational comparisons, Walter Wright likens Caroline to Flora of "Glasses," who is also happier in a pretense most would find absurd or pathetic (144–45). Donald Stone links her with Crawford of "Crawford's Consistency" as an idealist whose idealism may slide over into masochism (190). Powers groups Caroline with James's few lower-class characters in *The Princess Casamassima*, *The Bostonians*, and *In the Cage* (1969, 36).

The artist cousin is, Winner observes, like the painters in *Madame de Mauves*, *The Europeans*, and *The Ambassadors*, a significant although minor character because he represents the "possibilities of corruption or fulfillment" in a life that departs from the conventional duty to which the other characters subscribe (94). He is also, in Powers's argument, a true villain, which as he is also an American, shows a change from earlier works such as *The American* with its European villains (1970, 52). Kaplan also places him with the "great selfish agents" in James including Osmond and Marcher (255). (See also "Europe.")

Interpretation and Criticism

In 1879 Mrs. F. H. Hill found the story not a story: "It is a study, an episode, an interlude, not a sketch, because the lines are bitten in with too great depth and intensity. It is a sad etching" (18). James himself was proud of its conciseness, aiming to repeat its success in the 1884 "Pandora" (CN 24). He may have been inspired by an inquiry from editor Richard Watson Gilder of the *Century* for some stories as "short as *Four Meetings* & as good"—a compliment he passed on to his publisher James Osgood (Anesko 85). Appropriately given its relatively short length, both Cowdery and Vaid have classified the tale as an anecdote, Cowdery praising its "skillful balance" between narrative—or story—and development—or subject (Cowdery 25). While noting that the complexity of the heroine and her situation could have inspired a longer work, Vaid emphasizes its conventional chronological approach with the "teaser" frame that becomes clear only after a reading of the whole (36–41). Gerlach also analyzes its "conventional geometry" in its development over time, an ending that reverses its beginning, and "the natural termination, death." Such a design, Gerlach claims, fits the particular character and allows James to display it fully (82). Taking a different approach, Griffin pictures James using the various literary devices in the tale to weave together its episodic story and create a sense of Caroline as a "type" (45). Similarly, Vanderbilt sees this tale of the "death of the heart" as using an essentially musical form to contain its many themes as economically as possible, employing a four movement structure, supplemented by the use of leitmotifs (741–45).

Apart from the division of its three into four parts, the structure of "Four Meetings" remained largely the same through several revisions. Its many other changes, however, in Aziz's judgment, make it not one story but many. Although little attention has been paid (apart from Aziz) to the intermediate revisions, the changes from the original 1877 version to the New York Edition have generated considerable comment. Early on, James's secretary, Theodora Bosanquet, had sought to shape discussion following James's sense of things, arguing that the revised version "reveals states of mind much more definite" than the "wonderings and longings and vague appeals" of the original (17–18). Nevertheless, Rebecca West had already established a different school of thought in arguing that in the case of such early works as "Four Meetings," the revision "amounts to their ruin" (123). Tartella, however, follows Bosanquet, arguing that the story is strengthened but essentially unchanged by the revision of some twelve thousand words and the addition of nearly two thousand, concentrated primarily in four passages. He surveys several individual changes, showing how they contribute to an increased sophistication with a greater use both of the colloquial and of metaphor—the latter, he notes, occasionally incongruous with Miss Spencer's simplicity. Everything, he argues, is sharpened in the revision. While not addressing Tartella's conclusions, Aziz points out that he neglects to mention the intervening second text, in which some of the changes Tartella discusses were made (272).

One of the most significant changes is the elaboration of the passage on what the narrator originally called the "native American passion—the passion for the picturesque." In 1877 he continued only briefly, telling Caroline, "With us, I think, it is primordial—antecedent to experience. Experience comes and only shows us something we have dreamt of" (CT 4, 92). In the New York Edition, the description of what now becomes the "great American disease" is far more elaborate. It is

> . . . the appetite, morbid and monstrous, for colour and form, for the picturesque and the romantic at any price. I don't know whether we come into the world with it—with the germs implanted and antecedent to experience; rather perhaps we catch it early, almost before developed consciousness—we *feel*, as we look about, that we're going (to save our souls, or at least our senses) to be thrown back on it hard. We're like travellers in the desert—deprived of water and subject to the terrible mirage, the torment of illusion, of the thirst-fever. They hear the plash of fountains, they see green gardens and orchards that are hundreds of miles away. So we with *our* thirst—except that with us it's *more* wonderful: we have before us the beautiful old things we've never seen at all, and when we do at last see them—if we're lucky!—we simply recognise them. What experience does is merely to confirm and consecrate our confident dream. (274–75)

Certain critics including Geismar, Jefferson, and Vaid have cited the later version as representative of "early" James, a mistake for which Aziz calls them to account (260–62). Others including Geismar have used it to support the argument that James himself suffered deeply from the "American disease" (32).

The tale makes abundantly clear the depths of Caroline's suffering from the disease, and Edel declares the strength of the story is its portrayal of

Caroline's yearning for Europe (CT 4, 10). According to Tartella, "The story's excellence lies in the degree of significance with which James has invested the life of an insignificant woman" (28). The original response to Caroline, evident, for example, in Ford and West, appears to have been sympathy for her plight (Ford 25–27). Later, Stewart also judges the story "tragic as well as pathetic," seeing Spencer as doubly innocent: she is unable to distinguish a true artist or countess from a sham and she has "unimpaired moral standards" that make her believe it her duty to help. Her virtue therefore is her vulnerability: "She carries it to Europe and Europe betrays her" (83). Powers, who also takes a sympathetic view of Caroline while noting what a ready victim she makes, puts the blame not on Europe but on "the insufficiency of American civilization" that left her vulnerable to it (52). Similarly, Berland, using Arnoldian terminology, judges her a "touching" figure with an "innate predilection for culture, some special fine sensitivity, a sympathy for the full life," unfortunately born into an Hebraic society. In his view, the fact that she is "defrauded" does not detract from the story's depiction of the idea of culture (34–35, 140n.)

Other critics have held Caroline more responsible for her own misery, largely on the grounds of her romanticism. Fadiman, early on, argued that Caroline is brought down by her "narrow" view of Europe, her fascination with the "picturesque" allowing her to be taken in by her cousin's fakery. In the end, he says, she is "too weak, too mesmerized" to get rid of the Countess and yet "too sensitive" to approve of her (37–38). Similarly, Bewley points out that the "picturesque and romantic" Europe Caroline dreams of is only "an illusion of reality," which, he argues, she never moves beyond to see the life behind it (233–34). Kaplan observes that Caroline's misfortune is "in part engineered by her own great desires," but still offers her sympathy for their frustration (254–55). Gooder, too, remarks that Caroline's books have not prepared her for the truth of Europe, and indeed have made her its ready victim (xi–xiii).

Peterson examines the role of Puritanism in her behavior, writing that not only do her Puritanism and her hunger for romance feed on each other, but that she uses her Puritanism to justify her support of her cousin's romance because she has to suffer for it (63). Granville Jones also comments on how Caroline uses the family relationship to justify impoverishing herself for a romantic cause as a duty (114–15). The irony of Caroline's "credulous" sacrifice is increased, according to Leonidas Jones, by the tale's religious imagery. Caroline is a worshiper of culture, reading its "new gospel" of Byron. Vanderbilt also notes the religious imagery, but sees it placed alongside the romantic themes in order to intensify the picture of Caroline's romantic nature (747–48). Replacing the romantic with the sexual, Griffin sees Caroline's passion for Europe as a substitute for a more normal sexual passion, drawing attention to her flirtatiousness in her first conversation with the narrator (46–47). Such foibles have led critics such as Morgan to argue that Caroline is too easy a dupe to receive the reader's full sympathy (83; also Putt 120).

There is disagreement, too, over Caroline's state of mind at the end. Has she seen the foolishness of her dream? Why does she tolerate the countess? The disagreement often stems from the use of different texts. Such critics as Kraft, who use the earlier version, argue that Caroline either refuses or fails to accept the truth of her situation, renouncing reality instead (Kraft 101–2; also Powers 52; Peterson 63). But in the New York Edition, as Tartella notes, one of the most significant changes is the possibility of Caroline's "eventual enlightenment" (27). Gargano discusses the series of looks in the revised conclusion that brings about the change. At first, while the narrator signals his recognition to the Countess of her spuriousness, he refuses out of a genteel chivalry to respond to the appeal of Caroline's "little look." His "disgust," however, at the countess prompts another look, of which the narrator writes: "What passed between us, as from face to face, while she looked up at me, *that* at least our companion may have caught, that at least may have sown, for the after-times, some seed of revelation." Caroline is left "with the question of a moment before now quite cold in it" (311–12). Her knowledge, Gargano argues, is too much for Caroline, extinguishing what little life is left in her (310–13). Also using the New York Edition, Vaid argues that Caroline sees exactly what has happened to her, but with a new dignity acquired from her trials. "Her resignation, however," Vaid writes, "remains equal to her bitterness" and so she wastes her life (40). Putt depicts her as completely disillusioned with Europe as a result, without any longing ever to see it (120). Walter Wright argues for a more complex motive, contending that Caroline keeps the countess on because to make her leave would mean acknowledging the absurdity of her romantic ideals, which she recognizes but will not admit (144–45).

The cousin who dupes Caroline has received less attention, although James attached enough significance to his role to misidentify a translation in the *Revue des Deux Mondes* entitled "Cousin et Cousine"—actually "A Passionate Pilgrim"— as this tale even though it appeared earlier, in October 1876 (*Letters* 4, 360). Buitenhuis, indeed, found the tale flawed by its obvious villains (174). Kraft comments disparagingly on the putative artist's reliance on the adjective "nice" (100). According to Peterson, however, although he is as a Bohemian "pathetically banal," he is as equally a victim of "the passion for the picturesque" as Caroline, a kinship that allows him to fool her successfully (63). Kaplan qualifies the comparison by calling the cousin's greed an "ironic parody" of Caroline's passion (254). Kuhlman pictures the cousin and countess as shrewder people who live by recognizing and exploiting the illusions of others, cleverly basing their appeal to Caroline on the grounds of duty rather than pleasure (93–95). More generally, Putt comments on the importance of money in the story and the cruelty greed for it can elicit (119). Morgan, however, emphasizes Caroline's willingness to pay, noting the accuracy of the financial metaphor in the narrator's phrase, the "appetite . . . for the picturesque and the romantic at any price" (83). Kraft even gives some slight sympathy to the Countess, remarking on how, just as she is out of keeping with Caroline's dreams of Europe, so life at Caroline's must seem very inconsistent with her dreams of America (101). Looking over the four characters, Stewart reports that James here presents the Americans as good, Europeans as bad, and American Europeans as the worst (83).

The other American European besides the cousin is the narrator. Ford argues that in the original version the narrator appears as a "quiet, gentle, observant young New Englander," becoming only in the New York Edition a "sardonic, rather florid, rather garrulous, international American in the later years of his life." In either case, however, he writes that one will be most struck by the "singular pitilessness of the narrator." It never occurs to him, Ford writes, to help Caroline either with a small loan or some information. If he had and Caroline had accepted, Ford admits, "the story would have gone to pieces." "The real fact," he continues, "is that Mr. James knows very well that he was giving just an extra turn to the tragedy of the story by making his narrator so abnormally unhelpful" (26–27).

In later readings, even as there has been a general withdrawal of sympathy for Caroline, there has been an increased assigning of responsibility to the narrator. Early on, Rebecca West characterized the tale's chief virtue as the "detachment" evident in its narration (37–38). Similarly, Kelley praises the use of the "self-effacing narrator" to encapsulate the history of Caroline Spencer (260–61). Other critics have also praised James for keeping the narrator's role small, confining him, as Buitenhuis puts it, to making "appropriate remarks" (174). In the readings of Davis and Walter Wright, he is "only an intelligent observer" (Davis 183; Wright 41). Thorp and Kraft praise the authority and positioning of the narrator (Thorp xv; Kraft 99–100). Segal considers the tale a model of James's narratorial technique in which the narrator, privileged with none of the conventional narratorial omniscience, achieves through "complicated, groping processes of observation and evaluation" over a series of meetings a "comprehensive" sense of the situation (233). Booth, however, detected what he saw as a shift between the notebook entries and the story toward an involved narrator (344 n.8). His involvement has been increasingly viewed as harmful, Peterson, for example, calling him an "unaware victimizer," and arguing that he enjoys the spectacle of the progress of Caroline's pathetic delusion. In Peterson's reading, he remains objective only by remaining unhelpful (62–63). Similarly, Gooder attributes his final silence to a recognition of his deleterious involvement (xiii).

One of the most striking, if least likely, readings of both the narrator and Caroline attributes little virtue to either. According to Clair, Caroline is the servant of the Countess from the start of the tale. Seeking desperately to escape such servitude (perhaps including work as a prostitute), she flirts with the narrator and follows him to Europe, concocting a scheme of lies. She fails ultimately not because of her own weakness, but because of the narrator's egotism, which never allows him to see clearly either that she is pursuing him or that she is lying in order to do so (1–16). His analysis rests largely on a remark by the minister's wife about the length of the Countess's stay, somewhat slim evidence, as Wagenknecht points out (216–17). One can add that if Caroline were in fact living such a life as Clair attributes to her, she would never have been present at the home of the narrator's friend to begin with. Aziz bases his objection both to Clair's reading of Caroline as prostitute and Leonidas Jones's reading of her as saint on the grounds that both critics rely on the New York Edition (264–69). But while it seems likely that if James did not conceive of Caroline as a deceitful prostitute in 1877, he would not transform her into one in 1909, it does not seem equally unlikely that James in 1909 might decide to heighten her already established sacrificial nature through the addition of religious imagery.

Less sensationally, Kraft also argues for a possible romantic interest on the part of Caroline and the narrator, and finds fault with him for never venturing to forge a genuine relationship with her, to find out at least the truth of her sense of her situation, and thus leaving an incomplete record of it as well as a somewhat self-incriminating record of his response to it (102). As his approach to the two characters, Gurko seeks the missing word at the end of the narrator's pause in his regret at Miss Spencer's death, his recollection that she was "certainly not —!" He considers "alive" the best possible choice, as indicating her "psychic death." He, too, blames the narrator, even more harshly than Kraft, arguing that he puts on her at each meeting "more pressure than her nature can bear" so that "in effect" he kills her without realizing it. His fault, however, is not coldness or insincerity, but his very enthusiasm over Europe, his anger at her plight, his "sin" being an "excess of energy." He argues that James pointed up such a reading in the New York Edition, even having the narrator declaim at the end, "I could on the contrary but save the situation, my own at least. . . ."

Both Granville Jones and Seamon, however, seek to take some of the onus of responsibility from the narrator. Jones looks at how the narrator, who finds Caroline's accepting nature "alternately irritating and frustrating," attempts to be her "protector," to insinuate that the Countess is not what she seems, and when that fails, resolves at least to protect her from the "shock" of realizing her exploitation and so destroying her "faint faith in herself and in others." In Jones's reading, the narrator leaves only in order to keep from reminding her of the loss of her experience of Europe (114–15). Rejecting Clair's and Gurko's reading of the story as an "attack" on the narrator, Seamon, too, discerns in him a mixture of responsiveness and irritability.

Beginning with the narrator's original "mixture of condescension and indignation" at the news of Caroline's death, Seamon traces the four encounters that lead him to this stance. The first, he argues, is "replete with sexual and romantic possibilities," but at each meeting the narrator first responds to Caroline's need, whether sexual or material, then backs away. He becomes irritated partly at Caroline's indirection and passivity, and partly at his own failure to act, adopting a condescending air as cover for his failure. Still, in their final meeting, when Caroline asks only for the truth, Seamon judges his diffidence carried to "grotesque extremes," undercutting not only the story's sense of "the complicity of the characters" but its very probability. Although the narrator blames Europe, he, as an American, has been complicit in Caroline's sorry fate. Through it all, Seamon asserts, Caroline remains a mystery, and the consequent focus on the narrator is a sign of the tale's basic realism. Martin adds to Seamon, arguing that in the final scene the narrator retreats in part because, while feeling "painfully implicated," he cannot help Caroline, because to do so would require acknowledging his similarity with the countess. In order to avoid seeing himself as he is, he must also avoid Caroline. Martin argues that James heightened the narrator's responsibility in the New York Edition by heightening the initial conversation between Caroline and the narrator, making the Countess more clearly a fake, and labeling the narrator's exit a "retreat."

Vanderbilt, however, returns to an emphasis on Caroline's corruption, if one more modest than Clair's argument. In Vanderbilt's reading, Caroline's innocence is "rather precarious" from the start due to a submerged passion that surfaces in her strong response to her cousin's romantic tale. Initially a victim of European scheming, by the end, Vanderbilt maintains, Caroline has moved on to becoming herself a "procurer-and-collaborator," bringing Mr. Mixter into the circle of the countess to serve as her replacement dupe. Still, her collaboration brings her no great happiness, and in the end she inhabits what Vanderbilt depicts as a kind of "death-in-life." Throughout the narrator remains unaware of the full implications of Caroline's story. Far from an "intelligent observer," Vanderbilt argues, he sees largely through inadequate stereotypes (743–51).

Surveying the various theories, Wagenknecht provides a useful corrective to both Clair's attack on Caroline and to the attacks on the narrator by Gurko, Seamon, and Martin. He argues that blaming the narrator shifts the burden of responsibility to someone who is, after all, a mere acquaintance. Wagenknecht questions what he could have done to protect someone so ready to be taken in, and in response to Gurko's argument in particular, points out that at his first meeting with Caroline all the narrator did was to show her some pictures (11–12). It does seem an overstatement to produce a case for broken promises on the basis of a conversation at an evening's party. It is harder, as Ford notes, not to be struck by the narrator's failure at the second meeting to attempt, at least, saying a word to a woman abroad who has no other reliable adviser (26).

Ford's emphasis on the "pitilessness" of the tale has been taken up by subsequent critics. Swan repeats the term, and Putt cites as the conclusion to his analysis Ford's statement that the narrator's final remark about Caroline—"I could feel how right my poor friend had been in her conviction that she should still see something of that dear old Europe"—is "one of the most pitiless sentences ever penned by the hand of man" (Ford 27; Swan 12; Putt 120). Such discomfort with the narrator's attitude is, no doubt, responsible for the various attempts to strain the story to make a villain out of the narrator or Caroline. Despite the conflicting readings thus engendered, the story has continued to inspire generally consistent praise. In early reviews, the *Literary World* found it "admirably done" and the *Nation* judged it the "most pleasing" of the collection *The Author of Beltraffio*. More recently, Putt has faulted its American-European confrontation as "over-dramatic" (120). Zabel's assessment of the tale, however, as one of James's "earliest and most felicitous versions of the international theme, and a flawless example of his art in depicting the pathos of privation," is more representative (39). The tale's strength, as Edgar recognizes, is its mixture of "comedy and pathos" (25). In 1916 Rebecca West noted another mixture. Calling the tale James's first masterpiece, she spoke of it as "one of the saddest stories in the world, and one of the cleverest" (36–37). It is the blending of comedy and pathos, sadness and cleverness that continues to challenge the story's readers to do justice to all its elements in attempting to capture their essence.

Works Cited

Primary Works

James, Henry. 1877. "Four Meetings." *Scribner's Monthly* 15 (November): 44–56.

———. 1879. "Four Meetings." *Daisy Miller*. London: Macmillan.

———. 1883. "Four Meetings." Collective Edition. Vol. 13. London: Macmillan.

———. 1885. "Four Meetings." *The Author of Beltraffio*, 321–62. Boston: Osgood.

———. 1909. "Four Meetings." *The Novels and Tales of Henry James*. New York Edition. Vol. 16, 265–312. New York: Scribner's.

Secondary Works

Anesko, Michael. 1986. *"Friction with the Market": Henry James and the Profession of Authorship*. New York: Oxford University Press.

Anon. 1885. Review of *The Author of Beltraffio*. *The Nation* 40, no. 1028 (12 March): 226.

Anon. 1885. "Fiction." Review of *The Author of Beltraffio*. *Literary World* 16 (21 March): 102.

Aziz, Maqbool. 1968. "'Four Meetings': A Caveat for James Critics." *Essays in Criticism*, 18 (July): 258–74.

Berland, Alwyn. 1981. *Culture and Conduct in the Novels of Henry James*. Cambridge: Cambridge University Press.

Bewley, Marius. 1959. *The Eccentric Design: Form in the Classic American Novel*. New York: Columbia University Press.

Booth, Wayne C. 1961 [1983]. *The Rhetoric of Fiction*. Chicago: University of Chicago Press.

Bosanquet, Theodore. 1928. *Henry James at Work*. London: Hogarth Press, 1924; Garden City, NY: Doubleday. Revised in part from "The Revised Version." *Little Review* 5 (August 1918): 56–62.

Buitenhuis, Peter. 1970. *The Grasping Imagination: The American Writings of Henry James*. Toronto: University of Toronto Press.

Clair, John A. 1965. *The Ironic Dimension in the Fiction of Henry James*. Pittsburgh: Duquesne University Press.

Cowdery, Lauren Tozek. 1986. *The Nouvelle of Henry James in Theory and Practice*. Studies in Modern Literature 47. Ann Arbor: UMI Research Press.

Davis, Robert Gorham, ed. 1959. *Ten Modern Masters*. 2d ed. New York: Harcourt, 1953.

Edgar, Pelham. [1927] 1964. *Henry James, Man and Author*. New York: Russell & Russell.

Fadiman, Clifton, ed. 1948. *The Short Stories of Henry James*. New York: Modern Library.

Ford, Madox Ford. 1913. *Henry James: A Critical Study*. London: Martin Secker.

Gargano, James W. 1979. "The 'Look' as a Major Event in James's Short Fiction." *Arizona Quarterly* 35, no. 4 (Winter): 303–20.

Geismar, Maxwell. 1963. *Henry James and the Jacobites*. Boston: Houghton Mifflin.

Gerlach, John. 1985. *Toward the End: Closure and Structure in American Short Stories*. University: University of Alabama Press.

Gooder, Jean, ed. 1985. *Daisy Miller and Other Stories*. Oxford: Oxford University Press.

Griffin, Robert J. 1962. "Notes toward an Exegesis: 'Four Meetings.'" *University of Kansas City Review* 29 (October): 45–49.

Gurko, Leo. 1970. "The Missing Word in Henry James's 'Four Meetings.'" *Studies in Short Fiction* 7 (Spring): 298–307.

Hill, F. H. 1879. "Review of *Daisy Miller*." *The Daily News* [London] 21 March, 6. Reprinted in *Critics on Henry James*, ed. J. Don Vann, 17–18. Readings in Literary Criticism 18. Coral Gables, FL: Miami University Press, 1972.

James, William. 1983. *The Correspondence of William James*. Vol. 2: *William and Henry: 1885–1896*. Ed. Ignas K. Skrupskelis and Elizabeth M. Berkeley. Charlottesville: University Press of Virginia.

Jefferson, D. W. 1964. *Henry James and the Modern Reader*. New York: St. Martin's.

Jones, Granville H. 1975. *Henry James's Psychology of Experience: Innocence, Responsibility, and Renunciation in the Fiction of Henry James*. The Hague: Mouton.

Jones, Leonidas M. 1962. "James's 'Four Meetings.'" *Explicator* 20 (March): Item 55. Also reprinted in *The Explicator Cyclopedia*, vol. 3, ed. Charles Child Walcutt and J. Edwin Whitesell, 92–93. Chicago: Quadrangle Books, 1968.

Kaplan, Harold. 1972. *Democratic Humanism and American Literature*. Chicago: University of Chicago Press.

Kelley, Cornelia Pulsifer. [1930] 1965. *The Early Development of Henry James*. Urbana: University of Illinois Press.

Kraft, James. 1969. *The Early Tales of Henry James*. Carbondale: Southern Illinois University Press.

Kuhlmann, Susan. 1973. *Knave, Fool, and Genius: The Confidence Man as He Appears in Nineteenth-Century Fiction*. Chapel Hill: University of North Carolina Press.

LeClair, Robert Charles. 1955. *Young Henry James, 1843–1870*. New York: Bookman.

Lerner, Daniel. 1941. "The Influence of Turgenev on Henry James." *Slavonic Review* 20 (December): 28–54.

Long, Robert Emmet. 1979. *The Great Succession: Henry James and the Legacy of Hawthorne*. Pittsburgh: University of Pittsburgh Press.

McElderry, Bruce R., Jr. 1965. *Henry James*. New York: Twayne.

Martin, W. R. 1980. "The Narrator's 'Retreat' in James's 'Four Meetings.'" *Studies in Short Fiction* 17: 497–99.

Morgan, Alice. 1970. "Henry James: Money and Morality." *Texas Studies in Language and Literature* 12: 75–92.

Peterson, Dale E. 1975. *The Clement Vision: Poetic Realism in Turgenev and James*. Port Washington, NY: Kennikat.

Pound, Ezra. 1918. "A Shake Down." *The Little Review* 5 (August): 9–39.

Powers, Lyall H. 1970. *Henry James: An Introduction and Interpretation*. New York: Barnes & Noble.

———. 1969. *The Merrill Guide to Henry James*. Columbus, OH: Charles E. Merrill.

Putt, S. Gorley. 1966. *Henry James: A Reader's Guide*. Ithaca, NY: Cornell University Press.

Seamon, Roger. 1978. "Henry James's 'Four Meetings': A Study in Irritability and Condescension." *Studies in Short Fiction* 15: 155–63.

Segal, Ora. 1969. *The Lucid Reflector: The Observer in Henry James' Fiction*. New Haven: Yale University Press.

Stewart, John Innes Mackintosh. 1963. "Henry James." *Eight Modern Writers. Oxford History of English Literature*. Vol. 12, 71–121. New York: Oxford University Press.

Stone, Donald David. 1972. *Novelists in a Changing World: Meredith, James, and the Transformation of English Fiction in the 1880's*. Cambridge, MA: Harvard University Press.

Swan, Michael, ed. 1948. *Ten Short Stories of Henry James*. London: Lehmann.

Tartella, Vincent. 1960. "James's 'Four Meetings': Two Texts Compared." *Nineteenth-Century Fiction* 15 (June): 17–28.

Thorp, Willard, ed. 1962. *The Madonna of the Future and Other Early Stories*. New York: New American Library.

Tintner, Adeline. 1987. *The Book World of Henry James: Appropriating the Classics*. Ann Arbor: UMI Research Press. Revised in part from "Henry James and Byron." *Byron Journal* 9 (1981): 52–63.

———. 1986. *The Museum World of Henry James*. Ann Arbor: UMI Research Press.

Vaid, Krishna B. 1964. *Technique in the Tales of Henry James*. Cambridge, MA: Harvard University Press.

Vanderbilt, Kermit. 1973. "Notes Largely Musical on Henry James's 'Four Meetings.'" *Sewanee Review* 81 (Fall): 739–52.

Veeder, William. 1975. *Henry James—the Lessons of the Master: Popular Fiction and Personal Style in the Nineteenth Century*. Chicago: University of Chicago Press.

Wagenknecht, Edward. 1984. *The Tales of Henry James*. New York: Frederick Ungar.

Ward, Joseph A. 1967. *The Search for Form: Studies in the Structure of James's Fiction*. Chapel Hill: University of North Carolina Press.

West, Rebecca. [pseud]. 1916. *Henry James*. London: Nisbet.

Winner, Viola Hopkins. 1970. *Henry James and the Visual Arts*. Charlottesville: University Press of Virginia.

Wright, Nathalia. 1965. *American Novelists in Italy, The Discoverers: Allston to James*. Philadelphia: University of Pennsylvania Press.

Wright, Walter F. 1962. *The Madness of Art: A Study of Henry James*. Lincoln: University of Nebraska Press.

Zabel, Morton Dauwen, ed. [1951] 1968. *The Portable Henry James*. Rev. Lyall H. P. Powers. New York: Viking. Reprint. Harmondsworth: Penguin.

Foreign Language

Castiglione, Luigi. 1962. "Profilo di James." *La Fiera Letteraria* 17 (23 September): 5.

Hönnighausen, Lothar. 1967. *"The Velvet Glove* —Zur Erzähltechnik in Henry James's Spätwerk." *Germanisch-romanische Monatsschrift, Neue Folge* 48 (July): 307–22.

Iwase, Shitsuu. 1962. "Henry James: Revision of 'Four Meetings'—Point of View." *Queries* 3 (June): 9–22. [Japanese]

The Friends of the Friends

Publication History

This tale appeared first as "The Way It Came" on May 1, 1896, in *The Chap Book*, one of the new "little" magazines, published in Chicago and edited by Herbert S. Stone, and in *Chapman's Magazine of Fiction*, for whose editor, Oswald Crawford, James wrote the piece (N 241–44). James included it under the same title in that year's collection *Embarrassments*. When he revised the tale for inclusion in the New York Edition, he revised as well the original "colorless title" (*Criticism* 2, 1256).

Circumstances of Composition, Sources, and Influences

On February 5, 1895, James wrote in his notebook, "What is there in the idea of *Too late*," going on to consider the plight of two people who meet "only in time to feel how much it might have meant for them if they had only met earlier" and at the end proposing death as the "something else" that might intervene between them (CN 112). The entry is generally considered the source for both "The Beast in the Jungle" and "The Friends of the Friends" (N 184; CN 112). James formulated the latter tale more particularly on December 1, 1895, with "a scrap of a fantasy" of two people who, although they are constantly being told they ought to meet, do so at last only after one of them dies. In the notebook entry James concentrated mainly on the question of what form of narration the "rather thin little fantasy" should take. James continued the idea on January 10, 1896, having settled on the jealous "interested narrator" and working out how to divide the story according to the "divine principle of the 'scenario'" he had learned through the theatre (CN 144, 151–54).

James's experience in the theatre has also been held responsible for the tale's intense atmosphere and narratorial ambiguity, Wilson arguing that they are a lingering reaction to his public humiliation at the opening of *Guy Domville* (146; also Lind 237).

In recalling the origin of *The Turn of the Screw* during a country-house conversation, James remembered the general disapproval of "the new type" of ghost story—"the mere modern 'psychical' case, washed clean of all queerness as by exposure to a flowing laboratory tap, and equipped with credentials vouching for this," the sense that "the new type clearly promised little, for the more it was respectably certified the less it seemed of a nature to rouse the dear old sacred terror" (*Criticism* 2, 1182). Despite James's admonition, the tale, like other late James ghost stories, has been put in the context of the contemporary interest in the supernatural. (See "Sir Edmund Orme.") Kerr connects the ambiguity of the ghost to the debates over standards of evidence in the British Society for Psychical Research (145–46). Rawlings distinguishes the tale from the typical Poe ghost story on the grounds of its psychological focus (xvi). Whether more interested in the psychical or the psychological, James's brother William, who studied both, found the tale one of the two best in *Embarrassments* (411). The tale has also been placed in a more traditional line of ghost story by Edel, that of Defoe, and Voss specifies as the source his "A True Relation of the Apparition of One Mrs. Veal," where a person who has just died appears as a ghost and is mistaken for a living person (Edel 1970, 395; Voss 146; also Wagenknecht 96).

Relation to Other Works

"The Friends of the Friends" is a story told in a manuscript with a short framing introduction and an unnamed narrator recalling an event in the past, all points it has in common with "Sir Edmund Orme" (Lind 234–35). But more important for its critical history, it shares all these elements also with *The Turn of the Screw*, and has been drawn into the critical debate over the latter's narration (Lind 234–35; Edel 1970, 396; Shelden 4). It started with Wilson, who accused the female narrators here and in "The Marriages" and "The Path of Duty" of malicious meddling. Finding James's interest in "self-deception" in these tales evidence for his nonapparitionist reading of *The Turn of the Screw*, he argued that here, too, the ghostly is simply a production of the mind of the narrator (147). Lind objects to Wilson's Freudian reading as anachronistic, but still considers the narrator and the governess alike in their unconscious revelation of hysteria and their obsessive nature—also seen in Rose Armiger and the heroine of *In the Cage* (234–36). Geismar concurs, adding the narrator of *The Aspern Papers*, and, a bit oddly, the non-narrating mother of "The Author of Beltraffio" as suspect storytellers (165). Rimmon, for her part, considers the ambiguity here only a "pocket" in the larger narrative, as it is also in *The Aspern Papers* and *The Wings of the Dove* (xii). Earlier, Walter Wright had linked "The Friends of the Friends," *The Turn of the Screw*, *In the Cage*, and *The Sacred Fount* on the basis of the ambiguity faced not by the reader but by the main characters as they attempt to make sense of the situation around them. He reminds critics, however, that simply on the grounds of her belief in the ghost, the narrator is no madder than Ralph of *The Sense of the Past* (176).

Virginia Woolf first pointed out the similarity with the conclusion of *The Wings of the Dove*—where a dead woman again interrupts the relationship between a living couple. Unlike Krook later, she sees little difference between the ghostly and the realistic treatment, finding it a short way from the typical "extreme fineness" of James's characters to the supernatural (Woolf 322; Krook 331–32). Similarly, writing of James's ghost tales in general, Orage observed "how imperceptibly his method of dealing with real persons shades into his dealing with ghosts" (43).

The similarity in theme with "Maud-Evelyn" was first noted by Edgar, who considers "The Friends of the Friends" a "subtler elaboration" (192). Vaid considers them both inferior as a treatment of the "too late" theme to "The Beast in the Jungle" (224; also Matthiessen 139). Przybylowicz emphasizes what she sees as the man's fear of sexuality in each tale (103). The theme of "too late," as Banta points out, provides a link not only with "The Beast in the Jungle" but with *The Ambassadors* (181 n.23). Edel links the tale with "The Figure in the Carpet," seeing in James's bewilderment at Constance Woolson's death the inspiration for the view of death as forever sealing knowledge from the sight of a seeker as obsessed and frustrated as the narrator of *The Sacred Fount*. He adds that James finally broke the frustration with the final catastrophic revelation of "The Beast in the Jungle" (*Life* 447, 559; *Life* 4, 149–50; *Life* 5, 137). Adding to Edel's linking of "The Figure in the Carpet" and "The Friends of the Friends," Heller nominates not only "The Beast in the Jungle," but also "The Altar of the Dead" as having a similar theme (42–43).

The unexpected death of an unwanted husband occurs again in "The Path of Duty," where it also threatens an engagement. Here the interference is supernatural, and Putt contrasts it with the supernatural encouragement of marriage in "Sir Edmund Orme" (395). Jacobson dismisses the supernatural element introduced at the end as a "gratuitous gesture" added to the basic triangle of jealousy in order to gain popular appeal, and argues that James does the same in other late ghost stories including "Sir Edmund Orme" and "Owen Wingrave" (90).

Interpretation and Criticism

The value assigned the tale varies widely, from Dupee's questioning the inclusion of such an "overwrought" piece in the New York Edition to Edel's designating it "a perfect example of the Jamesian ghostly tale" (Dupee 241; Edel 1970, 396). In general, the story has lost out mainly in comparison with other similar stories, "The Beast in the Jungle" being held a superior treatment of the theme of "too late" (Vaid 224; Krook 332 n.5) and *The Turn of the Screw* of the unreliable narrator. In his preface James himself declared "The Friends of the Friends," like "The Jolly Corner," "one of those finished fantasies that, achieving success or not, speak best even to the critical sense for themselves" adding of it that it "allows probably for no other comment" (*Criticism* 2, 1264). But even as they demurred at his high estimate, critics have also refused to let the tale speak for itself, or to leave its ghosts in peace.

The story is a difficult one. It is even cumbersome to write about due to the lack of character names. From the beginning, James had a habit of leaving his narrators without names, but this is the sole story where no major character has a name. The title's plural also adds to the confusion, perhaps deliberately, as its three characters exist very much in isolation, so that it is hard to find enough characters to provide two who can be friends of another two without overlapping. As often with James, however, the main critical difficulty stems from the narration. As noted above, James first contemplated a third-person narration "according to my wont when I want something—as I always do want it—intensely objective." But James also wanted to avoid the direct depiction of the *post-mortem* interview" that "impersonal narration" would make necessary (CN 144). By the time of the next notebook entry, James had changed to the first-person narrator (CN 152). By the time of its publication, the tale had a framing introduction, and the woman friend an estranged husband. While Goetz argues that in switching to the first-person narrator, James kept the bar against "self-revelation," preventing his narrator from talking too much about herself, Booth contends that James's conception of the narrator evolved from an impartial observer to a "self-deceived and deceiving" one who becomes the main interest in the tale (Goetz 32; Booth 341–42).

The focus on the narrator has led, in turn, as with *The Turn of the Screw*, to a questioning of the authenticity of her narration. As early as the publication of the tale in *Embarrassments*, a critic was noticing that James left open a "natural explanation . . . to suit the skeptical reader." The story has continued to generate debate. Several critics consider the tale deliberately and irremediably ambiguous, such that it is impossible to tell whether the woman is to be trusted or not (e.g., Edel 1970, 395; Thompson 34). As Edel puts it, one's interpretation of the tale will rest upon one's interpretation of the narrator (CT 9, 11).

James himself, in his last notebook entry, pointed to an "ambiguity" in the tale, but referred only to the controversy between the engaged pair surrounding the dead woman's last appearance (CN 153). Rawlings distinguishes two uncertainties: whether the woman was alive or dead at her first visit, and whether she continued to visit after her death. He offers as a possible reading that the narrator imaginatively unites the two characters, achieving a "transcendent reconciliation" to the friends' "opposition" throughout the tale, but paying for it through the loss of *her* union to the man (xvi–viii). Shifting the debate, Auchard considers the question of the ambiguous timing less important than the question of whether love for the dead is perceived as valuable or as "morbid," stating that to James it was often the former (42–44).

Indeed, James's original projection that the pair separated by death would in fact be reunited by it has an air of triumph to it: ". . . they do meet, in spite of fate—they meet, and if necessary, they love.—They see, they know, all that would have been possible if they *had* met" (CN 144). To Woolf, who accepts the tale's ghosts, the communication of the living and dead is "beautiful" while "the spiritual and the carnal meeting together produce a strange emotion—not exactly fear, nor yet excitement." She sees James using the ghostly here to produce a shock, "the queerest of shocks—tranquil, beautiful, like the closing of chords in harmony; and yet, somehow obscene" (322). Some later critics have also kept the emphasis on the quality of that shock, and such critics tend naturally to believe the narrator. Segal argues that the narrator's decision not to marry the man is a simple judgment on the strength of his love for the dead woman, a judgment that, she argues, is strengthened not undermined by her intimacy with the man (236). Todorov, similarly, acknowledges the justification of the narrator's jealousy of the "incredible love" between the man and the dead woman. He states that while we have no information apart from the narrator, "she manages to convince us." The appeal of the ghost is the appeal of the absent and, according to Todorov, that is nearly irresistible (161–62). Markow-Totevy, who, like Todorov, has interpreted other ghosts in James on a strictly psychological basis, offers an intriguing reading by simply presenting the narrator's version of events, but without mentioning her, taking instead the man's point of view. He accepts the ghost without question, finding it a "peaceful" one who on her nightly visits is "joyfully welcomed" by the man (112).

There are unquestioned apparitions in this tale, those of the parents that appear to the man and woman. Andreas proposes that the narrator has imaginatively "bracketted" her two friends together on the basis of their supernatural experiences, making them "predestined lovers" (84). One might argue also that the knowledge of those experiences is part of what drew the narrator to her two friends, and so indicates again some kind of morbid sensibility or wish for one on *her* part. She says at the end, "I didn't pretend for a moment that he and she were common people. Pray, if they *had* been, how should I ever have cared for them? They had enjoyed a rare extension of being and they had caught me up in their flight" (CT 9, 400). Despite the fascination, she holds to a keen sense of betrayal in their relationship.

What one might call the common-sense school sees no reason to question the narrator's version of events. Walter Wright states that without the ghost, "there is simply no story" (176). Vaid, for his part, argues that questioning her narration inappropriately switches the central interest in the story from the other couple (93–95). Wagenknecht affirms that with a first-person narrator one must take a certain amount on faith, and sees the woman as clearly jealous, but not necessarily a liar (96–97).

Przybylowicz makes a little school of her own. Taking the postmortem meetings as authentic, but sexless, she asserts that despite the "vampiric hold" of the dead woman, the Jamesian male is capable of passion only when there is no possibility of its being consummated. In her view, the man is rejecting life and love for a dead woman. She does not explain why a man afraid of "women and sexuality" would pursue his engagement (103, 157).

The stated attitude of the man in the tale, at least at first, is that the ghost is entirely the idea of his fiancée: "It was an event of my history, a puzzle of my consciousness, not of his" (CT 9, 396). As James intended in the second notebook entry, the viewpoint of the woman and her fiancé diverge following the initial conversation about the death of the woman's friend. "The view we take" becomes "the view *I* take" so that "from here to the end, the attitude, on the subject, is mine . . ." (CN 153). According to the narrator, of course, her fiancé's attitude is a cover for his relationship with the dead woman. She declares of the "monstrous" facts and her "lucid perception of them": "The only thing allied to nature and truth was my having to act on that perception" (CT 9, 400).

Another school, however, finds little of "nature and truth" in the narrator's tale, blaming her for her own predicament. In such an interpretation, begun by Wilson, the woman is seen as manufacturing the apparition out of her own hysterical jealousy (147; also Lind 234). Blackmur pictures the narrator as creating her own destruction, since she, not her fiancé, answers an "irresistible call" in an obsession so extreme it borders on the merely "silly" ([1942] 1983, 52–53; [1948] 1983, 109). Gage certifies the narrator as straightforwardly mad, driven so by her frustrated desire for certainty. He adds that the characters' namelessness emphasizes the resemblances between her two friends as well as her fear of being replaced in her fiancé's affections by the other woman (27–30).

Even without entering into the question of the existence of the ghost, many critics deem the narrator unreasonably jealous. Geismar, who asserts that James identifies with the narrator's hysteria, states that she "destroys her lover for the sake of a dead woman" (140n, 165). Jones also emphasizes the destructiveness of her jealousy, which makes her unable even to believe in her own innocence, and so brings about the unhappiness of all (61–62). Banta acknowledges the ghost, stating that the tie between the dead woman and man is more powerful than that between the live woman and man, but also asserts that the narrator's attempted "possession" of her fiancé is more "violent" than that by the dead woman. Ironically, in Banta's view, the woman who cannot even see the ghost is the most haunted by the thought of it (181 n.23). In a way, such critics would say, she haunts herself.

In his notebook, James considered having the narrator make a last, late appeal for reconciliation with her fiancé, only to learn *"Il s'y soustrait par la mort"* (CN 154). Such an appeal does not appear in the final story and some have attributed the desire to put off the marriage to her. Shelden, who rejects the supernatural interpretation, notes that "ironically" the ghost functions as "wish-fulfilment." In her interpretation, the narrator is probably sublimating a fear of sex similar to Isabel Archer's into a "more socially acceptable" jealousy (8–11). Similarly, Edel argues that however one reads the ambiguities, the "deeper fact" is that the woman does not marry the man, but turns him away ([1949] 1963, 183). Akiyama, on the other hand, presents a narrator who is neither fearful nor jealous, but who, having prevented her friends from meeting, repents and refuses to marry her fiancé out of a recognition that he belongs with the dead woman, not her (45–47).

The possible interpretations seem endless. One might propose—perhaps by now someone has—a reading in which the two unnamed friends never appear together, and have no names, because they are really one and the same, or are simply the male and female version of the narrator, or perhaps do not exist at all.

Cowdery has placed the tale in the context of James's definition of the romance in the prefaces, remarking that a story that considers "the way it came" is dealing with "romantic intuition" rather than realistic storytelling. James, she records, defined the romantic as "the things that, with all the faculties in the world . . . we never *can* directly know: the things that can reach us only through the beautiful circuit and subterfuge of our thought and desire" (22–23). Perhaps the only thing one can surely and safely say of this tale is that it *is* a romance.

Works Cited

Primary Works

James, Henry. 1896. "The Way It Came." *The Chap Book* 4 (1 May): 562–93; *Chapman's Magazine of Fiction* 4 (May): 95–120.

———. 1896. "The Way It Came." *Embarrassments.* London: Heinemann; New York: Macmillan, 265–320.

———. 1909. "The Friends of the Friends." In *The Novels and Tales of Henry James.* New York Edition. Vol. 17, 321–64. New York: Scribner's.

Secondary Works

Akiyama, Masayuki. 1985. "James and Nanboku: A Comparative Study of Supernatural Stories in the West and East." *Comparative Literature Studies* 22, no. 1 (Spring): 43–52.

Andreas, Osborn. 1948. *Henry James and the Expanding Horizon: A Study of the Meaning and Basic Themes of James's Fiction*. Seattle: University of Washington Press.

Anon. 1896. Review of *Embarrassments. Athenaeum*, no. 3588 (1 August): 158.

Auchard, John. 1986. *Silence in Henry James: The Heritage of Symbolism and Decadence*. University Park: Pennsylvania State University Press.

Banta, Martha. 1964. "Henry James and 'The Others.'" *New England Quarterly* 37 (June): 171–84.

Blackmur, R. P. [1948] 1983. "Henry James." In *Studies in Henry James.* Ed. Veronica A. Makowsky, 91–124. New York: New Directions. Reprinted from *Literary History of the United States*, ed. Robert E. Spiller et al. New York: Macmillan.

———. [1942] 1983. *"The Sacred Fount."* In *Studies in Henry James.* Ed. Veronica A. Makowsky, 45–68. New York: New Directions. Reprinted from *Kenyon Review* 4: 328–52.

Booth, Wayne C. [1961] 1983. *The Rhetoric of Fiction.* Chicago: University of Chicago Press.

Cowdery, Lauren Tozek. 1986. *The Nouvelle of Henry James in Theory and Practice.* Studies in Modern Literature, 47. Ann Arbor: UMI Research Press.

Dupee, F. W. [1951] 1956. *Henry James.* Garden City, NY: Doubleday Anchor.

Edel, Leon, ed. 1970. *Henry James: Stories of the Supernatural.* New York: Taplinger.

———, ed. [1949] 1963. *The Ghostly Tales of Henry James.* New York: The Universal Library, Grosset & Dunlap.

Edgar, Pelham. [1927] 1964. *Henry James, Man and Author.* New York: Russell & Russell.

Gage, Richard P. 1988. *Order and Design: Henry James' Titled Story Sequences.* New York: Peter Lang.

Geismar, Maxwell. 1963. *Henry James and the Jacobites*. Boston: Houghton Mifflin.

Goetz, William R. 1986. *Henry James and the Darkest Abyss of Romance*. Baton Rouge: Louisiana State University Press.

Heller, Terry. 1989. *The Turn of the Screw: Bewildered Vision*. Boston: Twayne.

Jacobson, Marcia. 1983. *Henry James and the Mass Market*. University: University of Alabama Press.

James, William. 1983. *The Correspondence of William James*. Vol. 2: *William and Henry: 1885–1896*. Ed. Ignas K. Skrupskelis and Elizabeth M. Berkeley. Charlottesville: University Press of Virginia.

Jones, Granville H. 1975. *Henry James's Psychology of Experience: Innocence, Responsibility, and Renunciation in the Fiction of Henry James*. The Hague: Mouton.

Kerr, Howard. 1983. "James's Last Early Supernatural Tales: Hawthorne Demagnetized, Poe Depoetized." In *The Haunted Dusk: American Supernatural Fiction, 1820–1920*. Ed. Howard Kerr, John W. Crowley, and Charles L. Crow, 135–48. Athens: University of Georgia Press.

Krook, Dorothea. [1962] 1967. *The Ordeal of Consciousness in Henry James*. New York: Cambridge University Press.

Lind, Sidney E. 1970. "'The Turn of the Screw': The Torment of Critics." *The Centennial Review* 14: 225–40.

Markow-Totevy, Georges. 1969. *Henry James*. Trans. John Griffiths. London: Merlin.

Matthiessen, F. O. 1944. *Henry James: The Major Phase*. New York: Oxford University Press.

Przybylowicz, Donna. 1986. *Desire and Repression: The Dialectic of Self and Other in the Late Works of Henry James*. University: University of Alabama Press.

Orage, A. R. 1918. "Henry James and the Ghostly." *The Little Review* 5 (August): 41–43.

Putt, S. Gorley. 1966. *Henry James: A Reader's Guide*. Ithaca, NY: Cornell University Press.

Rawlings, Peter, ed. 1984. *Henry James's Shorter Masterpieces*. Vol. 2. Sussex: Harvester; Totowa, NJ: Barnes & Noble.

Rimmon, Shlomith. 1977. *The Concept of Ambiguity: The Example of Henry James*. Chicago: University of Chicago Press.

Segal, Ora. 1969. *The Lucid Reflector: The Observer in Henry James' Fiction*. New Haven: Yale University Press.

Shelden, Pamela J. 1976. "'The Friends of the Friends': Another Twist to 'The Turn of the Screw.'" *Wascana Review* 11 (Spring): 3–14.

Thompson, G. R. 1983. "Washington Irving and the American Ghost Story." In *The Haunted Dusk: American Supernatural Fiction, 1820–1920*. Ed. Howard Kerr,

John W. Crowley, and Charles L. Crow, 13–36. Athens: University of Georgia Press.

Todorov, Tzvetan. 1977. *The Poetics of Prose*. Trans. Richard Howard. Ithaca, NY: Cornell University Press.

Vaid, Krishna B. 1964. *Technique in the Tales of Henry James*. Cambridge, MA: Harvard University Press.

Voss, Arthur. 1973. *The American Short Story: A Critical Survey*. Norman: University of Oklahoma Press.

Wagenknecht, Edward. 1984. *The Tales of Henry James*. New York: Frederick Ungar.

Wilson, Edmund. 1960. "The Ambiguity of Henry James." In *A Casebook on Henry James's "The Turn of the Screw."* Ed. Gerald Willen, 115–59. New York: Thomas Y. Crowell.

Woolf, Virginia. [1921] 1988. "Henry James's Ghost Stories." In *The Essays of Virginia Woolf*. Ed. Andrew McNeillie. Vol. 3, 319–26. London: Hogarth Press. Reprinted from *Times Literary Supplement* (22 December).

Wright, Walter F. 1962. *The Madness of Art: A Study of Henry James*. Lincoln: University of Nebraska Press.

Foreign Language
Cesarini, Remo. 1986. "La maschera della medusa." *Belfagor* 41 (30 November): 605–20.

Gabrielle de Bergerac

Publication History

James published "Gabrielle de Bergerac" in the *Atlantic Monthly* from July to September 1869. He never reprinted it in his lifetime. It was first republished in 1918 by Mordell. Since Mordell presented it as a book unto itself, its appearance in Kenton's *Eight Uncollected Tales* remained appropriate.

Circumstances of Composition, Sources, and Influences

Because James wrote the tale in the fall of 1868 before his return to Europe, McElderry sees James in it anticipating his exposure to Europe's history

(McElderry 31; Edel, CT 2, 9). While awaiting its publication, James was concerned as to the quality of printing his text would receive at the *Galaxy* and whether or not he had misquoted a line from the Bible. Afterward, while he found it making a "decent figure" due to his father's efforts, he focused on the story itself, which struck him "as the product of a former state of being" (*Letters* 1, 114, 126) and which inspired him to some theorizing on the proper subjects of fiction. He wrote to his sister:

> It all strikes me as amusingly thin and watery—I mean as regards its treatment of the Past. Since coming abroad and seeing relics, monuments, etc I've got a strong sense of what a grim old deathly reality it was, and how little worth one's while it is to approach it with a pen unless your mind is *bourré* with facts on the subject—how little indeed it is worth-while at all to treat it imaginatively. You can *imagine* nothing so impressive as Queen Elizabeth's battered old tomb in Westminster. (*Letters* 1, 132)

Given his new knowledge, his sense was that fiction should focus on "the present and the immediate future," particularly the latter (*Letters* 1, 132). His remarks, according to Altenbernd, provide a notable counterbalance to the view of James as antiquarian (6).

Despite James's misgivings, the tale was his closest so far to popular success. Not only did worthies such as Howells and James Russell Lowell praise the tale (LeClair 1955, 422–24, 451 n.21), but, Howells wrote James in June, it was likely "to make a greater impression than anything else you've done in the Atlantic," and remarking on "a general waking-up" to James's worth, he asked him to remember him when his fame was "as great as Hawthorne's." In August Howells was still able to report to James T. Fields that James's story was "a great gain upon all that he's done before, in the popular estimation" (*Selected Letters* 1, 328, 330–31, 335; also Mordell 50). Howells evidently continued to think of its vein as James's most likely route to popularity, writing John Hay in 1877 of *The American*, that James's ability to write "likingly of such a fellow-countryman as Newman is the most hopeful thing in his literary history, since *Gabrielle de Bergerac*" (*Letters* 2, 158).

Kenton locates the seeds of the tale in James's youthful sighting of a ruin and a peasant that, in the "momentary measure" of a "small sick boy," he recalled in his autobiography, "signified and summarized" Europe for him (Kenton 7–8; *Life* 1, 121–22). Appropriately for a historical romance, the tale is full of allusions to literary history. Beach describes it as "a kind of *pastiche* of Scarron, Watteau, Rousseau, Walter Scott, with a spice of Hawthorne and other American writers" (186). Kenton notes numerous allusions to mid-eighteenth-century literature (12). Kelley stresses the influence of Sand, particularly her novel *Valentine* in its independent heroine and "open air spirit" (90; also Delbaere-Garant 231; Adams 463). In addition to "a passion for Virgil,"

Coquelin is a "firm admirer" of Jean-Jacques Rousseau, as, Shine observes, James was at the time, and she finds signs of his admiration in his romantic description of the wise, innocent child (CT 2, 105; 83–84). Delbaere-Garant marks Coquelin himself as "a kind of Noble Savage" (234; also Tintner 1987, 248; Adams 463). In Gabrielle, she sees combined Eugénie De Guérin, whose works James had reviewed, the heroines of George Sand, and the Celebrated Woman of Sainte-Beuve (233). Krook suggests that the tale is not merely French but anticipatory, however mildly so, of the class-crossing love affair of *Lady Chatterley's Lover*. The "humble but blissful" marriage that follows, with its political overtones, she aptly compares to that of Dorothea and Will Ladislaw in *Middlemarch* (87). Wagenknecht records a smaller debt to *Henry Esmond* (183–84).

Following Beach, LeClair also points to the influence of Scott in the tale's improved handling of description (1955, 424). Adams, however, qualifies the debt to Scott by putting it through the filter of Balzac, a great reader of Scott, and particularly an early novel, *L'Enfant maudit*, in which a young duke's son rejects a wealthy match for a lower class woman, only to be frightened to death with her when his father draws a sword as does James's baron. Adams adds that both heroes admire Petrarch and a heroine named Gabrielle (462–63).

The stories Coquelin tells are the classic fairy tales of Perrault and Madame d'Aulnay, and even in late years his student is able to recall their looking at the illustration by Doré of Sleeping Beauty's enchanted castle, with the woodcutters, which fit in turn "the old France, of La Fontaine's *Fables* and the *Médecin malgré lui*" (CT 2, 131). Tintner cites the allusion to La Fontaine, and takes "Sleeping Beauty" as the tale's dominant model. James begins with the initial somnolence of prerevolutionary rural France, followed by Gabrielle's awakening to love at a ruined castle, if not one covered in briars, and ends with the realistically tempered "happy" ending, which she sees as parallelling the threat to the fairy tale couple's children by an ogress (1989, 10–12, 51; 1986, 15–16). Gale points to the comparison of Gabrielle and the Dutchess in *Don Quixote* (109).

James evidently took the name Coquelin from a former schoolmate in France. As Kenton notes, by giving his noble family here the name of Bergerac, James oddly anticipated Coquelin's greatest role as Rostand's *Cyrano de Bergerac* (8; also Anderson 151; Edel, CT 2, 9). Making James even more perspicacious, Neff sees him drawing on the name of the seventeeth-century French dramatist Savinien Cyrano de Bergerac, who inspired the play (13).

Such a romance of aristocratic female and plebian tutor was the subject of a 1920 play by Ferenc Molnar, *The Swan*, later a Hollywood film, in both of which the lovers end alive but apart.

Relation to Other Works

The tale is unique in the James canon. Although some of its closest connections are with the other works set in the historical past, "The Romance of Certain Old Clothes" and "De Grey," it lacks their supernatural shadings. Still, Levy cites some of the tale's more vivid prose, its curses and inarticulate cries, to link it with the melodrama of "De Grey" (17–18). Beach points out that with "The Romance of Certain Old Clothes," it is the only James work set before 1800, while LeClair finds it superior to the earlier work, though similar in that its success lies in its treatment of character not setting (Beach 186; LeClair 1955, 424). It is often approached in the context of James's search for a proper mode of fiction, the various genres he tried out including this tale's historicism, the Gothicism of "De Grey," the contemporary realism of "Osborne's Revenge," until the return to modern Europe in "Travelling Companions" (Brodhead 123; Long 18). Kraft links the tale with "A Light Man" of the same year as showing James's movement to a focus on Europe, while Fox contrasts the romantic treatment of a bygone France here with the realistic treatment of a present-day France in *Madame de Mauves* (Kraft 37; Fox 9). Krook, for her part, dismisses the setting as superfluous, finding the Bergerac chateau simply a version of a British country house, with the characters French versions of various British characters elsewhere in James (85–86).

Krook considers Gabrielle herself intriguing as a precursor of Isabel, her arranged match with the Vicomte anticipating Isabel's relations both with Osmond and Warburton. While in Krook's view the Vicomte anticipates the intermediate M. De Mauves, Gabrielle has what James calls in Isabel "a certain nobleness of imagination" as well as an equally "presumptuous" independent view. Such independence her brother judges "perversity" when it leads her to choose Coquelin, even as, Krook notes, some of her friends judged Isabel's choice of Osmond perverse, and Mrs. Gereth judged Fleda's rejection of Owen. Still Gabrielle, she argues, also shares with Isabel, Fleda, and the governess of *The Turn of the Screw* a sense of self-doubt, and she cites the similarity between Gabrielle's confession to the Vicomte that "There are moments when I'm afraid of my nature," to Isabel's feeling, after Warburton proposes, "really frightened at herself." Meanwhile, the child narrator, Krook argues, anticipates Miles (85–88). Kenton earlier noted a resemblance to *The Turn of the Screw* in the image of Gabrielle looking up at the tower as Coquelin looks down, even as the governess will look up at Quint (8).

One of the central issues of the tale is that of class. In its exposure of the glamorous yet evil French aristocracy, Ward connects the tale to *The American* (13). Nevertheless, as Delbaere-Garant observes, Coquelin succeeds where Newman fails, bringing a French aristocrat to defy her family out of love for him (231). Putt, for his part, reads one indication of class, the con-

trast between Coquelin's lodge and the Bergerac chateau, more as an anticipation of the contrast of private and public in "Benvolio" (37). Anderson,
however, considers the treatment of class here as direct as in "A Passionate
Pilgrim" (156–57).

Although Anderson argues that James later abandoned such directness, it
is is also present in *The Princess Casamassima*, and Kenton compares the
tale with the novel in terms of their recognition of the near juxtaposition, and
the consequent antagonism, of upper and lower class, a recognition she
traces to the vision that inspired the tale, that of a peasant standing before a
ruined castle, as well as James's memory of hearing the servants of a noble
French family gossiping in the trains. She finds this contrast indicated in the
description of the ruin: "At the first glance we see nothing but the great proportions, the show and the splendor; but when we come to explore, we
detect a vast underground world of iniquity and suffering" (7–9). Krook has
praised the scene at the castle for its drama and "psychological verisimilitude," and Delbaere-Garant compares Coquelin's sense of the castle's evil to
Newman's sense of the Bellegardes' castle as an "evil-looking place to live in"
(Krook 87; Delbaere-Garant 274–75). She argues, however, that the use of
such a vision as a symbol, which appears also in *Madame de Mauves*, only
truly achieves an organic fitness in *The Ambassadors* with Strether's excursion into the country (380). Kraft, meanwhile, finds Coquelin's articulation of
his philosophy as "simply to make the most of life while it lasts" anticipating
Strether's (52).

The tale is told by an old man remembering his youth. As the first example
of James's adoption of the perspective of a child, Shine sees the story treating
unsuccessfully the theme of a child's exposure to "adult frailty" later handled
successfully in *The Pupil* (83–84). LeClair, however, praises the treatment of
the relationship between tutor and child, imagining James drawing on his
own experience (1955, 425).

Interpretation and Criticism

In August Minny Temple wrote her cousin, "My dearest Harry what a charming tale is Gabrielle de Bergerac! *Just* as pretty as ever it can be. I am proud of
you, my dear, as well as fond—have you any special objections?" (LeClair
1949–50, 45–46). Whatever James's objections, critics have continued to echo
Minny's opinion of the charm of the tale.

As indicated above, the story's setting in pre-Revolutionary France is one
of its most distinctive and significant characteristics. Kraft notes how James
presents Europe in the tale as possessing a different moral standard from
America's (44). Delbaere-Garant also points to a difference in values, and
argues that James chose to place his tale in France for that reason, because

it represented for him "the place where the highest refinement of manners was combined with the greatest social tyranny and injustice" (229). In her view, however, the characters of Gabrielle and Coquelin are anomalous in their setting. Observing that James had not yet returned to France as an adult, she sees Gabrielle's "moral energy" and Coquelin's kindness and enlightened views making them more American than French, giving them in fact the "moral complexity" of James's Americans (233–35). But while James had not yet returned to France, he helped lend credence to his hero's representation of American ideals by sending him to America for three years to fight with the French in the cause of American independence. As Kraft remarks, while James is making use of the values of feudal France here, he is also rejecting them, even when seen at their best in Coquelin's rival, the refined but worthless de Treuil. Dietrichson, too, comments on the "sinister" implications of wealth here, particularly in the concept of the mercenary marriage which ignores people's happiness (69–70). Coquelin himself shows his awareness that in the even more remote past, the only role for him would have been as a serf or a monk. The tale, Kraft argues, articulates instead an alternate vision of the "aristocratic democrat," and condemns rigid class structures as simply another form of parochialism or limited vision. The combination of the refined Gabrielle and the vital Coquelin become the ideal blending (51–52).

The "abominable past" that Coquelin refuses to romanticize, and which includes for readers the time period of the story itself, has also been a subject of criticism (CT 2, 144; e.g., Jones 116). Delbaere-Garant observes nevertheless how both he and Gabrielle feel bound, indeed preoccupied by the past at the start (230–31). It is the brother's unjust accusation that, according to Andreas, frees Gabrielle from her sense of loyalty to him and the past he represents, his false definition of her allowing her to choose her own (23). While Anderson sees James's attitude to the past here as mixed (151), most critics focus on the rejection of the past at the central scene at the Castle of Fossy.

Its setting and subject make it logical to speak of the story as a fairy tale, and Jones judges it a perfect one, with two good, beautiful, wise young people who reach across the divide of class to love and marry and even to die "romantically martyred" (116). Although Krook treats their romantic martyrdom as a "historical-romance flourish that need not be taken too seriously" (87), it has prompted some serious discussion. Their deaths are mentioned at the very beginning of the story by the frame narrator, but still retain the power of surprise at the end. Kelley speaks of the pair leaving together "only to die some years later on the scaffold as Girondists," although she adds more philosophically that one can read their deaths as an example of "the anomaly of happy disaster where one suffers for love" (90). Even less satisfied, Delbaere-Garant questions whether Gabrielle was ever happy (233).

Kraft takes a different, equally gloomy view. Since he reads the two as representing a new, better way of life, their deaths indicate to him that their voice "as artists of life, as true moralists" is "too subtle a combination to be heard," misunderstood by both the high and low, thus democratic revolutions prove "hopelessly destructive of the good they create" (51). Putt takes the combination not as subtle, but "socially unnatural" and so equally doomed because James did not know what to do with his characters once they had crossed class boundaries (37–38). It is James's brother William, however, who has the most distinctive reading of the ending. In October 1869 he wrote his brother that the tale was "Very exquisitely touched—but the denouement bad in that it did not end with Coquelin's death in that stormy meeting and her being sent to a nunnery. At least Co ought to have had a lettre de cachet and she, resisting still the Viscount, have ended in a nunnery. The ending is both humdrum and improbable" (103).

One could cite a chorus of critics who, despite its "humdrum and improbable" conclusion, write in praise of the tale. Beginning with Cary in 1905, James's sortie into historical romance has been enjoyed even by those acclimated to a very different James (Cary 34–35; also Beach 186; McElderry 31). Kelley, like Wagenknecht later, considered the tale the most "delightful" of James's early "experiments," even as she notes that the tale might have easily and more characteristically been treated realistically (Wagenknecht 183). Taking a different slant, Leyburn grounds its claims to superiority on its seriousness (6). Part of the reason for the acclaim is no doubt, as Kelley notes, due to its relative lack of the highstrung melodrama typical of James's early tales (88). Certainly, too, James had become a stronger writer by the time he wrote the tale, and Kraft, although he argues that James still fails to treat his subject successfully, senses in it a new certainty in its argument and values (37, 44, 51–52). LeClair, in particular, places great weight on the tale, regarding it as the end of James's apprentice period, a transitional work from his somewhat awkward tales of America to the more assured treatment of Europe, marked by a vast improvement in style (1955, 422–26). Most of the qualification to the general praise centers on the use of the young boy as narrator. Shine, for example, finds the use of a "narrator-in-retrospect" to be "clumsy and circuitous," while Vaid objects to the slowness of his prologue (Shine 83–84; Vaid 13; also Wagenknecht 184). Putt proffers a more inclusive dissent, speaking of the work as a "'French' exercise" and a "fairy tale with turgid passages" (37–38). Kelley's attitude seems more sensible. She acknowledges that James was wise not to be tempted by his first success, or Howells's encouragement of it, into becoming a facile imitator of past styles, to continue to work toward a new kind of literature that did more than entertain, but does not hold the tale itself responsible for the detour (90–91).

Works Cited

Primary Works

James, Henry. 1869. "Gabrielle de Bergerac." *Atlantic Monthly* 24 (July–September): 55–71, 231–41, 352–61.

———. 1918. *Gabrielle de Bergerac*. Ed. Albert Mordell. New York: Boni and Liveright.

Secondary Works

Adams, Percy G. 1961. "Young Henry James and the Lesson of his Master Balzac." *Revue de Littérature Comparée* 35 (July–September): 458–67.

Altenbernd, Lynn. 1977. "A Dispassionate Pilgrim: Henry James's Early Travel in Sketch and Story." *Exploration* 5, no. 1: 1–14.

Anderson, Quentin. 1957. *The American Henry James*. New Brunswick, NJ: Rutgers University Press.

Andreas, Osborn. 1948. *Henry James and the Expanding Horizon: A Study of the Meaning and Basic Themes of James's Fiction*. Seattle: University of Washington Press.

Beach, Joseph Warren. [1918] 1954. *The Method of Henry James*. Philadelphia: Albert Saifer.

Brodhead, Richard H. 1986. *The School of Hawthorne*. New York: Oxford University Press.

Cary, Elisabeth Luther. 1905. *The Novels of Henry James: A Study*. New York: Putnam's.

Delbaere-Garant, Jeanne. 1970. *Henry James: The Vision of France*. Paris: Société d'Editions Les Belles Lettres.

Dietrichson, Jan W. 1969. *The Image of Money in the American Novel of the Gilded Age*. Oslo: Universitetsforlaget; New York: Humanities.

Fox, Hugh. 1968. *Henry James, A Critical Introduction*. Conesville, IA: John Westburg.

Gale, Robert L. [1954] 1964. *The Caught Image: Figurative Language in the Fiction of Henry James*. Chapel Hill: University of North Carolina Press.

Howells, W. D. 1979. *Selected Letters*. Vol. 1: *1852–1872*. Ed. George Arms, et al. Boston: Twayne.

———. 1979. *Selected Letters*. Vol. 2: *1873–1881*. Ed. George Arms, Christoph K. Lohmann, and Jerry Herron. Boston: Twayne.

James, William. 1992. *The Correspondence of William James*. Vol. 1: *William and Henry: 1861–1884*. Ed. Ignas K. Skrupskelis and Elizabeth M. Berkeley. Charlottesville: University Press of Virginia.

Jones, Granville H. 1975. *Henry James's Psychology of Experience: Innocence,*

Responsibility, and Renunciation in the Fiction of Henry James. The Hague: Mouton.

Kelley, Cornelia Pulsifer. [1930] 1965. *The Early Development of Henry James*. Urbana: University of Illinois Press.

Kenton Edna, ed. 1950. *Eight Uncollected Tales of Henry James*. New Brunswick, NJ: Rutgers University Press.

Kraft, James. 1969. *The Early Tales of Henry James*. Carbondale: Southern Illinois University Press.

Krook, Dorothea. 1982. "Prefigurings of Isabel Archer." *Hebrew University Studies in Literature*: 80–98.

LeClair, Robert Charles. 1955. *Young Henry James, 1843–1870*. New York: Bookman.

———. 1949–50. "Henry James and Minny Temple." *American Literature* 21: 35–48.

Levy, Leo B. 1957. *Versions of Melodrama: A Study of the Fiction and Drama of Henry James, 1865–1897*. Berkeley: University of California Press.

Leyburn, Ellen Douglass. 1968. *Strange Alloy: The Relation of Comedy to Tragedy in the Fiction of Henry James*. Chapel Hill: University of North Carolina Press.

Long, Robert Emmet. 1979. *The Great Succession: Henry James and the Legacy of Hawthorne*. Pittsburgh: University of Pittsburgh Press.

McElderry, Bruce R., Jr. 1965. *Henry James*. New York: Twayne.

Mordell, Albert. 1961. *Discovery of a Genius: William Dean Howells and Henry James*. New York: Twayne.

Neff, John C. 1938. "Henry James the Reporter." *New Mexico Quarterly* 8 (February): 9–14.

Putt, S. Gorley. 1966. *Henry James: A Reader's Guide*. Ithaca, NY: Cornell University Press.

Shine, Muriel G. 1969. *The Fictional Children of Henry James*. Chapel Hill: University of North Carolina Press.

Tintner, Adeline R. 1989. *The Pop World of Henry James: From Fairy Tales to Science Fiction*. Ann Arbor: UMI Research Press. Revised from "Henry James and the Sleeping Beauty: A Victorian Fantasy of a Fairy-Tale Theme." *Topic* 37 (Fall 1983): 10–22.

———. 1987. *The Book World of Henry James: Appropriating the Classics*. Ann Arbor: UMI Research Press.

———. 1986. *The Museum World of Henry James*. Ann Arbor: UMI Research Press.

Vaid, Krishna B. 1964. *Technique in the Tales of Henry James*. Cambridge, MA: Harvard University Press.

Wagenknecht, Edward. 1984. *The Tales of Henry James*. New York: Frederick Ungar.

Ward, J. A. 1961. *The Imagination of Disaster: Evil in the Fiction of Henry James*. Lincoln: University of Nebraska Press.

Georgina's Reasons

Publication History

Along with "Pandora," "Georgina's Reasons" was one of two short stories James wrote for the New York *Sunday Sun*, where it appeared on July 20 and 27 and August 3, 1884, as well as being reprinted by various members of the *Sun* Syndicate. James himself reprinted both stories the next year in *The Author of Beltraffio* and *Stories Revived*, but he did not include "Georgina's Reasons" in the New York Edition. Its next appearance was therefore in Lubbock's edition of James's fiction in the 1920's. (See also "Pandora.")

Circumstances of Composition, Sources, and Influences

James wrote "Georgina's Reasons" in London the summer it was published, at the time he was working on *The Bostonians*. The source for the story, recorded March 26, 1884, came from an incident told James by Fanny Kemble. It had already traveled a circuitous route, coming through Kemble's brother-in-law from his daughter-in-law, whose father, for additional interest, was Ulysses S. Grant. Its "eminent, if highly convoluted" origins evidently so impressed Geismar that he erroneously describes the completed tale as "a melodrama of western American army life" (60). The original of Georgina had lived in "one of the far Western cities of America," had secretly married an officer, and subsequently abandoned first him and then their child and remarried (CN 26–27).

"Georgina's Reasons" seems designed to fit the newspapers, an unusual venue for James given his contempt for them. According to Ziff, the New York *Sun* under Charles A. Dana established the "tradition of personal journalism" (147). Edel speaks of James's "misguided belief" that the "sensational" subject was an appropriate one for the papers, but also supports James's view by quoting the headline from one paper reprinting the story:

Georgina's Reasons!
Henry James's Latest Story
A woman who commits bigamy and enforces silence on her husband!
Two other lives made miserable by her heartless action!   (*Life* 3, 119–20)

Tintner, at least, judges the story a success, arguing that James in his reach for the newspaper public, turned to the tradition of "sensation" stories as exemplified by Mary Elizabeth Braddon's *Lady Audley's Secret* and *Aurora Floyd* (which he had reviewed nearly twenty years before). Among the borrowings she identifies from Braddon are the theme of the secret; the use of a portrait as the means of discovering bigamy; and, for the character of Georgina, both Lady Audley's coldness and Aurora's queenly demeanor. At the same time, she argues, to keep to his standards as a literary artist, James retained his usual international setting, added a "correction" in his consideration of how the heroine's misdeeds affect the hero, and (in the most conjectural of Tintner's claims) updated Braddon by presenting his heroine's "insanity" according to contemporary medical understanding (1989, 159–64). Tintner quotes Oliphant on the challenge of producing high art in a popular publication to support her thesis that James sought to elevate the sensational story, but James's own description in his review of Braddon's "grim determination to succeed"—"Her purpose was at any hazard to make a hit, to catch the public ear. It was a difficult task, but audacity could accomplish it"— seems more in tune with his purposes to make a success of a new venue (*Criticism* 1, 741).

Jefferson, who finds in the tale "moral abnormality such as we should hardly expect to find in English fiction of the same period," leaves room for a foreign influence (108). In a review of the collection *The Author of Beltraffio* directly across from a reader's query as to the suitability of various French novels for "young people of both sexes," the reviewer for the *Literary World* pinned responsibility for James's dubious freedom in the tale on French influences. At the same time, the reviewer for the *Critic*, speaking of James's "abominable" Georgina as "another flower in these *fleurs du mal*," castigated him for adopting "the cast-off purple patches of a fast-decaying Frenchy school." Tintner less censoriously connects Georgina, along with Pandora Day and Olive Chancellor, as a deliberately "curious" heroine with the French decadent movement (1987, 266), an appropriate connection as James had been in Paris that February and found "'naturalism' . . . in possession *sur toute la ligne*" (*Letters* 3, 25). Maves points instead to Italy as a conventional justification for melodrama in English literature, including the similarly suspect behavior in Italy of George Eliot's Gwendolen Harleth and Trollope's Louis Trevelyan (82).

The narrator at one point provides a more classical source by speaking of the pair as "the Twelfth Street Juliet" and "her Brooklyn Romeo," drawing a connection with Shakespeare's story of passion and secret marriage (CT 6,

25). Melchiori notes, however, that unlike Shakespeare's heroine, Georgina has no aversion to bigamy (9). To Mrs. Portico, Georgina's "blooming hardness," as Gale recalls, seems "a king of Medusa-mask" (116).

Edel proposes a source from life, James's cousin Helen and her husband— a "dim little gentleman" as James spoke of him (*Life* 1, 105).

While acknowledging that the chronology precludes any influence, Jones draws a parallel between Georgina and Hedda Gabler of Ibsen's 1890 play: "For them both, their reputation is more real than their conscience" (1974, 194).

Relation to Other Works

Most of the connections focus on family roles as examined in works of roughly the same period. Viewing her in her role as a daughter, Jones considers Georgina's story as a "companion piece" to *Washington Square* (1884), with the same New York setting and situation, a young woman with a suitor her family dislikes. (Though Jones does not mention it, another link is in their common origin as stories told to James by Fanny Kemble.) Both Georgina and Catherine Sloper have confidantes outside the family, while keeping their passion hidden at home. But there, he notes, the differences begin: Catherine "respects" her society and wants to bring her lover into it; Georgina hates it and wants to escape it through hers. Georgina, Catherine's "antithesis," is completely at ease deceiving her family. But in a sense she, too, fails. As Jones points out, at the end Georgina is married to exactly the sort of man her parents wished for her at the start. Nevertheless, he sees a possible, secret satisfaction for her in her own awareness of her "bigamy and lies" (1974). Jefferson also links the two tales, offering a comparison not between the two heroines, but between Georgina and Catherine's father in their coldness and "moral abnormality" (108).

In Georgina's active, independent behavior, and especially in her desire to leave her family behind, there are also some echoes of the self-made girl defined in the companion story "Pandora," minus Pandora's affection. As Jefferson observes, Georgina can be read as "the final and most startling development of the independence of the American girl and her exploitation of the male," although he does not believe this to have been James's intent (108).

Jones briefly links the story to *The Wings of the Dove* and *The Golden Bowl*, finding that "Nowhere else in James's works . . . is sexual attraction so explicitly invoked" as in Georgina's challenge to Mrs. Portico—"Would you have liked me to—to not marry?" He comments further on her ability to marry against her parents' wishes, but her inability to challenge "her entire society's moral standards" (192). James's review of Braddon is interesting in this connection. She wrote, according to James, "with a strict regard to morality. If one of her heroines elopes with a handsome stable-boy, she saves the proprieties by marrying him. This may be indecent if you like, but it is not immoral" (*Criticism* 1, 746). Similarly, Jones links her with Christina Light, who always considers society's judgment in her rebellion against it (1975, 237). Stein finds Benyon's adherence to his marriage vows lacking the "moral authority" of Isabel Archer's (119).

Looking at her as a mother, Shine classes Georgina, whom she finds so "unbelievably cruel" that she puts the word "heroine" in quotation marks, with Mrs. Temperly, Mrs. Pallant, Mrs. Daintry of "A New England Summer," and Mrs. Mavis of "The Patagonia" as a mother who breaks James's rule that parents must not "manipulate their children in order to satisfy their own needs" (52). The story also has affinities with "The Author of Beltraffio," the germ for which was recorded on the same date in James's notebook. Both can be read as depicting the inscrutable behavior of a mother who sacrifices her child to her sense of respectability. A major difference is that Georgina is acting only for herself, while the mother in "The Author of Beltraffio" is seeking to save her child from something she considers worse than death. In a lesser way, Madame Merle gives up the possession, but not the care, of her child in order to safeguard her reputation.

The other main connection, again with *The Wings of the Dove*, is provided by the names of the Theory sisters. Matthiessen and Murdock, who record the "kinship of the names" in Minny, Mildred, and Milly, remark that the "Minny Temple theme was obviously already in his mind" (N 61). Edel sees Kate and Mildred Theory, with Benyon, as an "early form" of the characters of Kate Croy, Milly Theale, and Densher, and finds the anticipation "the most interesting part of the tale," at least for those familiar with late James and notes also the use of a portrait for a recognition scene in each (*Life* 1, 332; *Life* 3, 119–20; *Life* 5, 110–11; CT 6, 12). Cargill looks instead at the association between Georgina Roy and Kate Croy seen in their surnames and their characters, although he adds that by taking away Georgina's money James made Kate less unaccountable (347–48; also Putt 270; Powers 80). Samuels comments on how both women work to have both the man and the money they believe themselves entitled to (73). Looking at the surname, Habegger remarks that theories were one of the characteristics of "the American girl" that James particularly disliked (114). Edel also proposes a similarity with the triangular relationships of *The Golden Bowl* (*Life* 5, 212).

Donald Stone links Benyon in his choosing to renounce rather than face "dishonor" with Christopher Newman and Fleda Vetch (238).

Interpretation and Criticism

While Matthiessen and Murdock quote a contemporary reader who found the story a "masterpiece," and themselves call it an "interesting study," most subsequent critics have dissented from or at least qualified such praise (N 60). Most have acknowledged, as James felt, that the original idea, the basic "ugly narrative" as James once referred to it, represents a true "situation," but the fault that he found with it—"it sounds 'made up'"—has also continued to be held against the tale (*Letters* 3, 154; CN 26). Edgar, for example, finds in it "more contrivances of episode" than usual in or helpful to a James short story (46). Indeed, it may well be that the main difficulty readers face in the story—attempting to understand Georgina's behavior—stems in part from James's piling up of circumstance on circumstance so that Georgina becomes involved in an increasingly dense web of denial in order to avoid exposing her initial impulse to marry secretly.

Whatever the role played by such plotting, with its emphasis on reasons and understanding (two key words), the story circles about in an evident attempt to explain the motives of Georgina, beginning with her decision to marry Benyon. The first three sections of the story all repeat, with slight variation, her "off-hand" decision to marry Benyon: "Oh yes, I will marry you!" (CT 6, 17, 21, 23). Matthiessen and Murdock propose resistance to her family as her main object, but while that may be the motive for her initial acceptance of Benyon, it still seems inadequate to explain her subsequent actions or her basic "odiousness" that Matthiessen and Murdock call "the core of the work" (N 60). A final link with James's review of Braddon may be his description of her heroine as "simply foolish, or indiscreet, or indelicate—or anything you please to say of a young lady who runs off with a hostler"—an analysis that seems to anticipate the obscure behavior of his own heroine, if not to offer any illumination of it (*Criticism* 1, 744). In a poem praising James, Robert Louis Stevenson called Georgina a "trivial sphynx," writing James that while he found the first part of the story admirable, he was "not so well satisfied" with the second, perhaps because the absence of explanation becomes more nagging as the extravagant behavior multiplies (Smith 108, 172). A contemporary reviewer dismissed the heroine as "a moral monster" (*Independent*). Tintner, the story's strongest advocate, goes beyond Edgar's statement that Georgina's "caprice approaches madness," to declare her a psychopath in order to explain her behavior (Edgar 46; Tintner 1989, 162–64). Wagenknecht, while he still considers Georgina's reasons "hardly set forth adequately," discerns in her characterization a power beyond them, stating that she "remains a baleful, living character" (184).

Benyon's character has also been questioned. Putt calls him a "craven wretch" and considers his unwillingness to commit bigamy little more than "a protective alibi" against marriage (271). Similarly, Stein finds the work so "weak" in comparison to James's other mature treatments of marriage that Benyon's renunciation, unlike Isabel Archer's, "seems merely a somewhat foolish, quirky thing to do" (119 n.1). Wagenknecht, while not commiting himself, also comments that many readers find Benyon's continued sense of obligation to his vows to Georgina "incredible" given her behavior (184). Most pertinently, Jones, while arguing that the portrait of Georgina is the work's strength, examines Benyon in conjunction with her, seeing the combination of their weaknesses—Georgina's selfishness and Benyon's passivity—and their shared scrupulousness as the ingredients that turn their attraction to each other into a peculiarly doomed relationship (1974, 193; 1975, 101–2).

James himself, in an 1886 letter to John Hay, called it a "bad and unsuccessful story" (*Letters* 3, 154). In 1894, in response to a question from Frederic W. H. Myers, he wrote, "Of *Georgina's Reasons* I mainly remember that I thought them pretty bad at the time—I mean thought the tale a feeble one, and that impression has remained with me. I daresay it is one of the worst I was ever guilty of." He asserts that he is unable to find the book, and able only to remember the "limited anecdote" that prompted the tale. But James does not discount the worth of "Georgina's Reasons" alone. He continues with a scarcely more enthusiastic consideration of his attitude to other completed works: "I loathe them all! What I 'like' is the art—more than I can say; and the works have only a temporary tolerance—reflected from that" (*Letters* 3, 488–89). The tolerance accorded this story by James critics seems to have been more temporary than is usual, and although this may be shifting, it seems likely that its acceptance will not stem from a detective approach which finally gives a specific name or names to the heroine's mysterious reasons, but that Georgina and her story will remain, however "trivial," sphinx-like.

Works Cited

Primary Works
James, Henry. 1884. "Georgina's Reasons." *New York Sun* (20 and 27 July and 3 August) 1: 7 and 2.

———. 1885. "Georgina's Reasons." *The Author of Beltraffio*. Boston: James R. Osgood, 159–257.

———. 1885. "Georgina's Reasons." In *Stories Revived*. Vol. 2, 281–375. London: Macmillan.

———. 1921–23. "Georgina's Reasons." In *The Novels and Stories of Henry James*. Vol. 25. Ed. Percy Lubbock. London: Macmillan.

Secondary Works
Anon. 1885. Review of *The Author of Beltraffio*. *Independent* 37 (9 April): 459.

Anon. 1885. Review of *The Author of Beltraffio*. *Literary World* 16 (21 March): 102.

Anon. 1885. Review of *The Author of Beltraffio*. *The Critic* 6 (2 May): 206–7.

Cargill, Oscar. 1961. *The Novels of Henry James*. New York: Macmillan

Edgar, Pelham. [1927] 1964. *Henry James, Man and Author*. New York: Russell & Russell.

Gale, Robert L. [1954] 1964. *The Caught Image: Figurative Language in the Fiction of Henry James*. Chapel Hill: University of North Carolina Press.

Geismar, Maxwell. 1963. *Henry James and the Jacobites*. Boston: Houghton Mifflin.

Habegger, Alfred. 1989. *Henry James and the "Woman Business."* Cambridge: Cambridge University Press.

Jefferson, D. W. 1964. *Henry James and the Modern Reader*. New York: St. Martin's.

Jones, Granville H. 1975. *Henry James's Psychology of Experience: Innocence, Responsibility, and Renunciation in the Fiction of Henry James*. The Hague: Mouton.

———. 1974. "Henry James's 'Georgina's Reasons': The Underside of *Washington Square*." *Studies in Short Fiction* 11 (Spring): 189–94.

Maves, Carl. 1973. *Sensuous Pessimism: Italy in the Work of Henry James*. Bloomington: Indiana University Press.

Melchiori, Giorgio. 1965. "Locksley Hall Revisited: Tennyson and Henry James." *Review of English Literature* 6 (October): 9–25. Reprinted in Barbara Melchiori and Giorgio Melchiori, *Il Gusto di Henry James*. Turin: Guilio Einaudi editore, 1974.

Powers, Lyall H. 1970. *Henry James: An Introduction and Interpretation*. New York: Holt, Rinehart.

Putt, S. Gorley. 1966. *Henry James: A Reader's Guide*. Ithaca, NY: Cornell University Press.

Samuels, Charles Thomas. 1971. *The Ambiguity of Henry James*. Urbana: University of Illinois Press.

Shine, Muriel G. 1969. *The Fictional Children of Henry James*. Chapel Hill: University of North Carolina Press.

Smith, Janet Adam, ed. 1948. *Henry James and Robert Louis Stevenson*. London: Rupert Hart-Davis.

Stein, Allen F. 1984. *After the Vows Were Spoken: Marriage in American Literary Realism*. Columbus: Ohio State University Press.

Stone, Donald David. 1972. *Novelists in a Changing World: Meredith, James, and the Transformation of English Fiction in the 1880's*. Cambridge, MA: Harvard University Press.

Tintner, Adeline R. 1989. *The Pop World of Henry James: From Fairy Tales to Science Fiction*. Ann Arbor: UMI Research Press. Revised from "Henry James and Miss Braddon: 'Georgina's Reasons' and the Victorian Sensational Novel." *Essays in Literature* 10, no. 1 (Spring 1983): 119–24.

————. 1987. *The Book World of Henry James: Appropriating the Classics.* Ann Arbor: UMI Research Press.

Wagenknecht, Edward. 1984. *The Tales of Henry James.* New York: Frederick Ungar.

Ziff, Larzer. 1966. *The American 1890's: Life and Times of a Lost Generation.* New York: Viking.

The Ghostly Rental

Publication History

"The Ghostly Rental" appeared in September 1876 in *Scribner's*. It was not reprinted again until Leon Edel's 1949 edition of *The Ghostly Tales of Henry James.*

Circumstances of Composition, Sources, and Influences

James wrote "The Ghostly Rental" in 1876 while living in Paris and writing *The American* (Edel 1970, 103; see "Crawford's Consistency"). While Aziz questions James's reasons for writing such an American tale so shortly after coming to France, Buitenhuis sees in the tale evidence of James's continued fascination with America even when in Europe (Buitenhuis 87). Similarly, Martin and Ober, in response to Aziz, offer a reading of the tale as James's "apologia" for leaving America, a reflection of his ambivalence toward his native land. Noting that the tale was published in the centennial year of the Declaration of Independence, they find James comparing the Captain to Andrew Jackson to evoke the solid virtues of an America perhaps lost in the Civil War. Less allegorically, Edel finds James drawing on his memories of being a law student at Harvard in 1862–1863 and his friendship there with two students of divinity (*Life* 1, 194; 1970, 103–4).

The numerous literary allusions in the tale have drawn much attention, Kerr calling it James's "most consistently allusive" work apart from *The Turn of the Screw* (142; also Edel 1970, 105). About the only allusions that have not generated analysis are the mentions of Plotinus, Saint Augustine, and *The*

Arabian Nights. Edel briefly records the allusion in Miss Deborah's warning, "Remember Blue Beard's wife" ([1949] 1963, 71). Martin and Ober locate an allusion to Holmes's famous poem in a mention of an "old, one-horse chaise."

Kelley first noted the influence of E. T. A. Hoffmann signaled by the narrator's comparison of the Captain to "a figure out of one of Hoffmann's tales" (246 n.4). Briggs specifically cites the 1819 *Die Automate*, a tale of Adelgunda and the White Lady, as the "prototype" for the "faked haunting [that] rebounds upon its perpetrator when the real ghost appears" (149).

Andreach followed up on Kenton's suggestion of the possible significance of the student's readings of Pascal's *Thoughts* (1950, 12), formulating a reading of the tale based on Pascal's distinction between two ways of knowing—the "mathematical" and "intuitive"—both of which are necessary for true understanding, a stage the narrator fails to reach. One might add to his reading that the narrator's confidante, Miss Deborah, appears to have the "bonne vue" Pascal found necessary for intuitive vision. The narrator himself remains a rationalist, a fact various critics including Banta and Varnado have found indicated in his admiration for Channing, the rationalist theologian Banta 1972, 107; Varnado 80).

While Buitenhuis labels the Captain Dickensian (87), the story has been more typically seen as under the influence of two American writers, Hawthorne and Poe. Quentin Anderson, for example, calls it "second-rate Hawthorne" (38; also McElderry 1965, 115; 1949, 289). Buitenhuis himself finds James following Hawthorne in using the Gothic as a way of approaching an American setting as well as in the deliberate ambiguity in the appearance of the second ghost (85–87).

Banta, on the other hand, regards James in this story as still under the influence of Poe, but turning more to the "Dupinesque mode" of "intelligence and intuition" rather than Gothic emotion (1972, 107). Kerr sees it as a deliberate break with Poe, its haunted house encountered by a fearful narrator drawing on "The Fall of the House of Usher" only to overturn it, as it dissolves into "puddles" rather than a poetic tarn. Defending the legitimacy of the second ghost as serving "Poetic justice," he compares it to the appearance of Madeline Usher. Beneath the allusion to Jackson he discovers an evocation of one Robert Dale Owen, who published a series in the *Atlantic* chronicling his experience with a ghost later proved false. In Kerr's view, James here vindicates Owen's sincerity (140–46). Kenton notes that the house is spoken of as an "embodied mind" (1950, 17), a significance James could surely have found in Poe. Edel supports the general link by pointing out that James was reading Baudelaire on Poe at the time, but cautions that the echoes of Poe might stem directly from *his* sources in Hoffmann ([1949] 1963, 70).

Relation to Other Works

Although Kelley sees the tale as "outside the main stream of [James's] development," the natural connections are those McElderry rather disparagingly makes with the other early tales of the supernatural (Kelley 246 n.4; McElderry 1965, 27, 115). Wagenknecht, however, considers it to have the ghostly "atmosphere" the earlier "Romance of Certain Old Clothes" needed (185). Kerr links it with "Professor Fargo" in its break from the Gothic, its daughter who rebels against a military father, and its "voyeuristic" narrator (140).

Banta connects the tale with *The Bostonians* as a work that makes fun of contemporary spiritualism, but also assigns it more far-reaching significance, seeing its themes—"of the obsessed observer, of the burning desire for risk and adventure, and of the need for reverencing the dead"—throughout James's career (1972, 5, 7). Kenton, too, sees in it the "life-in-death" theme of James's later work (1950, 17). Edel perceives it as an early example of the haunter haunted, as in "The Jolly Corner" or *The Sense of the Past* (1970, 103; also Briggs 151). All three works also provide haunted houses, although Edel deems this tale a singularly "traditional" one, and in both short stories, as McCarthy has noted, the ghost appears at the bottom of the stairs (McCarthy 107). Edel expands the use of the house to James's symbolic use of houses both haunted, as in *The Turn of the Screw*, and otherwise, as in *The Spoils of Poynton*, particularly their connection with "family," as in *The Sense of the Past* (1970, 103–5). Banta links the tale with *The Turn of the Screw*, "Sir Edmund Orme," and the haunted Gardencourt of *The Portrait of a Lady* in James's use of the supernatural to challenge complacency and to prod self-awareness, particularly in the need for love to be generous (1972, 131–32).

Kenton groups the tale with such other early tales as "Travelling Companions," "Guest's Confession," "A Passionate Pilgrim," "Eugene Pickering," and "The Last of the Valerii" in its use of a first-person narrator who participates in the events he describes (1950, 18). Reaching farther, Putt and Kraft connect the tale with *The Sacred Fount* in its discussion of the validity of detached observation (Putt 390; Kraft 88). Andreach also classes the narrator with the inadequately self-aware narrators of *The Aspern Papers*, *The Turn of the Screw*, and *The Sacred Fount*, for instance. In contrast, he nominates Strether of *The Ambassadors* as a character who unites "feeling and thinking" (304–5).

Interpretation and Criticism

Critics such as Edel and Putt have classified "The Ghostly Rental" as a lowly "commercial" tale, while Banta judges it a "near failure" in any category (CT 4,

7; *Life* 2, 247; Putt 389; Banta 1972, 129). The tale is not, however, without its advocates. Beach deems it the best of the early tales, although inferior to the later ghost tales of the 1890s (185). Kraft gives the story one of its more generous assessments, characterizing it as "lightly written, humorous, and entertaining" (87–88). Even the majority, who judge the overall tale disappointing, locate in it elements of significance for the later work of James.

To start with, critics differ on what is real in the tale. McElderry calls the tale James's "most fanciful" early ghost tale, and accordingly takes the view of the locals that the house burns "mysteriously" (1965, 27). The story, however, also offers—in the manner of Hawthorne—the more straightforward explanation that the cause is the candle left burning by the frightened daughter, one more favored by critics. Critics also differ on whether the second ghost is supposed to be "real" or, as Martin and Ober put it, a "hallucination" brought on by the daughter's guilt (8). McElderry is alone in removing the *cause* for her guilt, stating that she intended to help her father by paying rent (1949, 289).

The second ghost, real or imagined, has been the cause of the most critical disagreement. In Todorov's reading, with the unmasking of the first ghost, the tale belongs to the category of the "supernatural explained" only to return to the ambiguous "fantastic" at the appearance of the second ghost (180). Putt judges the twist ending a "not unaffecting climax" (389). Varnado uses the terminology of Rudolf Otto to praise James's capturing of the "numinous" and his interest in the "ontology" of the supernatural. He finds James through the second ghost indicating his uncertainty whether he wishes to treat real ghosts or the perception of the ghostly (79–82). Andreach also considers the second ghost appropriate in its overturning of the narrator's insistence on the rational, and notes that the narrator, while sufficiently disturbed by his experience to give up his studies, never fully understands it. Jones states that it appropriately indicates the daughter's excessive vengeance (105).

Wagenknecht, on the other hand, objects to the story's "juxtaposition of true and false supernaturalism," as do McElderry and Banta (Wagenknecht 185; McElderry 1949, 289). In her earlier reading, Banta saw the tale as a warning to the living against "demeaning the dead by fraudulently taking over their role" (1964, 180 n.23). In that way the appearance of a real ghost would seem only just. Banta, however, took her reading another way, analyzing the psychological "inward haunting" induced in the narrator through his confrontation with the first, sham ghost, and remarking that James would take this idea even further later with the sense of hauntedness leading to knowledge rather than interfering with it, as here. The introduction instead of a real ghost for "shock" value, Banta argues, undercuts the more significant type of "haunting" (1972, 109–10).

Looking at the protagonist, Putt detects James's "earth-bound temperament" in the divinity student's comment that he had been "explicitly cultivat-

ing cheerful views of the supernatural" (389). His "inclination to coquet a little" with his "discovery," is, however, to Gale, unintentionally "erotic" (47
n.15). Kenton, while acknowledging the "saving light touch" in his character,
emphasizes his discovery through the encounter with the "spiritually blighted" Diamond house of less cheerful possibilities. She suggests, too, that his
religious studies make him a better confessor for Captain Diamond (1950, 17).

The greatest amount of critical attention, however, has focused on Miss
Deborah's boast of the powers of her imagination:

> Observe closely enough . . . and it doesn't matter where you are. You
> may be in a pitch-dark closet. All you want is something to start with; one
> thing leads to another, and all things are mixed up. Shut me up in a dark
> closet and I will observe after a while, that some places in it are darker
> than others. After that (give me time), and I will tell you what the
> President of the United States is going to have for dinner. (CT 4, 63)

Like Poe's Dupin solving cases far from the scene, the housebound Miss
Deborah's philosophy provides a link between this early James tale and what
Kenton calls the "familiar bouquet" of his later work (1919, 326).

Most critics, like Thorp, consider Miss Deborah to be speaking for the
author (viii). Kenton discerns in Miss Deborah's "system of observation" the
"reconciliation" James was then working toward between "passive wondering
and active inquiry" (1950, 14). Buitenhuis finds it a representation of the
growth of James's perceptive abilities, particularly of the American subject
(88). Beebe sees it as an early example of James's linking of observation and
inspiration by means of a "sympathetic response," and Putt as an early example of James's "propaganda for the speculative non-participant" (Beebe 205;
Putt 390).

Kraft demurs, seeing the "incompleteness and the irony" of the woman's
claim as showing James's awareness of the "*potential* hollowness" of observation and an art based on it alone, a hollowness that could only be avoided
through "consciousness and commitment." For Kraft the irony of the
woman's remarks supports the central theme of the tale, which contrasts the
student's study of religious theory and actual "spirits" to argue for the necessity of adding experience to observation (87–89). Banta, too, links her with
the narrator as a "prideful" rationalist whose rationalism cannot hold up to
events (1972, 108). Martin and Ober, as well, while noting her prophetess's
name, dismiss her at the end as a "mistaken local gossip" (8).

Walter Anderson, like Kraft, sees the story as stressing the limitations of
vision, although he considers the young narrator closest to James's own situation as a perceptive observer who struggles vainly to "close the gap"
between sight and experience. His reading stresses the final moment when
the possibility of knowledge literally goes up in smoke, leaving the narrator
with an unsolvable riddle (521–26).

An admirer of the tale, Buitenhuis reads it as James's reenacting his own encounter with America from the vantage point of Europe. The Captain's house stands for America, even as James, the one-time law student, is represented by the divinity student. In a reading of the sequence of events as metaphor, James at first fails to understand the mystery of America, recognizes it the second time as "merely human," only to discover there is still a ghost, one that according to Buitenhuis, James would set out to encounter many years later in "The Jolly Corner" (85–87, 219). Using the title as metaphor, Jay Martin criticizes the tale as an illustration of James's early belief that the ghostly could be treated lightly—"merely rented"—rather than "purchased" (126). Both he and Buitenhuis are indicating through their metaphors that the tale is one of much promise, treating issues central to James's approach to life and literature, but that will require much more working out before they are mastered. As an admittedly apprentice work, however, with a hero who remains forever at that stage, it still can intrigue.

Works Cited

Primary Works
James, Henry. 1876. "The Ghostly Rental." *Scribner's Monthly* 12 (September): 664–79.

Secondary Works
Anderson, Quentin. 1957. *The American Henry James*. New Brunswick, NJ: Rutgers University Press.

Anderson, Walter E. 1982. "The Visiting Mind: Henry James's Poetics of Seeing." *The Psychoanalytic Review* 69 (Winter): 513–32.

Andreach, Robert J. 1967. "Literary Allusion as a Clue to Meaning: James's 'The Ghostly Rental' and Pascal's *Pensées*." *Comparative Literature Studies* 4: 299–306.

Banta, Martha. 1972. *Henry James and the Occult: The Great Extension*. Bloomington: Indiana University Press.

———. 1964. "Henry James and 'The Others.'" *New England Quarterly* 37 (June): 171–84.

Beach, Joseph Warren. [1918] 1954. *The Method of Henry James*. Philadelphia: Albert Saifer.

Beebe, Maurice L. 1964. *Ivory Towers and Sacred Founts: The Artist as Hero*. New York: New York University Press.

Briggs, Julia. 1977. *Night Visitors: The Rise and Fall of the English Ghost Story*. London: Faber.

Buitenhuis, Peter. 1970. *The Grasping Imagination: The American Writings of Henry James.* Toronto: University of Toronto Press.

Edel, Leon, ed. 1970. *Henry James: Stories of the Supernatural.* New York: Taplinger.

———, ed. [1949] 1963. *The Ghostly Tales of Henry James.* New York: The Universal Library, Grosset & Dunlap.

Gale, Robert. [1954] 1964. *The Caught Image: Figurative Language in the Fiction of Henry James.* Chapel Hill: University of North Carolina Press.

Jones, Granville H. 1975. *Henry James's Psychology of Experience: Innocence, Responsibility, and Renunciation in the Fiction of Henry James.* The Hague: Mouton.

Kelley, Cornelia Pulsifer. [1930] 1965. *The Early Development of Henry James.* Urbana: University of Illinois Press.

Kenton, Edna, ed. 1950. *Eight Uncollected Tales of Henry James.* New Brunswick, NJ: Rutgers University Press.

———. 1919. "The Earliest Henry James." *Bookman* (August). Reprinted in Arthur Sherbo, "Henry James in *The Bookman* of New York." *Henry James Review* 13 (Fall 1992): 315–27.

Kerr, Howard. 1983. "James's Last Early Supernatural Tales: Hawthorne Demagnetized, Poe Depoetized." In *The Haunted Dusk: American Supernatural Fiction, 1820–1920.* Ed. Howard Kerr, John W. Crowley, and Charles L. Crow, 135–48. Athens: University of Georgia Press.

Kraft, James. 1969. *The Early Tales of Henry James.* Carbondale: Southern Illinois University Press.

McCarthy, Harold T. 1958. *Henry James: The Creative Process.* New York: Thomas Yoseloff.

McElderry, Bruce R., Jr. 1965. *Henry James.* New York: Twayne.

———. 1949. "The Uncollected Stories of Henry James." *American Literature* 21 (November): 279–291.

Martin, Jay. 1983. "Ghostly Rentals, Ghostly Purchases: Haunted Imaginations in James, Twain, and Bellamy." In *The Haunted Dusk: American Supernatural Fiction, 1820–1920.* Ed. Howard Kerr, John W. Crowley, and Charles L. Crow, 123–31. Athens: University of Georgia Press.

Martin, W. R., and Warren U. Ober. 1989. "Captain Diamond and Old Hickory: Realities and Ambivalence in Henry James's 'The Ghostly Rental.'" *Studies in Short Fiction* 26: 1–9.

Putt, S. Gorley. 1966. *Henry James: A Reader's Guide.* Ithaca, NY: Cornell University Press.

Thorp, Willard, ed. 1962. *The Madonna of the Future and Other Early Tales.* New York: New American Library.

Todorov, Tzvetan. 1977. *The Poetics of Prose*. Trans. Richard Howard. Ithaca, NY: Cornell University Press.

Varnado, S. L. 1987. *Haunted Presence: The Numinous in Gothic Fiction*. Tuscaloosa: University of Alabama Press.

Wagenknecht, Edward. 1984. *The Tales of Henry James*. New York: Frederick Ungar.

The Given Case

Publication History

In a letter to his agent, James B. Pinker, from Lamb House, on October 23, 1898, James worries at Pinker's failure to place three of his stories, one of which Edel identifies as "The Given Case" (*Letters* 4, 85). The tale took its place in *Collier's Weekly* in the December 1898–January 1899 issue, illustrated by Albert Herter, and in March in the English *Black and White*, illustrated by Lester Ralph (Anesko 194). The next year James revised it for his collection *The Soft Side*. It did not appear again until Lubbock's edition of James's fiction in the 1920s.

Circumstances of Composition, Sources, and Influences

James recorded the idea for "The Given Case" in his notebook on May 13, 1894 while in Venice. He had been "struck" reading an article from that month's *Fortnightly Review* on "English and French Manners" by the statement that the French consider "that 'flirting' is a dishonourable amusement and that a woman who has once listened to the overtures of a man considers it an act of justice to console him." He envisioned dramatizing this idea through two women "with their *opposed views of 'conduct'*" (CN 98).

James returned to the idea in December 1895 in a list of possible story topics. Again, the emphasis is on the opposition of attitudes seen between French and English conduct "as to the responsibility incurred by a flirtation: one thinking of the compensation *owed* (where the man is really touched), the other taking the exact line of backing out. 'It's serious'—they both see— but the opposed conclusion from that premise." His concern is how to treat the subject briefly, whether to use a correspondence, "a series of colloquies" (his eventual approach), or, as the notebook favors, his "usual third person: the observer, the *knower*, the confidant." He questions further whether to emphasize the two women or the two men, resolving that the women "seem, decidedly, the really designated characters" (CN 146–47).

In Tintner's opinion, the contrast between French and English manners in the story was replaced as a model by James's experience in August 1897 as a juryman on a divorce case. She notes that Barton Reeve is a lawyer, his expression described as "passionately legal," and that the "series of colloquies" resembles to the procedure of cross-examination (1989, 258–62). She also finds Edith Wharton picking up on the final dialogue here for the final dialogue of her novella *The Touchstone*, noting that the heroine in each ends asking the man to "pity" her as the one who has suffered most (1986, 5).

Without arguing for influence, Putt calls the tale "as artificial as the lovers' quartet in *A Midsummer Night's Dream* but without the excuse of fairies and love-philtres" (289). There are, however, no exchanges among the four as in Shakespeare's play. Also, although the loyalty of each woman is in question, those threatened by their changes of heart remain offstage.

Margaret's final pleading protest for her fiancé against the man she loves, "He trusted me. He trusted me," anticipates Lucy Honeychurch's "They trusted me," in E. M. Forster's *Room with a View*, in which the engagement is also ended by the unconscious deceit of a true passion (CT 10, 380; Forster 238).

Relation to Other Works

Putt classes it, as an "unsavoury" depiction of the "marriage-market," with two other tales of 1899: "The Great Condition" and (rather oddly) "Paste" (289). Edel also connects the tale with "The Great Condition" in its resumption of James's early interest in "supposedly fickle or flirtatious women" (CT 10, 11). Jones, on the other hand, puts the emphasis on their overactive sense of duty, finding both Mrs. Despard here and Lady Vandeleur in "The Path of Duty" causing suffering by sticking to proper behavior without regard to the feelings of others (121–22). The story also recalls "The Patagonia" in its consideration of the effects of a sudden calling to account after a long and distant engagement.

Interpretation and Criticism

"The Given Case" appears to have inspired almost no one to discuss it who has not been required to do so for reasons of inclusiveness, and given the treatment it receives in general assessments of James, that fact is not surprising. Edel and Matthiessen and Murdock all find the story "mechanical," Matthiessen and Murdock seeming to imply that using "direct narrative" in place of the "clever" observer suggested in the notebook entry may have been part of the problem (CT 10, 11; N 235). Wagenknecht also considers the presentation problematic, saying that the development "mainly through a series of confrontations" keeps the reader "busier figuring out relationships than the slight narrative adequately rewards him for" (185). McElderry points to the story's brevity as the problem: he feels more than its nine thousand words were needed to develop the tale's six characters, a tally that charitably includes the two male obstacles to romance (110). Without assigning any particular cause, Putt calls the tale "a tedious inconclusive sketch" and deems the women's virtue and the men's passion both so unimpressive that the conclusion lacks any significance (289). While one must acknowledge the confusion in reading, striking even for the late James, it seems unfair to deny that while it may seem suitable for Mrs. Despard to avoid the sordidness of the divorce court, there is also a pleasure in seeing Margaret breaking the ties of an unwanted engagement for a marriage of genuine love. While McElderry depicts the story as "a double demonstration of duty imposing the renunciation of love," Andreas sees Margaret learning through her hearing of Barton's case how to understand her own and Philip's and come to a compassionate conclusion (McElderry 110; Andreas 71–72). Similarly, Jones sees Margaret's acceptance of Philip an acceptance of responsibility for her actions (121). Gage is right that all is not happy at the end, but it is hard to picture Margaret and Philip's marriage as he does being "poisoned by guilt" (46). Indeed, the willingness of the second couple to resist the lure of Jamesian renunciation and stay together, rather than converting themselves with inadequate cause into a pair such as Kate Croy and Merton Densher, lends the story a certain charm and even a sense of success.

Works Cited

Primary Works

James, Henry. 1898–1899. "The Given Case." *Collier's Weekly* 22 (31 December 1898–January 1899): 14–16; *Black and White* (11–18 March): 302–04, 334–36.

———. 1900. "The Given Case." *The Soft Side*. London: Methuen; New York: Macmillan, 172–201.

———. 1921–23. "The Given Case." *The Novels and Tales of Henry James*. Vol. 27. Ed. Percy Lubbock. London: Macmillan

Secondary Works

Andreas, Osborn. 1948. *Henry James and the Expanding Horizon: A Study of the Meaning and Basic Themes of James's Fiction*. Seattle: University of Washington Press.

Anesko, Michael. 1986. *"Friction with the Market": Henry James and the Profession of Authorship*. New York: Oxford University Press.

Forster, E. M. 1908. *A Room with a View*. New York: Vintage.

Gage, Richard P. 1988. *Order and Design: Henry James' Titled Story Sequences*. New York: Peter Lang.

Jones, Granville H. 1975. *Henry James's Psychology of Experience: Innocence, Responsibility, and Renunciation in the Fiction of Henry James*. The Hague: Mouton.

McElderry, Bruce R., Jr. 1965. *Henry James*. New York: Twayne.

Putt, S. Gorley. 1966. *Henry James: A Reader's Guide*. Ithaca, NY: Cornell University Press.

Tintner, Adeline R. 1989. *The Pop World of Henry James: From Fairy Tales to Science Fiction*. Ann Arbor: UMI Research Press.

———. 1986. "Wharton and James: Some Literary Give and Take." *The Edith Wharton Newsletter* 3, no. 1 (Spring): 3–5, 8.

Wagenknecht, Edward. 1984. *The Tales of Henry James*. New York: Frederick Ungar.

Glasses

Publication History

"Glasses" first appeared in the *Atlantic* in February 1896 as one of two stories James delivered out of three he promised to the editor, Horace E. Scudder, in May of 1895 (CN 121). Later in the same year it appeared in the collection *Embarrassments*. It is the only story from that collection and the previous *Terminations* James chose not to include in the New York Edition. He did, however, agree to revise it for inclusion in the *Uniform Tales* edition issued by Martin Secker from 1915 to 1919. Thus, according to Herbert Ruhm, its revision was probably one of James's last literary efforts (174). It also appeared in Lubbock's edition of the novels and stories in the 1920s.

Circumstances of Composition, Sources, and Influences

On September 8, 1895, James recorded in his notebook his worry at being able to curtail "developments" enough to keep to the 10,000-word limit Scudder wanted, and ended by remembering the idea of *The Spectacles* as having "the needed singleness . . . if anything *can* have" (CN 130). But on October 4 James was writing Scudder "in much humiliation and distress" a long apology both for his failure to send a complete copy of the story and for his inability to keep the story within the space limit. "I find, in my old age," he wrote, "that I have too much manner and style, too great and invincible an instinct of completeness and of seeing things in all their relations, so that *development*, however squeezed down, becomes inevitable" (*Letters* 4, 22). Hoffmann speaks of the tale as an anecdote "stretched to the breaking point," proof that the form of the short novel has no intrinsic value (126).

Among the things being squeezed in were numerous impressions of his topic from varied sources. In 1883 James may have noticed in the April edition of the *Saturday Review* an oculist's advertisement presenting its readers with the choice: "SPECTACLES vs. BLINDNESS." In June of 1895 he certainly saw and recorded in his notebook as the possible germ for a story "a very pretty woman in spectacles . . . on the top of an omnibus" (CN 125–26). Given, then, that spectacles erase beauty, one is left with the basic opposition the story's heroine Flora Saunt faces: "BEAUTY vs. SIGHT." In a society where beauty is necessary for a woman for social acceptance, the dilemma is an awkward one, dangerous even in Flora's case as that acceptance is necessary for her financial survival.

In his notebook James writes that Maupaussant "would have called [the story] *Les Lunettes*, though I'm afraid that *The Spectacles* won't do" (CN 125). According to a 1976 essay by Tintner, the reason the title "won't do" is that there is already a story of that name by Edgar Allan Poe concerned like James's with love, vanity, and glasses. In it, a young man too vain to wear glasses falls in love with his great-great-grandmother at the opera, just as the narrator last sees Flora at the opera. In Tintner's reading, James shifts the flawed vision from hero to heroine, but keeps Poe's theme of the blinding effect of vanity and love.

In 1977, Tintner examined the description of Geoffrey Dawling's "variety of . . . inclinations," a phrase used by Gibbon to describe a Roman emperor. Tintner sees the allusion as intentionally ironic, pointing to "the usurping ironic glance" of the narrator (also Tintner 1979, 165). In the same note, Tintner remarks a resemblance between Walter Pater and the Oxfordian with whom Dawling studied, and points to a possible source for Dawling in Pater. In a 1982 essay, she elaborated on the connection between the two. Both, she argues, are unattractive men who dedicate themselves to a beautiful face: in Pater's case, the Mona Lisa, in Dawling's, Flora, who through her blindness, becomes like the Mona Lisa, who in James's words is "fixed for ever, rescued from all change and ransomed from all doubt" (1987, 155–56). Elsewhere, she refers to "Glasses" as "James's trial Symbolist story" (1979, 410).

One might also note an echo, in Dawling's name and in his role as the eventually rewarded faithful follower of an initially indifferent beauty, to Dobbin in Thackeray's *Vanity Fair*.

The opera in the story is *Lohengrin*, which also suggests a connection between Wagner's knight's rescue of the endangered Elsa and Dawling's of Flora. Tintner points to an invoking of Rostand's *La Princesse lointaine* featuring Sarah Bernhardt in pearls like Flora (1986, 139; also 1979, 408).

Dean puts forward the possibility that Mrs. Meldrum, who, she admonishes Putt, is *not* old, is based on Vernon Lee and that John Singer Sargent served as a model for the narrator, although she adds that James thought more highly of Sargent than of his narrator (192, 194). Tintner finds a particular parallel with Sargent's portrait of Mrs. Henry White and the final vision of Flora at the opera, noting that James had taken Mrs. White to the theatre the year before he wrote "Glasses" (1986, 93).

Relation to Other Works

Edgar, Putt, Allen, and Edel all connect "Glasses" with "The Wheel of Time" as examinations of the immense importance society assigns women's appearance (Edgar 156; Putt 285; Allen 121; Edel CT 9, 12). Putt finds repellent the adoption by James in the two tales of the "buyers' viewpoint" in the marriage market and judges the tale as distasteful as "The Visits" (284–86). Jones and Wagenknecht compare Flora's vanity to Lady Beldonald's (242–43; 134). Jones notes additionally how Flora, like "Poor" Richard Maule and Daisy Miller, feels driven to maverick behavior in her struggles with society (62).

As the study of an artist, Edgar deems it, like "The Tone of Time," "ineffective" compared with other stories of painters (158). Winner, on the other hand, links the tale's economic establishment of an artistic atmosphere with that in "The Liar" (125). A further correspondence between the artist in "The Liar" and the artist here lies in his putative disinterestedness and reliability, questioned in both cases by critics. More broadly, Gage sees it as fitting in with the general theme of the stories of *Embarrassments*, particularly "The Figure in the Carpet," by its emphasis on "problems of perception" (21–23).

Wagenknecht links the story with "Brooksmith" and "Greville Fane" as showing James's ability to sympathize with unlikely types (185). Although few other critics seem to have been impressed by the amount of sympathy James distributes here, there is a note of compassion in the description of Flora's "neglected childhood and queer continental relegations, with straying, squabbling, Monte-Carlo-haunting parents" rather analogous to the ill-fated Morgan Moreen of *The Pupil* (CT 9, 322).

Interpretation and Criticism

In 1904 Claude Bragdon singled out "Glasses" as a "typical example" of
James's modern tragedies, praising them as "more pertinent to modern life,
more true and vital" than the "outworn themes and situations of conventional romance" (148–49). Interest in the tale tends to divide between those who
find the story "unpleasant" and those who do not, with the former dividing
further between those who blame the story's unpleasantness on the narrator,
questioning his character and reliability as that of Lyon's in "The Liar" has
been, and those who blame it on James.

A contemporary reviewer, who judged the story the best in its collection,
praised the "strongly human element" evident in its analysis of the "over-
weening vanity of the female heart" (*Athenaeum*). Early critics such as Edgar
and McElderry also tended to take the story straight, accepting the narrator
as the one setting the values of the story (Edgar 156–58; McElderry 110).
Later critics such as Putt challenged the values while still identifying them
with James's. Edel suggests, however, that the "desperate curiosity of the narrator" may impress the reader even more than Flora's "destructive vanity"
and questions whether James recognized "how unpleasant and *sensitif* a narrator he had created" (CT 9, 12). Dean finds James here treating "the problem of artistic vision" and concludes that the narrator is not unreliable but
"myopic," examining "everyone but himself" (191). Gage, too, criticizes the
narrator's lack of perception (25). While Tintner speaks of the tale showing
the portrait painter's ability to "blast society," there is never any indication of
the painter here taking such an independent line (1986, 95).

It is hard, however, to pinpoint the evidence that the narrator is intended
to be the flawed character. Bishop contends that the narrator's "comparative
lack of circumspection is promptly telegraphed to the reader, if only by his
repeated gratuitous remarks about long-nosed Jews" (27). In the opening
description of Folkestone, for example, the narrator writes: "There were
thousands of little chairs and almost as many little Jews; and there was music
in an open rotunda, over which the little Jews wagged their big noses" (CT 9,
317). Such remarks, however, as Louis Harap has recorded, were representative of a general attitude toward Jews in English society—Levy sees the
remark as demonstrating "a thoroughly upper-class attitude"—and are present in other works by James (Harap 374; Levy 243). They are also strikingly
close to some of James's privately expressed views. Indeed, on August 27,
1895, James wrote to A. C. Benson from Folkestone, "Nothing more agitating
has happened to me—unless it be to have spent 3 days at Folkestone in the
very bosom and under the very nose of the ubiquitous Abraham. All Jewry
was there and I understand the rage of the persecutors—'Damned noser
hereditas' Du Maurier told me Burnand had called it" (17). Any discussion of
the putative unreliability of the narrator thus needs to take into account the

fact that at the time he wrote the story James was willing to espouse some of the same unattractive attitudes in response to the same group of people at the same place he set his story. The narrator's anti-Semitic caricatures cannot be held a sure sign of unreliability.

An argument might be made that the ingenuity of the verbal play on "glasses" seems to taste more of schoolyard jeers than the "elegant variation" Chatman judges is typical of James (85–86). But that may be equally a lapse by James as his narrator. Edel remarks on the odd gap between the "unperturbed prose" and its subject (CT 9, 12). Consider, for example, the description of Flora in her glasses: "The big gold bar crossing each of her lenses, over which something convex and grotesque, like the eyes of a large insect, something that now represented her whole personality, seemed, as out of the orifice of a prison, to strain forward and press" (CT 9, 354). One might point for a sign of authorial distance, in another direction, to the triteness of the narrator's sentimental descriptions of his mother: "There was one dear chair, creeping to its last full stop, by the side of which I always walked" (CT 9, 317).

A broader, surer sign of distance would seem to be the narrator's gleeful interference into others' lives, from his initial "cruel" question to Flora about her eyesight throughout his role as gossiping go-between for Flora, Dawling, and even Mrs. Meldrum, a role in which he feels free to analyze their behavior "perversely and rudely" in a manner that occasionally embarrasses even him, all despite what he claims is his "confirmed affection" for Dawling (CT 9, 327, 345–46). Looking at his encounters with Mrs. Meldrum and Dawling, Dean indicates how his recorded rudeness and interference "better explain" their reactions than his own attempted analysis (192–93).

Such voyeuristic concern is compounded rather than relieved by his persistent regarding of Flora as nothing more than a picture, an attitude little better than that of the scorned Lord Iffield. The narrator's attitude to Flora is not only superficial but harsh: when she begins to wear glasses, he considers her "extinguished" with her beauty "buried in the tomb her stern specialist had built" (CT 9, 363). That his judgment need not be consciously intended as unreliable can perhaps be seen in the way critics unconsciously echo it. For example, Voss is almost alone in recognizing that today glasses for women are commonplace (153). Edel, on the other hand, speaks of the sight that inspired the tale as "an attractive woman's face disfigured" by her large spectacles (*Life* 4, 145). Tintner, for her part, in talking of the blindness the glasses might have prevented seems to indicate that Dawling should have accepted the narrator's "warning" against Flora because of the risk to her eyesight, and refers to her elsewhere as "damaged for normal living" by her blindness, having become thereby "nothing *but* a face," "a complete burden" to Dawling (1977, 288; 1987, 156, 159). Such an attitude seems to imply not simply an awareness of the physical or social repercussions of blindness, but a sense that Flora is now somehow less of a person because she cannot see. More impressively, Dean points out how it is the narrator who seeks to "reduce Flora to an art object" at the end (194).

Indeed, whatever their view of the narrator, few readers seem to penetrate beyond his perspective sufficiently to gain a more objective view of Flora's situation. Only Gage notes his "obtuseness concerning the importance to Flora of the unimpeded beauty of her face" (25). As Bragdon noted, her face "is in a very literal sense her fortune" (149). Dietrichson points to her as an example that James recognized, despite his dislike of marrying for money, that it was necessary for some, although he notes that the generous character of Dawling offers a third, preferable approach (112–13). Andreas, on the other hand, sees James as blinding Flora in "symbolic revenge" for women who fail to value sufficiently men's love, failing to acknowledge the limitations of men's love as portrayed here (82). More aptly, Jones judges her both "pitiable and courageous" in her actions (62).

Part of the problem in analyzing the story is the common but dangerous confusion of the realities of blindness and its accreted symbolism—here in particular a confusion of a physical fact, the lack of vision, and a moral failing, vanity—much of which seems built into James's telling. A rationale for such mingling might be provided on the lines of Fielding's classic defense of physical humor in the preface to *Joseph Andrews*, that affectation is a legitimate source of the Ridiculous: "Much less are natural imperfections the object of derision: but when ugliness aims at the applause of beauty, or lameness endeavours to display agility, it is then that these unfortunate circumstances, which at first moved our compassion, tend only to raise our mirth" (7). Thus when sightlessness aims at sightedness it becomes absurd. Certainly Flora's behavior at the opera has sufficient of the grotesque, and one might argue that it is not her blindness, but her denial of it that is being condemned. But that a more sympathetic attitude even toward such denial is possible can be seen, for example, in John Mortimer's *Voyage Round My Father*, where the father also refuses to acknowledge his blindness. Instead, Flora seems to be blamed as much for her blindness as for her vanity.

Dawling also suffers both at the hands of the narrator and the critics (CT 9, 336). Perhaps relying on the allusions to Pater and Gibbon, Tintner seems to belittle Dawling for having diverse interests, although it is unclear why they are bad or even foolish. As Putt points out, Dawling is "jeered at" in the story for his bad looks, which, he adds, are "presented as almost as much his own fault as his acquired manner" while the "generous sympathy" he displays toward Flora is less noted (286). Although the narrator calls him "the interesting figure in the piece," only when he is painting Dawling's portrait is there a sense of his "soul" glimpsed (CT 9, 336–37).

Putt, who finds Mrs. Meldrum the only sympathetic character, considers the story "equally disquieting" whether one reads it from the perspective of the narrator who embodies society's false rules or the perspective of Flora, who acts in "cowed obedience" to those rules (286). While Jones includes Flora in a long list of Jamesian characters who, after suffering, do live "happily ever after" (157–58), Putt cannot move himself to care. Gale, however, who traces the bird imagery associated with Flora's sight, cites the mention of her "gratified passion" at the end to portray her "freed and sustained" by her husband's love (78).

James had begun the story with the idea of a Maupassantesque anecdote, and part of the problem may be that the story grew beyond him—so that, in a process similar to that Kozikowski claims for "The Liar," the narrator has both too much space to expose himself and too much material to present to explain himself (367). Similarly, McWhirter cites the story as an illustration of the difficult conflict in James's later work between the expansive, feminine "writer" and the masculine "author" concerned with the form of the completed work (60–61).

"Glasses" begins with the narrator musing:

> Yes indeed, I say to myself, pen in hand, I can keep hold of the thread and let it lead me back to the first impression. The little story is all there, I can touch it from point to point; for the thread, as I call it, is a row of coloured beads on a string. None of the beads are missing—at least I think they're not: that's exactly what I shall amuse myself with finding out. (CT 9, 317)

Approximately halfway through the story James has the narrator confirm that the beads are "all there," but there is reason to doubt his certainty (CT 9, 352). In discussing the subjective narration of *The Sacred Fount*, Rimmon cites the metaphor from "Glasses" and argues that the "central 'bead'" missing in *The Sacred Fount* is what creates its ambiguity (168). Here, too, is a similar ambiguity and the image seems to provide some clue to its understanding. As Gage notes, the image is echoed in the final description of Flora dressed in a "row of pearls" at the opera, an echo that according to Gage sounds all the way back to the pearls in "The Figure in the Carpet," which stood there for the secret to Vereker's work (25). Here the secret surrounds Flora and the narrator is just as unable to formulate it. The source for James's metaphor may well lie in a passage from Emerson's *Experience*: "Life is a train of moods like a string of beads, and as we pass through them they prove to be many-colored lenses which paint the world their own hue, and each shows only what lies in its focus. . . . Temperament is the iron wire on which the beads are strung" (345).

According to Emerson's metaphor, a person can show us only "what lies in [the] focus" of his moods at the same time that his temperament restricts that focus. Even so, in 1902 James's brother William would write "The axis of reality runs solely through the egotistic places,—they are strung upon it like so many beads" (500). To Dean, there is a bead missing, that of the narrator's genuine insight into his own behavior and the growth that would bring (192). It is a bead that his ego prevents him from stringing.

Adding another dimension, Gage associates the string of pearls with the rope that anchors the "balloon of experience" in James's preface to *Roderick Hudson* as images of the "connectedness or linkage" that provides coherence to the different parts of a work (7). Here the cord may have snapped. The metaphors quickly become muddled, but however one coordinates them, it appears that in this story the "writer" in James squeezed in too many "beads"—issues of blindness, society's obsession with beauty in women, vanity, the perspective of the artist—and let the "author" string them onto an inadequate thread, a narrator not only incapable of making sense of them all, but who compounds their confusion through his inadequate "focus." While William James judged the work "charming and genial" (390), there is something not just incomplete but repellent in the resultant "compromise," and so the story remains floating in the air suspended from the real life below.

Works Cited

Primary Works

James, Henry. 1896. "Glasses." *The Atlantic Monthly* 77 (February): 145–73.

———. 1896. "Glasses." *Embarrassments*. London: Heinemann; New York: Macmillan, 85–180.

———. 1916. "Glasses." In *The Uniform Tales of Henry James*. London: Martin Secker.

———. 1921–23. "Glasses." In *The Novels and Stories of Henry James*. Vol. 27. Ed. Percy Lubbock. London: Macmillan.

———. 1969. *Henry James: Letters to A. C. Benson and Auguste Monod*. Ed. E. F. Benson. New York: Haskell House.

Secondary Works

Allen, Elizabeth. 1984. *A Woman's Place in the Novels of Henry James*. New York: St. Martin's.

Andreas, Osborn. 1948. *Henry James and the Expanding Horizon: A Study of the Meaning and Basic Themes of James's Fiction*. Seattle: University of Washington Press.

Anon. 1896. Review of *Embarrassments*. *Athenaeum*, no. 3588 (1 August): 158.

Bishop, George. 1988. *When the Master Relents: The Neglected Short Fictions of Henry James*. Ann Arbor: UMI Research Press. Revised from "Shattered Notions of Mastery: Henry James's 'Glasses.'" *Criticism* 27, no. 4 (Fall 1985): 347–62.

Bragdon, Claude. 1904. "The Figure in Mr. James's Carpet." *Critic* 44 (Fall): 146–50.

Chatman, Seymour. 1972. *The Later Style of Henry James*. Oxford: Blackwell's.

Dean, Sharon. 1983. "The Myopic Narrator in Henry James's 'The Glasses.'" *Henry James Review* 4:191–95.

Dietrichson, Jan W. 1969. *The Image of Money in the American Novel of the Gilded Age*. Oslo: Universitetsforlaget; New York: Humanities.

Edgar, Pelham. [1927] 1964. *Henry James, Man and Author*. New York: Russell & Russell.

Emerson, Ralph Waldo. "Experience." In *Selected Writings of Ralph Waldo Emerson*. Ed. Brooks Atkinson, 342–64. New York: Modern Library.

Fielding, Henry. [1742] 1987. *Joseph Andrews*. Ed. Homer Goldberg. New York: Norton.

Gage, Richard P. 1988. *Order and Design: Henry James' Titled Story Sequences*. New York: Peter Lang.

Gale, Robert L. [1954] 1964. *The Caught Image: Figurative Language in the Fiction of Henry James*. Chapel Hill: University of North Carolina Press.

Harap, Louis. 1974. *The Image of the Jew in American Literature*. Philadelphia: The Jewish Publication Society of America.

Hoffmann, Charles G. 1957. *The Short Novels of Henry James*. New York: Bookman.

James, William. 1983. *The Correspondence of William James*. Vol. 2: *William and Henry: 1885–1896*. Ed. Ignas K. Skrupskelis and Elizabeth M. Berkeley. Charlottesville: University Press of Virginia.

———. [1902] 1987. *The Varieties of Religious Experience*. New York: Longmans.

Jones, Granville H. 1975. *Henry James's Psychology of Experience: Innocence, Responsibility, and Renunciation in the Fiction of Henry James*. The Hague: Mouton.

Kozikowski, Stanley J. 1979. "Unreliable Narration in Henry James's 'The Two Faces' and Edith Wharton's 'The Dilettante.'" *Arizona Quarterly* 35: 357–72.

Levy, Leo B. 1958. "Henry James and the Jews: A Critical Study." *Commentary* 26 (September): 243–49.

McElderry, Bruce R., Jr. 1965. *Henry James*. New York: Twayne.

McWhirter, David. 1989. *Desire and Love in Henry James: A Study of the Late Novels*. Cambridge: Cambridge University Press.

Putt, S. Gorley. 1966. *Henry James: A Reader's Guide*. Ithaca, NY: Cornell University Press.

Rimmon, Shlomith. 1977. *The Concept of Ambiguity: The Example of Henry James*. Chicago: University of Chicago Press.

Ruhm, Herbert, ed. 1961. *"Lady Barbarina" and Other Tales: "Benvolio," "Glasses," and Three Essays*. The Universal Library. New York: Vanguard.

Tintner, Adeline R. 1987. *The Book World of Henry James: Appropriating the Classics*. Ann Arbor: UMI Research Press.

―――. 1986. *The Museum World of Henry James*. Ann Arbor: UMI Research Press.

―――. 1982. "Pater in *The Portrait of a Lady* and *The Golden Bowl*, Including Some Unpublished Henry James Letters." *Henry James Review* 3, no. 2 (Winter): 80–95.

―――. 1979. "Henry James and the Symbolist Movement in Art." *Journal of Modern Literature* 7 (September): 397–415.

―――. 1977. "Why James Quoted Gibbon in 'Glasses.'" *Studies in Short Fiction* 14: 287–88.

―――. 1976. "Poe's 'The Spectacles' and James' 'Glasses.'" *Poe Studies* 9: 53–54.

―――. 1974. "Henry James Criticism: A Current Perspective." *American Literary Realism* 7: 155–68.

Voss, Arthur. 1973. *The American Short Story: A Critical Survey*. Norman: University of Oklahoma Press.

Wagenknecht, Edward. 1984. *The Tales of Henry James*. New York: Frederick Ungar.

Winner, Viola Hopkins. 1970. *Henry James and the Visual Arts*. Charlottesville: University Press of Virginia.

The Great Condition

Publication History

James received forty pounds for *The Great Condition* when it first appeared in the June 1899 issue of the handsomely produced *Anglo-Saxon Review*, edited by Lady Randolph Churchill. Its publisher, John Lane, had printed James's work before in *The Yellow Book*. James reprinted the story only once after that, in the 1900 collection *The Soft Side*. It next appeared in the 1920s in Lubbock's edition of James's fiction.

Circumstances of Composition, Sources, and Influences

Although Edel identifies "The Great Condition" as one of three stories whose chances for publication James worried about in an October 1898 letter to

James B. Pinker, James did not record the source for the story until February 10, 1899 (*Letters* 4, 85). The idea came from a conversation with the novelist George Meredith at Boxhill five days previous when Meredith told the story of "some woman . . . marrying a man who knew very little about her" and who, at a mention of her "past," promised to tell all if the man still wished to know six months hence. James approached the situation from the start as "*ironic*" and immediately began sketching out several pages of dialogue for the tale, interrupted by complaints of "extreme seediness" left over from a bout of influenza (CN 172–75). Although James recorded the germ at Lamb House, he left on the eighth of March for Paris, and two weeks later for a visit with the French novelist Paul Bourget and his wife at Costebelle, where he met Lady Randolph Churchill, who requested a story from him for her journal. He then wrote the tale later that spring while staying with Daniel and Ariana Curtis at the Palazzo Barbaro in Venice (*Life* 4, 285). (See also "Two Faces.")

Wagenknecht judges the marriage "test" constructed by Mrs. Damerel as effective as the one in Shakespeare's *The Merchant of Venice* (187).

Tintner cites the heroine's reading of Gardiner's *History of the Great Civil War* as an example of James's great interest in historical writing (1987, 165).

Relation to Other Works

Edgar argues that "The Great Condition" may be "loosely" tied with *The Pupil*, "Europe," and "Miss Gunton of Poughkeepsie" in its American heroine (56). Similarly, Wagenknecht finds the tale "international" only by virtue of its American heroine and English suitors (186).

Putt connects the tale with its near contemporaries "The Given Case" and "Paste," while Ziff links it not only with those two but all the tales of *The Soft Side* as demonstrating James's recognition of the necessity of passion, a willingness to give up one's "balanced life" for something greater (Putt 289–90; Ziff 61). Edel links it not only with "The Given Case" but the much earlier "The Diary of a Man of Fifty" as well, to show that over the years James's attitude toward women remained "ambiguous" (CT 10, 11). Zablotny, on the other hand, points to a definite change in James shown in this story in the implication that Braddle suffered a genuine loss by succumbing to fear (222). Wagenknecht objects to Edel's comparison with "The Given Case," marking in the story a clear contrast between Braddle, who is "quixotic, priggish, suspicious," and Chilver, who is capable of the trust necessary for love (187). Edel also, however, notes that Braddle is "defeated by his own suspicious nature," not James's (CT 10, 12). Tintner distinguishes it from both stories, finding its originality in its theme of time, dominant also in *The Ambassadors*, which James began shortly after "The Great Condition" (1984, 112–13).

Gage links its interest in a person's private past to several other stories in *The Soft Side*—"Paste" and "The Real Right Thing" and "John Delavoy." He connects it as well to "The Tree of Knowledge," whose protagonist also operates under an illusion about the character of the woman he loves (40–41, 46).

Interpretation and Criticism

The contrast between Braddle and Chilver, which Voss calls "exaggerated" (153), has absorbed most of the limited critical attention the story has received. Most praise Chilver's moral superiority seen in his remark to Braddle, which McElderry quotes as the moral of the story: "What I don't grasp . . . is your liking her so much as to 'mind' so much, without by the same stroke liking her enough not to mind at all" (110). Tintner, who dismisses earlier interpretations as "summary," locates the difference between the two men, and indeed the shaping theme of the story, in their attitudes to time. Using Bergsonian definitions, she pictures the "clock-watching" Braddle as trapped in "abstract time" obsessed by a "past" he can never experience, while through patience Chilver is able to make his home with the equally patient Mrs. Damerel in *durée*, or time as "concretely experienced" (1984).

Looking past the two contending suitors, Jones points to Mrs. Damerel as the one who arranges affairs to produce the "greatest happiness with the least suffering" (161). Matthiessen and Murdock, however, while agreeing with Mrs. Damerel's choice, find her "the one important character," Braddle being "simply a stupid man" and Chilver "relatively colorless" (N 273). Putt goes a step further and sees James showing a feminist contempt for both "high- and dirty-minded gentlemen," both of whom, he claims, "undoubtedly" suspected the heroine's past. Putt is nearly alone in his questioning of the legitimacy of Chilver's happiness, although his depiction of it is close to the self-satisfaction James attributes to Chilver in the notebook, where he describes Chilver as "highly pleased with his own magnanimity and delicacy" and even "'hugging' his sense of the beauty of his own behavior" (Putt 290; CN 175). Gage, too, takes note of Chilver's keeping to the "soft side": he "rests that is in the illusion that he has accepted ignorance of reality, a reality that in point of fact is not real at all" (41). Cary, however, locates in Chilver a "spiritual" rather than "surface" courtesy James gave only to his better, usually American, characters (75). As James records in the notebook: "They are happy," and if even the wise Mrs. Damerel can be happy with a marriage resting on such grounds, it seems quibbling to detract too much from it.

Works Cited

Primary Works

James, Henry. 1899. "The Great Condition." *The Anglo-Saxon Review* 1 (June): 7–38.

———. 1900. "The Great Condition." *The Soft Side*. London: Methuen; New York: Macmillan, 87–131.

———. 1921–23. "The Great Condition." In *The Novels and Stories of Henry James*. Vol. 27. Ed. Percy Lubbock. London: Macmillan.

Secondary Works

Cary, Elisabeth Luther. 1905. *The Novels of Henry James: A Study*. New York: Putnam's.

Edgar, Pelham. [1927] 1964. *Henry James, Man and Author*. New York: Russell & Russell.

Gage, Richard P. 1988. *Order and Design: Henry James' Titled Story Sequences*. New York: Peter Lang.

Jones, Granville H. 1975. *Henry James's Psychology of Experience: Innocence, Responsibility, and Renunciation in the Fiction of Henry James*. The Hague: Mouton.

McElderry, Bruce R., Jr. 1965. *Henry James*. New York: Twayne.

Putt, S. Gorley. 1966. *Henry James: A Reader's Guide*. Ithaca, NY: Cornell University Press.

Tintner, Adeline R. 1987. *The Book World of Henry James: Appropriating the Classics*. Ann Arbor: UMI Research Press.

———. 1984. "'The Great Condition': Henry James and Bergsonian Time." *Studies in Short Fiction* 21, no. 2 (Spring): 111–15.

Voss, Arthur. 1973. *The American Short Story: A Critical Survey*. Norman: University of Oklahoma Press.

Wagenknecht, Edward. 1984. *The Tales of Henry James*. New York: Frederick Ungar.

Ziff, Larzer. 1966. *The American 1890's: Life and Times of a Lost Generation*. New York: Viking.

Zablotny, Elaine. 1979. "Henry James and the Demonic Vampire and Madonna." *Psychocultural Review* (Summer–Fall): 203–24.

The Great Good Place

Publication History

According to Edel, "The Great Good Place" was one of the tales James in October 1898 worriedly wrote his new agent was delayed in finding a publisher. The tale found a home just three months later in *Scribner's Magazine*, and the same year in *The Soft Side*, a collection that James originally planned to entitle after this story (*Letters* 4, 85; *Correspondence* 194–96). James also included it in his New York Edition.

Circumstances of Composition, Sources, and Influences

"The Great Good Place" is usually traced to the notebook entry for May 12, 1892, which also gave rise to "The Middle Years" with its initial picture of "the old artist, or man of letters, who, at the end, feels a kind of anguish of desire for a respite, a prolongation." Toward the end, the story of "The Great Good Place" begins to emerge: "A young doctor, a young pilgrim who admires him. A deep sleep in which he dreams he *has* had his respite. Then his waking, to find that what he has dreamed of is only what he has *done*" (CN 68–69). "The Middle Years" has the doctor, but "The Great Good Place" has the pilgrim and the dream. Matthiessen and Murdock point to the presence of the name Dane in a list shortly following (N 123).

According to Krook, the tale is "semi-autobiographical," and many critics have pointed out resemblances between elements of the tale and James's life (352; e.g., Przybylowicz 40). According to Josephson, the young James had identified the "great good place" with Europe, but, now disillusioned, he realized that it "had no geography whatsoever" (88, 100). Bayley speaks of James's notebooks as his "great good place" (571; also CN xiii). Edel, however, offers a geographical site, seeing the tale as a peaceful "prevision of Lamb House," the home James was to move into that year, after having expressed his anxieties in *The Turn of the Screw* (*Life* 4, 240). Indeed, in 1899 James called Lamb House his "last long home"— a verbal echo of the title (*Letters* 4, 113). Rawlings cites a letter from his brother William at the time, referring to the purchase of Lamb House as "a great and good and holy and else a most prudent and financially sagacious thing" as perhaps suggesting the title, a source that lends an appropriateness to Horwitz's view that the story's peaceful brotherly relations reflect the resolution of James's strife with his brother (Rawlings xxi; Horwitz 488–89). Tintner sees the move as contributing to the sense of the tale in a different way, citing James's dismay at the "bewildering material detail," the consequent "acute sense of pressing work fatally retarded and blighted" (1986, 145). James's work schedule, Macnaughton notes, had been particularly cluttered in 1897 and 1898, including the demands of a series American Letters for *Literature* (45). Pearce, commonsensically, remarks that an "escape motif" is "probable and unremarkable in an overworked writer" (838).

Edel looks back in James's life to 1862 to point out that the Harvard Law School, during James's time there, was housed at Dane Hall, and that James wrote many years later of his leaving law for literature as "the turning point" of his life (1970, 568–69). More generally, Edel sees as autobiographical the tale's "wish for an exclusive man's world" with its "homo-erotic overtones" (*Life* 4, 240). Matthiessen, who evidently discounts "The Jolly Corner," remarks on the significance in James's closest approach to "a personal hallucination" being, unlike his father's and brother's visions of horror, one of "supernatural good." He finds, however, the "sickening" softness of "everything that is least virile" in the tale attributable to James's lack of religious stability as a child (1944, 144). The term "substitute" and Dane's concern for his "poor" substitute left behind to do the work recalls the use of "substitutes" paid for by those wishing to avoid service during the Civil War, a combat James missed on the grounds of his "obscure hurt" (CT 11, 25).

The novice brother says of "The Great Good Place" that it is as "open to as many interpretations as any other great work—a poem of Goethe, a dialogue of Plato, a symphony of Beethoven" (CT 11, 37). Following the musical parallel, Fadiman compares it to Mozart in its "perfection achieved with essentials" (413). Most comparisons, however, have been literary, and the American Romantics have been a prime source for them. A contemporary critic for the *Outlook* observed that the tale could have been thought of by James's "compatriot Hawthorne." Much later, Ward compared it to Poe's poem "Silence— A Fable" (1982, 129). A more frequently noted source has been Thoreau's *Walden* with its similar complaint that "life is frittered away by detail" and its search for a new simplicity of life and clarity of thought. Beebe was the first to judge the tale James's "personal *Walden*," one that Edel comments is "very comfortable" (Beebe 229; Edel 1970, 569; also Silverstein 464–65). Ward also notes a similarity in the emphasis on "negative" virtues, although he argues that unlike Thoreau, James sees idleness as an end in itself (1982, 129–30).

The English Romantics also contribute their share of source material. Martin and Ober record the use of a phrase from Wordsworth's *The Excursion*, "The vision and the faculty divine" (128 n.7). Rawlings sees not only the specific phrase, but the general sense of the artist "in retirement" drawing on Wordsworth, while also calling attention to the way allusions to

Goethe, Plato, and Germany contribute to the more general Romantic idealism underlying the tale (xxiii). Silverstein offers another link with the Romantics in the interest in childhood and private worlds (467). Without pointing to a particular verbal echo, many have glossed the meaning of the tale using Wordsworth's complaint that "the world is too much with us" (e.g., Putt 93; Kimbel 36; Wright 190). Both Wright and Vaid find echoes of Keats's "Ode to a Nightingale" (Wright 192–93; Vaid 206).

In that work Keats questioned whether he dreamt or woke. Swift's Gulliver wakes to find himself bound in Lilliput, and Zabel sees James recalling that incident in his description of Dane's frustrations: "It was a thing of meshes; he had simply gone to sleep under the net and had simply waked up there" (22–23). Many of the earlier English works cited as contributions belong to the tradition of the dream-vision. Whelan notes the similarity between Dane and Bunyan's burdened Pilgrim and his progress (213). Earlier Fadiman based the correspondence with *Pilgrim's Progress* and other such classic works as the *Divine Comedy* on the grounds that, on a small scale, James's tale also provides a "criticism of a whole culture" (413). Both Yeazell and Wright compare the tale to the dream-visions of Chaucer, Wright arguing that here as in Chaucer the dream is but "a device . . . for the clearer vision of reality" (Yeazell 16; Wright 190). Offering a different medieval source, Edgar mentions the dreamlike *Land of Cockayne* (192). Vaid finds Marvell's depiction of "the mind's withdrawal 'into its happiness'" applicable (190; also Silverstein 461). Pearce interprets the tale in the light of pastoral tradition, Dane and the Brother becoming the singers who praise the presumably "great good poet" of the "place," but he considers the general attitude toward the "pastoral fallacy"—that there is indeed a "happy land"—"highly ambivalent" (838).

The "Brotherhood" of the Pre-Raphaelites may also have helped inspire the tale, according to Tintner, who sees in Burne-Jones's painting "The Mill" a similar twilight world of vaguely Italian peace. Tintner also points as a possible model to Moreau's *Salomé Dancing before Herod*, which James called a "strange dream made visible" in the manner of "Kubla Khan" (1986, 132, 145–47). *The Dream of St. Ursula*, a painting written of by Ruskin, Silverstein suggests, may be the "early Tuscan" spoken of in the tale (462).

The works of Renan, Daugherty argues, also lie behind the use of various symbols in the tale and in the "quasi-religious significance" it assigns to the artist. She speculates that James in later life kept his admiration of Renan quiet because he feared people might note the same effeteness Renan was criticized for in his own work, a "non-virile" dreaminess that, as Daugherty notes, Matthiessen does indeed criticize in the tale (1979, 326–27; 1981, 133). Sicker, however, distinguishes James's "other worlds" from those of the aesthetes, and declares that James himself was never as enamored of them (84).

Tintner discovers some parallels with a 1898 novel, *New York*, dedicated to James by Edgar Fawcett, telling of a man named George Oliver, who, upon leaving prison, is sustained by an organization called "The Clasping Hand," which Tintner sees as analogous to James's Brothers. Nevertheless she proposes Balzac's *L'envers de l'histoire contemporaine* as the more significant source. Its young man finds solace for his "inner misery" through a lay charitable organization, characterized like James's retreat by solitude, anonymity, and peace (1989, 235; 1987, 292–99). Moon sees the work showing some of the same male comradeship as works by Whitman and Horatio Alger (259).

Dane's "world-weariness," according to Kimbel, anticipates twentieth-century existential angst, and several modern parallels have been put forward (36). Silverstein suggests that H. G. Wells's utopian tale "The Door in the Wall" may have been inspired in part by this tale (466). Identifying water as the element that keeps women out of the "masculine paradise[s]" in American literature, Fiedler sees the water imagery of the tale, while more reminiscent of "the bathtub or hydrotherapy," still taking its place with the lakes in Cooper, the oceans of Poe and Melville, and the fishing expeditions of Hemingway (357). Similarly, Hartsock points to Hemingway's "Big Two-Hearted River," where Nick finds "the good place" to restore his soul (1977, 28–29). Tintner argues that Wharton reversed the relation of literary master and disciple in her story "Full Circle" (1975, 376).

Relation to Other Works

"The Great Good Place," according to Blackmur, was James's only attempt to capture "the country of the blue" into which Ray Limbert escaped in "The Next Time"—and in which, he adds, James sometimes lived ([1943] 1983, 86). Appropriately, therefore, Edel places it among the artist tales, noting Dane's resemblance in name to Dencombe of "The Middle Years," who also wishes an escape, and to Doyne of "The Real Right Thing" (1970, 568). Dane's story illustrates, Geismar argues, one of James's favorite themes, "the punishment of success," present also in "The Death of the Lion," "The Lesson of the Master," and "The Middle Years" (194–95). Like Paraday and St. George, Silverstein observes, Dane is under siege, with women seeming particularly threatening. His rescuing young male admirer, Silverstein writes, also suggests similar, if less "magical," characters in "The Middle Years," "The Death of the Lion," and "The Author of Beltraffio" (460). Moon sees "scenes of male fosterage and male domesticity" in both "The Great Good Place" and "The Middle Years" (259).

The tale is something of a nonce word in James. Jones, however, places it in a line of development, in a list of several late works in which "metaphor overpowers linear narration" (233). Although the tale is not an allegory, it is certainly more abstract than any other story except "Benvolio." Dane and Benvolio themselves are similar, according to Edel, in their possession of at least a temporary retreat from urban pressures (1970, 569–70). Dane, Vaid asserts, is not only a "more integrated" Benvolio, but in his tale the earlier allegory is "refined into fantasy" (201–2). Both tales, despite their abstract formality, Putt argues, represent closely James's sense of himself at the time he wrote them: not only is George Dane's need for retreat foreshadowed in "Benvolio," so is his discovery that "everyone was a little someone else." Both feelings stem, in turn, according to Putt, from James's childhood sense that people were "so *other*" (87, 105). In Powers's reading, the two tales represent a fanciful solving of the problem of the artist in balancing the public and the private that James rarely depicted realistically, although he perhaps hinted at it in the conclusion to *The Tragic Muse* (111).

Numerous parallels have been offered, however, for the tale's theme of retreat. Edel notes both Rowland Mallet's visit to a monastery in *Roderick Hudson*, and Guy Domville's permanent return to one (*Life* 4, 241; 1970, 568–69). Sicker offers similar refuges elsewhere in James, at Poynton, and in Ralph Pendrel's retreat into the past in *The Sense of the Past* (84; also Perosa 135). Fox finds the stripping away of the external world to a "placid pastoral setting" in order to concentrate on the drama of consciousness anticipating the approach of *The Sacred Fount* (59–61). Przybylowicz also links the two, although she is less flattering about the withdrawal of the middle-aged artists into imaginary worlds, particularly Dane's, whose surreal experience reminds her, too, of *The Sense of the Past* (4, 39–41). Ward notes the seeking of the silence of a "private world" in other works including "The Altar of the Dead," "The Bench of Desolation," *The Ivory Tower*, *The Wings of the Dove*, and *The Ambassadors*, when Strether visits Notre Dame (1982, 131). Pointing to Strether's sense of Gloriani's garden as "a nursery of young priests," Ward observes that Catholic monasteries and churches are frequently refuges for James's characters (1961, 117, 178 n.8; also Silverstein 461). Tintner gives further examples of the Catholic idea of retreat in James, including Benvolio's half monastic life, the comparisons of the writer to a "disenfranchised monk" in "The Lesson of the Master," and in "The Next Time" to "the Trappists," and even the way Flora of "Glasses" goes "into goggles as repentant Magdalens go into the Catholic Church" (1987, 293).

By virtue of its retreat from "traditional realism," Miller includes the tale with "The Jolly Corner," "The Altar of the Dead," and *The Turn of the Screw* as a work that achieves a "transcendental reality" (601). McMurray sees in it as well as "The Real Thing" and "The Birthplace" the theme of reality as an imaginative construction (82). Banta includes it as one of James's few "psychical" tales involving "transposition of the self in time and place" with *The Sense of the Past*, *The Turn of the Screw*, and "The Private Life" (52). The latter, Wright remarks, illustrates the same split in a writer's role, which, Edel notes, is treated in each by the use of substitutes, a device Ralf finds indicating an "uncertainty about roles" (Wright 193; *Life* 4, 241; Norrman 145). Still, Przybylowicz observes, Vawdrey is more successful managing his different duties than is Dane initially (41).

The tale's insistence on the retention of the individual personality even in the spiritual world is typical of James, according to Matthiessen, who cites as further evidence James's 1910 essay "Is There a Life after Death?" (1947, 594; 1944, 148). Whelan takes a different tack, emphasizing the renunciation of egotism seen also in such works as "Broken Wings," "The Jolly Corner," "The Altar of the Dead," *Roderick Hudson*, *The Portrait of a Lady*, *The American*, and *The Tragic Muse*. The "great good place" itself he compares to the initial altar "of the spirit" of "The Altar of the Dead" (212–13, 217). Less positively, Geismar describes the religious atmosphere in both tales as "comfortable, respectable, upper middle class estheticism" (195). Still, according to Ford Madox Ford, both stories were classed by an embarrassed James with *The Turn of the Screw* as "indiscretions" for revealing his "particular interpretation of the Infinite" (1913, 121).

Interpretation and Criticism

In his preface, James declined the opportunity to explain the tale, remarking that "any gloss or comment would be a tactless challenge" to the "spirit" of the tale: "It embodies a calculated effect, and to plunge into it, I find, even for a beguiled glance—a course I indeed recommend—is to have left all else outside. There then my indications must wait" (*Criticism* 2, 1242). Zabel takes the refusal as an indication of James's "intimate" participation in the tale (22; also Wagenknecht 121). Indeed, according to the recollection of Ford Madox Ford, James regretted writing "The Great Good Place." He quotes the master as saying, "There are subjects one thinks of treating all one's life. . . . And one says they are not for one. And one says one must not treat them . . . all one's life. All one's life. . . . And then suddenly . . . one does . . . *Voilà*. . . . One has yielded to temptation. One is to that extent dishonoured. One must make the best of it" (1937, 11).

Smith has judged the tale representative of James's late period with its English setting, third-person narration, and most significantly, its themes of "fantasy, art, and identity" (160). Even so, it seems to require some special accounting for. Certainly when it appeared with the more worldly tales of *The Soft Side*, it was seen as an anomaly, the *Catholic World* welcoming its difference from the tales of life's "pleasure hall" (249). Taking a similar stance later on, Elton found its "soft rhythms of prose make us wish for more of this kind, even to the loss of the stories of a few 'trivial sphinxes' and adventuresses"

(368). The *Outlook* found it not only unlike the rest of *The Soft Side*, but "anything by the writer that we remember to have read" (280). Understandably, therefore, the story has garnered a great deal of critical attention, despite James's warning against analysis in the preface.

As critics have plunged in, they tend to have focused on the question of whether Dane seeks a permanent or temporary refuge; whether his "escape" is "escapist"; and on its realism, or alternately, its symbolism. The *Outlook* found the story depicting a "very real state of mind," but it is difficult to portray and to judge someone's dream world. Several critics have joined Matthiessen in dismissing the "great good place" as, in the mild words of Edgar, "somewhat lethargic" (192). Even Edel, who praises the story's establishment of atmosphere, notices a few "cloying" touches (1970, 570). Stevenson, like Matthiessen, casts the problem not simply as an aesthetic one, but a moral one as well, describing the dream world's "essential unhealthiness of perfect peace, segregated from the stew of life" (72). Rebecca West, placing the tale in the context of a deep spiritual exhaustion, saw in it the wish that "it would all stop," leaving one in an afterlife that would be nothing "but a climate," an eventless "peace of nothingness" (106). Virginia Woolf, who praised the detailed evocation of Dane's original rushed existence, felt that the story lost credibility and interest as it lost its connections with this world. In her view, James's imagination, far from "visionary," operates properly under "the pressure of reality." In its aim at the sublime, she wrote, the work becomes a "sweet soliloquy," an empty allegory, and something of an embarrassment (320–21). Citing Woolf, Ward argues that the problem she senses in the tale is quite simply its lack of any action to illustrate James's idea (1967, 53). Later Ward took his objections further. While noting that there are legitimate needs such a dream world provides, he argues that the emphasis here on negative goods, the new identity of "doing nothing" and "living" shows a disturbing susceptibility to the allure of the ease of dependency and even death (1982, 129–31).

Such views, however, have not stood unopposed. Dupee points out that, unlike the average Jamesian hero, Dane "has known only too much of robust experience" (154). Wright pictures him not as passive, but intensely aware in "creative meditation" on all around him. He emphasizes that it is his commitment to his writing that has brought upon Dane his many responsibilities (190, 192). Zabel, too, sees a man "beset . . . by his incurable avidity for life and art" and turning toward the "realm of hallucination" only to find that even the place he has escaped to is "nearer everything" than he expected, and so returning to reality (23–24). At the start, Dane's wish may well be for an end to activity. Putt indicates that both Dane's ready acceptance of life— which has produced the mountain of work facing him—and his "great sensitivity" combine to drive him to the extremity of a "brutal" desire for extinction (93–94). In words cited by Putt, however, Dane recognizes "that leaving was difficult, leaving impossible—that the only remedy, the true soft effacing sponge, would be to *be* left, to be forgotten. There was no footing on which a man who had liked life—liked it at any rate as *he* had—could now escape it" (CT 11, 14).

On his arrival Dane is soon counseled that "if one has a self worth six-pence," one's concern should be less with "putting [it] off" than "getting it back" (CT 11, 24). Once Dane has been left, and has gotten his self back, he will have the active will to return on his own. The trip to the great good place, as Putt remarks, helps this process along (93–94). Similarly, Hartsock objects to Matthiessen and Stevenson's criticism of the tale as a "fantasy of escape," perceiving the real message as "the discovery within oneself" of "resources" capable of sustaining one (1968, 307). Indeed most critics stress the temporary nature of Dane's retreat (e.g., Daugherty 1981, 133; Gage 35; Kimbel 36–37; Wagenknecht 123). In Andreas's reading, the "great good place" is simply a cleansing dream (128). As Horne points out, Dane leaves as soon as he is ready to work again and, upon his return, looks at his study and declares it "all right" (107–8).

In Vaid's reading, Dane does not escape the world but rather encounters the great good place within himself (205). Rawlings, however, sees Dane retreating both into self and the life that surrounds self. At first, Rawlings observes, Dane accepts his new surroundings happily enough primarily as the absence of things, but as he recovers, comes to ask the price of such a state and returns to the desire to create, to combine imagination and experience, to face even the literary market (xxiii–iv). McMurray also looks at the tale in terms of inner and outer worlds. He observes that Dane's desire to escape—"not to touch"—comes true at the great good place. At the end, however, the repetition of the phrase "it's all right" and the resemblance of the young man to the brother merge the two seemingly conflicting outer and inner worlds, demonstrating, McMurray argues, that the true reality is reas-suringly one created by man. In so doing, Jones writes, Dane is *"regaining, not losing"* his self. Jones's analysis rests on a distinction between two kinds of innocence: the young visitor is at a less advanced stage of innocence than Dane—still "deluded" in his eagerness. His intercession nevertheless allows Dane the necessary vacation to regain *his* lost innocence, a different, indeed superior, kind, based on experience and achieved through renunciation (248–49).

The beginning and end of Dane's experience is heralded by rain, and throughout the tale imagery serves to signal meaning. Remarking on the den-sity of figurative language in the tale, Tintner calls it the first of James's late prose poems (1987, 298). Three readings of the tale focus on its imagery to portray the great good place as a temporary escape, necessary to gather strength for a return to "real life." Shroeder uses "The Great Good Place," focusing on the description of Dane and his fellow brothers as "babes at the breast," to establish a key for reading the images of mothering and birth in other of James's stories. He detects running along the story's straight narrative a consciously symbolic one of exhaustion, retreat to the mother, and rebirth into the world. DeFalco offers a Jungian interpretation of the tale as a "dream sequence" that takes its protagonist on "a journey through the unconscious," where he "is healed by the tender care of the Great Mother archetype" and reborn. Such a "rupture," Dane comes to recognize, is necessary, a "ritualistic journey" to participate in the "collective unconscious." Its rewards, however, DeFalco writes, are not limited to the world of dreams. When Dane recognizes the young man as a "Brother," he brings "the awareness of brotherhood" into the "conscious world," making the "hollow hope" of the rain at the start "pleasant." Herx also puts the tale into the context of Jungian archetype and, most particularly, the hero's journey as set forth in Joseph Campbell's *The Hero with a Thousand Faces*. Dane's true story, she argues, is told through "dream symbols" which depict the traditional stages of departure, initiation into the spiritual, and return to the natural—a death of the old and a new rebirth.

Similarly, Przybylowicz uses psychoanalytic terminology for a reading of Dane's "withdrawal into madness." In his conversation with Brown, she bluntly declares, Dane appears "incoherent and insane," wishing for snow in May. Dane, she argues, is balking at the very conditions of existence, longing for a narcissistic fantasy world following his own desires. He rejects society and "the experience of time" for a "regression into the Imaginary" out of a desire to eliminate the differences society insists upon, "to unite self and other, to fuse the subjective and the objective worlds." During his "reassuring retreat," he initially experiences such oneness, seen in his similarity to the first Brother whom he meets, in the words of the story, "with closed eyes." He is tutored, however, by that very Brother (among others) that his desire to leave behind his identity is "a negative and annihilative act," that his "desire for pure plenitude, for the elimination of difference and alterity," is impossible in the real world. Discovering that "the desire to lose being-for-others amounts to losing being-for-oneself," he gradually prepares himself to return to the society he realizes he cannot totally escape. Showing his regained sense of "difference" in his parting talk with the novice, he returns to the world of responsibility, relinquishing at the same time, Przybylowicz contends, his search for fame in favor of the inner life (40–48).

Dane, as Przybylowicz points out, sees the hand of an artist behind the making of the great good place. Dane's very fantasy also, according to Przybylowicz, mirrors the process of art, as he remakes his surroundings. Every artist wants to remake his surroundings to seem "whole and coherent products of the central consciousness." Yet, she adds, while James, like Freud, recognized this drive, both men also recognized that if the artist did withdraw completely and permanently into his consciousness, he would lose the equally vital inspiration gained from contact with the outside world (41, 47–48). Other readings that focus on Dane's identity as an artist are more pragmatic. McElderry admits that the need for privacy and "inner resources" free from worldly business is "peculiarly intense" for writers, but also finds in the story a "wider application" (124–25). Similarly, while Horne calls the tale "an elaborate fantasy about the artist's need for solitude," she acknowledges that the tale does not discuss art itself, but rather the demands of life, particularly society, on the artist (105, 108).

While most critics see Dane's experience as a daydream, Przybylowicz sees the tale leaving indefinite whether it is a dream, a fantasy, or an actual stay at a hotel or sanatorium or such (40–41). In seeking to encapsulate his sense of the place, Dane himself speaks of it at various times not only as a Monte Cassino or a Grande Chartreuse, but "a box at the opera," a "bright country-house," a "hotel without noise," and "a club without newspapers" (CT 11, 24, 31). Such metaphors are disturbing to some. Matthiessen writes, "A fantasy of another world cast so overwhelmingly in the luxury products of this one betrays the vulgarity into which James could fall through the very dread of being vulgar" (1944, 144). To Blackmur, with its resemblance to an "unusually comfortable club," the place is unable to bear the significance James intended for it ([1948] 1983, 112). To Geismar it is "one of the oddest, most self-centered, luxury-loving and utterly selfish 'utopias' ever dreamed of," one entirely devoid of human emotion (193–96).

For Geismar and others, the cash basis of the place is one of the chief sticking points. Wright, Vaid, and Wagenknecht, however, read the fee metaphorically, Wright as "some form of creative meditation," Vaid as the "effort" necessary to reach such a state (Wright 192; Wagenknecht 123; Vaid 206). Taking it literally, Przybylowicz sees Dane's awareness of the fee as part of his healthy "return to the rationale and values of the natural-fact-world" (46). In general, the secular images, according to Vaid, stem from James's desire to keep his place from appearing "too utopian" (205–6). Still, Ward contends, the emphasis throughout is less on what is materially present than on what is absent (1982, 128–29). Kimbel, while acknowledging the upper-class conception of the refuge as "peculiarly Jamesian," insists it is "not narrow" in its appeal to those suffering from what James calls "the dreadful, fatal too much" (37). One might mark, too, the distinctions Dane draws between the place and the world, the Brother looking at him with "a look different from the looks of friends in London clubs" (CT 11, 21).

The requirement of a fee and the presence of servants keep the place, in Silverstein's view, from resembling a genuine monastery, although like a real monastery it is without women. For James, he states, the true path for the artist was the "path of celibacy." In his consideration, the consequences of such a path include a certain "psychological regression" as in the talk here of "babes at the breast" and kindergartens. He qualifies his indictment, however, to indicate that such regressiveness is "only a nuance" in James (464–67). Edel also mingles artistic and psychological issues, depicting the story as a combination of eroticized "infantile" longing for the comforting mother and a somewhat homoerotic desire for fraternal company—"churchly brotherhoods and Mother-Church"—the latter for James being art. Edel continues his reading by remarking on the longing for youth seen in the identification with the young visitor (1970, 567, 569; *Life* 4, 241). Their "mutual I-wish-I-were-you" is to Rawlings a key part of the tale's structure (xxiii). In the significance assigned the younger man's "devotion," Hartsock discerns a suggestion of homosexuality (1968, 307).

To Edel, the tale contains as much Freudian longing for "creature comfort" as any wish for the spiritual (1970, 567). The precise nature of the spirituality in the tale, if any, has continued to be a subject of dispute. Early on, Ford Madox Ford spoke of the story as showing James's "depth of religious, of mystical benevolence" (Page 19). The "strongest note" in James's character, according to Ford, was "a mysticism different altogether in character from that of the great mystics. It resembled rather a perception of a sort of fourth dimensional penetration of the material world by strata of the supernatural, of the world of the living by individuals from among the dead" (1937, 11). Fadiman, however, flatly declares that the tale is not religious (414). In response, Auden argued that both Matthiessen and Fadiman misinterpret the tale, which he takes as a "religious parable." The "great good place," he asserts, stands for a "spiritual state," its cash entrance fee for "sacrifice and suffering," a view later seconded by Zabel (Auden xxii; Zabel 23). Quentin Anderson locates in the tale the "religion of consciousness" James shared with his father (81 n.47). DeFalco's Jungian reading also points to such Christian imagery as the "baptism" of the rain and the functioning of the young man as a "savior." More markedly, Whelan sees the tale as deeply, if covertly, religious, the landlord of the "place" being God. Dane, as an artist, is an "analogue and image of that greater creator," the other Brothers simply projections of him as he learns to appreciate the ordinary as represented by his servant Brown and to renounce his own insistence on identity.

To Wagenknecht, Dane's experience might be just a dream or it might be a "mystical experience" (122). Such ambiguity does not bother Horne, who declares that one can read the tale as natural or supernatural without affecting its meaning (107). In Wright's reading, the place provides a secular version of grace, a sweetness that is then replaced by a sense of the "discipline" necessary to create such a place, and also to appreciate it as Dane does. In James's words, "The mere dream-sweetness of the place was superseded; it was more and more a world of reason and order, of sensible visible arrangement" (CT 11, 30; Wright 190–93, 209). While objecting to any strict religious interpretation, Vaid counters Matthiessen's criticism of the fantasy as stemming from James's "uprooted" and confused religious sense by seeing the tale as "rehabilitating that religious sense." Like Wright, he views the tale as a secular reworking of a religious experience in which Dane looks into the "heart of things" (205). His reading, however, is still too religious for Hartsock, who affirms, citing Wright, that there is no point in trying to interpret literally the finishing of the work by the young man, that the dream is just a device, the story staying "on the human level," with nothing changing in Dane's situation except his attitude toward it (1977, 26–28). While granting that the images of water, bells, and handshakes provoke a symbolic reading, Terrie maintains that there is no need to choose between Freudian, archetypal, or Christian readings as they all follow the same pattern of "disguise, retreat, and renewal" (12).

For those critics such as Geismar who dislike the tale, James's best defense is that he did not take his story as seriously as its commentators, that he was writing, as Ward terms it, a mere *jeu d'esprit* (Geismar 196; Ward 1982, 129). Those who admire the tale tend to take it more seriously. While calling the story a fairy tale, Fadiman strongly asserts that its depiction of an escape from the modern reality of needless rush and unneeded things makes it of James's tales "the one most densely charged with contemporary application" (413–15). In a more limited sense, as Terrie remarks, it "will always be an appealing fantasy for anyone who has been overwhelmed by paper" (12). Many critics, however, have read the tale as if they had never longed for the ending of a term or taken a summer vacation. In Frost's "Birches," the poet writes, "I'd like to get away from earth awhile / And then come back to it and begin over," but cautions, "May no fate willfully misunderstand me / And half grant what I wish and snatch me away / Not to return." In his irritation at the accumulations of modern life, James, too, did not want his wish half granted, any more than his protagonist Dane does. But he dreams of a respite. And while his dream may not have the simple imagery of a New England birch to hold its message, it is, to the dreamer as sweet and returns him to life refreshed.

Works Cited

Primary Works
James, Henry. 1900. "The Great Good Place." *Scribner's Magazine* 27 (January): 99–112.

———. 1900. "The Great Good Place." *The Soft Side*. London: Methuen; New York: Macmillan, 1–29.

———. 1909. "The Great Good Place." In *The Novels and Tales of Henry James*. New York Edition. Vol. 16, 223–63. New York: Scribner's.

———. 1993. *The Correspondence of Henry James and the House of Macmillan, 1877–1914*. Ed. Rayburn S. Moore. Baton Rouge: Louisiana State University Press.

Secondary Works

Anderson, Quentin. 1957. *The American Henry James*. New Brunswick, NJ: Rutgers University Press.

Andreas, Osborne. 1948. *Henry James and the Expanding Horizon: A Study of the Meaning and Basic Themes of James's Fiction*. Seattle: University of Washington Press.

Anon. 1901. Review of *The Soft Side*. *Catholic World* 73 (May): 249.

Anon. 1900. Review of *The Soft Side*. *Outlook* 66 (13 October): 423.

Auden, W. H., ed. 1946. *Henry James' "The American Scene" Together with Three Essays for Portraits of Places*. New York: Scribner's.

Banta, Martha. 1972. *Henry James and the Occult: The Great Extension*. Bloomington: Indiana University Press.

Bayley, John. 1987. "Beyond the Great Good Place." *Times Literary Supplement* 4391, 29 May, 571–72.

Beebe, Maurice L. 1964. *Ivory Towers and Sacred Founts: The Artist as Hero*. New York: New York University Press.

Blackmur, R. P. [1948] 1983. "Henry James." In *Studies in Henry James*. Ed. Veronica A. Makowsky, 91–124. New York: New Directions. Reprinted from *Literary History of the United States*, ed. Robert E. Spiller et al. New York: Macmillan.

———. [1943] 1983. "In the Country of the Blue." In *Studies in Henry James*. Ed. Veronica A. Makowsky, 69–90. New York: New Directions. Reprinted from *Kenyon Review* 5: 508–21.

Daugherty, Sarah B. 1981. *The Literary Criticism of Henry James*. Athens: Ohio University Press.

———. 1979. "James, Renan, and the Religion of Consciousness." *Comparative Literature Studies* 16 (December): 318–31.

DeFalco, Joseph M. 1958. "'The Great Good Place': A Journey into the Psyche." *Literature and Psychology* (University of Hartford) 8 (Spring): 18–20.

Dupee, F. W. [1951] 1956. *Henry James*. Garden City, NY: Doubleday Anchor.

Edel, Leon, ed. 1970. *Henry James: Stories of the Supernatural*. New York: Taplinger.

Edgar, Pelham. [1927] 1964. *Henry James, Man and Author*. New York: Russell & Russell.

Elton, Oliver. 1903. "The Novels of Mr. Henry James." *Quarterly Review* 198 (October): 358–79.

Fadiman, Clifton, ed. 1948. *The Short Stories of Henry James*. New York: Modern Library. Reprint. Louis G. Locke, William M. Gibson, and George Arms, eds. *An Introduction to Literature*. 5th ed. New York: Rinehart, 1967, 298–99.

Fiedler, Leslie. [1960] 1966. *Love and Death in the American Novel*. New York: Stein & Day.

Ford, Ford Madox. 1937. *Portraits from Life*. Boston: Houghton Mifflin.

———. 1913. *Henry James: A Critical Study*. London: Martin Secker.

Fox, Hugh. 1968. *Henry James, A Critical Introduction*. Conesville, IA: John Westburg.

Frost, Robert, 1969. "Birches." In *The Poetry of Robert Frost*. Ed. Edward Connery Latham, 121–23. New York: Holt, Rinehart.

Gage, Richard P. 1988. *Order and Design: Henry James' Titled Story Sequences*. New York: Peter Lang.

Geismar, Maxwell. 1963. *Henry James and the Jacobites*. Boston: Houghton Mifflin.

Hartsock, Mildred. 1977. "Another Way to Heightened Consciousness." *Humanist* 37 (July–August): 26–30.

———. 1968. "Henry James and the Cities of the Plain." *Modern Language Quarterly* 29 (September): 297–311.

Herx, Mary Ellen. 1963. "The Monomyth in 'The Great Good Place.'" *College English* 24 (March): 439–43.

Horne, Helen. 1960. *Basic Ideals of James's Aesthetics as Expressed in the Short Stories Concerning Artists and Writers*. Marburg: Erich Mauersberger.

Horwitz, B. D. 1977. "The Sense of Desolation in Henry James." *Psychocultural Review* 1: 466–92.

Jones, Granville H. 1975. *Henry James's Psychology of Experience: Innocence, Responsibility, and Renunciation in the Fiction of Henry James*. The Hague: Mouton.

Josephson, Matthew. 1964. *Portrait of the Artist as American*. New York: Octagon.

Kimbel, Ellen. 1984. "The American Short Story: 1900–1920." In *The American Short Story: 1900–1945*. Ed. Philip Stevick, 33–69. Boston: Twayne.

Krook, Dorothea. [1962] 1967. *The Ordeal of Consciousness in Henry James*. New York: Cambridge University Press.

McElderry, Bruce R., Jr. 1965. *Henry James*. New York: Twayne Publishers.

McMurray, William. 1977. "Reality in James's 'The Great Good Place.'" *Studies in Short Fiction* 14: 82–83.

Macnaughton, William R. 1987. *Henry James: The Later Novels*. Boston: Twayne.

Martin, W. R., and Warren U. Ober. 1983. "'Superior to Oak': The Part of Mora Montravers in James's *The Finer Oak*." *American Literary Realism* 16: 121–28.

Matthiessen, F. O. 1947. *The James Family: Including Selections from the Writings of Henry James, Sr., William, Henry, and Alice James*. New York: Knopf.

———. 1944. *Henry James: The Major Phase*. New York: Oxford University Press.

Miller, James E. 1976. "Henry James in Reality." *Critical Inquiry* 2 (Spring): 585–604.

Moon, Michael. 1989. "Disseminating Whitman." *South Atlantic Quarterly* 88: 247–65.

Norrman, Ralf. 1982. *The Insecure World of Henry James's Fiction*. New York: St. Martin's.

Page, Norman, ed. 1984. *Henry James: Interviews and Recollections*. New York: St. Martin's.

Pearce, Howard. 1975. "Henry James's Pastoral Fallacy." *PMLA* 90: 834–47.

Perosa, Sergio. 1983. *Henry James and the Experimental Novel*. New York: New York University Press.

Powers, Lyall H. 1970. *Henry James: An Introduction and Interpretation*. New York: Holt, Rinehart.

Przybylowicz, Donna. 1986. *Desire and Repression: The Dialectic of Self and Other in the Late Works of Henry James*. University: University of Alabama Press.

Putt, S. Gorley. 1966. *Henry James: A Reader's Guide*. Ithaca, NY: Cornell University Press. Revised from "'Benvolio': 'Everyone was a little someone else'" and "'Cher Maitre' and 'Mon Bon.'" In *Scholars of the Heart: Essays in Criticism*, 141–235. London: Faber, 1962.

Rawlings, Peter, ed. 1984. *Henry James's Shorter Masterpieces*. Vol. 2. Totowa, NJ: Barnes & Noble.

Shroeder, John W. 1951. "The Mothers of Henry James." *American Literature* 22 (January): 424–31.

Sicker, Philip. 1980. *Love and the Quest for Identity in the Fiction of Henry James*. Princeton: Princeton University Press.

Silverstein, Henry. 1962. "The Utopia of Henry James." *New England Quarterly* 35 (December): 458–68.

Smith, William F., Jr. 1973. "Sentence Structure in the Tales of Henry James." *Style* 7 (Spring): 157–72.

Stevenson, Elizabeth. [1949] 1981. *The Crooked Corridor: A Study of Henry James*. New York: Octagon.

Terrie, Henry, ed. 1984. *Henry James: Tales of Art and Life*. Schenectady, NY: Union College Press.

Tintner, Adeline R. 1989. *The Pop World of Henry James: From Fairy Tales to Science Fiction*. Ann Arbor: UMI Research Press.

———. 1987. *The Book World of Henry James: Appropriating the Classics*. Ann Arbor: UMI Research Press. Revised in part from "The Influence of Balzac's *L'envers de l'histoire contemporaine* on James's 'The Great Good Place.'" *Studies in Short Fiction* 9 (Fall, 1972): 343–51.

———. 1986. *The Museum World of Henry James*. Ann Arbor: UMI Research Press.

Revised in part from "Henry James's Salomé and the arts of the *Fin de Siècle*." *The Markham Review* 5 (Fall): 5–10.

———. 1975. "The Metamorphoses of Edith Wharton in Henry James's *The Finer Grain*." *Twentieth-Century Literature* 21: 355–79.

Vaid, Krishna B. 1964. *Technique in the Tales of Henry James*. Cambridge, MA: Harvard University Press.

Wagenknecht, Edward. 1984. *The Tales of Henry James*. New York: Frederick Ungar.

Ward, J. A. 1982. "Silence, Realism, and 'The Great Good Place.'" *Henry James Review* 3: 129–32.

———. 1967. *The Search for Form: Studies in the Structure of James's Fiction*. Chapel Hill: University of North Carolina Press.

———. 1961. *The Imagination of Disaster: Evil in the Fiction of Henry James*. Lincoln: University of Nebraska Press.

West, Rebecca. [pseud]. 1916. *Henry James*. London: Nisbet.

Whelan, Robert E., Jr. 1979. "God, Henry James, and 'The Great Good Place.'" *Research Studies* 47: 212–20.

Woolf, Virginia. [1921] 1988. "Henry James's Ghost Stories." In *The Essays of Virginia Woolf*. Ed. Andrew McNeillie. Vol. 3, 319–26. London: Hogarth Press.

Wright, Walter F. 1962. *The Madness of Art: A Study of Henry James*. Lincoln: University of Nebraska Press.

Yeazell, Ruth Bernard. 1976. *Language and Knowledge in the Late Novels of Henry James*. Chicago: University of Chicago Press.

Zabel, Morton Dauwen, ed. 1958. *Henry James: In the Cage and Other Tales*. Garden City, NY: Doubleday.

Greville Fane

Publication History

Illustrated by A. Forestier, "Greville Fane" was James's only story to appear in the *Illustrated London News*, where it was published in two instalments, on 17 and 24 September 1892. The next year James included it in the collection *The Real Thing*, and later in the New York Edition.

Circumstances of Composition, Sources, and Influences

In his preface, James recalled of the story's writing "only a dim warm pleasantness as of old Kensington summer hours. . . . a certain feverish pressure, in a cool north room resorted to in heavy London Augusts, with stray, rare echoes of the town . . ." (*Criticism* 2, 1239–40). The history of "Greville Fane," however, begins much earlier in the wintertime with two real-life examples. On January 22, 1879, James recorded in his notebook hearing that Anthony Trollope had raised his son to be a novelist. The son had instead become an Australian sheep farmer. Similarly, his friend Mrs. Ritchie, herself Thackeray's daughter, told James that she and her husband intended to raise their daughter in the trade. James projected a tale in which the "peculiar education" given a child leads to "some extremely prosaic situation," producing "a comment—a satire—upon the high parental views" (CN 9–10). When he returned to the idea ten years later he pictured a "weary battered labourer in the field of fiction," a "lady-novelist" with stupid and expensive children. The narrator, he had earlier decided, would meet her "at intervals, about the world, for several years" and serve as "a witness of her life—a friend." Initially, he envisioned the first-person narrator as a critic or journalist, but decided the following day to make the narrator a younger novelist "of the modern psychological type," for contrast (CN 48–49).

In the tale, Mrs. Stormer "had an idea that she resembled Balzac," while James himself in the notebook had attributed to her a "natural penchant to license *à la Ouida*" (CT 8, 437; CN 94). Not surprisingly, although McCarthy judges her a "highly representative . . . literary drudge," there have been several proposals for a specific source for Mrs. Stormer and her art (153).

Smith suggests Mary Elizabeth Braddon as a possible source of inspiration (137). The relationship of the younger novelist to the older may have some of the inflections of James's friendship with Mrs. Humphry Ward, whom, according to Edel, James liked personally while criticizing her novels as artless. In February of 1892 he wrote an appreciation of her for the *English Illustrated Magazine* which he later included in *Partial Portraits* (*Life* 4, 293). The tale itself, to Vaid, resembles one of James's "partial portraits" just as the narrator's "delightfully phrased" comments reflect James's own views (56). Stormer's children have a parallel in Howells, according to Dietrichson, who points out that the artist Beaton in *A Hazard of New Fortunes* (1889) sponges off his father in the same way as Greville Fane's children do off her (244–45). Edel sees Greville Fane's failure to "educate" her son as a novelist reflecting James's own sense that he could not "educate" himself to become a playwright, also reflected in "The Real Thing" (*Life* 4, 22).

In the most intricate search for an original, Rowe traces the model for Greville Fane back to a source in James's "transumption" of Anthony Trollope, of whom James had written an obituary in 1883, and who, like Greville Fane, treated literature as a "business." The character of Greville Fane, according to Rowe's theory, includes elements of Trollope's mother, Frances Trollope, and one of his brothers, Thomas Trollope, in ways that helped James caricature Trollope as more a "popular" artist than a great one. James's relationship to Trollope, Rowe argues, was complex. He admired the Englishman's acceptance of Americans in England, but felt it encroached upon his territory. He disapproved of Trollope's "type"—the "productive and commercial" writer—but longed for his success. Rowe stretches further to see George Eliot implicated in the portrait, arguing that from his anxiety of influence, James sought to diminish Trollope by portraying him as a woman, and George Eliot by portraying her as a romancer. The association comes in part through the name Greville, as it was Mrs. Richard Greville who introduced James to Tennyson the day before he met Eliot, although Rowe oddly does not indicate that it was also Greville who visited Eliot with him. In a "cluster" of associations, the "fane" or sacred place is linked with the name Greville to evoke the "tone of English history and tradition," back to the Renaissance poet Fulke Greville (76–82).

The picture Mrs. Stormer so admires at the Academy has, however, no specific source according to Tintner, although she argues that "Baby's Tub" fits the sentimental genre school popular at the time as well as Mrs. Stormer's vulgarity and her love for her children (154–55). Wharton's short story "The Pelican" tells of a widow who turns to lecturing to support her young son, using him as her excuse long after he is grown. Mrs. Stormer's faith in her unworthy children, and her disappointment, recalls Lear.

Relation to Other Works

The story begins following the death of its focal character, as do several other James stories, Gerlach pointing particularly to "Four Meetings" and "Brooksmith" as examples (88). Still the story, according to Shine, is an exception to the strength of James's anger at the "spoilers" she witnesses also in "Master Eustace," *Daisy Miller*, and *A London Life* (57–62).

Mrs. Stormer herself is, according to Edgar, another of James's examinations of "successful incapacity," such as Sir Northmore of "The Abasement of the Northmores," a story he judges superior in its "foreshortening." In its ability to inspire sympathy for its heroine, he judges "Greville Fane" inferior to "Broken Wings" as well (169–70). Of course, the heroine of "Broken Wings," who has also lost her popularity as a writer, is portrayed as a far more serious artist. As a woman writer "forced to disguise her identity for the sake of her work," her situation is seen by Rowe as another version of the theme of "The Private Life" (81). James is less sympathetic, according to Putt, who portrays him as looking down on Mrs. Stormer with the same comic contempt accorded such absurd characters as Mrs. Tarrant in *The Bostonians* (226). More moderately, Leyburn classes Mrs. Stormer with Mrs. Rooth in *The Tragic Muse* and Mrs. Stringham in *The Wings of the Dove* as romantics whom James rather likes, if he does not quite respect them (82).

The writer's children have inspired little respect or liking, Dietrichson deeming them even worse parasites than Ruck's wife and daughter in "The Pension Beaurepas" (107). The exploitative children, Leyburn observes, represent a change from the exploitative mother in "Europe," although they, too, are presented by a narrator who sides with their victims (84). Austin Wright also links the two stories, seeing in the daughters in "Europe" and in Greville Fane a baffled loneliness he judges characteristically modern (59–60). Rowe, on the other hand, argues that Greville Fane in a sense has "killed" Leolin even as James pictured in the notebook the parent "using" the child, and as the governess in *The Turn of the Screw* uses Miles (80). Certainly, several critics have pointed out how Mrs. Stormer cultivates in her children the tendencies she later suffers from, even as Louisa Pallant did.

Together mother and son demonstrate, according to Aswell, as in "The Real Thing," the absurdity of collaboration when "the various partners have no idea of how to differentiate between life and art," a message continued in "The Private Life" (191). The more supportive relationship between narrator and subject, despite a gap in generations, has elements of the friendship in "Flickerbridge," where the older woman is again bewildered by the younger man's ideas.

Interpretation and Criticism

In the preface James refers to the tale as a "minor miracle of foreshortening" by which he reduced a "developmental" subject into the form of an "anecdote" (*Criticism* 2, 1240). The tale, Vaid observes, has little "story" in it apart from the death of Fane herself, what little there is being relayed through "summary and report" so that it resembles most a "critical-biographical essay." What makes "Greville Fane" typically Jamesian, according to Vaid, is what also allowed James his "minor miracle," its framing prologue (55). The result, in Wright's formulation, is essentially a long flashback, producing a rough stream of consciousness (315). The narrator introduces his reminiscences with the remark that "the dear woman had written a hundred stories, but none so curious as her own" (CT 8, 436). Thus, Tintner indicates, "Greville Fane" is the story the narrator promises to write depicting the "new crime" the son has invented, a metafictional approach also taken by Rowe (Tintner 155, Rowe 79).

The story is also structured by the tensions Vaid examines between the narrator and Fane as writers, and Fane as writer and mother (56–57; also Wagenknecht 72). The tension is apparent also in what McElderry sees as the two missions of the narrator, and in the different moods that accompany the two. In telling the reader what he left out of his article, McElderry reports, the narrator treats both the badness of Mrs. Stormer's writing, a subject of satire, and her children, a subject of pathos (123). Although Leyburn classifies Mrs. Stormer's situation as "pathetic rather than tragic," she calls attention to the contrast between the narrator's humor at the expense of her writing, and the seriousness with which he takes her children's behavior (82–84). In response to the tale's mingled moods and genres, some have emphasized the comedy that Segal labels "farcical" and that Wright attributes to the chronological confusion (Segal 107; Wright 322; also Rowe 79). Others, such as the *Athenaeum*, which praised the way the tale's "restrained humour" heightened its "pathos," have emphasized the blending of the comic and the pathetic (601; also Matheson 225).

The tale has a definite element of satire, directed against the popular writers, mostly women, who were James's competition, a satire that James, according to Smith, pushed far too hard (Smith 137–38; also Geismar 118n.; Matheson 225). In Rowe's analysis, James has a more sophisticated sympathy with Greville Fane, since a woman's need to write under a man's name "recalls the constant theme in James of the 'secrecy' required of woman in a patriarchal culture" (82). Certainly a man capable of entitling works "Sir Dominick Ferrand" and "Sir Edmund Orme," or even *The Princess Casamassima*, should not be too harsh on the writer of romance. Still, the satire of Mrs. Stormer as a writer is clear: "She could invent stories by the yard,—but she couldn't write a page of English," her works treat endlessly one "formula"—"passion in high life" (CT 8, 436–37). In Matthiessen's estimate, however, the satire is "gentle" and balanced by "an appealing presentation" of Mrs. Stormer herself (N 94–95; also 1944, 4–5). In the notebook, James imagined that the narrator's reminiscences were to be "kinder still" than his already indulgent essay (CN 49). Accordingly, in the tale the narrator appears to emphasize the first half of his editor's directive to "Let her off easy, but not too easy" (CT 8, 433). Following his lead, many critics have characterized Greville Fane as a sympathetic figure (e.g., Hall and Langland 347; Dietrichson 80, 128; Vaid 60).

The sympathy accorded here comes more frequently from Greville Fane's travails as a mother than from her worries as a writer. Nevertheless, most critics acknowledge that, as Vaid puts it, her limits as a mother are "subtly intertwined" with her limits as an artist. In both fields of endeavor, according to Vaid, she is simultaneously innocent and ridiculous, giving a "comic-pathetic" impression (57–58). Her children clearly do not turn out well; Barzun writes that it is hard to specify their crime, apart from repeating the narrator's phrase "they go too far" (514). James himself confessed to the want of more "detailed notation of the behavior of the son and daughter" (*Criticism* 2, 1240). The *Illustrated London News* made its sense of things quite clear in the decorated title that headed the tale, incorporating an allegorical scene of a woman pushing a grindstone accompanied by a smiling boy with a whip and a smiling young woman with a fan. It is such indifference to their mother's efforts on their behalf that seems the root of what even Barzun acknowledges as their wickedness. Leolin, in particular, is classed appropriately as a parasite by Andreas (36). The fact that the narrator, who disapproves of her writing, can yet remain sympathetic to her personally intensifies, as Leyburn notes, James's criticism of the children's selfishness (82–84). Putt takes a different view. Sensing "first-hand acrimony behind the second-hand sympathy" of the story, he contends that James's disapproval of Mrs. Stormer's art overwhelms the sympathy for her as a person, so that the children become "cruel inventions" to a writer who fails to suffer the appropriate "torment of form" (225–26).

Others, while continuing the link between life and literature, have argued that the behavior and character of Greville Fane herself is the cause of her children's cruelty (e.g., Smith 137–38). In Dietrichson's view, her very generosity contributed to their parasitism (107). Shine points not to one of Mrs. Stormer's virtues, but to her "unforgivable failure of perception" as the key cause. Although sympathetic, Greville Fane is to blame for her children's failures: her romanticizing and her belief that one can "experience life vicariously" disable her son, and her snobbery—which Shine judges a sign of "heartlessness"—her daughter. Her weakness as an artist and mother mirror each other. Switching the emphasis from mother to son, Shine defines the "new crime" Leolin discovers as "his own destruction through his exploitation of her weakness." Despite the the narrator's statement that the mother "never saw" the truth of her son's crime, Shine suggests the possibility that Greville Fane did "in fact see a glimmer of the truth" (61). Similarly, Grossman states that she loses her ability to write of the "glamour of a vicious aristocracy" once she recognizes that the children she has so carefully molded are themselves "vicious aristocrats" (231). Grossman may attribute more discernment to her than she possesses, but in her last conversation with the narrator, Greville Fane's description of her daughter's inability to house her seems to have glimmers of understanding.

Like Shine, Aswell criticizes Mrs. Stormer for her upper-class sympathies, and sees her as getting an appropriate comeuppance. According to the narrator, "of all her productions 'my daughter Lady Luard' was quite the one she was proudest of" (CT 8, 441). Thus, Aswell writes, she regards her children as "extraordinary works of art," and as such, intends to exploit them in turn. When that fails, Aswell sees her reduced to the false sentimentality of such art as the "Baby's Tub." Ignorant, according to Aswell, of both life and art, her life "cruelly and ironically" imitates her dubious art. After her death, her children treat her in turn as simply a literary production, whether a collection of manuscripts to profit from or a "stock figure" to mold into posthumous respectability (189–91). In Matheson's reading, however, while her character combines the two types of mother and lady, more typically opposed, the mother in her is not only exploited but dominant throughout, using her art for the sake of her children. As such her case represents a twist on the "formula of the Woman as Mother exploiting the Artist" (225).

Rowe, however, although he speaks of James's concern for the "impotence" of women in "an essentially patriarchal culture," contends that the narrator exaggerates both the suffering of the "undisillusioned" Greville Fane and the criminality of Leolin. In his reading, the children—"parodies" of her characters—still expose her basic flaw as a writer, her "commodification of the literary spirit." More significantly, the narrator's telling of her story is influenced both by his sense of himself as vying with Leolin to be Greville Fane's heir, and a fear that he will become like Leolin a "literary ghoul . . . fetishizing . . . the mere artifacts of a dead literary tradition." These worries prompt him to replace Greville Fane's "*own* living story"—Leolin—with his literary version—the tale itself, a "sort of metaromance" (76–81).

James himself felt he had captured the "right effect" in his metaromance (*Criticism* 2, 1239–40). Similarly, Q. D. Leavis calls it one of James's "very good very short" stories (223). The polish and wit of its writing have been frequently complimented by critics (e.g., Zabel 40; Vaid 60). Still, the common judgment, even among those who dissect it, is that the tale is a "slight thing," a "trifle" (Wagenknecht 72; also Rowe 79).

If slight, the story is nevertheless amiable. In the notebook Greville Fane's "funny old art" was to elicit the "indulgence and humour" of the narrator, and it seems that critics who take her too strongly to task either for her writing or her parenting are straying from the spirit of the tale (CN 49). While Horne objects to the story for its focus on what she judges the psychology of an inadequate person, what the narrator continually emphasizes about Greville Fane is her "good faith"—"a serene good faith that ought to have been safe from allusion, like a stutter or a *faux pas*" (71–73; CT 8, 444, 447). Even the oft-criticized project of raising a writer was begun as a "joke" (CT 8, 442). The narrator's summary of her character is not without criticisms: "She was very brave and healthy and cheeful, very abundant and innocent and wicked. She was clever and vulgar and snobbish . . ." (CT 8, 437). And while critics have criticized her, it is significant that, while narrators in James are typically prime suspects for critical suspicion, few, apart from Rowe, have questioned the narrator who so likes her. There is indeed, as Smith observes, something "condescending" in his fondness, but he never stoops to condemnation, saying simply, "I didn't admire her, but I liked her" (137–38; CT 8, 433). There is, too, a sense in which he fails to recognize, or at least to emphasize, his greater freedom as a man, apparently without family, in which he prides himself on recognizing in her life the story she fails to see. But unlike other of James's narrators, it is hard to see how he could have helped her apart from being her friend. It is his triumph to have extended his sympathy to someone so different from himself, to have recognized the good person behind the bad writer. One needs really to care for her to care for the story. It seems hard not to find appealing the picture of a woman diligently "tracing the loves of the duchesses beside the innocent cribs of her children" (CT 8, 443), and to feel the poignancy of both duchesses and children later failing her. Contemporary literary criticism has rescued many of her real-life compeers, women writers of romance, from the condescension visited upon them, and it seems appropriate for it to recognize in Greville Fane a figure worth some respect.

Works Cited

Primary Works

James, Henry. 1892. "Greville Fane." *The Illustrated London News* 101, 17 and 24 September, 361–63, 393–95.

———. 1893. "Greville Fane." *The Real Thing*. New York and London: Macmillan, 1–41.

———. 1909. "Greville Fane." *The Novels and Tales of Henry James*. New York Edition. Vol. 16, 107–34. New York: Scribner's.

Secondary Works

Andreas, Osborn. 1948. *Henry James and the Expanding Horizon: A Study of the Meaning and Basic Themes of James's Fiction*. Seattle: University of Washington Press.

Anon. 1893. Review of *The Real Thing*. *Athenaeum* 3420 (13 May): 601–12.

Aswell, E. Duncan. 1966. "James's Treatment of Artistic Collaboration." *Criticism* 8: 180–95.

Barzun, Jacques. 1943. "James the Melodramatist." *Kenyon Review* 5 (August): 508–21. Reprinted in *The Question of Henry James*, ed. F. W. Dupee, 254–66. New York: Henry Holt, 1945.

Dietrichson, Jan W. 1969. *The Image of Money in the American Novel of the Gilded Age*. Oslo: Universitetsforlaget; New York: Humanities.

Edgar, Pelham. [1927] 1964. *Henry James, Man and Author*. New York: Russell & Russell.

Geismar, Maxwell. 1963. *Henry James and the Jacobites*. Boston: Houghton Mifflin.

Gerlach, John. 1985. *Toward the End: Closure and Structure in American Short Stories*. University: University of Alabama Press.

Grossman, James. 1945. "The Face in the Mountain." *Nation* 161 (8 September): 230–32.

Hall, James B., and Joseph Langland. 1956. *The Short Story*. New York: Macmillan.

Horne, Helen. 1960. *Basic Ideals of James's Aesthetics as Expressed in the Short Stories Concerning Artists and Writers*. Marburg: Erich Mauersberger.

Leavis, Q. D. 1947. "Henry James: The Stories." *Scrutiny* 14 (Spring): 223–29. Reprinted in *Collected Essays*. Vol. 2: *The American Novel and Reflections of the European Novel*, ed. G. Singh, 177–84. Cambridge: Cambridge University Press.

Leyburn, Ellen Douglass. 1968. *Strange Alloy: The Relation of Comedy to Tragedy in the Fiction of Henry James*. Chapel Hill: University of North Carolina Press.

McCarthy, Harold T. 1958. *Henry James: The Creative Process*. New York: Thomas Yoseloff.

McElderry, Bruce R., Jr. 1965. *Henry James*. New York: Twayne.

Matheson, Gwen. 1968. "Portraits of the Artist and the Lady in the Shorter Fictions of Henry James." *Dalhousie Review* 48: 222–30.

Matthiessen, F. O. 1944. "Introduction: Henry James' Portrait of the Artist." *Henry James: Stories of Writers and Artists*. Norfolk, CT: New Directions. Reprinted as "Henry James's Portrait of the Artist. *Partisan Review* 11 (1944): 71–87.

Putt, S. Gorley. 1966. *Henry James: A Reader's Guide*. Ithaca, NY: Cornell University Press.

Rowe, John Carlos. 1984. *The Theoretical Dimensions of Henry James*. Madison: University of Wisconsin Press.

Segal, Ora. 1969. *The Lucid Reflector: The Observer in Henry James' Fiction*. New Haven: Yale University Press.

Shine, Muriel G. 1969. *The Fictional Children of Henry James*. Chapel Hill: University of North Carolina Press.

Smith, Henry Nash. 1978. *Democracy and the Novel: Popular Resistance to Classic American Writers*. New York: Oxford University Press.

Tintner, Adeline R. 1986. *The Museum World of Henry James*. Ann Arbor: UMI Research Press.

Vaid, Krishna B. 1964. *Technique in the Tales of Henry James*. Cambridge, MA: Harvard University Press.

Wagenknecht, Edward. 1984. *The Tales of Henry James*. New York: Frederick Ungar.

Wright, Austin McGiffert. 1961. *The American Short Story in the Twenties*. Chicago: University of Chicago Press.

Zabel, Morton Dauwen, ed. [1951] 1968. *The Portable Henry James*. Rev. Lyall H. P. Powers. New York: Viking. Reprint. Harmondsworth: Penguin.

Guest's Confession

Publication History

"Guest's Confession" was published in the *Atlantic Monthly* from October to November 1872. It did not reappear until Mordell's 1919 *Travelling Companions*.

Circumstances of Composition, Sources, and Influences

While Henry was in Europe, his father read the proof for "Guest's Confession" (*Life* 2, 69). Edel argues for another family connection, stating that James represented in the narrator and his elder stepbrother his own resentment of his elder brother, William, and judges William's response to the story as particularly pointed in return. He overstates the case, however, when he writes that the elder brother humiliates Guest even though he knows his younger brother is in love with his daughter (*Life* 2, 40–41). Actually, at the time the elder brother is unaware of the romance, and even the younger brother is still unaware of the woman's identity. Putt also notes the importance of the fraternal strife, but argues against imputing too much autobiographical anxiety to it. In his view, Henry's split pairs draw more on his own dichotomous psyche than his relationship with William (38).

Kelley judges Saratoga, which James had visited two years before to write a travel essay, a rather crude setting for James, but still preferable to the vague location of other early American tales (127).

In the tale, David records his older brother Edgar's desire for "the vengeance of a very Shylock" (CT 2, 400). Tintner proceeds to find James drawing heavily on what James termed the "witless" story of *The Merchant of Venice*, doing so mainly in the spirit of technical bravura. In place of a wise Portia, the foolish Mrs. Beck provides the prize for competing suitors; Laura stands in for Jessica; and Guest plays both Antonio and Bassanio. More significantly, at the end David resists the temptation to play Shylock himself (19–23). In so doing, David shows greater mercy even than Portia, who saw to Shylock's punishment after his defeat. Kelley attributes James's depiction of conscience here more to Balzac than George Eliot (129). Edward Stone mentions David's likening of himself to "a legendary suitor of old" who might even slay a dragon (139). Gale is not very impressed by a comparison of Guest and Mrs. Beck to Samson and Delilah (156).

Relation to Other Works

While Mull and Dietrichson find the Westerner Crawford a forerunner of Newman, the more significant comparison, in what Thorp calls one of James's "earliest commemorations of the virtue of renunciation," is that noted by Wagenknecht and Buitenhuis between Newman's renunciation and David's (Dietrichson 118–19; Thorp xi; Wagenknecht 187; Buitenhuis 54). Mull judges David luckier in his opponent: the Bellegardes count on Newman's relenting, while Guest expects David to insist on revenge as he would. According to Mull David also anticipates the later suspect narrator or center of consciousness, as in *The Sacred Fount* or "The Liar," as Edgar partially anticipates Osmond (19–22). Jones compares David's stroll into the woods to that of another American confronting France, Longmore of *Madame de Mauves*. He also sees David exchanging his innocence for a maturity threatened by evil, but allowing for a happy marriage, while his evil brother loses everything in his egotism (99–100, 158).

Buitenhuis finds Mrs. Beck prefiguring Mrs. Luna of *The Bostonians* and Mrs. Worthingham of "Crapy Cornelia" (142, 221). Veeder notes that Mrs. Beck's "plumpness" denotes "moral softness" in James, as with Mme Merle and the Countess in "Four Meetings" (267 n.127). More seriously Buitenhuis finds the story depicting the "identity of the cheated with the cheater," present also in *The Ivory Tower* and "A Round of Visits" (236).

Interpretation and Criticism

Wagenknecht has drawn attention to the story's changing critical fortunes (187–88). Among the unenthusiastic, McElderry finds the tale does not live up to the promise of its premises, while Edel judges it highly "unpleasant," and Leyburn "revolting" (McElderry 288; CT 2, 11; Leyburn 6). One of its earliest critics, William Dean Howells relayed his own and his wife's praise to James, and indicated that it had in general been the best received of his work for the *Atlantic* (404). James's brother William "read and enjoyed" the tale, "admiring its cleverness though not loving it exactly." His main objection was to the style, including its French phrases, the tendency for "something cold, thin-blooded & priggish suddenly popping in and freezing the genial current" (176). Levy, alternately, sees it as rather theatrically melodramatic (16–77). Putt, for his part, praises the fresh wit of the writing, citing the description of Mrs. Beck as an example (40–41). Buitenhuis sees the wit balanced by an uncertainty about his American material seen in the Arcadian imagery depicting Mrs. Beck, which, however, is later transformed into the "pastoral, peaceful, and innocent" view of nature that influences David to mercy (53–54; CT 2, 442).

Buitenhuis analyzes the tale as an early example of James's dislike of businessmen and his interest in fraud, stemming from his fascination with "the psychological problem posed by the idea of possessions" (52). The problem is complicated here, as Dietrichson observes, by the fact that much of the elder brother's unpleasantness, toward David at least, stems from his envy of David's larger fortune (103). David calls his brother Edgar "the most consistent and incorruptible of egotists," and as such Kelley classes him with those who focus their sense of right and wrong more on the doings of others than their own. Even so, Kelley considers him unrealistically portrayed. Similarly, although Anderson and Allen cite the heroine as an early example of the Jamesian "American girl," Kelley dismisses her as unworthy of James (Anderson 125 n.2; Allen 212 n.9; Kelley 128–29).

Mull has argued that Edgar serves as little more than a "backdrop" for David's more subtle dilemma, and it is David's role that has generated the most discussion (21–22). Kelley observes that while he plays a more active role than usual for a narrator, it is his consciousness that provides much of the interest of the situation, an approach James would make more and more his own (129). Buitenhuis also calls attention to the increasingly "sophisticated" use of the narrator, who, first culpably passive—as David himself admits—then overly forceful, involves himself in Guest's own guilty behavior so that his ruminations on it become self-reflexive (55). Mull similarly sees much of the story's irony coming from the resemblance between Guest and David, both somewhat weak dandies concerned mainly with appearance. David, however, is always partly aware of his flaws and manages to redeem himself at the end (18–22). He moves away, in Kraft's view, from what Guest represents to "a more complex vision of life" (43). Andreas, for his part, sympathizes with Guest's unhappiness with the prospect of the marriage (51).

Howells's main objection to the tale was that "somehow the end does not come with a click," and that David was insufficiently "generous" to deserve "that good girl" (404). Walter Wright, too, casts doubt on the genuineness of the happy ending, attributing the narrator's behavior to shame (137). More reasonably, Kelley views the narrator as bringing about "a fairly satisfactory solution" to his problems (129). A 1919 reviewer, noting that he "involuntarily" identified James and the narrator, was pleasantly surprised when the narrator "burst into sympathetic song. How different do you suppose his later novels would have been if he had really done these things in his youth?" Without accepting the biographical commentary, one can still take the point that it is not always appropriate to interpret the young James by the lights of the old. It is certainly unusual for a James character to grow simultaneously in awareness and happiness, but it happens here, despite the inauspicious surroundings.

Works Cited

Primary Works

James, Henry. 1872. "Guest's Confession." *Atlantic Monthly* 30 (October–November): 385–403, 566–83.

———. 1919. *Travelling Companions*. Foreword by Albert Mordell. New York: Boni and Liveright.

Secondary Works

Allen, Elizabeth. 1984. *A Woman's Place in the Novels of Henry James*. New York: St. Martin's.

Anderson, Quentin. 1957. *The American Henry James*. New Brunswick, NJ: Rutgers University Press.

Andreas, Osborn. 1948. *Henry James and the Expanding Horizon: A Study of the Meaning and Basic Themes of James's Fiction*. Seattle: University of Washington Press.

Anon. 1919. Review of *Travelling Companions*. *New Republic* 19 (30 July): 422.

Buitenhuis, Peter. 1970. *The Grasping Imagination: The American Writings of Henry James*. Toronto: University of Toronto Press.

Dietrichson, Jan W. 1969. *The Image of Money in the Amrican Novel of the Gilded Age*. Osto: Universitetsforlaget; New York: Humanities.

Gale, Robert L. [1954] 1964. *The Caught Image: Figurative Language in the Fiction of Henry James*. Chapel Hill: University of North Carolina Press.

Howells, W. D. 1979. *Selected Letters*. Vol. 1: *1852–1872*. Ed. George Arms, Richard H. Ballinger, Christoph K. Lohmann, and John K. Reeves. Boston: Twayne.

James, William. 1992. *The Correspondence of William James*. Vol. 1: *William and Henry: 1861–1884*. Ed. Ignas K. Skrupskelis and Elizabeth M. Berkeley. Charlottesville: University Press of Virginia.

Jones, Granville H. 1975. *Henry James's Psychology of Experience: Innocence, Responsibility, and Renunciation in the Fiction of Henry James*. The Hague: Mouton.

Kelley, Cornelia Pulsifer. [1930] 1965. *The Early Development of Henry James*. Urbana: University of Illinois Press.

Kraft, James. 1969. *The Early Tales of Henry James*. Carbondale: Southern Illinois University Press.

Levy, Leo B. 1957. *Versions of Melodrama: A Study of the Fiction and Drama of Henry James, 1865–1897*. Berkeley: University of California Press.

Leyburn, Ellen Douglass. 1968. *Strange Alloy: The Relation of Comedy to Tragedy in the Fiction of Henry James*. Chapel Hill: University of North Carolina Press.

McElderry, Bruce R., Jr. 1949. "The Uncollected Stories of Henry James." *American Literature* 21 (November): 279–91.

Mull, Donald. 1973. *Henry James's "Sublime Economy": Money as Symbolic Center in the Fiction*. Middletown, CT: Wesleyan University Press.

Putt, S. Gorley. 1966. *Henry James: A Reader's Guide*. Ithaca, NY: Cornell University Press.

Stone, Edward. 1964. *The Battle and the Books: Some Aspects of Henry James*. Athens: Ohio University Press.

Thorp, Willard, ed. 1962. *The Madonna of the Future and Other Early Tales*. New York: New American Library.

Tintner, Adeline R. 1987. *The Book World of Henry James: Appropriating the Classics*. Ann Arbor: UMI Research Press.

Veeder, William. 1975. *Henry James—the Lessons of the Master: Popular Fiction and Personal Style in the Nineteenth Century*. Chicago: University of Chicago Press.

Wagenknecht, Edward. 1984. *The Tales of Henry James*. New York: Frederick Ungar.

Wright, Walter F. 1962. *The Madness of Art: A Study of Henry James*. Lincoln: University of Nebraska Press.

The Impressions of a Cousin

Publication History

"The Impressions of a Cousin" was published in two parts from November to December 1883 in the *Century* magazine. James collected it in book form only once, in *Tales of Three Cities* (1884). One of the few extant manuscripts of a James tale is a signed version in the Pierpont Morgan Library in New York. A brief part of the tale appearing in an article by Caroline Ticknor in 1900 in *Truth* magazine was one of only two holograph facsimiles to appear during James's lifetime (Edel and Laurence, 218). It did not appear as a whole again until the 1920s in Lubbock's edition of the novels and stories.

Circumstances of Composition, Sources, and Influences

James recorded the "germ of a story" for "The Impressions of a Cousin" in his notebook on January 17, 1881, in England. Its source was Anne Thackeray, Lady Ritchie, who, while writing a study of the letter writer Mme de Sévigné, told James of an example of her "unbecoming conduct" in taking the part of her daughter against her granddaughter, who, to cover for her father's having spent her inheritance, was to be sent to a convent. James changes the father to a "guardian or trustee," and in place of the mother's split loyalties creates a heroine torn between love and renunciation. At the end, the guardian, who has fallen in love with her, "discovers that she had been in love with him and that her love had made her eager to forgive the wrong he had done her, and to forego all reparation. But his dishonourable act had made her also blush for her passion and desire to bury it in the cloister" (CN 16).

James, busy at work on *The Portrait of a Lady*, appears to have done nothing more with the idea until another notebook entry dated May 30, 1883. There he has the impetus of a letter from Richard Watson Gilder of the *Century* magazine, needing two shorter tales to precede the already begun *Lady Barbarina*. Recalling the "sufficiently picturesque little *donnée*," he discards the convent (his tale is "too modern") but still has the girl retire "from the world with her property, her wound and her secret." He also adds the narrator cousin, a "type" who serves as companion to the heroine. Indeed, "it is only in her journal that the secret 'transpires'" (CN 22). Booth notes how adding a "reflector" to an already complete idea creates "a new heroine" who not only observes a romance, but is even given one of her own (340–41). Shine discovers another change in the heroine's increased awareness of evil (98–99).

James placed his tale in America, where he had been since the death of his father in December 1882. While Buitenhuis finds James's artistry suffering from his emotional state at the time, Edel sees James employing "vaguely" his difficult new experience as executor of his father's estate (132; *Life* 3, 70). Blackall describes Eunice's fondness for Wagner as an example of cultural local color (118).

Shortly before Mr. Caliph appears, Catherine records the basic configuration of characters: "[Adrian] is a charming creature—a kind of Yankee Donatello. If I could only be his Miriam, the situation would be almost complete, for Eunice is an excellent Hilda" (CT 5, 124). Following her lead, Buitenhuis notes the tale's "half-hearted" reworking and relocating of Hawthorne's *The Marble Faun* (129–30). Gale simply finds the "short, simple" comparison a sign of James's admiration of Hawthorne (107). Tintner argues for a stronger connection, maintaining that much of the story is "ambiguous or even absurd" unless you "insert" Hawthorne's tale in the gaps so that finally even James, feeling his readers could no longer be counted on to perform that operation, omitted the story from the New York Edition. Unlike Buitenhuis, Tintner sees a resemblance between Miriam and Catherine in her "morbid disposition," a description that is something of a joke in the story. More convincingly, she sees James imitating the two crimes of Hawthorne's novel: Adrian paying for a family crime as does Miriam and Catherine's challenge to Adrian echoing Miriam's unspoken command to Donatello to murder. Still, as Tintner concludes, "the moral *consequences*" here are out of proportion (1987, 180–81). Staying with the paradigm of *The Marble Faun*, one might argue that the evil Caliph resembles the mysterious model more than he does Kenyon. Even so, the Hawthorne model is not always helpful. For example, Tintner considers the cause of Catherine's "passionate love" for Adrian in the story absurd, but discarding the analogy there is no need to assume that Catherine is indeed passionately in love.

Like Buitenhuis, Tintner sees Caliph owing less to Hawthorne than to the *Arabian Nights*. An Haroun-al-Raschid, as Catherine calls him, Caliph's ultimate ancestor is, according to Tintner, actually the evil caliph of Beckford's *Vathek* who also inspired Byron. She locates additional contemporary sources for James's modern Caliph in Alphonse Daudet's *Le Nabab* and F. Marion Crawford's *Mr. Isaacs* (1989, 85–90). Caliph also stands in Tintner's reading partly for the Catholic Church that tempts the Americans in *The Marble Faun* (1987, 186). Buitenhuis sees Caliph more as the enemy of the Church, a Satan who reenacts with Catherine the tempting of Eve, and also notes his affinity with both the archetypal wandering Jew and Du Maurier's "exotic" types drawn for *Punch* (130–32). Tintner adds a parallel between Catherine and such Balzacian poor relations as Cousin Bette (1987, 179).

Relation to Other Works

Wegelin connects Caliph's role as an "unfaithful steward" with three works which arose from James's last visit to America: "A Round of Visits," "Crapy Cornelia," and *The Ivory Tower*, while Buitenhuis notes the interest in fraud in *Watch and Ward* and other early works. Wegelin writes that it was America's "lack of 'manners'" that most offended James, but as Buitenhuis notes, that is not Caliph's failing (Wegelin 191 n.10; Buitenhuis 130). In his mannered deceitfulness, he resembles Gilbert Osmond. Catherine's rebuke of him, "for a man who talks about taste!" echoes Isabel's rebuke of Osmond, "for a man who was so fine!" (CT 5, 176). Jones, on the other hand, judges him a complete villian similar to those in "A Light Man" or "Guest's Confession" (124). Harap includes Caliph with Miriam Rooth's father as a Jewish man interested in both art and money, while Levy places the "patriar-chal" character in a different stereotype of Jews as "sensuous and Eastern," seen in James's description of Fanny Assingham as resembling "a pampered Jewess," his "overpowering sexuality" evident also in Mr. Tischbein and Mr. Perriam of *What Maisie Knew* (372; 245).

Buitenhuis compares the artistic and carefree Adrian to Felix of *The Europeans*, while Havens finds his simple "niceness" linking him to Owen Gereth of *The Spoils of Poynton*, Mr. Wendover of *A London Life*, and possi-bly Lord Warburton (Buitenhuis 127; Havens 318). Even more laudatory, Labrie discovers in him the "mingling of aesthetic and moral awareness" James rated most highly, but usually assigned only to secondary characters such as Adrian, Mme Grandoni of *The Princess Casamassima*, or Ralph Touchett, who also secretly gave away a fortune (3–4). Appropriately then, Walter Wright characterizes Adrian as chivalric like Dawling of "Glasses" and Henry Wilmerding of "The Solution" (123).

Jones compares Eunice in her excessive and uncomfortable scrupulous-ness to such characters as Olive Chancellor and Laura Wing, and as someone whose scruples cause great harm, again to Wilmerding in "The Solution" (125–26, 142). Havens compares Catherine as an observer to Rowland Mallett (318; also Buitenhuis 127). Meanwhile, Mrs. Ermine reprises the foolish romance-hungry aunt in *Washington Square*, and Willie Woodley returns from *An International Episode* to be one of Eunice's dinner guests in New York (Gale 206).

Interpretation and Criticism

In his notebook James lamented, "The New York streets are fatal to the imag-ination," and although Edel finds the tale capturing some of the city's local color, Walter Wright has remarked on its "ugliness" (CN 22; CT 5, 11; Wright

73). Outside the city, Buitenhuis argues, the Hudson River provides James with something of the "schema" he normally derived from Europe, and the clichéd comparison Wegelin records Catherine making between the Hudson and the Rhine might be seen as linking the two (Buitenhuis 131; Wegelin 170 n.17). Wagenknecht implies that James gave himself more latitude by making his characters familiar with Europe, an international note Matthiessen and Murdock attribute to James's judging of his audience (188; N 53).

In his planning, James also complained of his theme as "thin and conventional, and wanting in actuality" (CN 22). A contemporary reviewer concurred, finding James not up to snuff as "an impressionist," producing "the most cold and tedious of any of his analyses" (*Critic* 491). The *Athenaeum* objected to James's "trick of always using tertiary hints and leaving the imagination of the reader to fill up the outline." The plot is, as McElderry observes, marked by "false leads" and "contrivance" or, as Putt terms them, the "bandying of emotional bargains," the main bargain being the suspended ending in which Catherine agrees to marry Adrian—if Eunice marries Caliph (McElderry 79; Putt 270). The resultant confusion has created, without any claims of ambiguity, an unusual amount of disagreement about how to "fill up the outline." Critics differ on whether Eunice still loves Caliph, whether Catherine ever loved Adrian, whether he previously loved Eunice, whether either pair will marry, and their chances for happiness if they do. Andreas confuses the matter further by reversing the names of the two cousins (69–70). Nevertheless, Shine predicts a "satisfactory future" for Eunice with Caliph, and Jones gives Catherine and Adrian a "fifty-fifty chance" of happiness (Shine 158; Jones 99). Walter Wright notes the mysteriousness of Eunice's love for Caliph, while Matthiessen and Murdock consider it to lessen when she no longer needs to sacrifice for him (Wright 157). Still, they sense a "strong suggestion" that both couples will marry and speculate that James softened the notebook ending to make the story more appealing to the public (N 53). Buitenhuis concurs, but considers it an "odd" step for Catherine as she has never indicated any particular feeling for Adrian (129). Certainly, as Jones observes, both pairs are formed of opposites, Eunice being driven by conscience, Caliph without one; Catherine driven by consciousness, Adrian by instinct (124).

The *Athenaeum* did acknowledge that James had "the materials of a striking tale." While two of its characters are rather one-note, if a genial one in the case of Adrian, both Catherine and Caliph present complicated cases, and have received weightier attention. Catherine's narration, which Putt calls "a remarkable *tour de force* for a male author," has received plaudits (269; also Tintner 1987, 187). Among the exceptions are Buitenhuis, who judges her an "inadequate" observer into whom James projected his own character, and Matthiessen and Murdock, who object to Catherine's central role, a criticism Havens dismisses as relying on the notebook, not the actual story

(Buitenhuis 127, 129, 132; N 53; also Stone 238). While Nathalia Wright emphasizes the importance to Catherine of her earlier experience of Italy, Havens praises the "gradual, unconscious self-revelation" of her character as it evolves from an "unattractive" self-centeredness to an outgoing appreciation for others, particularly Adrian (Wright 222; also Booth 341). Andreas praises her selflessness in encouraging Adrian to give his money to Eunice when she could have easily gotten it for herself by marrying him (70).

As an artist Catherine responds to the artistic Caliph and as a moralist she fears his lack of a "moral sense" (CT 5, 173). Her preoccupation with her "intimate conviction that he is a Jew" and therefore not a gentleman however, has not been figured into her character by critics (CT 5, 126). Nor has the characterization of Caliph generally been examined in terms of his Jewish identity. While both Buitenhuis and Tintner have pointed to his origin in Jewish stereotypes, Tintner sees him as converted to a "more exotic" Easterner and calls him an "original, florid, and fantastic" character (Buitenhuis 131; Tintner 1987, 185–86). Nevertheless, as Harap states, "the corruption of the Jew, Caliph, and the integrity of his non-Jewish half-brother, Adrian"—a split fitting with the "geminian theme" Putt discerns—is at the heart of the tale (Harap 373; Putt 269). Harap sees in James's fiction a "social condescension and an incapacity to see the Jew as an individual and not a type," a failure that is part of Catherine's makeup as well and that helps cast Caliph as the villain (368–69).

Buitenhuis at least criticizes the "fantasy" nature of Caliph's character. In his reading, James invented the character as a way of getting around the domination of women in American society, and wound up instead with the equally unsatisfactory triumph of the businessman (140). Dietrichson considers the tale notable in containing both men and women who demonstrate "high idealism," financially and emotionally (110). But for Buitenhuis, if the tale could sustain a coherent interpretation, it would read "Business will marry property, and art retreats to Europe" (132). Indeed, the strengths of this flawed tale, in which the characters are placed in a muddle cast in stereotypes, from which they have not completely extracted themselves at the end, do not include an overarching structure whether of literary allusion or independent allegory. Despite the stereotypes they are cast in, it is the characters who retain the most vitality, their motives and their impressions, sometimes revealed and often hidden, as they react to their muddle.

Works Cited

Primary Works

James, Henry. 1883. "The Impressions of a Cousin." *Century Magazine* 27 (November–December): 116–29, 257–75.

————. 1884. "The Impressions of a Cousin." *Tales of Three Cities*. Boston: Osgood; London: Macmillan, 1–117.

————. 1921–23. "The Impressions of a Cousin." *The Novels and Stories of Henry James*. Vol. 24. Ed. Percy Lubbock. London: Macmillan.

Secondary Works

Andreas, Osborn. 1948. *Henry James and the Expanding Horizon: A Study of the Meaning and Basic Themes of James's Fiction*. Seattle: University of Washington Press.

Anon. 1883. Review. "December Magazines." *Critic* (1 December): 491.

Anon. 1884. Review of *Tales of Three Cities. Athenaeum*, no. 2981 (13 December): 67.

Blackall, Jean Frantz. 1965. *Jamesian Ambiguity and "The Sacred Fount."* Ithaca, NY: Cornell University Press.

Booth, Wayne C. [1961] 1983. *The Rhetoric of Fiction*. Chicago: University of Chicago Press.

Buitenhuis, Peter. 1970. *The Grasping Imagination: The American Writings of Henry James*. Toronto: University of Toronto Press.

Dietrichson, Jan W. 1969. *The Image of Money in the American Novel of the Gilded Age*. Oslo: Universitetsforlaget; New York: Humanities.

Edel, Leon, and Dan H. Laurence. [1957] 1982. *A Bibliography of Henry James*. 3d ed. Oxford: Clarendon Press.

Gale, Robert L. 1965. *Plots and Characters in the Fiction of Henry James*. Hamden, CT: Archon.

————. [1954] 1964. *The Caught Image: Figurative Language in the Fiction of Henry James*. Chapel Hill: University of North Carolina Press.

Harap, Louis. 1974. *The Image of the Jew in American Literature*. Philadelphia: The Jewish Publication Society of America.

Havens, Raymond D. 1950. "Henry James' 'The Impressions of a Cousin.'" *Modern Language Notes* 65 (May): 317–19.

Jones, Granville H. 1975. *Henry James's Psychology of Experience: Innocence, Responsibility, and Renunciation in the Fiction of Henry James*. The Hague: Mouton.

Labrie, Ross. 1975. "The Good and the Beautiful in Henry James." *Greyfriar* 16: 3–15.

Levy, Leo B. 1958. "Henry James and the Jews: A Critical Study." *Commentary* 26 (September): 243–49.

McElderry, Bruce R., Jr. 1965. *Henry James*. New York: Twayne.

Putt, S. Gorley. 1966. *Henry James: A Reader's Guide*. Ithaca, NY: Cornell University Press.

Shine, Muriel G. 1969. *The Fictional Children of Henry James*. Chapel Hill: University of North Carolina Press.

Stone, Donald David. 1972. *Novelists in a Changing World: Meredith, James, and the Transformation of English Fiction in the 1880's.* Cambridge, MA: Harvard University Press.

Ticknor, Caroline. 1900. "Characteristic Manuscripts." *Truth* (May): 122–23.

Tintner, Adeline R. 1989. *The Pop World of Henry James: From Fairy Tales to Science Fiction.* Ann Arbor: UMI Research Press.

———. 1987. *The Book World of Henry James: Appropriating the Classics.* Ann Arbor: UMI Research Press. Revised from "'The Impressions of a Cousin': Henry James' Transformation of *The Marble Faun.*" *The Nathaniel Hawthorne Journal* (1987): 205–14.

Wagenknecht, Edward. 1984. *The Tales of Henry James.* New York: Frederick Ungar.

Wegelin, Christof. 1958. *The Image of Europe in Henry James.* Dallas: Southern Methodist University Press.

Wright, Nathalia. 1965. *American Novelists in Italy, The Discoverers: Allston to James.* Philadelphia: University of Pennsylvania Press.

Wright, Walter F. 1962. *The Madness of Art: A Study of Henry James.* Lincoln: University of Nebraska Press.

John Delavoy

Publication History

"John Delavoy" made its first public appearance in the January and February 1898 issues of the London-based *Cosmopolis*. The previous year, in November, James had had it printed as a separate volume—which he judged "very pretty"—by Macmillan in the United States, in order to protect its copyright (*Letters* 4, 66). James originally wanted it to be the "last tale but one" in the 1900 collection *The Soft Side*, but it eventually made its appearance there as the fourth from the last (*Correspondence* 189, 194). Passed over for the New York Edition, it returned to print in Lubbock's edition of the novels and stories in the 1920s.

Circumstances of Composition, Sources, and Influences

In February 1896 the *Century* magazine rejected James's essay "On the Death of Dumas the Younger" because it dared to discuss his works, the editor

Robert Underwood Johnson commenting that it would have been "unobjectionable" if it had remained "merely personal." James was struck by the contradictions of such an approach to great writers: "They want to *seem* to deal with him because he is famous—and he is famous because he wrote certain things which they won't for the world have intelligibly mentioned." To turn his outrage at the "whole loathsomely prurient and humbugging business" into a story, James imagined two young men of opposing views, a daughter of a "great defunct," and to give it "DRAMA" a "furious magazine-hunt, newspaper-hunt for a PORTRAIT," all told "this time" not by a first person narrator but an outside observer (CN 154–55). James's essay on Dumas would be published within a month by both the New York and Boston *Herald* as well as the *New Review*, before being included in his *Notes on Novelists* (*Life* 4, 156). Even that success did not revise his estimate of the young critic's chances, and Krook cites the story as showing why James was hesitant to treat the sexual themes of his stories fully, dependent as they were on magazine publication (369). James made the forces against him even stronger in the story by confronting him, as Matthiessen and Murdock observe, not with just another young man but a powerful editor (N 247). James made two additional cast changes, converting the daughter to a sister and the outside observer to a first-person narrator.

James was evidently not totally averse to the publishing of an author's portrait as long as the author's work was also treated. Among various magazine appearances of his likeness, his portrait by John Singer Sargent appeared in the second issue of *The Yellow Book* (Hyde 53). Emphasis solely on appearance, however, was bad in his view, and Tintner associates Beston's concern with surfaces with the Impressionist painters' emphasis on ocular vision (363).

Kermode points to the story's opening with the failure of a friend's play as drawing on memories of the opening of *Guy Domville* (29).

Relation to Other Works

In his notebook entry, James pictured the tale joining his "series of *small* things on the life and experiences of men of letters, the group of the little 'literary' tales" (CN 154). Putt observes that while "The Figure in the Carpet" soothes the neglected author and criticizes the critic, here the neglected critic is allowed his triumph (233).

Anderson associates the title *The Cynosure* with Ambient's reading of *The Observer*, both showing the egoism of those associated with them (147). Stevenson distinguishes the unpleasant journalists of such shorter works as *The Reverberator*, *The Papers*, and "John Delavoy," each of whom is shown as they work, from the heroes of the novels *The Wings of the Dove* and *The*

Ambassadors, who are shown primarily apart from their work (30). Tintner classes Beston with other "bad" editors—Morrow in "The Death of the Lion" and Bousefield in "The Next Time" (374). Edel also links it with "The Death of the Lion" as showing that the public want only a "monstrous newspaper image" of the writer, not his work (CT 9, 8).

Goetz connects the tale with "The Real Right Thing" and *The Aspern Papers* in that the "external mediator" or idol of the protagonist is safely dead, thereby removing the possibility of rivalry. Here, as in "The Death of the Lion," the narrator's love interest and his artistic ideal are conveniently contiguous, allowing the unusual happy ending (161–62). Similarly, Rawlings sees Beston and the narrator vying to supplant John Delavoy as the focus of Miss Delavoy's life, "to exorcise his spirit by having his work become known" (xx). Less cynically, Jones compares the way respect for the dead is rewarded with mutual happiness here and in "Sir Dominick Ferrand" (237).

In "The Death of the Lion," the narrator at the opera with Fanny Hurter taunts her to look at Paraday under the cover of the crowd. She stoically refuses. Both the narrator—being "momentarily gross"—and the woman with him here make full use of their opportunity at a play to gaze their fill at the sister of John Delavoy.

In tracing the evolution of James's use of point of view, Tintner sees this as the first tale to distinguish between superficial sight and perception. As a result she calls the tale a "trial run" for *The Sacred Fount*, where the in-depth examinations of the narrator are contrasted with the artist Obert's concentration on surfaces (363). (See "The Real Right Thing.")

Interpretation and Criticism

Remarking on the intensity James brings to the subject in the story, Wagenknecht wonders how James managed to get a magazine to publish the tale, given its attack on publishers (189). *Cosmopolis*, however, was hardly one of the "big" magazines Wagenknecht speaks of. Also, since, as McElderry observes, in his complaint against editorial restrictions James shows the editors as virtual slaves of their readers' ignorance and philistinism (124), it leaves room for a more heroic, independent editor. Such an editor would be indifferent to the profit that motivates Beston's concern for his readers. While there is little to choose from between Beston and his readers, whose taste is at least sincerely ignorant rather than mercenarily so, James had recent experience of other types of editors, including Henry Harland of *The Yellow Book* and Herbert Stone of *The Chap-Book* (Ford 78).

Such an expansive outlook, however, is present in the tale only in the characters of the narrator and Miss Delavoy, whom Delbaere-Garant accordingly sees as speaking for James (217). Kappeler indeed sees James in this tale demonstrating the "strong bond" between the writer and the "true" critic whose writing recognizes the distinction between an artist and his work (160–61). While Rawlings indicates that Miss Delavoy may not object to the fuss Beston creates about her brother as it brings him fame (xx), there is little indication of this in the story. Initially believing Beston to share her adulatory view of her brother, she comes finally to realize his actual opinion of his work, and declares bluntly, ". . . you make me very sick," breaking off relations with him and seeking to retrieve the portrait (CT 9, 437).

Putt also seeks to qualify the force of the tale by noting that John Delavoy shared many of James's own qualities as a writer, a fact he finds self-indulgent (233). It makes a certain sense, however, that James should create a writer he could admire to defend, although the writer that began the tale, Dumas the Younger, was not one James praised without exception. Far from viewing James as self-indulgent, Kermode sees him taking a "bantering, ironic" approach to a topic that might well have made him bitter (29–30). At the same time, Tintner's reading of the name "Delavoy" as evoking the French phrase "de la voie" (of the view) and the word "voir" (to see) connects him with a cardinal James virtue—perceptive sight. She reads the tale accordingly with a focus on point of view. In her reading, the depth of insight evidenced by Miss Delavoy and the narrator, who are the artist's adherents, is contrasted with the superficial view of Beston, who sports a monocle, is interested more in being seen—in being the "cynosure"—than in seeing, and circles round subjects rather than looking into them. Rawlings, for his part, concentrates on the initial failure in vision of the narrator shown in his mistaken suppositions about the identity of Miss Delavoy and Beston during the opening scene at the play (xix).

Anderson depicts the central contrast in the tale as that between true creation and static image-making, as represented in the editor's preference of the picture of Delavoy over his actual life's work (143, 194). James's opposite preference is clear. Gage points out how the picture's being "smaller than life" indicates that the sister is correct in her belief that "He *was* his work," not his personal life (47).

The enemy here is not, however, without resources. Kermode particularly praises the portrayal of Mr. Beston, who is both "powerful and dangerous" in his denial of sexuality for the sake of subscriptions (29–30). According to Tintner, he also gets his way, in a worldy sense at least, getting the "best" of Miss Delavoy (372). Gage also declares the editor victorious, although he remarks that while winning the battle over the picture he also loses Miss Delavoy. Although Gage may see that victory as less important—he finds the love triangle "superimposed" on the issue of identity (48–49)—it provides the final note of the tale.

One of the few mature artist tales not to be included in the New York Edition, its omission has been something of an issue. Edgar sees James leaving the tale out of the edition because it did not meet the standards of the other artist tales (158). Kermode, on the other hand, admires the tale, hypothesizing that James omitted it simply because there were already too many similar tales (29–30). Before the New York Edition came to be, a reviewer had found the tale masterful (*Speaker* 626). It is perhaps "smaller than life," like Miss Delavoy's portrait of her brother, a largely interior work of drawing rooms despite its opera scene. If much of the energy in the tale comes from Beston, its charm is that of the miniature, a beauty that does not put itself forward but is still felt, rather like the character of Miss Delavoy herself.

Works Cited

Primary Works

James, Henry. 1897. *John Delavoy*. New York: Macmillan.

———. 1898. "John Delavoy." *Cosmopolis Magazine* 9 (January–February): 1–21, 317–32.

———. 1900. "John Delavoy." In *The Soft Side,* 202–41. London: Methuen; New York: Macmillan.

———. 1921–23. "John Delavoy." In *The Novels and Stories of Henry James*. Vol. 27. Ed. Percy Lubbock. London: Macmillan.

———. 1993. *The Correspondence of Henry James and the House of Macmillan, 1877–1914*. Ed. Rayburn S. Moore. Baton Rouge: Louisiana State University Press.

Secondary Works

Anderson, Quentin. 1957. *The American Henry James*. New Brunswick, NJ: Rutgers University Press.

Anon. 1900. Review of *The Soft Side. The London Speaker*. Reprinted in *Current Literature* 29 (November): 626–27.

Delbaere-Garant, Jeanne. 1970. *Henry James: The Vision of France*. Paris: Société d'Editions Les Belles Lettres.

Edgar, Pelham. [1927] 1964. *Henry James, Man and Author*. New York: Russell & Russell.

Ford, Ford Madox. 1913. *Henry James: A Critical Study*. London: Martin Secker.

Gage, Richard P. 1988. *Order and Design: Henry James' Titled Story Sequences*. New York: Petter Lang.

Goetz, William R. 1986. *Henry James and the Darkest Abyss of Romance*. Baton Rouge: Louisiana State University Press.

Hyde, H. Montgomery. 1969. *Henry James at Home*. New York: Farrar, Straus.

Jones, Granville H. 1975. *Henry James's Psychology of Experience: Innocence, Responsibility, and Renunciation in the Fiction of Henry James*. The Hague: Mouton.

Kappeler, Susanne. 1980. *Writing and Reading in Henry James*. New York: Columbia University Press.

Kermode, Frank, ed. 1986. *The Figure in the Carpet and Other Stories*. London: Penguin.

Krook, Dorothea. [1962] 1967. *The Ordeal of Consciousness in Henry James*. New York: Cambridge University Press.

McElderry, Bruce R., Jr. 1965. *Henry James*. New York: Twayne.

Putt, S. Gorley. 1966. *Henry James: A Reader's Guide*. Ithaca, NY: Cornell University Press.

Rawlings, Peter, ed. 1984. *Henry James's Shorter Masterpieces*. Vol. 2. Totowa, NJ: Barnes & Noble.

Stevenson, Elizabeth. [1949] 1981. *The Crooked Corridor: A Study of Henry James*. New York: Octagon.

Tintner, Adeline R. 1985. "Henry James' Two Ways of Seeing." *AB Bookman's Weekly* 75, no. 3 (21 January): 363–74.

Wagenknecht, Edward. 1984. *The Tales of Henry James*. New York: Frederick Ungar.

The Jolly Corner

Publication History

As James was preparing "The Jolly Corner" for the New York Edition, it had not yet found a magazine home. In the end, however, it made its first appearance in December 1908 in the first issue of *The English Review*, whose editor, Ford Madox Ford, wanted a "not too long" story from James (Garnett x; Edel 1970, 724).

Circumstances of Composition, Sources, and Influences

The story was evidently finished in the summer, as Theodora Bosanquet records James causing "great tribulation" by losing the manuscript temporarily (Hyde 171). Edel identifies it with the tale James refers to in a letter to his agent Pinker in August 1906. James wrote, "I have an excellent little idea through not having slept a wink last night *all* for thinking of it, and must therefore at least get the advantage of striking while the iron is hot." Its title was originally "The Second House" (*Life* 5, 312–13).

In 1953 Edel found no notebook entry for the tale (584). The relevance of a notebook entry from February 5, 1895, was first noted by Krook and then Tremper (Krook 334n; Tremper 69–70). In this entry, James pondered "the situation of the man of genius who, in some accursed hour of his youth, has bartered away the finest vision of that youth and lives ever afterward in the shadow of the bitterness of the regret." He then adds the idea that the man recovers "a little of the lost joy, of the Dead Self" in some woman "who knows what that self was, in whom it still lives a little." It seemed to James banal, but possible if taken from the woman's point of view. He supposes that the man would have to die "in the flesh" in the tale, but ends by saying there probably "isn't much in it: it would take a deuce of a deal of following up" (CN 112–13). Fogel, while acknowledging differences between the tale and the entry, considers it the true source, arguing that to "rescue the idea from banality," James hit on the idea of making it the man's "worst" not "best" self that lives on (191–92). Perhaps prodded by Fogel, Edel and Powers connect the entry to the tale in their new edition of the notebooks (CN 113).

Edel and Powers also point to two earlier notebook entries in relation to the story. The first, on January 22, 1879, pictures a "long locked" door and a persistent knocking that coincides with the troubles of the house's occupant, who finally breaks open the door one day "and the trouble ceases—as if the spirit had desired to be admitted, that it might interpose, redeem and protect" (CN 10). An entry recorded in Rome on May 16, 1899 posits a similar idea of a young man followed "*everywhere*" by a knocking at his door (CN 183).

In 1900 Howells had requested from James a work of 50,000 words with an "international ghost"—a combination that also fits, as both Carl Smith and Strout have commented, with "The Jolly Corner" (Smith 417; Strout 1979, 51). The idea appealed to James, who had already been "attacking" the plot of *The Sense of the Past*, although James's first notebook entry on the topic indicates his worry that the space allowed would not admit of the complex subject. He recorded the need for "something *simpler*"—but not "of less dignity"—and turned to "something in the general glimmer of the notion of what the quasi-grotesque Europeo-American situation, in the way of the gruesome, may, *pushed to the full and right expression of its grotesqueness*, have to give," writing "that general formula haunts me, and as a *morality* as well as a terror, an idea as well as a ghost." He recalls having pictured while traveling by train "3 or 4 'scared' and slightly modern American figures moving against the background of three or four European *milieux*, different European conditions, out of which their obsession, their visitation is projected" as they search for "something or other," and he considers an American "terror" "to wind up" the series. The idea shares elements with "The Jolly Corner," and the trip back to America may have suggested to James that the desired simplification could come by keeping the tale in America. One could even stretch a resemblance between the name of his future protagonist and James's destination when the "picture" first came to him—Brighton (CN 189–91).

In 1914, returning to work on the unfinished novel *The Sense of the Past*, James recalled "filching" a piece from it for this tale (CN 505; see also Frantz 225 n.3). The tale, in Edel's phrase, is "derived" from the novel that was to remain unfinished (584). Both works, in turn, are generally connected to a dream James recalled in his 1913 autobiography of putting to flight a ghostly figure pursuing him through the Galerie d'Apollon of the Louvre. According to his recollection, "The lucidity, not to say the sublimity, of the crisis had consisted of the great thought that I, in my appalled state, was probably still more appalling than the awful agent, creature or presence." The idea of "turning the tables" from the dream recurs in both tale and novel, although Edel points out that in the tale Brydon is really more appalled than is the ghost (also Stevenson 161; Briggs 116). Edel sees the association nevertheless as appropriate, since Brydon like James and like Ralph Pendrel later is "searching for himself in a past which both attracts and appals." The fleeing figure he identifies with James's older brother, William, of whom James wrote, "I never for all the time of childhood and youth in the least caught up with him or overtook him. He was always round the corner and out of sight . . ." (also Rogers 1956, 435; Mackenzie 366–67). In the story, Edel writes, James is "laying the ghost of his old rivalry," realizing that "he did not have to be William; he could be himself." Edel speculates the dream may have marked the end of James's depression in 1910. If so, the story antedated the dream. However, as Edel records, James related a version of the dream in 1909 to Ottoline Morrell, when he also told her of a dream in which he encountered an old man in a chair and, conquering his initial fear, declared to him, "You're afraid of me, you coward" (1970, 724; *Life* 1, 75–79; *Life* 5, 315–16, 445). Lichtenberg offers the possiblility that the Galerie dream may have been an "old and recurring" one (87–89). Quentin Anderson comments on Brydon's need of Alice's help, in contrast to the solitary achievement of the dream figure, attributing it to the difference between artists and "lesser men" (180–81). James himself never directly associated dream and tale.

In Edel's assessment, the tale is one of James's "most autobiographical" (1970, 721). One aspect of its autobiography is its evaluation of America as a viable place for a sensitive man to live. At the time James wrote "The Jolly Corner," he was also at work on *The American Scene* and its treatment of his return to his homeland. In discussing its connection with the recent trip, Josephson discerns in the tale a "mood of confession, stirred by the remembered places revisited, the fated youth relived" (279). In June 1906 Hamlin

Garland visited James, who, according to Garland, declared that he had made a fundamental mistake in cutting himself off from America (*Life* 5, 312–13). Graham Greene writes, "The idea that he should have stayed and faced his native scene never left him; he never ceased to wonder whether he had not cut himself off from the source of deepest inspiration" ("Aspect" 37). According to Edel, James in the tale is trying "to see himself in the American past *as he might have been* had he stayed at home." While seeing James recognizing in the tale his own "ambivalence" toward the international theme, Edel emphasizes what he understands as the story's proving of the truth that James's cosmopolitan art found its appropriate fruit abroad. He objects consequently to Van Wyck Brooks's attempt to "invert" the meaning of the maimed fingers from what he sees as the indication that America would have "maimed" James and his writing (1967, 332–33; *Life* 4, 336; *Life* 5, 315; also Briggs 116). Buitenhuis counters that the loss is probably meant to be the result of a gun shot, as a symbol of America's violence (218). Earlier, Wilson read the missing fingers as having been "shot away" during the Civil War and sees the figure indicating that "'commitment' . . . to the war is supposed to have implied commitment to the commercialized society that followed it" (662–63). Strout suggests possible associations with James's brother's wounds in the Civil War or his own "obscure injury" at the time (1980, 106). Walter Wright, however, objects to reading the tale as an autobiographical treatment of the "pros and cons" of America vs. Europe, and attributes such readings to a false understanding of James's realism (50, 200).

In his analysis of the tale's treatment of "the central myth" of James's life, Edel links as its two parts the juxtaposition of America and Europe with "the question of his personal identity" (1970, 721). In the many readings of the tale, it is the personal—indeed the psychoanalytical—half of the myth that has received the emphasis. Most interpretations emphasize the psychoanalytic—rather than historical—angle of biography. Indeed, several critics see the tale as written in a manner that demands such a reading. Mackenzie, for example, judges some of it "so unrealistic as to be intelligible only as imaginative psychology" (359). Henry Nash Smith locates in the story a "combination of obscurity with almost hysterical strain in the language," which he attributes to "a charge of autobiographical emotion that James has failed to deal with fully" (125).

Several critics, however, have sought to make clear the obscurity. The earliest, Rosenzweig, looked at the tale in comparison with "The Story of a Year." The "ghost" in "The Jolly Corner," Rosenzweig writes, was brought into existence in the earlier tale with the death of John Ford, who himself stood for James. Similarly, Brydon's lost fingers represent Ford's wounds, which represented James's "obscure hurt." In a new century, Brydon and James are attempting, unlike Ford, who succumbed to his wounds, to "rectify the past."

James's memories of the war, Rosenzweig argues, were revived by his trip to America, even as his review of his work for the New York Edition reacquainted him with the early tale. Indeed, Rosenzweig asserts that "The Jolly Corner" represents in the New York Edition the "most radical revision" of an early tale, as James intended it to stand in for the absent "The Story of a Year" (103–5). Rosenzweig's reading has had considerable influence. Fadiman, although he offers a possibly "more general interpretation," summarizes Rosenzweig's reading enthusiastically—noting also that the tale's "auto-psychoanlysis," because unconscious, allows James "to treat his material artistically and with seeming detachment" (642–43). Edel, too, argues that James in the story had "banished" ghosts by writing of them, and could now "assert his recaptured self" in works that would continue to treat his American past (*Life* 5, 315–17).

Rogers follows the lead of Rosenzweig and Edel, reading the tale in terms of Freudian imagery to trace the "neurotic patterns which Henry James wove into the fabric of his art." Declaring Brydon's fear exaggerated, he attributes the disproportion to its reflection of the displaced "affects" of the Galerie dream. Translating the symbols, the house becomes the mother figure or womb, while the contrasting apartments are one of the tale's many phallic symbols. Moneymaking is associated with sexual activity, and with the active man or alter ego whom Alice "prefers" and toward whom Brydon is ambivalent. Brydon himself is characterized by a "childish interest" in sex, having renounced sexual relations for Alice as a mother figure. His failure to open the door is "indicative of impotence or castration" as is the "dangling double eyeglass" and the Id figure's missing fingers, which "belong in fact to the real Brydon." In the end, Brydon regresses, and returns to dependence on the mother, Alice. His situation reflects James's, according to Rogers, who sees James's early "obscure hurt" as psychosomatic, an excuse to avoid war and a "normal male role." James, he concludes, was "haunted by the beast" because he had failed to resolve his Oedipal complex satisfactorily and so remained fixated on his mother. Into "the phantasy of his writing" he poured "the tremendous energy" of his desire to possess the mother he could not possess in life (1956, 427–53). Later, Rogers would see Brydon's defense of "sexual repression" falling apart from the combined stimuli of his return home. Brydon then falls back on "projecting," attributing to the alter ego the virility he both desires and fears, hoping to gain control over it by separating it without "repudiating it." The end is still in regression (1970, 72). Roger's Freudian focus can seem narrow at times. He can see no reason, for example, why the alter ego should be encountered in the house apart from the sexual imagery he ascribes to it, and flatly declares of Brydon's mention of unopened letters, that it implies "but one thing, namely, that James never had sexual relations with a woman" (1956, 429, 441).

While continuing the reading of the tale as psychological autobiography, Geismar objects strongly to Rosenzweig and his followers, maintaining that

James is not reconsidering a choice that he never doubted, but egotistically deciding he could have succeeded at home or abroad. James returned to America, he contends, not to "work through" such traumas, but to "confirm" how right he was to leave. The house in the tale, he argues, does indeed represent the "locked room of the Jamesian unconscious," but not the "death of passion," as James never even got to that stage, but remained at an immature, even infantile level. Thus, we have Brydon voyeuristically revisiting the family bedrooms. Brydon's "jumping" at the idea of "discretion" to leave the door closed on the ghost, his avoidance of self-knowledge, Geismar takes as the key to James's works, which, he maintains, treat complex situations but evade acknowledging the human passions that motivate them (355–64).

Arguing that there is no need to adopt such "orthodox Freudian views" to recognize James's autobiographical depiction of a "hero fighting for a passionate as well as esthetical reintegration of himself," Bier still keeps the emphasis on the latter part of the tale's correspondences to James's "career and psychology." Observing that Alice shares the name of James's sister and his mother, Bier calls her a "double wish-fulfilling character—both the patient and knowing mother and also a fantasied version of his own ego, reconciling him to that part of himself which had kept him from her so long" (323–24). Delbaere-Garant gives even greater emphasis to the interplay between life and art, seeing the young James's "explorations" together with his brother in Paris as analogous to Brydon's in the jolly corner. In both is what James called a sense of "mystery"—something about to happen. For James the discovery would be of "style"—of "the reality of creation, with the enormous competitive power gathered there." Unlike Brydon in his encounter with "the thing *done*," James was young enough, writes Delbaere-Garant, to defeat the ghost (594).

Keeping the emphasis on James as artist, Mays returns it to the context of nationality. He reads the tale as a "kind of psychological parable of Henry James's lifelong anxieties about his personal success" in "specifically American and personal terms." The alter ego represents in Mays's view not only money but "life," making Brydon aware of "how equivocal a figure he has cut over the years." It was an awareness, Mays contends, shared by James, whose anxiety began with a sense of the "uniqueness" of the James family, cut off from typical American life by their spurning of business and conventional religion. Feeling inferior to both his business-minded peers and the soldiers of the Civil War, James saw both exemplifying the "active, competitive life, American style." At the same time, James himself was highly ambitious, not in business, but in art. Brydon, he asserts, is marked by the same "fear-desire" seen in the autobiography's description of the Louvre with its striking antitheses. While acknowledging the seeming difference in Brydon's collapse, Mays questions the reading of the tale as one of defeat. Its "curious coda," in which Brydon takes "refuge" with Alice, Mays suggests, follows

James's own experience. Even as James first sought money and fame in the theatre and then returned to the Muse, whose "tenderness of embrace" he spoke of in his notebooks, so Brydon returns to Alice, the muse of the story. Mays does not stop, however, with a reading of the conclusion as retreat, seeing art in James as also a "bridge to life." Brydon in the tale is said to return from his encounter with the alter ego with a "treasure of intelligence"; James wrote of himself that he had brought from his encounter with the theatre "a treasure of experience, of wisdom, of acquired material." At the Louvre, Mays writes, James saw art and life as one, even as his "success." Art can also reconcile the conflicts of life. Alice as muse says of the alter ego, "I *could* have liked him . . . I had accepted him," and so James learned that through art he could accept the businessman as a subject worthy of pity.

Mackenzie provides a less triumphant reading of the tale as James's "reviewing of his career at about this time, his 'dying of shame' for its conditional, pyrrhic monumentality, and his final, reluctant settling for it." Even so, he refers to the house and the skyscraper together as representing "James's own dynastic house of fiction" (359, 362). Lichtenberg follows Edel's reading of sibling rivalry in the memory of the Louvre, the dream about it, and the tale, but discerns two problems rather than one. The first, James's relationship to William, Lichtenberg writes, he never mastered, but the second, the relationship to the power and glory of art, he did. Still, Lichtenberg sees James characterized by a "lack of confidence" transcended in the dream and featured as the "central theme" of "The Jolly Corner." While the framing section is a "new invention," the middle section, as he points out, mostly elaborates on the imagery of the dream. But Lichtenberg points to another addition in the consideration of suicide. In his view, the issue stems not from James's youth or dream, but from his relationship with Constance Fenimore Woolson, who had died after a fall—or leap—from a window. Lichtenberg suggests that James imagined what could have led Fenimore to such an act, even as in the mention of "abject shame" he inserts some of his own feeling. The figure Brydon finally confronts offers resemblances not only to James himself, but to his brother and particularly his father, whom Lichtenberg sees left a "frightened, dysfunctional father" by his 1844 breakdown. Henry, as a result, turned to "grandiose figures" such as Napoleon for substitute fathers. In the memory of the trip to the Louvre Lichtenberg also detects signs of castration anxiety, homosexual inclinations, "primal-scene fantasies," and images of birth, arguing that in the story Brydon denies the alter ego in order to protect himself against his own sexuality. Even so, Lichtenberg acknowledges, this was not the way James himself would have read his dream, nor the main way in which he would have thought of his tale, which depicts not birth but "*rebirth*"—even as it switches from the "tragic-heroic" mode of the dream to an ironic one.

In Strout's view, it is not the tale but the dream of the Louvre that is wish fulfillment, the "turning of the tables" becoming in the story "only a passing thought." Citing Freud's belief that both love and work are "psychic imperatives," Strout focuses on the latter, along the way taking frequent exception to previous Freudian readings, which, he argues, are often intended simply to illustrate a theory and are invalid without the support of the patient's free associations—unattainable in James's case. More particularly, he finds that these readings "minimize" James's productivity, his "generous treatment of his siblings and friends," and his relative stability. He disagrees more particularly with Edel's casting of William as the ghost, and sees the "sibling rivalry" Edel locates in the tale less a matter of "oedipal terms" than a "larger identity issue" including one's choice of country (1980, 108). Conceding that Edel is "helpful" in connecting the ghost with the "enterprising side" of James, he sees James's try at the theatre as more relevant than his work on the New York Edition. Even so, he writes, the tale's criticism of Brydon's desire for power "functions autobiographically" as James's criticism of his own ambition for a "profitable success." But James's own recovery from theatrical failure, Strout contends, was "more heroic" than Brydon's adventure. It was not, however, permanent. Strout finds in James's renewed depression later, after the failure of the revival of his plays, an indication that he "did not fully exorcise the ghost in his soul." The flaw he could see in Brydon, he could not eliminate from himself. Thus, while contending that critics too often blur Brydon and James, Strout still sees a link between dream and tale in their "ambivalent vision of power." Noting the resemblance between the floor at the Louvre and the black and white squares of Brydon's family home, he observes how the Galerie in the dream is "the bridge over to style," just as the squares are Brydon's "education in style." In each tale, too, the recognition of the floor is part of the process of waking from a nightmare. Strout points to a punning rhyme between Napoleon—the symbol of power in James's dream —and the Galerie d'Apollon itself (1979, 47–52). One might add a further pun between Louvre and l'œuvre, a pun that returns the focus to the achieved work.

Miller writes that James appeared to experience his troubled relationship with America "as an aspect of his involvement with his family" (234). Strout also notes the link of "family feelings" and nationality, returning to the tale to examine the latter. The dates within the tale—Brydon leaves New York at twenty-three, returns at fifty-six after thirty-three years—provide a "numerical mirror image" of James, who left New York at thirty-two, returned at sixty-five, and published the story after thirty-three years. This Strout finds fitting in a tale of an alter ego. In the tale, Strout writes, James discovered a method of showing the "counterpoint between his repulsion from modern America and his lyrical nostalgic memories." By her sympathy for the other Brydon,

Alice becomes a "qualifying foil" for the condemnatory view of Brydon, demonstrating a "tolerance" that appears to come from her "insider's wisdom." Again Strout points to James's renewed depression in 1910, taking it as evidence that the reconciliation with America Edel sees in the tale was an uncertain one (1980, 106–8; also 1979, 51).

The tale, is, Strout admits, "profoundly autobiographical," a "psychoanalyst's gold mine," as if seeing his actual birthplace gone, James had allowed himself a "free fantasy of the hypothetic rescued identity" of home. At the same time, he cautions that the story is also a "quagmire," particularly in the differences between the hero and James, who returned from America to a bachelor writer's life in England. Not only can the story be read without the autobiographical "correspondences," asserts Strout, but the "correspondences" are "richer than the conventional Freudian categories" critics offer. He criticizes Rosenzweig, for example, for having "reduced" the ghost to "castration anxiety," arguing that it was William not Henry who had a "long, troubled, overidentification with his father" (1980, 105–8). Miller, too, while noting the tale's parallels to the oedipal "family romance" with the "hostile father," judges the tale typical of the era of "sons and lovers" (234). Earlier, Quentin Anderson had dissented from the view of the tale as "an account of uncontrolled experience" (180). Stovall objected more strongly that the autobiographical significance of the tale is "irrelevant." In his view, the tale is neither a reconciliation with America, as Rosenzweig argues, or, as others have argued, a justification for leaving it. It is, he contends, harder than that to tell James's attitude to "the real America." Even so, Stovall writes, James "could hardly have believed seriously that a life in America would have made of him something monstrous." His brother William, for example, was not monstrous. At the same time, James was not likely to have condemned his life and work in Europe as "wasted years." The story, he concludes, has "sufficient weight of meaning without our laying upon it the incubus of Freudian symbolism" (84).

Rovit declares that Brydon is "manifestly *not* Henry James." While he accedes to critics the right to use psychoanalytical approaches, he discredits the use of literature to psychoanalyze. Accepting some of the parallels between Brydon and James—he remarks on the relationship between Brydon's monocle, James's own monocle, William's poor eyesight, and his father's amputated leg—he still finds Edel's "too sweeping an identification." In particular, he thinks such an identification fails to account sufficiently for the implication that the alter ego tempts Brydon with suicide or for the relationship between Brydon and Alice (71 n.8; 72 n.12). Similarly, Hocks judges Edel's view that the relationship with William is illustrated in the story as not so much inaccurate as insufficient (246 n.25).

Other autobiographical readings focus more on the emotional life of the older James. In Tremper's view, the tale reflects James's new acknowledgment of and capacity for love, the result of his relationship with Jocelyn Persse. She also observes that Brydon in the tale is fifty-six, the age at which James met Hendrik Andersen. In the maternal image of Brydon and Alice at the end she sees "a touching expression of James's discomfort with or incomprehension of sexual love between man and woman" (70, 74). To Terrie, the terror in the story stems from James's own "troubled times" in the 1890s, marked by his failure as a playwright and the deaths of his sister, Alice, and of Woolson. As he approached his sixties, Terrie writes, James was plagued by "doubts about the shape of his life," particularly about leaving America (14–15). While taking exception to the general view that Woolson was in love with James, Moore sees "The Jolly Corner" as one of James's works that may show her influence. Although their relationship may have been closer to that represented in "The Beast in the Jungle," Moore suggests that James may have thought that with "more awareness on his part and more forcefulness on hers" it could have resembled the conclusion to "The Jolly Corner." She also sees James in the tale perhaps responding to Woolson's criticism that he did not show clearly enough that his heroines were "really in love" (87–90).

Focusing on James's professional life, Wegelin finds Brydon's discovery of his aptitude for making money echoing James's own learning that he could make money—"a pound a minute—like Patti!"—by his lectures in America (155). That James's own discovery was belated is natural, given that James's father was, as Tuveson writes, "uneasy about what most fathers wanted"— their sons' professional success. Instead, James writes in *Notes of a Son and Brother*, "What we were to do instead was just to *be* something, something unconnected with specific doing, something free and uncommitted, something finer in short than being *that*, whatever it was, might consist of." However, since Brydon's life of "being" is at first simply selfish "hedonism," Tuveson judges it uncertain whether the tale is for James "an act of atonement" for having wanted to succeed as a writer against his father's wishes (275–76). As Edel sees it, even as Brydon discovered his talent as a builder, James "remodel[ed]" his writings into the New York Edition (*Life* 5, 315–16). In revising his works, Caramello argues, James would have repeatedly confronted his ghosts even as Brydon does (305).

Seeing less of a parallel between Brydon with his "scandalous" life and his creator, Buitenhuis focuses instead on the shared sense of place. He particularly remarks on James's witnessing the destruction of his Washington Square birthplace and his Boston home in Ashburton Place (211–12). Shelden takes up the comparison by referring to the tale as the "commemorative table" James had wished for in *The American Scene* (124). Tintner discerns in the tale James's "regret at missing the experience of living in New York" as well as his sadness at the loss of Old New York and its architectural legacy. She locates in the tale tributes to still existing buildings, particularly the house of Mrs. Mary Cadwalader Jones, James's primary residence while in New York in

1905. A letter of thanks to Mrs. Jones, as Tintner remarks, anticipates the tale in its phrasing. In it James recalls the "dear East Eleventh Street 'first-floor-back' hours" and tells her: "it's astonishing, it's prodigious, how I find my spirit gratefully haunting them always or rather how insidiously turning the tables they, the mystic locality itself, haunt and revisit my own departed identity" (1976, 402, 406–9). There's an allusion to a Boston house as well, according to Edel, who sees James associating the name Alice with the idea of "home," the home of his sister-in-law, Alice, being on Irving Street even as the fictional Alice lives on Irving Place (1970, 723).

When James was a baby, his father had experienced what he called a "vastation"—a kind of breakdown in which he first sensed a presence in the house sending out from his "fetid personality influences fatal to life" and found himself "reduced from a state of firm, vigorous, joyful manhood to one of almost helpless infancy" (*Life* 1, 30). His brother William had a similar experience while viewing an epilectic patient, and realizing, "*That shape am I . . .* potentially." The relationship between Brydon's encounter with his frightening other self and the experiences of his father and brother have often been noted (e.g., Blackmur [1974] 1983, 99; Rogers 1956, 445; Banta 1972, 150; Sicker 117). All three, Strout observes, were associated with "vocational crises" (1980, 106). Yeazell adds to the series James's sister's recollection of loneliness pursuing her through the house like a "material presence" after their father's death. Alice, not unlike Brydon, "longed to flee in to the fire men next door" (24). Quentin Anderson points to correspondences with Henry James Sr.'s thinking as well as his experience. Brydon's awakening at the end of a "grey passage" he finds reminiscent of James Sr.'s "figure of man as a kind of conduit," even as his symbolic death and rebirth is reminiscent of his belief that death is "the state of those more in love with themselves than with God and their neighbors" (178–79). MacDonald cites Brydon's objections to everyone's demand for his opinions on the grounds that his "'thoughts' would still be almost altogether about something that concerns only myself" as a questioning of the value of objectivity with which William would sympathize (95). Hocks compares the image of the house as a "great glass bowl" to William's metaphor in "Human Immortality" of the brain as a "dome" of glass (211). Shelden connects the tale's images of the jungle with the frequent jungle imagery in sister Alice's journals (124 n.7).

Giving as the tale's subject "the return of an American expatriate," Quentin Anderson sees James's "overt commentary" on the expatriate in his biography of William Wetmore Story, who James wrote would have been a better artist in Boston, or even London. Brydon and Story, according to Anderson, were both dilettantes who led "greedy" lives, and Brydon is, "morally speaking, much closer" to Story than to James (175–77, 181). Mackenzie similarly compares Brydon to Story, whose career, James wrote, was "a sort of beautiful sacrifice to a noble mistake" (367). James pictured a "voice in the air" from

America telling Story, "You would have made an excellent lawyer"—a sense of "bifurcated desires" Przybylowicz finds in both biography and tale (236). Looking instead at the search for a "visitable past" in each, Maves points to a passage in the Story biography in which James describes a palace where one can imagine the "old-world Court . . . swimming, in advance, over the polished floors, with a ghostly click and patter" (124–25).

Tuveson associates the tale with the theories of F. H. Myers, whose work on the mind and the paranormal had been reviewed by William James. Myers proposed a view of the mind as "a vast complex structure of several 'selves,' only one of which can be evident at one time," and that includes an "unconscious" that he termed the "subliminal." In his collection *Phantasms of the Living* (1888), he recounted many stories of the several selves and the struggles among them for dominance. Tuveson detects also in Alice's dream of the alter ego an illustration of Myers's concept of "reciprocal hallucination" (271–78; also H. N. Smith 124). Martin, on the other hand, finds James presenting an almost "diagrammatic exhibition of the spatial concept of the unconscious" as articulated by Elizabeth Stuart Phelps in *The Gates Ajar* (1868), where the unconscious is the gate to the spiritual world (127).

The psychology of the tale has also been compared to Hawthorne. Thorberg likens its externalizing of the "mind's workings" through the metaphor of the house particularly to that in "Young Goodman Brown" (188). Travis, on the other hand, sees James reworking more realistically the allegorical "Egotism; or The Bosom Serpent," which also depicts a solipsistic protagonist, his snake-like alter ego, and his ultimate redemption by love (see also Strout 1979, 48). While Haggerty sees James drawing on Hawthorne's "chiaroscuro," he sees the ending as a "reversal of the ultimate Gothic concern" of "Rappaccini's Daughter" or James's own "Sir Edmund Orme." Because Alice accepts the horror without worrying about understanding it, Haggerty writes, James avoids Hawthorne's "epistemological confusion" (161–62, 166). More generally, Benert likens Brydon to "one of Hawthorne's crazed intellects, a man empty of feeling and relationship," while Bier offers the specific example of Owen Warland in "The Artist of the Beautiful" (Benert 123; Bier 326 n.10). Looking more at biography, Brodhead argues that James's "extravagant" claims for the artist, in contrast to Hawthorne's more modest ones, allowed him like Brydon "the achieved, the enjoyed, the triumphant life," so that he could "outdo" Hawthorne even as Brydon outdid *his* American counterpart (198).

According to Bier, it was as a combination of Hawthorne and his "anti-model or alter ego" Poe that the tale began. James, he argues, wanted Poe's "potent force" but not the vulgarity into which it could degenerate. Signs of Poe's influence include, according to Bier, the Poe-like cadences of the ghost's appearance with its "great grey glimmering margin": "It gloomed, it loomed, it was something, it was somebody, the prodigy of a personal presence." Hawthorne, however, is the "mediating ego" and James keeps to his more controlled third-person narration. While Bier seconds Banta's suggestion of "a new Gothicism" available to James in the "fusion" of Poe and Hawthorne, he pictures the puritan Hawthorne winning out over Poe in the end (321–28, 333).

William James left out Hawthorne to write his brother in January 1909 of his marvel at his "success in producing the Poe-like creepings of the flesh" (376). Gardner and Dunlap prefer James's "ingenious" schemas to Poe's, and praise the "organic" use of the symbolic setting of the house here over the artificially elaborate approach in "Ligeia" (v, 10). Poe's William Wilson, Huntley observes, searches for his other self through his school, even as Brydon searches through his house (230). In the end Wilson, like Brydon, Shelden notes, "'comes to' himself" (132). Tintner sees a smaller resemblance to "William Wilson," as well as to "The Black Cat" and *The Narrative of A. Gordon Pym*, presenting however "The Fall of the House of Usher" as a chief source for the tale. In both tales of "terror," the protagonist is obsessed with a family home that represents his own mind and is destroyed in the end, although Brydon, unlike Usher, is saved (1989, 193–200). Buitenhuis earlier noted affinities with "The Fall of the House of Usher" and pointed also to the use of doubleness to represent "the descent into the hell of one's self" in "A Descent into the Maelström" (220). Robinson places the story's treatment of "the sentient spirit of the ancestral house" in an American tradition of "Gothic house-building" including not only "The Fall of the House of Usher," but also Hawthorne's *The House of the Seven Gables* and Faulkner's *Absalom, Absalom* (184, 187).

Melville's "Bartleby" offers another example of an author serving "his defensive needs in a salubrious way," according to Rogers, and transmuting "libidinal components" into art (1970, 70, 85). Bier emphasizes Melville's and James's combination of Poe and Hawthorne, and their attack on "senseless American activity and busy-ness"(327–28 n.14). In Melville's *White Jacket*, Gale writes, his central character, like Brydon and Dane of "The Great Good Place," is "spiritually rejuvenated" by a "plunge" into the depths (28). Alice's residence on Irving Place, according to Bier, invokes Washington Irving, whose Rip Van Winkle also underwent a "psycho-allegorical exile" and whose first name evokes some of the patriotic concerns Fogel locates in the tale (Bier 322–23; Fogel 196–97). Bewley draws some comparisons with Cooper's Littlepage trilogy, while Banta sees some of both Brydon's facing down of the truth and his sense of doubleness in Thoreau (1959, 252–54; 1972, 141–42; Banta 1972, 260 n.17). Berthoff links James's evocation of Old New York with such local color works as *The Country of the Pointed Firs*, which also seek to honor the "'jolly corners' of American life" even as they are being extinguished by modernity (1971, 261).

Nat and Nathan Sumner note parallels with two poems by Emily Dickinson, both mentioned by Alice James in her diary. The first, entitled "Returning," begins "I Years had been from home,/And now, before the door,/I dared not open." The "I" eventually flees rather than face "a face/I never saw before." The second, "Ghost," begins by declaring, "One need not be a chamber to be haunted" as it is "Far safer, of a midnight meeting/External ghost,/Than an interior confronting/That whiter host" (also Terrie 15).

The *doppelgänger* was a popular figure at the turn of the century, as Strout insists one must recognize in reading the tale. Even so, Briggs sees James combining his "personal allegory" with the traditional figure. In the 1890s, Briggs points out, the double had begun to symbolize not a death outside oneself as earlier, but a division within oneself, as in *Dr. Jekyll and Mr. Hyde* and "Markheim" (84, 150). Strout also points to the association with Stevenson, who had died shortly before the failure of *Guy Domville*. As *Dr. Jekyll and Mr. Hyde* was in contrast a huge success, he argues it may have contributed to James's choice of a double "preoccupied with power" (50–51). Arguing that the title "The Jolly Corner" recalls "The Jolly Roger," Tintner sees it as a link to Stevenson's tales of adventure and piracy (1976, 409). Miller adds a possible reverse allusion, noting that James and Stevenson met in the year Stevenson wrote his novella, and that Henry Jekyll's name recalls James's (231)

Other examples of literary doubles are numerous. In addition to *Dr. Jekyll and Mr. Hyde*, Buitenhuis points to *The Secret Sharer* and *The Picture of Dorian Gray* as examples (219). Miller qualifies the comparison, however, noting that Brydon's life was not as depraved as those of Dorian Gray or the milder Stavrogin of Dostoyevsky's *The Possessed* (229–30). Rosenfield cites *Pierre*, *Wuthering Heights*, *Edwin Drood*, *The Secret Sharer*, and *Heart of Darkness*, Hogg's *Confessions of a Justified Sinner*, Goethe's *Faust*, and Mann's *Doctor Faustus*, O'Connor's *The Violent Bear It Away*, Knowles's *A Separate Peace*, Nabokov's *Pale Fire*, and three of Faulkner's works, *Go Down Moses*, *Sartoris*, and *Absalom, Absalom*, as well as Dostoyevsky's *Crime and Punishment* and *The Double*, the last also linked to the tale by Mackenzie (Mackenzie 55). Irwin places the tale in a line of doubles immediately following Mark Twain's *Pudd'nhead Wilson* and preceding Robinson Jeffers's *Tamar*. (14–17). Miller points to the similar talk of "black and white" in Bellow's story of a double, *The Victim* (354). Among the examples of the projection of "inner outer space" named by Knapp are Beckett's *Krapp's Last Tape* and Jean Vauthier's *The Character against Himself* (28). Purdy discusses the tale in connection with an episode of *Star Trek* that presents opposed doubles of the character Spock (50–55).

According to Levin, "any personage conceived by any writer" is to some degree his alter ego (5). Accordingly, Goetz traces how the use of doubles in

James's autobiographical tales such as "The Jolly Corner" and "The Beast in the Jungle" "complicates and partially disguises" the autobiography, just as does Joyce's use of doubles—Bloom and Dedalus—in *Ulysses* (159). Boren also looks at the connection between doubles and autobiography, seeing the "doubling" in the text "repeated in the act of authoring," allowing James to "exorcise—by making fun of—his own ambivalence" toward America (12).

The tale also has a place in the Gothic tradition. In Shelden's analysis, James is using the supernatural tale here as an outlet for his anxieties, even as in the eighteenth-century writers used the Gothic, portraying the story as the result of a nightmare like *The Castle of Otranto* or *Frankenstein*. Shelden identifies both the use of an "internal Doppelgänger" and the representation of the psyche through a house as Gothic devices, even as she classifies Brydon's seeking to confront the ghost as an extension of the "chase motif." The "twist" in the tale is that the true terror comes from within (125–26, 134). Miller also points to various Gothic conventions in the tale, including Mrs. Muldoon's Irish accent, the "exemplary journey," the swoon, the "attainment of a mother," and the doors closed by an "unknown hand," the last seen particularly in *The Mysteries of Udolpho* (230–32). Haggerty, however, attributes a greater courage to Brydon as he "presses on . . . to know what other Gothic heroes have fled in fear of." While Radcliffe's heroines, he writes, were "dwarfed" and "terrified" by their surroundings, Brydon "expands the dimensions of the house" by the importance he assigns the confrontation. While he considers the Gothic in Radcliffe "objective and isolated," he sees it becoming part of Brydon's "inner experience." Here, according to Haggerty, the reader cannot avoid the "Gothic intensity" by standing back and watching as one watches Frankenstein, Heathcliff, Usher, or Giovanni. At the same time, because the reader sees the ghost with Brydon, the story avoids what he sees as the baldness of earlier Gothic writers such as Lewis. By taking the Gothic out of the "realm of private fantasy," Haggerty contends, to give it "profound public significance," James legitimized the genre (162–64, 166).

According to Unrue, Brydon's confrontation with his alter ego recalls another Gothic convention, the threat of a "living portrait" seen in such works as *Melmoth the Wanderer*, *The Castle of Otranto*, and *The Mysteries of Udolpho* (1975, 46–50). Looking at his alter ego, Brydon thinks "no portrait by a great modern master could have presented him with more intensity, thrust him out of his frame with more art" (CT 12, 225). As the modern master, Winner suggests Sargent, whose portraits were also "brilliant, slightly dehumanized and sinister" (73–74). Tintner also discerns the influence of Sargent, pointing particularly to his portrait of Major Higginson, mentioned in *The American Scene*, and of the art dealer Asher Wertheimer (1986, 98, 187). In addition, Winner offers a painted parallel for Brydon's pursuit of his double in William Rimmer's 1872 *Flight and Pursuit* (87). The light outside the house meanwhile reminds Brydon "of the assault of the outer light of the

Desert on the traveller emerging from an Egyptian tomb," and Tintner comments on the allusion as reflecting twentieth-century taste, while Knapp sees it as recalling ancient mystical initiation rituals—Egyptian and Greek—which she sees reflected in Brydon's experience (CT 12, 202–3; Tintner 1986, 237–38; Knapp 28, 37–42). James himself never visited Egypt, having turned down an offer in 1897 to travel up the Nile with John Hay and Henry Adams as "perversely *impossible*" (*Life* 4, 233).

To Miller the title "The Jolly Corner" is "dualistic" like that of Dickens's *Bleak House*, in a reflection of the "mixed fortunes of family life"—the jolly corner "often proves bleak," while the bleak house has "jolly corners" (234). As Todorov points out, "thanks to the ghost," Brydon learns his lesson before death (189). The sequence is somewhat reminiscent of Scrooge's casting off of greed under a ghostly influence. Brydon, Tuveson writes, went abroad as if in response to Pater, but rather than living a life of "ascetic devotion to refined sensation," led one more like that of the narrator in Proust's *A la récherche du temps perdu* (274). The name Brydon suggests that of the Romantic poet Byron, who combined the "scandalous" life of Brydon with the artistic creativity of James. Auchard compares James's "sense of negation" in the tale with Keats's "negative capability," seeing in Brydon a greater egotism and a more tenuous connection to life (51–52). To Jacobs, the story is "a work about art itself" in the manner of Keats's "Ode on a Grecian Urn" and Yeats's "Byzantium" poems. Brydon faints into a "realm" like Byzantium, gaining a "glimpse" of "the essential truth of Keats's vision of beauty" (51, 59). After renouncing his search, Brydon looks out the window for "some comforting common fact . . . some night-bird however base. He would have blessed that sign of life"—an impulse reminiscent of Coleridge's *The Rime of the Ancient Mariner* (CT 12, 220).

As Brydon contemplates the closed door he faces "two alternatives," one of them leading to madness, a situation Honig compares to Hamlet's and producing, in Chapman's judgment, an equal "verbal agony" (CT 12, 218; Chapman 59). To Honig, indeed, the whole tale resembles an "interior monologue" (84–86). Brydon is not Macbeth, however, as Thorberg asserts that to take Brydon's interest simply in a life he had not led would be to reduce the quality of his curiosity to that of Macbeth's question-and-answer sessions with the witches (188). Looking at the name Spencer, Rovit finds it "punningly appropriate" as the tale is "not only a social but an internal 'Prothalamion'" (72 n.11). Wright locates the same paradox here as in Chaucer's "Pardoner's Tale"—turning from self-knowledge often leads one to it (205). In his survey of might-have-beens in a country churchyard, Gray imagined both "mute Miltons" and "Cromwells guiltless of their country's blood." James offers us a developer innocent of destruction.

The alter ego appears to Brydon at first like "one of those expanding fantastic images projected by the magic lantern of childhood," an image Edward

Stone associates with fairy tales (CT 12, 226; Stone 140). Appropriately then, Buitenhuis compares Alice's kiss to Sleeping Beauty's (218). Knapp relates Alice not only to Dante's Beatrice and Petrarch's Laura, but also to the medieval icon of the virgin taming the unicorn (43). To Banta, the tale, like *The Sense of the Past*, is a "new psychological retelling of knightly quest tales" (1972, 151). At one point in his search, Brydon feels like "Pantaloon, at the Christmas farce, buffeted and tricked from behind by ubiquitous Harlequin" (CT 12, 213). The Harlequin, Shelden argues, is the "repugnant self" Brydon can never fully acknowledge (132). Jacobs sees the image serving not only to show Brydon's "innate theatricality" but to represent the story's "complexity of perspectives"—including the reader's view of Brydon, Brydon's view of Alice, and the "undisclosed" perspective of Alice on Brydon (57). In Benert's reading, the allusion fits with Bakhtin's association of carnival and doubling (122). Clair tailors the allusion to fit his view of Alice, proposing that her name may suggest the "stave wielding clown" who tricks Brydon (28).

The tale has generated several mythological readings. Honig detects in it the pattern of Dionysus's sacrifice and rebirth. Brydon retreats from his other self to the jolly corner only to encounter him there, and finally escapes by sacrificing that other self to "the builders, the destroyers." Alice completes the sacrifice by declaring that the "stranger" was not Brydon (83–87). Pirie compares Brydon, "the wanderer returning home," to Ulysses, with Alice recalling Penelope (133). The alter ego, Unrue writes, is a more horrifying version of the "grotesque Dweller," a folk character who guards hidden knowledge. Brydon first sees its grotesqueness as an adverse reflection on his search, but after his faint he returns with a "treasure of intelligence," the traditional result of such a submergence into the unknown (1976, 299–300). Gutierrez places the tale in the context of the myth of the labyrinth. Brydon, like Theseus, seeks the minotaur in his maze-like house, although his search is an internal one for another self. Like Theseus, Brydon is rescued by his Ariadne, Alice (91–93). Such mythological associations, Tintner observes, are typical of James's late work. She points particularly to parallels between Brydon's alter ego and Pluto, ruler of Hades (1989, 138).

Freedman sees the tale as most reminiscent of Plato's "Allegory of the Cave," noting the mention of "Forms" in the tale, although they end here with a "monstrous rather than magnificent" vision. Knapp sees the house full of formless matter in motion like Democritus's atoms, the "void" in the house being reminiscent of the "void" before the beginning of the world. The Hebrew Kabbalist, according to Knapp, would see within such a "state of formlessness" the raw material of creation (30–33). Freedman points also to allusions to the New Testament: Brydon is revived like Lazarus, and is pictured at the end in the manner of Christ descended from the cross (108–9; see also Q. Anderson 181). Banta similarly compares the image of Alice holding Brydon to the *Pietà* (1972, 151; also Tremper 74; Knapp 43). Freedman notes allusions to Dante's *Inferno*, and Shulman also sees in the tale the "rhythms of some divine Comedy" as Brydon descends into the "underworld of the self" to return to "new life," assisted by a Beatrice figure (47). That figure, Alice, the reader is told, personally "trimmed her lamps" (CT 12, 196). Byers consequently compares her to the wise virgins in the parable preparing for the bridegroom, suggested in Brydon's name (92; also Fogel 202 n.12). The tale's stairs Knapp finds recalling Jacob's ladder, which reached from earth to heaven (41). To Rosenblatt, the "amassed scriptural context" makes the story "more solemn." He notes in addition to the specific parallels a "virtually overwrought insistence on the spirituality of the lovers' union." How the allusions add up he deems more uncertain, as Brydon appears at times as much a prodigal son as a returning Christ (see also Strout 1979, 48). Ultimately, however, he sees the story with its strong "moral opposites" following the example of the parable of the talents, by transforming "materialist values" into spiritual ones. In a similar vein, Fogel sees the scriptural allusions supporting an affirmative reading of the conclusion (202 n.20; also Pirie 137).

In Male's analysis, the parable of the prodigal son, the *Odyssey*, the *Divine Comedy*, and the allegory of the cave are all members of a category of stories he calls the "Exile's Return." American examples include not only "The Jolly Corner," but also "Rip Van Winkle," "Ethan Brand," Hamlin Garland's "The Return of a Private," Hemingway's "Soldiers Home," Dreiser's "The Old Neighborhood," Lionel Trilling's *The Middle of the Journey*, Frederick Buechner's "The Tiger," and Fitzgerald's "Babylon Revisited." Throughout them are found the recurrent themes of the "reunion" with the "feminine principle," the question of identity, and the conflict between responsibility and "egotism and escapism."

In his placing of the tale in the context of the American short story, Skaggs emphasizes its treatment of the "American self which is constantly in the process of redefinition" even into middle age (14–15). To Cady, the tale is James's main contribution to the realists' analysis of "the American Business Mind" (12). Similarly, Fadiman suggests that the ghost may represent the reality of the post-Civil War America of Dreiser and his followers—the closest, Fadiman argues, James ever came to facing its meaning, which he had recognized in *The American Scene* (643). Jacobs, too, sees the figure at the end as James's "awful vision" of the new American artist as it was taking shape in novels by Dreiser, Norris, and Howells (59–60). Tintner finds the concept of self-haunting here and in "The Beast in the Jungle" reflected in Wharton's 1910 tale "The Eyes," while Miller casts Alice as a more benign character out of Wharton's Old New York (Tintner 1975, 378; Miller 229, 277). Bewley acknowledges a preference for Fitzgerald's more complex response to the evils of the American economy (1959, 261). Henry Nash Smith calls the imagery of the hunt and the focus on a test of courage a "surprising anticipation of Hemingway" (124). But to Benert, the imagery, while anticipating "the moral world" of Hemingway and Faulkner, does not "hold up" (121). Alice is referred to in the tale as a "pale pressed flower," probably, Irwin hypothesizes, a narcissus, providing a link to *The Sound and the Fury* by way of Benjy's narcissus. The figure's maimed hand, Irwin argues, has a different "biographical resonance" in its indication of James's view of the writer as "non-participant, as passive observer," or, as one of Faulkner's characters said, "as eunuch" (15–17).

In Bier's view, for James, as for Stendahl, a happy ending was "an unguilty return . . . to the mother figure" (333 n.20). Stowell defines the tale not as a "quasi-ghost story" but one illustrating "the transformation of memory into a living person," in a manner similar to Chekhov's "The Lady with the Dog," which Miller views as another tale of the double life (Stowell 131; Miller 261). The beastly dream figure is connected by Rogers to that in Mann's *Death in Venice*, while Benert compares the frame dialogue to the one in Dostoyevsky's *The Underground Man* and Camus's *The Fall* (Rogers 1956, 446; Benert 119, 124). Henry Nash Smith sees "The Jolly Corner"—like James's final trilogy of novels—belonging not to the realm of "psychological realism," but to "a post-realistic mode of writing" which used modern psychology and parapsychology to show "how little rather than how much" is known of human behavior, in a manner anticipatory of Joyce's *Ulysses* and Gide's *The Counterfeiters* (127).

Several links have been proposed with the works of T. S. Eliot. Allott points to a passage in *The Family Reunion* speaking of "the loop in time" when "The hidden is revealed, and the spectres show themselves" (331). Matthiessen also connects the story to the play in which Harry, returning home to face his past, is told ". . . it will not be a very *jolly* corner." He points out, however, that Eliot deleted the next two lines, "I am sorry . . . for making an allusion/To an author whom you never heard of" (1958, 165, 176–77 n.6). Grover Smith qualifies the connection, saying Harry faces no doppelgänger here, only the "might have been" of an early relationship. He detects, however, a hint of "The Jolly Corner" in the encounter with the ghost in "Little Gidding" (205, 289). Buitenhuis finds Prufrock's invitation to "you and I" an exploration of self similar to Brydon's (220–21).

Tintner sees Philip Roth's *Zuckerman Unbound* as modeled on the tale. In it, the author is threatened by his alter ego, Alvin Pepler, who stayed behind in the old neighborhood and confronts Nathan outside a funeral parlor, the novella's "unjolly" corner (1982, 50–51).

Parrill discusses the series of prints by Peter Milton for a special edition of the tale by Quarius Press in 1971. He judges its depiction of a Brydon repressed in his erotic life as well as his professional by leaving behind the "vigor and power of America"—illustrated by way of men lounging on skyscrapers and a nearly naked Alice paired with Brydon's double—a "legitimate" extension of James's tale.

Relation to Other Works

James analyzed his reencounter with America in the nonfictional *The American Scene* as well as "The Jolly Corner," and according to Sanford one should read the two works together. Sanford specifically connects with the image of New York's "black over-scoring of a white page by science in *The American Scene* with the "black stranger" and the "criss-crossed lines" in "The Jolly Corner," which Esch compares in turn to the image of the streets like the "old ivory of an overscored table" in *The American Scene* (Esch 77). Sanford designates as the main theme of *The American Scene* the corruption of a land of "great natural beauty" by business and technology, and sees the same theme in the metaphor of the "corruption" of Brydon's "bud" into a "monstrous" flower (218). Mays also notes similar imagery in the two works, associating the "great ebony god of business" mentioned in *The American Scene* with the alter ego depicted in a "penumbra, dense and dark." Another nonfictional piece, an 1898 article on businessmen as a possible literary theme, Mays discovers, offers underwater imagery similar to that in the tale, comparing the businessman to "a diver for shipwrecked treasure" (470–71). Strout, too, points to "parallel imagery"—James looking at the site of his destroyed birthplace felt, he wrote, "amputated" of "half" his history, even as the alter ego is missing two fingers (1979, 51). Tintner cites from James's description of a skyscraper: "staring at them as at a world of immovably-closed doors behind which immense 'material' lurked, material for the artist, the painter of life, as we say, who shouldn't have begun so early and so fatally to fall away from possible initiations," and remarks on its closeness to Brydon's baffled search for his other self behind closed doors (1976, 402).

Himself the grandson of an immigrant, as Strout observes, James would still react to the newly arrived immigrants at Ellis Island as a "ghost in his supposedly safe old house" and hear "ghostly footsteps" in Ashburton Place—indications, according to Buitenhuis, of his failure to predict the changes that would occur in America, even as their phrasing anticipates Brydon's ghost (211). At Ellis Island James saw "no escape from the ubiquitous alien into the future, or even into the present . . . no escape but into the past"—a comment Morton and Lucia White tie to his attack on modern New York in both "The Jolly Corner" and "The Round of Visits" (90–92). Citing the tale's depiction of the city's "great builded voids," Benert sees a similar conception in the "great blank decency" of *The American Scene*. In *The American Scene*, James saw America handing over all its "socializing functions" to women, and Benert observes how Alice fulfils them here (123–24). The sense of relief at having escaped America Geismar finds the same in both works (360). Boren points to the similar "narrative design" marked by the use of "I." Although in the nonfiction work James's encounters are not by definition ghostly, they are still, she writes, "dreamlike, expressionistic and strangely poetic" (104).

According to Edel, "The Jolly Corner" is the only "American" work to appear in the New York Edition, a categorization that omits such works as "Four Meetings" or "Europe" or "Julia Bride" (*Letters* 4, 363). Wright, on the other hand, classes the tale's criticism of American ugliness not only with that in "A Round of Visits," but also such earlier works as "The Impressions of a Cousin," "A New England Winter," and "Pandora"—the last included in the New York Edition (73–74). To be fair, among the American tales, the work is most frequently compared with the other tales stemming from James's 1904 trip to America, two of which were published after the New York Edition. All four—"The Jolly Corner," "A Round of Visits," "Crapy Cornelia," and "Julia Bride"—share, according to Ward, the basic plot of an expatriate returning after long years abroad and being dismayed by the changes in American society, the increased materialism, the decreased humanity (165–66). Buitenhuis sees three central themes in the four tales, the "money passion," the ignorance of the past, and the search for the meaning of the self, observing that James's American characters have now become sensitive and perceptive (210). To Auchincloss, "The Jolly Corner" is the best of the tales because it deals with James's "real feeling" not "surface irritation" (143). Kimbel distinguishes the supernatural tales from the others on different grounds, finding that they represent a return to his earlier "social realism" (39). Millgate looks particularly at "The Jolly Corner" and "The Round of Visits" as indications of James's revulsion from—and inability to grasp—the American money world (11–12). The sense of betrayal seen in "The Round of Visits" is, however, according to Edel, absent here (CT 12, 8).

By virtue of being a woman, the heroine of "Crapy Cornelia," according to Matthiessen, is able to maintain her past and to shelter herself from the city better than Spencer Brydon (1947 *American*, xxiii). The same apparently is true of Alice. But while Stovall speaks of both as stories of "reawakened love," Geismar is contemptuous of their heroes for using age as a refuge from sexual demands (Stovall 83–84; Geismar 356). Alice is to Markow-Totevy a less central figure than Cornelia, although the hero's search for his youth in a modern New York is the same (107). Brydon's alleged business potential, however, is to Stone less convincing than White-Mason's acknowledged bewilderment (7). Both tales, Vaid observes, are marked in their telling by a similarly "dense imagery" (234).

James would leave behind at his death an unfinished novel, *The Ivory Tower*, which also depicts an expatriate American returning to encounter and be repulsed by America's greed (Wegelin 164; Buitenhuis 260; Auchincloss 146; Ward 165). The revulsion, in Matthiessen's judgment, is more effective here (1944, 137). Similarly Bewley contends that the tale is probably better than *The Ivory Tower* would have been if completed since Brydon's faint, effective in a short story, would not serve well as a response to evil through an entire novel (1959, 257). Edel, on the other hand, speaks of the projected work as intended to be a "concentration" of the tale in its treatment of "what America did to individuals and what one 'escaped' by being in Europe" (*Life* 5, 502). Pirie sees a difference between both late works and earlier ones where characters were "mainly unaware of, or at least unconcerned about" the sources of their wealth (133).

The American businessman came under attack in *The Ambassadors*, according to Van Wyck Brooks, who argues that Jim Pocock represents the "same face of horror" as Brydon's ghost (47; also cited Ward 114). Habegger looks back to see the ghost as the summation of James's endeavor to depict "aggressive male power," seen in the character of Basil Ransom of *The Bostonians* (193). In earlier works such as "The Pension Beaurepas," according to Ward, business was an obstacle to the imagination and the spirit, but not evil in itself, as it is in "The Jolly Corner" (30–31).

Przybylowicz groups together four works—"The Jolly Corner," *The Ivory Tower*, "Crapy Cornelia," and "A Round of Visits"—that treat a passive, cultured, thoughtful hero's "fascination with his alienated self" in a corrupt America. Disillusioned with the contemporary "depersonalized, technological society," and driven by a concern for the past marked by "fear and guilt," they seek to "justify" themselves, to see themselves in an "other" whom they can master and onto whom they can project their own "unconscious desire." Brydon, like Winch and White-Mason, she argues, ends by rejecting the other, although his other is only imagined, unlike Winch's or Fielder's. In three of the works—"Crapy Cornelia," "A Round of Visits," and *The Ivory Tower*—the heroes seek their other in society. Because their heroes do so, they, like *The Ambassadors*, are impressionistic works which show the external world through subjective impressions. Like them, "The Jolly Corner" asks the question of whether the "inner life can have a valid relationship with society." Unlike them, only parts of "The Jolly Corner" focus on the external world. Although Przybylowicz argues that these sections are stronger than the dream sections of the tale, it is the latter she sees giving the tale its essential character in their concern with the "phenomenological bases of knowledge." In her view, "The Jolly Corner" is the most "expressionistic" of James's "expressionistic" works, including also "The Beast in the Jungle," "The Great Good Place," *The Sense of the Past*, and *The Sacred Fount*. In each, because the sought other is imaginary, an "hallucinatory" relationship is created as the protagonist withdraws from the real world. Without the intervention of the third-person narrator available in the impressionistic works, the tension becomes greater, as are the distortions of time. Like the central characters of *In the Cage* or *The Ambassadors*, the protagonists in these works are "passive dispensers of visions," according to Przybylowicz, who attempt as Brydon does "to create the world around

[them] by transforming life into art." In examples of both the expressionistic and impressionistic works, characters project their fears on to an other in order to objectify them, and even transfer them, in a desire to escape time and death, an "impossible and deadly narcissistic pursuit." But as with the other expressionistic works, apart from *The Sacred Fount*, this tale, Przybylowicz argues, returns in the end from its timeless fantasy to present-day life (112–20, 140–47, 152–53, 163, 296–301).

The work most closely linked with "The Jolly Corner" is the unfinished *The Sense of the Past*, the basic situation of which—an American returning to his English ancestral home and encountering there another self—James reversed here (see Stovall 80–82; *Life* 5, 313; Keppler 169). Bewley sees a "reversal" in attitude as well, arguing that Pendrel is intended to be "more sensitive and intelligent" than the English, while "The Jolly Corner" is "anti-American with a vengeance" (1968, 73 n.1). Jones draws attention to yet another reversal, writing that Pendrel learns the "falsity of his romantic view of the European past" while Brydon learns to "accept both his American past and the route he has taken to get where he is" (256).

What James particularly recalls having "filched" from the unfinished work is its "most intimate idea . . . that my hero's adventure there takes the form so to speak of his turning the tables . . . on a 'ghost' or whatever, a visiting or haunting apparition otherwise qualified to appal *him*; and thereby winning a sort of victory by the appearance, and the evidence, that this personage or presence was more overwhelmingly affected by him than he by *it*" (CN 507; see also Edgar 182; Edel 1970, 721–24; Briggs 116; Byers 90). Many additional parallels have been noted. Allot focuses on the similarity between the family portrait in *The Sense of the Past* and the portrait-like ghost in "The Jolly Corner" and observes that Pendrel, unlike Brydon, had the chance to "live out his *vie manqué*" (326, 331). In both, Beach comments, while the apparitions are "purely metaphysical," they produce an incredibly strong "sense of the present, palpable reality of the physical situation" (cx–xi). Quentin Anderson points to the similar descriptions of the houses, each with black and white squares upon its floor, and compares both with James's Galerie d'Apollon dream (also Banta 1972, 136–37). All, according to Anderson, are emblems for "the archetypal human situation; Man first attempts to take possession of the house of life, but finally learns that it is his task to celebrate it" (178–79). James, according to Perosa, borrowed elements of the projected novel not only for "The Jolly Corner" but also for "The Great Good Place" with its sense of retreat, "The Third Person" with its period ghost, "The Tone of Time" with its mysterious portrait, and "Flickerbridge" with its retreat into the past (135–36, 156).

Others have commented on the use in both of the alter ego or double (e.g., Rogers 1970, 99; Bewley 1968, 73 n.1). Geismar, who sees in both works the same unwillingness to accept the alter ego as in *The Sacred Fount*, further criticizes James by contending it is in actuality his true self (438). Carl Smith pays attention instead to the way the hero in each pursues his alter ego "haunted" by the possibility of its existence (417). Miller observes how the dualism in each is linked with the issue both of dual nationalities and of family (239). Przybylowicz distinguishes between the two works, arguing that Pendrel both maintains his sense of self and his sense of his ancestor in the past while Spencer in the end rejects his other self, never having maintained both. In both works, she argues, James is asking whether it is better to be a "man of action" or a "man of imagination" (115, 160, 170). Purdy points to a different kind of "double consciousness" in both works, observing how the other characters understand that Brydon and Pendrel can see into another reality they cannot—a quality he notes also in *The Turn of the Screw* and somewhat in "The Beast in the Jungle" (47–48). In Schneider's reading, much of James's later fiction is an "elaborate paradigm of the situation" in "The Jolly Corner," with its two selves in conflict. After 1890 he notices an increasing tendency for the hero to fight rather than renounce (32–35). Hocks even detects a similarity in Brydon's relationship with the alter ego and James's description of his progress in facing mortality in the essay, "Is there a Life after Death?" (221).

While Carl Smith sees in the unfinished novel a stronger warning against returning to the past, Berthoff distinguishes between the encounters of the past and one's ghost self on the grounds that it produces "terror" in "The Jolly Corner" and "romance" in *The Sense of the Past* (Smith 417; Berthoff 1965, 125). In both, there is romance of another kind, and Stovall observes how the hero of each discards "a false self in order to discover the true self" and so "come[s] into the fulfillment of love" (80–82). Quentin Anderson gives greater credit to Nan and Alice for rescuing the hero (182; also Przybylowicz 161). To Clair, however, while Nan is selfless, Alice is not (18–19). Banta, too, sees both men rescued by the heroines, but is less happy about it. While, she writes, one can look at the conclusion of both in terms of "an evolving consciousness," since both men undergo "ordeals" sustained psychically by loving women, she senses a weakness when imagining the lives of the protagonists after the conclusion. In stories marked by "the strength of the desire for intensity of life," she finds a "suspicious stagnation" creeping in at the conclusion, that makes one wonder if the quests were to "come *only* to this." She contrasts such "sterile future[s]" unfavorably with the implied "future of private hells" indicated at the ending of *The Turn of the Screw* and "The Beast in the Jungle." It is not simply the "happy ending" that is the problem, she insists, offering similar objections to the ending of "Sir Edmund Orme" and such classic tragic works as *A Farewell to Arms* and *Sons and Lovers*. In essense, she finds both works, like "The Altar of the Dead" and "The Beast in the Jungle," "ultimately weakened by the nature of the women who stand waiting" (1972, 149–52, 208).

"The Passionate Pilgrim" also depicts a man in search of his other self, and of a home in Old England. To Edel they are simply different versions of the same tale. He points particularly to Searle's giving money to the Englishman wanting to emigrate to America as the same rejection of living in the past as in "The Jolly Corner" and *The Sense of the Past* ([1949] 1963, 391–92; *Life* 5, 315; also Vaid 233). Buitenhuis marks a difference, seeing the American setting having become for the older James the "romantic" setting (210–11).

In "The Beast in the Jungle" Marcher, after May's death, "wander[s] through the old years with his hand in the arm of a companion who was, in the most extraordinary manner, his other, his younger self . . . dependent on it not alone for a support but for an identity"—an image Jones parallels to Brydon's search for his other self (283). Other critics focus on the image of the beast in "The Jolly Corner" (e.g., Rogers 1956, 445; Kaston 152). As he walks the house by night Brydon imagines himself "stalking . . . a creature more subtle, yet at bay perhaps more formidable, than any beast of the forest" with the "rear of the house . . . the very jungle of his prey." Although the image, in Gale's view, does not "ring true here," the link with "The Beast in the Jungle" has proved fertile hunting ground indeed (72–73). To Fadiman the two tales are "the ones most profoundly connected" with James's own experience, and Rogers, who calls them "two versions of the same story," calls both "tragic lament[s] for a life unlived, for deeds undone" (Fadiman 642; Rogers 1956, 429, 432). Similarly, Sanford writes that the "symbolic autobiography" of both tales is the best illustration of James's "sense of personal failure" (216–17).

Sanford recognizes, however, as most critics do, the difference between Marcher's experience and Brydon's, its "untypically jolly counterpart" as Freedman puts it (Freedman 107; also Dupee 159; Stovall 80; Johnson 358; Moseley 86 n.29; Moore 89). Both men are "overtaken," in Kaston's phrasing, "by a sort of repressed Freudian id of a 'beast'" (151). Both have previously, in Quentin Anderson's formulation, sought to avoid "the guilt of experience," but Brydon, unlike Marcher, "actually brings his other self to bay" (176–77, 181). "Divided men" both, they learn, according to Mays, that the only thing more dangerous than to live is not to (469–70). Then, as Honig puts it, Brydon wakes to the "joy" of knowledge, while Marcher wakes to its "horror" (90). Strout, however, differentiates between the two men on the grounds that Brydon, unlike Marcher, "*has* lived" (1979, 50). Similarly, Winner emphasizes Brydon's active "stalking" of the ghost in comparison to Marcher's passive waiting, even as Edel calls the tale itself a "kind of active" "Beast in the Jungle" (Winner 214–15 n.5; *Life* 5, 314). Auchard, too, noting both characters' "imaginative interest in seemingly empty places," finds such places more active in "The Jolly Corner" (50–51). Stein takes a different line, seeing Marcher recognizing his selfishness in the end—an admission, Stein asserts, that Brydon will never make (63). Others look at the tales as "reverse" images of each other, Vaid pointing out how Marcher is "obsessed by what he will be," Brydon by "what would have been" (232; also Thorberg 189; Marys 469).

Nearly as many comparisons have been made between Alice Staverton and May Bartram as between Brydon and Marcher (e.g., Geismar 356; Krook 335 n.1). Sanford calls both women "Eve figure[s]"; Rogers classes them with Maria Gostrey as Jamesian mother figures who only appear "eligible" (Sanford 216–17; Rogers 1956, 432). Wright comments on how, like Milly Theale and the woman in "The Altar of the Dead," they are known through images and significant speech (42). Sharp classes both May and Alice with such selfless Jamesian confidantes as Mrs. Alsager of "Nona Vincent," and as exemplars of James's "ideals of friendship" with Fleda, Maria Gostrey, and Susan Stringham. Both women, she observes, are realists in love with men who "dodge reality." Like Chapman, however, she sees the relationship in "The Jolly Corner" as the less significant (Sharp 57, 59; Chapman 57). Yet Alice is less passive than May, Hocks argues, and even shares in Brydon's "psychic experience." She is, in fact, as "plucky" as the governess in *The Turn of the Screw*, although more aware (203–5). Sicker speaks of both Alice and May as "telepathic" women, and compares them to Ralph Touchett who also found "loving . . . a solitary lifelong occupation" (10, 123). Byers observes how the plots of both tales and of *The Ambassadors* require such a confidante figure, and Moore adds *The Wings of the Dove* to the list (Byers 92; Moore 90).

As the tale of a passive man's second chance with a more "practical woman," Jones places the tale with "Crapy Cornelia" and "The Bench of Desolation" (279). To Levy, the hesitating, self-examining heroes of "The Jolly Corner" and "The Beast in the Jungle" are part of a long line stretching back to "The Diary of a Man of Fifty" (32–33). Disagreeing with Edel that James's last tales are "angry" or despairing, Chapman instead sees such stories as "The Bench of Desolation," "The Beast in the Jungle," "The Jolly Corner," and even "A Round of Visits" as affirming the "redemptive power of human love" despite their limited heroes (50–51). Tremper puts together a trio of tales—*The Aspern Papers*, "The Beast in the Jungle," and "The Jolly Corner"—which, she argues, represent successive stages in the psychoanalytic cure from egotism and the inability to love that James himself followed, each tale marked by a confrontation with an alter ego. In the end, Aspern's editor is still unaware of his need for a cure; Marcher is more aware, but not "transformed"; only Brydon benefits fully from his recognition, and is left free to love in the end. Przybylowicz also notes Brydon's superior success in reaching out, despite his selfish use of a woman for a confidante, like that of Marcher, White-Mason, and Monteith. But while like Monteith, White-Mason, and Pendrel, he searches for himself in the past, Przybylowicz sees Brydon like Pendrel recognizing the need to fix oneself in the present (88, 94, 124).

"The Jolly Corner" and "The Beast in the Jungle," together with "The Altar of the Dead," make up for Vaid a "triptych depicting man in quest of his self" (214). Honig first examined the tales together, comparing Brydon's sacrifice of his alter ego which brings renewed life, Marcher's tragic sacrifice of May, and Stransom's more qualified sacrifice to the dead (90). In all three tales, Matthiessen argues, "'ghosts' of the dead seem to live through and beyond us"—a recurrent theme that he suggests may have originated with James's guilt over not having participated in the Civil War (247). Nevertheless, to Todorov "The Jolly Corner" is the "least despairing version" of the "new Jamesian figure" seen also in the other two tales, which shows the folly of searching for absence with a "presence"—the woman in each case—by your side (188–89). Connecting the quest in "The Jolly Corner" and "The Beast in the Jungle" to that in "The Figure in the Carpet," Peter Brooks points to James's use of the word "abyss" in all three to represent "the evacuated centers of meaning . . . that nonetheless animate lives, determine quests for meaning," and give life "the urgency and dramatics of melodrama" (173–74). Goetz compares the tale of Brydon and Marcher more generally to James's artist tales in which the artist serves as the "other" to the first-person narrators. Here the "other" is "internalized," at the same time as part of the protagonist's true self is projected onto the other, creating "an objectified image of the hero . . . that transcends his own single consciousness," which can be observed by the women in the tale and by the third-person narrator (164–65).

To Wright, it is "The Jolly Corner," "The Beast in the Jungle," and "The Great Good Place" that make up a trio, their concern the "identification of the self" aided by the confrontation with "other selves" (189, 209). Walter E. Anderson casts an even wider net, putting the scene of Brydon's hesitation before the closed door as the "climax" of James's presentation of a person "shut off from a promised life," stating that James would "attempt again and again to force that door in his fiction, but to the last it remained closed." As examples of parallel situations he offers the death and burial of May, the disappearance of the "ghost" in "The Ghostly Rental," and the encloistering of Claire in *The American*. He further places the image of letters burnt unopened in this tale with similar events in *The Aspern Papers* and *The American*. More particularly, he associates the "blighted" flower of Brydon's youth with the "flowers of experience" James asks for in a letter to Jocelyn Persse, and with "the fine flower of Newman's experience . . . 'cut off' and shut up to itself" (525–27). A soldier and businessman, Newman is, in Mays's analysis, a figure more like Brydon's alter ego than like Brydon (482).

The recurrent Jamesian theme of "too late" is a prominent one in both "The Jolly Corner" and "The Beast in the Jungle." Krook sees the theme again in "The Friends of the Friends" and *The Ambassadors*, the latter of which she argues may have been conceived about the same time as "The Jolly Corner."

In *The Ambassadors*, however, she argues, consciousness is presented as sufficient for a full life. Here love too is necessary, even as in "The Bench of Desolation" it is the saving grace of an otherwise desperate world (332–34). Such could prove difficult, given Rogers's characterization of Brydon, Marcher, and Strether as "incarnations of the passive, powerless Futile Man" (1956, 453). Both Strether and Brydon, however, Wright states, return to their former lives with "a great change of vision" (241). They begin, according to Banta, with an interest in "the unseen and the occult" like that of James (1972, 58). Goetz also sees in Strether something of his creator, and finds a parallel for Brydon and Marcher's search for an alter ego in Strether's search for "the pale figure of his real youth" (184). Similarly, as Przybylowicz records, Chad appears to Strether as "another self that had been long buried" (114).

Several critics have categorized "The Jolly Corner" with James's ghost stories (e.g., Rogers 1956, 446–53). To Matthiessen it is the "culmination" of the genre in the Jamesian canon (1944, 136; also Stovall 82). Martin locates its concept of the ghostly unconscious in several other James works as well, including "Sir Edmund Orme," "The Private Life," and "The Great Good Place," and most particularly *The Sense of the Past* (126–27). It has been linked most frequently, however, with *The Turn of the Screw*. To some, the two are the greatest of James's tales of the supernatural (Bewley 1959, 253; Briggs 150; Brooks, Lewis, Warren 1445). Auchincloss calls "The Jolly Corner" a "perfect ghost story," its ghostly figure more frightening than Quint (99–100). Pirie cautions, however, that James's concern is more profound and subtle than simply to "terrify the reader" (135). Ward sees both tales as versions of the motif of the "appalled appalling" stemming from James's nightmare of the Galerie d'Apollon, rendered also in *The Ambassadors* and "A Round of Visits" (159, 160). Przybylowicz makes the same connection, adding Maisie and Fielder as characters who "search for the self among the pressures exerted by other, stronger selves, by conditions of time and place" (215). The searches in the three ghostly works are all conducted in old houses, notes Huntley, who argues that both the governess and Brydon repudiate their doubles (230, 236). Moseley, however, links Brydon with Maisie against John Marcher and the governess, on the grounds that his imagination is receptive to new ideas (80). Certainly, as Springer indicates, the interest in both works is in each character's attitude to the ghost rather than the ghost itself. Brydon, unlike the governess, she points out, admits his role in shaping the ghost. For him, she writes, the danger is the opposite of the governess's, the possibility that he might dismiss what he saw as "only a ghost" (115–17, 120). Although Przybylowicz argues that Spencer rejects his "inner obsessions" to gain a false security, she sees him at least avoiding the madness the governess falls into by projecting her obsessions on others (147). Brydon's alter ego holds his head in his hands just as Miss Jessel does, Taylor points out, but she sees James protecting himself in the depiction of the confrontation with an "alien *other*" in "The Jolly Corner" and "The Beast in the Jungle" by avoiding first-person narration (173, 176). In Goetz's view, however, the first-person narrator is a problem in *The Turn of the Screw*, where the governess is unable to acknowledge her part in creating the ghosts. At the same time, he sees the "focalized, third-person narrative" of "The Jolly Corner" allowing for an equal amount of ambiguity (119, 165). Haggerty, on the other hand, sees none of the novella's ambiguity in the story, as it presents the "Gothic nature" of Brydon's "world strictly in terms of his own relation to it" (162). Finally, in Hocks's estimate, "The Jolly Corner" has come "full circle" from *The Turn of the Screw*, where the narrative failed to fit the protagonist's obsession, and even a step further from "The Beast in the Jungle," where it did, because its narrative is specifically constructed to fit Brydon's obsession, to show both its beginning and end (200–1).

James, writes Delbaere-Garant, was obsessed with "the thing *done*," an idea Gabriel Nash scorns in *The Tragic Muse*, and that Theobald in "The Madonna of the Future" is kept from achieving by his high ideals. But while choosing to do something shows one's limitations—as Isabel Archer's marriage does—it is the "only measure of man." Brydon's achievement thus becomes his return to the jolly corner (595–96). Armstrong also compares Brydon's choices and Isabel's, noting Isabel's worry that in accepting either Warburton or Goodwood she would give up "other chances" of living. Such chances, however, remain "empty possibilities" unless they are taken up, when they cause the sacrifice of still others. In the same way, he suggests, "The Jolly Corner" illustrates how the "unlived life always haunts the life we have lived as the ghost embodying the possibilities we have not selected." "The Beast in the Jungle," however, portrays the even greater danger of losing everything by not choosing (107). Auchard views both Brydon and Isabel as, like Marmaduke of "Maud-Evelyn," interested in the "other" simply as a "metaphoric emptiness into which an aspect of *self* may be projected" (52). Berland compares Brydon not to Isabel but to her suitors, seeing the contrast between Goodwood and Osmond reflected in the contrast between Brydon and his alter ego. All four have "ambition" and "will," but it comes out in Goodwood and the alter ego only in ways that the America of their time allowed. In Europe, he writes, Osmond and Brydon have not lost their ambition, simply the "American expression" of it (127). Wegelin compares both Isabel and Strether to the alter ego, seeing all three as victims of circumstance (155–56).

When Brydon enters the house, he enters "the other, the real, the waiting life; the life that, as soon as he had heard behind him the click of his great house-door, began for him, on the jolly corner" (208). It is his "private life." By working in the dark like a writer, he also recalls Vawdrey in "The Private Life," Dencombe in "The Middle Years," or even James, as Delbaere-Garant suggests, in comparing Brydon's shadowy search to James's own "beloved *chiaroscuro*" (591). Beebe focuses on the image of the writer in the preface to "The Private Life," working with his "turned back" to the reader, to picture Brydon as a "surrogate" for James, since he has lived with "his back so turned" to business. The image of the "turned back" recurs, Beebe records, in *Roderick Hudson*, "The Great Good Place," and "The Private Life." The last two stories also have doubles, like "The Jolly Corner," and in each case, Beebe remarks, what the protagonist takes as a ghost is really a part of himself, the alter ego here representing like the public Vawdrey the unartistic side (221–22). To Quentin Anderson, Brydon's discovery of his other self in "the house of life" and consequent discovery of his "form or style" represents "the classic Jamesian moral situation," with particular parallels to "The Birthplace," whose protagonist he judges worthy of greater respect (177).

Brydon's alter ego, in the judgment of Graham Greene, belongs with the other "pitiable" egotists in James, including Kate and Merton of *The Wings of the Dove* and Charlotte and the Prince of *The Golden Bowl* ("Private," 29). Brydon himself is classed by Malshri Lal with Maggie and Marcher and perhaps the governess not as a "conscious villain," like Mme Bellegarde or Osmond, but a person "whose demeanor is marked by good intentions" yet who is "strangely unaware of the portentous evil within" (169). Wilt and Lucas compare him to Scott Homer of "Mrs. Medwin," who as an American abroad also "followed strange paths and worshipped strange gods." They see the Europeanized Brydon, however, as triumphing in a manner that qualifies James's vaunting of American vitality in the earlier tale (xix). Delbaere-Garant attributes to Brydon a greater sense of reality in the world of imagination, akin to that of the telegraphist in *In the Cage* (591). His search for himself, Sicker contends, is both more intense and more successful than that of the heroes of James's later tales, "The Bench of Desolation," "Fordham Castle," and "The Velvet Glove" (172).

As Kaston observes, "The Jolly Corner," like *The Golden Bowl*, ends with an embrace (152). Quentin Anderson sees Maggie, like Alice, seeking to "redeem" a man she loves who has discovered his "other" self, whom she must replace. In the same way, even as Alice sees and accepts Brydon's alter ego, he writes, Milly Theale in *The Wings of the Dove* must see and accept Kate and Densher. Her doing so rids Densher of his other self, whose place she takes (237, 335). Esch draws attention to the mention of burning letters in both works (85). What he calls Alice's "forbearing, loving-kindly lie" denying that the alter ego is Brydon is, in Mackenzie's view, reminiscent of Maggie's "systematic humbugging" (370). The image of the "glass bowl" in "The Jolly Corner" and the title of *The Golden Bowl* are similar, Rogers suggests, in their "world of implication" (1956, 445). To Boren both images evoke "feelings of harmony, nostalgia, and unity" that are perhaps deceptive (13).

Buitenhuis concedes the presence of Freudian imagery in the tale and agrees that the two selves in the story can represent the id and ego, but differs with Rosenzweig over his identification of Ford and Brydon. He observes further a change in James's attitude to women, seen also in the character of Mme de Vionnet, in the difference between Lizzie and Alice (217). Rosenzweig, too, had noted the change from the faithless early heroine (104). Commenting on the maimed fingers, Gale finds James's only other "partially sexual image" with a castration motif in "The Bench of Desolation," where Dodd realizes he can't escape his troubled engagement "without losing a limb" (221 n.36).

Winner compares the "framing" of the vision of the alter ego to other recognition scenes in James, such as Milly viewing the Bronzino or seeing Kate on the balcony, and Hyacinth watching Millicent with the Captain (74). Tintner comments on the significance of doors in the tale and also in James's selections for the frontispieces of the New York Edition (1976, 404).

Interpretation and Criticism

Rosenblatt has called the tale a story about "property and ghosts" (284). Because the property is prime New York real estate, it has also been read as a story of New York and of business. When James's brother William wrote his praise, he added, "But *what* an insult to the type of the N. Y. business man— the country's pride! I don't see how your good name can recover" (376). The standard view of the tale has remained that it is, at least in part, an attack on an America characterized by "money-madness" (Dietrichson 140–41; Marder 18). That Brydon, with his "business ability and inclinations," is still better off a dilettante, writes Auchincloss, is a "pretty strong indictment of Wall Street" (142–43). Knapp pictures Brydon deliberately leaving America to flee the "crass" and "acquisitive" side of his personality, which left by itself becomes even more "vicious" just as Brydon's European side is more a "persona" or "mask" of the intellect alone than a real self (30, 35).

The ghostly alter ego, then, becomes the representative of a nation whose character Brydon would have taken on had he remained in New York (e.g., Lee 113; McElderry 144; Cowdery 31; Sanford 216; Auchincloss 100; Miller 232–33; Boren 11–12). Commenting on the difficulty of depicting the American businessman, Berthoff suggests that the "outright fantasy" of James's figure makes it perhaps the "most fully achieved image" of one—a solitary figure with no woman to accompany him and only his evening dress to link him to civilization (1965, 38). Such a figure is to some James's "last word on the subject" of an America which now seems more "sinister" than "innocent" (Wilt and Lucas xix; Swan 1957, 26; 1948 10–13; also Zabel 12–13). Mizener, however, points out that James would also criticize Londoners for a similar materialism (205). Even more acerbly, Wyndham Lewis wrote that the subsequent "proletarianization" of England and France in the manner of the United States would have caused James to show a face as shocking in its disappointment as the alter ego in its horror (228). Bewley discerns a further qualification to the seeming anti-American tenor of the tale by observing that Brydon is, after all, an American, even if an expatriate (1959, 253–54). With a less positive reading of Brydon, Quentin Anderson also offers a defense of his homeland, stating that in the story there is "no moral distinction between the greed of the American expatriate and that of the American millionaire." Indeed, writes Anderson, "the real sinner is the expatriate" (178, 181). As Anderson stresses, Alice accepts the other, more American, self, a fact Wegelin considers significant, seeing James, too, as pitying the figure. However, he asserts that she is charmed more by Brydon as he is, who achieves his triumph by virtue of being the product of a culture of superior "charm" (155–56). Taking a different point of view, Fogel works the dates of the tale, its writing and publication, to designate it a "centennial" story. Such a reading, writes Fogel, heightens the sense of Brydon's "apostasy," but in his reconciliation with Alice, who represents the American spirit at its best, and in his rejection of the apparition, which represents its "most destructive potentials," it presents a complex view of America.

In a reading built on Bakhtin, and drawing on the work of Nancy Chodorow and Carol Gilligan, Benert still sees the story as very much about James's response to America. The story, she writes, with its framing conversations, takes the form of a dialogue marked by gender difference. Unlike Alice, who focuses on "attachment," Brydon sees the world in a typically male polarized view, and the creation of a double is the mark of his particular midlife "crisis of identity and separation." In his conversations with Alice, Brydon seeks to "coopt" her answers, and to evade what she recognizes is the "real issue—his power," which takes shape in the double. After all, Brydon has taken advantage of the monstrous capitalism whose image he wishes to deny. The central section shifts from dialogue to imagery, which Brydon seeks to control as he pursues his alter ego. Unable ultimately to sustain the effort, he faints, only to be rescued by Alice, who, unlike him, "can transcend the polarities and face the realities." Brydon's house mirrors not only his self, argues Benert, but a society James viewed as empty of "public culture" and "humanizing" in either "manners or architecture," showing a bleak view of America's opportunities for men, if a happy resolution for Brydon in the "warmth and generosity" of Alice (116–24).

As Benert observes, one of the primary characteristics of the story's telling is its imagery. The chief image is that of the house on the jolly corner. To Matthiessen, the depiction of the house—lighted from the outside—represents a peak in James's "pictorial skills." Because the house is facing possible demolition, Matthiessen adds, it conveys a "peculiarly intimate sense" of

Brydon's own past being obliterated (*American* 1947, xxiii; 1944, 137). Most typically the house is seen as a reflection of Brydon's own mind (e.g., Delbaere-Garant 591; Thomson; Knapp 30). Miller pictures Brydon "burgling himself" within it as he "disputes the common ground of his childhood with a phantom fellow squatter" (230). In an extended reading of its "perfect metaphor," Knapp calls the house an "archetypal construct," the "great gaunt shell" in which Brydon can grow, a *temenos* or "sacred space" in which he can bring back to life his past, which still lives there in the form of "correspondences and analogies" of sight and sound (27–44). It is also an embodiment of the past—Levin cites from Melville's *Mardi* his observation that while travel represents space, architecture represents "duration" (5). Others, however, have cast the house as the house of fiction. Bier points to a possible pun on "storey" and "story" as well as the emphasis on "style," while Robinson pictures Brydon trapped within a "solipsistic house of fictional reflections" (Bier 323 n.5; Robinson 185). Terrie argues that the image of the house like a "great glass bowl" describes both the experience of Brydon entering the house, and a reader entering the tale (16).

The "great glass bowl . . . set delicately humming by the play of a moist finger around the edge" holds Brydon's "mystical other world" and gives forth the "sigh" of "all the old baffled foresworn possibilities" of his life (CT 12, 209). Grenander glosses the image as a glass armonica such as Mesmer used to hypnotize his subjects, arguing that Brydon's visits to the house elicit "a state of autohypnosis" in which he sees the ghost. While Haggerty praises its delicate impressionism, Knapp sees the "feminine" synesthetic image merging the black and white of the floor, Jacobs the conscious front of the house and the unconscious back (Haggerty 161; Knapp 39; Jacobs 350). Boren discourses on the way the "aural" image draws attention from the visual image of the alter ego, offering a "more innocent kind of imagination," the two counterpoised by James's voice as narrator. Such a "lyrical" approach is, in Boren's view, "subversive"—operatic—as multiple voices take over from the moral of "know thyself" and make certainty impossible (12–15).

When Brydon descends the staircase, the rooms below seem like "some watery under-world," the first floor like "the bottom of the sea" (CT 12, 223). At this point, according to Wright, the "images refuse to remain fixed" (205). Even so, Irwin sees the sea representing the "descent of the self into the narcissistic pool" (16). Thomson reads the image as an "eerily luminous submarine metaphor," appropriate as the ocean marks the division between America and Europe, so that Brydon is forced to use a "submerged link" to contact his past. Such a descent, he contends, is a "retreat from meaningful reality," but useful as his "revulsion" from its truth will allow him to escape.

The ocean floor of Brydon's house is paved with black and white squares whose absence from the television version Banta lamented, noting that they would have played off well against the apparition's black and white evening dress (1989, 130). Brydon refers to them as the "marble squares of his child-hood" and they have elicted other interpretations as well (CT 12, 223). Thomson sees Brydon choosing the white squares over the black in leaving for Europe, while Quentin Anderson contends that the fact that they served as a lesson in "style" shows that the "house of life" is not in Europe but in New York (177). To Bier, however, the marble is "morguelike" (332). Buitenhuis likens them to a game of chess, with the conflict between good and evil (218). The resemblance to a chess board, noted also by Tuveson, fits well with Esch's reading of the key phrase "turning the tables" as a reference to a game of chess (80). To Jacobs, the "polarized" perspective they represent complicates Brydon's bringing together of his two selves (55). Tuveson, how-ever, sees the squares connecting Brydon's two selves, representing not only "style" but family (279). Irwin treats the squares as connecting Brydon and James, representing "the black squares of print on the white squares of the page" through which "a writer must always encounter his other self in the growth of a personal style" (17).

The images used to describe Brydon, as Jones observes, are of "solitary fig-ure[s]" whether a Pantaloon, a hero of romance, or a hunter (256). His search, writes Delbaere-Garant, is actually a "violent game" described "in terms of physical action" (591–92). According to Terrie, James often used such violent imagery to depict the "interior life," as in the image of Brydon tracking his prey "like some monstrous stealthy cat" (15).

Although such readings demonstrate that the "figures" of the tale have been read in terms of meaning, not simply style, Esch argues for a reading that calls into question the whole concept of "figurative" and even "literal" meaning, citing Levin's reading of the tale as giving a "diagram" of the rela-tionship of the writer, the reader, and his material (Levin 5). To Esch, the tale "turns upon the consequences, for character, narrator, and reader, of 'strange figures' lurking in the text in the guise of familiar idioms." She focuses on two narratorial intrusions, one that seems to confess to the inadequacy of narra-tion, and a second that seems to assert its adequacy. Both, she writes, raise questions of the validity of figural writing. Brydon himself thinks figuratively, and the ghost starts as an "analogy" that Brydon literalizes through *prosopopoeia*—the making present of something abstract. The rigidly literal-izing Brydon, however, is constantly surprised by everything, suspecting at last "another agent" behind the turning of the ghost. The real "hazard," writes Esch, is "his conceivable loss of mastery over discourse . . . the possibility that his metaphors are out of his control." Because the figure "refuses to be restricted by the significance assigned it," a "new uncertainty" arises. The text shows language itself "susceptible to the very indetermination" that distinc-tions between literal and figurative seek to prevent. While Alice seems to see more clearly than Brydon, Esch questions her confirmation of the figure. Rather she takes Alice's earlier granting of independence to the figure as an "example for the reader of the tale" who can now see the central issue of the story as "the narrative's system of written signs." An intriguing reading thus ends rather disappointingly with the conclusion that reading is impossible.

The central "figure" in the tale, as Esch's reading makes clear, is the "ghost." Cameron, who observes the image of highway robbery in Brydon's complaint that everyone demands his opinion in a "stand-and-deliver way," proceeds to point out how Brydon "*is* delivered of his thought" by seeing his possible self—a visible embodiment of what he has thought privately (136n). To Purdy, Brydon's "double" is "indistinguishable from a ghost" (54). Perhaps, but the figure that appears to Brydon, one of the central images of the tale, has been the subject of much debate. Is it a supernatural phenomenon? a psychological one? Early on, Edgar remarked that a summary of the tale's events would convince a reader that Brydon was insane, although a reading of the tale itself brings the reader to share Brydon's experience so closely that he waives such judgment (183; see also Vaid 238–40). Henkle also sees James guiding his readers into an identification with Brydon, but adds that James then shows Brydon's vision to be not entirely reliable (82–84). Thompson calls the ambiguity deliberate (Thompson 34; also Fox 7). Most see the tale's supernatural enclosed in the psychological. Josephson writes that the story occurs, "one presumes, in the supernatural or really the fear-world of the dream" (280). Unrue speaks of Brydon's "trance-like states" (1976, 299). Wright calls the tale's events "symbolic," but argues that if one is to derive meaning from them, one "must still treat them as literal facts." In the tale one sees the "concrete embodiment" Brydon has given to the "inner workings" of his own mind until the penultimate scene, "when the supernatural fuses with the psychological and then finally yields to it entirely" (200–1). Briggs reverses the emphasis to state that even if the only reality in the tale is that of the "mind of man" still James projects it through space and time so freely that it enters the realm of the supernatural (48). Certainly, as McCarthy among others has commented, the apparition is a "vividly felt presence" (107). Although Buitenhuis, like Edgar, judges Brydon "very close to insanity" as he searches for the ghost he has created, he observes how James's "ambiguity of technique" naturally continues to elicit new interpretations (216). The ghost may be conjured up, or may be real, as seems to be confirmed by Alice, but for Brooks, Lewis, and Warren "the special quality of James's fairy-tale ghost stories [is] that these 'realistic' questions are quite beside the point" (1446).

Haggerty sees the tale as demonstrating "how we can live with the unknown," tracing the way an "unspecified 'it'" becomes "analogous" to a ghost and then that "analogical language" becomes "a version of the real." Thus Brydon imagines a ghost whose reality then terrifies him. Disagreeing with Przybylowicz's theory that Brydon has left the "natural-fact-world," he sees the realms of "subjective and objective," of "interior and exterior," of "physical and mental," the "languages of metaphor and metonymy," as blend-ed in the tale so that the "objective presence" of the ghost is of little concern. Even Alice, who could "dismiss" the ghost by her "cool rationality," serves instead to "contextualize the Gothic nightmare." The reader, Haggerty con-cludes, also accepts the figure as "an expression of Brydon's struggle with himself" (160–65).

While Norrman sees "not a whit of difference" between Brydon and the apparition, most critics stress a contrast (145–46). William Smith comments on the inequality of the relationship between Brydon and his alter ego, unlike that between Brydon and Alice, because the alter ego is dependent on them for his existence. He sees this treatment of multiple, diverse relationships reflected in the preponderance of compound-complex sentences in the tale (164). To Dietrichson, too, the ghost is inferior to Brydon—"grizzled, but foppish" (92). To many critics, the apparition is, as Brydon perceives it, "the face of a stranger. . . . evil, odious, blatant, vulgar" (CT 12, 226; e.g., Jefferson 95). Any alternate self must be hateful, states Andreas, even as he stops to pay tribute to the strength of Brydon's other self in surviving thirty-three years alone (150–51). Kimbel sees a universal significance in the vision of the "monstrous" other self going beyond the specific issues of country and capitalism to show the hidden, nocturnal side of the "human spirit" (40). Greene also sees the story moving beyond social criticism, not simply in its depiction of "man's ability to damn himself" but in its pitying such a damned soul ("Private," 29–30; "Aspect," 37). Voss similarly emphasizes the "pitiful" suffering of the figure (149).

Whatever its character, the ghost is generally read as a double or "other self" for Brydon. Blackmur sees the tale as being about "those partly living other selves, those unused possibilities out of the past, those unfollowed temptations of character, which if not struck down will overwhelm and engulf the living self." Such issues he writes were once dealt with by exorcism, nowadays by psychiatry, and in the tale itself by "imaginative exorcism" ([1942] 1983, 56–57). In his psychiatric approach, Rosenzweig judges the ghost typical of James in its representation not of "shadows of lives once lived, but the immortal impulses of the unlived life." The missing fingers of the "rejected self," he writes, stand "in some relation to the fact that the life was not lived or that, in other words, a kind of psychological death had occurred" (104). Rosenfield also discerns in the tale a kind of death, noting the suggestion of the "primitive belief that the sight of one's self may be an anticipation of death" (333). Edel pictures Brydon as a "man haunted by him-self, as he was and as he might have been," and who is afraid to face those selves even after he has conjured them up (1953, 584; *Life* 5, 316). Hocks calls the tale "unique" in its genuine reconciliation of "alter" and "ego," such that Brydon is "his own 'other self,'" attributing to it his own state of mind and changes of mood. The two, writes Hocks, are "empirically *con*joined in polarity." Given their close relationship, Hocks deems it likely that someone will eventually argue that Brydon is his own ghost, and states that one could in fact argue that Brydon and his ghost change places just before the turning point, with Brydon at the top of the stairs. Another variant he offers would be to see the point of view in the tale switching at the same point from "Brydon-*ego*" to "Brydon-*alter*." Hocks does not wish to argue such readings himself, simply to note their plausibility and inevitability in a tale that both features an alter ego and captures the "genuine polarity" of the "contraries" of identity which then "transform *into each other*" (206–8). Purdy emphasizes the time element, with Brydon looking "across the ends" of a "time fork" to see a double sprung originally from one side of his self, but grown increasingly far apart. In searching for his other self, Purdy writes, Brydon is seeking to "master his own identity," but by giving the ghost "incorporation in space and time"—however necessary the step—he risks his own existence (51, 55). As Goetz remarks, in the case of doubles, it always seems as if the original "does not possess his own identity" (159)

The character of a double, of course, is dependent on what it is doubling. If Brydon's double has been characterized as evil, Brydon as he is at the start of the tale has not escaped unblemished. Among the harshest critics, Stein sees Brydon as a man who has "accomplished little" given his gifts. Delbaere-Garant says bluntly, he "has made a hash of his life" (589). His chief weakness appears to be his egotism (e.g., Wright 201). If he has the makings of a good businessman, it may well be due to the same "ego" which caused him to leave New York and Alice to pursue his own way. In one conversation, Alice declares to Brydon, "You don't care for anything but yourself" (CT 12, 206). Her remark has been judged accurate and central to the tale (e.g., Shulman 47). Alice's mood at the time, Byers opines, is mainly one of exasperation, but he observes how Brydon immediately illustrates his selfishness by thinking that Alice is referring to his alter ego (93). Brydon's mistake, according to Delfattore, is part of his chronic "self-deceptive rationalization" by which he shifts the blame for his faults onto something "other" than himself (335–36). Even his boast of having lived a "frivolous, scandalous" life is taken issue with by Bier who calls it "only a mini-scandal of self-pampering" (330).

Still, Brydon has his defenders. Haggerty writes that he "at no time alienated us" (166). Moseley sees him treating both Alice and his other self "with good faith rather than egotism" and some courage as well (80–81). Additionally, Brydon's courage in seeking for his other self has generally received praise. Here, too, however, there is significant dissent, focusing in particular on Brydon's "discretion" in leaving closed the door behind which he suspects the ghost is hiding (CT 12, 218; e.g., Vaid 242; Tintner 1987, 193; Jacobs 57). Such discretion, according to Sanford, is but another example of "cowardly egotism"—in Vaid's words, a "rationalization" of Brydon's own fear, which Delfattore sees him transferring to the figure (Sanford 217; Vaid

242; Delfattore 337). One may point also to the passage where the narrator speaks of the "revelation he pretended to invite" (CT 12, 207).

Starting with a selfish and searching Brydon, critics have woven many different tales of multiple Brydons, their confrontation, and their resolution. Quentin Anderson depicts Brydon as a man who seemed "bold and free" in leaving home, but who left behind his talents. Reading the tale as a story of a man who discovers "what he *would have been*," Anderson writes, is a "trap," a term Vaid particularly objects to (Vaid 278–79 n.19). According to Anderson, Brydon discovers rather the selfishness in "what he *has been*" (176–77). Thorberg agrees with Anderson that the other self is what Brydon has been, judging the alternative "superficial." He draws attention, however, not to Brydon's selfishness but the "intensity" of his consciousness—"his great hunger for experience." The life Brydon has lived in Europe, writes Thorberg, "might have been sufficient" for someone else, but not for him. Thus through the years Brydon has been creating in his mind "another life . . . as real, indeed more real" because "inner and profounder" (188–89).

Wright begins by remarking on the odd significance of Brydon's seeming talent for construction, given that he has never created anything and that the new construction with its consequent destruction of the past is what most distresses him in the city. As Brydon explores the possibility of a different self, Alice looks ahead to the possibility of a third, superior one. The second self, in turn, has an identity to defend, and asserting that James's central concern is with "what *is*," Wright reads it as showing part of Brydon's "very nature" (200–9).

Earlier, Stovall offered not a double, but a triple Brydon, in an analysis designed to counter the "anti-American" readings of such critics as Van Wyck Brooks. Like Thorberg earlier, Stovall agrees with Anderson that Brydon has a "double consciousness," but not that it represents Brydon's "selfish and selfless aspects." The first ghost *is* what Brydon would have been if he had stayed in New York, *but* Brydon, Stovall maintains, never sees it, as it remains upstairs where the sense of the past is thickest. The figure that Brydon sees by the front door is "himself as he actually is"—namely a "false self" a "mask" he has worn throughout his years in Europe. The apparition by the door has characteristics of both selves, but Stovall associates its missing fingers not with American violence, but Old World big-game hunting. Consequently, Brydon's reaction to it does not indicate anything of his—or James's—final attitude to America.

Stovall's two-ghost reading has garnered few followers. Both Buitenhuis and Bier object that it adds new questions more than it reconciles old ones (Buitenhuis 216; Bier 322 n.3). Fogel also objects to Stovall's reading, offering instead his own. He first multiplies the possible selves, suggesting such choices as "Dead Self" vs. "Living Self," "False Self" vs. "True One," American vs. Europeanized, and then selects two, "worst self" which embodies not only parts of Brydon's unrealized American potential, but his actual European traits, particularly his egotism, and "best self" also only "partially realized." Both represent extremes: Brydon wishes to gain from the alter ego its power without accepting its evil or losing his own sensibility (192–93).

Returning to America, Brydon not only has to figure out the relationship between his different selves, but between himself and Alice. The addition of Alice, Strout notes, is the main change from the dream, and her presence "creates a dialogue . . . full of dramatic irony" (1979, 52). Her role is a key one, as many critics have insisted, and she contributes significantly to Brydon's conception of the ghost (e.g., Buitenhuis 213; Honig 84; Hocks 203; Moore 89). To Quentin Anderson, Alice becomes Brydon's "conscience," but at the same time she is neither "censorious" nor "coercive" (181). Fogel indicates a resemblance between the name Alice and the Greek word for truth, *aletheia* (202 n.12). As Kimbel describes her, she is one of James's "perfectly understanding and infinitely patient women," ready, writes Rosenzweig, to accept Brydon as he is or to help "reconcile" him to his other self (Kimbel 39; Rosenzweig 104; also Sharp 58). She is, as Pirie calls her, "sane" (134). She is not, however, stupid. Rosenblatt goes so far as to indicate that her irony indicates she is "more amused than charmed by Spencer Brydon's obsession" (282).

Alice appears only in the opening and closing section of the tripartite tale, so that as Delbaere-Garant puts it, Brydon's search for self is framed by sections that "illustrate the hero's relation to the external world" as illustrated by Alice (588). Springer further elaborates on Alice as a frame character. Like many critics she points out Alice's superior knowledge of Brydon's character. Alice recognizes that despite his contempt for the greed of modern New York, Brydon is "rather comfortable with it as a temporary curiosity," and that despite his belief that it has no connection with his "real life" abroad, it has in fact supported it. She is also proof that life in New York need not corrupt. "Too wise to oppose him openly," she chooses simply to be "*there*" for him. Her character, writes Springer, also serves as a testament to his, contributes to his eventual facing of his real self, and makes likely the success of their love at the end (116–23).

Terrie sees a "barrage of questions" arising from the tale's conclusion (16), and many of the questions have involved Alice. Brydon tells her at the end that the figure "has a million a year . . . . But he hasn't you" (CT 12, 232). Such a view seems to cast Alice as the reward for Brydon's struggle, and Schneider indeed writes that Brydon "receives, almost as compensation, Alice Staverton's love" (33; also Moseley 80–81). Dupee is one of the few to see Brydon as saving Alice, while Krook sees him saved by his power to receive her love (Dupee 159; Krook 334–35). Indeed, several critics cast Alice not simply as the seal, but the source, of Brydon's salvation (e.g., Blackmur [1942] 1983, 57–58; Thomson; Irwin 17). Edel has argued that Brydon does not conquer or recognize his ghost, but comes to accept him, and that only because Alice does ([1949] 1963, 395; see also Strout 1980, 108). Buitenhuis, similarly if less censoriously, observes how Brydon loses courage, refusing to recognize the self he has called up, but is saved by Alice's love, which accepts his flawed self (213–21; also Pirie 136–38). Hocks argues that Alice, having lived in New York, is not only less horrified by the alter ego, but aware that Brydon and the qualities he values in himself would not have been "irrevocably destroyed" had he stayed. Brydon does not know this even at the end, although to Hocks Brydon's living in Europe off his American rents is not hypocrisy, as Beebe sees it, but a healthy cooperation of his two selves (Beebe 221). Still, Hocks contends, Brydon, freed from his obsession and open now to love, "will presumably do so rather soon" (203–5). Similarly, Knapp sees Brydon avoiding the final moment of self-knowledge, while a sympathetic Alice, recognizing the "pain" of containing opposites for a sensitive man, does not force the issue on a Brydon who does at least now understand "the meaning of the heart" (43–44).

Alice, writes Jones, is Brydon's "guardian angel." Marked by "egocentric innocence," Brydon returns to a family home characterized by memories of "alienation, deaths" that he still patronizingly refers to as the "jolly corner." He rationalizes the ghost's hiding of his face as his triumph, and faints anyway, stripped of the pride that hampered him. But Alice kisses him and frees him of his guilt, signifying a reconciliation with the Old New York he once rejected. Having faced "the facts and the symbols of his whole way of life," he can now renounce them, and with Alice begin to "live an integrated life" (254–57). Fogel also assigns Alice a significant role, arguing that Brydon's remark at the end, "You brought me literally to life," applies "broadly" to her role throughout (192). To Haggerty, the horror of the "ghostly confrontation" is central, and it is only the presence of Alice who keeps it from being "devastating." As tutor, mother, and lover, she can accept the fact of "difference" that terrifies Brydon and overcome it with love (164–66).

Haggerty's reading contains a hint of a common qualification to Alice's achievement, and to the reading of the conclusion as a happy ending. Edel early on pictured Alice accepting Brydon "as a mother accepts her child" ([1949] 1963, 394; also Miller 231–32). Similarly, while acknowledging the possibility of Brydon's marrying Alice, Shroeder still finds their relationship at the end bearing many of the marks of the mother-child relationship, with Mrs. Muldoon serving as midwife (429). Although the "mother" label seems at times a way of dispatching superior women, such a reading need not reflect primarily on Alice. Delfattore argues that Brydon's relationship to Alice is a reflection of *his* "immaturity, self-centeredness, and ineffectuality" (341). To Strout, readings that focus on wombs, surrogate mothers, and symbolic rebirth are simply "psycho-babble" (1979, 50). Tremper offers a partial modification of such readings. She looks at the tale as the story of a man kept from commitment by a "self-contempt" he hides under his egotism, who is finally able to accept himself and the possibility of an adult relationship through Alice. Given the rareness of such romantic reconciliations in James's works, she argues, the overtone of a mother-son relationship, while a "taint," is "relatively minor and easily forgotten" (71–74). Knapp declares that while "the jolly corner" represents the realm of "the Great Earth Mother," Alice is not a mother figure (39–40, 44).

Rovit offers an added role for Alice in a reading of "The Jolly Corner" as a "closed" allegory, rather than an "open" symbolic work. Bothered by what he judges the damage done the realism of the tale by the supernatural element, Rovit focuses on the most intractable evidence of its existence, Alice's dreams of the ghost. To fit them into a psychological reading, Rovit suggests treating Alice "as a third part of a single total consciousness," Brydon's "conscience," even "the principle of divine love." Taking the entire tale as "interiorized action," according to Rovit, justifies the appearance of the ghost to Alice. Rovit recognizes possible objections, including the fact that Alice is presented as more "objectively real" than the alter ego. Rovit's reading focuses additionally on Brydon's relationship with his father, casting the tale as "a fictional rehearsing of the archetypal rebellion against the father," in which a guilty Brydon returns in part to face his dead father. The somewhat feminine Brydon is repulsed by the masculine power the fatherly alter ego represents, but has already released forces he cannot now avoid. Alice, then, as a mother figure, "intercedes" for the son with the father. Rovit criticizes Brydon's subsequent reunion with Alice as "dramatically disappointing" and "regressive," but nevertheless judges it as progress for Brydon. Brydon is now whole and capable of entering into a relationship with another.

Stovall casts Alice not as the third part of Brydon, but the person who helps him to put his three "selves" in order. Through the love Brydon has not yet recognized in a process he will never fully understand, she achieves "a common psychic experience" that frees him both from his "false" European self and his ghostly American self to achieve a "real self." Similarly Wright views the matter as not simply a choice between two selves, but a new transformed self that still contains parts of both former selves. Wright cautions, however, that while Alice will help him live with his new self-knowledge, he has not been metamorphosed into a "paragon of virtue." Rather he remains "very human," wanting to believe the figure was not himself, and "comically jealous" of Alice's acceptance of it. He has, however, found a "home," a significant achievement Wright notes, as in James life is "primarily a social matter" (202–9, 244). Tuveson again casts Alice not as the third part of Brydon, but as a woman who helps him to achieve a kind of third self. By her introduction of a new "element," Alice allows Brydon to "transcend both selves"—European and American—in "a kind of redemptive triumph." Tuveson pictures Alice supporting Brydon through her "psychically projected" love, even as his pity for the other self helps him give up his "lingering regret" that he was not a "success" and choose "being" instead (275–79). Similarly, Knapp speaks of Alice as "an anima figure," a "third force" who helps put together the two sides of Brydon (27, 31, 37).

It is Alice who tells Brydon at the end that the apparition "isn't—no, he isn't—*you!*" (CT 12, 232). The line has been read many ways, and to some it is an indication that Brydon never truly achieves the self-knowledge he pretends he has been seeking, and that Alice shelters him from this failure (e.g., Pirie 137–38). Sicker, for example, pictures Brydon at the end so exhausted by his encounter that he accepts her reassurance not as a lover, but "as a frightened child seeking his mother's comfort after a nightmare" (172). Differing with Sicker, Kaston sees a Brydon who has, in the words of the tale, "blighted" himself through repression, and so confronts a ghost associated with "love and sexuality." But Alice's confirmation that the ghost is not Brydon, she maintains, is less a rationalizing reassurance, than the recognition that Brydon is no longer a partial self. The final image of the tale, too, she points out, is not the maternal one of Brydon resting in Alice's arms, but the more active, romantic one of Brydon drawing Alice to him (150–52; also Fogel 199).

Sharp reads the ending differently, maintaining that Brydon rejects Alice because of her statement that she "liked" the apparition. It makes sense, Sharp adds, for Alice to like the other self who, by staying home, might have "given her the chance to marry him" (xviii, 59). Clair sees Alice as succeeding, but also portrays her as a woman interested primarily in securing her man, in part at least to fulfill her dreams of increased wealth and social standing. Taking issue with the usual readings of Alice as a "benevolent" but "minor" character, Clair assigns her a leading role as Brydon's "antagonist," a clever woman who recognizes that her only way to win the egotistic Brydon is by appealing to his incipient interest in a "ghost." According to Clair, she not only lies that she has seen the ghost in her dreams, but goes so far as to hire an imitation "ghost" to "haunt" Brydon's house. Her plan almost fails when her employee does not encounter Brydon until dawn, when the increased light makes it clear to Brydon that it is not his self he sees. In the final dialogue, which he calls "one of James's best comic scenes," Alice strives to figure out what Brydon actually saw, rearranging her story, including her premature arrival, in a manner that does not quite add up, but which Brydon accepts. The "unwitting dupe" throughout, Brydon still, in Clair's projection, is left better off than he started. Alice was not acting entirely selfishly— Brydon did need help. Her ruse, he adds, is not without a "tragic overtone," as Brydon considered suicide during the course of the night. For those who object to such a reading as "too-precious concealment," Clair stresses the tale's "*operative* irony," and contends that without the twist the tale would be simply "a sentimental, one-dimensional case history of a neurotic" (17–36).

Byers also calls Alice a liar. He does not go so far as to say she invents the ghost, but argues that, hoping for a proposal, she pretends to see it in order to keep up Brydon's interest in her. Still he judges her pursuit of him "very human," a deliberate "parallel and prelude" to Brydon's pursuit of his other self. Like Rovit, he sees Brydon's name suggesting a certain passive femininity, attributing to Alice a parallel active masculinity. In his reading, Brydon leaves America because it was "substance without style," to pursue in Europe "style without substance." The idea of another self is at first simply another "new sensation." Again, like Rovit, Byers identifies the alter ego with Brydon's "virile being." He emphasizes, however, the figure's desire to see Brydon, and its terror when it does so, facing a man Byers calls "sybaritic, parasitic, cowardly, selfish, and consequently evil." Like other critics, he sees the reassuring Alice at the end as a "mother-lover figure," but with a twist, he maintains that Alice is lying about the ghost's appearance, basing it on Brydon's own. Thus, while most critics read the missing fingers as confirming the truth of Alice's dream, Byers attributes the loss to Brydon himself. "Not a shred of presentable evidence" exists to support such a view according to Fogel, but others have shared it, including Rogers and Knapp (Fogel 201 n.10; Rogers 1956, 449–50; Knapp 42). Still, Byers's reading, like Clair's, provides a "bright future" in which Brydon learns with Alice to balance "the best of the two worlds—substance and style."

As such readings indicate, one approach to Brydon's crisis is to cast it as a sexual one. Sanford, for example, speaks of Alice restoring Spencer by conquering "the furniture of his childhood memories" so that he "passes through the door of sexual love" (217). In an extended analysis, Johnson comments on the "duality" throughout the tale with its two houses, two selves, "inner" and "outer" worlds, black and white squares, and contrasts of masculine and feminine. Brydon's insistent rigidity is poor equipment to face such complexity. He is bothered by his passive, sensual, feminine side in the face of aggressively masculine New York, even as he is ashamed of the "destructive potential" of the masculine, and yearns for a world of "childlike security." His relationship to Alice, in Johnson's view, is further complicated by his sense that it is "incestuous," forbidden because of her association with "hearth, home, family and mother." The alter ego triumphs over him because it possesses the strength Brydon lacks. This is not the end of Brydon, however, as Alice works with him to accept the "masculinity in his personality," and as he possesses "some latent capacity . . . to respond" and so to accept the ambivalence and complexity of his adult self.

In the television script by Arthur Barron, Brydon's "buried" self is his male sexuality, allowing for a similar recognition of Alice's own sexuality. Such an approach, in the view of Henry Nash Smith, makes Brydon's crisis "more understandable" (126). Banta, on the other hand, finds the emphasis on Alice the "fatal flaw" in Barron's script. Its "very safe ending," she argues, avoids the real encounter between Brydon and "his own 'possibilities' that eventually lead him toward a somewhat disturbing love relation with a woman who will 'possess' him as much as any ghost" (1989, 129). Earlier, Banta had objected to the ending of the tale itself as anticlimactic in its portrayal of a Brydon "saved" by the love of a woman. To her, the strength of the tale is in its tense depiction of the "great time of testing and victory." In her reading, she agrees with Stovall that there are two ghosts, and with Thorberg that while Brydon is "curious" about the one associated with his past, he is "appalled" by the one showing what he is. Thus, she writes, the tale has a "double climax," one for each ghost. The encounter with the first demonstrates that "a man's unused possibilities are forever a part of his imaginative life." By taking responsibility for this other self, Brydon "finally suffers" and, by forgiving it, finds a way to free himself from his guilt. Facing the second, Brydon sees "what he *is*," and is repelled by it. Both selves are simultaneously "other" and part of Brydon, but to "be freed completely into his conscious life," Brydon must "die" to both (136–41, 151–52).

Freedman, in contrast, emphasizes not the search but the arrival. He observes how the story starts in a "vocabulary of generalizations"—"everyone," "everything," and "all"—and that Brydon recognizes that for him, "'everything' is some sort of self-knowledge," but that knowledge does not become real until it becomes "something" in the vision of the figure, until in the end "everything" also becomes real by accepting some limits. The true end of the search, writes Freedman, is not the figure, but "having Alice and being himself—as he is" (106–7). Chapman also emphasizes the romantic element. Like others, she sees Brydon as essentially egotistic, interested much less in his former homeland than in his self that remained there. Upon seeing that self, however, he faints in horror, and is able to accept it only through Alice's aid. His painful victory, Chapman writes, reveals to him not only the "depths of his own character" but of Alice's love, in what she calls one of James's "tenderest love scenes" (56–60).

The typical reading of the tale is, like Chapman's, affirmative, with Brydon reborn to a new life (see Fogel 200 n.2). For many, the key to Brydon's victory is his ability to recognize the final apparition as himself (e.g., Dupee 159; Allott 332; Beebe 221–22). For others, the alter ego is not Brydon. Quentin Anderson, for example, sees Brydon's salvation predicated on his recognition of "the total *otherness* of the creature" which allows him to die "to selfhood." To accept the "portrait" figure as his own self would mean damnation. The living Alice replaces the false image as the story concludes by showing Brydon's "early conception of style" to be really "love of the images of life for the sake of life itself which has been represented by the persons whose love had filled the house." To Anderson, too, Brydon's relationship with Alice is no qualifier to his triumph. Brydon is now "delightedly dependent on fostering love" (178–80). Fogel also sees Brydon as achieving a "real moral victory" although he rejects the figure as his real self. It is after all, writes Fogel, his "worst self" and even the present Brydon is better than that. Most particularly, the "worst self" would never have looked for his other. Still, Fogel contends, Brydon denies his identification with the figure only momentarily. His acceptance of love and Alice then exorcises his former self, Alice's statement that the figure "isn't-*you*" being not false reassurance, but an affirmation that Brydon is not what he was. Such a reading, he adds, is supported by the revisions in the New York Edition (197–99, 203 n.22).

Vaid, while picturing a Brydon rejuvenated rather than crushed by the vision of his alter ego, spends more time explaining Alice's "acceptance" of the figure, which he takes primarily as a sign of her unconditional love for Brydon, and a "pity" for someone now dead. He discerns in the tale's final love scene a "profoundly peaceful tone," its kiss the completion of the depiction of Brydon as a hero of romance (244–46).

Shulman, while also treating the alter ego as "alien," projects a more qualified victory. To Shulman, the start of the tale is semicomic, with Alice "for no reason at all that we can see" suddenly literalizing an idiom and creating a ghost. Still, the essential situation is one in which both "life and happiness" are at risk due to Brydon's selfishness. Even in the end, when Brydon is able to care for someone outside himself, to Shulman the "process of knowing" remains "much too unequivocally painful" to be in any strict sense a comedy (46–47). Bier also emphasizes the pain of the struggle in a reading that, like Johnson's, sees Brydon searching for a "means between extremes," and encountering an alter ego that represents power, particularly sexual potency. Bier, however, stops short of depicting a fully integrated Brydon, even though he at first sees Brydon's "raw courage," combined with Alice's encouragement, bringing about an appropriately "manly synthesis" of "alter ego and ego." But although Bier judges it appropriate that the revived Brydon is given the "last gesture," he also objects to the "too exquisite and embarrassing" suggestions of the "infantile and maternal," and further sees Brydon as simply "too prostrated by his experience to convince us of the synthesis" (328–34).

Keppler similarly portrays Brydon as a man who has in his encounter with the ghost gotten "a little too much what he has been after." Casting the two selves not as "a Now-self and a Then-self" but "two Now-selves," she portrays a Brydon deeply dissatisfied with himself, and so seeking another self, only to discover that he cannot control it, even as he tries to speak for it. In Brydon's very assumption that he was victorious over the figure, she concludes "there are strong suggestions" that he was not (165–67).

Todorov pictures Brydon setting out to achieve "an impossible union of mutually exclusive elements," acting as if his life were a "narrative" in which he can bring together the self that is and the self that might have been. When the absent alter ego, however, becomes a presence, it turns out that it is "totally alien." It was only his when it was absent. Alice confirms the difference, making "*selfhood* . . . as uncertain as being." Doubtful of his own identity, Brydon has still believed in "the existence of an essence, at least with regard to others," particularly Alice. Searching for the "presence" of an "I," Todorov writes, Brydon discovers in her a present "you." The victory, if qualified, is also humane: "The relation with another, even the humblest presence, is affirmed against the selfish (solitary) quest for absence. The self does not exist outside its relation with others, with another; essence is an illusion" (159–60, 186–88).

For Mackenzie, too, "The Jolly Corner" is the chronicle of two struggles, one for self, which ends in a form of defeat, and one for relationship, which admits of a certain victory. In his view, the theme of the tale, as of much of James's work, is that of "shock"—"an unexpected exposure of the self to and before the self"—and its companion, shame. Here the rival who shames Brydon is his own other self, who shows his failure to live sufficiently. In self-defense, he denies his double as "totally other," and "patrols" the house as if to "*harrow*" it. At the same time, admitting the very existence of the double is a source of anxiety. Before the closed door, according to Mackenzie, Brydon renounces "prurient knowing" and so even as he reveals his fear, "honors the rival self." When he encounters the double again, it fails because "*there is finally only enough identity for one*." Neither has truly lived. Still, the figure's disfigurement reflects most on Brydon, being caused by his vengefulness, and he faints at the sight of it. Having "died" of shame, however, he is reborn to "knowledge" or rather the "secret" of his failure he still will not admit. Indeed, in a way Brydon has at last "lived" and "earned identity." Alice collaborates with his reconstruction by not questioning his denial of the other, serving as a mediator between the two selves. Alice, Mackenzie observes, has always sacrificed her rights to Brydon's, and will probably continue doing so. Since it is unclear if Brydon realizes how much he owes her, neither is at the end entirely free of shame. But Alice's self-sacrificing love represents a "higher" plane of experience than that of the question of Brydon's identity, which it sustains (371).

Another two-part reading is that of Robinson. He pictures Brydon as he confronts his ghost "trapped" in "mirror-gazing"—"at once solipsism's only cure and most telling symptom." Because Alice has shared his vision, however, Brydon's individual "revelatory vision" becomes a "*social* medium" allowing a way out of love of self into a love for others. Her "vocal presence . . . makes possible an interpretative dialogue," even as in the tale they speak of their "communities of knowledge." Such shared knowledge does not take Brydon "*out* of his solipsism," but it at least "composes a dialogical community in which to explore it"—a move from solitary vision to communal language (184–86).

Brydon's story is not, however, completely over, Ward contends. Remarking that his pride might well cause the ghost to cower, Ward argues that despite having routed it, Brydon must still "re-examine his past" and thereby himself (162–63). To others, Brydon is a complete failure, his chance at change over with. According to Rosenfield, Brydon gains some knowledge but "denies the major implication" of his experience, "that the possibility of such a horrible life still exists within him" (334). Auchard also emphasizes Brydon's failure, the "negation" throughout the tale, but fails to consider the effect of the final scene on his analysis (51–53). Levy, too, appears to take a negative view of Brydon, referring to him as not only seeing the "sterility" of his life in the vision of the ghost, but also being "repulsed by the ghost of the gross sexual self he has spent his life evading" (32–33). Reading the tale as one of evasion rather than confrontation, Geismar contends that although Brydon faces a "fleeting glimpse" of himself in the figure, the ending is "false" because Brydon is not forced to acknowledge its horror as himself (355–64).

Stein also presents a Brydon who refuses to face himself, and offers little sympathy for a man whom he sees as selfish from start to finish. Agreeing with Stovall and Anderson that the ghost is Brydon as he is, Stein points to its advanced aging as proof that it is also a "projection of what he will be." In his view Alice's love, while "potentially redemptive," will prove insufficient to change Brydon as he moves to a "complete dependence on her as a buffer to shield him from having to face the harsh facts of his life." Love becomes then only "the last refuge of a coward."

The same year as Stein, Shelden gave as the tale's basic contrast "woman's selflessness" versus "man's selfishness." Like Banta, she sees Brydon less afraid of the "potential self of the past" upstairs than the self he is downstairs, which he will not admit is him—even though, as Byers would later, she sees the missing fingers as tying Brydon the hunter and the figure. In her view, however, Alice, too, is playing a role at the end, that of "the clever protector, totally aware" but hiding her knowledge. An "all-forgiving, all-accepting mother figure," Alice offers Brydon another chance, but, according to Shelden, there is "no assurance that Brydon will take advantage of her offer" (128–34). Delfattore also views Brydon as remaining fundamentally ignorant of himself. Beginning with the false assumption that he would have been "substantially different" in New York, Brydon refuses to acknowledge the evidence that his other self is "not a nonexistent, but a hidden self" and that his own self is less than the "enjoyed, the triumphant life" he believes it to be. He is able to recognize his own fear only when he has projected it onto the ghost, and to see that face as his own only for an instant. As a result, he stays "essentially unchanged," still insisting the figure was a potential self, and a tycoon at that. His staying fast in his "passivity and psychological immaturity" leaves Alice again to a "motherly role."

Przybylowicz offers another reading of Brydon as a man who rejects maturity. Originally fascinated with the idea of the other self, Brydon still wishes to "control" it so as to become "one" again, making the relationship one of aggression. Indeed, at the climax of the tale, according to Przybylowicz, the other looks for Brydon in an "exchange of identities," which represents Brydon's own unconscious desires. But after first recognizing the other as his other self, he then insists it is not, as it is "antithetical" to his own image of himself. What truly frightens Brydon, she writes, is the figure's capacity for the passion which Alice wishes him to acknowledge. Alice's dream accordingly represents "her own repressed libidinal desires." The more frightened Brydon, however, punishes the other by picturing it as mutilated, denying at the same time "the truth of his own castration and division," and hoping to make himself appear "fulfilled" in contrast. While Przybylowicz pictures Brydon as accepting Alice's love and so acknowledging sexuality, she judges his acceptance "suspect" as "Spencer has become schizoid by refusing the castration that would give him access to the symbolic," or put another way, "remains riveted in the homosexualizing capture experienced by the ideal ego in the imaginary matrix of the primal scene." The move to Alice, then, is in part a return to the mother, with Brydon remaining at the narcissistic level, although his alliance with her, she acknowledges, is more than most of James's heroes achieve (23, 113, 116–25, 146, 228–29).

As Brydon walks down the stairs after his first encounter with a ghost, he thinks to himself of "the clear delight" with which he will now "sacrifice" his home: "They might come in now, the builders, the destroyers" (CT 12, 223). To those who read the tale affirmatively, his decision is often seen as a sign of Brydon's new freedom from the past (e.g., Rovit 69; Stovall 83; Tuveson 279; Byers 95). Purdy, however, sees the decision as raising the question of "whose identity" Brydon now has (116). Tintner makes the incident the basis for an interpretation by which the tale shows it is not "too late" for Brydon, but in an unfortunate sense. She argues that those who read the tale "as a piece of self-congratulation on the part of Brydon" neglect the significance of his decision. In her view, Brydon has chosen to become his alter ego, a rich businessman who, after all, has been accepted by Alice. Alice, Tintner argues, nurses his obsession out of the desire for a "powerful husband," although like many critics she sees Brydon as egotistically unaware of her influence (1987, 193–94; 1986, 185–86; 1976, 402–3, 406, 413).

Other critics, however, have pictured Alice and Spencer "setting up house in the house on the jolly corner," as Jones puts it, "peopled now with life" rather than ghosts (257; also H. N. Smith 123). Strout does not see things quite so simply, but he also takes exception to Tintner's reading. He contends that the story is best read with the ghost representing Brydon's other present self. When Brydon leaves the ghost behind the door he is ashamed, trying to think of himself as "noble," only to say he will let in the builders. "Having thus shamefully become a developer," he sees the ghost, but does not recognize it. What he argues Tintner ignores is the way in which Brydon's love for Alice is a "transcendence of his former egotism" as she represents his connection with Old New York. Strout draws attention to the depiction of Brydon as a man who "has gone to sleep on news of a great inheritance, and then after dreaming it away, after profaning it, with matters strange to it, has waked up to a serenity of certitude and has only to lie and watch it grow" (CT 12, 227). The comparison, he writes, indicates "a return to sanity rather than to a continuation of his nocturnal, panic-stricken decision" to give over his inheritance to the developers. Picturing Brydon as Tintner does, finally giving in to commercialism, he concludes, "makes a mockery out of his sense of having been restored to life," and turns the tale "upside down" (1978, 48–52).

In her reading, Delbaere-Garant casts Brydon as a man whose "hypothetical talent for construction" implies a parallel talent for artistic construction. Compelled to give shape to his "particular obsession," he projects himself into a "ghost," his imagination stirred by the "germ" of Alice's remark about his "gift." But while Brydon believes he might have been better in America, James signals the reader through the fact that Brydon owns both the modern American house and the European "jolly corner" that the two Brydons are one and the same. Faced by the "finished picture" of the ghost, Brydon, too, sees his self as "monstrous." He has been using the "title of artist" as an excuse for an "idle egotistical life" and now discovers that he is but a "would-be artist," his incapacity physically symbolized in his weak eyesight and maimed hand. His first "creation," writes Delbaere-Garant, is an illustration of his limitations as a creator. Again, however, Delbaere-Garant discerns in the tale a higher level, as in the last scene he is saved by Alice's love. "For the great artist" in James, she concludes, "love of art may replace love of man and transcend it. For the others, like Brydon, human love is the only alternative to death" (589–96).

Jacobs also puts the tale in the context of the conflict of art and life, with art able to offer a permanence in the face of death, but at the same time paradoxically serving in ways as a denial of life. "The Jolly Corner" is, he writes, a "parable of the artist as an unmistakable American," and he attributes to Brydon a "successful artistic career in Europe." Noting the many opposites in the tale and the upside-down "proportions," he see Brydon "uncomfortable" with the division in himself between pragmatic and aesthetic. Alice, in contrast, seems a "perfect achievement of art" but also "a still-life." Brydon retreats into a jolly corner he claims is full of life; but, Jacobs observes, with a hint of social criticism, it is actually the "unexplored life of the back," the servant quarters, that makes possible the "fine social forms in front." Brydon "shapes" his experience into the "form" of the alter ego so that his one self, who lives in the world of fancy, pursues the other, who lives in the world of fact, but is actually "a figment of the former." The figure is the "most perfectly realized creation of Brydon's artistic imagination"—"his finest self-portrait. . . . in which he may not recognize himself but in which others can identify him all too readily." While Brydon's "Europeanized sensibilities" collapse before it, the truth is, writes Jacobs, that both alternatives are "monstrous" in isolation as "examples of the distortion of self that results from an inability to reconcile the imagination with reality." While Alice accepts both selves, Brydon cleaves to the European, as Alice recognizes in her "No, he isn't—*you!*"

In writing to his agent Pinker, James spoke of the tale as a "miraculous masterpiece" of the "supernatural-thrilling" (*Life* 5, 316). Later, he was quite flattered at a praising letter about it from Max Beerbohm (*Letters* 4, 508). It continues to receive high praise. Auchincloss calls it a "great" story, while Italo Calvino once identified it as "the story I would have wanted to write" (Auchincloss 143; Esch 76). Todorov speaks of it as James's "last and densest ghost story," and its density continues to elicit comment, not always praising. Fadiman calls it "surely one of the most difficult" of James's stories, due to the late James style, while Miller pictures it as "written in a willed and laborious manner" (Fadiman 641; Miller 231). Still, Delbaere-Garant, while concurring with Fadiman that it is "one of the most difficult," also calls it "one of the most rewarding of James's late stories" (588). Garnett, who has little use for late James, refers to the tale as "the last he was *able* to write" (x). Others have lauded the writing. Indeed Blackmur sees the tale's "poetry" as its strength, while calling its "fable" a "little too pat" ([1942] 1983, 58–59).

The fable, as originally read, is according to Q. D. Leavis "a simple statement whose artistic effect depends entirely on playing on the reader's nerves" (226). As such, it has, in the view of Tuveson "broad cultural resonance," with Brydon as a "kind of Everyman" in a tale with particular meaning for Americans (280). As Edel writes, it is in part "a parable of every life—an inquiry into 'what might have been'" (1970, 721). The trouble for critics with such a tale is that a story everyone can understand leaves too little to write about, and so encourages them to go far afield in their search for something new to say—a little like Spencer Brydon. "The Jolly Corner," however, develops its everyday story in a richly textured manner that offers numerous fields for conjecture and explanation. As a result, there seems to be in the criticism less straining for new readings, even as the readings that follow traditional lines seem to acknowledge and enrich each other. For those who do not have to contend with the vast body of critical literature about the tale, the tale has the power to remain remarkably fresh, to draw one into the story of Brydon, to care what happens to him despite his flaws, to hope he may even become a better person through his searching, to follow the slow evolution of his relationship with his other self and with Alice, and to hope that, however his encounter with that self may turn out, that the story will leave him and Alice safely and happily together.

Works Cited

Primary Works

James, Henry. 1908. "The Jolly Corner." *The English Review* 1 (December): 5–35.

———. 1909. "The Jolly Corner." In *The Novels and Tales of Henry James*. New York Edition. Vol. 17, 433–85. New York: Scribner's.

———. 1919. *The Uniform Tales of Henry James*. London: Martin Secker.

Secondary Works

Allott, Miriam. 1953. "Symbol and Image in the Later Work of Henry James." *Essays in Criticism* (Oxford) 3 (July): 321–36.

Anderson, Quentin. 1957. *The American Henry James*. New Brunswick, NJ: Rutgers University Press. Reprinted in part in *Henry James: Seven Stories and Studies*, ed. Edward Stone. New York: Appleton-Century-Crofts, 1961.

Anderson, Walter E. 1982. "The Visiting Mind: Henry James's Poetics of Seeing." *The Psychoanalytic Review* 69 (Winter): 513–32.

Andreas, Osborn. 1948. *Henry James and the Expanding Horizon: A Study of the Meaning and Basic Themes of James's Fiction*. Seattle: University of Washington Press.

Armstrong, Paul B. 1989. *The Phenomenology of Henry James*. Chapel Hill: University of North Carolina Press.

Auchard, John. 1986. *Silence in Henry James: The Heritage of Symbolism and Decadence*. University Park: Pennsylvania State University Press.

Auchincloss, Louis. 1975. *Reading Henry James*. Minneapolis: University of Minnesota Press. Revised from "Henry James's Literary Use of His American Tour (1904)." *The South Atlantic Quarterly* 74 (1975): 45–52.

Banta, Martha. 1989. "Henry James and the Arts of Translation." *Henry James Review* 10: 127–34.

———. 1972. *Henry James and the Occult: The Great Extension*. Bloomington: Indiana University Press.

Beach, Joseph Warren. [1918] 1954. *The Method of Henry James*. Philadelphia: Albert Saifer.

Beebe, Maurice L. 1964. *Ivory Towers and Sacred Founts: The Artist as Hero*. New York: New York University Press. Reprinted in part in *Henry James: Seven Stories and Studies*, ed. Edward Stone. New York: Appleton-Century-Crofts, 1961. Revised in part from "The Turned Back of Henry James." *South Atlantic Quarterly* 53 (1954): 521–39.

Benert, Annette Larson. 1987. "Dialogical Discourse in 'The Jolly Corner': The Entrepeneur as Language and Image." *Henry James Review* 8: 116–25.

Berland, Alwyn. 1981. *Culture and Conduct in the Novels of Henry James*. Cambridge: Cambridge University Press.

Berthoff, Warner. 1971. *Fictions and Events: Essays in Criticism and Literary History*. New York: Dutton.

———. 1965. *The Ferment of Realism: American Literature, 1884–1919*. New York: Free Press.

Bewley, Marius. 1968. *The Complex Fate: Hawthorne, Henry James, and Some Other American Writers*. London: Chatto & Windus.

———. 1959. *The Eccentric Design: Form in the Classic American Novel*. New York: Columbia University Press.

Bier, Jesse. 1979. "Henry James's 'The Jolly Corner': The Writer's Fable and the Deeper Matter." *Arizona Quarterly* 35: 321–34.

Blackmur, R. P. [1942] 1983. "*The Sacred Fount*." In *Studies in Henry James*. Ed. Veronica A. Makowsky, 45–68. New York: New Directions. Reprinted from *Kenyon Review* 4: 328–52.

———. [1974] 1983. "Henry James." In *Studies in Henry James*. Ed. Veronica A. Makowsky, 91–124. New York: New Directions. Reprinted from *Literary History of the United States*, ed. Robert E. Spiller, et al., 1039–64. New York: Macmillan.

Boren, Lynda S. 1989. *Eurydice Reclaimed: Language, Gender, and Voice in Henry James*. Ann Arbor: UMI Research Press.

Briggs, Julia. 1977. *Night Visitors: The Rise and Fall of the English Ghost Story*. London: Faber.

Brodhead, Richard H. 1986. *The School of Hawthorne*. New York: Oxford University Press.

Brooks, Cleanth, R. W. B. Lewis, and Robert Penn Warren, eds. 1973. *American Literature: The Makers and the Making*. Vol. 2. New York: St. Martin's.

Brooks, Peter. 1976. *The Melodramatic Imagination: Balzac, Henry James, Melodrama, and the Mode of Excess*. New Haven: Yale University Press.

Brooks, Van Wyck. [1925] 1972. *The Pilgrimage of Henry James*. New York: Dutton. Reprint. New York: Octagon Books. Reprinted in part from "Henry James: The American Scene." *Dial* 75 (July 1923): 29–30.

Buitenhuis, Peter. 1970. *The Grasping Imagination: The American Writings of Henry James*. Toronto: University of Toronto Press.

Byers, John R., Jr. 1976. "Alice Staverton's Redemption of Spenser Brydon in James' 'The Jolly Corner.'" *South Atlantic Bulletin* 41, no. 2: 90–99.

Cady, Edwin H. 1971. *The Light of Common Day: Realism in American Fiction*. Bloomington: Indiana University Press.

Cameron, Sharon. 1989. *Thinking in Henry James*. Chicago: University of Chicago Press.

Caramello, Charles. 1981. "Performing Self as Performance: James, Joyce, and the Postmodern Turn." *Southern Humanities Review* 15, no. 4 (Fall): 301–5.

Chapman, Sara S. 1975. "Stalking the Beast: Egomania and Redemptive Suffering in James's 'Major Phase.'" *Colby Library Quarterly* 11: 50–66.

Clair, John A. 1965. *The Ironic Dimension in the Fiction of Henry James*. Pittsburgh: Duquesne University Press.

Cowdery, Lauren Tozek. 1986. *The Nouvelle of Henry James in Theory and Practice*. Studies in Modern Literature 47. Ann Arbor: UMI Research Press.

Delbaere-Garant, J. 1967. "The Redeeming Form: Henry James's *The Jolly Corner*." *Revue des Langues Vivantes* 33: 588–96.

Delfattore, Joan. 1979. "The 'Other' Spencer Brydon." *Arizona Quarterly* 35: 335–41.

Dietrichson, Jan W. 1969. *The Image of Money in the American Novel of the Gilded Age*. Oslo: Universitetsforlaget; New York: Humanities.

Dupee, F. W. [1951] 1956. *Henry James*. Garden City, NY: Doubleday Anchor.

Edel, Leon, ed. 1970. *Henry James: Stories of the Supernatural*. New York: Taplinger

——. 1967. "Henry James: The Americano-European Legend." *University of Toronto Quarterly* 36 (July): 321–34.

——, ed. 1953. *Henry James: Selected Fiction*. New York: Dutton.

——, ed. [1949] 1963. *The Ghostly Tales of Henry James*. New York: The Universal Library, Grosset & Dunlap.

Edgar, Pelham. [1927] 1964. *Henry James, Man and Author*. New York: Russell & Russell.

Esch, Deborah. [1983] 1987. "A Jamesian About-Face: Notes on 'The Jolly Corner.'" In *Henry James's Daisy Miller, The Turn of the Screw and Other Tales*. Ed. Harold Bloom, 75–91. New York: Chelsea House. Also in *Henry James*, ed. Harold Bloom, 233–50. Reprinted from *English Literary History* 50: 587–605.

Fadiman, Clifton, ed. 1948. *The Short Stories of Henry James*. New York: Modern Library.

Fogel, Daniel Mark. 1987. "A New Reading of Henry James's 'The Jolly Corner.'" In *Critical Essays on Henry James: The Late Novels*. Ed. James W. Gargano, 190–203. Boston: G. K. Hall.

Fox, Hugh. 1968. *Henry James, A Critical Introduction*. Conesville, IA: John Westburg.

Frantz, Jean H. 1959. "A Probable Source for a James 'Nouvelle.'" *Modern Language Notes* 74 (March): 225–226.

Freedman, William A. [1962] 1970. "Universality in 'The Jolly Corner.'" In *Twentieth*

Century Interpretations of "The Turn of the Screw" and Other Tales. Ed. Jane P. Tompkins, 106–9. Englewood Cliffs, NJ: Prentice-Hall. Reprinted from *Texas Studies in Language and Literature* 4 (Spring 1962): 12–15.

Gale, Robert L. [1954] 1964. *The Caught Image: Figurative Language in the Fiction of Henry James*. Chapel Hill: University of North Carolina Press.

Gardner, John, and Lennis Dunlap, eds. 1962. *The Forms of Fiction*. New York: Random House.

Garnett, David, ed. 1946. *Fourteen Stories by Henry James*. London: Rupert Hart-Davis.

Geismar, Maxwell. 1963. *Henry James and the Jacobites*. Boston: Houghton Mifflin. Reprinted in *Twentieth Century Interpretations of "The Turn of the Screw" and Other Tales*, ed. Jane P. Tompkins, 106–9. Englewood Cliffs, NJ: Prentice-Hall, 1970.

Goetz, William R. 1986. *Henry James and the Darkest Abyss of Romance*. Baton Rouge: Louisiana State University Press.

Greene, Graham. 1952. "Henry James: The Private Universe." In *The Lost Childhood*. New York: Viking, 21–30.

———. 1952. "Henry James: The Religious Aspect." In *The Lost Childhood*. New York: Viking, 31–44.

Grenander, M. E. 1975. "Benjamin Franklin's Glass Armonica and Henry James's 'Jolly Corner.'" *Papers on Language and Literature* 11: 415–17.

Gutierrez, Donald. 1984. "The Labyrinth as Myth and Metaphor." *University of Dayton Review* 16, no. 3: 89–99.

Habegger, Alfred. 1989. *Henry James and the "Woman Business."* Cambridge: Cambridge University Press.

Haggerty, George E. 1989. *Gothic Fiction/Gothic Form*. University Park: Pennsylvania State University Press.

Henkle, Roger B. 1977. *Reading the Novel: An Introduction to the Techniques of Interpreting Fiction*. New York: Harper & Row.

Hocks, Richard A. 1974. *Henry James and Pragmatic Thought: A Study in the Relationship between the Philosophy of William James and the Literary Art of Henry James*. Chapel Hill: University of North Carolina Press.

Honig, Edward. 1949. "The Merciful Fraud in Three Stories of Henry James." *The Tiger's Eye*, no. 9 (October): 83–96.

Huntley, H. Robert. 1977. "James' *The Turn of the Screw*: Its 'Fine Machinery.'" *American Imago* 34: 224–37.

Hyde, H. Montgomery. 1969. *Henry James at Home*. New York: Farrar, Straus.

Irwin, John T. 1975. *Doubling and Incest/Repetition and Revenge: A Speculative Reading of Faulkner*. Baltimore: Johns Hopkins University Press.

Jacobs, J. U. 1983. "The Alter Ego: The Artist as American in 'The Jolly Corner.'" *Theoria* 58: 51–60.

James, William. 1994. *The Correspondence of William James*. Vol. 3: *William and Henry: 1897–1910*. Ed. Ignas K. Skrupskelis and Elizabeth M. Berkeley. Charlottesville: University Press of Virginia.

Jefferson, D. W. [1960] 1971. *Henry James*. New York: Capricorn.

Johnson, Courtney. 1967. "James's 'The Jolly Corner': A Study in Integration." *American Imago* 24 (Winter): 344–59.

Jones, Granville H. 1975. *Henry James's Psychology of Experience: Innocence, Responsibility, and Renunciation in the Fiction of Henry James*. The Hague: Mouton.

Josephson, Matthew. 1964. *Portrait of the Artist as American*. New York: Octagon.

Kaston, Carren. 1984. *Imagination and Desire in the Novels of Henry James*. New Brunswick, NJ: Rutgers University Press.

Keppler, C. F. 1972. *The Literature of the Second Self*. Tucson: University of Arizona Press.

Kimbel, Ellen. 1984. "The American Short Story: 1900–1920." In *The American Short Story: 1900–1945*. Ed. Philip Stevick, 33–69. Boston: Twayne.

Knapp, Bettina L. 1986. *Archetype, Architecture, and the Writer*. Bloomington: Indiana University Press.

Krook, Dorothea. [1962] 1967. *The Ordeal of Consciousness in Henry James*. New York: Cambridge University Press.

Lal, Malashri. 1989. "*The Golden Bowl*: Two Definitions of Romance." In Amritjit Singh and K. Ayyappa Paniker, eds., *The Magic Circle of Henry James: Essays in Honour of Darshan Singh Maini*. New York: Envoy.

Lee, Brian. 1978. *The Novels of Henry James: A Study of Culture and Consciousness*. New York: St. Martin's.

Leavis, Q. D. 1947. "Henry James: The Stories." *Scrutiny* 14 (Spring): 223–29. Reprinted in *Collected Essays*. Vol. 2: *The American Novel and Reflections of the European Novel*, ed. G. Singh, 177–84. Cambridge: Cambridge University Press.

Levin, Harry. [1958] 1989. *The Power of Blackness*. Athens: Ohio University Press.

Levy, Leo B. 1957. *Versions of Melodrama: A Study of the Fiction and Drama of Henry James, 1865–1897*. Berkeley: University of California Press.

Lewis, Wydham. 1987. *Men without Art*. Ed. Seamus Cooney. Santa Rosa, CA: Black Sparrow.

Lichtenberg, Joseph D. 1987. "A Memory, a Dream, and a Tale: Connecting Themes in the Creativity of Henry James." In *Psychoanalytical Studies in Biography*. Emotions and Behavior Monographs 4. Madison, CT: International Universities Press, 85–109.

McCarthy, Harold T. 1958. *Henry James: The Creative Process*. New York: Thomas Yoseloff.

MacDonald, Bonney. 1989. "Acts of Life: The Family Vision of William and Henry James." *Henry James Review* 10: 94–98.

McElderry, Bruce R., Jr. 1965. *Henry James*. New York: Twayne.

Mackenzie, Manfred. 1974. "A Theory of Henry James's Psychology." *Yale Review* 63 (Spring): 347–71.

Male, Roy R. 1965. "'Babylon Revisited': A Story of the Exile's Return." *Studies in Short Fiction* 2 (Spring): 270–77.

Marder, Daniel. 1984. *Exiles at Home: A Story of Literature in Nineteenth Century America*. Lanham, MD: University Press of America.

Markow-Totevy, Georges. 1969. *Henry James*. Trans. John Griffiths. London: Merlin.

Martin, Jay. 1983. "Ghostly Rentals, Ghostly Purchases: Haunted Imaginations in James, Twain, and Bellamy." In *The Haunted Dusk: American Supernatural Fiction, 1820–1920*. Ed. Howard Kerr, John W. Crowley, and Charles L. Crow, 123–31. Athens: University of Georgia Press.

Matthiessen, F. O. 1958. *The Achievement of T. S. Eliot*. New York: Oxford University Press.

———. 1947. *The James Family: Including Selections from the Writings of Henry James, Sr., William, Henry, and Alice James*. New York: Knopf.

———, ed. 1947. *The American Novels and Stories of Henry James*. New York: Knopf.

———. 1944. *Henry James: The Major Phase*. New York: Oxford University Press.

Maves, Carl. 1973. *Sensuous Pessimism: Italy in the Work of Henry James*. Bloomington: Indiana University Press.

Mays, Milton A. 1968. "Henry James, or The Beast in the Palace of Art." *American Literature* 39 (January): 467–87.

Miller, Karl. 1985. *Doubles: Studies in Literary History*. Oxford: Oxford University Press.

Millgate, Michael. 1965. *American Social Fiction: James to Cozzens*. Edinburgh: Oliver and Boyd; New York: Barnes & Noble.

Mizener, Arthur, ed. 1966. *Modern Short Stories: The Uses of Imagination*. Rev. ed. New York: Norton.

Moore, Rayburn S. 1976. "The Strange Irregular Rhythm of Life in James's Late Tales and Constance Woolson." *South Atlantic Bulletin* 41, no. 4: 86–93.

Moseley, James G., Jr. 1975. *A Complex Inheritance: The Idea of Self-Transcendence in the Theology of Henry James, Sr., and the Novels of Henry James*. Missoula, MT: American Academy of Religion and Scholars Press, Dissertation Series 4.

Norrman, Ralf. 1982. *The Insecure World of Henry James's Fiction: Intensity and Ambiguity*. New York: St. Martin's.

Parrill, William. 1977. "Peter Milton, Henry James, and 'The Jolly Corner.'" *Innisfree* 4: 16–25.

Perosa, Sergio. 1980. *Henry James and the Experimental Novel*. New York: New York University Press.

Pirie, Gordon. 1974. *Henry James*. London: Evans.

Przybylowicz, Donna. 1986. *Desire and Repression: The Dialectic of Self and Other in the Late Works of Henry James*. University: University of Alabama Press.

Purdy, Strother B. 1977. *The Hole in the Fabric: Science, Contemporary Literature, and Henry James*. Pittsburgh: University of Pittsburgh Press.

Robinson, Douglas. 1985. "The House of Fiction." In *American Apocalypses: The Image of the End of the World in American Literature*, 184–86. Baltimore: Johns Hopkins University Press.

Rogers, Robert. 1970. *A Psychoanalytic Study of the Double in Literature*. Detroit: Wayne State University Press.

———. 1956. "The Beast in Henry James." *American Imago* 13 (Winter): 427–53. Reprinted in part in *Henry James: Seven Stories and Studies*, ed. Edward Stone. New York: Appleton-Century-Crofts, 1961.

Rosenblatt, Jason P. 1977. "The Bridegroom and Bride in 'The Jolly Corner.'" *Studies in Short Fiction* 14: 282–84.

Rosenfield, Claire. 1963. "The Shadow Within: The Conscious and Unconscious Use of the Double." *Daedalus* 92 (Spring): 326–44.

Rosenzweig, Saul. [1943] 1957. "The Ghost of Henry James: A Study in Thematic Apperception." In *Art and Psychoanalysis*. Ed. William Phillips, 89–111. New York: Criterion. Reprinted from *Character and Personality* 12 (December): 79–100. Also reprinted in *Partisan Review* 11 (Fall 1944): 435–55.

Rovit, Earl. 1965. "The Ghosts in James's 'The Jolly Corner.'" *Tennessee Studies in Literature* 10: 65–72.

Sanford, Charles L. 1961. *The Quest for Paradise: Europe and the American Moral Imagination*. Urbana: University of Illinois Press.

Schneider, Daniel J. 1978. *The Crystal Cage: Adventures of the Imagination in the Fiction of Henry James*. Lawrence: Regents Press of Kansas.

Sharp, Sister M. Corona. 1963. *The Confidante in Henry James: Evolution and Moral Value of a Fictive Character*. Notre Dame, IN: Notre Dame University Press.

Shelden, Pamela Jacobs. 1974. "Jamesian Gothicism: The Haunted Castle of the Mind." *Studies in the Literary Imagination* (Georgia State College) 7 (Spring): 121–34.

Shroeder, John W. 1951. "The Mothers of Henry James." *American Literature* 22

(January): 424–31. Reprinted in part in *Henry James: Seven Stories and Studies*, ed. Edward Stone. New York: Appleton-Century-Crofts, 1961.

Shulman, Robert. 1968. "Henry James and the Modern Comedy of Knowledge." *Criticism* 10 (Winter): 41–53.

Sicker, Philip. 1980. *Love and the Quest for Identity in the Fiction of Henry James*. Princeton: Princeton University Press.

Skaggs, Calvin, ed. 1977. *The American Short Story*. Vol. 1. New York: Dell.

Smith, Carl S. 1979. "James's International Fiction: Sources and Evolution." *Centennial Review* 23 (Fall): 397–422.

Smith, Grover. [1950] 1974. *T. S. Eliot's Poetry and Plays: A Study in Sources and Meaning*. Chicago: University of Chicago Press.

Smith, Henry Nash. 1977. "On Henry James and 'The Jolly Corner.'" In *The American Short Story*. Vol. 1. Ed. Calvin Skaggs, 122–27. New York: Dell.

Smith, William F., Jr. 1973. "Sentence Structure in the Tales of Henry James." *Style* 7 (Spring): 157–72.

Springer, Mary Doyle. 1978. *A Rhetoric of Literary Character: Some Women of Henry James*. Chicago: University of Chicago Press. Reprinted in part in "Henry James," in *A Library of Literary Criticism: Modern British Literature* 5, 2d supplement, comp. Denis Lane and Rita Stein, 249–54. New York: Frederick Ungar, 1985.

Stein, Allen F. 1974. "The Beast in 'The Jolly Corner': Spencer Brydon's Ironic Rebirth." *Studies in Short Fiction* 11 (Winter): 61–66.

Stevenson, Elizabeth. [1949] 1981. *The Crooked Corridor: A Study of Henry James*. New York: Octagon.

Stone, Edward. 1964. *The Battle and the Books: Some Aspects of Henry James*. Athens: Ohio University Press.

Stovall, Floyd. 1957. "Henry James's 'The Jolly Corner.'" *Nineteenth-Century Fiction* 12 (June): 72–84.

Stowell, H. Peter. 1980. *Literary Impressionism, James and Chekhov*. Athens: University of Georgia Press.

Strout, Cushing. 1980. "Psyche, Clio, and the Artist." In *New Directions in Psychohistory: The Adelphi Papers in Honor of Erik H. Erikson*. Ed. Mel Albin, 97–115. Lexington, MA: Heath.

———. 1979. "Henry James's Dream of the Louvre, 'The Jolly Corner,' and Psychological Interpretation." *Psychohistory Review* 8, no. 1–2: 47–52. Reprinted in *Literature and Psychoanalysis*, ed. Edith Kruzweil and William Philips, 217–31. New York: Columbia University Press.

Sumner, Nan, and Nathan Sumner. 1971. "A Dickinson-James Parallel." *Research Studies* 39 (June): 144–47.

Swan, Michael. 1957. *Henry James*. London: Longmans, Green.

———, ed. 1948. *Ten Short Stories of Henry James*. London: John Lehmann.

Taylor, Anne Robinson. 1981. *Male Novelists and their Female Voices: Literary Masquerades*. Troy, NY: Whitston.

Terrie, Henry, ed. 1984. *Henry James: Tales of Art and Life*. Schenectady, NY: Union College Press.

Thomson, Fred C. 1963. "James's 'The Jolly Corner.'" *Explicator* 22 (December): Item 28 .

Thompson, G. R. "Washington Irving and the American Ghost Story." In *The Haunted Dusk: American Supernatural Fiction, 1820–1920*. Ed. Howard Kerr, John W. Crowley, and Charles L. Crow, 13–36. Athens: University of Georgia Press.

Thorberg, Raymond. 1967. "Terror Made Relevant: James's Ghost Stories." *Dalhousie Review* 47 (Summer): 185–91.

Tintner, Adeline R. 1989. *The Pop World of Henry James: From Fairy Tales to Science Fiction*. Ann Arbor: UMI Research Press.

———. 1986. *The Museum World of Henry James*. Ann Arbor: UMI Research Press.

———. 1987. *The Book World of Henry James: Appropriating the Classics*. Ann Arbor: UMI Research Press. Reprinted from "Facing the 'Alter Ego': Edgar Allan Poe's Influence on Henry James." *AB Bookman's Weekly* 7, no. 2 (12 January 1987): 105–9.

———. 1982. "Hiding behind James: Roth's *Zuckerman Bound*." *Midstream* 28, no. 4: 49–53.

———. 1976. "Landmarks of 'The Terrible Town': The New York Scene in Henry James' Last Stories." *Prospects* 2: 399–435.

———. 1975. "The Metamorphoses of Edith Wharton in Henry James's *The Finer Grain*." *Twentieth-Century Literature* 21: 355–79.

Todorov, Tzvetan. 1977. *The Poetics of Prose*. Trans. Richard Howard. Ithaca, NY: Cornell University Press.

Travis, Mildred K. 1971. "Hawthorne's 'Egotism' and 'The Jolly Corner.'" *Emerson Society Quarterly* 63 (Spring): 13–18 .

Tremper, Ellen. 1976. "Henry James's Altering Ego: An Examination of His Psychological Double in Three Tales." *The Texas Quarterly* 19, no. 3: 59–75.

Tuveson, Ernest. 1975. "'The Jolly Corner': A Fable of Redemption." *Studies in Short Fiction* 12 (Summer): 271–80.

Unrue, Darlene. 1976. "Henry James and the Grotesque." *The Arizona Quarterly* 32: 293–300.

———. 1975. "Henry James's Extraordinary Use of Portraits." *Re: Artes Liberales* 1, no. 2: 47–53.

Vaid, Krishna B. 1964. *Technique in the Tales of Henry James*. Cambridge, MA: Harvard University Press.

Voss, Arthur. 1973. *The American Short Story: A Critical Survey*. Norman: University of Oklahoma Press.

Ward, J. A. 1961. *The Imagination of Disaster: Evil in the Fiction of Henry James*. Lincoln: University of Nebraska Press.

Wegelin, Christof. 1958. *The Image of Europe in Henry James*. Dallas: Southern Methodist University Press.

White, Morton and Lucia. 1962. *The Intellectual versus the City: From Thomas Jefferson to Frank Lloyd Wright*. Cambridge, MA: Harvard University Press and M. I. T. Press.

Wilson, Edmund. [1962] 1987. *Patriotic Gore: Studies in the Literature of the American Civil War*. New York: Oxford University Press; London: Hogarth.

Wilt, Napier, and John Lucas, eds. 1965. *Americans and Europe: Selected Tales of Henry James*. Riverside Editions. Boston: Houghton Mifflin.

Winner, Viola Hopkins. 1970. *Henry James and the Visual Arts*. Charlottesville: University Press of Virginia.

Wright, Walter F. 1962. *The Madness of Art: A Study of Henry James*. Lincoln: University of Nebraska Press.

Yeazell, Ruth Bernard, ed. 1981. *The Death and Letters of Alice James*. Berkeley: University of California Press.

Zabel, Morton Dauwen, ed. 1958. *Henry James: In the Cage and Other Tales*. Garden City, NY: Doubleday.

Foreign Language

Bereyziat, Jean. 1980. "Ironie, indices et dérobade: 'The Jolly Corner' et la question du sens." *Confluents* 6, no. 2: 7–56.

Boisson, Claude, Philipe Thoiron, and Paul Veyriras. 1980. "Du son au sens dan 'The Jolly Corner' de Henry James: Analyse d'un texte et esquisse d'une methode." *Confluents* 6, no. 2: 57–104.

Chang, Wang-Rok. 1984. "William James wa Henry James: Pragmatism eui hyangbang eul junksim euro." [Henry James as pragmatist]. In *Ubo Chang Wang-Rok baska hoegap kinyom nonmyngip* [Essays honoring the sixtieth birthday of Dr. Chang Wang-Rok]. Ed. Gangang Weewonhoe, 221–66. Seoul: Tap. [Korean with an English summary].

Chauchaix, Jacqueline, and Claudine Verley. 1986. "La Sémiotique de l'espace dans *The Jolly Corner* de Henry James." *La Licorne* 10: 17–29.

Gullón, Ricardo. 1965. "Imágenes de *El Otro*." *Revista Hispanica Moderna* 31: 210–21.

Kambara, Tatsuo. 1972. "James's Gothic: Gothic in American Novels (5)." *Bungakubu Kiyo* (Tokyo University of Education) 88 (March): 49–65. [Japanese]

Tochihara, Tomoo. 1965. "Henry James: 'The Jolly Corner'—Borderland between the Conscious and Superconscious." *Shakai-Gakubu Kiyo* (Kwansie Gakuin University) 11 (August): 37–45. [Japanese]

A Landscape Painter

Publication History

"A Landscape-Painter" appeared first in the February 1866 issue of the *Atlantic Monthly*. James included it in the 1885 *Stories Revived*, but never again reprinted it. It appeared for the first time after James's death as the title story of a 1920 collection, and not long after in Lubbock's edition of James's fiction.

Circumstances of Composition, Sources, and Influences

The tale was written during James's residence in Cambridge, and Buitenhuis postulates that James wrote it while looking from his window at Winthrop Square. James, Buitenhuis argues, was examining both the American landscape before him and that of his tale in terms of European art (20–22). The tale indeed is full of references to British culture, the Brontës, Wordsworth, Dickens, and Turner. LeClair sees James as drawing on memories of Newport for the setting (381). Bayley finds more significance in Newport as the place where James tried his hand as an artist, which he sees aiding him in his capturing of the diarist's painter's eye (42–43).

The narrator speaks at one point of "the young gentlemen who imitate Tennyson" (CT 1, 129), and it is Tennyson who provides probably the closest literary source. Allot traced the story of the appropriately named Locksley to a Tennyson poem "The Lord of Burleigh." In it the hero "is but a landscape-painter, / And but a village maiden she." He is really a lord, however, and after wedding him, disturbed by "the burthen of an honour / Unto which she was not born," the woman soon dies.

Kelley points to the influence of Goethe, but places the scheming heroine in the tradition of French authors or Thackeray (55–56). Similarly, Buitenhuis looks at the story as another tale of deadly women, its source like that of "A Tragedy of Error," in Mérimée's *La Vénus d'Ille*. He cites the remarks of the frame narrator on "the ultimate view taken by the great Nemesis of his [Locksley's] treatment of Miss Leary—his scorn of the magnificent Venus Victrix," arguing that Miriam, another sinister Venus, plays Nemesis (20–21). The diarist himself mentions Lady Macbeth in his first entry (CT 1, 101), another deadly woman who is, like Miriam, deadly through her ambitiousness. Zablotny compares Locksley to Oedipus in his failure in avoiding his "fate"—marriage to a mercenary woman (203)

Melchiori argues that the narrator's projected masterpiece is based on Manet's *Dejeuner sur la herbe*, still considered at the time a scandalous painting (cited in Winner 187 n.37).

Despite the many European allusions, the tale is allegedly American. Buitenhuis observes how the name changes in 1870—from the Dickensian Esther Blunt to the Hawthornesque Miriam and from Cragthorpe to Chowderville—attempt to make the tale more grounded in its setting (20–22). Long elaborates on James's taking the name and coloring of Miriam from *The Marble Faun* to create his own "dark lady" (16). At the same time, Matthiessen sees James as seeking here to "escape Hawthorne's bareness" through the use of an artist-narrator (535). Bayley looks at a contemporary of Hawthorne, in finding the "jaunty manner" of the narrator like that in Poe while judging that the opening question, "Do you remember how . . . ," anticipates the technique of Kipling and Stevenson (40–41).

Relation to Other Works

The tale is significant as the first of James's artist tales, although Kraft judges the artist theme here relatively insignificant compared to its appearance in later tales (16–17; see also Edel CT 1, 17). Matthiessen stresses that while the story itself is undistinguished, it is important as illustrating James's discovery that a "density of impression . . . might best be given unity if seen through a painter's eyes" (536; also Winner 94; McElderry 27). Winner notes that the narrator's desire to create a "national masterpiece" is similar to that of Roderick Hudson. She also includes him among James's narrating artists, such as the fellow diarist in "The Impressions of a Cousin" and the narrator of "Glasses" (94, 117).

Dupee judges the narrator typical of James's early heroes, such as John Ford of "The Story of a Year," in being unreasonably suspicious of life (50). Similarly, Poirier classes him as a weak hero along with Ford and also Roger

Lawrence of *Watch and Ward* (15–16). Along the same lines, Habegger finds James's changing of the names of his heroines for the 1885 *Stories Revived* here and in "A Most Extraordinary Case"—Blunt to Quarterman and McCarthy to Masters—reflecting a renewed fear after his father's death of "overmastering, masculinized" women (209). Edel, on the other hand, attributes the change to James's sense that the first version was simply too "blunt" and points out that he revised the ending to make it less so as well (*Life* 1, 256). The name Quarterman was ready to hand, as it appeared in a list of names in July 1884 (CN 66). Horrell records James's calling attention to her name's aptness in the narrator's remark, "Her name is Miriam, and it exactly fits her" (205).

Whatever her name, Esther or Miriam, the heroine here has evoked conflicting readings. Most typically, Arvin places Esther as the first of many mercenary females in James, a series that includes the Baroness of *The Europeans* and culminates with Kate Croy and Charlotte Stant, and a theme which recurs in *Lady Barbarina*, "Lord Beaupré," and *The Album* (439, 441; also Fox 12). More positively, Jones classes her with Angela of *Confidence*, Mrs. Damerel of "The Great Condition," and both hero and heroine of "Sir Dominick Ferrand" for withholding information out of a "legitimate sense of personal dignity" and a desire for happiness not only for oneself but others (161). Bayley also finds James sympathetic not only to Miriam, but to the often criticized heroine of "The Story of a Year" as well (56). In the 1868 version, Locksley concludes an early description of the heroine, "There you are, Miss Blunt, at full length,—emphatically the portrait of a lady" (Aziz 1, 63). Bayley and Jones might agree with the estimate and its anticipatory comparison with James's later lady, Isabel Archer, but most critics have considered her decidedly unworthy (e.g., LeClair 382). Evidently, James later did also, as he eliminated the epithet in the revised version (Aziz 1, 436).

Rimmon classes the story along with "Osborne's Revenge," "The Marriages," "The Path of Duty," and *Madame de Mauves* for presenting such a dramatic reversal that it requires a complete rereading of the character involved (82). Wagenknecht, on the other hand, considers the surprise ending better than the "trick" conclusion of "A Tragedy of Error" because, on thinking, the reader realizes that Miriam's behavior has been consistent throughout (190).

Calling attention to Locksley's description of his wealth as a "supreme curse," Delbaere-Garant points to the theme of money again in *The Wings of the Dove* and *The Ivory Tower* (106).

Levy puts the narrator's unconscious revelations in his diary at the start of James's use of the unreliable narrator, and combined with "an indulgent narrator" in the frame an anticipation of *The Turn of the Screw* in particular (409).

Interpretation and Criticism

The American setting has garnered little praise (e.g., McElderry 27; Jefferson 42). Winner notes that the narrator conceives of his planned masterpiece in terms of a "Renaissance *fête champêtre*," a work dependent on European tradition rather than a more distinctively American work (117). While Kraft praises the description of the "painterly" picnic so inspired, Fish considers there to be too much description of the American setting (Kraft 17; Fish 211). Even with the 1885 change of the British sounding Cragthorpe to the all-American Chowderville, Buitenhuis still argues that James does not handle the setting confidently (20). Kelley objects similarly to James's use of lower-class characters whose life was unfamiliar to him (58). Cantwell disagrees with Kelley, arguing that there was no need for James to be "content" to write only about his own class, although he adds that James later solved the problem of how to represent such unfamiliar territory by using "just a little" realism (498–99, 504).

The story is James's first attempt at using a diary to provide the narrative structure of a tale. Kelley sees James trying the diary form in order to keep tighter control of his story and provide it with a greater authenticity. In her view, however, there are gaps between James's intents and his accomplishments. In particular, she considers the frankness of the narrator in his diary unrealistic, although she praises James for having managed, despite the limitations of the diary form, to present a keener analysis of the heroine than the hero himself was aware of (55–57, 70). According to LeClair, the device allows James to effect the transition Kelley sees James striving for in the story from plot to psychology (Kelley 55; LeClair 381). Kraft, however, still judges the device awkward (17).

The diarist's main problem, in his view certainly, is his wealth. Dietrichson points to Locksley and his rather "naive idealism" as proof that early on James did not think of money as necessarily corrupting (144). Kraft has pointed to the contrast between appearance and reality in his courtship of Miriam (17), and Mull focuses the disparity on one of the self's covers, wealth. Mull argues that the narrator's desire to be judged simply for his self by stripping himself of his fortune is an impossible one; at the same time the heroine's focus on "externals" alone is also shown to be false. The story thus demonstrates the interdependency if not the identity of the self and its surrounding conditions (23–26).

According to Putt, the main significance of money here is as a "bar to married bliss" (38). As Arvin comments, the central irony in this tale is that Locksley falls for another mercenary woman so soon after spurning the first (439). Miriam may have a better excuse for her desire to marry well in her significantly lower social status. Still, while Kelley admits the unpleasantness of the heroine, she judges her deceptiveness unrepresentative and rather misogynistic on James's part (56). Others have offered readings that construe her actions in an even more positive light. McElderry declares that though the woman marries the man for his money, she marries him with "good will" (27). Jones goes further, praising the "intuitive" correctness of her reading the diary, which gives her the necessary knowledge of his wealth and fear of mercenary designs on it to behave properly in relation to him. Although he sees her act and her avowal of it as leaving them "completely free to be happy in complete trust," he does not comment on their failure to do so (162).

Critics have also responded to Miriam's defense by pointing out that Locksley stooped to deceit first (e.g., Kraft 17). Even Dietrichson qualifies his view of Locksley's idealism because of his deceit, which he judges selfish, although he argues that Miriam's mercenariness is worse (144). Fox pins the blame for Locksley's unhappy marriage primarily on a "selfish pride" that insists on being the grand benefactor in marriage (12). Originally, the tale had concluded somewhat abruptly with Miriam's injunction to Locksley, "Come, *you* be a man!" In the revision James added the promise, "Come, you may abuse me in your diary if you like—I shall never peep into it again!" James also narrowed the sweeping indictment of women in her claim that her act was not that of "a false woman," but "simply of a woman" to "it was the act of any woman—placed as I was placed" (Aziz 87, 444). Even without the softening of the revisions, Poirier considers the heroine's injunction to the narrator to "be a man" an understandable one given his behavior (15).

Both Jefferson and Kraft have praised the "witty" conversation of Miriam and Locksley (Jefferson 72) that seems to point toward a possible mutual understanding and equal strength that never materialize. While Kraft sees the dialogue as revealing most of Miriam's character, Zablotny objects to Locksley's bad jokes (Zablotny 206). Indeed, critics in general have seen Miriam as a stronger character than the narrator. Kraft discerns "power" in her, while characterizing him as "blasé" (17).

All three of the critics who have essayed in-depth analyses of the story blame Locksley for his faulty perception, a striking flaw in an artist. Levy sees in Locksley an affected, "pastoral," idealized view of nature representing an "outworn aesthetic doctrine." In his view, Locksley condescends to Miriam, thinking of her as a "figure in a landscape," himself as the painter. The contrast of Miriam's "intelligence and practical realism" and Locksley's artificiality becomes, according to Levy, more significant than the contrast of her greed and his lack of worldliness. Locksley falsely sees everything as "natural," while she accurately recognizes what is "artificial" in him. The frame narrator, meanwhile, being equally "bland" and "fatuous," has no corrective vision to offer (407–9).

Zablotny, like Mull before her, has pointed out that Locksley ought to have been able to perceive Miriam's true nature earlier, even as she grasped his

(Mull 23–26). In her reading, Locksley had many clues to Miriam's mercenary nature, including her frank admission before she knew of his wealth that she would "marry the first rich man who offers." But Zablotny portrays Locksley as aware only unconsciously of her nature, so that he becomes ill, but no wiser. Dressed, as Zablotny notes, in the white and blue of the Madonna, Miriam gradually changes her dress to more fitting darker colors, but still Locksley does not realize her true nature. In the end, Zablotny sees the title as a reflection on Locksley's inability to understand character, his capacity to understand only inanimate landscape. She nevertheless finds the tale unclear as to whether Locksley was happy or unhappy in his fate. But she remarks on the sinister insinuation of his early death, and pointing to James's numerous "vampire" tales, senses something in Miriam's nature that is best explained by the vampiric analogy, even while acknowledging the realism of this early work (205–7).

Bayley delivers the most praising reading of the tale, calling it a "remarkable performance, so remarkable that one may wonder whether James, even in his years of sophistication, ever produced a better, or a more characteristic one." Bayley, like Levy and Zablotny, reads the tale as one of perception. Bayley sees James as taking "an artful pleasure" in his hero's "sententiousness." But what the narrator sees as an ideal fantasy world in the Quartermans' "very happy little household" is, according to Bayley, quite real. The narrator is not wrong in valuing it highly, but in seeing it in solely aesthetic terms, even as at the end he "fatuously" looks forward to the "great aesthetic pleasure" of watching his new wife read the revelation of his wealth and superior status. In Bayley's view, it is "his romanticism, his artist's vision itself," his masculine vanity and his innocence, that keep him from seeing Miriam as she is.

Miriam herself, in Bayley's reading, is the character with whom James most identifies, although he finds James in the tale atypically responsive to the "physical presence and charm of women." Her deception, he argues, is both intelligent and well-intentioned. "Vividly suggested" by the narrator's description, she retains "an enigmatic life of her own," and, Bayley writes, James remains "deeply apprehensive" of her.

With Miriam's revelation, Bayley observes, the tale turns silent, the five years before Locksley's death producing no record, thus indicating that his experience with Miriam put an end to his "artist's vision." While the reader knows from the frame that Locksley is dead, Bayley contends that the knowledge "paradoxically" puts the reader more "in touch" with the diarist, his "vision of art, of happiness, of a possible life." The story provides a twist on the traditional "threshold" story which ushers a young person into life, by providing also a "ritual ending" to it. The missing five years, he argues, are "unnervingly" present in the unanswerable questions they stimulate.

The subject of the tale becomes, according to Bayley, not simply the obvious one of deception, but also the expulsion from innocence "into a world of marriage and death." Locksley is deceived, but so is everyone, for the deepest deception is "that practised by life itself." Accordingly, it is not Miriam, but marriage itself, that "silences" the diarist. Even before the revelation of Miriam's deception, Bayley asserts, the diarist is becoming aware of the end of his country Eden, as Miriam turns to interests in marriage and children and he is left with the "superfluous role of money-provider, cut off from art and from what fed it" (41–48, 56, 180). Wagenknecht notes that the tale begins misleadingly like "a sweet country love story" (190). As such it would follow in the manner of James's source, Tennyson's poem, but as Allott observes, James transforms Tennyson's sentimental story into a realistically rendered tale.

The narrator says of Locksley that he "wrote some rather amateurish verse, but he produced a number of remarkable paintings" (CT 1, 100). His prose, however, partakes of the insight attributed to the paintings, even as it reveals his failure to achieve that insight in his life, until the truths he was overlooking become painfully clear. There is a similar combination of strengths and weaknesses in James's tale. While it is capable of providing the basis for sophisticated theorizing, it retains many marks of a power not entirely under conscious control, but capable nonetheless of provoking not only abstraction, but interest, sympathy, and an appropriate bafflement.

Works Cited

Primary Works
James, Henry. 1866. "A Landscape-Painter." *Atlantic Monthly* 17 (February): 182–202.

———. 1885. "A Landscape Painter." *Stories Revived*. Vol. 2. London: Macmillan, 223–67.

———. 1920. *A Landscape Painter*. Preface by Albert Mordell. New York: Scott and Seltzer.

———. 1921–23. "A Landscape Painter." *The Novels and Stories of Henry James*. Vol. 25. Ed. Percy Lubbock. London: Macmillan.

Secondary Works
Allott, Miriam. 1955. "'The Lord of Burleigh' and Henry James's 'A Landscape Painter.'" *Notes & Queries* n.s. 2 (May): 220–21.

Arvin, Newton. 1934. "Henry James and the Almighty Dollar." *Hound & Horn* 7 (April–May): 434–43.

Bayley, John. 1988. *The Short Story: Henry James to Elizabeth Bowen*. Brighton: Harvester.

Buitenhuis, Peter. 1970. *The Grasping Imagination: The American Writings of Henry James*. Toronto: University of Toronto Press.

Cantwell, Robert. 1934. "A Little Reality." *Hound & Horn* 7 (April–May): 494–505.

Delbaere-Garant, Jeanne. 1970. *Henry James: The Vision of France*. Paris: Société d'Editions Les Belles Lettres.

Dietrichson, Jan W. 1969. *The Image of Money in the American Novel of the Gilded Age*. Oslo: Universitetsforlaget; New York: Humanities.

Dupee, F. W. [1951] 1956. *Henry James*. Garden City, NY: Doubleday Anchor.

Fish, Charles K. 1965. "Description in Henry James's 'A Light Man.'" *English Language Notes* 2 (March): 211–15.

Fox, Hugh. 1968. *Henry James, A Critical Introduction*. Conesville, IA: John Westburg.

Habegger, Alfred. 1989. *Henry James and the "Woman Business."* Cambridge: Cambridge University Press.

Horrell, Joyce Tayloe. 1970. "A 'Shade of a Special Sense': Henry James and the Art of Naming." *American Literature* 42: 203–20.

Jefferson, D. W. 1964. *Henry James and the Modern Reader*. New York: St. Martin's.

Jones, Granville H. 1975. *Henry James's Psychology of Experience: Innocence, Responsibility, and Renunciation in the Fiction of Henry James*. The Hague: Mouton.

Kelley, Cornelia Pulsifer. [1930] 1965. *The Early Development of Henry James*. Urbana: University of Illinois Press.

Kraft, James. 1969. *The Early Tales of Henry James, 1843–1870*. New York: Bookman.

LeClair, Robert Charles. 1955. *Young Henry James, 1843–1870*. New York: Bookman.

Levy, Leo B. 1981. "Consciousness in Three Early Tales of Henry James." *Studies in Short Fiction* 18: 407–12.

Long, Robert Emmet. 1979. *The Great Succession: Henry James and the Legacy of Hawthorne*. Pittsburgh: University of Pittsburgh Press.

McElderry, Bruce R., Jr. 1965. *Henry James*. New York: Twayne.

Matthiessen, F. O. 1943. "James and the Plastic Arts." *Kenyon Review* 5 (August): 533–50.

Mull, Donald. 1973. *Henry James's "Sublime Economy": Money as Symbolic Center in the Fiction*. Middletown, CT: Wesleyan University Press.

Poirier, Richard. 1960. *The Comic Sense of Henry James: A Study of the Early Novels*. London: Chatto & Windus.

Putt, S. Gorley. 1966. *Henry James: A Reader's Guide*. Ithaca, NY: Cornell University Press.

Rimmon, Shlomith. 1977. *The Concept of Ambiguity: The Example of Henry James*. Chicago: University of Chicago Press.

Wagenknecht, Edward. 1984. *The Tales of Henry James*. New York: Frederick Ungar.

Winner, Viola Hopkins. 1970. *Henry James and the Visual Arts*. Charlottesville: University Press of Virginia.

Zablotny, Elaine. 1979. "Henry James and the Demonic Vampire and Madonna." *Psychocultural Review* 3, nos. 3–4 (Summer–Fall): 203–24.

Foreign Language
Melchiori, Giorgio. 1964. "Il Déjeuner Sur l'herbe di Henry James." *Studi Americani*, no. 10:201–28. Reprinted in Barbara Melchiori and Giorgio Melchiori, *Il Gusto di Henry James*. Turin: Guilio Einaudi editore, 1974.

The Last of the Valerii

Publication History

In March of 1873, W. D. Howells wrote James that he had in hand his "Roman romance" and intended it to figure in the *Atlantic Monthly* "very soon," but it was January 1874 before the *Atlantic* published the tale. Its eventual appearance may owe something to Howells's fear that James would begin sending his work to the competing *Scribner's*, while the cause of delay may be indicated by his admission after the fact that the story "did not strike me so favorably in MS. as it does in print" (1979, 18, 39).

A pirated translation by Lucien Biart was published in the November 15, 1875, issue of the prestigious *Revue des Deux Mondes*, as James discovered on his arrival in Paris that same month. It was copied from there, he wrote his brother, in the *Independence Belge* (*Life* 2, 202–3; *Letters* 2, 13–14). James himself revised and reprinted the tale twice, in 1875 in the collection *A Passionate Pilgrim*, and ten years later in the 1885 *Stories Revived*. It next appeared over forty years later in Lubbock's edition of the novels and stories.

Circumstances of Composition, Sources, and Influences

When James's story appeared, he was in Italy for the third time, starting work on his Italian novel, *Roderick Hudson*. The previous year he had also explored Rome, visiting the ancient tomb of the Valerii beneath the church of San Stefano and watching the excavations throughout the city. James found a "peculiar fascination" in the excavated relics, writing, "It gives one the oddest feeling to see the past, the ancient world, as one stands there, bodily turned up with a spade" (Edel 1970, 69; *Life* 144).

A main source for James's story was Prosper Mérimée's *La Vénus d'Ille*. Introduced to the story in 1861 by John La Farge, James recalled later how the story set him "fluttering deliciously—quite as if with a sacred terror. . . . *La Vénus d'Ille* struck my immaturity as a masterpiece of art and offered to the young curiosity concerned that sharpest of all challenges of youth, the challenge as to the special source of the effect" (*Criticism* 2, 576). He wrote a translation and submitted it for publication to a New York weekly, which rejected it, not "in the least understanding it," as he recalled many years later (*Autobiography* 292). Ziolkowski has traced the myth of Venus and the Ring present in both tales back to the twelfth century in the *Chronicle of the Kings of England*, and notes additional treatments by William Morris in *The Earthly Paradise* and Leopold van Sacher-Masoch's *Venus in Furs*, among others. At its earliest, Ziolkowski states, the story represented the struggle of the new Christianity with the old paganism, a contrast he sees Mérimée and James transforming into a more secular contrast between paganism and civilization. Kelley, who judges James's version superior and more plausible, imagines James's early admiration for the story reanimated by his trip to Italy. Looking at the many changes James made to his source, Kelley points to the substitution of an active American girl for Mérimée's innocent bystander; Terrie sees James shifting the interest from the supernatural event to the response, and notes the corresponding change in narration from Mérimée's superior visiting artist to James's artistic but involved godfather; Wagenknecht sees James moving altogether from the supernatural to the psychological; and Maves considers the possibility that the change from Venus to Juno indicates a change in the view of the past's relation to the present, from a "dark primal force" to "a coherent alternative" (Kelley 154–55; Terrie 4; Wagenknecht 190; Maves 158 n.22). Delbaere-Garant, however, maintains that although James drew on Mérimée, their works are so different that they cannot be "fruitfully compared" (iv). Tintner, in turn, suggests that Heine's "Return of Pan" may also be a source (37).

Among the tale's earliest critics, Howells noted that in treating "the remaining paganism in Italian character," James was treading in the footsteps of Hawthorne ([1875] 1961, 72). While Kelley also likened Valerio to Donatello (155), it was Bewley who, objecting to the treatment of Mérimée as the sole source, insisted most emphatically on *The Marble Faun* as an alternative. Bewley emphasized the two works' "moral tone" in their exploration of the complex relationship between the Italian past and present (35). Subsequent critics have kept the emphasis on the theme and setting—Slabey remarks on the significance of St. Peter's in each (Slabey 91; also Kraft 77; Wegelin 33; Long 27–29). Edel adds a biographical note to the comparison, stating that in April 1873, while staying at the Villa Ludovisi, where Hawthorne had also visited, James had noticed on the premises a half-hidden head from a statue of Juno (1970, 69).

Of the Rome—"obsessed" characters in each work, as Charles Anderson refers to them, the emphasis has been on the heroine (13). Lohmann attributes to both an American sense of "mission" to redeem Europe, while Quentin Anderson argues that James's heroine has the greater "moral authority," and Churchill sees Martha entering into the life of Italy far more than Hilda ever did (Lohmann 331; Anderson 38; Churchill 159). Edel finds a change from both Mérimée and Hawthorne in the triumph of the American girl over the supernatural threat (*Life* 2, 103). Brodhead similarly argues that James in this story, through a "conscious act of literary imitation," achieves a command of and independence from Hawthorne by allowing his heroine through "a prodigious act of volition" to redeem her husband. It is to Hilda that Brodhead attributes the Hawthornesque recogniton that one must first "raise the past to consciousness" in order to clear it away to make room for the present. Looking instead at Valerio, Brodhead sees James using Mérimée in a "Hawthornesque" way, turning the "healthy physicality" of his hero into one with the primitive naturalness of Donatello (129–30).

Like Hawthorne's work, the tale draws on the Gothic, but moves beyond it. Long sees the innocent blonde bride in the eerie Italian castle echoing the Gothic, subordinated, however, to an "urbane intelligence" (29–30). Unrue characterizes the excavator as a "grotesque Dweller" from folklore and Gothic fiction who metaphorically guards the door into the unknown, until vanquished by the Countess's virtue (296–97; also Long 28–29). Briggs points out a similar but narrower "infatuation with the antique world" in Vernon Lee's *Hauntings* (122).

Tintner cites James's comparison of Valerio to the bust of the emperor Caracalla, and selects as the source for the excavated Juno a statue of Hera, also in the Vatican Gallery, their paganism, she notes, significantly contained within a Christian museum. At the same time she points out Valerio's objection to the encroachment of Christian on pagan in the Pantheon (35–37). Originally the archeologist had expected to unearth a Proserpine, who, like Martha, lives in two worlds, that of her birth and that of her marriage. Martha, Nathalia Wright remarks, hoped to discover a Minerva, the virginal goddess of wisdom, but found instead the wifely Juno, not, her godfather observes, a Venus (224). Long, meanwhile, records the association of the statue of Hermes already above ground with treasure, magic, dreams, and the erotic (29).

Cargill contrasts James's view of the "heavy heritage" of the past here— "the bloody medley of mediaeval wars"—with Henry Adams's idealizing of the Middle Ages and sees his much later work, *The Sense of the Past*, as an attack on the current worship of the past in the historical fiction popular at the time (486–87).

Edel cites an allusion to the tale in Constance Fenimore Woolson's "Miss Grief" (*Life* 2, 416). There is a chamber opera *The Voice of Ariadne* based on the tale (Boren 2).

Relation to Other Works

Unless one counts the wedding between British colonial and British subject in "The Romance of Certain Old Clothes," "The Last of the Valerii" presents the first of James's international weddings. Beach, followed by Edgar, noted the resemblances with the international marriage in James's next tale, *Madame de Mauves*, Beach emphasizing the contrast between the romanticism of the first and the realism of the second (Edgar 24; Beach 190). Stein compares the two as indications of James's sense of the great difficulty of overcoming differences of character and culture to achieve a marriage—itself an "alien territory"— that allows for individual growth (70, 76, 80). Levy also compares the two, offering Daisy Miller as an example of a less successful but equally innocent American girl abroad (29–30). Lohmann acknowledges a likeness to Euphemia and Daisy, but judges Charlotte of "Travelling Companions" and Mary Garland of *Roderick Hudson* closer parallels as Martha's fellow representatives of American womanhood abroad seeking to save a man threatened by the moral dangers of Europe (331–32). Allen, in turn, nominates Bessie Alden in *An International Episode*, contrasting her and Martha with Christopher Newman, who intends to take his symbol of Europe back home to the States (45). Nathalia Wright argues that Martha "temporarily" takes on the qualities of the "sensitive but immoral" type of collector best exemplified by Gilbert Osmond in her search for the statue (223–24). Martha has also been compared to the heroine of *The Golden Bowl*, Tanner pointing out that, like Maggie, she faces a surprisingly sinister Europe, while Wegelin observes in both the qualities to confront it, the "air and almost the habits of a princess" the narrator attributes to Martha and the crucial "active imagination" (56). Similarly, Brodhead sees Martha's ability to save rather than destroy her husband pointing forward to *The Golden Bowl* in contrast to the tendency in earlier tales such as "De Grey," where the heroine defies fate only to fall victim to it (131).

As the record of an encounter with Europe, Brodhead deems the tale a significant step forward from "A Passionate Pilgrim," with greatly improved narration and integration of setting (129). Quentin Anderson sees it conveying even more effectively the "exaltation and dread" Brooke of "Travelling Companions" felt in the face of the Roman past (153). Holder finds a similarly sympathetic yet questioning attitude toward such intense exploration of the past both early in "A Passionate Pilgrim" and later in *The Sense of the Past* (211). Edward Stone links it with "The Birthplace" in its "felicitous" association of place and person (153).

Looking at the husband, Levy classes Valerio among the numerous "pagan evildoers" James depicted in the 1870s including Mauves and the Marquis de Bellegarde of *The American*, while also observing that even at the time of *The Ambassadors*, James was still labeling characters, in this case Chad Newsome, "pagan" (28–29). Nathalia Wright points out that Valerio's visit to the Pantheon in a time of crisis puts him in the company of such James characters as Christina Light, and Morgan Moreen and his tutor. He is also, she argues, a representative Jamesian Italian, with an intellectual simplicity and seeming duplicity he shares both with lower-class characters such as Angelo of "Adina" and fellow aristocrats such as Prince Amerigo, who is, Maves remarks, also treated as an "expensive artifact" (Wright 227, 237; Maves 35).

Nathalia Wright perhaps compliments the narrator by including him with such Jamesian artists as Paul Overt and Jeffrey Aspern as one whose sensibility is heightened in Italy (222). McElderry suggests a very different resemblance, with the very American, inartistic Mr. Evans of "Travelling Companions" (32).

The hero here falls in love with a statue, and Kelley points to the parallel with "Rose-Agathe" where the man falls in love with a hairdresser's dummy (246 n.4; also Putt 78). Swan connects both tales with "The Special Type" to show James withdrawing from real life into a fascination instead with images (1957, 23–24; 1948, 7–8). Edel adds "Maud-Evelyn" as another inanimate love, while Jones points out that unlike Marmaduke, Camillo's departure from reality is only temporary ([1949] 1963, 70; Jones 136). According to Maves, Camillo, like Theobald in "The Madonna of the Future," falls so in love with perfect art that he neglects imperfect reality, but unlike Theobald, is saved, partly because Italy is his home, but more significantly because his self-esteem was less caught up in his delusion (38).

Interpretation and Criticism

In January James was able to write Howells, who had finally decided the tale was "excellent," thanking him for his good opinion, remarking that "It reads agreeably enough though I suppose that to many readers, it will seem rather idle" (Howells 1979, 39; *Letters* 1, 424). However idle the tale, critics have kept busy examining it and its many mixed elements. Edel has discerned in the tale an element of chiaroscuro, the "sunny warmth" on the surface a misleading cover for the dark past underneath (1967, 328; CT 3, 9). In Long's view an allegory of "American innocence" and "deep Roman knowlege" (30), the story is indeed one of contrasts: female versus male; American versus European; present versus past.

The masculine European past is represented here by the Count Valerio. While Wegelin criticizes the stereotyping, Putt finds the "caricature" of James's fascination with Rome in the character of Valerio one of the story's strengths (Wegelin 32–33; Putt 77–78). At any rate, according to both Edgar and Maves, the story's prime focus is on him and his "latent pagan strain" not on the Americans (Edgar 24; Maves 35). But the past that he represents is an ambiguous one, and many critics have seen it as sinister indeed. Holder, although he considers the narrator's description of Valerio's "heavy heritage" "overwrought," judges it representative of James's own attitude. The tale, he argues, illustrates James's belief that "the present could hold its own when compared with the past" and that one should not "slight" the present by dwelling too long in the past (210–11). Even more emphatically, Edel gives as the story's moral the belief that "the past is best left buried," the primitive subordinated to present civilization (1970, 70; also Levy 28–29). Taking a psychological approach, Long views the "underworld" of the past as the Freudian "id" (29). Jones, meanwhile, offers a defense for Camillo, whose "natural paganism," Jones argues, protects him from corruption, despite his obsession (136).

There is a suggestion that Camillo's behavior is due to supernatural influence, and Thorp goes so far as to speak of Valerio as actually going back in time to his ancestors. But most critics including Todorov have chosen to disregard such hints, and to read the tale as instead, in Kerr's phrasing, "a study in obsession" (Todorov 184; Kerr 135). Indeed, the living seem to call on the past here more than the past haunts the living.

Martha, whose character Kelley speaks of as "a most attractive and true portrait" (155), is the opposite of her husband. Generally she has been held to be his superior as well, Long, for example, distinguishing her innocent worship of her husband from his enslavement by the goddess (29). She has also generally been held to be superior to the goddess, Holder confirming the narrator's judgment that Martha is a "riper fruit of time" (210–11). At first, however, in what Smith calls a particularly American attitude, Martha seeks to protect Valerio's past, his ancestral home, from the encroachments of the present, viewing restoration as a "moral as well as aesthetic crime" (401). But her attitude changes, Kelley marking the evidence of Camillo's blood sacrifice as the turning point (155).

As her godfather, the narrator's loyalties are with Martha, but Stein sees his being both a bachelor and an artist a significant reflection on James's sense of the incompatibility of art and marriage, and his role if not his reliability has been questioned (75–76). Putt comments on his cynicism and his rather "farcical" voyeuristic viewing of Camillo's worship of the Juno (77–78). Similarly, Terrie finds his view of Martha's marriage and husband at times condescending and speaks of his "almost prurient interest" in their marriage as what gives the tale its interest. He also views the narrator, however, as working toward a Jamesian articulation of international contrasts (4–5). Wegelin, too, pictures the narrator as breaking from the American view to look less superficially and less superstitiously at Italian life (32–33).

At the end of the tale, Valerio tells a visitor admiring the preserved hand of the statue that, "It is the hand of a beautiful creature . . . whom I once greatly admired" (CT 3, 122). Pretty clearly an understatement of his original feeling, its accuracy as to his feeling at the end has also been doubted, although his open acknowledgment of it seems to undercut Wagenknecht's statement that he keeps the hand "surreptitiously" (190). While Holder attachs an "apparently" to the happiness of the ending, both early interpretations and late have typically paid less attention to the hand than to what Edel calls Martha's "quiet American efficiency" in achieving victory over the statue (Holder 211; Edel *Life*, 145; Edel 1967, 328; also Levy 29–30; Long 29–30). The title itself, which sounds ominous, may actually confirm the optimistic reading, as it follows up on the narrator's statement in the midst of Valerio's obsession that "He has proved himself one of the Valerii; we shall see to it that he is the last, and yet that his decease shall leave the Conte Camillo in excellent health" (CT 3, 117). Andreas, however, distinguishes the reader's reaction from the action in the tale, maintaining that the reader is left most vividly with the sense of the stimulation of the past rather than its exorcism (103).

Perhaps for this reason, more extensive analyses of the tale tend to stake out more complicated readings. Maves takes Camillo's rescue from atavism by American sense as "either insanely chauvinistic or charmingly Gothic" but not very probable in psychological terms. He proposes instead a reading which sees the spell of the statue for Camillo not so much as the world of the pagan past, but the perfect world of art, which awakens not a primitive self, but an unused intellect. Citing the narrator's reflection on Camillo, "That he should admire a marble goddess was no reason for his despising mankind; yet he really seemed to be making invidious comparisons between us," Maves admits that his fascination with the ideal unfits him for appreciating the actual. Throughout, Maves sees Camillo's role as a passive one, including his return to his wife, whom Maves argues simply assumes for him the role of Juno (34–39). Putt also examines the tension between art and life, seen in Martha's lament "His Juno's the reality; I'm the fiction!" (77). Walter Wright returns the contrast between imperfect and ideal to that between the present and past, as only the past can be perfect (168).

Although he derides Camillo as "almost too fatuous to be real," Sicker presents a serious and grim interpretation of his state. Looking at Valerio's moonlit visit to the statue, Sicker sees him giving up his strength to the Diana-like vampiric goddess. The blood left behind on the altar Sicker interprets along the lines of the narrator's "hideous conjectures," asserting that James "rather daringly insinuates" that Valerio has castrated himself in tribute to his pagan background and in search of "stasis." The burial of the statue, he argues, will not solve his obsession, simply repress it (39–40, 49).

Using the terminology of William James, Berkson diagnoses Camillo's complaint as "tender-minded" idealism in his view of women which causes him to retreat from his flesh-and-blood wife to the statue, significantly the wifely Juno. Martha, a "tough-minded" realist, recognizes the problem, and so buries the statue. However, because of Valerio's apparently lingering loyalty to the statue, Berkson sees in the title an indication that the marriage may remain symbolically barren.

Clark counters Berkson's reading by analyzing Valerio's contemplation of the statue of Hermes, a symbol of pagan sexuality. In his reading, Valerio, originally frightened of the statue under the repressive influence of Christianity, finds it when alienated from his wife "the friendliest, jolliest thing in the world," an attitude that tempts the narrator to knock off its nose (presumably a euphemistic substitution for the phallus) in what Clark takes as an imitation of an occasion in classical history when Hermae throughout Athens were similarly mutilated. Clark sees Valerio not as too "tender-minded" but too lustful for Christian marriage, necessitating the burying of the statue of Juno—if not Hermes—to bring things into order again.

The picture of marriage here strikes Stein as equally bleak. Beginning in a time-wasting childish idyll, the marriage, according to Stein, changes when the energetic American wife seeks to explore, literally to dig into, her husband's true nature. Revealing his nature to him through the discovery of the statue, she then discovers it is antithetical to their marriage and so denies it by burying it again. In so doing, Stein argues, she denies Valerio his proper identity and herself an occasion for growth. Recalling how she once wished to make some grand gesture for her husband, "to take some step, to run some risk, to break some law, even!" he now sees Martha retreating to their former childish relationship, leaving both of them trapped in a false peace based on a mutual denial of reality, of themselves, of beauty, and their own need for growth (70–76).

Charles Anderson calls the tale "conventional" and McElderry "odd" (Anderson 13; McElderry 32). Other critics, as seen above, have granted it quite serious attention, although not without acknowledging the evidence of its early date. McCarthy, for example, sees the romantic trappings as outweighing the "moral" interest, and both Swan and Walter Wright argue that the tale remains too much on the level of symbol (McCarthy 105; Swan 1957, 23–24; Wright 168–69). Swan, also, however, calls the tale the best of James's early tales (1957, 23–24), and it is one of the few early tales whose omission from the New York Edition has been questioned by critics. Beach prefers it to either "A Passionate Pilgrim" or "The Madonna of the Future," the earliest works James did include, judging both its sense of the past and of the "brooding loveliness" of the European present superior. He speculates that James did not acknowledge the tale either because its hero was not as interestingly "self-conscious" as in the other two tales or because of its conspicuous debts to Hawthorne and Mérimée (189–90). Kelley considers the latter possibility absurd, noting the equal dependence on its source of "The Madonna of the Future." She agrees with Beach, however, that the tale merited inclusion (156). In 1875 when Howells came to review the tale in *The Passionate Pilgrim and Other Tales,* he found it the lightest of the collection, but with a "surpassing charm" and "just the right hint of ideal trouble" (72). It is that "ideal trouble" that continues to give it charm today, and the seeming reality of the characters placed in it that continues to provoke controversy.

Works Cited

Primary Works

James, Henry. 1874. "The Last of the Valerii." *Atlantic Monthly* 33 (January): 69–85.

———. 1875. "The Last of the Valerii." *A Passionate Pilgrim.* Boston: Osgood, 125–77.

———. 1885. "The Last of the Valerii." *Stories Revived.* Vol 3. London: Macmillan.

———. 1921–23. "The Last of the Valerii." In *The Novels and Stories of Henry James.* Vol. 26. Ed. Percy Lubbock. London: Macmillan.

Secondary Works

Allen, Elizabeth. 1984. *A Woman's Place in the Novels of Henry James.* New York: St. Martin's.

Anderson, Charles R. 1977. *Person, Place and Thing in Henry James's Novels.* Durham, NC: Duke University Press.

Anderson, Quentin. 1957. *The American Henry James.* New Brunswick, NJ: Rutgers University Press.

Andreas, Osborn. 1948. *Henry James and the Expanding Horizon: A Study of the Meaning and Basic Themes of James's Fiction.* Seattle: University of Washington Press.

Beach, Joseph Warren. [1918] 1954. *The Method of Henry James.* Philadelphia: Albert Saifer.

Berkson, Dorothy. 1981. "Tender-Minded Idealism and Erotic Repression in James's 'Madame de Mauves' and 'The Last of the Valerii.'" *Henry James Review* 2: 78–86.

Bewley, Marius. 1952. *The Complex Fate: Hawthorne, Henry James, and Some Other American Writers.* London: Chatto & Windus.

Boren, Lynda S. 1989. *Eurydice Reclaimed: Language, Gender, and Voice in Henry James.* Ann Arbor: UMI Research Press.

Briggs, Julia. 1977. *Night Visitors: The Rise and Fall of the English Ghost Story*. London: Faber.

Brodhead, Richard H. 1986. *The School of Hawthorne*. New York: Oxford University Press.

Cargill, Oscar. 1961. *The Novels of Henry James*. New York: Macmillan.

Churchill, Kenneth. 1980. *Italy and English Literature, 1764–1930*. Totowa, NJ: Barnes & Noble.

Clark, Michael. 1989. "The Hermes in Henry James's 'Last of the Valerii.'" *Henry James Review* 10, no. 3 (Fall): 210–13.

Delbaere-Garant, Jeanne. 1970. *Henry James: The Vision of France*. Paris: Société d'Editions Les Belles Lettres.

Edel, Leon, ed. 1970. *Henry James: Stories of the Supernatural*. New York: Taplinger.

———. 1967. "Henry James: The Americano-European Legend." *The University of Toronto Quarterly* 36: 321–34.

———, ed. [1949] 1963. *The Ghostly Tales of Henry James*. New York: The Universal Library, Grosset & Dunlap.

Edgar, Pelham. [1927] 1964. *Henry James, Man and Author*. New York: Russell & Russell.

Holder, Alan. 1966. *Three Voyagers in Search of Europe: A Study of Henry James, Ezra Pound, and T. S. Eliot*. Philadelphia: University of Pennsylvania Press.

Howells, W. D. 1979. *Selected Letters*. Vol. 2: *1873–1881*. Ed. George Arms, Christoph K. Lohmann, and Jerry Herron. Boston: Twayne.

———. [1875] 1961. Review of *The Passionate Pilgrim and Other Tales*. Reprinted in *Discovery of a Genius: William Dean Howells and Henry James*, ed. Albert Mordell, 63–74. New York: Twayne.

Jones, Granville H. 1975. *Henry James's Psychology of Experience: Innocence, Responsibility, and Renunciation in the Fiction of Henry James*. The Hague: Mouton.

Kelley, Cornelia Pulsifer. [1930] 1965. *The Early Development of Henry James*. Urbana: University of Illinois Press.

Kerr, Howard. 1983. "James's Last Early Supernatural Tales: Hawthorne Demagnetized, Poe Depoetized." In *The Haunted Dusk: American Supernatural Fiction, 1820–1920*. Ed. Howard Kerr, John W. Crowley, and Charles L. Crow, 135–48. Athens: University of Georgia Press.

Kraft, James. 1969. *The Early Tales of Henry James*. Carbondale: Southern Illinois University Press.

Levy, Leo B. 1957. *Versions of Melodrama: A Study of the Fiction and Drama of Henry James, 1865–1897*. Berkeley: University of California Press.

Lohmann, Christoph K. 1974. "Jamesian Irony and the American Sense of Mission." *Texas Studies in Literature and Language* 16 (Summer): 329–47.

Long, Robert Emmet. 1979. *The Great Succession: Henry James and the Legacy of Hawthorne*. Pittsburgh: University of Pittsburgh Press.

McCarthy, Harold T. 1958. *Henry James: The Creative Process*. New York: Thomas Yoseloff.

McElderry, Bruce R., Jr. 1965. *Henry James*. New York: Twayne.

Maves, Carl. 1973. *Sensuous Pessimism: Italy in the Work of Henry James*. Bloomington: Indiana University Press.

Putt, S. Gorley. 1966. *Henry James: A Reader's Guide*. Ithaca, NY: Cornell University Press.

Sicker, Philip. 1980. *Love and the Quest for Identity in the Fiction of Henry James*. Princeton: Princeton University Press.

Slabey, Robert M. 1958. "Henry James and 'The Most Impressive Convention in All History.'" *American Literature* 30 (March): 89–102.

Smith, Carl S. 1979. "James's International Fiction: Sources and Evolution." *Centennial Review* 23 (Fall): 397–422.

Stein, Allen F. 1984. *After the Vows were Spoken: Marriage in American Literary Realism*. Columbus: Ohio State University Press.

Stone, Edward. 1964. *The Battle and the Books: Some Aspects of Henry James*. Athens: Ohio University Press.

Swan, Michael. 1957. *Henry James*. London: Longmans, Green.

———, ed. 1948. *Ten Short Stories of Henry James*. London: John Lehmann.

Tanner, Tony. 1963. "James's Little Tarts." *The Spectator* 210 (4 January): 19.

Terrie, Henry, ed. 1984. *Tales of Art and Life*. Schenectady, NY: Union College Press.

Thorp, Willard, ed. 1962. *The Madonna of the Future and Other Early Stories*. New York: New American Library.

Tintner, Adeline R. 1986. *The Museum World of Henry James*. Ann Arbor: UMI Research Press.

Todorov, Tzvetan. 1977. *The Poetics of Prose*. Trans. Richard Howard. Ithaca, NY: Cornell University Press.

Unrue, Darlene. 1976. "Henry James and the Grotesque." *The Arizona Quarterly* 32:293–300.

Wagenknecht, Edward. 1984. *The Tales of Henry James*. New York: Frederick Ungar.

Wegelin, Christof. 1958. *The Image of Europe in Henry James*. Dallas: Southern Methodist University Press.

Wright, Nathalia. 1965. *American Novelists in Italy, The Discoverers: Allston to James*. Philadelphia: University of Pennsylvania Press.

Wright, Walter F. 1962. *The Madness of Art: A Study of Henry James*. Lincoln: University of Nebraska Press.

Ziolkowski, Theodore. 1977. *Dissenchanted Images: A Literary Iconology*. Princeton: Princeton University Press.

The Lesson of the Master

Publication History

"The Lesson of the Master" appeared first in two issues (July 16 and August 15, 1888) of the *Universal Review*, the only of James's stories to appear in the new magazine, edited by Harry Quilter with a strong Pre-Raphaelite accent. James missed the first issue in May by just a few months, but the magazine itself would only last through 1890. To make sure that the tale was copyrighted in the United States, James sent a copy of the title page to Macmillan in July. It did not appear officially in the States until 1892, when James made it the title story of a collection (*Letters* 3, 237). He later included it as the lead story in volume 15 of the New York Edition and it appeared in the first volume of *The Uniform Tales*.

Circumstances of Composition, Sources, and Influences

The idea for "The Lesson of the Master" came to James in January 1888 as a result of a conversation with Theodore Child about "the effect of marriage on the artist, the man of letters." James mentioned British examples where marriage had proved "fatal" to the work, while Child spoke of cases in France, particularly Daudet, of whose memoir *30 Ans de Paris* Child said, "He would never have written that if he hadn't married." So James conceived of his older, ruined writer who, seeking to save a younger one "on the brink of the same disaster," performs "some act of bold interference—breaking off the marriage, annihilating the wife, making trouble between the parties" (CN 43–44). James wrote the tale after returning to London from an extensive trip to Italy (*Life* 3, 239).

After its publication, Lady Jersey wrote James asking if her country home, Osterley, was the original of Summersoft in the tale. James replied that the likeness was meant as "an affectionate and yet respectful reminiscence" and "was only a matter of the dear old cubic sofa-cushions and objects of the same delightful order, and not of the human furniture of the house" (*Letters* 3, 123). Tinter records additional similarities including a Gainsborough and an Adams ceiling (1986, 206–8), while also offering a weekend visit to the country house of the Dugdales ten years before as part of the inspiration for Summersoft (1989, 127–28).

James's brother William may have seen something of himself in the role of the master, writing Henry, "The lesson of the master is a true one and his marrying again is the truest part of it. One of the antinomies and paradoxes of life—art versus humanity. I hope my dear Alice won't take it as aimed at *her*!" (241). Critics tend, however, to emphasize the resemblance between St. George's advice and James's theories, or between Overt's character and James's, seeing in the story what Lee calls a "strong autobiographical element" (53). Like Overt in the end, James had once spoken of his life's "loneliness" as its essential element (*Life* 5, 186). As Leavis observes, however, both St. George and Overt represent "Henry James potentials" (224). The failure of both *The Princess Casamassima* and *The Bostonians*, in Marder's view, had led James to reexamine his devotion to art (16). His declining reputation led to a "restless period," according to Richardson, who sees James, with Overt, "envious[ly]" examining the "dexterity" of St. George, but still taking "consolation" in his art (487–88). To van Cromphout, however, James's bitter experiences in the 1880s left him sincerely feeling the artist's need for "spiritual independence" (134). Krook sees the story as presenting the rational argument for James's evident nonrational fear of sexual involvement, of marriage in particular. While she contends that James later came to reverse his view and argue that the denial of passion is more dangerous than its acceptance, Putt, despite his acknowledgement of the appropriateness for James of his choice as an artist to remain single, sees the consequent isolation as having "deplorable" results on James's later work (Krook 369; Putt 220). Miller, for her part, argues against biographical interpretations that generalize James's depreciation of life in favor of art from the tale's particular events, pointing out that James frequently argued the other way in his letters, writing Jocelyn Persse, for example, of his "Art of Life which beats any Art of mine hollow" (18–19).

St. George is a Henry. It may be that James is imagining himself as the novelist he might have been had he, too, been born an Englishman, without the benefits of the double vision given to him by his American birth. In 1904 Croly generalized from what he sees as James's rejection of marriage for the artist in the tale to a similar rejection of patriotism, as both create loyalties that interfere with what James referred to as the "saving and sacred sense of proportion" (33–34). In this connection it may be noteworthy that Overt is also an international writer, a course St. George counsels him against, telling him, "Hang abroad! Stay at home and do things here" (CT 7, 240). Even so,

James counseled Edith Wharton in 1906, after *Madame de Treymes*, against the "French or the 'Franco-American' subject" (Powers 1990, 67). In this case, however, James's advice, like St. George's, may be accused of shifting, as, after *The Custom of the Country* in 1913, he criticized Wharton for passing over what should have been its "main theme," the American girl among the French aristocracy (Wharton, 182).

The name of Henry's counterpart, Paul, Tyler suggests, may make him the "novelist's *St.* Paul," who could "triumph with the master's gospel." Tyler also points to the more conspicuous saintly allusion in the tale, seeing St. George slaying "the dragon of marriage" standing between Overt and his "*overt*" or potential fame (229). Horrell redistributes the legend's roles: St. George plays the dragon, but also rescues the young hero for literature by marrying the girl himself (210). In Posnock's casting, St. George is a dragon pure and simple who defeats the hero and takes the girl (95). In Tintner's reading, however, the first wife is the dragon and St. George the British saint who saves the young Overt from falling prey to another dragon-like woman, all for the glory of English literature (1989, 145–56). Tintner also connects the character of St. George with a painter of St. George and admirer of beautiful women—Edward Burne-Jones (1986, 144–45).

Early on, Huneker suggested George Meredith, whose later novels James had found wanting, as a model for St. George (367). Since then, he has been more frequently compared with Robert Browning (e.g., Macnaughton 27). Monteiro connects the St. George allusion with the British poet who rescued Elizabeth Barrett from her dragon father and likens St. George's attitude to marriage to Browning's Andrea del Sarto. Marian he finds like the heroine of "My Last Duchess" "too soon made glad," although his doubt of her worthiness ought perhaps to be modified by the unreliability of the charges against the Duchess in the poem. In all, he finds the tale a "more realistic" treatment of James's discomfort with the public Browning than "The Private Life," but observes, too, that when James himself became a master, he would revise his view, seeing Browning as one artist to whom St. George's advice was inapplicable (74–78). Posnock also sees in the tale a response to Browning, pointing out that the classical version of the St. George myth, Perseus and Andromeda, was a favorite of Browning's. Even more than Monteiro, his reading bypasses James's sense of Browning as a social mediocrity, for the vigorous, virile poet whose poems and whose marriage seemed to draw into question James's own advocacy of "sexual renunciation" for the sake of art. In order to rationalize his choice, Posnock sees James constructing in the tale a "myth of celibacy" to "exorcise" the burden of inferiority. Like James facing the "theatrical" Browning, Overt and the reader are at first baffled by the performance of St. George. In the end Overt "neutralizes" the double by separating St. George's "double imperative"—his "sexual authority" from his artistry. Still fearing that St. George will regain "unity" by starting to write again after his new marriage, he devotes himself busily to the life of art, a choice fueled greatly by anger and the desire for revenge. Even so, according to Posnock, James avenges himself on Browning by rewriting him. James, like Overt, however, becomes a master only by first allowing himself to be a "dupe," as he parodies his own creed of renunciation in the tale, and reveals his own anxieties about his celibate life (14–16, 19–25, 70–85, 93–104). (See further "The Private Life.")

The story, in Posnock's view, draws particularly on Browning's *The Inn Album*, a late work that James had reviewed rather harshly. St. George, Posnock writes, would be "at home" in the theatrical world of *The Inn Album* with its blurring of life and art. Such a blurring—the treatment of experience as "textuality"—Posnock writes, was to Browning a sign of modern man's corruption, which he "gloomily" accepted, while James embraced the "expressive, creative possibilities of the modern, denatured age" (70–80, 85).

Miller notes the allusion to Shakespeare's remark about poets in *A Midsummer Night's Dream*, in the "fine frenzy" missing from St. George's eyes, an association between inward genius and its appearance also present in the early "The Sweetheart of M. Briseux" and the late *The Ambassadors* (11).

The question of whether an artist is "a man all the same" is, Baxter argues, central to both Hawthorne and James, although Hawthorne expected an artist to be "more than a man," James "but partially a man" (225, 230–31). Similarly, James's view that isolation was good for the artist is opposite from that of Hawthorne, according to Bewley (223). Marder points particularly to Coverdale of *The Blithedale Romance*, another young writer who loses his love (180).

The opening passages of description, according to Buckler and Sklare, employ the technique of the French impressionists (415). Grover comments that the tale could have been written by a member of the "L'Art pour l'Art" movement, citing in particular treatments of the incompatibility of marriage with art by the Goncourts in *Manette Salomon* and *Charles Demailly*. In the first, the truest artist declares that celibacy is the only possible condition for the great artist. In the second, the artist marries a woman who, like Marian, seems to embody the spirit of his art, only to be destroyed by her. James's work differs, however, in Grover's view, because of the amiability of the characters and the indication that artistic awareness brings pleasure as well as pain (141, 143–44, 146–50). The surprises of the tale Leavis finds superior to the typical trick endings of Maupassant, Kipling, or W. W. Jacobs, in their sustained ambivalence (226).

In the preface to the tale, James defended his artistic "supersubtle fry" as his imaginary figures meant to offer "spiritual alternatives to the present as it is." According to Donadio, they thus represent a function usually associated with religion, switched here to art and the imagination in a manner similar to that of Matthew Arnold (102). Seltzer sees the same desire to invoke something better in *The American Scene* (138). Blackmur calls this desire "the pinnacle of principle" in James—a way of combining aesthetic and moral values into true art ([1943] 1980, 79).

To Beattie, Overt's lack of "gumption" designates him an ancestor of Eliot's Prufrock (99). Van Cromphout compares the advice he too readily heeds to the warning Prince Andrei offers Pierre against marriage in *War and Peace* (135). Tintner compares it to Lonoff's strictures about the "solitary life" of the writer in Philip Roth's *The Ghost Writer* (1981, 50). Budd finds both Roth and James using the novella form to treat some of the same themes arising from the same initial configuration of characters: aspiring author, established author, his wife, and young female admirer. Like Overt, the protagonist in Alberto Moravia's *L'Amore conjugale* learns, according to van Cromphout, that one cannot be both a great writer and a good husband (134). Stewart finds a parallel to St. George's lesson in Yeats's "Estrangement," which declares that more men are destroyed by their wives and children than by drink and harlots (98). The marriage of an idealistic man to a woman caught up in society and money recurs, Rentz observes, in *The Good Soldier* by Ford Madox Ford (113 n.16). Miller, however, distinguishes James's conception of the artist from Mann's romanticization of the decadent "inhuman, extra-human" artist in *Death in Venice* and "Tonio Kröger," although the latter presents, according to Lee, like "The Lesson of the Master," an artist who still wants to be a part of "the living" (Miller 19–20; Lee 52). Matthiessen in 1944 found the master's lesson rather dated in the light of the careers of such active artists as Malraux, but also noticed the increasing ease of "selling out" since James's day (1944, 2). Barry points to a parallel with Kawabata's *The Master of Go*, which also considers the issue of artistic commitment through a master and an aspirant (1983, 88–89).

In a biography of Edwin Arlington Robinson, Neff records that the poet read James's tale in 1896 when he was in his late twenties, and may have taken the final words about Overt's "intellectual" passion to heart, following the master's counsel of a lonely independence the rest of his life (also Ziff 327). Neff also points to particular parallels with Robinson's poems "The False Gods" and "Rembrandt to Rembrandt," in which the great painter wonders if he would have compromised his work had his wife lived. An interesting sidelight is Robinson's estimate of Browning's counterexample—though without any comparison to St. George—"Do you know I have a theory that Browning's life-long happiness is all humbug? . . . The man's life was in his art, but he was big enough to make the world think otherwise" (62–63, 201–2). Cynthia Ozick recalls her own early discipleship to the master: "Trusting in James, believing, like Paul Overt, in the overtness of the Jamesian lesson, I chose Art, and ended by blaming Henry James." Only at the cost of her youth, she records, did she learn that James himself had not started as a master, that the true lesson of the master is not Art, but Life.

Relation to Other Works

St. George's windowless study offers a striking contrast with the "wide window" of Benvolio, better adapted for an artist's observation, according to Beebe (204–5, 208). Luckily, Putt contends that such artless wedded bliss as St. George's, James and his characters such as Benvolio and Overt find "easy to walk away from" (220). Smith includes both artists' tales along with "A Day of Days," "The Author of Beltraffio," "The Next Time," *Lady Barbarina*, *The Portrait of a Lady*, and *The Tragic Muse* as evidence that James truly believed in the incompatibility of marriage and ambition (655). Taking a more general stance, Jones places both tales among those treating the conflict of art and life, seeing as the main message that life not only "provides the material for art" but "too much of it," and so endangers the artist. His other examples include *Roderick Hudson*, "The Madonna of the Future," "The Coxon Fund," and "The Death of the Lion." He specifically compares the spare study of St. George with the house in *The Sense of the Past*, which Ralph Pendrel worries will provide too many impressions (145–46).

Focusing on *Roderick Hudson*, Walter Wright finds St. George closer to James in his artistic views than Roderick, but still casts their counterparts Rowland and Paul as the "touchstone" of the works (91–92). Labrie observes the way in James that the artist is endangered by "the very sensitivity to life" that makes him an artist, the dire results of which, he argues, can be seen most dramatically in *Roderick Hudson* (168). Miller, on the other hand, contends that the "detachment" Roderick Hudson lacked was a more limited ability to concentrate on one's work than the total "detachment" from life advocated by St. George here (10).

Although Stewart finds "The Lesson of the Master" more mature than "The Author of Beltraffio," both are, according to Bass, early approaches to the themes of James's tales for *The Yellow Book* (Stewart 98–99). Bass notes particularly the presence of the young devotée in each (114). In Segal's reading, while the two tales show the same disjunction between life and "artistic convictions," elements that were "purely functional" in the earlier tale become central here (114, 121). Donald Stone points out that Ambient's marriage, however miserable, did not keep him from producing great works and notes the new limits assigned the artist here (252). Mottram, however, finds the lesson in both that the more a gentleman a writer is, the less an artist he becomes (179). Both St. George and Ambient are, in Goetz's view, relatively un-Jamesian as artists (150). (See also "The Author of Beltraffio.")

Others, including McElderry, link the two artist tales with James's novel of the artist, *The Tragic Muse*, all three showing, according to Long, the same argued-for necessity to sacrifice life to art in order to succeed (McElderry 80; Long 162). Gordon and Stokes judge both James's greater devotion to literature over the theatre or painting and his use of an "involved spectator" apprentice to make the treatment of the trap of the artist "much more sinister" in the tales than in *The Tragic Muse* (162). Macnaughton emphasizes the concern with "vocation" in the three works, while Powers contrasts their approval of giving up marriage for an artistic career to Verena's equally appropriate giving up of a sham career for marriage in *The Bostonians* (Macnaughton 27; Powers 1970, 120). Looking only at "The Lesson of the Master" and *The Tragic Muse*, Geismar points out the art-hating women in each, while Donald Stone compares the striking images in each of the artists left on their own in "ambiguous triumph" (Geismar 113; Stone 252, 318).

Wagenknecht speaks of "The Lesson of the Master" as the first of James's stories "about writers that really deals with writing as such" (50). Still, the contrast between the artist and society, according to Walter Allen, is the main subject here as opposed to such tales as "The Real Thing," where the contrast is between art and life (48). Walter Wright observes that St. George likes to think of himself as someone like Limbert, an artist done in by the "undiscerning" (91). But while Kermode observes that St. George and Limbert initially face the same problem of the married artist in need of an income, the resemblance between Overt and Limbert in their poverty, noted by Richardson, seems stronger in the end (Kermode 16; Richardson xix). Nathalia Wright classes Paul Overt with other Jamesian artists such as Jeffrey Aspern whose experience is significantly broadened by visiting Italy (222). Mottram finds the false artist illustrated in more detail in "Greville Fane," where the type is linked not simply with success, as here, but with deep vulgarity (169). As a genuine artist, however, Overt's tale is a superior "plea for something beyond cleverness" to that of the narrator of "The Figure in the Carpet," in the judgment of Horne (46–47). In Goetz's reading both tales begin with the typical contrast of the master with the mystery and the follower seeking to understand it; however, over the course of the story St. George is transformed into a "fallible" authority. At the same time, the story fails to follow what Goetz sees as the most likely course at the start, parallel to "The Death of the Lion," in which two young admirers—male and female—meet and marry. Unlike Paraday, St. George insists on becoming an "internal" rather than an "external" mediator" (163).

Labrie, however, sees the theme here as art versus life, particularly the need for a "normative balance between desire and detachment," evident also in "The Figure in the Carpet," *The Tragic Muse*, and "The Madonna of the Future" (161). Grover, too, places the tale in a line of works beginning with "The Madonna of the Future" and including *The Tragic Muse*, *Roderick Hudson*, and "The Death of the Lion," which treat the conflict between art and human love (15). Bass sees a similar choice in "The Coxon Fund" between loyalty to love and art, although the narrator in "The Coxon Fund" has less to gain personally, because, unlike Overt, he is not in line for either (117). Horne points to Gloriani in *The Ambassadors* as a man whose artistic greatness is based on a full experience of life as James's final word that the artist need not, indeed ought not, isolate himself from life (19). Marder, on the other hand, compares Overt not to another artist, but to Marcher, whom he charitably describes as a "timid lover" (180). Less kindly, Beattie classes him among James's "half-men," including such as Marcher and Winterbourne (99).

Edel finds the message that marriage kills creativity as early as "De Grey" and repeated in "The Next Time," and St. George's view that women are "the most dangerous distraction" Jones sees also in "Collaboration" (Edel 28; *Life* 2, 345–46; Jones 146–47; also Tanner 80). Similarly, Stein points to "The Birthplace" and "The Last of the Valerii" as well as "The Lesson of the Master" and "The Author of Beltraffio" as evidence that the "innate antipathy of a wife for art is virtually a given in James's marital fiction" (107). In the last two tales, writes Matheson, the artist is "opposed by his wife's maternal function," although the wife here is concerned with "Respectability" rather than "Morality," as was Mrs. Ambient (224). Miller argues, however, that the character of Maud Limbert in "The Next Time" provides a rebuttal to the argument that a wife will not put her husband's work before her family's prosperity (18; also Horne 83). Wagenknecht judges Marian's "aesthetic toggery" suspiciously similar to the dress of Gwendolen Ambient, as conventional as the Paris clothes of Mrs. St. George, but Barry portrays Marian as a superior version of Daisy Miller, her freedom tempered by a greater awareness and intelligence (Wagenknecht 53; Barry 1978, 387).

Leavis offers a connection with "The Jolly Corner" in the confrontations with "alternate selves," stemming from James's own attempts at self-justification. In Leavis's view, "The Lesson of the Master" is "a much finer and more complex story" because it addresses a far more significant contrast—as the James character faces not just a successful businessman, but the more tempting figure of the successful writer (225–26). Similarly, Kermode notes the use of "doubling" here, although he judges it less fantastic than in "The Jolly Corner" or "The Private Life" (15–16).

Both "The Liar" and "The Lesson of the Master," according to Walter Wright, suffer from the same kind of misinterpretation (96). In Segal's estimate, however, the relationship between observer and protagonist that caused the problematic "double-focus" in "The Liar" is resolved in "The Lesson of the Master" and "The Beast in the Jungle," where it becomes the central theme. On a lesser note, she compares the "nocturnal meetings" here with those in "The Figure in the Carpet" and *The Sacred Fount* (164, 237). The ambiguity of the tale Rimmon judges "less daring" than the "impossible objects" of "The Figure in the Carpet," *The Turn of the Screw*, and *The Sacred Fount*, as the ambiguity is apparent only in "retrospective," concerns only motives not "actual happenings," and is presented through a relatively simple "network of conflicting clues" with less "linguistic ambiguity." Rimmon also points to a resemblance between the ambiguity of Marian's character and that of Milly's sickness in *The Wings of the Dove* (56, 79, 93–94, 120–23).

In the view of Grossman, while James in "The Next Time" and "The Tree of Knowledge" successfully treated as comedy situations that seem essentially sad, here he mistakenly treats seriously a subject that calls for comedy (232). Indeed, Miller finds the tale more serious than the other artist tales collected in the New York Edition due to its absence of a mediating, ironic narration (10). Tintner goes so far as to call the tale a modern version of a saint's life, even as she sees "The Velvet Glove" as a modern mock epic (1989, 155–56). James, however, parodied the title of the tale, according to Adams, in the title to his 1905 lecture, "The Lesson of Balzac," where he called the French author "the master of us all" (458). Then again, it is in that lecture, writes Smith, that James "spells out his rigorous concept of the artist" (657).

Interpretation and Criticism

Two years after James's tale, the *Outlook* responded to another magazine's posing of the question "SHOULD literary men marry?" by asking their own questions: "Should publishers prosper?" "Should critics keep cool?" (346). The question has usually received more serious, if not always approving, treatment from the critics of this tale. As Baxter puts it, the "central issue" in the story is "the conscience of the artist, arrayed against the 'others,' struggling for survival amidst the longings of the natural man" (227). The tale, according to Vaid, is a "successful cross between the parable and the realistic tale" (212). What the "lesson" of that parable is, what the appropriate choice for the artist's conscience is, however, is not clear.

The issue is complicated by the presentation of the tale. As such critics as Segal and Kermode have recorded, it presents a "perfectly ambiguous situation" allowing for "mutually exclusive interpretations" (Segal 151; Kermode 15). James added the twist ending after the notebook entry, an addition Matthiessen and Murdock find makes "a neatly finished plot" but "possibly" confuses the original idea by raising the issue of St. George's sincerity (N 87). Leavis speaks of "the tension arising from the uncertainty the reader is kept in and finally left in." "The ambivalence," he continues, "which is personal and inside James himself, conditions the structure: the uncertainty Henry James felt remains to the end and is expressed in the final ambiguity—what indeed was the lesson of the Master?" (226). The tale itself, according to Holloway, is made up primarily of "conversation-episodes" that relay the facts of a series of events, only one of which is presented directly (62–63), an approach that further complicates reading. Certainly, as many have commented, Overt's name reflects his "openness" to the lesson (e.g., Posnock 85;

Kermode 15; Austin Wright 188). The question remains, if the giving of it is ambiguous, is the lesson?

In Rimmon's analysis, the tale follows the structure of the "inverted story," a variety of the classic *pointe* story, its "reversal scene" offering a complete inversion of the original reading. Unlike classic reversals, however, Rimmon contends, the tale leaves the motives of Henry St. George—and those of Marian as well—completely ambiguous. Rereading the tale, she argues, will produce an equal number of clues of St. George's possible sincerity—the "gratuitous nature" of his confession, its intensity—as of his possible deception—his interest in Marian, his contradictory attitude to his wife. The tale thus can be read either as a "story of rivalry" or of "salvation." The reversal scene itself, Rimmon observes, rather than a straight revelation, follows a "zigzag sequence" of "creditable and discreditable explanations," with St. George seeming at first "sincere—not a mocking fiend" and then indeed "the mocking fiend." When he enjoins Paul to look at him and "Consider, at any rate, the warning I am at present"—it could be either a boast or self-deprecation. The possibility that the master might write again is "particularly painful" because it would not only show St. George to be insincere, but his entire "lesson" to be inaccurate. As Rimmon notes, many critics cite the last line of the story as, "St. George was essentially right and that Nature dedicated him to intellectual, not to personal passion." In doing so they leave out a crucial introductory phrase, that Overt's attitude is "perhaps a proof" (79–94).

A further ambiguity, according to Wirth-Nesher, is Mrs. St. George's burning of her husband's "bad" book. Was it bad, she asks, because it was "evil" or because it was "badly composed"? She observes how Overt from the start is "ready for sacrifice," following the role of the "alienated artist," even as St. George is "convinced that any gains in life must entail losses in art." To Wirth-Nesher, St. George's discussion of the "happy" societies without art is particularly relevant in its taking up of the nineteenth-century question of whether art can replace religion. St. George appears to believe so, in his statement that the artist "has only to do with the absolute." If so, art needs also the "trappings of religion" such as priests and celibacy. But Wirth-Nesher argues that James, while linking the aesthetic and moral, did not believe art a sufficient religion, dependent as it was on both society and illusion. Out of its insecurity society does, Wirth-Nesher argues, want illusion, believing in "the magic of the individual product of the imagination" as does St. George. Thus, his advice is sincere even if he himself falls short of the standard, contenting himself with seeing others fulfill his ambitions. The letter about his wife after her death raises the issue, Wirth-Nesher argues, not of St. George's sincerity but of whether his work declined because of her interference, or rather because of her mistakenly "shielding him from quotidian life." Even more ambiguous, in her opinion, is St. George's final reference to himself as a "warning." His happiness, she argues, recalls Strether's advice to "live all you can; it's a mistake not to." In James, "zealous devotion to art" can lead to "decadence" as well as "holiness." The lesson, then, remains "undeciphered even at the end," just as in another story the "figure in the carpet" is never revealed (120–23).

Posnock takes issue with Rimmon's reading of the tale as "a deadlock of opposites." But in his analysis, too, James's intent was ambiguity. He notes the early certainty of St. George, Overt, and Marian that the perfection of art and the "world" are necessarily opposed. James, he writes, "encourage[s]" the reader to believe St. George, but then "forces us to revise our opinion." St. George "vulgarizes and simplifies" James's beliefs, as his "key term" of "perfection" was to James a "spurious goal." Renunciation for James was rather, in Posnock's view, a "temperamental need." The artist must work with reality, because "art is hopelessly involved with life." Like Wirth-Nesher, he views St. George's admission that societies without art are happier, as an acknowledgement that art, like the world, is flawed. Indeed, citing James's preface to *The Golden Bowl*, Posnock depicts art as exploiting its "raw materials"—its characters becoming "bleeding participants" in the novelist's "great game." This, he argues, is the "counterlesson" that contradicts St. George's advice to Overt. Naïvely, Overt misses it at first just as he misses St. George's early attentions to Marian. Overt's sense of St. George's "subtlety" and contradictions does not go far enough in recognizing St. George as a master of performance. Thus Overt feels "betrayed" at the end. Objecting to the "moralizing devaluation of the theatrical" in James criticism, Posnock offers a reading of St. George as someone who illustrates the "instability" of self the acceptance of which, according to Posnock, is the mark of the "truly civilized." Moving from James's belief in "manners" to the contention that James would recognize all social encounters as performances, he attributes St. George's "impersonal lucidity" to his "improvisational fluidity of a manner." To praise St. George's awareness without holding him responsible for the actions it leads him to, however, seems unlikely Jamesian morality. One need not resort to performance theory in order to recognize Overt as naïve in comparison to St. George, who can recognize, for example, both the attractiveness and the "immaturity" of Marian Fancourt. Posnock's analysis even offers a partial absolution of Mrs. St. George, presenting St. George's "impugning" of his wife as simply part of his "theatrically exaggerating" the artist's need of "independence." In fact, Posnock writes, Mrs. St. George is "ironically . . . the exception proving the rule that women intrude." Even so, Posnock suggests, the fact that Marian is so different from the first Mrs. St. George may indicate that St. George is "sincere" in protecting Overt from her. In the end St. George's "undecidability accounts for the ultimate ambiguity of the tale as a whole," the ambiguity being a "means of enacting a central theme of the tale: the heterogeneity of social reality," and focusing attention on the central concept of "social art" (78–93, 209 n.22).

Nuhn early, but briefly, declared that the famous Jamesian ambiguity is "entirely absent" in the tale (145). Putt rejects the famous ambiguity as a "simple ambiguity of plot" with little significance. In his reading, it is indeed Nature "not merely Henry St. George" that makes a celibate of Overt, whose very asking of advice indicates he is already heading that way (219–20). In 1978 Barry also protested against the critical focus on the tale's ambiguity, arguing that it did not matter whether St. George's advice was sincere, as either way the end was the same with Overt "saved" for art. In such readings, he argues, the tale remains "inert," with everyone agreeing that renunciation is necessary for the artist. He acknowledges that "part" of James's message is such renunciation, but sees it as "suspect"—a "convenient alibi" for James's own failures. James, he argues, is both more courageous and more subtle in the tale than most critics realize. Marian offers one challenge to renunciation, seeming to embody both "life" and artistic intelligence, but Barry contends that these characteristics are not clearly validated by James, and her role is really that of the American "pilgrim" whose "originality of thinking" is at least partly due to her situation. Rather, Barry locates a deeper ambiguity in the first Mrs. St. George. Barry points out that St. George is declared to be ruined only "in his own sight," and contends that Overt is "never completely happy" with his disapproval of her character from which James "withholds his authorial support." Thus it is Overt and not the narrator who "*assumes*" the book she burned was no good. Overt assigns St. George's decline, which he associates with his marriage, to the last ten years, but St. George has been married for "more than twenty" and seems as "enamoured of worldy success" as his wife. Most significantly, Barry points out that when Overt decides to stay abroad and finish his book, after having received St. George's letter praising his wife after her death, he is making his choice while believing both that Marian is free and that St. George has withdrawn his injunction against marriage. In Barry's view, "we must therefore accept that Overt's final state is one freely entered into." St. George's motives become insignificant. Both St. George's decline and Overt's decision come from within, making each responsible for his own fate. Such a reading, he argues, leaves open the debate between art and life: "We are given no guarantees that the married and vigorous St. George will not produce good work, or that the celibate Overt will." Thus James manages to speak "for art without taking sides against life" (385–89). By 1983 Barry saw the "lesson" of the tale further undercut, arguing that the master seems to have managed both art and life and that the evaluation of an artistic decline is necessarily subjective. Noting that critics generally disagree with the "lesson," he adds that James may have too (84–88).

Despite the muddle caused by the tale's ambiguity, most critics continue to take St. George's counsel to renounce as James's (e.g., Segal 109; Powers 1969, 15; Tintner 1989, 155; 1986, 83). Neither Markow-Totevy, who comments on the tale's humor, nor Richardson, who points to its "bitterness," sees those qualities as undercutting its basic message (Markov-Totevy 100–3; Richardson 488). While acknowledging the concluding irony that can leave the reader feeling as "sold" as Overt, Edel still affirms that James, too, saw success as "cheapening" and marriage as "death" to the artist (*Life* 2, 345–46; *Life* 3, 240; *Letters* 2, 79; [1949] 1963, 28). Stein goes so far as to argue that the ambiguity serves simply to make Overt question his renunciation. James, he writes, wanted to make "vivid for his reader the agonizing self-doubts about his lonely course that the artist must inevitably confront and that impart to his calling its quality of awful heroism . . . the absence of comfortable signposts." Even if the lesson *is* meant ironically, Stein maintains that "the very fact" that James "would think to associate terrible hindrances to art with marriage" is significant of his fears (108)

Others place some limits to the lesson. Mizener and Tanner, without disqualifying it, both place it in the context of the era James lived in, Mizener pointing to the worthlessness of London society in the tale (Mizener 205; Tanner 45–46; also Bantock 161, 165, 177). Horne, on the other hand, argues that the tension here is not between society and art, seeing St. George as comfortably representing "the social credit of literature." Horne instead places the conflict between art and life, and many critics uphold St. George's counsel to choose art as it applies to Overt's case (45–46). Blackmur, Andreas, and Dietrichson are among those critics who leave out the final "perhaps" to argue that St. George's lesson was right for Overt (Blackmur [1943] 1983, 88; Andreas 88; Dietrichson 127). While Marder, who attributes it to Overt, finds the reasoning doubtful, Lee, Smith, and Horne also agree that Overt seems meant for an "intellectual, not personal passion" (Marder 16; Lee 53; Smith 658; Horne 46; Labrie 158). Jones sees St. George's counsel as accurate given Overt's success and his decline. Jones pictures Overt on hearing this flattering explanation as "disappointed," not "angry" or "betrayed" but "stunned and frustrated by St. George's impeccable logic" (144–45). Geismar simply judges Overt unequal to a heroine such as Marian (114).

To Tyler, the tale is James's "clearest fictional statement about the undesirability of the artist's having any but the Muse for wife or any but the work of art for child." Even the fact that Overt's reward is simply the "prospect of success as an artist" Tyler sees as the "sign of James's own idealistic faith"— something the reader must take on faith (229). Similarly, Blackmur extends the judgment on Overt to all artists. The portrait of the artist as "the man, short of the saint, most wholly deprived" was indeed James's own. Blackmur, however, takes exception to it as a picture "natural to the man still in revolt" who "identifies the central struggle of life in society as the mere struggle of that aspect of his life of which he makes his profession," not having grasped that all professions are "mutually inclusive." Once an artist understands that, "his vision disappears in his work," which is why James can only portray the artist as a failure: "Otherwise there will be only the portrait of a man." James himself, "in his full maturity," according to Blackmur, would take the artist "for granted" and instead write of "men and women bent not on a privation but a fullness of being" ([1943] 1983, 88–89). Indeed, in 1948 he gives as the "moral of the fable" that the life of the artist is "the fullest possible human profession" ([1948] 1983, 106). The "odd corollary" of the tale, in Labrie's formulation, is that "one can only come to terms with life as an artist by not becoming deeply involved in it" (153). Such a separation from life is, in Grover's view, at the center of the tale. Even though art seeks to recreate the loveliness of life and its "fullest expression is found in a beautiful young woman," a choice is necessary because, he writes, "art is parasitical" (141).

Van Cromphout, on the other hand, disagrees with critics such as Matthiessen who argue James is advocating "withdrawal from life," contending that James meant a "dedication to art" only as opposed to compromises with "the world," not isolation from it. Marriage, he admits, is dangerous in James's view because it can lead to the "worship of false gods." But, he argues, artistic dedication does not mean that "the artist cannot *live*, cannot *experience* life" and he cites in defense St. George's saying that the true artist has "a passion, an affection, which includes all the rest." Indeed, van Cromphout argues, the tale makes it "quite clear" that to create art demands "the most intense experience of life" (133–35). In his reading of St. George's motives, Kermode comments that it was "common enough at the time to declare that marriage and children were the ruin of the artist." If ambiguous, it is still "permissible," Kermode adds, to see Overt as "lucky to misread the clues" and so to miss marriage, given the depiction of women in the tale. Nevertheless, Kermode points to the "striking" linking of the "two lives" of art and love in St. George's image that to betray art will bring regret "as a man thinks of a woman he has in some detested hour of his youth loved and forsaken." The tale, he writes, "honours both lives." While St. George's declaration that society is happier without art and that the artist is "in a false position" may be "special pleading," still Kermode sees it expressing the situation of the artist who is part of society, but dedicated to work that society ignores or scorns (15–18).

Other critics see the ambiguity as more seriously undercutting St. George's lesson. McElderry, for example, cautions the "unwary reader" against reading the tale as James's "rationalization" of his single state (81). Austin Wright sees the twist ending changing the story from a simple tale of "discovery" to one of "comic error," the source of Overt's vulnerability being his literary egotism, which Wright sees even in the concluding remark that Overt would applaud any further work of St. George despite its proving that he has been had (188–89). As Geismar points out, the change probably results from James's deepening rather than confusing his idea. The ambiguity, in his view, demonstrates James's ability to make light of his own seriousness. Geismar not only praises the "balance of emotions," but sees life "however 'stupid'" as triumphing despite the evident fear of women (112–14). Maintaining that James is "not an autobiographical writer," Wagenknecht dissociates St. George's views from James's. He observes that "it is hard to see how a celibate" could have bettered the working conditions Mrs. St. George provides her husband, and questions how she ruined him. Calling Overt a "simple soul," he sees the ending an "open" one, leaving unsure whether Overt will be great or whether St. George will write again (52–54). In Miller's reading, the Master is not necessarily duplicitous, but he is mistaken, perhaps not in his estimate of Paul, but in his general belief that art demands the abandonment of life. Rather, she argues, the tale shows life as the greater good, in Paul's deep sense of his loss and St. George's "vibrantly glowing" happiness. One simply cannot tell, she adds, whether Paul might have produced equally great works if he had married Marian (17–19). To Beattie, Overt is not man enough to recognize the true lesson for the artist that "there can be no lesson where the heart and sensibilities are concerned" (99).

In his analysis, Jones emphasizes that the tale is not simply a story of art but of two men (144). The relationship between the two is, in Geismar's judgment, "almost feudal" (112–13). Holloway points to the many "identity elements" intended to distinguish Paul from St. George, but finds some problematic (64–65). Like Posnock and Kermode later, Mackenzie casts St. George and Overt as doubles, providing a reading that emphasizes St. George's duplicitousness. Overt at the start is a "social and sexual aesthete," a beginner with claims to literary mastery. Socially and sexually established, St. George is still, for his part, in a false position with spurious claims to art. Mackenzie draws attention to the inconsistency of St. George's statements about his wife to Marian—that she was the making of him—and to Overt—that she has ruined him—and sees St. George as deliberately seeking to place Overt in a position as false as his own. Both are left incomplete, Overt's art "suicidally as well as sacrificially estranged from personal passion" and St. George still the sham master (67–70).

St. George's early masterpiece is *Shadowmere*, and to Lynd his entire claim as an artist—even a debased one—is shadowy. He writes that the story "fails to convince me of the reality of the chief character. I distrust most stories about pot-boiling writers who but for their wives might have been great geniuses. The successful pot-boiler is, as a rule, a born pot-boiler, and the man of genius cannot hope to compete with him in his particular market." The burnt book he equally doubts was "anything to grieve about" (116). Others stay more within the parameters of the tale in their critiques of his characer. Seed glosses three of the more arcane terms St. George uses to describe his work—*carton-pierre*, lincrusta Walton, and brummagaem—to show how all three "cheaply produced" items fit St. George's valuing of his work. Stewart blames St. George less for his literary compromises than for first allowing his wife a "ridiculous" degree of control over him and then blaming her for everything to a new acquaintance (99). Writing that critics who see St. George as James's spokesman and therefore denounce his second marriage as inconsistent oversimplify his character, Walter Wright seeks to provide a reading of the "consistently inconsistent" St. George who is more than "an illogically conceived allegorical device." In Wright's assessment Mrs. St. George is so clearly unsympathetic that it is easy to accept her husband's denunciation of her. He pictures St. George, however, as "sentimentally cynical," a man "quick to rationalize" his own compromises and attack others, someone whose sufferings consist largely of easy living and whose decline as an artist is his own doing. Overt's real lesson as an artist then is to learn to judge St. George, not simply the "general validity" of the master's criticism of the world but, more importantly and more positively, "something in his working at his own art that makes no sacrifice of his renouncing worldly things" (91–92).

Many, however, defend St. George from the intent to deceive, van Cromphout finding his advice "not unusual at all" (van Cromphout 135; also Jones 144). In 1943, Blackmur wrote that St. George married Marian "partly to save Overt," but in 1948 he added emphasis to the "partly" ([1943] 1983, 87; [1948] 1983, 106). Although she disagrees with Blackmur's contention, Horne also absolves St. George of deception in his marriage, arguing that it shows him giving up the attempt to compromise with art and redeeming himself by turning instead fully to life (44–45; also Mottram 180). Similarly, Labrie pictures a St. George who recognizes that while artistic dedication is the greatest good, it is not one to which he is "personally suited." While criticizing the "fifty standards" of women, St. George himself, Labrie remarks, has "not only accommodated himself to the viewpoints and needs of those around him, but he has enjoyed doing so" (157).

Some critics not only absolve St. George of blame, but attribute some good qualities to him. Speaking of his second marriage the *Bookman* asked why "such a good fellow, so full of the high spirits of success" *should* change. Observing that St. George seeks a "compromise between art and life," Horne contends that James does not designate in the story the "degree of asceticism necessary to the artist" (44, 48). Others seem sure that St. George, however attractive, is somewhat short of the necessary degree. As Grover points out, for the tale to work, St. George's life must be attractive, a genuine temptation. Indeed, Grover sees as the "special distinction" of the tale "the apparent grace, charm and physical well-being which accompany the artistic failure of Henry St. George" (140–44). Kaston sees the tale contrasting two types of imagination—masterly versus renunciatory. Seeing no suggestion that Overt is or will be a great artist, Kaston pictures St. George as "the supreme imaginer of *this* story, at least" (5–6). One may in fact question the value of what critics have set up as what would be the proper behavior for St. George. According to many the "creditable" motive for St. George's remarriage is his desire to "save" Paul. When questioned by him on his reasons, St. George admits that he did not marry "absolutely" to save him, "but it adds to the pleasure." The answer, writes Rimmon, upsets the "creditable interpretation" showing that "the marriage is not devoid of self-interest," but as she adds parenthetically, "why should it be?" (84). While deciding not to marry for the sake of one's art may seem practical even to those who do not see art as sacrosanct, to marry someone for the sake of someone else's art, without any personal reasons, seems highly suspect human behavior.

Both wives have received their own share of analysis. Grover blames the first Mrs. St. George for turning writing into "an industry like another" (142–44). Stein also faults the wife for applying business principles to literature, citing the description of St. George writing standing "like a clerk in a counting-house." The "bad book" she burns is, he assumes, one that is "too fine to sell well or that, perhaps, touches too closely on the Master's sense of artistic loss" (106–7). Kappeler provides a nearly opposite reading of Mrs. St. George's unfortunate influence. Following her contention that in James the artist must remain faithfully married to the Muse, she pictures St. George as a "living example of a polygamist on his way down." Mrs. St. George is a threat not because she is hostile to the Muse, but because she "condone[s], and even perversely delight[s] in a polygamous *ménage à trois*" with her husband and the Muse, providing the study for their meetings." Kappeler has the good sense to recognize that Mrs. St. George's devotion might be more to the economic results of her husband's relationship with the Muse than to the Muse herself. Even so, she concludes, "it is precisely the wife's 'understanding,' her excessive sanction of the lovers' affair, which renders her husband impotent with his mistress" (78–80). One might add, however, that strictly artistic impotence seems of little concern to her.

Marian herself, who in the phrasing of Blackmur, serves "as a nexus for the conflict of loyalties between the master and the disciple," has also been seen as an ambiguous character (1943, 87). To some she is what Paul first sees her as, a representative of life itself. Matheson, for example, speaks of her as the master of a "higher art than the literary, the art of living" (225). Others question the genuine interest and "intelligence in the arts" Blackmur attributes to her. William James, who objected to her French phrases—"how *can* you make that girl say such a thing as c'est d'un trouvé?!"—seemed to pin the blame on James's style rather than the character (241). *The Bookman*, however, recognized her as a familiar type, "bound to be, by her environment and her sex, a Philistine at bottom" (27). To Walter Wright, she is "conventional and naïve" (92). Wagenknecht sees her enthusiasm as merely provincial—she grew up in India—and characterizes her as "more interested in writers than she is in writing," a trait Posnock sees implied in the name "Fancourt" (Wagenknecht 54; Posnock 91). Grover points not only to the way Marian represents beauty and life in contrast with the "headachy fancies" of art, but also to her failure to recognize St. George's decline (141, 146). Tyler, too, sees Marian's marriage to St. George as proving she is "more attracted to past-mastery . . . than to speculative mastery . . ." and so is possibly insincere in "her own faith in love itself as an ideal" (230). Smith can judge Marian "delightful" and still find it necessary for Overt to sacrifice her (657). Tintner, on the other hand, while arguing that any wife, no matter how worthy, is bad for a writer—she points out that St. George had truly loved his wife—seems to feel compelled to prove that Marian is unworthy, mercenary and lacking in taste, in order to show that marriage would have been disastrous for Overt (1989, 152–55; 1986, 83).

Even Marian's superiority over the first Mrs. St. George has been questioned. Holloway notes the many differences James seeks to establish between the two. In the end, however, he argues, her assessment of Paul's work as the new Mrs. St. George—she and her husband call it "really magnificent"—seems no more authoritative (65–66). Labrie extends the comparison, seeing St. George's advice to Overt supported by the similarities between the two women, who both "quite distinctly, naturally, and readily subordinate aesthetics to the demands of life" (159–60).

Yet, as Rimmon indicates, for her character to fit the general ambiguity, it must have its good points. Accordingly, she points to positive assessments of Marian, not only by Paul and St. George, but by the narrator, citing particularly the narrator's comment on Paul and Marian's discussion of the "high theme of perfection": "And it must be said, in extenuation of their eccentricity, that they were interested in the business: their tone was genuine, their emotion real; they were not posturing for each other or for someone else" (CT 7, 252). Part of the problem in reading Marian is that, as Rimmon observes, the "creditable view" of her is mostly given, while her own talk seems, at times, less impressive (90–93). At the end, contemplating her choice of St. George, Paul himself senses an ambiguity in Marian, asking, "Why to him, why not to youth, to strength, to ambition, to a future? Why, in her rich young capacity, to failure, to abdication, to superannuation? . . . Didn't she know how bad St. George could be, hadn't she perceived the deplorable thinness—? If she didn't she was nothing, and if she did why such an insolence of serenity?" (CT 7, 279). As Rimmon reads his reaction, if Marian did not see St. George's deterioration, then she is not as intelligent as Paul thought, and so "would not have done as his wife." If she did, she "does not really care about perfection." Both views are "discreditable," leaving as the only reading "creditable" to her that she married to save Paul (86). But even more so than in the case of St. George, it seems bizarre to expect a young woman to marry one man in order to keep herself from marrying another, slated for artistic celibacy. This leaves a Marian less interested in art than St. George. Such is generally seen as a bad thing in most Jamesian criticism. Labrie, for example, while acknowledging the naturalness of the women's subordination to life, still uses a rather censorious tone in speaking of how "one suspects" Mrs. St. George was more interested in her husband than his work, and Marian in Paul (159–60). Miller pictures Marian, more simply, as placing life before art, and having come to love St. George as a man not an artist (16). James in "The Liar" portrayed sympathetically Mrs. Capadose, who chose a flawed man over a greater artist. Marian here seems to have done the same. Given that Overt, unlike Lyon, never even proposed, it seems hard to blame her.

In 1892 Robert Louis Stevenson acknowledged James's gift of the book version of the tale "with rapture" (329). William James not only called the collection "exquisite all through," but praised this particular tale as one of James's "most perfect things" (241, 244). Modern critics have also hailed the story's greatness (e.g., Leavis 226; Baxter 227; Richardson 487). Blackmur ringingly speaks of it as "the finest, surely the clearest, most brilliant, and most eloquent of all James's pleading fables of the literary life." Its strength to him is that it is "more nearly dramatic in character, more nearly joins the issue of the ideal and the actual" ([1943] 1983, 87). Indeed, without the drama of either the ideal or the actual, the story would be far less impressive. Edel sees St. George's failure to follow his own advice "treated largely as a joke," but it is not a joke to Overt (CT 7, 9). *The Bookman*, too, could afford to take things dispassionately, asserting that the trick ending keeps the tale from being a tragedy, thereby avoiding the emotions "so painful to a well-bred writer of fiction." But without its emotions, the tale risks being reduced to either a simple folksy moral of "lucky in art, unlucky in love" or inflated to a grandly abstract Emersonian scheme of "compensation." It is rather a human story, tracing the human encounter with art, in which both St. George's public displays and Overt's tentatively social, ultimately lonely misery play a part.

Works Cited

Primary Works
James, Henry. 1888. "The Lesson of the Master." *The Universal Review* 1 (16 July–15 August): 342–65, 494–523.

———. 1892. "The Lesson of the Master." *The Lesson of the Master*. New York and London: Macmillan, 1–80.

———. 1909. "The Lesson of the Master." *The Novels and Tales of Henry James*. New York Edition. Vol. 15, 1–96. New York: Scribner's.

———. 1915. "The Lesson of the Master." *The Uniform Tales of Henry James*. London: Martin Secker.

Secondary Works

Adams, Percy G. 1961. "Young Henry James and the Lesson of His Master Balzac." *Revue de Littérature Comparée* 35 (July–September): 458–67.

Allen, Walter. 1981. *The Short Story in English*. New York: Oxford University Press.

Andreas, Osborn. 1948. *Henry James and the Expanding Horizon: A Study of the Meaning and Basic Themes of James's Fiction*. Seattle: University of Washington Press.

Anon. 1892. Review of *The Lesson of the Master. Bookman* 2 (April): 27.

Anon. 1900. "Spectator." *Outlook*: 280.

Bantock, G. H. 1953. "Morals and Civilization in Henry James." *Cambridge Journal* 7 (December): 159–81.

Barry, Peter. 1983. "Citizens of a Lost Country: Kawabata's *The Master of Go* and James's 'The Lesson of the Master.'" *Comparative Literature Studies* 20, no. 1 (Spring): 77–93.

———. 1978. "In Fairness to the Master's Wife: A Re-Interpretation of 'The Lesson of the Master.'" *Studies in Short Fiction* 15: 385–89.

Bass, Eben. 1964. "Lemon-Colored Volumes and Henry James." *Studies in Short Fiction* 1 (Winter): 113–22.

Baxter, Annette K. 1955. "Independence vs. Isolation: Hawthorne and James on the Problem of the Artist." *Nineteenth-Century Fiction* 10: 225–31.

Beattie, Munro. 1967. "The Many Marriages of Henry James." In *Patterns of Commitment in American Literature*. Ed. Marston La France, 93–112. Toronto: University of Toronto Press.

Beebe, Maurice L. 1964. *Ivory Towers and Sacred Founts: The Artist as Hero*. New York: New York University Press.

Bewley, Marius. 1959. *The Eccentric Design: Form in the Classic American Novel*. New York: Columbia University Press.

Blackmur, Richard P. [1948] 1983. "Henry James." In *Studies in Henry James*. Ed. Veronica A. Makowsky, 91–124. New York: New Directons. Reprinted from *Literary History of the United States*, ed. Robert E. Spiller, et al. New York: Macmillan.

———. [1943] 1983. "In the Country of the Blue." In *Studies in Henry James*. Ed. Veronica A. Makowsky, 69–90. New York: New Directions. Reprinted from *Kenyon Review* 5 (Autumn): 595–617. Also reprinted in *The Question of Henry James*, ed. F. W. Dupee, 191–211, New York: Ronald, 1945; *Critiques and Essays on Modern Fiction*, 303–18, New York: Ronald, 1952.

Buckler, William, and Arnold B. Sklare, eds. 1960. *Stories from Six Authors*. New York: McGraw Hill.

Budd, John. 1982. "Philip Roth's Lesson from the Master." *NMAL: Notes on Modern American Literature* 6: Item 21.

Croly, Herbert. 1904. "Henry James and His Countrymen." Reprinted in *The Question of Henry James*, ed. F. W. Dupee, 28–39. New York: Henry Holt, 1945.

Dietrichson, Jan W. 1969. *The Image of Money in the American Novel of the Gilded Age*. Oslo: Universitetsforlaget; New York: Humanities.

Donadio, Stephen. 1978. *Nietzsche, Henry James, and the Artistic Will*. New York: Oxford University Press.

Edel, Leon, ed. [1949] 1963. *The Ghostly Tales of Henry James*. New York: The Universal Library, Grosset & Dunlap.

Geismar, Maxwell. 1963. *Henry James and the Jacobites*. Boston: Houghton Mifflin.

Goetz, William R. 1986. *Henry James and the Darkest Abyss of Romance*. Baton Rouge: Louisiana State University Press.

Gordon, D. J., and John Stokes. 1972. "The Reference of *The Tragic Muse*." In *The Air of Reality: New Essays on Henry James*. Ed. John Goode, 81–167. London: Methuen.

Grossman, James. 1945. "The Face in the Mountain." *Nation* 161 (8 September): 230–32.

Grover, Philip. 1973. *Henry James and the French Novel: A Study in Inspiration*. London: Paul Elek.

Holloway, John. 1979. "Identity, inversion, and density-elements in narrative: three tales by Chekhov, James, and Lawrence." In *Narrative and Structure: Exploratory Essays*, 53–74. Cambridge: Cambridge University Press.

Horne, Helen. 1960. *Basic Ideals of James's Aesthetics as Expressed in the Short Stories Concerning Artists and Writers*. Marburg: Erich Mauersberger.

Horrell, Joyce Tayloe. 1970. "A 'Shade of a Special Sense': Henry James and the Art of Naming." *American Literature* 42: 203–20.

Huneker, J. G. 1920. "The Lesson of the Master." *Bookman* 51 (May): 364–68.

James, William. 1992. *The Correspondence of William James*. Vol. 2: *William and Henry: 1885–1896*. Ed. Ignas K. Skrupskelis and Elizabeth M. Berkeley. Charlottesville: University Press of Virginia.

Jones, Granville H. 1975. *Henry James's Psychology of Experience: Innocence, Responsibility, and Renunciation in the Fiction of Henry James*. The Hague: Mouton.

Kappeler, Susanne. 1980. *Writing and Reading in Henry James*. New York: Columbia University Press.

Kaston, Carren. 1984. *Imagination and Desire in the Novels of Henry James*. New Brunswick, NJ: Rutgers University Press.

Kermode, Frank, ed. 1986. *The Figure in the Carpet and Other Stories*. London: Penguin.

Krook, Dorothea. [1962] 1967. *The Ordeal of Consciousness in Henry James.* New York: Cambridge University Press.

Labrie, Ernest Ross. 1969. "Sirens of Life and Art in Henry James." *Lakehead University Review* (Port Arthur, Ont.) 2: 150–69.

Leavis, Q. D. 1947. "Henry James: The Stories." *Scrutiny* 14 (Spring): 223–29. Reprinted in *Collected Essays.* Vol. 2: *The American Novel and Reflections of the European Novel,* ed. G. Singh, 177–84. Cambridge: Cambridge University Press.

Lee, Brian. 1978. *The Novels of Henry James: A Study of Culture and Consciousness.* New York: St. Martin's.

Leavis, Q. D. 1947. "Henry James: The Stories." *Scrutiny* 14 (Spring): 223–29. Reprinted in *Collected Essays.* Vol. 2: *The American Novel and Reflections of the European Novel,* ed. G. Singh, 177–84. Cambridge: Cambridge University Press.

Long, Robert Emmet. 1979. *The Great Succession: Henry James and the Legacy of Hawthorne.* Pittsburgh: University of Pittsburgh Press.

Lynd, Robert. 1952. "Literary Life." *Books and Writers.* Foreword by Robert Church. New York: Macmillan.

McElderry, Bruce R., Jr. 1965. *Henry James.* New York: Twayne.

Mackenzie, Manfred. 1976. *Communities of Honor and Love in Henry James.* Cambridge, MA: Harvard University Press.

Macnaughton, William R. 1987. *Henry James: The Later Novels.* Boston: Twayne.

Marder, Daniel. 1984. *Exiles at Home: A Story of Literature in Nineteenth Century America.* Lanham, MD: University Press of America.

Markow-Totevy, Georges. 1969. *Henry James.* Trans. John Griffiths. London: Merlin.

Matheson, Gwen. 1968. "Portraits of the Artist and the Lady in the Shorter Fictions of Henry James." *Dalhousie Review* 48: 222–30.

Matthiessen, F. O. 1944. "Introduction: Henry James' Portrait of the Artist." *Henry James: Stories of Writers and Artists.* Norfolk, CT: New Directions. Also reprinted as "Henry James's Portrait of the Artist." *Partisan Review* 11 (1944): 71–87.

Miller, Vivienne. 1980. "Henry James and the Alienation of the Artist: 'The Lesson of the Master.'" *English Studies in Africa* 23, no. 1 (March): 9–20.

Mizener, Arthur, ed. 1966. *Modern Short Stories: The Uses of Imagination.* Rev. ed. New York: Norton.

Monteiro, George. 1977. "Henry James and the Lessons of Sordello." *Western Humanities Review* 31: 69–78.

Mottram, Eric. 1985. "'The Infected Air' and 'The Guilt of Interference': Henry James's Short Stories." In *The Nineteenth-Century American Short Story.* Ed. by A. Robert Lee, 164– 90. London: Vision; Totowa, NJ: Barnes & Noble.

Neff, Emery. 1948. *Edwin Arlington Robinson.* New York: William Sloane.

Nuhn, Ferner. 1942. *The Wind Blew from the East: A Study in the Orientation of American Culture.* New York: Harper.

Ozick, Cynthia. 1982. "The Lesson of the Master." *New York Review of Books* 29, no. 13 (12 August): 20–21.

Posnock, Ross. 1985. *Henry James and the Problem of Robert Browning.* Athens: University of Georgia Press.

Powers, Lyall H., ed. 1980. *Henry James and Edith Wharton. Letters: 1900–1915.* New York: Scribners.

———. 1970. *Henry James: An Introduction and Interpretation.* New York: Holt, Rinehart.

———. 1969. *The Merrill Guide to Henry James.* Columbus, OH: Charles E. Merrill.

Putt, S. Gorley. 1966. *Henry James: A Reader's Guide.* Ithaca, NY: Cornell University Press.

Rentz, Kathryn C. 1982. "The Question of James's Influence on Ford's *The Good Soldier.*" *English Literature in Transition* 25: 104–14, 129–30.

Richardson, Lyon N., ed. [1941] 1966. *Henry James: Representative Selections, with Introduction, Bibliography, and Notes.* New York: American Writer Series; Urbana: University Press of Illinois.

Rimmon, Shlomith. 1977. *The Concept of Ambiguity: The Example of Henry James.* Chicago: University of Chicago Press.

Seed, David. 1980. "James's 'Lesson of the Master.'" *Explicator* 31, no. 1 (Fall): 9–10.

Segal, Ora. 1969. *The Lucid Reflector: The Observer in Henry James's Fiction.* New Haven: Yale University Press.

Seltzer, Mark. 1984. *Henry James and the Art of Power.* Ithaca, NY: Cornell University Press.

Smith, Charles R. 1969. "The Lesson of the Master: An Interpretive Note." *Studies in Short Fiction* 6 (Fall): 654–58.

Stein, Allen F. 1984. *After the Vows were Spoken: Marriage in American Literary Realism.* Columbus: Ohio State University Press.

Stevenson, Robert Louis. 1905. *The Letters of Robert Louis Stevenson.* Ed. Sidney Colvin. Vol. 2. New York: Scribner's.

Stewart, J. I. M. 1963. "Henry James." In *Eight Modern Writers. Oxford History of English Literature.* Vol. 7, 71–121. New York: Oxford University Press.

Stone, Donald David. 1972. *Novelists in a Changing World: Meredith, James, and the Transformation of English Fiction in the 1880's.* Cambridge, MA: Harvard University Press.

Tanner, Tony. 1985. *Henry James: The Writer and His Work.* Amherst: University of Massachusetts Press.

Tintner, Adeline. 1989. *The Pop World of Henry James: From Fairy Tales to Science Fiction.* Ann Arbor: UMI Research Press. Revised from "Iconic Analogy in 'The Lesson of the Master.'" *Journal of Narrative Technique* 5 (1975): 116–27.

———. 1986. *The Museum World of Henry James.* Ann Arbor: UMI Research Press.

————. 1981. "Henry James as Roth's Ghost Writer." *Midstream* 27 (March): 48–51.

Tyler, Parker. 1964. *Every Artist His Own Scandal: A Study of Real and Fictive Heroes.* New York: Horizon.

Vaid, Krishna B. 1964. *Technique in the Tales of Henry James.* Cambridge, MA: Harvard University Press.

van Cromphout, G. 1968. "Artist and Society in Henry James." *English Studies* 49 (April): 132–40.

Wagenknecht, Edward. 1984. *The Tales of Henry James.* New York: Frederick Ungar.

Wharton, Edith. 1934. *A Backward Glance.* New York: Appleton-Century.

Wirth-Nesher, Hana. 1984. "The Thematics of Interpretation: James's Artistic Tales." *Henry James Review* 5: 117–27.

Wright, Austin McGiffert. 1961. *The American Short Story in the Twenties.* Chicago: University Press of Chicago.

Wright, Nathalia. 1965. *American Novelists in Italy, The Discoverers: Allston to James.* Philadelphia: University of Pennsylvania Press.

Wright, Walter F. 1962. *The Madness of Art: A Study of Henry James.* Lincoln: University of Nebraska Press.

Ziff, Larzer. 1966. *The American 1890's: Life and Times of a Lost Generation.* New York: Viking.

Foreign Language
Castiglione, Luigi. 1962. "Profilo di James." *La Fiera Letteraria* 17 (23 September): 5 [Italian].

Cestre, Charles. 1945. *La Littérature Américaine.* Paris: Librairie Armand Colin.

The Liar

Publication History

"The Liar" was first published in the May and June issues of *Century* Magazine in 1888. The next year James included it in *A London Life*, and it also appeared in the periodical *Vestnik Yevropy*, translated into Russian. Later, it also took its place in the New York Edition.

Circumstances of Composition, Sources, and Influences

On June 19, 1884, James recorded the possibility of a tale about the predicament of a fine-spirited woman married to an incorrigible liar. Finally, forced to lie herself to support him, she comes to hate him. He appended at the end of the entry the title *Numa Roumestan*, an 1881 work by Daudet containing basically the same situation (CN 28). In the preface to the tale, however, he declares his "personal experience . . . immediately accountable" for the tale's germ, in particular a London dinner where there were also "a gentleman, met for the first time, though favourably known to me by name and fame, in whom I recognised the most unbridled colloquial romancer the 'joy of life' had ever found occasion to envy" and his "veracious, serene and charming" wife, unable to meet the eyes of the others at table (*Criticism* 2, 1190). The disparity between the two accounts has drawn frequent comment, although Matthiessen and Murdock attribute the substitution simply to the more dramatic impact of the presumably later experience, speculating that James may not even have remembered the entry (N 62). No nominees have been offered so far for the real-life liar.

Kane first noted the debt to Hawthorne's "The Prophetic Pictures," in which a gifted portrait painter reveals the true character of a less-than-perfect husband in a way perceptible at first only to the sensitive wife. Rosenberry elaborates on the connection, seeing James filling out and modifying the Daudet source by way of the Hawthorne, the introduction of the painter taking the attention away from the couple and revising the ending. The stories also, according to Rosenberry, share an ambivalence toward the power of the observer, both painters committing "the unpardonable sin—the violation of the human heart." He notes, too, that in contrast to their unperceptive husbands, the women share the insightfulness of the painters, who, while they triumph in art, lose the moral victory to the wives (also Powers 1961, 366). (See also "The Story of a Masterpiece.")

Bell links the Hawthorne and James tales with one by Edith Wharton, "The Portrait," which treats a similar theme, but in which the painter spares the subject out of love for his daughter (230). Bewley discusses the tale within the context of the theme of "appearance and reality" in *The Scarlet Letter* (80, 84–87). Edward Stone follows up on Bewley's comparison, finding in both works "the progressive degeneration and self-corruption of a rejected and malicious leech" pursuing his revenge against someone who seems, in comparison, more and more innocent. He distinguishes the tale, however, from Hawthorne's in that Lyon's original outrage is absurd, while Chillingsworth's is legitimate, and in that Everina's lie at the end, while harmless, is a slip that makes her less "sublime" than her counterpart Dimmesdale (80–87).

Lyon himself is a reader whose allusions have been analyzed. The hopelessness of his love is evident, according to Jeffares, in his comparison of Everina to Thackeray's Ethel Newcome (181 n.47). His dangerous "susceptibility to the sensational" is equally apparent, Powers argues, from his enjoyment of LeFanu (1961, 364). Before the tale begins, he had painted Everina as the heroine of Goethe's *Werther*, a choice Ron links with the view that the tale represents Lyon's "symbolic suicide." At the same time, he suggests a significance in Lyon's remembering the innocence of that portrait while Capadose recalls one of Everina as a Bacchante (229).

The structure of the tale, according to West and Stallman, is theatrical. They see the stock characters and melodramatic elements as those of a "Restoration Heroic drama," where "Love triumphs over Honor," and locate elements as well of the classical Greek theatre, with Lyon as the "*eiron* or underdog" who defeats the "*alazon*, his bullying antagonist and rival," bringing him down by the weight of his own flaws (210–13).

Edward Stone is less complimentary of Lyon's revenge, comparing its obsessiveness with that plotted by Dostoyevsky's Underground Man against a man who does not even know him (87 n.). Ron compares Lyon to another revenger, Shakespeare's Hamlet. In his reading, Lyon's observation of the Capadoses before the portrait echoes the bedroom scene in *Hamlet*, where Hamlet seeks to persuade his mother of her husband's guilt and her tainting by it. Here, however, Hamlet's spoken dagger is a real one held by the guilty party and its effect turns on its owner—Lyon who, like Hamlet, has only projected his own "criminal desire" on another (229). Kavka also detects a mother-son relationship behind the tale, asking whether James was expressing in the tale his own mixed feelings toward his mother, toward whom, he asserts, James "may have had some cause for contempt." Kavka follows Edel and Strouse, among others, to portray Mrs. James as seeking control through "self sacrifice." The mixed messages of such behavior, he argues, left James permanently "struggling with female ambivalence," as he does here (226–27, 242–57).

Lyon's chosen method of revenge—the revelation of Capadose as a liar through a painting—has been judged implausible by McElderry and Fadiman (McElderry 81; Fadiman 186). Tintner, however, points to a contemporary story about John Singer Sargent, who was said to have exposed a woman's lying just that way. She draws attention also to Lyon's model for his portrait, the *Portrait of a Man* in the National Gallery by Moroni, appropriately enough a sixteenth-century painter, given that Lyon likens Capadose to a Venetian of that time (81, 93, 238; see CT 6, 400, 420).

James's portrait of Capadose anticipates, according to Edel, the genial real-life inventions of Ford Madox Ford (*Life* 5, 42). Edel also calls him, as did Fadiman earlier, "an easygoing English Munchausen" (CT 6, 11; Fadiman 185). Lyon's dismissal of unwelcome truths as "vulgar," on the other hand, is compared by Norrman to that of Howells's Editha (111).

Relation to Other Works

In planning *The Sense of the Past*, James considered having Ralph's secret made visible in his portrait, but then hesitated, "I don't want to repeat what I have done at least a couple of times, I seem to remember, and notably in The Liar" (CN 530). The less notable tale James was remembering may have been the 1868 "The Story of a Masterpiece," and beginning with Kenton, many critics have noted the closeness of the parallel (Kenton 5; e.g., Segal 101 n.6; Winner 94). In 1885 James published his *Stories Revived*, and Martineau argues that in preparing the collection James would have read through his 1868 tale "The Story of a Masterpiece," with its trio of an artist, his former love, and her current fiancé, and the resultant stabbing of a portrait. James, Martineau asserts, took the man's false charge to the artist there, "You loved her, she was indifferent to you, and now you take your revenge," imagined what would have happened had it been true, and combined the theme with that of the compulsive liar to produce this tale. Still, Martineau emphasizes the differences between the tales: Capadose destroys his own portrait; the portrait is not a triumph of realism but a "corrupt masterpiece"; and Capadose destroys it out of concern for his wife (19–22). Similarly, Jeffares contrasts the rejection of the painter's "astute portrait" here with the more typical praising acceptance seen in "The Story of a Masterpiece" (176 n.41). Delbaere-Garant, on the other hand, sees the portrait, like that in "The Story of a Masterpiece," as possessed of an artistic power of disclosure stemming from the artist's "curiosity and interest" unbearable by its subject (52). Bowden connects the two portraits with the portraits of Miriam in *The Tragic*

Muse, seeing all three assisting "clarity of vision and insight" (70; also Delbaere-Garant 52). Ron places "The Liar" within what he sees as the characteristic Jamesian situation of someone wanting something that belongs to another—in this case Everina—and so seeking to discover that person's "skeleton in his closet" only to reveal his own. "The Story of a Masterpiece," he argues, presents a variant of the situation, with Baxter "cheapen[ing]" the desired person through the "unflattering" portrait (233–34). Gale appends the comment that James's own portrait by Sargent "curiously" was slashed, although subsequently repaired (127–28).

In 1918 Beach would see the third-person narration here as "objective" like that in "The Two Faces" and "Pandora," Lyon simply an "observer" with little role as actor in the story (69). Bewley, however, would point to Lyon as a self-deceived and deceitful forerunner of the governess in *The Turn of the Screw*, a view Wilson would come to accept (Bewley 87, 135–36; Wilson 153). Norrman calls the two works "double-exposure" tales in which the original sense of honest teller and culpable subject is reversed, although the reversal never completely erases the first reading—a technique he uses to argue for the equivalency of the two couples—adulterous lovers vs. daughter and father—in *The Golden Bowl* (149, 169, 174). Ron, commenting on the failure of the nonapparitionist readers of *The Turn of the Screw* to come to the defense of Lyon, attributes their reluctance to the disparity between the quality of their opponents: the Capadoses marked by their devoted married love; Quint and Jessel by a scandalous illicit relationship (227).

Lyon's indictment as an unreliable reflector has placed him in the company of numerous suspect characters. Walter Wright, Geismar, and Donald Stone have all noted a particular resemblance to *The Aspern Papers*, with Wright observing how looking at either tale with the view that it is wrong "to tamper recklessly with the souls of others" changes the seeming story of the protagonist's "ingenuity" (Wright 59; Geismar 86; Stone 250). Segal remarks that neither man has at the end "fully assimilated" his lesson, and compares them to the obsessed narrator not only in *The Turn of the Screw*, but also in "The Figure in the Carpet." She argues, however, that the search here is a moral one, not simply intellectual as in "The Figure in the Carpet" as well as in *The Sacred Fount*, where the "real, inescapable difficulty" produces "epistemological uncertainty" not simply "dramatic irony." As a "characteristic transitional work" Segal places the tale between such works as *Madame de Mauves* and *The Portrait of a Lady*, where the narrator is simply contributory to other themes, and such others as *The Sacred Fount*, where the narrator is the focal point (94, 96, 99, 106, 151). Berland also constructs a sequence linking Lyon with such characters as Longmore of *Madame de Mauves*, Winterbourne of *Daisy Miller*, Littlemore of *The Siege of London*, Vanderbank of *The Awkward Age*, and the narrator of *The Sacred Fount*. Berland also argues, however, that James was generally unaware that his use of an observer had created a character of culpable egoism. For example, while Berland faults the observers in *The Sacred Fount* and "The Liar" for thinking that following "honourable" rules in ferreting out secrets will produce honorable results, he does not believe that James would necessarily find them wrong (41–43). In Norrman's view, James in such ambiguous works had discovered "a new victim—the reader" (161).

Jefferson locates a milder version of Lyon's investigations in Robert Acton, who in *The Europeans* "almost wished that he could make her [Eugenia] lie and then convict her of it" (36). Bishop, however, detects a sexual innuendo in the two men's fascination with women who "lie" (53–54). In Segal's view, Lyon, like Longmore, Touchett, and Strether, is "half in love" with the heroine and so wants to "save" her (149–50). If so, his attempt brings disillusionment, and in Ron's analysis, Lyon's discovery of the Capadoses before the portrait is "the melodramatic equivalent" of Strether's discovery of Chad abroad with Mme de Vionnet, or Isabel's discovery of Osmond at home with Mme Merle (229).

Lyon is an artist as well as a man. In both capacities, Martineau argues, he is an egotist and, like Marcher of "The Beast in the Jungle," so wrapped up in his illusions that he cannot see outside himself and is defeated, if not beyond pity (22; also Berland 40–42). In Lyon's saga, Segal sees James's interest in the "dialectics of artistic excellence versus moral evil," evident also in "The Author of Beltraffio," *The Aspern Papers*, and *The Sacred Fount* (101). But while Everina refers to Lyon more than once as "maître," Powers sees Lyon as failing to stick to the "lesson of the master," the necessary solitude of the artist. He also compares the artists here and in "The Real Thing," arguing that the artist there sacrificed his personal concerns to his art and so "improved" the couple he dealt with, while Lyon by sacrificing his art to his personal concerns makes his "somewhat worse" (1961, 367–68). The artists in both, Mackenzie asserts, have to learn a lesson in what the "real thing" is from the couple they originally look down on (188–89 n.30). Still, according to Terrie, it is life that "intrudes" on art in "The Real Thing" while in "The Liar" art "intrudes" on life (8). In Ron's reading, the failure of the artist's pictures of the Monarchs demonstrates that the subject cannot be dominant in true art, although he adds that art can represent "the ego" of *"any person"* involved in its creation including painter, model or patron, pointing to "The Real Thing," "Glasses," "The Tone of Time," as well as "The Liar" for examples (230–31).

Capadose is also a kind of artist, and as such Horne compares him to Brooksmith, Saltram of "The Coxon Fund," and even Theobald of "The Madonna of the Future," who is also "possessed" by his gift. The narrator himself thinks at first that he is "the liar platonic. . . . He has an inner vision of what might have been. . . . He paints, as it were, and so Do I!" (CT 6, 412). Still, as Horne observes, the narrator later rejects him as an artist without purpose, creating "by inclination only" (119–20). Jones compares Capadose to Gedge in "The Birthplace," who also embroiders the truth (203). A less flattering resemblance between artists may be implicit in Sir David's description of Capadose's lying as a "natural peculiarity—as you might limp or stutter or be left-handed," which recalls Greville Fane's "serene good faith that ought to have been safe from allusion, like a stutter or a *faux pas*" (CT 6, 407; CT 8, 444).

Mrs. Capadose, according to Bewley, discovers the truth beneath the lies, and so anticipates Maggie in *The Golden Bowl*, a work which he judges, like this one, to be deeply pragmatic (87, 135, 148). Segal also has praise for Mrs. Capadose for holding up, unlike Miles, under pressure (104). (See particularly "The Tree of Knowledge.")

Interpretation and Criticism

In 1984, Wagenknecht made the remarkable statement that "The Liar" "has not attracted much commentary" (226 n.11). The tale is, however, the subject of a controversy similar to that over *The Turn of the Screw*. The debate is lodged both over the reliability of the tale's center of consciousness, Oliver Lyon, and over the relative virtue of the three central characters—Lyon, Anton Capadose, and his wife, Everina. When in 1896 an Anton Capadose surfaced to object to James's use of his name, James explained he had simply collected it somewhere, probably from *The Times*, adding that he wished he had given it to "a more exemplary individual! But my romancing Colonel was a charming man, in spite of his little weakness" (*Letters* 4, 39). The man through whom we learn of Capadose in the tale, the painter Lyon, is not, as he has sometimes been said to be, the narrator of the story, but his consciousness is clearly in control throughout much of the tale. In 1905, Cary praised the initial description of Stayes, likening it to a "rich example of Venetian painting" (109). It is probably the painter's eye of Lyon that makes it that way, and his character serves to shape the reader's perceptions of people as well.

Following Lyon's lead, Edgar, writing in 1927, was able simply to summarize the story as seen from his point of view as an exploration and confirmation of Mrs. Capadose's "contamination" by her husband (175–77). Fadiman also seemingly reads the story through Lyon's eyes. Although he sees the Colonel's lying as a "passion" not a "vice," one viewed with a "continuous play of sympathetic humor," Fadiman judges the Colonel's relationship to his wife more seriously. Calling the tale a "love story," he pictures the couple's relationship as loving, but almost sadomasochistic in the Colonel's "training" of his wife and her willingness to do anything to protect him (184–85).

Matthiessen and Murdock saw Everina's constant love for her husband resembling the "'possession' of a pure spirit by an impure one" (N 62). In the reading of West and Stallman, the tale is framed by the "ironic focus" of Lyon's "central intelligence," which in turn gives the tale its meaning. The problem of the tale they see as a moral one, the conflict between love and honor. Lyon, they write, succeeds in proving Everina "ashamed" through her reaction to the portrait, and proves her changed by her husband through her lie. But while the Capadoses are shown up by the portrait, West and Stallman also see Lyon as punished in the end, having violated in his search for truth the social mores necessary for the preservation of society, however hypocritical these may be. But while the critics cast Lyon as the ultimate victim of the tragic irony of the tale, they make him a noble one, painting under the inspiration of the "Muse of Truth" while Capadose lies in obedience to the "Muse of Deceit." In their view, Lyon is the only character with any illusions left, while both Capadoses are experts at the art of social "masking." Both, in other words, are liars. To expose them as such costs Lyon his ideal, his view of Everina as supremely moral. They do not question, however, the validity of his testing her, seeing in her refusal to confess to him—a possible first step to redemption—a sign that just as she proudly asserts she "possesses the original" of Lyon's painting, "the original possesses her" (CT 6, 440). Their picture of Lyon, however, as the artist who follows life, who "seeks out the truth or full meaning of his subject," seems in contrast to Lyon's own sense of himself as someone who sees "nothing else" in the Colonel apart from his lie (CT 6, 419; 209–216).

Later, Powers would attribute such readings to a mistaken acceptance of the authority of narration, what Norrman calls the "double allegiance of language" (1970, 141; Norrman, 149). Looking at the tale in 1952, Bewley set as the story's central question, "Who is the liar?" In his view the answer is ambiguous, and its ambiguity is "intricately embedded" in the narration. Piling up the evidence against Lyon, he asserts that almost at the start Lyon realizes the Colonel's lying is harmless and that his wife sincerely loves him. Still, he proceeds against them, originally intending his exposé to be discernable only by the "initiated," but then moving beyond that intent to paint for the "meanest intelligence" to see. Lyon's whole pretense of friendship with the Colonel, Bewley writes, is a lie. The incrimination of the model, on the other hand, he dismisses as unlikely to bring about serious harm. Mrs. Capadose then becomes the one who sees the truth, despite Lyon's concluding allegations. Lyon may have also "taken himself in completely," but he is not therefore, in Bewley's judgment, innocent. Rather, he is guilty of the worst crime, "violating the integrity of another man's personality, of seeking to take possession of it through false images and conventional laws" (84–87, 135). In 1959 Wilson, who had originally seen the wife "protect[ing]" her husband with an "'authority'" similar to that of the governess in *The Turn of the Screw*, revised his view following Bewley's argument, now arguing that Lyon's view, like that of the governess, is distorted by his emotions (120, 153).

In another pivotal reading, Booth, too, turned Lyon's story against him. James typically, Booth wrote, complicates his stories by telling them through involved narrators who transform them into the "story of one's story." Here James went one step further, Booth asserts, by making a center-of-consciousness unaware of his motives, and who becomes "a vicious agent in the story" unlike any James discussed theoretically. Trying to reconstruct the story independent of Lyon's viewpoint, Booth presents an Everina who sensibly refused Lyon not for his poverty, but his self-centeredness, and a Colonel whom "everyone else in the story likes" and whom even James called a "charming man." Lyon, in contrast, he writes, plays the role of West and Stallman's servant of "the Muse of Truth" only in the notebook. The actual story "consists largely" of his lies, many of them cruel. His behavior throughout is sneaky, and his role as an artist is no excuse, his art "perverted more and more" by his desire to expose the Colonel. His elimination of all the good traits from his portrait of the Colonel produces a malicious caricature. It is, Booth concludes, "impossible to reconcile this picture of the artist's task with any notion James ever espoused."

Noting that Bewley had argued the same point of view, Booth goes on to ask why everyone has not read the tale the same way. He provides several answers: the general similarity between Lyon's voice and James's, the fact that Lyon is a great artist, the "natural tendency to agree with the reflector." As a result, he sees in the tale "some inevitable ambiguities, ambiguities which James almost certainly did not intend," although he also remarks four interjections of the "reliable narrator" which show the real Lyon. In general, he argues, Lyon is not acting as an artist or an idealist but as a "disappointed lover." That motive also raises the question of whether Lyon has a right to feel betrayed. Everina, Booth remarks, in her final lie may have endangered the model, but she also protected a "relatively harmless man from a predator." In the New York Edition, Booth argues, James painted Lyon more clearly as the villain. In 1888, for example, "Lyon lashed him [Capadose] on"; in 1908 he "lashed his victim on." Nevertheless, Booth still finds James's attempted capture of the "complexity of life" insufficiently bounded. In his estimate, if one reads the story with Lyon as the liar, it is "still partially unrealized," while if one reads it with Lyon as "the noble artist struggling for truth against a philistine culture," it is weak (347–54).

The responses to the readings of Bewley and Booth have been many. Vaid proclaims that there is no reason to believe the Colonel is not the liar of the title, even if a "harmless one." In objecting to Wilson and Bewley's characterization of Lyon as a first-person narrator, however, he offers no interpretation of Lyon apart from that (271 n.9). While cautioning that Lyon is not an "unre-

liable narrator, because he is not a narrator at all"—a fact Booth acknowledges—Martineau agrees with Booth's basic argument against Lyon. She cites
the final portrait scene in particular as pointing ironically against Lyon, his
"vindictiveness" toward Everina contrasting with the Colonel's tender care for
her (21–22). Rimmon's dissent is limited to Booth's assertion that the story is
ambiguous. In her view it is ambiguous only to its center of consciousness,
who is "the butt of our irony" (xii, 15). Kozikowski takes a similar exception
to Booth's reading, pointing to the pun in Lyon's name as evidence James
deliberately intended Lyon's "vicious inconscience." Comparing Booth's
remarks to Edith Wharton's criticism in her essay "Telling a Short Story,"
Kozikowski sees James leaving Lyon so free to analyze others' characters, that
he is kept too busy to analyze his own (358 n.4, 367). Disregarding the controversy, Bell simply observed of the tale that James "wished his reader to be
in unbroken contact with the mind of his character so that his action might
be seen not as the result of a single conscious decision, but as a gradual
unconscious growth" (235). If so, Booth may be right that James misjudged
his choice. Donald Stone, for example, finds "justifiable" the "critical annoyance" at the choice of Lyon as reflector (250).

Wagenknecht, however, disagrees wholeheartedly with what he characterizes as Booth's "savage attack" on the painter, and quotes at face value Lyon's
view of himself: "He had exposed his friends to his own view, but without
wish to expose them to others, and least of all to themselves." In its place, he
gives a fairly middle-of-the-road reading, noting that James added to his notebook conception, finding both sides "wanting" while keeping his focus on
the faults of the Capadoses. The portrait, he writes, reveals to Mrs. Capadose
her husband's "moral nakedness." Nevertheless, he points to a question that
the destruction of the painting leaves unanswered: Would Lyon have subjected the Capadoses to the public exposure of the Academy? (44–46, 226 n.11).

Other critics also seek for a balance between the two camps. McElderry,
who mistakenly says "they" destroy the painting, finds James achieving a difficult balance in the tale: the reader is shocked at Mrs. Capadose's lie, but
more shocked at Lyon's cruel vengefulness. He points out also that James
gives Mrs. Capadose the last—spoken—word (81). Berland, too, is somewhere in the middle, judging Lyon suspicious in his passionate search for the
"truth" and deceitful in his pretended friendship, but still seeing James as
valuing Lyon's dedication to art more highly than Everina's dedication to her
husband—a contrast the complexity of which he does not believe James does
justice to (42–43).

Others remain stoutly against Lyon, who in the words of Edel is "unable to
grasp the simple truth" that Everina loves her husband (CT 6, 11). Similarly,
Putt, who sides with the Bewley camp, notes Lyon's inability to see that "married love recognizes and overcomes such shortcomings" as Capadose's. Putt
also points to the "odious rectitude" with which Lyon produces the painting

(274–75). Lyon's view of Everina as "trained" by her husband, Rosenberry calls "self-consolatory rationalization" (238). As Winner remarks, in the tale the painter "inadvertently" exposes himself (94).

That Lyon should hold a grudge for so long against Everina, Edward Stone judges absurd. He attributes Lyon's obsession not so much to love as to curiosity. Arguing that Everina originally refused Lyon because of his suspiciousness, he cites her insightful remark to him at the country house, "When you come to see me in London . . . I shall see you looking all around" (81, 86–87). At the start, Voss finds Lyon's interest in Everina's state of mind "natural enough," but by the end, he too sees it as culpably deceitful. However, he concedes to Lyon finally more awareness than most readings, more indeed than the story implies, saying that his success turns "to ashes in his mouth" as he realizes "the power of her love" (142–43).

Such readings have not stemmed the criticism of the Capadoses. Nathalia Wright finds it significant that they are compared to "Italian types," since James typically portrayed Italians as possessing "an air of duplicity" (237). In glossing an observation of Lyon's on Everina's "abyss" added to the New York Edition, Purdy translates her "abyss" as "her unhappiness and the moral debasement." Part of Everina's "tragic situation," in his view, is having been made a liar through her love for her husband (428). Purdy does not offer an evaluation of Lyon. Jones, however, responds to Bewley and Putt's charges against Lyon by arguing that Lyon would have forgiven the destruction of the painting, but cannot forgive the naming of the model. At the same time, however, he notes how much of Lyon's "self-esteem" rides on his assessment of Everina. He concludes that Lyon could have still forgiven Everina if "she at any time [had] taken him into her confidence or given him even a hint of her discomfort or disgust with her husband," his disappointment at the end showing more disillusionment than jealousy (196–97). Such a reading, however, follows Lyon's dubious assumption that Everina is in some way accountable to him, and owes him a loyalty greater than that to her husband.

Many of the more extended analyses trace a development in Lyon's character or motivations. In Powers's reading, Lyon begins as a genuine, moral artist who keeps himself clear of personal involvement. Indeed, Powers compares him and Capadose in his commitment to the "ideal" over the real. His artistic objectivity is evident, Powers observes, in his portrait of Sir David, and Powers locates his fundamental error not so much in his valuing the artistic over the personal as his straying from art's necessary disinterestedness out of jealousy. His portrait of Capadose—"a teller of tall tales for the fun of it"—is a spiteful caricature of the man as a "dreadful liar." Faced with the portrait, Powers writes, Capadose damns not himself but Lyon. Thus, his slashing of the portrait, according to Powers, is not the symbolic suicide some have seen it as, but a violent response deliberately triggered by Lyon, making it more of a willed suicide on the artist's part. He observes, too, that

Capadose never lies to harm another until driven to it by Lyon. He agrees with Bewley that throughout, Everina's vision is the "clearest," and that she probably had good reasons long ago for refusing Lyon. "Lyon's warped little mind," on the other hand, and the "multitude of subtle touches" that reveal it form in Powers's estimate the chief interest of the tale (1961, 363–68; 1969, 24; 1970, 113–14, 141).

Like Booth, Walter Wright notes the transformation of James's original notebook entry brought about by the introduction of Lyon. He cites the narratorial comment that, "If our friend hadn't been in love with her [Everina] he would surely have taken the Colonel's delinquencies less to heart. As the case stood they fairly turned to the tragical for him . . ." (CT 6, 411). Lyon is not, however, in Wright's view, to blame for his initial human jealousy, his hope that she will "repent." Unlike Powers, he does see the Colonel's destruction of the portrait as a figurative suicide, but sees his destroying it for Everina as showing a trust in her which she rewards. Because its tone is "casual, sometimes ironically playful," concentrating on the "ingenuity" of Lyon's attempt, Wright finds in the story a "special intensity of horror." He writes of Lyon, "The measure of his own evil is, of course, his abysmal failure to see it." Everina's superior insight again receives praise. Observing that the Colonel, too, was once poor, he remarks that Everina may well have been "sparing the feelings of the egoist" when telling Lyon she needed to marry well. Still, he detects in the concluding remark that the Colonel had "trained her" a possible "ironic truth": "The colonel has helped to make her what she is by earning her love." The two live, Wright concludes, in a "precarious Eden," one that Lyon, however, has been unable to harm (96–98, 124–25).

While seeming to exaggerate the extent of Everina's own lying, Beattie still judges it the "sign and seal of her devotion" (108). Everina is also the victor in Segal's reading, and Lyon a "self-deceived observer" who fails because of his "excessive emotional involvement." Calling him an "extraordinary mixture of acuteness and bad faith, sensitivity and cruelty, genuine compassion and vindictiveness," she decides he could not be intended as trustworthy because of his "ungenerous egotism," seen particularly in his desire to wring a confession out of the proud Mrs. Capadose. In James, she remarks, such "an open avowal" with the "intimate bond . . . the community of knowledge" it would create would constitute a "a betrayal" of the Colonel. The issue, she writes, is not simply an intellectual one, but moral as well, as James explores the "dialectics of artistic excellence versus moral evil." The portrait, she asserts, is a good one, but Lyon does not mind its destruction because he did not have a "properly artistic motive" in painting it. The "failure" of his imagination, morally and intellectually, is evident in his failure to consider the possiblity that Everina could know that her husband was a liar and still love him. His truly "unforgivable sin," however, is not stopping with the proof of his theory offered by its destruction. In seeking to shame Mrs. Capadose, he ironically makes his victory a "pyrrhic" one. Mrs. Capadose, she states, in her last remarks "gently but firmly" demonstrates to Lyon both her love for her husband and her pity for him. Her ability to do so obliquely, her "mock-ironic" salute *cher maître* mark her, in Segal's view, as "a master of the Jamesian irony." Still, while Segal dismisses Lyon's experience as the "stuff of an ironic comedy," she judges Everina's case "sad and touching." She is, however, at least aware of it, while even at the end, Segal argues, Lyon has "not yet fully assimilated" the lesson she teaches him, as seen in his insult about the training (93–106, 151).

Mackenzie emphasizes the psychological in his explanation of Lyon's pursuit of Everina. He pictures Lyon as a man suffering a "crisis of self-doubt" in discovering that the woman he loved chose a man with such an obvious flaw. In order to regain his place, he launches his quest to make Everina acknowledge his superiority. Indeed, in his painting of the child, Mackenzie writes, he nearly "expropriate[s]" her. The Colonel is his "double" and he hopes, in painting him, to expose his double, but such an effort necessarily produces catastrophe. In what Mackenzie considers a "characteristic voyeurist" scene, the Colonel's destruction of the painting shows his condemnation both of himself and Lyon, leaving Lyon an opening to take his place. Lyon even imitates the Colonel in telling a lie about the destruction, and so, like the Colonel, commits a symbolic suicide. The Colonel, however, in *his* lie is simply becoming more rather than less himself, and Everina in hers simply more the loving wife. Lyon, thus, is the loser. While Mackenzie considers the possibility that Everina may be stooping to revenge in her boast of possessing the original, he finds her remark more important as a moral statement (96–97).

Similarly, Norrman sees Lyon as imitating Capadose throughout, including in his lies. Since the two are so frequently equated, the text is suggesting either that Lyon's painting is bad just as the Colonel's lies are, or that the Colonel's lies are art just like Lyon's paintings—or a little of both. Thus, the portrait of the Colonel is also a self-portrait, Lyon's attempt to "kill" the colonel through it also a form of suicide. Norrman, however, does not take sides between the two, seeing by the end of the tale "two complete but mutually exclusive sets of values"—one exposing Lyon, one exonerating him (150, 162–69).

Gargano bases his judgment of Lyon on the significant "looks" in the tale, arguing that the tale's "eye-play" helps elucidate many obscurities. The first, and most important, look is Mrs. Capadose's look of love at the Colonel at the dinner table at Stayes. Coupled with her refusal to look at Lyon, it clearly indicates her loyalties, and Lyon's failure to recognize them shows his "decided lack of sensitivity" in Gargano's estimate. Instead, Lyon keeps looking for a second look of confession, seeking "a secret sharing, and an intellectual intimacy" that will rival her commitment to her husband. Failing to receive that look, Lyon creates another, the lying "look" of her husband's portrait, misusing his art in a way, Gargano writes, that James would judge "contemptible." In the end, as she stands by her husband's lies, Lyon remembers "that first glimspe of her he had at Stayes—of how he had seen her gaze across the table at her husband"—a memory that shows how futile was all he had attempted in the meantime (CT 6, 440). It also, according to Gargano, shows Mrs. Capadose as wise in early recognizing Lyon as "a man who could not understand love" (313–15).

Stein goes counter to such readings that vaunt the loyalties of the Capadoses to each other. Far from a "precarious Eden," Stein pictures the couple's marriage as an "insidious bastion," which sustains Capadose in his lies and subordinates Everina to their demands. Like Mackenzie, Stein traces in the tale a "doppelgänger motif," but he sees it as indicting Capadose by comparison with Lyon. Both men, he emphasizes, are artists—"Capadose" being close to "capodopera" or "masterpiece" in Italian—who collaborate on the Colonel's portrait. Both are liars, Lyon motivated by a more culpable, "utterly malignant curiosity." Most important, Stein concludes, both through their artistic need for "self-assertiveness" exploit and demean Everina (97–101).

Terrie, who finds James absenting himself almost entirely from his third-person narration, argues that the tale can be read so as to avoid the either-or indictment of Capadose or Lyon, although his interpretation does come down rather heavily against Lyon. Reading the tale as "a complex study of lying as a human social phenomenon," he sees neither Ashmore's acceptance of Capadose's lying nor Lyon's scorn for lying as "the least heroic of vices" leaving any room for judging the context or significance of the individual lie. Looking at the individual lies, Terrie argues that Capadose's are indeed harmless, until pressed into the incrimination of the model by Lyon. Similarly, Everina's lie to support her husband is understandable, in his view, as telling the truth would have justified Lyon. On the other hand, while Terrie excuses Lyon despite his deceitfulness, he casts him as the "Father of Lies," noting that despite his condemnation of Capadose, he is, as he once recognized, not far removed from him as an artist (7–8).

Taking a double approach to the tale, Ron begins by placing it in the context of James's general theoretical approach to art, his stated belief that art is both particular and universal, and that the "great portrait" therefore—whether of pen or brush—is the greatest work of art. He takes note of the tale's celebrated ambiguity—which he attributes to its use of "free indirect discourse" that blurs the perspective of the character with the authorial narration. At the same time, he follows Mackenzie's theory of the symmetry between the two men so galling to Lyon, and argues that Lyon's portrait is a piece of attempted sabotage that turns on the perpetrator. One can extrapolate, in turn, he argues, some general truths from this reading that apply to art, namely that the portrait destroys its subject, as old Sir David fears, and that "Every portrait is also a self-portrait," as Lyon's dinner companion intimates. Thus, presumably, every portrait destroys its painter. These truths he notes, are the direct opposite of James's stated beliefs about the truth of portraits and the greatness of artists, and so James suggests them only through indirect means. The particular portrait in the tale, Ron argues, reveals both the Colonel's own "self-infatuation," his desire "to shine in society" through his lies, and at the same time Lyon's own "unavowed self-infatuation." While Lyon has reacted to his "absolute sameness" with the Colonel by seeking "violently . . . to establish an absolute difference," the result simply underlines their basic identity. Thus, despite James's indirection, the tale's destructive portrait must be taken not as the exception to the artistic practice Booth reads it as, but rather the exemplification of it. In conclusion, Ron remarks that the "fondness of fiction" of the characters in the tale is evidenced also in the discrepancies between the notebook entries, the completed tales, and the prefatory remarks for both "The Liar" and "The Tree of Knowledge."

In contrast to such critics, Kavka is an enthusiastic advocate of Lyon, chastising even Matthiessen and Murdock, and West and Stallman for failing to appreciate him. Occasionally, his eagerness to defend Lyon trips him up, as when he states—as is never stated in the story—that Lyon was once engaged to Everina. Lyon's project to gain Everina's confidence he speaks of as "restorative techniques in the maintenance of his own self-esteem," although he admits his plan is not necessarily in "the best interests of others and possibly cruel and destructive." Still, in response to Booth's charges of egoism, he points out that Capadose, too, is self-centered. In the portrait, Kavka sees James illustrating how "the artist is a mirror of evil in life," even as he questions the basic device of a portrait's power to reveal the character of a liar. Although he argues that it is "psychologically naive" to believe that Lyon is still in love with Everina, he also sees an "exhibitionistic drive" in the portrait, an attempt to "arouse" Everina, an indication, he suggests, that Lyon was impotent and seeking to compensate for his impotence through art. The artist is "vindicated" in her horror, his "penultimate triumph—to see that he has had a powerful effect," although he writes that Lyon is left at the end in a "double bind," unsure whether Everina really hated the painting. Of their final meeting, Kavka writes, "James is dealing with how women need to lie to themselves about their men and become enraged when these lies are exposed." His essay also seeks to connect the psychology of Lyon in relation to Everina with that of James in relation to his mother. Thus Everina is to pay not only for her decision to be separate from Lyon but also for what Kavka sees as James's confusion at his separation from his mother. It seems, ultimately, that it is Kavka rather than James who is insistent that Everina bear the brunt of being female.

Although he cites a dozen of the critical discussions of the tale, Bishop still places the story on "the razor's edge" between canonicity and rejection. He castigates the story's previous critics for their focus on morality, their use of "the language of judgment." He rejects, too, the solution of ambiguity, and, more respectfully, Segal's reading of the power of "love," seeing the latter sinking into "the kingdom of tautology." Finally, he dismisses all the previous readings for their reliance on the New York Edition, although he never points to what in his reading is specific to the earlier text. Bishop proposes, instead, a reading that in its focus on the consciousness of Lyon is consistent, in essence, with many of the previous negative readings. Lyon, Bishop asserts, is "first and foremost an artist" who wants to paint perfect portraits even before he wants revenge. In Bishop's view the artist who sums up his fellow diners in capsule metaphors, who, ruled by logic, simplifies Everina to make her comprehendable, coming across Capadose, discovers his powers of summary to be inadequate. The difference between the two men is seen in the incident of the model. Lyon quickly reduces the intrusive Geraldine to a category, while the Colonel amplifies, creating a fictive history for her, as he does in general with his lies. Through her connection with the Colonel, Everina moves out of the simple classification to which Lyon had earlier assigned her, moves from Charlotte to a Bacchante. Lyon cannot handle the transition, and finally his logic and his mastery break down (41–55). One might append, however, that to show Lyon as driven by aesthetic motives does not necessarily, as Segal demonstrates, show that the following through on such motives will be free of moral implications.

As many critics have remarked, the names in the tale serve almost as labels. The Colonel is whatever he is *cap a dos*—from head to toe. Everina's name, too, implies consistency. Lyon's name is open to more ambiguity. Does it, as some suggest, tag him as the tale's liar, or does it simply mark him as an artistic lion? In the tale, Lyon exhibits the stress of such conflicting potentials. Certainly his character goes through the most changes over the course of the story, or at least these changes are the most evident. The fallacies in his thinking are apparent. It is hard not to see Lyon as a man who, disappointed by an individual, pretends he wishes her to have stayed true to an abstraction, while wishing she had stayed true to him. His sense of control is often less than it seems, or than he thinks it. He does not even tell the story that seems to come from his mind. It is, as Fadiman calls it, one of James's "wittiest" (185). The wit is not, however, all Lyon's. Urbane and sophisticated as he seems, his chief claim to sympathy at the end seems to be not so much his superiority to the Colonel or to Everina, as his vulnerability to, his love for, a woman who is wise enough to reject him not just once, but twice, and kindly.

Works Cited

Primary Works
James, Henry. 1888. "The Liar." *Century* 36 (May–June): 123–35, 213–23.

————. 1889. "The Liar." *A London Life*. London and New York: Macmillan.

————. 1908. "The Liar." *The Novels and Tales of Henry James*. New York Edition. Vol. 12, 311–88. New York: Scribner's.

Secondary Works
Beach, Joseph Warren. [1918] 1954. *The Method of Henry James*. Philadelphia: Albert Saifer.

Beattie, Munro. 1967. "The Many Marriages of Henry James." In *Patterns of Commitment in American Literature*. Ed. Marston La France, 93–112. Toronto: University of Toronto Press.

Bell, Millicent. 1965. *Edith Wharton and Henry James: The Story of their Friendship*. New York: George Braziller.

Berland, Alwyn. 1981. *Culture and Conduct in the Novels of Henry James*. Cambridge: Cambridge University Press.

Bewley, Maurice. 1952. *The Complex Fate: Hawthorne, Henry James and Some Other American Writers*. London: Chatto & Windus.

Bishop, George. 1988. *When the Master Relents: The Neglected Short Fictions of Henry James*. Ann Arbor: UMI Research Press.

Booth, Wayne C. [1961] 1983. *The Rhetoric of Fiction*. Chicago: University of Chicago Press.

Bowden, Edwin T. [1956] 1960. *The Themes of Henry James: A System of Observation through the Visual Arts*. Yale Studies in English 132. New Haven: Yale University Press.

Cary, Elisabeth Luther. 1905. *The Novels of Henry James: A Study*. New York: Putnam's.

Delbaere-Garant, Jeanne. 1970. *Henry James: The Vision of France*. Paris: Société d'Editions Les Belles Lettres.

Edgar, Pelham. [1927] 1964. *Henry James, Man and Author*. New York: Russell & Russell.

Fadiman, Clifton, ed. 1948. *The Short Stories of Henry James*. New York: Modern Library.

Gargano, James W. 1979. "The 'Look' as a Major Event in James's Short Fiction." *Arizona Quarterly* 35, no. 4 (Winter): 303–20.

Geismar, Maxwell. 1963. *Henry James and the Jacobites*. Boston: Houghton Mifflin.

Horne, Helen. 1960. *Basic Ideals of James's Aesthetics as Expressed in the Short Stories Concerning Artists and Writers*. Marburg: Erich Mauersberger.

Jeffares, Bo. 1979. *The Artist in Nineteenth Century English Fiction*. Atlantic Highlands, NJ: Humanities.

Jefferson, D. W. 1964. *Henry James and the Modern Reader*. New York: St. Martin's.

Jones, Granville H. 1975. *Henry James's Psychology of Experience: Innocence, Responsibility, and Renunciation in the Fiction of Henry James*. The Hague: Mouton.

Kane, R.J. 1950. "Hawthorne's 'The Prophetic Pictures' and James's 'The Liar.'" *Modern Language Notes* 65 (April): 257–58.

Kavka, Jerome. 1987. "Who is 'The Liar' in Henry James's Short Story? A Comparative Analysis." In *Psychoanalytic Studies in Biography*. Emotions and Behavior Monographs 4. Ed. George Maraitis and George H. Pollock, 219–61. Madison, CT: International Universities Press.

Kenton, Edna. 1934. "Some Bibliographical Notes on Henry James." *Hound & Horn* 7 (April–May): 535–40.

Kozikowski, Stanley J. 1979. "Unreliable Narration in Henry James's 'The Two Faces' and Edith Wharton's 'The Dilettante.'" *Arizona Quarterly* 35: 357–72.

McElderry, Bruce R., Jr. 1965. *Henry James*. New York: Twayne.

Mackenzie, Manfred. 1976. *Communities of Honor and Love in Henry James*. Cambridge, MA: Harvard University Press.

Martineau, Barbara. 1972. "Portraits Are Murdered in the Short Fiction of Henry James." *Journal of Narrative Technique* 2: 16–25.

Norrman, Ralf. 1982. *The Insecure World of Henry James's Fiction: Intensity and Ambiguity*. New York: St. Martin's.

Powers, Lyall H. 1970. *Henry James: An Introduction and Interpretation*. New York: Holt, Rinehart.

———. 1969. *The Merrill Guide to Henry James*. Columbus, OH: Charles E. Merrill.

———. 1961. "Henry James and the Ethics of the Artist: 'The Real Thing' and 'The Liar.'" *Texas Studies in Literature and Language* 3 (Autumn): 360–68.

Purdy, Strother B. 1970. "Henry James's Abysses: A Semantic Note." *English Studies* 51 (October): 424–33.

Putt, S. Gorley. 1966. *Henry James: A Reader's Guide*. Ithaca, NY: Cornell University Press.

Rimmon, Shlomith. 1977. *The Concept of Ambiguity: The Example of Henry James*. Chicago: University of Chicago Press.

Ron, Moshe. 1985. "The Art of the Portrait according to James." *Yale French Studies*, no. 69: 222–37. Reprinted as "L'Art du portrait selon James," trans. Ruth Amossy and Nadine Mandel. *Littérature* 57 (February): 93–108.

Rosenberry, Edward H. 1961. "James's Use of Hawthorne in 'The Liar.'" *Modern Language Notes* 76 (March): 234–38.

Segal, Ora. 1969. *The Lucid Reflector: The Observer in Henry James's Fiction*. New Haven: Yale University Press. Revised in part from "'The Liar': A Lesson in Devotion." *Review of English Studies* n.s. 16 (August 1965): 272–81.

Stein, Allen F. 1984. *After the Vows were Spoken: Marriage in American Literary Realism*. Columbus: Ohio State University Press.

Stone, Donald David. 1972. *Novelists in a Changing World: Meredith, James, and the Transformation of English Fiction in the 1880's*. Cambridge, MA: Harvard University Press.

Stone, Edward. 1964. *The Battle of the Books: Some Aspects of Henry James*. Athens: Ohio University Press.

Terrie, Henry, ed. 1984. *Henry James: Tales of Art and Life*. Schenectady, NY: Union College Press.

Tintner, Adeline R. 1986. *The Museum World of Henry James*. Ann Arbor: UMI Research Press.

Vaid, Krishna B. 1964. *Technique in the Tales of Henry James*. Cambridge, MA: Harvard University Press.

Voss, Arthur. 1973. *The American Short Story: A Critical Survey*. Norman: University of Oklahoma Press.

Wagenknecht, Edward. 1984. *The Tales of Henry James*. New York: Frederick Ungar.

West, Ray B., Jr., and Robert Wooster Stallman, eds. 1949. *The Art of Modern Fiction*. New York: Rinehart. Reprinted in part in Edward Stone, *Seven Stories and Studies*. New York: Appleton-Century-Crofts, 1961.

Wilson, Edmund. 1960. "The Ambiguity of Henry James." In *A Casebook on Henry James's "The Turn of the Screw."* Ed. Gerald Willen. New York: Thomas Y. Crowell. Reprinted and revised from *Hound and Horn* 7 (April–June 1934): 385–406.

Winner, Viola Hopkins. 1970. *Henry James and the Visual Arts*. Charlottesville: University Press of Virginia.

Wright, Nathalia. 1965. *American Novelists in Italy, The Discoverers: Allston to James*. Philadelphia: University of Pennsylvania Press.

Wright, Walter F. 1962. *The Madness of Art: A Study of Henry James*. Lincoln: University of Nebraska Press.

Foreign Language

Aoki, Tsugio. 1969. "Lies in 'The Liar.'" *Eigo Seinen* [The Rising Generation] (Tokyo), 115 (April): 26–27. [Japanese]

Stanzel, Franz K. 1986. "Wandlung und Verwandlung eines Lügners: 'The Liar' von Henry James." In *Theorie und Praxis im Erzählendes 19. und 20. Jahrhunderts: Studien zur englischen und amerikanischen Literatur zu Ehren von Willi Erzgräber*. Ed. Winfried Herget, Klaus Peter Jochum, and Ingeborg Weber, 283–93. Tübingen: Gunter Narr.

A Light Man

Publication History

James first published "A Light Man" in the July 1869 issue of *Galaxy*. In 1873 James wrote his mother of his first projected volume of short stories, declaring that of his pre-1870 tales, "A Light Man" was the "only one . . . I should not rather object to reissue. That showed most distinct ability" (*Letters* 1, 357). *A Passionate Pilgrim* appeared, however, without the tale, which did not appear again until 1884, when Scribner's invited James to contribute to their series *Stories by American Authors*. Aziz argues that James chose an early tale because the other contributions were "not very distinguished." Even so, James revised the tale heavily, with over five hundred new readings, a change so extreme, in Edel's estimate, "as to amount almost to a rewriting of the story" (Aziz 1, xlv; Edel [1957] 1982, 207). It may have been its publication there that prompted James to consider including the story in the 1885 collection, *The Author of Beltraffio* (*Correspondence* 93–94). He included it instead, perhaps more appropriately, in the 1885 *Stories Revived*, with a much smaller number of changes this time. It next appeared after James's death in the 1920 collection *Master Eustace*, and following that in Lubbock's *The Novels and Stories of Henry James*.

Circumstances of Composition, Sources, and Influences

The date of composition, according to Kelley, falls before James's departure for Europe in March of 1869. In fact, she argues that his dissatisfaction with the tale's realism contributed to his decision to see more of the world (91, 112 n.1; also Aziz xlii).

The relationship between Maximus and Theodore has often been seen as representing James's relationship with his older brother, William. According to Edel, James identifies with Maximus, an indication that by remaining at home while William was away in Europe, Henry was enjoying the strength of his position in the family (*Life* 1, 251). In Feinstein's reading, James distributes qualities of himself and William to both Maximus and Theodore as they struggle for the favor of Sloane, whom Feinstein takes to be a harsh satire of James Sr. He also adds a comparison between the later James at Rye with his acolytes and the retired Sloane (233–35). Martin and Ober give a different twist to the sibling rivalry by seeing it transformed into a nonsexual fraternal love (310).

The tale's epigraph comes from Browning's dramatic monologue "A Light Woman": "And I—what I seem to my friend, you see— / What I soon shall seem to his love, you guess. / What I seem to myself, do you ask of me? / No hero, I confess" (CT 2, 61). Browning was one of James's favorite poets, and Edel cites from an 1865 review James's praise of Browning as the master of the technique of telling a story through the viewpoint of an "imaginary hero" as different as possible from oneself (CT 2, 8). While taking Browning as his model here, however, James makes his title the opposite of the master's, a habit with James, as Tintner notes (1987, 53). Indeed, apart from Vaid, who points to the applicability of the confession of Browning's narrator that he is "No hero" to the narrator here, critics have focused on the changes from Browning (92–93). Monteiro looks at James's replacement of Browning's two men vying for a woman with two men vying for a man, the narrator in both poem and tale claiming to be acting for the sake of his friend (72; also Feinstein 233). Wagenknecht remarks that Sloane could also be read as the light man (191).

The character of Maximus has been traced by Long to Hawthorne, on the grounds that Maximus commits the Unpardonable Sin in his exploitation of Sloane and Theodore (18–19). Habegger points to a novel entitled *Opportunity* (1867), by Anne Crane Seemuller, that focuses on the contrast between two opposed types of men, one of which—the "languidly selfish" one—James praised in his review (111). Vaid suggests a more remote predecessor for the tone of Max's diary in Iago's soliloquies (92).

Theodore reads both Emerson and Voltaire, but Sloane can tolerate only the French philosopher, and indeed may, according to Tintner, owe his character to him (CT 2, 69). Tintner points to parallels in his appearance, his skepticism, his lakeside residence, even his niece and duelling secretaries, one faithful and one exploitative. Tintner offers essays on Voltaire by Carlyle and Sainte-Beuve as intermediate sources for James's knowledge of the original *Mémoires sur Voltaire et sur ses ouvrages, par Longcham et Wagnière, ses secrètaures* (1987, 208–11). Other sources proposed for Sloane include William Beckford and Swinburne, who, Wagenknecht remarks, share his "curious blend of sensuality and impotence" (191). Martin and Ober present the possibility that Sloane's name stems from that of the collector Hans Sloane (306).

Focusing on Max, Martin and Ober consider Augustine's *Confessions* as ultimately the most significant source, developing a reading in which Max, whose name, Austin, is a form of Augustine, moves from sin to salvation. In the course of their argument, they point to the similar autobiographical form of each narrative, the presence of "pagan" father figures, and the mirroring in Max and Theodore's friendship of that of Augustine and Alypius.

Among other allusions, Martin and Ober cite references to Horace, to Saint Paul, and the Bible stories of the Prodigal Son and Jacob and Esau (308–9). Maximus himself invokes his "brief career" in terms of a Hogarth series, which he adds would be most appropriately entitled "So-and-So's Progress to a Mercenary Marriage," an allusion Tintner opines would be handled more subtly in *A London Life* (CT 2, 74; 1986, 23).

Somers conjectures a possible influence on Sherwood Anderson of James's unreliable narrator here and in *The Aspern Papers* (92).

Relation to Other Works

James had first used the form of a diary three years earlier in "A Landscape Painter," and Voss finds James becoming more effective in using the form in this tale (128). Ten years later, James used the technique again in "The Diary of a Man of Fifty," and Vaid links the two tales as rare examples of James presenting a first-person narrator telling his own life story. He also classes the tale with *The Aspern Papers* and "The Figure in the Carpet" as one of the few ironic treatments of such a narrator (16, 249). Peterson refers to both "A Light Man" and "The Diary of a Man of Fifty" as "self-incriminating," adding that he finds James's narrators in general more suspect than does Vaid (144 n.27).

The tale the diary tells is, according to Edel, the culmination of the theme of "reversal of role and usurpation" seen earlier in "De Grey" and "The Romance of Certain Old Clothes" (*Life* 1, 250). The usurping Max is, in Kraft's estimate, a "materialistic European-American" in the style of Gilbert Osmond (46). Long also classes Maximus with Osmond as an "egotist-violator," as well as with Dr. Sloper of *Washington Square*, while arguing that James leads the reader to identify with such characters by the force of their intelligence (19–20). Habegger associates him with a Jamesian type of "*homme fatal*," including such examples as Hubert Lawrence of *Watch and Ward*, Morris Townsend of *Washington Square*, Sir Claude of *What Maisie Knew*, Vanderbank of *The Awkward Age*, and Prince Amerigo of *The Golden Bowl* (111). Edel also locates the themes of "treachery and fraternal humiliation" in *The Ivory Tower*, as well as in "Guest's Confession" (*Life* 5, 505). Haddick sees the plot both of *The Ivory Tower* and *The Wings of the Dove* reworking the plot here, but with a woman added to the triangle. At the same time, he sees *Roderick Hudson* and *The Bostonians* as treating the same concept of a "kept friend" of the same sex (20). LeClair finds the relationship between the men a less subtle treatment of the theme of homosexual love than *The Pupil* or *The Turn of the Screw* (423).

Theodore, in Stevenson's judgment, is as poor a portrait of a divinity student as Hubert Lawrence was (36). Kraft views him as an early version of Lambert Strether, and Sloane as a predecessor of Abel Gaw and Frank

Betterman of *The Ivory Tower* (46). Gale, for his part, judges James's "high-priests" such as Theodore, Eugene Pickering's father, and Bender of *The Outcry* as "dull" (152).

Interpretation and Criticism

James, Edel argues, must have had a "particular fondness" for the tale given its reprintings, quite numerous for such an early story. He attributes the fondness to James's pleasure in the tale's "technical skill," the successful carrying out of the self-revealing diary (*Life* 1, 25; CT 2, 7). While Thorp also praises the use of the diary to carry out its ironic revelation of the "despicable" nature of its writer, other critics have been more qualified in their praise of the technique (xiv). Leyburn, for example, judges James generally successful, but occasionally too obvious in making his point (8). Kelley, more critically, contends that James chose the diary form in an attempt to add more art to his analysis, and then undid his attempt with an "impossible" diarist (91). Finally, Beach calls it so "desperate a venture" that James never again attempted it (180).

In 1884 James had Maximus add to his diary assessments of the tale's three characters: Sloane is a "humbug," Theodore a "prig," and himself an "adventurer" (Aziz 1, 503). Jones translates these terms into moral absolutes: Max is "the most unconscionably heartless character" in James; Sloane such a selfish fool that he merits Max's abusive treatment; and Theodore, whose legitimate work on Sloane's memoirs he stresses, is a "paragon of virtue and dependability" (97–98). Other critics have generated a greater range of reactions, and Max has his defenders even as Theodore has his detractors.

Sweeney, who locates in the tale James's first use of the term the "New England conscience," views James as "fully sympathetic" with its possessor here, Theodore. He sees in Theodore's worries about providing for his family, and about shaming himself in doing so, a "mark more of rectitude than morbidity" (255–57). Tanner, on the other hand, argues that Theodore's "pious pseudoreligious dedication" hides the same "ruthless competitive egotism" as Sloane's (12). Stevenson, who remarks that James was "helpless" depicting American clergy, sees Theodore as having "only a certain hangdog modesty as the badge of his profession." His behavior she finds equally as cynical as Max's (36). Leyburn prefers the portrayal of the evil Sloane and Max to that of Theodore, whom she judges too "insipid" to inspire much sympathy. As a result, she contends, James's attempt to combine comedy and tragedy falls short of any true tragic sense (8–10).

Max receives his most positive reading from Martin and Ober, who argue that his character is at a point of transition. Sloane represents the man he is in danger of becoming, while Theodore, also undergoing his hour of temptation at Sloane's, has earlier pointed another way. Dismissing the common view that Max is staying on at Sloane's to try to marry the niece and gain her fortune, they argue that Max by the end is a changed character as evidenced by his ability to feel compassion even for Sloane, and in his refusal to burn the will, allowing Theodore to destroy it instead as a way of allowing him to restore *his* self-respect. Together Max and Theodore, both mixed characters, represent in their view different but "necessary" values, which are best combined.

Martin and Ober are perhaps overly positive. The more common reading of Max was established early on by Howells, who wrote James of the light man, "I confess the idea of him fascinated me. He's one of your best worst ones . . ." (328). A highly conscious character, Maximus is, according to Long, too conscious, indeed too mocking, of his role as a seeker of Sloane's inheritance. He judges Maximus with his great wit and absent morals an ambiguous character, but asserts that while the tale's irony keeps Maximus from being a "fiend," he is still judged for his behavior. While he wishes to think of himself as a "man of fact" facing a "man of fancy," he is in actuality "worldliness reduced to an essence of negativity" (18–20). Rimmon and Vaid, however, dismiss the idea that his character is at all ambiguous (Rimmon 15; Vaid 92–93). Similarly, Levy limits the value of Max's consciousness. Although Max has the ability to discern Theodore's "moral blindness" and Sloane's "pretensions," Kraft writes, he "exists only in his own consciousness of wickedness" (17). Edel, perhaps, does the most possible for Max in finding him at least "a cheerful scoundrel" (*Life* 1, 250)

The third man, Sloane, is cast by Putt as a "father-figure" (38) and by Edel as a "kind of father-mother" to both Max and Theodore (*Life* 1, 250; also Kraft 126 n.16). Martin and Ober even consider the possibility that Max is Sloane's natural son, noting Sloane's statement to Max: "I knew you in knowing your mother," and his invitation to "come and be a son to me" (309). As sparring siblings, both Max and Theodore manage to lose. As Edel observes, Maximus attempts to replace Theodore, but succeeds only in removing him (*Life* 1, 250–51). By failing, McElderry adds, they are both "relieved of the pretenses they had been forced into" (28).

The contest between Theodore and Maximus has been analyzed in terms of money, sex, and nationality. The story is, as Putt observes, marked throughout by monetary imagery (38). In Max's image, Sloane "wraps himself in his money as in a wadded dressing-gown, and goes trundling through life on his little golden wheels" (CT 2, 76). Dietrichson sees the central theme as the temptation of "the wealth of others" to those without, and the way wealth can smooth the path of those, however unpleasant, who possess it. But if Sloane is unpleasant in his use of money, Max, whom Mull calls "surely the least subtle of James's first-person villains," is no more so. Motivated solely by greed, Max thinks of love as "a combination of lust and financial gain" and justifies his behavior by the "specious" argument that he has never pretended to be any better. Mull finds Theodore more complex if "obscure," because he rationalizes his greed as seeking "the natural reward of conscientious service" for the sake of his sister (15–17).

LeClair and Mull both note the suggestion of homosexual attraction between the two men, but do not analyze it (LeClair 423–24; Mull 16–17). Fish, who analyzes Sloane's library to find it—like its compiler—"more flamboyant than sound," notes that his wickedness was originally described as being "of a feminine turn." He argues, however, that James means to characterize him not as a homosexual but as a combination of "sensuality and impotence." Speaking in terms of "unnatural passion" and "sexual deviation," Fish adds, in disagreement with LeClair, that if anyone is meant to be so characterized, it is Sloane, not Max, who is simply incapable of "disinterested friendship" (213–14). Similarly, Martin and Ober, although they use the earlier text, never consider the possibility of a sexual attachment. Feinstein, however, calls the tale "transparently homosexual and at times even pornographic." In his reading, Max makes up to Sloane, is thwarted, then unconvincingly tells Theodore he does not "understand" love between men (233). Habegger and Haddick also read the work as a clearly gay tale (Habegger 111; Haddick 19–20).

The extensive revisions in 1884, however, include, as Monteiro observes, the editing out of most of the suggestions of homosexuality (72). Subject to particular revision was what Leyburn characterizes as the "fine recognition scene" between Max and Theodore (see Ruhm 678). In 1869 Max tells Theodore, "You say you loved me; if so, you ought to love me still. . . . I never pretended to love you. I don't understand the word in the sense you attach to it. I don't understand the feeling, between men. To me love means quite another thing" (Aziz 1, 372). In the 1885 version, Max states, "You say you were such a friend of mine; if so, you ought to be one still. . . . I never pretended to take one's friendship so seriously. I don't understand the word in the sense you attach to it. I don't understand the feeling of affection between men. To me it means quite another thing" (CT 2, 95). Kraft sees the earlier sexual inuendo as unintentional and unfortunate (46). Whether intentional or not, James was evidently uncomfortable with it. Either version, if taken as representing a homosexual relationship, seems to portray Theodore's love for the sophisticated Max as unfortunate, characterized by unease and ended by betrayal. One might add that Max appears a sexual opportunist, equally willing to woo the heiress for her money as Sloane or Theodore.

Others have read the relationship of Max and Theodore in terms of nationality. Although LeClair argues that the theme of American identity will be treated better later in James's career (423), Kraft still finds the greatest significance of the tale in its national or international theme. In his view Max was corrupted by Europe while Theodore, an American innocent, is "really no better," trapped like Max in a limited perspective that make it impossible for either to understand the other. Sloane combines character traits of both men, but remains a fool. James, Kraft argues, is showing the need for a better, stronger combination (44–47). Similarly, seeing the tale representing the breakdown of New England culture under the pressure of European influence, Cantwell points to James's construction of two "social types" to illustrate the clash. One, Max, is "flippant, irresponsible, continental"; the other, Theodore, is "a descendent of the New England tradition, upright and conscience-ridden." In his estimate, however, the plotting undermines the symbolism (303).

Maves gives the tale high marks as an early work, judging it with *Madame de Mauves*, "Four Meetings," and "The Madonna of the Future" as the best of James's work before *Daisy Miller* (157 n.15). Similarly, Schelling calls it a "fine, if forbidding, piece of psychological insight" (174). Most critics, however, are more negative, Cantwell judging it "strikingly bad," Kraft unsuccessful, and Putt "unpleasant" (Cantwell 303; Kraft 46; Putt 38). As LeClair indicates, most of what the tale does James will do better later, in other works (423–24). The characters, if intriguing, are hardly likeable, and it seems probable that the tale will continue to be read more for its indications of James's psychology than his artistry.

Works Cited

Primary Works
James, Henry. 1869. "A Light Man." *Galaxy* 8 (July): 49–68.

———. 1884. "A Light Man." *Stories by American Authors*. Vol. 5. New York: Scribner's.

———. 1885. "A Light Man." *Stories Revived*. Vol. 1. London: Macmillan.

———. 1920. "A Light Man." *Master Eustace*. Preface by Albert Mordell. New York: Thomas Seltzer.

———. 1921–23. "A Light Man." *The Novels and Stories of Henry James*. Vol. 25. Ed. Percy Lubbock. London: Macmillan.

———. 1993. *The Correspondence of Henry James and the House of Macmillan, 1877–1914*. Ed. Rayburn S. Moore. Baton Rouge: Louisiana State University Press.

Secondary Works
Beach, Joseph Warren. [1918] 1954. *The Method of Henry James*. Philadelphia: Albert Saifer.

Cantwell, Robert. 1934. "A Little Reality." *Hound & Horn* 7 (April–May): 494–505.

Dietrichson, Jan W. 1969. *The Image of Money in the American Novel of the Gilded Age*. Oslo: Universitetsforlaget; New York: Humanities.

Edel, Leon and Dan H. Laurence. [1957] 1982. *A Bibliography of Henry James*. Oxford: Clarendon Press.

Feinstein, Howard M. 1984. *Becoming William James*. Ithaca, NY: Cornell University Press. Reprinted in part from "A Singular Life: Twinship in the Psychology of William and Henry James." In *Blood Brothers: Siblings as Writers*. Ed. Norman Kiell, 301–28. New York: International University Press, 1983.

Fish, Charles. 1965. "Description in Henry James's 'A Light Man.'" *English Language Notes* 2 (March): 211–15.

Gale, Robert L. [1954] 1964. *The Caught Image: Figurative Language in the Fiction of Henry James*. Chapel Hill: University of North Carolina Press.

Habegger, Alfred. 1989. *Henry James and the "Woman Business."* Cambridge: Cambridge University Press.

Haddick, Vern. 1976. "Colors in the Carpet." *Gay Literature* 5: 19–21.

Howells, W. D. 1979. *Selected Letters*. Vol. 1: *1852–1872*. Ed. George Arms, et al. Boston: Twayne.

Jones, Granville H. 1975. *Henry James's Psychology of Experience: Innocence, Responsibility, and Renunciation in the Fiction of Henry James*. The Hague: Mouton.

Kelley, Cornelia Pulsifer. [1930] 1965. *The Early Development of Henry James*. Urbana: University of Illinois Press.

Kraft, James. 1969. *The Early Tales of Henry James, 1843–1870*. New York: Bookman.

LeClair, Robert Charles. 1955. *Young Henry James, 1843–1870*. New York: Bookman.

Levy, Leo B. 1957. *Versions of Melodrama: A Study of the Fiction and Drama of Henry James, 1865–1897*. Berkeley: University of California Press.

Leyburn, Ellen Douglass. 1968. *Strange Alloy: The Relation of Comedy to Tragedy in the Fiction of Henry James*. Chapel Hill: University of North Carolina Press.

Long, Robert Emmet. 1979. *The Great Succession: Henry James and the Legacy of Hawthorne*. Pittsburgh: University of Pittsburgh Press.

McElderry, Bruce R., Jr. 1965. *Henry James*. New York: Twayne.

Martin, W. R., and Warren U. Ober. 1986. "Refurbishing James's 'A Light Man.'" *Arizona Quarterly* 42, no. 4 (Winter): 305–14.

Maves, Carl. 1973. *Sensuous Pessimism: Italy in the Work of Henry James*. Bloomington: Indiana University Press.

Monteiro, George. 1977. "Henry James and the Lessons of Sordello." *Western Humanities Review* 31: 69–78.

Mull, Donald. 1973. *Henry James's "Sublime Economy": Money as Symbolic Center in the Fiction*. Middletown, CT: Wesleyan University Press.

Peterson, Dale E. 1975. *The Clement Vision: Poetic Realism in Turgenev and James*. Port Washington, NY: Kennikat.

Putt, S. Gorley. 1966. *Henry James: A Reader's Guide*. Ithaca, NY: Cornell University Press.

Rimmon, Shlomith. 1977. *The Concept of Ambiguity: The Example of Henry James*. Chicago: University of Chicago Press.

Ruhm, Herbert. 1963. "The Complete Tales of Henry James." *Saturday Review* 71: 675–80.

Schelling, Felix E. 1922. "Some Forgotten Tales of Henry James." In *Appraisements and Asperities: as to Some Contemporary Writers*. Philadelphia: Lippincott, 169–74.

Somers, Paul P. Jr. 1977. "Sherwood Anderson's Mastery of Narrative Distance." *Twentieth-Century Literature* 23, no. 1 (February): 84–93.

Stevenson, Elizabeth. [1949] 1981. *The Crooked Corridor: A Study of Henry James*. New York: Octagon.

Sweeney, Gerard M. 1981. "Henry James and the New England Conscience—Once Again." *New England Quarterly* 54: 255–58.

Tanner, Tony. 1985. *Henry James: The Writer and His Work*. Amherst: University of Massachusetts Press.

Thorp, Willard, ed. 1962. *The Madonna of the Future and Other Early Tales*. New York: New American Library.

Tintner, Adeline R. 1987. *The Book World of Henry James: Appropriating the Classics*. Ann Arbor: UMI Research Press.

———. 1986. *The Museum World of Henry James*. Ann Arbor: UMI Research Press.

Vaid, Krishna B. 1964. *Technique in the Tales of Henry James*. Cambridge, MA: Harvard University Press.

Voss, Arthur. 1973. *The American Short Story: A Critical Survey*. Norman: University of Oklahoma Press.

Wagenknecht, Edward. 1984. *The Tales of Henry James*. New York: Frederick Ungar.

Longstaff's Marriage

Publication History

"Longstaff's Marriage" appeared first in the "Midsummer Holiday Number" of *Scribner's Monthly* in August 1878. James collected it the next year for *The Madonna of the Future* and also included it in his 1883 Collective Edition. He did not, however, reprint it again. Its next appearance was in Mordell's 1920 *Master Eustace*. It also appeared in Lubbock's edition of the novels and stories.

Circumstances of Composition, Sources, and Influences

Edel finds James recreating in the story his feelings of mingled fear and admiration for his cousin Minny Temple, and particularly his relief at the easing of those fears caused by her death seven years before, arguing that Longstaff recovers not, as he believes, from hurt pride, but from a similar relief. To Edel, Longstaff *is* James (*Life* 1, 327–30). Edel also sees, in James's letter to his brother describing himself "slowly crawling from weakness and inaction and suffering into strength and health and hope: she sinking out of brightness and youth into decline and death," a reflection of his "vampire" myth present here (1970, 28). Krook, too, traces the genesis of the tale to Minny's death, although she discerns more of an "expiatory impulse" (138).

James himself draws attention to the appropriateness of Diana's name for a heroine who is "passionately single, fiercely virginal," and most critics have followed his lead, Horrell finding the allusion a bit heavy-handed (CT 4, 210; Horrell 209). Sicker notes that in early James the heroines almost inevitably appear to the hero "an incarnation either of Diana or Mary" (35). Tintner, however, sees Diana here as being "punished" for aspiring to divinity (1986, 42). Kraft is among the few who point to the invocation of the Endymion myth (89). One may find indications of the Pygmalion myth as well in the manner by which Diana is transformed by love: "The beautiful statue had grown human and taken on some of the imperfections of humanity" (CT 4, 234).

Kelly notes what she considers the unfortunate influence of the romantic novelist George Sand (246 n.4). Tintner views Longstaff as a "tepid" reincarnation of the Byronic hero, his romance with Diana being based on Byron's relationship with Mme. de Staël as described in *Corinne*, which along with *Childe Harold* forms some of the heroine's reading material (1987, 97–99).

Relation to Other Works

In discussing the troubled marriages of James's early works, such as those in "Crawford's Consistency" and *Madame de Mauves*, Stein picks the marriage here—where the bride barely survives the ceremony—as "revealingly, the most convincing untroubled marriage" (86 n.26). Similarly, Edel comments on the ease with which both Longstaff and Marmaduke of the later tale "Maud-Evelyn" become widowers (*Life* 1, 330).

Looking at the Italian setting of the tale's conclusion, Nathalia Wright points out that like other of James's lovers who met at St. Peter's in *Daisy Miller*, *The Portrait of a Lady*, and *Roderick Hudson*, Longstaff and Diana's romance ends unhappily. She also draws a parallel between the shabby old palaces of Diana, the Bordereaux in *The Aspern Papers*, and the Moreens in *The Pupil* as fitting residences for such characters, and adds that Diana's choice of such a palace for her death anticipates Milly Theale's (226–27, 231).

Mackenzie finds it noteworthy that what he takes as the earliest instance of the vampire theme focuses on an international marriage and what he calls "its problem of social and sexual aestheticism" (191 n.54). He also includes both Diana and Longstaff among the early examples of "extraordinary cases" in James whose self-inflicted shame causes them physical suffering (36). Looking at some of the same tales, including "Poor Richard" and "The Most Extraordinary Case," Sicker characterizes love in early James as "self-induced disease." In contrast to Edel, however, he argues that the seeming vampirism portrayed in such tales is really separate death wishes, hero and heroine being too trapped in ego to feed on one another. Sicker also sees in the tale a suggestion of "the worship of the dead" typical of works of the 1890s such as "The Altar of the Dead," "The Tone of Time," and *The Awkward Age* (35, 99–100, 110). (See also "De Grey.")

Levy compares Diana with Christina Light and Angela of *Confidence*, saying that all start as "dangerous coquette[s]," but only Angela breaks free from the role (37–38). Edel implies a parallel between Diana and Isabel Archer, whose name also alludes to the virgin goddess, and between the two sickly lovers Longstaff and Ralph Touchett (*Life* 1, 331). Cargill reinforces the connections between tale and novel, and adds a resemblance between the two faithful followers Agatha and Henrietta (84). Mull focuses the comparison more closely, seeing the story as presenting a conception of money different from the early stories and closer to *The Portrait of a Lady*, where Ralph magnanimously wishes to endow Isabel, a gesture intended to express his love without diminishing the freedom she values. Similarly, Longstaff offers Diana his worldly goods, saying, "It can only give you a larger liberty" (26). Krook develops the relationship not only to *The Portrait of a Lady*, but also to the later *The Wings of the Dove*, seeing the final turn where Diana dies, according to her friend, in order to leave Longstaff "at liberty" as prefiguring Milly's death, which leaves Densher free to marry Kate. Krook emphasizes the forgiving nature of the gesture in *The Wings of the Dove*, although Longstaff would seem to have less need to be forgiven (137–39). Samuels also connects the tale with *The Wings of the Dove*, as one of several "renunciation fantasies" in which sickness and love are allied and dying becomes "a more significant proof of love than living" (72–73). Putt objects to what he sees as the same "possessiveness" hidden behind self-sacrifice here and in *The Golden Bowl* (268).

Mackenzie likens Agatha's "sublime hypocrisy" to Fleda's lie to Mrs. Gereth in *The Spoils of Poynton* (CT 4, 239–90 n.35). One might find the initial peacefulness of female friendship interrupted by a man analogous to that of the comparatively lighthearted "The Third Person."

Interpretation and Criticism

James wrote in March of 1879 to his brother William his surprise at William's thinking "Longstaff's Marriage" ought to have been included in his 1879 collection, *Daisy Miller*. He writes that it was too late to do so, but adds there was still plenty of time to reprint it in his next "if it has any virtue," calling it "a poor affair" (*Letters* 2, 216). He did reprint it in his next collection, making some revisions, including changing the comical sounding name Gosling to Josling, perhaps to prevent readers from thinking of her as Horrell does, as a "rather stupid goose of a woman" (208). Nevertheless, subsequent readers have still tended to side more with Henry's original opinion than William's. The tale has had many commentators but few admirers. At its reissuing, Schelling contented himself with doubting the likelihood of its symmetrical plot (173–74). Since then representative opinions have included Wagenknecht's description of it as "one of James's oddest, most abnormal, and least convincing tales" (191). Sicker has labeled it "one of [James's] most unpleasant tales," while Krook stays with the briefer label "silly" (Sicker 41; Krook 139).

Kraft is unusual in finding the tale "almost perversely interesting." He argues that its twining of love and death is a genuine if unusual potential of human relationships, and it is for the most part that mixture that bring critics who disparage the tale to analyze it (89). Most attack its emotional ethics. Jones finds the most significant mixture the hero and heroine's striking quantities of both "selfishness and conscience" (104). Putt particularly challenges the claimed magnanimity of Diana's death as the "nastiness of competitive sacrifice" (268). Sicker charges that both hero and heroine, rather than looking outward to love the other, are so "trapped" within that all they love is the idea of their own death (41–42). Cargill, however, warns that James is not in sympathy with Diana's "limitation," that her belated passion for Longstaff is intended as punishment for her initial rejection of him, as she herself believes (84, 106). More commonsensically, Samuels finds Diana's reluctance to marry a man she does not love understandable, and notes the irony of her dying at the point that *both* wish the marriage (73). While Andreas calls it "cruel" (77), her comment to the allegedly dying Longstaff, that "if he could die with it, he can die without it," seems to point shrewdly to the weakness in a man who can die for love, but not be cured by it.

Wagenknecht observes how the beginning seems to promise a comedy but the conclusion is tragic (191). And indeed, despite the description of its strenuous heroine, the story seems at first unlikely to follow such convoluted paths. While Sicker argues that by loving "the image of a virgin" Longstaff is doomed to, indeed desirous of, romantic disappointment (35), it is helpful to keep in mind that most heroes of the age loved virgin heroines, and that many heroines made the transformation to matron quite successfully—a process charted by James in his early "Travelling Companions." Indeed, both Longstaff's and Diana's preoccupations seem more assigned than innate as they are overwhelmed by events that befall them. Whether James meant them to stand so allegorically is unclear. Kelley found the attempted romanticism, which did not suit well with prosaic Americans, the cause of the story's failure (246). The international setting, which McElderry considers merely "incidental," may have been intended to make the characters and plot seem more in proportion (77). The result, as Mackenzie labels it, is a "fantasy," and in the end a rather unpleasant one (36). McElderry rather laconically describes the tale's conclusion as "a delayed and unsatisfactory marriage" (77). One might say nearly the same of the many elements set in motion here.

Works Cited

Primary Works
James, Henry. 1878. "Longstaff's Marriage." *Scribner's Monthly* 16 (August): 537–50.

———. 1879. "Longstaff's Marriage." *The Madonna of the Future and Other Tales*. London: Macmillan.

———. 1883. "Longstaff's Marriage." Collective Edition. Vol. 13. London: Macmillan.

———. 1920. "Longstaff's Marriage." *Master Eustace*. Preface by Albert Mordell. New York: Thomas Seltzer.

———. 1921–23. "Longstaff's Marriage." *The Novels and Stories of Henry James*. Vol. 24. Ed. Percy Lubbock. London: Macmillan.

Secondary Works

Andreas, Osborn. 1948. *Henry James and the Expanding Horizon: A Study of the Meaning and Basic Themes of James's Fiction*. Seattle: University of Washington Press.

Cargill, Oscar. 1961. *The Novels of Henry James*. New York: Macmillan.

Edel, Leon, ed. 1970. *Henry James: Stories of the Supernatural*. New York: Taplinger.

Horrell, Joyce Tayloe. 1970. "A 'Shade of a Special Sense': Henry James and the Art of Naming." *American Literature* 42: 203–20.

Jones, Granville H. 1975. *Henry James's Psychology of Experience: Innocence, Responsibility, and Renunciation in the Fiction of Henry James*. The Hague: Mouton.

Kelley, Cornelia Pulsifer. [1930] 1965. *The Early Development of Henry James*. Urbana: University of Illinois Press.

Kraft, James. 1969. *The Early Tales of Henry James, 1843–1870*. New York: Bookman.

Krook, Dorothea. 1986. "Isabel Archer Figures in Some Early Stories of Henry James." *Henry James Review* 7, nos. 2–3 (Winter–Spring): 131–39.

Levy, Leo B. 1957. *Versions of Melodrama: A Study of the Fiction and Drama of Henry James, 1865–1897*. Berkeley: University of California Press.

McElderry, Bruce R., Jr. 1965. *Henry James*. New York: Twayne.

Mackenzie, Manfred. 1976. *Communities of Honor and Love in Henry James*. Cambridge, MA: Harvard University Press.

Mull, Donald. 1973. *Henry James's "Sublime Economy": Money as Symbolic Center in the Fiction*. Middletown, CT: Wesleyan University Press.

Putt, S. Gorley. 1966. *Henry James: A Reader's Guide*. Ithaca, NY: Cornell University Press.

Samuels, Charles Thomas. 1971. *The Ambiguity of Henry James*. Urbana: University of Illinois Press.

Schelling, Felix E. 1922. "Some Forgotten Tales of Henry James." *Appraisements and Asperities: as to Some Contemporary Writers*. Philadelphia: Lippincott, 169–74.

Sicker, Philip. 1980. *Love and the Quest for Identity in the Fiction of Henry James*. Princeton: Princeton University Press.

Stein, Allen F. 1984. *After the Vows Were Spoken: Marriage in American Literary Realism*. Columbus: Ohio State University Press.

Tintner, Adeline R. 1987. *The Book World of Henry James: Appropriating the Classics*. Ann Arbor: UMI Research Press. Revised from "Henry James and Byron." *Byron Journal* 9 (1981): 52–63.

———. 1986. *The Museum World of Henry James*. Ann Arbor: UMI Research Press.

Wagenknecht, Edward. 1984. *The Tales of Henry James*. New York: Frederick Ungar.

Wright, Nathalia. 1965. *American Novelists in Italy, The Discoverers: Alliston to James*. Philadelphia: University of Pennsylvania Press.

Lord Beaupré

Publication History

The tale was first published as "Lord Beauprey" in three issues of *Macmillan's Magazine* from April to June 1892. James revised it for *The Private Life* where it appeared in 1893 as "Lord Beaupré." It next appeared in Lubbock's edition of James's novels and stories.

Circumstances of Composition, Sources, and Influences

James recorded the germ for the tale in late 1891 as "an *idée de comédie* . . . on the subject of the really terrible situation of the young man, in England, who is a great *parti*—the really formidable assault of the mothers, and the *filles à marier*" (CN 64) Originally it was to have been Beaupré's mother who steered him to the shelter of a false engagement. It is ironic, as Matthiessen and Murdock point out, that it becomes Mary's, so that he is in a sense trapped by the sort of designs he hoped to avoid (N 115–16).

   Tintner reads Bolton-Brown's contemplation of the Assyrian bull in the British Museum as symbolic of his attempting to figure out the riddle of Mary's engagement to Lord Beaupré (102).

Relation to Other Works

Jones sees Guy as initially like Graham Fielder in *The Ivory Tower*, feeling prey to the plotting of others because of his simplicity. Jones also observes how in *The Awkward Age*, the multiple layers of knowlege enveloping Vanderbank and Nanda prevent their union just as they prevent Guy and Mary's here (122–23). Both men let the women go through what even James called "too great delicacy" (CN 64). Edel links the tale with "Collaboration" as illustrating "the difficulty of men with women" (CT 8,10). One might of course say that Beaupré's life was perfectly simple in its relations with women until the addition of his fortune. Unlike Verver, however, who accepts a marriage of convenience to preserve his peace, Beaupré tries first for a simple engagement.

Focusing on the woman's perspective, Allen links the tale with "The Visits," "The Chaperon," and "The Patagonia" as demonstrating the way women, who can only attain power by marrying well, must work against each other to succeed, behavior seen clearly in Mary's mother and several of the other women characters. In contrast perhaps, Allen sees in Mary the "intelligence and sympathy" shared by such other Jamesian women as Mrs. Ryves in "Sir Dominick Ferrand," Fleda in *The Spoils of Poynton*, and the heroine of *In the Cage* (123).

Interpretation and Criticism

A contemporary reviewer for the *Athenaeum* found that while the tale's basic concept contained "elements of humor . . . the joke is a little far-fetched" (61). Subsequent estimates have not gone much higher than Wagenknecht's assessment that it is "easy to read and entertaining" (191), or Edgar's view that it is "sparkling" but lacking in "firmness of texture" (155).

Allen notes the irony of such a passive, weak man setting into motion so much scheming, possible only in a society that assigned women so little independent status (121–22). In such a situation, it is Beaupré's behavior that absorbs most of the blame. The reviewer for the *Athenaeum* particularly objected to his offer of a false engagement, and critics have continued to question it. Edgar remarks that Guy has used Mary "for his convenience" (155), no small crime in Jamesian terms. Putt, who finds the tale "chillingly unreal," labels him a "complacent" nonmarrier (283). Yet James's sympathy for Beaupré's situation in the notebook entry with its repeated "reallys" is apparent, and he also records there that Guy "doesn't dream he's hurting her" (CN 64). Indeed, most of the remorse in the original conception is Guy's. James changed this somewhat in the story itself, eliminating Beaupré's belated discovery that he was the one Mary loved after all. Andreas sees both Guy and Mary as victims of the confusion of marriage and money (80–81).

Beaupré's clever idea is a joke that gets out of hand, that doesn't take sufficient account of its human players including himself. While to say the same of James's story would not be accurate, the critical assessment seems to display an uneasiness with the way James combined the lightness of the false engagement and the solemnity of the emotions it brings into play. This yoking of unequal temperaments is, however, meant to be part of the story in its contrast of Mary's seriousness and Beaupré's frivolity. In the end, the harm done is hard to take too seriously. The projection of continued unhappiness and probable infidelity for Guy and Mary by Mary's mother (similar to that at the conclusion of "The Path of Duty") has been aptly questioned by Wagenknecht and Matthiessen (Wagenknecht 192; N 115). Tintner contrasts the formal landscape of Beaupré's estate with the natural landcape which frames the American Bolton-Brown's talk with Mary (101–2), and one can see the appeal for Mary of escaping from the artificial to the real. Bolton-Brown is also an amateur sketcher, "a sign of gentility or 'niceness'" in Jamesian vocabulary according to Winner (94). On the whole the story is something of a tempest in a teapot, and follows the lead of its lighthearted, passive hero more than its thoughtful heroine.

Works Cited

Primary Works

James, Henry. 1892. "Lord Beauprey." *Macmillan's Magazine* 65–66 (April–June): 64–74, 133–44, 465–74.

———. 1893. "Lord Beaupré." In *The Private Life*. London: Osgood, Mcilvaine; New York: Harper, 79–198.

———. 1921–23. "Lord Beaupré." *The Novels and Stories of Henry James*. Vol. 27. Ed. Percy Lubbock. London: Macmillan.

Secondary Works

Allen, Elizabeth. 1984. *A Woman's Place in the Novels of Henry James*. New York: St. Martin's.

Andreas, Osborn. 1948. *Henry James and the Expanding Horizon: A Study of the Meaning and Basic Themes of James's Fiction*. Seattle: University of Washington Press.

Anon. 1893. Review of *The Private Life*. *Athenaeum* 3428 (8 July): 60–61.

Edgar, Pelham. [1927] 1964. *Henry James, Man and Author*. New York: Russell & Russell.

Jones, Granville H. 1975. *Henry James's Psychology of Experience: Innocence, Responsibility, and Renunciation in the Fiction of Henry James*. The Hague: Mouton.

Putt, S. Gorley. 1966. *Henry James: A Reader's Guide*. Ithaca, NY: Cornell University Press.

Tintner, Adeline R. 1986. *The Museum World of Henry James*. Ann Arbor: UMI Research Press.

Wagenknecht, Edward. 1984. *The Tales of Henry James* New York: Frederick Ungar.

Winner, Viola Hopkins. 1970. *Henry James and the Visual Arts*. Charlottesville: University Press of Virginia.

Louisa Pallant

Publication History

James first published "Louisa Pallant" in the February 1888 issue of *Harper's New Monthly Magazine*, where it appeared with illustrations by C. S. Reinhart. He collected it that same year in *The Aspern Papers*, and later included it in the New York Edition.

Circumstances of Composition, Sources, and Influences

"Louisa Pallant" began in Florence on January 12, 1887, with "the idea of a worldly mother and a worldly daughter," perfectly trained by her mother, who has become "appalled at her own work." James then created a narrator who is an uncle of the boy the daughter is pursuing and an "old flame" of the mother. At the notebook stage James had the narrator clearly aware of the daughter's mercenariness. When the mother makes the announcement of her plan to denounce the girl to the young man, "He admires her, and he must describe this in a good tone." Still, he feels sorry for the girl, so that the mother tells him "She will still get a prince!" The story ends with the narrator telling of the girl's marriage. James contemplated possible settings, including Florence, but settled on Hamburg and began writing (CN 34–35). In his preface James recalled the Florence setting he had rejected for the tale, speaking of the "light and the colour and the sound of old Italy" that accompanied his writing that February, by the Arno (*Criticism* 2, 1207).

Advised by Howells that he did "the 'international' far better than anything else," James decided to make his characters Americans abroad (CN 34). His willingness to take such advice stems in part, according to Donald Stone, to his desire to regain the popularity lost by *The Bostonians* and *The Princess Casamassima* (247).

In their European sojourn, the Americans move from Hamburg to Lake Geneva. Edel finds James perhaps imitating the narrator's discretion in staying on the other side of the lake from the Pallants in his staying across Lake Geneva from Constance Fenimore Woolson later that year, rather than at the same hotel (*Letters* 3, 247; *Life* 3, 251). The second locale lends an additional appropriateness to Fadiman's comparison of Louisa to Dr. Frankenstein, who also regrets having created a monster, as Switzerland was the site where Mary Shelley created her monster (124).

The narrator, according to Levine, belongs to a line of "participant-observors" —a type she notes is not solely modern, as it also includes the narrators of Poe's "The Fall of the House of Usher," Melville's "Bartleby the Scrivener," and Hawthorne's *The Blithedale Romance*. She characterizes all four of them as sharing a sense of detachment, superiority, and judgmental curiosity without any sense of responsibility, and as exhibiting a consequent failure to grow in character. She concludes that all four authors are "doing more than simply faulting these narrators for their lack of objectivity: they are criticizing the value of objectivity itself" because "it is involvement, not objectivity, which leads to understanding" (33, 40). These are stirring words, but as none of the narrators, in her reading, ever succeeds at being objective, the works might be seen more as criticisms of a false complacency that one is objective—given as a rationale for one's lack of involvement—rather than as objectivity itself. Nicoloff compares Archie to Giovanni in "Rappaccini's Daughter" (416). Gale compares Louisa, in turn, to Hawthorne's Lady Eleanore (174).

James acknowledged taking Dumas's play *Le Demi-Monde* as the starting point for his tale *The Siege of London*. Grover adds this tale and the earlier "The Diary of a Man of Fifty" as additional James works based on Dumas. Here James presents an "adventuress" like Dumas's and the rescue of an innocent man from her clutches. At the same time, Grover argues, James brings into question the reliability of the "assured judgments made by one character on the basis of what he understood of the past actions of others" assumed in the French play, assigns his adventuress an active conscience, and changes her penalty for worldliness from social censure to private remorse.

Relation to Other Works

"Louisa Pallant" Shine sees—along with "Mrs. Temperly," "A New England Summer," "Georgina's Reasons," and "The Patagonia"—as condemning "maternal manipulation" (52). Similarly, Wasserstrom compares Linda to Christina Light of *Roderick Hudson*, asserting that both young women are made evil beyond hope of change by the aspirations of their mothers, and so suffer from the same "waste of life" (57). Fadiman takes James's presentation of such a deliberate shaping of a person, visible not only in the characters of Linda and Christina, but also Prince Amerigo, as a reflection of James's interest in art (125). Jones marks the possibility that Louisa, like the mother of Christina Light and like Duchess Jane in *The Awkward Age*, has passed on her ambitions for herself to ambitions for her daughter (95). Louisa herself claims to have come to the recognition that she has created a "bad" child, as does the mother in "Master Eustace."

Wegelin finds the young American here, with Christopher Newman, one of the few instances when James used a male character to represent the "promise" of American strength and innocence, although here he finds no international contrast (78, 181 n.17).

The narration in this story has been frequently characterized as unreliable, Marks giving the tale and "The Path of Duty" as good examples of the later Jamesian ambiguity, seen also in *The Turn of the Screw* and *The Spoils of Poynton* (12–13). Levy writes that here, as in *The Turn of the Screw*, the reader is aware of an "absolute" evil, but cannot tell who is its source (57). Tintner remarks that the narrator here and in "The Figure in the Carpet" and *The Sacred Fount* have a similar problem locating the meaning of their stories (69). Nicoloff also compares the narrator here to the narrator in *The Sacred Fount* and in "The Diary of a Man of Fifty," although he observes that the young man in the latter tale was wise enough to break free from his misguided mentor and to marry. He comments, too, that Roger Lawrence avoided the need for such suspicions by raising his own wife in *Watch and Ward* (418–20). Tintner argues that the tale is a reversal of "The Diary of a Man of Fifty," the suspected woman here being shown as indeed suspicious (73). The strategy she assigns Louisa—slandering a family member in order to preserve her for one's own purposes—is the same as that taken by Adela Chart in "The Marriages."

Intepretation and Criticism

The famous first line to the tale, present already in James's notebook entry, declares, "Never say you know the last word about the human heart" (CT 6, 233). It has taken on a life of its own apart from the story. Knights, for example, cites it in his argument that James's complexities of style may stem from his attempt to portray complex human situations, indeed the "final 'unknowableness' of other lives" (27–28). Certainly "Louisa Pallant" seems a good example of such "unknowableness." It seems equally certain that the last word about *it* will not be said any time soon.

In James's last word on the subject, in his preface, he wrote of the genesis of the tale that "'Louisa Pallant,' with still subtler art [than *Madame de Mauves*], completely covers her tracks—her repudiation of every ray of legend being the more marked by the later date (1888) of her appearance. Charitably affected to her and thus disposed, if the term be not arrogant, to hand her down, I yet win from her no shadow of an intelligible account of herself" (*Criticism* 2, 1207). Whether it is the tale or the character that is being so mysterious James leaves unclear.

Earlier James had been somewhat more direct. One of the tale's mysteries is what precisely Mrs. Pallant said of her daughter to warn off Archie. In his reply to a letter from a Laura Wagniére, James stated that it must have been something "pretty bad," but that the "particular thing is a secondary affair." He did, however, indicate that he thought it unlikely Linda "had been not as young ladies should be," as Wagniére presumably suggested, because she would have been "too careful of her future to have sacrificed to that extent to the present." Such behavior "wouldn't have paid in comparison with keeping straight and marrying—with patience—a lord or a millionaire." So, although he admits it possible, he thinks it unlikely, and if it *were* true, her mother would not have told the young man (*Letters* 3, 225). In the notebook he pictures her denouncing the girl "after a fashion" (CN 34).

A deeper mystery is Louisa's motivation for the denunciation. According to James, in his letter to Mme Wagniére, Louisa "in a fit of exaltation and penitence over her own former shabby conduct, wished to do something heroic and sacrificial to repair her reputation with her old lover." He abuses her, James writes, "affectionately" (*Letters* 3, 225).

The traditional view follows James seeing Louisa, with a newly moral sense, acting in what Andreas calls "symbolic reparation" for having jilted the narrator (58–59; also Canby 232; McElderry 78). While acknowledging the "purity" of her act, Fadiman, however, points to the "irony" in the last sentence that she could not have acted well in the end without having first acted badly (124–25). Grover locates a different irony in her act, her need to be "an unnatural mother and sacrifice her child" in her very attempt to act rightly in atonement for her past behavior (593–95). Putt, however, sees all the complications as simply producing another Jamesian "non-marrying victory" (274). While Fadiman judges the mercenary attitude toward marriage the lesser of the story's themes, Dietrichson emphasizes the story's condemnation of such mercenariness, such that even Louisa's plea of poverty as a motive is insufficient (Fadiman 124; Dietrichson 78).

In Fadiman's reading, the evil is not so much in Louisa herself as in her relationship with her daughter, whom she made evil (124). Similarly Geismar locates the "deeper implications" of the tale in the rivalry between the mother and daughter, which, he argues, James abandoned in order to portray a newly noble Louisa (70n.). Levine adds a feminist note in remarking that the narrator feels free to dismiss Louisa's attack on her daughter because it goes counter to traditional definitions of the role of the mother (37).

Louisa has not escaped censure for her unusual act. Even though she believes the charges against Linda, Wasserstrom laments "the absurdity and horror" of the "waste" it produces, and sympathizes with Linda as her mother "warns off the best kind of American suitor" (57). Edel speaks of the reader's "uneasy feeling that the mother has compounded her complicated history by a grossly meddlesome act" (CT 6, 11). Pound significantly describes the tale as "a study in the maternal or abysmal relation" (29).

James is treating, according to Canby, his "favorite theme of the aware and the unaware in dramatic contrast." Canby argued that the mother was aware here, while the narrator was not (231). The assignment of awareness, and of responsibility and even honesty, however, has been widely distributed by critics. As Grover, who believes Louisa to be truthful, puts it, the story leaves questions unresolved because the marriage between Linda and Archie might have worked out (593–95). The narrator, too, may be suspect. He has informed the reader that Louisa originally broke with him because of his excessive jealousy. Perhaps she was right. Taking another approach, Levy argues that the mother's charges against the daughter are "simply projections" of her own sense of guilt (57)

Complicating interpretation even further, Walter Wright calls into question not the narrator's intention, but his understanding. The tale, he argues, is a "mulling over of evidence in the search for certainty about human motives, a certainty which the narrator can never achieve." "Every incident," Wright asserts, "is capable of two or more interpretations." Louisa herself may be acting, or may be sincere and right about Linda, or yet again may be sincere and wrong, because she is "projecting" on Linda her own guilt in order to produce her own atonement. Or a bit of each motive may play a role in her actions. Because Louisa is so ambiguous, Wright continues, the reader is led to question the other characters as well. Linda, he observes, seems simple and genuine, but may only be polished in her cunning, or may even be "free of malice and eager to please" while being a complete egotist and schemer. Archie could be either naïve or secretive (158–59).

Nicoloff, too, takes Louisa as a starting point for a reevaluation of the tale's events. Finding no "hard evidence" for her "hysterical accusations," he turns to the narrator. Unlike Wright, he characterizes the narrator as more "aroused" than "baffled" by events. He is, indeed, in Nicoloff's reading "the hidden protagonist," interested not in protecting his nephew, but serving his own embittered interests. As Nicoloff sees it, Louisa finds Archie an unappealing match and so works to get rid of him through the narrator, whose egotism and lingering sense of injury she correctly assesses. Knowing that the narrator will leave as soon as he is convinced "that her sacrifice is being performed solely for himself," she plots the elaborate charade of indicting her daughter. Thus the narrator, who ought to have had the knowledge to serve as "the ideal guardian," twice falls victim to Louisa, and so sacrifices Archie's happiness at the same time.

Without blaming the narrator, Jones also considers the possibility that Louisa is again playing a false game, lying to the narrator and to Archie in order to keep her daughter free for a great marriage (94–95). Similarly, Tintner judges the narrator not unreliable, but "gullible." Looking to Archie's mother's condemnation of Louisa's interference as a key to the tale's meaning, Tintner argues that the mother sees the truth that far from atoning for it, Louisa has simply repeated her original offense. With little desire for a family tie to the narrator and a great longing for her daughter to achieve the title she failed to gain, Louisa lies to scare off Archie, who is genuinely in love.

Wagenknecht, however, finds Louisa probably sincere, especially given James's remarks in his letter to Mme Wagniére. Still, while admitting that the reader has little direct knowledge of Linda, he also observes that little of what one does see appears wicked. He questions, too, why Linda would spend so much time on Archie if she were really mercenary. Returning to the mother, he argues that her extremism makes her less trustworthy, and asserts that even if she is reformed, there is no indication that she is "less dangerous." She herself may not understand all her motives, and may, even without realizing it, sacrifice her daughter to her desire to atone—as Archie's mother may sense in condemning her at the end (33–36).

Levine returns the deception to the narrator, at the same time as she argues that the taciturn Linda is indeed evil. In her reading, the narrator, whose whole life has been dominated by his rejection by Louisa, wants Archie to pursue Linda precisely because Louisa does not. In her view, the plot logically should focus on Linda, but the narrator stubbornly keeps his gaze on Louisa. The narrator, she argues, believes himself objective because he is writing of others, but in reality he is writing about himself, and his writing makes clear his need to maintain his view of himself as someone aggrieved beyond reparation, a view that allows him a freedom from responsibility or commitment. In the end, according to Levine, he sees Louisa as "sincere," but keeps alive his condemnation of her by projecting it onto his sister.

With a simpler approach, Geismar characterizes the tale as "a rather nice story in James's old-fashioned and sentimental vein" (70n.). Matthiessen and Murdock praise the less gentle "singleness of effect" given the story by Louisa's denunciation of her daughter to the uncle (N 75). The general impression of the tale is closer, however, to Wright's focus on its "multiplicity of ambiguities" (160). Arguing for an even greater convolution, Wagenknecht deems the tale not ambiguous but "enigmatic," and asserts that James has not given sufficient information to unravel the enigma. All of these tangled relationships have, in the evaluation of Edgar, nothing significant to say about "the general problem of manners" (47). Wright, however, although he agrees that the events are "atypical of life," argues that the frustrating search for order is a basic human experience (160). At times, it seems as if critics in their search for order simply strain for yet another permutation in the basic relationships here. Yet such a search seems part of James's intention, as he invites his reader to accompany the narrator, however fallible, in seeking to adjudicate the rights and wrongs of Louisa and Linda, of Archie and himself.

Works Cited

Primary Works
James, Henry. 1888. "Louisa Pallant." *Harper's New Monthly Magazine* 76 (February): 336–55.

————. 1888. "Louisa Pallant." *The Aspern Papers*. London and New York: Macmillan, 139–96.

————. 1908. "Louisa Pallant." *The Novels and Stories of Henry James*. New York Edition. Vol. 13, 493–550. New York: Scribner's.

Secondary Works:
Andreas, Osborn. 1948. *Henry James and the Expanding Horizon: A Study of the Meaning and Basic Themes of James's Fiction*. Seattle: University of Washington Press.

Canby, Henry Seidel. 1951. *Turn West, Turn East: Mark Twain and Henry James*. Boston: Houghton Mifflin.

Dietrichson, Jan W. 1969. *The Image of Money in the American Novel of the Gilded Age*. Oslo: Universitetsforlaget; New York: Humanities.

Edgar, Pelham. [1927] 1964. *Henry James, Man and Author*. New York: Russell & Russell.

Fadiman, Clifton, ed. 1945. *The Short Stories of Henry James*. New York: Random House.

Gale, Robert L. [1945] 1964. *The Caught Image: Figurative Language in the Fiction of Henry James*. Chapel Hill: University of North Carolina Press.

Geismar, Maxwell. 1963. *Henry James and the Jacobites*. Boston: Houghton Mifflin.

Grover, P. R. 1973. "Henry James and the Theme of the Adventuress." *Revue de Littérature Comparée*: 47 (October–December): 586–96.

Jones, Granville H. 1975. *Henry James's Psychology of Experience: Innocence, Responsibility, and Renunciation in the Fiction of Henry James*. The Hague: Mouton.

Knights, Lionel Charles. 1976. "Henry James and Human Liberty." *Explorations* 3: 24–37. Pittsburgh: University of Pittsburgh Press.

Levine, Peg. 1987. "Henry James's 'Louisa Pallant' and the Participant-Observer Narrator and Responsibility." *Mid-Hudson Language Studies* 10: 33–41.

Levy, Leo B. 1957. *Versions of Melodrama: A Study of the Fiction and Drama of Henry James, 1865–1897.* Berkeley: University of California Press.

McElderry, Bruce R., Jr. 1965. *Henry James.* New York: Twayne.

Marks, Robert. 1960. *James's Later Novels: An Interpretation.* New York: William-Frederick.

Nicoloff, P. L. 1970. "At the Bottom of All Things in Henry James's 'Louisa Pallant.'" *Studies in Short Fiction* 7 (Summer): 409–20.

Pound, Ezra. 1918. "A Shake Down." *The Little Review* 5 (August): 9–39.

Putt, S. Gorley. 1966. *Henry James: A Reader's Guide.* Ithaca, NY: Cornell University Press.

Shine, Muriel G. 1969. *The Fictional Children of Henry James.* Chapel Hill: University of North Carolina Press.

Stone, Donald David. 1972. *Novelists in a Changing World: Meredith, James, and the Transformation of English Fiction in the 1880's.* Cambridge, MA: Harvard University Press.

Tintner, Adeline R. 1985. "The Use of Stupidity." *Journal of Narrative Technique* 15 (Winter): 69–74.

Wagenknecht, Edward. 1984. *The Tales of Henry James.* New York: Frederick Ungar.

Wasserstrom, William. 1959. *Heiress of All the Ages: Sex and Sentiment in the Genteel Tradition.* Minneapolis: University of Minnesota Press.

Wegelin, Christof. 1958. *The Image of Europe in Henry James.* Dallas: Southern Methodist University Press.

Wright, Walter F. 1962. *The Madness of Art: A Study of Henry James.* Lincoln: University of Nebraska Press.

Foreign Language

Blake, Nancy. 1982. "'*Never say*': l'art du non-dit dans 'Louisa Pallant.'" *Delta* 15: 115–23.

Martin, Jacky. 1982. "Les relations énonciatives dans 'Louisa Pallant.'" *Delta* 15: 125–31.

Richard, Claude. 1982. "La Romance de Louisa Pallant." *Delta* 15: 103–13.

The Madonna of the Future

Publication History

"The Madonna of the Future" appeared first in the March 1873 issue of the *Atlantic Monthly* and was reprinted by James first in 1875 in *A Passionate Pilgrim*, again in 1879 in England in a collection bearing its title, and yet again in the 1883 Collective Edition. It is, after "A Passionate Pilgrim," the earliest of James's stories to appear in the New York Edition. It also appeared as "Le Madone de l'avenir" in the *Revue des Deux Mondes* on April 1, 1876 (Niess 93).

Circumstances of Composition, Sources, and Influences

On January 14, 1873, James's father wrote Henry that he had read the tale to the family, that "Willy pronounced it very *distingué*, Mother charming, Alice exquisite," while he himself "was very much struck with it as a whole, and admired it greatly also in parts." He had, however, to inform Henry that Howells was upset by two episodes, judging Theobald's discussion of his love and visit from his "madonna" and "his subsequent disgust of her worthlessness" to be "risky," and a final discussion by the narrator and his neighbor unnecessary. The family, the senior James relayed, thought Howells generally "too timid" but right in these cases, Alice and Mother finding the episodes "scary" and the father "disagreeable." So James's father took it upon himself to consent to their deletion in return for having the tale published in one issue (Matthiessen 1947, 122). William wrote his brother himself that he judged the revision to the tale's "advantage": the first scene might have been acceptable minus "its some what cold & repulsive details," but the second was an unnecessary "excrescence" (189–90).

Far from the scene in Paris, James was understandably dismayed at hearing that Howells thought parts of his tale "too much fashioned upon French literature" (Matthiessen 1947, 122). He wrote his father, "As far as I can remember the 'immoral' episodes don't artistically affront. With such a standard of propriety, it makes it a bad look out ahead for imaginative writing. For what class of minds is it that such very timorous scruples are thought necessary?" Nevertheless, he considered his father "very right to make all convenient concessions" and acknowledged Howells's superior knowledge of public taste (*Letters* 1, 333–34). On March 10 Howells wrote James that the story was a success, and himself applauded its "well-managed pathos." But while he spoke of it as "a bravely solid and excellent piece of work," he confessed he still objected to the refrain of "cats and monkey" as its "sole blemish" (1979, 17–18).

As the incident above perhaps indicates, James was not yet a fully established writer of fiction. Putt finds it noteworthy that such an early art tale is one of failure, and several critics have read in the story a reflection of James's anxiety about his career as he moved out of his apprenticeship (214; e.g., Brodhead 131; Tanner 1963; Geismar 17). Matthiessen more particularly ties James's fears to his ill-health at the time, while Horne calls to mind James's early attempt to be a painter (*Major* 1944, 29; Horne 35). Remarking on the disjunction between idealism and artistry in the tale, Kraft sees in it James's worries that he could not write as "effectively" as "less idealistic" artists can (78). Vaid sees in it James's attempt to sort out issues of popularity and perfectionism, which, he adds, certainly failed to impede James's own production. The tale is not, Vaid judges, autobiographical (14, 27). Similarly, Theobald's absolute idealism is, according to Maves, more extreme than James's early romanticism (28). Horne, however, argues that the characters are so scantly developed that the ideas in the tale "appear clearly" as James's, particularly Theobald's distinction between the "critical and the ideal" methods of viewing art (26, 30)

While Josephson and Kelley mark in the tale James's love for Italy, Charles Anderson cites to different effect James's remarks to his brother William in 1872, that if he stayed too long in Italy he would cease to be creative (Josephson 95; Kelley 151; Anderson 13). Jefferson, on the other hand, contrasts Theobald's despair over the lot of American artists with James's more optimistic declaration in an 1867 letter to T. S. Perry that being born an American is "a great blessing . . . an excellent preparation for culture." Still, he acknowledges that James's attitude may have fluctuated between the two extremes ([1960] 1971, 10, 16). According to Lebowitz, James at the time was seeking to "rescue" from America what was useful in it for his art, namely the "moral elevation of relationship" there (113). As Buitenhuis points out, James returned to America not long after writing the story, writing in 1881 of his decision, that he thought "it my duty to attempt to live at home before I should grow older, and not take for granted too much that Europe alone was possible; especially as Europe for me then meant simply Italy, where I had some very discouraged hours" (69–70).

James's experience offered other sources for Theobald. Falk points to two possibilities: the American expatriate artist William Wetmore Story and a "seedy and sickly American" James once encountered in the Uffizi (70). Similarly, Edel points to James's meeting in Venice on the night of his arrival an American painter, who impressed James with his innocent appreciation of the beauty around him (*Life* 2, 74). Tintner offers three possible models: the appropriately named Raffaello Boniauti, who could never complete his *Temptation on the Mount*; his American student Elihu Vedder; and Washington Allston, whose unfinished masterpiece *Belshazzar's Feast* impressed on James the need for the American artist to head for Europe (1986, 29; 1987, 69–70).

The unsympathetic Mrs. Coventry dismisses the work of Theobald as likely to be "scarce more than in that terrible little tale of Balzac's—a mere mass of incoherent scratches and daubs, a mumble of dead paint!" (CT 3, 28). As Kelley first noted, Mrs. Coventry is referring to *Le Chef-d'oeuvre inconnu*; however, beginning with Kelley's analysis of the change in paintings from portrait to madonna, critics have tended to emphasize the differences between the two tales (149–51). According to Vaid, Theobald's poverty makes his situation "more terrible" than that of Balzac's artist, Frenhofer, while Voss stresses the new dimension added by making Theobald an American (Vaid 26; Voss 130). Adams, however, emphasizes the identity of the "disease" that kills both artists—their idealistic approach to art (464). The contrast between the two types of artist within the tale is, Falk notes, an addition to Balzac, but he adds that some of the "fleshy underpinning" of Balzac's influence may have been lost to Howells's editing (70–72). To Grover, while both Frenhofer and Theobald are artistic idealists, Frenhofer remains in a "Hobbesian" world of struggle and unanalyzed desire, while James's artist occupies a "Kantian and idealistic" world of moral choice consciously articulated if not resolved (24–28). Charney looks at the change in the type of model: in Balzac the purpose of the model's life ended with the artist's, while here Serafina is part of the life that goes on without Theobald (72). Adding another layer to the influence, Niess offers James's tale as an intermediate source for Zola's *L'Œuvre*, usually judged to be indebted to the Balzac tale, pointing out that Zola's failed painter's only good work was of his dead son, even as Theobald's only work is of Serafina's dying son.

The narrator is more sympathetic than Mrs. Coventry. Citing not Balzac but "that charming speech of the Florentine painter in Alfred de Musset's *Lorenzaccio*," he quotes to Theobald the description of the painter's days in his studio with sorties only to church and the home of his "sweetheart" (CT 3, 30). Again, Kelley first drew attention to the allusion and the influence of Musset in depicting Theobald's artistic isolation (149–51; also Matthiessen "Portrait" 1944, 12; Falk 70; Edel CT 3, 8). Nevertheless, Kelley argues that James drew on Balzac and Musset only to round out his story, which was inspired primarily by "the Madonnas of Florence" (151)

Theobald himself quotes lines from Browning's "Pictor Ignotus." Telling the narrator "I've never sold a picture!," he declares, "At least no merchant traffics in my heart!" (CT 3, 16). In Ross's view, however, both James's artist and Browning's are deceiving themselves by hiding their failures under the guise of principle, and Theobald is not only less productive than the "pictor ignotus" but more concerned with fame. In fact, to Ross, Theobald is more reminiscent of Browning's Andrea del Sarto, who opined, "In this world, who can do a thing, will not; / And who would do it, cannot, I perceive: / Yet the will's somewhat—somewhat, too, the power / —And thus we half-men struggle." Theobald has the will, Andrea the power—neither are whole, in contrast to Raphael, the artist against whom each measures himself and falls short. Wagenknecht adds that Theobald's failure is in not taking Browning's lesson on "the glory of the imperfect" (3).

Matthiessen cites Harry Levin on the contrast between Balzac's *Le Chef-d'oeuvre inconnu* and Hawthorne's "The Artist of the Beautiful," the first emphasizing vitality, the second spirituality, and traces the difference to the intensity of American artists stemming from the general indifference of their country to art ("Portrait" 1944, 13). Other critics have drawn parallels between the two American tales. While Vaid emphasizes the greater realism of James's work, Long finds the concluding refrain recalling the mocking of Owen Warland (Vaid 26–27; Long 26–27). Vielledent argues that while the two artists are alike in their perfectionism, Theobald is hampered not only by his superior spirituality but by his inferior intelligence, unable to recognize that Seraphina is no frail butterfly (35). Charles Anderson, who reports the existence of a "legend" of "the American 'artist-failure'" in Italy, draws a connection with another of Hawthorne's artists, Hilda, who in *The Marble Faun* abandons her original painting to produce copies of classic paintings, suffering like Theobald from the overwhelming influence of the Italian past (13).

Matthiessen sees James as arguing that such idealism as Theobald's is insufficient in itself. Faced with the examples of the many transcendentalists in the generation before him, including his own father, whose genius never quite transcribed itself into concrete form, James, Matthiessen argues, may well have been afraid of joining their ranks ("Portrait" 1944, 13; 1943, 533). Rovit also sees James distancing himself from the previous generation of American writers, arguing that in his tales of artists of the 1870s and 1880s James portrayed such artists as Theobald, Henry St. George, and even Aspern as somehow "deficient" as people, even as he was deciding that the American artists Hawthorne and Emerson were "deficient as artists because they seemed so successful as human beings" (438). Although he does not seem to regard the comparison as intentional, McCarthy contrasts Theobald's obsessive approach to his art with James's assessment that George Sand achieved true "style" through "performing the act of life" (41).

Overtones of Ruskin have been noted in the tale (Beebe 201; Winner 103). More particularly Berland points to the influence of Pater's 1873 *Studies in the History of the Renaissance* in the "elaborate impressionistic" description of the Raphael "Madonna of the Chair" (26). In the narrator's words, "The figure melts away the spectator's mind into a sort of passionate tenderness which he knows not whether he has given to heavenly purity or to earthly charm" (CT 3, 19–20). Thus, Curtsinger finds the significance of the painting its combination of earth and heaven, which eludes Theobald (23). Tintner judges it a particularly dangerous example to follow, "nothing of manner, of method, nothing, almost, of style; it blooms . . . as if it were an immediate exhalation of genius," and so requires an equal genius to match it (CT 3, 19). Mrs. Coventry, who goes about wearing a brooch copied after the painting, Tintner finds absurd in her artistic affectation (1986, 27–30). Similarly, Long denotes both Mrs. Coventry with her copy and the ironically named Serafina as "spurious" Madonnas (25). Kaplan emphasizes the implied contrast between Raphael, whose models were his lovers, and Theobald, who refuses to acknowledge his model's earthiness (258). More sympathetically, Horne senses a "strong" if unintentional "Platonic flavour" in the tale and in Theobald's idealism, his desire not to avoid reality for ideas, but to "present the Idea behind reality" (31). The tale also makes mention of Cellini's Perseus, and Tintner draws attention to the appropriateness of its reference to the memoirs in which Cellini recalled the many difficulties of the statue's production (1987, 54–55).

The phrase "cats and monkeys" Melchiori associates with the "goats and monkeys" of Shakespeare's *Othello* (9). Powers points to loftier echoes from the Renaissance, seeing in Theobald's declaration that "just as the truly religious soul is always at worship, the genuine artist is always in labor" a reflection of the tradition that identifies artistic and human creation, as in Sidney's speaking of himself as "great with child to speak" (1970, 107). The relationship between Theobald and Seraphina recalls some of the miscommunication and admiration between Don Quixote and his Dulcinea.

"The Madonna of the Future" produced its own ripples of influence. In December 1886 James reported to Charles Eliot Norton his pleasure at Philip Burne-Jones's having painted "a very beautiful little picture" on the subject of "The Madonna of the Future," which not only sold quickly but produced another commission for the same subject (*Letters* 3, 147). Jeffares provides further evidence of the reception of James's idea from a 1884 novel by Blanche Willis Howard, *Guenn, A Wave on the Breton Coast*, which assigns to its group of artists "unrevealed . . . half-finished romances, tragedies with the fifth act undetermined, unwritten poems, pathetic Madonnas of the future" (130).

Edith Wharton also responded to the tale, according to Bell, who notes, however, that while the American painter in "The Recovery" is initially crushed by the weight of European art, as are Theobald and Lance Mallow of "The Tree of Knowledge," he recovers by following the remedy prescribed by the narrator—"the only thing that helps is to do something fine"—and so declares, "Nothing left? . . . There's everything!" (232–33). Bellman discerns several parallels—including madonnas, struggling painters, and contrasting suitors—between James's tale and two modern works, Bernard Malamud's "Still Life" and Robert Towers's *The Monkey Watcher* (52).

Relation to Other Works

In 1875 James would send another American artist, Roderick Hudson, abroad to seek success, only to be in the words of Nathalia Wright "virtually paralyzed both artistically and sexually" by Italy (223). Roderick, like Theobald, Maves writes, idealizes Italy and art, particularly as represented by a woman, and is destroyed by the discovery of that woman's imperfections (49). The initial problem of both men, according to Winner, is their "superstitious valuation of Europe" (116). Despite Roderick's tragic end, Horne sees James as having moved in the novel from the asceticism of the tale toward a view that the artist must seek experience (33). According to Anderson, James himself acknowledged the connection between Roderick and Theobald in an 1874 letter to Howells, which said of the novel that it treated "a theme I have had in my head a long time and once attempted to write something about." For both novel and story, Anderson cites the description in James's biography of William Wetmore Story of an Italy that provided its resident Americans with

> a sense of the sterner realities as sweetened as if, at the perpetual banquet, it had been some Borgia cup concocted for the strenuous mind. But the sensitive soul in general drained it, and, for the most part, at first, in innocent delight, without a misgiving or a reserve. Moreover, as most of those who sickened or died of it never knew they were ill or dead, the feast had never the funeral air, and the guests sat at table to the end.

Anderson finds Theobald "almost a case history" of such a "sensitive" and "sickened" soul and Roderick, despite his eventual collapse, a representative of "the strenuous mind" equal to it (13, 24; also Jeffares 44–45). Auchard, on the other hand, judges Theobald's failure more honorable than Roderick's, while Markow-Totevy objects that James handled the encounter between American artist and European past unsuccessfully in both (Auchard 36; Markow-Totevy 27). Commenting on the particular dangers of Italy for the artist as presented in tale, novel, and biography, Holder remarks that while James did not fall apart like Roderick or Theobald, he found it difficult to write in Rome (271). Edel draws particular attention to a passage in which Roderick worries, "What if the watch should run down and you should lose the key? . . . Such things have been, and the poor devils to whom they happened have had to grin and bear it. The whole matter of genius is a mystery" (*Life* 2, 176–77). Several critics, beginning with Walter Wright, have found resemblances between the realism of Gloriani in the early novel and that of the cats-and-monkeys sculptor (Wright 90; also Stone 193; Winner 103; Maves 53).

One theme of *Roderick Hudson* and "The Madonna of the Future"—the overwhelming influence of the past in Italy—can also be found treated, less effectively according to Anderson, in "Adina" and "The Last of the Valerii" (13, 24). Churchill also sees the two supernatural tales as underscoring the message of "The Madonna of the Future" that American creativity and Italian sources of inspiration are essentially incompatible (159). Still, according to Maves, the tale is superior to the earlier "Travelling Companions" and "At Isella" because it separates narrator and protagonist. Thus the "haze" or romanticism is all Theobald's, although Maves remarks that even as it shows the danger of idealizing Italy and Art, the tale leaves the two "nearly synonymous" (26–28, 32). Theobald himself laments that "the soil of American perception is a poor little barren artificial deposit," a view that may be echoed in Madame Merle's dismissal of Americans as "mere parasites without our feet in the soil" (CT 3, 15). Theobald also anticipates Little Bilham of *The Ambassadors*, to whom "study had been fatal."

Even without the international element, "The Madonna of the Future" as the story of an artist has much company in the Jamesian canon, although Segal considers it unique in its focus on the artist's art, as opposed to a focus on his relationships, seen in such tales as "The Story of a Masterpiece" and "The Liar" (112). McElderry links it not only with two other European tales about art, "The Sweetheart of M. Briseux" and "Benvolio," but with the English "Broken Wings" and "The Tree of Knowledge," which treat the failed artist more lightly (33–34, 122–23). Auchard sees in both this tale and "The Real Thing" a "preoccupation" with "absence" shared with the ghost tales, finding in Theobald an ability to dress up a blank imaginatively similar to Isabel Archer's, who loved Osmond "for his very poverties" (36, 39, 61). Osmond himself is included by Kaplan as a member of Theobald's "famished race," along with the narrator of *The Aspern Papers* and the "cold, philistine Newsomes," all of whom are unable to balance nature and culture (263, 272). Like Dr. Sloper of *Washington Square*, Stone argues, Theobald takes his proud realism to extremes (203).

To Horne this tale, like "The Tone of Time" and "The Middle Years," demonstrates the need for an artist to produce out of a direct experience of life, even as it shows, like "The Real Thing," that "the represented," however preferable to the real, relies upon it. The idea of the "divine afflatus" in the story, she indicates, is more unusual in James, except for "The Next Time," in which Limbert's case also exhibits the coming together of James's "morality of art and his morality of life" in a view that consistency dedicated to a high standard is the chief virtue. It is also, she adds, a demanding one, according to which St. George of "The Lesson of the Master" fails (29–31, 33). Both

"The Madonna of the Future" and "The Figure in the Carpet," according to Feidelson, show the "breakdown of imaginative life" into "opposite versions." While the later tale, he asserts, is "less grim," its conclusions are more sweeping, casting doubt not only on "the genesis of art," but the very concept of "imaginative reality" (52, 55).

Theobald's injunction that "a great work needs silence, privacy, mystery even" is cited by Kappeler in connection with the narrator's private pursuit in *The Sacred Fount* (118–19). If one put together Theobald and the maker of statuettes "there would have been no problem," writes Horne, who sees the split between two halves of an artist again in "The Private Life." Still, she observes in the tale the "same plea" for a proper appreciation of art as in "The Lesson of the Master," "The Figure in the Carpet," and "The Next Time," and the same indictment of society's actual use of art, sharpened in this tale by comparison with the fruitful collaboration of art and society during the Italian Renaissance. James's own rejection by the unappreciative public, Horne writes, was clearly "painful" for him, as evident in "The Figure in the Carpet" and "The Lesson of the Master" (29, 35). Similarly, Powers locates the conflict between the world's valuing of productivity in the artist and the true artist's emphasis on being also in "The Next Time," "The Coxon Fund," and "The Tree of Knowledge." Mrs. Coventry, like Mr. Highmore and George Gravener, wants to know what the artist has to "show." Mallow, Highmore, and the sculptor have plenty to "show," but Limbert and Theobald are the true artists (1970, 104–6; also Horne 148).

To Gabriel Nash in *The Tragic Muse* "having something to show's such a poor business. It's a kind of confession of failure." In Powers's view, *The Tragic Muse* and other later works help dispel the ambiguity of the early tale by putting the artist's conflict in terms of public and private duty (1962, 129–32). Nash's theorizing, however, works against him, according to Stevenson, who argues that James illustrates through both Theobald and Gabriel the need for the artist to have something to show for his ideas (72). Similarly, Lebowitz links Nash and Theobald as exhibiting an "artistic waste" similar to the missed opportunities of Strether and Marcher (18). While the usual comparison is between Theobald and Gabriel, Berland compares Theobald's situation to that of Nick Dormer at the novel's end (e.g., Stone 320; Berland 184 n.49).

Neither a tale of the artist or of the international, "The Beast in the Jungle," Hoffmann observes, shares many of the elements of this tale—the hero's *idée fixe*, his failure, and its revelation—while still illustrating the difference between the short story and the novella (103). McCarthy sees in both the same admonishment to seize the day using the materials at hand, and the same "desolate" end for the hero who fails to do so (40). In his linking of Theobald and Marcher, Auchard asserts that James is more censorious of the latter, remarking that the "cats and monkeys" refrain represents an emptier approach to life than Theobald's, while the tiger of "The Beast in the Jungle" represents Marcher's own emptiness (37).

The portrayal of the narrator H—, according to Tanner, shows James working to perfect "the urbane speculative narrator" (1963). Sharp observes how he serves as a male confidant for the protagonist, like the narrator of "Eugene Pickering" (xxv, 4). His lack of experience, however, Jones contends, invalidates his vision, making him comparable to the narrator of "The Diary of a Man of Fifty" (198). Cornwell's attack is even sharper. She holds the narrator responsible for Theobald's death through his well-intentioned determination that the artist see his work honestly, even as the narrator of "The Author of Beltraffio" convinced Ambient's wife to reexamine his work and so contributed to the death of the son (146–47). Similarly, Segal classes both the observer here and in "The Author of Beltraffio" with those of *Lady Barbarina* and *The Turn of the Screw* on the grounds that they bring on each tale's crisis (236). Vaid, however, maintains that the narrator here is "not a monster of curiosity" as in *The Sacred Fount* and *The Aspern Papers*. And with an enviable critical naïveté, while defending the narrator of *The Turn of the Screw*, he cites the failure of critics to offer equally "perverse" readings of other tales, including both this tale, "The Author of Beltraffio," and "Four Meetings," all of which had had or would soon have their narrators challenged (15, 252).

The character of Serafina, in contrast, as Nathalia Wright points out, is portrayed with an intellectual simplicity typical of James's Italians (237). Without considering her nationality, Sharp considers the "distinctly maternal" Serafina an "outstanding exception" to James's typical portrayal of intelligent women (xiv).

Interpretation and Criticism

Facing the richness of Florence's past, the American Theobald declares to the American narrator:

> We are the disinherited of art! We are condemned to be superficial! We are excluded from the magic circle. The soil of American perception is a poor little barren, artificial deposit. . . . An American, to excel, has just ten times as much to learn as a European. We lack the deeper sense. We have neither taste, nor tact, nor force. How should we have them? Our crude and garish climate, our silent past, our deafening present, the constant pressure about us of unlovely circumstance, are as void of all that nourishes and prompts and inspires the artist, as my sad heart is void of bitterness in saying so! We poor aspirants must live in perpetual exile. (CT 3, 14–15)

To Geismar the speech not only expresses James's own view, it also betrays the "bitterness" Theobald disavows (17–18). McElderry, in contrast, sees its attribution to Theobald as discrediting (33). Horne, more generally, objects to critics' emphasis on the international in the tale and sees Theobald's own Americanness as evidence against his complaint of America's "artistic unfruitfulness" (27 n.2, 34–35). If Theobald seems a less than satisfactory counterexample, the narrator offers a rebuttal: "Nothing is so idle as to talk about our want of a nutritive soil, of opportunity, of inspiration, and all the rest of it. The worthy part is to do something fine! There's no law in our glorious Constitution against that. Invent, create, achieve! No matter if you've to study fifty times as much as one of these! What else are you an artist for?" (CT 3, 15).

This second speech, less frequently cited, as Buitenhuis observes, is in his opinion evidence against those who claim that the first proves James's dismissal of America. Buitenhuis, however, also maintains that the narrator in it "ignores" the real issues Theobald, and James, faced. He points, too, to the ambiguity implicit in the barrenness of American perception, a fact that could refer either to America itself or to its past writers, who had failed to create adequate "schemata" for treating it (69–70). Unrue, however, pictures the narrator as proving the "inefficacy" of Theobald's complaint (249). Lebowitz also cites both speeches. The first, she states, shows that Theobald is not sustained by his European idealism. The American view of the narrator, on the other hand, she writes, is supported by Roderick Hudson's declaration that "It's a wretched business . . . this virtual quarrel of ours with our own country," and his proclamation of "an American day" (112–13). Holder, too, takes the rebuke as evidence that art was possible in America (64; see also *Life* 2, 36–37).

Maves, in contrast, highlights the tension between the two views, and contends that James did not yet want to resolve the issue. He sees him in this tale extending "his view of Italy as artifice" through his first depiction of an artist in Italy, or rather "an artist *manqué*," even as he paints for the first time a realistic Italy, not simply the Italy of tourists. The relationship of the "passionate pilgrim," according to Maves, to his "idol" is now one of "victim and victimizer": Theobald is his "own worst enemy," but not, Maves judges, alone responsible for his fate, as Serafina is complicit in supplying her foolish American with romance (27–30).

While Nathalia Wright points out that Theobald's "high aesthetic fever" marks him as an American, Buckler and Sklare contend that it is not an "absolute requirement" for the tale's aims that Theobald and the narrator be American (Wright 223). In their reading, the setting of Florence by itself contributes to the central theme, namely, what is necessary for a Renaissance, a theme they acknowledge was designed with "particular meaning" for

American readers. James, they write, believed a "widespread devotion to a vision of artistic perfection" was needed for a second Renaissance (416–18). In Vaid's reading, the issue is not between America and Europe but "reality and art." Although he acknowledges that the narrator connects Theobald's "extreme idealism" and his Americanness, Vaid points out that in Theobald's final speech, summing himself up as a "dawdler," he does not mention his nationality and so takes on the larger role of the "disillusioned artist" (20–21, 25–26).

In turning the issue to Theobald as an individual rather than an American, McElderry, like Vaid, considers Theobald's complaint against America less significant than a later speech lamenting his own inactivity: "We talents that can't act, that can't do nor dare! We take it out in talk, in plans and promises, in study, in visions! But our visions, let me tell you . . . have a way of being brilliant, and a man has not lived in vain who has seen the things I have!" Still, as McElderry observes, the narrator, despite his recognition of Theobald's weakness, protects him by shielding his canvas from Mrs. Coventry (34). Critics seem less certain whether to shield Theobald or to expose him. Andreas, for example, argues that Theobald possesses the gift of expressing his enthusiasm, but also sees that power, which can only treat "created art" not create it, as ultimately unsatisfying. Theobald, he adds, procrastinates not only artistically but sexually as well, in his relationship to Serafina (146). Edel gives as the moral of the tale that the only way for an artist to avoid wasting his life is to be virtually the opposite of Theobald, "hard, unyielding, resolute, masculine, and if necessary an egotist" (CT 3, 8). For Kaplan, the artist tales show that the "problems of art and life are the same"—both require balance, a combination of imagination and actuality. By these rules, Theobald, who refuses to "be fed by gross substance," fails in relationships both with his model and his art. Because he fails to distinguish between the ideal subject and the imperfect model, Kaplan asserts, he "cannot reconcile them either" (257–58).

To many critics, despite his failure, Theobald is an admirable character. Winner, for example, contends that such critics as Falk "overemphasize the anti-idealism" of the tale (185 n.4). In his defense, Dietrichson emphasizes Theobald's poverty (125). Horne, meanwhile, objects to Andreas's reading as a "misinterpretation" that does not "do justice" to his love for Serafina. An awareness of the tale's espousal of a "higher vision" in art, she argues, explains the narrator's relationship with Serafina as platonic not simply in the "non-sexual" sense, but in the sense that Theobald has seen in the "particular" of Serafina a Platonic "absolute." Thus, in response to McCarthy, who criticizes Theobald for waiting for his "ideal impression," Horne affirms that Theobald has already received that impression from Serafina. What holds him back is simply the lack of "inner confidence" to express it. The reader, she asserts, is "not allowed to doubt" that Theobald is artist enough to do so, as his powers are evident in his drawing of the Bambino. Still, like all defenders of Theobald, she must eventually account for the blank canvas. Citing Theobald's distinction between artists "who were pure because they were innocent and those who were pure because they were strong," she places Theobald in the first category, and agrees with Stevenson that the artist must be willing to lose his innocence to experience life, in order to render it as art. Even as Theobald speaks of "the irrepressible discord between conception and result," he acknowledges its silencing in Raphael, who serves, Horne writes, as evidence that it is "possible to express one's self adequately in art." The moral of the tale becomes an admonition that the "artist must not hold himself back from his work." Nevertheless, in her view, Theobald invokes more pathos than criticism. Nor does he, she contends, "die entirely broken." His strength is his power of perception, which serves as "the link between art and life" (26–34). Similarly, according to Auchard, James does not "sharply condemn" Theobald, despite his immaturity and incompleteness. Theobald, Auchard argues, through his passion lives "sufficiently" (37).

Buckler and Sklare also see James as praising Theobald, and see James's demonstrating through him the "notion that art of consummate, sublime perfection is the product of a deep intuitive perception." The transfer of idea to canvas is, they write, in comparison a "mechanical act": Theobald has taken "the truly important first step." James's respect for Theobald, Buckler and Sklare write, is evident in the contrast between the narrator's attitude to him with that of Mrs. Coventry and Serafina. The superiority of the "vision" of first-rate art over "completed second-rate," meanwhile, is seen in the contrast with the sculptor. In their conclusion, Theobald's "mildly psychotic dedication to art is an evangelical protest against the indifferent-to-art world in which he finds himself. The Madonna of the future—the spiritual motherhood needed for sublime artistic rebirth—is still to appear, but not until there are fewer Mrs. Coventrys and Serafinas and more Theobalds and believers in Theobald" (416–18).

The "mildly psychotic" Theobald, with his passion for beauty and for art, has also generated a fair number of mixed reviews. Beebe argues that the tale shows James's belief that the artist needs not only dreams but craft (201–2). Perosa shifts the emphasis even further, arguing that the tale demonstrates James's opinion that art needed "technical application more than a tumultuous experience of life" (93–94 n.18). Grover, in contrast, observes that "the power to have visions is part of the creative process. Art is forever an attack upon the inarticulate—because it cannot be expressed." Still he points to an all-important "gap" in the tale "between aspiration and performance" (27). Maini sees James showing the "ambivalent nature of art" in Theobald's ridiculous "inflated aestheticism," which cannot totally erase admiration for "a passion so pure and abiding" if not productive (119). Citing the narrator's view of Theobald—"A creature more unsullied by the accidents of life it's impossible to conceive"—Jones indicates his sense that such innocence may keep Theobald's inspiration from being "relevant" or perhaps even "communicable," a fact Theobald himself recognizes in forgiving the narrator for his harsh news (198–99). Similarly, Sicker, while judging Theobald himself as a sympathetic character, sees James illustrating through him the danger of static images of love that deny the change necessary to life, however frightening such change may be (30–32).

Like Grover, Maves points to a "gap" in the tale between ideal and actual, one emphasized by the detachment of the narrator from the subject. Both the title and the treatment are, in his view, ironic. The tale is a "study in extremes," and the idealist Theobald, having lost the connection between the world and art, is a sterile half. When the narrator shows him what really is, Maves records, he destroys Theobald's ideal, and so Theobald. Serafina, a cynical pragmatist, on the other hand, is "perfectly right about Theobald." Like Andreas, Maves sees a sexual as well as an artistic incompleteness about Theobald, and points to the failed synthesis between the sculptor's animalism and Theobald's idealism about sex. The possible combination of extremes, Maves argues, glimpsed in Theobald's cry for his "other half," is still "hypothetical" in the tale (26–32).

The presence of the contrasting maker of statuettes serves an important purpose in the tale. According to Edgar's early judgment, "his vulgar facility brings into still stronger relief" Theobald's "incapacity" (175). Putt, however, stresses the bitterness with which his success is treated, and brings to bear James's disdain for the "life-like" in art (215). Most critics, indeed, see Serafina's lover serving to make the flawed Theobald look good by comparison (e.g., Matthiessen "Portrait" 1944, 13; McElderry 34; Wagenknecht 3). As Tyler writes, despite the warning against Theobald's idling, the portrait of his compeer "leaves no doubt as to which path of 'truth' James considered the most honorable" (226–27). In Powers's analysis, the reader is at first tempted to impatience with Theobald and approval of the productive maker of cats and monkeys, who turns out, however, to be simply too crude, as is exemplified in his treatment of Serafina, while the unrealistic Theobald at least understands what an artist ought to *be*, and treats his muse Serafina with respect (1970, 104–5; 1962, 128–31). Falk speculates that Howells's censorship may have further skewed the case against the modeler, but admits that Theobald's "pathetic" idealism would in any case have remained preferable to the modeler's productive cynicism (71–72).

Howells continued his objection to the sculptor's refrain, "Cats and monkeys, monkeys and cats; all human life is there," dismissing it as of "but wandering purport," out of key with the otherwise poignant tale, notable only for its "excess" ([1875] 1961, 71). Other critics, however, such as Maves, have emphasized the necessity of the sculptor, not simply as a contrast to Theobald, but as his missing, complementary half. Horne argues that his presence "turns the story from a romantic fantasy into a powerful ironic treatment of the problem of artistic creation" because the two men together represent the necessary halves of an artist (28–29). The story, Powers contends, advocates not a choice between the two men, but a compromise between the two extremes of action and artistry (1969, 6). Tanner provides an interesting, if mistaken, gloss on the split, stating that Theobald, incapable of a masterpiece, is "better" at making the cynical pieces: "a kind of vengeful anti-idealism to make up for that vacant canvas" (1985, 15).

Feidelson makes perhaps the strongest case for the sculptor. In his reading, Theobald "scarcely does justice to him or to his half of the world." The sculptor has imagination, variety, and, like Theobald, deals in "types." He represents a genuine world of experience, and his values "point toward something positive." Theobald, in contrast, finds it difficult to "conceive of the secular mode except in its lowest form." Even Theobald recognizes that Raphael's Madonna was once, in the narrator's words, "some pretty young woman." The type of the Madonna, Feidelson contends, is itself not "one of the eternal needs of man's heart" as Theobald asserts, but only a product of a certain time. Feidelson takes as particularly significant the tale's presentation of contrasting images of human strength in Michelangelo's David and Cellini's Perseus. Theobald himself "momentarily glimpses the artist as Perseus" in his recognition that Michelangelo, in his statue of Lorenzo d'Medici, "did his best at a venture, and his venture's immortal." Still, Feidelson acknowledges, if Michelangelo's statue is simply a higher version of the sculptor's commercial concerns, "there must be a basic shift of emphasis somewhere." While Theobald's constant idealistic "work" produces nothing, the sculptor's produces nothing of value. In the meantime, the narrator's knowledge of Theobald's case casts a sad light on the masterpieces of the past. Even as they continue to stand for the possibility of genuine completed art, Feidelson observes, the narrator sees in them now some "fatal flaw at the heart of all imaginative triumph" that speaks of the element of chance and "sheer fabrication" in art. Even if "contrived," the conflict here, Feidelson concludes, helps elaborate James's sense of the "problematical in art" in a genuine way (52–55).

The narrator himself, according to the approving Thorp, is James's first use of a "fine central intelligence" to mediate between the reader and the author (xv). Looking at the use of various points of view to dramatize the tale's artistic problems, Wegelin considers the narrator's closest to James's, "detached" but ultimately sympathetic to Theobald (33). In Vaid's assessment, the narrator, as typical of James, is "more of a method and less of a character." A bit of "the busybody," he "sheds his skepticism" along with the reader. When the narrator tells Theobald that Serafina is old, however, Vaid states, he "becomes instrumental to the drama" and introduces a new element of "remorse." In the end, despite "his own intellectual superiority," the narrator moves from "amused disapproval" to "compassion," a move the reader is intended to imitate. Throughout, Vaid asserts, the narrator remains a "thoroughly reliable witness," his involvement in the plot at one point serving simply to "justify" his presence. It would, he affirms, be "perverse" to blame the narrator for Theobald's death (14–25, 252). Nevertheless, Stone, while casting the narrator as a rational midpoint between Theobald's romanticism and the sculptor's cynicism, also argues that his implication in Theobald's death creates a perhaps unintentional ambiguity (190).

Serafina's role in Theobald's life is a large one, but a smaller one in criticism. Howells, however, particularly praised James's restraint in the portraiture of the vulgar madonna, the way in which he kept her from becoming a caricature by showing her "dim sense" of Theobald's value (1961, 71). Slabey is also charitable to her character, pointing out that she is not a hypocrite in her relationship to Theobald, but sincerely kind and generous (98). Matheson sees her role as more circumscribed, writing that she "plays almost to the point of absurdity the role of Woman as Inspiration." Serafina, she asserts, "could represent the eternal Feminine, combining in herself both its benign and sinister aspect" typical of Jamesian "dualism" (230 n.2). Both Serafina and Mrs. Coventry, Jefferson observes, give evidence of James's "growing mastery of national types," Mrs. Coventry representing, according to Winner, the "lip service" society gives to art ([1960] 1971, 15; Winner 118).

The tale begins not in the voice of the narrator, H—, but with a framing prologue Vaid finds significant in its indication of the tale's "pathetic conclusion" (13–14). Although James used similar double frames in such works as *The Turn of the Screw*, Buckler and Sklare call it an "afterthought" or "incompletely executed forethought" since it is not returned to in the end (416). Vaid also finds fault with the conclusion, finding the tale after the visit to the Pitti Palace "unnecessary" and too neat (26). Similarly, Daiches argues that the death of Theobald is badly handled, a problem he finds typical of the early stories (573). Typical also of the style of the early tales, according to Smith, is the tale's use of mostly simple sentences rather than compound or complex ones. Smith judges their use appropriate here as the simple sentence emphasizes the "uniqueness of things." The unique thing here—the projected painting—never comes to be, an indication, Smith speculates, that James came to see "the failure of uniqueness," a recognition he later reflected in a turn away from the simple sentence (162–63).

From his friends and family, James's tale received high marks. Howells praised its "unity and completeness" and his brother William called it "altogether . . . a masterpiece" (Howells 1979, 18; James 190). Early critics such as Beach and Edgar praised it for its depiction of Florence, and of the artist Theobald (Beach 187; Edgar 175). Howells declared, "Every figure in it is a real character, and has some business there" (1979, 18). Others, however, such as Buckler and Sklare, charge that the characters, including Theobald, remain undeveloped, leaving the tale's focus on ideas (416; also Matthiessen 1943, 533). Still, "The Madonna of the Future" has been judged one of the best of the tales of the early period (e.g., Richardson 485–86; Buitenhuis 69; Maves 26). Stone, indeed, speaks of it as James's first masterpiece (189). Rebecca West called the tale "admirable," but like Garnett "uncharacteristic" of James (West 28; Garnett viii). Kraft locates more serious flaws in the tale, charging that such high estimates are inflated by the story's biographical interest (78).

Even as the tale's success has received varying estimates, so has Theobald's. Feidelson speaks of the "indubitable fact of successful art" that seems so to witness against Theobald. But in the story there is also the evidence that Theobald himself could create art in the drawing he did of Serafina's dying child. Designating the story's theme as "the vanished muse" in the modern world, Curtsinger sees the sculptor failing by disregarding the need for a muse. In contrast, Theobald's search to capture a muse, he writes, while vain, gains the sympathy of the narrator and of James. Curtsinger also observes that Theobald is given the ability to capture Serafina's baby in a drawing, if not a painting, of "dimpled elegance and grace . . . and boldness" reminiscent of Correggio if not of Raphael (22–27; CT 3, 34). Beebe, too, comments on how Theobald's portrait of the child shows him to be both sincere and talented (201–2; also Horne). In drawing the baby, Theobald has completed half his masterpiece, even as he sees himself as half an artist. Later, in *The Tragic Muse*, James would have his characters speak of portraiture as ruling out love; in "The Liar" and "The Story of a Masterpiece," he would show the dangerous consequences of the mixture of the two. In painting the child, not the mother, Theobald is, perhaps, avoiding the complications of mature sexuality and artistry. But he produces an endearing human testament, even as the drawing of the young Gabrielle de Bergerac, the masterpiece of the man who loved her, survives the death of both artist and subject. In *The Portrait of a Lady*, the very modern Harriet Stackpole's favorite painting is a madonna by Correggio in which Mary claps her hands at the infant Christ. The mingling of art and life are evident in the drawing, even as the mingling of sadness and triumph. The drawing of the baby shows one of the chief purposes of art, one that even Feidelson might recognize as "one of the eternal needs of man's heart," the preservation of the human images we love.

Works Cited

Primary Works
James, Henry. 1873. "The Madonna of the Future." *Atlantic Monthly* 31 (March): 276–97.

———. 1875. "The Madonna of the Future." *A Passionate Pilgrim*. Boston: Osgood, 261–97.

————. 1879. "The Madonna of the Future." *The Madonna of the Future and Other Tales*. London: Macmillan.

————. 1883. "The Madonna of the Future." Collective Edition. Vol. 14. London: Macmillan.

————. 1908. "The Madonna of the Future." *The Novels and Tales of Henry James*. New York Edition. Vol. 1, 435–92. New York: Scribner's.

Secondary Works

Adams, Percy G. 1961. "Young Henry James and the Lesson of his Master Balzac." *Revue de Littérature Comparée* 35 (July–September): 458–67.

Anderson, Charles R. 1977. *Person, Place and Thing in Henry James's Novels*. Durham, NC: Duke University Press.

Andreas, Osborn. 1948. *Henry James and the Expanding Horizon: A Study of the Meaning and Basic Themes of James's Fiction*. Seattle: University of Washington Press.

Auchard, John. 1986. *Silence in Henry James: The Heritage of Symbolism and Decadence*. University Park: Pennsylvania State University Press.

Beach, Joseph Warren. [1918] 1954. *The Method of Henry James*. Philadelphia: Albert Saifer.

Beebe, Maurice. 1964. *Ivory Towers and Sacred Founts: The Artist as Hero*. New York: New York University Press.

Bell, Millicent. 1965. *Edith Wharton and Henry James: The Story of their Friendship*. New York: George Braziller.

Bellman, Samuel I. 1965. "Henry James' 'The Madonna of the Future' and Two Modern Parallels." *California English Journal* 1: 47–53.

Berland, Alwyn. 1981. *Culture and Conduct in the Novels of Henry James*. Cambridge: Cambridge University Press.

Brodhead, Richard H. 1986. *The School of Hawthorne*. New York: Oxford University Press.

Buckler, William, and Arnold B. Sklare, eds. 1960. *Stories from Six Authors*. New York: McGraw Hill.

Buitenhuis, Peter. 1970. *The Grasping Imagination: The American Writings of Henry James*. Toronto: University Press of Toronto.

Charney, Hanna. 1978. "Variations by Henry James on a Theme by Balzac." *New York Literary Forum* 2: 69–75.

Churchill, Kenneth. 1980. *Italy and English Literature, 1764–1930*. Totowa, NJ: Barnes & Noble.

Cornwell, Ethel F. 1962. *The 'Still Point': Theme and Variations in the Writing of T. S. Eliot, Coleridge, Yeats, Henry James, Virginia Woolf, and D. H. Lawrence*. New Brunswick, NJ: Rutgers University Press.

Curtsinger, E. C. 1986. *The Muse of Henry James*. Mansfield, TX: Latitudes Press.

Daiches, David. 1943. "Sensibility and Technique (Preface to a Critique)." *Kenyon Review* 5 (August): 569–79.

Dietrichson, Jan W. 1969. *The Image of Money in the American Novel of the Gilded Age*. Oslo: Universitetsforlaget; New York: Humanities.

Edgar, Pelham. [1927] 1964. *Henry James, Man and Author*. New York: Russell & Russell.

Falk, Robert. 1965. *The Victorian Mode in American Fiction, 1865–1885*. East Lansing: Michigan State University Press.

Feidelson, Charles, Jr. 1970. "Art as Problem in 'The Figure in the Carpet' and 'The Madonna of the Future.'" *Symbolism and American Literature*. Chicago: University of Chicago Press. Reprinted in *Twentieth Century Interpretations of "The Turn of the Screw" and Other Tales*, ed. Jane P. Tompkins, 47–55. Englewood Cliffs, NJ: Prentice-Hall, 1970.

Garnett, David, ed. 1946. *Fourteen Stories by Henry James*. London: Rupert Hart-Davis.

Geismar, Maxwell. 1963. *Henry James and the Jacobites*. Boston: Houghton Mifflin.

Grover, Philip. 1973. *Henry James and the French Novel: A Study in Inspiration*. London: Paul Elek.

Hoffmann, Charles George. 1957. *The Short Novels of Henry James*. New York: Bookman.

Holder, Alan. 1966. *Three Voyagers in Search of Europe: A Study of Henry James, Ezra Pound and T. S. Eliot*. Philadelphia: University of Pennsylvania Press.

Horne, Helen. 1960. *Basic Ideals of James's Aesthetics as Expressed in the Short Stories Concerning Artists and Writers*. Marburg: Erich Mauersberger.

Howells, W. D. 1979. *Selected Letters*. Vol. 2: *1873–1881*. Ed. George Arms, Christoph K. Lohmann, and Jerry Herron. Boston: Twayne.

———. [1875] 1961. "The Passionate Pilgrim and Other Tales." In *Discovery of a Genius: William Dean Howells and Henry James*. Ed. Albert Mordell, 63–74. New York: Twayne.

James, William. 1992. *The Correspondence of William James*. Vol. 1: *William and Henry: 1861–1884*. Ed. Ignas K. Skrupskelis and Elizabeth M. Berkeley. Charlottesville: University Press of Virginia.

Jeffares, Bo. 1979. *The Artist in Nineteenth Century English Fiction*. Atlantic Highlands, NJ: Humanities.

Jefferson, D. W. [1960] 1971. *Henry James*. New York: Capricorn.

———. 1964. *Henry James and the Modern Reader*. New York: St. Martin's.

Jones, Granville H. 1975. *Henry James's Psychology of Experience: Innocence, Responsibility, and Renunciation in the Fiction of Henry James*. The Hague: Mouton.

Josephson, Matthew. 1964. *Portrait of the Artist as American*. New York: Octagon.

Kaplan, Harold. 1972. *Democratic Humanism and American Literature*. Chicago: University of Chicago Press.

Kappeler, Susanne. 1980. *Writing and Reading in Henry James*. New York: Columbia University Press.

Kelley, Cornelia Pulsifer. [1930] 1965. *The Early Development of Henry James*. Urbana: University of Illinois Press.

Kraft, James. 1969. *The Early Tales of Henry James, 1843–1870*. New York: Bookman.

Lebowitz, Naomi. 1965. *The Imagination of Loving: Henry James's Legacy to the Novel*. Detroit: Wayne State University Press.

Long, Robert Emmet. 1979. *The Great Succession: Henry James and the Legacy of Hawthorne*. Pittsburgh: University of Pittsburgh Press.

McCarthy, Harold T. 1958. *Henry James: The Creative Process*. New York: Thomas Yoseloff.

McElderry, Bruce R., Jr. 1965. *Henry James*. New York: Twayne.

Maini, Darshan Singh. [1973] 1988. *Henry James: The Indirect Vision*. Ann Arbor: UMI Research Press.

Markow-Totevy, Georges. 1969. *Henry James*. Trans. John Griffiths. London: Merlin.

Matheson, Gwen. 1968. "Portraits of the Artist and the Lady in the Shorter Fictions of Henry James." *Dalhousie Review* 48: 222–30.

Matthiessen F. O. 1947. *The James Family: Including Selections from the Writings of Henry James, Sr., William, Henry, and Alice James*. New York: Knopf.

———. 1944. "Introduction: Henry James' Portrait of the Artist." *Henry James: Stories of Writers and Artists*. Norfolk, CT: New Directions. Also reprinted as "Henry James's Portrait of the Artist." *Partisan Review* 11 (1944): 71–87.

———. 1944. *Henry James: The Major Phase*. New York: Oxford University Press.

———. 1943. "James and the Plastic Arts." *Kenyon Review* 5 (August): 533–50.

Maves, Carl. 1973. *Sensuous Pessimism: Italy in the Work of Henry James*. Bloomington: Indiana University Press.

Melchiori, Giorgio. 1965. "Locksley Hall Revisited: Tennyson and Henry James." *Review of English Literature*, 6 (October): 9–25. Reprinted in Barbara Melchiori and Giorgio Melchiori, *Il Gusto di Henry James*. Turin: Guilio Einaudi editore, 1974.

Niess, Robert J. 1956. "Henry James and Emile Zola: A Parallel." *Revue de Littérature Comparée* 30 (January–March): 4–6.

Perosa, Sergio. 1983. *Henry James and the Experimental Novel*. New York: New York University Press.

Powers, Lyall H. 1970. *Henry James: An Introduction and Interpretation.* New York: Holt, Rinehart.

———. 1969. The Merrill Guide to Henry James. Columbus, OH: Charles E. Merrill.

———. 1962. "Henry James's Antinomies." *University of Toronto Quarterly* 31 (January): 125–35.

Putt, S. Gorley. 1966. *Henry James: A Reader's Guide.* Ithaca, NY: Cornell University Press.

Richardson, Lyon N., ed. 1941. *Henry James: Representative Selections.* New York: American Book Company.

Ross, M. L. 1974. "Henry James's 'Half-Man': The Legacy of Browning in 'The Madonna of the Future.'" *Browning Institute Studies* 2: 25–42.

Rovit, Earl. 1964. "James and Emerson: The Lesson of the Master." *American Scholar* (Summer): 434–40.

Segal, Ora. 1969. *The Lucid Reflector: The Observer in Henry James's Fiction.* New Haven: Yale University Press.

Sharp, Sister M. Corona. 1963. *The Confidante in Henry James: Evolution and Moral Value of a Fictive Character.* Notre Dame, IN: Notre Dame University Press.

Sicker, Philip. 1980. *Love and the Quest for Identity in the Fiction of Henry James.* Princeton: Princeton University Press.

Slabey, Robert M. 1958. "Henry James and 'The Most Impressive Convention in All History.'" *American Literature* 30 (March): 89–102.

Smith, William F., Jr. 1973. "Sentence Structure in the Tales of Henry James." *Style* 7 (Spring): 157–72.

Stevenson, Elizabeth. [1949] 1981. *The Crooked Corridor: A Study of Henry James.* New York: Octagon.

Stone, Donald David. 1972. *Novelists in a Changing World: Meredith, James, and the Transformation of English Fiction in the 1880's.* Cambridge, MA: Harvard University Press.

Tanner, Tony. 1985. *Henry James: The Writer and His Work.* Amherst: University of Massachusetts Press.

———. 1963. "James's Little Tarts." *The Spectator* 210 (4 January): 19.

Thorp, Willard, ed. 1962. *"The Turn of the Screw" and Other Short Novels.* New York: New American Library.

Tintner, Adeline R. 1987. *The Book World of Henry James: Appropriating the Classics.* Ann Arbor: UMI Research Press.

———. 1986. *The Museum World of Henry James.* Ann Arbor: UMI Research Press.

Tyler, Parker. 1964. *Every Artist His Own Scandal: A Study of Real and Fictive Heroes.* New York: Horizon.

Unrue, Darlene. 1984. "The Complex Americanism of Henry James and William Faulkner." In *The Origins and Originality of American Culture.* Ed. Tibor Frank, 247–53. Budapest: Akadémia Kiadó.

Vaid, Krishna B. 1964. *Technique in the Tales of Henry James.* Cambridge, MA: Harvard University Press.

Vielledent, Catherine. 1985. "Representation and Reproduction: A Reading of Henry James's 'The Real Thing.'" In *Interface: Essays on History, Myth, and Art in American Literature.* Ed. Daniel Royat, 31–49. Montpellier: Publishers de la Recherche, University Paul Valéry.

Voss, Arthur. 1973. *The American Short Story: A Critical Survey.* Norman: University of Oklahoma Press.

Wagenknecht, Edward. 1984. *The Tales of Henry James.* New York: Frederick Ungar.

Wegelin, Christof. 1958. *The Image of Europe in Henry James.* Dallas: Southern Methodist University Press.

West, Rebecca. [pseud]. 1916. *Henry James.* London: Nisbet.

Winner, Viola Hopkins. 1970. *Henry James and the Visual Arts.* Charlottesville: University Press of Virginia.

Wright, Nathalia. 1965. *American Novelists in Italy, The Discoverers: Allston to James.* Philadelphia: University of Pennsylvania Press.

Wright, Walter F. 1962. *The Madness of Art: A Study of Henry James.* Lincoln: University of Nebraska Press.

Foreign Language

Castiglione, Luigi. 1962. "Profilo di James." *La Fiera Letteraria* 17 (23 September): 5.

Sarber, Aladà. 1975. "Henry James: A pa'lya e's tanulsa'gai." ["Henry James: lessons of a career."] *Filolo'gia Kozlony* 21:58–78.

The Marriages

Publication History

James first published "The Marriages" in the *Atlantic Monthly* on August 1891. He included it the next year in the collection *The Lesson of the Master*, and later in the New York Edition.

Circumstances of Composition, Sources, and Influences

"The Marriages" was the first result of three story ideas James recorded while in Florence on January 12, 1887, the other two becoming *The Aspern Papers* and "Louisa Pallant." The idea came from a letter from his sister, Alice, telling how Sir John Rose, widower of one of the Temples, was to marry the Dowager Lady Tweedaddle, so that "he blushes whenever her name is mentioned," and one daughter "says it is simply forty years of her mother's life wiped out" (CN 32). Alice recorded the reaction of one of the daughters in her diary: "You can't imagine how strange it was to see Father in love and to see her sitting upon his poor old knee" (157–58). In real life, however, the daughters were grown and married, and the marriage eventually took place.

The date of the writing of the story has been variously placed. Matthiessen and Murdock speculate that the story was written about the same time as the notebook entry, its publication held up in a general delay James complained of to Howells (N 71). Edel argues for a later date based on Alice's recording in April 1891 of the case of a Lady Gower, who died three years after her mother's death and her father's remarriage to "an abomination in the shape of woman," making Alice ask, "Will there be no stirrings of remorse in her father's bosom for the brutalities which rent that delicate fiber?" Edel speculates that James may have been prompted to return to his earlier source upon hearing of Lady Gower's story (Alice James 195–96). Richards, however, contends that the timing is too close for a story published across the Atlantic in August, and argues for an intermediate date of late 1889 or 1890, on the basis of James's drawing on an anecdote from the diary of Lady Knutsford published in 1889 and a term from his brother William's 1890 *Principles of Psychology* (318, 322).

As the "little drama" evolves in the notebook, the father, too, is ashamed of his engagement, until after his daughter takes it upon herself to warn off the woman, when he turns resentful, wondering what the daughter said. The daughter goes to apologize only to learn that the woman has already become engaged to someone else. James already intended that the woman should see through the lies, but considered at this stage having her mistakenly believe that the father was behind them (CN 32–33).

Tintner records the striking similarities between the plot here and one of the subplots in George Meredith's *Emilia in England* (1864), in which a widower's children lie in order to prevent his marriage to a rich vulgar widow, Mrs. Chump. While in both narratives there is a brother whose sympathies waver, only in James's work does the sister have to act alone, and her psychology, Tintner maintains, becomes the focus of the new tragic treatment (1987, 125–28). As another indication that Victorian daughters not infrequently objected to a parent's remarriage, Richards cites Gaskell's *Wives and Daughters*, reviewed by James in 1866 (322).

"What a falling off was there / from me," laments Hamlet's dead father of his widow's new husband, and Adela sees her father's choice as representing a similar decline. Dale Kramer and Cheris Kramer compare Adela not only to Hamlet, but also to Ophelia in her "complacent thought of going mad" (78; also Moon 43).

James, according to Moon, saw a "falling off" also in the changing order from aristocracy to commercial wealth the marriage represents, and he notes the same dismay in Dickens and Du Maurier, and particularly in Booth Tarkington's 1918 novel, *The Magnificent Ambersons*, which also combines psychoanalytic and social themes (42, 44).

Relation to Other Works

Adela has generally been placed in the unfortunate category of the obsessed, the excessively conscientious, linked in particular with Fleda Vetch of *The Spoils of Poynton*, and in her concern and dismay over her family's behavior with Laura Wing of *A London Life*. Tanner faults both Adela and Laura for failing to consider a stoic acceptance of their situations (276). Donald Stone adds Charlotte Wentworth of *The Europeans* to the three (199n), while Jones contributes Mme de Mauves, Olive Chancellor of *The Bostonians*, the governess of *The Turn of the Screw*, and Agatha Grice of "The Modern Warning," remarking that like Laura's and Agatha's, and also Guy Domville's, Adela's conscience is controlled by family concern (35, 121, 127, 137, 142). Wilson stresses the resemblance to Olive Chancellor, picturing both women as unaware of the true motives that cause them to meddle in others' lives, although he sees the treatment here, in contrast to that of *The Bostonians*, as "frankly comic" (121). Edward Stone links Adela not only with Olive, but also Beatrice Ambient of "The Author of Beltraffio" and the governess of *The Turn of the Screw*, as "morbid" and "deceitful" (1969, 52; 1964, 54). Putt, however, emphasizes her status as a child, comparing her "preternatural meddling" to that of Maisie in *What Maisie Knew* (279).

Looking at the connection to *The Turn of the Screw*, Tilton contends that Adela is portrayed as plainly neurotic, and so clears the ambiguously portrayed governess (ix). Richards, for his part, finds the scene in which Adela is alone in the country in charge of her younger siblings and faints at the unexpected arrival of her brother's wife as the basis of *The Turn of the Screw*, "in miniature" (321).

Adela's behavior has also been taken more sympathetically. Edgar compares her to Stransom in "The Altar of the Dead" because of her grieving in a London uninterested in grief: "Remembrance there was hammered thin—to be faithful was to make society gape. The patient dead were sacrificed; they had no shrines, for people were literally ashamed of mourning" (101). Stransom's revulsion at his friend Creston's remarriage to a vulgar American woman of "monstrous character" is particularly apposite (CT 9, 235). Pointing to the contrast the new marriages illustrate between vulgar present and hallowed past, Moon, however, sees both Adela and Stransom as turning to extremes in their response (43; also Tanner 275).

Others have emphasized the imaginative side of Adela's acute consciousness. Donald Stone notes the links between her ambiguous character and James's artist figures (247). Choosing one of the less savory Jamesian artists, Tanner sees her "diseased, hypertrophied imagination" as anticipating that of the narrator of *The Sacred Fount* (276).

Adela is not simply a psyche or an imagination, but a representative of a social class, and Moon places the tale with *A London Life*, *What Maisie Knew*, *The Siege of London*, and *The Awkward Age* not as psychological studies, but as examinations of the decline of England's upper class. Mrs. Churchley he sees as representing an intermediate stage between the attractively vulgar Mrs. Headway of *The Siege of London* and the objectionable Mrs. Worthingham of "Crapy Cornelia" (35).

When James began writing *The Golden Bowl*, he judged it a "pity" he had already used the title "The Marriages" (CN 146). Several critics have seen the works as related by more than title, including Edel and Powers, Cargill, and Wasserstrom (CN 33, 75; Cargill 402–3; Wasserstrom 89–90). Equally intense father-daughter relationships are located by Jones in *Washington Square* and *The Portrait of a Lady* (190; also *Life* 5, 211). Similarly, Wasserstrom observes how the Victorian patriarchs here and in *Washington Square* ruin their daughters' futures (89). Sharp places Colonel Chart somewhat differently in the galaxy of Jamesian fathers, with Mr. Ruck of "The Pension Beaurepas" and Ed Brookenham of *The Awkward Age* as a "completely ruined man" (284).

Examining the tale in the context of volume 18 of the New York Edition, Gage locates a change in the manner of meddling. While in *Daisy Miller* or

"The Patagonia" the older generation meddles with the younger, here the younger interferes with the older. At the same time the sense of meddling is intensified because it occurs within the family (153, 165). Gage also compares what he judges the inadequate epistemology of Adela to the Monarchs of "The Real Thing." In his analysis, Adela rejects Mrs. Churchley as too vulgar to be her father's companion, even as the Monarchs reject Miss Churm as too vulgar to be a model, although both are better suited to the roles than their critics (171, 176–78).

Interpretation and Criticism

In his preface, James had written that "The embodied notion, for this matter, sufficiently tells its story; one has never to go far afield to speculate on the possible pangs of filial piety in face of the successor, in the given instance, to either lost parent, but perhaps more particularly to the lost mother, often inflicted on it by the parent surviving. . . . it's but a question of 'first catching' the example of piety intense enough. Granted that, the drama is all there—all in the consciousness, the fond imagination, the possibly poisoned and inflamed judgment, of the suffering subject; where, exactly, 'The Marriages' was to find it" (*Criticism* 2, 1282). Faced with this passage, critics have had a tendency to pass over James's sense of the naturalness of the subject, to "go far afield" instead with a distinct emphasis on the "poisoned and inflamed judgment" with a frequent neglect of the "possibly," Richards being one of the few critics to draw attention to it (322). In the general view, Adela was destined by James from start to finish for an ironic treatment (e.g., Rimmon 15).

Despite the almost universal habit of interpreting the story along Freudian lines, it was written without the benefit of Freud's work, a fact that has been taken to render James's application of it, as McElderry phrases it, "startling," rather than critics' drawing on it anachronistic (112). Edel writes, "James's achievement in this tale is to have seen clearly all its psychological values: for what he makes equally apparent—and wholly without benefit of Freud—is the girl's driving need to take possession of her father, and her fear of having this possession violated" (CT 8, 9). Matthiessen and Murdock even contend that James did not go far enough, writing, " . . . a later writer would not have skirted the 'unsympathetic' element, and would have probed more deeply into the sexual pathology latent in the theme" (N 71). Elsewhere Matthiessen, in arguing that James saw the father-daughter relationship in *The Golden Bowl* as "exceptionally close" and "naively innocent," but with no sense of "pathological fixation," asserts that James often seemed unaware of what modern psychology would consider problematic in the relationships of his characters (92–93). In the notebook, James had said the daughter would need to have worshiped her mother "to make her opposition natural" (CN 32). Most critics, however, take her devotion to her mother's memory as just a cover for her Electra complex, her desire to keep her father for herself (e.g., Gage 155, 164). Even the usually mild-mannered McElderry speaks of her "almost incestuous possessiveness" (112).

In his notebook, James presents Adela's lie as what makes her a questionable character. Indeed James decided to make the fiancée doubt Adela's tale in order to make her action "a little less odious," although he still laments, "It wouldn't be a very 'sympathetic' tale" (CN 33). William James, however, wrote his brother that the tale "was one of the most perfect little things you ever did—a chef d'oeuvre. It seems to be generally regarded as such, but, strange to say, Howells says that it gave rise at the Interval House to a great casuistical controversy about lying" (185). Since then, such is the concentration on Adela's original resentment that the issue of her lie receives scant critical attention. Andreas is one of the few to criticize Adela's meddling without psychoanalyzing it (59). Like him, Wagenknecht acknowledges Adela's meddling, and James's dislike of such interference, but judges the usual condemnation of Adela extravagant (63). More typically, Jones considers it "immaterial" whether Adela's concern for her mother is her motivation, given that her goal is to stop the marriage (109–10).

The amount of critical ill-will toward Adela is remarkable. Cargill calls her "deranged"; Levy judges her a "magnificent study of pathological evil"; Cheris and Dale Kramer speak of the "ultimate viciousness in Adele's [sic] hard and intolerant egoism" (Cargill 403; Levy 88; Kramers 79). Gage blames her for her "unwarranted" suspicions, even though her suspicion—that her father is courting Mrs. Churchley—is right (155–56). While Cheris and Dale Kramer give as the tale's theme "the comfort of having human sympathy while facing crises of life and while facing life itself," critics generally ignore the possibility of Adela's own need for sympathy (79). Richards is an exception, calling Adela a "touching case-study of a young woman interested in preserving the family unit she has known." He notes that her "case" can be treated in psychological terms, but argues that James saw her as a person (321–22). Donald Stone takes a middle route. Recognizing the "torments" that the "self-righteous" Adela causes her family, he still argues that the story's ambiguity prevents any clear conclusion on Adela, whether to condemn her or see her as understandably concerned in protecting her mother's memory (247).

It seems at times that the idea of the sexually repressed spinster is so appealing to critics, that when they see a candidate, they can allow her no other qualities or capacities. Adela claims to be acting out of love for her dead mother, and one of the reasons Adela has received so little credit for such a motive is that such motives are given little credit today. We are in an age, like Adela's, unsympathetic to mourning, that values the rights of parents over those of children, and the rights of the dead not at all. Accordingly, to

Tanner, Adela is mistaken in her "ardour for the dead mother instead of concern for the happiness of the living father" (275). Gage objects to her sense of superiority in her faithfulness as a "prideful and dangerous feeling predicated on no concrete evidence of Londoners' callousness or her own virtue" (157). James, however, as is evident in his notebooks and letters, also valued the dead and regretted modern society's callousness toward them. Admittedly, few would find Adela sympathetic in her response to her brother's remark that their father is not "very happy." "Of course he isn't," she replies, "any more than you or I are; and it's dreadful of him to want to be" (CT 8, 39). Her view of life is more strenuous than most people would find comfortable. Such was the response of James's contemporary R. L. Stevenson, who presented James with his tribute to the story in a verse beginning, "Adela, Adela, Adela Chart, / What have you done to my elderly heart?" and remarking of the "delightful" "maniac," "I thank my dear Maker the while I admire / That I can be neither your husband nor sire" (282).

While Adela might well have objected to any new wife for her father, she faces a very specific nominee in Mrs. Churchley. No matter one's analysis of Adela, one must keep in mind that we see her nemesis, as Richards cautions, largely through Adela's prejudiced eyes (322). Tintner, however, appears to agree with Adela, finding Mrs. Churchley "place[d]" by her "enormous red fan of red feathers" (1986, 238). Even more strongly, Wagenknecht judges Mrs. Churchley such "a dreadful person" that Adela's father is lucky to have escaped marrying her (63). Sharp is more tolerant. Calling Mrs. Churchley "one of those vulgar and gaudy women who so amused James," Sharp argues that she "is not really a bad person," is indeed "stronger" than the Colonel, and is possessed of "some insight (the cardinal Jamesian virtue)" (284). Beattie speaks of the "comfort and companionship" offered the colonel by the "well-to-do widow," without any further look at her personality (107). Moon argues that while lacking taste, Mrs. Churchley possesses a certain wisdom and the integrity essential to James, as is seen in her not telling Chart why she objects to Adela (41). However, her decision to spare Chart the knowledge of his child's lie also means she expects him to cast off his daughter for no clear reason, hardly evidence of the "greater humanity" Moon imputes to her. To apply contemporary standards to her behavior, as most critics have done with Adela, one could argue that insisting on one's husband's tossing out his daughter is not the proper start for the stepparent relationship. Even at the time, it could have hardly seemed kind.

Both Gage and Dietrichson make the case for Mrs. Churchley's "kindness" partly on the grounds of her willingness to help Godfrey (Gage 163; Dietrichson 111–12). Similarly, Tanner calls Mrs. Churchley "not ungenerous," and contrasts Adela's contempt for her with her brother's liking (275–76). The brother's opinion, however, is an even more definite example of prejudice, because he is relying on Mrs. Churchley's money to bail him out of his marriage. Godfrey's situation brings to mind the title's plural, which might refer to Chart's previous marriage, but is more likely a reference to the son's present marriage. Gage sees Adela as failing to see irony in the superiority of Mrs. Churchley to the woman Godfrey marries (162). But the irony can be directed the other way. One might accept Chart's choice if it were not for the light thrown on it by his son's.

Looking at the two men's behavior together helps explain a problem in structure first pointed to by Edgar, who argued that the melodrama of Godfrey's marriage upset the "finer effect" of the main situation (101). Indeed, speaking of James stories "so monstrously ill-constructed that if they were buildings they would have fallen down long ago," O'Faolian gives "The Marriages" as his example (170). As McElderry observes, however, the sub-plot emphasizes Adela's state (112). Kramer and Kramer elaborate, seeing the link between the "two essentially unrelated plots" as the insight they shed on Adela's "egocentric personality," which misreads the behavior of both men, and cite her brother's charge that she is a "raving maniac" (75–76). The brother, however, is speaking in angry desperation at the possible loss of Mrs. Churchley's bribe money, and is hardly a reliable witness. Moon, who notes Godfrey's "self-serving eagerness" for the wedding, also sees his wife as an intensification of Mrs. Churchley (47).

The rashness of the two men's choices indicates that they may be more driven than Adela. Although they remain true Victorians in insisting on mar-riage, their choices seem to have little to do with the women as persons, rather than as outlets for sexual energy. Perhaps Adela simply takes marriage more seriously than her brother, or her father, or Mrs. Churchley, whose name implies that she is heading for church no matter with whom, and who has managed to find a new fiancé by the end of the story.

The father's role in all this seems largely passive after the initial engage-ment. He is, as several critics have noted "patient, loyal, and loving" toward his daughter (Tilton ix; Edgar 101; Cargill 402; Kramers 79). Gage admittedly says that the father defends his daughter "ignorantly," and offers the possibil-ity that "he himself cherishes an unhealthy affection for his daughter" that places them, in the end, in an "unhealthy" marriage "in fact, if not in name" (153, 164–65). Picturing him as James's closest portrait of the "Victorian paterfamilias," Sharp locates more mundane limitations in Chart. Like Putt, who comments on his stumbling conversation with his daughter, Sharp sees Chart representing "the insurmountable 'otherness' of fatherhood." He is forced to live in isolation because the current definition of "paternal love" did not admit intimacy. His strength is restricted to a "pathetic dignity," to "prop-ping a shaky facade" both in regard to Adela, whom he never accuses, and his son (Sharp 284–85; Putt 279–80).

The isolation of the father also isolates the children. Since Adela has no knowledge of her father's actions, she is reduced to suspicions. Having no forum in which to approach him, she is driven to covert actions. She is at once both immensely vulnerable to, and without influence over, the actions of her father. In her rebellion Adela encounters a new sensation, "a singular and almost intoxicating sense of power." When she believes she has stopped the marriage, the narrator records, "These results were in important and opulent lives; the stage was large on which she moved her figures. Such a vision was exciting . . ." (CT 8, 54). Sharp goes so far as to argue that Adela acts not primarily out of devotion but "restiveness under the paternal dispositions," and that in the end, "chastened and wiser," she takes over her father's place of control (285). Both Gage and Edel have criticized Adela's relish of her new power, Gage arguing that it undercuts the reader's sympathy for her (Gage 160–61; CT 8, 9). One does not need to argue with Sharp that power is her motive, however, to understand why a proper Victorian daughter, who is left at home while her brother and father go off to form new alliances, might enjoy some sense of control. One sees the same reaction in the governess Miss Flynn during her one opportunity to act.

Other critics have blamed her not for abandoning her role, but for behaving in accordance with it. Dale and Cheris Kramer, for example, are suspicious of Adela's taking over her mother's place in the running of the household and the care of the younger children (78). Wasserstrom puts some of the blame on the father, stating that his demands on Adela have contributed to her distorted emotional focus on him, with the result that in the end she has no prospect for independence through marriage, but is "delighted" by what will be in essence her "marriage" to her father (89). In speaking of *The Golden Bowl*, however, Edel points out that in the Victorian scheme of things such intense devotion between father and daughter was "expected," and he points to examples James was familiar with including that of his sister, Alice, who ran the James household after the death of her mother (*Life* 5, 210–11).

While generally united in the view that Adela acted wrongly, critics split on whether she ever recognizes her wrongdoing. Austin Wright emphasizes her "comeuppance," her learning that her father has been kinder to her than she to him, that she has acted from "vanity" (187–88). Walter Wright argues that Adela is redeemed by her father's behavior, but, more important, is still unable to repair the harm she has done (95). Tilton and Wilson, on the other hand, see Adela as unable ever to understand the complications she helps to create, remaining satisfied that she acted correctly (Tilton ix; Wilson 122). In the view of Dale and Cheris Kramer, James meant to emphasize the romantic, self-styled tragic Adela's ironic "self-discovery" through the tale's events, rather than the events themselves. Still they argue that her "self-delusion quickly reasserts itself" upon learning the cause of Churchley's leaving (75–79).

Objecting to the assumption of her unreliability and attributing it to a mood of anti-Victorian "debunking," Moon sets out to deliver Adela from her years on the "Procrustean bed" of the "psychoanalytical couch." In essence, however, Moon simply shifts the source of Adela's unreliability from her repressed sexuality to her defensive class-consciousness, which he views as a more complex motive. In Moon's reading, Adela's action is the "manifestation of a larger disaster," one of class, afflicting the Charts. While he leaves in some standard criticism of her as "vestal virgin" and speaks of her "sadistic interference with the potential sexual fulfillment of her father," he argues that her interference does not stem from an obsession with her father. Still, he finds it necessary to offer up another female victim, Adela's dead mother, as cause for the family's "deterioration." Behind James's description of "the incomparable mother, so clever, so unerring, so perfect," Moon senses a "mordant authorial distaste." Her representation of her class, which Adela seeks to uphold, becomes the reason for the father's pursuing the vulgar Mrs. Churchley and Godfrey's taking on a "masochistic marriage" to an unacceptable Cockney. According to Moon "the predators" win, Godfrey's wife receiving a handsome allowance and Mrs. Churchley a better match. The Kramers offer an additional note on class, pointing out the heroism of the governess in "athletically contending" with Godfrey's wife after Adela faints (78).

An element of class conflict is undoubtedly in the story and was present as well in Alice's record of the case of Lady Gower, who was dismayed that "the Queen would not receive" her father's second wife. While sympathetic to her loyalty to her mother, such "an absolute standard of the possible and the impossible bred in her bone" made Alice glad to have escaped "any such *entravement* of one's personal prerogative" (196). Her brother, too, was glad to be free of any class label in British society, but he was also increasingly disconcerted by what he called, in 1895, "The demoralization of the aristocracy . . . their general vulgarization" (CN 117).

The story treats complex issues of class, sex, and family structure. Its complexity has not been adequately captured in the criticism, which has somewhat distortedly concentrated on the possible distorting influence of James's center of consciousness. The story, however, is a strong one and can stand on its own.

Works Cited

Primary Works
James, Henry. 1891. "The Marriages." *Atlantic Monthly* 68 (August): 233–52.

———. 1892. "The Marriages." *The Lesson of the Master*. New York and London: Macmillan, 81–122.

———. 1908. "The Marriages." In *The Novels and Tales of Henry James*. New York Edition. Vol. 18, 255–304. New York: Scribner's.

————. 1969. *Henry James: Letters to A. C. Benson and Auguste Monod*. Ed. E. F. Benson. New York: Haskell House.

Secondary Works

Andreas, Osborn. 1948. *Henry James and the Expanding Horizon: A Study of the Meaning and Basic Themes of James's Fiction*. Seattle: University of Washington Press.

Beattie, Munro. 1967. "The Many Marriages of Henry James." In *Patterns of Commitment in American Literature*. Ed. Marston La France, 93–112. Toronto: University of Toronto Press.

Cargill, Oscar. 1961. *The Novels of Henry James*. New York: Macmillan.

Dietrichson, Jan W. 1969. *The Image of Money in the American Novel of the Gilded Age*. Oslo: Universitetsforlaget; New York: Humanities.

Edgar, Pelham. [1927] 1964. *Henry James, Man and Author*. New York: Russell & Russell.

Gage, Richard P. 1988. *Order and Design: Henry James' Titled Story Sequences*. New York: Peter Lang.

James, Alice. 1964. *The Diary of Alice James*. Ed. Leon Edel. Harmondsworth: Penguin.

James, William. 1983. *The Correspondence of William James*. Vol. 2. *William and Henry: 1885–1896*. Ed. Ignas K. Skrupskelis and Elizabeth M. Berkeley. Charlottesville: University Press of Virginia.

Jones, Granville H. 1975. *Henry James's Psychology of Experience: Innocence, Responsibility, and Renunciation in the Fiction of Henry James*. The Hague: Mouton.

Kramer, Dale, and Cheris Kramer. 1966. "James's 'The Marriages': Designs of Structure." *University of Kansas City Review* 33 (October): 75–80.

Levy, Leo B. 1957. *Versions of Melodrama: A Study of the Fiction and Drama of Henry James, 1865–1897*. Berkeley: University of California Press.

McElderry, Bruce R., Jr. 1965. *Henry James*. New York: Twayne.

Matthiessen, F. O. 1944. *Henry James: The Major Phase*. New York: Oxford University Press.

Moon, Heath. 1984. "A Freudian Boondoggle: The Case of James's 'The Marriages.'" *Arizona Quarterly* 40: 35–48.

O'Faolian, Sean. 1948. *The Short Story*. London: Collins.

Putt, S. Gorley. 1966. *Henry James: A Reader's Guide*. Ithaca, NY: Cornell University Press.

Richards, Bernard. 1979. "The Sources of Henry James's 'The Marriages.'" *Review of English Studies* 30: 317–22.

Rimmon, Shlomith. 1977. *The Concept of Ambiguity: The Example of Henry James.* Chicago: University of Chicago Press.

Sharp, Sister M. Corona, O. S. U. 1966. "Fatherhood in Henry James." *University of Toronto Quarterly* 35: 279–92.

Stevenson, Robert Louis. 1905. *The Letters of Robert Louis Stevenson.* Ed. Sydney Colvin. New York: Scribner's.

Stone, Donald David. 1972. *Novelists in a Changing World: Meredith, James, and the Transformation of English Fiction in the 1880's.* Cambridge, MA: Harvard University Press.

Stone, Edward. 1969. *A Certain Morbidness: A View of American Literature.* London: Feffer & Simons; Carbondale: Southern Illinois University Press.

———. 1964. *The Battle and the Books: Some Aspects of Henry James.* Athens: Ohio University Press.

Tanner, Tony. 1965. *Reign of Wonder: Naivety and Reality in American Literature.* Cambridge: Cambridge University Press.

Tilton, Eleanor, ed. *Henry James: "The Marriages" and Other Stories.* A Signet Classic. New York: New American Library.

Tintner, Adeline R. 1987. *The Book World of Henry James: Appropriating the Classics.* Ann Arbor: UMI Research Press. Reprinted from "Henry James' Debt to George Meredith." *AB Bookman's Weekly* 70, no. 12 (20 September): 1811, 1812, 1814, 1816, 1818, 1820, 1822, 1824–27.

———. 1986. *The Museum World of Henry James.* Ann Arbor: UMI Research Press.

Wagenknecht, Edward. 1984. *The Tales of Henry James.* New York: Frederick Ungar.

Wasserstrom, William. 1959. *Heiress of All the Ages: Sex and Sentiment in the Genteel Tradition.* Minneapolis: University Press of Minnesota.

Wilson, Edmund. 1960. "The Ambiguity of Henry James." In *A Casebook on Henry James's "The Turn of the Screw."* Ed. Gerald Willen, 115–53. New York: Thomas Y. Crowell.

Wright, Austin McGiffert. 1961. *The American Short Story in the Twenties.* Chicago: University of Chicago Press.

Wright, Walter F. 1962. *The Madness of Art: A Study of Henry James.* Lincoln: University of Nebraska Press.

Master Eustace

Publication History

"Master Eustace" was first published in the November 1871 issue of *Galaxy*. James reprinted it only once, in the 1885 *Stories Revived*. Its next appearance was as the title story of Mordell's 1920 collection, and it appeared not long after in Lubbock's editon of the novels and stories.

Circumstances of Composition, Sources, and Influences

James evidently wrote "Master Eustace" on his return from Europe, contemporaneously with "Guest's Confession" and *Watch and Ward* (Kelley 127; also Kraft 37). Edel sees reflected in Eustace's outrage at his return home James's own sense of having been displaced by his brother on his return to the family home in Cambridge (*Life* 2, 39–40).

Eustace declares of his mother's suitor, Mr. Cope, "I am like Hamlet—I don't approve of mothers consoling themselves" (CT 2, 363). Naturally enough, critics have picked up on the allusion, using a Freudian interpretation of the play appropriate for the tale, emphasizing the son's attachment to the mother and resentment of his stepfather. Following his analogy, Eustace plays the title role, his mother becomes Gertrude, and Mr. Cope is Claudius (*Life* 2, 39; Putt 37; Levy 17). Tintner, who has provided the most elaborate exposition of the connection, finds James inspired by Goethe's revision of the play in *Wilhelm Meister*, and points to a major change in James's making his Hamlet Claudius's bastard son (1987, 4–10; 1989, 25, 30). Lerner points to a tale by Turgenev, "The Dream," of Freudian implications, containing like this one a son who while fixated on his mother idealizes his unknown father only to hate his father when he ultimately appears (41). Tintner argues that Eustace's jealousy is underscored by the tale's allusion to Bluebeard, although she remarks here it is the wife hiding a man (1989, 25, 29; 1986, 18).

Kelley points to George Sand as the model for the treatment of passion here as in "De Grey," judging it an inappropriate one for Americans, an opinion seconded by Buitenhuis (Kelley 128; Buitenhuis 52). McElderry similarly considers the tale "foreign in mood and motivation" (1949, 289).

Perosa comments on the use of the term "tussle," taken from popular literature, and also used in next year's "Guest's Confession" (58, 249 n.83).

Relation to Other Works

The "perspective of foreign travel," according to McElderry, allows James to seem "more at home" here as in "De Grey" and "A Light Man" (1965, 28). Mull compares Eustace to Max of "A Light Man" in their shared "cynicism, charm, and complete egotism" (17).

Putt likens the "Hamlet-like doom" to that in "The Romance of Certain Old Clothes" (37). Tintner finds a resemblance to Graham Fielder in *The Ivory Tower* through their shared source in Hamlet (1987, 17–19).

Stevenson records that the narrator, though "colorless," is one of the earliest of many Jamesian governesses, represented later in *A London Life*, *What Maisie Knew*, and, of course, *The Turn of the Screw* (30). Krook elaborates on the last example, noting in both that a governess of "romantic disposition" tells the story of the beautiful but demonic child she cared for. The relationship between Mrs. Garnyer and the governess, according to Krook, prefigures the adoption of a poor girl by a wealthy woman seen in such other early tales as "De Grey," "A Most Extraordinary Case," and "The Sweetheart of M. Briseux," as well as later works from *The Portrait of a Lady* to *The Spoils of Poynton* and *The Wings of the Dove* (5–9, 11).

Krook compares the mother's belief in the absoluteness of love to Maggie Verver's and finds her as a "Doting Mother" similar to Daisy Miller's mother, a type that becomes scarce later in James, she argues, due to its Americanness (10–11). Edel considers the treatment of sexuality more explicit if perhaps less conscious in James's first novel, *Watch and Ward*, published that same year (*Life* 2, 44).

Interpretation and Criticism

Critical appreciation often splits between praise for the characterization of Eustace and disparagement of the melodrama that surrounds him, particularly in the tale's conclusion. Edel, for example, singles out for praise James's capture of Eustace's psychology (CT 2, 11). Krook is atypical in finding Eustace's mother the more interesting character (9), but the mother's role is also crucial in analyses of the tale as she is the one who shapes Eustace's character. Shine discusses the story as an example not only of James's concern with the "spoiled" child, but with the parental "dereliction" responsible for it, an approach, she argues, that took him from the depiction of children by themselves into a more subtle consideration of the way children and adults affect each other. She blames the mother's stated belief that "love, love, pure love, is the sum and substance of maternal duty, and that the love which reasons and requires and refuses is cruel and wicked" for Eustace's flaws (33–35). As a result, according to Kraft, Eustace "refuses to accept reality and truth" (43). Mull similarly observes that it is her "devotion" that has created in Eustace the proud possessiveness that leads him to consider her as just another possession, not a person (17). Edel, in turn, argues that Eustace's view of himself as a rival to his new father begins with his mother's treatment of him as a lover, not a child (*Life* 2, 38–39). Putt, while blaming the mother like the others, nevertheless finds the depiction at least of Eustace's selfishness "almost charming" (37). Schelling and Levy are almost alone in their criticism of James's characterization of Eustace (Schelling 171; Levy 22).

Mrs. Garnyer declares of love: "It's either a passion . . . or it's nothing. You can know it by being willing to give up every thing for it—name and fame, past and future, this world and the next" (CT 2, 347). But the conclusion reveals that she has actually been a careful protector of her name in hiding her affair with Mr. Cope. In the end she also decides not "to give up everything" for her passion for Eustace, deciding she can be both loving mother and loving wife. Kelley views the tale as one of two passions, mother for son, and son for absent father (128). The mother had not paid sufficient heed to the latter, while allowing Eustace to worship the dead man he believes to be his father. Andreas gives a certain plausibility to her behavior by noting the wrong done Mrs. Garnyer, forced into marriage by her parents. Indeed, he provides a full elaboration of the never-quite-stated events behind events. Mrs. Garnyer, he asserts, was forced to marry when pregnant with Eustace by Mr. Cope, who went to Australia and married, only to return promptly when widowed (39–40).

The commotion produced by Mrs. Garnyer's second marriage is certainly melodramatic, marked by revelations, gunshots, attempted suicides, and sudden deaths. Such critics as Putt and Wagenknecht who praise the characterization of Eustace find the tale undercut by its overwrought conclusion (Putt 37; Wagenknecht 193; see also Leyburn 5). Even Levy, who criticized Eustace as lacking in "psychological unity," judges the Hamlet-like psychology superior to the "external" melodrama that overwhelms it. He also points out, however, that the surprise of Eustace's illegitimacy was a plot device "perennially attractive" to James, a reading that seems a more accurate view than Gerlach's claim that James later moved away from such surprise "revelation of circumstance" (Levy 17; Gerlach 74). Beach's judgment is perhaps harshest in objecting to both the "unmodified banality" of Eustace's character and the "loud-voiced passion" of the tale (173–74). Kelley at least praises James's use of foreshadowing to prepare for its revelations (128). It is after all not surprising for a person brought up to believe life is to be made easy for him to throw something of a fit when the first time he is ever crossed it is on such a crucial matter. Similarly, Rimmon comments that the twist at the end of the story here does not require a reworking of our earlier understanding of the characters involved (82).

Looking at setting, McElderry judges the story the least beholden to its American locale of James's early stories (1965, 28). More disparagingly, Edel finds the story badly affected by the "torpor of Cambridge" (CT 2, 11), while Buitenhuis criticizes the vagueness of the American setting (52). Looking at the narration, Schelling applauds James for staying within "the limitations" of the governess narrator throughout (174). In Beach's view, however, James simply assigns the governess his own omniscience and so achieves nothing by the device (179–80). Actually there is a frame narrator who accepts tea along with the tale and speaks somewhat condescendingly of the "old-maidish precision" with which it is served. Similarly, at the tale's conclusion, he dismisses her "triumphant air," declaring he had "foreseen it half-an-hour ago." But even he admits to being "rather at a loss how to dispose of our friend Eustace" (CT 2, 341, 373). The story never does seem quite to sort itself out, and there is much in the tale that is "out of place" or inconsistent with its mild-mannered narrator. The character of the mother in particular needs to be assembled after the fact, even though she is the prime mover in the tale and Mr. Cope never develops beyond his walk-on role at the end. Perhaps James was looking for the sort of romance produced by the old servant Mrs. Dean speaking to Mr. Lockwood of the tempestous Heathcliff and Cathy. The characters in this tale, however, fall somewhat short of mysteriousness without quite achieving complete believability, leaving the tale not entirely one thing or another. Although possessed of a certain graciousness of style and a certain amount of psychological insight, it is still a work that fails to create an entirely convincing reality, even though it produces the necessary interest and suspense to want it.

Works Cited

Primary Works
James, Henry. "Master Eustace." 1871. *Galaxy* 12 (November): 595–612.

———. "Master Eustace." 1885. *Stories Revived* 3. London: Macmillan.

———. "Master Eustace." 1920. *Master Eustace.* Preface by Albert Mordell, 7–54. New York: Thomas Seltzer.

———. 1921–23. *The Novels and Stories of Henry James.* Vol. 26. Ed. Percy Lubbock. London: Macmillan.

Secondary Works
Andreas, Osborn. 1948. *Henry James and the Expanding Horizon: A Study of the Meaning and Basic Themes of James's Fiction.* Seattle: University of Washington Press.

Beach, Joseph Warren. [1918] 1954. *The Method of Henry James.* Philadelphia: Albert Saifer.

Buitenhuis, Peter. 1970. *The Grasping Imagination: The American Writings of Henry James*. Toronto: University of Toronto Press.

Gerlach, John. 1985. *Toward the End: Closure and Structure in American Short Stories*. University: University of Alabama Press.

Kelley, Cornelia Pulsifer. [1930] 1965. *The Early Development of Henry James*. Urbana: University of Illinois Press.

Kraft, James. 1969. *The Early Tales of Henry James*. Carbondale: Southern Illinois University Press.

Krook, Dorothea. 1983. "Prefiguring in Two Early Stories of Henry James." *Modern Language Studies* 13, no. 4 (Fall): 5–21.

Lerner, Daniel. 1941. "The Influence of Turgenev on Henry James." *Slavonic Review* 20 (December): 28–54.

Levy, Leo B. 1957. *Versions of Melodrama: A Study of the Fiction and Drama of Henry James, 1865–1897*. Berkeley: University of California Press.

Leyburn, Ellen Douglass. 1968. *Strange Alloy: The Relation of Comedy to Tragedy in the Fiction of Henry James*. Chapel Hill: University of North Carolina Press.

McElderry, Bruce R., Jr. 1965. *Henry James*. New York: Twayne.

———. 1949. "The Uncollected Stories of Henry James." *American Literature* 21 (November): 279–91.

Mull, Donald. 1973. *Henry James's 'Sublime Economy': Money as Symbolic Center in the Fiction*. Middletown, CT: Wesleyan University Press.

Perosa, Sergio. 1983. *Henry James and the Experimental Novel*. New York: New York University Press.

Putt, S. Gorley. 1966. *Henry James: A Reader's Guide*. Ithaca, NY: Cornell University Press.

Rimmon, Shlomith. 1977. *The Concept of Ambiguity: The Example of Henry James*. Chicago: University of Chicago Press.

Schelling, Felix E. 1922. "Some Forgotten Tales of Henry James." *Appraisements and Asperities: as to Some Contemporary Writers*. Philadelphia: Lippincott, 169–74.

Shine, Muriel G. 1969. *The Fictional Children of Henry James*. Chapel Hill: University of North Carolina Press.

Stevenson, Elizabeth. 1949, 1950. *The Crooked Corridor: A Study of Henry James*. New York and London: Macmillan.

Tintner, Adeline R. 1989. *The Pop World of Henry James: From Fairy Tales to Science Fiction*. Ann Arbor: UMI Research Press.

———. 1987. *The Book World of Henry James: Appropriating the Classics*. Ann Arbor: UMI Research Press. Reprinted from "Henry James's *Hamlets*: 'A Free Rearrangement.'" *Colby Library Quarterly* 18, no. 3 (September 1987): 168–82.

———. 1986. *The Museum World of Henry James.* Ann Arbor: UMI Research Press.

Wagenknecht, Edward. 1984. *The Tales of Henry James.* New York: Frederick Ungar.

Maud-Evelyn

Publication History

"Maud-Evelyn" appeared first in the April 1900 issue of the *Atlantic Monthly*. It was a late addition that same year to James's collection *The Soft Side* (*Correspondence* 1993) but was never reprinted by James. It next appeared in Lubbock's edition of the novels and tales.

Circumstances of Composition, Sources, and Influences

In the summer of 1894, while at Torquay, James first learned from Paul Bourget the outline of a story by Luigi Gualdo, telling of a couple who commission a painting of the child they are unable to have. That September James recorded his desire to write his own story on the "charming little subject" (CN 131; 1970, 598). In a list on May 7, 1898, he split the idea into two variations—the other half would become "The Tone of Time." "Maud-Evelyn" was first spoken of as "Gualdo's story of the child *retournée*—the acquisition, construction (by portrait, etc. ???) of an ANCESTOR instead of *l'Enfant*. The setting up of some one who must *have* lived: un vrai mort." James decided, however, not on an imagined ancestor, but an imagined marriage. The situation of the young man, James decided, would be the focus as he "succumbs to suggestion" so strongly that he dies in order to "rejoin his wife," even while leaving his money to the live girl he doesn't marry. James ended the entry with the injunction "35 pages. (Subject—subject.)," the parenthetical remark in red ink (CN 169). Immediately following the entry, as Tintner notes, James recorded the significant name Dedrick (1986, 170). The original germ would eventually result in a third tale, James's only extant unfinished story, "Hugh Merrow." According to Bishop, all three tales depict the same theme—"the artistic construction of identity"—in different frames (86–87).

In its story of a beloved dead girl, Matthiessen finds the tale bordering on Poe's "ghoulish extremes," missing them just barely because, unlike some of Poe's heroines, Maud-Evelyn at least stays dead (140). Auchard points a different link with Poe, arguing that because Marmaduke had become such a part of the family before he "wed" Maud-Evelyn, his marriage to her combines "morbidity . . . with the hint of incest" in the manner of "The Fall of the House of Usher" (49).

In Browning's "Evelyn Hope," the speaker cries out to the dead young girl, "I claim you still, for my love's sake," and Sicker sees James illustrating the effects of such a claim (100–1). In D'Avanzo's view, James turns the forward-looking love of Browning's speaker toward the past. Indeed, D'Avanzo sees James's story, with its allusions to Shelley and Wordsworth, as a general critique of the Romantic imagination, which can be both "a sublime and sick power." D'Avanzo locates another romantic source in the opening description of Lady Emma telling the tale by firelight by connecting it to Hawthorne's discussion of reality and imagination in "The Custom House" preface to *The Scarlet Letter*. The name of the dead girl, he writes, comes from Mary Magdalene, the source for the "maudlin," an association pointed to in Lady Emma's reading of a novel by Wilkie Collins, which D'Avanzo speculates is *The New Magdalene*. According to Fiedler, who places the tale in the context of the American romance, it exhibits a typical necrophilia in its "final consummation of the American asexual affair with the Pure Maiden" (304).

Briggs finds a similarity with one of Villiers de l'Isle Adam's *Contes Cruels*, "Vera" (1883), where a Count pretends his dead bride is alive (81). Tintner discovers a parallel in a short story by Henry Harland, "The House of Eulalie," which appeared in a collection James reviewed in April 1898. The story tells of a young man who rents from an old couple the house they built for their dead daughter, Eulalie-Josephine-Marie. Like the Dedricks, they pretend that their daughter once lived in the lovely home, and the young man, although he does not enter into their pretense as does Marmaduke, comes to decide sympathetically that "there are illusions that are not falsehoods." More generally, Todorov traces the "romantic theme" that "death is the source of life" and love to Théophile Gautier's "Spirite" (162). The allusion to Burns's poem "John Anderson, My Jo," noted by Gale (113), may in its evocation of the Dedricks' devotion to each other, be meant to emphasize the relationship Marmaduke and his "wife" do not have.

Others connect the tale more to James's life than his reading. Edel cites the refuge from love in death in James's relationship to his cousin Minny Temple, and Bronfen similarly sees the tale's preference of a dead woman for inspiration illustrated in James's reaction to Minny's death (*Life* 5, 110, 117; Bronfen 111–13). Looking as well at James's relationship to his brother William, Edel sees the tale indebted to James's sense that he, too, was being left outside, like Lavinia (*Life* 4, 326). Santangelo also considers William an influence, but more as a philosopher than a brother. In his reading, the tale acts out the pragmatist belief that "the truth of an idea is not a stagnant property inherent *in* it. Truth *happens* to an idea. It *becomes* true, is *made* true by events." Similarly, Santangelo argues, in its treatment of time and its dual reality, the story illustrates William's idea that even the past is shaped by present consciousness, its "only value being its uses in the present as a reality" (51–53).

Contending that James may have been familiar with Freud's work through William, Houston argues that, whether knowingly or not, James attributes to the Dedricks and to Marmaduke the classic symptoms of *folie à deux*. Houston mentions other later literary treatments of the psychosis, including *Lilith* by J. R. Salamanca, *We Have Always Lived in the Castle* by Shirley Jackson, and *The Sterile Cuckoo* by John Nichols (28–30).

Relation to Other Works

Because of its treatment of devotion to the dead, the tale is frequently linked with "The Altar of the Dead" (e.g., Fiedler 304). In both, those who mourn are isolated in the midst of a vast, unnoticing city. In Q. D. Leavis's estimate, both tales are "unprofitably unpleasant" and "morbid" (223). McElderry, however, finds the treatment of the theme more sympathetic in "The Altar of the Dead" and more effective in *The Wings of the Dove* (116). Similarly, Bishop argues that "The Altar of the Dead" is less unpleasant, possibly because its dead are "real," while in "Maud-Evelyn" the dead are fabricated (89). Przybylowicz focuses on the role of Lavinia and the unnamed woman in "The Altar of the Dead" as preservers of the temples established by Marmaduke and Stransom (159). Edel also compares the tale to *The Wings of the Dove* in the hero's renunciation of a live woman for a dead one, as well as to "De Grey" and "Longstaff's Marriage" in its relationships broken by death (*Life* 1, 330; *Life* 5, 110, 117). Sicker classes together Marmaduke, Stransom, and Densher, along with Longdon and Nanda of *The Awkward Age* and Mary Tredick of "The Tone of Time," as people who seek "stability . . . in the perpetual adoration of a dead image" (100, 140). Houston discerns in both "Maud-Evelyn" and "Longstaff's Marriage" depictions of the particular psychosis *folie à deux* (29).

Another frequent comparison is with "The Beast in the Jungle." Banta, indeed, finds "Maud-Evelyn" an "ironic reversal" of "The Beast in the Jungle": there a living man acts as if he were dead, here the dead are treated as if they were living (181 n.23). Edel links the tale to both "The Altar of the Dead" and "The Beast in the Jungle," calling Marmaduke the "least interesting of James's haunted people" due to his "extreme passivity" (1970, 599). Briggs senses in all three tales a death to life far worse than any genuine ghost, a pall finally cast off in "The Jolly Corner" (150). Santangelo, however, judges Marmaduke a more positive character than Marcher, because he does not avoid commitment, adding that the expansion of experience through consciousness illustrated in *The Ambassadors* will be even greater (53). Wagenknecht and Przybylowicz add *The Sense of the Past* to the list of related works, with Przybylowicz stressing the necessarily doomed attempt to find in the past the perfection that cannot be attained in the present (Wagenknecht 193; Przybylowicz 159).

Among the tales of the supernatural, Edel contrasts the tale's morbidity with the geniality of the ghostly "Third Person" (*Life* 502), while Gage compares the romanticization of the dead in both (51). In McCarthy's classification, "Maud-Evelyn," "The Beast in the Jungle," and "The Great Good Place" all deal with the supernatural in the form of an *idée fixe* (107). Todorov observes how in ghost tales such as "Sir Dominick Ferrand," "Sir Edmund Orme," "Nona Vincent," and this one, James draws attention to the "absent and essential" character in the title (162).

In his turning away from life, Stevenson sees Marmaduke as simply the most extreme example of such fantasists as Stransom, Dane of "The Great Good Place," Theobald of "The Madonna of the Future," Gabriel Nash of *The Tragic Muse*, and Gedge of "The Birthplace" (73). Like Gedge, one might observe, Marmaduke becomes caught up in a make-believe world that he originally enters primarily for profit. In Jones's analysis, the way Marmaduke's imaginary world completely takes over his real life moves the tale a step further than the subordination of real life to the speculative in *The Papers* and *In the Cage* (135). Auchard also links the imaginative construction of Maud-Evelyn to the fantasies of the girl in the telegraph cage. He adds a comparison with Isabel Archer, asserting that all imagination in a way "gives 'life' where life is not" and that Isabel, in marrying a "complete nonentity," chooses like Marmaduke the imaginary over the real (49–50). Powers records many other examples of James's presentation of an "*imagined* or created experience" designed to compensate for one missed, including not only "Hugh Merrow" and "The Tone of Time," but "The Beast in the Jungle," *The Ambassadors*, *The Turn of the Screw*, and *The Sacred Fount* (117–18).

In his idolization of a nonexistent woman, Jones compares Marmaduke to Sanguinetti of the early "Rose-Agathe." Judging the folly of both innocent, he nevertheless compares their happiness unfavorably to that of Felix in *The Europeans*, which stems from a "very real involvement in a very real world" (148, 169). Less favorably, Tintner examines the similarities between the "grotesque" collecting of the Dedricks and Sanguinetti, placing the woman in "The Altar of the Dead" along with them as keepers of a shrine (1986, 169–70).

In remaining deliberately constant with his fianceé's worst view of him as "half a man," Marmaduke, according to Mackenzie, resembles the hero of James's early "Crawford's Consistency" (93). D'Avanzo, on the other hand, finds Marmaduke superior to the Byron-loving Caroline Spencer of "Four Meetings" in his balance of Romanticism and worldliness (31–32). (See also "The Friends of the Friends.")

Interpretation and Criticism

A story that James could refer to as "the Young Man who has Married the dead Daughter" has naturally attracted a fair amount of attention, much of it disapproving (CN 170). Reporting that his family read the tale aloud "with great pleasure," brother William found the story "very exquisite but hardly realistic" (114, 118). To Edel it is "unpleasant"; to Sicker "perhaps the most bizarre and perplexing tale in James' entire canon" (*Life* 5, 110; Sicker 100).

The tale is told by Lady Emma to a society friend. Beach comments on her extreme distance from the story's actors, but also maintains that the real action of the story is its revelations to its hearers—and readers (40–41). Lady Emma tells the tale as an interesting anecdote, and in Vaid's judgment her "frivolous tone" brings a "false note" into the story from the start (61). Stevenson, too, speaks of the tale's "deathly chill . . . islanded in the tone of easy gossip." In addition, as Stevenson indicates, assigning the narration to Lady Emma keeps the reader from ever seeing Marmaduke alone with the Dedricks, an insight that would help in assessing his character (73).

Distant as the view of him may be, the character of Marmaduke is at the center of the controversy over the tale. While the Dedricks come to their grief naturally, Marmaduke begins as a bystander, and his transformation into a participant has provoked skepticism. Some, such as Wilson, see him as insincere, interested largely in the material advantages of cooperating with the Dedricks (147). Others find him sincere, but no less culpable. Many, including Edel and Putt, have found him, as Edgar puts it, "anaemic" for choosing a ghost over a live woman (Edel 1970, 598–99; Putt 292; Edgar 191–92). Taking a somewhat different tack, Stein pictures Marmaduke's devotion to a delusion simply as "a disquieting literalization" of the many self-deluded, destructive marriages in James (114). Stevenson, who calls Marmaduke "ineffectual," sees evidence of both flaws in him, remarking that while he is more comfortable with the dead than the living, he is also partly impressed by the Dedricks' money (73). To Blackmur, Marmaduke is a "cad" whom James enjoys punishing. Obsessed with the past, he wrongly uses the Dedricks' "true obsession . . . to fill out his own false obsession" ([1942] 1983, 53–54). Bronfen is less certain. Remarking on how Marmaduke's "omnipotence" eclipses even Maud-Evelyn, she argues that one still cannot tell whether his behavior is pure "self-deception" or "really beautiful" (114–16). While such critics question Marmaduke, Gage is one of the few to portray Marmaduke himself as questioning his role in the Dedricks' fantasy (51).

Other critics are kinder in their readings of the would-be son-in-law. While acknowledging something "awry" in Marmaduke's *modus vivendi*, Andreas contends that Marmaduke's obsession with the past has "some internal sanity of logic which makes his life as complete as other and more normal lives" (102). Both Jones and Sicker see Marmaduke as essentially kind and harmless (Jones 148). Indeed, Sicker declares, "so innocuous is his dementia, so contented is he in his fantasy love, and so exemplary is his conduct that he arouses our wonder more than our disapprobation" (101). D'Avanzo makes his case for Marmaduke by arguing that, while mercenary at the start, he becomes sincerely involved in the imaginative cult of Maud-Evelyn by the end. Still, he sees in Marmaduke's final "stoutness" James's indication that such imagination is an ambiguous force. Walter Wright also emphasizes the changes in Marmaduke, citing Lady Emma's statement that Marmaduke "had grown like a person with a position and a history" and arguing that, in taking up with the Dedricks, Marmaduke was not abandoning real life, because before he had "almost no life" to abandon (125). Similarly, in Powers's estimate, Marmaduke may fatten on his fortune, but such prosperity is not his aim. Like a good pragmatist, Marmaduke focuses on the "practical result" without worrying overly about actuality. Powers sees the good results shared round: Emma moves from antipathy to sympathy and Lavinia is given assurance that Marmaduke will not marry *and* a generous inheritance. One may point out, however, that Lavinia's share seems rather meager.

Lavinia, whom Edgar judges a "charming" woman, appears to have her own difficulties in adjusting to reality (191–92). Certainly her happiness at the fact that the man she has rejected is safe from the arms of any other woman by his marriage to a dead girl is one of the strangest ever examples of the classic bed trick, by which a lady saves her virtue by finding another woman to serve her lover's fleshly desires. What her true motives are in doing so, and whether she is happy in the results, however, is not certain, partly because of the veil cast by the sheer politeness of her conversation. Not surprisingly, Richardson remarks on her "frustration" (490). In Putt's view she is a victim, bearing the brunt of Marmaduke's strange behavior and receiving as a "consolation prize" Maud-Evelyn's riches (292). Houston, while drawing on a dated definition of homosexuality as a "personality disorder," sees signs of latent homosexuality in Marmaduke's rejection of Lavinia for the "distant, unreal femininity" of Maud-Evelyn (38). Similarly, Bronfen points out how Marmaduke uses the dead girl to keep Lavinia "at bay," gaining much greater imaginative freedom by loving a dead girl who cannot talk back (114–16). Wright, however, who judges the giving of the treasures to Lavinia a final gentlemanly deed on Marmaduke's part, emphasizes the "imaginative excitement" her vicarious participation in his experience has allowed. In this way he sees the tale itself as a twist on the "reality" that imaginary characters take on for their creators (126). In Jones's view, Lavinia is "awed" into silence (135–36).

Lady Emma, as participant and narrator, is less silent. Estimates of her true attitude vary from Jones's assertion that she remains outside, never believing or understanding, to D'Avanzo's argument that she moves from cynicism to acceptance (Jones 135–36). D'Avanzo, indeed, takes the tale as partly "a study of her own education." Lady Emma is at the farthest end of the tale from Maud-Evelyn, and the ultimate significance of her story is sharply debated, in part because of the different levels of experience it depicts. Wagenknecht, for example, finds the Dedricks "touching and believable" in hanging onto the possibilities of their dead daughter's life, while Marmaduke, whether sincere or insincere, is both unpleasant and implausible. The story, in his view, simply goes too far (193; also N 267). McElderry argues that such, with hopes for a greater success, was James's intent: he took a natural emotion, sympathy for the dead and the mourning, and saw how far he could stretch it (116). More acceptingly, Todorov analyzes the levels of engagement James portrayed from the nearly absent Maud-Evelyn through her "naïve" parents, who believe Maud-Evelyn still "literally" exists, to the "poetic" Marmaduke, who is not particularly interested in Maud-Evelyn, but accepts death as the "most extraordinary" experience possible, then to the "estheticizing" Lavinia, who is interested only in Marmaduke's particular case, and the "realistic" Lady Emma, who finds them all foolish. The tale thus, in Todorov's view, glorifies the past, and the life the search for it brings, even through death (162–64).

The Dedricks turn to illusions in response to a grievous loss, Marmaduke out of a felt lack, leaving the story open to interpretation not as a story of death, but as a more general treatment of illusion. D'Avanzo, for example, argues that the tale is not morbid, but stands for the value of illusion, however er private, as a "vital and sustaining force" in an overly practical world. Other critics are less certain James meant to stand behind the process he depicts. Norrman, for example, finds James's attitude to such "rewriting of history" uncertain (183). Given the uncertainty, the story becomes to Edel a tale not simply of death, but "death-in-life and life-in-death" (1970, 599). Focusing on the final hint that Lavinia will also enter the imaginary world of Maud-Evelyn, Sicker sees the tale portraying how the "imagination can create process as well as stasis," not only preserve the past but create it. Still, he concludes, "to endow a figment of our own creation with life, even in the sphere of our own fantasy, is ultimately to destroy the thing we love" (101). Przybylowicz also notes the ambiguous value of imagination in the tale, even as it asks, "What is more real"—imagination or reality? The answer she gives seems clearly slanted toward reality, as she states how giving life to Maud-Evelyn "paradoxically" removes the characters from the realm of "physical reality," rendering all their relationships "unfulfilling" as they are but "relationships to a ghost." In seeking the unattainable, they leave barren what they already possess (158–59). Similarly, Auchard maintains that while the imagination here at first invigorates, it ultimately brings on collapse (49).

Keeping the emphasis on the theme of death, Blackmur criticizes even the preoccupation of the Dedricks, who, he writes, "made a temple of death in order to profane it, to stretch its precincts to cover the living world" ([1948] 1983, 108–9). In Putt's view, not only Maud-Evelyn, but all the characters in the story seem "half-dead" (292). Jones, on the other hand, argues that James, in general sympathetic to the plight of the elderly, empathizes with them again here, citing Marmaduke's explanation that the Dedricks, unable to do much with the future, "had to do what they could with the past" (275). The ambiguity extends also to the parallel theme of the past. Todorov, for example, cites Marmaduke's proclamation "The more we live in the past, the more things we find in it" as an admirable sentiment. Tintner, however, stresses the materialism of the "things" of the past in the tale and their power to sway otherwise reasonable people (1986, 170). Houston also notices the significance of the economic motif, although he argues that Marmaduke's interest in the Dedricks' money wanes as he gets caught up in their delusion (37–38). One might indeed argue that the things get the last word, as Lady Emma ends her tale by saying to her listener, "Tell you about them you say. My dear man, everything" (CT 11, 75). While Houston reads Lady Emma's relish in the things as possibly indicating that she, too, has been taken in by the cult of Maud-Evelyn (39), it seems more likely that she has been pleased in its resolution in a material form she can appreciate.

Hoping to rescue the tale from its "seeming vapidity and mawkishness," Houston offers a more concrete view of Marmaduke's personality. Judging him guilty of "gross violations" of nineteenth-century manners, he also finds him suffering from a "full-blown psychosis" in his acceptance of the Dedricks' fantasy. While Wagenknecht asserts that Houston's article is more relevant to students of psychology than of literature (194), Houston's view that James leads the reader to experience "vicariously . . . the complex delusions of the story" only to catch him in "another *amusette*" appears a useful corrective to some of the more fine-spun readings of the tale.

Santangelo also offers a psychological reading, picturing Marmaduke's choice of a "safe non-sexual union" with Maud-Evelyn as "certainly a strange neurotic sexual regression," and noting also Lavinia's probable fear of the sexual. He focuses, however, on the forms these regressions take, in "ghostly elements" and "attenuated, non-sexual involvements," and the way these forms suggest "the nature of consciousness and reality" (46). Like Todorov, he draws attention to the various "interlocking locutors" between the reader and Maud-Evelyn. Disagreeing with Vaid, he considers Lady Emma an effective narrator, because James needed someone "initially skeptical" to bring the reader to consider the idea at all. Additionally, through her contributions to the telling of the dead girl's story, Santangelo argues, Lady Emma comes to a "qualified acceptance" of it, and an understanding of it that surpasses even Lavinia's. In the end, she recognizes what Santangelo gives as the moral of the tale, that "life is what the mind makes it to be." Marmaduke's behavior is simply an "exaggerated" example of the normal human effort "to make a meaningful existence." As a result, Santangelo concludes, "the value of Maud-Evelyn is not her having once lived and died, but her actuality in the present. She has been *made* an object of consciousness . . . " (53). The last, however, sounds a rather sinister operation to perform on a person.

Bishop also focuses on the tale's creation of fictional reality. In his view, if it is "unpleasant" for Marmaduke to be "engaged in the construction of some-one he never knew," then so is "the artist's construction of personality." Pointing like Santangelo to Todorov's analysis of the narration, Bishop sees the "telescoping series of fictions" not as a wheel with spokes but as concentric circles that circumscribe Maud-Evelyn until she "finally disappears, replaced by other deaths, other absences." James in such fictions "plays with the possible permutations of narrative art as a deflection and container of those who are lost." Looking at the role of the "things" at the end, Bishop acknowledges that not everyone will approve of the implied emphasis on money in their "value." Still he conceives of their main significance as signals of fictional operations, their transference from Marmaduke to Lavinia herald-ing the opening up of her fiction as his closes, even as Lady Emma's promise at the end to tell the young man about the treasures promises "continuance" of "the cycle of fiction-construction"—yet another circumscribing story. In the end he sees mainly lingering questions: death is "unknowable," judgment uncertain, and the "boundaries between critic and fictionist" threatened (89–92, 97–98).

In the 1970s Houston and Santangelo could argue that the tale had not received the attention it merited. Since then, it has accumulated a fair body of criticism, some of it approaching Houston's valuing of it as "one of the best illustrations of James's psychological craftmanship and art" (28). Similarly, Richardson earlier praised the tale as "a good story," which works out its themes "with true ingenuity" (490). But while Gage judges it a *"tour-de-force"* in working out its outré theme, one can still feel the merit of Matthiessen's assessment that James "overreached himself" here, that the tale is "ghastly in a sense he did not intend" (Gage 51; Matthiessen 139). Indeed, for all their complex schema, the later analyses do not erase the feeling that the tale is simply, as Edel calls it, "gruesome" in its depiction of the relations of the living and the dead (1970, 598–600). Perhaps for this reason the tale has inspired fewer subversive readings than have many more conventional texts. Houston, indeed, noting some confusion over the ages of the Dedricks, remarks that "one might suspect by the enigmatic chronology that Maud-Evelyn may never have existed at all" (40 n.17). Otherwise, however, it seems that whether for the Freudian or the poststructuralist, James has provided all the oddity necessary or even desirable. The result is something of an acquired taste. James has so distanced the original loss in the tale, the unknown young girl, that the story gains most of its interest, its sole solidity, from the examination of how people, themselves possessed of varying degrees of normality, deal with the oddities of human behavior in those they know.

Works Cited

Primary Works

James, Henry. 1900. "Maud-Evelyn." *Atlantic Monthly* 85 (April): 439–55.

———. 1900. "Maud-Evelyn." *The Soft Side*. London: Methuen; New York: Macmillan, 279–310.

———. 1921–23. "Maud-Evelyn." *The Novels and Stories of Henry James*. Vol. 28. Ed. Percy Lubbock. London: Macmillan.

———. 1993. *The Correspondence of Henry James and the House of Macmillan, 1877–1914*. Ed. Rayburn S. Moore. Baton Rouge: Louisiana State University Press.

———. 1987. "Hugh Merrow." In *The Complete Notebooks of Henry James*. Ed. Leon Edel and Lyall H. Powers, 589–96. New York: Oxford University Press.

Secondary Works

Andreas, Osborn. 1948. *Henry James and the Expanding Horizon: A Study of the Meaning and Basic Themes of James's Fiction*. Seattle: University of Washington Press.

Auchard, John. 1986. *Silence in Henry James: The Heritage of Symbolism and Decadence*. University Park: Pennsylvania State University Press.

Banta, Martha. 1964. "Henry James and 'The Others.'" *New England Quarterly* 37 (June): 171–84.

Beach, Joseph Warren. [1918] 1954. *The Method of Henry James*. Philadelphia: Albert Saifer.

Bishop, George. 1988. *When the Master Relents: The Neglected Short Fictions of Henry James*. Ann Arbor: UMI Research Press.

Blackmur, Richard P. [1942] 1983. "*The Sacred Fount*." In *Studies in Henry James*. Ed Veronica A. Makowsky. New York: New Directions. Reprinted from "*The Sacred Fount*." *Kenyon Review* 4: 328–52.

———. [1948] 1983. "Henry James." In *Studies in Henry James*. Ed. Veronica A. Makowsky, 91–124. New York: New Directions. Reprinted from *The Literary History of the United States*, ed. Robert E. Spiller, et al., 1039–64. New York: Macmillan.

Briggs, Julia. 1977. *Night Visitors: The Rise and Fall of the English Ghost Story*. London: Faber.

Bronfen, Elisabeth. "Dialogue with the Dead: The Deceased Beloved as Muse." *New Comparison* 6: 101–18.

D'Avanzo, Mario L. 1968. "James's 'Maud-Evelyn': Source, Allusion, and Meaning." *Iowa English Yearbook* 13 (Fall): 24–33.

Edel, Leon, ed. 1970. *Henry James: Stories of the Supernatural*. New York: Taplinger.

Edgar, Pelham. [1927] 1964. *Henry James, Man and Author*. New York: Russell & Russell.

Fiedler, Leslie. [1960] 1966. *Love and Death in the American Novel*. New York: Stein & Day.

Gage, Richard P. 1988. *Order and Design: Henry James' Titled Story Sequences*. New York: Peter Lang.

Gale, Robert L. [1954] 1964. *The Caught Image: Figurative Language in the Fiction of Henry James*. Chapel Hill: University of North Carolina Press.

Houston, N. B. 1973. "Henry James's 'Maud-Evelyn': Classic *Folie à Deux*." *Research Studies* 41: 28–41.

James, William. 1904. *The Correspondence of William James*. Vol. 3: *1897–1910*. Ed. Ignas K. Skrupskelis and Elizabeth M. Berkeley. Charlottesville: University Press of Virginia.

Jones, Granville H. 1975. *Henry James's Psychology of Experience: Innocence, Responsibility, and Renunciation in the Fiction of Henry James*. The Hague: Mouton.

Leavis, Q. D. 1947. "Henry James: The Stories." *Scrutiny* 14 (Spring): 223–29. Reprinted in *Collected Essays*. Volume 2: *The American Novel and Reflections of the European Novel*, ed. G. Singh, 177–84. Cambridge: Cambridge University Press.

McCarthy, Harold T. 1958. *Henry James: The Creative Process*. New York: Thomas Yoseloff.

McElderry, Bruce R., Jr. 1965. *Henry James*. New York: Twayne.

Mackenzie, Manfred. 1976. *Communities of Honor and Love in Henry James*. Cambridge, MA: Harvard University Press.

Matthiessen, F. O. 1944. *Henry James: The Major Phase*. New York: Oxford University Press.

Norrman, Ralf. 1982. *The Insecure World of Henry James's Fiction: Intensity and Ambiguity*. New York: St. Martin's.

Powers, Lyall H. 1988. "James's 'Maud-Evelyn.'" In *Leon Edel and Literary Art*. Ed. Lyall H. Powers, 117–24. Ann Arbor: UMI Research Press.

Przybylowicz, Donna. 1986. *Desire and Repression: The Dialectic of Self and Other in the Late Works of Henry James*. University: University of Alabama Press.

Putt, S. Gorley. 1966. *Henry James: A Reader's Guide*. Ithaca, NY: Cornell University Press.

Richardson, Lyon N, ed. [1941] 1966. *Henry James: Representative Selections, with Introduction, Bibliography, and Notes*. New York: American Writer Series; Urbana: University of Illinois Press.

Santangelo, Gennaro A. 1975. "Henry James's 'Maud-Evelyn' and the Web of Consciousness." *Amerikastudien* 20, no. 1: 45–54.

Sicker, Philip. 1980. *Love and the Quest for Identity in the Fiction of Henry James*. Princeton: Princeton University Press.

Stein, Allen F. 1984. *After the Vows Were Spoken: Marriage in American Literary Realism*. Columbus: Ohio State University Press.

Stevenson, Elizabeth. [1949] 1981. *The Crooked Corridor: A Study of Henry James*. New York: Octagon.

Tintner, Adeline R. 1986. *The Museum World of Henry James*. Ann Arbor: UMI Research Press.

———. 1983. "A Source for James's 'Maud-Evelyn' in Henry Harland's 'The House of Eulalie.'" *NMAL* 7, no. 2 (Fall): Item 13.

Todorov, Tzvetan. 1977. *The Poetics of Prose*. Trans. Richard Howard. Ithaca, NY: Cornell University Press.

Vaid, Krishna B. 1964. *Technique in the Tales of Henry James*. Cambridge, MA: Harvard University Press.

Wagenknecht, Edward. 1984. *The Tales of Henry James*. New York: Frederick Ungar.

Wilson, Edmund. 1960. "The Ambiguity of Henry James." In *A Casebook on Henry James's "The Turn of the Screw."* Ed. Gerald Willen, 115–53. New York: Thomas Y. Crowell.

Wright, Walter F. 1962. *The Madness of Art: A Study of Henry James*. Lincoln: University of Nebraska Press.

The Middle Years

Publication History

"The Middle Years" appeared first in May 1893 in *Scribner's Magazine*, the only new tale James published that year. He collected it in book form in *Terminations*, which appeared in May 1895 in London, published by Heinemann, and in June the same year in New York, published by Harper and Brothers. He revised it in 1909 for volume 16 of the New York Edition.

Circumstances of Composition, Sources, and Influences

The written record of James's short story, "The Middle Years," begins with a notebook entry dated May 12, 1892:

> The idea of the old artist, or man of letters, who, at the end, feels a kind of anguish of desire for a respite, a prolongation—another period of life to do the *real* thing that he has in him—the things for which all the others have been but a slow preparation. He is the man who has developed late, obstructedly, with difficulty, has needed all life to learn, to see his way, to collect material, and now feels that if he can only have another life to make use of this clear start, he can show what he is really capable of. Some incident, then, to show that what he *has* done *is* that of which he is capable—that he has done all he can, that he has put into his things the love of perfection and that they will live by that. Or else an incident acting just the other way—showing him what he might do, just when he must give up forever. The 1st idea the best. A young doctor, a young pilgrim who admires him. A deep sleep in which he dreams he *has* had his respite. Then his waking, to find that what he has dreamed of is only what he has *done*. (CN 68)

There is in this entry and in the story, critics generally concur, "much literary autobiography" (Richardson 488; Wegelin 639). So much so that Horne judges Dencombe to be less a character in his own right than a mouthpiece for James (64). James had turned forty-nine on April 15, less than a month before. In a letter that day to Robert Louis Stevenson, he describes himself as "more and more companionless in my old age—more and more shut up to the solitude inevitably the portion, in these islands, of him who would really try, even in so small a way as mine, to *do* it" (*Letters* 3, 384). Edel has pointed to the presence of "acolytes" such as Morton Fullerton and Logan Pearsall Smith in James's circle at this time as types for Dr. Hugh as well as his earlier friendship for Wolcott Balestier, who had died young two years before (*Life* 3, 312–13; *Life* 4, 48). Wegelin suggests some of James's younger writer friends including Conrad, Stephen Crane, and Ford Madox Ford (640). But James was still in the midst of his unsuccessful siege of the theatre, having abandoned novels altogether due to the failure of his last three (*The Bostonians, The Princess Casamassima*, and *The Tragic Muse*) and Edel sees James as looking still to the theatre for his "second chance" (*Life* 3, 389). In 1888 he had written Howells that he had "entered upon evil days," that the demand for his work had been reduced to "zero" (*Letters* 3, 209). As he set to evaluate his accomplishments with fifty looming before him, he still felt himself to be in their grip. Edgar judges the mingled faith and despair in Dencombe's rereading of his work an exact reflection of James's own sense of his career at the time (163). James finally gained that "better chance," according to Edel, with the revisions for the New York Edition (*Life* 5, 325–26; also Anesko 144).

The notebook entry also follows by two months the death of his sister, Alice, who had been living an invalid's life in England. No doubt Alice's death also served to turn his attention to mortality. As Matthiessen noted in connection with the story, it, too, "heightened his feeling of isolation" (6). James had been with her at the time of her death and the memory of it may underlie some of his depiction of Dencombe's deathbed. When the already ailing Alice had first arrived in England in 1884, she had gone to Bournemouth, where she was attended by her companion, Katherine Loring, whose attentions were, like Dr. Hugh's, divided between the two invalids, Alice and Katherine's sister, also in residence at Bournemouth. That same year James would meet at the seaside resort an invalid more resembling Dencombe, the writer Robert Louis Stevenson (*Life* 4, 128–29).

Horne notes how the way Dencombe makes up a story about the three characters—the Countess and her retinue—approaching him echoes James's use of a "germ" from life to begin his stories (70). Similarly, Lycette attributes to Dencombe James's own "dramatic method," but sees the story illustrating the dangers of relying on it alone or on the "illusion" of art apart from life (60–61).

In his preface to the twelve tales of volume 16 of the New York Edition, rather than discussing the stories' themes, James focuses on the effort necessary to produce such "concise anecdote[s]." He even underestimates by approximately 2,000 words the length of "The Middle Years," the first he discusses, which is nearly 8,000 not 5,550 words (N 122). His metaphors, too, show the strain of enforced compression: the task is similar to "the anxious effort of some warden of the insane engaged at a critical moment in making fast a victim's straitjacket." The process, he records, monopolized an entire month (*Criticism* 2, 1238–39). Cowdery comments that James first creates the difficulty—by his distinction between the anecdote and nouvelle—and then prides himself on having solved it (30). His pride in having made the jacket fast, however, shows not only in the public preface but in an 1895 notebook entry where he cites "The Middle Years" as one model for the working out of a "single incident" without "developments" (CN 130). Austin Wright has analyzed the weaving together of scene and narrative that made such concision possible (394–95).

As is appropriate for a story whose length frequently leads it to being categorized as a "parable," two of its nominated sources are biblical. Babin points to a parallel between Dr. Hugh's situation and the New Testament injunction that "No man can serve two masters. . . . You cannot serve God and mammon," and the admonition to the rich young man to sell all he had before he could follow Christ (511).

Poole has characterized the story as having a "grave and tender late-Shakespearean tone" and points to verbal links with *Antony and Cleopatra* and *The Tempest* (203n). Caramello sees in Dencombe's declaration that "The rest is the madness of art" a union of Lear's "that way madness lies" and Hamlet's "the rest is silence" (305). Tintner has argued more extensively that *The Tempest* is a primary source for the story, in ways that reinforce the autobiographical connection. In Tintner's reading, Dencombe plays the magician Prospero, Dr. Hugh is his Ariel, and the Countess the witch Sycorax, from whom he frees Ariel. Significant among the supporting evidence she offers are the shared music motif (the Countess is an opera singer, Miss Vernham a pianist) and the pervasive imagery of the sea. "Above all," she writes, "the mood is that of the play and of the relinquishing of the magic of art near the sea." Drawing on a 1907 essay on *The Tempest* by James, Tintner sees him as exploring here how a "faculty so radiant" as Shakespeare's could have voluntarily stopped writing, and quotes Virginia Woolf's recollection of James's "assertion that never, never so long as he lived could there be any talk of completion: the work would end with his life" (1987, 44–49). Dencombe dives into his book "where, in the dim underworld of fiction, the great glazed tank of art, strange silent subjects float" (CT 9, 56)—a phrase that anticipates Woolf's description of the literary imagination—"the pools, and depths, the dark places where the largest fish slumber"—and provides a link between the seas of Shakespeare, James, and Woolf (Woolf 281).

Brooks contrasts Dencombe's doctrine of the "madness of art" with the antimelodramatic school of Flaubert (198). Rovit sees the same doctrine as indebted to the "exhortations" of Emerson's "The Poet," and views as Emersonian also Dencombe's final understanding that "frustration doesn't count" (438).

Relation to Other Works

From its first reviews in 1895 as one of the four stories in *Terminations*, "The Middle Years" was classed with "those studies of the artistic temperament which Mr. James has grown to be fond of" (*Critic* 67).

The bulk of James's stories on writers appeared during his "evil days" when he felt the lack of popularity most keenly. They became for him a period of sorting out his relationship with the reading public and the publishing world through his fiction. Van Cromphout groups "The Middle Years" with "The Death of the Lion" and "The Next Time" as stories referring to James's "frustration" with the age's "indifference" to literature (136). The early reviews bear out this sense. The *New York Times* wrote that "He has had experience" of "the difference between popularity and merit in literature." Less sympathetically, *The Nation* locates an "autobiographical smart" in his work and proceeds to criticize his lack of a worthy subject. Allen links the search for certainty about one's work here not only with the other artist tales, but with the *The Sacred Fount*'s demonstration of the way artistic perception can go astray (120).

The Literary World in 1895 saw "The Middle Years" along with "The Death of the Lion" more particularly as tales of literary "hero worship." Similarly, the critic for the *New York Times* suggested as an appropriate text for the two stories a declaration in William Dean Howells's new work, "My Literary Passions," that "the adoration which a young writer has for a great one is truly a passion surpassing the love of women." Edel has placed it as the first of the tales with a great writer and an admiring follower and observes that it is always the follower who makes the sacrifice for the writer as in "The Death of the Lion" and "The Coxon Fund" (*Life* 3, 313, 385). Given that Dr. Hugh is not a writer, Dupee may be more correct in linking the tale with "The Jolly Corner," *The Pupil*, "The Altar of the Dead," and "The Beast in the Jungle" as a treatment of the "unlived life" and classing Dencombe among their "poor sensitive gentlemen" with their "implicit desire of being loved, along with a disposition to substitute less intimate for more intimate kinds of love" (153–54, 157). It is important to note, however, that James has Dencombe tell Dr. Hugh not that he has not lived, but that he has "outlived," having survived a wife and son. Swan has connected the sense of what "might have been" here with *The Ambassadors* and "The Jolly Corner," seeing Strether suffering from the "same slight sense of disappointment" as the tale evidences (1957, 26; 1948, 10). Berthoff sees the tale linking the interest in the suffering of the artist in tales such as "The Death of the Lion" and "The Figure in the Carpet" with the more general crisis of middle age in "The Altar of the Dead" (112). To Wegelin, both "The Figure in the Carpet" and "The Middle Years" portray James's belief in the mystery of art, an art that "feeds on life" (645–46).

Rawlings, while also focusing on the relationship between Dencombe and Dr. Hugh, finds similarities with "Nona Vincent" in its portrayal of an "artistic communion . . . which both creates the conditions for and is a consequence of a deeper dependency" (xix). Gage links it in its concern with inheritance with "The Coxon Fund" (18–19).

An obvious connection is with James's own unfinished volume of memoirs, *The Middle Years*. Babin writes that it charts his change of consciousness in 1869 as he took up, in James's words, "the extraordinary gauge of experience," thereby becoming an observing artist rather than a direct participant in his own life. Edel, who uses the phrase to entitle the third volume of his biography of James, covering the years 1882 to 1894, sees James using the term to mean the "'middle' span" of life—the late twenties to late fifties (*Life* 3, 18). James's borrowing of the earlier title shows his recognition that he had lived beyond his own middle years, a recognition seen also in a notebook entry shortly following the failure of *Guy Domville*: "Large and full and high the future still opens. It is now indeed that I may do the work of my life. And I will" (CN 109). As Isle notes, unlike his hero, James had his second chance (19). Rahv puts it differently, picturing a James who "understood that for the artist there can be no second chance," but who himself grew into a "full maturity" (xii). Brodhead stresses how much James associated such a maturity with a "late style." Here in what Brodhead calls James's "transition anxiety," James projects what will be his deliberate adoption of a late style as a hedge against "natural time itself" (170–71).

But in writing "The Middle Years" James was not yet on the other side. In a discussion of *The Portrait of a Lady*, Quentin Anderson traces the concept of "the middle years" to James's father, who conceived of them as a dark period of soul building. Thus, "the middle years" wrap about Isabel as she returns to England toward the suspended ending of the novel. Later Jamesian characters such as Lambert Strether and Adam Verver are seen reaching the other side of their "middle time." A successful passage may lead to the glory James found in the Galerie d'Apollon. To the artist, this period is the "needful subjective preparation for his subsequent objective or aesthetic expansion." In Dencombe's case, although he found the preparation so protracted it left little room for expansion, Anderson writes, the artist nevertheless "comes to accept the loss of his selfhood; he dies into his work, into creation . . . " (192–93). Dencombe is "saved," writes Lycette, in a manner similar to Strether (61–62). Dencombe finds his own "glory" at the end: "It *is* glory—to have been tested, to have had our little quality and cast our little spell. The thing is to have made somebody care" (CT 9, 75).

The phrasing of the last sentence illustrates another connection between tales. In his notebook entry James had spoken of "the *real* thing that he has in him" (CN 68). It was a phrase with resonance for James, whose short story "The Real Thing" had appeared the month before on April 16, the day after his birthday. The narrator of "The Real Thing" suffered from "an innate preference for the represented subject over the real one," and finds his art suffers when he allows caring to interfere. Here the lesson appears reversed. According to Rovit, however, the artists in both learn that the artist must be "a human being first." For them the "real thing" becomes "the moral completeness of the lives they live," a completeness that demands a close union between their art and experience (438). Lycette also compares the life-affirming morals of the two tales, "The Real Thing" demonstrating the inadequacy of the "pictorial perspective" alone, "The Middle Years" the inadequacy of the dramatic (62).

The tale is linked with "The Great Good Place" by virtue of its common source. There is no dream here, although it may have left its traces in Dencombe's faintings and convalescent rest. Jones notices that both men turn their cares over to younger men (248). Also, to a certain extent, he does realize at the end that what he has dreamed of he has done.

Gerlach points out that James's use of his protagonist's death is found in many of James's short stories, including "The Altar of the Dead," which also concludes just following its protagonist's dying words (82, 88). The hope for a second chance is found also in *The Sacred Fount* where the narrator asks "What's a greater one [miracle] than to have our youth twice over? It's a second wind, another 'go'—which isn't the sort of thing life mostly treats us to" (29).

Interpretation and Criticism

The difference in tone is in large measure what sets it apart from the other tales of writers. Wagenknecht remarks on the difference, for example, between the "satirical and ironic" "The Death of the Lion" and the "pure poetry" of the "profoundly sad and deeply moving" "The Middle Years" (75–76). Segal speaks of its "elegiac lyricism" (107). Fadiman states that "The Middle Years" is unlike all the other tales about writers in that it is *not* "diluted by a certain infusion of self-pity" (316; also Gage 19). Poole illustrates how James underscored Dencombe's selflessness in his revisions for the New York Edition by changing his "murmur" at Hugh's sacrifice to a "wail." Poole, noting two similar changes in *The Aspern Papers* and "The Private Life," remarks that Dencombe is the only one to wail at another's loss, rather than his own (210).

There has been dissent. Edward Stone finds the tale bordering on the "possibly silly" (171). Mackenzie presents a reading in which Dencombe dies at the shock of facing his own insufficient identity made evident to him through the encounter with and misdirected efforts of his double, the healthy Dr. Hugh (107–10). Westbrook argues that Dencombe's story is an "egotistical distortion of what actually happened" and supplies a detailed alternative plot—Dr.

Hugh himself wrote the praising review and only pretended to have sacrificed the fortune for the mercenary Dencombe. Intriguing as this argument may be, Westbrook fails to provide any of the "subtle but unmistakable clues" for it (134–36). Although Dr. Hugh is "off-stage" at the right times, there is no particular need or benefit to reading the story this way.

Westbrook's goal in withdrawing narratorial sympathy from Dencombe is to makes James appear "less of a prig" and "pompous self-pitier" (134). Putt in decrying the tale's "explicit" self-pity (225) provides a justification for Westbrook's motive if not his method. Jones takes the middle ground by postulating a progression in Dencombe out of an original "personal despair" that he mistakes for philosophical renunciation (199). Vaid, however, while accepting Dencombe as a recipient of James's sympathy, argues that James fails "to render artistically the transfiguration of self-pity into self-acceptance." Basically, Vaid resents James's choice to "dramatise" the story. Although he labels James's description in the Preface of working from the "outer edge in, rather than from its centre outward" unclear, it is clear that this approach is the cause of most of Vaid's dissatisfaction. Even as Putt would reform the "staginess" of Dencombe and Dr. Hugh's original encounter (225), Vaid wants fewer "unnecessary concession[s]" to external realism such as the Countess and Miss Vernham, and more of Dencombe's inner "transfiguration" (207–10). While Matheson assigns significance to Miss Vernham, and to the Countess and Dr. Hugh's unseen patroness as the representatives of a womanhood hostile to art and the artist, Ward sees the significance of Miss Vernham at least in how her attempt to save Dr. Hugh, the "brutality of her good conscience" as James called it, instead destroys Dencombe (Matheson 226; Ward 65–66). Geismar adopts a halfway position, praising at first James's presentation of the universal melancholy at the passing of time, but finding in the end the tale's lesson still too confined to the artistic experience, rather than the experience of life itself (132–36, 439).

Whatever self-pity there is in the story is not really a question of insufficient fame, but of absolute accomplishment. The notebook entry pays no attention to the extent of Dencombe's audience and the narrator tells us flatly at the start that he "had a reputation." Dupee has perhaps located the distinction in his statement that "This time the question of public recognition is united with the question of a writer's acceptance of himself" (153; also Markow-Totevy 97). Horne sees the story as disproving Dencombe's belief that "a first existence was too short—long enough only to collect material; so that to fructify, to use the material, one should have a second age, an extension." Dencombe, she argues, learns that art not only has to be produced in the midst of life, but is better for the "fervour" such struggle brings to it (69–70). The distinction is also due to the way James has connected here, as Hoffmann observes, the theme of art versus life to the "problem of middle age" (53). Dencombe's greatest threat is not neglect, but death. Gale has discovered "a clever little joke" by James emphasizing this theme. In the New York Edition, the story begins with a roman numeral I, setting up the ultimately frustrated expectation of a II. The readers, then, like Dencombe, must face the realization that "a second chance" is a "delusion." Austin Wright sees Dencombe in this realization and the acceptance of it reaching a stance that "verges on exaltation" demanding a simultaneous "enlargement" of the reader's sensibility for its proper effect (178).

An indication of the expanding focus can be seen in the change in James's manner of entitling his story collections. The three previous collections all take their names from a story concerned with art: *The Lesson of the Master* (1892), *The Private Life* (1893), and *The Real Thing* (1893). But even though two of the three other stories accompanying "The Middle Years" in book form concern artists, James grouped all four thematically by the deaths they portray—*Terminations*. His concern with age shows too in the notebook entry immediately following that for "The Middle Years" sketching out "The Wheel of Time."

Kermode points out that Dencombe is still "poor" Dencombe in the last sentence as he is in the first—and as, according to Gosse, most people were for James (Kermode 20; Charteris 176). Life is still in the end, for each of us individually, a tragedy. When frustration passes, so does life. In 1895 James had lamented to Howells of "a new generation, that I know not, and mainly prize not" (*Letters* 3, 511). Through Dr. Hugh, Dencombe not only gains a sense of his accomplishment in terms of the things that last—art and the imagination—but sees it accepted by another generation. Although he initially misreads Dencombe's book so badly that Rawlings sees the implications for reading as "profoundly pessimistic," Dencombe is able to educate him in "creative reading" (xix). Babin writes that Hugh "chooses to determine the worth of things in a way to which he has been opened by art, by life, and particularly by Dencombe" (511). Lycette stresses Dencombe's initial misreading of the relationships between the other characters. His recognition of his mistakes and his friendship with Hugh bring him out of the isolation of his art into life, and so teach him the lasting value of that art (61–62). Wegelin sees Dencombe learning that true art defies conscious aims, and learning his lesson through his "experience among human beings," particularly Dr. Hugh (643–44).

The relationship between Dr. Hugh and Dencombe has also been interpreted as possessing what Matheson calls "an almost erotic intensity" (226). Beattie characterizes Dencombe's "devotion" as "almost wifely," while Haddick takes it as an "unequivocal" homosexual relationship (Beattie 98; Haddick 20). Jacobson also finds in the "impassioned eloquence" of Dencombe's great apologia a "transference" of his love for Dr. Hugh (96–97). Hartsock argues that Dr. Hugh's "caring" for Dencombe is at the heart of the work and that without a homosexual basis, his "devotion" "goes beyond any credibility" (306–7). The last argument is disturbing in that it bases the case for the homosexual relationship not on the quality of affection between the two men, but on an assumption that it makes no sense for someone to renounce without gain, even as Jacobson seems to assume that no one could care that much for art. At the start, Hugh is in the uncomfortable situation of waiting attendance on a woman he does not like in hopes of material gain. Meeting Dencombe brings him back to his moral senses. Instead of being adopted by the Countess, Dr. Hugh takes his inheritance from Dencombe.

Perhaps for this reason, James's story has served as a fruitful source for later writers as well as critics. James Thurber took the title to use for his 1930 parody of James (Stone 170–74). Robinson has recorded how Budd Schulberg blended James and Fitzgerald to create the lead character in his 1952 novel *The Disenchanted*, Manley Halliday, a writer who attempts a comeback as Dencombe did and is befriended by a young screenwriter, his Dr. Hugh. As he dies, he sees "like a deadly subtitle" the lines from James, "A second chance. That's the delusion. There never was but one." Philip Roth pays tribute in his novel *The Ghost Writer*, which contains nearly five pages of plot summary and two of quotation from James's work. Roth's middle-aged writer Lonoff, according to Oakes, is a "modern version" of James's, while Tintner compares the imagined scene of Anne Frank reading her diary to Dencombe's reading his book (Tintner 1981). Wegelin, in turn, compares Zuckerman's imaginings to Dencombe's when first observing the Countess and her entourage (644). Lonoff's inspiration, pinned to his study wall, is some of James's most famous words—a passage that Walter Wright calls "strikingly rare" for James in its poetry and that Tintner unwisely essays to paraphrase: "We work in the dark—we do what we can—we give what we have. Our doubt is our passion and our passion is our task. The rest is the madness of art" (Wright 50; Tintner 1987, 48).

Works Cited

Primary Works

James, Henry. 1893. "The Middle Years." *Scribner's* 13 (May): 609–20.

———. 1895. "The Middle Years." *Terminations*. London: Heinemann; New York: Harper & Brothers, 151–84.

———. *The Sacred Font*. New York: Scribner's.

———. 1909. "The Middle Years." *The Novels and Tales of Henry James*. New York Edition. Vol. 16, 75–106. New York: Scribner's.

Secondary Works

Allen, Elizabeth. 1984. *A Woman's Place in the Novels of Henry James*. New York: St. Martin's.

Anderson, Quentin. 1957. *The American Henry James*. New Brunswick, NJ: Rutgers University Press.

Anesko, Michael. 1986. *"Friction with the Market": Henry James and the Profession of Authorship*. New York: Oxford University Press.

Anon. 1895. Review of *Terminations*. "Mr. James in a Sombre Mood." *New York Times*, 26 June, 3.

———. 1895. Review of *Terminations*. *Literary World* 26 (13 July): 218.

———. 1895. Review of *Terminations*. *Nation* 41 (25 July): 63.

———. 1895. Review of *Terminations*. *Critic* 27 (3 August): 67–68.

Babin, James L. 1977. "Henry James's 'Middle Years' in Fiction and Autobiography." *The Southern Review* 13, no. 3 (July): 505–17.

Beattie, Munro. 1967. "The Many Marriages of Henry James." In *Patterns of Commitment in American Literature*. Ed. Marston La France, 93–112. Toronto: University of Toronto Press.

Berthoff, Warner. 1965. *The Ferment of Realism: American Literature, 1884–1919*. New York: Free Press.

Brodhead, Richard H. 1986. *The School of Hawthorne*. New York: Oxford University Press.

Brooks, Peter. 1976. *The Melodramatic Imagination: Balzac, Henry James, Melodrama, and the Mode of Excess*. New Haven: Yale University Press.

Caramello, Charles. 1981. "Performing Self as Performance: James, Joyce, and the Postmodern Turn." *Southern Humanities Review* 15, no. 4 (Fall): 301–5.

Charteris, Evan. 1931. *The Life and Letters of Sir Edmund Gosse*. New York: Harper.

Cowdery, Lauren Tozek. 1986. *The Nouvelle of Henry James in Theory and Practice*. Studies in Modern Literature 47. Ann Arbor: UMI Research Press.

Dupee, F. W. [1951] 1956. *Henry James*. Garden City, NY: Doubleday Anchor.

Edgar, Pelham. [1927] 1964. *Henry James, Man and Author*. New York: Russell & Russell.

Fadiman, Clifton, ed. 1945. *The Short Stories of Henry James*. New York: Random House.

Gage, Richard P. 1988. *Order and Design: Henry James' Titled Story Sequences*. New York: Peter Lang.

Gale, Robert L. 1963. "James's 'The Middle Years.'" *Explicator* 22 (November): Item 22.

Geismar, Maxwell. 1963. *Henry James and the Jacobites*. Boston: Houghton Mifflin.

Gerlach, John. 1985. *Toward the End: Closure and Structure in American Short Stories*. University: University of Alabama Press.

Haddick, Vern. 1976. "Colors in the Carpet." *Gay Literature* 5: 19–21.

Hartsock, Mildred E. 1968. "Henry James and the Cities of the Plain." *Modern Language Quarterly* 29 (September): 297–311.

Hoffmann, Charles G. 1957. *The Short Novels of Henry James*. New York: Bookman.

Horne, Helen. 1960. *Basic Ideals of James's Aesthetics as Expressed in the Short Stories Concerning Artists and Writers.* Marburg: Erich Mauersberger.

Isle, Walter. 1968. *Experiments in Form: Henry James's Novels, 1896–1901.* Cambridge, MA: Harvard University Press.

Jacobson, Marcia. 1983. *Henry James and the Mass Market.* University: University of Alabama Press.

Jones, Granville H. 1975. *Henry James's Psychology of Experience: Innocence, Responsibility, and Renunciation in the Fiction of Henry James.* The Hague: Mouton.

Kermode, Frank, ed. 1986. *The Figure in the Carpet and Other Stories.* London: Penguin.

Lycette, Ronald L. 1977. "Perceptual Touchstones for the Jamesian Artist-Hero." *Studies in Short Fiction* 14: 55–62.

Mackenzie, Manfred. 1976. *Communities of Honor and Love in Henry James.* Cambridge, MA: Harvard University Press.

Markow-Totevy, Georges. 1969. *Henry James.* Trans. John Griffiths. London: Merlin.

Matheson, Gwen. 1968. "Portraits of the Artist and the Lady in the Shorter Fictions of Henry James." *Dalhousie Review* 48: 222–30.

Matthiessen, F. O. 1944. "Introduction: Henry James' Portrait of the Artist." *Henry James: Stories of Writers and Artists.* Norfolk, CT: New Directions. Also reprinted as "Henry James's Portrait of the Artist." *Partisan Review* 11 (1944): 71–87.

Oakes, Randy W. 1984. "Faces of the Master in Roth's *The Ghost Writer.*" *NMAL: Notes on Modern American Literature* 8 (Autumn): Item 11.

Poole, Adrian, ed. 1983. *The Aspern Papers and Other Stories.* Oxford: Oxford University Press.

Pound, Ezra. 1918. "The Middle Years." *The Little Review* (August): 5–41.

Putt, S. Gorley. 1966. *Henry James: A Reader's Guide.* Ithaca, NY: Cornell University Press.

Rahv, Philip, ed. 1944. *The Great Short Novels of Henry James.* New York: Dial.

Rawlings, Peter, ed. 1984. *Henry James's Shorter Masterpieces.* Vol. 1. Sussex: Harvester; Totowa, NJ: Barnes & Noble.

Richardson, Lyon N., ed. 1941. *Henry James: Representative Selections, with Introduction, Bibliography, and Notes.* New York: American Writer Series; Urbana: University of Illinois Press.

Robinson, J. J. 1952. "Henry James and Schulberg's 'The Disenchanted.'" *Modern Language Notes* 67 (November): 472–73.

Rovit, Earl. 1964. "James and Emerson: The Lesson of the Master." *The American Scholar* (Summer): 434–40.

Segal, Ora. 1969. *The Lucid Reflector: The Observer in Henry James' Fiction.* New Haven: Yale University Press.

Stone, Edward. 1964. *The Battle of the Books: Some Aspects of Henry James.* Athens: Ohio University Press.

Swan, Michael. 1957. *Henry James.* London: Longmans, Green.

————, ed. 1948. *Ten Short Stories of Henry James.* London: Lehmann.

Tintner, Adeline R. 1987. *The Book World of Henry James: Appropriating the Classics.* Ann Arbor: UMI Research Press.

————. 1981. "Henry James as Roth's Ghost Writer." *Midstream* 27, no. 3: 48–51.

Vaid, Krishna B. 1964. *Technique in the Tales of Henry James.* Cambridge, MA: Harvard University Press.

van Cromphout, G. 1968. "Artist and Society in Henry James." *English Studies: A Journal of English Letters and Philology* 49, no. 2 (April): 132–40.

Wagenknecht, Edward. 1984. *The Tales of Henry James.* New York: Frederick Ungar.

Ward, J. A. 1961. *The Imagination of Disaster: Evil in the Fiction of Henry James.* Lincoln: University of Nebraska Press.

Wegelin, Christof. 1987. "Art and Life in James's 'The Middle Years.'" *Modern Fiction Studies* 33: 639–46.

Westbrook, Perry D. 1953. "The Supersubtle Fry." *Nineteenth-Century Fiction* 8 (September): 134–40.

Woolf, Virginia. [1942] 1984. "Professions for Women." In *The Virginia Woolf Reader.* Ed. Mitchell A. Leaska, 276–82. New York: Harcourt, Brace. Reprinted from *The Death of the Moth and Other Essays,* 235–42. New York: Harcourt, Brace.

Wright, Austin McGiffert. 1961. *The American Short Story in the Twenties.* Chicago: University of Chicago Press.

Wright, Walter F. 1962. *The Madness of Art: A Study of Henry James.* Lincoln: University of Nebraska Press.

Miss Gunton of Poughkeepsie

Publication History

James sold the story in December of 1899 and it appeared in New York from May to June 1900 in *Truth* with illustrations by W. L. Jacobs, and in London in May in the *Cornhill Magazine*, where Miss Gunton's earlier compatriots Daisy Miller and Mrs. Headway had also made their first European bow (*Life* 4, 338). It was the latest of the tales James added to that year's collection, *The Soft Side* (*Correspondence* 195 n.2), and was also included in the New York Edition.

Circumstances of Composition, Sources, and Influences

The initial situation of "Miss Gunton" was based on the experience of the daughter of James's friend Katherine Bronson, who encountered a similar stalemate when engaged to the Count Rucellai of Florence. Although she eventually gave in and "wrote first," James, in his notebook in February 1895, while in London, considered the ramifications of a girl's continuing to refuse to do so (CN 116). The name "Gunton" appears in a list James made in November 1899 shortly before the story appeared (CN 187). James made his Italian a Roman prince, while converting the expatriate American to a tourist from Poughkeepsie, a town James may have remembered from trips by the river between his grandmother's home in Albany and New York City.

Relation to Other Works

Maves finds "Miss Gunton of Poughkeepsie" and "The Solution" serving as a "miniature prologue" to James's later international works (102). More specifically, the tale, with its American girl and Italian prince, is most often read as a short, simple "prologue" to *The Golden Bowl* (e.g., Maves 102). Elizabeth Allen links Miss Gunton with Maggie Verver, arguing that both see in their prince his "history," not his "self" (182). Wegelin detects more of a contrast, arguing that unlike Miss Gunton and her prince, Maggie and hers share a "common intelligence" that makes reconciliation possible, an ending that Wegelin judges more representative of what James saw as the future of

internationalism and that contrasts with what Putt sees as a return in the tale
to the resentment of *The American* (Wegelin 149; Putt 134). Nathalia Wright
classes Miss Gunton instead with Maggie's father as well as with Gilbert
Osmond, among others, as a collector of cultural prizes, while Putt sees her
anticipating Charlotte Stant (Wright 223–24; Putt 134). Sharp adds Lady
Champer as a "finger exercise" for Fanny Assingham, since both
Englishwomen negotiate between American and Italian attitudes in an
attempt to keep a couple together (216). The prince's fear of his mother's
reaction to his marriage choice ties him in part to the daughters in "Mrs.
Temperley" and *The American*.

At the end of the tale Lady Champer exclaims, "With Americans one is
lost!" (CT 11, 92). Her cry, according to Walter Allen, "echoes and re-
echoes" through James's international works such as *Madame de Mauves*,
and this shorter tale itself contains the essence of his international theme
(43–44). Accordingly, although James placed the tale in volume 16 of the
New York Edition, which opens with "The Author of Beltraffio," he reserved
discussion of it for volume 13, which contains *Lady Barbarina*, *The Siege of
London*, and *An International Episode*, and for volume 18 with the other
"international young ladies" (*Criticism* 2, 1277). Critics such as Maves and
Putt have accordingly picked up on the similarities with Daisy Miller and
Bessie Alden (Maves 103; Putt 134). Both Daisy and Pandora had, like Lily
Gunton, their starts in small towns in upstate New York, while Mrs.
Penniman in the uncollected *Washington Square* accepts residence at her
brother's in the city "with the alacrity of a woman who had spent the ten
years of her married life in the town of Poughkeepsie," and, unlike Miss
Gunton, evidences no desire to return. Ward cautions that when an
American gains a victory over Europe as here and in *An International
Episode*, *The Siege of London*, and *The Reverberator*, it is because he has
dealt only with its "surface" (39). Jones is more impressed with Lily's victory, and remarks on its superiority to the fate of Daisy Miller, Mme de
Mauves, and even Bessie Alden (103). Like Tanner, however, who finds Lily
"hard and socially ambitious" unlike the "fresh, open" Daisy, Jones is not
impressed with Lily herself, finding her as selfish in her demands as
Georgina of "Georgina's Reasons" (Tanner 124; Jones 102–3, 157–58). Voss,
on the other hand, judges Lily's reasons for refusing the prince "not so different" from Bessie's for refusing Lord Lambeth (137).

Interpretation and Criticism

Wegelin observes that in contrast with most of the late international tales, in
which the international theme is subordinate, the contrast between cultures
is the focus here, the puzzle for the prince and his confidante being the

American character: "Is it . . . a supreme sense of what aristocracy means, or is it the lack of all such sense?" (53–54).

Vaid notes that the story presents Lily's "case" with only a "mildly ironical" cast, courtesy of the narrator. At the same time, he considers the tale a rare instance in which James managed to present a situation fully without interior analysis of the characters, producing a "simple and uninvolved" result (193). The character of Lily, however, has generated questions. Most harshly, Putt speaks of her "grotesque egotism" and her "vulgar and quite unprovoked" demands on her intended family (134). Wegelin asks why, if Lily is so attracted by the prince's aristocratic "position," she objects to the display of it by his mother (53). Matthiessen and Murdock explain it by seeing Lily as so admiring the prince's tradition that it makes her stand up for her own as well (N 190). As James put it in his notebook, she has "taken her stand on her own custom—her own people." It is an "*idée fixe*" (CN 116). Also, as Lily herself says quite openly, "Unless he wants me more than anything else in the world I don't want him" (CT 11, 79). Evidently, part of the appeal of an aristocrat for her was the sight of nobility humbling itself for her sake, of herself as the only superior to a man who acknowledged no others (Jones 103). Perhaps, too, she realized she should not marry a man she cared about less than she did a letter. In addition, as Andreas points out, the European tradition implies an "absorption" of the woman into her new family, while the American preserves more of a sense of the wife as an individual (142–43). Tilton provides a more practical rationale, arguing that international differences had shrunk so much since James began writing his international tales, that he needed to give his heroine "a special stubbornness" to create sufficient conflict (x).

Another part of the puzzle for Lady Champer and the Prince is their inability to grasp that Lily does not recognize what they consider a given: the inferiority of Poughkeepsie to Italy, and therefore the relative insignificance of her wishes. The same inability appears to hold for many critics. Jones speaks of Lily wanting the Prince's mother to "compromise society's code," failing to acknowledge that there are two societies and two codes operating here (103). Gage criticizes her clinging to her American identity as "soft" (53–54). As a result, while Austin Wright explicitly questions how much of Lily's behavior is sincere and how much pretense (407), most critics tend to assume her behavior is mostly the latter. Walter Allen is an exception, seeing in the tale the "clash of conventions . . . each proper in the context of its own society but irreconcilable with the other" (44).

Most critics are also struck, as was the Prince, by her seemingly limitless ability to "draw" on her funds (e.g., Jefferson 78). Fowler goes so far as to portray her link to her grandfather as simply an economic one (42–43). However, if she is characterized primarily by her wealth, the prince is characterized primarily by his desire for it, an attitude Matthiessen and Murdock consider "an amusingly vulgar touch" (N 190). While Maves judges him a more interesting character than the traveling art student American (103), he has in himself little more to show. Significantly, only one critic, Gage, sees him as suffering because of his love for Lily, even though Wegelin and Wagenknecht argue that he loses more than she: not only her and her money, but even his mother's good will (Wegelin 124; Wagenknecht 103). Gage speaks of a general lack of "grace and generosity" in the tale (53–54). It is certainly not all Lily's doing. In a contemporary review wishing for a little more "real heart" in his tales, Carolyn Shipman wished, not that Lily would give in, but that the Prince would be "spontaneous," follow her to America, and marry her there (299). It is not entirely unfair that, as Maves points out, this is the first tale in James to show Italy losing to America (104). While Sharp notes that Lady Champer has at least the "satisfaction" of having been right (216), Lily sounds at the end as if she intends to be happy.

Works Cited

Primary Works

James, Henry. 1900. "Miss Gunton of Poughkeepsie." *Cornhill Magazine* n.s. 8 (May): 603–15.

———. 1900. "Miss Gunton of Poughkeepsie." *Truth* (June): 116–18, 142–43.

———. 1900. "Miss Gunton of Poughkeepsie." *The Soft Side*. London: Methuen; New York: Macmillan, 311–26.

———. "Miss Gunton of Poughkeepsie." *The Novels and Tales of Henry James*. New York Edition. Vol. 16, 371–92. New York: Scribner's.

———. 1993. *The Correspondence of Henry James and the House of Macmillan, 1877–1914*. Ed. Rayburn S. Moore. Baton Rouge: Louisiana State University Press.

Secondary Works

Allen, Elizabeth. 1984. *A Woman's Place in the Novels of Henry James*. New York: St. Martin's.

Allen, Walter. 1980. *The Short Story in English*. New York: Oxford University Press.

Andreas, Osborn. 1948. *Henry James and the Expanding Horizon: A Study of the Meaning and Basic Themes of James's Fiction*. Seattle: University of Washington Press.

Fowler, Virginia C. 1984. *Henry James's American Girl: The Embroidery on the Canvas*. Madison: University of Wisconsin Press.

Gage, Richard P. 1988. *Order and Design: Henry James' Titled Story Sequences*. New York: Peter Lang.

Jefferson, D. W. 1964. *Henry James and the Modern Reader*. New York: St. Martin's.

Jones, Granville H. 1975. *Henry James's Psychology of Experience: Innocence, Responsibility, and Renunciation in the Fiction of Henry James*. The Hague: Mouton.

Maves, Carl. 1973. *Sensuous Pessimism: Italy in the Work of Henry James*. Bloomington: Indiana University Press.

Putt, S. Gorley. 1966. *Henry James: A Reader's Guide*. Ithaca, NY: Cornell University Press.

Sharp, Sister M. Corona. 1963. *The Confidante in Henry James: Evolution and Moral Value of a Fictive Character*. Notre Dame, IN: Notre Dame University Press.

Shipman, Carolyn. 1900. Review of *The Soft Side*. *The Book Buyer* 21 (November): 299–300.

Tanner, Tony. 1985. *Henry James: The Writer and His Work*. Amherst: University of Massachusetts Press.

Tilton, Eleanor, ed. *Henry James: "The Marriages" and Other Stories*. A Signet Classic. New York: New American Library.

Vaid, Krishna B. 1964. *Technique in the Tales of Henry James*. Cambridge, MA: Harvard University Press.

Voss, Arthur. 1973. *The American Short Story: A Critical Survey*. Norman: University of Oklahoma Press.

Wagenknecht, Edward. 1984. *The Tales of Henry James*. New York: Frederick Ungar.

Ward, J. A. 1961. *The Imagination of Disaster: Evil in the Fiction of Henry James*. Lincoln: University of Nebraska Press.

Wegelin, Christof. 1958. *The Image of Europe in Henry James*. Dallas: Southern Methodist University Press.

Wright, Austin McGiffert. 1961. *The American Short Story in the Twenties*. Chicago: University of Chicago Press.

Wright, Nathalia. 1965. *American Novelists in Italy, The Discoverers: Allston to James*. Philadelphia: University of Pennsylvania Press.

The Modern Warning

Publication History

James first published this tale under the title "Two Countries" in the June 1888 issue of *Harper's New Monthly Magazine*, where it was accompanied by illustrations by C. S. Reinhart, the subject of one of James's essays in his 1893 *Picture and Text*. When he included it the same year in the collection *The Aspern Papers*, he gave it the more urgent title "The Modern Warning." He never again reprinted the tale, which next appeared in Lubbock's edition of the novels and stories in the 1920s.

Circumstances of Composition, Sources, and Influences

James recorded in a notebook entry on July 9, 1884, his inspiration for "The Modern Warning," a reading of Sir Lepel Henry's 1884 book *The Great Republic*, a conservative warning against the United States (N 66). Thus the story began with the "type" of Sir Rufus, whom James quickly imagined in love with a properly patriotic "American Girl," whom he then attaches to a "violently American" anglophobic brother. The "interest" was to come from the woman's "difficulty of choice and resignation" (CN 29). Edel states that the story was written in 1886, one of the stories James complained of being held back by their publishers, noting that the cause was often the time taken up by illustration (*Life* 3, 167, 243).

Fowler and Ziff both link heroine and author, Ziff seeing James treating through his heroine his own decision to leave America for England (Fowler 149 n.7; Ziff 55). Edel sees James as drawing on his talks with Clover Adams and her suicide, though not her character (*Life* 3, 167). James's sister, Alice, in a letter to their brother William wrote of the tale, "I feel as if *I* were the heroine." Yeazell sees Alice's sense of her "Irish blood," shared by the heroine, as a link, but also remarks on Alice's strong "attachment" to her brother. Agatha's response to her brother's visit, she concludes, "strangely antici- pates" Alice's "hysteria" at a surprise visit by William the next year (149).

Tintner, building on the Greek allusions in Agatha Grice's name, sees James, perhaps inspired by Frederick Leighton's painting of the subject, pro- ducing a modern tragic version of Euripides's *Alcestis*, complete with scurry- ing servants, and featuring Macarthy as Death, Sir Rufus as Herakles, and

Agatha as Alcestis deciding to die so that her husband can have his happiness. Since Tintner calls Agatha's actions "irrational," it is understandable that Tintner's explanations of Agatha's behavior are not always convincing. It does not make sense, for example, that once Agatha has consented to the book's publication, Sir Rufus would need her further "out of the way"; nor does it seem logical that the brother would be less angry with Sir Rufus rather than more so after her death, even if it does break their relationship (1989, 123–30). Tintner also compares Agatha and her brother to Byron and his sister (1987, 100–1). She implies an association between the suicide here and in "The Patagonia" and that of Tolstoy's Anna Karenina (1987, 239).

Relation to Other Works

Fowler compares Agatha's insecurity to Isabel Archer's and Milly Theale's and notes that Agatha is made to feel she is "betraying" her brother if she marries, just as Maggie Verver feels she will be betraying her father when she weds (51). Vaid finds the suicide flawed by "unintentional melodrama," as are the deaths in *Roderick Hudson*, *The American*, and *Daisy Miller* (164). Buitenhuis comments that James generally used suicide as the only way around a "fictional deadlock" as in this tale, *Roderick Hudson*, and *The Princess Casamassima*, whose pictures of British misery Dietrichson finds repeated here (Buitenhus 140; Dietrichson 67 n.32; also Stevenson 141). James himself rejected suicide for the heroine of *A London Life* on the grounds that it was "too rare" and that he had just used it in what he still called "Two Countries" (CN 38).

Putt finds the tale's start promising in the manner of *Daisy Miller*, its book-inspired death as absurd as that in "The Author of Beltraffio," and its Anglo-American contrasts in general "heavy and laboured" in contrast to the "light and effective" "The Point of View" (132–34). Part of the last change, as Buitenhuis indicates, is that the multiple voices of the early story dwindle down to two opposed voices, both extreme (139–40). Wegelin likens the contrast between Macarthy and Chase to that between Caspar Goodwood and Lord Warburton, who both possess the best qualities of their countries, British "culture" and American "character" (80, 182 n.18; see also Ziff 55).

Interpretation and Criticism

Donald Stone points to James's statement in his notebook that the thin subject "is always enough if the *author* sees substance in it" as an example of the dangerous confidence that sometimes afflicted James (181). Apart from one contemporary critic who felt that marrying into a family of "monomaniacs" was bound to produce some sort of disaster, most readers have centered their objections to the tale on Agatha's suicide, and have followed the view of William James, who condemned it as "rather abrupt & shocking . . . a piece of wanton tragedy as it seems" (James 99; e.g., Sherbo 51; Stevenson 141; Voss 136–37).

Nevertheless, critics have gone on to attempt to explain her decision. Some do so by characterizing Agatha as fundamentally weak, or as Edgar puts it, "easily distracted" (53). Others point to the story's two central themes of patriotic and familial loyalty. Analyzing the family constellation, Stevenson notes Agatha's "morbid love" for her brother, but finds it inadequately developed as a motive (141; also Tintner 1987, 100–1).

Looking at the conflict between the two countries, McElderry finds that the lack of specific information about the charges against America in Sir Rufus's book renders the patriotic motive unconvincing (77). Buitenhuis argues that James may simply have lost interest in the international theme, as indicated in the notebook entry, while Edel indicates that at the time James was coming to an increasing sense of the "futility" of dwelling on the dwindling differences between America and Britain rapidly becoming "a big Anglo-Saxon total" (140; CT 6, 9; *Life* 3, 241). Ziff argues, however, that James is showing his own misgivings about such "a big Anglo-Saxon total" as he called it to his brother William and indicating even in a story that favors the English, what one loses in losing one's Americanness (54–56). Wegelin believes that James's lack of interest in "political principles" weakened his presentation of American attitudes, such as the dislike of British snobbery or the concern over the desertion of American women for titled marriages (80–81). Matthiessen and Murdock, on the other hand, believe the brother's criticisms do "balance" the debate, while the presence of what Walter Wright calls "brief but damning" pictures of English poverty in the tale indicate that James expended at least some effort bolstering the American case (N 66; Wright 76; also Wagenknecht 194).

Putt seeks to separate the strands of familial and cultural conflicts, arguing that it is their overlapping that causes the story to fail. To him, the excessive emotions generated in response to the husband's book become a sign of the story's basic unreality (133–34). The most successful analyses of the story, however, rest precisely on the recognition of how the two themes reinforce each other. Edel and Fowler both note how, for Agatha, brother and country become identified (CT 7, 9; Fowler 49). As Vaid observes, without the international context, the story makes no sense (275 n.2). Indeed, Agatha thinks of herself as marrying "partly to bring [Chasemore] over to the admiration of her country" (CT 7, 55). Jones sees Agatha as an illustration of the destructiveness of patriotic and personal devotion unbalanced by a strong sense of self (110–11). Fowler examines Agatha's plight, more specifically, as representative of the typical American girl. She sees the brother's patriotic objections as a cover for his desire that his sister abandon all attempts to establish an independent identity and be as devoted to his domestic comfort as he is committed to his business. Despite its excessiveness, Agatha cannot shake her sense of his claim on her (47–51).

In her indictment of the American businessman brother, Fowler lets the British husband off the hook; Jones, too, finds him "considerate and patient" (111). According to Ziff's analysis, the reader is at first glad that Agatha goes against her domineering brother to marry the superior Sir Rufus, but the story makes clear after the marriage that there is a certain freedom associated with America not seen in England (56). Though Tintner may be putting it a bit strongly in saying that Rufus values his book more than his wife, certainly he holds his views equal to her, and is capable of such condescension as informing his wife that "she knew nothing whatever" about her own country (1989, 130; CT 7, 71).

Wagenknecht accurately pictures Agatha as "crushed between" the two men, Sir Rufus's being "unusually intelligent" as if to even the conflict (194; also Buitenhuis 140). Allen, too, indicts both men, pointing out James's awareness of the way women, forced to serve as representatives of others, are "ideally blanks." In her reading, Agatha is caught, unable to "abandon her American identity and her relation to her American brother, in order to represent England and her English husband." She is also unable, too, to find a way through language to negotiate such complex social codes, as Allen notes some of James's women do (43). In Ziff's phrasing, she "cannot strike an adequate balance" (56). Nathalia Wright has pointed to the significance of Agatha and Rufus's meeting in Italy (217). Its main importance might well be that it allows the two to meet on neutral territory, but the common ground it provides proves illusory. Between them the two men insist on her making a choice between the "two countries," and Agatha dies under the strain.

Works Cited

Primary Works
James, Henry. 1888. "Two Countries." *Harper's New Monthly Magazine* 77 (June): 83–116.

———. 1888. "The Modern Warning." *The Aspern Papers*. London and New York: Macmillan, 197–290.

———. 1921–23. "The Modern Warning." *The Novels and Stories of Henry James*. Vol. 26. Ed. Percy Lubbock. London: Macmillan.

Secondary Works
Allen, Elizabeth. 1984. *A Woman's Place in the Novels of Henry James*. New York: St. Martin's.

Buitenhuis, Peter. 1970. *The Grasping Imagination: The American Writings of Henry James*. Toronto: University of Toronto Press.

Dietrichson, Jan W. 1969. *The Image of Money in the American Novel of the Gilded Age*. Oslo: Universitetsforlaget; New York: Humanities.

Edgar, Pelham. [1927] 1964. *Henry James, Man and Author*. New York: Russell & Russell.

Fowler, Virginia. 1984. *Henry James's American Girl: The Embroidery on the Canvas*. Madison: University of Wisconsin Press.

James, William. 1983. *The Correspondence of William James*. Vol. 2: *William and Henry: 1885–1896*. Ed. Ignas K. Skrupskelis and Elizabeth M. Berkeley. Charlottesville: University Press of Virginia.

Jones, Granville H. 1975. *Henry James's Psychology of Experience: Innocence, Responsibility, and Renunciation in the Fiction of Henry James*. The Hague: Mouton.

McElderry, Bruce R., Jr. 1965. *Henry James*. New York: Twayne.

Putt, S. Gorley. 1966. *Henry James: A Reader's Guide*. Ithaca, NY: Cornell University Press.

Sherbo, Arthur. 1990. "Jamesian Gleanings." *Henry James Review* 11: 42–57.

Stevenson, Elizabeth. [1949] 1981. *The Crooked Corridor: A Study of Henry James*. New York: Octagon.

Stone, Donald David. 1972. *Novelists in a Changing World: Meredith, James, and the Transformation of English Fiction in the 1880's*. Cambridge, MA: Harvard University Press.

Tintner, Adeline R. 1989. *The Pop World of Henry James: From Fairy Tales to Science Fiction*. Ann Arbor: UMI Research Press.

———. 1987. *The Book World of Henry James: Appropriating the Classics*. Ann Arbor: UMI Research Press.

Vaid, Krishna B. 1964.*Technique in the Tales of Henry James*. Cambridge, MA: Harvard University Press.

Voss, Arthur. 1973. *The American Short Story: A Critical Survey*. Norman: University of Oklahoma Press.

Wagenknecht, Edward. 1984. *The Tales of Henry James*. New York: Frederick Ungar.

Wegelin, Christof. 1958. *The Image of Europe in Henry James*. Dallas: Southern Methodist University Press.

Wright, Nathalia. 1965. *American Novelists in Italy, The Discoverers: Allston to James*. Philadelphia: University of Pennsylvania Press.

Wright, Walter F. 1962. *The Madness of Art: A Study of Henry James*. Lincoln: University of Nebraska Press.

Yeazell, Ruth Bernard, ed. 1981. *The Death and Letters of Alice James*. Berkeley: University of California Press.

Ziff, Larzer. 1966. *The American 1890's: Life and Times of a Lost Generation*. New York: Viking.

Mora Montravers

Publication History

"Mora Montravers," like James's preceding two stories, appeared in Ford Madox Ford's *English Review*, in the August and September issues of 1909. James collected it the next year in *The Finer Grain*. After James's death, Lubbock added the tale to his edition of the collected novels and stories.

Circumstances of Composition, Sources, and Influences

James recorded the germ for "Mora Montravers" on August 2, 1901, at Lamb House. It was taken from a conversation with George Ashburner, who told the story of Sir John Simon's niece who had "bolted." The man she was now living with told Sir John, "If I marry her I lose all control of her." The uncle insisted they marry and they did, and the new husband subsequently lost all control of the niece. Taking the germ, James wondered what would happen if "one of the parties interested or connected *doesn't* insist, while the other does" (CN 197).

The story was meant to be a "short thing" (CN 198). Of course, it was not. Neither was the time from its inception to publication. It was eight years later that James wrote his agent, Pinker, of the completion of the tale on April 13, making it the last of the tales finished for *The Finer Grain* (Tintner 1975, 361).

At one point in the contretemps over their niece Traffle thinks of his wife, "I've only to go, and then come back with some 'new fact' *à la Dreyfus*, in order to make her sit up in a false flare that will break our insufferable spell" (CT 12, 302). Tintner takes the reference, bolstered by the subsequent repetition of the words "facts" and "truths," to read the tale as a treatment of the Dreyfus case, with Mora's innocence vindicated ultimately by new information even as was Dreyfus's (1989, 271–74).

For James, the Dreyfus case was, according to Tintner, connected with his sense of Edith Wharton's difficult marriage, about which he also looked for "any definite 'new fact.'" As a result, she argues, Traffle's "amused view" toward Mora's behavior echoes James's own attitude toward Wharton's marital difficulties. Tintner compares Mora and Wharton as "working artists" who "defy the conventional moralities." Among the other characters, Traffle plays James, Wharton's friend Walter Berry appears as Walter Puddick, and Bernard Berenson has a cameo as Sir Bruce Bagley. She also notes a specific allusion to Wharton's "The Mission of Jane," in which an incompatible couple come to terms with each other as they deal with the difficult girl they have adopted (1975, 362–65).

Tintner also suggests an allusion to George Bernard Shaw's response to James's play *The Saloon*. Shaw had written James that repressed families such as the one in his play were "smashed every day . . . by one girl who goes out and earns her living or takes a degree somewhere." Accordingly, the repressive Traffle family is "smashed into smithereens by [Mora's] leaving their roof" (1975, 362–63). Martin and Ober detect another Shavian note with roots in Nietzsche in the reversal of values the tale represents, the respectable Jane being the "monster," Mora her superior (123).

When Mora leaves home, she marries, but in a markedly modern way. Martin and Ober find her approach to marriage even more "radical" than that in the novels of D. H. Lawrence (125). Wagenknecht reaches farther back to compare her unconventionality toward marriage to that of Cathy in *Wuthering Heights* (165–66). Beattie sees James venturing into "H. G. Wells territory," and Tintner points specifically to his *Ann Veronica* as another treatment of the theme of the "new woman" (Beattie 103; 1989, 283). In 1919 Hackett referred to the story as Nora Montravers, and Tintner calls its heroine "Nora-Mora" (Hackett 79; Tintner 1971–1972, 368). Both variations imply a connection with another famous "new woman" who also exits her "doll house." Krook, on the other hand, sees Ibsen's "depressed, deprived women" best represented in Jane (346–47).

Mora's experiences help to develop in Traffle "the vision and the faculty" (CT 12, 332), a phrase Martin and Ober trace to Wordsworth's *The Excursion* (127). They also cite from the lines describing those with "the vision and the faculty divine": "All but a scattered few, live out their time, / Husbanding that which they possess within, / And go the grave, unthought of" (Book I, lines 77–91). The word "husbanding" almost points to the way Traffle's marriage stifles his imaginative development.

The Traffles are respected in their set for having "so much good old mahogany and so many Bartolozzis" (CT 12, 268). Their collection of the eighteenth-century Italian engraver who was enjoying quite a vogue at the turn of the century is, however, to Dyson, an indication that Sidney is more interested in art's social rather than aesthetic value, so that he chooses Bartolozzis over Puddick on meretricious grounds (1980).

Traffle also has a "precious little old Copley Fielding" (CT 12, 288). Fielding, too, Tintner asserts, was a second-rate artist, a watercolorist in the style of Turner. Nevertheless she writes that the picture serves to give Traffle a "sense of freedom" from his suburban setting (1986, 124). For the Metsu that inspires Traffle while visiting the National Gallery, Tinter proposes *The Music Lesson* (1986, 225). Martin and Ober deem its depiction of courtship, "with its combination of realism and romance, of life and art," suitable for Traffle and Mora (124)

Traffle's name is slightly reminiscent of Tommy Traddles in *David Copperfield*, who as a boy specializes in drawing skeletons.

Relation to Other Works

Eshuis notes how Traffle, like Milly in *The Wings of the Dove*, seeks peace in the placidity of Dutch art at the National Gallery. In both works, Eshuis observes, the Dutch room also serves as a different sort of "sanctuary" for the clandestine lovers Mora and Sir Bruce and Kate and Merton, respectively (43–44).

In the National Gallery Traffle tells Mora, "If my living to do something myself hadn't been the most idiotic of dreams, something in *his* [Metsu's] line—though of course a thousand miles behind him—was what I should have tried to go in for" (CT 12, 306). Consequently, Traffle has often been seen, as Voss puts it, as a "lesser Strether," who realizes with regret the life he has failed to live, although Voss sees both men, unlike Marcher, gaining some recompense from their knowledge (150; also Eshuis 43–44; Edgar 181; Tintner 1986, 224–25; Wagenknecht 166). Tintner finds that Mora's different mission in the gallery—to meet a lover—at least ties her to life (1986, 242). Krook finds in Traffle not only a Stretheresque consciousness, but a Pocock philistinism (346). Similarly, Wagenknecht judges Traffle's imagination not only "modest," but "much less dignified" in comparison to Strether's (166). Stein locates the difference in Strether's eventual acceptance of "a redemptive renunciatory vision" that Traffle never achieves (118).

Among the tales of *The Finer Grain*, Edel points to this one and "The Bench of Desolation" as showing a more "compassionate and pitying side" than the rest in their treatment of "human waste, mistaken lives, wrong decisions, lost opportunities" (CT 12, 10). Martin and Ober also link the two tales, arguing that while "The Velvet Glove" and "A Round of Visits" present "victories of the imagination," they illustrate both its failure—in Jane and in Dodd—and victory—in Mora and Sidney and in Kate (122). They connect, however, Traffle's image of Mora—"as if she had just seated herself in the car of a rising balloon that would never descend again to earth" (CT 12,

313)—to the image of Diana in her "chariot of fire" in "The Velvet Glove," Mora here representing the imagination (125). Gage further connects the image of the two romantic women to that of romance in the preface to *The American*. Even as James in the preface speaks of cutting the cable of romance "for the fun of it," Traffle seeks the "fun" here of watching Mora. The two final images, of Traffle looking "out of the glimmering square of the window" and Berridge watching the Princess disappear "in the great floridly-framed aperture," he connects to the image of the house of fiction with its many windows in the preface to *The Portrait of a Lady*. Gage offers additional comparisons in the use of Olympian imagery and in the admiration of the hero for the vitality of the young lovers, maintaining that the basic contrast of respectability and vitality in "Mora Montravers" is a version of the contrast between the contemplative and active lives in "The Velvet Glove" (218–19, 226–28, 230).

Also looking at the tale in the context of the later works, Tanner sees Traffle as a typical character, "shocked or stupefied into immobility and silence," but absolves him of the egoism of John Marcher and Dodd while granting him the compensation of "his private almost Jamesian mind and imagination" (124–25). Jones places Traffle among a group of elderly innocents including the mothers of Daisy Miller and Roderick Hudson, Mrs. Rooth and Mr. Carteret of *The Tragic Muse*, Mr. Longdon of *The Awkward Age*, as well as Mrs. Portico of "Georgina's Reasons," Mrs. Drack of "Julia Bride," and Adam Verver of *The Golden Bowl*. Mora, for her part, Jones places with Maisie and Morgan in *The Pupil* among James's youthful innocents (123, 193).

The setting of Wimbledon is the same as in "The Coxon Fund," where it gives a context to a similar tension between society and art. The representative of stuffy Wimbledon, the wife Jane Traffle, is, Martin and Ober argue, of the same stuff as the vulgar Mrs. Worthingham in "Crapy Cornelia" (123). The "sardonic, bitter-indulgent tone" consequently directed toward her Krook finds new in James (347), but one can see it also in "The Birthplace," where the wife was progressively forced toward practicality as the husband took over the imaginative ground. Martin and Ober characterize the marital split in "The Birthplace" as "neo-tragic" but see it treated here as "sardonic comedy" (123). Looking at the husbands only, Jones remarks how both Traffle and Gedge learn to live with their "nurtured private impressions" (204). Mora, however, acknowledges no distinction between her uncle and her aunt, and like the brother in "Guest's Confession" he must suffer by association for his timidity in failing to stand up for his different standards at a time of crisis.

Walter Wright places the story with such other works of James as "The Figure in the Carpet" and *In the Cage*, which also treat "the fascination of guessing" (128). Jane's awareness of "only one kind of irregularity" brings to mind the philistine argument in "The Story in It" that an adventure must be illicit to be of interest (CT 12, 275).

Interpretation and Criticism

Traffle says of her niece, "She is, one does feel, her name" (CT 12, 278). While Horrell objects that his observation leaves the relationship between name and person vague, Bender quotes Traffle at greater length showing his sense of how its "grand air" puts "a premium on adventures . . . points the whole career for you" (Horrell 205; Bender 254). According to Martin and Ober, Mora's last name suggests "crossing"—perhaps even something like a Nietzschean transvaluation. They gloss the first name as a reference to *Mora excelsa*, a "lofty tree . . . . superior to oak." Thus Mora becomes the "finer grain" (127), in contrast it may be to the Traffles' mahogany. Perhaps seeing Mora as a more conventional transgressor, Lynd mistakenly refers to her as "Mora Maltravers" (11).

The name "Mora" also echoes the adjective "moral," and Mora's morality is one of the story's chief issues. Wagenknecht backs Mora's honesty as consistent with her unconventionality, and states that James makes it easier for the reader to accept such an unusual character by keeping her offstage for a large part of the story (165–66). As a new woman, Tintner notes, Mora is both independent but willing to use her femininity to her advantage (1989, 283). She is, as Edgar observes, "competent to create her own current even in the most stagnant pool" (181).

With what Dyson calls an "explicitly romantic name," Mora is contrasted by name most closely perhaps with what Dyson calls "prosaically denominated Walter Puddick" (CT 12, 278; 1979, 68; also N 8). Although Wright calls Puddick "really an admirable man," Martin and Ober suggest that Puddick, whose works make "so straight a push for the Academy," is not a "true artist" (Wright 128; Martin and Ober 125). The key contast in the tale, however, is usually located in the previous generation in what Matthiessen and Murdock denominate the "ironic interplay" and Edgar the "counterpoise" between the perspectives of Mora's aunt and her uncle (N 310; Edgar 181; also McElderry 146). While Mora's identification of uncle with aunt forces Traffle to realize that "He should stand or fall with fatal Jane," he insists on differentiating himself, presenting her fatal effect in a manner that underlines their opposition: "It was in fact with fatal Jane tied as a millstone round his neck that he at present knew himself sinking" (CT 12, 102)

In Traffle's estimate of himself, he has moved away from his wife's sense of things through the growth of his imagination in following his niece's own evolution. The growth is a mixed blessing, he recognizes: "What would have been the use, after all, of so much imagination as constantly worked in him. Didn't it let him into more deep holes than it pulled him out of? Or didn't it at the same time . . . give him all to himself a life, exquisite, occult, dangerous and sacred, to which everything ministered and which nothing could take away?" (CT 12, 331–32). His late awakening to a new sense of life, emphasized by Matthiessen and Murdock, has traditionally been seen as receiving the imprimatur of the author even when it is criticized, as Fox puts it, as "only a sense of decency" limited by Traffle's role as observer and outsider (N 310; Fox 81).

In the midst of the turmoil caused by Mora, Traffle says to his wife, "If we're having the strain and the pain of it let us also have the relief and the fun" (CT 12, 279). It is a remark and an attitude that Wright judges fully Jamesian. He sees Traffle remaining a "troubled mortal," feeling inferior to Puddick, left out of his wife's new interest in the artist at the same time as he shares a fair amount of her Puritanism, but still a "fascinated spectator" who "live[s]" in his observation of Mora's career (330–32). Jones, too, portrays Traffle as a flawed if sympathetic character, humiliated by his failure to stand up for his niece, aware that Mora was right to leave his oppressive house, that he as well as his wife had felt "threatened" by Mora's vitality, that his own incomplete artistry is a sign of having compromised. In the end he sees Traffle left with nothing but "a rather prurient 'elderly innocence,'" and his imagination, unlikely ever to change his life outwardly. In the meantime his cooperation with Jane's plotting has caused Puddick to lose all connection with a woman he truly cares for and "corrupts the innocence [in Mora] her aunt never believed she had" (154–56). Similarly, Gage sees Sidney as the tale's victim, abandoned in the end even by Jane, who gives her newly developed compassion to Walter—even though she is, Gage observes, a dubious companion for either man. Still Gage sees his "loneliness and isolation" as that of "the richly imaginative man," which provides the few "hints of compensation" in the tale (229–30).

In Wright's estimate, James, by keeping the focus on Traffle, "leaves out what some readers most want," namely an explanation of Mora's behavior (129). Martin and Ober keep the focus on Traffle, seeing the story as Traffle's "gradual realization of the power of the imagination—the artistic consciousness," but also emphasize the role of Mora as his "model of behavior." Mora breaks free from convention in pursuit of "higher social truths" that are "not unrelated" to artistic ones. Jane they cast as the villain, the "denial and death of the imagination." She represents the forms Mora bravely defies, marrying Puddick "with a serene and dispassionate offhandedness that looks like—but is not—cynicism," and allying herself with Sir Bruce, whom they see as a champion of art superior to Puddick. Traffle, they argue, in a prodigious balancing feat manages to honor Mora without betraying his wife, his "pretenses" being cleared of "duplicity" on the grounds that they are forced on him by the unchanged Jane. His is the true consciousness of "those who lead enlightened and enlightening lives." Mora meanwhile "enhances not only her life," but Puddick's, Sir Bruce's, and Traffle's (122–25). In 1972 Tintner similarly portrayed Traffle as a Jamesian observer, but cast Mora as the story's true rebel (1972, 362–65).

By 1989, however, Tintner was referring to Traffle as "an impotent old voyeur" (1989, 22). Earlier, Winner had seen Traffle remaining the "would-be artist, the gentleman, who exemplifies middle-class propriety" in contrast to "the real artist, who is socially outside but artistically very much inside the pale" (108). In 1979 Dyson directly addressed the question of whether Traffle is to be taken as one of the standard-bearers of the Jamesian imagination or as an inadequate observer. Despite his possession of a certain sensitivity, Traffle according to Dyson is from the start "ill at ease with the world outside him." As events progress, Dyson argues, the romantically-minded Traffle is unable to adapt his imagination to account for them, and so imagines himself "excluded" on the grounds of his fineness. Dyson notes the initial contrast set up between Traffle and his "rigidly middle-class" wife. Nevertheless, he argues that Jane, despite a mistaken estimate of Mora and even herself, proves superior to Traffle in the end, able to fashion a new imaginative formula to meet the new facts. She remains involved, unlike Traffle, who, Dyson contends, distances himself from Mora because he is not truly interested in her or anything apart from his own imagination, and so cannot present a "real" version of her story (68–70).

Other critics have also judged Jane superior or at least honorable. Ward, for example, while he initially saw the tale as lacking in self-analysis, later examined its narrative in terms of the implied analysis of Traffle. Traffle, he maintains, is shown to be an "aesthetic idler" and egotist who looks at others only for the sake of "comic diversion," and proves lacking while everyone else in the tale is shown to be better than they seemed at first. The puritanical Jane turns tolerant, Mora and Puddick "quite innocent" (1961, 165; 1967, 57). Similarly, Wagenknecht observes the way in which Jane also "has her inning at the end" by adopting Puddick: "We see a new dimension of her, the existence of which she had until now no more suspected than we had ourselves" (166; also Tintner 1971, 498). Jones, however, while noting Jane's acquisition of sympathy in her friendship with Puddick, sees it unlikely to produce any significant change (156). Krook views the ending as a "super-sardonic *dénouement*," arguing that Jane deliberately contradicts herself in an attempt to get ahead of her husband (347).

In Stein's reading, neither Jane nor Sidney comes in for any sympathy in what Stein calls the "sardonic account of the multiple self-deceptions engendered by an especially luckless union." Like Jones, he acknowledges Jane's change in befriending Puddick, but he sees her attempt to gain a "new identity and new freedom" unlikely to succeed. Similarly, he sees Traffle's bid to escape from convention as too little too late, "a self-deception every bit as pathetic as the one from which he has only just been awakened and far more ludicrous." His attempt to establish a new life through Mora's escape, he argues, is undercut by several facts: the possibility that Puddick himself is not a true artist, that Mora is possibly selfish in taking up with Sir Bruce, and, finally, that he is motivated by an "illicit, unconscious passion for Mora." Still, Traffle's fate is not portrayed tragically, Stein argues, as Traffle remains a "dreamer and bumbler" (115–18).

The critical differences about what the story is saying are reflected also in the differences over how well it says them. While Edgar finds "Mora Montravers" sharing in the "rare perfection of finish" of all the stories in *The Finer Grain* (180), Putt finds its style "deadened by the conditional mood," its prose "of such viscosity that the reader has to struggle through sentences that no parodist of James would dare invent, and no guide, however, conscientious, wish to quote." Putt senses a deadness in the tale as well, the real feelings of its characters being "somehow, sloughed off in their escape from the whole atmosphere and *milieu* of their own story" (301). Jones, however, judges it an "interesting tale" and argues that its "psychological complications raise it to the level of serious art" (156). Wright also points to serious implications in its portrayal of the continual mystery of life in which we can never explain the behavior of others, nor cease trying to do so. Still he calls it a "humorous story" (128, 130). It may be partly the mixture of tones that produces the critical disparity. As Martin and Ober observe, without disparagement, much of the source of the comedy is in Traffle's differences with his wife (121). Precisely because she is presented as so uncomprehending, however, she seems an unfair target for the abuse heaped on her both by her husband and the critics. The tale's combination of humor and seriousness comes together more easily and satisfactorily in the characters of the extravagant Mora and the constantly sentient if baffled Sidney.

Works Cited

Primary Works

James, Henry. 1909. "Mora Montravers." *The English Review* 3 (August–September): 27–52, 214–38.

———. 1910. "Mora Montravers." *The Finer Grain*. New York: Scribner's; London: Methuen, 47–138.

———. 1921–23. "Mora Montravers." *The Novels and Stories of Henry James*. Vol. 28. Ed. Percy Lubbock. London: Macmillan.

Secondary Works

Beattie, Munro. 1967. "The Many Marriages of Henry James." In *Patterns of Commitment in American Literature*. Ed. Marston La France, 93–112. Toronto: University of Toronto Press.

Bender, Bert. 1976. "Henry James's Late Lyric Meditations upon the Mysteries of Fate and Self-Sacrifice." *Genre* 9: 247–62.

Dyson, John Peter. 1980. "Bartolozzi and Henry James's 'Mora Montravers.'" *Henry James Review* 1, no. 3 (Spring): 264–66.

————. 1979. "Romance Elements in Three Late Tales of Henry James: 'Mora Montravers,' 'The Velvet Glove,' and 'The Bench of Desolation.'" *English Studies in Canada* 5: 66–77.

Edgar, Pelham. [1927] 1964. *Henry James, Man and Author*. New York: Russell & Russell.

Eshuis, Enny de Boer. 1984. "Reflections on Holland in the Works of Henry James." *Henry James Review* 6, no. 1 (Fall): 39–45.

Fox, Hugh. 1968. *Henry James, A Critical Introduction*. Conesville, IA: John Westburg.

Gage, Richard P. 1988. *Order and Design: Henry James's Titled Story Sequences*. New York: Peter Lang.

Hackett, Francis. 1919 "Henry James." *Horizons: A Book of Criticism*. New York: Huebsch, 74–82.

Horrell, Joyce Tayloe. 1970. "A 'Shade of a Special Sense': Henry James and the Art of Naming." *American Literature* 42: 203–20.

Jones, Granville H. 1975. *Henry James's Psychology of Experience: Innocence, Responsibility, and Renunciation in the Fiction of Henry James*. The Hague: Mouton.

Krook, Dorothea. [1962] 1967. *The Ordeal of Consciousness in Henry James*. New York: Cambridge University Press.

Lynd, Robert. 1952. "The Return of Henry James." *Books and Writers*. New York: Macmillan, 8–12.

McElderry, Bruce R., Jr. 1965. *Henry James*. New York: Twayne.

Martin, W. R. and Warren U. Ober. 1983. "'Superior to Oak': The Part of Mora Montravers in James's *The Finer Oak*." *American Literary Realism* 16 (Spring): 121–28.

Putt, S. Gorley. 1966. *Henry James: A Reader's Guide*. Ithaca, NY: Cornell University Press.

Stein, Allen F. 1984. *After the Vows Were Spoken: Marriage in American Literary Realism*. Columbus: Ohio State University Press.

Tanner, Tony. 1985. *Henry James: The Writer and His Work*. Amherst: University of Massachusetts Press.

Tintner, Adeline R. 1989. *The Pop World of Henry James: From Fairy Tales to Science Fiction*. Ann Arbor: UMI Research Press.

————.1986. *The Museum World of Henry James*. Ann Arbor: UMI Research Press.

————.1975. "The Metamorphoses of Edith Wharton in Henry James's *The Finer Grain.*" *Twentieth-Century Literature* 21: 335–79.

————. 1971–72. "James's Mock Epic: 'The Velvet Glove,' Edith Wharton, and Other Late Tales." *Modern Fiction Studies* 17 (Winter): 483–99.

Voss, Arthur. 1973. *The American Short Story: A Critical Survey.* Norman: University of Oklahoma Press.

Wagenknecht, Edward. 1984. *The Tales of Henry James.* New York: Frederick Ungar.

Ward, Joseph A. 1967. *The Search for Form: Studies in the Structure of James's Fiction.* Chapel Hill: University of North Carolina Press.

————. 1961. *The Imagination of Disaster: Evil in the Fiction of Henry James.* Lincoln: University of Nebraska Press.

Winner, Viola Hopkins. 1970. *Henry James and the Visual Arts.* Charlottesville: University Press of Virginia.

Wright, Walter F. 1962. *The Madness of Art: A Study of Henry James.* Lincoln: University of Nebraska Press.

A Most Extraordinary Case

Publication History

"A Most Extraordinary Case" appeared first in the April 1868 issue of the *Atlantic Monthly*. James collected it in 1885 in his *Stories Revived*. It next appeared, after James's death, in Albert Mordell's 1920 *A Landscape Painter*, and shortly thereafter in Lubbock's edition of *The Novels and Stories of Henry James*.

Circumstances of Composition, Sources, and Influences

In 1861, toward the start of the Civil War, James suffered an "obscure hurt" that kept him from the war, and critics, beginning with Edel, have seen a connection between that "hurt" and Mason's "extraordinary" illness that keeps him from love and kills him even after he has recovered (*Life* 1,

179–80; also Putt 35–36). The tale was written, in Aziz's estimate, in the fall of 1867, long enough after the war's end for James to have seen some of its effects on its participants (Aziz 1, xl). Dupee speaks of the Civil War veterans as a "Lost Generation" and sees James in the tale not only describing his own hurt, but moving outside himself to identify with them (50). Similarly, Wilson notes that James had "observed in others the destructive effects of the war even on those who succeeded in surviving it," although he finds the "invalidism half-acquiesced-in" here entirely James's (662). Buitenhuis diagnoses in both James and Mason a sense of "frustrated inaction": the sense of promise—Mason's aunt calls him "the most gifted, the most promising young man of his generation"—and the lack of a sufficient outlet as valuable time passes (33, 36–37). LeClair sees James as drawing on his hesitant relationship to Minny Temple, which ended in her dying as he moved into health (404). Sicker judges such autobiographic connections therapeutic, as James purged himself of his insecurities through portraying them in tales such as this (42).

James revised the tale rather heavily for his *Stories Revived* (Aziz 1, xlvi), so much so that Ruhm objects to Edel's choice of the 1885 *Stories Revived* text, pointing to the many changes in style, including one long cut that removed such pearls of observation as the description of "the great satisfaction [for Mason] of discussing with the woman on whom of all others his selfish and personal happiness was most dependent those great themes in whose expansive magnitude persons and pleasures and passions are absorbed and extinguished, and in whose austere effulgence the brightest divinities of earth remit their shining" (678–79). It is a phrase Walter Wright cites as evidence of the unfortunate influence of Mrs. Radcliffe in James's work (113–14).

The tale is set in the Hudson River valley, long familiar to James, and Buitenhuis notes the confidence the setting gives the tale. The "long settled, almost legendary region" had associations for James with his youth, with Washington Irving, and with the Hudson River School of landscape painters. All three sources thus worked together, according to Buitenhuis, to provide James the schema he often felt wanting in the States (34–36).

Looking at European sources, Buitenhuis locates in the tale further echoes of Mérimée's "La Venus d'Ille," Caroline here figuring as a Diana who grants her lover a final, fatal interview (33–34). Habegger compares her to a fatal Lorelei in her singing of German lieder by the Hudson (172). Tintner calls the tale a "partially successful tribute" to Stendhal's *La Chartreuse de Parme* with Clelia, the young woman the hero loves, becoming Caroline here, but with the same fatal consequences, and the relationship between Mason and his aunt reflecting the relationship between Fabrice and his aunt the Duchess of San Severino (246–48).

Relation to Other Works

The character of Mason has been taken by Mackenzie for a "type" character seen also in the heroes of "De Grey," "A Passionate Pilgrim," the heroine of "Poor Richard," and both the hero and heroine of "Longstaff's Marriage," as well as Roderick Hudson. All, according to Mackenzie, are invalids who turn their desire for revenge against others for their shame, not against those who have wronged them but against themselves (36). Sicker, too, places him with "Poor Richard" and Searle of "A Passionate Pilgrim," as well as the suicide lover of "Osborne's Revenge," for seeking death not love (37–38, 40). Wright sees Mason more benignly as a timid lover anticipating Ralph Touchett, a sensitive man who like Ralph and Severn of "Poor Richard" dies, and unlike the rare example of Roger Lawrence of *Watch and Ward*, who is sensitive and thrives (113–15; also Kraft 18). Krook also compares the tale to *The Portrait of a Lady*, seeing in the relationship of Caroline and Ferdinand an anticipation of that between Isabel and Ralph, "as it might have been experienced by Ralph with a no-nonsense aunt in each case" (134–36). Putt emphasizes the renunciative motive, with Mason's dying of love and leaving his money to his supplanter a slight anticipation of Milly Theale's renunciation in *The Wings of the Dove*, while Krook locates in both an interest in the "problem of pain" (Putt 34; Krook 136; also Samuels 72–73). Kraft puts the link with Milly somewhat differently, stating that like her, Mason "wants to live and that circumstances of love stop him" (18). Morgan, however, while comparing the linkage of charity and failure in love to Rowland Mallet's situation in *Roderick Hudson*, judges the failure of each man not a deliberate renunciation but a result of circumstances (77–78). Levy traces an evolution from unwilled to willed renunciation. Designating the problem for Mason as well as Hyacinth Robinson as one of the "accessibility to experience," Levy places the tale at the start of a strain in James leading to "The Beast in the Jungle" and "The Jolly Corner" as well as *The Ambassadors*, in which a man deliberately turns away from the possibilities of life offered him (32, 63).

Buitenhuis gives Mason a reason, emphasizing the danger of love here, which he argues exhibits the same exchange of strength found in *The Sacred Fount* (34). Similarly, Sicker classes Caroline for her "sisterly" feelings toward Mason among James's early "belles inhumaines" (36–37; also Krook 136). Dupee, more generously, sees Caroline's great hopes for the future as being her link with later James heroines (50–51). Caroline's aunt receives praise from Kraft as an example of the Jamesian "type" of the "fairy godmother" like Mrs. Touchett or Mrs. Stringham in *The Wings of the Dove* (18).

James's brother William wrote him a long analysis of the tale stating that he thought he had now figured out James's intention—"to give an impression like that we often get of people in life: Their orbits come out of space and lay themselves for a short time along of ours, and then off they whirl again into the unknown, leaving us with little more than an impression of their reality and a feeling of baffled curiosity as to the mystery of the beginning and end of their being, and of the intimate character of that segment of it wh. we have seen." He finds it a "very legitimate method" with "a great effect when it succeeds," but argues that "the gushing system is better to fail in" since it is warmer, noting the scepticism, almost impudence, "implied in your giving a story which is no story at all" (46–47). Stafford argues that William's remark is appropriate when applied to the later James, but is "really too rich" for the early tale, which does not actually merit such strong praise (342; also Kraft 19). William did apply the theory to later James, although more critically. Matthiessen records William's description of the conclusion of *The Tragic Muse* as "rather a losing of the story in the sand, yet that is the way in which things lose themselves in real life." Matthiessen also points to James's defense of his approach in his statement in the preface to *Roderick Hudson* that "Really, universally, relations stop nowhere," that the artist simply works to make them "happily *appear* to do so" even as he had attempted to do in *The Portrait of a Lady*, which does not conclude but "groups together"—works that have more of the richness Stafford does not find in the tale (1944, 181–82). (See "The Story of a Year.")

Interpretation and Criticism

In 1885, while preparing *Stories Revived* for publication, James sent Grace Norton a copy of several of the early tales, including this, which he recalled talking about with Grace and her sister Jane "one evening at Shady Hill, a thousand years ago, and our having an immense, interminable laugh over [it]. The heroine in it nibbled a cake, which you didn't like; and in this revision I have suppressed the cake and the nibbling, thinking of you, but with the feeling, throughout, that the lady must be hungry" (*Letters* 3, 76–77).

James's brother William also commented on the cake, finding the scene one of the tale's "plastically conceived situations" (47). Since then, however, critics have not commented on the cake issue, nor have they generally found the story, like William, "bright & sparkling" (47), but have, without much laughter, judged it lacking—even as they have discerned in it significant beginnings of later Jamesian themes.

A representative judgment is that of McElderry, who finds the situation "promising," but the treatment inadequate (288). As Edel phrases it, James here has a sense of "his material while still awkwardly trying to melt it into life" (CT 1, 19). Daiches more particularly faults the death of Mason as "inorganic" despite the extensive preparation for it, an indication of James's inadequate control of technique (573). Kelley is even less impressed, finding James overanalyzing characters he does not "care for," ignoring the need for any plot, and spending too much time trying to be witty (83). Kraft is more positive, judging the tale "effectively written" (18). Similarly, Leyburn calls it "one of the most convincing" of the early tales, pointing out in particular one of Mason's "self-mocking retort[s]" (CT1, 360) as evidence of James's "awareness of the presence of mirth in sadness." But even she finds this sign of strength poorly integrated into the overall tale (5).

The extraordinary "case" of this tale, Mason, has drawn the bulk of critical attention. Wagenknecht sees his absolute passivity as the story's main flaw (195). LeClair, on the other hand, judges its one interest the "acutely sympathetic" depiction of Mason, who in James's words refuses to "go a wooing in his dressing-gown and slippers" (403–4). The cause of Mason's refusal has been much examined. Andreas contends Mason is simply seeking to recover his strength before he will declare himself to Caroline, a delay that allows Caroline to love elsewhere, the disappointment at which brings about his death (83). Kraft speaks approvingly of James's recognition of "war as that which accentuates the human condition, releasing our weaknesses in 'wounds'" (17–18). Wilson, accordingly, sees him as too weakened by the war to rally and cites Mason's speech on his outing with Caroline—"there are moments when this perpetual self-coddling seems beneath the dignity of a man, and I'm tempted to purchase one short hour of enjoyment, of happiness—well, at the cost of my life if necessary," and his subsequent "symbolic gesture" of poking his stick at a tear in her dress (661–62). But even for a Jamesian protagonist his "one short hour of enjoyment" seems mild. Levy pictures Mason as surrendering even earlier, overwhelmed by Caroline's "beauty and vitality" in contrast to his own weakness. He cites the analysis the doctor gives to Mason of his case that he "took things too hard" even as he was "devoured with the mania of appearing to take things easily": "You played your part very well, but you must do me the justice to confess that it *was* a part" (32; CT 1, 340). Dupee, too, while calling Mason "curiously prim" in his hesitance, nevertheless argues, especially in the light of Caroline's "air of expecting great things of life," that his death "follows naturally enough from his given circumstances" (50–51). Among the harsher judgments, Putt considers Mason's leaving his money to the doctor an almost relieved celebration of his own impotence (35). Sicker sees Mason's search for love as a mask hiding his love of death. Collapsing further after each moment of contact with Caroline, Mason, according to Sicker, "wills his relapses during moments of intimacy because they impose the barriers to sexual union upon which his self-flagellant imagination thrives" (36–37).

The other characters in the tale have drawn less attention, apart from their anticipation of later James. William James admittedly found Caroline a vivid character, who gave "the impression of having roots spreading somewhere beyond your pages" (46–47). In Habegger's reading, the depiction of Caroline is at first ambiguous, as there seems much in her to admire, but she is gradually revealed as a "hard and self-sufficing woman" who wears down the hero to the point of death. While Habegger argues that Mason is forgiven the fancies he weaves about her, he sees Caroline unfairly held responsible for failing to return the affection he never directly declares (168). The aunt has received even less comment, although Tintner, characterizing her attitude toward her nephew as "loving and erotic," argues he would have been better off responding to her than to Caroline (247).

In the tale James is clearly working at the management of point of view, making Mason his center of consciousness and trying to tell his story within those bounds. In his brother's formulation, James was trying by means of "a few external acts and speeches" and the "magic" of his art to make "the reader *feel* back of these the existence of a body of being of which these are casual figures" (46). According to Wright, however, the approach necessitates awkward passages of "silent communication," as James tries to convey the interior thoughts of other characters without breaking with the limited point of view. James thus has to pretend that Caroline's thoughts can be discerned from her attitude when he wants to indicate what she is thinking (114). Still, Buitenhuis, who notes that James even calls attention in one place to his decision not to shift the viewpoint, finds this greater control of point of view intended to allow a realistic treatment of a melodramatic situation (34).

The point of view is, indeed, like the rest of the techniques employed in the tale, a skill still being developed. But from the moment when the aunt visits her nephew's lonesome hotel room and offers him a new chance at life, there is a sense of expectation, even as there would be later when Isabel Archer is offered a new world by her aunt. Edel calls attention to the scene and to Mason's tears at his aunt's reminder of "the exquisite side of life" (CT 1, 19). Mason's subsequent slow lapsing into death after a seeming recovery succeeds in irritating readers only because his character and his chances have first succeeded in engaging them.

Works Cited

Primary Works
James, Henry. 1868. "A Most Extraordinary Case." *Atlantic Monthly* 21 (April): 461–85.

————. 1885. "A Most Extraordinary Case." *Stories Revived*. Vol 3. London: Macmillan.

————. 1920. "A Most Extraordinary Case." *A Landscape Painter*. Preface by Albert Mordell. New York: Scott and Seltzer.

————. 1921–23. "A Most Extraordinary Case." *The Novels and Stories of Henry James*. Vol. 26. Ed. Percy Lubbock. London: Macmillan.

Secondary Works:
Andreas, Osborn. 1948. *Henry James and the Expanding Horizon: A Study of the Meaning and Basic Themes of James's Fiction*. Seattle: University of Washington Press.

Buitenhuis, Peter. 1970. *The Grasping Imagination: The American Writings of Henry James*. Toronto: University of Toronto Press.

Daiches, David. 1943. "Sensibility and Technique (Preface to a Critique)." *Kenyon Review* 5 (August): 569–79.

Dupee, F. W. [1951] 1956. *Henry James*. Garden City, NY: Doubleday Anchor.

Habegger, Alfred. 1989. *Henry James and the "Woman Business."* Cambridge: Cambridge University Press.

James, William. 1992. *The Correspondence of William James*. Vol 1: *William and Henry*. Ed. Ignas K. Skrupskelis and Elizabeth M. Berkeley. Charlottesville: University Press of Virginia.

Kelley, Cornelia Pulsifer. [1930] 1965. *The Early Development of Henry James*. Urbana: University of Illinois Press.

Kraft, James. 1969. *The Early Tales of Henry James*. Carbondale: Southern Illinois University Press.

Krook, Dorothea. 1986. "Isabel Archer Figures in Some Early Stories of Henry James." *Henry James Review* 7, no. 4 (Fall): 5–21.

LeClair, Robert Charles. 1955. *Young Henry James, 1843–1870*. New York: Bookman.

Levy, Leo B. 1957. *Versions of Melodrama: A Study of the Fiction and Drama of Henry James, 1865–1897*. Berkeley: University of California Press.

Leyburn, Ellen Douglass. 1968. *Strange Alloy: The Relation of Comedy to Tragedy in the Fiction of Henry James*. Chapel Hill: University of North Carolina Press.

McElderry, Bruce R., Jr. 1949. "The Uncollected Stories of Henry James." *American Literature* 21 (November): 279–91.

Mackenzie, Manfred. 1976. *Communities of Honor and Love in Henry James*. Cambridge, MA: Harvard University Press.

Matthiessen, F. O. 1944. *Henry James: The Major Phase*. New York: Oxford University Press. Also reprinted in *Essays in Modern Literary Criticism,* ed. Ray B. West, 469. New York: Rinehart, 1952.

Morgan, Alice. 1970. "Henry James: Money and Morality." *Texas Studies in Language and Literature* 12: 75–92.

Putt, S. Gorley. 1966. *Henry James: A Reader's Guide*. Ithaca, NY: Cornell University Press.

Ruhm, Herbert. 1963. "The Complete Tales of Henry James." *Saturday Review* 71: 675–80.

Samuels, Charles Thomas. 1971. *The Ambiguity of Henry James*. Urbana: University of Illinois Press.

Sicker, Philip. 1980. *Love and the Quest for Identity in the Fiction of Henry James*. Princeton: Princeton University Press.

Stafford, William T. 1959. "William James as Critic of his Brother Henry." *The Personalist* 40: 341–53.

Tintner, Adeline R. 1987. *The Book World of Henry James: Appropriating the Classics*. Ann Arbor: UMI Research Press. Reprinted from "In the Footsteps of Stendhal: James's 'A Most Extraordinary Case' and *La Chartreuse de Parma*." *Revue de Littérature Comparée* 55 (1981): 232–38.

Wagenknecht, Edward. 1984. *The Tales of Henry James*. New York: Frederick Ungar.

Wilson, Edmund. [1962] 1987. *Patriotic Gore: Studies in the Literature of the American Civil War*. London: Hogarth.

Wright, Walter F. 1962. *The Madness of Art: A Study of Henry James*. Lincoln: University of Nebraska Press.

Mrs. Medwin

Publication History

"Mrs. Medwin" was James's entry into the hallowed British *Punch*, where it was stretched out over four issues from August 28 to September 18, 1901. It appeared next in the 1903 collection *The Better Sort*. Following that, when a reshuffling of material left a space in the New York Edition, it was, Anesko writes, "resuscitated," or, as James put it in the preface, "accommodated" "for convenience" (Anesko 161; *Criticism* 2, 1286).

Circumstances of Composition, Sources, and Influences

"Mrs. Medwin" evolved over the course of several notebook entries beginning on May 7, 1898, in a list of possible topics as "The Miss Balch and Lady G. incident" (CN 169). Originally, the "poor fine lady" who accepted money to place a "*tarée* one" was to have killed the person who interferes with the job, although as James acknowledged, "The killing is difficult" (CN 170). He returned to the idea on February 15, 1899, with the idea that having his protagonist "turning . . . the tables" might be even more dramatic. He fixed on a cousin to be the "upsetter" and wished he could make *him* a murderer. Interrupted by influenza, he returned to work the next day to settle on a stepbrother who presents first the complication then the solution to Miss B.'s predicament, his crime "probably" cards, a spurious allegation at that (CN 177–79). In Rome that May and again in October he focused on the use of "talk" to keep the story manageable—"concentrat*issimo*" (CN 184–85). Following the last entry, he included Wantridge and Medwin among one of his lists of names, and in November, back at Lamb House, speculated about writing a play with Miss B. as a "*man*—an amiable London celibate" (CN 187).

Richards has offered as the original Miss Balch Elizabeth Balch, an American who wrote such works as *Glimpses of Old English Homes*, and for Lady G., Lady Grantley, a native of New York and participant in a scandalous divorce case in 1879. For the stepbrother, Scott, he suggests Minny Temple's brother Robert, whom James described as a character out of Dickens or Thackeray, making him an appropriate character for James's first publication in *Punch* (229). James's picture of Robert as "inimitable, inimitably droll, inimitably wasted, wanton, impossible" but saved by "his genius for expression" fits Scott well. Even his lack of the "[inward] elements" suits a story told primarily through dialogue (*Autobiography* 324–25). Rather more dramatically, Tintner depicts Scott as a devil figure, if a charming one, the "flower" of an evil society (1989, 78).

Relation to Other Works

Fadiman links the story with *The Princess Casamassima* and *The Ivory Tower* as a work that demonstrates the satire beneath James's alleged "snobbery" (xv). McElderry sees English society similarly but more harshly dealt with in *A London Life* and *The Awkward Age* (143; also Ward 81). Putt, who finds the story a more successful social satire than "The Two Faces," parallels Scott Homer, who is expected to provide the "sexual excitement" at a country-house weekend, and Straith and Harvey in "Broken Wings," who are expected to bring artistic interest (293). Among the other unsavory social climbers in James, Gage names Mrs. Bridgenorth of "The Tone of Time," while Markow-Totevy nominates the Moreens of *The Pupil* (Gage 79; Markow-Totevy 48). Jones adds Saltram of "The Coxon Fund" as an outsider society is brought to accept, and compares Mamie to Rose Tramore of "The Chaperon" in her bringing about the acceptance (238).

Edgar links the tale with "Flickerbridge" and "Fordham Castle" as the three last "American" tales before James's 1904 trip to the States (62). Macnaughton links the three with "The Beldonald Holbein" as evidence that James, tired of London by itself after the writing of *The Awkward Age*, was newly interested in the international following his trip to the continent the summer of 1899 (61). Quentin Anderson links Mamie Cutter as a Europeanized American who introduces others to Europe with Maria

Gostrey, Fanny Assingham, and Mme Merle (31 n.6). Stevenson classes Scott among the "American exploiters"—the reverse of the innocent abroad type—with Chad Newsome and Mrs. Headway (60; also Wilt and Lucas xix).

Gage sees the story as the pivot of *The Better Sort*. The first story without a single character interested in renunciation, it turns the theme from the conflict of individuals toward the conflict between society and the individual. In the context of volume 18 of the New York Edition, where it is the concluding story, he sees it as presenting a truce between society's curiosity and an individual's privacy (61, 190, 286–87).

Interpretation and Criticism

James envisioned his story as "really a little cynical comedy," its focus to be not "the very *usé* element" of the woman trying to get into society, but the Cutter character, "the way she *works* her *relations*, etc., etc." (CN 178). Critics have followed his lead, praising the story's cynical portrayal of upper-class society (e.g., Wagenknecht 132; Geismar 255–56). Fadiman values the "rather frail" tale as proof that James was not so overwhelmed by "snobbery and Anglomania" that he could not see the flaws of the British upper class even if he gave it only "the most glancing of blows." In Fadiman's reading, the Europe whose culture had earlier sustained traveling Americans now has come to live off their greater vitality. The heart of the story thus lies in Scott's declaration of the aristocrats, "They're dead . . . *we're* alive." Appropriately, Tintner observes that Mamie, who collects people, lives in rooms like a museum (1986, 171).

Putt judges the story "a well constructed four-part morality farce," and noting a similarity between the immoral society James depicts here and that depicted by Proust in *Cities of the Plain*, argues that James's intention is to criticize society's hypocritical claiming of rules it has abandoned rather than the rules themselves (293–94). As Dietrichson states, they can be bought (122). Gage argues that the ending is "ambiguous," the victory of neither vice nor virtue, as both sides—British and American—are deeply flawed (94, 106). Bernard observes the elegant obliqueness with which *all* the characters converse, referring to their sordid subjects with vague pronouns as they efficiently arrange their compromises. Jones, on the other hand, attaches a certain "poignance" to the plight of the outsiders, and Richards notes some genuine feeling in Scott's "painful" homesickness (Richards 230). Jones also remarks that Scott's misdeeds are at least intriguingly mysterious while the details of Mrs. Medwin's scandal are well known to her compatriots (238). As Austin Wright puts it, Scott's moral failings make his exposure of the British all the more satisfying (191). It is perhaps appropriate then that, as Wilt and Lucas argue, James grants "the last laugh" here to the Americans (xix).

Works Cited

Primary Works

James, Henry. 1901. "Mrs. Medwin." *Punch* 121 (28 August–18 September): 160–61, 178–79, 196–97, 214–15.

———. 1903. "Mrs. Medwin." *The Better Sort*. London: Methuen; New York: Scribner's, 116–42.

———. 1908. "Mrs. Medwin." *The Novels and Tales of Henry James*. New York Edition. Vol. 18, 471–506. New York: Scribner's.

Secondary Works

Anderson, Quentin. 1957. *The American Henry James*. New Brunswick, NJ: Rutgers University Press.

Anesko, Michael, 1986. "Friction with the Market": *Henry James and the Profession of Authorship*. New York: Oxford University Press.

Bernard, Kenneth. 1963. "Henry James's Unspoken Discourse in 'Mrs. Medwin.'" *Discourse* 6 (August): 310–14 .

Dietrichson, Jan W. 1969. *The Image of Money in the American Novel of the Gilded Age*. Oslo: Universitetsforlaget; New York: Humanities.

Edgar, Pelham. [1927] 1964. *Henry James, Man and Author*. New York: Russell & Russell.

Fadiman, Clifton, ed. 1945. *The Short Stories of Henry James* New York: Random House.

Gage, Richard P. 1988. *Order and Design: Henry James' Titled Story Sequences*. New York: Peter Lang.

Geismar, Maxwell. 1963. *Henry James and the Jacobites*. Boston: Houghton Mifflin.

Jones, Granville H. 1975. *Henry James's Psychology of Experience: Innocence, Responsibility, and Renunciation in the Fiction of Henry James*. The Hague: Mouton.

McElderry, Bruce R., Jr. 1965. *Henry James*. New York: Twayne.

Macnaughton, William R. 1987. *Henry James: The Later Novels*. Boston: Twayne.

Markow-Totevy, Georges. 1969. *Henry James*. Trans. John Griffiths. London: Merlin.

Putt, S. Gorley. 1966. *Henry James: A Reader's Guide*. Ithaca, NY: Cornell University Press.

Richards, Bernard. 1980. "The Sources of Henry James's 'Mrs. Medwin.'" *Notes and Queries* 27: 226–30.

Stevenson, Elizabeth. [1949] 1981. *The Crooked Corridor: A Study of Henry James*. New York: Octagon.

Tintner, Adeline R. 1989. *The Pop World of Henry James: From Fairy Tales to Science Fiction*. Ann Arbor: UMI Research Press.

———. 1986. *The Museum World of Henry James*. Ann Arbor: UMI Research Press.

Wagenknecht, Edward. 1984. *The Tales of Henry James*. New York: Frederick Ungar.

Ward, J. A. 1961. *The Imagination of Disaster: Evil in the Fiction of Henry James*. Lincoln: University of Nebraska Press.

Wilt, Napier, and John Lucas, eds. 1965. *Americans and Europe: Selected Tales of Henry James*. Riverside Editions. Boston: Houghton Mifflin.

Wright, Austin McGiffert. 1961. *The American Short Story in the Twenties*. Chicago: University of Chicago Press.

Mrs. Temperly

Publication History

"Mrs. Temperly," James's first short story published after a gap of two years, appeared originally as "Cousin Maria" in three installments of *Harper's Weekly* with "ugly big pictures" by Charles S. Reinhart in August 1887 (*Correspondence* 149). In 1889 James revised it for publication in the collection *A London Life*, but never subsequently reprinted it. Indeed, in planning *A London Life*, he originally included then forgot the work, apologizing to his publisher, Macmillan: "It was stupidly oblivious of me . . . to drop out the *Cousin Maria*—which for the moment, I not only forgot that I had named to you, but forgot that I had written!" (*Correspondence* 149). It next appeared in Lubbock's edition of the novels and stories.

Circumstances of Composition, Sources, and Influences

"Mrs. Temperly" is the first production of what Leon Edel terms James's "Italian phase"—"a new period of happy creation" experienced while in Florence and Venice, following the prolonged labor on the two serials *The Bostonians* and *The Princess Casamassima* of 1885 and 1886, and preceding *The Tragic Muse* of 1889 and 1890 (*Life* 3, 214–15; CT 6, 7). Indeed, although it was his only fiction to appear that year, he was writing a great deal. In a letter to his brother in October he proclaimed, "I *am* productive, and in the course of this autumn shall have sent off the eighth or ninth fiction of about the length of 'Daisy Miller' since I quitted England on the first December last" (*Letters* 3, 201). Similarly, that December he wrote Robert Louis Stevenson, speaking of his productivity and blaming the "beastly periodicals" for holding his work back (*Letters* 3, 206). "Cousin Maria," on the other hand, James had expected would appear in *Harper*'s holiday number, so its appearance was somewhat earlier than anticipated (CN 35).

There is a suggestion of Cinderella in "Mrs. Temperly." Benyon is "ashamed" at viewing Dora as "the Cinderella of the house, the domestic drudge, the one for whom there was no career," but nevertheless acknowledges the justness of the parallel, with the two sisters and especially the mother, who wishes to marry off the other daughters first, "like the mother in the fairy-tale . . . a *femme forte*" (CT 6, 221). By this analogy, of course, Benyon ought to play the prince, but James does not extend it that far, perhaps recognizing that Benyon has neither the riches nor the force of will to change the mother's determination, even as he cannot convince his Cinderella to go against her mother's wishes. Tintner, who points to Louisa May Alcott's 1860 "A Modern Cinderella," explores the parallels further, calling particular attention to the absence of a fairy godmother in James's realistic tale. She also presents a Freudian reading, seeing the tale as reflecting James's attitude to his mother, Mary (hence Maria), tangled up as it was at the time in his relationship to Constance Fenimore Woolson (30–36, 214).

Q. D. Leavis draws attention to the similarity of the original title, "Cousin Maria," and Hawthorne's title "My Kinsman, Major Molineux," which "conveys the same intimation" (162).

Relation to Other Works

Apart from its opening two scenes in New York, "Mrs. Temperly" is set in Paris, and has echoes of *The American*. This time, however, the Americans seeking to establish themselves among the French aristocracy are female and hospitably received. While in *The American* "the greatest lady of France" is the formidable Duchess, the "most distinguished woman in France" here is the young, charming Marquise, Madame de Brives. Both fail to help the Americans. The immorality of the French upper classes remains a barrier, as Mrs. Temperly is determined that none of her daughters will find herself in a situation such as James represented in *Madame de Mauves*. The heroine of next year's *The Reverberator* (which also contains a Madame de Brives) is perhaps luckier. Though she loses her social acceptance in the Parisian society Mrs. Temperly survives in, she keeps her Franco-American fiancé.

Ingredients of the characters of both mother and daughter can again be found in *The American*. When Christopher Newman asks Claire why she consents to give him up, she replies "I'm afraid of my mother," and her mother tells Newman, "My power . . . is in my children's obedience" (215, 217). Neither mother nor daughter speaks as openly in "Mrs. Temperly."

Raymond's formulation of Dora's attittude, made only to himself, is nearly opposite— "Elle adore sà mere!"—but it has the same effect. Dora refuses to say or hear anything to contradict such a view (CT 6, 227). Because Dora never speaks, her mother can continue to prevent her marriage, claiming Dora has chosen "not to make a choice" (CT 6, 226).

In Edel's reading, Mrs. Temperly belongs to a type of "power-driven matron" frequent in James. She is, in the words of the narrator "a man as well as a woman—the masculine element was included in her nature" (CT 6, 13). Levy finds the mother's parallel in the sternly paternal Dr. Sloper of *Washington Square* (55). Although he calls her the "most conventionally innocent person" in the story, Jones finds in Mrs. Temperly's treatment of her daughter Dora a similar possessiveness to Mrs. Rimmle in the 1899 "Europe." At the same time, because Dora cooperates passively with her mother, he places her with Caroline Spencer of "Four Meetings," Owen Wingrave, and Grace Mavis of "The Patagonia" in a long list of victims of family responsibility (113–14). One might add Pansy Osmond of *The Portrait of a Lady*, possessor of a similarly weak if pretty name, to Jones's list.

Edgar considers "Mrs. Temperly" and next year's "Louisa Pallant" together, but sees them as "two colourless romances" that say nothing worthwhile about manners (47). Although he also finds the story "light," Putt argues that an understanding of contemporary manners helps one to appreciate it and such tales as "Louisa Pallant." Indeed, his description of the way mothers "walked abroad with marriageable daughters chained to their will like bibles to old fashioned lecterns" fits Mrs. Temperly well (272–73).

Q. D. Leavis, who conceives of the story as a parable about art, sees Mrs. Temperly not only as a parent who interferes with her daughter's happiness, as Osmond in *The Portrait of a Lady* does, but also, in anticipation of Adam Verver, a collector who in her patronage of fashionable art and her dismissal of her unsucessful artist cousin is, unlike Rowland Mallet who is willing to assist an beginner, an "anti-artist" like Julia Dallow of *The Tragic Muse* (162–64). Winner draws a similar comparison between Julia and Mrs. Temperly, while also noting her resemblance to Mrs. Coventry of "The Madonna of the Future," another devotee to the fashion of art who has little use for the struggling artist (118–20).

Like three tales before it—"The Impressions of a Cousin," *Lady Barbarina*, and "Georgina's Reasons"—"Mrs. Temperly" has a conspicuously suspended ending, changing in the last sentence from past to present tense, and providing one of the few jarring notes in the smoothly written tale: "It may be added that Tishy is decidedly a dwarf and his probation is not over" (CT 6, 232). It is a sentiment that justifies Donald Stone's labeling the story "a grotesque comedy" (247).

Interpretation and Criticism

While Howells praised "Mrs. Temperly" among other tales of the late 1880s as one of "a massing of masterpieces," it has since received little individual attention, although Edel in his introduction quotes and agrees with Howells, finding it "a graceful anecdote," a worthy companion to *The Aspern Papers*. Ezra Pound, too, found the story an "excellent delineation" of its theme, proof that James could be an "excellent hater" (29). Edel puts his finger on the source of the story's interest—the gradual process through which Dora's suitor comes to understand her mother's character and to recognize her plan to keep Dora for use as, in James's words, "a precocious duenna" (CT 6, 10–11, 225). It is the daughter's continued loyalty to her mother despite this plan that Wagenknecht finds baffling (195). Andreas offers an explanation, seeing Dora, acting from a devotion to unworldly artistic values, more interested in frustrating her mother's desire for social success through her daughters' marriages than she is even in Raymond himself (109–10). It is an intriguing argument, although far less is often enough to stifle action on the part of a Jamesian character.

Works Cited

Primary Works

James, Henry. 1887. "Cousin Maria." *Harper's Weekly* (6, 13, and 20 August): 557–58, 577–78, 593–94.

———. 1889. "Mrs. Temperly." *A London Life*. London and New York: Macmillan.

———. [1877] 1978. *The American*. Ed. James W. Tuttleton. New York: Norton.

———. "Mrs. Temperly." In *The Novels and Stories of Henry James*. Vol. 26. Ed. Percy Lubbock. London: Macmillan.

———. 1993. *The Correspondence of Henry James and the House of Macmillan, 1877–1914*. Ed. Rayburn S. Moore. Baton Rouge: Louisiana State University Press.

Secondary Works

Andreas, Osborn. 1948. *Henry James and the Expanding Horizon: A Study of the Meaning and Basic Themes of James's Fiction*. Seattle: University of Washington Press.

Edgar, Pelham. [1927] 1964. *Henry James, Man and Author*. New York: Russell & Russell.

Jones, Granville H. 1975. *Henry James's Psychology of Experience: Innocence, Responsibility, and Renunciation in the Fiction of Henry James*. The Hague: Mouton.

Leavis, Q. D. 1985. "The fox is the novelist's idea: Henry James and the house beautiful." In *Collected Essays*. Vol. 2. Ed. G. Singh, 158–76. Cambridge: Cambridge University Press.

Levy, Leo B. 1957. *Versions of Melodrama: A Study of the Fiction and Drama of Henry James, 1865–1897*. Berkeley: University of California Press.

Pound, Ezra. 1918. "A Shake Down." *The Little Review* 5 (August): 9–39.

Putt, S. Gorley. 1966. *Henry James: A Reader's Guide*. Ithaca, NY: Cornell University Press.

Stone, Donald David. 1972. *Novelists in a Changing World: Meredith, James, and the Transformation of English Fiction in the 1880's*. Cambridge, MA: Harvard University Press.

Tintner, Adeline R. 1989. *The Pop World of Henry James: From Fairy Tales to Science Fiction*. Ann Arbor: UMI Research Press.

Wagenknecht, Edward. 1984. *The Tales of Henry James*. New York: Frederick Ungar.

Winner, Viola Hopkins. 1970. *Henry James and the Visual Arts*. Charlottesville: University Press of Virginia.

My Friend Bingham

Publication History

"My Friend Bingham," published in March 1867, was the third of James's tales to appear in the *Atlantic Monthly* and the second of those he never chose to reprint subsequently. It appeared for the first time after his death in 1950 in Kenton's *Eight Uncollected Tales*.

Circumstances of Composition, Sources, and Influences

James evidently wrote the tale in early 1867 while in Cambridge, and drew the picture of Bingham and his friend from friends there including Sargeant Perry, as well as from himself and his brother. The setting, which Buitenhuis finds "suspiciously" like Newport, LeClair identifies as the nearby Swampscott, which James had visited the previous spring (Buitenhuis 23; LeClair 384, 393).

The allusion to Coleridge's *The Rime of the Ancient Mariner* has been most fully analyzed by Martin and Ober, who note James's unironic transformation of the "symbolic" killing of a bird into the realistic death of a boy, the result of the "boredom" of the narrator, who like the Mariner is eventually redeemed by sympathy—in Bingham's case for Mrs. Hicks (also Buitenhuis 26). Fogel takes the allusion further, noting that Bingham's marriage parallels the blessing of the water snakes in Coleridge's poem—the acceptance of something once rejected, a reconciliation with the natural order—at the same time as the marriage's childlessness parallels the mariner's continued need for penitence (144–45).

While Bingham designates Tennyson as the heroine's likely reading (CT 1, 170), Tintner points out the Wordsworthian associations of her name, Lucy, to link the allusions to Romantic poetry with allusions to American painting. The hero, Bingham, shares his name with George Caleb Bingham, who frequently painted hunters, and the heroine shares hers with Edward Hicks, who painted numerous depictions of "the peaceable kingdom," where the lion and the lamb live peaceably together led by a little child. Even so, in the story, Tintner argues, the death of the child, a representative of Christ, unites the hunter and the minister's widow (1986, 179–81; 1987, 70). Buitenhuis proposes another American source, tracing the theme of the ennobling effect of suffering to Hawthorne (26).

Bingham himself concentrates on the French critics (CT 1, 168), and modern critics have looked to the continent for influences. Peterson argues that the technique of the "norm-setting friend narrator" may have come from either Turgenev or Mérimée (42). Tintner points to the similarity in title with Turgenev's "My Neighbor Radilov," which also starts with a hunting scene (1986, 22). Kelley attributes the use of a passion as the center to George Sand, while Adams finds resemblances between the tale and the part of *Le Député d'Arcis* not written by Balzac (Kelley 69; Adams 466).

Relation to Other Works

The character of Bingham himself Walter Wright finds in the same key as James's later "poor sensitive gentlemen," and he speculates that his stoutness at the end may provide a link with Marmaduke of "Maud-Evelyn" (112–13). Fogel compares Bingham and Strether in their "double consciousness" and diffidence (144). McElderry finds Bingham, like Crawford of "Crawford's Consistency," a "thoughtful" bachelor who undergoes a strange, barely believable experience (285).

McElderry also sees a similarity with "Crawford's Consistency" in the use of the understated narration of a friend (285). Vaid, for his part, judges the first-person narration, like that in such other early tales as "Guest's

Confession" and "Adina," unsophisticated in comparison to that of "A Passionate Pilgrim" (27).

The role of the child has been most fully examined by Shine, who sees it being used, as in "A Tragedy of Error," to inspire "tenderness," but additionally as a "trigger" to the action, though without any real character or even a name. A more significant development, she finds, is the first example of the sacrifice of a child, generally male, for the benefit of adults, a theme seen later in "A Problem," "The Author of Beltraffio, *The Pupil*, and *The Turn of the Screw* (29–30). Putt connects the death of the child to that in *The Other House* as well (34, 215).

Finding parallels with the earlier "A Landscape Painter," LeClair notes a reversal in that the progatonist there had jilted his fiancée while the protagonist here has been jilted. The heroine he finds an improvement on Esther Blunt, but he argues that James's early heroines lacked something in their restriction to the American setting (393–94).

McCarthy states that in this tale and "Poor Richard" James was drawing less on his own emotions than seeking to base his story on "sweet reasonableness" as he found it in his favorite authors (54). Perhaps as an example of such "sweet reasonableness," Jones sees both this tale and "A Problem" as producing happy endings equivalent to that of "Travelling Companions," death in each preparing the way for love (157).

Interpretation and Criticism

At the start of his tale, the narrator tells us of his friend that he was "*par excellence* a moralist, a man of sentiment" (CT 1, 167). In its concluding lines, he informs us that Bingham "is a truly incorruptible soul; he is a confirmed philosopher; he has grown quite stout" (CT 1, 190). But whether that is evidence of a transformation, or how precisely that transformation is wrought is unclear to many readers. Bayley simply accepts the mystery, pointing to the concluding glimpse of Bingham as a result of James's "experimenting with varieties of tone and ending," a statement which rounds off the tale while still leaving intact the mystery of the character (60–61). Others question further. Wright asks, for example, what James means by "moralist," and finds little in Bingham of the possible answer (112–13). Stein, too, indicates that the tale could be meant to show an initially frivolous Bingham matured through his contact with suffering. Or, Stein argues, it might be intended to show how Bingham remains insensitive, his marriage to the mother of the child he killed an indication that he simply has no capacity for taking such calamity seriously or personally, an interpretation Stein finds likely given the stress laid on the horror of the child's death and Bingham's quick recovery from his guilt (64–67). Certainly, at the start, his character seems far from deep. Dietrichson calls him a "sentimental idler," who though he looks down on those rich like him, is still like them in "that home-keeping benevolence which accompanies a sense of material repletion" (68–69). (See also "A Problem.")

Love is supposed to be the cause of Bingham's transformation, if such it is, and some critics have accepted both the love and the transformation as valid. But perhaps because, as Bayley puts it, James fails to "convey the innerness" of his idea, the strange relationship between Mrs. Hicks and Bingham created by her child's death, critics have continued to differ (60). Shine's reading attributes the best motives to all: Bingham falls in love with Mrs. Hicks while "trying to make amends," she returns the feeling, and "after a decent interval, they marry and are presumed to live happily ever after" (29). Fogel, too, provides a logical explanation: Bingham's remorse stirs Mrs. Hicks's pity; both emotions then evolve into love (145). Thorp sees the key as an "inevitable love" that "overcomes the tragedy," and finds James successful in treating realistically a melodramatic subject (xiv). Buitenhuis discerns in the tale a notable advance in James's treatment of love and death. As usual, he argues they are closely associated, but this time the child functions as a scapegoat so that the marriage can be happy, although "through some principle of equity," as the narrator puts it, they have no children (26; also Martin and Ober 48).

Those who find the love unconvincing generally blame the narrator. Bayley judges his tone "laborious and arch" (60). Beach argues that James made a mistake in choosing a narrator who can tell us so little of the thoughts of Mrs. Hicks and even Bingham, or their behavior together, leaving the story basically untold. He points to the description of Bingham's response to her acceptance—"What honest George Bingham said, what I said, is of little account. The proper conclusion of my story lies in the highly dramatic fact that out of the depths of her bereavement—out of her loneliness and her pity—this richly gifted woman had emerged, responsive to the passion of him who had wronged her all but as deeply as he loved her" (CT 1, 189)—as a last-ditch attempt to substitute the idea for its presentation (177–78). Kelley also considers the story harmed by James's unwillingness to portray directly the turn from guilt and sorrow to love, arguing that a tale about such an unusual love "should be lighted and warmed by some of the glow, at least, of that love." The choice of the observer to tell the tale, while probably intended to give an added reality, she contends, denies the tale the passion necessary to make the events seem other than freakish (69–70; also Kraft 393; Wagenknecht 196). Buitenhuis is nearly alone in finding the narrator, though "anonymous and passive," useful in helping James manage his subject more effectively (27).

Levy, perhaps as a way around the confusion, proposes a reading in which the narrator's envy of Bingham supplies the complexity of the tale, Bingham's love being a simple one unmotivated by guilt. The narrator, in his reading, seeks to disrupt and disparage Bingham's courtship as he wishes to win Mrs.

Hicks for himself (409–10). Martin and Ober object that the narrator is not the center of the tale (47 n.7). There is also the objection that the death of a child is not an easy matter to overlook, even if there is no envious Iago about to remind one. Bingham and Mrs. Hicks's love may well be genuine, but it is hardly simple.

In the concluding passage cited by Beach, the narrator attempts to substitute the transformation of Mrs. Hicks for that of Bingham as the real subject of the tale. Buitenhuis points to the issue of class raised here, the narrator being a member of the idle rich, Mrs. Hicks a poor widow. The question of a "misalliance" is avoided, however, Buitenhuis argues, because of her metamorphosis, as she becomes in the words of the narrator "potentially at least, a woman of the world" (26). Martin and Ober disagree with Buitenhuis that Mrs. Hicks is transformed, seeing any change simply "altered perception," and fault James for failing to provide a character for her sufficient to explain her "unblinkingly" marrying her son's killer (48). Among other analysts, LeClair sees her interest hampered by her Americanness; Dietrichson argues that she "fully deserves her good fortune in the end"; and Bayley sees James coming close to identifying with his heroine, but leaving her a "mysterious figure" for all that (LeClair 394; Dietrichson 68–69; Bayley 60).

Even Buitenhuis, who provides a rationale for some of the tale's failings, judges the tale overall "quite slight" (26; also McElderry 285). LeClair discerns some improvement in the tale, finding the action improving and a new "authority" in certain passages (392–93). Kraft, too, labels certain passages as "delicately written," but also points to unintentional slips into humor in the handling of the melodrama (21–22). Similarly, Bayley, who characterizes the tale as "engagingly bad," speaks of the crucial scene of the death of the child as being written with "wonderful ineptitude" (59–60). The problem of style no doubt contributes to the central difficulty, which is that while James starts with "a pretty psychological problem," as Beach calls it, he is simply not, as Wagenknecht observes, fully equal to his theme (Beach 177; Wagenknecht 196). In February 1867 James, writing to his sister, spoke of "My Friend Bingham" as a "slight romance from my facile pen" (*Letters* 1, 69). But such a theme with its strange commingling of love and death demanded more than slightness and even facility, and James at this point, at least in this tale, did not command the needed depth and difficulty.

Works Cited

Primary Works

James, Henry. 1867. "My Friend Bingham." *Atlantic Monthly* 19 (March): 346–58.

———. 1950. "My Friend Bingham." *Eight Uncollected Tales of Henry James*. Ed. Edna Kenton. New Brunswick, NJ: Rutgers University Press.

Secondary Works

Adams, Percy G. 1961. "Young Henry James and the Lesson of His Master Balzac." *Revue de Littérature Comparée* 35 (July–September): 458–67.

Bayley, John. 1988. *The Short Story: Henry James to Elizabeth Bowen.* Brighton: Harvester.

Beach, Joseph Warren. [1918] 1954. *The Method of Henry James.* Philadelphia: Albert Saifer.

Buitenhuis, Peter. 1970. *The Grasping Imagination: The American Writings of Henry James.* Toronto: University of Toronto Press.

Dietrichson, Jan W. 1969. *The Image of Money in the American Novel of the Gilded Age.* Oslo: Universitetsforlaget; New York: Humanities.

Fogel, Daniel Mark. 1981. *Henry James and the Structure of the Romantic Imagination.* Baton Rouge: Louisiana State University Press.

Jones, Granville H. 1975. *Henry James's Psychology of Experience: Innocence, Responsibility, and Renunciation in the Fiction of Henry James.* The Hague: Mouton.

Kelley, Cornelia Pulsifer. [1930] 1965. *The Early Development of Henry James.* Urbana: University of Illinois Press.

Kraft, James. 1969. *The Early Tales of Henry James.* Carbondale: Southern Illinois University Press.

LeClair, Robert Charles. 1955. *Young Henry James, 1843–1870.* New York: Bookman.

Levy, Leo B. 1981. "Consciousness in Three Early Tales of Henry James." *Studies in Short Fiction* 18: 407–12.

McCarthy, Harold T. 1958. *Henry James: The Creative Process.* New York: Thomas Yoseloff.

McElderry, Bruce R., Jr. 1949. "The Uncollected Stories of Henry James." *American Literature* 21 (November): 279–91.

Martin, W. R., and Warren U. Ober. 1987. "James's 'My Friend Bingham' and Coleridge's 'Ancient Mariner.'" *English Language Notes* 25, no. 2 (December): 44–48.

Peterson, Dale E. 1975. *The Clement Vision: Poetic Realism in Turgenev and James.* Port Washington, NY: Kennikat.

Putt, S. Gorley. 1966. *Henry James: A Reader's Guide.* Ithaca, NY: Cornell University Press.

Shine, Muriel G. 1969. *The Fictional Children of Henry James.* Chapel Hill: University of North Carolina Press.

Stein, Allen F. 1984. *After the Vows Were Spoken: Marriage in American Literary Realism.* Columbus: Ohio State University Press.

Thorp, Willard, ed. 1962. *Henry James: The Madonna of the Future and Other Early Stories.* New York: New American Library.

Tintner, Adeline R. 1986. *The Museum World of Henry James*. Ann Arbor: UMI Research Press.

―――. 1987. *The Book World of Henry James: Appropriating the Classics*. Ann Arbor: UMI Research Press.

Vaid, Krishna B. 1964. *Technique in the Tales of Henry James*. Cambridge, MA: Harvard University Press.

Wagenknecht, Edward. 1984. *The Tales of Henry James*. New York: Frederick Ungar.

Wright, Walter F. 1962. *The Madness of Art: A Study of Henry James*. Lincoln: University of Nebraska Press.

A New England Winter

Publication History

"A New England Winter" appeared first in 1884 in the August and September issues of *Century* magazine. James included it the same year as the Boston tale in *Tales of Three Cities* but never reprinted it again. It returned to print in the 1920s in Lubbock's edition of the novels and stories.

Circumstances of Composition, Sources, and Influences

On January 18, 1881, James recorded the basic situation that would become "A New England Winter": the solicitous mother, the son returning from Europe to visit, and the young woman brought in to keep him amused. James first proposes that the son will fall in love with the girl, be refused, and return to Europe to marry a woman he has a "connection" with there. If that appears "too harsh," he then considers having the son marry the girl. In both cases the loss of the son's company is considered "just retribution" for the mother's scheming indifference to the fate of the girl (CN 17). Matthiessen and Murdock note, on the other hand, that the final version is not only not "harsh" but not "serious" (N 21). On finishing the tale James wrote apologizing to his editor, Richard Watson Gilder, for making the story, the last of three promised to the *Century*, long enough to require two installments after the previous one, *Lady Barbarina*, had already stretched into three (*Letters* 3, 23–24).

In between the conception of the tale and its writing, James had been twice to America, returning to London in September 1883, so that the story's impressions of Boston were fresh (*Life* 3, 66–67). Tintner identifies Isabella Gardner, at whose Beacon Street home James visited on those trips, as the source for Mrs. Mesh, and notes that two years later Gardner also "monopolize[d] an impressionist," John Singer Sargent, who had appropriately enough provided some of the inspiration for Florimond (1986, 92, 199–200). Tinter also cites James's allusion to the American impressionist J. Appleton Brown (1986, 106).

Looking at European influences on the tale, Tintner sees James drawing on Balzac's *Le Cousin Pons* in his creation of the character Rachel and in the mention of a Watteau fan that James uses here to demonstrate the superiority of Rachel's knowledge of art to Florimond's (1974; 1987, 251). Elsewhere, Tintner casts Mrs. Mesh as Circe with Florimond for an Odysseus (1989, 108–9, 141). Grover detects the influence of Gautier, Flaubert, and the Goncourts in James's descriptive technique, while Buitenhuis attributes the technique to the influence of Daudet, who helped James overcome his initial disapproval of Impressionism (Grover 125–27; Buitenhuis 134–36, 142).

The conspicuous names "Daintry" and "Florimond" were recorded in a list taken mostly from the London *Times* on January 2, 1884, with a final comment, "Very rich" (CN 23). The even less substantial "Dainty" had appeared three years earlier in a similar list (CN 13). Donald Stone sees an echo of the name of Pater's 1878 "imaginary portrait" of Florian Deleal in "The Child in the House," and considers the character a "parody" of Pateresque aestheticism as well as a "self-parody" of the Pateresque in James (43). Tintner meanwhile points to the similarly named Prince Florizel of Robert Louis Stevenson's 1882 *The New Arabian Nights* and traces the link made by Rachel Torrance's name with the renowned actress Rachel, and by her "tortuous thinness" with Sarah Bernhardt (1989, 90).

In an 1885 letter to Macmillan, James mistakenly referred to the collected volume as "Tales of Two Cities" (*Letters* 3, 81)—mixing Dickens's title and his own. Earlier, the reviewer for the *Athenaeum* noted the allusion and warned James not to make comparisons that would work against him (767).

Relation to Other Works

Most comparisons have been made with the two novels of New England that bracket the tale, *The Europeans* (1878) and *The Bostonians* (1885). Levy fits the depiction of Boston here as a "corrosive vision of lifeless gentility" with that in *The Bostonians* and even the less harsh "ironic" view in *The Europeans*, all of which contrast sharply with the "pastoral" retrospective an older James granted Boston's homogeneity in *The American Scene*, in response to what he felt as a frightening intrusion of the "alien" (247). Gale links the title and the story with the "Grimwinter" of "Four Meetings" and the Wentworths in *The Europeans* to suggest that James thought of Americans as "essentially chillier types" than Europeans (34). Quentin Anderson, on the other hand, judges the tale a "pleasant genre piece," an exception to James's usual rule of identifying New England and "self-righteousness" as in the character of Susan Stringham in *The Wings of the Dove* (30 n.3). Heimer takes a middle road, arguing that the tale "bridges" the light tone of *The Europeans* and the harsh satire of *The Bostonians*, giving as it does a clear victory to the natives (24 n.40). James himself described the tale as "most *lacteal* in its satire" although he anticipated it would not "be liked" in Boston (*Letters* 3, 24).

More specifically, Long links the description of Boston as a "city of women" in both the tale and the later novel (124, 158). In the tale, Florimond compares Boston to "a country stricken by a war, where the men had all gone to the army" (CT 6, 142). As Jacobson points out, his observation is partly accurate because Boston was still feeling the effect of the casualties of the Civil War (28), but that does not account for his dismissive attitude. Although Edel sees James as sharing his protagonist's views, Auerbach observes that Florimond's dismay at the preponderance of women—Jefferson remarks on the absence of husbands—is undercut by his inferiority to the women he criticizes (*Life* 3, 67; Auerbach 209 n.39; Jefferson 76). Donald Stone, however, who points to the same observation in *The Europeans* and *The American Scene*, observes that James was not alone in his view, as De Tocqueville also sensed a lack of "manly candor" in the States (239, 260).

Buitenhuis offers another link between the tale and *The Bostonians* in the use of "impressionist schemata" James discovered here, while Winner finds the use of impressionism here "solidly worked" into the tale, as in *The Reverberator* (Buitenhuis 142; Winner 126). Buitenhuis notes that in "The Art of Fiction" of the same year James spoke of good fiction as "a direct impression of life" (136). Grover considers the description somewhat less dependent on Florimond's gaze than that in *The Ambassadors* is on Strether's (126). Jefferson, for his part, classes Florimond with such characters as Gaston Probert and Rowland Mallet, who possess great taste without the corresponding talent (68). In 1890 James considered writing another tale of a "very modern impressionist painter" familiar with Europe returning to America, but evidently never did (CN 54–55).

Interpretation and Criticism

When questioned in 1901 by a woman seeking addresses for the characters in *The Bostonians* and "A New England Winter," James could recall only that Mrs. Daintry lived in Marlborough Street (*Letters* 4, 195). Nevertheless, the story's portrait of the city has been the focus of criticism from the start.

Among the contemporary reviews of *Tales of Three Cities*, which generally found the volume either thin or "polished" or both, almost the only specific mention of "A New England Winter" was *Lippincott's* praise of its "absolutely accurate" picture of Boston (215). The response was appropriate as James himself, in writing to Howells, described the story as "not very good," but significant for giving "form" to "a certain impression of Boston" (*Letters* 3, 27). Howells was more enthusiastic, praising the description both of the physical Boston in its "savage sunshine" and the cultural city, writing, "The fashionableness which is so unlike the fashionableness of other towns—no one touches that but you; and you contrive also to indicate its contiguity, in its most etherial intangibility, to something that is very plain and dully practical" (109). Apart from Edgar, who considers it an "ineffective" portrait of the city, later critics have followed Howells's lead, praising the "atmospheric" evocation of a "period" Boston, Matthiessen indeed finding little else to the tale (Edgar 44; Matthiessen xiii; also Winner 113; Putt 271; Jefferson 61). Buitenhuis writes that the tale's picture of a frosty New England and the title itself not only describe the place but symbolize it (138–39).

While Howells went on to praise the characters as well, and Edel once described the tale taken as a whole as "charming" (*Life* 3, 67), later critics such as Wagenknecht have often found that the rest of the story does not live up to its setting (196). The main problem is with Florimond as protagonist, of whom James confides in a rather Thackerayesque manner to the reader, "A hero fails us here" (CT 6, 117). Not impressed by James's claims of presenting an antihero, Putt dismisses Florimond as a "tenuous string" on which to build a story (271–72). Margolis provides an explanation for his tenuousness, seeing James in this "transitional" tale attempting through the new type of "aesthete" to break away from the international theme, but still indicates he hasn't given Florimond enough to do (61).

Nor is Florimond particularly pleasant in what little he does. Indeed, in Andreas's view the character is intended to satirize the American assumption that European residence produces necessarily superior beings (132). Instead, Florimond is, as James recorded in his notebook, simply "clever and selfish" (CN 17). As such he is an exception for James, according to Winner, one of his few callous trained artists, a fact she attributes to James's conception of impressionism as valuing "quick perception" over "depth of feeling" (113–14; also Tintner 1986, 106). Both Stone and Buitenhuis have pointed to the contempt in the portrayal of Florimond, although Buitenhuis qualifies it as "indulgent" (Stone 43; Buitenhuis 133). As Rimmon remarks, the twist at the end does not demand that the reader revise his view of Florimond (82). Whether flirting with a woman he would not marry because of her social position or could not marry because of her marital status, he is rather cowardly as well as frivolous. A married woman may even have seemed a safer refuge from commitment. Buitenhuis has remarked on "the comic improbability of a European-style adulterous affair in Boston" (133, 138). As a result, as Putt notes, Florimond gets out of his various entanglements quite freely at the end (271–72). It is perhaps only the humorously ironic presentation of Florimond's views that saves his character. And it does take a certain amount of inspiration to present a character that is, as Howells put it, himself so "wholly uninspired" (109).

James initially considered telling the story through a diary kept by the mother (CN 17) and her character as Jefferson notes is crucial to the contrast of cultures (69). What Shine describes as her "foolish diplomatic maneuvering" is evident in the very first scene where she hesitates on her own front steps trying to decide the rights of asking her maid to wait to shut the door until she is out of sight (52). She is torn between her uncertainty that "this was an act of homage that one human being had a right to exact of another" and her desire to impress her form-conscious son (CT 6, 87–91). As with the aesthetic son there is a comic angle to the mother's character. While for Mrs. Daintry, responsibility is her "nearest approach to a joy" (CT 6, 90), for the reader, as Buitenhuis remarks, there is comedy in her New England conscience (134).

In her responsibility to her son, however, she does approach a genuine misuse of another person. Called an unduly manipulative mother by Shine (52), she is perhaps more significantly lacking the proper concern about the effect of her manipulations on others. While Edel speaks of Mrs. Daintry as searching for a wife for Florimond, she is explicitly looking for someone to amuse but *not* to marry him (CT 6,11). James appears to have kept to his notebook interpretation that Mrs. Daintry is remiss in not being concerned that the girl "may be sacrificed" (CN 17).

Her sister-in-law is concerned, however, and Matthiessen and Murdock note how James uses the "shrewd" Miss Daintry to provide contrast to the mother and son (N 21). Howells reported that her character gave "universal satisfaction," inspiring women readers to inspect their roofs as had the maiden aunt (109). While Miss Daintry is a tougher sort of New Englander, it is ironically Florimond's lightness, his preference for the frivolous Pauline over the talented Rachel, that saves Mrs. Daintry from paying for her lack of consideration. Mrs. Daintry remains vulnerable, according to Jones, in her insistence on her son's innocence and her wilful ignorance of the full extent of his conceit (246). The rather negligible Pauline, spoken of by Howells as "a great triumph," has inspired little further comment (109). The independent Rachel, too, has been greeted mainly by critical silence, even as she escaped the comprehension of Florimond and his mother.

Looking at the tale as a whole, Buitenhuis contends that it treats too much, and wavers in its approach (138–39). The locale of Boston serves, however, to hold the story in hand. The "Frenchified" Florimond returns to America "to see how it looks" and learns that "even amid the simple civilisation of

New England there was material for the naturalist" (CT 6, 114, 140, 146). He is unable to make much of it, however, except, as James indicates, a somewhat imitative Europe, prompting a Parisian friend to ask about his watercolors on his return "if Massachusetts were really so much like Andalusia" (CT 6, 115). James himself made more of his trip home, producing a Boston and inhabitants unlikely to be mistaken for Andalusia or any place other than itself.

Works Cited

Primary Works

James, Henry. 1884. "A New England Winter." *Century* 28 (August–September): 573–87, 733–43.

———. 1884. "A New England Winter." *Tales of Three Cities*. Boston: Osgood; London: Macmillan, 267–359.

———. 1921–23. "A New England Winter." *The Novels and Stories of Henry James*. Vol. 25. Ed. Percy Lubbock. London: Macmillan.

Secondary Works

Anderson, Quentin. 1957. *The American Henry James*. New Brunswick, NJ: Rutgers University Press.

Andreas, Osborn. 1948. *Henry James and the Expanding Horizon: A Study of the Meaning and Basic Themes of James's Fiction*. Seattle: University of Washington Press.

Anon. 1885. Review of *Tales of Three Cities*. *Lippincott's* 35 (February): 215–16.

Anon. 1884. Review of *Tales of Three Cities*. *Athenaeum* 2981 (13 December): 767.

Auerbach, Nina. 1978. *Communities of Women: An Idea in Fiction*. Cambridge, MA: Harvard University Press.

Buitenhuis, Peter. 1970. *The Grasping Imagination: The American Writings of Henry James*. Toronto: University of Toronto Press.

Edgar, Pelham. 1964. *Henry James, Man and Author*. New York: Russell & Russell.

Gale, Robert L. [1954] 1964. *The Caught Image: Figurative Language in the Fiction of Henry James*. Chapel Hill: University of North Carolina Press.

Grover, Philip. 1973. *Henry James and the French Novel: A Study in Inspiration*. London: Paul Elek.

Heimer, Jackson W. 1967. *The Lesson of New England: Henry James and his Native Region*. Ball State Monograph 9. Muncie, IN: Ball State University.

Howells, W. D. 1980. *Selected Letters of William Dean Howells*. Vol. 3. Ed. Robert C. Leitz III, with Richard H. Ballinger and Christoph K. Lohmann. Boston: Twayne.

Jacobson, Marcia. 1983. *Henry James and the Mass Market*. University: University of Alabama Press.

Jefferson, D. W. 1964. *Henry James and the Modern Reader*. New York: St. Martin's.

Jones, Granville H. 1975. *Henry James's Psychology of Experience: Innocence, Responsibility, and Renunciation in the Fiction of Henry James*. The Hague: Mouton.

Levy, Leo B. 1958. "Henry James and the Jews: A Critical Study." *Commentary* 26 (September): 243–49.

Long, Robert Emmet. 1979. *The Great Succession: Henry James and the Legacy of Hawthorne*. Pittsburgh: University of Pittsburgh Press.

McElderry, Bruce R., Jr. 1965. *Henry James*. New York: Twayne.

Margolis, Anne T. 1985. *Henry James and the Problem of Audience: An International Act*. Ann Arbor: UMI Research Press

Matthiessen, F. O., ed. 1947. *The American Novels and Stories of Henry James*. New York: Knopf.

Putt, S. Gorley. 1966. *Henry James: A Reader's Guide*. Ithaca, NY: Cornell University Press.

Rimmon, Shlomith. 1977. *The Concept of Ambiguity: The Example of Henry James*. Chicago: University of Chicago Press.

Shine, Muriel G. 1969. *The Fictional Children of Henry James*. Chapel Hill: University of North Carolina Press.

Stone, Donald David. 1972. *Novelists in a Changing World: Meredith, James, and the Transformation of English Fiction in the 1880's*. Cambridge, MA: Harvard University Press.

Tintner, Adeline R. 1989. *The Pop World of Henry James: From Fairy Tales to Science Fiction*. Ann Arbor: UMI Research Press.

———. 1987. *The Book World of Henry James: Appropriating the Classics*. Ann Arbor: UMI Research Press.

———. 1986. *The Museum World of Henry James*. Ann Arbor: UMI Research Press.

———. 1974. "Henry James and a Watteau Fan." *Apollo* 99: 488.

Wagenknecht, Edward. 1984. *The Tales of Henry James*. New York: Frederick Ungar.

Winner, Viola Hopkins. 1970. *Henry James and the Visual Arts*. Charlottesville: University Press of Virginia.

The Next Time

Publication History

Appearing in July 1895, "The Next Time" was the third and final story James placed in *The Yellow Book*. He collected it the next year in *Embarrassments*, and also included it in his New York Edition.

Circumstances of Composition, Sources, and Influences

In January 1895 James's play *Guy Domville* had its disastrous premiere. Later that month he recorded in his notebook "the idea of the poor man, the artist, the man of letters, who all his life is trying—if only to get a living—to do something *vulgar*, to take the measure of the huge, flat foot of the public." James saw himself thus "twenty years ago, and so it has been ever, till the other night, Jan. 5th, the *première of Guy Domville*" (CN 109–10). Twenty years earlier, in 1876, James was the writer of a regular letter from Paris for the *New York Tribune*. He was not entirely happy with the job, feeling quite strongly "the vulgarity and repulsiveness" of the newspaper (*Life* 193). He continued the work, however, and in the summer asked his editor, Whitelaw Reid, for a raise. Reid, however, wrote James that he had had in mind "a suggestion of a quite different nature": "that the letters should be made rather more 'newsy' in character, and somewhat shorter, and that they should be sent somewhat less frequently" (Lind 898). On August 30 James responded by offering to end the series of letters, as he could not make them any more "'newsy' and gossipy": "I am too finical a writer and I should be constantly becoming more 'literary' than is desirable. To resist this tendency would be rowing upstream and would take much time and pains. If my letters have been 'too good' I am honestly afraid that they are the poorest I can do, especially for the money!" (*Letters* 2, 64). These were the two experiences James would turn into fiction.

Needing "an action" to fit his subject, he began with a contrast with a successful, vulgar woman writer, who "*thinks* she's fine." He considers making her the narrator "with a fine grotesque *inconscience*" so the tale "becomes a masterpiece of close and finished irony," but then decides the narrator needs to "be *conscient*, or SEMI-CONSCIENT, perhaps, to get the full force of certain efforts," although he projects him still the "opposite" of the central character (CN 109–10). Vaid cites the development of the narrator as showing the importance to James of having at least a "semi-conscient" narrator (251–52). James returned to the idea that June in a long notebook entry which settles on a narrator like that in "The Death of the Lion" or "The Coxon Fund." James then seeks to settle the three or four cases that will best show his hero's predicament, and to give the story urgency focuses on what his failure keeps him from—"marrying, living, keeping his head above water." While in his experience "everything didn't depend upon his success," for his "imagined little hero everything *does*" (CN 123–25).

In his preface, James says of the artist tales that they could only be "intelligently fathered but on his own intimate experience," and Lind observes how very much this one is. While she writes that it "seems strange" that James retained such a strong impression from his experience with the *Tribune*, she observes of the two notebook entries that they show how James regarded his failure in journalism and in the theatre "as failures of equal intensity"—"part of a persistent literary problem, his inability to achieve 'adequate vulgarity.'" Lind charts how the "crucial phrases" of his exchange with Reid appeared again and again in James's works. Variations on the idea that work can be "too good" and yet the worst possible "for the money" appear not only in James's 1881 recalling of the event in his notebooks, but in his planning for the play of *The American*, in "The Death of the Lion," *The Papers*, and especially in this story, "The Next Time." Similarly, Matthiessen and Murdock cite a letter to William James in which Henry contrasts his play to the one following it, *The Masqueraders*, and Wilde's concurrent play, *An Ideal Husband*, as illustrating the contrast between his own work and the popular idea. It includes a metaphor for the difference, "you can't make a sow's ear out of a silk purse," which appears again in both notebook entries as well as in the story (Lind 901, 904; N 180–81; also CN 110 n.2; Powers 1970, 27).

Further parallels between James and Limbert, Lind observes, abound. Limbert, like James, is always being called "ingenious," although the sales of his books, like those of James's most recent novels, are disappointing. In Limbert's first failure at the *Beacon*, she sees little attempt to hide the autobiographical parallel; in the second as an editor, she sees James treating "under a veil" his more recent encounter with the "cerebral treachery" of the theatre. She suggests, too, that Limbert's "adventure-story" may be the stand-in for *The Aspern Papers* or *The Reverberator*. Limbert's third stage represents the future James projected for himself as he moved past his humiliation, seen in his letter to Howells promising "far better work than ever I have done before," a promise Lind sees James keeping in his final trilogy of novels (901–10). Beebe also sees Limbert's entry into the "country of the blue" as reflecting James's own state after the failure of *Guy Domville* following the "rededication" in his notebooks (225). Even the deleterious influence of the narrator has an autobiographical parallel. An article in the November

1882 *Century* by William Dean Howells, praising James among the new novelists over several of the old, produced a backlash of criticism. Since James had also written on Howells, the two were accused by the critic of the *Academy* of being "linked in the most drivelling mutual admiration." At the time James wrote Howells not to let the "matter bother you; it is infinitesimally small and the affair of three fourths of a minute." In February, however, James would still be writing to a friend of the "truly idiotic commotion" of Howells's "ill-starred amiabilities to me" (*Letters* 2, 391–92, 406).

While Lind writes that the tale does not need the biographical background to be of interest, she sees it adding "meaning and significance" to the story, showing how James used "fantasy" to approach his problems (905). Most critics, indeed, have commented on the biographical parallel (e.g., Bass 119; Rawlings xii). Still, Edel contends that James's experience at the *Tribune* was different from Limbert's, since he failed only in a medium not his own, while Limbert also failed—financially—in his own (*Life* 2, 244–45). The observation applies equally to James's experience with the theatre, which he clearly regarded as an alien field. Even so, while Richardson writes that James, like Limbert, "can write nothing but 'charming masterpieces' of highest beauty" (489), one might note that James's plays, unlike Limbert's novels, are not generally judged to be masterpieces. Indeed, in Geismar's assessment, unlike Limbert, James had not only been willing but also successful in cheapening his art, producing truly vulgar, if not popular, plays (140). Such willingness is seen in James's letter to the editor of the *Illustrated News* shortly before the appearance of *The Other House*: "I should be very glad to write you a story energetically designed to meet your requirements of a "'love story' . . . I shall endeavour to be thrilling'"(*Life* 4, 156–57). Given such eagerness, it makes sense that Powers sees the tale as designed to "reassure" James that he will remain a true artist, even if like Limbert he tries "flirting with prostitution" of a literary order (1969, 17). He did, however, according to his sister Alice, once turn down an offer to write some stories for the *New York World* from Joseph Pulitzer, who asked that they not have "anything literary" in them (154). As James acknowledges, and Lind points out, James lacked Limbert's motivation (906). Limbert had the excuse of a wife to win and a family to feed that the bachelor James lacked in his search for fame and fortune.

Despite its closeness to his own experience, James's story has generally received high marks for avoiding self-pity, being instead, according to Matthiessen, "wryly comic" (*Major* 12). In the judgment of Edel and Lind, James treats his "sense of being a rejected author" in the tale "with an easy cheerfulness and mocking irony which cushioned inner heartbreak." At the same time, they find the tale anticipating the pressures on twentieth-century artists, and so achieving a "universal" relevance, proclaiming "the sovereignty of style, the sacred uniqueness of the creative consciousness" (xxxiii, xxxvii). Beebe, too, commends James's "ability to transcend the personal," directing his satire at Limbert's hopes for success, not at his art (225). Shulman not only sees James transforming his defeat into comedy, but sees him making the comedy out of techniques he had learned in the theatre, the "few big familiar effects" he had criticized the public for wanting in their plays: the "simple and obvious" contrast between Mrs. Highmore and Limbert, and the "geometric symmetry of stage comedy" in their repeated failure and successes (43).

Mordell, however, locates in the tale a "sensitiveness, nay pain," and, as Lind indicates, James in the 1890s was disappointed not only by his reception in the theatre world (Mordell 14). Rebecca West early remarked on the amnesia demonstrated by the obituaries of James, which spoke of him as a writer who had never been popular, despite his popularity in the late 1870s and early 1880s (46). Smith, too, points out that unlike Limbert or John Delavoy, who seem "totally unknown to the public," James, while a poor seller, was always rated high critically (144). However, by 1900 a reviewer could speak bluntly of the influences that "have brought Mr. James so thoroughly (magnificently, he would say) to throw the public over" (*Nation*). To Isle, the tale signals James's abandonment of "any serious effort to gain popular success" (21). Mordell calls the tale James's "apology for his whole career in writing novels which the public did not relish" (13–14). The feeling would linger. Edgar cites a letter to Edmund Gosse in which James describes himself as Ozymandias surveying the New York Edition, a failure despite the "deep and exquisite" nature of its "artistic problem," as an indication that James felt like Limbert "the victim of his own genius" (166; *Letters* 4, 777).

There were, however, other struggling artists in James's time, and other parallels for Limbert have been proposed. Dietrichson notes the similarity between Limbert's situation and that of Théophile Gautier as James described it in an 1874 essay:

> [his] exquisite literary work, though relished by the delicate of taste all over the world, never procured him anything but a decent subsistence. He could never treat himself to that supreme luxury of the artist,—the leisure to do a certain fine thing to please himself. . . . In this daily pressure of labor and need, it is immensely to Gautier's credit that he never, for three words together, was false to his rigid literary conscience. (133 n.15)

James's friend Robert Louis Stevenson, who had died only months before, is, according to Tintner, another source. Like Limbert, Stevenson supported a large family, and although he made a success of his adventure stories, he was like Limbert at work at the time of his death on what would have been another "high success" (139–41). Delbanco finds Limbert's situation anticipating that of Stephen Crane, while Smith compares his aim with his magazine to Melville's writing *Pierre* for two seemingly opposite audiences—the large public and the select few (Delbanco 58–59; Smith 140). Kappeler points to the allusion to Flaubert's hatred of society (86). Dietrichson proposes a parallel with P. B. S. Ray in Howells's *The World of Chance*, who loses his assignment with a local newspaper for not being gossipy enough (270, 281 n.20).

Jane Highmore, on the other hand, is a stunning popular success, and, as Gale points out, both her initials and many of her other qualities are the reverse of James's (1963, 397). Kermode comments that the choice of a woman foil may have been meant to strengthen either the contrast or the realism of the tale (23). In his notebooks James rejected the idea of having her married to a publisher as making her too like Mary Elizabeth Braddon, author of *Lady Audley's Secret* (CN 124). Edel sees James's satire of her ambitions coming from his view of Mrs. Humphry Ward, the popular writer and niece of Matthew Arnold, whom James found a "dear," although admitting, "Somehow I don't, especially when talking art and letters, *communicate* with her worth a damn" (*Life* 4, 293). At one point Limbert's wife remarks to the narrator, "Of course if she could have chosen she would have liked him to be Shakespeare or Scott, but that failing this she was glad he wasn't—well, she named the two gentlemen, but I won't" (CT 9, 227). Gale nominates as the two unnamed gentlemen the popular writers Thomas Anstey Guthrey and Frances Marion Crawford (1962).

After Limbert's marriage, his mother-in-law lives with him unable to "resentfully revert again from Goneril to Regan," Regan being in this case his sister-in-law Mrs. Highmore (CT 9, 224). Just before his death, Limbert wakes up "again in the country of the blue" (CT 9, 229). Kermode presents the possibility that the phrase has its root in one of the marginal glosses to *The Ancient Mariner* describing the stars: "Everywhere the blue sky belongs to them, and is their appointed rest, and their native country" (452 n.14). Limbert's death van Cromphout finds "strongly reminiscent" of the death of Goethe (137).

Shulman places James's tale in a modern genre of comedy based on intellectual uncertainty, an approach he traces back to such works as *Tristram Shandy*, *Candide*, *The Confidence-Man*, and "My Kinsman, Major Molineux," and forward to such works as *Herzog*, *Waiting for Godot*, and *The Tin Drum* (41). In a study of Walter de la Mare, Reid invokes James's tale in relating how the author, attempting to write a popular "shocker" in *The Return* and win popular success, won instead the Polignac Prize (84–85). Powers sees the character of Richard Silenski in Baldwin's *Another Country* as the opposite of Limbert, having only a "sow's ear to work with" (1984, 662).

Relation to Other Works

Defending his "supersubtle fry" in "The Death of the Lion," "The Next Time," and "The Figure in the Carpet," James wrote that he intended in these tales both an ironic criticism of what was and an "affirmation" of the good that could be (*Criticism* 2, 1229–30). In Wallace's sense of things, the biographical connections of Paraday, Limbert, and Vereker have kept critics from paying proper attention to the "method" of the tales, namely the comic-satiric approach that shifts the focus from the author in the tale to his society (161–63). Allen, however, keeps the focus on the writer, linking "The Middle Years," "The Death of the Lion," and "The Figure in the Carpet" on the basis of the striving of the artist in each for knowledge and his fear of having worked in vain (121). Berland pictures the artist in the last three as martyrs in the religion of art (32). While Gage nominates misperception as the general theme of *Embarrassments*, Dupee says of its two artist tales, that while James may still see life and art as "unalterably opposed . . . he is now less inclined to preach the importance of the disjunction than to smile bitterly over its consequences for artist and public alike" (Gage 26; Dupee 151). In both "The Next Time" and "The Figure in the Carpet" Geismar finds "passages of farce and satire" (139).

In his notebook entry, James thought of the tale as a "mate" to "The Death of the Lion" (CN 109). In the later tale, Matthiessen argues, James again deals with his own situation, in a more comic but still direct way ("Portrait" 5). While Jefferson speaks of Limbert doing without the social immersion other Jamesian authors consider desirable, Limbert, according to Blackmur, seeks unsuccessfully to make society his prey, while in "The Death of the Lion" society makes the writer its prey, a fate van Cromphout finds worse than the "public indifference" Limbert encounters (Jefferson 1964, 120–21; Blackmur 85; van Cromphout 139). Wallace points to additional resemblances, calling the "inversion" of the concepts of "success" and "failure" a similar device to the "reversal of the sexes" in "The Death of the Lion," and noting the narrator's unconscious contribution in each to the artist's demise (169, 172). Austin Wright observes that while other productive Jamesian artists also suffer from a lack of public acceptance, most are at least able to support themselves—Saltram of "The Coxon Fund," he notes, is not productive. This may account for the difference he discerns between the amount of interest in the relatively comfortable Vereker's desire for understanding and in Limbert's desire for a popular success (53 n.19; 61 n.38). Stevenson contrasts Limbert's inability to earn money by his writing to Saltram's inability to write once he has money (69). Limbert does try to earn his money, as does Mrs. Harvey of "Broken Wings." Edel and Lind put both in the same "pattern" with the reporters in *The Papers*, Limbert in his writing for *The Blackport Beacon*, and Mrs. Harvey—also "attempting something beyond her talents"—in her writing for the similarly named *The Blackport Banner* (xxxii).

Mrs. Highmore, in contrast, Vaid writes, is an "avatar" of Greville Fane, even as a subordinate theme of her tale—"the contrast between the good and the bad writer" and their disparate success—is central here (63). "The

Next Time," according to Matheson, "reverses" the theme of "Greville Fane," but still presents in Mrs. Highmore a "spiritual sister" to Greville Fane (225–26). Bass and Wallace contrast the depiction of Mrs. Highmore with the harsher caricature of the popular writers Dora Forbes and Guy Washington in "The Death of the Lion" (Bass 120; Wallace 169). Mrs. Highmore's manager husband, Matheson adds, is akin to Mrs. St. George of "The Lesson of the Master" (225–26). Limbert, on the other hand, Richardson observes, "lacks the adaptability" of St. George (489–90).

Limbert's constraint by family duties, Stewart observes, is typical of the artist tales (99). Walter Wright sees Limbert, like Gedge of "The Birthplace," as an artist hemmed in both by an unsympathetic society and the conventionality of family obligations (79). Unlike St. George, Bass remarks, he is incapable of being "cheapened into a domestic provider." The tension between "personal and intellectual passions"—present also in "The Coxon Fund"—Bass sees reduced by the transformation of "the irksome problem of the object of the personal passion" into a "loyal, rather uninteresting and inconspicuous wife." Although he remarks that the disciple here, for once, is of the same generation as the artist, he "gracefully accedes" his love to Limbert (119). Kappeler observes that it is Limbert's mother-in-law, rather than his wife, as in St. George's case, whose "vested interest" in his art is satirized (81).

"The Next Time" was the last of three artist tales to appear in the "lemon-coloured" *Yellow Book*, and Bass draws attention to the description of Limbert's *The Major Key* in its three "lemon-coloured volumes" as an image connected in James's mind with a youthful idealism about art that, he argues, is recovered in *The Ambassadors* when Strether sits reading a "lemon-coloured" novel—evidence that art survives even the artist (121–22). Bender locates the story's poignancy in what the narrator calls Limbert's "assumption that a man could escape from himself," a belief that Bender sees running opposite to Strether's realization that "one's consciousness is poured" like a "helpless jelly" into the "tin mould" of one's life (255).

Shulman places the tale with "Flickerbridge," "The Figure in the Carpet," *What Maisie Knew*, and *The Awkward Age* as examples of James's "comedy of knowledge" that derive humor from the modern concern with epistemology. Their search for knowledge turns serious in "The Jolly Corner," and produces tragic mistakes in "The Beast in the Jungle" and *The Wings of the Dove* (42–46). Limbert's end in the "country of the blue" Bender takes as one of the "fantastic otherworlds" James enjoyed creating for his writers, evident also in "The Great Good Place" and "The Private Life" (253). Such seclusion as Limbert establishes here, however, Rawlings remarks, is shown to be dangerous for the artist in "The Great Good Place" (xii).

Interpretation and Criticism

According to Richardson, the "narrative focus" of "The Next Time" is "unswervingly directed" toward Limbert (489). Other critics, however, have directed some of that attention toward the narrator himself. In the notebooks James fixed on the idea of the narrator's praise harming the writer's prospects, so that he tries to stop in order to help. In James's words, "This attitude of mine is a part of the story." James continued to project the narrator as unable to give up the "risk" of writing the last review, even as the writer's life is dependent on it, calling him the "*blighting* critic" who "dish[es]" the writer. He does not, however, address the issue of why the narrator cannot keep his mouth shut (CN 124–25). Bell, in looking at the "final shift from the enunciated to the enunciating subject," sees the "I" "consciously" taking on a "double duty" so that "the writer is his own reader" (151). To Matthiessen and Murdock, the narrator's character "contributes a double refinement" to the tale, his helpless devotion mirroring Limbert's unavoidable greatness (N 204). Lind, in her reading, picks up on James's use of the first-person in the notebooks for the narrator, saying of the narrator in the tale that he is James, the only one adequately "conscient" to tell the tale. Since Limbert is also James, she concludes, "the irony of James's commentary on James becomes increasingly delicious as we follow its implications throughout the story." In the narrator's recognition that Limbert could not succeed because then he would have thought "less well of him," she sees an "all too endearingly human compulsion to rationalize" (906, 908).

In his examination of the notebook entries, Booth also focuses on the ironic. Remarking on James's unusually explicit awareness of the effect an ironically unaware narrator such as the Mrs. Highmore character might have, Booth notes how he rejects such a character for a "real ironic painter," one who will be "ironic not as victim of the ironies but as master of them." However, Booth contends, James does not stop there, but makes his ironic master another involved narrator, as the interest in the narrator's attempt to restrain himself from writing about Limbert quickly becomes the focal drive of the tale that leads to its dénouement (342–44).

Still, Blackall includes the narrator in a list of narrators with "no personal stake" in their subject (155). Vaid offers a more detailed defense, speaking of the narrator's connection to the central characters as a "silken thread." He acknowledges the narrator as a rejected suitor of Maud, but asserts that the fact is "not indispensable to his function as a narrator." It serves simply to "lend flavor," a sign that James could use his narrators to add interest to a tale without compromising it (64–65). Similarly, Seed, in response to what he calls the critical "commonplace" that the narrator in James should *not* be identified with James, asserts that James himself does not distinguish himself sharply from his narrators. Citing the notebook entry to "The Next Time," Seed views the Jamesian narrator in general as a "persona" for James without any intended effect on the "objectivity" of the work (503).

Other critics continue to focus on the harm the narrator does Limbert, and the motive behind it. To Bass and Kermode, the issue is primarily a literary one. To Bass, the narrator is there mainly to provide a "useful distance" on a subject "full of sentimental and emotional attachment," but his presence also "shapes" events. A "Cassandra-like reviewer," he "does real harm to Limbert's reputation," a fact "obvious" even to the "inept" Limbert (120). Kermode says of the narrator that he becomes Limbert's enemy "willy-nilly but in the manner of his profession." No personal grudge is required (24). Goetz records that the narrator and Limbert were once romantic rivals, while Wallace states that the rivalry is resolved before the story starts (Goetz 162; Wallace 170–71). Gage, however, places that fact at the center of the tale, seeing James as complicating his original subject by making the narrator a rejected suitor. As Gage remarks, the narrator recognizes his "baleful influence" as a critic, even writing, "Mine was in short the love that killed" (CT 9, 188). He does not, however, Gage contends, understand the reasons for his own behavior, instead moving "back and forth" between two beliefs: his "half-real half-illusory belief that he loves Limbert and his masterpieces, and the half-real and half-illusory truth" that he is jealous of Limbert and happy in his failure. The issue then becomes one's perception of one's identity (26). To do him justice, it is also the narrator who passes on to Limbert the job with the *Beacon*. In this story, however, the narrator's sincerity or insincerity does not damage the central message. Whatever the motives for the narrator's inconvenient inability to be silent, they do not dimish the value of Limbert's continued devotion to his work, nor do they seem intended to damage the narrator sufficiently as a character to draw into question his high estimate of Limbert's work.

The role of Mrs. Highmore is clearer. As Dietrichson remarks, she is a "foil" to Limbert (127). In Vaid's estimate the "antithesis" between the two is not as "mechanically worked out" as one might expect, because James keeps the focus on Limbert, while Mrs. Highmore's "failure" serves simply as an "ironic backdrop" (63). Even so, Goetz argues that the addition of Mrs. Highmore "alchemically transformed" James's original autobiographical inspiration so that it becomes of "purely ironic and differential value" (157). Bass notes the irony within Mrs. Highmore's name—the story gives a "*low* view" of "Mrs. *High*more's" writing—but discerns a greater subtlety in her character in her "sensitive and kindly" treatment of Limbert (120). Even so, given her success, Matheson finds it "highly ironical and paradoxical" that Limbert's unborn popular success is called a "male heir," while his masterpieces are "but another female child" (226).

Limbert himself has several flesh-and-blood children in addition to a wife. Seeing James's sense of the incompatibility of marriage and art in the tale, Stein comments on how Limbert's marriage exacerbates his desperation and his desire to lower his art, while accepting himself allows him "a greater freedom with his wife" (109; CT 9, 211). While Limbert writes at the "garden level," his wife and mother-in-law inhabit the "Upstairs": "It was Upstairs that the thunder gathered, that Mrs. Stannace kept her accounts and her state, that Mrs. Limbert had her headaches, that the bells for ever jangled at the maids, that everything imperative in short took place" (CT 9, 204). The "impression of domestic pressures" here is, as Vaid puts it, "created synoptically." As Vaid also observes, the story for once credits a wife's "acceptance of her husband's genius" (66, 69). In the words of the narrator, the "strangeness" was that "she had really seen almost better than any one what he could do. The greatest strangeness was that she didn't want him to do something different." In the end, he records, "she was essentially one of us" (CT 9, 198, 226). Less expansively, Wagenknecht describes Mrs. Limbert as being "as understanding as a wife could be under the circumstances" (84). In Kappeler's view the happy marriage is part of the problem. Not only does his marriage with its "domestic squalor" bear "the seal of sacrifice," but Maud "unfortunately" is interested in his art, although luckily her children keep her too busy to interfere, switching the "function of the 'evil wife'" onto her mother. The problem, in Kappeler's folkloric reading, is that Limbert, like any true artist, is married first to his muse. By putting Maud first, he has "degraded" his muse "to the status of concubine," and even worse, sadistically seeking to lower his art further, "takes to the whip." The "most disconcerting failure in the story," Kappeler finds, is the Muse's "unfailing loyalty" to Limbert "as if she too found a certain perverse pleasure in the relationship" (81–82). All of which seems to be taking a metaphor too far. Limbert's marriage to Maud never harms his art, and while his final comfort is alone "in the country of the blue," it is not a cause of regret that he had some human company along the way.

Andreas calls the tale James's "revenge on his own public" (149). As Horne writes, it is taken for granted here that the public is stupid (82). Most critics, like Matheson, see the presentation of the "artist who is too good to be popular," the contempt for popular literature reflecting not only James's experience, but his beliefs as a novelist (225; also Smith 139; van Cromphout 138). As Dietrichson observes, only the expectation of death allows Limbert to write as he wishes (127). Limbert fails, in Blackmur's words, "because he cannot help remaining the harmless, the isolated monarch of his extreme imaginative ardent self" (85).

The idea that Limbert is "possessed by" his talent, rather than its "possessor," is, as Horne observes, unusual in James (82). Rawlings also looks at how the work of the artists in the tale is disturbingly independent of their control, and of their critics, yet dependent on their editors. He also remarks on the various definitions of "success" in the tale, from something "achieved . . . when of a beautiful subject his expression was complete" to Mrs. Highmore's market views (xi–xii). The whole story, according to Kappeler, is a "study in pragmatism and cynicism." Taking the narrator's remarks on "the inexorable limits of his circulation" as almost a "Marxian economic analysis," she provides one of her own. To the literati, art has an "intrinsic," "pure-use value," but they offer only "appreciation and understanding" in exchange. She cites, for example, the description of Limbert's friends, who "appeared to have a mortal objection to acquiring [the books] by subscription or by purchase: they begged or borrowed or stole, they delegated one of the party perhaps to commit the volumes to memory and repeat them, like the bards of old, to listening multitudes." Kappeler does not acknowledge the exaggeration of the description, but is more on the mark in speaking of Limbert's need of a larger public willing to buy. In their attempts to boost circulation, to accommodate the product to the marketplace, Limbert and the narrator, she writes, are "on the verge of grasping the full complexity of the literary work as commodity" (86–88).

Instead, he sails into the "country of the blue," which, Blackmur writes, "is a very lonely place to be, for it is very nearly empty except for the self, and is gained only by something like a religious retreat, by an approximation of birth or death or birth-in-death" (86). In Edgar's words, the story "illustrates with tragic irony the embarrassments that accumulate on the path of a man of genius" (165). Segal succinctly refers to the tale's "sad humor" (107). But if Limbert in the tale is unable to turn his high art into popular success, he seems also unable to turn the comedy of his art into the tragedy of his life. To Kermode, despite Limbert's death, the tone of the tale remains that of "social comedy" not tragedy (24). The story covers a wide range of moods, according to Smith, from "comic fantasy" to "intense seriousness" (140–41). Lind notes not only the "poignancy" and "suspense" achieved by Limbert's "fierce financial pressure," but also the tale's "amusing satire" of the "richly textured" story (904–5).

Some critics emphasize the humor. Geismar calls the tale an "entertaining satire," McElderry an "ironic representation of the popular press as the enemy of artistic quality" (McElderry 123; Geismar 139). Edel judges it "ironic" and "at moments savagely witty," and, with Lind, a "little pathetic comedy" of "high contrasts" (CT 9, 8; xxxiii). Matheson further emphasizes the harshness of the comedy in the tale's "bitterly ironic and yet almost burlesque manner" (225) Norrman, on the other hand, finds it "funny"—to James at least—in a way that undermines its role as a serious commentary on art. He describes it as a "pure" example of James's beloved chiastic situations, so that the meaning of words becomes inverted, failures are "exquisite," and popular success a "hard doom." According to Norrman, once James began working within such a balanced framework, no matter what the initial inspiration, the parallelism tended to take over (150–51). For his part, Putt prefers the satire of those who frustrate Limbert to the "self-pity" and high-flown praise of those who side with him (231).

Others classify the tale as a different kind of comedy. To Vaid, Limbert's situation "humanized" James's original idea, and although his "exaggeratedly protracted defiance of his genius, which itself is exaggerated," is a source of humor, as is the public that ignores him, the "chief source" of comedy in the tale is not Limbert's failure. It is his triumph, seen in the tale's "final twist" in which Limbert gives up his quest for public approval and so regains his "good conscience." The tone "remains that of high comedy," but with a serious intent, shown in the narrator's increasingly serious mood toward the conclusion of the story (68–70). In Horne's estimate, the tale fits many genres. It is a "fairy-tale," with all the "charm and atmosphere of a fable" and a "delightfully ironic style." Primarily, however, she characterizes it as a "true comedy" with pathos, but no tragedy (80–81).

Many critics, including Kappeler and Horne, have noted the constant "inversion" of values in the tale, particularly the play on the word "success" (Kappeler 82; Horne 80). To Shulman, these inversions are one of the characteristics of its genre—the "comedy of knowledge." In his reading, James leads the reader into sharing the laughter "of a small group or coterie at odds with the values of the mass"—those illustrated in the "high" figure of Mrs. Highmore. The coterie—and the story—has its own implicit values that survive the constant playing with the terms of "success and failure, good and bad and worst." The "mistakes" in the story are comic as they show "two intelligent, discriminating, imaginative men" constantly getting things wrong, a comedy multiplied by the way in which the narrator doubles Limbert, and both double James. As the story continues there are more and more "elements of tragedy or pathos," but the tale remains a comedy, because the reader, like the narrator, still wants Limbert to be a success "in a genuine and not a commercial way." With Limbert's final "success," the "comedy is enlarged and deepened and carried to its furthest limits." In the end, the joke "becomes a rather grim one" but produces a "kind of apotheosis," reaching a "borderline where pathos, tragedy, and comedy converge." Shulman even points to the tale's subtle religious vocabulary as deepening the attack on the public and the elevation of the "comically but nonetheless painfully crucified" Limbert (43–49)

In his reading of the tale, Wallace also notes the "logic turned topsy-turvy" in the lamenting of both masterpieces and best-sellers. The mechanical "laws" that frustrate Limbert and guide the symmetrical plot he finds fitting Bergson's definition of the comic as "the mechanical encrusted on the living." The situation, in his view, is "doubled by the presence of the narrator," who is equally unable to be anything other than an "exquisite failure." The satire, however, is directed primarily at the public. By the end, Limbert is "not really a comic figure," he argues, as one "cannot help feeling the sad irony of his situation." Still, the story represents James's "detached and humorous view of his own frustrating situation." Like Shulman he, too, finds the ending "more sad than happy" and yet "affirmative" (170–79).

Richardson places the tale among James's best (489). To Bass, it shows James's "increasing restraint and control with a highly personal subject" (120). Putt objects to the story as stretching its subject too far, although like Wallace, he praises its wit (Putt 231; Wallace 172). Certainly, James took his subject further than his original biographical inspiration. Unlike Limbert, James was not beleaguered by the thought of a wife and children to feed, much less a disapproving mother-in-law. When he felt the need to travel, he could. One might argue that in embellishing his own situation, James was like Limbert in trying to bow to the tastes of a vulgar public little interested in solitary artistic effort. Or, if one stayed with the biographical approach—an approach by no means necessary for an appreciation of the work—one might rather note how such dramatic effects seemed to James a fitting objective correlative for his own frustration at what the narrator calls the "grotesque want . . . of adequate relation" between a writer's effort and the public's response (CT 9, 223; Lind 909).

Works Cited

Primary Works
James, Henry. 1895. "The Next Time." *The Yellow Book* 6 (July): 11–59.

———. 1896. "The Next Time." *Embarrassments*. London: Heinemann; New York: Macmillan, 183–202.

———. 1909. "The Next Time." *The Novels and Tales of Henry James*. New York Edition. Vol. 15, 155–216. New York: Scribner's.

Secondary Works
Allen, Elizabeth. 1984. *A Woman's Place in the Novels of Henry James*. New York: St. Martin's.

Andreas, Osborn. 1948. *Henry James and the Expanding Horizon: A Study of the Meaning and Basic Themes of James's Fiction*. Seattle: University of Washington Press.

Anon. 1900. Review of *The Soft Side*. *The Nation* 71 (29 November): 430.

Bass, Eben Edward. 1964. "Lemon-Colored Volumes and Henry James." *Studies in Short Fiction* 1 (Winter): 113–22.

Beebe, Maurice. 1964. *Ivory Towers and Sacred Founts: The Artist as Hero in Fiction from Goethe to Joyce*. New York: New York University Press.

Bell, Ian F. A., ed. 1985 *Henry James: Fiction as History*. Totowa, NJ: Barnes & Noble.

Bender, Bert. 1976. "Henry James's Late Lyric Meditations upon the Mysteries of Fate and Self-Sacrifice." *Genre* 9, no. 3 (Fall): 247–62.

Berland, Alwyn. 1981. *Culture and Conduct in the Novels of Henry James*. Cambridge: Cambridge University Press.

Blackall, Jean Frantz. 1965. *Jamesian Ambiguity and* The Sacred Fount. Ithaca, NY: Cornell University Press.

Blackmur, R. P., ed. [1943] 1962. "In the Country of the Blue." In *Studies in Henry James*. Ed. Veronica A. Makowsky, 69–90. New York: New Directions. Reprinted from *Kenyon Review* 5: 508–21.

Booth, Wayne C. [1961] 1983. *The Rhetoric of Fiction*. Chicago: University of Chicago Press.

Delbanco, Nicholas. 1982. *Group Portrait*. New York: Morrow.

Dietrichson, Jan W. 1969. *The Image of Money in the American Novel of the Gilded Age*. Oslo: Universitetsforlaget.

Dupee, F. W. [1951] 1956. *Henry James*. Garden City, NY: Doubleday Anchor.

Edel, Leon, and Ilse Dusoir Lind, eds. 1961. Introduction. *Henry James: Parisian Sketches, Letters to the New York Tribune, 1875–1876*. New York: Collier, 9–27.

Edgar, Pelham. [1927] 1964. *Henry James, Man and Author*. New York: Russell & Russell.

Gage, Richard P. 1988. *Order and Design: Henry James' Titled Story Sequences*. New York: Peter Lang.

Gale, Robert L. 1963. "Henry James's J. H. in 'The Real Thing.'" *Studies in Short Fiction* 14: 396–98.

———. 1962. "James's 'The Next Time.'" *Explicator* 21 (December): Item 35.

Geismar, Maxwell. 1963. *Henry James and the Jacobites*. Boston: Houghton Mifflin.

Goetz, William R. 1986. *Henry James and the Darkest Abyss of Romance*. Baton Rouge: Louisiana State University Press.

Horne, Helen. 1960. *Basic Ideals of James's Aesthetics as Expressed in the Short Stories Concerning Artists and Writers*. Marburg: Erich Mauersberger.

Isle, Walter Whitfield. 1968. *Experiments in Form: Henry James's Novels: 1896–1901*. Cambridge, MA: Harvard University Press.

James, Alice. 1964. *The Diary of Alice James*. Ed. Leon Edel. Harmondsworth: Penguin.

Jefferson, D. W. 1964. *Henry James and the Modern Reader*. New York: St. Martin's.

Kappeler, Susanne. 1980. *Writing and Reading in Henry James*. New York: Columbia University Press.

Kermode, Frank, ed. 1986. *The Figure in the Carpet and Other Stories*. London: Penguin.

Lind, Ilse Dusoir. 1951. "The Inadequate Vulgarity of Henry James." *PMLA* 66 (December): 886–910.

McElderry, Bruce R., Jr. 1965. *Henry James*. New York: Twayne.

Matheson, Gwen. 1968. "Portraits of the Artist and the Lady in the Shorter Fictions of Henry James." *Dalhousie Review* 48: 222–30.

Matthiessen F. O. 1944. "Introduction: Henry James' Portrait of the Artist." *Henry James: Stories of Writers and Artists*. Norfolk, CT: New Directions. Also reprinted as "Henry James's Portrait of the Artist." *Partisan Review* 11 (1944): 71–87.

———. 1944. *Henry James: The Major Phase*. New York: Oxford University Press.

Mordell, Albert, ed. 1957. *Literary Reviews and Essays by Henry James*. New York: Grove.

Norrman, Ralf. 1982. *The Insecure World of Henry James's Fiction: Intensity and Ambiguity*. New York: St. Martin's.

Powers, Lyall H. 1984. "Henry James and James Baldwin: The Complex Figure." *Modern Fiction Studies* 30: 651–67.

———. 1970. *Henry James: An Introduction and Interpretation*. New York: Holt, Rinehart.

———. 1969. *The Merrill Guide to Henry James*. Columbus, OH: Charles E. Merrill.

Putt, S. Gorley. 1966. *Henry James: A Reader's Guide*. Ithaca, NY: Cornell University Press.

Rawlings, Peter, Jr. 1984. *Henry James's Shorter Masterpieces*. Vol. 2. Sussex: Harvester; Totowa, NJ: Barnes & Noble.

Reid, Forrest. 1929. *Walter de la Mare: A Critical Study*. New York: Henry Holt.

Richardson, Lyon N, ed. [1941] 1966. *Henry James: Representative Selections, with Introduction, Bibliography, and Notes*. New York: American Writer Series; Urbana: University of Illinois Press.

Seed, David. 1981. "The Narrator in Henry James's Criticism." *Philological Quarterly* 60 (Fall): 501–21.

Segal, Ora. 1969. *The Lucid Reflector: The Observer in Henry James' Fiction*. New Haven: Yale University Press.

Shulman, Robert. 1968. "Henry James and the Modern Comedy of Knowledge." *Criticism* 10 (Winter): 41–53.

Smith, Henry Nash. 1978. *Democracy and the Novel: Popular Resistance to Classic American Writers*. New York: Oxford University Press.

Stein, Allen F. 1984. *After the Vows Were Spoken: Marriage in American Literary Realism*. Columbus: Ohio State University Press.

Stevenson, Elizabeth. [1949] 1981. *The Crooked Corridor: A Study of Henry James.* New York: Octagon.

Stewart, J. I. M. 1963. "Henry James." In *Eight Modern Writers. Oxford History of English Literature.* Vol. 7, 71–121. New York: Oxford University Press.

Tintner, Adeline R. 1987. *The Book World of Henry James: Appropriating the Classics.* Ann Arbor: UMI Research Press.

Vaid, Krishna B. 1964. *Technique in the Tales of Henry James.* Cambridge, MA: Harvard University Press.

van Cromphout, G. 1968. "Artist and Society in Henry James." *English Studies* 49 (April): 132–40.

Wagenknecht, Edward. 1984. *The Tales of Henry James.* New York: Frederick Ungar.

Wallace, Ronald. 1975. *Henry James and the Comic Form.* Ann Arbor: University of Michigan Press.

West, Rebecca. [pseud].1916. *Henry James.* London: Nisbet.

Wright, Austin McGiffert. 1961. *The American Short Story in the Twenties.* Chicago: University of Chicago Press.

Wright, Walter F. 1962. *The Madness of Art: A Study of Henry James.* Lincoln: University of Nebraska Press.

Nona Vincent

Publication History

"Nona Vincent" was published in the February and March 1892 issues of the *English Illustrated Magazine*, accompanied by illustrations by W. J. Hennessy, and included the next year in *The Real Thing*. It next appeared in print after James's death, in Lubbock's edition of the novels and stories.

Circumstances of Composition, Sources, and Influences

"Nona Vincent" was written in the midst of James's involvement with the theatre, which may well explain why this is the first of three mature tales not recorded in the notebooks (N ix). There are still indications of it, however, in that source as the names of Wayworth, Nona, and Alsager all appear in an entry on July 27, 1891 (CN 60). Later, on October 22, James recorded his disappointment with the stage version of *The American* and his continuing faith in the "absolute and interesting success" possible as a dramatist, even as he paid tribute to the sustaining force of his art as a fiction writer. At the same time, he reminded himself of his promise of a story to the editor of the *English Illustrated Magazine*, Sir Clement Kinloch-Cooke. Given his preoccupation with playwriting at the time, it is not surprising that he substituted a tale of the theatre for the sketched idea of a woman, her lover, and her dying husband (CN 61–62).

Matthiessen and Murdock point to an earlier entry from January 27, 1888, concerning the actress Isabel Bateman, who had been replaced by Ellen Terry in *Hamlet* only to be asked to return to the play later for the sake of the director, as showing James's interest in tales of the theatre. One could also see a connection between the story's theme—"the special sort of sacrifice made by a woman" in giving up her pride for the play's success—and the character of Mrs. Alsager (N 11).

Although McElderry finds relatively little of the "atmosphere" of the theatre in the tale (121), James is clearly identifying with the struggles of his neophyte playwright protagonist. Brooks and McCarthy cite Wayworth's enthusiasm for the "scenic idea" as representing James's own (Brooks 111; McCarthy 92). Putt even finds the tale harmed by the professional preoccupation of an "over-anxious" James (224). Edel assigns specific roles, seeing James embodying the uneven acting of Elizabeth Robins, the woman who had played Claire de Cintré, in Violet Grey. As the model for Mrs. Alsager, Edel's prime candidate is Florence Bell, a woman of leisure, playwright, and frequent reader of James's plays; another possibility is Mrs. Mahlon Sands to whom James wrote of Robins's performance, "I wish she could see *you*!" (*Life* 4, 21, 25, 32, 40–41; *Letters* 3, 358; 1970, 175–76). Perhaps the most touching bit of autobiography in the story is the modest career James, struggling for a hit, projects for his representative at the end—"His plays sometimes succeed" (CT 8, 187). Rawlings and Aswell both take a dim view of even such limited expectations, arguing that the reliance on the supernatural for the success of Wayworth's first play augurs badly for both his and James's dramatic careers (Rawlings xvii–xviii; Aswell 180–81).

James read his play of *The American* to the imperious Isabel Gardner, as Wayworth reads his plays to the humbler Mrs. Alsager (*Life* 3, 41). In earlier years he had complained of an evening in Rome spent listening to William Wetmore Story reading a five-act tragedy (*Life* 2, 127; *Letters* 1, 353).

Edel offers a biographical source for the supernatural touch in the tale as well, remarking that James presented his brother's paper on a medium to the British Society of Psychical Research in October 1890 (1970, 174–75). Wagenknecht invokes the Pygmalion myth, calling the imagined character of

Nona Vincent Wayworth's Galatea (224). James had recorded the year before the germ for what would become Du Maurier's *Trilby*, a tale that combines aspects of the supernatural and of the shaping artist of the Pygmalion myth (CN 51–52).

Relation to Other Works

"Nona Vincent" has been frequently paired with "Sir Dominick Ferrand," most pejoratively by Edgar, who labels them both "slack-fibred" (156). Aswell locates in both a reliance on the supernatural to sustain an artistic collaboration (185–86). Considering the supernatural element more generally, Todorov judges the two, along with "The Great Good Place," as examples of tales that exhibit quasi-supernatural experiences and so make the categorizing of James's "ghost" stories quite difficult (184). As Edel observes, the two have no ghosts, but do offer examples of "extra-sensory perception," here in the suggestion of "thought-transference" in the simultaneity of Wayworth's vision of Nona with Mrs. Alsager's visit to Violet (CT 8, 11–12; 1970, 176). Pound argues that in both James was pushing his art just "beyond the right curve," an overextension that he would later correct (30). Briggs adds "The Real Right Thing" to the list (150).

Putt discerns similarities with "The Real Thing" in the concern with the disjunction between what is real in ordinary life and what appears to have reality in art (224). One might add that Philip Vincent, the author whose "*édition de luxe*" the artist is illustrating in "The Real Thing," makes an appropriate relation for the imaginary Nona. Rawlings offers a correspondence between the limited "fragile" community of art here and in "Brooksmith" (xviii, xxvi).

Looking at the two heroines, Wagenknecht compares Violet to Miriam Rooth as an example of an actress realistically portrayed, without reliance on stereotypes (196). Mrs. Alsager as a confidante anticipates Maria Gostrey, according to Sharp, who observes that, as in *The Spoils of Poynton* and *The Golden Bowl*, the hero marries someone other than his confidante. She also links the tale with "Flickerbridge" and with "The Death of the Lion" as late, light tales with more serious shadows, that use a confidante and talk of art (28–29).

Interpretation and Criticism

Ezra Pound dismissed the tale as one that might have been written by "a person of eighteen doing first story" (34). A contemporary critic for the *Athenaeum* contented himself with calling the tale "feeble" and seems to have anticipated most of the later objections of the relatively small amount of criticism the story has received since. Sounding almost like James, the review-er commented: "There is no particular reason why Wayworth should have married Violet Grey at the end, or why he should not; if anything, the balance of circumstances would have suggested his not doing so; but he does" (601–2). Part of the problem may well be that James waited until the last para-graph to announce the marriage, a technique criticized by both Wagenknecht and Putt (Wagenknecht 197; Putt 224).

The *Athenaeum* also objected to the use of "second-sight" as "hardly wor-thy" of James (602). Wagenknecht judges unconvincing not only the super-natural but also Nona's transformation as an actress (197). Sharp senses throughout the tale an air of "preternatural reality," particularly in the ideal-ized relationship between Wayworth and Mrs. Alsager (30, 32). She plays a dual role as both muse and audience for Wayworth's play, a combination that Rawlings argues embodies James's view of the necessary closeness between the artist and his sources. At the same time, in Rawlings's view, she repre-sents a "compromise" similar to that between "process and product" that James saw represented by the theatre (xvi–xx).

Mrs. Alsager is anchored somewhat to earth by her marriage to a vulgar, wealthy newspaperman. Indeed, Barzun cites the description of her hus-band's appreciation of her different "tastes" because "that seemed to give a greater acreage to their life" as an example of the potential bitterness of James's humor (516 n.1). Sharp points out that James also grounds the rela-tionship between Wayworth and Mrs. Alsager realistically by basing it on female self-effacement and male self-centeredness. Aswell also notes Wayworth's complacent insensitivity toward Mrs. Alsager, and like Sharp locates in it a certain amount of self-portraiture by James (Sharp 30, 32). While Rawlings speculates on the possibility of an affair between Mrs. Alsager and Wayworth, there is little indication of such a physically intimate relation-ship (xvi–xx). Rather, as Aswell puts it, Wayworth transforms Mrs. Alsager into an "imaginary creation," making his experiencing her as a supernatural apparition appropriate (183–84). Mrs. Alsager is indeed put more in the role of an ideal than a person. As Jones says of her, she "contributes herself to the world of art" (242). Wayworth accepts the contribution. At the same time, according to Andreas's theory, he creates in Nona Vincent an image of an unmarried Mrs. Alsager and once Nona's identity is assumed by Violet Grey is able to marry his ideal (126).

Toward the start of his tale, James says of Mrs. Alsager that while "she had the artistic chord . . . She had not the voice—she had only the vision" (CT 8, 155). The lack of a voice makes it appropriate that Nona's visit is soundless. It also allows Wayworth, as Aswell writes, to do something for Mrs. Alsager; he provides her in his work with the "voice" that realizes her vision (183–84). Jones is also correct in discerning in the tale a sense of a certain shared responsibility for each other between Mrs. Alsager, Violet, and Wayworth (242). Kappeler makes a defense of her as the "truest artist" of the three, pointing out that the story calls her "even more literary and more artistic" than Wayworth, who, looking at the expression in her face, asks, "How in the world could she express better?" (98–99; CT 8, 155). But while Wayworth's work may have flaws, the perfection assigned Mrs. Alsager here treats her somewhat condescendingly as a special case, both as a woman and as a non-producing artist who is above criticism precisely because she produces nothing to criticize. She is, however, a woman of great sensitivity and joy in art, and in the end, although she must renounce her monopoly on Wayworth to achieve it, his success is not for her without its rewards.

As Markow-Totevy notes, while the apparition of Nona arises from Wayworth's anxieties, it offers reassurance, not fear (112–13). The reassurance is justified as Violet's next performance is a stunning success. Despite the dire predictions read into the tale from James's career, the tale in itself is like its apparition both mild and soothing. In a letter to Florence Bell, who may have modeled for Mrs. Alsager, James called the tale, of which she had just read the first installment, "a very small and simple *fantaisie*" (*Letters* 3, 373). No one since has thought to give it higher praise, but as something small and simple, it fills its role well.

Works Cited

Primary Sources

James, Henry. 1892. "Nona Vincent." *The English Illustrated Magazine* 9 (February–March): 365–76, 491–502.

———. 1893. "Nona Vincent." *The Real Thing*. New York and London: Macmillan, 131–78.

———. 1921–23. "Nona Vincent." *The Novels and Stories of Henry James*. Vol. 26. Ed. Percy Lubbock. London: Macmillan.

Secondary Sources

Andreas, Osborn. 1948. *Henry James and the Expanding Horizon: A Study of the Meaning and Basic Themes of James's Fiction*. Seattle: University of Washington Press.

Anon. 1893. Review of *The Real Thing*. *Athenaeum* 3420 (13 May): 601–2.

Aswell, E. Duncan. 1966. "James's Treatment of Artistic Collaboration." *Criticism* 8: 180–95.

Barzun, Jacques. 1943. "James the Melodramatist." *Kenyon Review* 5 (August): 508–21. Also reprinted in *The Question of Henry James*, ed. F.W. Dupee, 254–66. New York: Henry Holt, 1945.

Briggs, Julia. 1977. *Night Visitors: The Rise and Fall of the English Ghost Story*. London: Faber.

Brooks, Van Wyck. 1928. *The Pilgrimage of Henry James*. London: Jonathan Cape.

Edel, Leon, ed. 1970. *Henry James: Stories of the Supernatural*. New York: Taplinger.

Edgar, Pelham. [1927] 1964. *Henry James, Man and Author*. New York: Russell & Russell.

Jones, Granville H. 1975. *Henry James's Psychology of Experience: Innocence, Responsibility, and Renunciation in the Fiction of Henry James*. The Hague: Mouton.

Kappeler, Susanne. 1980. *Reading and Writing in Henry James*. London: Macmillan.

McCarthy, Harold T. 1958. *Henry James: The Creative Process*. New York: Thomas Yoseloff.

McElderry, Bruce R., Jr. 1965. *Henry James*. New York: Twayne.

Markow-Totevy, Georges. 1969. *Henry James*. Trans. John Griffiths. London: Merlin.

Pound, Ezra. 1918. "A Shake Down." *The Little Review* 5 (August): 9–39.

Putt, S. Gorley. 1966. *Henry James: A Reader's Guide*. Ithaca, NY: Cornell University Press.

Rawlings, Peter, ed. 1984. *Henry James's Shorter Masterpieces*. Vol. 1. Sussex: Harvester; Totowa, NJ: Barnes & Noble.

Sharp, Sister M. Corona. 1963. *The Confidante in Henry James: Evolution and Moral Value of a Fictive Character*. Notre Dame, IN: Notre Dame University Press.

Todorov, Tevetan. 1977. *The Poetics of Prose*. Trans. Richard Howard. Ithaca, NY: Cornell University Press.

Wagenknecht, Edward. 1984. *The Tales of Henry James*. New York: Frederick Ungar.

Osborne's Revenge

Publication History

"Osborne's Revenge" was the lead story in the July 1868 issue of *Galaxy*. It was accompanied by an illustration by W. J. Hennessy showing a foppish Osborne watching as Henrietta Congreve, looking like a ship's figurehead, tears up Graham's letter (Aziz 1, 331). The story was not reprinted until 1950 in Edna Kenton's *Eight Uncollected Tales*.

Circumstances of Composition, Sources, and Influences

LeClair finds James working here with materials from his own life and circle, depicting talented and leisured people in a Newport setting familiar to him, the treatment of which Jefferson nevertheless judges "featureless" in comparison to next year's travel sketch (LeClair 407; Jefferson 42). Despite its locale both Buitenhuis and Kraft see the tale as moving away from its American setting (Buitenhuis 49; Kraft 37).

Miss Congreve shows herself a "true artist" at an amateur performance Osborne attends (CT 2, 27). She appears in "powders and patches," and while the piece is French, her name (Wagenknecht for some reason calls her Cosgrove) evokes the world of Restoration comedy, and its role-playing and concealments, and the strong-minded woman and the baffled man of the tale have their sympathies with such characters as Mirabell and Millamant in Congreve's *Way of the World*. Tintner considers the names Graham and Osborne to come from Maria S. Cummins's *The Lamplighter* (206).

Jefferson finds the only American characteristic assigned the heroine here a theological learning she shares with Poe's Morella (73). Walter Wright considers her range of learning to surpass even that of the heroines of Mrs. Radcliffe (113).

Relation to Other Works

The story is usually seen in the context of James's other early tales. Looking at the story's technical structure, Torgovnick draws attention to the use of a "quasi epilogue" such as he also used in "De Grey" (186–88). Kelley links the tale with "The Problem" in their topic of jealousy (84). Along similar lines,

LeClair groups the tale with four other tales of 1869 in its treatment of revenge, and finds Osborne's rescue of Henrietta's nephew recalling the death of the child in "My Friend Bingham" (406–7; also Leyburn 6 n.3). Shine also focuses on the nephew, seeing his purpose to bring together Osborne and Henrietta, in a similar manner to Daisy Miller's more convincingly portrayed brother. The encounter itself she sees "felicitously" constructed in the manner of one of James's frequent framed pictures, a scene that also contributes to the story's theme. Nevertheless, she considers the tale the last of James's to use a child incidentally, rather than in a significant role of its own (30–32). Although Shine does not elaborate on the thematic significance, Osborne's rescuing the boy from what he sees as Henrietta's neglect may mirror his attempt to avenge his dead friend against her coldness. If so, Osborne proves a better rescuer than avenger.

Levy sees the story as a "longer and more complicated version" of "My Friend Bingham" and "The Landscape Painter," noting that like "My Friend Bingham," it concerns two friends and their relationship to one woman, and that as Locksley repeats his experience with a mercenary woman, Osborne repeats the experience of his friend Graham (410–11). Sicker sees the tale like "The Story of a Masterpiece" presenting a "double focus" with two men who love the same woman, but one rationally, the other romantically. In the irrational Graham, Sicker detects the same mixture of love and a longing for death treated also in "Poor Richard," "A Most Extraordinary Case," and "A Passionate Pilgrim" (37–38, 42, 99). Jones emphasizes the selfishness of Graham's passion, comparing him to Longstaff in "Longstaff's Marriage" (104). Fox considers such selfishness part of James's constant concern in such early tales as "A Landscape Painter" and "Poor Richard" (12).

Kraft, while remaining in the early tales, looks forward to placing the story at the start of a new group of tales all of which examine the issue of distorted vision, written from 1868 to 1872, a "period of uncertainty" for James (43, 125–26 n.13). Wagenknecht also anticipates, finding in Osborne's, and the reader's, attempt to comprehend Henrietta a foreshadowing of the prolonged study of Angela Vivian in *Confidence* (197). Segal points to a connection with "The Diary of a Man of Fifty," where a man also believes a woman to be heartless, but learns that the character flaw is his own (222–23 n.8). One might also offer a parallel in Winterbourne's misguided reading of Daisy, who, Fox asserts, Henrietta resembles (12). Similarly, Edel locates in Osborne's false readings of Graham and then Henrietta an early treatment of the difficulty of discerning between appearance and reality seen in *The Turn of the Screw* (*Life* 1, 258). Rimmon meanwhile finds the disconcerting "replacement" of such an original reading by one "diametrically opposed," not only in such early tales as "The Landscape Painter" and *Madame de Mauves*, but also such later works as "The Marriages" and "The Path of Duty" (82). Jones finds Henrietta an intriguing but insufficiently realized character, arguing that if James had treated her type again later she might have been the equal of Isabel, Milly, and Maggie as a "vital young woman ignorant of the very thing" she most needs to know (104).

Interpretation and Criticism

Few critics argue for the story as a neglected masterpiece. Torgovnick states simply that it is "not major"; McElderry calls it "confused and inept," faulting the story primarily on the grounds of its ending (Torgovnick 188; McElderry 1949, 285). Kelley was the first to blame the sudden switch from a culpable Miss Congreve to an innocent one for splitting the story in two, frustrating the need for revenge, and so leaving the reader feeling nearly as "tricked" as Osborne (84). LeClair, drawing heavily on Kelley, concurs, finding the story, which he calls neither sufficiently realistic nor romantic, showing the young James's difficulty treating American themes (406–8). Wagenknecht stands alone in his assessment of the twist ending as a "piece of ironic comedy as well as a study in morbid psychology" (197). Leyburn also gives it high marks for its combination of the comic in the different types of foolishness represented by Mrs. Dodd, Mr. Stone, and Osborne, and the tragic in the underlying fact of Graham's suicide, learned at the end by Henrietta, although the story turns again to the comic in the twist ending (6–8).

As with most of the early stories, critics find its significance in its revelation of James's development. His brother William found it showing progress by moving from James's "previous somewhat too great daintiness" to "a mere 'chasted'ness" (52). Kenton gives its importance in its being James's first use of a "central consciousness." The story is told so exclusively from Osborne's point of view, she argues, that all its mistakes in analysis are his (15–16). Although Levy objects to Kenton's claim that the story could have easily been told in the first person without affecting it, like most subsequent critics, he follows her focus on Osborne's character and consciousness (412). Edel has seen the story as analyzing the "paradox of human identity" (CT 1, 7). Along the same lines, Levy views the story as exploring the way a "sane" man, Osborne, finds himself unable to avoid the mistakes of a "neurotic" man, Graham. Reality is too confusing and too powerful even for the ordinary man to comprehend competently. So wherein lies the difference between the two (410)? Wagenknecht, for his part, finds the only flaw in the disparity between the men—he finds it hard to believe Osborne's attachment "to such a poor creature" as Graham (197). Brodhead moves the emphasis from the individual context, but similarly sees the tale as "a charade of social misprision" (123).

Levy and Torgovnick focus on the concluding paragraph and its revelation that Osborne has married a woman with a "striking likeness" to the photograph he had earlier used to tease Henrietta. Both feel the final twist reflects badly on Osborne, Levy seeing it as an attempt, following the failed "fantasy of revenge," to substitute another fantasy instead of facing reality. Torgovnick also sees in it a "willed consistency" to make the past lie true (Torgovnick 188). In so doing, neither acknowledge the long tradition, from *The Magic Flute* to Mark Twain's *Autobiography*, of falling in love with a picture, which at least supplies Osborne's behavior with a precedent. McElderry ingenuously bypasses the issue, claiming Osborne marries Henrietta herself (1965, 27).

Torgovnick also somehow sees the ending as implicating Henrietta for her failure to inform Osborne of her engagement (188), although given Osborne's treatment of her the omission is understandable. One might almost title the story "Henrietta's Revenge" on two wilfully misunderstanding men. Critics, however, have given Henrietta comparatively little attention, although McElderry notes her "intellectual joy," a trait she shares with many of James's heroines (1949, 285). What attention she receives is generally as the "other" of Osborne's observation. Edel records the early description of her as a vampire who "drained honest men's hearts to the last drop and bloomed white upon the monstrous diet," an image that he notes is shown to be entirely without basis (*Life* 1, 257; also Gale 56). Putt nevertheless still draws the moral of the story from Graham's case, not Osborne's: "Death . . . follows love" (36). In the end, the criticism seems to follow the story in being, like so many of James's, not the portrait of a lady, but the chronicling of one man's portraiture.

Works Cited

Primary Works
James, Henry. 1868. "Osborne's Revenge." *Galaxy* 6 (July): 5–31.

Secondary Works
Brodhead, Richard H. 1986. *The School of Hawthorne*. New York: Oxford University Press.

Buitenhuis, Peter. 1970. *The Grasping Imagination: The American Writings of Henry James*. Toronto: University of Toronto Press.

Fox, Hugh. 1968. *Henry James, A Critical Introduction*. Conesville, IA: Westburg.

Gale, Robert L. [1954] 1964. *The Caught Image: Figurative Language in the Fiction of Henry James*. Chapel Hill: University of North Carolina Press.

James, William. 1992. *The Correspondence of William James*. Vol. 1: *William and Henry: 1861–1884*. Ed. Ignas K. Skrupskelis and Elizabeth M. Berkeley. Charlottesville: University Press of Virginia.

Jefferson, D. W. 1964. *Henry James and the Modern Reader*. New York: St. Martin's.

Jones, Granville H. 1975. *Henry James's Psychology of Experience: Innocence, Responsibility, and Renunciation in the Fiction of Henry James*. The Hague: Mouton.

Kelley, Cornelia Pulsifer. [1930] 1965. *The Early Development of Henry James*. Urbana: University of Illinois Press.

Kenton, Edna, ed. 1950. *Eight Uncollected Tales of Henry James*. New Brunswick: NJ: Rutgers University Press.

Kraft, James. 1969. *The Early Tales of Henry James*. Carbondale: Southern Illinois University Press.

LeClair, Robert C. 1955. *Young Henry James, 1843–1870*. New York: Bookman.

Levy, Leo B. 1981. "Consciousness in Three Early Tales of Henry James." *Studies in Short Fiction* 18: 407–12.

Leyburn, Ellen Douglass. 1968. *Strange Alloy: The Relation of Comedy to Tragedy in the Fiction of Henry James*. Chapel Hill: University of North Carolina Press.

McElderry, Bruce R., Jr. 1965. *Henry James*. New York: Twayne.

———. 1949. "The Uncollected Stories of Henry James." *American Literature* 21 (November): 279–91.

Putt, S. Gorley. 1966. *Henry James: A Reader's Guide*. Ithaca, NY: Cornell University Press.

Rimmon, Shlomith. 1977. *The Concept of Ambiguity: The Example of Henry James*. Chicago: University of Chicago Press.

Segal, Ora. 1969. *The Lucid Reflector: The Observer in Henry James' Fiction*. New Haven: Yale University Press.

Shine, Muriel G. 1969. *The Fictional Children of Henry James*. Chapel Hill: University of North Carolina Press.

Sicker, Philip. 1980. *Love and the Quest for Identity in the Fiction of Henry James*. Princeton: Princeton University Press.

Tintner, Adeline R. 1989. *The Pop World of Henry James: From Fairy Tales to Science Fiction*. Ann Arbor: UMI Research Press.

Torgovnick, Marianna. 1978. "James's Sense of an Ending: The Role Played in its Development by the Popular Conventional Epilogue." *Studies in the Novel* 10 (Summer): 183–98.

Wagenknecht, Edward. 1984. *The Tales of Henry James*. New York: Frederick Ungar.

Wright, Walter F. 1962. *The Madness of Art: A Study of Henry James*. Lincoln: University of Nebraska Press.

Owen Wingrave

Publication History

"Owen Wingrave" was the only story James published in *The Graphic*, where it appeared in the Christmas issue of 1892, illustrated by Sahr. He collected it the next year in the British *The Private Life* and the American *The Wheel of Time*. James also included it in the New York Edition.

In 1907 James began to rework the tale as a play. He offered the play unsuccessfully to the Forbes-Robertsons and to Harley Granville-Barker. Eventually, after a further rejection by the Incorporated Stage Society, "The Saloon" (as it was called) was produced as a curtain-raiser at The Little Theatre in London, in 1911, by the actress Gertrude Kingston (Edel 1949, 642).

Circumstances of Composition, Sources, and Influences

As with "The Liar," "Owen Wingrave" had both a written source, recorded in the notebooks, and an observed one, recorded in the prefaces (see N xiv–xv, 120). In the notebooks, the tale treating "the idea of the *soldier*" takes its impetus from a reading of the memoirs of Marbot, one of Napoleon's generals in March 1892. The hint of the supernatural appears in the second sentence where the "idea" becomes "the image, the type, the vision, the character, as a transmitted, hereditary, mystical, almost supernatural force, challenge, incentive, almost haunting, apparitional presence, in the life and consciousness of a descendant." The descendent is of entirely different pacifist sympathies, but "subjected to a supersititous awe" of the military tradition, and so evolves the story's contradiction: the hero performs "a brave soldierly act . . . in the very effort to evade" the ugliness of soldiering. James returned to the idea that May, reminding himself that since the story was intended for *The Graphic* it must not be "'psychological'—they understand that no more than a donkey understands a violin." He adds the woman, considers a setting during the Napoleonic wars, and decides on "some *haunting* business" (CN 66–68; see also *Life* 4, 101–3; Edel 1970, 311–13).

According to the preface, however, "Owen Wingrave" took its start one summer afternoon while James was sitting in a penny chair at Kensington Gardens and saw "a tall quiet slim studious young man, of admirable type," who "settled to a book with immediate gravity." The "seedless fable" of Owen

Wingrave was shortly "bristling with pretexts" (*Criticism* 2, 1262). Wagenknecht finds the use of the image an "excellent example" of what James called "the suddenly-determined *absolute* of perception" (1973, 15). Earlier, in her essay on James's ghost stories, Virginia Woolf cited James's depiction of the "conscious" process as an illustration of one of "our critical fables" (323). Nevertheless, she appears to advocate the same process, with a turn to the involuntary, in her 1924 essay "Character in Fiction" when she speaks of "a character imposing itself upon another person . . . making someone begin almost automatically to write a novel about her" (425).

Just as the young hero here refuses to become a soldier, so had James back in 1861, and Edel thus looks to more personal, psychological sources. Edel stresses that the defiant Owen is a second son like James, his preference for literature over war echoing James's giving up both law and science for writing, despite the urging of his family. Edel observes that James planned the story shortly after the death of his sister, Alice, and he sees the thoughts of family her death gave rise to, combined with the reading of Marbot, reminding James of his experiences during the Civil War (1970, 312–13; *Life* 4, 101, 104). The psychological reading began with Rosenzweig, who saw James in the story exorcising the ghosts left over from the conflicts he felt at the start of the Civil War. James, according to Rosenzweig, has his hero wounded like his predecessor, even as James was wounded like his father, both pairs, biographical and fictional, receiving their wounds away from actual battle (101).

Rowe, examining James's representation of the story's genesis in his preface, links it with the psychological analysis, picturing James as repeating the scene of Owen reading from the story to fill the gap left by his inability to recapture the transformation of the glimpsed young man and the "character" of Owen. This inability, according to Rowe, is associated with James's drawing for the character on his own experiences, his escape from the Civil War, his having chosen the alternate challenge of literature even as Owen chooses the ghostly room. This shared "psychic history," Rowe writes, "is at once invoked for the sake of art and at the same time strategically repressed" (241–44). One might see both James and Owen grasping for what James's brother William was to call the "moral equivalent of warfare."

James's attitude to soldiering was a complicated one. In Edel's formulation, James admired bravery, but abhorred violence (1970, 313). The mixed emotions can be seen in an early essay on "The British Soldier" James wrote after visiting a military camp, in which James avowed a "lively admiration of the military class," praising the participation of the upper class and the "simple and beautiful idea of British valor." He declares war itself a "detestable thing," but holds out that "there is something agreeable in possible war" (see Edel [1949] 1963, 142). Edel draws attention also to his admiration of the memoirs of Field Marshal Viscount Wolseley, whom James called on their first meeting an "excellent specimen of the *cultivated* British soldier" (1970, 312; *Life* 225, 436). James's friend Kipling may have grasped something of James's ambivalence. According to Tintner, he caricatured James as a man fascinated but repelled by the military in "A Conference of the Powers," a story that she argues prompted James to build out of military terms a pacifist work in which a man can prove his heroism without harming others (249–51).

Among other literary sources, Tintner points to allusions to *Paul et Virginie* (1787), appropriate since its author, Bernardin de Saint-Pierre, was a military man under Napoleon (251). Briggs finds a parallel in Walter Scott's "The Tapestried Chamber" (1828), which also compares the bravery necessary to face battle and to face the supernatural (35–36). Matthiessen and Murdock trace Colonel Wingrave back to Hawthorne (N 120). Delbanco finds a similarity between Owen Wingrave and Crane's Henry Fleming of *The Red Badge of Courage*, published three years later, and indeed Crane himself (51). "An ironic white feather" is the only missing ingredient in the tale, according to the unimpressed Putt (391). Perhaps A. E. W. Mason drew on James's tale in his 1901 *Four Feathers* for his story of a man who shows his bravery twice, first in confessing his actual fear to his father, then in war itself.

Looking more at the times, Edel finds the addition in 1893 of the adjective "proved" to Mrs. Coyle's question, "Do you mean to say the house has a *ghost?*," an acknowledgement of the psychical research of the time (1970, 314). Spender, however, approaches the ghost tales of James, including *The Turn of the Screw* and "Owen Wingrave," as a bridge to the spiritualism of Yeats (113).

Relation to Other Works

Comparisons to other tales of the supernatural are naturally common. Allen sees James turning to the supernatural as a way of treating the question at the center of the artist tales— the "relativity of perception"—in such tales as this, "The Real Right Thing," and especially *The Turn of the Screw* (121). Edgar, however, contrasts the tale with *The Turn of the Screw*, saying that the more normal world here and the lack of suspense make "Owen Wingrave" a less successful supernatural tale (189). Todorov compares the underplayed ending with the explicitly supernatural conclusion to "The Romance of Certain Old Clothes," with its equally murderous ghost (182–83). The lateness of the introduction of the supernatural in both tales recurs, McCarthy observes, in such tales as "Nona Vincent," "The Ghostly Rental," and "The Friends of the Friends" (107). Rowe links Owen's fatal ordeal in the haunted room with Spencer Brydon's more successful night in a haunted house, both of which stories he sees as working "cathartically to justify for James his own will to authority" (243). Edel associates both confrontations with James's dream of such a ghostly confrontation in the Galerie d'Apollon (1970, 724).

Remarking on the scarcity of soldiers in James's works, Edel observes that of the few, two—the heroes of "A Most Extraordinary Case" and "The Story of a Year"—are broken by their military experiences (1970, 313). Rosenzweig finds this tale repeating the basic situation of "The Story of a Year," with an emphasis on war and the paternal rather than the maternal relationship, as was the case in the earlier tale. Kate Julian plays a similar role to Elizabeth Crowe, but James allows his protagonist victory, even if it is only to "win" his "grave" (100–1). Rowe similarly links the two works as springing from the same anxieties, Owen encountering now a supernatural rather than a flesh and blood enemy. He finds inferior the realism of the early work, where Jack chides Elizabeth for her romanticism, evident in her reading of Goethe's *Faust*, contrasted with the more mature James's realistic awareness that Owen's turn from the military to Goethe's poems is equally a form of "romantic escape" (243). Levy, however, compares the story with "Collaboration," which also criticizes patriotism and valorizes art (249).

Edel likens Owen, as a rebel against family, with Guy Domville, another peaceful second son who resists the uncongenial fate his family determines for him, and so ends the family line ([1949] 1963, 142–43; 1949, 641). Jones, on the other hand, contrasts Owen's failed rebellion against family with the successful rebellion in the early tale "Gabrielle de Bergerac" (116). Several other of the superior, second sons in whose company Edel places Owen also fail: Roderick Hudson, Morgan Moreen, Valentin Bellegarde, and one second sibling, Kate Croy (*Life* 1, 58–59). Bender also classes Owen with John Marcher and Mora Montravers in having his fate given by his name: Owen, which means "young soldier" in Welsh, wins his grave (254; also Edel 1970, 311). The idea of the won grave leads other critics to emphasize Owen's moral victory rather than his physical defeat. Accordingly, Fox classes Owen with Isabel Archer and Lambert Strether among the many of James's heroes and heroines who gain victory through stoic endurance (77). Bender, noting the "quasi-religious" basis of several of James's late tales, compares specifically Owen and Limbert of "The Next Time" as Jamesian martyred saints who are rewarded for their sacrifices (252–56).

Looking at the spectators and participants in the sacrifice, Norrman finds the way Coyle changes sides—an element of "chiastic inversion"—preparation for Strether's similar about face in *The Ambassadors* (146). Walter Wright similarly likens Coyle's "imaginative understanding" to that of the young couple in "The Birthplace," who offer Gedge a sympathetic audience (122). In contrast, Jefferson compares the "absoluteness" with which Owen's family cuts him off to the manner in which Mr. Carteret cuts off Nick Dormer, both being "truly English" reactions (117). Dietrichson judges such financial pressure unusual in James, and Unrue links the Wingraves with the worst of

James's villains from *The American*, *The Bostonians*, and *The Portrait of a Lady* in their commiting of the ultimate Jamesian crime, the denial of another's free choice (Dietrichson 105; Unrue 50).

Focusing on the women, Edel links the tale with *The Pupil* as a story with autobiographical associations depicting the death of a young man who sees the flaws in his family and so dies at their hands. In each case, he points out, a woman is primarily to blame, the mother there, the fianceé here (*Life* 4, 96). Noting what is called in "Fordham Castle" "the greater energy of women," Przybylowicz particularly compares the destructive women and passively peaceful protagonists of "Owen Wingrave" and "The Bench of Desolation" (101).

Interpretation and Criticism

Writing for the *Dial*, Payne found it "gratifying" to discover "anything of so startling a character" in a James story as a "mysterious death," even if the murderer is a ghost (344). Later critics have found the death and the ghost somewhat less gratifying, but both continue to generate discussion.

In the first notebook entry James pictured his hero as "winning (in a tragic death?) the reward of gallantry—winning it from the apparitional ancestor" (CN 67). The merit of such a victory, however, is debatable, and when James submitted "The Saloon" to the Incorporated Stage Society, it became the subject of a famous exchange of letters. George Bernard Shaw wrote the letter of rejection, objecting vehemently to the death of the young man, asking James, "What do you want to break men's spirits for?" by showing such a man as Owen killed by "the rubbish" of his family traditions. In truth, Shaw declared, "families like these are smashed every day and their members delivered from bondage, not by heroic young men, but by one girl who goes out and earns her living or takes a degree somewhere." In a long response to Shaw's "delightful" letter, James first pleaded the play's humble origins, but then took his stand against Shaw's view that literature should "preach" and "encourage," his story having come from a higher source, the "play" of imagination. Shaw was not satisifed: "The question whether the man is to get the better of the ghost or the ghost of the man is not an artistic question: you can give victory to one side just as artistically as to the other." James began his reply, "This is but a word to say No . . . ." "Really, really," James insisted, "we would have howled at a surviving Owen Wingrave who would have embodied for us a failure—and an ineptitude." Instead, James argues that Owen gets "*the best of everything.*" He succeeds in cleansing the house and in creating "for us, spectators and admirers, such an intensity of impression and emotion about him as must promote his romantic glory an edifying example forever. . . . He wins the victory—that is he clears the air, and he pays with his life" (Edel 1949, 642–47). Looking over the exchange, Dupee argues that James, although vulnerable to Shaw's direct attack on "whatever was self-indulgent in his habitual death-and-transfiguration scheme," was able to triumph by rejecting the limitations in Shaw's equation of "help" and "works of art" (197). Murphy has called "The Saloon" the best, most Jamesian of James's plays, and the Jamesian insistence on an aesthetic complexity is the keynote of James's letters to Shaw (92).

In revising the tale for the New York Edition, James changed the final line, "He looked like a young soldier on a battlefield," to "He was all the young soldier on the gained field." Garnett, who dislikes the conventionality of the conclusion, considers the revision a distinct loss (vii–viii). As Edel notes, the change strengthens Owen's victory (1970, 314–15; *Life* 4, 105). Still, critics have continued to debate who won the victory, at what cost, and to what gain. Edel calls the tale James's most "deterministic," depicting a world that allows one only to "win his grave" as honorably as possible (CT 7, 9). Bender writes, "The wonder is the paradox that Owen does, but does not, reverse his fate" (255). James was well aware of the paradox, which lies at the heart of the story. In his second notebook entry, he writes that Owen " . . . for his own view—acts the soldier, *is*, the soldier, and of indefeasible soldiery race—proves to have been so—even in this very effort of abjuration" (CN 68). He reaffirms this view in his second letter to Shaw, writing, "The whole point of the little piece is that he, while protesting against the tradition of his 'race,' proceeds and pays exactly like the soldier that he declares he'll never be" (Edel 1949, 646–47). Blackmur awards the victory to Owen, who, as the last Wingrave, defeats his family by his death. The battle, writes Blackmur, is between Owen's "individually achieved" conscience and the family's group conscience, which activates the ghost that had stayed quiet when Owen slept in the room without their knowledge (50–52). Other critics split the victory, Edel calling it a Pyrrhic victory both for Owen, who is killed by his family, and for his family, whose line comes to an end through his death (1970, 315). Similarly, Jones casts Owen as both victim and victor, his sense of pride, a family legacy, contributing to his death (115–16).

Other critics, such as Stevenson, unreceptive to James's paradox, grant the Wingraves complete victory over Owen (139). Speaking of the play, Fox reads the ending as "the triumph of tradition" as it "completely destroys Reform, the past completely engulfs the Present." While acknowledging that for James the stoic endurance of Owen was adequate victory, he judges such a triumph over the past inadequate in the modern era (76–77). Virginia Woolf criticizes the death on other grounds, as cutting short the possibilities of Owen's richly peopled situation (323–24).

Looking at the family arrayed against Owen, Wagenknecht offers "no forgiveness" to the Wingraves, who violate not simply manners but the rights of others (1948, 131). An ally of the Wingraves, Kate is dismissed by Wagenknecht as a "silly chit" (1984, 74). Others have found her more significant, Briggs judging her "far more sinister" than the unseen ghost (150). Piper offers some defense for Kate, arguing that she was equally the victim of her upbringing and that there must have been "another side" to her or Owen would not have loved her (14). Similarly, Virginia Woolf sensed in Kate a "subtlety and oddity" presented as if in preparation for some act more significant than the taunting of Owen (324).

Coming to Owen's side against his family is Owen's tutor, Coyle. Banta has noted among the story's themes "the fumbling attempts by innocence to save which actually lead to catastrophe" (180 n.23). Coyle is just such a fumbling innocent, and while his character has been criticized as flat by O'Faolian, Jefferson judges him a good choice for the point of view, as his ability to combine a finer sensitivity with a military loyalty "vouches for Owen" (O'Faolian 151–52; Jefferson 162–63). Jones, while he notes Coyle's sympathy with Owen, finds him, too, proud as he looks at the dead Owen of having trained such a brave young man (115–16).

The ghost that destroys Owen is a family ghost, or as Edel articulates it, "the ghost of family" (1970, 311). Most critics have preferred James's treatment of Owen's family situation to his supernatural embodiment of it. Even James was upset by a too obvious depiction of the supernatural. At hearing of the representation of an actual ghost in the 1908 presentation of "The Saloon," he wrote the producer, "There is absolutely no warrant or indication for this in my text and I view any such introduction with the liveliest disapproval" (1970, 314). A contemporary, M. Sturge Gretton, similarly mentioned in his review of the New York Edition that by showing the ghost, the production had gone against James's habit of presenting not the "supernatural" but "rare and delicate but 'natural' psychological experiences" (508). Blackmur concurs, noting that the power, even the presence of the ghost, comes simply from the belief of Owen and his family that it "*ought* to appear and *ought* to obsess" (50). In stressing the human basis of the supernatural in "Owen Wingrave," critics have occasionally denied the supernatural altogether. Edgar, for example, asserts that in the tale "forces purely human collide" (189). Markow-Totevy considers Owen the victim not of the ghost but his own conscience, torn as it was by conflicting duties (112–13). Q. D. Leavis takes the ghost as a symbol representing the "oppressive atmosphere of moral pressure" (224).

Throughout, as Todorov argues, the interest of the supernatural is subordinated to the true conflict in the tale between Owen's desire to remain faithful to his ideals and to his family (182–83). Even Wagenknecht, who argues that there is no alternative offered for a non-supernatural interpretation, acknowledges that it is the initial situation of the conscientious objector that is more likely to engage interest (1984, 72–74). In Stevenson's view, the tale is a good example of James's method of building the ghostly on a "reasonable account" of a real-life situation (139).

Indeed, the appearance of the supernatural is confined to the tale's conclusion. Early on, as Unrue remarks, the family portraits may seem to Owen to "glower" at him (50), but there is no supernatural presence outside the character's mind. O'Faolian, who finds that the story "unfolds itself rather than reveals itself," indicates that it is only its abrupt conclusion that makes it a short story (151). To Virginia Woolf, the supernatural conclusion interrupts the tale "rudely, incongruously" just as the reader is "settling in for a long absorbing narrative." It does not even, she adds, have the merit of being frightening (323–24). So, too, Jacobson charges that the ghostly killing is not only a "perfunctory" conclusion to the story's real debate over militarism, but also a "careless" one leaving unclear who kills Owen (90).

Whoever killed Owen, his death has generally been accepted as an argument against killing. Levy, for example, calls the story an "impassioned defense of pacifism and the pacifist temperament," characterizing James, along with his brother William as an "outspoken foe of imperialism and militarism" (249). Even more impassionedly, Matthiessen and Murdock speak of the work as James's "single eloquent denunciation of the stupidity and barbarism of war" (N 120; also Matthiessen 9). In a more qualified view, Jefferson argues that James only achieved his graceful presentation of the "somewhat idealistic conception of the young pacifist" by putting in Coyle for balance (163).

The "idealistic conception of the young pacifist" and his revolt against the military mind was, however, signal to Benjamin Britten, who in 1971 composed the music for an operatic version of the tale to premiere on television. Writing during the Vietnam War, Britten, who had himself been a conscientious objector during World War II, evidently identified with James's failure to fight in the Civil War and responded deeply to the tale as a manifesto against all war, the young man "victorious in his own private battle" not to fight. The librettist Myfanwy Piper had, however, noted the danger of the characters becoming caricatures, and to some critics the work appeared dated, the closeness of television emphasizing its melodrama (Graham 54–55; Evans 228–37; Piper 13–15; Fingleton 249–50).

If Britten's opera and James's play have failed to establish themselves, the original story has remained current among James's readers despite some dismissive comments by critics, such as Putt, who finds it morbid (391). Q. D. Leavis judges it "respectable," but asserts it does not "rise to its possibilities" (223), while F. R. Leavis, even more pejoratively, deems it "one of James's feebler things" (234). Jefferson may be closer to the mark when, while acknowledging that "Owen Wingrave" is not one of James's "most substantial" tales, he speaks of it as a "very delicate piece of art" (163). As such, it may seem to require delicate treatment, but the story is rather like its hero, stoutest when arguing against stoutness itself.

Works Cited

Primary Works

James, Henry. 1892. "Owen Wingrave." *The Graphic* (28 November): 11, 14, 15, 18, 22, 26, 30.

———. 1893. "Owen Wingrave." *The Private Life*. London: Osgood.

———. 1893. "Owen Wingrave." *The Wheel of Time*. New York: Harper.

———. 1909. "Owen Wingrave." *The Novels and Tales of Henry James*. New York Edition. Vol. 17, 267–319. New York: Scribner's.

———. 1878. "The British Soldier." *Lippincott's Monthly Magazine* 22 (August): 214–21.

Secondary Works

Allen, Elizabeth. 1984. *A Woman's Place in the Novels of Henry James*. New York: St. Martin's.

Banta, Martha. 1964. "Henry James and 'The Others.'" *New England Quarterly* 37 (June): 171–84.

Bender, Bert. 1976. "Henry James's Late Lyric Meditations upon the Mysteries of Fate and Self-Sacrifice." *Genre* 9: 247–62.

Blackmur, R. P. [1942] 1983. *"The Sacred Fount."* In *Studies in Henry James*. Ed. Veronica A. Makowsky, 45–68. New York: New Directions. Reprinted from *Kenyon Review* 4: 328–52.

Briggs, Lynda S. 1977. *Night Visitors: The Rise and Fall of the English Ghost Story*. London: Faber.

Delbanco, Nicholas. 1982. *Group Portrait*. New York: Morrow.

Dietrichson, Jan W. 1969. *The Image of Money in the American Novel of the Gilded Age*. Oslo: Universitetsforlaget; New York: Humanities.

Dupee, F. W. [1951] 1956. *Henry James*. Garden City, NY: Doubleday & Anchor.

Edel, Leon, ed. 1970. *Henry James: Stories of the Supernatural*. New York: Taplinger.

———, ed. [1949] 1963. *The Ghostly Tales of Henry James*. New York: The Universal Library, Grosset & Dunlap.

———, ed. 1949. *The Complete Plays of Henry James*. Philadelphia: Lippincott.

Edgar, Pelham. [1927] 1964. *Henry James, Man and Author*. New York: Russell & Russell.

Evans, John. 1984. "Owen Wingrave: A Case for Pacificism." In *The Britten Companion*. Ed. Christopher Palmer, 227–37. London: Faber.

Fingleton, David. 1971. "*The Knot Garden* and *Owen Wingrave*: Operatic Development or Experiment?" *Contemporary Review* 219 (November): 246–51.

Fox, Hugh. 1968. *Henry James, A Critical Introduction*. Conesville, IA: John Westburg.

Garnett, David, ed. 1946. *Fourteen Stories by Henry James*. London: Rupert Hart-Davis.

Graham, Colin. 1979. "Staging first productions." In *The Operas of Benjamin Britten*. Ed. David Herbert, 44–58. New York: Columbia University Press.

Gretton, M. Sturge. 1912. "Mr. Henry James and his Prefaces." *Contemporary* 101 (January): 69–78. As reprinted in *Henry James: The Critical Heritage*, ed. Roger Gard, 503–12. London: Routledge & Kegan Paul.

Jacobson, Marcia. 1983. *Henry James and the Mass Market*. University: University of Alabama Press.

Jefferson, D. W. 1964. *Henry James and the Modern Reader*. New York: St. Martin's.

Jones, Granville H. 1975. *Henry James's Psychology of Experience: Innocence, Responsibility, and Renunciation in the Fiction of Henry James*. The Hague: Mouton.

Leavis, F. R. 1947. "The Appreciation of Henry James." *Scrutiny* 14 (Spring): 229–37.

Leavis, Q. D. 1947. "Henry James: The Stories." *Scrutiny* 14 (Spring): 117–19. Reprinted in *Collected Essays*. Vol. 2: *The American Novel and Reflections of the European Novel*, ed. G. Singh, 177–84. Cambridge: Cambridge University Press.

Levy, Leo B. 1958. "Henry James and the Jews: A Critical Study." *Commentary* 26 (September): 243–49.

McCarthy, Harold T. 1958. *Henry James: The Creative Process*. New York: Thomas Yoseloff.

Markow-Totevy, Georges. 1969. *Henry James*. Trans. John Griffiths. London: Merlin.

Matthiessen, F. O. 1944. *Henry James: The Major Phase*. New York: Oxford University Press.

Murphy, Brenda. 1983. "James's Later Plays: A Reconsideration." *Modern Language Studies* 13, no. 4 (Fall): 86–95.

Norrman, Ralf. 1982. *The Insecure World of Henry James's Fiction: Intensity and Ambiguity*. New York: St. Martin's.

O'Faolian, Sean. 1948. *The Short Story*. London: Collins.

Payne, William Morton. 1893. Review of *The Wheel of Time*. *Dial* 15 (1 December): 344.

Piper, Myfawny. 1979. "Writing for Britten." In *The Operas of Benjamin Britten*. Ed. David Herbert, 8–21. New York: Columbia University Press.

Przybylowicz, Donna. 1986. *Desire and Repression: The Dialectic of Self and Other in the Late Works of Henry James*. University: University of Alabama Press.

Putt, S. Gorley. 1966. *Henry James: A Reader's Guide*. Ithaca, NY: Cornell University Press.

Rosenzweig, Saul. [1943] 1957. "The Ghost of Henry James: A Study in Thematic Apperception." In *Art and Psychoanalysis*. Ed. William Phillips, 89–111. New York: Criterion Books. Reprinted from *Character and Personality* 12 (December): 79–100; also reprinted in *Partisan Review* 11 (Fall 1944): 435–55.

Rowe, John Carlos. 1984. *The Theoretical Dimensions of Henry James*. Madison: University of Wisconsin Press.

Spender, Stephen. 1936. *The Destructive Element*. Philadelphia: Albert Saifer.

Stevenson, Elizabeth. [1949] 1981. *The Crooked Corridor: A Study of Henry James*. New York: Octagon.

Tintner, Adeline R. 1989. *The Pop World of Henry James: From Fairy Tales to Science Fiction*. Ann Arbor: UMI Research Press.

Todorov, Tzvetan. 1977. *The Poetics of Prose*. Trans. Richard Howard. Ithaca, NY: Cornell University Press.

Unrue, Darlene. 1975. "Henry James's Extraordinary Use of Portraits." *Re: Artes Liberales* 1, no. 2: 47–53.

Wagenknecht, Edward. 1984. *The Tales of Henry James*. New York: Frederick Ungar.

———. 1973. *The Novels of Henry James*. New York: Frederick Ungar

———. 1948. "Our Contemporary Henry James." *College English* 10 (December): 123–32.

Woolf, Virginia. [1921] 1988. "Henry James's Ghost Stories." In *The Essays of Virginia Woolf*. Vol. 3: *1919–1924*. Ed. Andrew McNeillie, 319–26. London: Hogarth.

———. [1924] 1988. "Character in Fiction." In *The Essays of Virginia Woolf*. Vol. 3: *1919–1924*. Ed. Andrew McNeillie, 420–38. London: Hogarth.

Wright, Walter F. 1962. *The Madness of Art: A Study of Henry James*. Lincoln: University of Nebraska Press.

Pandora

Publication History

"Pandora" appeared first in the unusual venue of the New York *Sun* on June 1 and 8, 1884. In speaking of the project to Thomas Bailey Aldrich, editor of the *Atlantic Monthly*, James calls it *"a complete and sacred secret,"* but one that should produce for him "the enjoyment of a popularity" that will enable him to name a high price for the serialization of *The Princess Casamassima* he was then negotiating (*Letters* 3, 25). According to Kenton, it may have been the first of such syndicated stories in America. The tale was to be part of a series, with Howells writing the second story and Bret Harte the third. In the end, Howells did not participate, and James's "Georgina's Reasons" was the third tale, after one by Harte (536). James collected "Pandora" in 1885 in the American volume *The Author of Beltraffio* and the British *Stories Revived*. He also included it in the New York Edition. (See also "Georgina's Reasons.")

Circumstances of Composition, Sources, and Influences

In January of 1884 while in New York, James decided to treat the "self-made girl," considering placing her first in New York, then in Washington, or both, giving him a chance to *"do"* Washington, "even *do* Henry Adams and his wife" (CN 24–25). James recalled the entry in his preface as "one of the scantest of memoranda" prompted by seeing a young lady "at a certain pleasure party, but present in rather perceptibly unsupported and unguaranteed fashion, as without other connexions, without more operative 'backers' than a proposer possibly half-hearted and a slightly sceptical seconder." Upon inquiry James found that she "was an interesting representative of a new social and local variety, the 'self-made,' or at least self-making, girl." He was struck by the one requirement that, like "Little Bo-Peep," she was required to leave her "tail" or family behind, until she was sufficiently launched to demand their acceptance. Still, in recalling the source of the tale, James in 1905 was most struck by the fact that "proceeding from a brief but profusely peopled stay in New York, I should have fished up that none so very precious particle as one of the pearls of the collection," a fact that leads him to enlarge on the difficulties for an American writer of being unable to deal with the downtown side of

American life, namely Wall Street and "the supremely applied money-passion" (*Criticism* 2, 1272–75).

In "doing" the Adamses, James, according to Monteiro, drew particularly on his 1882 visit to their home in Washington. Gooder links the Adamses and Bonnycastles as "witnesses" to politics (xxii). In a study of Adams, Harbert praises James's capturing of Adams's "unusual position" in Washington in his statement that Bonnycastle "was not in politics, though politics were much in him" (21). Monteiro argues that the portrait was designed to be recognized only by the Adamses and their circle. He cites as an allusion for the knowing Vogelstein's inexact memory of Randolph Miller's name as "Madison, Hamilton, or Jefferson," which recalls Adams's works *John Randolph* and the *History of the United States of America During the Administration of Jefferson and Madison* (1975, 41–43). Gale points to the transformation of the Adamses' "genial house"—as James called it in a letter—to a "bonny castle," a name Monteiro deems "pleasantly allegorical" (Gale 223). In giving Mrs. Bonnycastle a first name, James also paid Marian a compliment, naming her according to Gooder after Shakespeare's charmingly satirical heroine in *Much Ado about Nothing* (xxii). The portrait of the pair, despite the satire that surrounds it, is generally conceded to be, in Edel's term, "friendly" (CT 5, 10; Monteiro 1975, 43; N 56). Vandersee speaks of Mrs. Bonnycastle's laughter in the New York Edition as Dickensian (103). The picture of the confident and lively pair, however, is given a retrospective poignancy by the suicide of Marian Adams less than two years after the story's original publication.

Although Buitenhuis asserts the city made a vivid impression on James, the portrait of Washington also draws on Adams's knowledge (114, 126; also Jacobson 32). In a review of Adams's *Democracy*, Edmund Wilson remarks on the similarity between the two works in their descriptions of Washington, but finds James's work in comparison insufficiently dramatic, in part because while Adams was a resident in Washington, James "as elsewhere, was an intelligent visitor" (203). Critics differ over whether James's view of the capital was in fact as negative as his narrator's. Walter Wright argues that it was (74). Buitenhuis, however, while he acknowledges James's description of an oddly barren, often vulgar monumentality, judges more significant the view of Washington given from the terrace of the Capitol: "bristling and geometrical; the long lines of its avenues seemed to stretch into national futures" (125–26). Also taking the middle ground, Tintner asserts that James did not necessarily share either Vogelstein's denigration of Washington's "impoverished Neoclassicism" or Pandora's equally partisan but opposite assessment (1986, 47–48).

James's own knowledge of politics was limited—he was embarrassed early in his residence in England by being unable to name the members of the Cabinet (*Autobiography* 30). Gale, however, sees James in this tale as perhaps seizing the moment to appeal to an election-year interest in politics. In his analysis, the president in the tale represents Garfield (222–24). Edel, however, argues that James is drawing on his meeting with President Arthur (CT 5, 10). Gale indeed cites a letter from James after an after-dinner talk with President Arthur, showing an unusual political ambitiousness on James's part. Talking to the president, James wrote his mother, that he had thought to himself "if I had any smartness in me, I ought, striking while the iron was hot, to apply for a foreign mission, which I should doubtless promptly get" (223; see also *Life* 3, 32). Instead James passed along the impulse and the moment to his heroine. Indeed, the tale is more significant in capturing what Gooder calls "a moment of American social history" (xiv) than its political one.

Pandora's reading in the tale is more French than American, consisting mainly of works "in fresh yellow paper" by such writers as Sainte-Beuve, Renan, and, for relaxation, Alfred de Musset (CT 5, 368). Accordingly, while the contemporary reviewer for *The Literary World* appeared to find the hearty Pandora a relief from the decadence of the other tales making up *The Author of Beltraffio*, Tintner traces the influence of the French "decadent" novel in the characterization of Pandora as well, pointing to additional allusions to Byron and to Balzac's "La Fille aux yeux d'or" (1987, 266, 270).

Vogelstein's learning is naturally more Germanic, including a reference to Hegel when he speaks of Washington as a "monstrous, mystical *Werden*" (CT 5, 388). Gooder points to his citing of a dictum of Goethe, which she identifies as the appropriate counsel, "Let no one think that he can conquer the first impressions of his youth." Still, Gooder argues, Vogelstein's tiresome conversation with an earnest Bostonian girl about the novels of Spielhagen indicate that Boston can be even more earnest than Prussia (278, 280).

The title itself is an allusion, which Horrell judges "self-explanatory" in its reference to the heroine's "sweetly troublesome" nature (209; also Auerbach 126). In his reading of Pandora's "exposure," Mackenzie points to not one but two boxes—the customs box and the letter from the Department of State (31–33). Taking Pandora's family name as an allusion to its classical source, Hesiod's *Works and Days*, Tintner reads the tale as a new version of the myth. Pandora, she notes, has read Goethe, who had written two plays on the Greek myth, which was also prominently reflected in the contemporary art scene. In 1883, she records, there were six paintings of Pandora on display in London, the most significant being Rossetti's yellow-eyed femme fatale. In her analysis, Vogelstein plays many roles: Epithemeus abandoned by Pandora; Pandora consumed by curiosity; and even the box whose emotions when released bring turmoil. Newly returned from Greece, Pandora here is "self-made," while in the original myth she was made by the gods. The German retellings, Tintner asserts, emphasize the gifts rather than the trouble brought by Pandora, and she sees James combining the more positive interpretations with the traditional warning against curiosity seen in Hawthorne's *The Wonder Book* (1989, 110–22; 1987, 266, 270). Similarly, in

Vandersee's reading, "the lavish box of American opportunity" is full not of evils but the "latent powers and perceptions" of the self-made girl (108). Gooder appends a contemporary reference in the use of the name for the doll-sized mannequins then used in the couturiers of Paris (277).

The name of Mrs. Steuben is taken by Gooder as a reference to Baron Steuben, a Prussian, like Vogelstein, who served under Washington during the Revolution (280). Charles Anderson finds James's depiction of the type of the Southern lady in her unimpressively dependent on stereotype (249). Vandersee sees her as combining two stereotypes, the Southern lady and the poetess (103).

Relation to Other Works

In planning the tale in his notebook, James sought a heroine to "rival" his earlier Daisy Miller, and to repeat her success (CN 24). Making the connection apparent enough even for his newspaper readers, he has Vogelstein read the book, an allusion critics have picked up eagerly. Donald Stone and Margolis both note the self-parody in James's allusion to his own work, Stone linking it to similar passages in "The Point of View" and "The Art of Fiction" (Stone 23, 239). According to Margolis, James was already bored with the international theme, but she, like Monteiro, sees James still pushing himself to create new variations on it in order to sustain his literary success (Margolis 61; Monteiro 1975, 39). Pandora, however, was not as popular as Daisy. Indeed, the *Independent* found her a "highly disagreeable" version of the earlier heroine. Examining the changed reaction to Pandora, despite her "obvious superiorities" to Daisy, Wagenknecht conjectures that Daisy's personal failure made the success of her work, while Pandora's personal success prevented the success of hers (32). Her inadequate popularity may be the reason, according to Edel, that "Pandora" and *Lady Barbarina* form the end of the line of international tales (*Life* 3, 85).

Pandora, Powers observes, is a Daisy "safely in America" (77). Gooder, however, points out the contrast between their behaviors even while in Europe, as Pandora deliberately advances herself through travel while Daisy wanders randomly (xv). According to Shine, James created his "successful Daisy Miller" as a way of trying to make the "case" for the American girl, although the parallel remains "tongue in cheek" (50–51). James intended Pandora and Daisy to be distinct types, as Monteiro points out, but the bewildered Vogelstein continues drawing on the comparison (1975, 39–41). In Buitenhuis's analysis, Vogelstein's application of his reading illustrates "how perception of reality is conditioned by literary schemata." Part of his problem, according to Buitenhuis, is that while he eventually recognizes that Pandora is *not* Daisy, he fails to recognize that he is very like Winterbourne (122).

Indeed, Gage contends that in both stories the interest in the view of the "stiff" man supplants the interest in the woman he attempts to understand, even as the issue of class takes over from the earlier issue of innocence. A significant difference, as both Gage and Gooder point out, is that Vogelstein's failure in comprehension, unlike Winterbourne's, hurts only himself (Gooder xxvi). Gage notes other small roles carried over from the earlier story: Mrs. Dangerfield takes over the tasks of the earlier Mrs. Costello and Mrs. Walker, while the President stands in for Giovanelli in his intimate talk with Pandora (127–137, 186–87). Similarly, Shine compares the "vague" parents of both heroines and judges Pandora's brother a half-hearted "rehabilitation" of Daisy's (50).

Buitenhuis places the two tales in a Jamesian "trilogy" of the American girl, also containing the late novella "Julia Bride." In the later tale, the family irrelevant to Daisy and Pandora become a significant impediment to self-advancement, even as the methods of self-advancement, once "direct and honest," become "devious and sordid" (122, 229, 232–33).

Pandora has been compared with other heroines as well. Shine sees her as the earliest Jamesian heroine forced to be her "own parent," shaping her own life, like Rose Tramore of "The Chaperon" (51–52). Less favorably, Wegelin classes her with the snobbish provincials Mrs. Church and Clement Searle, and Rentz includes her among James's "anti-heroines," such as Sophy Ruck of "The Pension Beaurepas" and Georgina (Wegelin 60; Rentz 106). Also negative in his view, Edel emphasizes the acquisitiveness of both Daisy and Pandora in comparison to Isabel (24). Much later, according to Edel, James would still see in a friend of his niece Peggy "all the negative qualities" of Daisy and Pandora (CN 386). Using "Pandora" as a model for a different type of negativity, Mackenzie argues that it illustrates James's "psychological subject"—namely, "the varieties of shame" (35). Delbaere-Garant, on the other hand, writes that despite the plainness of American life James found its young women, such as Pandora, Bessie Alden of *An International Episode*, and Francie Dosson of *The Reverberator*, "young and unformed enough to be worth saving" and so saved them (292).

If James aimed for the success of *Daisy Miller* in "Pandora," he aimed also for the "concision" of "Four Meetings," imitating its structure in seeking to make it, too, a "'little gem'" (CN 24–25). It turned out, however, at over 18,000 words, closer to a "nouvelle" (N 56). (See also "The Modern Warning" and "The Point of View.")

Interpretation and Criticism

The text of "Pandora" exists in four versions. According to Vandersee, in 1885 James revised the original newspaper text separately for publication in

Boston—with twenty changes—and London—with forty changes. It was the Boston text that he used for the New York Edition. In the final revision, Vandersee argues, James makes both Vogelstein, who becomes slower, and Mrs. Bonnycastle, who becomes sharper, more into types. In addition, he finds the criticism of the United States strengthened even as the distance between the German and the American widened. Throughout, Vandersee asserts, the "discreet satire" changes into a "broad burlesque," with an increase in the colloquial and informal, and a greater sense of the author's mediating role. In his analysis of the revision for the New York Edition, Matthiessen finds the changes mostly in style and the addition of detail. As an example, he points to the American accent given the initially bland phrase "persons of leisure" as it becomes "that body which Vogelstein was to hear invoked, again and again, with the mixture of desire and deprecation that might have attended the mention of a secret vice, under the name of a leisure-class" (xiv–xv).

Even if leisure-class aspirations are a vice, Pandora possesses them. The tale is, in Geismar's phrase, a "leisure-class version of the Horatio Alger success story" (57n). According to the story, "She was simply very successful, and her success was entirely personal." But both Pandora's individuality and her personality have been sharply scrutinized by critics. Early on, the *Literary World* praised James for his restraint, his Pandora "neither crude nor loud." Others have echoed the praise, Jefferson for example judging her "delightful" (46). Jones adds a new element, deeming her both "shrewd and charming," innocent with age-old wisdom (159). Shine, however, finds her bid for sympathy ineffective, arguing that James believed too strongly in tradition to accept the idea of a "self-made" girl, so that Vogelstein's doubts speak for the author more than he acknowledges (51). Wright similarly tries to capture something of the complexity of James's attitude to the "self-made girl," seeing the portrayal of Pandora as simultaneously "satiric and compassionate." Her learning is "perhaps a little too obvious," but still superior to that of her parents. Still, Wright comments, what James most lamented was that such a type as Pandora was the best American culture had to offer (73). Her "impossible" parents, as James called them in the notebook, also require of Pandora a tenuous stance. James indicated in the notebook that she is making a social position not only for herself but "indirectly" for them as well (CN 25). Still, that requires her distancing herself from them for a time. As Wagenknecht comments, "Her attitude toward her parents is in its way exemplary." But despite her devotion to them, as he notes, she keeps them strictly under control (32).

One of the reasons Pandora generates such mixed reactions and remains such an unexplained character is, as Buitenhuis observes, that we are limited to viewing her through the eyes of Count Vogelstein (125–26). After she leaves the ship, Pandora calls to the Count, "I hope you'll judge us correctly."

The Count of course does not. Gage calls her remark the key to the tale, pointing the reader to the possible inaccuracy of his judgment (131). In his notebook, James projected for his "hero" a foreign secretary, "inquiring and conscientious" (CN 24–25). But while Edel characterizes him as "literal-minded but not insensitive," most other critics have been less sympathetic (*Life* 3, 120). Andreas, for example, considers him cowardly subservient to public opinion, giving up his love for Pandora because of Mrs. Dangerfield's low estimate of her (26). If he is a coward, he pays the price for it, and Jones sees a final humiliation in Pandora's winning for her nobody fiancé a rank he may never achieve (159). Gage, however, sees Vogelstein's feelings at the end as mixed: although he is sorry to lose Pandora, he is relieved that she will never run his career as she does her fiancé's (135).

As a representative of Europe, McElderry notes, Vogelstein is not simply for tradition but against democracy (75). James himself casts doubt on the value of his conservatism, following his identification of him as a "Junker of Junkers" with a description of the huddled masses in steerage, "Their numbers . . . were striking," the narrator writes, "and I know not what he thought of the nature of this particular evidence" (CT 5, 359). Europe evidently has aspects that Vogelstein does not acknowledge. Indeed, Rebecca West argues that Vogelstein's inflexible character makes him of dubious value as an observer of Pandora, pointing particularly to his surprise at her unsurprising success (49). Knights, however, praises James for capturing Vogelstein's devotion to organizing his observations (27). Similarly, Shine judges that James does "a credible job" of putting Vogelstein's stiff manners in contrast with looser American attitudes (50).

Certainly, Pandora and Vogelstein are opposites. Wegelin remarks on Vogelstein's bafflement at how little her experience of Europe appears to have changed her (60). Pandora thrives, Gooder observes, on the formlessness that the exact Vogelstein finds himself lost in (xxvi). In his analysis, however, Mackenzie emphasizes the mutuality of their plight, seeing the story's theme of "exposure" unfolded through a series of tense encounters between hero and heroine. Coming to America, Mackenzie writes, Vogelstein faces forfeiture of his European social identity and so reads *Daisy Miller* to fortify himself. Pandora, in turn, is exposed at customs by Bellamy's failure to show and Vogelstein's failure to take up his protective role. When Vogelstein sees her again in Washington, Pandora has become the "willing cynosure of all eyes." In the scene at shipboard, Vogelstein is exposed for the last time "to himself" as he is left outside, in "a voyeurist relationship to the lovers." Bellamy's appointment is to Vogelstein a "kind of secret reproach" revealing his failure to live "either socially or sexually." Still, according to Mackenzie, Pandora is also a victim at the end, her celebrity largely compensation for her exposure by the snobbish Vogelstein, a hurt so painful that the desire for revenge may continue to be the compelling factor in the rest of her career

(29–35). The conclusion certainly emphasizes reversal. As Tintner states, the promotion of Pandora's fiancé, ironically, makes her of even higher status than the two women who have looked down on her (1989, 117, 122). There is little evidence at the end, however, that Pandora is suffering or that this triumph is bitter to her, and even Vogelstein's failure seems relatively mild in comparison to the heavy overtones of Mackenzie's reading, which would better suit a greater tragedy.

In examining the role of Bellamy, Tintner also steps up the rhetoric, seeing him as accepting "a passive female role in relation to his aggressive fiancée," Pandora, who is "driven by perverse male drives" in seeking the ambassadorship for him (1987, 266). In a somewhat lower key, Auerbach speaks of Bellamy's "obliging facelessness" and finds that the conclusion realizes the earlier "nervous jokes" about Pandora's becoming a foreign minister herself (126). Similarly, Wagenknecht observes that Pandora most likely will manage Bellamy as she has her parents (32).

In its chronicle of Pandora's success, Buitenhuis argues, even given its "element of romance," the tale remains a "significant *exemplum* of American experience," an analysis of society and politics. Even though it does not take on a depiction of "downtown," Buitenhuis finds that the tale implicitly criticizes it by showing how at odds it was with the uptown element, thereby making room for the corruption illustrated in such personalized politics as Pandora's (125–26). Dietrichson, however, views James as taking a more benign, "accepting attitude" to the elastic, egalitarian society described here, seeing even his presentation of the spoils system as devoid of criticism (54–55). Certainly, the depiction of the distribution of the spoils here is rather blurred. As Harris remarks, we do not actually hear how Pandora achieves her success, James in typical fashion diverting the reader's attention through an intermediate "point-of-view character" (87). In Edel's estimate, the critique James is offering of America is a good-natured one, not to be identified with that of Vogelstein (*Life* 3, 120–21). Putt also finds the international contrast more balanced this time, stating that it is largely Vogelstein's factual bent that produces his criticisms. He also points out that James allows America to defend itself, commenting, for example, on his description of America's "social distinctions . . . delicate shades, which foreigners are often too stupid to perceive" (132). Powers, in turn, describes the story's satire as reflexive, as the criticism Vogelstein directs toward America reflects equally on him (77–78).

In Irwin's analysis, however, the tale disrupts the very contradictions in social values that structure it. He notes that Vogelstein is criticized by Mrs. Dangerfield and Mrs. Bonnycastle for asking about people's "social position," but then learns that the secret to Pandora is her belonging to a particular type, however new: the "self-made girl." Irwin also finds the concluding appointment of Pandora's fiancé undercutting the earlier criticism of

European hierarchy, questioning whether James fails to recognize Pandora's flirtatious string-pulling for what it is (18–19). The last suggestion, however, seems rather improbable.

In general, the tale has been well received, Ezra Pound, who approved of its demonstration of "why Germany will never conquer the world," going so far as to call it "of the best" (25, 28). While *The Literary World* praised its "delightful humor," it was, Monteiro records, "less than an unqualified success in its own day," and in 1975 he still found the critical assessment unequal to its worth (1975, 43). Before then, Putt had, while praising the tale's observations on America, judged it as a story "frail indeed" (131). More recently, Wagenknecht has spoken of it as "a happy example of [James's] lighter manner" (32). Edel appropriately locates its strength in James's mastery of the international tale (*Life* 3, 120–21). More curiously, Margolis faults it on the grounds that Pandora's marrying Bellamy, not Vogelstein, whose observations are the focus of the tale, creates an "abrupt and somewhat disappointing conclusion," which she argues signals James's imaginative exhaustion on the subject of the international American girl (61).

The self-made girl was the natural product of a self-made nation, and Monteiro cites some interesting evidence as to the allure of the second phenomenon from none other than Sir George Trevelyan, who writes of being engrossed in such reading as the "Letters and Diaries of John Hay," James's life of William Story, and particularly the autobiography of Henry Adams, declaring, "What a period it was! What a policy! What men, and what a literature as the outcome of it!" (1965, vii). The "inner circle" of Adams's world that fascinated Trevelyan may have seemed small, its environment sparse to James, but the Victorian literary London that so impressed the young James would later strike Virginia Woolf as distinguished by *its* "smallness" (169–70). While Putt notes the opportunity that writing "Pandora" gave James to sketch "the lack of cultural resonance" in Washington (131), he also seems to have taken the occasion to consider for a moment how it would feel to have one's own "brave, new world" to create—to "be vulgar and invite the president"—and to enjoy if not entirely to praise, the homegrown efforts of his fellow citizens to do so.

Works Cited

Primary Works
James, Henry. 1884. "Pandora." *The New York Sun* (1 and 8 June): 1: 7, 2.

———. 1885. "Pandora." *Stories Revived*. Vol. 1. London: Macmillan.

———. 1885. "Pandora." *The Author of Beltraffio*. Boston: Osgood.

———. 1908. "Pandora." *The Novels and Tales of Henry James*. New York Edition. Vol. 18, 95–168. New York: Scribner's.

Secondary Works

Anderson, Charles R. 1955. "Henry James's Fable of Carolina." *South Atlantic Quarterly* 54 (April): 249–57.

Andreas, Osborn. 1948. *Henry James and the Expanding Horizon: A Study of the Meaning and Basic Themes of James's Fiction*. Seattle: University of Washington Press.

Anon. 1885. Review of *The Author of Beltraffio*. *Independent* 37 (9 April): 459.

Anon. 1885. Review of *The Author of Beltraffio*. *Literary World* 16 (21 March): 102.

Auerbach, Nina. 1978. *Communities of Women: An Idea in Fiction*. Cambridge, MA: Harvard University Press.

Buitenhuis, Peter. 1970. *The Grasping Imagination: The American Writings of Henry James*. Toronto: University of Toronto Press. Revised in part from "From Daisy Miller to Julia Bride: A Whole Passage of Intellectual History." *American Quarterly* 11 (Summer 1959): 136–46.

Delbaere-Garant, Jeanne. 1970. *Henry James: The Vision of France*. Paris: Société d'Editions Les Belles Lettres.

Dietrichson, Jan W. 1969. *The Image of Money in the American Novel of the Gilded Age*. Oslo: Universitetsforlaget; New York: Humanities.

Edel, Leon. 1960. *Henry James*. Minneapolis: University of Minnesota Press.

Gage, Richard P. 1988. *Order and Design: Henry James' Titled Story Sequences*. New York: Peter Lang.

Gale, Robert L. 1964. "'Pandora' and Her President." *Studies in Short Fiction* 1 (Spring): 222–24.

Geismar, Maxwell. 1963. *Henry James and the Jacobites*. Boston: Houghton Mifflin.

Gooder, Jean, ed. 1985. *Daisy Miller and Other Stories*. Oxford: Oxford University Press.

Harbert, Earl N. 1977. *The Force So Much Closer Home: Henry Adams and the Adams Family*. New York: New York University Press.

Harris, Wendell V. 1979. *British Short Fiction in the Nineteenth Century: A Literary and Bibliographic Guide*. Detroit: Wayne State University Press.

Horrell, Joyce Tayloe. 1970. "A 'Shade of a Special Sense': Henry James and the Art of Naming." *American Literature* 42: 203–20.

Irwin, Michael. 1989. "Henry James and the Vague *Nouvelle*." In *The Modern American Novella*. Ed. Robert A. Lee, 13–29. New York: St. Martin's.

Jacobson, Marcia. 1983. *Henry James and the Mass Market*. University: University of Alabama Press.

Jefferson, D. W. [1960] 1971. *Henry James*. New York: Capricorn.

Jones, Granville H. 1975. *Henry James's Psychology of Experience: Innocence, Responsibility, and Renunciation in the Fiction of Henry James.* The Hague: Mouton.

Kenton, Edna. 1934. "Some Bibliographical Notes on Henry James." *Hound & Horn* 7 (April–May): 535–40.

Knights, Lionel Charles. 1976. "Henry James and Human Liberty." In *Explorations* 3, 24–37. Pittsburgh: University of Pittsburgh Press.

McElderry, Bruce R., Jr. 1965. *Henry James.* New York: Twayne.

Mackenzie, Manfred. 1976. *Communities of Honor and Love in Henry James.* Cambridge, MA: Harvard University Press.

Margolis, Anne T. 1985. *Henry James and the Problem of Audience: An International Act.* Ann Arbor: UMI Research Press

Matthiessen, F. O. 1947, ed. *The American Novels and Stories of Henry James.* New York: Knopf.

Monteiro, George. 1975. "Washington Friends and National Reviewers: Henry James's 'Pandora.'" *Research Studies* 43: 38–44.

———. 1965. *Henry James and John Hay: The Record of a Friendship.* Providence, RI: Brown University Press.

Pound, Ezra. 1918. "A Shake Down." *The Little Review* 5 (August): 9–39.

Powers, Lyall H. 1970. *Henry James: An Introduction and Interpretation.* New York: Holt, Rinehart.

Putt, S. Gorley. 1966. *Henry James: A Reader's Guide.* Ithaca, NY: Cornell University Press.

Rentz, Kathryn C. 1982. "The Question of James's Influence on Ford's *The Good Soldier.*" *English Literature in Transition* 25: 104–14, 129–30.

Shine, Muriel G. 1969. *The Fictional Children of Henry James.* Chapel Hill: University of North Carolina Press.

Stone, Donald David. 1972. *Novelists in a Changing World: Meredith, James, and the Transformation of English Fiction in the 1880's.* Cambridge, MA: Harvard University Press.

Tintner, Adeline R. 1989. *The Pop World of Henry James: From Fairy Tales to Science Fiction.* Ann Arbor: UMI Research Press.

———. 1987. *The Book World of Henry James: Appropriating the Classics.* Ann Arbor: UMI Research Press.

———. 1986. *The Museum World of Henry James.* Ann Arbor: UMI Research Press.

Vandersee, Charles. 1968. "James's 'Pandora': The Mixed Consequences of Revision." *Studies in Bibliography* 21: 93–108.

Wagenknecht, Edward. 1984. *The Tales of Henry James*. New York: Frederick Ungar.

Wegelin, Christof. 1958. *The Image of Europe in Henry James*. Dallas: Southern Methodist University Press.

West, Rebecca. [pseud]. 1916. *Henry James*. London: Nisbet.

Wilson, Edmund. 1925. "A Novel by Henry Adams." *New Republic* 44 (October 14): 203.

Woolf, Virginia. "The Old Order." *The Essays of Virginia Woolf.* Vol. 2: *1912–1918*. Ed. Andrew McNeillie, 167–76. New York: Harcourt, Brace.

Wright, Walter F. 1962. *The Madness of Art: A Study of Henry James*. Lincoln: University of Nebraska Press.

A Passionate Pilgrim

Publication History

"A Passionate Pilgrim" first appeared in the *Atlantic Monthly* in March and April of 1871. Nearly fifty years later, Howells recalled the privilege of accepting it (1920, viii). James reprinted the tale several times, making it in 1875 the title story for his first collection of stories. In 1883 he substituted it for "The Pension Beaurepas" in the Tauchnitz edition of *The Siege of London*, where it appeared with a note that the tale "has been, in the matter of language, much altered and amended" (Edel and Laurence 58). Having rewritten it for Tauchnitz, he proposed to Macmillan in 1885 including it as one of two "ancient" tales with four recent ones in the British collection *The Author of Beltraffio*, as it had never yet been reprinted in England and was "often . . . asked for" (*Correspondence* 93–94). It appeared instead the same year with the older tales of *Stories Revived*. Finally, it had the signal honor of being the earliest work in the New York Edition.

Circumstances of Composition, Sources, and Influences

In his preface to the tale, James declared of it and "The Madonna of the Future" that it was "in the highest degree documentary for myself." While he also spoke of both tales as "sops instinctively thrown to the international Cerberus formidably posted where I doubtless then did n't [sic] quite make him out"—"dodg[es]" to avoid dealing with the business-man and the downtown realism of American literature—his motives were clearly more than practical. Connecting the tale with his adult discovery of England, he writes of himself that he "had, perceptively and æsthetically speaking, taken the adventure of my twenty-sixth year 'hard,' as 'A Passionate Pilgrim' sufficiently attests." Back in America, "the nostalgic poison had been distilled for him": "I had from as far back as I could remember carried in my side, buried and unextracted, the head of one of those well-directed shafts from the European quiver to which, of old, tender American flesh was more helplessly and bleedingly exposed, I think, than to-day" (*Criticism* 2, 1204–5). The only tale to come from his 1869 trip to England, "A Passionate Pilgrim" draws on actual passages from letters James wrote to his brother back home, and Edel takes it as one of the "record[s]" of James's travels (*Letters* 1, 111, 114 n.3, 237). Consequently, while James wrote Grace Norton that he had written the tale for her father and his "more than anyone," most critics see James's "own emotion" at his trip as the basis of the tale (*Letters* 1, 257; also Josephson 94). Stevenson points particularly to the narrator's description of the "rare emotion" of the traveler greeting the English scene "as children greet the loved pictures in a story-book, lost and mourned and found again" as James's own (108–10, 114). Edel points to the way Searle's envy of the transformation of "vulgar idleness" in America to "elegant leisure" in England reflects James's own sense of the lack of appreciation for the leisured literary life in America (*Life* 2, 24). Sweeney, who asserts that Searle has venereal disease, argues for a more particular connection between his illness and James's "obscure hurt" (16).

James's phrase "a passionate pilgrim" has often been applied to James himself. In his day, it was soon a part of the cultural vocabulary. In 1881 J. G. Holland wrote in *Scribner's*, "All Americans are by nature 'Passionate Pilgrims' . . . The Old World is a lodestone that is always drawing them to it" (Mott 258). It is a term Mulvey judges generally appropriate for American travelers in Europe at the time. The tale itself, in his assessment, captures both the "phases" such travelers pass through as they encounter Europe and the moment of "magical synthesis" in which the American first "feel[s]" England. Even the relative passivity of the narrator he finds fitting for a portrayal of the tourist experience. James's own perspective was, according to Mulvey, still that of a tourist, as he had not yet chosen England over Italy as a possible residence (59, 107–13).

James, in Bewley's view, would later successfully weather the transition to England as an American's proper home, even though his attempts to portray it in fiction were either tragic as in "A Passionate Pilgrim" or unfinished as in *The Sense of the Past* (70). His view of England, too, Altenbernd argues, was more dispassionate. While noting that even the "more robust" narrator is like Searle under the sway of Old England's charm, Altenbernd contends that both represent only part of James. James, he argues, was not the "unreserved adolator" of Europe critics would make him by citing what he calls the formulaic gush of his travel writing. The tale is indeed "documentary," not as a romanticized version of England, but as a step toward the truth illustrated in Searle's recognition that he bears a greater affinity to the tramp and the impoverished Rawson than to the ruling class. The moral of the tale, according to Altenbernd, is that, however unlovely America, that is where the real future is. Nevertheless, Altenbernd acknowledges that the story does not resolve James's dilemma as a would-be expatriate—a dilemma that would become his great theme. In 1920 Howells, commenting on the autobiographical interest of the tale, notes that James's own "Americanism" had ended eventually in his giving up his American citizenship (viii).

"Clement" evokes "claimant" as Gill notes, and the tale also appeals to interest in a more particular kind of traveler abroad, the "American claimant," which Howells noted in 1875 was a "very common motive" (Gill 38; Howells 65). James's distinction, according to Segal, was to transform the claimant's "dispossession" from the realistic level to the symbolic (2). James himself in his 1908 preface would evoke the type in his depiction of his young self with but a "single intense question" of his future: "Was he to spend it in brooding exile, or might he somehow come into his 'own'? —as I liked betimes to put it for a romantic analogy with the state of dispossessed princes and wandering heirs" (*Criticism* 2, 1205). Such "wandering heirs" had appeared in a tale by N. P. Willis, in Hawthorne's fragment *Doctor Grimshawe*, and would later figure in Mark Twain. As late as 1896 the *Atlantic* would contain an article on unclaimed estates in England and fraudulent operators who claimed to locate them (Everett). While Mulvey praises James for producing in Searle the "most complete fictional representation" of the type of the "American claimant," the model of Hawthorne was to James particularly significant (116). His *Our Old Home*, as Wegelin points out, offered not only the general American sense of being at home in England, but also Hawthorne's recollections of his experience as a consul dealing with actual claimants (34, 37–38). Of the first, Long points particularly to Hawthorne's comment in the *English Notebooks* on himself in England: "I feel as if I might have lived here a long while ago, and had now come back because I retained pleasant recollections of it" (21). Buitenhuis cites the specific examples James made use of from Hawthorne: one of an American who was stranded after having failed to gain his claim, another of an American finding an ancestral portrait like himself (49). Matthiessen points to a different source in Hawthorne for the portrait, *The House of the Seven Gables* (1943, 535). Even so, Brodhead argues, James is becoming more independent in his use of Hawthorne, incorporating his own material into the source. Still, he remarks an "affinity of imagination" between the two authors on the basis of parallels between James's tale and Hawthorne's unfinished and then unpublished *The Ancestral Footstep*. In selecting "A Passionate Pilgrim" as the first tale for his first collection, James, Brodhead argues, was seeking to show himself not just the heir of Europe, but of Hawthorne, in a tale fittingly about inheritance (128–29, 133–34). Rebecca West, however, while acknowledging James's debt to Hawthorne for the international subject, found the tale to be "very clumsy Hawthorne" (25–26). Geismar is also negative in his judgment, seeing James as the "real 'American Pretender'" in British society (430).

Other American Romantics play a role. In the description of Searle after he sights the family ghost: "his transcendent gravity, and a certain high fantastical air in the flickering alternation of his brow . . . like the vision-haunted knight of La Mancha, nursed by the Duke and Duchess," Segal remarks first the "grimness of a Hawthornesque allegory," a development she sees signaling a significant change in the story from the "romance of England" to the "romance of New England." The allusion to Don Quixote, which Tintner ties to Doré's illustration of the scene, she finds takes it into a larger arena, as Don Quixote was to the Romantics "the perfect symbol" of an exalted madness (Tintner 1987, 207). The allusion, in Segal's view, however, leaves the narrator as a "sober Horatio" not a Sancho, second fiddle to Searle's "madness" (12). Banta discerns a general influence of the "gothic and the ghostly," while Sweeney detects more particularly the influence of Poe's "The Fall of the House of Usher" (Banta 1972, 82; Sweeney 15). At the end of his tale, Searle speaks with admiration of "a certain heroic strain in those young imaginations of the West, which find nothing made to their hands, which have to concoct their own mysteries and raise high into our morning air, with a ringing hammer and nails, the castles in which they dwell" (CT 2, 294). His stirring imagery recalls Thoreau, who in his conclusion to *Walden* enjoined the reader to advance "confidently in the direction of his dreams": "If you have built castles in the air, your work need not be lost; that is where they should be. Now put the foundations under them" (493).

In the midst of his meditation on the beauties of St. John's, its "delightful lie," Searle notices one student reading Artemus Ward (CT 2, 294). While some such as Veeder remark on the allusion (236 n.3), most critics, perhaps responding to Searle's sense of the incongruity of reading American writers under "windows of Elizabeth," have concentrated on the allusions to English writers (e.g., Tintner 1987, 81). The narrator has come to England, equipped by reading Dickens, Smollett, and Boswell (CT 2, 228). The town near Lockley Hall appears to the narrator appropriate to the heroines of Jane Austen, with Miss Searle as a "potential heroine of Miss Burney" (CT 2, 252, 260). A Mistress Margaret Searle of older times is called "a sort of Beatrix Esmond" (CT 2, 278). Indeed, the atmosphere of the tale as a whole strikes Geismar as smacking too much of James's reading (16).

Searle, for his part, is reminded of "Tennyson's Talking Oak" in the grounds at Lockley Hall (CT 2, 253). The name Lockley itself points to

Tennyson's "Locksley Hall," which James would later, to his disappointment, hear Tennyson read aloud. Melchiori observes how the tale places Searle in the role of the speaker of the poem, but discerns in it a "new and bitter" tone because Searle—as an American in Europe—has already abandoned the faith in progress that eventually comforts Tennyson's speaker. In the New York Edition, James changed the name to Lackley. According to Melchiori, the new name is due to James's desire to move away from Tennyson, now that his admiration for him had dimmed (1965, 16–20).

In its mention of a "moated grange," the tale alludes also to Tennyson's "Mariana," itself, as Melchiori observes, a subject from Shakespeare. Citing allusions to *Hamlet* and *Macbeth*, Melchiori judges the more interesting parallel with *Othello*, seeing the tale as a restrained nineteenth-century version of Shakespeare's play with the American here the "outsider," using "witchcraft" to woo an insider (1967, 56; 1965, 11). The title of the story itself he finds fitting James's work far better than the 1599 miscellany attributed to Shakespeare by its publisher (1965, 11).

Of Miss Searle, the narrator writes at first, "[she] was to the Belle au Bois Dormant what a fact is to a fairy-tale, an interpretation to a myth" (CT 2, 258–59). Later, when Searle kisses her hand, he records "The Belle au Bois Dormant was awake" (CT 2, 264). The allusion has been noted by several critics, including Gale, who judges it "ordinary enough" (e.g., Gale 118; Stone 141; Long 22). Tintner has traced the parallels most extensively, and comments on how Searle also undergoes an awakening under the influence of England, and how the awakening of both characters recalls James's own adult introduction to Europe. She notes, too, how as a realist James refuses to grant his characters the fairy tale's happy ending (1989, 12–14; 1986, 18). If her name, Margaret, alludes to the Marguerite of *Faust* one could construct a reading with Searle as Faust and the narrator as the devil.

Lockley Hall boasts a gallery containing works by Vandyke, Rubens, Rembrandt, Claude, Murillo, Greuze, and Gainsborough, as well as the key family portrait by Joshua Reynolds (CT 2, 254–56). As such, Tintner judges the Lockley gallery the greatest in all of James's country houses, perhaps excepting Dedborough in the art-focused *The Outcry* (1986, 25, 89).

The narrator comes from Sargasso, Illinois, an appropriate homeplace, as the Sargasso Sea near Bermuda is the still center of strong currents, entangled by seaweed. Not at home in England, the narrator is truly cast in a Saragassian sea.

Relation to Other Works

In his *Atlantic* review of 1875, Howells paired "The Madonna of the Future" with "A Passionate Pilgrim" as the best of James's early collection on the ground that each "touches the heart" (70–71). Over twenty-five years later, James paired them again by choosing them as the earliest tales in the New York Edition. Discussing together the "brace of infatuated 'short stories,'" James sees them both betraying their consolatory use for a man who had briefly regained the Old World and wished to make it his: "The deep beguilement of the lost vision recovered, in comparative indigence, by a certain inexpert intensity of art—the service rendered by them at need, with whatever awkwardness and difficulty—sticks out of them for me to the exclusion of everything else and consecrates them, I freely admit, to memory" (*Criticism* 2, 1206). While Kraft objects to both tales as overrated on the grounds of their autobiographical connections, critics have continued to compare the two, adding similarity to similarity (78).

Beach linked both as early romantic works, although he found less story in "The Madonna of the Future," which Stewart finds in turn a "more deliberate study in the romantic attitude" (Beach 167, 186–87; Stewart 77). Segal contrasts the "genuinely romantic" title of "A Passionate Pilgrim" with the "ironic overtones" of "The Madonna of the Future" (13–14). Long, however, sees in the theme of pilgrimage and quixotism in each a mixture of realism and romance (24). Ford emphasizes the grim, taking Searle's lament that "The soul is immortal certainly—if you've got one; but most people haven't!" and the sculptor's cry of "cats and monkeys" as the "final, sad message" of James, the proof that he was never, even early on, completely naïve (139–40). While finding the "saving feature" in each the criticism of the "romantic malaise of the hero," Vaid assigns to "The Madonna of the Future" more "universal" themes. While in his characterization "The Passionate Pilgrim" is simply the "portrait of an American as an expatriate," "The Madonna of the Future" is the "portrait of an American as an artist" (36). Similarly, Wagenknecht judges Theobald's creative ambition nobler than Searle's, and his tale superior in focus, although he still considers both tales hampered by the strain of the protagonist's "aberrant if not unbalanced behavior" on the reader's sympathy (2).

As a protagonist, Theobald is, as Jefferson among others note, another "passionate pilgrim" (1964, 62). He is also, as Buitenhuis observes, like Searle an "aesthetic invalid abroad" (69). Both works, in Edel's formulation, treat the separation of the American from his European past, and in each the American protagonist dies fevered and dispossessed (*Life* 2, 34–37). Both characters, Powers argues, sought in Europe the "appropriate incarnation and activity" to fulfill their unsatisfied spirits (1969, 5–7). Instead, Spender writes, they are both "reduced to torpor by the intoxication of the tradition that they seek too avidly to make part of themselves" (421). Still, Theobald, in Kelley's view, is closer to James than Searle is, although she qualifies the resemblance by noting that Theobald remains a failure whereas James was a striver (152). Searle and Theobald, according to Baxter, go beyond the "partial isolation"

James portrayed as proper to the artist in such works as "The Middle Years." As a consequence, he contends, they move from the category of the "misunderstood" to the less sympathetic "type" of the "outcast" (228).

Kraft maintains that both Searle and Theobald are "too absurd to be representative and too romantic to be real," and further that the narrator in each story is unable to keep the balance (78). Others also focus on the narrator and his relationship with the protagonist. Wegelin argues that the narrators, while sympathetic to each hero and his extreme absorption in Europe, keep themselves a more balanced attitude, one closer to James's own (34). Vaid also points to the similarities between the speechifying protagonists and their recording narrators, but distinguishes between the two tales on the grounds that the attitude of the narrator is clearer in "The Madonna of the Future," the conversation better handled, and the death of the protagonist less central (28–29). To Sicker, however, not only "A Passionate Pilgrim" and "The Madonna of the Future," but also "The Last of the Valerii" share the same tone—a "curious mixture of sympathetic identification and ironic detachment"—and type of narrator—one "deeply concerned about the protagonist's welfare and acutely aware of his delusion" (42).

As a tale of the "discovery of Europe," "A Passionate Pilgrim" does not stand alone, but is sandwiched between two other tales of the discovery of Italy, "Travelling Companions" and "At Isella" (CT 2, 9). Dupee writes of the new "light" that "shone" over these international works (67). The heroine of the first is, as Lanzinger observes, also a passionate pilgrim, even as Isabel Archer will be later (139). In that light, Rahv places Searle at the head of the line of many Jamesian pilgrims from Daisy to Maggie, and Edel places the story at the head of the international tales, with their contrast of American rawness and European civilization (Rahv 1944, viii; Edel 1960, 14). Nevertheless, James, according to Winner, had not yet mastered the form, and this tale remained as "overloaded" with description of art as "Travelling Companions" (78). Searle himself, according to Walter Wright, although described by the narrator as typically American in his "perplexing interfusion of refinement and crudity," his "delicate" perceptions and "his opinions, possibly, gross," is in actuality without vulgarity, like such other American pilgrims in James as Caroline Spencer, Isabel Archer, Milly Theale, and the real-life William Wetmore Story, but not, Wright insists, Miranda Hope of "A Bundle of Letters." Wright denotes a difference in James's manner of presenting the adventures of Searle and those of such later travelers as Milly and Strether and Pendrel. Early on, Wright argues, James left his pictures static without any of the analysis or crystallization that characterizes the later works, a deficiency Wright senses James seeking to remedy in his revision for the New York Edition (116–18).

Two common sources for comparisons among the early international works are *The American* and *Madame de Mauves*. According to Ford, it was in the latter novella and in the tales "The Madonna of the Future" and "A Passionate Pilgrim" that James was "beginning to find himself" (128). Matthiessen emphasizes the thematic continuity of James's works, envisioning Searle as following the "challenge to *live*" that recurs to James's characters from Christopher Newman to Roderick Hudson, Isabel Archer, Lambert Strether, and even John Marcher (1944, 25). Wegelin highlights a contrast with the clash of cultures depicted in *Madame de Mauves* and *The American*, asserting that their criticism of the aristocracy in France is moral; the criticism of that in England social (38). Dietrichson contrasts the impecunious travelers Clement Searle and Caroline Spencer with Newman, who intends to buy what he wants of Europe, unlike Searle, who is drawn more simply to the experience of Europe (137). Samuels, however, sees the novel like the tale demonstrating the superiority of Americans to Europe, and even taking such superiority one step further, by making Newman renounce Europe deliberately, while Searle does so only through death (45). In Segal's view, because the perspective here remains American it is closer to such a work as *The American* than to such works as *An International Episode* and *Lady Barbarina*, which better balance the conflict of cultures (3).

When Searle recognizes his own features in the old family portrait, he is anticipating the action of a much later compatriot in England, Ralph Pendrel of *The Sense of the Past*. Accordingly many critics have noted the similarity not only in the particular device, but between the central characters and themes of the two works (e.g., Matthiessen 1943, 535; Edel and Powers CN 502; Geismar 425; Briggs 114–15). The protagonists of both, Jones observes, are displaced, without a home in time or place (207). Bewley finds the recurrence of the device, and James's evident unawareness that he was repeating himself, evidence of James's "ancient" concern with such themes (73 n.1). Others have emphasized the differences between the two works (e.g., Perosa 142). Even though, as Holder puts it, the novel "converts Searle's delusion into a reality" because Pendrel is a legitimate heir, Pendrel, unlike Searle, eventually chooses the present over the past (211; also *Life* 4, 332). Thus, Stevenson contends, the message of the work is essentially different from the early tale in which the pilgrim passively dies of his "sick desire" (117–18). Similarly, Cargill distinguishes a "great gulf" between the two men, remarking that James satirizes Pendrel's love of the past (488). Finally, Pendrel, in Edward Stone's view, lacks the symptoms of Searle's derangement (186n.).

Given the close links between *The Sense of the Past* and "The Jolly Corner," it is not surprising to find critics associating all three works. In Banta's analysis, "A Passionate Pilgrim" anticipates the two later works both in the "excited sense of living" the hero experiences facing a ghost and in his declaration that he could haunt himself (1964, 180 n.23). Kraft offers a more particular connection to "The Jolly Corner," citing the narrator's reference to Searle's "haunted tenement" (127–28 n.21). Casting Searle as an early example of

James's "poor sensitive gentleman" such as Brydon, Marcher, Strether, Stransom, and Herbert Dodd of "The Bench of Desolation," Segal comments on how the international theme would later blend with the theme of "too late" treated in the stories of Brydon, Strether, and Marcher (2).

Even so, the "haunted" Searle is, in the estimate of Levy, a more "plausible" character than the equally overwrought heroes of such early tales as "Guest's Confession" and "Master Eustace," possessing a new "psychological unity" Levy attributes to James's passion for his new subject (22). Similarly, Segal finds the "device of the confession" used in the former tale as well as in such other early tales as "The Sweetheart of M. Briseux" and "Eugene Pickering" less artificial here. Searle's confessions are made to a limited narrator, a technique Segal finds an advance over the "almost Trollopian manner" of "The Story of a Year" (4, 7). Unlike Segal, who emphasizes that the narrator is a "traditional confidant" not yet a detective, Macnaughton, while he judges James basically sympathetic to the narrator, maintains that he is already working toward the suspect narrator in *The Aspern Papers* (148–49). Cowie, who notes that James disliked first-person narration, simply observes that it is kept well in check here, as in "The Pension Beaurepas" (729).

Segal records how James picks up on the expression "a generous mistake" the narrator uses of his marriage for a significant phrase in *The Portrait of a Lady* (53 n.15). The country houses in both are similarly named, as Lanzinger points out, Lockleigh and Lockley Park (138). Jones looks at Searle, like Taker of "Fordham Castle" and Dencombe of "The Middle Years," as a man who hopes for a second chance, only to fail twice (206–7). In attempting the sympathetic treatment of a doomed person, James, according to Vaid, would fail here, as he would in *Roderick Hudson*, before succeeding in *The Wings of the Dove* (28).

Interpretation and Criticism

In 1873 Howells suggested that James entitle his first collection of tales *Romances*, and his father had gone to the publisher Osgood to discuss the possibility of such a book, but James wanted to wait. He wrote four more tales, keeping only one earlier romance, and, Matthiessen observes, showing his awareness of the reception of "A Passionate Pilgrim" and his evolving theme, kept it to use for the head of a collection "on the theme of American adventurers in Europe" (Matthiessen 1947, 122–26; *Letters* 1, 357).

In a review of the collection Howells would praise James's description of setting in the tale (1875, 67). Indeed, according to Buitenhuis, in this tale James first solved the problem of setting (49). It is largely because of this achievement that the tale has traditionally been viewed as, in Edgar's phrasing, James's "first production of power." Edgar was not, however, unqualified in his praise. Although he accepted the purple passages of travel writing as a necessary part of James's subject, he judged the dialogue often too "bookish" (17–18). The strength of the tale, as McElderry notes, is its description, and the reason for all the description—even if too lengthy as in Voss's estimate or "commonplace" as in Walter Wright's—is that the English setting and Searle's response to it are key to the story (McElderry 32–33; Voss 130; Wright 116). But if, as Canby observes, the tale is "hot with passion" for its subject, it is also in his view written by "a dilettante in story telling," most interested in "his own emotions in a place of pervasive beauty." As a result, he finds that even if the tale is "engaging," its plot and characters are absurd (68). Later critics have lodged similar, if sometimes contradictory complaints. In the tale Howells found "eminently dramatic," Briggs finds too much plot, and Walter Wright too little (Howells 1882, 116; Briggs 115; Wright 117–18). One element of plot, the last-minute death of Miss Searle's inconvenient brother, Wagenknecht judges "deeply, one might even say crassly, ironical" (3). Quentin Anderson and McElderry offer similar criticisms, the first finding the tale "rambling and rhapsodic," the second "cluttered and indecisive" (McElderry 32–33). The reason for the disorganized abundance of themes, Anderson argues, in contrast to Buitenhuis, is that James was still uncertain "what was to be done with Europe" (156). Still, in Wright's view, the story manages to create an effect greater than its disparate parts (117).

Walter Wright uses the original magazine text to criticize the tale, but many critics have relied on James's late New York Edition version as a basis for their judgments. Gegenheimer, in fact, argues that the high critical opinions of the tale may depend on the "much better style" of the New York Edition revision. According to his comparison, the numerous changes in the later version, contrary to popular wisdom, offer a less flowery, more concrete and exact style. They also contribute, Gegenheimer contends, to a greater sophistication in the telling of the tale, seen in the increased criticism of the English, from the universities they attend to the Burgundy they serve, and a greater softness toward America. Similarly, Falk sees James in the revision taking away some of the "passion" from his pilgrim (81).

Lockley Park is the center of what Ford Madox Ford originally judged the tale's "apotheosis of the turf, the deer, the oak trees, the terraces of manor houses" (110). The tale, according to Howells, begins with the atmosphere of a novel but becomes a romance at Lockley Park, and several subsequent critics have called attention to the tale's "essentially romantic" manner (Howells 1875, 66; e.g., Stewart 77). Beach found the tale's "obviously and technically romantic manner" reflecting James's own youthful excitement in discovering himself amid the "romance" of Europe (120, 167). Similarly, Putt sees James in the tale as full of "eager innocent" praise of England, his "fresh propagandist enthusiasm" tempered only by perfunctory social criticism (1966, 61–64; 1985, 7). Powers finds in the tale an "almost mythical quality," as it treats what

James called the "latent preparedness of the American mind" for English life, the "fatal and sacred" emotion of the American's enjoyment of England (1970, 44–45; 1969, 5–6).

But while Beach argued that James's rapturous romanticism "cannot fail to captivate any reader who is still capable of enthusiasm," Segal questions whether the tale is "a nostalgic romance" or "an ironic antiromance" (Beach 187, Segal 3). Indeed, several critics have challenged the tale's romanticism, some arguing that James himself undercut his romantic approach, others that he should have. Taking James's analogy in the preface to *The American* about the balloon of experience and the way the romancer must unobservedly cut its cord, Marder examines Searle and his lack of connection to reality. In Marder's view, Searle is "destroyed by his egotistic prejudices," which keep him from seeing England as it is (14). Lanzinger similarly argues that James is showing how Americans' "romantic notions about England" are likely to produce disillusionment. In his reading, the tone of the tale is "ironic and sarcastic," Lockley Park suggests not a paradise, but through its name, something "locked-in, confined, or excluded" (136–39).

In his reading of the tale's fatal romanticism, Marder emphasizes Searle's death scene, presumably his giving of money to Rawson, with its turn to the West as the hope for civilization (14). Previously, Edel had also pointed to the story of Rawson, the penniless young son who goes to America to "replace" the pilgrim, as evidence of James's acknowledgement of the virtues of American democracy, his giving tribute to the American future after his obsession with the European past (1960, 14; *Life* 2, 36). Similarly, Jones sees in the gesture Searle's giving up not only his claim on England, but his claim for England (207). At the time, however, Howells, in praising the use of Rawson, cautioned that his hope of America was "as hopeless and unfounded" as Searle's of England (1875, 66).

Other critics have also pointed to Rawson as a significant qualification of the tale's romanticization of England (e.g., Lanzinger 139). Wegelin notes that both Rawson's penury and Searle's "ferocity" offer evidence of James's recognition that England was not all roast beef and prosperity. He sees Searle as a "cultural snob" whose quest for "the best" in England "ends ironically in the discovery of social injustice" (35, 60). Dietrichson adds the implicit criticism in the encounter with a beggar at Hampton Court (158, 193). Long traces how James undercuts the romantic view of Searle through a series of encounters, the first with the American Simmons at the Johnsonian inn, then with the beggar, the locked doors of Lockley Park, and finally, Rawson. It all adds up, Long contends, to a view of England characterized by "enclosure and a narrow confinement" and leaves Searle "caught between two worlds, one which he rejects and the other which rejects him" (22–23). Although McElderry considers the encounter with Rawson insufficient to balance the romance cast about England in the rest of the tale, both Falk and Vaid praise the use of the beggar and Rawson, who serve in Vaid's reading as "doppel-gänger[s]" to Searle, to provide balance to James's enthusiastic response to England (McElderry 33; Falk 80–81; Vaid 33–35).

The issue of the tale's romantic attitude to England has become entwined with the issue of the tale's alleged autobiography. Early critics who saw the tale praising England tended to see the praise as reflecting James's own. Even later critics such as Fox and Geismar saw the tale, in its fascination with old England, as what Canby called a "record of James' state of mind at this moment" (Fox 14; Geismar 15–17; Canby 68). Melchiori comments both on the "painful . . . intensity" of James's search for his roots in the English past, and on the "happy intuition" of the narrator's epiphany at Hampton Court when he sees England in the "dark composite light that I had read in all English prose" (1965, 11–13). Kelley was among the first to disagree, taking on not only West, Ford, and Brooks, but James's own testimony in *The Middle Years* and in the preface that the tale is autobiographical. Her analysis emphasizes the role of the narrator, who, she says, is "genially interested" in Searle's case and "may well" represent James but "is *not* a case for psychologists," as Searle is. She points to the difference between the narrator's "intelligent" enjoyment of England and Searle's sense of mistreatment by it, and sees in the tale James's "scorn" for those English who failed to appreciate their own country. Like Gegenheimer later, she attributes some of the misreading to a reliance on the New York Edition. By the time of the revision, she argues, James had come to identify more with Searle, as he was then himself disappointed in his adopted country (117–20). LeClair added his voice to Kelley's in arguing against the view of James as an "intoxicated" Anglophile, stating that James is not to be identified with Searle or even with the narrator. As evidence he cites James's criticism of the English lack of "moral wit" and observes that at the time James was still more interested in writing about the Continent than England (442, 453 n.31). Similarly, Nathalia Wright notes that despite the story's setting, the narrator is equally "enthusiastic" about Italy, an attitude that mirrors James's own feelings at the time (217).

Others, while connecting the views of the tale and James's own, stress James's ambivalence at the time toward his European experience. Jefferson remarks that James's "eloquence and also wit" at the expense of Americans' "immense susceptibility" to England was an indication of his own ambivalent feelings (1964, 43; also [1960] 1971, 14). Kraft also sees an ambivalence in the tale reflecting James's own. The tale, in his view, illustrates the contrast between the different failures of American and European society, the one lacking in "color and subtlety," the other in "opportunity and freedom." At the same time, according to Kraft, the tale remains "annoying" because the reader cannot tell whether he is to look admiringly or condescendingly at Searle, who is clearly mad, but who also speaks at times for James. He blames not James's "impartiality," but his indecision, contending that if Searle is mad, he is not "representative," and is as much to blame for his condition as America is. James would later himself, according to Kraft, follow the narrator's advice to Searle—"You have lived hitherto in yourself. The tenement's haunted! Live abroad! Take an interest"—and leave behind such muddles (47–49). Long argues that while James may portray Searle as suffering from some of the same problems as the writer in America, James takes an ironic perspective on him and the other characters as well (24).

Such readings do not necessarily mean that Searle is to be bereft of all sympathy. In 1875 Howells wrote that the reader will feel an "instant tenderness" for Searle, the "gentle visionary" character done with the "finest sense of its charm and its deficiency". Although some have criticized his dwelling on death, Searle's illness, in Walter Wright's view, serves not only to justify his present activity, but also to strengthen the pathos of his attachment to life (e.g., Segal 9; Wright 115–16). Later, Rahv would find him tragicomic in his desire to "appropriate the fruits of civilization" without losing his "new-world innocence" (1944, viii). Other critics would highlight the comedy. Jefferson judged the tale's humor a relief from its general sadness, while Kraft objected that Searle's madness occasionally seemed "unintentionally humorous instead of pathetic" (Jefferson [1969] 1971, 14; Kraft 48; also Vaid 33). Even Howells noted an "unwonted interfusion of humor" in the tale, which he judged "a little too scornful" (68)

Both the tragedy and the comedy of Searle's situation stem from his standing between two cultures, the American and the English. During the course of the story, Bewley contends, Searle learns "not that he is both American and English, but that he is neither in any significant way" (70). Ward points the moral a different way, attributing the "evil" in the tale to America, seeing Searle with his need for "a richness of culture and manners" ruined by "the aesthetic poverty of America" (33). Tanner is close to Ward, stating that Searle "comes into his own" metaphorically if not legally upon visiting Lockley, although, ironically, what kills him later is "the sudden onset of too much material" (1985, 11; 1987, 106). Mackenzie, however, returns Searle to the crossfire, observing that Searle's "posthumous life" in England takes from him what little remaining identity he has as an American while not giving him a true British identity. His death is caused thus, Mackenzie argues, by his "being and refusing to be American," his shame at "his not being and his claiming to be English." Even so, his evolving role as a "disembodied observer" makes him a "problematical figure," which Mackenzie finds bearing on James himself (12, 44–45).

England for James, and for Searle, represents the past. Indeed, West laments, James's love of the past limited even his love of England, through a mistaken belief that the life of the past had been as fine as its buildings leading him to a "distrust" of the present (26–28). Andreas, however, portrays nonjudgmentally Searle's choice to yield to his sense of the past, as evident in

its monuments, as giving him a "final climactic intensity of life" (98). Searle is
so taken up by his sense of the past, Briggs observes, that he even reacts to
the ghost that warns of his own death with the ironic declaration "This is life!
This is living!" (112). Such a love of the past becomes in Holder's view
"pathological" (211). Sicker's reading is also censorious, characterizing Searle
as "really in love with death" (38).

Miss Searle, just like her brother, like Rawson and the beggar, represents
certain aspects of England. Howells judged her in her "dullish kindness" an
even better character than Searle, done with "peculiar sweetness and firmness" (65–66). The less enthusiastic Putt dismisses her as "merely the most
precious item in the narrator's collection of curiosities" (1966, 63–64).
Similarly, McElderry considers the romance between her and Searle unlikely
and unnecessary (32–33). Long, however, while judging the brother overly
melodramatic, considers the romance of Searle and Margaret affecting in part
because they are, like their portraits, somewhat otherworldly (22–23). While
most critics see her as a static type, Rahv gives her character a further dimension, contending that she, too, is a "passionate pilgrim," a role unusual for an
Englishwoman (1943, 51).

To Lanzinger, however pathetic Searle may be, he remains the narrator's
"*alter ego*" (137–38). The narrator indeed is the character most closely tied to
Searle. Early on, McElderry judged his purpose "ill-defined," and several critics have stepped in since to define it (33). Geismar, while acknowledging him
as saner than Searle, sees him as even more taken by the evidences of old
England, and so as representing James's own fantasy of England (15–17). In a
more sustained analysis, Vaid objects that the contrast between the narrator
and Searle is not explicit. Searle, he argues, is so sick and so poor that his
character is "overburdened with an ironic pathos" that shields him from
objective analysis. The narrator he sees as a static character, a "sympathetic
companion" who because he never argues with Searle, creates an imbalance
between the two. Like Searle, he is a passionate pilgrim. His lyrical descriptions of England provide an "objective correlative" to Searle's responses, even
as his " greater discrimination" creates an "implicit contrast" evident also in
his intention to return to America. As a result, Vaid admits, the tale manages
to achieve a "midposition between severity and total approval," which gives it
some success. Even Searle himself, he adds, having at first blamed America
for his failure, realizes later that his own weakness played a part (29–35).

Segal, too, views the narrator as a parallel pilgrim, arguing that his greater
cultivation and intelligence make him the "perfect mirror" for the more
intense and rather pathetic Searle. Segal, however, sees their relationship
undergoing a significant evolution from its initial "gently ironic distance." At
Lockley Park, she contends, a gradual reversal between the two begins. Searle
becomes more simple, impressing the narrator, even as the narrator himself
becomes more effusive in his literary dreaming. Part of the change, according

to Segal, is the new comparison set up between Searle and his unimpressive British counterpart. Searle's "madness" thus takes on a new grandeur, upstaging the narrator. His "highest moment of truth"—the recognition of the "romance of the American imagination"—comes when he is mad. With this recognition, Segal contends, the "ironic distance" between the two characters disappears, and the original "ironic detachment" is subsumed if not erased by "a sad admiration" for the American not as a pilgrim, but a "romantic kind of 'wise fool.'" Even the increased sophistication of the narrator documented by Gegenheimer, she argues, does not transform the story into a "wholly ironic" one, rather it simply upsets the crucial balance between narrator and protagonist (1–14).

The contrast between narrator and protagonist is also at the center of Gill's analysis. Neither, he says, speaks precisely for his author. Still, while noting the greater sense of the narrator, he also points to Searle's strengths, his understanding that Lockley Park is also a "house of life," not just an aesthetic object as in the narrator's sight. The "house of life," however, also contains a ghost whose mistreatment in the past, Gill argues, suggests that evil, too, is present there. In its contrast between the ideal and the real England, Gill writes, the tale goes beyond a mere exposé, the death at the end of both Searle and his rival cousin signifying a "stalemate" (38–41).

Like Gill, Macnaughton refuses to see either American as representing James. In his reading, however, the narrator is not trustworthy, but swayed by a fascination with the English picturesque evident in a constant disjunction between what he sees and what is. Searle, in contrast, he maintains, sees not only his own faults but England's, his sin being not an unclear vision, but a reluctance to act. By the time the narrator pushes him to act, Searle has become dangerous—a "sick man in an alien society." Like Segal, he sees a change in the behavior of both at Lockley. There, Searle takes on a new dignity, while the narrator increasingly begins to meddle. His attitude, Macnaughton admits, is "not despicable" and has one good result, letting Searle live intensely for once, but shows a double attitude to Searle as "both a friend and a picturesque object." The narrator, Macnaughton argues, is Searle's "doppelgänger" with the youth, health, and resources to fulfill Searle's dream. While he comes to England intending to stay only six weeks, he is still there a year later when Miss Searle "has begun to wear colors" (CT 2, 306). Indeed, Macnaughton concludes, "consciously or unconsciously" the narrator wants Lockley himself, and helps along Searle's death to make it possible for him to inherit through a marriage to Miss Searle. Macnaughton also presents an alternative reading of Miss Searle's brother, arguing that James shows him not as a type of "melodramatic villainy," but a man who has suffered losses, loves his home, and so distrusts Searle. In sum, Macnaughton asserts, the picture of England is one that refuses to equate Europe and corruption, which shows the danger of the love of the picturesque even as it shows its "charm" (148–53).

Jones is more moderate in his incrimination of the narrator, but views him as intervening in key moments to spur Clement on, and particularly blames him for paying no attention to Miss Searle's innocence and so bringing about an end to it, as well as to her contentment (206–7). Sweeney, too, deals a good share of blame to the narrator, chastising him for his failure to interfere to protect Margaret from Searle and to recognize the true cause of Searle's sickness. The sickness, however, is his main focus. While the narrator and most critics have typed Searle as a hypochondriac, Sweeney diagnoses him as suffering from syphilis. He cites Searle's confession that in New York, "I respected Pleasure, and she made a fool of me," and points to symptoms including paleness, insanity, and even swollen knuckles, as well as indications of Searle's passionate nature as evidence. Searle's proposal to Miss Searle therefore becomes particularly wrong, even though Sweeney gives him the excuse of being drunk at the time. Such a reading, he contends, alters the interpretation of the tale, reinforcing how Americans are not so much destroyed by Europe, as by the "seeds of their own destruction" that they bring with them.

In the 1870s James had many thank you's to write to friends for their praise of his tale, including Charles Eliot Norton, Elizabeth Boott and her father, and, of course, Howells. To Howells, he wrote, "If kindness could kill I should be safely out of the way of ever challenging your ingenuity again." More significantly, he concluded, "I lift up my hanging head little by little & try to earn the laurel for the future, even if it be so much too umbrageous now" (*Letters* 1, 255, 257, 262, 475). Through the years Howells continued to rank the tale high. In 1882 he viewed it as being "for certain rich poetical qualities, above everything else that he has done," and in 1920 he included the 1875 text in an anthology of "great modern American stories," writing that it has "a life, a feeling, a color, and above all a prompt distinctness, altogether absent from his later, and, if one will, more masterly work" making it "an intense piece of American fiction, such as the author has never since surpassed" (1882, 116; 1920, viii).

Later critics have tended to echo Howells's high praise, while restricting their comparisons to early James. Hart calls it James's "first important fiction," Dupee his "first really good story," and Ford his first masterpiece (Hart 374; Dupee 47; Ford 111). More moderately, Canby points to it as the only apprentice tale "worth reading" (68). For such critics, and even for Vaid, who thinks less highly of it, its significance is primarily its adoption of the international theme (Vaid 27–28; e.g., Segal 1). Donald Stone is one of the dissenters to the story's pride of place, judging it inferior to "At Isella," and awarding the palm of first masterpiece to "The Madonna of the Future" instead (189).

Other critics have been harsher. Kraft calls it a failure (48). Rebecca West offers the opinion that "in those days Mr James could not draw normal events" (26). Arguing against the "glamour" accorded the tale by its placement in the New York Edition, Kelley cautions that the tale, even its very setting in England, is atypical of early James (120). Melchiori chastises the elderly James for including the inferior tale largely for "sentimental value" (1965, 11). As often with James criticism, the truth probably lies somewhere in the middle. If the tale is not an exact record of James's first adult impression of England, it is certainly significant as his first fictional treatment of the relationship between Americans and England. In later works, the relationship would become more complex, but even here it is not simple. In one of his letters from Oxford in 1869, James had written of the "happy belief the world is all an English garden and time a fine old English afternoon" (*Life* 1, 291). His phrasing indicates he was already aware that the world is not, and even that English gardens can contain as much grief as gardens anywhere else. Critical reaction to the tale initially followed the critics' support or dislike of this "happy belief," whether they romanticized old England or disapproved of it, as much as James's. James got a march on his critics, however, by putting both sides in the tale.

Works Cited

Primary Works

James, Henry. 1871. "A Passionate Pilgrim." *Atlantic Monthly* 27 (March–April): 352–71, 478–99.

———. 1875. "A Passionate Pilgrim." *A Passionate Pilgrim*. Boston: Osgood, 15–124.

———. 1884. "A Passionate Pilgrim." *The Siege of London*. Leipzig: Bernhard Tauchnitz.

———. 1885. "A Passionate Pilgrim." *Stories Revived*. Vol. 1. London: Macmillan.

———. 1908. "A Passionate Pilgrim." *The Novels and Tales of Henry James*. New York Edition. Vol. 13, 333–434. New York: Scribner's.

———. 1993. *The Correspondence of Henry James and the House of Macmillan, 1877–1914*. Ed. Rayburn S. Moore. Baton Rouge: Louisiana State University Press.

Secondary Works

Altenbernd, Lynn. 1977. "A Dispassionate Pilgrim: Henry James's Early Travel in Sketch and Story." *Exploration* 5, no. 1: 1–14.

Anderson, Quentin. 1957. *The American Henry James*. New Brunswick, NJ: Rutgers University Press.

Andreas, Osborn. 1948. *Henry James and the Expanding Horizon: A Study of the Meaning and Basic Themes of James's Fiction*. Seattle: University of Washington Press.

Banta, Martha. 1972. *Henry James and the Occult: The Great Extension.* Bloomington: Indiana University Press.

———. 1964. "Henry James and 'The Others.'" *New England Quarterly* 37 (June): 171–84.

Baxter, Annette K. 1955. "Independence vs. Isolation: Hawthorne and James on the Problem of the Artist." *Nineteenth-Century Fiction* 10: 225–31.

Beach, Joseph Warren. [1918] 1954. *The Method of Henry James.* Philadelphia: Albert Saifer.

Bewley, Marius. 1968. *The Complex Fate: Hawthorne, Henry James, and Some Other American Writers.* London: Chatto & Windus.

Briggs, Julia. 1977. *Night Visitors: The Rise and Fall of the English Ghost Story.* London: Faber.

Brodhead, Richard H. 1986. *The School of Hawthorne.* New York: Oxford University Press.

Buitenhuis, Peter. 1970. *The Grasping Imagination: The American Writings of Henry James.* Toronto: University of Toronto Press.

Canby, Henry Seidel. 1951. *Turn West, Turn East: Mark Twain and Henry James.* Boston: Houghton Mifflin.

Cargill, Oscar. 1961. *The Novels of Henry James.* New York: Macmillan.

Cowie, Alexander. 1948. *The Rise of the American Novel.* New York: American Book Company.

Dietrichson, Jan W. 1969. *The Image of Money in the American Novel of the Gilded Age.* Oslo: Universitetsforlaget; New York: Humanities.

Dupee, F. W. [1951] 1956. *Henry James.* Garden City, NY: Doubleday Anchor.

Edel, Leon. 1960. *Henry James.* Minneapolis: University of Minnesota Press.

Edel, Leon, and Dan H. Laurence. 1982. *A Bibliography of Henry James.* Oxford: Clarendon.

Edgar, Pelham. [1927] 1964. *Henry James, Man and Author.* New York: Russell & Russell.

Everett, H. Sydney. 1896. "Unclaimed Estates." *Atlantic Monthly* 77 (February): 240–50.

Falk, Robert P. 1965. *The Victorian Mode in American Fiction.* 1865–85. East Lansing: Michigan State University Press.

Ford, Ford Madox. 1913. *Henry James: A Critical Study.* London: Martin Secker.

Fox, Hugh. 1968. *Henry James, A Critical Introduction.* Conesville, IA: Westburg.

Gale, Robert L. [1954] 1964. *The Caught Image: Figurative Language in the Fiction of Henry James.* Chapel Hill: University of North Carolina Press.

Gegenheimer, A. F. 1951. "Early and Late Revisions in Henry James's 'A Passionate Pilgrim.'" *American Literature* 23 (May): 233–42.

Geismar, Maxwell. 1963. *Henry James and the Jacobites.* Boston: Houghton Mifflin.

Gill, Richard. 1972. *Happy Rural Seat: The English Country House and the Literary Imagination.* New Haven: Yale University Press.

Hart, James D. 1983. *The Companion to American Literature.* Oxford: Oxford University Press.

Holder, Alan. 1966. *Three Voyagers in Search of Europe: A Study of Henry James, Ezra Pound and T. S. Eliot.* Philadelphia: University of Pennsylvania Press.

Howells, W. D., ed. 1920. *The Great Modern American Stories.* New York: Boni and Liveright.

———. 1882. "Henry James, Jr." *Century* (November). Reprinted in *Discovery of a Genius: William Dean Howells and Henry James,* ed. Albert Mordell, 112–25. New York: Twayne, 1961.

———. 1875. "James's *Passionate Pilgrim and Other Tales.*" *Atlantic* 35 (April): 490–95. As reprinted in *Discovery of a Genius: William Dean Howells and Henry James,* ed. Albert Mordell, 63–74 . New York: Twayne, 1961, and *Critics on Henry James,* ed. J. Don Vann, 10–16. Readings in Literary Criticism 18. Coral Gables: University of Miami Press, 1972.

Jefferson, D. W. 1964. *Henry James and the Modern Reader.* New York: St. Martin's.

———. [1960] 1971. *Henry James.* New York: Capricorn.

Jones, Granville H. 1975. *Henry James's Psychology of Experience: Innocence, Responsibility, and Renunciation in the Fiction of Henry James.* The Hague: Mouton.

Josephson, Matthew. 1964. *Portrait of the Artist as American.* New York: Octagon.

Kelley, Cornelia Pulsifer. [1930] 1965. *The Early Development of Henry James.* Urbana: University of Illinois Press.

Kraft, James. 1969. *The Early Tales of Henry James.* Carbondale: Southern Illinois University Press.

Lanzinger, Klaus. 1989. *Jason's Voyage: The Search for the Old World in American Literature: A Study of Melville, Hawthorne, Henry James, and Thomas Wolfe.* New York: Peter Lang.

LeClair, Robert Charles. 1955. *Young Henry James, 1843–1870.* New York: Bookman.

Levy, Leo B. 1957. *Versions of Melodrama: A Study of the Fiction and Drama of Henry James, 1865–1897.* Berkeley: University of California Press.

Long, Robert Emmet. 1979. *The Great Succession: Henry James and the Legacy of Hawthorne.* Pittsburgh: University of Pittsburgh Press.

McElderry, Bruce R., Jr. 1965. *Henry James.* New York: Twayne.

Mackenzie, Manfred. 1976. *Communities of Honor and Love in Henry James*. Cambridge, MA: Harvard University Press.

Macnaughton, W. R. 1974. "The First-Person Narrators of Henry James." *Studies in American Fiction* 2 (August): 145–64.

Marder, Daniel. 1984. *Exiles at Home: A Story of Literature in Nineteenth Century America*. Lanham, MD: University Press of America.

Matthiessen F. O. 1947. *The James Family: Including Selections from the Writings of Henry James, Sr., William, Henry, and Alice James*. New York: Knopf.

———. 1944. *Henry James: The Major Phase*. New York: Oxford University Press.

———. 1943. "James and the Plastic Arts." *Kenyon Review* 5 (August): 533–50.

Melchiori, Giorgio. 1967. "Shakespeare and Henry James." *Shakespeare Newsletter* 17 (December): 56.

———. 1965. "Locksley Hall Revisited: Tennyson and Henry James." *Review of English Literature* 6 (October): 9–25. Reprinted in Barbara Melchiori and Giorgio Melchiori. *Il Gusto di Henry James*. Turin: Guilio Einaudi editore, 1974.

Mott, Frank Luther. 1938. *A History of American Magazines, 1865–1885*. Cambridge, MA: Harvard University Press.

Mulvey, Christopher. 1983. *Anglo-American Landscapes: A Study of Nineteenth-Century Anglo-American Travel Literature*. Cambridge: Cambridge University Press.

Perosa, Sergio. 1983. *Henry James and the Experimental Novel*. New York: New York University Press.

Powers, Lyall H. 1970. *Henry James: An Introduction and Interpretation*. New York: Holt, Rinehart.

———. 1969. *The Merrill Guide to Henry James*. Columbus, OH: Charles E. Merrill.

Putt, S. Gorley, ed. 1985. *An International Episode and Other Stories*. Harmondsworth: Penguin.

———. 1966. *Henry James: A Reader's Guide*. Ithaca, NY: Cornell University Press. Revised in part from "'The Passionate Pilgrim': An Aspect of Henry James," *The Wind and the Rain* (London) 4, 230–32.

Rahv, Philip. 1944. *The Great Short Novels of Henry James*. New York: Dial.

———. 1943. "The Heiress of All the Ages." *Partisan Review* 10 (May–June): 227–47. Also reprinted in *Image and Idea*, 51–76. Norfolk, CT: New Directions, 1957.

Samuels, Charles Thomas. 1971. *The Ambiguity of Henry James*. Urbana: University of Illinois Press.

Segal, Ora. 1969. *The Lucid Reflector: The Observer in Henry James' Fiction*. New Haven: Yale University Press.

Sicker, Philip. 1980. *Love and the Quest for Identity in the Fiction of Henry James*. Princeton: Princeton University Press.

Spender, Stephen. 1934. "The School of Experience in the Early Novels." *Hound & Horn*. 7 (April–May): 417–33. Reprinted in *The Destructive Element*, 23–46. Philadelphia: Albert Saifer, 1953.

Stevenson, Elizabeth. [1949] 1981. *The Crooked Corridor: A Study of Henry James*. New York: Octagon.

Stewart, J. I. M. 1963. "Henry James." In *Eight Modern Writers*. Oxford History of English Literature. Vol. 7, 71–121. New York: Oxford University Press.

Stone, Donald David. 1972. *Novelists in a Changing World: Meredith, James, and the Transformation of English Fiction in the 1880's*. Cambridge, MA: Harvard University Press.

Stone, Edward. 1964. *The Battle and the Books: Some Aspects of Henry James*. Athens: Ohio University Press.

Sweeney, Gerard. 1988. "The Illness of the Passionate Pilgrim." *American Literary Realism* 21: 3–18.

Tanner, Tony. 1987. "The Watcher from the Balcony: *The Ambassadors*." In *Henry James*. Ed. Harold Bloom, 105–23. New York: Chelsea House. Reprinted from *Critical Inquiry* 8, no. 1 (Spring 1966): 35–52.

———. 1985. *Henry James: The Writer and His Work*. Amherst: University of Massachusetts Press.

Thoreau, Henry David. [1854] 1963. Walden. In *Eight American Authors: An Anthology of American Literature*. Ed. Floyd Stovall, et al., 419–500. New York: Norton.

Tintner, Adeline R. 1989. *The Pop World of Henry James: From Fairy Tales to Science Fiction*. Ann Arbor: UMI Research Press. Revised in part from "Henry James and the Sleeping Beauty: A Victorian Fantasy of a Fairy-Tale Theme." *Topic* 37 (Fall 1983): 10–22.

———. 1987. *The Book World of Henry James: Appropriating the Classics*. Ann Arbor: UMI Research Press.

———. 1986. *The Museum World of Henry James*. Ann Arbor: UMI Research Press.

Vaid, Krishna B. 1964. *Technique in the Tales of Henry James*. Cambridge, MA: Harvard University Press.

Veeder, William. 1975. *Henry James: Lessons of the Master: Popular Fiction and Personal Style in the Nineteenth Century*. Chicago: University of Chicago Press.

Voss, Arthur. 1973. *The American Short Story: A Critical Survey*. Norman: University of Oklahoma Press.

Wagenknecht, Edward. 1984. *The Tales of Henry James*. New York: Frederick Ungar.

Ward, Joseph A. 1961. *The Imagination of Disaster: Evil in the Fiction of Henry James*. Lincoln: Univeristy of Nebraska Press.

Wegelin, Christof. 1958. *The Image of Europe in Henry James*. Dallas: Southern Methodist University Press.

West, Rebecca. [pseud]. 1916. *Henry James*. London: Nisbet.

Winner, Viola Hopkins. 1970. *Henry James and the Visual Arts*. Charlottesville: University Press of Virginia.

Wright, Nathalia. 1965. *American Novelists in Italy, The Discoverers: Allston to James*. Philadelphia: University of Pennsylvania Press.

Wright, Walter F. 1962. *The Madness of Art: A Study of Henry James*. Lincoln: Nebraska University Press.

Foreign Language
Nakazato, Haruhiko. 1962. "Henry James's 'A Passionate Pilgrim.'" *Rikkyo Daigaku Kenkyu Hokoku* 12 (August): 1–22. [Japanese]

Paste

Publication History

"Paste" first appeared in *Frank Leslie's Popular Monthly* in December 1899 with illustrations by Howard Chandler Christy. As Kenton discovered, Howells had written James the year before that the editor there was "revamping" the magazine and that he had advised him to solicit a tale from James. He advised James in turn to "fix a good price, and demand cash" (Howells 182–83; Kenton 538). The story appeared again the next year in *The Soft Side*. James also included it in the New York Edition.

Circumstances of Composition, Sources, and Influences

According to a rather jaundiced account by Thomas Beer, James's friend and fellow novelist Mrs. Humphry Ward once "fell speechless and scarlet" at being told that the very proper James had taken one of his tales from Maupassant (106). Since then, the source of James's "Paste" has continued, if less dramatically, to be a subject of contention.

It appears simple enough in the preface to the New York Edition, where James records the source of "Paste" as "but . . . the ingenious thought of transposing the terms of one of Guy de Maupassant's admirable *contes*"—"La Parure" (1883):

> It seemed harmless sport simply to turn that situation round—to shift, in other words, the ground of the horrid mistake, making this a matter not of a false treasure supposed to be true and precious, but of a real treasure supposed to be false and hollow: though a new little 'drama,' a new setting for *my* pearls—and as different as possible from the other—had of course withal to be found. (*Criticism* 2, 1242–43)

In 1964 T. M. Segnitz offered a new source, arguing that James's "new setting" was already present in Maupassant, who had himself made the transposition of "La Parure" in "Les Bijoux," a story with numerous similarities to "Paste." In it a government clerk discovers after his wife's death that her treasured imitation jewels were in fact real, the gift of some lover. Segnitz points out also that while James writes in his preface that the necklace in "La Parure" was pearls, it was not, but the wife in "Les Bijoux" was particularly fond of pearls. He also points to James's mention in his essay on Maupassant of a nonexistent story, "*Le Collier*," as one of his "little perfections," as indicating a possible "unconscious association" in James's mind between *colle* (paste) or *coller* (to paste) and *collier* (necklace). Tintner also connects the two stories, pointing to the shared themes of the theatre, jewels, and infidelity, as well as the allusion to Maupassant in Mrs. Guy's name (230–33).

Earlier, while not arguing for a direct influence, Davis had also placed "Paste" in relation to "Les Bijoux," including the Maupassant story in his anthology as a parallel to James's, along with another parallel story, Somerset Maugham's "Mr. Know-All" in which Mr. Kelada, a man obnoxious to his fellow shipboard travelers equally for his claims of knowledge and his evident foreign extraction, nevertheless performs a service for the pretty wife of an American diplomat by backing down on his claim in a bet that the necklace she told her husband she had bought for eighteen dollars in New York was in fact genuine pearl. At the end Kelada says, "Were the pearls real? If I had a pretty little wife I shouldn't let her spend a year in New York while I stayed at Kobe" (Davis 490). Gilbert Highet, in a review of James's notebooks, while linking the story, following James, with Maupassant's "La Parure," also makes the connection with "Mr. Know-All," saying that James's plot has been seen "more recently, and more vividly, revised" in Maugham's story, which had been filmed in 1948 as part of *Quartet* (189–90). Terrie also comments on the connections between the three, and adds that Maugham was probably familiar with both the James and Maupassant works (10). All three stories, unlike "La Parure," not only have the real pearls substituted for paste, but the issue of their genuineness subordinated to their indication of sexual misbehavior. Bayley, looking at "Paste" in connection with "Mr. Know-All" and "La Parure," argues that even James failed to create "a true inner dimension" to its consideration of "value" because of the contrived nature of the plot (180–81).

There is no notebook entry to substantiate a connection with either Maupassant tale. Matthiessen and Murdock, followed by Davis, do indeed cite a November 18, 1894, entry as a possible "hint" for the story's consideration of the different ways family members respond to the revelation of family disgrace, although the entry does not mention Maupassant. It also rejects "the unchaste woman" as probably "too stale and threadbare" to serve as the needed disgrace (N 197). Edel and Powers, in their edition of the notebooks, do not connect the entry with the story.

Relation to Other Works

McCarthy links it with "The Last of the Valerii" as another reworking of the possibilities of a classic story (71).

Edgar offers Mme Merle as a kindred spirit to the worldy Mrs. Guy (291).

Austin Wright compares the tale to "The Lesson of the Master," arguing that readers of both are unsure whether to approve the moral victories of those who renounce or to laugh at the effects of their renunciation (358). Jones distinguishes Charlotte, who considers herself innocent of contributing to the crime against her, with Mark Monteith of "A Round of Visits" and Graham Fielder of *The Ivory Tower*, who both come to feel implicated in the wrongs done them (93).

Interpretation and Criticism

Much of the interpretation of the story has rested on the comparison with Maupassant. Among those who accept the "La Parure" source, Edgar, while qualifying it with an "avowedly," judges James's story ingenious in its reworking of Maupassant, but lacking the original's "tragic irony" (148–49). Q. D. Leavis, who calls its source "one of Maupassant's slickest stories," finds James's version "hardly less shallow than its model" (223). Putt, on the other hand, claims the "unsavoury" story "out-Maupassants Maupassant," although the moral he derives from it—"naked cupidity is stronger even than self-protective hypocrisy"—can also be applied to "Les Bijoux" (290–91). Gerlach footnotes the identification of the source as "Les Bijoux," but discusses the story in comparison to "La Parure," finding it superior because the title's indication that the jewels may be real allows James to treat Charlotte's whole character, rather than just "the single emotion of a character" as Maupassant was forced to do in his reliance on the surprise ending (74–75, 174 n.1). Segnitz and Terrie, who use "Les Bijoux" as the source, come to similar conclusions, arguing that James outdid the plot-oriented Maupassant in the strength of his psychological portraiture (Segnitz 217–18; Terrie 10–11). On the other hand, Rawlings considers the story "slight" and written with an eye on the market, and uses the "Les Bijoux" source to show that even James's "transposition" was not original (xx). McCarthy records both possibilities and without analyzing what James made of them comments on James's fascination with reworking the subject matter of others (71).

The characters have absorbed most of the remaining critical attention. Wagenknecht names the two villains, Arthur and Mrs. Guy, as the most vivid portraits (119). Arthur is the easy one to criticize. As Andreas formulates it, Arthur's truthfulness is so corrupted by his Puritan values that he violates them in order to preserve their appearance (135–36). Charlotte, like a good Jamesian heroine, has also been subjected to judgment. Putt, while condemning the hypocritical Arthur, places Charlotte, however honorable, with James's "selfless ninnies," and argues that only the worldy Mrs. Guy "manages for a brief instant to win the reader's assent" in her advice to Charlotte to keep the pearls (291). Similarly, Kuhn's questions suggest that Mrs. Guy is "more mature" than either Arthur or Charlotte and less burdened by pride. Ziff, too, contends that Charlotte's lack of passion makes her less deserving of the pearls than the admittedly unpleasant but passionate Mrs. Guy (62). Segnitz judges Charlotte as "morbid from unfulfilled desire," not as in Maupassant, "from shamed pride." Through the comparison with the wife in "Les Bijoux," he even attempts a retrospective analysis of the late Miss Bradshaw, claiming that she "cherished" her necklace as representing "the fullest experience and enjoyment of life" and may have married the vicar as "an act of penance" (217–18). Austin Wright argues that the reader's pleasure in seeing Charlotte suffer the consequences of her "excessive scrupulousness" outweighs any pity produced from her plight. To keep the tale a comedy, however, he rather minimizes the loss she sustains, referring to it simply as an embarrassment(170–72). Given the picture of her impoverished circumstances, however, the pearls may have been her one chance of improving her position.

Taking exception to such criticism of Charlotte, Knieger argues that she deals competently with complex issues and was unlikely to have been any happier if she kept the jewels; that Mrs. Guy, like Arthur, is a liar; and that Arthur's hypocrisy, not Charlotte's "scrupulousness," is the story's central issue. Gerlach, while keeping Charlotte at the center, is like Knieger more positive in his reading, seeing her, despite her many scruples, as a survivor with a certain "moral consistency" in contrast to her corrupt surroundings (75). Jones also indicates that Charlotte was unlikely to have behaved differently even had she known Arthur's potential for deceit, and notes she keeps her integrity if not her innocence (93). As Voss acknowledges, it is an "unhappy truth" that being honest can also be seen as "inviting" the dishonest to make use of one's honesty (152). Terrie also refrains from condemning Charlotte, and most significantly cites her "final uncertainty," which extends the life of the story beyond its brief bounds (11). It is indeed really only Charlotte's sharp yet hesitant awareness that keeps the story from the patness of a textbook tale.

Works Cited

Primary Works
James, Henry. 1899. "Paste." *Frank Leslie's Popular Monthly* 49 (December): 175–89.

———. 1900. "Paste." *The Soft Side*. London: Methuen; New York: Macmillan, 52–70.

———. 1909. "Paste." *The Novels and Tales of Henry James*. New York Editon. Vol. 16, 313–37. New York: Scribner's.

Secondary Works
Andreas, Osborn. 1948. *Henry James and the Expanding Horizon: A Study of the Meaning and Basic Themes of James's Fiction*. Seattle: University of Washington Press.

Bayley, John. 1988. *The Short Story: Henry James to Elizabeth Bowen*. Brighton: Harvester.

Beer, Thomas. [1923] 1945. "Henry James and Stephen Crane." In *The Question of Henry James*. Ed. F. W. Dupee, 105–7. New York: Henry Holt.

Davis, Robert G., ed. 1953. *Ten Modern Masters: An Anthology of the Short Story*. New York: Harcourt, Brace.

Edgar, Pelham. [1927] 1964. *Henry James, Man and Author*. New York: Russell & Russell.

Gerlach, John. 1985. *Toward the End: Closure and Structure in American Short Stories*. University: University of Alabama Press.

Highet, Gilbert. 1953. "Paste." *People, Places, and Books*. New York: Oxford University Press, 189–90.

Howells, W. D. 1981. *Selected Letters.* Vol. 4: *1892–1901*. Ed. Thomas Wortham, et al. Boston: Twayne.

Jones, Granville H. 1975. *Henry James's Psychology of Experience: Innocence, Responsibility, and Renunciation in the Fiction of Henry James*. The Hague: Mouton.

Kenton, Edna. 1934. "Some Bibliographical Notes on Henry James." *Hound & Horn* 7 (April–May): 535–40.

Knieger, Bernard. 1971. "James's 'Paste.'" *Studies in Short Fiction* 8 (Summer): 468–69.

Kuhn, B. M. 1957. "Study Questions and Theme Assignments on Henry James's 'Paste.'" *Exercise Exchange* 4 (April): 4–5.

Leavis, Q. D. 1947. "Henry James: The Stories." *Scrutiny* 14 (Spring): 117–19. Reprinted in *Collected Essays*. Vol. 2: *The American Novel and Reflections of the European Novel*, ed. G. Singh, 177–84. Cambridge: Cambridge University Press.

McCarthy, Harold T. 1958. *Henry James: The Creative Process*. New York: Thomas Yoseloff.

Putt, S. Gorley. 1966. *Henry James: A Reader's Guide*. Ithaca, NY: Cornell University Press.

Rawlings, Peter, ed. 1984. *Henry James's Shorter Masterpieces*. Vol. 2. Totowa, NJ: Barnes & Noble.

Segnitz, T. M. 1964. "The Actual Genesis of Henry James's 'Paste.'" *American Literature* 36 (May): 216–19.

Terrie, Henry, ed. 1984. *Henry James: Tales of Art and Life*. Schenectady, NY: Union College Press.

Tintner, Adeline R. 1987. *The Book World of Henry James: Appropriating the Classics*. Ann Arbor: UMI Research Press.

Voss, Arthur. 1973. *The American Short Story: A Critical Survey*. Norman: University of Oklahoma Press.

Wagenknecht, Edward. 1984. *The Tales of Henry James*. New York: Frederick Ungar.

Wright, Austin McGiffert. 1961. *The American Short Story in the Twenties*. Chicago: University of Chicago Press.

Ziff, Larzer. 1966. *The American 1890's: Life and Times of a Lost Generation*. New York: Viking.

The Patagonia

Publication History

James first published "The Patagonia" in the August and September 1888 issues of *The English Illustrated Magazine*. The next year he included it in *A London Life* and later in the New York Edition.

Circumstances of Composition, Sources, and Influences

James first recorded the "admirable little dismal subject" that was to become "The Patagonia" in his notebook on January 5, 1888. Its source was Fanny Kemble, provider of the gossipy germs for three other James works of the 1880s, who told of a friend's brother, Barry St. Leger, who on ship from India took part in a flirtation with a young woman traveling under the protection of the captain that so scandalized passengers she jumped overboard (CN 43). Gargano notes how James immediately Americanized the British participants and changed the French nature of the plot to a more Anglo-Saxon one by making the woman not married but engaged, a difference the narrator alludes to in the story (51; CT 7, 315)

Relation to Other Works

McElderry includes the story among the many James wrote at the same time about jilted lovers, while Edgar links it with *A London Life* as the end of James's American stories from the 1880s (McElderry 78; Edgar 53). Jones adds "The Visits," in that the heroines of all three suffer from having committed an "indiscretion," although Jones sees Grace as punished from without rather than within, as in the other tales (112).

Grace is in Mrs. Nettlepoint's words "an extraordinary girl not brought up at all"—a would-be "self-made" girl like Pandora, eclipsing her ignorant mother and inspiring mean-spirited gossip (CT 7, 309). Wagenknecht sees in her the recklessness of Daisy Miller, but not her youth or charm, as she faces in the women aboard ship even fiercer critics than did Daisy (1984, 55). Gage remarks similarities between all three tales, with their social categories, mysterious heroines, and confused observers, and contrasts the dockside conclusions of

"Pandora" and "The Patagonia," one marked by triumphant reunion, the other tragic separation (138–44, 150–52). He considers the narrator suspicious like Adela Chart in "The Marriages," and Winterbourne of *Daisy Miller* and sees him like the narrators of "The Real Thing" and "Brooksmith" flattering himself on his superior understanding of those he observes. He also links the suicides of Brooksmith and Grace, both members of a lower class who have enjoyed exposure to a better way of life and come to their watery ends, while the upper class continues undisturbed (156, 164, 185). Looking at the other side, Mrs. Nettlepoint uses Grace to keep her son amused for the dull voyage in a manner similar to Mrs. Daintry's intended use of Rachel Torrance to amuse her son over the course of a dull visit in a "New England Winter." Walter Wright classes Jasper in his irresponsible egotism with others whose weakness causes harm including Owen Gereth of *The Spoils of Poynton*, Chad Newsome, Lord Gwyther of "The Two Faces," and Tony Bream of *The Other House* (88). Dietrichson, who is perhaps the only critic to offer any sympathy to the "unfortunate" Mr. Porterfield, compares him and Grace to the couples in *The Golden Bowl* and *The Ivory Tower*, whose marriages are also delayed by poverty (111). Gooder notes that Caroline Spencer's cousin in "Four Meetings" is a fellow student of his at the École des Beaux Arts in Paris (282).

Tanner, Putt, and Samuels all compare the narrator here to the narrator of *The Sacred Fount*, Samuels adding the narrators of such tales as *The Turn of the Screw*, "The Liar," "A Light Man," and "Louisa Pallant" (Tanner 331; Putt 277; Samuels 26). The narrator's description of a sea voyage's freedom from "letters and telegrams and newspapers and visits and duties and efforts, all the complications, all the superfluities and superstitions that we have stuffed into our terrene life," is reminiscent of "The Great Good Place" (CT 7, 314), and as Tanner remarks, of the country-house weekend of *The Sacred Fount* (332).

Interpretation and Criticism

James's use of setting in the tale has received generally favorable notice. Edel and Wagenknecht praise the evocative picture of Boston in the August heat, which is indeed the "triumph of robust and vivid concision" James aimed for in his notebook (CT 7, 9; Wagenknecht 1984, 55; CN 45). Putt, in turn, praises the atmospheric description of shipboard life (277).

As Gargano observes, by the time of the second notebook entry James had made his narrator the center of his tale, so that it is no longer "an account of a sensational suicide" but "a documentation of sensations" (49). Indeed, a contemporary critic for *The Cambridge Review* found James's careful adherence to the limited point of view the main strength of the story (Sherbo 52).

Edel speaks of the tale as a "perfect" illustration of James's "'indirect method'" (CT 7, 9). Labrie appropriately chooses the narrator to illustrate the significance to James's characters of such subtle enjoyments as being conscious of their own consciousness while observing others. Labrie also distinguishes between consciousness and knowledge, remarking that the narrator is very conscious of Jasper and Grace but really knows little about them (524–25).

In his own words, the narrator is "an inveterate, almost a professional observer"; in Mrs. Nettlepoint's he is "cold-blooded" (CT 7, 305, 308). As Gargano states, once James chose a first-person narrator he risked making him appear parasitical. In Gage's argument James then added the far more virulent Mrs. Peck and removed the threat of the narrator acting as an informer to the fiancé in order to soften the character somewhat (55). Nevertheless, Wagenknecht's view that the story is a "simple, straightforward narrative" and Beach's view of the narrator as a simple "outside observer" have come to be the minority opinion (1984, 54; Beach 69). Sharp places him among the "more closely involved" Jamesian observers (xxii).

Putt takes a middle road, judging the narrator's role "ambiguous" and calling him a "benevolent busybody" (278). Tanner is his greatest defender, comparing his role to that of an artist. In his view, the narrator makes order out of disorder, and provides a final "benediction," the "sympathetic generosity of appreciation," on a woman he could not save. Taking Mrs. Peck as a foil, he distinguishes the narrator's insightful observation from her murderous attention (331–33). The narrator himself draws the comparison, saying he "had not looked at them so continuously and hungrily as Mrs Peck," or as he puts it even more strongly in the New York Edition, "I had taken really no such ferocious, or at least, competent, note . . ." (Gooder 296). Nevertheless, Samuels disagrees with Tanner, contending that the narrator's judgment is severely compromised, partly because James was unwilling to face head-on the evils of an upper-class world he had invested himself in emotionally (25, 39; also Gage 141). Gage also blames the narrator for "luxuriating" in his observations and for allowing his behavior to be influenced by jealousy of Jasper, adding that interfering with Grace's romance was far crueller than letting it take its natural course (142, 146, 151). Gargano keeps the metaphor of the artist, but not the nobility Tanner ascribes to it, emphasizing their shared vulnerability to being surprised by the characters they observe, and calling the narrator a "mixture of the ridiculous, the officious, and the clairvoyant" (50, 56). James himself made the narrator a less voluntary observer in the New York Edition, changing his boast about his observing that "It puts it in my power, in any situation, to *see* things" to the more passive "It makes me, in any situation, just inordinately and submissively *see* things" (Gooder 296).

Shine puts the blame elsewhere, viewing the tale as one of "parental laxity" both in Grace's mother's promotion of her marriage and in Mrs. Peck's preference of gossip over the care of her badly behaved children, whom Shine sees as representing "the dreary, uncivilized existence" Grace wishes to flee (53). As Gargano indicates, the introduction of class differences to the tale's "germ" provides more opportunites for indifference and misunderstanding (53). Certainly, it seems that Jasper's revelation to Grace that her new home in the Batignolles will simply be the Parisian equivalent of Merrimac Avenue plays a part in her increasing dissatisfaction (CT 7, 320). Jasper is the tale's natural villain. Wagenknecht points to him as one of James's least forgivable characters and Barzun classes him with James's "shaded" and "shady" villains from melodrama (Wagenknecht 1948, 131; Barzun 514). The narrator too, Gargano writes, comes to recognize that Jasper's "predatoriness" not Grace's behavior is the real root of the scandal (62). While James in his notebook pictured him "overcloud[ed] . . . forever more" (CN 46), in the tale Jasper is out of sight in his cabin at the end.

Jones distributes the guilt among all three of Grace's watchers: Mrs. Nettlepoint for abdicating her responsibility as chaperon, Jasper for failing to consider Grace's position, and the narrator for irresponsibly undertaking more than he can carry out in his belated efforts to help Grace (113). As Gooder puts it, this tale of "collective responsibility" analyzes "how a group works" as over the course of the voyage the passengers become either actors or spectators (xxvi–viii).

Ezra Pound disqualified the tale for greatness largely because "the sense of the finale intrudes all along," because there seemed no other ending possible (29). Wagenknecht argues that if Grace had not encountered Jasper, she might have gone on to a reasonably satisfactory marriage (1984, 56). But as Gargano correctly observes, the prospect is "hateful" to her (26). Still, from the very beginning critics have noted that the conclusion, which Pound saw looming over the story from the start, fails to solve its mysteries (Sherbo 51–52). Gargano emphasizes James's symbolic use of darkness, particularly the veil in which Grace hides her face (57–64; also Samuels 30; Jones 113). As Gage points out, the form of narration similarly keeps us from seeing inside the "veil" of her thoughts (140, 145). We are left only with speculation. Jones pictures Grace, like Daisy, a "victim of her openness in a closed world" (113). Gargano pictures her "foolishly or not" having "a brief splendor, a heightened escape into love" before her "escape into death" (63). Less high-flown, Andreas speculates that she could have gone through with her marriage, if only the shipboard gossips had let her have her "little romance" in peace (27–28). Perhaps most appropriate are Allen's comments on Grace's powerlessness given her unmarried status and low social position (121). James himself, in the notebook, indicated that her poverty compels her to go to a marriage she no longer wants, and judged her death, her desire to "escape," "more touching" if she was only engaged, not married (CN 44). Her brief escape seems an unsatisfactory compensation, however, especially as Grace—in the glimpses one has of her—displays an honesty and integrity none of the other characters possesses. In the end she treats herself as the others have treated her, as disposable. The commentary her death provides on the society she lives in points as much to the poverty of its imagination as the bleakness of her own.

Works Cited

Primary Works

James, Henry. 1888. "The Patagonia." *The English Illustrated Magazine* 5 (August–September): 707–18, 769–83.

———. 1889. "The Patagonia." *A London Life*. London and New York: Macmillan.

———. 1908. "The Patagonia." *The Novels and Tales of Henry James*. New York Edition. Vol. 18, 169–254. New York: Scribner's.

Secondary Works

Allen, Elizabeth. 1984. *A Woman's Place in the Novels of Henry James*. New York: St. Martin's.

Andreas, Osborn. 1948. *Henry James and the Expanding Horizon: A Study of the Meaning and Basic Themes of James's Fiction*. Seattle: University of Washington Press.

Barzun, Jacques. 1943. "Henry James, Melodramatist." *Kenyon Review* 5 (August): 508–21. Also reprinted in *The Question of Henry James*, ed. F. W. Dupee, 254–66. New York: Henry Holt, 1945.

Beach, Joseph Warren. [1918] 1954. *The Method of Henry James*. Philadelphia: Albert Saifer.

Dietrichson, Jan W. 1969. *The Image of Money in the American Novel of the Gilded Age*. Oslo: Universitetsforlaget; New York: Humanities.

Edgar, Pelham. [1927] 1964. *Henry James, Man and Author*. New York: Russell & Russell.

Gage, Richard P. 1988. *Order and Design: Henry James' Titled Story Sequences*. New York: Peter Lang.

Gargano, James W. 1984. "'The Patagonia': Henry James at Work." *Arizona Quarterly* 40, no. 1 (Spring): 49–65.

Gooder, Jean, ed. 1985. *Daisy Miller and Other Stories*. Oxford: Oxford University Press.

Jones, Granville H. 1975. *Henry James's Psychology of Experience: Innocence, Responsibility, and Renunciation in the Fiction of Henry James*. The Hague: Mouton.

Labrie, Ross. 1968. "Henry James' Idea of Consciousness." *American Literature* 39:517–29.

McElderry, Bruce R., Jr. 1965. *Henry James*. New York: Twayne.

Pound, Ezra. 1918. "A Shake Down." *The Little Review* 5 (August): 9–39.

Putt, S. Gorley. 1966. *Henry James: A Reader's Guide*. Ithaca, NY: Cornell University Press.

Samuels, Charles Thomas. 1971. *The Ambiguity of Henry James*. Urbana: University of Illinois Press.

Sharp, Sister M. Corona. 1963. *The Confidante in Henry James: Evolution and Moral Value of a Fictive Character*. Notre Dame, IN: Notre Dame University Press.

Sherbo, Arthur. 1990. "Jamesian Gleanings." *Henry James Review* 11: 42–57.

Shine, Muriel G. 1969. *The Fictional Children of Henry James*. Chapel Hill: University of North Carolina Press.

Tanner, Tony. 1965. *The Reign of Wonder: Naivety and Reality in American Literature*. Cambridge: Cambridge University Press.

Wagenknecht, Edward. 1984. *The Tales of Henry James*. New York: Frederick Ungar.

———. 1948. "Our Contemporary Henry James." *College English* 10 (December): 123–32.

Wright, Walter F. 1962. *The Madness of Art: A Study of Henry James*. Lincoln: University of Nebraska Press.

The Path of Duty

Publication History

"The Path of Duty" appeared first in the December 1884 issue of *The English Illustrated Magazine*. James included it the year after that in the collection *The Author of Beltraffio*, and the year after that in his *Stories Revived*. Percy Lubbock was the next to publish the story in his edition of James's fiction in the 1920s.

Circumstances of Composition, Sources, and Influences

On January 2, 1884, James recorded, among others, the names Vandeleur and Ambrose in his notebook. Later in the month he recorded a "situation" he had heard of at Mrs. Tennant's. A young Lord Stafford had been hopelessly in love with the married Lady Grosvenor. No sooner had Stafford engaged himself at last to marry elsewhere than the inconvenient Lord died. What was the young man to do? In James's mind there was little doubt: "The question, as a matter of ethics, seems to me to have but one answer; if he had offered marriage . . . by that offer he should abide." But he also recognized "several different turns" the situation might lend itself to. He rejects one possibility—the fiancée's acceptance out of ambition of an unfaithful husband—considering it more the province of the French naturalists, a reaction Geismar criticizes as failing to take full advantage of the freedom James claimed for literature (60). In the end James settles on an approach close to the one in the tale, although with a man as narrrator (CN 23–24).

James earlier had praised in Turgenev's *A Nest of Noblemen* a less ironic approach to a similar predicament. There, the heroine Liza discovers that the man she loves is still married. However, "Her love . . . is a passion in its essence half-renunciation. The first use she makes of the influence with him which her own love gives her is to try to reconcile him with his wife." She does not stay about to do so, as does Lady Vandeleur, but enters a convent (*Criticism* 2, 982).

The London James portrays here seems a newly decadent, ugly one, a transformation Kimmey traces to James's disillusionment brought on by the Dilke and Campbell divorce scandals. The latter brought James to speak of upper-class London as "like the heavy, congested and depraved world upon which the barbarians came down" (37, 41; *Letters* 3, 146). Twenty years later he wrote in regard to the translation of *The Siege of London* of 1882 that Mrs. Dolphin's remark, "It's like the decadence of the Roman Empire," is meant only to "caractériser la personne qui parle," that it is "*in* character la sorte de chose qu'elle est assez niaisement sujette à dire et que neuf Amèricaines sur dix, jugeant la société européene toujours à l'aide de leurs *cheap* souvenirs littéraires, trouveraient d'un bon effet. C'est enfin, non pas une parole d'auteur, mais de personnage, et naturelle au personnage" (*Letters to Benson* 105–6). But he uses such a comparison again, as Gale observes, seemingly sincerely in the later "The Two Faces" (154). It is not clear then which view one should take of the American narrator's comparison of Joscelind in London society to "a Christian maiden in the Roman arena" (CT 6, 176).

Relation to Other Works

Kimmey marks the transition from the "simple" view of England in such early works as "A Passionate Pilgrim" and *An International Episode* and later works with their criticism of the upper class, including "The Path of Duty," *Lady Barbarina*, *The Siege of London*, and especially *A London Life*. In the latter he locates a similar situation, with an American woman interfering with someone else's marriage and winding up isolated by her "overwrought sense of duty," although Kimmey absolves Laura of what he sees as the narrator's hypocrisy (38, 43–44).

A dozen years later James would present, in *The Spoils of Poynton*, another young woman in love with a man engaged to someone else. There, Fleda's response to Owen's asking her if he must marry a woman he hates is clear: "You mustn't break faith. Anything is better than that . . . The great thing is to keep faith. Where *is* a man if he doesn't? If he doesn't he may be so cruel" (140).

This tale is one of several that have been made part of the controversy over *The Turn of the Screw*. Wilson judges the narrator as unreliable as the governess in *The Turn of the Screw*, stating that her unreliablity is rendered quite clearly, while it is more problematic in the novella (146). Marks goes so far as to use the tale, with "Louisa Pallant," to prove that the technique of *The Turn of the Screw* is not exceptional, but typical in James (12). Bewley, on the other hand, considers the narrator here reliable in contrast to "The Liar" (82–84; also Jefferson 108).

Bewley links the tale with "The Liar" and *The Golden Bowl* on other grounds as well, arguing that Maggie is at first shut out like Joscelind, but goes on to an understanding of the deception around her that Joscelind never reaches, even as the "lie" that links Maggie and the Prince is a valid version of the spurious "duty" that links Tester and Lady Vandeleur (88, 95). Putt discerns "moral blackmail" in both tales (274). Looking at the links between novel and tale, Segal sees both pairs of lovers brought together by their own conception of nobility, and implying an international contrast of manners in both, states that James uses the first-person narrator in the tale to express his own "amused and ironic" view of their high-mindedness, while in the novel he lets the lovers express their own view of their behavior without narratorial interference (177–79). Levy compares the renunciation in Isabel's return to Osmond and Tester's marriage to Joscelind as examples of James's belief in "the beauty of self-immolation" (52–55). Bewley pictures Lyon in "The Liar" hoping for an "adulterous liason of the spirit" similar to that portrayed at the end here (87).

Interpretation and Criticism

Bewley speaks of the tale as "undistinguished" (83) and it is certainly neither one of James's best nor his worst tales. Nevertheless, while a contemporary reviewer for the *Independent* found the morality of the tale "scarcely debatable," seeming to object to James's discussing it, it has generated considerable debate. The reviewer for *Literary World* similarly objected to James's discussion of "sexual relations in their baser aspects" and indicated further that if discussed one would at least "prefer the free, bold treatment of a Fielding to the morbid vein of analysis that Mr. James has assumed." It is the narrator that supplies most of the morbid vein in this tale, and it is not surprisingly the narration that has generated most debate. The form is rather unusual even for James: the woman writes it out as for an American friend, despite her decision, recorded in the preface, never to show him what she has written (CT 6, 154). In the notebook entry James had envisioned the narrator casting "the light of the pathetic" on the unwitting wife (CN 24), and she states in the tale that her sympathy for Joscelind "colours" her rendering (CT 6, 163). In 1947, however, Matthiessen and Murdock found that the "lightness" of the narrator left the tale "rather cool," without any clear sympathy or disapproval for any of the characters (N 56). The next year Wilson proposed that the narrator, far from being cool, was herself in love with Tester and trying to marry him off to Joscelind in order to prevent any of the others from being happy while she was not. Wilson maintains that she hides her motives, even from herself, under the veil of "duty," with just enough sense that her behavior is questionable to decide not to share her written account with her friend (146–47).

Vaid acknowledges the "mixed motives" of the narrator but takes issue with Wilson, who he feels pulls the narrator too much to the center of the tale, maintaining that the tale is "completely unambiguous" in its irony (93–94). Rimmon classes the tale as a "twist" story that requires a complete reinterpretation on the grounds of the new information at the end, but as she does not specify either the information (none of which is entirely new) or the characters implicated, it is hard to tell if she means to point it against the narrator or against Tester and Lady Vandeleur (82). Kimmey also argues that the narrator is in love with Tester and sees her as "at odds with everything," including herself and London, although he does see some of her disapproval of London, however "squeamish," as James's own (41–42).

Looked at objectively, the narrator, who is already married—a fact infrequently noted by critics—appears relatively honest in her narration. She records her flirtation with Tester, although in a manner that does not seem to imply it is of great import. She also acknowledges his charm, but at the same time is capable of mocking him as a type, like an Englishman in a novel (CT 6, 158). Certainly she seems to have realized the mistake of her interference by the end. Recognizing Joscelind's misery, she asks, "Why couldn't I be content to be wrong? to renounce my influence . . . and let my young friend do as he liked?" (CT 6, 169). Jones, who notes the narrator's contribution to Joscelind's misery, still sees it as coming about from her desire to protect the young woman (122).

The case against the narrator is often bolstered by critics' sense that all her bother about a broken engagement is absurd. In evaluating her judgment, the mores of London are no help in the matter as the city simply "prefers the spectacle that is more entertaining," in this case Joscelind's jilting (CT 6, 176). James's attitude, however, is clear from the notebooks where he declares that the one "rigidly honourable" approach is to go through with the marriage (CN 24). If in the tale he seems to have switched the emphasis from "honourable" to its modifier, "rigidly," it is still clear from tales such as "The Wheel of Time" or "The Visits" that in James young ladies *do* die as a result of broken relationships. Thus the narrator's claim that Tester's jilting her "would just kill" Joscelind is neither absurd nor extreme (CT 6, 169). As Blackmur declares in speaking of "Sir Edmund Orme," "The act of jilting was for James, throughout his work, an act of moral abasement, for in performing it one damaged one's integrity" (52).

One may of course question James's general view of jilting. Geismar, for example, objects to James's stressing of duty "at the expense of both psychology and social reality" (60). In this case, however, James appears to be showing Tester as culpably selfish, not simply unconventional, in his behavior. He is selfish even in his choice of Joscelind. As the narrator remarks in a rather worldly way, most men marrying for convenience would not have chosen, as does Tester, a woman most would have chosen for love. To increase the sense of damage, James has the narrator present a touching picture of Tester's courting Joscelind in the Row (CT 6, 167).

While Wilson felt the irony against the narrator here "obvious," Bewley seems more accurate in arguing that the "irony" seen in the title and in the name of the country house "Doubleton" is directed not against the narrator, but against London society's confusion of appearance and reality—particularly Lady Vandeleur and Sir Tester's belief that they are virtuous because they so carefully keep up the appearance of virtue (Wilson 146). As Vaid indicates, this is where the emphasis of the story belongs. While there is some justice in Andreas's blaming Tester's father for demanding that his son marry, it is Tester and Vandeleur who make the significant decisions in the tale, regardless of who advises them (41).

The narrator realizes from early on that Tester is most in love with his own virtue (CT 6, 166). What she does not know is where that will take him, that it would lead to what Putt calls a "refined sadism" (272). As Wagenknecht observes, Tester and Vandeleur at the end are not only still in love with each other, but also "more dangerously, with their own nobility" (198–99). Edel categorizes the tale as "a study in the psychology of self-deception," and Tester's self-deception, according to Stein, is reinforced by the shield marriage offers him (CT 6, 11; Stein 115). Tester and Vandeleur's self-deception is one they take pleasure in constantly reinforcing.

James gives some powerful words to the commonsensical opposition to such behavior. The narrator worriedly thinks of writing Tester before his marriage the following warning: "There is, after all, perhaps, something worse than your jilting Miss Bernardstone; and that is the danger that your rupture with Lady Vandeleur may become more of a bond than your marrying her would have been. For heaven's sake, let your sacrifice *be* a sacrifice; keep it in its proper place!" (CT 6, 192). This seems to put the rights and wrongs of the situation in a clear moral hierarchy. It also implies that Tester and Vandeleur's behavior does not qualify as proper Jamesian resignation, although Levy argues unapprovingly that James wished his readers to take it as morally valuable (53–55). Nor is there any indication afterward that their relationship has cooled, as Kimmey maintains (41).

The ending description of the two who have "soared into the blue, and . . . wear in their faces the glory of those altitudes" cries out for an ironic reading (CT 6, 194). As Walter Wright says after quoting the line, "The story is comic, of course; but, then, hypocrisy *is* comic" (101). Bewley moves beyond the issue of irony to find a danger to the writer of himself becoming "detached" from human values, the actuality of virtue or cruelty, by his recognition of the way such values reveal "deeper truth" when reversed (84). But on the reverse side of the comic hypocrisy, is another final description, this time of the drooping Joscelind "absolutely white with uneasiness," which shows an awareness of human values (CT 6, 193). Although Levy argues that James intended otherwise, James's description of the wife who has born two children to a man who prefers the platonic companionship of an ever-present consort seems a clear indictment of him. Tester and Vandeleur's nobility has made Joscelind as much a victim and an outsider as the conscious cruelty of another cast-off lover will the bewildered wife in "The Two Faces." Wagenknecht may put the decisions of the conscious three in proper perspective by referring to it as "a nice little Jamesian problem of conscience" (196). But the unenlightened suffering of Joscelind provides the heart of the tale.

Works Cited

Primary Works
James, Henry. 1884. "The Path of Duty." *The English Illustrated Magazine* 2 (December): 240–56.

———. 1884. "The Path of Duty." *The Author of Beltraffio*. Boston: James R. Osgood, 261–317.

———. 1885. "The Path of Duty." *Stories Revived*. Vol. 1. London: Macmillan.

———. 1921–23. "The Path of Duty." *The Novels and Stories of Henry James*. Vol. 25. Ed. Percy Lubbock. London: Macmillan.

———. 1969. *Henry James: Letters to A. C. Benson and Auguste Monod*. Ed. E. F. Benson. New York: Haskell House.

———. [1897] 1963. *The Spoils of Poynton*. Harmondsworth: Penguin.

Secondary Works

Andreas, Osborn. 1948. *Henry James and the Expanding Horizon: A Study of the Meaning and Basic Themes of James's Fiction*. Seattle: University of Washington Press.

Anon. 1885. Review of *The Author of Beltraffio. Independent* 37 (9 April): 459.

Anon. 1885. Review of *The Author of Beltraffio. Literary World* 16 (21 March): 102.

Bewley, Marius. 1952. *The Complex Fate: Hawthorne, Henry James, and Some Other American Writers*. London: Chatto & Windus.

Blackmur, R. P. [1942] 1983. "*The Sacred Fount.*" In *Studies in Henry James*. Ed. Veronica A. Makowsky, 45–68. New York: New Directions. Reprinted from *Kenyon Review* 4: 328–52.

Gale, Robert L. [1954] 1964. *The Caught Image: Figurative Language in the Fiction of Henry James*. Chapel Hill: University of North Carolina Press.

Geismar, Maxwell. 1963. *Henry James and the Jacobites*. Boston: Houghton Mifflin.

Jefferson, D. W. 1964. *Henry James and the Modern Reader*. New York: St. Martin's.

Jones, Granville H. 1975. *Henry James's Psychology of Experience: Innocence, Responsibility, and Renunciation in the Fiction of Henry James*. The Hague: Mouton.

Kimmey, John. 1986. "James's London Tales of the 1880's." *Henry James Review* 8, no. 1 (Fall): 37–46.

Levy, Leo B. 1957. *Versions of Melodrama: A Study of the Fiction and Drama of Henry James, 1865–1897*. Berkeley: University of California Press.

Marks, Robert. 1960. *James's Later Novels: An Interpretation*. New York: William-Frederick.

Putt, S. Gorley. 1966. *Henry James: A Reader's Guide*. Ithaca, NY: Cornell University Press.

Rimmon, Shlomith. 1977. *The Concept of Ambiguity: The Example of Henry James*. Chicago: University of Chicago Press.

Segal, Ora. 1969. *The Lucid Reflector: The Observer in Henry James' Fiction*. New Haven: Yale University Press.

Stein, Allen F. 1984. *After the Vows Were Spoken: Marriage in American Literary Realism*. Columbus: Ohio State University Press.

Vaid, Krishna B. 1964. *Technique in the Tales of Henry James*. Cambridge, MA: Harvard University Press.

Wagenknecht, Edward. 1984. *The Tales of Henry James*. New York: Frederick Ungar.

Wilson, Edmund. 1960. "The Ambiguity of Henry James." In *A Casebook on Henry James's "The Turn of the Screw."* Ed. Gerald Willen, 115–53. New York: Thomas Y. Crowell.

Wright, Walter F. 1962. *The Madness of Art: A Study of Henry James*. Lincoln: University of Nebraska Press.

The Pension Beaurepas

Publication History

"The Pension Beaurepas" debuted in the July 1879 issue of the *Atlantic Monthly*. James reprinted it first in the 1881 edition of *Washington Square*, and two years later both in *The Siege of London* and in the Collective Edition. He also included it in the New York Edition.

Aziz traces the revision of the tale from the "minor corrections" in the 1881 version to the numerous changes for the New York Edition that, he argues, were made to sharpen the tale's satire. The sleepy pension Beaurepas, for example, becomes the Chamousette or "louse" (268–71).

Circumstances of Composition, Sources, and Influences

The narrator comes to the pension in the footsteps of Balzac and Stendhal. Delbaere-Garant notes how James and his narrator take the example of Stendhal, who wrote his sister in 1874, "I have a passionate desire to know human nature, and a great mind to live in a boarding-house, where people cannot conceal their real characters" (136; also Mordell 371). Balzac's *Le Père Goriot* also shows the real characters of people as exhibited in a boarding-house, and Kraft finds James following Balzac's work here in the focus on class and money (104). Tintner links all three authors, recalling that as Balzac wrote a preface for *La Chartreuse de Parme*, James quotes Stendhal as a preface for his reworking of Balzac. Tintner demonstrates how James makes Balzac's Parisian pension Swiss and places one American, Mr. Ruck, in the title role of the businessman bled dry by his family, and another, the narrator, in the role of Rastignac (1987, 248, 251–56). Wagenknecht points out that James need not have gone abroad for an example of the boardinghouse format, as he would have found it also at home in Oliver Wendell Holmes's *The Autocrat of the Breakfast Table* (19).

James actually wrote the tale in the middle ground of England (*Life* 2, 310). He drew, however, as Putt records, on his own observations of Geneva (1966, 123), and he regrets in the New York Edition preface not having made more use of the "prodigiously archaic and incredibly quaint" pension, where "the precious treasure of a sense that absolutely primitive pre-revolutionary 'Europe' had never really been swept out of its cupboards, shaken out of its curtains, thumped out of its mattresses" (*Criticism* 2, 1224). Other critics, including Kelley and Aziz, have seen James drawing on his own personality as well in shaping the narrator (Kelley 273; Aziz 269). Walter Wright, for example, notes that the narrator is enamored of the "picturesque," just as the early James was (119). Donald Stone, however, finds the unnamed narrator a descendent of Hawthorne's Coverdale, whose "tragedy" also lay in his "detached vision" (197).

Offering a classical precedent for modern behavior, Tintner parallels the "sacred rites" of the Rucks' shopping to these in Euripides's *Bacchae* (1989, 132). Barzun speaks of Ruck as one of James's "Cinderella-fathers" (513).

The tale has also been discussed along with the work of Edith Wharton. Jefferson compares Sophy Ruck to Undine Spragg of *The Custom of the Country*, and Millgate extends the comparison to their families, seeing the Rucks and the Spraggs both illustrating the divorce between the interests of American men and women (Jefferson 1964, 95; Millgate 59).

Relation to Other Works

"The Pension Beaurepas" is the first of three works that share characters and concerns, the others being "A Bundle of Letters" of the same year and "The Point of View" of 1882. They are generally seen as studies in international manners (e.g., Jefferson 1964, 66; Delbaere-Garant 287). Indeed, their focus is so much on manners that they have been frequently discounted as stories, "A Bundle of Letters" and "The Point of View" consisting solely of letters, while Aziz has spoken of this tale as consisting primarily of "conversations" (270). Their publisher, Frederick Macmillan, spoke of the first two as "charming sketches" likely to be popular with the public (*Correspondence* 59). Tanner refers to all three as mere "vehicles" for James's contrast of America and Europe, while Edgar considers them nevertheless enlivened by their capturing of different characters, and Jefferson notes the appropriateness of placing Americans in a cosmopolitan setting as a way of analyzing their characters (Edgar 29; Jefferson [1960] 1971, 18–19). Kelley focuses the attention to character on the American girls in the stories, as James attempted an "all round view" of the type, including the incompletely Europeanized Aurora, the intrepid Miranda, and the spoiled Miss Ruck and Miss Ray (273–75). Assigning a more pronounced slant to their portraits, Wright sees James analyzing the center stage position occupied by women and children in American society (72–73). Dupee looks instead at the juxtaposition of American girl and European setting, as each girl confronts "the world of fact" as embodied in Europe, a process seen also in "The Patagonia" and *The Reverberator* (96).

The three tales were all included in volume 14 of the New York Edition as companion pieces to three longer international tales, *Lady Barbarina*, *The Siege of London*, and *An International Episode*, and critics have also placed them in the broader context of James's international works. Rebecca West argues that the works of the period immediately following *Daisy Miller* and including "The Pension Beaurepas," along with "Pandora," *The Siege of London*, *Lady Barbarina*, and *The Reverberator*, are all harmed by the transition James was undergoing when he "had lost America and had not yet found Europe" (48–50). Similarly, while Stone considers this tale "almost as good" as *Daisy Miller* (197), Jones judges all three "inconsequential," fragmented treatments of the same attitudes already treated successfully in *Daisy Miller*, which was held together by the use of innocence as an "ordering principle" (Stone 197; Jones 59–60). Wegelin, however, places *Daisy Miller* with the three tales, *An International Episode*, and even *The Portrait of a Lady* as part of James's early "collection of social data" for his treatment of the international theme (59). While Levy sees James in "The Pension Beaurepas" and in *An International Episode* as moving from the portrayal in *The American* of the superiority of American values over European to a more "ironic" comparison of the two, Delbaere-Garant extends the early, American stage even further, judging all the tales between *The American* and *The Reverberator* more significant for their depiction of Americans than Europeans—arguing, for example, that the French men are "exaggeratedly light" and stereotypical in their preoccupation with women (Levy 28; Delbaere-Garant 290–91).

Citing James's preface to *The Reverberator*, Millgate points out that in his early works James pictured his businessmen such as Mr. Dosson, Mr. Westgate of *An International Episode*, and Mr. Ruck not at their work, which he knew little of, but in their dealings with women. He comments on the early appearance here of the "gulf" between American men and women that James would remark on so forcibly in an 1892 notebook entry, and traces it as well in the careers of Christopher Newman and Adam Verver. Mr. Ruck, however, Millgate contends, is more along the lines of Jim Pocock of *The Ambassadors*, an "obscure rather than . . . epic" businessman (5–8, 16–17). As such, Delbaere-Garant considers him a more successful picture of the American businessman than the "composite" Newman (282). Ward observes that he is less "morally deranged" than such later businessmen as Pocock and Waymarsh (114). In comparing the tale to *The Reverberator*, Leyburn argues that its story of the wealthy Dossons is dependent on the European setting, as is that of the impecunious Churches here, but that the Rucks could have played out their tragedy even in America (56–57). Tintner, meanwhile, follows the Rucks back to America to place them at the center of the series, citing Aurora's mention of them in the last letter of the last tale, "The Point of View," as having disappeared from New York in what Aurora calls "the strange way in which people over here seem to vanish from the world" (1987, 257).

The Rucks *filles* have also drawn comment in themselves. Leyburn sees them as a living example of Mrs. Westgate's famous dictum that "An American woman who respects herself . . . must buy something every day of her life" (54). Accordingly, as Wegelin notes, like the Rays of "A Bundle of Letters," they approach Europe solely as a shopping destination. It is not surprising, then, that he finds Sophy—like Selina Wing of *A London Life*—one of the few exceptions to James's "intelligent responsible" American girl, or that Kelley finds both Sophy and Viola Ray resembling Daisy Miller, but without her charm (Wegelin 60, 64; Kelley 275). Nevertheless, Greene characterizes the satire here and in *Daisy Miller* as "so gentle, even while so witty, that it has the quality of nostalgia," a sense of innocence even in the greed (28).

The daughter who studies instead of shopping, Aurora, suffers from a confusion of nationalities similar to that of Gaston Probert in *The Reverberator*, although she encounters more difficulties than he did in turning to romance for rescue. As Putt observes, Aurora wishes to be the kind of "simple" American girl that Daisy was, and in failing to be, lives while Daisy died (1966, 124). Still, Quentin Anderson includes her, "the lost little American," with the other children in James sacrificed to their parents' "distorted" interpretations of life, such as Dolcino Ambient and Pansy Osmond, and the majority of the *"jeunes filles"* (34). Her sacrificing mother, the affectedly Europeanized Mrs. Church, has been connected by Wegelin to the Europeanized Americans who scorned Daisy Miller, and by Delbaere-Garant to Louis Leverett of "A Bundle of Letters" and "The Point of View" (Wegelin 61; Delbaere-Garant 290–91).

The narrator of "At Isella" had been fascinated to find himself witness to a very Italian, illicit elopement. The narrator here, in a more tepid Switzerland, facing an insufficiently Europeanized heroine, is offered the chance to participate actively in one, but cannot quite bring himself to do so. The ironic stance he takes instead has led Stone to link him with Robert Acton of *The Europeans* and Rowland Mallet (199).

As a novella centered on a place of confined action, Irwin connects the tale with *In the Cage* and "The Birthplace" (13).

Interpretation and Criticism

Surrounded by a contrast between American and European, the tale focuses on its contrast between American and American, although admittedly one between Americans Euopeanized and stubbornly domestic, no matter how much foreign travel. The story is, as critics have noted, full of types, or as a contemporary reviewer put it, "parodies with an element of truth" (*Literary World*). Still the types have provoked a great deal of comment and some disagreement. The most obvious stereotypes, the tale's two genuine Europeans, Madame Beaurepas and M. Pigeonneau, have received comparatively little attention. As Kraft writes, they may appear more wise in their lack of illusions, but they also miss out on most of the interest in life, such as the narrator finds in the fortunes of the Rucks and the Churches (108). It is as a way of setting off the interest of their fortunes that, as McElderry notes, James uses his European setting (76). Kraft points out how James actually uses two settings—the closed garden and the open terrace—to illustrate the differences between the two American families, the Europeanized Churches and the American Rucks, although, as he notes, even Mr. Ruck won't look at the still more open mountains (108). As Wegelin reads the story, it portrays two kinds of provincialism, the Rucks' total ignorance of culture in their concentration on buying and Mrs. Church's cultured snobbery (60–61).

A provincial himself, Mr. Ruck is the victim of the first type of provincialism, as exhibited by his wife and daughter. Ward notes how he is ironically "broken down" first by too much money and then by not enough (31). As Jefferson observes, however, even before his bankruptcy Ruck is incapable of enjoying anything other than business (1964, 76–77). James, feeling himself incapable of treating Ruck in his natural habitat in business "down-town," had to take him, as Tilton puts it, "out of his natural habitat," and it is this displacement that seems to prompt James's sympathy for his "awkward and unhappy" businessman (viii–ix). His displacement puts him in the company of women, and while Kraft writes that it is his money that "creates their reality," they appear to have little interest in his reality. According to Kraft, the sympathy James gives Ruck is not typical of his attitude to men of business, nor is the dignity Ruck displays (107). In the view of McElderry such character in the absence of culture was a "typical" combination for James (76).

According to Fowler, however, Ruck has contributed to the difficulty of his position through his ignorance of everything apart from business. In the absence of any other bond, Fowler contends, the main tie between male and female in the Ruck family is economic. Sophy Ruck carries over this purely monetary interest from her treatment of her father to her consideration of potential suitors (43–45). Jefferson, who points to the effectiveness of their idiomatic speech in portraying their vulgar assurance, notes the extremely rough-hewn way in which Sophy and her mother keep up the claim of American women to being cultural custodians in their spending and quick opinions (1964, 77–78). In Barzun's view James, while he does not condemn the women's coldness outright, creates a sense of it in the reader by the story's "accumulation of trifles" that all speak against them (513). Aziz sees

James heightening the unattractive vulgarity of the Rucks in his revision for the New York Edition (273–74).

Without a father to abuse, the Churches provide a contrast with the Rucks mainly in their approach to economy and education. Dietrichson contrasts the spendthrift Ruck ladies with the thrifty Mrs. Church, noting that the behavior of each with money harms others (144). While her thrift no doubt stems from her need as the head of an all-female household to be the sole provider for her daughter, it also contributes to a restricted vision, compounded by a rather dubious pretense to European culture. In contrasting the two mothers and their daughters, Kraft judges both the informal lessons of Mrs. Ruck and Mrs. Church's carefully regulated ones as disasters. Due to them, Sophy becomes—like her mother—a thoughtless exploiter of her father, and Aurora becomes—like hers—a homeless "hybrid" of American and European. Kraft is one of the few to argue for a more sympathetic interpretation of Mrs. Church, maintaining that James respects Mrs. Church for her persistence through difficulties and her hope for a decent marriage for her daughter even if he quarrels with her "pretentious, materialistic vision," which is little better than the Rucks' (104–7). Aziz, however, sees James taking the character in a different direction in the last revision for the New York Edition, making her even colder and more absurd as she exposes her affectations (277–81).

Like her fellow victim Mr. Ruck, the more "ambiguous" Aurora escapes in large part James's satire, as Leyburn states, if not his analysis (52). Wegelin pictures James sympathizing even more with Aurora than with Mr. Ruck, both because of her youth and superior capacity and because the forces against her are more pernicious than the Rucks' vulgarity (60–61). In Wagenknecht's view, the other women are despicable, Aurora simply pitiable (20). She is attempting to mold herself to fit a definition of the American girl that Veeder argues James himself did not wholeheartedly believe: that the American girl is an "intelligent, reasonable creature" (159). The narrator's admonition that an American girl "wouldn't reason out her conduct," as Aurora does, leaves her with the formula that "to do very simple things that are not at all simple—that is the American girl!" (CT 4, 369). But while Sophy Ruck provides her with a clear example of the unreasoning American girl, there is no model for her of a positive simplicity, no Isabel Archer or even a Daisy Miller here to illustrate what American womanhood can, ideally, be. Aurora is faced, instead, with what Rebecca West judged "extraordinarily cold-blooded and, to women of to-day, extremely unsavoury discussions of how a girl ought to behave if she wants to be married," discussions she found disturbing to the pathos of the tale (48). Views of Aurora's eventual fate vary, and the tale offers no clear picture of it. As Jefferson notes, Aurora's mother has "driven her to desire her own country" ([1960] 1971, 46), and it is in America in "The Point of View" that her tale continues if not concludes. Kraft does not consider "The Point of View" and so repeats Mme Beaurepas's prediction that Aurora will run off someday (104–7). Tilton, for her part, argues that one does not need the second story to realize that a girl of Aurora's training will be unable to marry (ix).

If the keynote of the tale is contrast, one that catches Aurora in the middle, the narrator is the one who presents that contrast to us. Like Beach before him, Putt finds him "inoffensive"—a "neutral recorder" with a proper appreciation for Europe that steers clear of the errors in perspective of both the Rucks and the Churches (Beach [1918] 1954, 68–69). "Tolerant" and "well-disposed" in McElderry's assessment, he has, Putt argues, the "superior wisdom" necessary to portray both sides, although he has no way to translate his sympathy into action (Putt 1966, 123–24; McElderry 76; also Kraft 104). Indeed, while the narrator considers being "a hero of romance," he cannot bring himself to become one (CT 4, 384). Consequently, Tintner objects to him as being "cold as a fish" (1987, 255). Stone is more sympathetic to his position. Noting that he is "momentarily tempted" to rescue Aurora, Stone finds his general attitude of spectatorship nevertheless both "necessary and poignant" given his character (197–98). Far from faulting his coldness, however, Leyburn finds him somewhat short of objective, arguing that his being "half in love" with Aurora complicates the picture of her, although not excessively. She questions, too, the directness of his appeal for pity for Mr. Ruck (51–55). Despite these qualifications, the narrator is certainly not unreliable in any way that jeopardizes our basic sense of the characters.

The narrator's distance from his tale also fits with James's evident desire to avoid definite conclusions. In McElderry's phrase, the tale is an "inconclusive juxtaposition" (76), and Kraft notes how the narrator contributes to the story's refusal to come down conclusively on the side of any one of the various perspectives (108). Beach includes the Rucks with the stereotypically vulgar Americans James was content to satirize gently (1921, 99). A contemporary reviewer for the *Atlantic* had noted in contrast the novelty of the Churches as "foreign Americans," calling them "individuals, but scarcely types" (707). Their distinctiveness, Putt asserts, causes James to transfer the main burden of satire from the familiar type of the innocent abroad with its "comparatively harmless" greed to Mrs. Church's affectations of culture, which he judges equally American (1966, 124; 1985, 8–9; also Aziz 281). Still, it is clear that in the contest between the Rucks and the Churches, James holds no brief for either.

The narrator's voice is also the source of the story's tone. The story has been especially praised for the way it combines humor, pathos, moral concerns, and social issues, particularly in the portrayal of the Rucks (e.g., Kraft 104; Stone 198). Early on, in praising both Mr. Ruck and Mrs. Church as new comic types, Howells remarked on how James subordinates his humor to more serious issues (115). Both Putt and Kraft comment on the tension between the tale's surface placidity and the "outraged compassion," the "desperation" beneath (Putt 1966, 123; Kraft 104). As Ward observes, the story of Ruck the comic businessman becomes tragic in the end. The mixed effect stems from the linking Ward sees in James between vulgarity and morality, the way those who have no perceptiveness in matters of culture—a designation that includes Mrs. Church—tend to have no awareness of the needs of others (28–29). Similarly, in Leyburn's view, the Rucks remain comic, but demonstrate how James saw such light characters as producing tragedy for characters of greater value, despite—or perhaps because of—their stunning lack of awareness (54–55). James himself referred to the work as a "mere pretext" in writing to Howells (*Letters* 2, 243). However, as is frequent in James, the victims give weight to the work, preventing it from being simply what Geismar saw it as, "an entertaining satire of western American wealth" (50), and making it a more complex, if no less entertaining, consideration of some of the types of human character and their contexts.

Works Cited

Primary Works

James, Henry. 1879. "The Pension Beaurepas." *Atlantic Monthly* 43 (April): 388–92.

———. 1881. "The Pension Beaurepas." *Washington Square*. London: Macmillan.

———. 1883. "The Pension Beaurepas." Collective Edition. Vol. 12. London: Macmillan.

———. 1883. "The Pension Beaurepas." *The Siege of London*. Boston: James R. Osgood.

———. 1908. "The Pension Beaurepas." *The Novels and Tales of Henry James*. New York Edition. Vol. 14, 391–476. New York: Scribner's.

———. 1993. *The Correspondence of Henry James and the House of Macmillan, 1877–1914*. Ed. Rayburn S. Moore. Baton Rouge: Louisiana State University Press.

Secondary Works

Anderson, Quentin. 1957. *The American Henry James*. New Brunswick, NJ: Rutgers University Press.

Anon. 1883. Review of *The Siege of London*. *The Atlantic* 51 (May): 706–7.

Anon. 1883. Review of *The Siege of London*. *The Literary World* 14 (24 March): 90.

Aziz, Maqbool. 1973. "Revisiting *The Pension Beaurepas*: The Tale and Its Texts." *Essays in Criticism* 23 (July): 268–82.

Barzun, Jacques. 1943. "James the Melodramatist." *Kenyon Review* 5 (August): 508–21. Also reprinted in *The Question of Henry James*, ed. F. W. Dupee, 254–66. New York: Henry Holt.

Beach, Joseph Warren. 1921. "Henry James." In *The Cambridge History of American Literature*. Vol. 3. Ed. William Peterfield Trent, et al., 96–108. New York: Putnam's.

———. [1918] 1954. *The Method of Henry James*. Philadelphia: Albert Saifer.

Delbaere-Garant, Jeanne. 1970. *Henry James: The Vision of France*. Paris: Société d'Editions Les Belles Lettres.

Dietrichson, Jan W. 1969. *The Image of Money in the American Novel of the Gilded Age*. Oslo: Universitetsforlaget; New York: Humanities.

Dupee, F. W. [1951] 1956. *Henry James*. Garden City, NY: Doubleday Anchor.

Edgar, Pelham. [1927] 1964. *Henry James, Man and Author*. New York: Russell & Russell.

Fowler, Virginia. 1984. *Henry James's American Girl. The Embroidery on the Canvas*. Madison: University of Wisconsin Press.

Geismar, Maxwell. 1963. *Henry James and the Jacobites*. Boston: Houghton Mifflin.

Greene, Graham. 1952. "Henry James: The Private Universe." In *The Lost Childhood and Other Essays*, 21–30. New York: Viking.

Howells, William Dean. [1882] 1961. "Henry James, Jr." As reprinted in *Discovery of a Genius: William Dean Howells and Henry James*, ed. Albert Mordell, 112–25. New York: Twayne. Reprinted from *Century* 3 (November): 25–29.

Irwin, Michael. "Henry James and the Vague *Nouvelle*." In *The Modern American Novella*. Ed. Robert A. Lee, 13–29. New York: St. Martin's.

Jefferson, D. W. 1964. *Henry James and the Modern Reader*. New York: St. Martin's.

———. [1960] 1971. *Henry James*. New York: Capricorn.

Jones, Granville H. 1975. *Henry James's Psychology of Experience: Innocence, Responsibility, and Renunciation in the Fiction of Henry James*. The Hague: Mouton.

Kelley, Cornelia Pulsifer. [1930] 1965. *The Early Development of Henry James*. Urbana: University of Illinois Press.

Kraft, James. 1969. *The Early Tales of Henry James*. Carbondale: Southern Illinois University Press.

Levy, Leo B. 1957. *Versions of Melodrama: A Study of the Fiction and Drama of Henry James, 1865–1897*. Berkeley: University of California Press.

Leyburn, Ellen Douglass. 1968. *Strange Alloy: The Relation of Comedy to Tragedy in the Fiction of Henry James*. Chapel Hill: University of North Carolina Press.

McElderry, Bruce R., Jr. 1965. *Henry James*. New York: Twayne.

Millgate, Michael. 1964. *American Social Fiction: James to Cozzens*. Edinburgh: Oliver and Boyd.

Mordell, Albert, ed. 1957. *Literary Reviews and Essays by Henry James*. New York: Grove.

Putt, S. Gorley, ed. 1985. *An International Episode and Other Stories*. Harmondsworth: Penguin.

————. 1966. *Henry James: A Reader's Guide*. Ithaca, NY: Cornell University Press.

Stone, Donald David. 1972. *Novelists in a Changing World: Meredith, James, and the Transformation of English Fiction in the 1880's*. Cambridge, MA: Harvard University Press.

Tanner, Tony. 1963. "James's Little Tarts." *The Spectator* 210 (4 January): 19.

Tilton, Eleanor, ed. *Henry James: "The Marriages" and Other Stories*. A Signet Classic. New York: New American Library.

Tintner, Adeline R. 1989. *The Pop World of Henry James: From Fairy Tales to Science Fiction*. Ann Arbor: UMI Research Press.

————. 1987. *The Book World of Henry James: Appropriating the Classics*. Ann Arbor: UMI Research Press. Revised from "Henry James's 'The Pension Beaurepas': 'A Translation into American Terms' of Balzac's *La Père Goriot*." *Revue de Littérature Comparée* 57, no. 3 (July–September 1983): 369–76.

Veeder, William. 1975. *Henry James: Lessons of the Master: Popular Fiction and Personal Style in the Nineteenth Century*. Chicago: University of Chicago Press.

Wagenknecht, Edward. 1984. *The Tales of Henry James*. New York: Frederick Ungar.

Ward, J. A. 1961. *The Imagination of Disaster: Evil in the Fiction of Henry James*. Lincoln: University of Nebraska Press.

Wegelin, Christof. 1958. *The Image of Europe in Henry James*. Dallas: Southern Methodist University Press.

West, Rebecca. [pseud]. 1916. *Henry James*. London: Nisbet.

Wright, Walter F. 1962. *The Madness of Art: A Study of Henry James*. Lincoln: University of Nebraska Press.

Foreign Language
Onishi, Akio. 1963. "Henry James: Trilogy of International Theme." *Bungaku Ronshu* (Kansai University) 12 (January): 1–45. [Japanese]

The Point of View

Publication History

"The Point of View" first appeared in the December 1882 issue of *Century* magazine, and that same year in a separate edition privately printed for copyright, James having learned his lesson from the earlier piracy of "A Bundle of Letters." The next year it was reprinted in both the collection *The Siege of London* and James's Collective Edition. It also appeared that year in the land of Lejaune in the prestigious *Revue des deux mondes*, translated by the French critic Th. Bentzon, along with an essay by her that discussed "The Pension Beaurepas" and "A Bundle of Letters" as well (Austin 82–83). Along with the two earlier stories using the same characters, the tale appeared in volume 14 of the New York Edition.

Circumstances of Composition, Sources, and Influences

The story's theme is generally traced to an abstractly terse notebook entry recorded on March 1880, "Description of a situation, or incident, in an alternation of letters, written from an aristocratic, and a democratic, point of view;—both enlightened and sincere" (N 15; CN 13). Two months before that James had entered the idea of an epistolary story on an unrelated theme, showing his renewed interest in the technique (CN 11).

The idea evidently lay fallow until his first trip to America for five years in 1881, a trip that included his first visit to the capital. As James recalled in his New York Edition preface, upon his return he "inevitably, on the spot, had impressions." "A Bundle of Letters" began then in the "faded iridescence of a far-away Washington spring," but James put the tale aside, preserving its "thread" until his return to Washington in 1882 inspired him to complete the piece. Looking back from a different century, he recalled how his room there had "exhaled for me, to pungency, the domestic spirit of the 'old South.'" In his recollection, he manages to preserve some of its most harmful stereotypes of "smiling, shuffling, procrastinating persons of colour," at the same time as he declares that their plight "anciently" was in his view "so badly the matter . . . that a deluge of blood and fire and tears had been needed to correct it." The house itself having been destroyed, he retains the story as a "magic ring" or "talisman," a "swinging, playing lantern, with a light that

717

brought out the past," in a passage whose affirmation of art in the face of the destruction of the physical Krupnick traces (*Criticism* 2, 1221–23; Krupnick 38–39).

The month before the story's appearance, James's friend William Dean Howells had published an essay in the *Century* praising him as part of a new school of literature far superior to that of Dickens and Thackeray. That James himself was not to be held innocent of his friend's claims is seen in the *Tribune*'s review of "The Point of View," which exclaimed that "even Thackeray had a finer art than this!" The *Literary World* lodged a similar complaint, writing that "the letters are all strangely alike, so to speak, in their handwriting," and asking, "Why . . . should anybody read Henry James?" Looking at the reviews, Monteiro perceives a shift in the general attitude toward James as a result of Howells's too enthusiastic praise in his essay and James's criticism of America in his tale, the start of a decline in James's popularity (1973, 71–75, 81). In discussing the relative failure of *The Bostonians* and *The Princess Casamassima*, Edel indicates that what the public wanted from James were more international tales such as "The Point of View" (1960, 26). At the time, however, as Monteiro demonstrates, they did not seem to want that either. The response at least lent some accuracy to James's boastful prediction to his father that the tale would "probably call down execration on my head" (*Life* 3, 50; also Macnaughton 4). Nevertheless, by 1883 the *Nation* could refer to it sedately, along with its predecessor "The Pension Beaurepas," as a "most amusing study of international life."

James's hosts in Washington were Henry Adams and his wife, Marion Clover Hooper Adams, who he wrote were "always at the centre of a distinguished circle" (Monteiro 1983, 4). Clover's acid wit, according to Edel, influenced James's views in the story (*Life* 3, 29, 49). Monteiro sees not only James's views but his tone as indebted to the Adams wit, distinguished by "piercing social observation and the mordant *bon mot*" (1983, 4). To her father, however, Clover would own up to only one of the witticisms, the reference to a British "Hares and Rabbits Bill and Deceased Wife's Sister" (Monteiro 1973, 74). Marcellus himself, however, according to Tilton, might be a portrait of Henry Adams (ix). David Stone proposes a different Henry, James's father, as the source for Marcellus's faith in democracy (235).

The supersensitive Bostonian Leverett has generally been allied with James himself, both Edel and Josephson citing Leverett's discomfort in his hotel to picture James's own (*Life* 3, 19–20; Josephson 115). Most, however, qualify the comparison, Tilton calling it a "satiric self-portrait" (ix). Similarly, Buitenhuis detects in Leverett some of James's own "exaggerated emotions" on returning to America, exaggerated even further for a comic effect (121). Watson, however, dismisses altogether the idea that Leverett is James, seeing the comedy coming from James's "inversion" of the "Boston-Harvard parochialism and pretensions" he so disliked and with which he did not identify (176).

The robust Marcellus, or "crowing Cockerel" as Watson calls him, stems from a different strand of Brahminism, according to Watson, who sees in him Emerson and Thoreau's brand of patriotism with a particular parallel to Thoreau's promise to "brag as lustily as Chanticleer in the morning" (183 n.6). Monteiro leaves New England to locate in Marcellus a "residue of the frontier tradition" present also in Cooper's Natty Bumppo, although here, he argues, the frontier has switched from that between man and nature to that between the cultures of old and new world (1983, 5).

Aurora refers to Lejaune as "the first French writer of distinction who has been to America since De Tocqueville" (CT 4, 474). Accordingly, Lynn puts the tale as a "comic counterpart" to Tocqueville's *Democracy in America* (390–91). Basil Ransom, Tintner notes, is also a reader of Tocqueville, whose work, she states, underlay *An International Episode* as well (168). Lejaune notices mainly what America lacks in litanies of "no's" that, Wegelin argues, "travesty" James's own similar passage in his 1879 biography of Hawthorne, which in turn came from a notebook entry (179 n.17). Delbaere-Garant finds Lejaune's criticism that in America "there is nothing to appreciate" echoing James's own view, but sees him leaving out James's sense that the young venturing Americans were "worth saving" (292). In his *Hawthorne*, James remarked that what was left to the American was "his secret, his joke, as one may say," his "consolation" being "that 'American humour' of which of late years we have heard so much" (*Criticism* 2, 352). Lejaune's name indicates his "jaundiced" attitude, and so, as Watson notes, he leaves out the joke (177–78). Austin also distinguishes James from Lejaune in his possession of the "saving grace of the American humorist, the ability to make fun of himself." At the same time, according to Austin, James, because he shares Lejaune's dislike of American newspapers, mocks through him not only French stereotypes but American ones (4–5). Monteiro contends that James's agreement with Lejaune on the newspapers is a limited one, pointing, for example, to James's willingness to publish his tales in them. He notes another congruity in taste, however, in Lejaune's scorn for the way a visitor can walk into the Capitol "as you would into a railway station" (1983, 6–8). The same complaint about the openness of public buildings persisted, Holder notes, appearing again in the late *The American Scene* (30).

Lejaune singles out one American novelist as having "pretensions to literature," whose subjects are the "chase for the husband" and "rich Americans in our corrupt old Europe," the former of which Stone observes is acted out by Aurora in the tale (235). The novelist is clearly James himself, and Lejaune's estimate of his work as *proprement écrit* but "terribly pale" reflects, according to Swan, the opinion of James's peers Flaubert and Turgenev, and is also, according to Wegelin, representative of his reviews at the time (CT 4, 506; Swan 6; Wegelin 179 n.17).

Watson pictures Aurora and her mother heading west "like an incongruous pair of Huck Finns lighting out for the territories" (181).

Relation to Other Works

James's two trips in 1881 and 1882 gave rise to at least three other American tales: "The Impressions of a Cousin," "New England Winter," and "Pandora." Among James's other Americans returning home, there is a resemblance not only between the roles of Catherine of "The Impressions of a Cousin" and Harriet Sturdy, as Buitenhuis has noticed, but between their no-nonsense attitudes (127). One of Miss Sturdy's objections is to the overindulgence of American children, and Jefferson points to similar criticism in "A New England Winter" and in James's essay on Saratoga (69–71). Edel cites Daisy Miller's young brother Randolph as a good example of such spoiling, to which James also objected (*Life* 2, 307). Monteiro, meanwhile, finds Aurora partial kin to Daisy herself (1983, 5).

Aurora's frustrating experience in being accepted in America is, according to Lynn, a strong theme in James's fiction of the time, present also, for example, in *The Siege of London* and *Lady Barbarina*. Lynn remarks also that while James left Aurora still struggling in the States, he himself left America for twenty years after finishing the tale (391–92). Significantly, the two characters James imported into his tale from previous tales of Americans abroad are the two Europeanized Americans whose frustrating experiences might resemble his own.

Many connections have been noted with *The Bostonians*, James's next novel. Veeder judges the criticism of American society in both "strongly grounded" in their time, Jacobson citing particularly the consideration of the position of women (Veeder 147; Jacobson 21). Long also connects the novel with Leverett's satire of Boston, where his old rooms are now inhabited by "a mesmeric healer" (126). Miss Sturdy, Monteiro argues, is a forerunner of Dr. Prance (1983, 4). Lejaune, as one of James's conservative characters, is linked by Buitenhuis and Long with Ransom, and by Buitenhuis with Sir Rufus of "The Modern Warning" and Count Vogelstein in "Pandora" as well (142). Long includes Leverett in the same list of "antidemocratic" characters in James (126).

Both works, with their tolerance of opposing points of view, are in Stone's view comic (234). Arguing along the same lines, Segal finds a "balance" between the opposing views here and in "A Bundle of Letters," *Lady Barbarina*, and *An International Episode*, that she does not find in *Madame de Mauves*, where the international marriage ends in suicide (16).

Pointing to a later tale of international marriage that also ends in suicide, "The Modern Warning," Buitenhuis argues that it is James's use of letters to tell the tale that allows him to avoid the "destructive consequences" of the collision of opposites here (117, 140).

Marcellus's definition of "high civilization" is "the union of the sense of freedom with the love of knowledge" (CT 4, 514). Both Holder and Berland have remarked on the similarity to Isabel Archer's earlier definition of the "aristocratic life" as "the union of great knowledge with great liberty, the knowledge would give one a sense of duty and the liberty a sense of enjoyment" (Holder 285; Berland 123 n.24).

Looking at later works, Matthiessen sees Antrobus's worries about the growth of "an idle and luxurious class" borne out in *The Ivory Tower* (xiii, xxvi; also Dietrichson 76). Watson finds Spencer Brydon's venture into the "jolly corner" completing the "journey of self-discovery" Aurora embarks on as she heads west at the end of the tale (181–82). (See also "The Modern Warning" and "Pandora.")

Interpretation and Criticsm

"The Point of View" has been James's ticket of admission to the hall of American humorists. Despite its objections to James's "distorted" view of America, the *Literary World* still judged it "amusing." Admittedly, Bier considers humor not James's "natural bent," and characterizes his as that of "chill sophistication," a mixture of British and American technique (390–91). Putt more simply finds it makes one laugh out loud (45). The tale is, as Ward calls it, a "social comedy" based on the collision of manners and mores (18).

In its humor, the tale is remarkably multivoiced for James. Its range includes the blunt aphorisms of Mrs. Sturdy, the boasting of Marcellus, the effete wit of Lejaune, the deadpan of Antrobus, and what Holder calls the "uncharacteristic but memorable" combination of "comic hyperbole with a sense of nightmare" in Leverett's horror at his Boston hotel (24). Still, contemporary reviews charged that they all sounded like James and spoke "Jamesese" (Monteiro 1983, 4). At the same time, they also debated which of the characters spoke for the "real" James, a debate that has continued. Critical opinion seems, however, to have settled down, rather sensibly, to the view that James expresses many of his own ideas through the characters, but that no single one is his mouthpiece, and that, ever so delightfully, many of the views contradict and are not resolved, creating what Monteiro calls a "multiple reality" (Monteiro 1983, 4–7; see also, e.g., W. Wright 69; Stone 234). Austin Wright sees James making fun of all the characters in turn in a "plain but skillful blancing" (4–5). Tanner finds the "fermenting ambivalence" of James's attitude to his subject producing delightful, lively contradictions between ideas as well as individual statements of great insight. Lynn discerns more of a "bite" to the tale, coming from the complexities of James's recent trips to the States, marked both by his gratifying welcome as an established author and the death of his parents (390–91).

Most critics then and now were interested in trying to disinter from the contradicting opinions James's complaints about America. Calling the tale "a convenient compendium of several of James's dissatisfactions" with America, Holder notes that he also includes a defense (24). Geismar, not surprisingly, sees James's using the different points of view simply as cover for his own view of America as a nightmarish blankness, articulated both by Leverett's fervently emotional, physical distress and Lejaune's coldly intellectual disdain (51–54). More surprisingly perhaps, Edel refers to it as James's "most sharply critical" tale about America, citing not only Sturdy and Antrobus for support, but also Lejaune and even Mrs. Church as indicating James's disappointment with America's democratic mediocrity. He defends James against his critics, however, arguing that James was simply fulfilling his duty as an artist in describing his land to itself (*Life* 3, 47–50).

There is general agreement, however, that James sides with Miss Sturdy in her disapproval of the "juvenile takeover" in America, which despite its comic treatment Shine emphasizes James felt showed the danger of a disdain for maturity. Both Shine and Matthiessen see James pointing to a genuinely problematic tendency, but his criticism was not well taken (Matthiessen xiii, Shine 48–49). John Hay wrote Howells of arguing with people who claimed, "'Miss Sturdy is James himself. . . . she says children are uproarious in America and women's voices are higher toned than their manners, there is no forgiveness for the writer" (Monteiro 1973, 80). James's attitude toward American provinciality critics judge more complex, Bier noting his ambivalence toward both "sophisticates and provincials" (392). Stevenson cites Miss Sturdy's "humorous discourse . . . on the serious need in America of a little honest coarseness, which the country lacked, in place of the overnice vulgarity which it had in abundance." She recalls his complaint of the "vulgar, vulgar, vulgar" Americans in Rome and deems his attitude overall one of "loving disrespect" (58–59). Matthiessen links the remark with T. S. Eliot (xiii). Indeed, Miss Sturdy has found almost universal acceptance as the most reliable witness of America, representing the closest to James's own point of view, her opinions occasionally overlapping with those James expressed in his personal letters (see Wagenknecht 22; Matthiessen xiii; Stone 235; Buitenhuis 118; Shine 47–48; Watson 180; Putt 46). Jefferson emphasizes Miss Sturdy's moderation, finding her qualified acceptance of the free upbringing of American women preferable to Lejaune's absurd disdain for women who have "no imagination, no sensibility, no desire for the convent" (76).

In Watson's reading, the "most caustic anti-Americans"—namely Mrs. Church, Leverett, and Lejaune—are also the "most ridiculous" characters. He calls attention to Leverett's "fatuous egotism" in fussing about Aurora, who does not take him at all seriously. While Watson considers Antrobus "humorous and appealing" if often the butt of jokes, Buitenhuis judges the Englishman as much of a caricature as Lejaune, seeing only through his own prejudices, but finds Lejaune the most amusing because, unable to speak English, he judges without being able even to communicate with the subjects of his study (Watson 174–77, 179; Buitenhuis 119–20). Jefferson dismisses Mrs. Church as a caricature as well (86–87). In Fowler's view, however, she expresses James's own bewilderment at the "virtually meaningless" relationships between young men and women in which the sexual was either completely absent or ignored (45–46). In the view of Holder, her complaints, such as her indignation that in America the "individual has quite ceased to be recognized," are ones James sometimes voiced in his own right, but not consistently (49). Mrs. Church's similar lament that "in this country the people have rights, but the person has none" is contradicted, according to Stone, by James's statement in an 1882 letter that it was "pleasant to be in one's native land, where one is someone and something," and in *Hawthorne* that America emphasized "the importance of the individual" (234).

Unlike her mother, Aurora eagerly seeks the promise of America, and so comes to represent in Buitenhuis's view the "pathos of expatriation" (119). According to Lynn, James is "concerned" most about her, because of his increasing interest in the way America "frustrated or rebuffed" some who sought it (391). Watson also sees Aurora as bearing the "chief emotional burden of rediscovering America," and Jefferson argues that Aurora's sense of "anticlimax" in her new freedom is more telling than that of her less hopeful mother (Watson 181; Jefferson 86–87). Critics differ on the likelihood of her eventually succeeding in her search for a husband. Monteiro and Jones see it as probable, Monteiro observing that her "rare" type will be appealing in the west (Monteiro 1983, 5; Jones 60). Buitenhuis, on the other hand, asserts that she will "obviously" be unsuccessful (119). Lynn and Watson confine themselves to paying tribute to Aurora's initiative, Lynn seeing her continuing "gamely" out west, Watson finding her like the dawn her name invokes still youthful, hopeful, and westward moving (Lynn 391; Watson 181).

In defending James's patriotism to his fellow countrymen, Hay sought to argue that Marcellus was James's spokesperson. He wrote Howells: "How James is catching it for his 'point of view.' In vain I say to the Howling Patriot The Pt. of Vw is clearly and avowedly the pt. of vw of a corrupted mother and daughter, spoiled by Europe, of a filthy immoral Frenchman, of a dull, well-meaning Englishman. The author gives his sympathy only to the Roaring American." It is a claim Monteiro finds "highly questionable" (1973, 80). Indeed, several critics including the original reviewer for the *Atlantic* found the character's "luxury of praise of things American" impressive, particularly as evidence of what Tilton calls James's ability to "enter into a quite alien point of view" (*Atlantic* 707; Tilton ix; also Matthiessen 1947, xiv). Similarly, Putt sees as most significant James's ability to voice Marcellus's pungent criticisms of Europe, of its "stultified peasants of whom it takes so many to make a European noble" (46). Accordingly, Wagenknecht classes Cockerell with Lejaune and Antrobus as critical national caricatures (22). Ward and Monteiro point out his particular faults, Ward calling him "vulgar and self-satisfied" as he "complacently rejects all of Europe," and Monteiro arguing that he overstates, particularly about the papers (Ward 28; Monteiro1983, 5).

Emphasizing the positive, Watson points to Marcellus's lack of the personal vanity so marked in the other characters (178). Buitenhuis discerns in Marcellus some of James's own ambivalence in his observations on Europe's need for democracy and the significance of America's growth, but remarks that James still used mainly "negatives" in constructing his case for America (120). Andreas takes the case even further, arguing not only that James approves of Marcellus, but also that he is the "only one who understands what he sees," namely the "tremendous social drama" of the growth of American democracy (142). There is, as the *Atlantic* early observed, "a downright quality about Mr. Cockerel's speech, a vehemence of American assertion, which invests him with a singular individuality" (707). As Dietrichson formulates it, Marcellus's views cannot be identified with James's, but still possess a "ring of sincerity and conviction" in their condemnation of "the fashionable European topics" as "petty and parochial" when contrasted to the sweeping tide of democracy (54). Marcellus declares at one point, "There are bad manners everywhere, but an aristocracy is bad manners organized" (CT 4, 515). Marion Adams would quote the definition approvingly, and even Edel acknowledges that James gave Marcellus not only "largely" the last word but one of the best lines (*Life* 3, 49).

In his preface James recognized the difficulty of writing a story with such a multiplication of views. He wrote of "the burden bequeathed by such rash multiplications of the candid consciousness. They are splendid for experience, the multiplications, each in its way an intensifier; but expression, liking things above all to be made comfortable and easy for it, views them askance." Still he spoke of the tale as "the little rounded composition" (*Criticism* 2, 1222–23). Ford agreed, arguing that the work is a "true short story" given its "account of conflicting irresolutions ending in a determination" (168). The determination is, however, rather open-ended even for James, and Matthiessen judges the work "hardly a story" (xiii). To Buitenhuis the technique of beginning and ending with Aurora's letters gives the tale only "a certain factitious unity" (118). Putt simply refers to the tale as "an animated series of exceedingly witty essays" (45). Without making a case for the tale's formal structure, McElderry considers the wit of the observations to compensate for any looseness, judging for example the inclusion of Mr. Antrobus "gratuitous" but enjoyable (76).

Such a form indeed seems more appropriate for the subject. In the preface, James also recalls his joy in Washington of noting that "Impressions could mutually conflict—which was exactly the interest of them." He continued, "'The Point of View,' in fine, I fear, was but to commemorate, punctually enough, its author's perverse and incurable disposition to interest himself less in his own (always so quickly stale) experience, under certain sorts of pressure, than in that of conceivable fellow mortals, which might be mysteriously and refreshingly different" (*Criticism* 2, 1222). In the view of the *Atlantic*, he captured his subject well in a series of what they call "instantaneous mental photographs," letters "so agile, so true to every wind of doctrine that blows, so prospective, retrospective, and introspective, that the reader is lost in admiration" (707).

The photographs themselves, Buitenhuis argues, are "primarily satiric" though "good-humoured." In his view, they cumulatively present a view of the States as "very trying" to those used to Europe, and contain a more serious message in their recognition of the distorting power of stereotypes, as well as their indication that an "ultimate and objective truth in judgment" is unattainable (117–18, 120–22). Watson, however, deems the tale a "light-hearted *tour de force*," an "intricate comedy" of both American and European provincialism (183). As in the story, both assessments are probably right, as James showed his ability to find "mysteriously and refreshingly different" a wide spectrum of his fellow mortals and their views.

Works Cited

Primary Works
James, Henry. 1882. "The Point of View." *Century* 25 (December): 248–68.

———. 1882. *The Point of View*. Copyright Edition.

———. 1883. "The Point of View." *The Siege of London*. Boston: James R. Osgood.

———. 1883. "The Point of View." Collective Edition. Vol. 12. London: Macmillan.

———. 1908. "The Point of View." *The Novels and Tales of Henry James*. New York Edition. Vol. 14, 535–607. New York: Scribner's.

Secondary Works
Andreas, Osborn. 1948. *Henry James and the Expanding Horizon: A Study of the Meaning and Basic Themes of James's Fiction*. Seattle: University of Washington Press.

Anon. 1883. Review of *The Siege of London*. *The Atlantic* 51 (May): 706–7.

Anon. 1883. Review of *The Siege of London*. *The Nation* 36 (5 April): 301.

Anon. 1883. Review of *The Siege of London*. *Literary World* 14 (24 March): 90.

Austin, James C. 1978. *American Humor in France: Two Centuries of French Criticism of the Comic Spirit in American Literature*. Ames: Iowa State University Press.

Berland, Alwyn. 1981. *Culture and Conduct in the Novels of Henry James*. Cambridge: Cambridge University Press.

Bier, Jesse. 1981. *The Rise and Fall of American Humor*. New York: Octagon.

Buitenhuis, Peter. 1970. *The Grasping Imagination: The American Writings of Henry James*. Toronto: University of Toronto Press.

Delbaere-Garant, Jeanne. 1970. *Henry James: The Vision of France*. Paris: Société d'Editions Les Belles Lettres.

Dietrichson, Jan W. 1969. *The Image of Money in the American Novel of the Gilded Age*. Oslo: Universitetsforlaget; New York: Humanities.

Edel, Leon. 1960. *Henry James*. Minneapolis: University of Minnesota Press.

Ford, Ford Madox. 1913. *Henry James: A Critical Study*. London: Martin Secker.

Fowler, Virginia C. 1984. *Henry James's American Girl: The Embroidery on the Canvas*. Madison: University of Wisconsin Press.

Geismar, Maxwell. 1963. *Henry James and the Jacobites*. Boston: Houghton Mifflin.

Holder, Alan. 1966. *Three Voyagers in Search of Europe: A Study of Henry James, Ezra Pound, and T. S. Eliot*. Philadelphia: University of Pennsylvania Press.

Jacobson, Marcia. 1983. *Henry James and the Mass Market*. University: University of Alabama Press.

Jefferson, D. W. 1964. *Henry James and the Modern Reader*. New York: St. Martin's.

Jones, Granville H. 1975. *Henry James's Psychology of Experience: Innocence, Responsibility, and Renunciation in the Fiction of Henry James*. The Hague: Mouton.

Josephson, Matthew. 1964. *Portrait of the Artist as American*. New York: Octagon.

Krupnick, Mark L. 1976. "Playing with the Silence: Henry James's Poetics of Loss." *Forum* (University of Houston) 13, no. 3: 37–42.

Long, Robert Emmet. 1979. *The Great Succession: Henry James and the Legacy of Hawthorne*. Pittsburgh: University of Pittsburgh Press.

Lynn, Kenneth S., ed. 1958. *The Comic Tradition in America*. New York: Doubleday.

McElderry, Bruce R., Jr. 1965. *Henry James*. New York: Twayne.

Macnaughton, William R. 1987. *Henry James: The Later Novels*. Boston: Twayne.

Matthiessen, F. O., ed. 1947. *The American Novels and Stories of Henry James*. New York: Knopf.

Monteiro, George. 1983. "'He Do the Police in Different Voices': James's 'The Point of View.'" *Topic* 37: 3–9.

————. 1973. "The *New York Tribune* on Henry James, 1881–1882." *Bulletin of the New York Public Library* 67: 71–81.

Putt, S. Gorley. 1966. *Henry James: A Reader's Guide*. Ithaca, NY: Cornell University Press.

Segal, Ora. 1969. *The Lucid Reflector: The Observer in Henry James' Fiction*. New Haven: Yale University Press.

Shine, Muriel G. 1969. *The Fictional Children of Henry James*. Chapel Hill: University of North Carolina Press.

Stevenson, Elizabeth. [1949] 1981. *The Crooked Corridor: A Study of Henry James*. New York: Octagon.

Stone, Donald David. 1972. *Novelists in a Changing World: Meredith, James, and the Transformation of English Fiction in the 1880's*. Cambridge, MA: Harvard University Press.

Swan, Michael, ed. 1948. *Ten Short Stories of Henry James*. London: Lehmann.

Tanner, Tony. 1963. "James's Little Tarts." *The Spectator* 210 (4 January): 19.

Tilton, Eleanor, ed. *Henry James: "The Marriages" and Other Stories*. A Signet Classic. New York: New American Library.

Tintner, Adeline R. 1987. *The Book World of Henry James: Appropriating the Classics*. Ann Arbor: UMI Research Press.

Veeder, William. 1975. *Henry James: Lessons of the Master: Popular Fiction and Personal Style in the Nineteenth Century*. Chicago: University of Chicago Press.

Wagenknecht, Edward. 1984. *The Tales of Henry James*. New York: Frederick Ungar.

Ward, J. A. 1961. *The Imagination of Disaster: Evil in the Fiction of Henry James*. Lincoln: University of Nebraska Press.

Watson, C. N. 1975. "The Comedy of Provincialism: James's 'The Point of View.'" *Southern Humanities Review* 9 (Spring): 173–83.

Wegelin, Christof. 1958. *The Image of Europe in Henry James*. Dallas: Southern Methodist University Press.

Wright, Austin McGiffert. 1961. *The American Short Story in the Twenties*. Chicago: University of Chicago Press.

Wright, Walter F. 1962. *The Madness of Art: A Study of Henry James*. Lincoln: University of Nebraska Press.

Foreign Language
Onishi, Akio. 1963. "Henry James: Trilogy of International Theme." *Bungaku Ronshu* (Kansai University) 12 (January): 1–45. [Japanese]

Poor Richard

Publication History

"Poor Richard" appeared first in the *Atlantic Monthly* from June to August in 1867. When arranging his *Stories Revived* for publication in 1885, James was particularly concerned, as he wrote Macmillan, that there be space for his revised version of the "longish" tale (*Correspondence* 95). He never printed it again, however, its next appearance not coming until the 1920 posthumous collection *A Landscape Painter*. Lubbock also included it in his 1920s collection of James's fiction.

Circumstances of Composition, Sources, and Influences

In terms of James's career, the tale's chief claim to fame has often been seen as the fact that it was his first story accepted by William Dean Howells, now assistant editor at the *Atlantic* (Kelley 72–75; Dupee 49; *Life* 1, 269). In his autobiography James recalled addressing "the most presuming as yet of my fictional bids" to Howells at his "positive invitation" (494). Indeed, the tale moved Howells to write, in a letter to E. C. Stedman, that he found James "extremely gifted—gifted enough to do better than any one has yet done toward making us a real American novel" (1979, 271). The tale was, as Wagenknecht observes, James's longest so far, the first to be published in more than one instalment (199). To his brother William, however, who spoke of it as the "$200 story," its chief significance appeared to be monetary (22, 28).

According to Edel, the source of the tale is James's 1865 visit with Oliver Wendell Holmes and John Gray, both still in uniform, to New Hampshire where Minny Temple was also staying. Edel sees James as sharing his hero's sense of inferiority in the presence of rivals, and notes that like his hero James had also suffered from typhoid. The alternation of strength between hero and heroine he also sees as deriving from James's sense of his relationship with Minny (*Life* 1, 236–38, 327). Kraft qualifies the parallel, discerning in Gertrude a "negativism" not apparent in Minny. He locates, however, a more general autobiographical application in the question of what the feeling man is to do in an indifferent world (7–8). LeClair records that James's cousin Gus

Barker was killed by guerillas as is Severn, and speculates that James probably knew independent women similar to Gertrude (397).

In Kelley's view, the characters derive not from James's personal circle, but from the passionate novels of George Sand. James also, she argues, sought to use the model of the more reasonable George Eliot in the tale's analysis of character and general "humanity" (69–71). Adams offers a source from Balzac, *La Vielle fille*, which contains an independent woman and three lovers, including a sickly young man like Richard and a fortune hunter like Luttrell. In Balzac's tale, however, the woman marries the third, most likely, suitor and the young man kills himself. Adams locates a further source for the young man in each, in Werther or the Rousseau of Madame de Warens (461–62). Unlike Mordell, who considers the autobiographical sources more important than the literary ones (404), LeClair follows Kelly in picturing the characters as indebted more to George Sand than to life, calling the story a good "joining" of literature and life (397). Buitenhuis likewise sees the real-life models being put through the influence of George Sand. He also finds the sorrowful hero reminiscent of Goethe, and the heroines of George Eliot, making the tale a mixture of passion and philosophy (31–33). Sicker finds Richard, in his unheroic heroism, a departure from traditional English heroes (6).

The title alludes to an American classic, Benjamin Franklin's *Poor Richard's Almanac*, an allusion that at first appears ironic, as, Buitenhuis observes, James's Richard is unable to practice the kind of industry Franklin advocates (32). Marks, however, emphasizing Richard's success at the end, sees the modifier in the titles of each indicating a different kind of irony (62). Levy also views the title as ironic, but in a more complicated sense. Giving as the motif of Franklin's work the "search for control over the conditions of his life," he locates a similar search for "self-discipline" at the heart of "Poor Richard," a search in which Gertrude serves as the Franklinesque adviser. Richard succeeds in gaining manhood when he confesses his lie to Gertrude. Levy stresses how little James is interested in his material prosperity, concentrating instead on the "stoic calm" that accompanies it, which shows not that Franklin was wrong in his "way to wealth," but that the way might not be quite the simplifying factor his readers believed it to be. Zablotny also complicates the allusion, citing the safe, priggish, Franklinesque Richard at the end as "hoarding his own emotional wealth" (216).

Other American sources include Hawthorne, James revising his hero's surname in 1885 from Clare to that of the unfortunate Maules in *The House of the Seven Gables*, a change Buitenhuis argues James intended to make the tale more American (33; also Long 16). Veeder also locates the influence of Hawthorne in the use of such type epithets as a "man of refined tastes," "of observation," and "of action" (59). Tintner and Habegger both trace the name Gertrude to the heroine of Maria S. Cummins's *The Lamplighter* (Tinter 206;

Habegger 13). The name, however, is also that of Hamlet's mother, and Zablotny finds the character appropriately "mature" and "maternal" in relation to Richard (212). As Gale records, Gertrude herself alludes to Whittier in her fear that to Severn she is "at the very most a sort of millionaire Maud Müller" (CT 1, 207; Gale 113).

Relation to Other Works

Gertrude provides the main link with later James. Back in 1875 Howells placed her at the head of a series of James's heroines, including the heroines of "Guest's Confession" and "Gabrielle de Bergerac," which culminates in the "truly American" and "womanly" Mme de Mauves ([1875] 1961, 70). Jefferson, however, judges Gertrude, apart from her "independence and moral ascendancy" over men, less of a representative American girl than Adela of "A Day of Days" (73). Habegger compares Gertrude to another early heroine, Nora of *Watch and Ward*, seeing as the main weakness of both their distaste for their own independence (255 n.2). Looking ahead, Kraft sees a clearer picture of the sensitive American girl, inspired by Minny Temple, in Milly Theale (7), while Nathalia Wright puts Gertrude with Jane Rimmle as a spinster finding a larger world in "Europe" (222).

Others, including Edel, have seen Gertrude as a study for Isabel Archer, who, in *The Portrait of a Lady*, faces three suitors just as Gertrude does here (*Life* 1, 237; Fox 12). Cargill objects to the linking, on the grounds that Gertrude and Nora, with whom Edel also compares Isabel, are "far less palatable" characters (112 n.21). Similarly, Kraft sees her as James's first attempt at an American girl with the "intellectual grace" and "moral spontaneity" of Minny Temple, but finds the sense of them still vague here before the introduction of an international perspective (7–8). Edel himself, however, judges Gertrude wanting in interest compared to Isabel (*Life* 1, 237). Krook accepts the comparison, seeing Gertrude most notably anticipating Isabel in her interior monologues, and in her worry that she has not suffered enough and does not feel enough. In lesser ways, she finds Severn preparing for Warburton; Lutrell for Osmond; and Richard for Goodwood as well as Roderick Hudson. She also notes in both works the use of deception and at the end, an air of unhappiness (131–33).

Jones classes the relationship between Gertrude and Richard with a host of Jamesian examinations of the relationship between a sophisticated "somebody" and a relative "nobody," including Winterbourne and Daisy Miller, Rowland and Roderick Hudson, and Roger Lawrence and Nora (63–64). Edel sees Richard as preparing not only for Roderick, but also for Eugene Pickering (*Life* 1, 237). Richard also has an affinity with Rowland, who, like him, discovers his love for a woman evaporating when she becomes available.

As a Civil War story, McElderry judges both this and "A Most Extraordinary Case" less effective than "The Story of a Year" (26). As Kraft notes, however, it shares with "The Story of a Year" an emphasis on what James called "the reverse of the picture" in wartime (5). (See also "De Grey.")

Interpretation and Criticism

Critics have quickly dismissed the American setting here as thin in order to concentrate on the tale's themes and characters (e.g., Buitenhuis 33; Marks 61). Both are complex. As Edel observes, it is James's "most ambitious" early tale (1960, 11). Beach is also speaking for many readers when he finds James approaching his materials as if he were writing a novel and promptly getting in over his head (175). According to Kelley, what swamps James is the abundant analysis, which, she argues, hampers not only the story's structure but also its plausibility, as James attributes so much of the character analysis to the characters themselves that Richard and Gertrude should either "think less deeply or act more wisely" (71).

James puts his characters together in complicated scenes that are meant to express a range of emotions in the manner of an operatic trio or quartet, and his success at this has generally been praised, with the exception of Beach, who objects that the scenes go nowhere (Wagenknecht 199; Beach 177). LeClair singles out the after-dinner scene in which Richard seeks to make himself felt in the presence of his rivals, a scene Zablotny also judges "painfully funny" (LeClair 396; Zablotny 211).

It is, however, as solo characters or halves of a duet that the characters have received the most attention. Richard, the nominal hero, has received largely mixed reviews from critics. Edel, for instance, speaks of him as "rather loutish," a "sad case" (CT 1, 19). In their approach to Richard, critics have looked particularly at his moment of deceit. Edel, who sees in his "brilliantly done" lie to Severn "genuine dramatic power," still does not endorse its rightness (CT 1, 19). Holding him responsible for the results of his lie, Fox blames his selfishness for Gertrude's unhappiness (12; also Marks 62). Wilson, however, protests against Richard's excessive sense of responsibility for his rash act, "I do not understand . . . unless it is a case of neurotic guilt—why Richard should declare he has *killed* the Colonel" (660).

Richard is admittedly a character self-consciously in the process of transformation. As Kraft puts it, he is "potentially decent" and works to keep himself from becoming the successful and insensitive type Lutrell represents (6). Marks charts the transformation, seeing his task as the mastery of language as he moves from his dependence on Gertrude to adulthood, and from a romantic subjective view to a realistic, communal one. Along the way, he falls prey to the temptation to use the power of speech improperly in his lie to Severn, but his illness serves as a "symbolic catharsis" and he shows his new mature speech, she argues, in his confession to Gertrude. His falling out of love with Gertrude signals, to Marks, a "final repudiation" of his immature romanticism (62–64). Sicker, on the other hand, misrepresents Richard's character by ending his analysis with his drinking and illness, rather than his rehabilitation (37), while Jones acknowledges the change, but finds it unconvincing (64).

In place of Marks's focus on language, Zablotny emphasizes a different kind of orality. In her reading, Richard's relationship with Gertrude is in one sense "a disturbed relation between mother and child," with Richard initially at the stage of the nursing infant who, fearing he will drain his mother dry or that she will do the same to him in revenge, refuses to drink at all. Thus Richard rejects Gertrude's "rather patronizing friendship" and at the same time seeks to break his addiction to alcohol. Discerning the lack of a "real explanation" for his later falling out of love with Gertrude, Zablotny suggests that Richard's lie gave him a "hateful sense of collusion" with Lutrell, in whom he saw his "own emotional greediness." Noting that typhoid comes from infected milk or water, she also suggests that his response is connected with an infant's fear that a mother will give him bad milk if she is angry. According to Zablotny, "[O]n an unconscious level Richard is moved by such infantile fantasies and is therefore unable to accept the motherly young woman who loves him." So the Richard who is at the start at least "a man of passion" is at the end a safe, moderate drinker "completely self-contained and self-imprisoned" (211–16). While the psychoanalytic reading at times seems strained, the tale does present a rather limited view of love, or rather a view of love as a limited quality, which seems as much a product of the imagination of its characters as the infant's alleged failure to recognize that its mother can provide it with as much milk as it needs. But while Zablotny sees James trapped in the same infantile fears as Richard, viewing man and woman in a vampiric relationship in which the "sacred fount" is never replenished, but rather drained dry, it is not clear that James thinks Richard is better off at the end to be free of Gertrude.

Gertrude herself has also received some of the blame for the failure of the relationship. Kelley argues that her character became James's primary interest in the tale, and she is certainly as complex as Richard (71). In Kraft's analysis, although Gertrude genuinely loves Severn, she may be interested in him as someone who "will help to make Richard man enough to be someone she could marry." He offers no conclusion about her motives in the matter, citing the narrator's comment that "Gertrude's private and personal emotions were entertained in a chamber of her heart so remote from the portals of speech that no sound of their revelry found its way into the world." Nevertheless, he does fault her for her unwillingness to risk her pride for love. Gertrude, he notes, recognizes her fault, asking herself, "If you won't risk anything how can you demand of others that they shall?" (9–11). What seems less plausible is Richard's interpretation as rendered by Edel, who pictures him as falling out of love with Gertrude because she has been diminished by her interest in Severn, and by her engagement to Lutrell has lost even her "moral force" (*Life* 1, 237). Also noteworthy is that while Edel finds it "difficult to see her as anything but wealthy and motherly," Gertrude herself recognizes she is viewed in such a way and resents it, blaming her relationship with Richard for the problem. In love with Severn, she finds the love of Richard, "an intemperate, uneducated boy . . . a cheerless prospect, for it seemed to convert her into a kind of maiden-aunt" (CT 1, 219).

The conjunction of "wealthy and motherly" is significant, however, as part of Gertrude's problem is her money, which makes Luttrell pursue her and Severn hesitate. In Mull's analysis, Gertrude feels at first "smothered" by her wealth. He argues that when Gertrude recognizes how her money has determined the course of her relationships with the others, she comes to love Richard, the only one of her suitors unconcerned with her fortune. When he no longer loves her, she turns back to her money for what James terms "a most efficient protection" (22–23). Dietrichson, however, parcels out the blame further, asserting that just as Luttrell is to blame for wishing to marry Gertrude for her money, Severn is to blame for not being willing to marry her because of it (108). Again Gertrude is aware of the problem, and both critics cite her "vague suspicion that her money had done her an incurable wrong," causing her to feel "cruelly hedged out from human sympathy by her bristling possessions" (CT 1, 239).

In the end, Kraft observes, only the immoral Luttrell is able to get what he wants, a conclusion many critics have found an unsatisfactory resolution of the issues of the tale (6). Many question in particular why Richard falls out of love with Gertrude, Levy writing, "[I]t is as if James had not yet discovered the reasons for the behavior he would demand of his characters" (554). Other critics attribute the ending less to James's weak technique than his strong fatalism, both in the sense that love is fatal, as Buitenhuis contends Severn's death illustrates (32), and that it is fated, or as Barzun states, in James, "Free will makes the wrong choice . . . simply because it is will" (515). Thus Mull invokes Bayley's "Proust's Law" that A will cease to love B as soon as B loves A (23). Assigning somewhat more power to the characters, Tanner speaks of how they "contrive to secure unhappiness for each other" (10). Kraft, too, while acknowledging the harsh conditions of the world Richard and Gertrude inhabit, represented by the Civil War, still sees the failure as personal because "the world is always cruel." Even so, he states, James believes one must not flee it in fear as hero and heroine do here, but go out to encounter it and so to grow and learn. Instead, Kraft argues, "they seem to have lived all the life they will ever have" (9–11).

Still other critics see the conclusion as intended to be, however modestly, a happy one. Putt, noting the signs of early "emotional cannibalism," points to the escape from love as evidently advantageous (35). Dupee cites James's summary of the final situation—Gertrude "felt that he was abundantly a man, and she loved him. Richard, on his side, felt humbly the same truth, and he began to respect himself"—apparently finding it preferable to James's usual tragedy (51).

Even after his next two tales, James's brother William judged this "the best of your stories because there is warmth in the material," with "hardly a trace of that too diffuse explanation of the successive psychological steps wh. I remember attacking you for when you read it to me." It was, he wrote, a tale he would have enjoyed even if Henry had not been the author (31, 36–37, 47). The *Nation*, however, wholeheartedly dismissed the tale as containing "nothing new or striking," a review that caused Howells to conclude that James "must in a very great degree create his audience. In the meantime I rather despise existing readers." Even Howells concentrated his praise on the "remarkable strength in the last scenes," and most subsequent critics have also qualified their praise (1979, 283–84). Beginning with his brother's sense that it was "thin" given its length, its length has often created expectations of greater depth, and sometimes caused the story to be viewed as, in Krook's words, "rambling, sprawling, ill-shaped" instead (131). Kraft finds the tale strengthened by its simple telling, its freedom from the intrusions of a first-person narrator (8–9). But the absence of such a narrator still left the tale enough diverse elements for Jones to object to the intrusiveness of Gertrude's romance with Severn and Richard's saga of development on what he takes as the central relationship between Gertrude and Richard, and for Buitenhuis to find its relative effectiveness surprising (Jones 33; Buitenhuis 33). LeClair judges the tale an improvement over James's previous stories, particularly in terms of characterization, although, like Beach, he argues that James was still telling more than showing (LeClair 396–97; Beach 175). Zablotny attributes the greatest significance to the tale, calling it "crucially important" for its insight into the Jamesian hero (211). Wagenknecht similarly locates its main strength in its anticipation of James's later ethical concerns (199). The tale has all the frustration of late James as one watches intelligent, aware characters unable to make their own happiness, and much still of the frustration of early James in which one is uncertain whether their inability is the result of their own or their author's limitations, so that the ambiguity surrounding their motives seems perhaps more that of a lack of skill than the mystery of human behavior.

Works Cited

Primary Works
James, Henry. 1867. "Poor Richard." *Atlantic Monthly* 19 (June–August): 32–42, 166–78, 694–706.

———. 1885. "Poor Richard." *Stories Revived*. Vol. 2. London: Macmillan.

———. 1920. "Poor Richard." *A Landscape Painter*. Preface by Albert Mordell. New York: Scott and Seltzer.

———. 1921–23. "Poor Richard." *The Novels and Stories of Henry James*. Vol. 25. Ed. Percy Lubbock. London: Macmillan.

———. 1993. *The Correspondence of Henry James and the House of Macmillan, 1877–1914*. Ed. Rayburn S. Moore. Baton Rouge: Louisiana State University Press.

Secondary Works

Adams, Percy G. 1961. "Young Henry James and the Lesson of His Master Balzac." *Revue de Littérature Comparée* 35 (July–September): 458–67.

Barzun, Jacques. 1943. "James the Melodramatist." *Kenyon Review* 5 (August): 508–21. Also reprinted in *The Question of Henry James*, ed. F.W. Dupee, 254–66. New York: Henry Holt.

Beach, Joseph Warren. [1918] 1954. *The Method of Henry James*. Philadelphia: Albert Saifer.

Buitenhuis, Peter. 1970. *The Grasping Imagination: The American Writings of Henry James*. Toronto: University of Toronto Press.

Cargill, Oscar. 1961. *The Novels of Henry James*. New York: Macmillan

Dietrichson, Jan W. 1969. *The Image of Money in the American Novel of the Gilded Age*. Oslo: Universitetsforlaget; New York: Humanities.

Dupee, F. W. [1951] 1956. *Henry James*. Garden City, NY: Doubleday Anchor.

Edel, Leon. 1960. *Henry James*. Minneapolis: University of Minnesota Press.

Fox, Hugh. 1968. *Henry James, A Critical Introduction*. Conesville, IA: John Westburg.

Gale, Robert L. [1954] 1964. *The Caught Image: Figurative Language in the Fiction of Henry James*. Chapel Hill: University of North Carolina Press.

Habegger, Alfred. 1989. *Henry James and the "Woman Business."* Cambridge: Cambridge University Press.

Howells, W. D. 1979. *Selected Letters*. Vol. 1: *1852–1872*. Ed. George Arms, et al. Boston: Twayne.

———. [1875] 1961. Review of *The Passionate Pilgrim and Other Tales*. Reprinted in *Discovery of a Genius: William Dean Howells and Henry James*, ed. Albert Mordell. New York: Twayne. Reprinted from *The Atlantic Monthly* (April).

James, William. 1992. *The Correspondence of William James*. Vol. 1: *William and Henry*. Ed. Ignas K. Skrupskelis and Elizabeth M. Berkeley. Charlottesville: University Press of Virginia.

Jefferson, D. W. 1964. *Henry James and the Modern Reader*. New York: St. Martin's.

Jones, Granville H. 1975. *Henry James's Psychology of Experience: Innocence, Responsibility, and Renunciation in the Fiction of Henry James*. The Hague: Mouton.

Kelley, Cornelia Pulsifer. [1930] 1965. *The Early Development of Henry James*. Urbana: University of Illinois Press.

Kraft, James. 1969. *The Early Tales of Henry James*. Carbondale: Southern Illinois University Press.

Krook, Dorothea. 1986. "Isabel Archer Figures in Some Early Stories of Henry James." *Henry James Review* 7: 131–39.

LeClair, Robert Charles. 1955. *Young Henry James, 1843–1870*. New York: Bookman.

Levy, Leo. 1980. "Ben Franklin." *Southern Review* 16 (July): 552–59.

Long, Robert Emmet. 1979. *The Great Succession: Henry James and the Legacy of Hawthorne*. Pittsburgh: University of Pittsburgh Press.

McElderry, Bruce R., Jr. 1965. *Henry James*. New York: Twayne.

Marks, Patricia. 1979. "Culture and Rhetoric in Henry James's 'Poor Richard' and 'Eugene Pickering.'" *South Atlantic Bulletin* 44, no. 1: 61–72.

Mordell, Albert, ed. 1957. *Literary Reviews and Essays by Henry James*. New York: Grove.

Mull, Donald. 1973. *Henry James's "Sublime Economy": Money as Symbolic Center in the Fiction*. Middletown, CT: Wesleyan University Press.

Putt, S. Gorley. 1966. *Henry James: A Reader's Guide*. Ithaca, NY: Cornell University Press.

Sicker, Philip. 1980. *Love and the Quest for Identity in the Fiction of Henry James*. Princeton: Princeton University Press.

Tanner, Tony. 1985. *Henry James: The Writer and His Work*. Amherst: University of Massachusetts Press.

Tintner, Adeline R. 1989. *The Pop World of Henry James: From Fairy Tales to Science Fiction*. Ann Arbor: UMI Research Press.

Veeder, William. 1975. *Henry James: Lessons of the Master: Popular Fiction and Personal Style in the Nineteenth Century*. Chicago: University of Chicago Press.

Wagenknecht, Edward. 1984. *The Tales of Henry James*. New York: Frederick Ungar.

Wilson, Edmund. [1962] 1987. *Patriotic Gore: Studies in the Literature of the American Civil War*. London: Hogarth.

Wright, Nathalia. 1965. *American Novelists in Italy, The Discoverers: Allston to James*. Philadelphia: University of Pennsylvania Press.

Zablotny, Elaine. 1979. "Henry James and the Demonic Vampire and Madonna." *Psychocultural Review* 3, nos. 3–4 (Summer–Fall): 203–24.

The Private Life

Publication History

"The Private Life" made its first appearance in the April 1892 issue of the *Atlantic Monthly*. James collected it the next year as the title story of a collection, and also included it in the New York Edition.

Circumstances of Composition, Sources, and Influences

On July 27, 1891, while in Kingston, Ireland, James began a brief entry in his notebook with title and idea complete for "The Private Life," and immediately launched into the opening lines with their invocation of the Alps. Six days later he returned to the idea, acknowledging it as a "rank fantasy," but still if "very brief—very light—very vivid" possibly "amusing and pretty." He ends by adjuring himself: "[B]ut I *see* it: begin it—begin it! Don't talk *about* it only, and around it" (CN 60–61).

In the notebooks, James points to his sources by initials, "F.L and R.B." (CN 60). In the preface, James acknowledged his use of actual people, recalling the "highly distinguished man . . . whose peculiarity it was to bear out personally as little as possible (at least to *my* wondering sense) the high denotements, the rich implications and rare associations, of the genius to which he owed his position and his renown." For relief, James recalled, he turned to " . . . the whimsical theory of two distinct and alternate presences, the assertion of either of which on any occasion directly involved the entire extinction of the other. This explained to the imagination the mystery: our delightful inconceivable celebrity was *double*, constructed in two quite distinct and 'water-tight' compartments" (*Criticism* 2, 1253–54).

The way to "dramatise" the explanation came to James in the reminder of its antithesis:

> . . . that most accomplished and most dazzling of men of the world whose effect on the mind repeatedly invited to appraise him was to beget in it an image of representation and figuration so exclusive of any possible inner self that, so far from there being here a question of an *alter* ego, a double personality, there seemed scarce a question of a real and single one, scarce foothold or margin for any private and domestic *ego* at all. (*Criticism* 2, 1254–55)

The "explanatory secret" here was "a clear view of the perpetual, essential performer, consummate, infallible, impeccable, and with his high shining elegance, his intensity of presence, on these lines, involving to the imagination an absolutely blank reverse or starved residuum, no *other* power or presence whatever." The "harmless formula" for the two types led James naturally to the idea to "'play them against each other'" (*Criticism* 2, 1255).

At the end of his description of the "double" artist in the preface, James identifies his inspiration as the poet Robert Browning. Lind cites the nearly exact description of Browning in London in James's biography of William Wetmore Story: "[I]t is impossible not to believe that he had arrived somehow, for his own deep purposes, at the enjoyment of a double identity. It was not easy to meet him and know him without some resort to the supposition that he had literally mastered the secret of dividing the personal consciousness into a pair of independent compartments." One was the "man of the world—the man who was good enough for the world, such as it was" who "showed himself" in public; the other was the "inscrutable" poet who "sat at home" (Lind 317).

Lind, however, offers in addition to the biographical model an autobiographical motive. While the narrator is, like James, an unhappy playwright, Lind sees Vawdrey essaying the difficulties of a first play for the actress as the James stand-in. He points for support to a sketch, "The Golden Dream: A Little Tale," which James would write in 1899 in the album of the actress Mary Anderson depicting an author who wished to write a play, but was only asked "too late." The key resemblance, however, in Lind's view is the division James himself practiced between a social and creative self, seen in James's tale "Benvolio," and also in the Browning poems "House" and "Shop" (319–20; also Wright 34).

Bargainnier vigorously objects to Lind's reading of the tale as autobiography, countering with further information on James's knowledge of Browning to prove that the biographical model is sufficient. He cites a letter from James to his sister, Alice, upon first meeting Browning in 1876 indicating an early sense of his two halves: "Robert B. I am sorry to say does not make on me a purely agreeable impression . . . . But evidently there are two Brownings—an esoteric and an exoteric. The former never peeps out in society, and the latter has not a ray of suggestion of *Men and Women.*" James and Browning, he acknowledges, were similar in the separation of their public and private lives, and in their belief in the privacy of the artist, and he notes the "ironic" reversal of the usual sense that one's work is public and one's social life private (154).

In the preface, James described Browning as "loud, sound, normal, hearty"—a description that certainly does not fit Vawdrey. Indeed, the sometimes embarrassed public Vawdrey seems to have more in common with the "poor gentlemen" James clearly disassociates Browning from (*Criticism* 2,

1253). Still, Poole remarks that while James was shocked by how very much the laureate Tennyson was "not Tennysonian," his disappointment in Browning was "tempered by a sense of a saving awkwardness" or "'restlessness'" in the poet (xvi). Nor does Vawdrey's conversation resemble James's, according to at least one contemporary witness who wrote, "There is only . . . one thing which Henry James could never do in any conversation—he never could be commonplace" (Tanner 1963). Indeed, according to Rogers, "part of the fun" of the tale is the knowledge that James was proficient both in the study and in society (100; also Miller 241). Still, we know that James like Vawdrey was fond of a good gossip.

In the intricate reading of Posnock, "The Lesson of the Master" is a better presentation of James's reaction to Browning, and the focus of both is "the exclusion of a younger writer from the private life of sexuality." In his view, James remained dissatisfied with his theory of the "two Brownings" first articulated in 1877, because it did not get at the heart of what disturbed him in Browning, the "uncanny" poet who, James wrote, surprises by walking on "the novelists' side of the street," even as, Posnock observes, Vawdrey surprises by writing in the dark. Posnock follows the theories of Girard to see both James and the narrator here as under the pressure of "the double bind of mimetic desire," the contradictory message that the disciple takes from his master, to imitate and not to imitate. In response, Posnock argues, James took Browning—with his fame both as poet and lover—and divided him differently and less formidably into the artist and mundane socialite. The first James imitated, the second he rejected. Most significant to Posnock, however, is the omission of the sexual element.

Thus, "The Private Life," according to Posnock, is James's "confession of failure to solve the riddle" of Browning, with himself cast as the observer narrator. Indeed, to Posnock, the tale is flawed by the lack of an "objective correlative" for the narrator's intense fascination with Vawdrey, a flaw he attributes to James's closeness to his material. Vawdrey is a "compelling figure" to the narrator only because James was really talking about himself and Browning in the tale. Even the "uncanny" air of the tale, Posnock argues, reflects James's sense of puzzlement at the richness and "theatricality" of Browning, as well as his "repression" of the sexual element in Browning. He concedes that James did intend the possible "nonmimetic" reading, but only to "divert readers from the real interest and drama of the tale"—his response to Browning. James's method in the tale then resembles that of Blanche, relating James to her as well as to the narrator, as both seek to hide their "private, personal relations." Despite what he sees as the tale's failure, Posnock also judges the tale, with its "severely ironic parody" both of James and his "theory," as an act of "implicit self-awareness" by which James recognized his anxiety about Browning and so provided himself genuine "relief" (4, 18–19, 25–27, 41–42, 56–61, 69, 104, 204 n.18).

Posnock particularly links the tale with Browning's poem "One Word More," the coda to *Men and Women* that addresses Browning's wife in his own person, and articulates a concept of the "two soul-sides." Remarking a transformation similar to that noted by Bargainnier, Posnock points to the difference between the attributes of public and private from poem to tale. In Browning the public self includes the poetic, while the private is a sexual realm shared only with one woman, but with elements of poetry in it. Thus the private life, for Browning, in Posnock's construction, is "the union of love and art" as represented in his marriage to Elizabeth Barrett. James, Posnock writes, disregards this view as it contradicts his own belief in the necessary deprivation of the artist. James instead, Posnock notes, would adopt as his model Browning's opposite, the "galley-slave" Balzac, who James declared wrote simply out of imagination, not experience. Because to James, Browning "never seems to have paid for his art," Posnock writes, he was too great a challenge to "the foundation of James's moral life: the necessity of renunciation." Indeed, to Posnock, James's awareness of the counterexample of Browning makes his adoption of an ascetic life an "excuse" for the avoidance of sexuality (62–68).

Understandably enough, James did not name the original of Lord Mellifont. Matthiessen and Murdock early on, however, glossed F.L as a reference to the popular Victorian painter Frederick Leighton (N 110). Lind also finds a parallel for James's sense of Mellifont's emptiness in his description of Leighton's funeral three years after the tale: "The day was suave and splendid, congruous, somehow, with the whole 'note' of Leighton's personality." The sense of "*commital* of the public spirit" James sensed in it eventually issued in "simply nothing at all" (318; also Edel 1970, 211). Poole cites James's description of Leighton at a prize-giving: "He *represents* admirably" (xv). The portrait of Mellifont may not give one all of the man, according to Jeffares, who points to more admiring depictions of Leighton in two works of 1870, Adelaide Sartoris's *A Week in a French Country House* and Disraeli's *Lothair*. Indeed, Jeffares suggests that Leighton's idealism and success called forth James's malice (138). Bargainnier points out that Browning and Leighton were longtime friends (155 n.22). Tinter furthers the rehabilitation of Leighton, suggesting that James may never have identified his source because he felt the characterization of him in Mellifont was "over harsh." At the same time she contends that Mellifont is the "real hero" of the story—"he never lets anyone down." In conclusion, she points to evocations of Leighton's paintings in the tale, including the initial tableau before the Alps ("Leighton").

Apart from Lind, other critics have linked James with the "double" artist of the tale. Edel and Canby both see Vawdrey as a stand-in for James, although in more limited applications. Canby compares Vawdrey's "wrestling . . . with a never-ending task," to James's constant efforts to keep the short story under control (227). Edel sees the division as representing James's simultaneous work as a solitary literary artist and as a writer for the public stage (*Life* 3, 277; 1970, 211). Przybylowicz, who points out that James also described Story in terms of a "double, or perhaps rather a triple inner life," sees James as projecting his own "psychological obsessions" on his subjects (236–37). Even without invoking "The Private Life," Warren interprets James as double, the diner-out combined with the artist, the exterior in the mold of Charles Eliot Norton or James Russell Lowell, the interior more like Hawthorne or Emerson (566). Donald Stone contrasts James's sense of the split between private and public as unavoidable with that of George Meredith, who worked to reconcile the two (20).

Seeing James as only partially subject to the "schizoid condition," Vaid asserts its commonness among writers including Balzac, Flaubert, and later Thomas Mann (270 n.7). Similarly, Beebe traces quite a history of artistic doppelgängers including Thoreau, Coleridge, and Disraeli (7–9). According to Jacobson, interest in split personalities was strong at the time, and James was trying to appeal to the popular interest (88). Tanner attributes such interest to the "latent schizophrenia" of the Victorian age in its heavy emphasis on public behavior divorced from private feeling (1985, 79–80). The split self was accorded serious moral treatment in such contemporary works as *Dr. Jekyll and Mr. Hyde* and *The Picture of Dorian Gray*, but as Stone notes, James took a comic approach (316n). Tintner finds a precedent for James's use of the humorous double in Edward Everett Hale's tale "My Double; and How He Undid Me," published in 1859 in the *Atlantic Monthly*. In Hale's story a minister hires a man to fulfill the irksome social duties of his profession so that he can be free to work on his writing. James, Tinter remarks, contributed the idea of a "*double* double" to Hale's conception (*Pop* 206–13).

The *Athenaeum* found James's mixing of the supernatural, the "apologue," and a realistic setting reminiscent of Hawthorne, but still "ingenious without being convincing" (61). However Hawthornesque the tale, the narrator is disappointed to find little of the Byronic in Vawdrey. Trapped with Vawdrey in a mountain storm, exposed to "the fury of the elements," he laments that the writer produces no "Manfred attitude" but only London gossip (CT 8, 225).

Blanche Adney is forever acting in the plays of one Bowdler. Kermode doubts her Bowdler is the famed expurgator of Shakespeare, proposing instead that James intended to suggest an imaginary playwright of similarly timid quality (450 n.7). Miller sees her as "a divine embodiment" of the theatre in which James was seeking to establish himself at the time (241).

The confident titled Englishman, the timid observer, the suggestion of illicit romance, the European setting, the symmetrical pairs, the false appearances, all seem to anticipate Ford Madox Ford's *The Good Soldier*.

Relation to Other Works

From early on, the tale has been connected with *The Sacred Fount* (Edgar 192; also *Life* 3, 277, Wagenknecht 1984, 68). While Q. D. Leavis calls the story an "exercise" for the similarly "silly" novella (223), Blackall constructs the relationship less judgmentally. She sees "The Private Life" as the kind of tale *The Sacred Fount* might have been if James had confined it to a short story as he originally intended. It, she argues, remains "figurative" with an emphasis on the exterior, while *The Sacred Fount* shows James's progress in searching for a way of accounting "in realistic terms" for the "fantastical equation" (157). Posnock depicts both narrators as "loners, surveying at a distance the private lives of people" and making up theories to explain them. The narrator in the short story he finds even more pitiful, as he "mindlessly mistakes his theory for fact," while in the novella the narrator recognizes his theories as theories (55–56). Yet Macnaughton attributes to both the narrator here and in *The Sacred Fount* a sympathy for the subjects of their observations (157). In their rejection of "the detective and the keyhole," Segal contends, they also resemble the narrator of *The Aspern Papers*, although Poole considers the unnamed narrator here a "more mildly inquisitive predator" than in *The Aspern Papers* (Segal 153; Poole xvi). Blackall also discusses all three works, but likens "The Private Life" more particularly to "The Figure in the Carpet" on the grounds that the intellectual snooping in the two tales creates "more suspense than damage," in contrast to both *The Sacred Fount* and *The Aspern Papers* (162–64). Geismar casts an even wider net, including not only the "scholar-spy" of *The Aspern Papers*, but also the "voyeur-analysts" of later tales (118). Nominating as the "paradigmatic Jamesian plot . . . the attempt of two lovers to keep their affair hidden from a third person," Posnock sees "The Private Life" as a "variation on the pattern," in that the secret is never brought into the open. Still he finds in the narrator's "uncanny experience" the same "shock of sudden revelation" as in such discovery scenes as Strether's discovery of Chad and Marie together (207 n.45).

The artist himself, Vawdrey, is able to solve relatively easily the problems that so bedevil such other Jamesian artists as Dencombe and Paraday, an exemption noted by Delbaere-Garant (218). He can even write "in the dark" as Dencombe pictured writers doing, and, Tintner reports, as James was once said to do (*Pop* 210). Similarly, Posnock sees Vawdrey writing with his back turned to the narrator recalling James's comments on the difficulty of picturing the "artist *in triumph*" in the preface to *The Tragic Muse*. Of him, wrote James, the reader can see only "the back he turns to us as he bends over his work" (206 n.28). Nevertheless, Horne locates the same message here of the incompatibility of artistic and social demands as in "The Coxon Fund," and she points to the way Lord Mellifont repeats the distinguished appearance and empty insides of the Monarchs of "The Real Thing" (122).

Despite Mellifont's negative example, the artist for James, Allen contends, had a single role, while people in general were defined by their relations with others, a fate she sees even the independent-minded Isabel Archer unable to avoid (70). Similarly, Stone notes the same conflict between the free private self and public constraint in both "The Private Life" and *The Portrait of a Lady* (20).

In approaching his subject through the concept of "alternate identities," James was aware, Matthiessen and Murdock argue, that he was coming close to the world of his supernatural tales (N 110). Similarly, Geismar argues that the tale's concluding "baroque and fantastic note" connects it with the "twilight world" of James's late "mad" tales (118). According to Goetz, "The Private Life" and "The Real Right Thing" provide a transition from the artist tales, which offer a contrast of master and disciple, to the psychological ghostly tales of "The Beast in the Jungle" and "The Jolly Corner," which contrast different selves of the same person (163–64).

Blanche, according to Beach's categorization, belongs with such early confidantes as Mrs. Tristram in *The American* and Mrs. Draper of *Madame de Mauves* (70). Lady Ringrose, of whom Vawdrey gossips, is possibly the same Lady Ringrose who figured earlier as the subject of scandal in *A London Life* (CT 8, 225). (See particularly "Benvolio.")

Interpretation and Criticism

James had begun his tale with the idea of a contrast, and the symmetry with which he worked it out has provoked substantial comment. Not only are the two central characters paired, but as Geismar remarks, there is a pair of observers to watch them (118). Norrman places the tale's split personalities under the domain of James's favorite device—"chiastic inversion" (145). The result, according to Vaid, possesses "the balance of an extended dramatized epigram." He examines its division into two parts: the first containing the truth about Vawdrey, discovered fittingly by another writer; the second the truth about Mellifont, discovered fittingly by an actress (71). To Todorov the symmetry is not only typical of James, but in this case "perfect." Vawdrey is the double of Mellifont who is "not even single." Mellifont's personality thus illustrates that "presence is empty," while Vawdrey's work demonstrates that "absence is a plenitude" (170).

While most critics concur on the tale's use of symmetry as a device, they split on its genre. The standard view of the tale has been as a story of the supernatural, Edel calling it "one of the most fanciful of James's stories of the benign-occult" (1970, 210). An early critic, Elton, noted the blending in the tale of the "uncanny" and the realistic—a "sharp and light satire"—to produce a "certain kind of preternatural story" perfected by James. Although

744   The Private Life

Mellifont, he wrote, is "virtually a hallucination on the part of other people," the supernatural in his character is "only a symbol here; we have all known such people, or something like them" (365). Even earlier Payne noted a similar combination of "verisimilitude" with a "fanciful thesis," and also pointed to a third element that modern critics have found most disturbing. In his words, "[T]he allegory lurks beneath, and his readers can never quite forget that" (228). McElderry confines himself to the observation that the tale is "almost allegorical" (121). To Ezra Pound, its allegory is its ruin. The tale is "not life, not people, allegory." It was, indeed, "waste verbiage at the start, ridiculous to put all this camouflage over something au fond merely an idea" (31).

To other critics, the allegory is not so much the ruin of the tale, as of the supernatural in the tale. According to Todorov, the allegory is "so obvious" that it allows no hesitancy about the reality of its events, disqualifying the tale from the realm of the "fantastic" (182). Similarly, Rimmon argues that the allegory here eliminates the "potential ambiguity" (14). Bargainnier and Posnock agree that it is not a ghost story (Bargainnier 156; Posnock 57–58). Other critics, however, such as Lind and Wagenkncht, have placed it in the in-between category of the fantasy, or like Matthiessen and Murdock associate it with the ghost stories by virtue of its "method" (Lind 321; Wagenknecht 1984, 66; N 110). In Walter Wright's estimate, the tale has "just enough of a ghostly atmosphere" to illustrate "the uncanny nature of the mind" being allegorized (157). Blackmur, while noting "the very conventionality of its fantasy—its *glaring* incredibility," goes on to philosophize, "Of this little piece what does one say but that the ghost story is the most plausible form of the fairy tale; it makes psychological penetration ominous because not verifiable" (83). Gale, for his part, points to a "sequence of drama figures" that structure the tale's entrances and exits (135–36).

The setting of the tale is Switzerland, and the narrator finds the locale "more human" than London (CT 8, 190). Commenting on the lack of "nature" in James, Stevenson, however, argues that its conversations could as easily have taken place in London (26; also Jefferson 54). James took a low view of such society, according to Lee, who points to the narrator's observation that "when the world was old and stupid . . . [Vawdrey] would have been a fool to come out." In such a world, Lee concludes, the "only hope" James leaves for the artist is a dual self (52).

This dual self has been, for many critics, the key to examining Vawdrey. To Lind, Vawdrey's double cannot properly be called a doppelgänger because it "*supplements*" his actions rather than "*duplicates*" them (321). Whatever their titles, Norrman discerns a basic uncertainty about roles lying behind the tale's split personalities (145). In presenting them, Ward sees James limiting himself, attempting only to "dramatize" Vawdrey's split, not to "resolve" it (50). In the view of Delbaere-Garant, however, the split is an easy solution to the demands of the writer's life (218). Kappeler, too, while reading the tale as an "allegory of the writer's dilemma," stresses its solution. Observing that Vawdrey needs his public self as a researcher for his work, she cites the remark of the narrator, "After all they're members of a firm, and one of them couldn't carry on the business without the other" (91).

James himself, looking back at the tale's treatment of opposites in 1894, pointed to its use of an "*image*" to support it (CN 84). James does not specify what image he is referring to, and it may well have been the whole concept of the contrast of appearing and disappearing personalities. However, critics who focus on the single nature of Vawdrey as a writer would undoubtedly point to the image of him in his room working in the dark. Andreas presents as the lesson of the tale that to know a person truly one must see them when at their true work (127). To Blackmur, the "fantastic statement" of the tale "so far as it has a serious side" is "of the inviolable privacy of the man of genius" (83–84). Characterizing the tale simply as a "literary daydream," Lind dismisses Blackmur's interpretation as overdone (321). Subsequent critics, however, have also emphasized the tale's view of Vawdrey the solitary genius (e.g., Miller 240–41). Tintner calls the tale a "justification of the writer's isolation and dedication" (1989, 212). Both Todorov and Kermode in their analyses emphasize the image of Vawdrey at his desk. Todorov writes of "the special place" belonging to the work of art: "more essential than the hidden, more accessible than the ghost, more material than death, it affords the one means of experiencing essence. That other Clare Vawdrey, sitting in the dark, is secreted by the work itself, is the text writing itself, the most present absence of all" (170–71). Kermode seconds Blackmur in locating a serious center within the tale's lightness: "For the image of the artist Vawdrey working alone in the dark is genuinely a figure for the operation of the imagination as James understood it" (19).

If Vawdrey is serious, Mellifont is light. His character is also, in Vaid's view, of a greater general application (72). While Przybylowicz writes that James "deplores" such men who exist only in public, other critics have had more fun with his character (41). Payne remarks of Mellifont that he is "not a reality, but a mere reaction," adding that he reappears at the "appearance of some one (may we say some one else?) upon the scene" (228). He is not, however, without his advocates. According to Jefferson, Mellifont needs a great deal of rest because of his intense social art and activity, and so is driven to the opposite extreme of a "temporary cessation of being." Jefferson also takes an unconventional view of Vawdrey, whom he criticizes as "so addicted to the routines of society" that he relegates his writing to a different self (55). Without attacking Vawdrey, Edel also detects something of the artist in Mellifont, writing that he "put[s] more art into everything than was required" (*Life* 3, 277). As Todorov acknowledges, Mellifont's conversation in the tale, unlike Vawdrey's is "rich, relaxed, and instructive." But, Todorov cautions, it is necessary for Mellifont to be good at his part for the contrast to work (170).

Looking at the two opposites, Blackmur observes, "Life, the actuality, lies somewhere between; and it is a relief to think that your dull man of genius keeps a brilliant ghost in his workroom, just as it is a malicious delight to figure that your brilliant public man is utterly resourceless without a public" (83). The people seeking relief and delight in the tale are the two observers, the narrator and Blanche, the "conspiracy" between whom, Kermode remarks, "thickened" the tale's lightness (19).

In 1894 James spoke of the tale's narration as "impressionistic, with the narrator of the story as its spectator" (CN 82–84). While Wagenknecht potrays the narrator as assiduous in his pursuit, and Lind sees him as typically gratuitous in his curiosity, he has for the most part avoided the scapegoating of many James narrators (1984, 68; Lind 319). In Edel's formulation both he and Blanche are "neither haunted nor obsessed; they are merely curious" ([1949] 1963, 211–12). Blackall notes how the narrator gives up his pursuit simply at the interruption of Lady Mellifont (163). To Jones, the same incident is a deliberate renunciation calling off a meddling search, and he cites the narrator's response to Lady Mellifont's worries, "From the moment my experiment could strike her as an act of violence, I was ready to renounce it" (CT 8, 223). In his reading, the narrator's renunciation, the benign nature of Blanche's capture of Vawdrey's other self, and Lady Mellifont's sacrifice of her own curiosity to her duty all combine to defuse a potentially harmful situation (236). With less concern, Rogers finds Lady Mellifont's worries over her husband—whether he will return each time he leaves—part of the comedy of the tale (100).

The character of the narrator's co-conspirator, Blanche Adney, has drawn but sparse comment. Geismar, for example, judges her "a rather good character," while Wagenknecht sees in her a "Dickensian vividness" (Geismar 118; Wagenknecht 1948, 128). Her role as a second detective is appropriate in the "nicely orchestrated" tale, as Poole remarks, given that there are two mysteries. Poole also remarks on the significance of the contrast the successful Blanche provides to the narrator, "another loser" (xvi).

In two fuller analyses, Blanche's role has been highlighted. In Aswell's reading, however, it is not an inspiring one. The symmetry of the tale, to Aswell, serves to provide a contrasting view of collaboration—the futile, that between Blanche and the narrator, and the fruitful, that between the two selves of Vawdrey. Both Blanche and the narrator, Aswell writes, miss the "central truth revealed by their snooping." Aswell, however, is harder on the narrator, writing of him as "an intrusive meddler" given to "frantic posturings" and "pointless intellectual exercises that parody the activity of true artists," a man so ignorant of himself that he cannot even remember his own birthday. While Vawdrey can balance his two selves, the narrator's "get in each other's way" and so prevent any true work, making his "shadowy double life" a parody of the other writer's. His attempt to collaborate, ironically, leaves him more alone than before. Blanche, on the other hand, Aswell sees as a "complement" to Vawdrey, as both use society to rest from their true labor, and so the private Vawdrey is willing to communicate with her. But because she does not recognize her similarity to him, she also goes astray in her search, losing interest in the public Vawdrey. Mellifont and Vawdrey, in the meanwhile, are not unique cases, but simply "exaggerated" versions of everyone's need to balance the private and public self. The true artist recognizes that he "must work alone." The artist's works, in turn, "not only assure him of continued contact with humanity, but they protect him from the urge to intrude into the lives of others" (181, 191–95).

Blackmur and other critics followed the suggestions of the narrator to see Blanche as having fallen in love with Vawdrey's private self (83). In Posnock's interpretation, however, Blanche's pretense of interest in the private Vawdrey is only a cloak for her adulterous relationship with Mellifont, which the narrator originally and correctly suspected. In his reading, the narrator is marked at the start by the "need for a response from others that will define his identity," particularly from Vawdrey as "a fellow playwright, *the* playwright of his time, and a figure of immense authority." To the narrator, Posnock writes, Vawdrey's "blandness" is "infuriating" since it seems to deny him this "confirmation." When he finds Vawdrey at his desk, the narrator experiences the "uncanny" something "simultaneously familiar and unfamiliar." It is for the narrator a "psychologically bruising experience," because Vawdrey fails to respond to him. Indeed, Posnock compares the strength of the scene to the "primal scene" of Freud, and argues that in its emphasis on privacy it is "not without sexual overtones." It is this unsettling moment, Posnock contends, his refusal to believe what he saw, that prompts the narrator to see Vawdrey as dual. Because Blanche uses his confusion to cover her affair, the tale again links the private life of the artist with the sexual. The narrator, however, is excluded by Blanche and Vawdrey from both. He is, in Posnock's assessment, "hopelessly deluded" to the end, preserving his peace of mind by becoming Blanche's "dupe." Still, to Posnock, what is "most memorable" in the tale is not the narrator's "dearly bought equanimity," but his "emotional torment" over Vawdrey (43–56). Posnock's reading is partially undermined by his assertion that Vawdrey is famed as a playwright, while the tale presents him as a "great mature novelist" uncertainly approaching a new genre (CT 8, 198).

More calmly than his narrator, James acknowledged the "small game" of the contrasting types in "The Private Life," writing in his preface, "I fear I can defend such doings but under the plea of my amusement in them—an amusement I of course hoped others might succeed in sharing" (*Criticism* 2, 1253–56). In Wagenknecht's view, James succeeded in his task, "One step in the wrong direction, at any point in its development, would have ruined 'The Private Life,' but James's hand never falters, and the tone is just right" (1984,

68). To Edgar, however, the tale is a tad "too ingenious" in its treatment of "certain mysterious facts of personality" (192). Payne similarly speaks of the opposites as "ingenious," but also senses a "charm" in the tale, which "although hopelessly elusive, is not without a certain power of fascination." Putt is harsher, calling the work perhaps "the most dismal of all of James's self-pitying tales" in its attack on the actor and canonization of the observer (391–92). Pound gives less emphasis to the portrait of Mellifont, and finds it more enjoyable, writing that James's "tilting against the vacuity of the public figure is naturally, pleasing" (31). Others have emphasized the fun of the tale, Poole calling it a "high-spirited comedy," Geismar an "interesting *jeu d'esprit*"; Miller a "comedy of errors" (Poole xvi; Geismar 118; Miller 241). The tale is, as Edel puts it, "comic and ironic," or in the phrasing of Vaid "a kind of joke as well as a kind of truth" (1970, 210; Vaid 72). It encompasses not only the "vacuity" of Mellifont, the befuddled observations of the narrator, but also the shrewder sense of Blanche, and most significantly, the quiet diligence of Vawdrey.

Works Cited

Primary Works

James, Henry. 1892. "The Private Life." *Atlantic Monthly* 69 (April): 463–83.

———. 1893. "The Private Life." *The Private Life*. London: James R. Osgood; New York: Harper, 3–78.

———. 1909. "The Private Life." *The Novels and Tales of Henry James*. New York Edition. Vol. 17, 215–66. New York: Scribner's.

Secondary Works

Allen, Elizabeth. 1984. *A Woman's Place in the Novels of Henry James* New York: St. Martin's.

Andreas, Osborn. 1948. *Henry James and the Expanding Horizon: A Study of the Meaning and Basic Themes of James's Fiction*. Seattle: University of Washington Press.

Anon. 1893. Review of *The Private Life*. *Athenaeum* 102 (8 July): 60–61.

Aswell, E. Duncan. 1966. "James's Treatment of Artistic Collaboration." *Criticism* 8: 180–95.

Bargainnier, Earl F. 1977. "Browning, James, and 'The Private Life.'" *Studies in Short Fiction* 14: 151–58.

Beach, Joseph Warren. [1918] 1954. *The Method of Henry James*. Philadelphia: Albert Saifer.

Beebe, Maurice. 1964. *Ivory Towers and Sacred Founts: The Artist as Hero from Goethe to Joyce*. New York: New York University Press.

Blackall, Jean Frantz. 1965. *Jamesian Ambiguity and The Sacred Fount*. Ithaca, NY: Cornell University Press.

Blackmur, R. P. [1943] 1983. "In the Country of the Blue." In *Studies in Henry James*. Ed. Veronica A. Makowsky, 69–90. New York: New Directions.

Canby, Henry Seidel. 1951. *Turn West, Turn East: Mark Twain and Henry James*. Boston: Houghton Mifflin.

Delbaere-Garant, Jeanne. 1970. *Henry James: The Vision of France*. Paris: Société d'Editions Les Belles Lettres.

Edel, Leon, ed. 1970. *Henry James: Stories of the Supernatural*. New York: Taplinger.

———, ed. [1949] 1963. *The Ghostly Tales of Henry James*. New York: The Universal Library, Grosset & Dunlap.

Edgar, Pelham. [1927] 1964. *Henry James, Man and Author*. New York: Russell & Russell.

Elton, Oliver. 1903. "The Novels of Mr. Henry James." *Quarterly Review* 198 (October): 358–79.

Gale, Robert L. [1954] 1964. *The Caught Image: Figurative Language in the Fiction of Henry James*. Chapel Hill: University of North Carolina Press.

Geismar, Maxwell. 1963. *Henry James and the Jacobites*. Boston: Houghton Mifflin.

Goetz, William R. 1986. *Henry James and the Darkest Abyss of Romance*. Baton Rouge: Louisiana State University Press.

Horne, Helen. 1960. *Basic Ideals of James's Aesthetics as Expressed in the Short Stories Concerning Artists and Writers*. Marburg: Erich Mauersberger.

Jacobson, Marcia. 1983. *Henry James and the Mass Market*. University: University of Alabama Press.

Jeffares, Bo. 1979. *The Artist in Nineteenth Century English Fiction*. Gerrards Cross: Colin Smythe.

Jefferson, D. W. [1960] 1971. *Henry James*. New York: Capricorn.

Jones, Granville H. 1975. *Henry James's Psychology of Experience: Innocence, Responsibility, and Renunciation in the Fiction of Henry James*. The Hague: Mouton.

Kappeler, Susanne. 1980. *Writing and Reading in Henry James*. New York: Columbia University Press.

Kermode, Frank, ed. 1986. *The Figure in the Carpet and Other Stories*. London: Penguin.

Leavis, Q. D. 1947. "Henry James: The Stories." *Scrutiny* 14 (Spring): 223–29. Reprinted in *Collected Essays*. Vol. 2: *The American Novel and Reflections of the European Novel*, ed. G. Singh, 177–84. Cambridge: Cambridge University Press.

Lee, Brian. 1978. *The Novels of Henry James: A Study of Culture and Consciousness*. New York: St. Martin's.

Lind, Sidney E. 1951. "James's 'The Private Life' and Browning." *American Literature* 23 (November): 315–22.

Macnaughton, W. R. 1975. "The Narrator in Henry James's *The Sacred Fount*." In *Literature and Ideas in America: Essays in Memory of Harry Hayden Clark*. Ed. Robert Falk, 155–81. Ohio University Press.

McElderry, Bruce R., Jr. 1965. *Henry James*. New York: Twayne.

Miller, Karl. 1985. *Doubles: Studies in Literary History*. Oxford: Oxford University Press.

Norrman, Ralf. 1982. *The Insecure World of Henry James's Fiction: Intensity and Ambiguity*. New York: St. Martin's.

Payne, William Morton. 1893. Review of *The Private Life*. *Dial* 15 (October): 228.

Poole, Adrian. 1983. *Aspern Papers and Other Stories*. Oxford: Oxford University Press.

Posnock, Ross. 1985. *Henry James and the Problem of Robert Browning*. Athens: University of Georgia Press.

Pound, Ezra. 1918. "A Shake Down." *The Little Review* 5 (August): 9–39.

Przybylowicz, Donna. 1986. *Desire and Repression: The Dialectic of Self and Other in the Late Works of Henry James*. University: University of Alabama Press.

Putt, S. Gorley. 1966. *Henry James: A Reader's Guide*. Ithaca, NY: Cornell University Press.

Rimmon, Shlomith. 1977. *The Concept of Ambiguity: The Example of Henry James*. Chicago: University of Chicago Press.

Rogers, Robert. 1970. A Psychoanalytic Study of the Double in Literature. Detroit: Wayne State University Press.

Segal, Ora. 1969. *The Lucid Reflector: The Observer in Henry James' Fiction*. New Haven: Yale University Press.

Stevenson, Elizabeth. [1949] 1981. *The Crooked Corridor: A Study of Henry James*. New York: Octagon.

Stone, Donald David. 1972. *Novelists in a Changing World: Meredith, James, and the Transformation of English Fiction in the 1880's*. Cambridge, MA: Harvard University Press.

Tanner, Tony. 1985. *Henry James: The Writer and His Work*. Amherst: University of Massachusetts Press.

———. 1963. "James's Little Tarts." *The Spectator* 210 (4 January): 19.

Tintner, Adeline R. 1989. The Pop World of Henry James: From Fairy Tales to Science Fiction. Ann Arbor: UMI Research Press.

———. 1989. "Lord Leighton and his Paintings in Henry James's 'The Private Life.'" *Journal of Pre-Raphaelite and Aesthetic Studies* 2: 1–10.

Todorov, Tzvetan. 1977. *The Poetics of Prose*. Trans. Richard Howard. Ithaca, NY: Cornell University Press.

Vaid, Krishna B. 1964. *Technique in the Tales of Henry James*. Cambridge, MA: Harvard University Press

Wagenknecht, Edward. 1984. *The Tales of Henry James*. New York: Frederick Ungar.

———. 1948. "Our Contemporary Henry James." *College English* 10: 123–32.

Ward, J. A. 1975. "The Ambiguities of Henry James." *Sewanee Review* 83 (Winter): 39–60.

Warren, Austin. 1943. "Myth and Dialect in the Later Novels." *Kenyon Review* 5 (August): 551–68.

Wright, Walter F. 1962. *The Madness of Art: A Study of Henry James*. Lincoln: University of Nebraska Press.

Foreign Language
Gullón, Ricardo. 1965. "Imágenes de El Otro." *Revista Hispanica Moderna* 31: 210–21.

Kambara, Tatsuo. 1972. "James's Gothic: Gothic in American Novels (5)." *Bungakubu Kiyo* (Tokyo University of Education) 88 (March): 49–65. [Japanese]

Walch, Günter. 1980. "'The Private Life': Das Motiv des gedoppelten Menschen in der englischen Literatur der Jahrundertwende." *Zeitschrift für Anglistik und Amerikanstik* 28, no. 2: 101–12.

A Problem

Publication History

The first and only appearance of "A Problem" in James's lifetime was in the June 1868 *Galaxy*, where it received the tribute of a full-page illustration by W. J. Hennessy (see Aziz 1, 275). It was not reprinted again until Kenton's 1950 *Eight Uncollected Tales*.

Circumstances of Composition, Sources, and Influences

Scharnhorst has located a contemporary source for the clergyman Mr. Clark in the Reverend William Rounseville Alger, whose book *The Friendships of Women* James had criticized for its sentimentality the year before, in a review for the *Nation*. Noting that in "A Day of Days" James had treated a young minister straightforwardly, Scharnhost attributes the satire (seen in such comments as "Gentlemen of his profession have these little parcels of sentiment ready to their hands") to his scorn for Alger, reflected later in the minister Babcock of *The American* and Brand of *The Europeans*.

McElderry find James's use of Hawthorne as a model here typical of his early supernatural tales, while Brodhead compares the story specifically to Hawthorne's "The Threefold Destiny," which also depicts a "supernatural fate" coming about in a surprising, but natural manner (McElderry 1965, 27; Brodhead 125). Fox comments that the fortune-teller could have stepped out of "Young Goodman Brown" (6). Thorp sees the model of Hawthorne leading James to his American subject matter, signalled in this tale in the presence of the Indian women (xi). Wagenknecht classifies it not as a supernatural tale but "a psychological study" similar to William Dean Howells's 1890 *The Shadow of a Dream* (199).

Relation to Other Works

McElderry, who feels the lack of any "depth or perspective" to the couple's woe, such as the Civil War provided the couple in "The Story of a Year," offers the consideration of "a sense of impending doom" in the story as a tie to the much later "The Beast in the Jungle," although in the earlier work the theme is only "mechanically" treated (1949, 283). Elsewhere he classes it with "The Ghostly Rental" and "The Romance of Certain Old Clothes" as an early sign of James's interest in the supernatural (1965, 27). Brodhead also links the tale with "Romance" in its use of Hawthorne, while Kelley points out its similar framework and inferior atmosphere (Brodhead 125; Kelley 84).

Stein and Shine link the story with "My Friend Bingham," Stein focusing on the depiction of marriage while Shine finds in both the theme of the sacrificial child (Stein 67). According to Shine, this time the child is a victim of fate, not chance, her death necessary to reunite her parents, making her death more important in itself than in "My Friend Bingham," even if she remains an "idea" without any individual character (29–30).

Interpretation and Criticism

Stein has noted in "A Problem" a range of possible readings similar to those he remarked in "My Friend Bingham." On one hand, the story seems intended to portray marriage as both a valid encounter with the world and the consolation for the pains such an encounter brings. On the other hand, as written the story seems instead to display the "ghastliness" of marriage. Putt takes the latter view, pointing out the misery James here associates with marriage (37). Stein offers a third possibility, however: that the weaknesses of

James's claims for marriage may simply be the result of inadequate story-telling. Thus, the choice of such a "childish, insipid pair" as hero and heroine and a conclusion that depicts marriage as "little more than an evasion of painful realities" may not have been James's intent (64, 67–69).

A contemporary reviewer confined himself to describing the story as showing James's skill "not so forcibly" as earlier work "but still very well," and even praised his comparative lessening of "voluptuousness" in its depiction of women. With the exception of Wagenknecht, however, who writes that the tale treats "both narrative and characterization satisfactorily though without distinction" given its length (199), most modern critics align themselves along Stein's third possibility, concentrating so much on the failure of technique that there is little room for the consideration of meaning. To Putt, it is a "flimsy sketch"; to Kraft "one of James's oddest and most banal tales" (Putt 37; Kraft 120). James's structuring of the story around the seemingly conflicting prophecies, while it may have seemed a clever device, appears to have been insufficient in itself to sustain the story, which remains rather hollow in the middle. Kelley sees James fixing on the idea of the prophecies in an attempt to curb his tendency toward excessive analysis and relying on the suspense it would generate to sustain interest. Like McElderry, she finds its handling mechanical and she objects in particular to the cavalier treatment of the child's "conveniently" dying. She recommends more analysis as the solution to the story's lack of atmosphere or sympathy (83). Similarly, LeClair sees the structure as having given James such a sense of overconfidence that he neglected to add any atmosphere or sympathy for the characters, even at the death of the child; but he finds the analysis of psychological motives *too* thorough, putting the blame on the conflict between romance and realism at this time in James's career (406). McElderry, who labels the story romantic "in the more external sense," also finds its unfolding unconvincing. Emma's jealousy, he insists, is illogical, the reconciliation "inevitable and automatic," the "few possibilities" of the situation left unexplored, leaving the reader feeling tricked, as in an O. Henry story (1949, 282–83). Kraft, finally, sees the story as seeming to have "no other purpose than to prove that fortunetellers can be right, although not exactly as we think" (20).

Cargill juxtaposes James's two stories—"A Problem" and "The Solution"—and Kenton places the story in a similar context, pointing to a 1867 review of two historical novels by James where he discusses "the problem of opposites as a task for story-tellers" and states, "There is no reason" why the novelist, like the historian, "should not imprison his imagination, for the time, in a circle of incidents from which there is no arbitrary issue, and apply his ingenuity to the study of a problem to which there is but a single solution" (14–15). Two years after writing "A Problem," James was to refer to Minny Temple's death as the solution to "a sadly insoluble problem" (*Life* 1, 222). The problem in both cases would seem to be the too easy satisfaction with what *is* an arbitrary issue to a case that *could* have produced other solutions. The problem in this story turns out to be *too* solvable.

Works Cited

Primary Works
James, Henry. 1868. "A Problem." *Galaxy* (June): 697–707.

Secondary Works
Anon. 1868. Review of "A Problem." *The Nation* (28 May): 434.

Brodhead, Richard H. 1986. *The School of Hawthorne.* New York: Oxford University Press.

Cargill, Oscar. 1965. Foreword. *Plots and Characters in the Fiction of Henry James* by Robert L. Gale. Hamden, CT: Archon.

Fox, Hugh. 1968. *Henry James, A Critical Introduction.* Conesville, IA: John Westburg.

Kelley, Cornelia Pulsifer. [1930] 1965. *The Early Development of Henry James.* Urbana: University of Illinois Press.

Kenton, Edna, ed. 1950. *Eight Uncollected Tales of Henry James.* New Brunswick, NJ: Rutgers University Press.

Kraft, James. 1969. *The Early Tales of Henry James.* Carbondale: Southern Illinois University Press.

LeClair, Robert Charles. 1955. *Young Henry James, 1843–1870.* New York: Bookman.

McElderry, Bruce R., Jr. 1965. *Henry James.* New York: Twayne.

———. 1949. "The Uncollected Stories of Henry James." *American Literature* 21 (November): 279–91.

Putt, S. Gorley. 1966. *Henry James: A Reader's Guide.* Ithaca, NY: Cornell University Press.

Scharnhorst, Gary. 1986. "Henry James and the Reverend William Rounseville Alger." *Henry James Review* 8: 72.

Shine, Muriel G. 1969. *The Fictional Children of Henry James.* Chapel Hill: University of North Carolina Press.

Stein, Allen F. 1984. *After the Vows Were Spoken: Marriage in American Literary Realism.* Columbus: Ohio State University Press.

Thorp, Willard, ed. 1962. *The Madonna of the Future and Other Early Tales.* New York: New American Library.

Wagenknecht, Edward. 1984. *The Tales of Henry James.* New York: Frederick Ungar.

Professor Fargo

Publication History

"Professor Fargo," which James published in *Galaxy* magazine in August 1874, suffered the same fate as its immediate predecessor, "Adina," and the earlier "At Isella." Like them, it was never reprinted by James, but was collected in Mordell's 1919 selection *Travelling Companions*, and later published with a sensationalized title, "Spiritual Magnetism," under the aegis of Little Blue Books from Girard, Kansas, in 1931.

Circumstances of Composition, Sources, and Influences

There is some debate about the dating of the tale's composition. Kelly, considering "Professor Fargo" inferior to the other stories of 1873–1874, argues that it may have been written earlier in 1870 or 1871, when James was in America between trips to Europe, and "resurrected" when the demand for his stories began to grow (168). Tintner, on the other hand, argues that it was written in Europe when James was contemplating a permanent return to America (1987, 201). Putt places it even earlier, before James's first trip to Europe (132).

The world of public entertainment was one familiar to James in his New York youth. As Putt notes, his autobiography fondly recalls the music halls and mediums of his boyhood (33). Like Thackeray and Emerson, who both visited with the James family when they were in the city to lecture, James's father was a public speaker. Habegger has stressed the fanaticism of James Sr., while Edel seeks to correct his view to fit the eyes of the child James was during those years (Habegger 83–84; Edel 92). While Henry and his siblings never got to attend their father's lectures, James would recall in *A Small Boy and Others* his father's "mysterious," "legendary" departure for the lecture hall as an evening ritual in the years before their 1855 departure to Europe. His father's leaving at bedtime "lent to the proceeding—that is to *his*—a strange air of unnatural riot, quite as of torch-lighted and wind-blown dissipation." The image of his father "at the door of the carriage and under the gusty street-lamp" evokes the second, urban setting of the story (*Autobiography* 355). The visionary nature of James Sr. is also present in the Colonel, who tries to impress on audiences his world vision. If Selah Tarrant

755

in *The Bostonians* is, as Putt sees him, "a medium for a double assault on the less rooted forms of public life," one must keep in mind the similarly rootless life James grew up in (182).

A more limited, but perhaps relevant, experience may have contributed to James's choice of a mathematician for his feckless idealist. In *A Small Boy and Others*, James recalls his "great public exposure" at the "wonderful exhibition of Signor Blitz, the peerless conjurer":

> On my attending his entertainment with W. J. [his brother William] and our frequent comrade of the early time "Hal" Coster, [Signor Blitz] practised on my innocence to seduce me to the stage and there plunge me into the shame of my sad failure to account arithmetically for his bewilderingly subtracted or added or divided pockethandkerchiefs and playing cards; a paralysis of wit as to which I once more, and with the same wan despair, feel my companions' shy telegraphy of relief, their snickerings and mouthings and raised numerical fingers, reach me from the benches. (*Autobiography* 67)

Nor was his bewilderment that night unusual as he recalls as part of the winter of 1854 in his New York school "the dreadful blight of arithmetic, which affected me at the time as filling all the air" (*Autobiography* 127). That particular blight, however, seemed more associated with the numbers of business—"ledgers, daybooks, double-entry, tall pages of figures"—more suitable to the Professor than the Colonel, the sort of study that might have driven Spencer Brydon away before he learned he could master it.

In the germ for his play *The Reprobate*, recorded on October 23, 1891, James wrote of "the idea of the *hypnotization* of a weak character by a stronger, by a stronger will, so that the former accepts a certain absolute view of itself, takes itself from the point of view of another mind, etc., and then, by the death of the dominant person, finds itself confronted with the strange problem of liberty" (CN 62). The second half of the germ is not relevant here, but the first captures the situation of the Colonel's daughter in relation to the Professor. Edel and Powers also note James's interest in mesmerism in connection with his recording of the plot of Du Maurier's *Trilby* on March 25, 1889, and in *The Bostonians* (CN 51–52).

Critics have found two major literary sources for the story, one European and one American. Buitenhuis points to the model of Hawthorne's *The Blithedale Romance*, which provides the rural New England setting as well as some New York scenes, the topic of mesmerism, and the mesmerist villain. Buitenhuis observes, however, that James treated the elements realistically rather than romantically, and like Long finds the change in treatment strengthens the story (Long 30–32). Walter Wright, on the other hand, considers the transformation from romance to realism unsuccessful (93).

Buitenhuis also uses the tale as an intermediate work to reduce James's debt for *The Bostonians* to Hawthorne (141–42). Kerr, while adding a parallel to Maule's "magnetic ravishment" of Alice Pyncheon, also sees the tale as a reworking and rejection of *The Blithedale Romance*. In James's tale, he argues, mesmerism is not broken by love, but humbuggery confirmed by sexual seduction, the heroine a diminished version of Priscilla (135–39). Vanderbilt points to parallels with Howells's 1880 *The Undiscovered Country*—and sees Howells's changing the name of his scientist Gifford to Ford, perhaps in response to his recognition of the other similarities (47n; also Long 146–47; Banta 90–100). Kuhlmann links Hawthorne's, Howells's, and James's works as placing the theatrical mesmerist-confidence man "in the context of New England reform and the convulsions of social experiment" (82). Such a context returns the work to the autobiographical parallels with James's father; Banta associates the tale with "the decay of transcendentalist dreams" (90).

Early in the tale, the unnamed narrator reads *Don Quixote* and so recognizes Colonel Gifford later as "Don Quixote in the flesh" (CT 3, 268). Kelly early noted the influence of *Don Quixote*, but was unimpressed by it, finding the characters "unnatural, not even parallel to the figures of literature" James had in mind (168). Later, after Gale enumerated the many references to the work in James (108), Tintner set out to explore them fully in this tale. Tintner locates in "Professor Fargo" the start of a "life long narrative habit" of rewriting classics, the story being "built" around *Don Quixote* in the edition illustrated by Doré (1986, 18–19). Here, she argues, the first two sections refer to *Don Quixote* while the third presents a modern retelling (1987, 201–8).

Influences can also be found in Turgenev, according to Lerner, who links James's work to Turgenev's 1869 "A Strange Story," which also focuses on the "psychology of sex" as a young girl falls under the influence of a medium (40; also Long 30). Lerner acknowledges the change from the religious fanatic in Turgenev to the sham professor in James, and while Buitenhuis and Peterson consider that the transformation from Turgenev's "sober study" to James's "satiric" portrayal disqualifies the comparison, the central enchaining of a young girl by a mesmerist remains the same (Buitenhuis 72n; Peterson 142 n.6). Lerner also connects the girl's deaf-mute condition with Turgenev's "Mumu" (40; also Buitenhuis 72n).

Looking at other sources, Kelley judges the comparison of the daughter to Mignon far from compelling (168). Wagenknecht is more impressed by the likeness of Fargo to Melville's *Confidence Man* and the various tricksters in the work of Mark Twain (200). Long points also to Bayard Taylor's 1860 "Confessions of a Medium," with its mesmerist maiden victim (186 n.6). Looking to the future, Wright finds it similar but inferior to Thomas Mann's "Mario and the Magician" (93).

Relation to Other Works

The Bostonians has provided most of the connections. Among the ties are the American setting, the vulnerable daughter, and, most specifically, the subject of mesmerism and vulgar American quackery. Several critics have pointed out the way the Colonel's daughter prepares for Verena Tarrant and Fargo for her father, Selah (e.g., Putt 44; Long 147).

Other comparisons also focus on the American setting. Putt points to another mesmerist in "The Point of View," and earlier remarks some of the same "love-hate feeling" toward "mountebanks" in the sketch of the heroine's background in James's *Watch and Ward*, both of which portray a low, "grubby" New York, to become sinister later in "The Jolly Corner" (32–33, 45, 52; also Wagenknecht 200). The geographical name of the Professor connects him with the same West that provided *Watch and Ward* with the shady Fenton. The New York here contains a "little Jew" who owns the hall the Professor rents and who evicts him to bring instead "the Canadian Giantess," an evident attempt at humor like the Jewish tourist in the stage version of *Covering End* (CT 3, 296). To Putt, there is a "raw, wounded" air in James's dismissal of his native country, a distaste seen again in "Pandora." He also notes, however, the contrasting "reluctant appreciation" of rural New England seen later in *The Europeans* and in "The Point of View" (44–45, 132). As a link between the two themes of the supernatural and America, it is instructive to contrast it with James's "The Last of the Valerii," where the supernatural influence of the classical past, though seemingly as destructive as the mesmerism of the American present, is nevertheless overcome.

Wright compares Dr. Sloper's cruel possessiveness in *Washington Square* to Professor Fargo's behavior here, stating that both far from being "case studies" are primarily "characters in 'fairy tales'" (93–94).

Interpretation and Criticism

The dismissive opinion conveyed by James's neglect of his story has been imitated by many critics, even his own father, who, William informed Henry, judged it "not one of your genuine ergo good ones" (242; e.g., Wagenknecht 199). Kelly links what she sees as its failure to its American setting: "Surely its effect must have been to prove to James that he had better leave America; leave freaks and odd sticks, alone" (168–69). Edel echoes her judgment, calling the tale "clearly one of James's recurrent potboilers," but departs from Kelly by finding it significant "in the thematic sequence of James's fiction" through its recognition "that there exist already in the New World forms of corruption distinctly American" (CT 3,10). Other, usually later, critics have been less condemnatory and have, like Edel, discovered merit in the very Americanness Kelly decries. Putt objects to Edel's dismissal, finding strengths in the tale's "really vibrant horror of American vulgarity" conveyed with "a freshness of observation" (44). Buitenhuis contends that although James could not use the American setting effectively for romance, when he used it for a vulgar subject as here, he managed well (74)

Banta also disagrees with Kelley, defining the work as minor but not un-Jamesian, focusing not so much on the setting as on the theme of spiritualism (243 n.13). Martin sees Gifford expressing James's early rationalism, but adds that in his later ghostly tales James had moved from his satiric attitude toward supernaturalism closer to Fargo's (126–27). Banta suggests that the narrator becomes interested in Fargo because Fargo *is* a fraud, and as such supports his spiritual skepticism (92).

The professor's powers, however, are indeed not what they seem. While some critics such as McElderry have accepted the Professor's claim to have won the daughter through mesmerism, others have indicated that the power the Professor uses is sexual (e.g., Banta 91, 96; Wagenknecht 200; Kerr 138). The Colonel is tricked, as Buitenhuis indicates, when he accepts the bet because he does not realize the Professor is seducing his daughter (73). Long looks at the coercive nature of the seduction and the grim picture of the couple's life together in the future, which he characterizes as primarily a "social shudder" at the disorderly democracy that produces such characters as Fargo (31–32).

The Colonel, in contrast, is according to Kraft a true genius, and he sees the tale accordingly embodying the overwhelming of genius in America by vulgar greed. In his reading, the daughter's surrender to Fargo indicates that things will only get worse (78–79). Jones admits the possibility of such a reading, but presents alternatives as well, for example that Gifford is misled in putting all his faith in objective science and denying the power of Fargo's "spiritual magnetism." He marks, too, the failure of the Colonel to provide an upbringing for his daughter that could support his teachings, leaving her vulnerable to Fargo's persuasion, although he questions the extent of her innocence in her dealings with the Professor (24–25). Banta also questions the Colonel as ideal. While stating that the story illustrates "the eternal incompatibility of science and spirituality," she emphasizes the feeble version represented of each. The Colonel is "quixotically ignorant" of life, the spiritual corrupt (93–94).

Despite her intricate analysis of the tale, Banta finds little mystery in its neglect, given that the story is simply "not well written" (91). Most other evaluations are similarly mixed. Buitenhuis is perhaps the tale's strongest advocate, attributing to the story "considerable artistic success" primarily due to its use of Hawthorne (74). Back in 1919, however, without any attention paid to themes or sources, an anonymous reviewer gave a fairly accurate picture of what was already an obscure tale: "The figures have bones and flesh on their bones, and the author, by taking pains, does kindle a tiny fire of human relations between them, which burns faintly in a still air" (*New Republic*).

Works Cited

Primary Works

James, Henry. 1874. "Professor Fargo." *Galaxy* (August): 233–53.

———. 1919. "Professor Fargo." *Travelling Companions*. Foreword by Albert Mordell. New York: Boni and Liveright.

———. 1931. "Spiritual Magnetism." Little Blue Books 1674. Girard, KS: Haldeman-Julius.

Secondary Works

Anon. 1919. Review of *Travelling Companions*. *New Republic* (30 July): 422.

Banta, Martha. 1972. *Henry James and the Occult: The Great Extension*. Bloomington: Indiana University Press.

Buitenhuis, Peter. 1970. *The Grasping Imagination: The American Writings of Henry James*. Toronto: University of Toronto Press.

Edel, Leon. 1989. "The James Family." *Henry James Review* 10 (Spring): 90–94.

Gale, Robert L. [1954] 1964. *The Caught Image: Figurative Language in the Fiction of Henry James*. Chapel Hill: University of North Carolina Press.

Habegger, Alfred. 1989. "In Darkest Henry James, Sr." *Henry James Review* 10 (Spring): 81–84

James, William. 1992. *The Correspondence of William James*. Vol. 1: *William and Henry: 1861–1884*. Ed. Ignas K. Skrupskelis and Elizabeth M. Berkeley. Charlottesville: University Press of Virginia.

Jones, Granville H. 1975. *Henry James's Psychology of Experience: Innocence, Responsibility, and Renunciation in the Fiction of Henry James*. The Hague: Mouton.

Kelley, Cornelia Pulsifer. [1930] 1965. *The Early Development of Henry James*. Urbana: University of Illinois Press.

Kerr, Howard. 1983. "James's Last Early Supernatural Tales: Hawthorne Demagnetized, Poe Depoetized." In *The Haunted Dusk: American Supernatural Fiction, 1820–1920*. Ed. Howard Kerr, John W. Crowley, and Charles L. Crow, 135–48. Athens: University of Georgia Press.

Kraft, James. 1969. *The Early Tales of Henry James*. Carbondale: Southern Illinois University Press.

Kuhlmann, Susan. 1973. *Knave, Fool, and Genius: The Confidence Man as He Appears in Nineteenth-Century Fiction*. Chapel Hill: University of North Carolina Press.

Lerner, Daniel. 1941. "The Influence of Turgenev on Henry James." *Slavonic Review* 20 (December): 28–54.

Long, Robert Emmet. 1979. *The Great Succession: Henry James and the Legacy of Hawthorne*. Pittsburgh: University of Pittsburgh Press.

McElderry, Bruce R., Jr. 1965. *Henry James*. New York: Twayne.

Martin, Jay. 1983. "Ghostly Rentals, Ghostly Purchases: Haunted Imaginations in James, Twain, and Bellamy." In *The Haunted Dusk: American Supernatural Fiction, 1820–1920*. Ed. Howard Kerr, John W. Crowley, and Charles L. Crow, 123–31. Athens: University of Georgia Press.

Peterson, Dale E. 1975. *The Clement Vision: Poetic Realism in Turgenev and James*. Port Washington, NY: Kennikat.

Putt, S. Gorley. 1966. *Henry James: A Reader's Guide*. Ithaca, NY: Cornell University Press.

Tintner, Adeline R. 1987. *The Book World of Henry James: Appropriating the Classics*. Ann Arbor: UMI Research Press. Revised from "Professor Fargo and Don Quixote." *American Literary Realism 1870–1910*, no. 3 (Spring 1987): 42–51.

———. 1986. *The Museum World of Henry James*. Ann Arbor: UMI Research Press.

Vanderbilt, Kermit. 1968. *The Achievement of William Dean Howells: A Reinterpretation*. Princeton: Princeton University Press.

Wagenknecht, Edward. 1984. *The Tales of Henry James*. New York: Frederick Ungar.

Wright, Walter F. 1962. *The Madness of Art: A Study of Henry James*. Lincoln: University of Nebraska Press.

The Real Right Thing

Publication History

James first published "The Real Right Thing" in the December 1899 issue of *Collier's Weekly*, where it was illustrated by Howard Pyle. He included it the next year in the collection *The Soft Side*, and after that in the New York Edition.

Circumstances of Composition, Sources, and Influences

"The Real Right Thing" began in London with James's hearing Augustine Birrell talk at Lord Rosebery's of the experience of writing a biography of Sir Frank Lockwood, Solicitor-General when Rosebery was Prime Minister, "soon after his death and amid all his things . . . and 'feeling as if he might come in.'" (N 265). James recorded the germ on May 7, 1898, and included it the next May, while in Rome, in a list of possible topics as "The Biographer (after death: A. B. and F. L.)" (N 292). Although Edel links the tale and entries in his edition of the supernatural tales (1970, 552), their connection is not cited in Edel and Powers's edition of the notebooks (CN 168, 184).

As Edel notes, the issue of biography was particularly present to James at the later date, as he set about writing a biography of William Wetmore Story—a man he did not particularly admire—for Story's family, and so he expressed his anxieties about his role both in this tale and his 1899 essay on George Sand (1970, 551–52; *Life* 5, 143). Indeed, Edel points out, James recorded a beginning for the Story biography the same day as the reminder for the tale ([1949] 1963, 339). Przybylowicz remarks that James followed through on his principles both in his biography of Story and in the burning of his own letters (232).

Perhaps acknowledging its antecedents, James in 1911 sent a copy of *The Soft Side*, noting particularly "The Real Right Thing," to Mary Elizabeth Braddon, author of *Lady Audley's Secret* (*Letters* 4, 579).

Tintner sees the tale as a *fin de siècle* poster, both in its description of the black-garbed widow like "some 'decadent' coloured print, some poster of the newest school," and in its appearance in *Collier's*, where the text and illustration make a single image (137).

As with the phrase "the real thing," this tale's title also became a part of James's vocabulary. In 1915, for example, James wrote Edith Wharton in response to her war letters, calling them "wondrous wafts of the real right thing" (Bell 193).

Relation to Other Works

Generally the tale has been placed in the context of others that address issues of literary publicity, particularly making public the private lives of dead writers, seen also in such tales as *The Aspern Papers* and "John Delavoy" (e.g., Jones 236). Sharp contrasts the story's biographer with the "publishing scoundrel" of *The Aspern Papers*, who fails to respect the privacy of the dead (258; also Przybylowicz 232). Edel points out that the burning of the letters there is "the great thing" as it is "the real right thing" here to leave them undisturbed, or in "The Coxon Fund" unread (CT 10, 12; also Delbaere-Garant 216). Przybylowicz notes at the same time that the dead author becomes, for his biographer, a presence almost like that of the poet in "The Birthplace" for Gedge, or his own alter ego for Spencer Brydon (156). While Withermore, as Telotte observes, like Brydon, is seeking to track down some tangible sign, he ultimately, as Walter Wright records, decides not to intrude on the ghostly (Telotte 11; Wright 204). Powers notes the same "misdirection of attention" from the work of the artist to his life as in *The Tragic Muse*, "The Death of the Lion," and "Broken Wings" (102).

In entitling his tale, James was adding the "real right thing" to the "real" one, and Tinter accordingly calls it a "parody" title (137). Telotte distinguishes the two tales on the basis of title, arguing that in "The Real Thing" the "real thing" was too real, leaving no space for the artist's subjectivity, while here James is concerned with the "right" approach to reality (13–14).

Quentin Anderson links the tale with "John Delavoy" and *The Tragic Muse*, among others, as works in which characters discover the difference between the identity the world assigns and the truer work the creative artist does (194–95). Gage also sees the story as concerned with identity, a concern he designates as the central theme of the collection *The Soft Side*. Here Withermore and Doyne's widow discover it is better to stay ignorant of Doyne's true self than to violate it (38–39).

Allen suggests that James uses the supernatural as another way to represent the difficulty of absolute knowledge explored in the artist tales of the 1890s (121). Wagenknecht judges it a rather "pale" ghost story, whose place in the New York Edition might better have been filled by "The Third Person" (119–20). Markow-Totevy classifies the ghost as "hostile," like the violent ghost of the sister in "The Romance of Certain Old Clothes" who also guards what is hers (111). (See "Nona Vincent" and "Sir Dominick Ferrand.")

Interpretation and Criticism

The story has throughout the ghostly air of James's original inspiration, the sense that the subject of the biography "might come in." In a traditional reading, Edel marks the story's turn from the mere "occult" to the "ghostly" at the end with the apparition of Doyne (1970, 551). Vaid writes that the remoteness of the ghost makes for a rather mild supernaturalism, which in the end "convinces us without moving us" (212–13). Todorov, on the other hand, judges it unlikely the reader will believe, stating that because they see the characters from outside, readers are more likely to attribute the phenomenon to the "woman's hypernervous state," which also affects the would-be biographer (181). Banta casts the widow, who, Tintner remarks, is a "somewhat equivocal" character, as a comic ghost haunting her own house in her obsession with a dead husband she had no interest in while he was alive (Banta 181 n.23; Tintner 137).

The motives of the two thus haunted have been duly questioned. Wagenknecht posits that given her evident neglect of him in life, the wife's interest in a biography of her husband is not without an ulterior motive (120). Wright pictures her as seeking to possess without the interference of his artistic genius the man who eluded her in life (99). In Telotte's reading, Withermore has ulterior motives of his own. He sees him approaching Doyne's work looking for "self-assurance and self-assertion," as he is not only a man interested in Doyne's work but a young writer with his own name to make. He wants something concrete and "communicable," but Doyne's work—like that of any great artist— "defies true duplication," just as reality does. To translate it into biography would be to simplify its ambiguities, to present only part. Withermore becomes haunted as he seeks to commune with the dead Doyne, but what haunts him is the dark "ambiguity of the real"—the "ghosts of what has been left out, overlooked, or has simply defied apprehension." Therefore, as Telotte argues, it is appropriate that his vision of him is "unutterable," and that his conversation with him is "wordless." In the end, Withermore is at least wise enough to leave alone the reality he cannot capture. The issue is not simply reality, but as the title emphasizes the "right" and wrong construction of reality, which is never "neat."

The tale moves from the viewpoint of the biographer to his subject. And as Andreas formulates it, the lesson Withermore learns is that biography can harm the identity of the artist created in his work (148). The dead author's name here, Doyne, seems to emphasize that his work is done and needs no further meddling, while the name of the would-be biographer, Withermore, seems to carry the threat of blight. McElderry finds evident in the tale "James's distrust of biography" (122). It was a distrust he felt both as writer and subject, and Putt uses the tale's injunction "The artist was what he *did*—

he was nothing else" to admonish those who would read James's notebooks as diaries (419). In the preface to his study of James, one of the earliest, Edgar invokes this tale, acknowledging that James—like Doyne—may well have meant his works to stand as "sufficient provision" for "the legitimate curiosity of posterity." Heeding therefore "the menacing figure on the threshold," he confines himself to discretion in his use of James's biography (9–10). Most subsequent critics have braved the ghost. What James would say is impossible to tell.

Works Cited

Primary Works
James, Henry. 1899. "The Real Right Thing." *Collier's Weekly* 24 (16 December): 22, 24.

———. 1900. "The Real Right Thing." *The Soft Side*. London: Methuen; New York: Macmillan, 71–86.

———. 1909. "The Real Right Thing." *The Novels and Tales of Henry James*. New York Edition. Vol. 17, 409–31. New York: Scribner's.

Secondary Works
Allen, Elizabeth. 1984. *A Woman's Place in the Novels of Henry James*. New York: St. Martin's.

Anderson, Quentin. 1957. *The American Henry James*. New Brunswick, NJ: Rutgers University Press.

Andreas, Osborn. 1948. *Henry James and the Expanding Horizon: A Study of the Meaning and Basic Themes of James's Fiction*. Seattle: University of Washington Press.

Banta, Martha. 1964. "Henry James and 'The Others.'" *New England Quarterly* 37 (June): 171–84.

Bell, Millicent. 1965. *Edith Wharton and Henry James: The Story of Their Friendship*. New York: George Braziller.

Delbaere-Garant, Jeanne. 1970. *Henry James: The Vision of France*. Paris: Société d'Editions Les Belles Lettres.

Edel, Leon, ed. 1970. *Henry James: Stories of the Supernatural*. New York: Taplinger.

———, ed. [1949] 1963. *The Ghostly Tales of Henry James*. New York: The Universal Library, Grosset & Dunlap.

Edgar, Pelham. [1927] 1964. *Henry James, Man and Author*. New York: Russell & Russell.

Gage, Richard P. 1988. *Order and Design: Henry James' Titled Story Sequences*. New York: Peter Lang.

Jones, Granville H. 1975. *Henry James's Psychology of Experience: Innocence, Responsibility, and Renunciation in the Fiction of Henry James*. The Hague: Mouton.

McElderry, Bruce R., Jr. 1965. *Henry James*. New York: Twayne.

Markow-Totevy, Georges. 1969. *Henry James*. Trans. John Griffiths. London: Merlin.

Powers, Lyall H. 1970. *Henry James: An Introduction and Interpretation*. New York: Holt, Rinehart.

Putt, S. Gorley. 1966. *Henry James: A Reader's Guide*. Ithaca, NY: Cornell University Press.

Przybylowicz, Donna. 1986. *Desire and Repression: The Dialectic of Self and Other in the Late Works of Henry James*. University: University of Alabama Press.

Sharp, Sister M. Corona. 1963. *The Confidante in Henry James: Evolution and Moral Value of a Fictive Character*. Notre Dame, IN: Notre Dame University Press.

Telotte, J. P. 1984. "The Right Way with Reality: James's 'The Real Right Thing.'" *Henry James Review* 6, no. 4 (Fall): 8–14.

Tintner, Adeline R. 1986. *The Museum World of Henry James*. Ann Arbor: UMI Research Press.

Todorov, Tzvetan. 1977. *The Poetics of Prose*. Trans. Richard Howard. Ithaca, NY: Cornell University Press.

Vaid, Krishna B. 1964. *Technique in the Tales of Henry James*. Cambridge, MA: Harvard University Press.

Wagenknecht, Edward. 1984. *The Tales of Henry James*. New York: Frederick Ungar.

Wright, Walter F. 1962. *The Madness of Art: A Study of Henry James*. Lincoln: University of Nebraska Press.

The Real Thing

Publication History

"The Real Thing" appeared first, illustrated by Rudolf Blind, in an April 1892 issue of *Black and White*. The same month, the story was also distributed, Nordloh has discovered, by the S. S. McClure syndicate, which also handled such works as William Dean Howells's *The Quality of Mercy*. It appeared as a two-part serial with illustrations by F. C. Drake in at least eight newspapers from the New York *Sun* to the Indianapolis *News*. The next year James made it the title story of a collection and later he included it in the New York Edition.

Circumstances of Composition, Sources, and Influences

In his notebook James recorded his friend the illustrator George Du Maurier's having told him of a lady and gentleman who had called on him for work as models, sent on to him by the painter William Frith. What James was "struck with" was "the pathos, the oddity and typicalness of the situation," seeing it at the same time as a way to represent "the everlasting English ama- teurishness—the way superficial, untrained, unprofessional effort goes to the wall when confronted with trained, competitive, intelligent, *qualified* art." Rejecting the possibility of making the center of interest the husband's jeal- ousy of the painter as "vulgar and obvious," he turns to the idea of a contrast between the established models, lower-class professionals, who regard the genteel newcomers with "derisive amazement," and the couple who respond with their own "more silent amazement." He next increases the "action" by making the artist also face a trial, so that more depends on the issue of the contrast. Along the way, his terminology for the piece shifts about. At first, "it must be an idea—it can't be a 'story' in the vulgar sense of the word. It must be a picture; it must illustrate something." Toward the end, he asks, "Frankly, however, is this contrast enough of a *story*, by itself? It seems to me Yes—for it's an IDEA." James also felt it was about all he could fit into his word limit and his aim from the start was to keep the thing short (CN 55–57). He did indeed bring it in at under 10,000 words.

In his preface for the New York Edition, James retraces the genesis of the story. The "strange and striking couple," fallen like the Monarchs on hard times, he recalls, pled "with well-bred ease and the right light tone, not to say with feverish gaiety, that (as in the interest of art itself) *they* at least should n't have to 'make believe.'" James now recalls having debated with Du Maurier what they saw as the key question in "the rather lurid little passage": "whether their not having to make believe *would* in fact serve them, and above all serve their interpreter as well as the borrowed graces of the comparatively sordid professionals who had had, for dear life, to *know how* (which was to have learnt how) to do something." Interestingly, in the preface James stresses how the hiring of the new couple would hurt a pair already employed, "would have entailed the dismissal of an undistinguished but highly expert pair, also husband and wife"—"exceedingly modest members of society" who "earned their bread" through their modeling (*Criticism* 2, 1283). James's professional models are not married, and Shaw notes the change as a way James signals their independence compared to the Monarchs. Ron implies that James's emphasis in the preface on the longstanding employment of the first couple shows him forgetting that his "image of the happy studio" had actually "been engendered by the story" (192).

Oddly, given the usual reading of the tale, James once contemplated writing a tale as a "pendant" to "The Real Thing" with the opposite moral. According to it a woman turns out to be an excellent model because she is really "a deposed princess!," a conceit that occurred to him from hearing that a painter had once declared that only Empresses know how to pose (CN 70). Tintner, who also cites the above anecdote, sees James as drawing on the real-life Prince Edward and Queen Alexandra as models for his Monarchs. She sees in the fictional couple's lack of proper occupation a reflection on the royal couple's, evident in Edward's involvement in the card-playing scandal of the day, the Baccarat case, and Alexandra's frequent posing for photographs. She argues further that James's conception of out-of-work royalty was influenced by Daudet's 1879 *Les Rois en exil* and an 1857 work by a Dr. Doran, *Monarchs Retired from Business* (1989, 253–58).

The narrator's versions of Mrs. Monarch, which always come out "too tall," are reminiscent of Du Maurier's own drawings of women, as Tintner observes, which might indicate some criticism of his friend's work, except that Du Maurier's illustrations are generally meant comically (1989, 254). The scale of Du Maurier's later drawings was due to his eye troubles. Du Maurier had been told in the early 1870s, before James met him, that if he wished to avoid blindness, he should increase the scale of his drawings. According to Kelly, Du Maurier was unable to adjust to the new scale, and "disappointed with himself" he grew repetitious in his work, which declined in quality.

Others connect the artist most closely to James. Edel argues that the lesson here that the "real thing" cannot learn to be something else reflects James's realization that he could not educate himself to be a playwright, that "art is not simply a learning of particular laws" (*Life* 4, 22). Marder also connects the tale with James's playwriting endeavors, contending that literary art became a "ghost" at this time in his fiction, citing as examples the narrator's preference for the model over the "real thing" and the disappearing Lord Mellifont of "The Private Life" (17). Richardson notes that James like the painter wanted the "germ" of an event, "not the whole 'real thing'" (xli). Ron particularly cites James's irritation at Mrs. Anstruther Thompson for telling too much of the "germ" to *The Spoils of Poynton* (198). In the case of this story, as Beach observes, James had no interest in the way the original situation worked out (16).

The narrator at one point remarks that there are "few serious workers in black-and-white," which Gale takes as a dig at contemporary illustrations, and even at the magazine *Black and White* itself where his story "Brooksmith" had recently appeared as he recalled in the notebook entry for the tale. The issue in which the story first appeared Gale judges "otherwise totally undistinguished," even as he calls the illustrations "incredibly wretched" (1963). Similarly, Bogardus finds the stiffness of the illustrations producing an "unintended irony" (78). Shaw, on the other hand, sees the order of pictures in the magazine nicely reproducing the contrast between the amateur and professional models (71). James's first essay in his collection *Picture and Text* was entitled "Black and White," and James in 1883 suggested the phrase among several possible titles for what was to become the *English Illustrated Magazine* to its publisher Macmillan (*Correspondence* 75). James generally disliked illustrations, according to Edel, who cites his remark when preparing for the New York Edition, that he "wanted to be spared such a tribute." The publishers had suggested the illustrator Albert Sterner, to which James replied "I like Albert Sterner; but are twenty Albert Sterners desirable or even thinkable—???" (*Life* 5, 333–34). Nevertheless James included some of the illustrations to *Daisy Miller* in his decorations for Lamb House (*Life* 468). For the New York Edition, James turned to photography, rather oddly, as Beaver comments (54). James, observes Higgins, generally disliked photography even more, and it is the inartistic Monarchs who register "like a photograph, or a copy of a photograph" (662).

James's New York Edition was still several years in the future. The artist in the tale, however, is already setting to work to illustrate "the projected *édition de luxe* of one of the writers of our day—the rarest of the novelists—who, long neglected by the multitudinous vulgar and dearly prized by the attentive . . . had had the happy fortune of seeing, late in life, the dawn and then the full light of a higher criticism" (*CT* 8, 237). The novelist is an imagined one, Philip Vincent, although James had in the notebooks imagined him as Fielding, the trial work *Joseph Andrews*, and in the tale the work is a "historical" novel (*CN* 56). Still, the parallel with James's own collected edition pertains, and Matthiessen and Murdock see James "indulging in oblique, playful concern" the thought of it, while Higgins sees it as a less concerned "wishfulfilling" projection (N 105; Higgins 662).

James would revise "The Real Thing" itself for the New York Edition. In examining the successive revisions of the tale, Wilson sees the earlier revision for *The Soft Side* concentrating on "linguistic detail" while that for the New York Edition offers more interpolations and larger changes as James worked to emphasize the tale's relationships and escape what Wilson sees as the restrictions of first-person narration for the James of the major phase (293–96).

When James fired his alcoholic servant couple, the Smiths, in 1902 with two months' pay, he wrote of the event to his sister-in-law Alice: "They will never turn round; they are lost utterly; but I would have promised *anything* in my desire to get them out of the house before some still more hideous helplessness made it impossible" (*Life* 545). His mood is reminiscent of the narrator's here.

As a source of Jack Hawley's initials (the reverse of James's) and something of his cold, critical, unproductive character as well, Gale proposes John Hay (1977).

The artist's need "to impose his own imaginative order upon his selected materials," according to Edel and Lind, was evident in James as early as his art criticism from Paris in the 1870s (xxi). The issue of "imitation," however, goes back to Plato and Aristotle, as Terrie observes, noting that the distinction of this tale is to treat the artistic issue in "distinctively human terms" (8). The failure of the Monarchs, according to Lainoff, is designed to illustrate the failure of the eighteenth-century concept of the *beau idéal* articulated in Reynolds's *Discourses*. The artist's having to resort to servants as models instead, demonstrates further, Lainoff argues, James's belief that no better standard had yet appeared in mannered, upper-class society. Indeed, in Lyon's analysis, the tale should be placed in the context of a general hostility to art in the nineteenth century. The Monarchs, who claim to be reality, are in actuality "inimical to art." Their photographic accuracy "leaves everything out" and they live only within James's prose. The Major is properly satirized as one of Arnold's barbarians, but his hostility to the imagination, Lyon writes, was also typical of the middle class. In James's treatment of such characters, Lyon discerns a reflection of Santayana's distress at American business, as well as some of his philosophy in James's pondering of the "old conundrum about the reality of the ideal and the ideality of the real" (41–43). Pendleton locates echoes of the pragmatic philosophy of James's brother William, which asserted that "the final truth or falsity of an idea depends upon the actual difference the idea will make when it is applied to a concrete or practical situation" (3–4). Hocks also locates several of William's ideas in the tale, including his conception of "experience and human consciousness" (124–25).

Banta places the tale in the context of the nineteenth-century debate between realism and idealism or romanticism, remarking on the general interest in "real things" or "types" at the turn of the century seen in such philosophers as William James, Josiah Royce, Kenyon Cox, Charles Sanders Pierce, and John Dewey. She sees the same interest in the literature of the time as well, pointing, for example, to the similarities in theme and setting with Du Maurier's *Trilby*, whose heroine combines qualities of both women in James's tale, being both a Cockney and a *real* lady. Other works she mentions as dealing with the distinction between the "real thing" or type and the stereotype, or lady and artist include William Ordway Partridge's 1900 *The Angel of Clay* and Robert Chambers's 1911 *The Common Law* (9, 19–26). Roditi points to a short story by Oscar Wilde that appeared a decade earlier entitled "The Model Millionaire" as less successfully examining the relationships between artist, model, and reality through the device of a millionaire posing as a beggar model (71–72). Beaver sees Hawley's philosophy reminiscent of that of Oscar Wilde with a debt as well to Ruskin's search for "the innocence of the eye" and an anticipation of Berenson's cultivation of it, as well as a Wildean split life and art (57–58, 68). Shaw notes that gentility selling itself can find a market and so be comically treated as in W. S. Gilbert's Duke and Duchess of Plazatoro in *The Gondoliers* (66–67).

James's approach of taking only the "germ" of the subject is also, according to Richardson, Hawthorne's "method of romance" (xli). Sanders offers a particular parallel with "The Prophetic Pictures," both in the challenging of fate, and in the arrogance of the artist who fails to see "the disorder" of his own life (361). Gerlach finds the rejection of the Monarchs a "metaphorical" death similar to those in such Hawthorne tales as "Wakefield" (88). Kaplan sees the Monarchs facing of starvation treated with the "stoic clarity" of Melville (257)

Walter Wright compares the narrator's fixed fascination with the Monarchs to that of the listening wedding guest in *The Ancient Mariner* (1957, 88). In Beaver's view, the artist needs in his models the "negative capability" of Keats's poet (56). Banta has stated that while Miss Churm is indeed possessed of a genuine "Shakespearean negative capability," Mrs. Monarch suffers from a disabling "Wordsworthian ego" (12). The narrator says of Major Monarch "his occupation was gone," and Beaver sees the artist rather hyperbolically and snidely turning him into a "neurotic Othello" (65). In her reading, Lester sympathetically notes "the artist's reluctance to grow up by sacking the Monarchs" (37). The idea of the necessary dismissal of a representative of make-believe recalls Prince Hal's "sacking" of his companion Falstaff as he becomes king.

James cited Maupassant in his notebooks as a model of conciseness, and Ron calls the early 1890s James's "Maupassant phase" (190 n.1). Tintner finds James taking inspiration from a specific tale then attributed to the French writer, "The Real One and the Other," about a politician, his "real" wife, who cannot properly play the role of politician's wife, and his mistress, who adeptly impersonates her as she should be (1987, 221–25). Delbaere-Garant loosely associates James's criticism of the French realists with that of the lifeless modelling of the Monarchs (50).

Oronte, upon first seeing Mrs. Monarch, stares at her "with the rapt, pure gaze of the young Dante spellbound by the young Beatrice" (CT 8, 248). Wegelin notes the allusion, as well as another in Hawley's reference to "*coloro che sanno*"—the "maestro" of "those who know" in Dante being Aristotle (255 n.2). The latter, writes Beaver, is intended to place the narrator with Hawley in the aesthetic "elect" (58). Oronte, however, according to Lester, remains a "blatantly stock character—the clever servant who gets his master out of a jam," even as he sees his emphatically Italian nature recalling the Roman comedies which were the origin of the type (37).

Given that Kehler reads Churm's name as a Cockneyfied pun on "charm," it is appropriate that Briden finds her a prototype of Shaw's Eliza Doolittle. Ryan, who argues that the narrator's lesson here "validate[s]" for him the value of the unreal, sees the issue of the connection between the real and the unreal—the "invisible bridge" between them—also in Musil's *Die Verwirrungen des Zöglings Törleß* (308).

Relation to Other Works

The phrase that provides the story's title was a frequent refrain for James. In "Flickerbridge" Granger to Miss Wenham is "too exactly the real thing." In "The Beldonald Holbein" the narrator-painter threateningly promises to do a portrait of the heartless Lady Beldonald that will be "the real thing." In "The Two Faces" the country house Mundham is "theatrically, the real thing." In a letter to Fullerton, James spoke of himself as the "real thing" (*Life* 511). In *The Ambassadors* the revelation of Mlle de Vionnet's engagement has "something ancient and cold in it—what he would have called the real thing" (312). Miller, in a discourse on the significance of the word "thing" calls it "a name for something all that surface complexity hides, or only obscurely reveals" pointing to the titles of "the real thing," and "the right real thing" or the dying James's greeting of death as "the distinguished thing at last" (104–5).

The Ambassadors, as a whole, is to Ryan a "more sophisticated version" of the tension between the real and the unreal as Strether puzzles out the truth about the relationship between Chad and Mme de Vionnet (308–9). Quentin Anderson argues that Strether fails to learn, as the artist here does, the difference between appearance and reality (211). Discovering in "The Real Thing" no interest in Miss Churm's own story or identity, Banta writes, James would tell "*that* story" through the character of Mme de Vionnet (12)

Mme de Vionnet is, of course, from a very different class than Miss Churm. She would fit more with the Monarchs, whom Dietrichson classes with such contemptuously portrayed upper-class characters as Selina of *A London Life* and the Duke of Green-Erin of *An International Episode*, as the narrator finds in them "everything he most objected to in the social system of his country." Later, he classes them among the *"pauvres honteux"* who most appreciate what money can bring, but still finds the contempt outweighing the pity of their portrait (59–60, 79–80). The Monarchs, in the view of the narrator, are "insurmountably stiff," and Mrs. Monarch in particular reminds Gage of the equally "stiff" Winterbourne, who looked down on Daisy, as Mrs. Monarch does on Miss Churm, her inability to comprehend her talent similar to to Vogelstein's "bewilderment" at the success of Pandora Day. The comparison to Daisy he finds heightened by the addition of Oronte, who with Miss Churm makes a pair reminiscent of Daisy and Giovanelli. The issue here, Gage observes, is switched in this tale from their acceptability by society to their utility in art. In "The Real Thing," however, he concludes the upper-class characters come to a greater insight (170–76).

As members of the lower class, Oronte and Churm, writes Salzberg, resemble Mr. Mudge of *In the Cage* in their successful plasticity, while the Monarchs resemble Mr. Everard in his attractive but limited nature (76 n.8). Boren places Churm with Noémie Nioche of *The American*, Henrietta Stackpole, and Daisy Miller as a character with a voice of her own free to "cavort" linguistically apart from the Jamesian "idealized" speech (86–87). The Monarchs are on the way to the lower class, and Dietrichson contrasts their impoverished but loving marriage with that of the Dodds in "The Bench of Desolation" (116). Richardson points to the shared theme of declining fortunes in "Brooksmith" (489). Jones compares their graceful exit to that of Brooksmith, but makes the point that while Brooksmith is an "anomaly," they are "anachronisms." Neither is able, he adds, to make the sort of compromise that Gedge does in "The Birthplace" (202–3). While Gage emphasizes the similarity between the short Oronte and the too short Brooksmith, the more relevant comparison may be with the Monarchs whose height also interferes with their employment—they keep coming out too tall. In contrast with the dissatisfied and doomed Brooksmith, Gage adds, Churm and Oronte remain "comfortable" (180, 188).

In Grover's view, "The Real Thing" is a "philosophical parable" on the same themes James discusses abstractly in "The Art of Fiction" (127). The themes often contain a moral element, and Quentin Anderson places the tale with "The Birthplace" as being "of central importance in defining Henry James's moral horizon" and "the *metaphysical* role which the creative imagination plays in his work" (1950, xiii). Walter Wright sees the view that James is "obsessed with art to the neglect of moral character" as supported only by a "misreading" of the tale, noting that in *The Portrait of a Lady*,

James condemned "mere esthetes" as he does Chad in *The Ambassadors* (1957, 89). Lackey focuses on the danger of confusing "moral responsibility" with the "aesthetic impulse" and the consequent "desire for control," a danger also illustrated in the behavior of Adam Verver and Mrs. Gereth (192).

In "The Liar," the professional model says to Capadose, "You don't sit so well as us," a remark Horne cites as representing Churm's attitude to the Monarchs (60). The narrator's own famed "innate preference for the represented subject over the real one" Bowden likens to James's depiction of Italian art in *Roderick Hudson* in which he values a "quality of life" represented by European art over art itself (25). James, Cowie indicates, believed art should "represent" life not "reproduce" it (731). Auchard calls James "a shakey realist," and so portraying both the narrator's acceptance of the "real thing" in the Monarchs and Roderick's acceptance of the "actuality" of Christina Light as inappropriate choices (36–38). Falk contrasts the early treatment of the gap between illusion and reality in "The Madonna of the Future" illustrated by two extremes, with the subtler treatment here. He argues that "The Madonna of the Future" makes clear that the "real thing" is nothing without the artist's imagination, but that James by embodying the "real thing" through the "surface action" of the sympathetic Monarchs, makes his point more complex if no less definite (69). While Van Nostrand sees James portraying through Theobald the "limitations of idealism," he writes that James "had no quarrel with the validity of subjective impressions." Thus "mere actuality is not sufficient" indeed its insufficiency leads the painter "to construct a more perfect reality" (150–51).

In its comparison of art to "wasteful reality," Beebe places the tale with "The Sweetheart of M. Briseux" and "The Birthplace" (215 n.50). Perosa contrasts the tale's successful dramatization of the "predominance of art over life" with the technical failure of *The Sacred Fount* (93). Edel reads the masks in *The Sacred Fount* as pointing to the same truth he sees in "The Real Thing"—that "the 'real thing' was simply itself, photographic. Art transfigured reality" (*Life* 4, 343). Putt finds "The Real Thing" a more successful treatment of the same theme as "The Author of Beltraffio" because of the greater life of the representative characters and their lack of self-consciousness, adding that Ambient may well be too much the "real thing" for that story (1966, 223).

James was drawn, according to Lycette, to a "pictorial style" illustrated by such characters as Mme Merle, Osmond, Mrs. Costello and the Monarchs whose identities are "clearly represented in their poses and 'appurtenances,'" unlike Isabel Archer, Roderick Hudson, and Strether. The Monarchs, she writes, exhibit the same "doll-like function" with which Osmond "traps" Isabel. James and his artist-heroes, on the other hand, from Roderick through Strether, "realize a transformation of consciousness to transcend the shells of the stereotyped existence." To such as Isabel, Lambert, and even Miss Churm it is "variety, scope, and adaptability" that are important to art (56–59). The relationship of the artist with those who cannot understand art, Baxter argues, is a theme shared by this tale, "The Author of Beltraffio," and "The Lesson of the Master" (227). Quentin Anderson also sees the theme of the portrait as false art in this tale, "The Author of Beltraffio," and "The Figure in the Carpet" (149).

The use of contrasting cases, Monarchs and professional models, Goetz argues, can produce only a relative meaning, an approach typical of James's artist tales including "The Next Time" and "The Private Life." Goetz notes also the prevalence of first-person narration in the artist tales including in addition to those above *The Aspern Papers*, "The Death of the Lion," and "The Figure in the Carpet" (31, 156). The last line here, speaking of the narrator's "harm" and his "precious memory" recalls the last line of *The Aspern Papers*: "When I look at it I can scarcely bear my loss—I mean of the precious papers." Bishop connects the tale with "The Tone of Time," the unfinished "Hugh Merrow," and "The Liar," the narrator here exhibiting the same egotism as the artists of the last two, the issue of "artistic rendering" as a "reflector of sensibility" the same as in the last. He traces, too, how this tale and "Hugh Merrow" share the same kind of "determinative first paragraph" showing the initial encounter of painter and sitters (92–94, 96–97).

The Tragic Muse, Q. D. Leavis observes, also treats the "theory of the function of artist and actress and their pre-eminence in a world of politics and society" (227). Edward Stone notes the tale's paradox in the novel as well where the actress Miriam Rooth, in order to project "personality" on the stage, must not possess too much of it off stage (107; also Gordon and Stokes 162). More positively Delbaere-Garant finds in Miriam and the two professional models the same "plasticity," and the same lack of it in Miriam's mother and the Monarchs (322). Calling the Monarchs "too respectable to be of any use artistically," Grover compares Mrs. Monarch's objections to Russian princesses with Miriam's mother's worries that her daughter portray a "bad" woman, to which the great French actress replies, "To be too respectable to go where things are done best is, in my opinion, to be very vicious indeed; and to do them badly in order to preserve your virtue is to fall into a grossness more shocking than any other" (76).

Swan classifies the tale with "The Beldonald Holbein" and "The Velvet Glove" as one of James's "lighter" works, a view the Monarchs or Mrs. Brash might find it hard to sustain (1948, 9–10).

Inglis sees the chiastic exchange of roles between the Monarchs and the models typical of late James, similar to the exchange of roles between Nanda and Vanderbank in *The Awkward Age* in which *she* lets him "down easily" and of Milly and Sir Luke in *The Wings of the Dove* (82).

In an analysis of significant looks in *Madame de Mauves*, "Four Meetings," and "The Liar," Gargano contrasts the heroism and recognition of Mrs.

Monarch's epiphanal look with the more limited vision of both Caroline Spencer and Oliver Lyon (315).

Interpretation and Criticism

In 1896 Horace Scudder, in a review of a novel by James's friend Mrs. Humphry Ward, notes the problem caused by Ward's primary interest being not in her created characters but in "the people of the actual world . . . whom she tries to transfer to her novel." Remarking on the need in art of "making anew," Scudder cites James's "luminous parable" in which the painter discovers that those "real enough in actual life" are "inferior models," a moral he had applied also in a review of Owen Wister's fiction.

The traditional reading of the tale follows just such a distinction. Norrman sees James as having being unable to resist the possibilities for "chiastic inversion" in his initial situation, creating two contrasting pairs of characters and qualities (147). One, as Beach puts it, has plasticity but no gentility, the other gentility but no plasticity(16). Throughout the tale such opposites recur. Lebowitz, for example, summarizes the theme as "the tragedy of object posing as subject, costume as mind, 'fool' as 'free agent'" (79). Even the narrator has a complement in Hawley, who, writes Marquardt, "completes the symmetrical arrangement" of pairs (6). The insistent symmetry is for some overdone. O'Faolian, for example, sees in Oronte a "mere repetition" of Miss Churm (189).

The traditional moral is antimimetic. Reality is not the best inspiration for art. As Winner cites the narrator, "in the deceptive atmosphere of art even the highest respectability may fail of being plastic" (108). Mrs. Monarch proudly observes that "the drawings you make from *us*, they look exactly like us," but the type of realism advocated here, as Lainoff observes, is the giving of "the *shape of reality* or the air of reality to that which may not be real" (193). Thus, writes Wagenknecht, "art is not life but the distilled essence of life" (69–70). Nalbantian sees the preference for the imaginary an example of the specialized aesthetic of the decadent artist who has to "postpone" the real in order to produce the ideal. By dealing directly with the real—the Monarchs—the narrator, according to Nalbantian, deprives himself of the necessary exercise to produce anything other than copies of life of the realistic school (48).

According to Walcutt, the "*idea* of gentility is the real thing" but "its embodiment in actual people weights it with a millstone of human inadequacy" making it "stiff and crass" (178). Other critics tend to emphasize the completeness of the Monarchs that leaves little room for the work of the artist (e.g., Telotte 13; McCarthy 81; Auchard 37–38; Kaplan 256). Writes Todorov,

"The absence of 'real' qualities" in Churm and Oronte is more conducive to the artist who prefers "the represented subject" to the real. The work of art must be "primary" with "nothing antecedent to it" (167–69). Others such as O'Faolian emphasize the rigidity of the Monarchs (163). As the narrator complains of Mrs. Monarch, "She was the real thing, but always the same thing." In the face of such rigidity, McElderry sees the tale arguing for the superiority of impressionism to "literal Realism" given that "details stifle" and "suggestion stimulates" (123).

The only thing more complete than the Monarchs is a photograph. Indeed, to Andreas, the message of the tale is the ironic fact that "photographic naturalism and reportorial art" are "less realistic" than "representational art" (147). Bogardus, on the other hand, sees illustration as the tale's subject and comments that, while the narrator could have painted the Monarchs well enough because the painter is free to follow his imagination, he has difficulty using them as the subject of illustrations because an illustrator must follow the text. Still, the view of photography in the tale, he notes, is even more negative (78, 120–21).

The tale is a "parable," as Markow-Totevy articulates it, showing the differences between "creation" and "literal imitation," art and reality, the vision of the artist and the ordinary person (96). Banta sees the tale as offering the reader "two kinds of identity" to "assess": Mrs. Monarch's "singleness" and Miss Churm's "infinite variety." Banta's own preference is clear, while noting that Mrs. Monarch has "moral value" and that she preserves "the privacy of an inner life," by posing only for the figure, she still remarks of the two Monarchs that "they have been up for sale for some time." "A raving egoist when it comes to identity," Mrs. Monarch in Banta's formulation has priced herself out of the market. The more modest and "suggestive" Miss Churm is more useful in the studio, offering "art, not nature" (10–12).

Beginning with James's statement in "The Art of Fiction" that "The only reason for the existence of a novel is that it does attempt to represent life," Grover also examines the nature of realism in the tale. In the essay, as Grover indicates, James made specific parallels between the art of painting and of fiction, making the experience of the artist in the tale relevant for the writer as well. In the essay, James asserts, the "picture *is* reality." Real in what way, asks Grover. Pointing to the common assumption that a representation must "resemble" its subject, as the Monarchs assume, he emphasizes the difference between resemblance and representation. In "The Art of Fiction," after all, James also spoke of a novel as "a personal, a direct impression of life . . . which is greater or less according to the *intensity* of the impression." Such impressions "produce" reality. The story in turn plays on the "difference between appearance and reality," turning around the general assumption that "appearances are deceptive and should be rejected in favour of the real."

But here, as the narrator asserts, Miss Churm can look like a princess without any resemblance at all, "when I *make* her." Art, concludes Grover, is about "signs" not "referents" because the latter bears greater fruit.

Similarly Quentin Anderson sees the tale depicting the "moral primacy" of "dramatic values" over "pictorial." The Monarchs have "limited, fixed, pictorial values," while the models can "project themselves in dramatic situations." He speaks of the difference in the terms of James's father's philosophy, as an opposition between the "identity" given us by the world and the "individuality" that we create ourselves. Anderson further ties the Monarchs' limitations to their class, calling the aristocrat a "licensed image of conformity." The Monarchs are "frozen into the forms of a caste society," and the artist is right to break away from them (43, 142, 146).

The class of the Monarchs has attracted much comment. O'Faolian declares that they are "evidently of a type that James particularly likes, people with a splendid facade, of elegance and worldliness, which conceals poverty and vacuity" but "nice" (163). Most critics, however, have seen little liking in the portrayal of the Monarchs' type. The narrator speaks of the Monarchs having "in their faces, the blankness, the deep intellectual repose of the twenty years of country-house visiting" which he evokes further in terms of "their leggings and waterproofs, their knowing tweeds and rugs, their rolls of sticks and cases of tackle and neat umbrellas" (CT 8, 236). It is a picture of an unimaginative, materialistic world Gill among others sees as representing James's own view in the 1890s (77, 79; also Ward 30–31). As Holder points out, James was particularly irritated by the ignorance of art among such people, "the everlasting English amateurishness" (295). James once spoke of its "gilded bondage": the "waste of time in vain sitting and strolling about is a gruesome thought in the face of what one still wants to do with one's remnant of existence" (*Letters* 3, 146). He did not exempt the Monarchs: in the notebook entry for their tale he spoke of them "all their life stupid and well-dressed" able only to "*show*" themselves, clumsily, for the fine, clean, well-groomed animals that they were, only hope to make a little money by—in this manner—just simply *being*" (CN 55). In Jefferson's assessment, despite their value as people, the Monarchs are "completely and damningly" the products of their environment (52–54). Putt takes exception, however, to Leavis's reading of James's contempt in the tale "for the English country-house culture and its social values," seeing James taking more of an "amused affectionate tone" (Leavis 227; Putt 1966, 223).

Vielledent assigns a greater value to what she calls the Monarchs' "social" artistry. In her reading, the narrator is soured throughout by his initial disappointment that the Monarchs were not paying customers. More comfortable with Churm and Oronte to whom he can safely condescend, he does not notice the Monarchs' ability to transform themselves, first into decent models then into servants (40–43). Similarly, Walcutt raised the question of whether the Monarchs by virtue of acquiring the "manners and trappings of aristocracy" had "not themselves achieved artistic creations." If they are frauds, he adds, the artist should have recognized them as such from the start (179). Mackenzie also faults the narrator for his preference of the servile Oronte and his humiliation of the Monarchs out of a sense of social anxiety, characterizing the way the "precluded, servant-like artist revolts, nominally on behalf of actual servants against the masters, the 'social people.'" Still, it is not their gentility that makes the Monarchs the real thing in Mackenzie's reading, but what the narrator himself calls their "real marriage" (188–89 n.30). Even that strength, however, can be a weakness, in the view of Stein, who sees James's sense of a conflict between art and marriage reflected in the Monarchs, whose marriage, while not the cause of their inadaptibility, contributes to it because "in their touching mutual support each reinforces the other's shortcomings as a model" (108–9).

Farnsworth, on the other hand, emphasizes the appeal of the Monarchs' world to the narrator, whose social ambitiousness is evident in his desire to become a portraitist. Although their very name "suggests a dead set of social values, something quaintly inappropriate to the new world," it seems attractive to an artist who finds the present world "frequently grubbily commercial." As a result, the narrator paints pictures of a Mrs. Monarch "seven feet high" and is keenly aware of his "own very much scantier issues." He is saved, however, in Farnsworth's view, by Hawley's "wise criticism." James, however, shows his own "nostalgia" in the final revelation of the Monarchs' humanity as they take over the role of servants. By doing so, Farnsworth contends, the Monarchs justify the narrator's treasuring of their memory. There is yet another irony, however, he writes, in the narrator's paying off the Monarchs, which draws into question his newly acquired compassion.

The task of the narrator in the tale, according to Kaplan, is to discover "what *does* represent life." Here ironically he is "misdirected" by the very "real thing," as the "given truth blocks the way to a discovered truth." In Kaplan's view the imagination is best "aroused by a subject moving in transit between one possibility and another." Miss Churm in her miming illustrates the "hopeful aspect" of such a capacity, rising to play a princess, while the Monarchs show the "reverse" as they descend in the social scale. However unfortunate, it is this movement that allows the Monarchs to become "real," to "win a victory over their own artifice." The story thus becomes a "lesson in freedom as well as art" as it shows the power of art to break through form in a manner that "parallels" the "democratic imagination." The "real 'real thing,'" however, is the Monarchs' desire to avoid starvation, and Kaplan sees in the tale James's recognition of the vulnerability of life, art's role being to create a "frame of judgment" based on a "stoic knowledge of contradictions" (256–57).

On first looking at the tale, Ron finds it so "obliging" in its "explictness" that there seems little to say. He turns nevertheless to examine first two central "polarities," those of "master/slave and art/life." In the studio where life is "converted into art" the model or "slave" becomes the master, by the "dynamic element" of "professionalism" through the agency of the artist. This system, however, is *"jammed"* by the arrival of the Monarchs, who introduce a third polarity, that of "sign/meaning." At the same time, because there are now "too many models" a *"struggle"* begins, enacted by a shifting of "function[s]" in the hierarchy of the studio, from model to servant. The Monarchs, according to Ron, seem at first a "demystification" of the theory of realism, as they "short circuit" what James calls the "alchemy of art." The problem is that they are types, and a type is "poor economy" because, in contrast to the flexible Miss Churm, it can represent only one thing. Even so, Ron insists, there must be more of a reason why the real thing will not work in art. He looks then at class, and sees the reality the Monarchs represent as that of a class whose power they do not share, so that there is a "disparity" between them as real and as pictured. They represent more *"appearance"* than reality. The gap, writes Ron, may seem "symptomatic" of James's era, a sign of its decadence, but, he argues, it should not be limited to any particular time period as it indicates "the congenitality of the illness that is culture" at all times. The Monarchs, however, claim to be the "real thing," metaphor not metonymy, while the models claim no such "continuity." Their insistence interferes with the "monopoly," and since, citing Toor, Ron sees the narrator as unreliable, the narrator naturally reacts badly to such interference. But Ron also sees the narrator's mistreatment of the couple masking his fear in what he characterizes vaguely as an "Oedipal situation" whereby the narrator is "excluded" from the Monarchs by their marriage. Although their power is "entirely illusory," it is enough to induce in the narrator what Barthes calls a "Noah complex" in which Hawley plays the son who laughs at the parent's nakedness, and the narrator the one who looks away. The worst "wound," however, he sees the narrator sustaining is not that of the bitter "memory" the Monarchs leave him with, but the recognition that "being itself is already a representation." Thus, the narrator's identity is also deconstructed. Ron's first two polarities merge as in *mimesis* "life is to art what master is to slave." James, Ron admits, kept an "allegiance" to the "ideal of metaphysics," but he himself hopes his own work "betray[s] some of its profound inauthenticity." One does, too, as despite the intricate and insightful reading of the interrelationships of the studio, one does not necessarily wish therefore to subscribe to the view that interpretation is most likely "an act of violence."

As Ron's reading illustrates, however, the Monarchs are not only types but individuals. James himself in his notebook remarked on the "tragedy" of their situation (CN 55). In discussing the tale with Ford Madox Ford, James had spoken of them as "reduced, literally, to complete vagueness as to the provenance of their next day's breakfast, lunch, tea, and dinner . . ." (1937, 8–10). Critics often see in the tale what Walcutt calls an "interesting dominance of theme over event and character" (178). Swan, for example, counsels that the "particular instance" in the tale probably should not be taken "too literally" as James was primarily concerned with the "general truth" it illustrated about the "odd side of the artistic imagination" (1957, 25–26). Beach also spoke of the tale as "a sort of problem in human reactions" rather than a "particular case" (16). But as Tanner observes, although "something of an ontological joke," the story has "serious resonances" (80). Many readers have noted a genuine emotionalism in the tale. In a letter to John Galsworthy, Joseph Conrad defended James from the charge of coldness, saying of "The Real Thing" in particular that it "seems to flow from the heart" (Gard 279–80). The *Athenaeum*, too, found in the tale "pathos" as well as "humor" (602). Gage detects an "elegiac" note in Mrs. Monarch's passing glory, and Richardson similarly draws attention to the "poignant elaboration" of the Monarchs' "fallen fortunes" (Gage 167; Richardson 489). McElderry notes that while they provoke humor when contrasted with the models, they evoke pathos when they stand alone (123).

While O'Faolian speaks of the Monarchs as "little more than social types" accorded "virtually no characterisation," many critics have praised their vividness (187). Indeed, a reviewer in 1945, Stevens, called Major Monarch one of the few James characters who seems "alive on any terms" (32). Tilton, while acknowledging James's satire of the "clean and stiff and stupid" Monarchs, as the narrator calls them, also sees them as so appealing that there is a danger of the reader missing the satire (x). Similarly, Putt argues that James rose far beyond the paradoxes posed by his narrator, making the Monarchs, particularly the "knowing but tongue-tied" Major, far more "real" than necessary for their roles in the artistic argument (1976, 8).

Others are less sympathetic. Ford writes that "we may doubt whether . . . the artist . . . isn't as much to be commiserated for having them descend upon him and so nearly ruin his work" and remarks that James in treating the conflict between the "oppressor and the oppressed" always shows that "even in the act of oppressing, the oppressor isn't having a very much better time than his victims" (1913, 81–82). Voss writes that while the artist can admire and pity the Monarchs, he can also be "bored" and "irritated" by their incapacity in the world of art (142).

Walter Wright, however, contends that the obvious "antithesis between art and life" is not the main point of the tale. The tale instead gains its meaning from what he sees as its focus on the Monarchs. Why, he asks, would the narrator keep on the Monarchs at the risk of his career? He keeps them, because they are the "real thing" "stripped . . . of all . . . external supports"; ". . . their love has been tried by the kind of misfortune that often degrades and it has never been shaken." They are not dead, but intensely alive, exemplifying the "art of living," and James gives them in the end his "benediction." The narrator learns from them as he never will from Churm or Oronte, contends

Wright. Like James, a "portrait painter *in* words," he gains from them the memory he records in the tale (1957, 85–90). Miller gives a different reading of those "words." Observing how the narrator "ends his memorial record of a strange episode in his life which has damaged his art" by speaking of the "price" he paid, he writes "the doing of the thing, in this case, is the composition of its written record or memorial inscription, the record or accounting of the price paid for the value banked in the memory" (105).

Wright's reading is in part a response to the influential reading of Fadiman, who raised the issue of morality in the Monarchs' lack of plasticity and, he charged, vitality. Their equal failure morally and artistically demonstrates, Fadiman asserted, the congruence of the two qualities for James (216–17). Labor, however, dismisses Fadiman's reading as making the tale into "an esthetic cliché." He discerns in the tale three "major thematic levels": social, aesthetic, and moral. The social, he states, is "quite explicit"—the Monarchs "have been and still are the real thing." The real thing in society, however, is not necessarily the real thing for the artist who needs rather "the ideal thing." The first two levels of the tale, then, are in "conflict," giving the story its "tension." Hawley's judgment on the Monarchs, for example, is perfectly correct from an artistic standpoint, but otherwise "heartless." The "third level" comes into play in the last line, when the narrator admits he has given up some of his art for a "memory." It is the narrator, not the Monarchs, Labor asserts, who undergoes the greatest change from an initially "commercial" stance through a "detached, even slightly cruel, amusement" to a newly humane one. If he has "lost something" as an artist, he has "gained infinitely more as a man." He has learned compassion. Paradoxically, the moral level "justifies the artist's willingness to renounce his talent" even as such a willingness is necessary for true artistic greatness. Bernard combines Fadiman and Labor, to depict the artist learning through the Monarchs that his art has *not* been a true transformation of reality, but of the artificial, the posturings of models to whom he has no true commitment, and that the real thing in art, not just life, that will allow him to make that transformation, is compassion (31–32).

Others, while acknowledging the role of human emotion in the tale, see it as inferior to art. To Baxter the Monarchs represent "the uncomprehending 'others' who must be renounced," even though their departure is a "personal loss" for the narrator, a "surrendering [of] companionship in the superior interests of his art" (227). Jones, too, points to the narrator's personal sympathy for the Monarchs, but his inability to compromise himself as an artist (201–2). Lester, drawing on the theories of Northrop Frye, reads the tale as a "comedy" but comes to similar conclusions about the relationship of the artist to the Monarchs. Part of the narrator's experience, she writes, is a "renewed commitment to visual make-believe," even as the tale explores "the value of all artistic fictions" by way of the analogy of painting and fiction. She sees the narrator as self-consciously trying to "impress" the Monarchs. But as an artist, he needs to "keep his own point of view," which is difficult in view of the Monarchs' attempt to "import" their own point of view—that they are the "real thing"—into the studio. The narrator's suppressed worry shows up in his pictures where the over-sized Monarchs appear like parents, parents who draw bounds to creativity and whom the narrator seeks to "exorcise" with "childish malice." To get rid of the actual Monarchs is not so easy, and Lester sees James deepening both the dilemma and the comedy by the Monarchs' genuine love for each other. The narrator first shows his authority in choosing Oronte over the Major, although he faces the problem fully only when his own survival is at stake, declaring to the Major, "I can't be ruined for *you!*" The end is a mixture of tragedy—the departure of the Monarchs—and comedy—the posing of Churm and Oronte as "a charming picture of blended youth and murmured love." Looking at both, the narrator has gained his maturity and and with it a sense of "the proper and independent sphere of art, and personal control over it."

Marquardt also sees the narrator learning a lesson through the Monarchs, arguing that he recognizes their unsuitability as models all along. At the start, however, the narrator is overly respectful of "delicate shades of principle (or perhaps pretension) in others" and a poor protector of his own interest. Even when his doubts about the the lifeless Monarchs are confirmed by Miss Churm and Hawley, he seeks to reconcile the conflict between the professional and the personal approach. The struggle is an important one, as the artist tries to combine the "broad humanity and sensitivity of the great artist" with "the professional exactitude of the lesser artist." His success is dependent on the Monarchs, and when they rise to their fate, "the story ends ideally for both the reader and the narrator—and even for the Monarchs."

In Shaw's reading, too, the artist's encounter with the Monarchs is a "personally valuable, humanizing one." She sees the tale following an "alternating rhythm of arrivals and poses, movement and stillness" as it settles the fate of both artist and Monarchs. The Monarchs, she observes, become "sitters" in the sense of "squatters." Like Lester, she focuses on the recognitions of the final scene, after the narrator's choice has been made, and the crisis seemingly past. In the Major's desperate offer, "we'll do *anything*," she notes an echo of his initial offer to "be *anything*," a change that shows his realization that "'being' will not 'do.'" Her reading, however, focuses not on the departure of the Monarchs but on the "mood of fundamental stability and calm" they leave behind. The artist has had his "belief in art as a supreme and autonomous value" "challenged," but he is still hard at work in the end (67–75).

Such is precisely the way it should be in the view of Raeth, who has little sympathy for Marquardt's sympathy for the Monarchs. In her view, they are both "intellectually dead and spiritually bankrupt," alive only to their suffering, unfit even to represent the "alive and vital" high society of *Rutland Ramsay*. The Monarchs may try to convince the artist of their worth, but he rejects them and his initial sympathy for them. Insofar as he does allow himself to become "emotionally involved," Raeth contends, "his art suffers." To accept the Monarchs would be to adopt the surface art of the photographer. The story, she concedes to Marquardt, is not just about art and reality, for it shows art as "not an end in itself but a symbol of truth."

In "The Art of Fiction," James had maintained that it was an "incident for a woman to stand up with her hand resting on a table and look out at you in a certain way" (*Criticism* 1, 55). Here, the central look often referred to in adjudicating the rights and wrong of the models and Monarchs is the look Mrs. Monarch gives the narrator when she goes to fix Miss Churm's hair. It is a look, the narrator recalls, "I should like to have been able to paint . . ." (CT 8, 257). As Marquardt reads the scene, Mrs. Monarch becomes in it "not merely a suitable model but even a worthy subject of art," as she encounters "perhaps for the first time, a great challenge" (8). Berkelman sees the episode affirming Mrs. Monarch's magnanimity in contrast to Miss Churm's earlier resentment at having to serve tea to the Monarchs. With her gesture, the tale moves from the "real thing" in art to the "real thing" in life, showing that while art offers "ingenious make-believe," life illustrates "quiet heroism." Thus, concludes Berkelman, the narrator is content to pay the price for the memory. Gargano also focuses on the two incidents, describing the tale as "a quiet one in which people make the most important decisions of their lives by gazing at one another 'in a certain way.'" In her final look, he writes, Mrs. Monarch shows not only her awareness of Miss Churm's fear, but of her value, and a resignation to her own reduced role. The narrator's description, meanwhile, Gargano writes, is his "crowning success as a portraitist" (315–18). Gage, too, sees the moment as one of epiphany in which Mrs. Monarch, by overcoming her envy, "paradoxically becomes a fit subject for the artist," transcending her limitations at the very moment of recognizing them (176). To Mackenzie, her heroism is a primarily a lesson for the narrator (188–89 n.30).

Powers, too, focuses on the human or "ethical" dimensions, and on the growth of the Monarchs. Arguing that the Monarchs are bad models because they are lifeless as people, he argues that they learn life through their humiliation in the artist's studio, by the artist's refusal to take them on the basis of their appearance alone, their need to serve in lowly tasks. He sees a happy ending for all—the artist faithful to his work keeps his work as do the true models, Churm and Oronte (1970, 112–13). It is hard, however, to see what the Monarchs gain by acquiring "real life" given that they have no means to sustain it, once the artist who has given it to them exiles him from the studio. Earlier, Powers noted that the narrator was a bit "rough" in his lessons to the Monarchs, but found them "humanized" at the end, such that "[w]e are left at ease, then, in accepting the necessity of the little sacrifice of the Monarchs." As Powers does point out, however, the narrator's decision to let the Monarchs go is made more understandable given the threat to his own well-being if he keeps them (1960, 360–62).

Horne also attributes generally commendable qualities to all characters, while seeing both the narrator and the Monarchs growing over the course of the story. She emphasizes the two levels in the artist—practicing illustrator, potential portraitist—and sees him by the end wanting to go further in his art, having come to see art more clearly through the Monarchs. They fail to suit him, she writes, "only as a craftsman." The Monarchs, in turn, begin by conceiving of art simply in terms of "attractiveness." Along the way, the artist becomes angry with the Monarchs for failing to realize that their work together is a failure. At the end, they have, however, come to realize that "art is not what they had supposed it to be." Even better, in Horne's view, "they have heroically come back to be useful in any way they can, and come back to the person who caused their painful humiliation." When the artist says he would like to paint Mrs. Monarch's glance, he, too, gains something new, a respect in place of his former pity. The glance—"art at its purest"—shows the artist "what he *could* do" and he can now set out to achieve it (56–63).

The future Bernard projects for the narrator is less rosy. Taking Fadiman's statement that the tale shows art as a *"transformation* of reality," Bernard turns the definition against the artist. The narrator's success, he writes, in dismissing the Monarchs is *"only the measure of his failure."* The narrator has indeed learned the difference between first- and second-rate art, but has also learned "the degree to which he is bound, perhaps forever, to the latter." Before his encounter with the Monarchs, he was an "unfeeling" man; "deeply moved" by them, he is cured as a person, but not necessarily as an artist. The Monarchs are "real," but the narrator seems unable to work with them. He needs to turn his models "into something artificial" before he can use them, removing any "emotional commitment." It is the awareness of this limitation that does him the "permanent harm" he writes of, although he is still glad at least for the painful truth, as it puts him closer to "true art," even if he cannot produce it.

Foff and Knapp also incorporate some criticism of the narrator's art into their examination of the tale, even as they return to an insistence on the failure of the Monarchs. The Monarchs, they write, even *"conceive* of themselves as types" and so cannot model. They not only wear masks, they have "become the masks." Churm and Oronte, on the other hand, are "artists by virtue of their unusual plasticity—a plasticity that is theirs only because they are not trying to *be* an artificiality but to *imitate* it." Still, inside the Monarchs is "a kind of 'real thing'" their artificiality has destroyed, and so they are figures of pathos. The painter, meanwhile, is able, in their view, to "balance" his compassion for them and his needs as an artist. But they point also to a "final irony" in the fact that the drawings the Monarchs were inadequate models for, are "not sketches designed to reveal *life*"—only "illustrations for a society novel." In the end, they conclude, one almost believes more in the Monarchs than the professional models, "for the truth is that though the Monarchs are artificial, the successful sketches of the artist are imitations compounded of imitations." Similarly, Banta observes that it is unclear "what quality of realism" is represented in *Rutland Ramsay* as the narrator is "perhaps naive" such that his concern may be "ironically dedicated to productions patently scanty in human reference" (10).

Lycette also rebukes both Monarchs and artist, although she sees the artist as learning more over the course of the tale than the couple. According to Lycette, James was both attracted and dismayed at people who, like the Monarchs, cultivate "a premeditated, highly discriminated and selective life style." They are "too perfect," superficial, and monotonous. The Monarchs' shallowness, he asserts, is evident in their snobbish attitudes toward Churm and Oronte. The narrator, for his part, sees the Monarchs at first "as they view themselves," namely "as things." Out of "his own selfish career motivations," he manipulates his models with a complete lack of "moral responsibility." However, he comes to sense their "shame and their personal tragedy," and although they are incapable of change, he can change by acquiring a compassion for them. The "resolution" of the tale "involves a conscious transition from the trained eye of the artist, who systematically and impersonally views individuals as things, to the 'fresh eye' which seeks variety, expressiveness, and a more profound sensitivity for the self concealed behind its shells" (56–59).

Initially, most critics read the narrator as a relatively neutral character. Walter Wright, for example, called him only an "intelligent observer" to the action (1962, 41). Richardson wrote that James used a first-person narrator simply to gain "intimacy" and "the illusion of reality" (489). The germ James received from Du Maurier focused on the Monarch characters, but the story gives equal weight to the narrator. Because the narrator in the tale articulates views on art similar to those held by James, the traditional approach has been to accept his authority (e.g., Putt 1966, 222–23). There may seem little reason at first to question it. In his notebook James provided a rationale for the narrator taking on the Monarchs: he "feels—sceptically, but, with his flexible artistic sympathy—the appeal of their type." And the narrator here is not a meddler, for the Monarchs come to him. He also faces a genuine crisis. Walcutt writes that while the Monarchs are "actually hungry," the artist may go hungry if he keeps them on and loses the contract so that he "does not really confront a serious decision" (179). Banta speaks of his "care for the people whose grasp around his neck he must unloosen" (20)

Toor, however, presents a full-scale indictment of the narrator as unreliable. While noting that the Monarchs are rather farcical repesentations of types James cared little for, he sees also in their situation something that goes beyond farce and that the narrator is unwilling to admit. In short, the Monarchs are "the real thing," but the painter is not. James did indeed believe art must "transcend life," but if the narrator's drawings of the Monarchs fail to do so, it is possible, Toor suggests, that the fault lies wth the artist, who shifts the blame to the Monarchs. Toor emphasizes the self-avowed "perversity" in the narrator's preference for the represented over the real. As an artist, he states, the narrator is an admitted hack, if one with greater aspirations. Such aspirations do not impress Toor, who sees the narrator interested mainly in the associated "honours," "emoluments," and "fame." What the narrator has is mainly a "talent for imitation," and he is "almost" jealous of the Monarchs even as he seeks to make them scapegoats for his own failure. His attributing to them a "permanent harm" to his work is a way of blaming someone else for his own lack of the "real thing."

Responding to Toor, Hocks seeks to create a more complex reading by putting together Toor's conception of the narrator as unreliable, the tale's parallels with "The Art of Fiction," and its emphasis on "conscience" (the last from the analysis of Virgil Scott). He observes how the Monarchs evolve from the original static idea of the notebooks, "unstiffen[ing]" even as James "unstiffen[s]" his idea once "engaged" with it. The Monarchs become more "living" characters, as they "dominate a story the main point of which is that they lack interest." Indeed, it is the pathetic charm of their stiffness that gives them interest. Still, a writer needs a "germ"—a concept recalled in Miss Churm's name—which Hocks locates in the artist's ambition to be a portraitist. While he demurs from explicitly calling him unreliable, he does note the "resonating plurality"of the narrator's character who gives us a "portrait" of the Monarchs. His "distortion[s]," Hocks maintains, are never in his presentation of the Monarchs, but in his refusing to recognize how his attitude to them as models is shaped by his own ambitions to do another kind of work. James *conjoins* the two issues "on the identical terms by which they are *disjoined* by his narrator." The narrator does not recognize the linking, showing it only through his drawings of the two. The narrator also learns through the Monarchs, and their final act of heroism which causes his work to "blur," and shows that there is "always character and meaning to be found in even what appears the quintessential case of surface." The narrator may not become a great portraitist in paint, but he has already, Hocks asserts, produced in "The Real Thing" a great portrait (120–34).

The same year as Toor, however, Sanders also offered a portrait of the artist as a failure, whose behavior at times "reeks to high heaven." At the same time, like Bernard, he admits the possibility of the narrator's tragic recognition of his own failure. In Sanders's reading, the narrator is a "classic example" of an inferiority complex. His problem is that he looks at people as types, not as individuals. His liking for the Monarchs is "hollow," and he prefers Churm and Oronte because they are less of a threat to his sense of superiority, even as he chooses Hawley for a friend because he is an inferior painter. But by avoiding type, the narrator himself *"becomes* a type." This creates in the tale, according to Sanders, an "aesthetic pathos." It may be that the reader with his new understanding is meant "genuinely" to pity the artist, or that the narrator also gains a new understanding, seeing his "snobbery" reflected in the Monarchs' toward the model, making him if not a hero a "tragic protagonist." But if he has enough strength to seek to overcome his ambition, Sanders does not grant him sufficient strength to win. The reverse of the Monarchs, he will not accept his failure, but he does accept his fate, that of a "commercial book illustrator"—something other than the "real thing." Nor does he have the final insight to consider that *he* may have harmed the Monarchs (335–61).

Beaver also looks at the way James's choice of narrator affects his presentation of a story that appears at first to argue for an "absolute hierarchy" of art." To him, the narrator is an "often inadequte and fatuous" advocate of his views. Following Barthes, he sees the concept of "representation" as key. The narrator works by a process beginning with his model's own "graceful mimicry" which he, in turn, interprets. The Monarchs it seems at first have "exhausted their fictional imagination." Mrs. Monarch proves, however, that she is "capable of further transformation" in fixing Miss Churm's hair, a fact that seems to support the incompatibility of art and morals. The narrator, however, is also a plagiarist of aesthetic conventions, a fact seen magnified in the self-consciously bohemian Hawley. He, too, imposes inappropriate "sentimental values" on art in an attempt to convince himself that he is not the hack he is. Like the Monarchs, he is "attached to the vision of luxury," represented here by the *édition de luxe.*" A "lickspittle middle-class humbug," in Beaver's phrase, he cannot recognize the "sheer decency and pathos" of the Monarchs, even as the Monarchs themselves never recognize him as an equal. The narrator cannot even fulfill the artist's task, "to change structures," following Barthes. So he passes that task on to his models, remaining dependent on a type, a "schema" to work from. In his sentimentalized memory, he suppresses the slur on his art, and accepts the final "divorce of life from art." James, however, Beaver concludes, shows through the narrator's story, that "art, far from possessing a privileged status, must itself be viewed simulataneously as a dependent term."

Such critiques of the narrator have, indeed, become almost the standard view. Terrie points to his "limited talent" as an illustrator of fiction who "makes imitations of imitations of life." The Monarchs, in contrast, he points out, have at least a "personal history" and more important, "a true marriage." An "honest memory" of his encounter with them, Terrie concludes, would bring the narrator a "very limited consolation." The artist therefore "suppress[es] his humanity" and returns to his "artificial world" (8–9).

Terrie also returns attention to the issue of class, and Lackey, in her portrait of an "unreliable" narrator, focuses on the issue. She takes the tale as a "parable of mastery" in which the narrator's need for a sense of "class mastery" in order to attain "artistic mastery" is upset by the arrival of the Monarchs. Like Sanders, she sees the narrator feeling comfortably superior to Churm and Oronte, but unable to make use of the Monarchs because his "social defenses" interfere. He tries instead to "type" them, to deny them "an identity beyond the sum of their accouterments," and so produces "grotesque caricatures" of them. At one point, he speaks of them as "a pair of patient courtiers in a royal antechamber," and Lackey sees him postponing "the climactic dismissal" as a way of "settling a political grudge." In the tale, however, as "form shatters against substance," his "artifice is exposed" and even the "apolitical purview of art turns out to be another cozy manufacture of desire" (192)

The narrator's friend Hawley has also come under attack. O'Faolian objects to his very existence, finding his "intrusion . . . quite indefensible" (189). Many critics point to the fact that he is a bad artist (e.g., Vielledent 43). In Goetz's view, the tale is unique among James's artist works because it has no "master" figure, Hawley being even "less masterly" than the narrator (158). Hawley has been abroad searching for a "fresh eye," a concept Marquardt dismisses as a "superficial expedient" that will result in little change, unless Hawley gains some human understanding as well (6). Sanders also sees Hawley as an inadequate guide, providing the narrator with rationalizations for his failure with the Monarchs, rather than the truth (356). Hocks, while judging Hawley right about the Monarchs' effect on the narrator's illustrations, his word backed up by the publishers, sees him as too "facile," paying no attention to concerns apart from art (131). Raeth, however, objects that Hawley is not an "inferior" critic who looks only at technique. She sees Hawley coming back from his travels with a genuinely "fresh eye," paying attention as he looks at the pictures from the Monarchs for the first time to the "problems of meaning and content" they raise (5).

Other readings take the tale as a struggle between competing perceptions. In Austin Wright's view, the Monarchs, whom he judges the protagonists of the tale, never realize that they are inadequate and so are sustained throughout by their belief in their superiority (190 n.13). Mueller splits the blame between the two sides, viewing the tale as a "perceptual tug-of-war" in which the phenomenal selves of the Monarchs, based on their experience, clash with the phenomenal self of the narrator based on his. Neither side, according to Mueller, can really "see" the evidence that their view of themselves is flawed, causing some painful readjustment as both refuse to budge from their self-conception. In the end, Mueller argues, circumstances force all three to face the truth and so lose part of their selves, the Monarchs their belief that they can support themselves, the narrator his belief that he is not the sort of person who would sacrifice others to his needs. Because the narrator as a portrait painter is, according to Mueller, particularly vulnerable to the personality of sitters, he suffers as he recognizes "permanent harm" to his art.

In response to Mueller's view that "perceptual field is reality," Uroff asserts that in the contention between the two readings of the tale—a serious argument for realism or a "light-hearted spoof" of artistic pretension—both can't be right. Picturing the narrator as unreliable and the Monarchs self-deceived, he calls the tale an "object lesson in perceptual hazards." The narrator is a "poseur," an illustrator who thinks of himself as a portraitist, the Monarchs sham genteel. Held together by their "clouded vision," the collaboration between the two types will necessarily turn out to be fruitless. At the root of the conflict, however, Uroff places money, or rather the lack of it, which "contracts the world view." The "memory" left to the narrator at the end, writes Uroff, is less likely to be of the Monarchs than of the fruitlessness of their collaboration. He gives them up because he needs to keep his contract, providing a "negative example" of James's view that an artist needs independence and integrity.

Pendleton adds a pragmatic slant to his reading of perceptions in the tale. As he reads it, there are four "basic sources of desire" or forces in the tale, the publisher, the artist, the Monarchs, and the models. All of them need to see the world "as clearly as possible in order to respond to it efficiently" in order to survive, even as they want to see it "in a certain way." They seek, in turn, the "key" to their own survival in others, whose desires they therefore endeavor to understand. Because the publisher here has the ultimate power, he is the one who sets the standards for "coherent, purposeful action." Functioning in a largely "subjective" field, the artist relies on others to set such standards. He also has, however, "humanitarian values," which he has not realized conflict with artistic goals until the Monarchs arrive. The Monarchs are most directly concerned with survival, trying to adjust to change, although adhering to their "concept of the universe," which had worked before, and which they try to bring with them into the world of the studio. There they come into competition with Churm and Oronte, whose rule of order is chaos. Observing and taking part in this "evolutionary game of survival of the fittest," the artist learns that the "reality or falsity of any entity rests in its meaning to and its use by some superior imaginative force." Unlike the Monarchs, he recognizes the need to be flexible, and "true to his pragmatic responsibility" adapts to what he can't change, sending away the less flexible Monarchs.

The perceptions of Churm and Oronte have generally received less attention. Nevertheless, they play a necessary role in the production of art, one that has not always received adequate attention in readings that focus on the transforming power of the artist's imagination, or even on its failure. Edel, for example, writes that the Monarchs are "useless to the artist who imagines reality better than life itself," but the artist does not rely only on his imagination (CT 8, 9). Matthiessen points to the "anti-transcendental 'lesson'" in the tale, that shows art relying on imitation. He speaks in particular of Oronte's "brilliant mimetic gift," while Holder praises Miss Churm's ability as an actress (14; Holder 295). Typically, critics have noted the models' plasticity. O'Faolian notes an association of such flexibility with the lower class, while Nathalia Wright sees it, in Oronte's case, a reflection of James's belief that Italians possessed a "histrionic and instrumental character" (O'Faolian 187; Wright 237). Walcutt, however, sees the professional model like an artist, treating "the idea as an idea, as an inspiration for creative expression" (178).

If the model is already an artist, there is less work left for the painter. Witness the narrator's description of Churm and Oronte posing for a scene from *Rutland Ramsey*: "The pair were vividly before me, the piano had been pulled out; it was a charming show of blended youth and murmured love, which I had only to catch and keep" (CT 8, 237). Aswell points to the description as showing the narrator's "ridiculously exalted" opinion of his own work, but it also fits with Aswell's analysis of the tale's "light-hearted" treatment of the "problem of collaboration." For the artist here does not work alone. He is rather, Aswell writes, "dependent on his models for inspiration" at the same time as he is "so uncertain as to how to use them" that he cannot produce genuine art (186–89).

Why then, asks Walcutt, are the Monarchs harder to draw from? As he remarks, "Either set of models would seem to demand a reincarnation as they passed from life through the mind of the artist and onto his canvas." The "important creative act" is supposed to come "after the model, who is only a convenience of colors and shape" (179). Some see the difference in the professional models' need to transform themselves to imitate the upper-class figures. This, Delbaere-Garant argues, stimulates the artist's own transformation. Because the Monarchs are statically correct, they provide no spark (50–51). Similarly, Gage sees both Miss Churm and the Monarchs as "ineffective" when they play characters on their own "social level," Miss Churm serving tea or the Monarchs as figures in high society. The tale argues, in his view, "that good art can be created and exist only by a dissonance or separation between reality and the representation of that reality" (172–77). Such readings, however, seem to support Wagenknecht's suggestion that James may be placing "a heavier responsibility on the imagination of the model than upon the artist himself" (70). So, too, Munson compares the narrator to a beginning novelist who tries to use real people as characters, while the real artist uses real life only for "hints," as seen in the narrator's sense that Mr. Monarch would make a good footman or Oronte a good gentleman (264).

The Monarchs are often seen to be interesting because of their change in status, their fall from a high place. Churm and Oronte are already there, and therefore receive less attention. Ron, for example, writes of Miss Churm that she yields "much (in art) for little (in life)" (199). The presumption is that there is no more in the two than the narrator can see, a presumption that is likely to be erroneous, however much encouraged by the telling of the tale. Similarly, critics tend to follow the sentimentality of the narrator's conclusion, allowing it to focus them on the narrator's loss rather than the far more tangible one of the Monarchs. Edel says of "The Real Thing" that it demonstrates that "'make believe' has a reality of its own" (1953, vi). The story also seems to show, however, that reality has a "make-believe" of its own. A contemporary reviewer noted that the story would "bear two interpretations," namely, "either a model can never be, but must only suggest, the real thing in art, or that the real thing in human nature scorns the conscious patronage of art" (*Chautauquan* 486). It is such "irony and ambiguities" that place the tale, as Allen notes, among James's "most disturbing stories" (48).

In 1942 Nuhn could mention "The Real Thing" with "The Lesson of the Master" as stories that "have not received their due" (145). It is now not only one of James's most frequently anthologized tales, but also one of the most common objects of criticism. However interpreted, it receives nearly universal praise as one of James's best (e.g., Berkleman 95). Norrman speaks of it as a "little masterpiece of its kind," and its comparative brevity—for James—has also generally been held in its favor (147). It is, according to Shaw, "an impressive example of his ability to deal with a group of characters without releasing more suggestions than the narrative could hold" (66). Even so, the tale has received a multiplicity of readings that are a credit to its compact richness. As Q. D. Leavis observes, it is "much deeper than it looks and will bear endless pondering" (227). There have been exceptions to the approval. Early on the *Athenaeum* judged the work "too thin and spun out" (602). Similarly, Berthoff sees it as a "slighter" work like many of the later magazine tales, objecting specifically that after having nicely set up his situation and subject, James failed to treat the climax fully enough (109–10). O'Faolian provides one of the more amusing negative judgments. Writing that James had "almost no power of indirect suggestion," he sees the tale as lacking form, "moulded" as it is about an idea "which James chases hither and over like a retriever." In James, he writes, "stories dangle from his point like tapestry trailing from a hook." To help James out, he offers a cut version of the tale, indicating that one could cut it even further—in half—without any loss (188). Most readers would prefer "The Real Thing."

Works Cited

Primary Works

James, Henry. 1891. *The Tragic Muse*. London: Macmillan.

———. 1892. "The Real Thing." *Black and White* 3 (16 April): 463–83.

———. 1893. "The Real Thing." *The Real Thing*. New York and London: Macmillan, 1–41.

———. 1908. "The Real Thing." *The Novels and Tales of Henry James* New York Edition. Vol. 18, 305–46. New York: Scribner's.

———. 1993. *The Correspondence of Henry James and the House of Macmillan, 1877–1914*. Ed. Rayburn S. Moore. Baton Rouge: Louisiana State University Press.

Secondary Works

Allen, Walter. 1980. *The Short Story in English*. New York: Oxford University Press.

Anderson, Quentin. 1957. *The American Henry James*. New Brunswick, NJ: Rutgers University Press.

Andreas, Osborn. 1948. *Henry James and the Expanding Horizon: A Study of the Meaning and Basic Themes of James's Fiction*. Seattle: University of Washington Press.

Anon. 1893. Review of *The Real Thing*. *Athenaeum* 3420 (May): 601–2.

Anon. 1893. Review of *The Real Thing*. *Chautauquan* 17 (May): 485–86.

Aswell, E. Duncan. 1966. "James's Treatment of Artistic Collaboration." *Criticism* 8: 180–95.

Auchard, John. 1986. *Silence in Henry James: The Heritage of Symbolism and Decadence*. University Park: Pennsylvania State University Press.

Banta, Martha. 1984. "Artists, Models, Real Things, and Recognizable Types." *Studies in the Literary Imagination* 16: 7–34.

Baxter, Annette K. 1955. "Independence vs. Isolation: Hawthorne and James on the Problem of the Artist." *Nineteenth-Century Fiction* 10: 225–31

Beach, Joseph Warren. [1918] 1954. *The Method of Henry James*. Philadelphia: Albert Saifer.

Beaver, Harold. 1983. "'The Real Thing' and Unreal Things: Conflicts of Art and Society in Henry James." *Fabula* (Villeneuve d'Ascq) 1 (March): 53–69.

Beebe, Maurice L. 1964. *Ivory Towers and Sacred Founts: The Artist as Hero*. New York: New York University Press.

Berkelman, Robert. 1959. "Henry James and 'The Real Thing.'" *University of Kansas City Review* 26 (Winter): 93–95.

Bernard, Kenneth. 1962. "The Real Thing in James's 'The Real Thing.'" *Brigham Young University Studies* 5 (Autumn): 31–32

Berthoff, Warner. 1965. *The Ferment of Realism: American Literature, 1884–1919.* New York: Free Press.

Bishop, George. 1988. *When the Master Relents: The Neglected Short Fictions of Henry James.* Ann Arbor: UMI Research Press.

Bogardus, Ralph F. 1984. *Pictures and Texts: Henry James, A. L. Coburn and New Ways of Seeing in Literary Culture.* Ann Arbor: UMI Research Press.

Boren, Lynda S. 1989. *Eurydice Reclaimed: Language, Gender, and Voice in Henry James.* Ann Arbor: UMI Research Press.

Bowden, Edwin T. [1956] 1960. *The Themes of Henry James: A System of Observation through the Visual Arts.* Yale Studies in English 132. New Haven: Yale University Press.

Briden, E. F. 1976. "James's Miss Churm: Another of Eliza's Prototypes?" *Shaw Review* 19: 17–21.

Cowie, Alexander. 1948. *The Rise of the American Novel.* New York: American Book Company.

Delbaere-Garant, Jeanne. 1970. *Henry James: The Vision of France.* Paris: Société d'Editions Les Belles Lettres.

Dietrichson, Jan W. 1969. *The Image of Money in the American Novel of the Gilded Age.* Oslo: Universitetsforlaget; New York: Humanities.

Edel, Leon, ed. 1953. *The Sacred Fount.* New York: Grove.

Edel, Leon, and Ilse Dusoir Lind, eds. 1961. *Henry James: Parisian Sketches, Letters to the New York Tribune, 1875–1876.* New York: xxxi–vi.

Fadiman, Clifton. 1945. *The Short Stories of Henry James.* New York: Modern Library. Reprinted in *Reading for a Liberal Education*, ed. Louis Glenn Locke, et al. New York: Rinehart, 1948. Vol. 2, 1948, 333–34; vol. 2, 1952, 330–31.

Falk, Robert. 1965. *The Victorian Mode in American Fiction, 1865–1885.* East Lansing: Michigan State University Press.

Farnsworth, Robert M. 1967. "The Real and the Exquisite in James's 'The Real Thing.'" *The Literary Criterion* 7, no. 4: 29–31.

Foff, Arthur, and Daniel Knapp. 1964. "Analysis of 'The Real Thing.'" In *Story: An Introduction to Prose Fiction*, 366–68. Belmont, CA: Wadsworth.

Ford, Ford Madox. 1937. *Portraits from Life.* Boston: Houghton Mifflin.

———. 1913. *Henry James: A Critical Study.* London: Martin Secker.

Gage, Richard P. 1988. *Order and Design: Henry James' Titled Story Sequences.* New York: Peter Lang.

Gale, Robert. L. 1977. "Henry James's J. H. in 'The Real Thing.'" *Studies in Short Fiction* 14: 396–98.

———. 1963. "A Note on Henry James's 'The Real Thing.'" *Studies in Short Fiction* 1 (Fall): 65–66.

Gard, Roger, ed. 1968. *Henry James: The Critical Heritage.* London: Routledge & Kegan Paul.

Gargano, James W. 1979. "The 'Look' as a Major Event in James's Short Fiction." *Arizona Quarterly* 35, no. 4 (Winter): 303–20.

Gerlach, John. 1985. *Toward the End: Closure and Structure in American Short Stories.* University: University of Alabama Press.

Gill, Richard. 1972. *Happy Rural Seat: The English Country House and the Literary Imagination.* New Haven: Yale University Press.

Goetz, William R. 1986. *Henry James and the Darkest Abyss of Romance.* Baton Rouge: Louisiana State University Press.

Gordon, D. J., and John Stokes. 1972. "The Reference of *The Tragic Muse.*" In *The Air of Reality: New Essays on Henry James.* Ed. John Goode, 81–167. London: Methuen.

Grover, P. R. 1989. "Realism, Representation, and 'The Real Thing.'" In *The Magic Circle of Henry James.* Ed. Amritjit Singh and K. Ayyappa Paniker, 122–31. New York: Envoy.

Higgins, Charles. "Photographic Aperture: Coburn's Frontispieces to James's New York Edition." *American Literature* 53: 661–75.

Hocks, Richard A. 1974. *Henry James and Pragmatic Thought: A Study in the Relationship between the Philosophy of William James and the Literary Art of Henry James.* Chapel Hill: University of North Carolina Press.

Holder, Alan. 1966. *Three Voyagers in Search of Europe: A Study of Henry James, Ezra Pound and T. S. Eliot.* Philadelphia: University of Pennsylvania Press.

Horne, Helen. 1960. *Basic Ideals of James's Aesthetics as Expressed in the Short Stories Concerning Artists and Writers.* Marburg: Erich Mauersberger.

Inglis, Tony. 1976. "Reading Late James." In *The Modern English Novel: the Reader, the Writer, and the Work.* Ed. Gabriel Josipovici, 77–94. London: Open Books.

Jefferson, D. W. [1960] 1971. *Henry James.* New York: Capricorn.

Jones, Granville H. 1975. *Henry James's Psychology of Experience: Innocence, Responsibility, and Renunciation in the Fiction of Henry James.* The Hague: Mouton.

Kaplan, Harold. 1972. *Democratic Humanism and American Literature.* Chicago: University of Chicago Press.

Kehler, Harold. 1967. "James's 'The Real Thing.'" *Explicator* 25: Item 79.

Kelly, Richard. 1983. *George Du Maurier*. Boston: Twayne.

Labor, Earl. 1962. "James's 'The Real Thing': Three Levels of Meaning." *College English* 23 (Fall): 376–78. Reprinted in *Twentieth Century Interpretations of "The Turn of the Screw" and Other Tales*, ed. Jane P. Tompkins, 29–32, Englewood Cliffs, NJ: Prentice-Hall, 1970; Ray B. Browne and Martin Light, "Henry James," in *Critical Approaches to American Literature*, vol. 2: *Walt Whitman to William Faulkner*, 159–65, New York: Crowell, 1965; and *Tales of Henry James*, ed. Christof Wegelin, 472–75, New York: Norton.

Lackey, Kris. 1989. "Art and Class in 'The Real Thing.'" *Studies in Short Fiction* (Spring 26): 190–92.

Lainoff, Seymour. 1956. "A Note on Henry James's 'The Real Thing.'" *Modern Language Notes* 71 (March): 192–93.

Leavis, Q. D. 1947. "Henry James: The Stories." *Scrutiny* 14 (Spring): 223–29. Reprinted in *Collected Essays*. Vol. 2: *The American Novel and Reflections of the European Novel*, ed. G. Singh, 177–84. Cambridge: Cambridge University Press.

Lebowitz, Naomi. 1965. *The Imagination of Loving: Henry James's Legacy to the Novel*. Detroit: Wayne State University Press.

Lester, Pauline. 1978. "James's Use of Comedy in 'The Real Thing.'" *Studies in Short Fiction* 15: 33–38.

Lycette, Ronald L. 1977. "Perceptual Touchstones for the Jamesian Artist-Hero." *Studies in Short Fiction* 14: 55–62.

Lyon, Richard C. 1966. "Santayana and the Real Thing." *Shenandoah* 17, no. 3: 41–60.

McCarthy, Harold T. 1958. *Henry James: The Creative Process*. New York: Thomas Yoseloff.

McElderry, Bruce R., Jr. 1965. *Henry James*. New York: Twayne.

Mackenzie, Manfred. 1976. *Communities of Honor and Love in Henry James*. Cambridge, MA: Harvard University Press.

Marder, Daniel. 1984. *Exiles at Home: A Story of Literature in Nineteenth Century America*. Lanham, MD: University Press of America.

Markow-Totevy, Georges. 1969. *Henry James*. Trans. John Griffiths. London: Merlin.

Marquardt, William F. 1949. "A Practical Approach to 'The Real Thing.'" *English "A" Analyst* (Northwestern University), no. 14: 1–8.

Matthiessen, F. O. 1944. "Introduction: Henry James' Portrait of the Artist." *Henry James: Stories of Writers and Artists*. Norfolk, CT: New Directions. Also reprinted as "Henry James's Portrait of the Artist. *Partisan Review* 11 (1944): 71–87.

Miller, J. Hillis. 1987. *The Ethics of Reading: Kant, de Man, Eliot, Trollope, James, and Benjamin*. New York: Columbia Univeristy Press.

Mueller, Lavonne. 1968. "Henry James: The Phenomenal Self as the 'Real Thing.'" *Forum* (University of Houston) 6 (September): 46–50.

Munson, Gorham. 1950. "The Real Thing: A Parable for Writers of Fiction." *University of Kansas City Review* 16 (Summer): 261–64.

Nalbantian, Suzanne. 1983. *Seeds of Decadence in the Late Nineteenth-Century Novel: A Crisis in Values.* New York: St. Martin's.

Nordloh, David J. 1984. "First Appearances of Henry James's 'The Real Thing': The McClure Papers as a Bibliographical Resource." *Papers of the Bibliographical Society of America* 78, no. 1: 69–71.

Norrman, Ralf. 1982. *The Insecure World of Henry James's Fiction: Intensity and Ambiguity.* New York: St. Martin's.

Nuhn, Ferner. 1942. *The Wind Blew from the East: A Study in the Orientation of American Culture.* New York: Harper.

O'Faolain, Sean. 1948. *The Short Story.* Collins: London. Reprinted in part in Edward Stone, ed., *Henry James: Seven Stories and Studies,* New York: Appleton, 1961, 135–36, and in Georgianne Trask and Charles Burkhart, eds., *Storytellers and Their Art,* 193, 343–44, 351–52. Garden City, NY: Doubleday, 1963.

Pendleton, J. D. 1973. "The James Brothers and 'The Real Thing': A Study in Pragmatic Reality." *South Atlantic Bulletin* 38 (November): 3–10.

Perosa, Sergio. 1983. *Henry James and the Experimental Novel.* New York: New York University Press.

Powers, Lyall H. 1970. *Henry James: An Introduction and Interpretation.* New York: Holt, Rinehart.

———. 1961. "Henry James and the Ethics of the Artist: 'The Real Thing' and 'The Liar.'" *Texas Studies in Literature and Language* 3 (Autumn): 360–68.

Putt, S. Gorley, ed. 1976. *The Aspern Papers and Other Stories.* Harmondsworth: Penguin.

———. 1966. *Henry James: A Reader's Guide.* Ithaca, NY: Cornell University Press.

Raeth, Claire. 1949. "The Real Approach to 'The Real Thing.'" *English "A" Analyst* (Northwestern), no. 15: 1–5.

Richardson, Lyon N., ed. [1941] 1966. *Henry James: Representative Selections, with Introduction, Bibliography, and Notes.* New York: American Writer Series. Urbana: University of Illinois Press.

Roditi, Edouard. 1947 [1986]. *Oscar Wilde.* New York: New Directions.

Ron, Moshe. 1979. "A Reading of 'The Real Thing.'" *Yale French Studies* 58: 190–212. Reprinted in *Henry James: Daisy Miller, Turn of the Screw, and Other Tales,* ed. Harold Bloom, 43–60. New York: Chelsea House, 1987.

Ryan, Judith. 1989. "Validating the Possible: Thoughts and Things in James, Rilke, and Musil." *Comparative Literature* 40: 305–17.

Salzberg, Joel. 1979. "Mr. Mudge as Redemptive Fate: Juxtaposition in James's *In the Cage.*" *Studies in the Novel* 11 (Spring): 63–76.

Sanders, Thomas E., ed. 1967. *The Discovery of Fiction*. Glenview, IL: Scott, Foresman.

Scudder, Horace E. 1896. Review of *Owen Wister: Red Man and White*. *Atlantic* 77 (February): 265.

———. 1896. "Review of Mrs. Humphry Ward. *Sir George Tressady*." *Atlantic* 78 (December): 841–43. Cited in Helen McMahon, *Criticism of Fiction: A Study of Trends in "The Atlantic Monthly," 1857–1898*. New York: Bookman.

Shaw, Valerie. 1983. *The Short Story: A Critical Introduction*. London and New York: Longman.

Stein, Allen F. 1984. *After the Vows Were Spoken: Marriage in American Literary Realism*. Columbus: Ohio State University Press.

Stevens, George. 1945. "The Return of Henry James." *Saturday Review of Literature* 28 (3 March): 7–8, 30, 32–33.

Stone, Edward. 1964. *The Battle and the Books: Some Aspects of Henry James*. Athens: Ohio University Press.

Swan, Michael. 1957. *Henry James*. London: Longmans, Green.

———, ed. 1948. *Ten Short Stories of Henry James*. London: John Lehmann.

Tanner, Tony. 1985. *Henry James: The Writer and His Work*. Amherst: University of Massachusetts Press.

Telotte, J. P. 1984. "The Right Way with Reality." *Henry James Review* 6, no. 4 (Fall): 8–14.

Terrie, Henry, ed. 1984. *Henry James: Tales of Art and Life*. Schenectady, NY: Union College Press.

Tilton, Eleanor, ed. 1961. *Henry James: "The Marriages" and Other Stories*. A Signet Classic. New York: New American Library.

Tintner, Adeline R. 1989. *The Pop World of Henry James: From Fairy Tales to Science Fiction*. Ann Arbor: UMI Research Press.

———. 1987. *The Book World of Henry James: Appropriating the Classics*. Ann Arbor: UMI Research Press.

Todorov, Tzvetan. 1977. *The Poetics of Prose*. Trans. Richard Howard. Ithaca, NY: Cornell University Press.

Toor, David. [1967] 1970. "Narrative Irony in Henry James's 'The Real Thing.'" In *Twentieth Century Interpretations of "The Turn of the Screw" and Other Tales*. Ed. Jane P. Tompkins. Englewood Cliffs, NJ: Prentice-Hall, 33–39. Reprinted from *University Review* (Kansas City) 34 (Winter): 95–99.

Uroff, M. D. 1972. "Perception in James's 'The Real Thing.'" *Studies in Short Fiction* 9 (Winter): 41–46 .

Van Nostrand, A. D. 1968. *Everyman His Own Poet: Romantic Gospels in American Literature*. New York: McGraw Hill.

Vielledent, Catherine. 1985. "Representation and Reproduction: A Reading of Henry James's 'The Real Thing.'" In *Interface: Essays on History, Myth, and Art in American Literature*. Ed. Daniel Royat, 31–49. Montpellier: Publications de la Recherche, Université Paul Valéry.

Voss, Arthur. 1973. *The American Short Story: A Critical Survey*. Norman: University of Oklahoma Press.

Wagenknecht, Edward. 1984. *The Tales of Henry James*. New York: Frederick Ungar.

Walcutt, Charles Child. 1966. *Man's Changing Mask: Modes and Methods of Characterization in Fiction*. Minneapolis: University of Minnesota Press.

Ward, Joseph A. 1967. *The Search for Form: Studies in the Structure of James's Fiction*. Chapel Hill: University of North Carolina Press.

Wegelin, Christof, ed. 1984. *Tales of Henry James*. New York: Norton.

Wilson, R. B. J. 1981. *Henry James's Ultimate Narrative: The Golden Bowl*. St. Lucia: University of Queensland Press.

Winner, Viola Hopkins. 1970. *Henry James and the Visual Arts*. Charlottesville: University Press of Virginia.

Wright, Austin McGiffert. 1961. *The American Short Story in the Twenties*. Chicago: University of Chicago Press.

Wright, Nathalia. 1965. *American Novelists in Italy, The Discoverers: Allston to James*. Philadelphia: University of Pennsylvania Press.

Wright, Walter. 1962. *The Madness of Art: A Study of Henry James*. Lincoln: University of Nebraska Press.

———. 1957. "'The Real Thing.'" *Research Studies* 25 (March): 85–90.

The Romance of Certain Old Clothes

Publication History

"The Romance of Certain Old Clothes" appeared first in the February 1868 issue of the *Atlantic Monthly*. In 1875 James included it in his first collection of stories, *A Passionate Pilgrim*, and ten years after that he included it in the third volume of *Stories Revived*. It appeared next in 1898, in volume 18 of the *International Library of Famous Literature*, although James later claimed himself "at a loss" to explain how. He did, however, as Havens discovered, "absolutely object" in response to a query from J. A. Hammerton to having "the little old thing . . . disinterred" once again for a 1914 collection, casting aspersions on the editorial judgment of anyone who would select such an early, unrepresentative work over what was by then his complete corpus of short stories (131–32). It appeared next in Lubbock's edition of the novels and stories.

Circumstances of Composition, Sources, and Influences

James wrote the tale while living at his family home in Cambridge, his brother William away on his first European tour. Edel therefore argues that the tale's concern with usurpation stems from James's sibling rivalry with William, detecting a link even with the theme of clothes in James's ordering of a suit in the same cloth as William had previously chosen (*Life* 1, 249–50). Mackenzie also ties the tale to the relationships of brothers, calling it a "Jacob and Esau fantasy of sexual rivalry" (76). Speaking of it as a tale of "undifferentiated twinship," Feinstein deems the rivalry here particularly rancorous, with James not usurping but feeling usurped as William not only had gone to Europe as he had hoped to, but was attempting to write criticism there. Feinstein points to the the foolish older brother as the first picture of William, but sees William represented most fully in Viola, the more appropriate wearer of the contested clothes. The attempt of the younger Perdita, Henry's stand-in, to keep "some separateness" from her sister produces only violence. Feinstein adds a further twist, however, by seeing the husband as "merely a pretext for displaying the attachment between two siblings of the same sex," James's relationship to William being marked, in his view, by "fraternal incestuous strivings." According to Feinstein, the portraits are "so thinly disguised" that William's restraint in his comments on the story is "remarkable" (231–33). His restraint may perhaps be a clearer indication of the tale's biographical significance—or lack of it.

Allott has discovered a common plot and a common source for "The Romance of Certain Old Clothes" in Alfred Lord Tennyson's poem "The Ring" (1899). In both, the elements of the plot are the same: the rivalry, the marriage, the death in childbirth, the promise, the second marriage, the breaking of the promise, and the supernatural death. Both writers took the plot from James Russell Lowell, who told of the events in connection with a house he had once lived near. Allott notes that James returned to the Lowell story when planning *The Sense of the Past* with its rival sisters, and that he underlined the connection by imagining the American minister who would hear the tale as Lowell.

Despite the closeness to Tennyson, from the days of Rebecca West the most frequent comparison has been with Hawthorne, Quentin Anderson remarking that the tale "sounds like an addition to Hawthorne's 'Legends of the Province House'" (West 24–25; Anderson 37; also Dupee 48; Briggs 118; Thorp x; McElderry 115; McCarthy16). Buitenhuis specifically compares the description of the dead Viola to that of the dead Colonel Pyncheon (42). Edel finds the use of the term "romance" accurately Hawthornesque, combining "the marvelous" with the real, but he points out that James reserves his use of "the marvelous" for the end, while the rest of the story has a resolutely "real" atmosphere (3; also Long 17). Matthiessen and Kelley both emphasize that James would soon move beyond the use of Hawthorne for a model, while Kelley argues that Howells was instrumental in the temporary turn toward romance á la Hawthorne (Matthiessen viii; Kelley 82). (See also "De Grey.")

In revising the tale for *Stories Revived*, James changed the names Wingrave to Willoughby and Viola to Rosalind. The first change removes the association St. Armand points out with Harriet Prescott Spofford's 1860 gothic ghost story "The Amber Gods," whose exotic heroine was a Willoughby (118 n.16). The second change Edel finds appropriate not only because violets shrink while roses have thorns, but—following the Shakespearean allusion—because his Rosalind was "more aggressive" than Viola (4; also Melchiori 9). Feinstein considers the fact that Shakespeare's Viola disguised herself as a man significant (233). The younger sister also has a Shakespearean name, Perdita, given her in memory of a middle sister who died as a baby. Like the Perdita of *The Winter's Tale*, she is lost, or at least loses, but unlike Shakespeare's heroine, there is no reversal in her fortune.

Edel originally called the chest a Pandora's box (4; also Akiyama 45). In Hawthorne's telling of the tale in *The Wonder Book*, the chest is indeed a large piece of furniture, not a mere box or jar. More elaborately, Mackenzie pictures Viola as dying of humiliation, the open chest serving as an emblem of a "seriously wounded personality" laid open to exposure (35–36). Edel also compares Viola to another archetypal female who cannot resist opening forbidden things, Bluebeard's wife (*Life* 1, 249).

Akiyama compares the treatment of jealousy and revenge in this tale and two later ghost stories, "The Friends of the Friends" and "Sir Edmund Orme," with *Tokaido Yotsuya Kaidan*, a ghost story by the Japanese author Nanboku. He asks why Perdita does not avenge herself on her faithless husband rather than her sister, but judges the choice of the other woman as victim appropriate, an approach also seen in Lafcadio Hearn's "Of a Promise Broken" (51).

Relation to Other Works

"The Romance of Certain Old Clothes" was the earliest of the tales James included in his 1875 collection, *A Passionate Pilgrim*, which in title and selection emphasized his turn to the international theme. This tale marks instead the start of another Jamesian line of development, the use of the supernatural. As such, it and "The Last of the Valerii" were the only tales of the collection Howells judged "purely romantic" (1875, 72). In its dependence on Hawthorne for its sense of romance, the tale is often linked with "De Grey" of the same year, Banta and Kerr judging both instances unfortunate (Banta 1972, 107; Kerr 135, 139; also Briggs 118). Cowie links the two more positively as solid traditional work, if unlike the later James (727). Long, for his part, explains the Hawthornesque romanticism of both as an attempt to achieve a wider popularity and to remedy a certain thinness in James's earlier tales. Still, he finds this tale too imitative (17–18).

It is Hawthornesque also in its historical atmosphere, and Wagenknecht connects it with "Gabrielle de Bergerac" of the same year, and the much later *The Sense of the Past*, as James's only historical works, although he finds little historical atmosphere (200; also Beach 186).

The tale has been compared mostly with later works. Levy links the last image of the dead Viola with Claire's fear of her mother in *The American* as anticipations of James's later examinations of the abysses of evil (37). Looking at two later examples of such evil, Walter Wright compares Viola's revenge and the jealousy that inspires it to the similar, but strictly human revenge of Mrs. Grantham in "The Two Faces" and Lord Mark in *The Wings of the Dove* (87). Wegelin also notes a later movement away from the pure supernatural, contrasting the omniscient telling of the appearance of an unquestioned ghost with the subjective narration of an ambiguous haunting in *The Turn of the Screw*, in which the interest has switched from the ghost to the consciousness that perceives it (485–86). Mackenzie also discusses the tale, with *The Turn of the Screw* and *The Spoils of Poynton* as well, as illustrations of the enactment of "secret revenge for secret injury" (75–76).

A more direct similarity of plot, as Edel notes, is with *The Other House*, where the heroine, dying in childbirth, makes the hero promise not to remarry while their child lives. The promise there has equally disastrous consequences, as the woman who wishes to marry the widower kills the child in order to free him from his promise (4).

Interpretation and Criticism

Despite James's own late disavowal of the work, the story has garnered considerable critical attention, a fair amount of it favorable. James's brother William wrote him of the story that it "is in a different tone fr. any of yours, seems to have been written with the mind more unbent & careless, is very pleasantly done, but is, as the Nation said, 'trifling' for you." William also found in it, however, "a certain neatness & airy grace of touch wh. is characteristic of your productions" as well as "a greater suppleness & freedom of movement in the composition" (36–37). Howells, who called it "admirable" to Norton (1979, 283), found it a model in dramatic storytelling that, he argued, even James himself could benefit from paying attention to. The tale was "written with heat" as it "rapidly advances from point to point, with a constantly mounting interest" and without the usual over analysis, or what Howells called the "assumed narrator" who often supplied it (1875, 73). Kelley's view of the story as an exception among the early works—"a vivid jewel, even though an imitation one, among pebbles"—is representative (82–84; e.g., Edgar 15).

The review by the *Nation* William cited had actually first called the work "a tantalizing story," but finding that "the end turns out trivial," saw it as "trivial altogether." Much criticism focuses on the story's dramatic conclusion, the description of the dead Viola, which it seems almost a requirement to quote: "On her limbs was the stiffness of death, and on her face, in the fading light of the sun, the terror of something more than death. Her lips were parted in entreaty, in dismay, in agony; and on her bloodless brow and cheeks there glowed the marks of ten hideous wounds from two vengeful ghostly hands" (CT 1, 318–19).

The explicit description makes it clear that we are not dealing with any supernatural ambiguity—the "fantastic" in Todorov's terminology. Instead, the hands mark the tale as clearly "marvelous" (183). As LeClair observes, James keeps the foreshadowing sufficiently "light" for it to remain "natural" (400), and the reception of James's turn at the end to the overtly supernatural has not always been welcomed. Kraft argues that the conclusion is "so contrived and slight, and so long in coming," that it fails to shock as it ought; Long judges it forced (Kraft 20; Long 17). Even more pejoratively, Garnett cites it as an example of the "sort of nonsense" James got away from by moving to Europe (ix).

Others concentrate more on what James was aiming for in the conclusion. Swan sees it as the first demonstration of James's commitment to connecting the supernatural and the natural (23). Buitenhuis judges the description itself excellent but out of place. The story ultimately fails, he feels, because James, while taking Hawthorne as his model, did not adequately create the necessary ambiguous romance world, but merely imported his own realistic approach into the historical past, using detail in place of image or symbol. The result, Buitenhuis argues, is that the story fulfills more of its promise of "costume drama" than romance (42).

One reason for the focus on the final lines may be that the story is, as Rebecca West puts it, "seven-eighths prelude" with only the small bit of "catastrophe," which she judges of both "too short and small a report" (25). Beach also sees the ending with its intrusion of the romantic as the focus of the tale, even though he judges it totally out of keeping with what goes before (184). Levy notes a similar disjunction, but contends that the "image of Gothic terror" compensates for what is otherwise the story's "faded gentility" (31).

Kelley is alone in considering the concluding picture to be but the last in a series of "highly colored, impressionistic paintings" through which James successfully tells his story and keeps down the superabundant analysis of his previous, more realistic tales. She sees the wedding clothes as serving as a central symbol to hold the story together and to provide for a graceful transition between the views of Viola and Perdita. The ghostly death caps the picture of the destuctiveness of jealousy, in her view, and in all she judges James's first excursion into romanticism occasionally "extravagant" but successful (81–82).

The story told in this series of pictures contains, as Banta notes, "hoary themes": "rivalry, possessiveness, and jealousy between sisters" (1964, 180 n.23). Howells praised both the bold depiction of the rivalry and the individual characters of the sisters, the "selfish, luxurious" Viola and the poignant Perdita (1875, 73). While Wagenknecht finds the dead Perdita both "petty" and "conventional" in her behavior, Jones argues that Viola acts from a belief that Arthur's protecting of the clothes is an indication of his continuing memory of Perdita, which gives a greater significance to the behavior of both sisters, living and dead (Wagenknecht 200; Jones 60). Mackenzie's reading posits two sisters with "sufficient identity only for one," an insufficiency he reads into the tale's two mirror scenes, so that the desires of each are driven underground into secret resentment as they seek to displace the other. The dying Perdita feels she has "never lived sufficiently," and so tries to gain an extended existence through the protection of her clothes; the now-married Viola feels she is living insufficiently due to the decline in Willoughby's fortunes and the lack of a child of their own. The encounter of the two, according to Mackenzie, in Viola's attack on the box, rather than giving either victory simply provides the conclusion to their inadequacies (75–78).

The husband so battled for has inspired little enthusiasm among readers, beginning with William's low opinion of him (47). His experiences, however, and those of his two wives, certainly would seem to indicate a reason to fear marriage, a motive Putt locates beneath the supernatural costuming (37).

How well James combines such human fears with a supernatural treatment has been frequently debated. Howells praised the choice of a colonial New England late enough for "splendor" and remote enough for romance (1875, 72–73). McCarthy, however, finds that the romanticism combined with the story's explicitness keeps the tale superficial by preventing the reader from becoming involved in the story. He further asserts that the tale violates James's theory that a ghost story should be connected to common life, and that properly the "dramatic interest of crime 'lay in the fact that it compromised the criminal's moral repose'" (104–5). Similarly, Banta finds it a "conventional" work, its use of "physical vampirism" less impressive than James's later consideration of the vampire-like "power struggles" engaged in by real people (1972, 89). In Edel's view, however, the natural and supernatural are better combined here, as James "places the real before us, squarely and objectively, and then skillfully mingles it with the unusual and the eerie" (CT 1, 20).

According to LeClair's formulation, both the "natural" jealousy and the "supernatural" vengeance it inspires are more effective because they are not explained (401). Indeed, the story covers a wide range of images, from the homely description of the resented stepdaughter, "a little girl who sat in a high chair and ate bread-and-milk with a wooden spoon" (CT 1, 316), to the gruesome description of the dead Viola. We are granted some insight behind the images, perhaps more than the narrator would like to think. We are clearly told, for example, that Viola's love for Willoughby is a "passion" from start to end, but shortly afterward we are informed that "Viola's desires, as the reader will have observed, have remained a good deal of a mystery" (CT 1, 312, 314). It may be that James wanted his story even more mysterious than it is. Vaid speaks of it as a "simple allegory," but considers that James's keeping his theme and plot contained makes the tale relatively successful (134, 259). The tale is, perhaps, like most of James's early works, most successful in parts, but it also sustains a curiosity and a suspense about its configuration of characters, which he ambitiously caps with what must be one of his least ambiguous endings ever. James may have objected to seeing the tale "disinterred," but a reader today need not be embarrassed to enjoy it.

Works Cited

Primary Works

James, Henry. 1868. "The Romance of Certain Old Clothes." *Atlantic Monthly* (February): 209–20.

———. 1875. "The Romance of Certain Old Clothes." *A Passionate Pilgrim*. Boston: James R. Osgood, 327–62.

———. 1885. "The Romance of Certain Old Clothes." *Stories Revived*. Vol. 3. London: Macmillan.

———. 1921–23. "The Romance of Certain Old Clothes." *The Novels and Stories of Henry James*. Vol. 26. Ed. Percy Lubbock. London: Macmillan.

Secondary Works

Akiyama, Masayuki. 1985. "James and Nanboku: A Comparative Study of Supernatural Stories in the West and East." *Comparative Literature Studies* 22, no. 1 (Spring): 43–52.

Allott, Miriam. 1955. "James Russell Lowell: A Link between Tennyson and Henry James." *Review of English Studies* 6 (October): 397–99.

Anderson, Quentin. 1957. *The American Henry James*. New Brunswick, NJ: Rutgers University Press.

Anon. 1868. Review of "The Romance of Certain Old Clothes." *The Nation* (30 January): 94.

Banta, Martha. 1972. *Henry James and the Occult: The Great Extension*. Bloomington: Indiana University Press.

———. 1964. "Henry James and 'The Others.'" *New England Quarterly* 37 (June): 171–84.

Beach, Joseph Warren. [1918] 1954. *The Method of Henry James*. Philadelphia: Albert Saifer.

Briggs, Julia. 1977. *Night Visitors: The Rise and Fall of the English Ghost Story*. London: Faber.

Buitenhuis, Peter. 1970. *The Grasping Imagination: The American Writings of Henry James*. Toronto: University of Toronto Press.

Cowie, Alexander. 1948. *The Rise of the American Novel*. New York: American Book Company.

Dupee, F. W. [1951] 1956. *Henry James*. Garden City, NY: Doubleday Anchor.

Edel, Leon, ed. 1970. *Henry James: Stories of the Supernatural*. New York: Taplinger.

Edgar, Pelham. [1927] 1964. *Henry James, Man and Author*. New York: Russell & Russell.

Feinstein. Howard M. 1984. *Becoming William James*. Ithaca, NY: Cornell University Press. Reprinted in part from "A Singular Life: Twinship in the Psychology of

William and Henry James," in *Blood Brothers: Siblings as Writers*, ed. Norman Kiell, 301–28. New York: International University Press, 1983.

Garnett, David, ed. 1946. *Fourteen Stories by Henry James*. London: Rupert Hart-Davis.

Havens, Raymond D. 1981. "Henry James on One of his Early Stories." *American Literature* 23 (March): 131–33.

Howells, W. D. 1979. *Selected Letters.* Vol. 1. *1852–1872*. Ed. George Arms et al. Boston: Twayne.

———. 1875. Review of *The Passionate Pilgrim and Other Tales. The Atlantic Monthly* (April). Reprinted in *Discovery of a Genius: William Dean Howells and Henry James*, ed. Albert Mordell, 63–74. New York: Twayne.

James, William. 1992. *The Correspondence of William James*. Vol. 1: *William and Henry*. Ed. Ignas K. Skrupskelis and Elizabeth M. Berkeley. Charlottesville: University Press of Virginia.

Jones, Granville H. 1975. *Henry James's Psychology of Experience: Innocence, Responsibility, and Renunciation in the Fiction of Henry James*. The Hague: Mouton.

Kelley, Cornelia Pulsifer. [1930] 1965. *The Early Development of Henry James*. Urbana: University of Illinois Press.

Kerr, Howard. 1983. "James's Last Early Supernatural Tales: Hawthorne Demagnetized, Poe Depoetized." In *The Haunted Dusk: American Supernatural Fiction, 1820–1920*. Ed. Howard Kerr, John W. Crowley, and Charles L. Crow, 135–48. Athens: University of Georgia Press.

Kraft, James. 1969. *The Early Tales of Henry James*. Carbondale: Southern Illinois University Press.

LeClair, Robert Charles. 1955. *Young Henry James, 1843–1870*. New York: Bookman.

Levy, Leo B. 1957. *Versions of Melodrama: A Study of the Fiction and Drama of Henry James, 1865–1897*. Berkeley: University of California Press.

Long, Robert Emmet. 1979. *The Great Succession: Henry James and the Legacy of Hawthorne*. Pittsburgh: University of Pittsburgh Press.

McCarthy, Harold T. 1958. *Henry James: The Creative Process*. New York: Thomas Yoseloff.

McElderry, Bruce R., Jr. 1965. *Henry James*. New York: Twayne.

Mackenzie, Manfred. 1976. *Communities of Honor and Love in Henry James*. Cambridge, MA: Harvard University Press.

Matthiessen, F. O., ed. 1947. *The American Novels and Stories of Henry James*. New York: Knopf.

Melchiori, Giorgio. 1965. "Locksley Hall Revisited: Tennyson and Henry James." *Review of English Literature* 6 (October): 9–25. Reprinted in Barbara Melchiori and Giorgio Melchiori, *Il Gusto di Henry James*. Turin: Guilio Einaudi editore, 1974.

Putt, S. Gorley. 1966. *Henry James: A Reader's Guide*. Ithaca, NY: Cornell University Press.

St. Armand, Barton Levi. 1983. "'I Must Have Died at Ten Minutes Past One": Posthumous Reverie in Harriet Prescott Spofford's 'The Amber Gods.'" In *The Haunted Dusk: American Supernatural Fiction, 1820–1920*. Ed. Howard Kerr, John W. Crowley, and Charles L. Crow, 101–19. Athens: University of Georgia Press.

Swan, Michael. 1957. *Henry James*. London: Longmans, Green.

Thorp, Willard, ed. 1962. *The Madonna of the Future and Other Early Tales*. New York: New American Library.

Todorov, Tzvetan. 1977. *The Poetics of Prose*. Trans. Richard Howard. Ithaca, NY: Cornell University Press.

Vaid, Krishna B. 1964. *Technique in the Tales of Henry James*. Cambridge, MA: Harvard University Press.

Wagenknecht, Edward. 1984. *The Tales of Henry James*. New York: Frederick Ungar.

Wegelin, Christof. 1973. "Henry James and the Treasure of Consciousness." *Die Neueren Sprachen* 72: 484–91.

Wright, Walter F. 1962. *The Madness of Art: A Study of Henry James*. Lincoln: University of Nebraska Press.

Rose-Agathe

Publication History

Originally entitled "Théodolinde," this story was the first by James to appear in the Philadelphia *Lippincott's Magazine*, since *Scribner's* and the *Atlantic* had sufficient of his material at the time, causing James a "stoppage of chance to publish," as he wrote his mother (*Letters* 2, 155). He may also have been attracted by *Lippincott's* higher fees. It was, however, the last of James's stories to appear there, a fact influenced, one might speculate, by the rejection of *Daisy Miller*, "without comment," two months before "Théodolinde" took its place in the May 1878 issue (Aziz 3, 14–16). James reprinted the story only in his 1885 *Stories Revived*. It appeared after his death in the 1919 collection *Travelling Companions* and in Lubbock's edition of the novels and stories.

Circumstances of Composition, Sources, and Influences

Aziz proposes the summer of 1877 for the composition of the tale, seeing it along with "Four Meetings" and "Longstaff's Marriage" as inspired by James's year in Paris and written shortly thereafter, following his move to London (3, 14).

The story may be read as an incomplete version of the Pygmalion myth, one in which the unaspiring artist is quite content that his Galatea remain a statue. A more contemporary, less lofty source of inspiration may be George Sand's *Dernières Pages*, which James reviewed for the *Nation* in 1877 and which contains a history of her puppet shows. Of them James wrote, "[M]ust we be French and frivolous to care about ingenious and artistic pastimes? We should almost recommend that the article be translated, and circulated as a tract, for the benefit of domestic circles infected with what Matthew Arnold calls 'dreariness'" (*Criticism* 2, 736). One might say the same of James's story.

Delbaere-Grant is one critic who has correctly appreciated the "French and frivolous" nature of the story, helpfully placing it in the context of James's "ironical view of the French" (290). In particular, she provides a rationale for the narrator's striking sensory sensitivity, particularly to smells, in the first paragraph:

> there was a sort of vernal odour in the street, mingling with the emana-
> tions of the restaurant across the way . . . with the delightful aroma of the
> chocolate shop . . . and . . . with certain luscious perfumes hovering
> about the brilliantly - polished windows of the hairdresser's establish-
> ment . . . Presently . . . my right-hand nostril was exposed to the titillation
> of a new influence. It was as if a bottle of the finest hair-oil had suddenly
> been uncorked. (CT 4, 119–20)

All this, she argues, can be read as a parody of French writers, Zola in especial
(289; see also Wagenknecht 201). Less approvingly, Donald Stone sees James as
aiming here for a typical "well-made" French story (191). In a more restricted
criticism, Gale considers the three comparisons to the Madonna "unfortunate" when the subject is a hairdresser's dummy ([1954] 1964, 157).

Relation to Other Works

Jones places the central character, Sanguinetti, "as a connoisseur and collector of beautiful objects," in a collection of James's characters whose "taste"
dominates their lives. He sees him as happier in his taste than Hyacinth
Robinson or Graham Fielder, more human than Christina Light, Mme Merle,
or Mrs. Gareth, a small-scale Adam Verver, whose waxen statue provides the
connection between life and art spoken of by Henry St. George. Most
markedly, he contrasts him with Osmond, who attempts to turn human
beings into art objects, while Sanguinetti simply attributes human characteristics to art objects. He does acknowledge, however, his difference from the
other collector in *The Portrait of a Lady*, Ned Rosier, who disposes of his collection in an attempt to win his real-life love. Thus, he concludes that
Sanguinetti, with Marmaduke in "Maud-Evelyn," achieves a happiness less
harmful to others than the artists of "Collaboration" or Nick Dormer, if also
less significant than the happiness achieved by Felix Young of *The Europeans*
(147–48, 169). Putt also notes briefly the comparison (not the difference)
with Rosier, adding "the more frivolous bric-a-brac side" of Gabriel Nash as a
further parallel (268).

Delbaere-Garant offers a comparison between Sanguinetti and Gaston
Probert of the 1888 novella *The Reverberator*, both being "Parisianized"
Americans who regard the world largely as a visual phenomenon. She quotes
Probert's early statement about his fiancée—"And think of the delight of hav-
ing that charming object before one's eyes—always, always!"—to show how
easily it could be Sanguinetti speaking far more appropriately, of the dummy.
She notes, however, Probert's change to a more admirable human attitude
(311–12). He moves, one might say, from the stance of an Osmond to a
Rosier, while Sanguinetti stays in the middle.

Interpretation and Criticism

Delbaere-Garant and Jones apart, the general attitude toward the tale has been one of dismissal, although McElderry acknowledges its "finish" (72). In 1922 Schelling found it "trivial, almost banal," although "forgivable for the charming description of a very pretty woman" (171–74). Edel has labeled it a "trifle"; Putt finds it "absurd"; and it is the only one of the ten stories written from 1876 to 1880 that Kraft considers unworthy of discussion (CT 4, 7; Putt 268; Kraft 86). More appreciatively, Wagenknecht has called it "the *jeu d'esprit* par excellence about James's *jeux d'esprit*" (201).

Generally, criticism focuses on the character of Sanguinetti. Delbaere-Garant's and Jones's basically positive readings should be apparent from above. Putt, on the other hand, finds him a "trim self-satisfied dilettante," whose collecting is simply an extreme example of the typical avoidance of marriage by the men in James's work (268). Similarly, Tintner argues that "something went wrong" in his development (170).

A better appreciation of the story and its protagonist is gained through a recognition of its setting, its first-person narration, structure, and general lightness of tone. Paris, the narrator recognizes, is the "city in which even the humblest of one's senses is the medium of poetic impressions" (CT 4, 119). However, because he also regards it as "the city of gallantry," he quickly falls into the mistaken belief that his friend Sanguinetti's new object of affections must be the hairdresser's wife not his display dummy, even though he is aware that so far his "affections had no object save . . . faded crockery and . . . angular chairs" (CT 4, 122, 124).

As Delbaere-Garant writes, only in Paris could a man "speak of a beautiful object in exactly the same terms as he would speak of a beautiful woman" (290). An uninitiated American, the narrator should perhaps catch the distinction in Sanguinetti's conversation and behavior, but does not. Knowing only what the narrator does, the reader is intended to share his mistake. Indeed, although the reader may sense that more is suspect than Sanguinetti's morals alone, James does an admirable job of crafting dialogue that can apply to either the woman or the dummy, thereby producing in the tale's discussion of the negotiations for purchase an artificial frankness that also parodies the French school. The story has one of James's few textbook surprise endings, so that the confusion is perpetuated up to the last paragraph—a confusion incorrectly dispelled in Gale's description of Sanguinetti as a "Paris collector of hair dresser dummies" (1965, 183).

Later critics have taken the tale as a more pointed social metaphor. Niemtzow reads its comedy as a critique of marriage as a process of acquisition, with women the objects bargained for, like the mannequin in the tale (388–89). Sicker takes Sanguinetti as a parody of all James's earlier "imaginative lovers" seeking to evade the changes of life by escaping reality through a focus on a dead, fixed image (45).

McElderry notes the story may be read as teaching the "power of preconception," but adds that James seems to assign it no "heavy moral" (72). The narrator (identified in the magazine version as a Bostonian), who believes that "it is one's duty to take things seriously," has really been taking them too seriously, and perhaps leading the reader to as well. As Jones points out, "to both the narrator and the reader [Sanguinetti] may seem absurd; but to himself and perhaps to James—he is simply and purely what he is" (147). The story may poke fun at Sanguinetti (and the narrator as well), but it is hard to see it condemning him, unaware as he is of the moral quandary he has thrown the narrator into. Frivolity here is not immoral, simply artistic and "French"—an antidote to "dreariness." The story is perhaps a "trifle," but one content to be so, a pretty knickknack or bibelot.

Works Cited

Primary Works

James, Henry. 1878. "Théodolinde." *Lippincott's Magazine* (May): 533–63.

———. 1885. "Rose-Agathe." *Stories Revived*. Vol 2. London: Macmillan.

———. 1919. "Rose-Agathe." *Master Eustace*. Preface by Albert Mordell. New York: Thomas Seltzer.

———. 1921–23. "Rose-Agathe." *The Novels and Stories of Henry James*. Vol. 25. Ed. Percy Lubbock. London: Macmillan.

Secondary Works

Delbaere-Garant, Jeanne. 1970. *Henry James: The Vision of France*. Paris: Société d'Editions Les Belles Lettres.

Gale, Robert L. 1965. *Plots and Characters in the Fiction of Henry James*. Hamden, CT: Archon.

———. [1954] 1964. *The Caught Image: Figurative Language in the Fiction of Henry James*. Chapel Hill: University of North Carolina Press.

Jones, Granville H. 1975. *Henry James's Psychology of Experience: Innocence, Responsibility, and Renunciation in the Fiction of Henry James*. The Hague: Mouton.

Kraft, James. 1969. *The Early Tales of Henry James*. Carbondale: Southern Illinois University Press.

McElderry, Bruce R., Jr. 1965. *Henry James*. New York: Twayne.

Niemtzow, Annette. 1975. "Marriage and the New Woman in *The Portrait of a Lady*." *American Literature* 47, no. 3 (November): 377–95.

Putt, S. Gorley. 1966. *Henry James: A Reader's Guide*. Ithaca, NY: Cornell University Press.

Schelling, Felix E. 1922. "Some Forgotten Tales of Henry James." In *Appraisements and Asperities: as to Some Contemporary Writers*, 169–74. Philadelphia: Lippincott.

Sicker, Philip. 1980. *Love and the Quest for Identity in the Fiction of Henry James*. Princeton: Princeton University Press.

Stone, Donald David. 1972. *Novelists in a Changing World: Meredith, James, and the Transformation of English Fiction in the 1880's*. Cambridge, MA: Harvard University Press.

Tinter, Adeline R. 1986. *The Museum World of Henry James*. Ann Arbor: UMI Research Press.

Wagenknecht, Edward. 1984. *The Tales of Henry James*. New York: Frederick Ungar.

Foreign Language
Izzo, Donatella. 1989. "'Rose-Agathe': Henry James e la donna-ogetto." *Merope* 1 (November 1): 101–20.

A Round of Visits

Publication History

"A Round of Visits," Henry James's last published short story, appeared first in the *English Review* in April and May of 1910, and was collected that same year in *The Finer Grain*. He recorded two payments from Pinker in his cash accounts, one in May at £8, the other in June at £29. 16. 0. (CN 602). After James's death, the story was next printed by Lubbock in his edition of *The Novels and Stories of Henry James*.

Circumstances of Composition, Sources, and Influences

On February 17, 1894, James recorded in his notebook "the notion of a young man (young, presumably), who has something—some secret sorrow, trouble, fault—to *tell* and can't find the *recipient*" (CN 88). The entry trails off into a series of x's. Two months later in Venice, James returned to the idea, articulating the "misery" the young man carries about in search of "the ideal sympathy," until, meeting a superior appeal, "a *demand* where he had at last been looking for a supply," he forgets his own sorrow in pity. At that point, James judged the idea "perhaps as pretty as another," seeming to gain more confidence in it by imagining the last person a woman whose encounter he sketches (CN 94–95). Nevertheless, he did nothing with the idea until May 1898, when he included it in a list of possible topics. The next February, reminding himself not to lose track of the "little *concetto*," he heightened the atmosphere of "the great heartless preoccupied" London, only to conclude that the idea of one forgetting his sorrows in another's "obvious and banal . . . 'goody' and calculable beforehand." Instead he contemplated having someone "*tide over* some awful crisis by listening to him. He learns afterwards what it has been" (CN 169, 179).

Another ten years would elapse before the writing of the tale, years that contained James's last visit to America. Although Auchincloss argues that James simply "transfers" his anger of London society to America, Matthiessen sees the American trip as shaping James's idea, his sense of dislocation in the "harsh and violent" city strengthening the picture of Monteith's isolation (Matthiessen 1947, xxii; N 281). Wegelin, however, sees the fact that Winch is refined rather than disfigured by greed harking back to the story's original setting in the more mannered London (157). American manners by contrast, in Ward's estimate, provoke in James a horror that, "subdued" in *The American Scene*, becomes "emphatic" here (1988, 152). Graham Greene traces the horror to an earlier date, arguing that James felt he had failed not just his country but his ill-fated brothers Wilky and Bob by not serving in the Civil War, and that his sense of guilt lies behind his recurrent theme of betrayal at the hands of friends (27–28).

The chief setting in the tale is Monteith's hotel, a "microcosm" of New York according to Bradbury (212–13). Its name, the Pocohantas, points to the personal dimension of the encounter of cultures, but its original was the Waldorf, and Lee comments on the appropriateness of such "a prodigious public setting" to underscore Monteith's isolation (113). Similarly, Ward observes, as an emblem of American devotion to wealth, it is an appropriate frame for a tale which shows the misery and violence that are its results (1988, 152). In *The American Scene*, James had compared the Waldorf to Pandemonium in *Paradise Lost*, evidence, in Tintner's view, that James believed the skyscraper was a devilish invention (1976, 401, 426, 434). Tintner, who originally characterized the tale as a "hotel story," would later broaden the scope of her label, characterizing it as a "skyscraper story," noting that James disapproved of the way such housing was replacing the private home (1986, 186–87). Before his birth, of course, James's own family had made their home in what was then New York's new hotel, the Astor House, where his older brother, William, was born in 1842 (*Life* 1, 40). On a lighter note, Tintner attributes the animal imagery here and in the other late New York tales to a visit to the Central Park Zoo (1976, 416–17).

People as well as buildings served as sources for the tale, and Tintner sees in it a response to the work and personality of Edith Wharton. She notes the influence of an 1899 Wharton tale, "A Cup of Cold Water," which features embezzlement and attempted suicide, as well as the 1905 novel *The House of Mirth*, which described the New York hotel world's "torrid splendour." Mrs. Ash, Tintner writes, not only reflects in her name Wharton's compulsive smoking, but shares her marital turmoil and need for a confidant (1975, 365–68). Mrs. Ash may also owe a debt to the widow Mrs. Philip Livingstone Van Rensellaer, who, according to Edel, "charmed" Henry abroad, but bored him later when she came to England (*Life* 263). As a source for the name, but not the character, of Bloodgood, Martin and Ober point to Dr. Joseph Colt Bloodgood of Johns Hopkins Medical School, who may have been one of the "gallant young Doctors" James recalled as his guides in *The American Scene* (1984). Buitenhuis points to a less august, nameless person as a source, the murderer James met upon a visit to a prison, who, he recalled in *The American Scene*, was notable for the "refinement wrought in him by so many years of easy club life" there (237).

Martin and Ober argue for a more controlling literary source. In their reading, Monteith's residence on the tenth story of his hotel echoes the ten divisions of Dante's Inferno, the setting for his "round" of visits being the circles of Dante's hell. Noting the same time span in each from Thursday to Sunday, they speculate that the March Sunday here may also be Easter, and see the tale's message as one of forgiveness, despite the surprise of the final suicide. They place Mrs. Folliot in the first circle of the lustful, identify the doctor as Virgil and Winch's sister-in-law as Beatrice, and remark that betrayers like Bloodgood occupied the bottom level of hell, a frozen lake reproduced in the frozen city of the tale. In their reading, when Monteith breaks through his "circle" of ego to pity Bloodgood, Winch realizes that he, too, can be forgiven, and has the courage to commit suicide and face God. Thus they take Winch's line "You saved my life" as spoken without irony and Monteith's final line as spoken "with more gladness or pride than regret." In all, they view the tale as something of a "last testament" for James (1981).

Such a religious reading Wagenknecht finds "curious and high-flown" (260 n.19). Earlier, in 1971, Tintner had noted the religious imagery, but also its context in a "thoroughly secularized" New York "ritualize[d]" only by "the feasts of lunch, tea, and dinner" (498–99; also Bradbury 214). In 1976 she reasserted James's "secular" outlook, but formalizing the secular ritual of the tale, proposed in place of the religious calendar a secular "bible," *The New York Directory* with its opening almanac, as the framework for the tale (427–28).

Both Martin and Ober and Tintner acknowledge other literary sources for the story. Martin and Ober point to a parallel with Zola's *Thérèse Raquin*, in which two lovers escape a hellish life through mutual suicide (1981, 52). Tintner argues that as a victim of richer relations, Monteith's story, like that of "Crapy Cornelia," can be seen as a version of Balzac's *Les Parents pauvres* (1975, 358). Other critics point to Hawthorne as an influence, Buitenhuis seeing him as a source for the idea of "education by sin and suffering," and Matthiessen and Murdock more generally characterizing the abstract beginnings of the tale as Hawthornesque (236–37; N xiv).

More modern sources include, according to Tintner, the opera *Salomé* and its source in Wilde's play. Casting Winch's sister-in-law in the title role on the grounds that her conversation brings to Monteith's mind "profane modern music," Tintner argues that she inadvertently brings about Winch's death (1986, 135). Vaid finds Monteith's "burden of grief" reminiscent of Chekov's "Lament" (235). Przybylowicz compares Monteith's relationship to Winch with Graham's relationship to the corrupt Horton in *The Ivory Tower*, placing both in the context of such works by Conrad as *Heart of Darkness* and *The Secret Sharer* (113). Tintner sees the tale itself as a potential source for the series of visits in Louis Auchincloss's *The Book Class* (1989, 333).

Relation to Other Works

As a tale of New York, "A Round of Visits" has many late associates. In Tintner's view, it is the "crescendo" to the "horror" of the late New York tales, including the chapter "The Married Son" from the multiauthored *The Whole Family*. She chronicles how the family home slated for destruction in "The Jolly Corner," redecorated in "Crapy Cornelia," and abandoned in "Julia Bride," is utterly gone here (1976, 401, 424, 434). Purdy, too, judges "A Round of Visits" as the most despairing New York tale, pointing out that while White-Mason found New York society "false," Monteith finds it "criminal." At the same time, he remarks, Monteith lacks the linguistic sophistication that provided White-Mason the tool to come to terms with New York (421–22). Drawing closer links with "Julia Bride," Berthoff comments on the "moral ugliness" of both stories, Menikoff on the use of "interior narration" in each, and Tintner on the manner in which each protagonist seeks sympathy, but must give it instead (Berthoff 125; Menikoff 439–40; Tintner 1976, 428).

A prime connection has been with "The Jolly Corner," which, Hocks laments, has overshadowed this less famous tale (203). Wegelin sees in Monteith's recognition of Winch's guilt an "image" like that of Brydon's other self in "The Jolly Corner," illustrating James's own recognition on his last trip to America of the "education of business" that lay behind even such American fortunes as Milly Theale's or Christopher Newman's (156–57). Similarly, while pointing to the differences in the conclusions, Vaid sees both Bloodgood and Winch as showing what Monteith might have become in America, even as the ghost shows Brydon, a theory that Buitenhuis objects takes the connection too far (Vaid 235; Buitenhuis 235–37). Mays points to the similarity between Alice's sympathy for the scarred ghost and Monteith's for Bloodgood, observing that like the ghost Winch in the end is "disfigured," while Monteith like Brydon remains comparatively unmarked by the business of life (472–73).

Elaborating on the connection, Bradbury places "A Round of Visits" with *The Ivory Tower* as a pair parallel to that of "The Jolly Corner" and *The Sense of the Past*, while noting shared elements also with the two late works of nonfiction, the *Autobiography* and *The American Scene* (211–12). Particular resemblances with *The Ivory Tower* include, according to Geismar, the "sensibility of high finance" and concern over tainted money, and, according to Edel, the stealing of inherited wealth in a "great predatory competitive world" (Geismar 421; *Life* 5, 501; also Buitenhuis 237). Still, Jones traces the complex morality by which the protagonists in both, by "shirking their responsibility to know and to act," become "simultaneously sufferers and sinners" (92). Similarly, Przybylowicz observes how Fielder and Monteith, as "temptingly fatuous" clients more concerned with morality than money, are victimized by "duplicitous other[s]" (113, 133–34).

Among the tales of *The Finer Grain*, Hocks judges the air of this one and "The Bench of Desolation" in particular akin to that of the ghostly tales, with its "phantasmogoric" social setting, in which Monteith encounters Winch almost as one would meet a ghost (197). Looking at the protagonists, Tintner argues that Monteith's "ineffectuality" is even greater than Dodd's, while Gage finds the "self-destructive urge" of both Winch and Bloodgood similar to Dodd's (Tintner 1976, 433; Gage 261). At the same time, Gage compares the final isolation of the characters to that of Traffle in "Mora Montravers," although Gage argues that unlike Traffle or Berridge of "The Velvet Glove," Monteith not only seeks to respond to reality, but is changed by it (242, 245). Tintner describes the contrast with Berridge's tale more sweepingly: "The Velvet Glove" is "euphoric, comic, and pagan"; "A Round of Visits" is "depressed, tragic, and Christian" (1971, 498–99).

Certainly, Monteith's betrayal is more tragic. As Greene observes, Monteith, like Milly Theale, Maggie Verver, and Isabel Archer, is betrayed by a friend (118–19). In Ward's reading, however, Monteith is also like Milly, Maggie, and Stransom in giving up his sense of betrayal to sympathize with his betrayer (1961, 160). Krook also notes the particular edge given to betrayal by the closeness of the betrayer here, in *The Golden Bowl*, and in *The Ivory Tower* as well. Citing Monteith's concluding insight—"Of such convenience in pain, it seemed, was the fact of another's pain, and of so much worth again disinterested sympathy," she sees it teaching the same lesson as *The Golden Bowl*, that there can never be "disinterested sympathy" because people are able to give only in as much as they need to receive, so that in behavior the selfish and the selfless motive end up not far apart (338, 342–43). The theme of betrayal, as Vaid remarks, was persistent in James from his first tale, "A Tragedy of Error," to his last, accompanied by violence in both (279 n.25). Segal nevertheless distinguishes a more positive change, the transformation of Jamesian observers from meddlesome snoops to sympathetic listeners reflected in the emphasis on the need to share the burden of suffering (217–18).

The change that Winch has undergone in the tale, Ward notes, is similar to that imputed to the characters of *The Sacred Fount*, and Przybylowicz points out that Winch likewise is shown as good beneath his "mask" following the conceit of the novella (1961, 160; Przybylowicz 135). Other striking transformations in James are those of Chad in *The Ambassadors*, noted by Hocks and Wagenknecht, and of Kate in "The Bench of Desolation," noted by Gage and Ward (Hocks 197; Wagenknecht 260 n.18; Gage 262–63, 276; Ward 1961, 161).

Monteith also has his spiritual kin. Buitenhuis compares him to Mason of "A Most Extraordinary Case" as an invalid alone in an indifferent New York (234). Matthiessen notes that James had portrayed similarly isolated individuals in London, such as Hyacinth Robinson (1944, 114). The round of visits in "The Visits" also ended in a disaster—the death of the young heroine—chronicled by the witnessing narrator.

Additional comparisons include Edel's contrast of the burdened hero here with the free spirit of Saltram in "The Coxon Fund," whose germ was recorded the same year (*Life* 3, 374–75). Looking also at the notebooks, Matthiessen contrasts the tale's development with that of "The Special Type." While "A Round of Visits" began with an abstraction, James's trip to America, Matthiessen argues, provided the tale with a vigor and violence in its depiction of the abuses of wealth, whereas "The Special Type" began with an actual case only to become unconvincingly "etherialized" (1944, 111–13). Purdy compares the final conversation here as a "set scene," which determines life or death to similar scenes in "Owen Wingrave" and *The Other House* (422). Ward points to the metaphor of the "panther" in the "jungle" of the hotel here in relation to the "beast" of "The Beast in the Jungle" (1988, 152). The name Newton, Buitenhuis comments, recalls the "insufferably forward and selfish" son of Mrs. Luna in *The Bostonians* (234–35).

Interpretation and Criticism

"There was nothing like a crowd," Monteith discovers in New York, "for making one feel lonely" (CT 12, 434). The story is accordingly marked by the sense of a solitary man pitted against what Edgar calls the "unfeeling restlessness" of the city (73). In the tale, Matthiessen observes that the corruption of the downtown world has "seeped" into the uptown one James staked as his territory (1947, xxiv). Nevertheless, as Bradbury writes, money itself is not the focus, but the "patterns of selfishness and irresponsibility" associated with it (215–16). The issues such a concern give rise to are by no means simple. While Edel once facilely dismissed Monteith's misery by declaring that in "our time" he would simply have consulted a psychoanalyst (*Life* 3, 374–75), Monteith's questions are not those that produce easy answers in any age.

For all its loneliness, the story is structured following a series of visits, primarily *tete à tetes*, and the moral decisions of individuals are at the heart of the tale. James suited his style of narration accordingly. Menikoff discusses how James as a compromise between first- and third-person narration uses the "subjective pronoun"—"he"—for Monteith, to "attach" the reader to Monteith while preserving objectivity. The informal tone thus created, Menikoff argues, also provides a "reflective narrative" able to treat the story's past and present events. Looking more particularly at the conversation between Monteith and Winch's sister-in-law, Hocks similarly notes the typically Jamesian conflation of different "fields of consciousness": the sister-in-law talking to Winch, telling Monteith of it, and Monteith recalling it (79–80). The actual detailing of conversation, particularly in the final scene, is, as Purdy observes, increasingly subordinated to the depiction of consciousness that accompanies it (423–26, 430)

The city itself is described in striking, often commented on, images of the jungle, of "the Tropics" and "the Pole" (e.g., N 281; Bradbury 212–13). The contrast between the latter two extremes of heat and cold—according to Matthiessen one of James's "most brilliant" metaphors—embodied in the hotel and the blizzard, expresses in Buitenhuis's view the basic contrast between appearance and reality, while in Tintner's view it represents the extremity of the control of the city over its people (Matthiessen 1947, xxiv; Buitenhuis 234; Tintner 1976, 433). Early on Allott saw the imagery also indicating the "powerful fascination" of the jungle, the lure of its "opulence" bringing Mark to ruin and Newton to scandal and suicide (333). The violent imagery, according to Chapman, gradually disappears (131–32). Through a Freudian analysis of the tale's language, Gregory constructs a reading focused on "death, revenge, and the figurative/literal aspect of language." Thus Monteith "mark[s]" the world around him, unaware that he is the ape or panther he imagines accompanying him, as his name—"mark my teeth"—indicates; Mrs. Folliot runs to folios in a "self-referential" society; and Winch is wound up by many "turns" of the screw. Gregory's reading, however, is hampered both by the need to translate English words into French for the proper pun, and by a general vagueness about what he sees as James's inspired repression.

The main impression created by the tale's imagery is of an uninhabitable city, and the women in the tale do little to make it habitable, although Monteith remains of the persuasion that such is their task. As Przybylowicz remarks, Monteith, like the typical James hero, "egotistically requires feminine devotion and self-denial" (134). Still, as Edel states, the women here are notably unsympathetic, and accordingly portrayed without pity (CT 12, 8–9). All—with the possible exception of Winch's sister-in-law—fail in comparison to the men. As Ward observes, they simply never attain the same level of understanding or empathy (1961, 159–61; also Gage 233, 236). Bradbury points out, for example, how Mrs. Ash's "manicured hands" contrast with Winch's hands "refined by age" (214–15). Mrs. Folliot, Krook makes clear, is flawed both by her self-absorption and her inability to understand Monteith's "vicarious anguish" for Bloodgood (338). Seeing a difference in Winch's sister-in-law, Chapman calls her one of the last of James's American girls, citing her "conciliatory words" to Monteith: "Well then, feel for others. Fit him in. Tell him why!" (134).

Monteith, more typically for a James character, has had both many admirers and detractors. The traditional view could be represented by Dietrichson, who praises Monteith for his "moral perceptiveness" in his desire to understand the man who betrayed him, and his recognition of that man's suffering (149). Others, however, seizing on the description of Monteith as "a client temptingly fatuous," contend that by living off unearned wealth, he has left himself open to exploitation, almost encouraged it, by those who actually work—with however white a collar—to produce that wealth. Thus, Bradbury sees Mark taking responsibility for Winch's death as partial atonement for his "earlier abnegation of responsibility which permitted his friend to become involved in fraud" (216). Even those who do not hold him responsible for his own deception often note in him a strong egotism (e.g., Gage 237) in need of a strong check to break through it.

Most critics have found the guilty Winch the more interesting character, perhaps because of the amazing transformation Monteith marks in him, the evident result of the "education of business" (CT 12, 457). Bewley has argued that it is Winch's swindling that has "refined" him, and questions whether this is due to "simple perversity" or to James's belief that America has so little to offer that he has to make his "phoenix to rise out of such ashes" (240–42). Most critics, however, like Matthiessen initially, attribute Winch's change to suffering (1944, 116–17). Thus Walter Wright distinguishes between Winch's "reflections" on his crimes, which produce the change, and the crimes themselves, and Buitenhuis, in objecting to Bewley, affirms that business here corrupts, and it is guilt not sin that refines (Wright 140; Buitenhuis 235–37). Such suffering, in Ward's view, is portrayed in the tale as "the ultimate experience," which pays no regard to distinctions of guilt or innocence (1961, 159–61). Still, Wegelin can characterize the change as something of a "Fortunate fall" in the greater awareness it brings (157). In Winch's metamorphosis, Mays sees the signs of James's ambivalent attitude toward American businessmen. While business seems to have made a "beast" of Bloodgood, it has refined Winch (471–73).

Winch's transformation, however, ends in suicide, a death that Mays states makes him again a "horrible figure" (472–73). In the tale, the shot sounds with the fall so "as to make all one violence," and the story's violent end fits its depiction of a callous world (CT 12, 459). It demonstrates strikingly, as Matthiessen argues, James's sense of a world "so corrupted by money that the only escape seemed to be by violence" (1944, 116–17). It shocked James's first readers, however, who were more used to what the critic for *The Times Literary Supplement* called James's "subtle and immaterial" work. The introduction of pistols and police left the critic "almost as much shocked by this whiff of the melodramatic real as the pious by the entry of a dog into church." Again, in 1919, Hackett criticized James's depiction of the scene as lacking "common emotion," observing that James was "too urban, too urbane" for such violence (81).

The sudden act is not without preparation. Bradbury cites some of the foreshadowing, including Monteith's remark that he would "go like a shot" to visit Bloodgood (215). Matthiessen, however, while he praises the device of the "single unexplained concrete detail" in Monteith's sighting of the "tiny flash" of the hidden gun to bring the drama to a head, objects that the use of the gun "breaks the situation to pieces rather than resolves it" (1944, 116–17). The conclusion is undeniably abrupt, ending with Monteith's response to the policeman with the "severe pair of eyes." Asked whether he could not have prevented Winch's death he answers, "I really think I must practically have caused it" (CT 12, 459). Did their conversation cause Winch's death? Could it have prevented it? Would it have been good if it had? As Wagenknecht remarks, even while making some claim for the healing nature of Monteith's visit, James provides no clue as to the "spirit" of the last line, leaving it "one of the most ambiguous endings he ever achieved" (176)

Critics of James, however, have rarely left an ambiguity alone. The joint issues of Monteith's guilt and Winch's motive have lain at the heart of much of the criticism of the story. Early on, McElderry saw "the very absence of a quarrel" such a strain on Winch that it led to his suicide (144). Andreas, on the other hand, sees Monteith's sympathy for Bloodgood as changing Winch's motive from fear of arrest to "remorse and self-judgment" (60). Similarly, Jones sees him as committing suicide because he realizes his own victims may be as kind and forgiving as Monteith, which also makes him realize his own contrasting evil (92).

In his analysis of what he judges an "almost colorless" yet blundering final conversation, Purdy locates a hope at one point that the conversation may change Winch's mind, previously resolved for suicide. Monteith, however, makes too much of Winch's first show of concern, and so begins a conversation that continues at cross purposes. Winch, in turn, is less interested in Monteith himself than in Monteith's reaction to such betrayal as Winch's. Thus, Purdy argues, Winch takes Monteith's remark about "the sort of hell"

Bloodgood must be experiencing, intended as sympathetic to Bloodgood, as hostile, a particular point that Gage objects to as simplifying the ambiguity of Winch's response (Gage 240). In any case, Purdy maintains that Winch throughout remains concerned primarily with his own case, hoping Monteith may still serve to calm him enough to keep him from killing himself and so declares, "You save my life." When Monteith finally understands both Winch's guilt and his intent, his assent to Winch's declaration "We *are* wonderful" gives him, Purdy argues, "such a sense of kindred involvement" that he says he caused the suicide. Indeed, according to Purdy, the story depicts a "horror-in-communication that has as its result the truly shocking prospect of one man so brought into harmonic 'vibration' with another that he can be said to have *committed* the *other*'s suicide."

Another scenario also pictures Monteith flubbing a critical question. When Winch asks Monteith if he would be willing to go to Bloodgood "in kindness," Monteith qualifies the phrase, answering, "Well—to understand," and—led on by Winch—expatiates on the "services" Bloodgood owed to his past kindnesses (CT 12, 452). According to Tintner in 1971, his answer reflects a continued self-preoccupation with himself and ends all possibility of his influencing Winch to live. In Tintner's view, this "lack of mercy" on Monteith's part makes him the "lesser man," a murderer "saved only by the knowledge of his guilt" (498–99). In 1976, however, Tintner pictured Winch simply as "killing time" in his attention to Monteith, although she continued her criticism of Monteith as a "spiritless man," citing his last remark as evidence of his lack of caring (428, 432).

Buitenhuis takes a more positive view both of Monteith's influence and of Winch's suicide. He speculates that Mark gave Winch the courage he had lacked before to kill himself, although he also suggests that Winch is in part paying Mark back for being so ready a victim, by the timing of his death, which Buitenhuis argues Monteith anticipates and yet cooperates with. The suicide itself he sees as a deliberate "act of resignation, even of expiation" (235–37). Similarly, Chapman reads the tale as an account of "spiritual development" from egotism. In her reading, while she acknowledges Monteith as an egotist at the start, a "shirker" who preserved his innocence by noninvolvement, she sees him in the end as recognizing the common humanity of the others he has encountered, even the selfish women, and even sees in the tale itself a "qualifed hope" for the individual to survive. Chapman stresses the parallels established between Winch and Monteith, and while noting Winch's initially superior perceptiveness, finds in the concluding sentence an acceptance of responsibility for a share of Bloodgood's guilt, and a "new potential" to recognize himself in others and to see the links between himself and others.

Such links are less productive in Sicker's reading of James's "nightmare" New York, where human ties are only "visits" that offer no release from isolation. Thus, when Monteith breaks through the barriers to offer Winch sympathy, his achievement only brings grief, as Winch now learns the suffering he has caused others, a bitterness increased by Monteith's forgiveness. Even his suicide does not end the misery, as one of its results is to switch the "burden of guilt" to Winch (172–74).

Equally bleak about New York, but less praising of Monteith, Przybylowicz argues that Monteith could have saved Winch, but "subconsciously exults" in the "cathartic release" of his anger at Bloodgood by transferring it to Winch. Still, in her analysis of the final conversation, she sees Winch acting as "analyst" for Mark while gaining at the same time "self-knowledge," so that the relationship is "therapeutic" for Monteith and "expiatory" for Winch. She emphasizes the links between all three men, the way Monteith merges Winch with Bloodgood in his thinking. Winch, however, she argues, also represents for Monteith his "other" antithetical self, and so his suicide represents Monteith's destruction of that other self in his desire to sustain "an illusory sense of self-unity." The story, while destroying the businessman, Przybylowicz argues, also impugns his "passive artistic 'victim,'" as even Monteith recognizes his responsibility for leaving Winch alone at a critical moment (113, 134–36).

The strong links among the three men, present and absent, have been a recurrent critical theme. Matthiessen early noted the parallel structure of Monteith's conversation with Winch, whereby Winch sees in Monteith a representative of those he has harmed, even as Monteith comes to imagine what Bloodgood must be suffering (1944, 116–17). The web of involvement becomes even tighter in Gage, who sees all three tied together in Winch's exclamation "We *are* wonderful." The betrayal again is the link, with Bloodgood causing Monteith's despair, and Winch perceiving it. Gage, however, sees Monteith's role as redemptive, his forgiveness of Bloodgood sustaining Winch, and his sense of involvement altering his own understanding (239–45).

A story that leaves readers a choice between suicide as despair or redemption has certainly strayed far from the comic vision. The picture of New York in the tale remains starkly pessimistic, as the encounters within it evolve from the near caricature of Monteith's female conversationalists to the unspoken subtleties and ambiguous hints of the final encounter with Winch. The latter, in Purdy's words, is of "a complexity . . . requiring a response to both speech and gesture that is at the outer limits of human capacity" (432). Taking perhaps the lightest approach to such concerns, Geismar objects to much of the praise for the tale, which he calls a "sentimental" view of the new financial world combined with an old concern for investments (364–65). Putt and Wagenknecht both take the tale more seriously, although their different conclusions mark the various poles of interpretation. Putt sees the moral of the tale "that nobody is really interested in anybody else," and that "it is more blessed to be deceived than to deceive" (305). Wagenknecht, however, while acknowledging the "painful impression" of the tale and the presence of pain throughout it, argues that as the last tale published by James, it represents not a grim end to a career, but a notable achievement for an "aging writer" to "conceive of Monteith rising above his own woes as he does at the end" (173, 177). Certainly, however, unless one takes the leap into the spiritual, as Martin and Ober do, the implication of the story appears to be that such transformations as Monteith and Winch undergo, from the selfish to the sensitive, fall on hard ground. A powerful vision, the tale is hardly a comforting one. Like one of Shakespeare's problem plays, it raises more issues than it resolves, comforts some, and leaves others to their doom.

Works Cited

Primary Works

James, Henry. 1910. "A Round of Visits." *The English Review* 5 (April–May): 46–60, 246–60.

———. 1910. "A Round of Visits." *The Finer Grain*. New York: Scribner's; London: Methuen.

———. 1921–23. "A Round of Visits." *The Novels and Stories of Henry James*. Vol. 28. Ed. Percy Lubbock. London: Macmillan.

Secondary Works

Allott, Miriam. 1953. "Symbol and Image in the Later Work of Henry James." *Essays in Criticism* (Oxford) 3 (July): 321–36.

Andreas, Osborn. 1948. *Henry James and the Expanding Horizon: A Study of the Meaning and Basic Themes of James's Fiction*. Seattle: University of Washington Press.

Anon. 1910. Review of *The Finer Grain*. *The Times Literary Supplement* (13 October): 377.

Auchincloss, Louis. 1961. "A Reader's Guide to the Fiction of Henry James." In *Reflections of a Jacobite*, 209–20. Cambridge: Riverside.

Berthoff, Warner. 1965. *The Ferment of Realism: American Literature, 1884–1919*. New York: Free Press.

Bewley, Marius. 1959. *The Eccentric Design: Form in the Classic American Novel*. New York: Columbia University Press.

Bradbury, Nicola. 1979. *Henry James: The Later Novels*. Oxford: Clarendon Press.

Buitenhuis, Peter. 1970. *The Grasping Imagination: The American Writings of Henry James*. Toronto: University Press of Toronto.

Chapman, Sara S. 1973. "The 'Obsession of Egotism' in Henry James's 'A Round of Visits.'" *Arizona Quarterly* 29: 130–38.

Dietrichson, Jan W. 1969. *The Image of Money in the American Novel of the Gilded Age*. Oslo: Universitetsforlaget; New York: Humanities.

Edgar, Pelham. [1927] 1964. *Henry James, Man and Author*. New York: Russell & Russell.

Gage, Richard P. 1988. *Order and Design: Henry James' Titled Story Sequences*. New York: Peter Lang.

Geismar, Maxwell. 1963. *Henry James and the Jacobites*. Boston: Houghton Mifflin.

Greene, Graham. 1952. *The Lost Childhood and Other Essays*. New York: Viking.

Gregory, Robert. 1983. "Henry James and the Art of Execution." *Topic* 37 (Fall): 43–48.

Hackett, Francis. 1919. "Henry James." In *Horizons: A Book of Criticism*, 74–82. New York: Huebsch.

Hocks, Richard A. 1974. *Henry James and Pragmatic Thought: A Study in the Relationship between the Philosophy of William James and the Literary Art of Henry James*. Chapel Hill: University of North Carolina Press.

Jones, Granville H. 1975. *Henry James's Psychology of Experience: Innocence, Responsibility, and Renunciation in the Fiction of Henry James*. The Hague: Mouton.

Krook, Dorothea. [1962] 1967. *The Ordeal of Consciousness in Henry James*. New York: Cambridge University Press.

Lee, Brian. 1978. *The Novels of Henry James: A Study of Culture and Consciousness*. New York: St. Martin's.

McElderry, Bruce R., Jr. 1965. *Henry James*. New York: Twayne.

Martin, W. R. and Warren U. Ober. 1984. "Henry James and 'Bloodgood.'" *American Notes & Queries* 23, nos. 1–2 (September–October): 14–15.

———. 1981. "Dantesque Patterns in Henry James's 'A Round of Visits.'" *Ariel: A Review of International English Literature* 12: 45–54.

Matthiessen, F. O., ed. 1947. *The American Novels and Stories of Henry James*. New York: Knopf.

———. 1944. *Henry James: The Major Phase*. New York: Oxford University Press.

Mays, Milton A. 1968. "Henry James, or, the Beast in the Palace of Art." *American Literature* 39 (January): 467–87.

Menikoff, Barry. 1971. "The Subjective Pronoun in the Late Style of Henry James." *English Studies* 52: 436–41.

Przybylowicz, Donna. 1986. *Desire and Repression: The Dialectic of Self and Other in the Late Works of Henry James*. University: University of Alabama Press.

Purdy, Strother B. 1969. "Conversation and Awareness in Henry James's 'A Round of Visits.'" *Studies in Short Fiction* 6: 421–32.

Putt, S. Gorley. 1966. *Henry James: A Reader's Guide*. Ithaca, NY: Cornell University Press.

Segal, Ora. 1969. *The Lucid Reflector: The Observer in Henry James' Fiction*. New Haven: Yale University Press.

Sicker, Philip. 1980. *Love and the Quest for Identity in the Fiction of Henry James*. Princeton: Princeton University Press.

Tintner, Adeline R. 1989. "The Jamesian Tradition in *The Book Class*: Louis Auchincloss's *A Small Boy and Others*." In *The Magic Circle of Henry James: Essays in Honour of Darshan Singh Maini*. Ed. Amritjit Singh and K. Ayyappa Paniker, 326–41. New York: Envoy.

———. 1986. *The Museum World of Henry James*. Ann Arbor: UMI Research Press. Revised in part from "Henry James's Salomé and the Arts of the *Fin de Siècle*." *The Markham Review* 5 (Fall 1975): 5–10.

———. 1976. "Landmarks of 'The Terrible Town': The New York Scene in Henry James' Last Stories." *Prospects* 2: 399–435.

———. 1975. "The Metamorphoses of Edith Wharton in Henry James's *The Finer Grain*." *Twentieth-Century Literature* 21: 355–79.

———. 1971–72. "James's Mock Epic: 'The Velvet Glove,' Edith Wharton, and Other Late Tales." *Modern Fiction Studies* 17 (Winter): 483–99.

Vaid, Krishna B. 1964. *Technique in the Tales of Henry James*. Cambridge, MA: Harvard University Press.

Wagenknecht, Edward. 1984. *The Tales of Henry James*. New York: Frederick Ungar.

Ward, Joseph A. 1988. "The Amazing Hotel-World of James, Dreiser, and Wharton." In *Leon Edel and Literary Art*. Ed. Lyall H. Powers, 151–60. Ann Arbor: UMI Research Press.

———. 1961. *The Imagination of Disaster: Evil in the Fiction of Henry James*. Lincoln: University of Nebraska Press.

Wegelin, Christof. 1958. *The Image of Europe in Henry James*. Dallas: Southern Methodist University Press.

Wright, Walter F. 1962. *The Madness of Art: A Study of Henry James*. Lincoln: University of Nebraska Press.

Sir Dominick Ferrand

Publication History

Under the title of "Jersey Villas," this tale was one of two stories James published in the *Cosmopolitan Magazine*, where it appeared in July and August of 1892 with illustrations by Irving R. Willis. James included it in the 1893 collection *The Real Thing* under the new title "Sir Dominick Ferrand." It next appeared, after his death, in Lubbock's edition of *The Novels and Stories of Henry James*.

Circumstances of Composition, Sources, and Influences

This rather light tale began quite augustly in a notebook entry on March 26, 1892, with "The idea of the *responsibility* of destruction—the destruction of papers, letters, records, etc., connected with the private and personal history of some great and honoured name and throwing some very different light on it from the light projected by the public career." James quickly added "a young man poor enough to be tempted" and then "a girl—a woman—poor like himself," so that by the end he declared, "I see the rest of this so clearly now that I will go straight on with it" (CN 66). Given the short period of time prior to its publication, he evidently did just that.

Edel points also to the previous notebook entry recording the idea of a servant accused of "reading of letters, diaries, peeping, spying, etc." (1970, 250). It is an unjust accusation of "the base things people in London take for granted servants do" (CN 65). Edel notes that the entry appeared shortly after his sister, Alice's, death that March, and that James was concerned over the fate of her diary, that it might indeed be read by the wrong people. Edel records also that James later burnt many of his own letters, and spoke of his friend Mrs. Proctor's burning of her no doubt interesting but personal papers as "strange and sad—or blessed and beneficent" (1970, 250–51). James, who early in his career had reviewed several volumes of letters by writers, was not always averse to their publication. In February 1895, asked about publication of Stevenson's letters by Sidney Colvin, he replied "Publish them—they make the man so loveable" (McElderry 104).

The use of the supernatural may also have a link with Alice James, according to Edel, who notes that she used hypnosis for her constant pain toward the end of her illness (1970, 250). Elsewhere Edel indicates that the secret letters might have a suggestion of the Parnell Case (*Selected Letters* xxv), which would be appropriate, as Alice was keenly interested in the movement for Irish Home Rule. As another connection with the story's supernaturalism, Edel cites a notebook entry on October 23, 1891, referring to hypnosis, an echo of James's recording in 1889 of George Du Maurier's germ for *Trilby* (1970, 250). Whatever their source, the woman's psychic powers are an addition to the notebook prospectus, one that Jacobson sees as catering to popular interest in such semi-supernatural processes (88).

It was also in the spring of 1892 that Constance Fenimore Woolson had evidently been discussing with James the possibility of collaborating on a play, a discussion that Aswell indicates may have affected his treatment of artistic collaboration (180–81; *Life* 3, 318–19). The turn of his protagonist from unsalable short stories to songwriting may also reflect James's turn from the small profits of the novel to the theatre. Perhaps another contribution to theme was the sudden success James's friend Francis Boott, an amateur composer, had experienced the year before following the mention in one of Woolson's stories of his musical setting of a poem by John Hay (*Life* 3, 294–95).

An 1872 ghost story, "Sir Dominick's Bargain" by Sheridan LeFanu, may be an additional source. In it the hero agrees to serve Satan after a term in which Satan first serves him. Such a Faustian bargain is the kind offered to Baron by his editor, who promises to publish Baron if he may publish the letters in Baron's possession, and one may speculate that had he given in to his temptation, Baron would have been dealt the same death—morally speaking—as LeFanu's hero received in fact.

Bell notes that Edith Wharton shared James's interest in the "peculiar conflict of claims which is involved in the guardianship of the past, of reputations," and published a story *The Touchstone*, where the protagonist gives in to the temptation to publish and so suffers. She notes, too, that in Wharton the man knows the author of the letters, so that his temptation is "cruder" and James's "more tenuous and abstract" (228–29).

Edel ties the desk with that in Maupassant's ghostly "*La Chevelure*" (1970, 251).

Relation to Other Works

"Sir Dominick Ferrand" was the first of two James stories to approach the rights of the literary dead through the suggestion of the supernatural, the other being the 1899 "The Real Right Thing" (McCarthy 107; Banta 181 n.23). Lind takes Blackmur's characterization of the theme of "The Private Life"— the "inviolable privacy" of genius—which he finds inappropriate there, and applies it instead to both these tales and two other works treating dead geniuses—an 1872 review of Hawthorne's *French and Italian Notebooks* and *The Aspern Papers* (321). Edel remarks that in the latter, Tina Bordereau, like Baron, also meticulously burns the letters in her possession (CT 8, 12; also Wagenknecht 201). Dietrichson notes the applicability of Juliana Bordereau's insult—"you publishing scoundrel!"—to Mr. Locket (145–46). Certainly the title of Locket's magazine, *The Promiscuous Review*, makes James's view clear. Edel adds *The Reverberator*, "The Abasement of the Northmores," and "John Delavoy" to complete the list of James's attack on the publicizing of the private (1970, 250; *Life* 5, 141; also Jones 236). Walter Wright cites a whole host of dislikable journalists, from Mr. Pardon of *The Bostonians* on through the unperceptive critics of the artist tales (77–78). Todorov compares Sir Dominick and Captain Everard of *In the Cage* as central characters with some hidden secret who are never presented directly, but contrasts the final clearing-up of Sir Dominick's character with the lingering ignorance about Captain Everard (148–49, 154).

Tintner sees the work connected to *The Spoils of Poynton* on the basis of its hero and his meticulously described davenport, James having passed on his love for the proper desk to his young writer Baron (166–69).

Briggs links it with "Nona Vincent," "The Real Right Thing," and "Owen Wingrave" as stories James begin with an abstract "idea" and then vitalized through the use of the supernatural (15). (See also "Nona Vincent.")

Interpretation and Criticism

As Caesar with Gaul, the critics have generally divided the tale into three parts—and have gone on to find the combination faulty. There is the supernatural element, the literary theme, and the love story. Ward calls the tale an "extreme" example of James's occasional "inability to construct an organic plot," which James himself diagnosed in *The American*. Dividing the literary subject further, Ward discerns no connection between the "idea" of the papers that gave rise to the tale and the story of Baron's fortunes (52–53; also Tintner 168; Putt 284). Horne reads the literary themes as added on to the supernatural love story (121–22). Todorov gives a name to one of the tale's juxtapositions, calling the seemingly coincidental revelation of a close relationship between apparently distant characters—Mrs. Ryves and Sir Dominick—melodramatic (147). Aswell, for his part, offers some links, noting a relationship between Baron's weakness as a writer—keeping a character together—and his temptation—to take one apart and so endanger his own (185).

The heroine says of the letters, "They haunt me," and so, as Edel says, they become the ghost of the tale (1970, 251). Andreas remarks on the "parallelism" in the behavior of Mrs. Ryves and Baron, which signals to the reader the presence of the occult (70–71). Markow-Totevy offers as a possible explanation for the intuitive understanding of the characters James's belief in an overarching scheme of justice beyond the reach of individuals that presumably rewards Baron for his better feelings (117–18). Banta provides another explanation, seeing the "second sight" given to protect against the "spiritual snatching" that is the story's theme, the breaking in on the privacy of another's soul, particularly blamable here as the dead have no defense against it (180 n.23). Norrman notes that the occult here serves a purpose, providing some reason not to look at the letters, unlike the usual obscurity about reading letters in James (130).

In one sense, Baron's dilemma over the letters clearly places money and success against ethical behavior (e.g., Dietrichson 145–46). Critics, however, have questioned the legitimacy of his decision not to allow them to be published. Putt calls the "suppression of truth" "mawkish" (284). Wagenknecht points out that burning the letters not only keeps private Ferrand's private life, to which the public has no right, but also information about his public doings, to which they are "entitled" (201–2). Wright, however, points to the significant factor against publishing the letters as their incompleteness—they leave out his kindnesses. Even before that, however, as Wright points out, a Jamesian sympathy for the dead makes Baron feel that exposing Ferrand is "for himself not an imperative task" (98–99). Jones goes so far as to include Baron's moral duty to the public among his "temptations" (161–62). It seems likely that James would have sympathized most with Wright's and Jones's attitude.

Todorov finds most significant in the tale the absence of the one central character, Sir Dominick, and notes that when his mystery is explained, the narrative it motivated necessarily stops (146–47). What remains after that point is the happy ending, an ending many critics would gladly do away with. Aswell finds it unconvincing, maintaining that the value accorded the pair's initial earnings shows more the "fairy-tale atmosphere" of their successful collaboration than the true interests of James at a time of stressful isolation (185–86). Labrie provides a particularly harsh reading. While applauding his burning the letters, he sees Baron yielding to popular standards in his songwriting, the "tawdriness" of which is "only partially mitigated by his love" (167–68).

The story is not, however, unmitigatedly sentimental. Putt, who has little else to say in defense of the tale, finds merit in the observation on the impoverished Mrs. Ryves's ability to hire a sitter for her child: "There is nobody so bereft of joy as not to be able to command for twopence the services of somebody less joyous" (284). Mrs. Ryves, then, is not a porcelain heroine. She has, Allen states, both "intelligence and sympathy" (123). As Rimmon observes, the revelation of Mrs. Ryves's identity, while a surprise, in no way upsets one's initial understanding of her character (82). While Aswell contends that their occupation as songwriters diminishes the pair, it may be that James is simply seeking to establish an idea of moderate success (186). At the end of the tale, too, as Wagenknecht emphasizes, Baron is still writing stories while supporting himself through the songs (201). As James puts it, Baron still "tries his hand at prose" and is even occasionally published, though not at the *Promiscuous* (CT 8, 405). There is a legitimate relief for both Baron and Mrs. Ryves in reaching outside themselves both in their songs and their love. The tale seems to be one of those occasions, such as the very early "Travelling Companions" and perhaps the late *The Golden Bowl*, where James is trying to present a workable resolution of the complex duties of life, art, and love. The tale is, as Wagenknecht acknowledges, overly contrived, but it is also, as he puts it, "absorbing and extremely clever," or perhaps even better, in the phrasing of William James's sister-in-law Mary Gibbens—*"fine!"* (Wagenknecht 201; W. James 232).

Works Cited

Primary Works
James, Henry. 1892. "Jersey Villas." *Cosmopolitan Magazine* 13 (July–August): 314–28, 433–49.

———. 1893. "Sir Dominick Ferrand." *The Real Thing*. New York and London: Macmillan.

———. 1921–23. "Sir Dominick Ferrand." *The Novels and Stories of Henry James*. Vol. 26. Ed. Percy Lubbock. London: Macmillan.

Secondary Works
Allen, Elizabeth. 1984. *A Woman's Place in the Novels of Henry James*. New York: St. Martin's.

Andreas, Osborn. 1948. *Henry James and the Expanding Horizon: A Study of the Meaning and Basic Themes of James's Fiction*. Seattle: University of Washington Press.

Aswell, E. Duncan. 1966. "James's Treatment of Artistic Collaboration." *Criticism* 8:180–95.

Banta, Martha. 1964. "Henry James and 'The Others.'" *New England Quarterly* 37 (June): 171–84.

Bell, Millicent. 1965. *Edith Wharton and Henry James: The Story of Their Friendship*. New York: George Braziller.

Briggs, Julia. 1977. *Night Visitors: The Rise and Fall of the English Ghost Story*. London: Faber.

Dietrichson, Jan W. 1969. *The Image of Money in the American Novel of the Gilded Age*. Oslo: Universitetsforlaget; New York: Humanities.

Edel, Leon, ed. 1974. *Henry James: Selected Letters*. Cambridge, MA: Belknap Press of Harvard University Press.

————, ed. 1970. *Henry James: Stories of the Supernatural*. New York: Taplinger.

Horne, Helen. 1960. *Basic Ideals of James's Aesthetics as Expressed in the Short Stories Concerning Artists and Writers*. Marburg: Erich Mauersberger.

Jacobson, Marcia. 1983. *Henry James and the Mass Market*. University: University of Alabama Press.

James, William. 1992. *The Correspondence of William James*. Vol. 2: *William and Henry: 1885–1896*. Ed. Ignas K. Skrupskelis and Elizabeth M. Berkeley. Charlottesville: University Press of Virginia.

Jones, Granville H. 1975. *Henry James's Psychology of Experience: Innocence, Responsibility, and Renunciation in the Fiction of Henry James*. The Hague: Mouton.

Labrie, Ernest Ross. 1969. "Sirens of Life and Art in Henry James." *Lakehead University Review* (Port Arthur, Ont.) 2: 150–69.

Lind, Sidney E. 1951. "James's 'The Private Life' and Browning." *American Literature* 23 (November): 315–22.

McCarthy, Harold T. 1958. *Henry James: The Creative Process*. New York: Thomas Yoseloff.

McElderry, Bruce R., Jr. 1965. *Henry James*. New York: Twayne.

Markow-Totevy, Georges. 1969. *Henry James*. Trans. John Griffiths. London: Merlin.

Norrman, Ralf. 1982. *The Insecure World of Henry James's Fiction: Intensity and Ambiguity*. New York: St. Martin's.

Putt, S. Gorley. 1966. *Henry James: A Reader's Guide*. Ithaca, NY: Cornell University Press.

Rimmon, Shlomith. 1977. *The Concept of Ambiguity: The Example of Henry James*. Chicago: University of Chicago Press.

Tintner, Adeline R. 1986. *The Museum World of Henry James*. Ann Arbor: UMI Research Press.

Todorov, Tzvetan. 1977. *The Poetics of Prose*. Trans. Richard Howard. Ithaca, NY: Cornell University Press.

Wagenknecht, Edward. 1984. *The Tales of Henry James*. New York: Frederick Ungar.

Ward, Joseph A. 1967. *The Search for Form: Studies in the Structure of James's Fiction*. Chapel Hill: University of North Carolina Press.

Wright, Walter F. 1962. *The Madness of Art: A Study of Henry James*. Lincoln: University of Nebraska Press.

Sir Edmund Orme

Publication History

Illustrated by John H. Bacon, "Sir Edmund Orme" appeared first in 1891 in the Christmas issue of the new magazine *Black and White*, following the British tradition of ghost tales for the holiday. The next year James included it in the collection *The Lesson of the Master* and in 1909, "heavily revised," according to Edel, in the New York Edition (1970, 141–42).

Circumstances of Composition, Sources, and Influences

James recorded the idea for the tale on January 22, 1879. It began with a focus on the young girl, not the mother, and with the fear that the girl may become aware of the ghost that follows her. The relationship of the ghost to the mother is revealed only after her death through the discovery of a miniature. The notebook proposes a happy ending: the girl falls in love, and so as the "theory" predicted, sees the ghost, which never appears again after she accepts her suitor (CN 10). In his preface, James recalls choosing "the old, the mid-Victorian, the Thackerayan Brighton" as his setting in order to emphasize the sense of "the strange and sinister embroidered on the very type of the normal and easy" (*Criticism* 2, 1264).

In October 1890, Henry James read a letter by his brother William before the British Society of Psychical Research, an event Beidler argues may have stimulated his interest in the supernatural (159). McCarthy also remarks on the connection between the interests of the two brothers at the time, but finds James in his ghost tales avoiding the "scientific" explanation popular at the time, and sees Henry, like William, coming to an interest in the supernatural from an interest in psychology (106). Jacobson explains James's writing ghost tales as an attempt to profit from the newly fashionable genre, due in part to the recent founding of the Society for Psychical Research, but also in part to an increased demand for short stories in general. She notes, too, that the ghost here is a "charming" one, like the popular ghosts of John Kendrick Bangs (87–88, 90). Edel offers the most practical explanation, attributing James's turn to the ghost story in the context of his attempt at dramatic success, when he gave up the writing of novels for a time as he concentrated on the stage (1970, 141).

Tinter finds James drawing here on Kipling's "The Phantom Rickshaw" (1888), in which a young man is haunted by a married woman he has jilted (239–45). Haggerty discerns a parallel with Hawthorne's "Rappaccini's Daughter," Charlotte being here like Beatrice the innocent subject of "experiment and speculation" (149–50).

Relation to Other Works.

The idea for "Sir Edmund Orme" was to sit undisturbed in James's notebook for twelve years, leaving a significant gap between his previous ghost story, "The Ghostly Rental," in 1876 and this, sufficiently long for the man whose chief claim to popular fame is now another Christmas ghost story—*The Turn of the Screw*—to surprise his readers. The reviewer for the *Bookman* found the "graceful habitué of *salons*" most out of place, writing "Perhaps Mr. James once made a vow to write a ghost story. He has got the vow off his mind now. . . . Let us hope Mr. James feels no obligation to make further attempts in this direction" (27). Jacobson finds them generally inferior tales, different from the early ghost stories in being "less brooding . . . less moral," less under the influence of Hawthorne and more under the influence of current popular ideas about the supernatural (87–88). Edel, less pejoratively, also observes a change in the type of ghost tale, the ghost here being James's "first characteristic daylight ghost" (1970, 141; CT 8, 11).

According to Jones's analysis, there is less of a break: James picks up where he left off in "The Ghostly Rental" with a supernatural treatment cloaking a theme of guilt (105). Edel also focuses on the theme of guilt, speaking of it as a ghostly reworking of "Louisa Pallant" with a mother who seeks to appease her guilt, this time by protecting rather than sacrificing her daughter, its focus still on family relationships not the supernatural (1970, 142; CT 8, 12).

Blackmur includes it in his list of ghost tales that prepare through their obsessive hallucinations for the complexity of *The Sacred Fount* (48). Also looking ahead, Haggerty speaks of the tale as the "reverse" of "Owen Wingrave" because it adopts the perspective of those who torment the young with their own "haunted personalities" rather than that of the young victim (149). The most common comparison, however, is with *The Turn of the Screw* (e.g., Lind 234–35). Todorov notes that, like the governess, the mother is less afraid of the ghost than of its appearing to someone under her care (159). Similarly, Briggs points to how the narrator and Mrs. Marden both seek to prevent Charlotte from seeing the ghost, just as the governess seeks to prevent Miles and Flora from sharing her apparitions (157). Taylor concentrates on the conclusions, finding them similar, but that of "Sir Edmund Orme" too simple, the tale as a whole less interesting in its lack of ambiguity

(176, 223). Beidler also parallels the conclusions, seeing Orme's cry at the end indicating the exorcism of his spirit and Miles's his dispossession, arguing that both events are ambiguously portrayed (206–7).

Briggs locates the issue of the selectivity of such supernatural vision not only in *The Turn of the Screw* and "Sir Edmund Orme," but also in *The Portrait of a Lady* (157). Isabel Archer, as Banta first formulated the comparison, must undergo an emotional education to receive the privilege of seeing the dead, even as, she argues, the narrator here must (1972, 111, 248 n.7). The narrator's comment of the "things I shouldn't escape knowing" (CT 8, 126) recalls Isabel Archer's sense that she cannot "escape" unhappiness.

Looking back at even earlier James, Rosenzweig considers the tale a healthier treatment of the complex relationships, particularly the relationship with the mother, of "The Story of a Year," arguing that James now free of the burdens of America felt capable of allowing his hero to triumph (100–1). Jones contrasts Charlotte's recapturing of innocence with the more efficacious renewal of Adela Moore in the early tale "A Day of Days," finding it more like that of Newton Winch in "A Round of Visits" in its being shortly ended by death (156).

Interpretation and Criticism

Despite being, as Tintner puts it, James's first tale with a "palpable . . . visible" ghost (240), the ghost has been subjected to the doubt typically accorded the Jamesian ghostly. Early on, Elton referred to the tale's "actual ghost" in contrast to the phenomena of "The Private Life" (365). Putt, too, calls the haunting here "conventional" (390). But Todorov finds the story's too obvious "moral lesson" weakening the "fantastic" nature of the tale. He further argues that readers feel no obligation to believe the sighting of ghosts by such first-person narrators and notes the "hesitation" of the narrator himself, omitting the others who see him (156, 181–82). Similarly, Voss finds the story putting a "considerable strain on the reader's credulity" (145). In rebuttal, Walter Wright states that as the narrator is neither "neurotic" nor guilty, there is no need for him to lie or fantasize (123). Indeed, Taylor goes so far as to argue that the narrator's clear vision robs the story of any real interest (176). No one has made much of the fact that the frame narrator calls into question the authenticity of the document he presents, although Wagenknecht records the fact (66).

Both those who doubt and those who do not, however, concentrate on the psychological significance of the apparition. Characterizing the ghost as a typically Jamesian "convenient symbol" for a psychological state, Q. D. Leavis sees the ghost here representing Mrs. Marden's sense of guilt (224; also McElderry 115; Jones 105). Like Woolf, who saw the ghost of Orme not only as the mother's guilty conscience but also as "the guardian of the rights of lovers," Banta and Markow-Totevy broaden his symbolism by pointing out that he appears to the different characters with different motives—to the mother his appearance is a punishment, to the daughter it is a threat, to the suitor a friendly recognition of the value of his love (Woolf 291; Markow-Totevy 113; Banta 1972, 111–14; also Beidler 159). Tintner adds another dimension, noting the significance of the daughter's sense of her mother's guilt (243). In his many aspects, the ghost is, as Edel notes, a combination of the two magics ([1949] 1963, 108).

Surprisingly few modern critics have found Orme's haunting inadequately motivated, repeating the charge that Mrs. Marden was a coquette and ruined Orme's happiness. Andreas, for example, writes that the "blow to her conscience" Mrs. Marden sustained from her jilting of Sir Edmund causes her to live in terror that her daughter might also become a jilter (60). James, whose works take jilting quite seriously, refers in the preface to "some hardness or baseness in the mother's youth," and he increases at the same time Mrs. Marden's consciousness of the wrong she has does Orme by revising her simple statement "But he did love me" to add "and I knew—that is almost knew!—how much" (*Criticism* 2, 1263; CT 8, 143). But her own telling of events suggests that far from being hard or generally flirtatious, she fell in love with one man, Charlotte's father, which decided her to break her engagement to Orme, an engagement arranged not by her but her family in seeking an advantageous match. She is hardly to blame for Orme's decision to kill himself, and even waits a decent interval, five years, to marry Marden after his death. Unlike the mother in "Louisa Pallant," who jilted her lover for a more prosperous marriage, the mother here rejects money for love. Both stories show the proclivity Putt comments on in James toward symmetrical plots, multiple generations with a shared plight (391). But the working out of events seems perhaps to follow more that of "The Diary of a Man of Fifty" where a similar examination of the daughter proves not only her innocence, but the prior innocence of her mother. Thus the contemporary critic who complained of Orme as "a malicious bore who ruins an old lady's piece of mind for no adequate reason whatsoever" had a valid point (*Bookman*).

Perhaps Orme is simply seeking to see that Charlotte gets engaged to the right man the first time around. He does not appear until her debut, following Captain Marden's death. At any rate, Edgar is writing for the majority when he calls Orme "an exceptionally refined ghost" (191). Similarly, Blackmur calls him "an object and guiding principle of human sympathy," while Akiyama goes so far as to call him "lovable" (Blackmur 52; Akiyama 49, 51). His entrance into the story is certainly genteel enough, as he walks into the narrator's pew at church. Indeed, later critics have found him almost too "respectable," Virginia Woolf being the first to admit that she was not frightened (324, also Briggs 150).

Orme is also, as Edel calls him, a "policing" agent, and while Edel reads him as primarily a good cop, others have questioned both his and the narrator's assumption of superiority to Charlotte, their management of her life (1970, 141). Banta speaks without judgment of the way "the living and the dead fight silently for possession" of Charlotte (1964, 180 n.23). Haggerty, however, takes exception to the behavior of the narrator, and such interpretations of it as Todorov's, which emphasize his search for understanding, as "particularly inhumane." In his reading, the ghost—seen or unseen—is not "a measure of narrative confusion but . . . a measure of Charlotte's victimization" (149–50, 178 n.7). More typically, Tintner points to the web of protection about her, in which the ghost shields the narrator, and the narrator shields Charlotte (243). Wright, too, links the ghost and the narrator in their kindly suspension of judgment of Charlotte, adding that the story can be read as a study of the narrator's sympathetic observation (123). Why precisely such "a beautiful, liberal creature," as the narrator calls Charlotte, should need so much suspended judgment is never evident, and gives some credence to Haggerty's analysis (CT 8, 124).

The mother's relationship to the daughter has also been subjected to scrutiny. Early on, Edgar had noted "a community of nervous interest" between the mother and the narrator (191). Przybylowicz suggests additional, odder alliances in the tale, between ghost and lover, love and death, the ghost here serving to make the narrator feel "connected" (157–58). Contending that the narrator is more interested in the mother than the daughter, and the mother too interested in the daughter's marrying, Jacobson finds the original situation "provocative," and argues that the introduction of the ghost disrupts its treatment (90). In his preface, however, James recalls the mother-daughter configuration as stemming from his idea of doing something different, more refined, with the ghost story by dealing with the idea of "*unconscious* obsession," someone being haunted without being aware of it. The aware mother then watches in fear that the object of the haunting will lose her "blest ignorance" producing the suspense in the tale (*Criticism* 2, 1263). The situation obviously calls for a third person to witness it.

The witness is, however, also a participant. Matthiessen and Murdock trace how the "theme of unconscious obsession by a deadly presence" leads to its "release through love" (N 10). The latter particularly impresses Putt, who comments on the atypical encouragement of marriage in James (391). One might qualify Putt's enthusiasm by recalling, as Wagenknecht does, that the marriage lasts only one year before the wife dies in childbirth (66). Banta attributes Charlotte's death to James's recognition of natural threats in a story of the supernatural, although she also objects to the neatness, the freedom from future challenge, it produces (1972, 114, 152). Jones, on the other hand, goes so far as to take it as the completion of Sir Edmund's revenge (105).

Certainly the satisfaction of the reader in the concluding words telling the reader of "the last of Sir Edmund Orme" is partly undercut by their remembering from the prefatory frame that the last of Charlotte will soon follow.

The one remaining ghostly debate is over whether Charlotte finally sees the ghost, and if so what that sight means. In the notebook, her seeing the ghost is a sign of the genuineness of her love (CN 10). Wright questions whether Charlotte does, in fact, see the ghost, asserting that if she does, the ghost has found her guilty of "coquetry" even as he has so scared her she will never be guilty of it again, a reading Wagenknecht considers reasonable but "beyond the range of the story" (Wright 123, 157; Wagenknecht 66). Banta also judges Charlotte's sight of the ghost as ambiguously rendered, but still a sign of the superiority of experience, even of the terrifying, over innocence to James, an importance the narrator ironically acts against in his attempt to shield her (1972, 113, 248 n.9, n.10). The narrator does, however, clearly state that as Charlotte moves to give him her hand, "with the definite act she saw" (CT 8, 150). Both Blackmur and Jones read the scene accordingly, seeing Charlotte now in a position to jilt the narrator, but also learning to renounce such a power and so exorcising the ghost of Orme (Blackmur 52; Jones 105).

When James's brother William read "Sir Edmund Orme" in *The Lesson of the Master*, he immediately classed it with the title story as one of James's "most *perfect* things . . . which I enjoyed *extremely*" (241). Similarly, Edel once called it one of James's finest ghost stories ([1949] 1963, 107). He later dropped the superlative, however, and critics in general have not placed the tale in the first rank of James's work (1970, 141–42). Indeed, it has received some harsh estimates, Leavis, for example, calling it a "feeble, uncharacteristic effort" (223). Despite such slurs it is, with its ghosts and its tightly knit characters and their complicated and conscious relationships, quite characteristic, and quite capable of inspiring interested reading, if not demanding intense criticism.

Works Cited

Primary Works
James, Henry. 1891. "Sir Edmund Orme." *Black and White* (25 November): 8, 11–15.

——. 1892. "Sir Edumund Orme." *The Lesson of the Master*. New York and London: Macmillan, 266–302.

——. 1909. "Sir Edmund Orme." *The Novels and Tales of Henry James*. New York Edition. Vol. 17, 365–408. New York: Scribner's.

Secondary Works
Akiyama, Masayuki. 1985. "James and Nanboku: A Comparative Study of Supernatural Stories in the West and East." *Comparative Literature Studies* 22: 43–52.

Andreas, Osborn. 1948. *Henry James and the Expanding Horizon: A Study of the Meaning and Basic Themes of James's Fiction*. Seattle: University of Washington Press.

Anon. 1892. Review of *The Lesson of the Master*. *Bookman* 2 (April): 27.

Banta, Martha. 1972. *Henry James and the Occult: The Great Extension*. Bloomington: Indiana University Press.

———. 1964. "Henry James and 'The Others.'" *New England Quarterly* 37 (June): 171–84.

Beidler, Peter G. 1989. *Ghosts, Demons, and Henry James: The Turn of the Screw at the Turn of the Century*. Columbia: University of Missouri Press.

Blackmur, R. P. [1942] 1983. "*The Sacred Fount*." In *Studies in Henry James*. Ed. Veronica A. Makowsky, 45–68. New York: New Directions. Reprinted from *Kenyon Review* 5: 328–52.

Briggs, Julia. 1977. *Night Visitors: The Rise and Fall of the English Ghost Story*. London: Faber.

Edel, Leon, ed. 1970. *Henry James: Stories of the Supernatural*. New York: Taplinger.

———, ed. [1949] 1963. *The Ghostly Tales of Henry James*. New York: The Universal Library, Grosset & Dunlap.

Edgar, Pelham. [1927] 1964. *Henry James, Man and Author*. New York: Russell & Russell.

Elton, Oliver. 1903. "The Novels of Mr. Henry James." *Quarterly Review* 198 (October): 358–79.

Haggerty, George E. 1989. *Gothic Fiction/Gothic Form*. University Park: Pennsylvania State University Press.

Jacobson, Marcia. 1983. *Henry James and the Mass Market*. University: University of Alabama Press.

James, William. 1992. *The Correspondence of William James*. Vol. 2: *William and Henry: 1885–1896*. Ed. Ignas K. Skrupskelis and Elizabeth M. Berkeley. Charlottesville: University Press of Virginia.

Jones, Granville H. 1975. *Henry James's Psychology of Experience: Innocence, Responsibility, and Renunciation in the Fiction of Henry James*. The Hague: Mouton.

Leavis, Q. D. 1947. "Henry James: The Stories." *Scrutiny* 14 (Spring): 223–29. Reprinted in *Collected Essays*. Vol. 2: *The American Novel and Reflections of the European Novel*, ed. G. Singh, 177–84. Cambridge: Cambridge University Press.

Lind, Sidney E. 1970. "'The Turn of the Screw': The Torment of Critics." *The Centennial Review* 14: 225–40.

McCarthy, Harold T. 1958. *Henry James: The Creative Process*. New York: Thomas Yoseloff.

McElderry, Bruce R., Jr. 1965. *Henry James*. New York: Twayne.

Markow-Totevy, Georges. 1969. *Henry James*. Trans. John Griffiths. London: Merlin.

Przybylowicz, Donna. 1986. *Desire and Repression: The Dialectic of Self and Other in the Late Works of Henry James*. University: University of Alabama Press.

Putt, S. Gorley. 1966. *Henry James: A Reader's Guide*. Ithaca, NY: Cornell University Press.

Rosenzweig, Saul. [1943] 1957. "The Ghost of Henry James: A Study in Thematic Apperception." In *Art and Psychoanalysis*. Ed. William Phillips, 89–111. New York: Criterion. Reprinted from *Character and Personality* 12 (December 1943): 79–100; also reprinted in *Partisan Review* 11 (Fall 1944): 435–55.

Taylor, Anne Robinson. 1981. *Male Novelists and their Female Voices: Literary Masquerades*. Troy, NY: Whitston.

Tintner, Adeline R. 1989. *The Pop World of Henry James: From Fairy Tales to Science Fiction*. Ann Arbor: UMI Research Press.

Todorov, Tzvetan. 1977. *The Poetics of Prose*. Trans. Richard Howard. Ithaca, NY: Cornell University Press.

Voss, Arthur. 1973. *The American Short Story: A Critical Survey*. Norman: University of Oklahoma Press.

Wagenknecht, Edward. 1984. *The Tales of Henry James*. New York: Frederick Ungar.

Woolf, Virginia. [1921] 1988. "Henry James's Ghost Stories." In *The Essays of Virginia Woolf*. Vol. 3: *1919–1924*. Ed. Andrew McNeille, 319–26. London: Hogarth.

Wright, Walter F. 1962. *The Madness of Art: A Study of Henry James*. Lincoln: University of Nebraska Press.

Foreign Language
Kambara, Tatsuo. 1972. "James's Gothic: Gothic in American Novels (5)." *Bungakubu Kiyo* (Tokyo University of Education) 88 (March): 49–65. [Japanese]

The Solution

Publication History

The month before the appearance of this tale, James wrote Edmund Gosse, who was filling in for the regular editor at the *New Review*, T. N. Archibald Grove, in his "wild & verbose" grief at Gosse's decision to allow the "most ineffective" first chapter to be published as a single instalment after much prior negotation with Grove had seemingly forestalled that disaster. Calling himself "a deeply injured man," James may also have been lingeringly irritated at Grove's failure to include the tale in the first issue of his new review as promised (*Selected Letters* 66–68). Grove, in turn, may have been irritated at James's inability to produce a story of the requested length, which Matthiessen and Murdock point out he ran over by some 4,000 words (N 93). Perhaps as a result, "The Solution" was the only story James published in *The New Review*, where it appeared in three issues from December 1889 to February 1890. James included it in the 1892 collection *The Lesson of the Master*. Its next appearance was in Lubbock's edition of James's fiction in the 1920s.

In the winter of 1890 James revised the story into a play, eventually entitled *Disengaged*, and intended for Ada Rehan in the leading role. Augustin Daly optioned the work, which Edel has characterized as "a series of unmotivated entries and exits," but never produced it (*Life* 291; see also Edel 1949, 295–99 and Kossman 54–58). William James wrote of it, "I should think it might be effective enough with Mrs. Jasper embodied in Rehan flesh and dimples; but for reading, the *matter* is so slight, that my only wonder is that you could have carried it through with such nerve, being on the whole in a line so unlike the spontaneous bent of your genius" (Matthiessen 335). Much of the matter was the same as the tale. Such as it was, James included it in his first series of *Theatricals*.

Circumstances of Composition, Sources, and Influences

James's original note on the idea for "The Solution" is lost, but he returned to it on February 28, 1889, as being better than the idea for "Greville Fane," which he had written out the day before, to fulfill his obligation to the *New Review* (N 93). The situation came from Fanny Kemble, who told James of a young diplomat in Rome whose colleagues had tricked him into marrying a girl he did not like by making him think he had compromised her. His initial idea was to treat their "after life" together, but after fixing on the setting, the form of narration, and even the characterization, James still asked himself, "But what is the drama—the denouement—*voyons?*" He saw a glimmer of light with the introduction of a second woman, although even then he found the idea of a widow "rather conventional" (CN 50).

Edel finds appropriate James's memory of his friendship with Sarah Wister during his "golden morning of life" in the early 1870s, in Rome, molding his characterization of Mrs. Rushbrook (*Life* 121–22; also CT 7, 10), as her mother was the source for the tale. Maves also associates the tale with James's earlier experience of Rome, finding the depiction here similar to that in his biography of William Wetmore Story (120). Perhaps it was his memories of Rome that led him to give to his hero, Wilmerding, his own name. James may also have taken some hints for the character from a friend in London in the later 1870s, Nadal, a second secretary of legation whom James described as an "amiable" failure in London society and a "wonderful specimen of American innocence" (*Life* 2, 320–24).

Gale remarks on the Roman imagery in the tale (115). Tintner finds James associating the Americans in the story with the honorable Romans of the Republic (an association also evident in American statuary of the period), while the behavior of the Europeans is more in keeping with the corruption of the papal Rome (37–41). Berland notes the use of Arnoldian terminology in James's calling Mrs. Goldie a "Barbarian" (29).

Relation to Other Works

Rimmon compares the tale to "The Tragedy of Error," "Gabrielle de Bergerac," and *The Siege of London* as a *"pointe"* or "twist" tale in which the reader is happy to see the character—the British narrator here—unhappily surprised (82). McElderry points out that the topic of jilting is treated comically here in contrast to tales of the past three years such as "Mrs. Temperly," "Louisa Pallant," and "The Patagonia" (78). Putt looks particularly at the contrast with the last, as both rely melodramatically on the vulnerability of Victorian women to "compromise," which in neither case produces the called-for wedding (278–79). Maves remarks a resemblance to "The Diary of a Man of Fifty" in setting, theme, and frame (94). Powers judges the story most interesting for its use of a narrator who fails to understand the events he is narrating, like Lyon in "The Liar" (141).

Maves compares the "dovelike" Henry at the mercy of European sophistication to the similarly situated Milly Theale; Jones adds Daisy Miller, Isabel Archer, and Mme de Mauves as others who remain true to their American

innocence, and also Eugene Pickering, who, like Henry, manages to be innocent without being stupid, and whose fidelity, like Henry's, brings him happiness (Maves 96–97; Jones 125–26). Although few people mention it, the
narrator sharply limits the happy ending: "The subsequent life of this ingenious woman was short: I doubt whether she liked America as well as she
had had an idea she should, or whether it agreed with her" (CT 7, 306). The
implication is that the woman who gave up much for "a knight of romance"
ended up feeling about her consequent situation much as Lady Barbarina did
about hers, although some of this may be the narrator's sour grapes (CT 7,
383). Jones finds Wilmerding deceived in a manner similar to the Italian
Angelo of the early "Adina." Although he distinguishes Henry from Angelo by
saying he never seeks revenge (125), he does, like Angelo, marry the woman
his tormentor had hoped to, which serves well enough.

Matthiessen and Murdock point out that the name Goldies had also
appeared in *The Aspern Papers* (N 96).

Interpretation and Criticism

Robert Louis Stevenson wrote James from Australia after reading the first
part, telling him, "It is an exquisite art; do not be troubled by the shadows of
your French competitors: not one, not de Maupassant, could have done a
thing more clean or fine; dry in touch, but the atmosphere (as in a fine summer sunset) rich with colour and with perfume" (370). The story has continued to receive high praise from many readers who have read past the first
part, particularly for its setting, which Putt judges "vividly accurate" (278).

The convoluted plot, however, while well paced, according to Putt, has
been the focus of most negative criticism (279; e.g., Geismar 121). Powers
finds the twist ending too much of an O. Henry surprise (141). Matthiessen
and Murdock, too, see James as turning from the more serious possibilities
considered in the notebook to an overextended treatment of a practical joke
turned back on the joker (N 96). As a result, in Maves's view, the plot soon
swallows up the character of its hero (97).

The hero, such as he is, is placed in a familiarly international context. Swan
notes in the story the traditional split between innocent American and knowl-
edgeable Europeans (13). Walter Wright categorizes Henry as "noble" for his
"quiet virtue" (123). Jones notes, however, that while Henry seems at first a
natural victim at the hands of the Europeans, it is one of them, indeed "the
most cultivated" of them all, Mrs. Rushbrook, who rescues him (126). Henry
fits another American stereotype, however, in his riches, and Dietrichson
attributes the joke to "mischievous envy" of Wilmerding's fortune (79). If so,
the fortune helps him out of its consequences. Although Swan says we never
learn what the "solution" is (14), it clearly involves the payment of cash. It is

striking that the noble Henry and Mrs. Rushbrook seem so at ease bribing their way out of their predicament. The British Goldies, who accept the payment, never seem quite the same size as the rest of the characters—the narrator recalls that the mother made him believe in the caricatures of Thackeray (CT 7, 355). Their name and characterization are intended, no doubt, to make the reader believe these are people it is perfectly proper to buy off. Nevertheless, the fact remains, as Wright points out, that Veronica is an "innocent victim" who undergoes an unnecessary humiliation as part of someone else's joke (101, 138).

According to Edel, the "suavity" of its telling cloaks the "lightness" of the tale, which is nevertheless marked by a darker subject: "the fear of entanglement and the fear of women" (CT 7, 10). Such a view, however, overlooks the fact that women here are also victims and that it is the men that cause the entanglement. There is, however, a deeper source of darkness. The story is framed by a narrator who begins by quoting the narrator of the tale's permission to write it down because "every one's dead" (CT 7, 351). Vaid asserts that the narrator of the frame is identical with the narrator of the tale (37). But he is actually a London friend who informs us that the tale's narrator is dead as well, a fact that provides a certain distance between reader and teller, and as Maves notes, a certain "morbid" touch. Maves finds James in the tale itself going a step beyond his usual nostalgic approach to Rome, finding its almost funereal tone overwhelming the otherwise "charming social comedy" (94–97). Perhaps the approach is meant to fit in with what Swan calls, using the terminology of Meredith, its "High Comedy," a comedy based on "loss" (14). Indeed, the story is based on loss. While Wright judges the narrator as something of a foolish cad for not realizing from the start the cruelty of his joke (101), he creates enough sympathy for himself for the reader to recognize his loss of the woman he loves as significant. Henry loses both his innocence and his fortune to gain her; she loses her life not long after; and even the narrator of the frame has the loss of his friend to lament. While Wagenknecht considers the tale "a delightful, perfectly managed trifle" (202), there are elements in it that project the darker mood of James in the 1880s and that are not always at ease with its perfection.

Works Cited

Primary Works

James, Henry. 1889–1890. "The Solution." *The New Review* 1 and 2 (December–February): 79–90, 161–71, 666–90.

———. 1892. "The Solution." *The Lesson of the Master*, 202–65. New York and London: Macmillan.

———. "The Solution." *The Novels and Stories of Henry James*. Vol. 26. Ed. Percy Lubbock. London: Macmillan.

———. 1988. *Selected Letters of Henry James to Edmund Gosse, 1882–1915, A Literary Friendship.* Ed. Rayburn S. Moore. Baton Rouge: Louisiana State University Press.

Secondary Works

Berland, Alwyn. 1981. *Culture and Conduct in the Novels of Henry James.* Cambridge: Cambridge University Press.

Dietrichson, Jan W. 1969. *The Image of Money in the American Novel of the Gilded Age.* Oslo: Universitetsforlaget; New York: Humanities.

Edel, Leon, ed. 1949. *The Complete Plays of Henry James.* Philadelphia and New York: Lippincott.

Gale, Robert L. [1954] 1964. *The Caught Image: Figurative Language in the Fiction of Henry James.* Chapel Hill: University of North Carolina Press.

Geismar, Maxwell. 1963. *Henry James and the Jacobites.* Boston: Houghton Mifflin.

Jones, Granville H. 1975. *Henry James's Psychology of Experience: Innocence, Responsibility, and Renunciation in the Fiction of Henry James.* The Hague: Mouton.

Kossman, Rudolph R. 1969. *Henry James: Dramatist.* Groningen: Wolters-Noordhoff.

McElderry, Bruce R., Jr. 1965. *Henry James.* New York: Twayne.

Matthiessen, F. O. 1947. *The James Family: Including Selections from the Writings of Henry James, Sr., William, Henry, and Alice James.* New York: Knopf.

Maves, Carl. 1973. *Sensuous Pessimism: Italy in the Work of Henry James.* Bloomington: Indiana University Press.

Powers, Lyall H. 1970. *Henry James: An Introduction and Interpretation.* New York: Holt, Rinehart.

Putt, S. Gorley. 1966. *Henry James: A Reader's Guide.* Ithaca, NY: Cornell University Press.

Rimmon, Shlomith. 1977. *The Concept of Ambiguity: The Example of Henry James.* Chicago: University of Chicago Press.

Stevenson, R. L. 1995. *The Letters of Robert Louis Stevenson.* Vol. 6. Ed. Bradford A. Booth and Ernest Mehew. New Haven: Yale University Press.

Swan, Michael, ed. 1948. *Ten Short Stories of Henry James.* London: John Lehmann.

Tintner, Adeline R. 1986. *The Museum World of Henry James.* Ann Arbor: UMI Research Press.

Vaid, Krishna B. 1964. *Technique in the Tales of Henry James.* Cambridge, MA: Harvard University Press.

Wagenknecht, Edward. 1984. *The Tales of Henry James.* New York: Frederick Ungar.

Wright, Walter F. 1962. *The Madness of Art: A Study of Henry James.* Lincoln: University of Nebraska Press.

The Special Type

Publication History

Illustrated by Charlotte Harding, "The Special Type" was the last of three stories James published in *Collier's Magazine*, where it appeared in June 1900. James later included it in the 1903 collection *The Better Sort*. Its first posthumous publication was in Lubbock's *Novels and Stories of Henry James* in the 1920s.

Circumstances of Composition, Sources, and Influences

On December 21, 1895, while at his home in London, James recorded as a possibility for stage or story some gossip about the divorce of William Kissam Vanderbilt I, who while in Paris had hired a "*demi-mondaine*" (actually Nellie Neustretter of Nevada) to provide him the grounds of divorce. James immediately added a third woman, the one the man actually wishes to marry but at the same time to shield from the divorce court, and considered the possibility that the *demi-mondaine* may develop "a tremendous, disinterested fancy" for the man. The same day, he put it in a list of possible story topics. It was included in two more such lists, in 1898 and 1899, before he finally wrote it up into a story (CN 145–46, 168, 181, 184).

Tintner finds the artist-narrator reflecting Sargent, who had painted more than one Vanderbilt (*Museum* 94–95). She also finds the confusion of person and portrait both here and in "The Tone of Time" reflected in Wharton's short story "The Moving Finger," whose portraitist declaims, "*I* turned my real woman into a picture" ("Wharton," 4–5).

Relation to Other Works

There are numerous resemblances between this tale and "The Tone of Time," both of which feature a portrait painter and a "*cocotte*" (CN 184). Jones emphasizes the renunciatory heroines in both (204–5), while Edel places his emphasis on the themes of jealousy and revenge seen in the struggle for the portraits (*Life* 4, 325). Winner observes that the two women are allowed at least the "presumably consoling" portraits of the men they loved and lost, in contrast to Fleda Vetch, who is denied any memento of her experience in *The Spoils of Poynton* (152). Gage, remarking on the powerful influence of society in motivating the small cast of characters in each tale, points out that Alice Dundene alone is free of any resentment, even though the story enacts her mistreatment rather than simply recalling it as in "The Tone of Time," and even though she must live with the knowledge that the man she loves is alive and loves another (76–77, 105–6). He considers, however, that both Mary Tredick and Alice gain "a spiritual union of sorts" by means of the portraits, in contrast with John Marcher, who, in "The Beast in the Jungle," is completely cut off from May after her death, and he places Alice at the opposite end from Marcher in her acute consciousness of others combined with only a slight consciousness of her own value (90, 110).

Krook argues that the plan to achieve Mrs. Cavenham's happiness at the expense of Mrs. Dundene's foreshadows Kate Croy's plan to secure her future through Milly Theale (331). The pretended affair designed to shield the true one here is somewhat reminiscent of the pretended engagement in "Mrs. Temperly." Putt points to the new acceptance of divorce reflected in the story (292), and the two remarrying Brivets are reminiscent of Maisie's parents in *What Maisie Knew*. (See also "The Beldonald Holbein.")

Interpretation and Criticism

Wagenknecht gives perhaps the most laudatory verdict, declaring that "James never wrote a more touching story" and praising the way James here took his source "out of the gutter" and made it into "something fine" (203). Matthiessen, however, judges the same transformation unfortunate as it "etherialized" the original idea, removing its "human substance" (N 233; 1944, 11–13). Other critics have sided with Matthiessen, including Putt, who considers the tale "mawkish" (291).

The sentimental focus of the tale is the renunciatory Alice Dundene, who loses her remaining reputation for a man she has never been alone with. McElderry finds the title referring to "the kind of woman who will for a fee allow herself to be compromised" (110), but as the story makes clear, it soon takes on another meaning. Andreas emphasizes Alice's "capacity for unacquisitive feeling," which makes her superior to those who make use of it for acquisitive means (49). Gage calls her the best of "the better sort" and her tale the "climax" of the theme of renunciation in James's volume. More in line with Matthiessen, he does admit that she is "somewhat hard to credit as a character" (77, 101–2). Edel judges her keeping the picture as "her own quiet revenge," a motive that seems perhaps more human, but not that assigned her in the tale (*Life* 4, 325).

If Alice is a victim, Brivet is her victimizer. Most have noted the egotism and indifference to others the tale portrays, a theme that runs throughout *The Better Sort* (CT 11, 8). In a description judged particularly apt by Stafford, William James said of the collection, "It is hard enamel finish" (James 229; Stafford 349). The phrase certainly covers Frank Brivet. Both the notebook and the tale offer an explanation for Brivet's desire for divorce in the "odious" nature of his wife, and it is his appearance that appeals to Alice, leading her to declare, "I should have liked to love him for himself" (CN 145; CT 11, 174–75). But it is his money that makes him feel confident he can first use Alice and then go on to claim Mrs. Cavenham. Accordingly, Dietrichson sees the tale as a critique of the unethical use of wealth (84). Speaking of Brivet's blithe egotism, Walter Wright declares that in James "Hell was less often a place of conscious suffering than of complete absence of understanding" (102). While Putt speaks of the tale as another variation on avoiding marriage (291), Brivet's motivation at least is his desire to marry again. Mrs. Cavenham, his intended replacement, however, if not odious, is certainly far from significant apart from her striking appearance.

At the end of the tale, the narrator characterizes Brivet as having the "awkwardness of a man in dispute between women" (CT 11, 192). Throughout the tale the narrator himself is caught up in the dispute, as Brivet juggles three women, the current Mrs. Brivet, Mrs. Cavenham, and Mrs. Dundene. Generally critics have confined his role to the relaying of that dispute (e.g., Blackall 155) and have praised his sensitive analysis of it. Wagenknecht, for example, depicts the narrator as the only character to recognize that Mrs. Dundene is far finer than Brivet or Mrs. Cavenham, noting too his willingness to anger the latter two and to sacrifice his masterpiece in order to give Mrs. Dundene the portrait (203; also Gage 102).

Macnaughton, however, gives some spice to the tale's alleged mawkishness by implicating the narrator in Brivet's selfishness. In his judgment, the narrator "partially realizes" the immorality of the episode, but rather than face the facts as the impartial reader will see them, blames Mrs. Cavenham inordinately, and to make Mrs. Dundene's sacrifice seem acceptable makes it "heroic." Thus, in Macnaughton's view, he is as compromised as the society he criticizes (156–58). For if Mrs. Dundene achieves a moral victory, society—represented in Brivet—is both cruel and, according to Gage, "fully triumphant" (94, 106).

At the start the narrator speaks of himself as Brivet's "machinery" and "willing enough to turn his wheel" (CT 11, 175). After the plot is set afoot, he declares:

> I felt from the first so affected by the business that I desired to wash my hands of it. There was something I wished to say to him [Brivet] before it went further, but after that I cared only to be out of it. I may as well say at

once, however, that I never *was* out of it; for a man habitually ridden by the twin demons of imagination and observation is never—enough for his peace—out of anything. (CT 11, 179)

This is the typical Jamesian implication of the observer, and how one reads it no doubt has something to do with whom one takes for the liar in "The Liar" or the possessed in *The Turn of the Screw*. The narrator here is something in between a go-between and an innocent bystander, but one with an acute sense for what he observes. He seems, however, to make less of a contribution to events, which are set in motion by other people than himself, and to have less of an opportunity to influence them, given the determination of the other characters, than in some other tales where the observer's role has also been questioned. As Jones puts it, he has a sense of responsibility for the situation without any control over it (205). In analyzing the narrator's role one ought also to take into account James's depiction of himself in *The American Scene* in the same terms: "hag-ridden by the twin demons of observation and imagination" (Swan 6).

In his praise of *The Better Sort*, William James had told his brother, "You certainly excel in stories of that size" (229). James's own evaluation of the tale as written to his editor, Pinker, in September 1899 also notes its brevity: "It happens to be one of the very best short tales I've ever written; the best, in fact, I think of any equally brief" (Macnaughton 156). Matthiessen and Murdock see James as later leaving the tale out of the New York Edition because it was "too special" a type (N 233). It may, however, have simply been left on the cutting-room floor because there were simply too many other tales of artists, betrayers, and renouncers. Seen among the whole of James's work, this one, however well done, ceased to be special enough.

Works Cited

Primary Works
James, Henry. 1900. "The Special Type." *Collier's Magazine* 25 (16 June): 10–11, 14.

———. 1903. "The Special Type." *The Better Sort*. London: Methuen; New York: Scribner's, 93–115.

———. 1921–23. "The Special Type." *The Novels and Stories of Henry James*. Vol. 28. Ed. Percy Lubbock. London: Macmillan.

Secondary Works
Andreas, Osborn. 1948. *Henry James and the Expanding Horizon: A Study of the Meaning and Basic Themes of James's Fiction*. Seattle: University of Washington Press.

Blackall, Jean Frantz. 1965. *Jamesian Ambiguity and* The Sacred Fount. Ithaca, NY: Cornell University Press.

Dietrichson, Jan W. 1969. *The Image of Money in the American Novel of the Gilded Age*. Oslo: Universitetsforlaget; New York: Humanities.

Gage, Richard P. 1988. *Order and Design: Henry James' Titled Story Sequences*. New York: Peter Lang.

James, William. 1992. *The Correspondence of William James*. Vol. 3: *William and Henry*. Ed. Ignas K. Skrupskelis and Elizabeth M. Berkeley. Charlottesville: University Press of Virginia.

Jones, Granville H. 1975. *Henry James's Psychology of Experience: Innocence, Responsibility, and Renunciation in the Fiction of Henry James*. The Hague: Mouton.

Krook, Dorothea. [1962] 1967. *The Ordeal of Consciousness in Henry James*. New York: Cambridge University Press.

McElderry, Bruce R., Jr. 1965. *Henry James*. New York: Twayne.

Macnaughton, W. R. 1974. "The First-Person Narrators of Henry James." *Studies in American Fiction* 2 (August): 145–64.

Matthiessen, F. O. 1944. *Henry James: The Major Phase*. New York: Oxford University Press.

Putt, S. Gorley. 1966. *Henry James: A Reader's Guide*. Ithaca, NY: Cornell University Press.

Stafford, William T. 1959. "William James as Critic of his Brother Henry." *The Personalist* 40: 341–53.

Swan, Michael, ed. 1948. *Ten Short Stories of Henry James*. London: John Lehmann.

Tinter, Adeline R. 1986. *The Museum World of Henry James*. Ann Arbor: UMI Research Press.

———. 1986. "Wharton and James: Some Literary Give and Take." *Edith Wharton Newsletter* 3, no. 1 (Spring): 3–5, 8.

Wagenknecht, Edward. 1984. *The Tales of Henry James*. New York: Frederick Ungar.

Winner, Viola Hopkins. 1970. *Henry James and the Visual Arts*. Charlottesville: University Press of Virginia.

Wright, Walter F. 1962. *The Madness of Art: A Study of Henry James*. Lincoln: University of Nebraska Press.

The Story in It

Publication History

In his preface for "The Story in It" in the New York Edition, James recalled that the tale despite its brevity, "haunted, a graceless beggar, for a couple of years, the cold avenues of publicity." He gave it finally "at no cost to himself but the cost of his confidence" to an old friend, who was starting a new magazine that, he recalls, only lasted one more number (*Criticism* 2, 1284–85). Indeed, in 1906 LeRoy Phillips, preparing the first James bibliography, was unable to locate a copy of the January 1902 issue of the *Anglo-American Magazine*, where the story appeared (N 287). Still, James included it the next year in *The Better Sort*, and after that in the New York Edition.

Circumstances of Composition, Sources, and Influences

On October 18, 1895, while at Torquay, James wrote down as a possible subject "the study of a romantic mind" (CN 136). Three years later on May 8, while in London, he wrote *"L'honnête femme n'a pas de roman*—beautiful little 'literary (?)' subject to work out in short tale. The trial, the exhibition, the proof:—either it's not a *'roman,'* or it's not *honnête*. When it becomes the thing it's guilty; when it doesn't become guilty it doesn't become the thing." The same day, he included Blessingbourne in a list of names (CN 170–71). In between the two entries he presumably took part in the conversation with "a distinguished friend, a novelist not to *our* manner either born or bred," usually identified as the French novelist Paul Bourget (N 277; also McFarlane 157–58). The novelist, James recalled, was asked why his heroines "were so perversely and persistently but of a type impossible to ladies respecting themselves." The reply was "not unnaturally . . . that ladies who respected themselves took particular care never to *have* adventures," that such "reserve" while admirable "was yet fatally detrimental to literature, in the sense of promptly making any artistic harmony pitched in the same low key trivial and empty" (*Criticism* 2, 1285). At Lamb House on February 15, 1899, James returned to the idea, fleshing it out with the basic situation of the love triangle and a fair amount of the actual dialogue, with a London setting, and the man at this stage "a man of letters, an artist," who is equally as conscious as Maud of their "relation" (CN 176–77). He reminded himself of the tale again in May, in Rome, and again in October admonished himself, *"Ne lâchez donc pas, vous savez, mon bon*, that idea of the little thing on the *roman de l'honnête femme"* (CN 184, 186).

Maud reads not only French novels, but those of the Italian author D'Annunzio. Tremper links the tale to James's 1903 essay on D'Annunzio, whom he criticized for treating the erotic "isolated from 'life,' in the larger sense of the word." Here James shows how to write an "aesthetic case" without vulgarity, a moral aestheticism (13–16). Tintner also sees James drawing on the work of D'Annunzio, particularly *Il Piacere*. Indeed, she argues that Colonel Voyt is modeled after him, but that James, seeking the "finer possible combinations" he looked for in vain in D'Annunzio, provides a "corrected" version of his work that would keep his heroine from an affair (1982). Less persuasively, Roditi links Maud with the heroines of Oscar Wilde, on the grounds of their shared taste for "naughty" literature (55).

Lebowitz argues that James acknowledged more degrees than the French, and that in his discussion of whether a novel could be both "good" and interesting was included his view that one could be both "bad" and uninteresting, as he thought *Madame Bovary* was (19).

Interestingly, it is in response to an English writer, George Eliot, that one sees James discussing the concept of a one-sided relationship. In his 1876 "Conversation" on *Daniel Deronda*, James's spokesperson Constantius says of its heroine that "Poor Gwendolen's falling in love with Deronda is part of her own luckless history, not of his" (*Criticism* 1, 984). Much later James recalled his first meeting with Eliot, and the "relation" it created for him, qualifying the claim saying, "My 'relation'—for I didn't go so far as to call it 'ours'" (*Autobiography* 578).

Relation to Other Works

Several critics have seen James setting himself the task of producing the kind of a work Maud looks for, the novel of a "decent woman" (CT 11,317). Vieilledent proposes that he had already penned one in the 1875 *Madame de Mauves* (189). Gage points to "The Beast in the Jungle" as James's proof that Maud's type of story "without passion, adventure, or romance" can be great literature, seeing both stories as treating "renouncers who lose their loves in favor of an internal and purer vision, a passion manqué" (61, 91). The majority of critics, for instance Putt, look to James's final three novels for examples (297; also Tintner 1982, 201). Macnaughton first connects the tale with his asking in his essays on D'Annunzio for "finer possible connections," and then sees James himself seeking to provide them in *The Golden Bowl*. The first half of the novel, Macnaughton writes, is like the French books Maud reads, the second half portrays Maggie as the interesting yet decent heroine the French omit (103, 109; also Tremper 15). Lebowitz also links the works, but calls Maud a "Maggie who never grows up," arguing that a heroine needs to leave behind her innocence as does Maggie to be "interesting" (19). Lambert Strether in *The Ambassadors* is seen by Delbaere-Garant as a male Maud, who in his decency is more interesting than the lovers whose affair is recorded through his consciousness (351–53). Relating the story more narrowly to the theme of missed opportunity in *The Ambassadors*, Tintner uses it to support the validity of Strether's experience (1986, 118). Finally, Krook compares the condescending "admiration" Mrs. Dyott and the Colonel bestow on Maud to Kate Croy's attitude toward Milly Theale in *The Wings of the Dove* (331). Stowell categorizes the story with the three novels on different grounds, calling all four—as well as "Flickerbridge" and "The Beast in the Jungle"—late impressionistic works similar in tone and approach (27).

More support for Maud is offered by Beach, who notes that his description of her adventures in the preface as "all beautifully, a matter of interpretation and of the particular conditions" echoes his description of Isabel's: "Without her sense of them, her sense *for* them, as one may say they are next to nothing at all." Their subjectivities provide "the beauty and the difficulty"—even as, Beach points out, Miriam Rooth in *The Tragic Muse* recognizes the greater challenge of speeches and scenes "open to interpretation" (152–53). Bender traces a development in James's concept of "story," a term he used conventionally in the titles to the early tales "The Story of a Year" and "The Story of a Masterpiece," but uses "questioningly" here. Voyt's inability to see a "story" in Maud's situation, Bender argues, is a "caricature" of critics who could not see the "story" in James's tales (249). Perosa chooses Voyt's definition of art—"Art is our flounderings shown"— to apply to the narrator's floundering search for relations in *The Sacred Fount* (89).

Focusing on Maud's life more than her art, Jones places this tale among some of James's "more intense" pieces, in which the ideas of innocence and life give way to that of renunciation, including also *The Ambassadors*, "The Altar of the Dead," and "The Beast in the Jungle," all of which he calls "painless but excruciating portraits of transfigured renouncers" (260–61). In Horne's more negative view, Maud is a reader cut off from life just as Mary Tredick, in "The Tone of Time," is an artist cut off from life, a connection also made by Gage, who adds Alice Dundene as a woman left loving an image rather than a reality in "The Special Type" (Horne 109; Gage 103). Similarly, Edel characterizes Maud's passion as a kind of "worship of icons," seen also in "Maud-Evelyn" (CT 11, 8).

Concentrating on its form, Vaid compares the tale to the nonfiction dialogues "Daniel Deronda: A Conversation" and "After the Play" (213).

Interpretation and Criticism

"The Story in It" is, in part, a theoretical conversation, an example of the "frequent metaliterary turn" Vieilledent notes in James's late stories (189). In his preface, James wrote that "what sort of performance" could be produced by "a picture of life founded on the mere reserves and omissions and suppressions of life" would need to be "really luminous," grounded "on some such perfect definition of terms as is not of this muddled world" (*Criticism* 2, 1285). In the story, however, as Kappeler and Vieilledent observe, terms are continually questioned and redefined (Kappeler 103; Vieilledent 192–93).

Such theoretical quibbling has not been to every reader's taste. Tremper calls the tale an exercise (13); Putt refers to it as a "dispirited . . . diagram" (297). Rebecca West goes so far as to dismiss the entire collection *The Better Sort* as a "twittering over teacups" (106). More moderately, Edgar questions whether the "brilliant trifle" has a story at all (149). Even less censoriously, McElderry judges the tale, with its "amusing dialogue," to be "a light statement" of a "fundamental conviction" (145–46). Cowdery, however, takes the title as a serious challenge to readers to find the story (23). Such can be difficult, as Horne and Gage emphasize, because the tale offers no plot or action, only character and situation (Horne 108; Gage 85). It is the configuration of the three characters and their intertwined relationships that enact the issues of the debate.

Limited as it may be, the tale has received much praise, particularly for its presentation. James was working for a very short story here, aiming first for 3,000 to 4,000 words and actually managing to bring it in at close to 6,000 (CN 176). As such, it is in Horne's estimate a "little masterpiece of James' later style" (108). Stowell analyzes the tale in terms of its "pictorial impressionism," beginning with the "painterly" description of a rainy day—which Tintner attributes to the influence of D'Annunzio (Tinter 1982, 208). While likening it to a one-act play, Stowell sees impressionism throughout the story, James giving only the surface of things, the "oblique and nuanced" dialogue, and so, with a style suited to his subject, preserving the "mystery of the world" and of Maud's feelings (28–30).

Speaking for the minority, Matheson finds the connection to the life of the artist here "remote" (230 n.6). Matthiessen calls the tale a "condensed parable of [James's] material and method" (14) and in general critics have approached its characters by estimating the congruity of their opinions with James's. This is particularly the case with Maud, to whom most critics have assigned the victory in the debate, even though she does not entirely persuade the Colonel and Mrs. Dyott, on the grounds that her views most closely resemble James's (e.g., N 278; Andreas 120; Vaid 213). As Voss indicates, the story shows James's belief that "it is felt experience which evokes art and that only art can give the experience meaning and significance," and it was to such dramas as Maud's that James chose to give "life, interest, and importance" (141). As a spokeswoman, Maud combines boldness in literary opinions with a reserve about personal matters. James emphasized this in the change from notebook to story, by having Mrs. Dyott guess Maud's love for Voyt rather than having Maud declare it, further evidence of the circuitousness of both author and characters (N 277). According to Austin Wright, Maud is "almost wholly admirable," her revelation of her passion making her interlocuters seem "foolish and shallow" in comparison, while she avoids appearing either forlorn or pitiable (60, 199). Tintner, while arguing that James here refrains from judging "moralistically" so that Mrs. Dyott too is a "good woman" though in a bad situation, nevertheless sees James's sympathies as being "unmistakably" with Maud. While she argues that Maud does have an "adventure," Tintner indicates she is distinctly avoiding the "great relation" and wisely so, given the pain it causes Mrs. Dyott (1982, 201, 205, 214).

In James's solving of his "problem," Beach discerns a "Puritan cleanliness" and "Yankee ingenuity" (19). Both qualities are somewhat discounted today, and those critics who do not want to accept what Geismar calls the "basic Jamesian equation of moral virtue with emotional inhibitions" in the tale take the victory from Maud (255n). Stowell gives it to the Colonel, seeing him in his disquisition on "relationships" as the spokesperson for both impressionism and James (29). Stating that in James the "supreme ethical concern" is "commitment to human relationship," Lebowitz argues that James is here comparing human and artistic commitment, and that for James both require the giving up of innocence. Thus, in her reading, the "realistic" Colonel, while far from perfect, still speaks for James in his demand for "dynamic" relationships, while Maud suffers from a "fatal separation between life and art" (18–19). Similarly, Gage judges Maud's renunciation ambiguous on the grounds that she has abandoned "human experience in favor of fictional human experience as it is presented in literature," without any real recognition of what she is giving up. This lack of knowledge, evident in what he sees as her inability to answer Voyt, "reduces her to comic dimensions" (103).

Others split the contest, or characterize it as even more ambiguous. Edgar, for example, describes the Colonel as arguing "winningly" and Maud "stoutly" (149–50). Tremper acknowledges Maud as James's voice in the tale, but adds that the Colonel also has a "good argument" (14). In Horne's reading, it is not Maud's relationship with Voyt, but Voyt's relationship with Mrs. Dyott that holds together the story. Maud and Voyt both believe with James that the British novels are false to life, and that there should be a significant relationship between art and life. Maud, however, Horne argues, looks to literature to replace life, while Voyt reads it more appropriately as art. Horne admits that the tale can be read as a defense of James's concept of the "drama of consciousness." But because James did not adopt his approach from a concern with morality, as Maud does, Horne argues that Maud is disqualified as a spokeswoman. Maud is not, however, the subject of James's condemnation, Horne insists, noting the ambiguous irony of the tale's concluding remarks. In conclusion, Horne comments, because the story is presented as a drama, not a treatise, one simply cannot deduce from it James's "true" view (108–11).

Arguing that it does not so much matter who wins the central argument as much as "the subjective basis" of their ideas, Gargano sees in the story two stories. One is the "stereotyped French romance" of the Colonel and Mrs. Dyott with its storms, secrecy, and burned letters. Gargano observes how they mislead and condescend to Maud, but argues that they are not without redeeming values. Dyott in particular recognizes and appreciates Maud's romance, which is the tale's other story. James, Gargano argues, treats Maud with "tender parody," making clear her misreading of the Colonel and her desire to become herself "a Platonic concept." Gargano himself sides with the Colonel, whom he calls many-sided and "not surprisingly, attractive" to both women.

Wagenknecht accepts Gargano's reading that the story describes its characters "*in terms of* what they believe about literature." He points, however, to some mixed signals, particularly Maud's fondness for French literature and Colonel Voyt's "high respect for the decent woman in life," if not in literature (135–36). The latter, given that the Colonel is married, seems a good example of the old-fashioned double standard (CT 11, 324)

In her analysis, Kappeler concentrates on the opposition between literature and life. At first, it seems that Mrs. Dyott is meant to represent "Life" and Maud "Art." But Maud defies such categorizing. She does not support the French over the English as the Colonel expects her to. She is not looking simply for "a relation more curious" as the Colonel and Mrs. Dyott presume. The Colonel, whose fighting instincts Kappeler remarks on, seeks to get to the heart of Maud's ideas, and is followed in the hunt by Mrs. Dyott. By changing Maud's concept of "interest" into one of "story," however, Kappeler argues, he misses the point. In her view, Maud "intuits the fallacy" of the strict opposition of life and art, representing in herself a "practical synthesis." Like Gargano, Kappeler states that Maud fails to see the Colonel clearly, being in love instead with an "impression" of him, although her emphasis is on how this protects Maud (101–5).

Vieilledent's reading returns the focus to the debate between French literature and Anglo-Saxon, seeing James as seeking some other possibility outside the stereotypes of "scandalous adultery and naive respectability." In her analysis, the skillful wordplay throughout unsettles the clichés of both literatures, and leaves Maud the victor, her "version of passion" being more impressive than that of the lovers, even as her innocence is more informed than that of the enforced ignorance of the English novel. The lovers' case, she suggests, is undermined by their "overly satirical" names: Dyott suggests "diet"—one might add "die"—and Voyt "void." While Vieilledent suggests that the tale's "'nihilistic' ungrounding of authority" may problematize the text as a whole, she argues that it also serves Maud's cause because its restoration of "the exchange of the fictive and the real" allows for new categories. Maud's favorite category, she concludes, dismissed by Voyt as a "small, scared, starved, subjective satisfaction," is also one of James's, and is surprisingly rich.

It requires Colonel Voyt's learning of Maud's passion to give it recognition, even if only as "a kind of a shy romance," and so one might argue that Maud's romance is dependent on the knowledge of the Colonel. It is also dependent on the presentation of the author. Luckily for Maud, James held that "It is, not surprisingly, one of the rudiments of criticism that a human, a personal 'adventure' is no *a priori*, no positive and absolute and inelastic thing, but just a matter of relation and appreciation—a name we conveniently give, after the fact, to any passage, to any situation, that has added the sharp taste of uncertainty to a quickened sense of life. Therefore the thing is, all beautifully, a matter of interpretation and of the particular conditions . . ." (*Criticism* 2, 1285). In this tale, James used the robust physical passion of the Colonel and Mrs. Dyott to provide the "particular conditions" that best highlight Maud's "quickened sense of life." In what Tintner argues may be James's "most sophisticated tale" (1982, 204), James appears to be arguing that the greatest sophistication is a certain simplicity.

Works Cited

Primary Works
James, Henry. 1902. "The Story in It." *Anglo-American Magazine* 7 (January): 1–13.

———. 1903. "The Story in It." *The Better Sort*. London: Methuen; New York: Scribner's, 168–88.

———. 1908. "The Story in It." *The Novels and Tales of Henry James*. New York Edition. Vol. 18, 407–35. New York: Scribner's.

Secondary Works
Andreas, Osborn. 1948. *Henry James and the Expanding Horizon: A Study of the Meaning and Basic Themes of James's Fiction*. Seattle: University of Washington Press.

Beach, Joseph Warren. [1918] 1954. *The Method of Henry James*. Philadelphia: Albert Saifer.

Bender, Bert. 1976. "Henry James's Late Lyric Meditations upon the Mysteries of Fate and Self-Sacrifice." *Genre* 9: 247–62.

Blackall, Jean Frantz. 1965. *Jamesian Ambiguity and* The Sacred Fount. Ithaca, NY: Cornell University Press.

Cowdery, Lauren Tozek. 1986. *The Nouvelle of Henry James in Theory and Practice*. Ann Arbor: UMI Research Press.

Delbaere-Garant, Jeanne. 1970. *Henry James: The Vision of France*. Paris: Société d'Editions Les Belles Lettres.

Edgar, Pelham. [1927] 1964. *Henry James, Man and Author*. New York: Russell & Russell.

Gage, Richard P. 1988. *Order and Design: Henry James' Titled Story Sequences*. New York: Peter Lang.

Gargano, James W. 1976. "James's Stories in 'The Story in It.'" *NMAL: Notes on Modern American Literature* 1: Item 2.

Geismar, Maxwell. 1963. *Henry James and the Jacobites*. Boston: Houghton Mifflin.

Horne, Helen. 1960. *Basic Ideals of James's Aesthetics as Expressed in the Short Stories Concerning Artists and Writers*. Marburg: Erich Mauersberger.

Jones, Granville H. 1975. *Henry James's Psychology of Experience: Innocence, Responsibility, and Renunciation in the Fiction of Henry James*. The Hague: Mouton.

Kappeler, Susanne. 1980. *Writing and Reading in Henry James*. New York: Columbia University Press.

Krook, Dorothea. [1962] 1967. *The Ordeal of Consciousness in Henry James*. New York: Cambridge University Press.

Lebowitz, Naomi. 1965. *The Imagination of Loving: Henry James's Legacy to the Novel*. Detroit: Wayne State University.

McElderry, Bruce R., Jr. 1965. *Henry James*. New York: Twayne.

McFarlane, I. D. 1950. "A Literary Friendship: Henry James and Paul Bourget." *Cambridge Journal* 4 (December): 144–61.

Macnaughton, William R. 1987. *Henry James: The Later Novels*. Boston: Twayne.

Matheson, Gwen. 1968. "Portraits of the Artist and the Lady in the Shorter Fictions of Henry James." *Dalhousie Review* 48: 222–30.

Matthiessen, F.O. 1944. "Introduction: Henry James' Portrait of the Artist." *Henry James: Stories of Writers and Artists*. Norfolk, CT: New Directions. Also reprinted as "Henry James's Portrait of the Artist." *Partisan Review* 11 (1944): 71–87.

Perosa, Sergio. 1983. *Henry James and the Experimental Novel*. New York: New York University Press.

Putt, S. Gorley. 1966. *Henry James: A Reader's Guide*. Ithaca, NY: Cornell University Press.

Stowell, H. Peter. 1984. "Impressionism in James's Late Stories." *Revue de Littérature Comparée* 58, no. 1 (January–March): 27–36.

Tintner, Adeline R. 1986. *The Museum World of Henry James*. Ann Arbor: UMI Research Press.

———. 1982. "Henry James's 'The Story in It' and Gabriele D'Annunzio." *Modern Fiction Studies* 28, no. 2 (Summer): 201–14.

Tremper, Ellen. 1981. "Henry James's 'The Story in It': A Successful Aesthetic Adventure." *Henry James Review* 3, no. 1 (Fall): 11–16.

Vaid, Krishna B. 1964. *Technique in the Tales of Henry James*. Cambridge, MA: Harvard University Press.

Vieilledent, Catherine. 1989. "Literary Pornographics: Henry James's Politics of Suppression." *Henry James Review* 10, no. 3 (Fall): 185–96.

Voss, Arthur. 1973. *The American Short Story: A Critical Survey*. Norman: University of Oklahoma Press.

Wagenknecht, Edward. 1984. *The Tales of Henry James*. New York: Frederick Ungar.

West, Rebecca. [pseud]. 1916. *Henry James*. London: Nisbet.

Wright, Austin McGiffert. 1961. *The American Short Story in the Twenties*. Chicago: University of Chicago Press.

The Story of a Masterpiece

Publication History

Accompanied by two illustrations, one by Gaston Fay and one by W. J. Hennessy, "The Story of a Masterpiece" appeared in the *Galaxy* in the January and February 1868 issues. Never reprinted by James, it did not appear again until Kenton's 1950 *Eight Uncollected Tales*.

Circumstances of Composition, Sources, and Influences

On October 2, 1867, James wrote the editor of the *Galaxy*, Francis P. Church, to inquire as to the whereabouts of a manuscript he had sent two weeks before (Aziz 1, xl). Before the end of the month, James was able to write thanking him for payment. He objected, however, to Church's request for an added concluding paragraph, explaining, "It doesn't seem to me necessary. Silence on the subject will prove to the reader, I think, that the marriage *did* come off. I have little fear that the reader will miss a positive statement to that effect and the story closes in a more dramatic manner, to

my apprehension, just as I have left it" (*Letters* 1, 74). Fish argues that James
was working here toward his later "indirect" manner of presentation from a
belief that the author should share the work with readers, just as he admonished George Eliot in his 1866 review of *Adam Bede* that she should have let
the reader assume Adam and Dinah married, rather than making a "positive
statement." Church, however, was evidently unimpressed, and the story
appeared with an added paragraph, which LeClair argues weakens the tale
(399). Still, as Martineau comments, James's grudging transition—"I need
hardly add"—makes his opinion clear (25 n.2). In Fish's judgment, James
made the best of a forced job: losing the "spell" of the abrupt ending, he
kept a "tough-minded rejection of sentimentality," its irony typical of his
early tales (242–43).

LeClair suggests that the story benefits from James's drawing on his
acquaintances for his characters, with Miss Everett a shallow "composite" of
his female Temple cousins, Gilbert a reflection of the admired William Hunt,
the mentor of John La Farge, who is represented in turn by Baxter. The connection thus established with James's Newport days, the site of Lennox and
Marian's meeting, is strengthened, LeClair states, by the allusion to Browning,
as James and his circle there were admirers of Browning (399).

Baxter says to Lennox of his portrait inspired by "My Last Duchess," "This
is simply an attempt to embody my own private impression of the poem,
which has always had a strong hold on my fancy. I don't know whether it
agrees with your own impression and that of most readers" (CT 1, 264).
Kenton states that reading the poem will give the critic "a more satisfying
sense" of Baxter's impression, but offers no sense of what that will be (12).
Interestingly, while Lennox finds an "exquisite significance" in Marian's being
chosen to represent Browning's heroine, critics such as Edel who have commented on the relationship seem to imply that it is unfortunate (*Life* 1, 256).
Sicker speaks of Marian having, like Browning's Duchess, a "heart too soon
made glad"—a shallowness that loves everyone and so no one (28). In
Browning's poem, however, the implication is clear that the Duchess was a
loving young woman misinterpreted by a sour old man. If the poem were followed directly, then Marian would be intended as a woman misunderstood
by men who wish her to think of them as her universe. While an intriguing
possibility, it is more likely that Tintner is right that the story reworks the
poem only imperfectly (1987, 202).

In its review, the *Nation* found the idea of the revelation of character
through a portrait the most intriguing part of the tale. The device is also used
by Hawthorne in his tale "The Prophetic Pictures," in which an artist paints
the portrait of an engaged couple. Beebe argues for a similarity in the artist's
revelation of a soul for the sake of art here and in James's "The Liar," holding
both artists culpable for a "sin as reprehensible as that of Roger Chillingworth

. . . or Gilbert Osmond" (206). Buitenhuis detects a change in emphasis, in James, from the mysterious to the psychological (39). Long charts a similar change, from romance to realism, indicating, for example, that Lennox responds to the portrait not because of its powers, but because it confirms his unacknowledged suspicion of Marian (16–17). To Buitenhuis, however, the "Balzacian insistence on fact" fits uneasily with Hawthorne (40). Brodhead sees in Lennox both Elinor's apprehension and Walter's aggression, although he stabs only the portrait, not the actual woman as does Walter (128)

Looking at the conceit of the revealing portrait, Putt, while dismissing it as "exceedingly unpromising," notes its "inexplicable fascination" at the time, as seen also in Wilde's *The Picture of Dorian Gray* and *Father Strafford* by Anthony Hope (39; also Sicker 30). Jeffares locates additional examples in Leitch Ritch's 1854 *Wearyfoot Common* as well as *Romola*, and later in George Gissing's *Thyrza* (1878) and Vernon Lee's *Oke of Okehurst* (1890) (95–96). Veeder, meanwhile, locates other artistic Gilberts, including Gilbert Osmond, Gilbert Stuart, and the painter in the popular *The Wide, Wide World* (120).

Tintner calls attention to the numerous quotations from Gibbon, the French poets, and Horace (1989, 141).

Relation to Other Works

All three of the main characters have inspired comparisons. Baxter, Winner observes, is the opposite of Roderick Hudson in that, in the narrator's terms, his "artist half" holds dominance over his "human half" (105). Baxter is also more perceptive than the earlier artist Locksley in "A Landscape Painter," according to Zablotny, who sees the closer resemblance between the two heroines (221). Bayley draws attention to the way the hero in each, once he has come to doubt that he is loved, also begins to doubt that he is in love (62). Marian herself, Jones argues, is a "naturally heartless though innocently frivolous creature" totally unaware of her character, similar to Elizabeth Ingram of "Crawford's Consistency" and Lady Barbarina (100). Kraft judges Marian shallow not sinister, like Daisy Miller, a woman whose beauty has led her to expect and enjoy the attention of men. He remarks, however, that being less simple, she is also more successful (30).

The focus on the artist's use of models and "types," in Kenton's analysis, begins a significant theme in James, seen also in "The Real Thing" and the preface to *The Portrait of a Lady*, even as the use of real people as models will be treated in the preface to "The Coxon Fund" (5, 14). (See particularly "The Liar.")

Interpretation and Criticism

"The Story of a Masterpiece" appears to have been greeted, initially, with enthusiasm. In a review of it, only the sixth of James's signed tales, the *Nation* not only judged it James's best, but proclaimed him "within the somewhat narrow limits to which he confines himself . . . the best writer of short stories in America." They continued, "He is never commonplace, never writes without knowing what he wants to do, and never has an incident or a character that is not in some way necessary to the production of such effects as he aims at." James's brother William also praised the tale, finding in it and James's next, "The Romance of Certain Old Clothes," not only Henry's characteristic "neatness & airy grace of touch" but also "a greater suppleness & freedom of movement in the composition" (36).

McElderry continues the praise, judging the tale the best of the early stories because of its use of Europe and art (287). Most modern critics, however, have been less commendatory. Putt, for example, considers it a generally "unrewarding exercise" (39). As a rule, the blame has been put on the technique. In Kelley's analysis, a "few hints" would have sufficed to give readers what they needed of Marian and Baxter's romance, but James provides a lengthy flashback, taking away the reader's attention from the hero, Lennox (81). Later critics have lodged similar objections (Vaid 133–34; Wagenknecht 204; Thorp xiv; LeClair 398–99). Buitenhuis sees the awkwardness as part of a general problem with point of view, a disparity of approaches also evident in the poor fit of the melodramatic conclusion with the contemporary realism of the rest of the tale (39–40).

The treatment of character has generally drawn higher praise (e.g., Voss 128). William, however, reserved his interest for the heroine, dismissing the other characters as comparatively uninteresting (47). Nevertheless, he also found the tale itself "unsympathetic" by virtue of being "one of those male versus female subjects you have so often treated," having "something cold about it, a want of heartiness or unction" without any compensatory "rare picturesque elements" or action (36). As a tale of "male versus female," there certainly seems a lack of sympathy in the story toward the female, as represented here by the heroine, Marian. James declares her shallow so early on that Buitenhuis finds he undercuts any possible suspense (31). Levy sees the treatment of Marian's character illustrating James's sense of the great gap between good and evil, along with his belief in the ease with which evil can masquerade as beauty (31). Certainly Marian is set up as a type, first by Baxter in his portrait of "My Last Duchess," and when she fails to fit that role, into that of the faithless woman. Bayley, however, asserts that James is well aware of the "many modes of feeling and behaving" between loving a man for his money or for himself (61). Walter Wright, for his part, argues that James first assigns Marian a type, and then attributes to her characteristics that do not fit that type, a mix he finds "more inconsistent than intriguing" (156). Marian, for example, has refused two rich suitors as well as the impecunious Baxter, and displays a certain intelligence and wit even at her most fickle. While it is unclear whether the young James was quite so immune to typecasting as Bayley would have him, he does not seem consistent in its application.

Marian's fiancé, Lennox, has been alternately sympathized with or scorned, partly on the basis of the critic's reading of Marian. Dietrichson, for example, who sees Marian as a golddigger, praises Lennox as a man better characterized by his sensibility than by his wealth, who had wished to be loved for himself (69). Segal, on the other hand, writes that Lennox's suspicions are "not surprisingly" confirmed by the picture painted by a "previous rejected lover," and says of this tale among other early ones that it "is clearly intimated" that his fears are "groundless" (222 n.8). The fact that his previous marriage necessitated a "trying and salutory probation" for his temper may reflect on his understanding of women (CT 1, 259).

It is Lennox's jealousy of Baxter, in Kelley's judgment, that is the story's real subject, and she argues on that ground that the conclusion in which his "pent up" jealousy is "graphically" revealed is the story's one "artistic" achievement (80). Baxter does seem to turn in that scene from a condemnation of Marian to a condemnation of the painter. Bayley writes, "Lennox behaves as if art were so much outside life that the removal of what was uncomfortable in it could make life comfortable again . . ." (62). In the narrator's account, Lennox "lacked the brutal consistency necessary for taking away Marian's future. If he had mistaken her and overrated her, the fault was his own, and it was a hard thing that she should pay the penalty. Whatever were her failings, they were profoundly involuntary, and it was plain that with regard to himself her intentions were good. She would be no companion, but she would be at least a faithful wife" (CT 1, 294–95). The "it was plain" seems an unlikely indication of the rationalization Bayley detects, rather a recognition of the exaggerations—whether idealizations or demonizations—of art, and of the hard facts of life. When Lennox destroys the painting, he may be destroying not a symbol of Marian, but of someone else's version of her, their attempted possession of her. He declares, "Come, Marian may be what God has made her; but *this* detestable creature I can neither love nor respect" (CT 1, 295). The implication is that Marian is *not* what the picture represents. While Wright takes the portrait as a faithful one, he still sees Lennox as an impressive character with a greater understanding than Baxter. In Wright's terminology, Lennox is a "romantic realist," who "will accept Marian both as she is and as she believes she wishes to be," while Baxter fails to recognize "that what Marian wishes to be is part of what she is." The tale thus illustrates, he argues, James's method of inclosing an "artist register" within a larger "artistic creation," the tale itself (130–31).

Still, as the Jamesian artist, Baxter has naturally garnered his share of praise. Wagenknecht argues that the exposure of Marian in the painting is due to Baxter's greatness as an artist, not his malice as a person (203). Indeed, Baxter is depicted as working with "something more than knowledge—with imagination, with feeling. He had almost *composed*; and his composition had embraced the truth" (CT 1, 285). Baxter represents what critics such as Buitenhuis have taken as the story's most significant theme, the "psychology of art" (40). Zablotny, however, while noting the implication in the tale that Baxter has "chosen the better course" in choosing art over dubious love, remarks that James will revise that view in later works (221). There is still another turn, however, in that Baxter has gained love as well, being newly engaged at the start of the tale.

Kraft, who is perhaps the tale's chief advocate, sees James as disapproving of both Marian and Lennox. Marian, with a superficial beauty esteemed by society, is at least not to blame for her superficiality; Lennox, however, has sufficient understanding that his standards should be higher. Lennox's marrying Marian, according to Kraft, shows instead his acceptance of the standards of his class and its limited vision, and his inability to accept the vision of art. Only the artist transcends class and sees truly. The tale, however, as Kraft observes, is open-ended, because James does not tell us anything of the quality of Lennox's marriage.

James, Kraft contends, is seeking to "make the reader see for himself" the truth of the story, just as Baxter does in his paintings. Although he appears to present "the work of art" as the true reality, James acknowledges that reality is a "many-sided phenomenon." As a key example of the tale's ambiguity, Kraft points to Lennox's meeting with Baxter's fiancée, who is looking at the portrait. Lennox judges her "evidently an excellent person" mainly on her appearance, and Kraft remarks that James may be "facetious" here or may be suggesting that her appearance to Lennox "is actually an ideal—art refines on life, as does the portrait, and then life refines on art, as does the fiancée standing in front of the portrait." James, he argues, was not yet sure, and may have destroyed the portrait because it was "too much" for him (23–35).

Martineau, while recognizing some awkwardness, also has a high estimate of the tale, calling it a "remarkably fine specimen" of early James. She, too, focuses her discussion on the "relation between actuality and artistic representation." While contending that Lennox receives some authorial sympathy, she sees Baxter, as the representative of "*the* artist," receiving the bulk of it. Thus, she argues, while Lennox's destruction of his portrait seems adequately justified, its real cause is Lennox's dislike of "brutality." Such "brutality" to Baxter is "truth" or "reality," but Lennox is unable to face it, and so destroys it. Because Lennox accepts Marian, but destroys the portrait, Martineau views the conclusion as failing to bring together the two main conflicts in an appropriate "dramatic resolution." Part of the failure, in Martineau's view, stems from the fact that as types of the "artist" and "hollow woman," both Baxter and Marian are "flat figures." Like Kraft, Martineau points to questions the tale leaves unanswered: how the loss of his work will affect Baxter, and how long the relief Lennox experiences in destroying the portrait will last (16–19).

Lennox's inability to face the truth is also emphasized by Sicker. In his analysis, the story presents, through its two heroes, the two responses possible to the destruction of a "love-image." Both Baxter and Lennox are initially taken in by the outward image of Marian, which Baxter presents in his first portrait in highly idealized form. Baxter comes to see her lightness, which he represents in the second portrait. When this portrait teaches Lennox the truth as well, Sicker writes, there is no possible way of repairing the damage. While painting the portrait freed Baxter from his love, Lennox's destruction of the painting has no such salutary effect, for it is a denial of his own recognition and so of his own self. Lennox's marriage, in Sicker's view, is simply part of the "self-induced hallucination" his life becomes in his attempt to avoid the truth (27–30).

In seeking to explain the tale's "unsympathetic" air, William supposed that his brother was reacting to the "sloppy and gushing" literature current in the *Atlantic* (36). Similarly, LeClair argues that James was searching to produce in his writing what Baxter produces in his portraits, an objective execution revealing an "inner truth" (398–99). Yet, as Baxter paints his portrait, the narrator tells us he assumed Lennox already recognized his wife's shallowness: he "knew nothing of the serious nature of the poor man's passion, nor of the extent to which his happiness was bound up in what the painter would have called his delusion" (CT 1, 286). Such ignorance seems to show an inadequate understanding of human nature. Throughout, as the tale juggles its terms of "real," "brutal," and "actual" noted by Martineau, James not only fails to make his female's fickleness sufficiently "real," he also makes his artist's truth a tad too "brutal." In James's early tales, Bayley writes, the author, reader, and characters are all almost on a level so that—as Howells said—they are "like a nice informal little social gathering" (61). The author here provides much entertainment and food for thought but, perhaps feeling the lack of the necessary confidence as host, is occasionally pushy toward his guests.

Works Cited

Primary Works
James, Henry. 1868. "The Story of a Masterpiece." *Galaxy* 5 (January–February): 5–21, 133–43.

Secondary Works
Anon. 1868. "The Magazines for February." *Nation* 6 (30 January): 94.

Bayley, John. 1988. *The Short Story: Henry James to Elizabeth Bowen*. Brighton: Harvester.

Beebe, Maurice L. 1964. *Ivory Towers and Sacred Founts: The Artist as Hero*. New York: New York University Press.

Brodhead, Richard H. 1986. *The School of Hawthorne*. New York: Oxford University Press.

Buitenhuis, Peter. 1970. *The Grasping Imagination: The American Writings of Henry James*. Toronto: University of Toronto Press.

Dietrichson, Jan W. 1969. *The Image of Money in the American Novel of the Gilded Age*. Oslo: Universitetsforlaget; New York: Humanities.

Fish, Charles K. 1965. "Indirection, Irony, and the Two Endings of James's 'The Story of a Masterpiece.'" *Modern Philology* 62: 241–43.

James, William. 1992. *The Correspondence of William James*. Vol. 1: *William and Henry: 1861–1884*. Ed. Ignas K. Skrupskelis and Elizabeth M. Berkeley. Charlottesville: University Press of Virginia.

Jeffares, Bo. 1979. *The Artist in Nineteenth Century English Fiction*. Atlantic Highlands, NJ: Humanities.

Jones, Granville H. 1975. *Henry James's Psychology of Experience: Innocence, Responsibility, and Renunciation in the Fiction of Henry James*. The Hague: Mouton.

Kelley, Cornelia Pulsifer. [1930] 1965. *The Early Development of Henry James*. Urbana: University of Illinois Press.

Kenton, Edna, ed. 1950. *Eight Uncollected Tales of Henry James*. New Brunswick, NJ: Rutgers University Press.

Kraft, James. 1969. *The Early Tales of Henry James*. Carbondale: Southern Illinois University Press.

LeClair, Robert Charles. 1955. *Young Henry James, 1843–1870*. New York: Bookman.

Levy, Leo B. 1957. *Versions of Melodrama: A Study of the Fiction and Drama of Henry James, 1865–1897*. Berkeley: University of California Press.

Long, Robert Emmet. 1979. *The Great Succession: Henry James and the Legacy of Hawthorne*. Pittsburgh: University of Pittsburgh Press.

McElderry, Bruce R., Jr. 1949. "The Uncollected Stories of Henry James." *American Literature* 21 (November): 279–91.

Martineau, Barbara. 1972. "Portraits Are Murdered in the Short Fiction of Henry James." *Journal of Narrative Technique* 2: 16–25.

Putt, S. Gorley. 1966. *Henry James: A Reader's Guide*. Ithaca, NY: Cornell University Press.

Segal, Ora. 1969. *The Lucid Reflector: The Observer in Henry James' Fiction*. New Haven: Yale University Press.

Sicker, Philip. 1980. *Love and the Quest for Identity in the Fiction of Henry James*. Princeton: Princeton University Press.

Thorp, Willard, ed. 1962. *The Madonna of the Future and Other Early Tales*. New York: New American Library.

Tintner, Adeline R. 1989. *The Pop World of Henry James: From Fairy Tales to Science Fiction*. Ann Arbor: UMI Research Press.

———. 1987. *The Book World of Henry James*. Ann Arbor: UMI Research Press.

Vaid, Krishna B. 1964. *Technique in the Tales of Henry James*. Cambridge, MA: Harvard University Press.

Veeder, William. 1975. *Henry James: Lessons of the Master: Popular Fiction and Personal Style in the Nineteenth Century*. Chicago: University of Chicago Press.

Voss, Arthur. 1973. *The American Short Story: A Critical Survey*. Norman: University of Oklahoma Press.

Wagenknecht, Edward. 1984. *The Tales of Henry James*. New York: Frederick Ungar.

Winner, Viola Hopkins. 1970. *Henry James and the Visual Arts*. Charlottesville: University Press of Virginia.

Wright, Walter F. 1962. *The Madness of Art: A Study of Henry James*. Lincoln: University of Nebraska Press.

Zablotny, Elaine. 1979. "Henry James and the Demonic Vampire and Madonna." *Psychocultural Review* 3 (Summer–Fall): 203–24.

The Story of a Year

Publication History

"The Story of a Year" was the first signed story James published and the first of his many tales to appear in the *Atlantic Monthly*, taking its place there in the March 1865 issue. Never reprinted by James, it next appeared in Matthiessen's 1947 collection, *The American Novels and Stories of Henry James*.

Circumstances of Composition, Sources, and Influences

In March 1864 James wrote his friend Thomas Sergeant Perry of the as yet untitled tale, "I have given it my best pains: bothered over it too much. On the whole, it is a failure, I think, tho' nobody will know this, perhaps, but myself. Do not expect anything: it is a simple story, simply told"—the last, perhaps in comparison to the previous "A Tragedy of Error." He told Perry he would have the *Atlantic* send their reply to him, James not feeling up to the "pressure of avowed authorship" again for a while, and cautioned him not to mention the story to William (*Letters* 1, 50; *Life* 1, 219). In acknowledging news of its acceptance from Perry, James agreed with him that the welcome news was "'not unmingled with misfortune.' But I suppose I ought to be thankful for so much and not grumble that it is so little." Edel speculates the misfortune may have been a request for rewriting or the offer of a smaller payment than James had expected (*Life* 2, 219). Habegger interprets the phrase as an allusion to the tale's having been held up for publication, the *Atlantic* wanting a shorter work. James, he argues, accordingly revised the tale in November (171–72).

James's father, however, wrote William that the tale was "considered good" (Matthiessen *Family* 315). His terseness might have been a reflection of the painful memories for the James family embedded in the tale. Despite Matthiessen's caution against reading "any deep personal significance" into the tale, there is certainly some in it (*American* vii). Edel places the tale in 1863, the year in which one of James's cousins had been killed in battle and his brother Wilky had been brought home gravely wounded (*Life* 2, 220). James's description of the wounded Ford—"Death is not thinner, paler, stiller"—may well have reminded the family of Wilky's state upon his return. Buitenhuis comments on the resemblance to William's sketch of Wilky, which James reproduced in his *Notes of a Son and Brother* (18; also *Life* 2, 186–87).

The tale contains, as Kenton observes, a preponderance of family names: Robertson, Robert, James, Elizabeth, and John. Kenton detects additional family references in the allusion to Elizabeth's reading of Jane Porter's *Scottish Chiefs* and to Robert Bruce as her own "Scottish chief," noting that James's ancestory was part Scottish on his mother's side (11). Edel also draws attention to the Scottish motifs and their family associations, and notes as well the emphasis in *Scottish Chiefs* on sectional strife, appropriate for a tale of civil war (*Life* 2, 220; CT 1, 17).

Rosenzweig sees James dealing with his passive status through Ford by drawing attention to the passage in his autobiography where James, still suffering from his recent "obscure hurt," went "measuring wounds against wounds" on an 1861 visit to a camp of wounded soldiers. Maintaining that James emphasizes love not war as the cause of Ford's hurt, Rosenzweig argues that Ford's death represents James's own "passional death," which James "materialize[d]" in 1875 by moving to Europe. He adds that the "possessive mother," Elizabeth's status as a ward or "cousin," and Bruce's personality most likely had autobiographical roots also, although he does not have the information necessary to establish them. Ford's father, he speculates, may be absent from the tale, because James's own relationship with his father, with whom he identified on the grounds of their shared injuries, was "too sacred" to include (95, 98–99). Beebe disagrees with Rosenzweig's reading, stating that Ford does not represent James and does not doubt himself or Elizabeth. Nor, Beebe adds, is he the center of the tale. Elizabeth is, and her sense of "relief" at being absolved of responsibility may, in Beebe's view, speak for James (533–34; also LeClair 379). Buitenhuis points particularly to Lizzie's dream as a possible reflection of James's guilt about his failure to participate in the war himself (19).

Habegger, on the other hand, rejects such interpretations. He sees James beginning by wanting to be "just *literary*," as he later declared of himself, and to leave behind all autobiographical turmoil. He points to two specific contemporary works—Rebecca Harding Davis's "A Story of To-day" and Anne Moncure Crane's *Emily Chester*, which James had reviewed in January 1865—as spurring him to write his tale to counter the approval of the sympathy accorded the wavering affections of their heroines by showing their disastrous results on the hero thus abandoned (170–72). Habegger points to another debt in the tale's "jabbing, spasmodic" style, typical of such contemporary women writers as Elizabeth Stoddard (94). Other debts noted to popular literature include Tintner's suggestion of James's dependence on Alcott's *Hospital Sketches* for the war atmosphere, and her location of a flirtatious Mr. Bruce in the popular novel *The Lamplighter* (1989, 206, 213–14).

James, according to Kenton, makes it clear in his opening paragraph that he means to take on the contemporary Civil War literature (11). But some critics, including Matthiessen, have remarked little superiority to the work of what Matthiessen calls the "literary ladies" of the time (*American* vii). Kelley notes, for example, that James ends up doing what he had criticized Seemuller for in *Emily Chester*, going around a moral problem—in each story a love triangle—through the death of one of the characters, instead of solving it (36).

Long judges the tale Hawthornesque, noting particular parallels with the suppressed *Fanshawe*: the detachment of the hero, the light and dark imagery, the psychological probing of Lizzie by Ford and his mother, whom James compares to "the chilly spectator on the dark side of the [window] pane" (15–16). Fox links the tale with Hawthorne differently, seeing the opening image of Lizzie like "the damsel in the fairy-tale . . . empowered to utter diamonds and pearls" but told to "hold her tongue," allying her with "Poe's Fays and Hawthorne's human angels" as a heroine of romance rather than reality (8). Tintner identifies the allusion as referring to Perrault's "The Fairies" (1989, 6; also Stone 137).

Beach finds James attempting a George Eliot seriousness in treating the psychology of a basically simple woman, but failing in his aim to create a new Maggie Tulliver or Hetty Sorrel (173). Buitenhuis likens the heroine to the destructive Venus of Mérimée (18). The ending, with the importunate Mr. Bruce, Kelley also judges French (35). Matthiessen sees James seeking to carry out his advice to Harriet Prescott Spofford, to follow Balzac, treating "objects as they are," but only presenting things when "they bear upon the action"—although he finds the setting here rendered only in "the faintest crayon strokes" (*American* vii–viii). Edel also associates the tale with Balzac, seeing the decision to stay with the home front, the narrator's "taste" for "the reverse of the picture," echoing Balzac's preface to the *Comédie Humaine* (CT 1, 18).

Martin discovers resemblances to *Hamlet*, particularly its play-within-the-play of "The Mousetrap," with the protesting but unfaithful Lizzie resembling the Player Queen and the solicitous soldier Ford the King. By extension they represent Hamlet's mother and dead father, while the civilian Bruce stands in for a "not quite villainous" Claudius.

Leaving for war, Ford says he will think of Lizzie as "Catholics keep little pictures of their adored Lady in their prayer books" (CT 1, 54). Later, his view of her metamorphoses to become "not unlike an old wounded Greek," who crawls inside a temple to die "in idle admiration of sculptured Artemis" (CT 1, 97). Edel notes how the change allows Lizzie to be "the masculine-active yet all-mothering" divinity, but not human (*Life* 2, 221). Both views, Sicker argues, transform Lizzie into a static art image, while Long finds the chaste Artemis a more appropriate lover for Ford than Lizzie (Sicker 32–33; Long 15). Tintner traces the Greek references to James's early experiences in the Galerie d'Apollon (1986, 21–22).

In the use of war imagery, Buitenhuis finds the tale "strangely prophetic" of *The Red Badge of Courage* (19; also Wagenknecht 204). The story's triangle of soldier, sweetheart, and disapproving mother also appears in another late Civil War tale, Howells's 1905 "Editha."

Relation to Other Works

"The Story of a Year" is the first of three early stories set around the Civil War. Thorp finds James, due to his lack of military experience, confining himself here, as he will later in "A Most Extraordinary Case," with the war's "effects" (x). At the same time in the two tales and such other early works as *Watch and Ward*, he began, Quentin Anderson argues, his forays into the "deeper psychology" of "inward conflict" that he would later treat through the symbolic conflicts of the international theme (47). Segal places the heroes of both tales at the start of a Jamesian pattern of high-minded renunciation, while Edel emphasizes their surrender to death (Segal 222 n.8; *Life* 1, 221; also Long 15; Jones 60). Samuels argues that Mason's renunciation is even more extreme than Ford's, as he not only gives up the girl but gives her his fortune as well (72). Fogel sees Ford's forgiveness of Lizzie's defection as anticipating the later generosity of Milly Theale, who like Mason gives away a fortune (142). The ceded fortune provides a link with Ralph Touchett, and Habegger classes all three men into a "sickly and specifically male type" who dies when the woman he loves comes to love someone else (167–68, 171–73). The death of the hero Buitenhuis sees as James's subject still in *The Bostonians* (147). Poirier stays with the early work to offer Ford, with Locksley of "The Landscape Painter" and Lawrence of *Watch and Ward*, as examples of what Dupee called James's "powerless-feeling young men" (15–16).

Rosenzweig sees the death of Ford—identified, as he argues it is, with James's own "passional death"—as giving rise to the "ghost" in his later tales, including "Sir Edmund Orme," "Owen Wingrave," and "The Jolly Corner" (99–101). Vaid considers Rosenzweig's theory about the connections with "The Jolly Corner" "far-fetched" (233), while Beebe objects to his connection with "Sir Edmund Orme" (534).

In Edel's reading, the three main characters of mother, ward, and son were to recur in such works as *Roderick Hudson* and *The Portrait of a Lady* (*Life* 1, 220–21). Buitenhuis, for reasons he does not explain, sees Lizzie like Gertrude Wentworth of *The Europeans* as a foretype of Olive Chancellor (142). Habegger links Lizzie with Miss Birdseye of *The Bostonians* as contemptuously portrayed "birdbrained" women (210). Kraft calls her the first of the shallow Daisy Miller heroines (22). LeClair, on the other hand, sees hints of the sympathy James would give to Maggie or Maisie in his treatment of Lizzie (379). (See particularly "Owen Wingrave.")

Interpretation and Criticism

In his letter to Perry, James played with the various possible terms for the work, starting by calling it a "modern novel" and asking, "Why use that vile word novelette. It reminds me of chemisette. Why not say *historiette* outright?" It is, in Edel's terminology a "long short story" (*Life* 1, 219–20). Both Kelley and Matthiessen observe that James began his first signed tale with enough material for a novel. James, according to Kelley, was following the receipt for proper fiction that he had developed in his reviews, seeking to include all the necessary ingredients. Both Matthiessen and Kelley also argue, however, that all that material was simply too much for a short story, and that most of it remains undeveloped (*American* viii; Kelley 34; also Buitenhuis 20).

James begins his tale with the narrator stating, "My story begins as a great many stories have begun within the last three years, and indeed as a great many have ended; for, when the hero is despatched does not the romance come to a stop?" (CT 1, 49). Buitenhuis sees the remark as James's signal to the reader of his determination to break with sentimental expectations and an ironic indication of the conclusion (17). At the start of the tale's second section, the narrator continues to break expectations, avowing his preference for "unwritten history" or "the reverse of the picture" over public events (CT 1, 62). Kenton observes that while the preference of "ideas" over "things" will become James's standard approach, it is "nonetheless amazing" to watch the process of him "throwing away 'things,' really the novelist's stock in trade" (10; also Kraft 5). LeClair sees James's declarations here partly as a cover for his inadequate description and partly as an indication of his true interest, although he finds the character analysis of Lizzie an inadequate substitute for the plot's thinness (378). Buitenhuis, however, considers James's concentration on character and consciousness the signal strength of the tale (18). The focus on character goes against what Kelley sees as the implication in the title of a focus on action. Further, in the treatment of character, Kelley argues, James concentrates more on the phrasing of his characterizations than their depth (34–36).

The style itself Kelley judges too "flowery" to be effective, as has Kraft (Kelley 36; Kraft 22). The writing is generally held to be awkward at times, and Edel acknowledges its "stilted moments and quaint formal expression" (*Life* 1, 220; also Matthiessen *American*, viii). Barzun points instead to the terse last two paragraphs with their "propensity toward violence" made manifest in speech, and questions how many readers would be likely to identify them as James's, although he asserts that they are typical of his manner (518).

The style is marked by the voice of the narrator, and Vaid states that James's inadequate control over the tale is especially notable in the "garrulous bonhomie" of the omniscient narrator, who even calls attention to his own inabilities (132–33). Similarly, Wagenknecht finds the story told "loosely and somewhat naively" (204). Many of the narrator's speeches could easily be deleted, according to Thorp, producing a more traditional omniscient narration (xv). In Buitenhuis's view, however, the ungainly Victorian omniscience is partly offset by James's use of dialogue until it is mostly replaced by his use of Lizzie's consciousness for point of view (20).

One particularly purple pasage has drawn the most attention, a description of a sunset Ford and Lizzie watch before he goes to war: "There were columns charging and columns flying and standards floating,—tatters of the reflected purple; and great captains on colossal horses, and a rolling canopy of cannon smoke and fire and blood" (CT 1, 51). Kenton notes how at the time of "A Passionate Pilgrim" James was still, he recalled in his autobiography, fond of "more or less associational cloud-scenery to promote the atmosphere of literary composition," and finds the same technique here, which she takes as an "interesting hint" of James's road to style (11). Matthiessen attributes to the tale the start of James's "gift for conveying his characters' thoughts in terms of visual images," but judges this particular passage the "kind of set-piece of moralizing that he would not have allowed himself later" (*American* viii). Fox looks backward to note how it fits into the "transcendental tradition" of showing nature in "correspondence" with mankind (7–8). In Fish's view the description serves to anticipate "the private and public calamity of civil war" (211). Kelley considers the passage "amateurish and awkward" (36). Buitenhuis, however, deems it useful, ascribing the unusual use of allegory to James's need to amplify his military tale without military knowledge (19). Even so, Geismar complains that James lacked sufficient knowledge of either the military or passion for his subject (14).

Critics have also located broader symbolism within the tale. Buitenhuis observes how James uses the symbolism of the yearly cycle: Ford woos Lizzie in the spring and dies at the end of the winter, while Lizzie moves on to Bruce (20). Appropriately, Long points to the description of Bruce—"a tall figure beneath the budding trees of the garden"—as linking him with "germination and the natural world" (15). Fogel reads the story in terms of opposites—the two suitors who contend for Lizzie, as James puts it, "like opposing knights, (the black and the white)"—an image based, according to Gale, on a "faulty" knowledge of chess (217). In a manner prefigured by the view of the "opposing squadrons" of clouds yielding their "shabby compromise," Lizzie herself, in Fogel's view, follows a spiral pattern typical of James's late works as she moves from the light of her love for Ford through the darkness of her infidelity to a new love for Bruce. Fogel contends, however, that the power of the pattern is undercut by the narrator's contemptuous insistence on Lizzie's shallowness (141). Similarly, Leyburn remarks on the unhelpful way James follows Lizzie's dream of the corpse with a passage poking fun at his heroine, and argues that James had not yet learned how to combine the tragic and comic successfully (4–5). Rosenzweig praises the dream as "one of the highlights of the tale" showing James's "early mastery of certain psychological processes" not yet formalized, reading its "clear images" as an indication that Ford's death is brought about by Lizzie's "faithlessness," his mother's opposition, and his own "self-doubt" (98–99).

That Lizzie is faithless the story makes clear. Indeed, both LeClair and Habegger comment on the explicitness with which James indicts his heroine (LeClair 377; Habegger 168). While McElderry sees James as proceeding "without the least vindictiveness," Putt pictures the reader's sympathies as "forcibly wrenched" by James's editorial comments, including references to Lizzie as a "little fool" (McElderry 1956, 26, 28; Putt 35). Jefferson notes her promise early on in the typically American "intellectually ambitious" talk between her and Ford, showing that she has at least enough intellectual capacity to interpret the "shabby compromise" of the clouds (72). But when Ford is wounded, and his mother takes command, the narrator writes of Lizzie: "And now it was a relief to have responsibility denied her. Like most weak persons, she was glad to step out of the current of life, now that it had begun to quicken into action. Even to the sensitive spirit there is a certain meditative rapture in standing on the quiet shore (beside the ruminating cattle), and watching the hurrying, eddying flood, which makes up for the loss of dignity" (CT 1, 76–77). Indeed, Lizzie seems at times so under the command of others, that she does not appear to be accountable for her behavior. As Kelley points out, James takes all decisions out of Lizzie's hands and gives them to Ford or his mother or Mr. Bruce (35). Similarly, McCarthy finds the emphasis on her temptations and her lack of resources undermining whatever moral lesson her experience might provide (54). Because of Lizzie's powerlessness, Jones argues, James does not blame her for her actions (61).

There is some disagreement over whether Lizzie is genuinely bad or simply shallow. Buitenhuis judges her name's invocation of the crow "gruesomely apt," as is seen in the dream of the unburied corpse (19). Matthiessen, too, sees James tackling the power of evil in her character, although he acknowledges the complexity of her attitude, which he judges inadequately portrayed (*American* viii). Kraft, however, finds James—with "unusually certain insight" for a young author—giving a vivid picture of the destructively shallow Lizzie (23). In Habegger's reading, James blames her for refusing to fulfill her traditional duty to a traditionally-minded man (170–71). Most critics, however, such as LeClair and Wagenknecht, find Lizzie "well-meaning" if shallow—neither clever enough to plot, nor strong enough to be faithful (LeClair 377; Wagnknecht 204). McElderry argues that Lizzie receives with the rest of the characters James's "restrained, judicial sympathy," arguing that she is shallow but capable of being hurt by her awareness of her shallowness (1949, 281–82). Bayley proposes an even greater authorial sympathy, seeing James on Lizzie's side, "sympathetically aware of the difficulty, for the girl, of keeping up the *idea* of their love" and aware, too, of the meddling influence of the mother, and Lizzie's resentment of her. Lizzie's grief he sees as real, even as it requires her to "act the part" of grief and even though it will naturally lose out to "unemotional necessities" such as marriage (56–57).

LeClair locates the true indication of James's promise in treating the "interplay of human relationship" not between Ford and Lizzie, but between Lizzie and his mother (378). Edel cites James's describing the mother biting a thread at the news of her son's engagement as if "executing a human vengeance" (*Life* 1, 221). At times it seems that that is what she is doing. As Edel also points out, Ford gives his mother an advantage by telling her of the engagement, while not letting Lizzie know she has been told (*Life* 1, 221). In Wilson's retelling of the tale, he emphasizes the role of the mother in bringing about the dissolution of Lizzie and Ford's relationship (659–60). As Buitenhuis remarks, the mother is "dominant, wise" but also "slightly sinister" (18). It seems quite possible that the outcome would have been different, if Lizzie had had the mother's support, rather than her opposition.

Kraft argues that James's focus is blurred by his fascination with Lizzie's character. In his reading, James began with a focus on Ford, and his parallel destruction by men on the battle field and women on the home front, only to lose his "sociological" thread in favor of the "psychological" with the concentration on Lizzie (23). Jones, on the other hand, sees the tale as Lizzie's, but finds her story "paled by the glow of Jack Ford's renunciation" (61). Banta locates the story's central theme in Ford's question, "What rights has a dead man?" The answer is "none" unless the living care to grant them (180 n.23). In his relinquishing of his rights, Ford strikes such critics as Beebe and LeClair as "realistic," a refusal to bow to "tawdry sentiment" after James's own heart (Beebe 533–34; LeClair 378). Similarly, McElderry argues that Ford simply lives up to his earlier disavowal of false sentiment about the dead in setting Lizzie free out of "genuinely unselfish concern" (1949, 281–82). But other critics question Ford's willingness to renounce. His reasons for renouncing so quickly, Dupee charges, are as a given, rather than justified by any cause (50). Looking at Ford's observation that a wounded soldier looks more like a woman than a man, Rosenzweig argues for "feminine elements" in Ford's personality. In his view, Ford dies of psychic not physical wounds, "a lover forsaken by his psychological fate." His death, Rosenzweig argues, serves as the means whereby James can show the personal significance of war (97–99, 102–3). Kraft agrees with Kelley, however, that Ford's death is "an evasion, not a solution" (22).

The man who triumphs in his stead, Mr. Bruce, although LeClair finds him "admirable and earnest," is not your usual Jamesian hero (377). Dietrichson emphasizes his identity as a wealthy businessman, and Martin speculates that Bruce's "immense" business may even be some kind of profiteering (Dietrichson 68; Martin 137).

Evaluating the tale and its history, McElderry praises both the *Atlantic* for having published such an unsentimental tale during the war, and Matthiessen for having "exhumed" the tale from the *Atlantic* in 1947 (1965, 26, 28; 1949, 281). Kelley also contrasts the tale to the usual sentimental fiction of the *Atlantic*, finding it superior to it, if inferior to later James (37). Matthiessen observes, however, that the "triangle against the background of the war is certainly conventional enough" (*American* vii). In contrast, Edel praises both the originality of its conception and its execution (*Life* 1, 220). McElderry, too, finds the real Jamesian "intelligence" in operation here, with the story's "sense of a situation" and "felt life" a significant accomplishment for a young author (1965, 26, 28; 1949, 281). Comparing the tale with James's earlier work, his critical reviews, LeClair emphasizes the "difference between precept and practice" demonstrated by the divergences between the astute reviews and the sometimes inept early tales, which were not yet able to exemplify their dicta (377–78). Matthiessen and Vaid also stress how much James had yet to learn, Vaid dismissing the tale as of "historical interest only"

(133). Matthiessen, while affirming that James "was to develop very slowly" also writes, " . . . it is always of interest to observe where a great writer started" (vii–viii). James's start here displays much of his true self, if not his accomplished manner. Its chief strength, Buitenhuis argues, in addition to its portrait of Lizzie, is "its grim sense of loss and waste," a sense that James would evoke many times over the course of his career (20).

Works Cited

Primary Works

James, Henry. "The Story of a Year." 1865. *Atlantic Monthly* 15 (March): 257–81.

Secondary Works

Anderson, Quentin. 1957. *The American Henry James*. New Brunswick, NJ: Rutgers University Press.

Banta, Martha. 1964. "Henry James and 'The Others.'" *New England Quarterly* 37 (June): 171–84.

Barzun, Jacques. 1943. "James the Melodramatist." *Kenyon Review* 5 (August): 508–21. Also reprinted in *The Question of Henry James*, ed. F. W. Dupee, 254–66. New York: Henry Holt, 1945.

Bayley, John. 1988. *The Short Story: Henry James to Elizabeth Bowen*. Brighton: Harvester.

Beach, Joseph Warren. [1918] 1954. *The Method of Henry James*. Philadelphia: Albert Saifer.

Beebe, Maurice L. 1954. "The Turned Back of Henry James." *South Atlantic Quarterly* 53 (October): 521–39.

Buitenhuis, Peter. 1970. *The Grasping Imagination: The American Writings of Henry James*. Toronto: University of Toronto Press.

Dietrichson, Jan W. 1969. *The Image of Money in the American Novel of the Gilded Age*. Oslo: Universitetsforlaget; New York: Humanities.

Dupee, F. W. [1951] 1956. *Henry James*. Garden City, NY: Doubleday Anchor.

Fish, Charles. 1965. "Description in Henry James's 'A Light Man.'" *English Language Notes* 2:211.

Fogel, Daniel Mark. 1981. *Henry James and the Structure of the Romantic Imagination*. Baton Rouge: Louisiana State University Press.

Fox, Hugh. 1968. *Henry James, A Critical Introduction*. Conesville, IA: John Westburg.

Gale, Robert L. [1954] 1964. *The Caught Image: Figurative Language in the Fiction of Henry James*. Chapel Hill: University of North Carolina Press.

Geismar, Maxwell. 1963. *Henry James and the Jacobites*. Boston: Houghton Mifflin.

Habegger, Alfred. 1989. *Henry James and the "Woman Business."* Cambridge: Cambridge University Press.

Harris, Wendell V. 1979. *British Short Fiction in the Nineteenth Century: A Literary and Bibliographic Guide*. Detroit: Wayne State University Press.

Jefferson, D. W. 1964. *Henry James and the Modern Reader*. New York: St. Martin's.

Jones, Granville H. 1975. *Henry James's Psychology of Experience: Innocence, Responsibility, and Renunciation in the Fiction of Henry James*. The Hague: Mouton.

Kelley, Cornelia Pulsifer. [1930] 1965. *The Early Development of Henry James*. Urbana: University of Illinois Press.

Kenton, Edna, ed. 1950. *Eight Uncollected Tales of Henry James*. New Brunswick, NJ: Rutgers University Press.

Kraft, James. 1969. *The Early Tales of Henry James*. Carbondale: Southern Illinois University Press.

LeClair, Robert Charles. 1955. *Young Henry James, 1843–1870*. New York: Bookman.

Leyburn, Ellen Douglass. 1968. *Strange Alloy: The Relation of Comedy to Tragedy in the Fiction of Henry James*. Chapel Hill: University of North Carolina Press.

Long, Robert Emmet. 1979. *The Great Succession: Henry James and the Legacy of Hawthorne*. Pittsburgh: University of Pittsburgh Press.

McCarthy, Harold T. 1958. *Henry James: The Creative Process*. New York: Thomas Yoseloff.

McElderry, Bruce R., Jr. 1965. *Henry James*. New York: Twayne.

———. 1949. "The Uncollected Stories of Henry James." *American Literature* 21 (November): 279–91.

Martin, W. R. 1989. "*Hamlet* and Henry James's First Fiction." *American Notes and Queries*, no. 4 (October 2): 137–38.

Matthiessen F. O. 1947. *The James Family: Including Selections from the Writings of Henry James, Sr., William, Henry, and Alice James*. New York: Knopf.

———, ed. 1947. *The American Novels and Stories of Henry James*. New York: Knopf.

Poirier, Richard. 1967. *The Comic Sense of Henry James*. New York: Oxford University Press.

Putt, S. Gorley. 1966. *Henry James: A Reader's Guide*. Ithaca, NY: Cornell University Press.

Rosenzweig, Saul. 1957. "The Ghost of Henry James: A Study in Thematic Apperception." In *Art and Psychoanalysis*. Ed. William Phillips, 89–111. New York: Criterion. Reprinted from *Character and Personality* 12 (December 1943): 79–100. Also reprinted in *Partisan Review* 11 (Fall 1944): 435–55.

Samuels, Charles Thomas. 1971. *The Ambiguity of Henry James*. Urbana: University of Illinois Press.

Segal, Ora. 1969. *The Lucid Reflector: The Observer in Henry James' Fiction*. New Haven: Yale University Press.

Sicker, Philip. 1980. *Love and the Quest for Identity in the Fiction of Henry James*. Princeton: Princeton University Press.

Stone, Edward. 1964. *The Battle and the Books: Some Aspects of Henry James*. Athens: Ohio University Press.

Thorp, Willard, ed. 1962. *The Madonna of the Future and Other Early Tales*. New York: New American Library.

Tintner, Adeline R. 1989. *The Pop World of Henry James: From Fairy Tales to Science Fiction*. Ann Arbor: UMI Research Press.

———. 1986. *The Museum World of Henry James*. Ann Arbor: UMI Research Press.

Vaid, Krishna B. 1964. *Technique in the Tales of Henry James*. Cambridge, MA: Harvard University Press.

Wagenknecht, Edward. 1984. *The Tales of Henry James*. New York: Frederick Ungar.

Wilson, Edmund. [1962] 1987. *Patriotic Gore: Studies in the Literature of the American Civil War*. London: Hogarth.

The Sweetheart of M. Briseux

Publication History

James at first intended "The Sweetheart of M. Briseux" to appear in *Wood's Household Magazine*, edited by Mary Abigail Dodge. The magazine, however, "exploded," so James was spared the "degrading connection" and requested that his father send the story on to the *Galaxy*, where it appeared in June 1873. He forebore sending it to the *Atlantic* because, he wrote Howells, "it hinges on a picture," as did the recent "The Madonna of the Future" (W. James 180–82; *Letters* 1: 334). Never reprinted by James, it next surfaced in Mordell's 1919 collection, *Travelling Companions*. One of four early tales issued in the Little Blue Books series out of Girard, Kansas, in 1931, it was the only one to appear under its original title.

Circumstances of Composition, Sources, and Influences

Tintner reads the characterization of the heroine here following Walter Pater's 1869 interpretation of the Mona Lisa, while Boren finds it challenging Pater's reading (Tinter 1987, 105–6; Boren 100). Tinter also finds James recreating the battle between the Neoclassicists led by Ingres, the model for Staines's teacher Martinet, and the Romantic colorists led by Delacroix, whose *Apollo Overcoming the Python* provides some of the imagery. She nominates the Romantic painter Henri Regnault as the main source for Briseux, and also calls attention to the allusion to the Romantic poet Shelley (1986, 9–10, 49–51). Winner observes that Staines's taste for Guido Reni and Caravaggio, noted by Tintner, is in James generally a bad sign (Tintner 1986, 122, 60; Winner 80). Boren argues that the heroine poses herself like Madame de Staël's portrait in a yellow shawl (98).

Balzac's "Le Chef d'Oeuvre Inconnu" provides another source. Kelley notes that in both the issue of one painter's fiancée sitting for a portrait to another breaks an engagement (153). Adams adds that the scene in which Briseux grabs the ineffectual Staines's brush also has its model in the Balzac story (464).

Quentin Anderson finds the relation between artist and lady drawing on James's sense of his relationship to Minny Temple, demonstrated more fully in "Travelling Companions" (141).

Relation to Other Works

Most comparisons lie among the tales of other artists. Kelley links the story with "The Madonna of the Future," as does Edel, who sees the artist here as having the necessary hardness Theobald lacks (Kelley 153; Edel CT 3, 7). Kraft adds "The Story of a Masterpiece," observing that in all three a painting reveals hidden truths (78). Thorp finds what he calls "The Secret of M. Briseux" anticipating *The Aspern Papers* (xii). Winner sees James representing respectability and creativity as antithetical here as in *Roderick Hudson*, "Mora Montravers," and "The Real Thing" (108; also Beebe 525; Jones 154). Putt and Tintner discern faint foreshadowings of Roderick Hudson in Briseux; Tintner proposes Angela of *Confidence* as another Mona Lisa figure (Tintner 1986 10; 1987, 145). Putt sees Gilbert Osmond in Staines; Norrman adds that in early James the woman is sensible enough to reject the Osmond figure (Putt 78). The "collusion between victim and victimiser" that Norrman sees in such later works as *The Golden Bowl* is here the more innocent attraction of opposites (176). As in "A New England Winter," the mother uses a young woman for the sake of her upper-class artiste son, although in this case she hopes for their marriage.

Interpretation and Criticism

William James wrote his brother that he read the tale "without the delight I have so often got from your things" (210). James, in reply, was sorry he didn't like the tale, which he himself had thought "sufficiently pleasing" (*Letters* 1, 394). While Tintner speculates that James later omitted it from the New York Edition because it did not adhere closely enough to its sources, the story is so clearly an imperfect apprentice work that there is little need to search for so idiosyncratic a reason (1986, 51). The technique is not strong. Vaid, Kraft, and Putt all criticize the narrative prologue for taking up too much of the tale (Vaid 13; Kraft 78; Putt 78).

While Putt finds Staines's mother the only lifelike character in the tale, the usual emphasis is on the two artists and the nameless woman they paint (78). Staines is aptly described by Wagenknecht as "all surface" (205). In Nathalia Wright's view he "denies the vitality of art" by copying rather than creating, while Anderson sees him attempting to make his fiancée a "dependent ornament" (Wright 223; Anderson 140–41). Even Tintner acknowledges that Staines is "silly" in considering he can copy the Mona Lisa (1981, 108). He is given one sympathetic moment, however, when he protests against his fiancée not for rejecting him but for judging him.

According to Nathalia Wright, the heroine is prepared in Italy by her broken engagement for a "larger" experience in her encounter with M. Briseux (223). While Kraft finds in her "a deeply sensitive nature," Tintner originally, perhaps in the interest of keeping to the Mona Lisa analogy, was extremely negative in her reading, stating that the woman "ruins her own life as well as that of her fiancé in order to achieve a kind of immortality" (Kraft 78; Tintner 1981, 105). Later she softened her view, remarking simply that like the Mona Lisa she is "enigmatic" and "accused" of "slyness" (1987, 145). Walter Wright's reference to the story's "selfish" lover is ambiguous, but certainly suits Staines better than the heroine (87, 126).

While Kelley wishes for more treatment of the artists and less of the woman, the story's significance is precisely in the woman's ability to speak for herself, to tell a tale of the other side of the easel (153). Boren points out that Briseux learned his art painting meat and approaches the portrait similarly, concentrating on the scarf rather than the model (99). He is, however, a genuine artist, unlike Staines. Briseux's name, as Tintner glosses it, indicates that he is a "stone-breaker," an "innovator" (1986, 50). He succeeds in breaking not only the mold of the old art but an old engagement, liberating both the artistic form represented in "The Lady with a Yellow Shawl" and a young woman who finds a newly independent life before her. While McElderry mistakenly speaks of the woman as marrying Briseux, Anderson focuses on the contrast between the legend that the painting is of the artist's sweetheart, a "subject woman," and the fact that it is of an independent woman, as illustrating James's constant theme of the disparity between what is seen and what is known, a distinction the true artist can appreciate (McElderry 34; Anderson 140–41). While the woman speaks of herself as descending into the "dusky limbo of unhonoured victims" in people's ignorance of her identity, Boren notes that James gives her the final victory, a victory to which Briseux in his superior perception perforce contributes. The frame narrator recognizes in the painting not simply Briseux's artistry, but her "passionate desire to escape the bondage of the yellow shawl," summing it up as the "picture of a mind, or at least of a mood" (100). In life, too, while Norrman finds her single state an "alternative type of sterility" (176), she seems far from pitiable, with ample friends and relations, far better off than she would be in the stifling pretense of a marriage to Staines. Jones who praises her choice, still sees it as a renunciation of life in the service of art, but there was little in the life she renounced she valued (154). Kelley sees the story as lacking passion (153), but the woman still looks out with an intense gaze from both the masterpiece the story describes and the apprenticework it is.

Works Cited

Primary Works

James, Henry. 1873. "The Sweetheart of M. Briseux." *Galaxy* 15 (June): 760–79.

———. 1919. "The Sweetheart of M. Briseux." *Travelling Companions*. Foreword by Albert Mordell. New York: Boni and Liveright.

———. 1931. "The Sweetheart of M. Briseux." Little Blue Book 1672. Girard, KS: Haldeman-Julius.

Secondary Works

Adams, Percy G. 1961. "Young Henry James and the Lesson of his Master Balzac." *Revue de Littérature Comparée* 35 (July–September): 458–67.

Anderson, Quentin. 1957. *The American Henry James*. New Brunswick, NJ: Rutgers University Press.

Beebe, Maurice L. 1954. "The Turned Back of Henry James." *South Atlantic Quarterly* 53 (October): 521–39.

Boren, Lynda S. 1987. "Undoing the *Mona Lisa*: Henry James's Quarrel with da Vinci and Pater." *Mosaic* 20 (Summer): 95–111.

James, William. 1992. *The Correspondence of William James*. Vol. 1: *William and Henry: 1861–1884*. Ed. Ignas K. Skrupskelis and Elizabeth M. Berkeley. Charlottesville: University Press of Virginia.

Jones, Granville H. 1975. *Henry James's Psychology of Experience: Innocence, Responsibility, and Renunciation in the Fiction of Henry James*. The Hague: Mouton.

Kelley, Cornelia Pulsifer. [1930] 1965. *The Early Development of Henry James.* Urbana: University of Illinois Press.

Kraft, James. 1969. *The Early Tales of Henry James.* Carbondale: Southern Illinois University Press.

McElderry, Bruce R., Jr. 1965. *Henry James.* New York: Twayne.

Norrman, Ralf. 1982. *The Insecure World of Henry James's Fiction: Intensity and Ambiguity.* New York: St. Martin's.

Putt, S. Gorley. 1966. *Henry James: A Reader's Guide.* Ithaca, NY: Cornell University Press.

Thorp, Willard, ed. 1962. *The Madonna of the Future and Other Early Tales.* New York: New American Library.

Tinter, Adeline R. 1987. *The Book World of Henry James.* Ann Arbor: UMI Research Press.

———. 1986. *The Museum World of Henry James.* Ann Arbor: UMI Research Press.

———. 1981. "Henry James's Mona Lisas." *Essays in Literature* 8: 105–8.

Vaid, Krishna B. 1964. *Technique in the Tales of Henry James.* Cambridge, MA: Harvard University Press.

Wagenknecht, Edward. 1984. *The Tales of Henry James.* New York: Frederick Ungar.

Winner, Viola Hopkins. 1970. *Henry James and the Visual Arts.* Charlottesville: University Press of Virginia.

Wright, Nathalia. 1965. *American Novelists in Italy, The Discoverers: Allston to James.* Philadelphia: University of Pennsylvania Press.

Wright, Walter. 1962. *The Madness of Art: A Study of Henry James.* Lincoln: University of Nebraska Press.

The Third Person

Publication History

"The Third Person" was originally written for the *Atlantic Monthly*, but James later wrote his agent, Pinker, that it would not suit the magazine, and, feeling it was too long to sell elsewhere, that he would reserve it for *The Soft Side* (Ferguson 293). Even in planning that collection with his American publishers, Macmillan, however, he was willing to sacrifice the tale if space made it necessary (*Correspondence* 194). There was sufficient space, however, and "The Third Person" duly appeared in 1900 in *The Soft Side*, its only publication in James's lifetime. It next appeared in Lubbock's edition of *The Novels and Stories of Henry James*.

Circumstances of Composition, Sources, and Influences

There is no clear notebook entry for the tale. Bishop argues that the tale represents the metamorphosis of an idea James worked out in notebook entries from 1894 to 1899 but seemingly never wrote up, called "The Publisher's Story," concerning a woman hack writer who attacks in print the work of a man she secretly loves, combined with his idea in May 1899 for "The Sketcher"—"some little drama, situation, complication, fantasy, to be worked into small Rye-figure of woman working away (on my doorstep and elsewhere)" (73–75). The connection, however, seems tenuous at best.

James wrote the tale while his brother and sister-in-law William and Alice were visiting him at Rye in December 1899. Edel speculates that the ailing William figures as the hanged ghost and Henry and Alice as the two women, or alternatively Henry or William as the outsider ghost following the triangles Edel sees in their childhood (*Life* 4, 327; *Life* 503).

The setting of Rye plays a large part in the tale. Edel contrasts the "extraordinary avoidance of picture" James complained of in Thackeray's novel of Rye and Winchelsea, *Denis Duval*, with James's careful painting of Rye's "huddled, red-roofed, historic" appearance, both in the tale and the nearly contemporaneous essay "Winchelsea, Rye and 'Denis Duval.'" The house of the two Frushes is James's Lamb House itself and their smuggling ancestor is glimpsed in the essay:

> a part of the small romance of Rye [is] that you may fondly fancy such
> scant opulence as rears its head to have had its roots in the malpractice
> of forefathers not too rude for much cunning—in nightly plots and
> snares and flurries, a hurrying, shuffling, hiding, that might at any time
> have put a noose about most necks. (Edel 1970, 630–32)

While Edel notes that *Denis Duval* contains two smugglers, one who is eventually hanged ([1949] 1963, 356), Briggs offers a less literary, less romantic
source for James's ghost in one Allan Grebell, who was stabbed to death by a
butcher (117).

Edward Stone finds James drawing on Hawthorne's "Custom House" preface to *The Scarlet Letter*. Set in the similarly decayed sea port of Salem, it presents Hawthorne as the "third person" in a conversation with his ancestors,
Colonel and Major Hawthorne, whose guilt he first offers to atone for, as Miss
Susan seeks to atone for Cuthbert's, only to discover that it is their disgust
that their descendent is "a writer of story-books!" that will serve as "sufficient
retribution" to free them. Stone finds James departing through Susan's smuggling from Hawthorne's model, because it imitates rather than offsets the
ancestor's action (213–19). Still, it is a book in each case that is the instrument of liberation.

Wagenknecht finds the Frush women slightly reminiscent of the women of
Gaskell's *Cranford* (205).

Relation to Other Works

Briggs notes that James also presented Lamb House, his "great good place,"
as Longdon's home in *The Awkward Age* (117), or so it is pictured in the New
York Edition.

Looking primarily at the living, Walter Wright finds Strether's pronounce-
ment to "Live all you can" animating this tale as well (86). Gage sees the two
women's competition over the ghost coming close to the *"ménage a trois"* in
"John Delavoy," where two people seek the identity of a third, or "Maud-
Evelyn" (49).

Looking primarily at the influence of the dead, Perosa compares the
haunted house to that in *The Sense of the Past* (135). While Edel senses a less
sinister relationship to the past, akin to that in "Flickerbridge" (CT 11, 9),
another association is with *The Turn of the Screw*. Wright uses the determination of the ghost here to finish his last act to support the governess's view
that Quint and Miss Jessel are attempting to finish some incomplete evil after
their deaths (181). Bishop offers a more extensive comparison with *The Turn
of the Screw*, demonstrating that—with significantly different forms of narration—both present a confidante, unread letters, and exorcisms, one through

a configuration of two spinsters and one ghost, the other with one ghost and two spinsters (60).

Interpretation and Criticism

Most critics have taken kindly to this tale, its "domesticated" ghost and sympathetic spinsters, and wax lyrical about its charm. Briggs, for example, praises its "mellow, gently humorous vein, reminiscent of a warm afternoon in late summer" (117). It is generally acknowledged as "the most harmless" and "the sunniest and most humorous" of the ghost tales (Edgar 159; Edel 1970, 630–32; also Putt 1966, 395). Wagenknecht observes also its "sly delicacy, deftness, and sophistication" (205).

In analyzing such perfection, Bishop, who objects to both Edel and Stone's interpretations as requiring "extratextual" material to support them, treats the text as metafiction. He focuses on the two Miss Frushes, whose occupations of writing and sketching are treated somewhat comically, then subsumed into a return to the "country," which is then narrowed into a focus on the house, particularly on the "reading" of it rather than the creation of any new work about it of pen or brush. Bishop proposes that the first appearance of the ghost to Susan in her mirror not only suggests that she is seeing herself—she also usually holds her head "on one side"—but also that as an artist she is placing the figure in a "frame." Amy, on the other hand, searches for the "meaning" in her first sighting, as befits a literary critic. With the discovery of the letters, the ghost becomes the "text" over whose interpretation they jealously spar, while Mr. Patten, whom Bishop judges most unreliable, enjoys jokingly turning it about and upside down. The title of the tale, however, Bishop reads as James's indication that through his omniscient narration he is maintaining ultimate "authority" for the reading of the text. Even the smuggling of the Tauchnitz, which Bishop assumes to be a James work, reinforces in Bishop's view by its trifling nature both the essential mildness of the Frushes and the contrasting authority of James (60–73).

Earlier, Todorov also emphasized the narratorial distance that, he argues, undermines the reality of the ghost, the vision of which he implies is due to the Frushes' being "smothered by a life of idleness and boredom" (181). Edel also originally questioned the ghost, but then argued, somewhat condescendingly, that the reader accepts the ghost for providing a "certain richness of experience" to the manless women ([1949] 1963, vi).

Other readers have questioned the ghost less, but still have found serious themes amid the cheerful tone. Banta points to the themes of the appeal of the dead for help, rivalry, "the excited delight found in facing the dead, and the adventurous act as the exorcising deed which can save the dead and the living alike" (181 n.23). Throughout, as Putt indicates, the interest is less in the ghost than in his effect on the women (1969, 6). While Andreas mistakenly attributes the desire to be rid of the ghost to fear of village gossip (103), Ziff accurately speaks of the need to transform the rivalry he has sparked to the former harmony (62). Edel adds a charitable motive, stating that the two women seek to aid the "rather unhappy" specter who seems almost equally "haunted" by exorcising him (1970, 632).

It is easy at first, as Bishop observes, to confuse the two Miss Frushes, who seem to share a blurred identity as English old maids of a feather. But Bishop also notes their significant differences of personality as well as occupation, Amy being "the more conniving, more vindictive," and thus the originator of the jealousy over the ghost (61). Susan is perhaps sufficiently characterized by Winner's noting that in James the hobby of sketching was a "sign of gentility or 'niceness'" (95). She also has, however, as Jones notes, to offset Amy's dashing nature, her own distinctive "hyperactive conscience" (245). The two different women naturally come up with differing solutions to their ghostly predicament. In Gage's reading their ghostly ancestor represents a part of the identity of each. The more provincial Susan, he argues, by trying to expiate the crime, seeks to deny that identity, while Amy actively accepts it through her miniature crime (49–50). Wright goes so far as to compare Amy's morality to Antigone's in its recognition of responsibilities beyond the law. Susan fails because she acts as a puritan. Amy succeeds because she thinks from the perspective of the dead man, a "frustrated romantic," seeing that what haunts him is the incomplete last attempt. She risks what is for her equivalent to his life, her reputation, and in so doing lives life as the "creative adventure" James considered it (18–19, 86). Ziff similarly notes the greater value assigned the "act of passion" over that of conscience (62). Nevertheless, as Jones observes, both are left in the end feeling "purged and proper" (245).

So, too, perhaps is the reader. The concluding smuggling has not gone without its critics, beginning with Garnett, who objected to it as "a feeble joke and out of place" (viii). Similarly, Edel complains that the tale "peters out in a joke" (*Life* 503). Putt, however, while acknowledging the conclusion as an "anticlimatic crisis," appears to approve of the "hilarious perspective" it applies to smuggling (1969, 6). What draws attention to the conclusion is probably its specificity, which is also largely what makes the tale comic, and perhaps un-Jamesian. James is not working here to make the reader "think the evil for themselves" as he was in *The Turn of the Screw*, to imagine heaven knows what vague horrors of depravity, but offers them instead a clearly named, bloodless crime. It is, for all the passion with which Amy may have approached it, a delightfully easy exorcism. The tale is marked by what an early reviewer calls "the smiling affectation of seriousness and reality" (*Outlook* 280). As such it may not appeal to those who insist on "the real thing" and not its affectation, and perhaps James himself neglected it on such grounds. But for those who enjoy a good-humored "spoof on spooking," as Putt calls it, it fits the bill quite nicely (1969, 6).

Works Cited

Primary Works

James, Henry. 1900. "The Third Person." *The Soft Side*. London: Methuen; New York: Macmillan, 242–78.

———. 1921–23. "The Third Person." *The Novels and Stories of Henry James*. Vol. 27. Ed. Percy Lubbock. London: Macmillan.

———. 1993. *The Correspondence of Henry James and the House of Macmillan, 1877–1914*. Ed. Rayburn S. Moore. Baton Rouge: Louisiana State University Press.

Secondary Works

Andreas, Osborn. 1948. *Henry James and the Expanding Horizon: A Study of the Meaning and Basic Themes of James's Fiction*. Seattle: University of Washington Press.

Anon. 1900. Review of *The Soft Side*. *Outlook* 66 (13 October): 423.

Banta, Martha. 1964. "Henry James and 'The Others.'" *New England Quarterly* 37 (June): 171–84.

Bishop, George. 1988. *When the Master Relents: The Neglected Short Fictions of Henry James*. Ann Arbor: UMI Research Press.

Briggs, Julia. 1977. *Night Visitors: The Rise and Fall of the English Ghost Story*. London: Faber.

Edel, Leon, ed. 1970. *Henry James: Stories of the Supernatural*. New York: Taplinger.

———, ed. [1949] 1963. *The Ghostly Tales of Henry James*. New York: The Universal Library, Grosset & Dunlap.

Edgar, Pelham. [1927] 1964. *Henry James, Man and Author*. New York: Russell & Russell.

Ferguson, Alfred R. 1949. "Some Bibliographical Notes on the Short Stories of Henry James." *American Literature* 21: 292–97.

Gage, Richard P. 1988. *Order and Design: Henry James' Titled Story Sequences*. New York: Peter Lang.

Garnett, David, ed. 1946. *Fourteen Stories by Henry James*. London: Rupert Hart-Davis.

Jones, Granville H. 1975. *Henry James's Psychology of Experience: Innocence, Responsibility, and Renunciation in the Fiction of Henry James*. The Hague: Mouton.

Perosa, Sergio. 1983. *Henry James and the Experimental Novel*. New York: New York University Press.

Putt, S. Gorley, ed. 1969. *The Turn of the Screw, and Other Stories*. Harmondsworth: Penguin.

———. 1966. *Henry James: A Reader's Guide*. Ithaca, NY: Cornell University Press.

Stone, Edward. 1964. *The Battle of the Books: Some Aspects of Henry James*. Athens: Ohio University Press.

Todorov, Tzvetan. 1977. *The Poetics of Prose*. Trans. Richard Howard. Ithaca, NY: Cornell University Press.

Wagenknecht, Edward. 1984. *The Tales of Henry James*. New York: Frederick Ungar.

Winner, Viola Hopkins. 1970. *Henry James and the Visual Arts*. Charlottesville: University Press of Virginia.

Wright, Walter. 1962. *The Madness of Art: A Study of Henry James*. Lincoln: University of Nebraska Press.

Ziff, Larzer. 1966. *The American 1890's: Life and Times of a Lost Generation*. New York: Viking.

The Tone of Time

Publication History

James published "The Tone of Time" in the November 1900 issue of *Scribner's Magazine*, and reprinted it in the 1903 *The Better Sort*. It next appeared after James's death in Lubbock's edition of the novels and stories.

Circumstances of Composition, Sources, and Influences

Matthiessen and Murdock start the trail of "The Tone of Time" on September 2, 1895, with an allusion in James's notebook to "Gualdo's charming little subject on *The Child*" (N 213), which also gave rise to "Maud-Evelyn" (1900). When next mentioned on May 7, 1898, in a list of topics, "Gualdo's story of the child *retournée*" is followed by "The woman who wants to have *been* married—to *have become a widow*." The story is to be in the "same key" as the previous and so involves the procuring of a portrait in place of a person who never lived (CN 169). In a second entry in February the next year, he adds the second, female, portrait painter who paints the lover it turns out she had lost to the first woman, now an "ex-*femme galante*." James considered the possibility of having the painter then keep the portrait and pretend its subject was *her* late husband, but thought the last touch "perhaps a little extravagant and *de trop*" (CN 179–81). Evidently he continued to think so, as he left off that final twist in the plot. He listed it one more time in May 1899, before finally writing the tale (CN 184).

The inspired painting so like life is compared by Kappeler to the painting in Wilde's *The Picture of Dorian Gray* (92).

Relation to Other Works

Bowden finds that the portrait here serves, as the portrait in *Confidence* fails to, as the "means . . . by which the central characters are to make discoveries of the hidden relations between each other," and so, like the portraits of Miriam in *The Tragic Muse*, as "an axle" or focal point for the story's events (37, 71). Fadiman judges the intense emotions produced by the painting here similar to those produced by the antiques at Poynton (457–58). Sicker compares the portrait to that in "The Story of a Masterpiece," where again both the painter and the purchaser have loved the subject (100). Gage notes that the pictures of Stuart Straith in "Broken Wings" also age quickly (74). Horne compares the tale to "The Tree of Knowledge" of the same year, which she judges a more effective psychological study with artist characters (99).

Banta connects the tale with the ghost stories, commenting that while there is no actual ghost, the dead man's "presence" has an almost haunting effect on the two women he abandoned (181 n.23). Similarly, Todorov links the tale with "The Friends of the Friends" and "Maud-Evelyn" in its focus on the dead, as the love and hate of a dead man here control the actions of the living (164–65). In comparing the tale to "Maud-Evelyn," Edel calls it comic, arguing that Mrs. Bridgenorth is "indulging a fancy no more supernatural than the daydreams of a girl who waits for a romance" (600), a synopsis that leaves out Mary Tredick and thus most of the theme's development. Perosa finds the "worldly" treatment of the supernatural and the "mysterious portrait" tying the tale to *The Sense of the Past* (135).

Macnaughton links the narrator with John Marcher in his lack of self-knowledge (160). Sicker contrasts Tredick with Stransom of "The Altar of the Dead" and Longdon of *The Awkward Age*, stating that unlike them she cannot learn to share the object of her worship (100). Gage compares the treatment of jealousy and revenge to that in "The Two Faces" (69–75). Horne finds James missing the effective "transformation" of character with Mary Tredick that he achieved with Mrs. Monarch of "The Real Thing" (100–1). In a reading that seems more appropriate for Mrs. Bridgenorth than the

Merrows, Powers distinguishes this tale and "Hugh Merrow" from "Maud-Evelyn" as treating characters who seek to "mask" experiences that were "mistaken," rather than simply to replace "missed" experience (117–18). (See also "The Beldonald Holbein," "The Special Type," and "Maud-Evelyn.")

Interpretation and Criticism

As seen above, the story has frequently been linked with James's tales of the supernatural, partly because of its focus on the past, a preoccupation that Horne is alone in finding a flaw (100). Walter Wright finds the characters' mingled emotions of love and hate also bordering on the supernatural, or at least the "strange" (157). No doubt another factor is what Edgar calls the "staggering" nature of the story's main coincidences (159). Millet sees James dealing "frankly" with them, and Wagenknecht asserts that James is able to produce through them an effective portrayal of character (Millet 199; Wagenknecht 206). Horne, however, finds that the coincidence undercuts the tale's irony (101).

The subject thus portrayed has generally been given as jealousy, a veritable "battle" in Geismar's terms (McElderry 122; Fadiman 457–59; Geismar 255n). The two jealous rivals, however, never meet, and Wagenknecht judges James wise in omitting the confrontation scene between the two women planned in the notebook (206), a route he followed in *The Portrait of a Lady* as well. Instead, the narrator serves as intermediary between the two women in their feud over the portrait.

Horne points to the relationship between the two painters, male and female, as holding together the story, but says little about the relationship itself (101). Bishop sees hints early on that there is some sort of romantic relationship between the narrator and Mary Tredick, but states that this is then abandoned, perhaps because they are both professional artists, and that the narratorial distance from the two women which frames their story produces at the end simply a chronicle of unanswered questions (88–89, 94). Macnaughton implicates the narrator more deeply, judging James's characterization of him as weak, and arguing that if the story is read simply as presented by the narrator it is weak, too. In his reading, there is no coincidence: the narrator is himself the subject of the painting. Another of James's unreliable narrators or imperceptive observers, he fails to recognize his portrait and is protected from the knowledge by the very women he has condescended to, though even they are surprised by his failure. According to Macnaughton, he is "mildly troubled" and therefore slightly improved by his experience, but only slightly. At the end of the tale, years later, he still remarks, "No one, strange to say, has ever recognised the model, but everyone asks his name. I don't even know it" (CT 11, 215). He does recognize in the portrait "a guarantee" that its subject "will die without having suffered" (CT 11, 202), and as Horne points out that indicates a removal from reality dangerous in James (202). If the narrator is the subject of the portrait, his only suffering would seem to be his lingering doubt about the portrait's identity. If, as seems more likely, he is not, he still seems to possess the same shield against reality despite his self-avowed interest in "the given, the presented case" (CT 11, 194).

At the start, his counterpart, Tredick, is a sympathetic, independent, professional woman, but her composure is unsettled as she sets herself to reencounter a past wrong. Sicker gives quite a harsh estimate of her, attributing her decision to keep the painting to a "perverse cruelty" and "a self-absorption so extreme that it sought not only to enshrine a dead image, but to guard it from the rest of the world" (100). With an emphasis on art, Kappeler observes how Tredick's repression of her hate kept her from producing a masterpiece, until she released her passion in the one portrait, and indicates that James may have felt it necessary for the artist to keep her passion for art (92). Wagenknecht is also easier on Tredick, who he says frees herself from her hatred through painting the portrait, which she holds on to, as she says herself, "in joy" (206). Gage also finds it hard to condemn Mary for keeping the portrait, citing the narrator's early description of her as having "given up everything but her work . . . given up too much." In his view, through the portrait she gains at least a sort of "reunion" with its subject, but as Gage adds, given the quality of man he was, it is something of a dubious acquisition (73). Horne points out that her portrait is superior to the rest of her work because it is painted with passion, not just skill. She complains, however, that while James shows her as she was before, having cut herself off from life, and her return to life as she paints the portrait and holds to it, he does not show what becomes of her afterwards (100–1).

Mrs. Bridgenorth, the third party, has received somewhat less attention. Andreas stresses the lingering strength imputed to the pains of love and implies that Mrs. Bridgenorth's desire for the portrait was motivated by her love for the man she lost (84–85). Horne, however, finds Mrs. Bridgenorth merely a type, and objects that Andreas is ignoring her original motive, her desire for respectability in the shape of a dead husband, regardless of the identity (101 n.1). Gage, however, maintains that she too has suffered and deserves a certain sympathy as well. Indeed, he argues that her losses, some of them suffered at the hands of Mary, are greater: she loses not only the man, but the portrait of him, and the bid for social acceptance she hoped to make through it (69–75, 102). Linking the two women, Horne observes that both fail in their attempts to shape life according to their desires through the portrait (102). As a result they both end up, according to Jones, relegated to the past (204–5).

The tale has usually been judged excellent if not, within James's work, exceptional. James's brother William and his wife, Alice, found it "a charming and interestingly wrought out bit of fancy" (142–43). Millet proclaims the story "in almost every respect, characteristic of the art of Henry James at its ripest" (199). Like him, Fadiman, though he thinks little of James's sense of art in the tale, questions James's decision to omit it from the New York Edition (457–59). Horne and Putt, on the other hand, have little good to say of the tale, and Putt considers the final lines of dialogue designed to hearten the mockers of James's late style (Horne 99–102; Putt 233–34). Certainly it is typical late James, though hardly as rarified as some, and with an intriguing revelation of what happens when deeply held and deeply hidden emotions are accidentally disturbed.

Works Cited

Primary Works

James, Henry. 1900. "The Tone of Time." *Scribner's Magazine* 28 (November): 624–34.

———. 1903. "The Tone of Time." *The Better Sort*. London: Methuen; New York: Scribner's, 68–92.

———. 1921–23. "The Tone of Time." *The Novels and Stories of Henry James*. Vol. 27. Ed. Percy Lubbock. London: Macmillan.

Secondary Works

Andreas, Osborn. 1948. *Henry James and the Expanding Horizon: A Study of the Meaning and Basic Themes of James's Fiction*. Seattle: University of Washington Press.

Banta, Martha. 1964. "Henry James and 'The Others.'" *New England Quarterly* 37 (June): 171–84.

Bishop, George. 1988. *When the Master Relents: The Neglected Short Fictions of Henry James*. Ann Arbor: UMI Research Press.

Bowden, Edwin T. [1956] 1960. *The Themes of Henry James: A System of Observation through the Visual Arts*. Yale Studies in English 132. New Haven: Yale University Press.

Edel, Leon, ed. 1970. *Henry James: Stories of the Supernatural*. New York: Taplinger.

Edgar, Pelham. [1927] 1964. *Henry James, Man and Author*. New York: Russell & Russell.

Fadiman, Clifton, ed. 1945. *The Short Stories of Henry James*. New York: Random House.

Geismar, Maxwell. 1963. *Henry James and the Jacobites*. Boston: Houghton Mifflin.

Gage, Richard P. 1988. *Order and Design: Henry James's Titled Story Sequences*. New York: Peter Lang.

Horne, Helen. 1960. *Basic Ideals of James's Aesthetics as Expressed in the Short Stories Concerning Artists and Writers*. Marburg: Erich Mauersberger.

James, William. 1992. *The Correspondence of William James*. Vol. 3: *William and Henry: 1897–1910*. Ed. Ignas K. Skrupskelis and Elizabeth M. Berkeley: Charlottesville: University Press of Virginia.

Jones, Granville H. 1975. *Henry James's Psychology of Experience: Innocence, Responsibility, and Renunciation in the Fiction of Henry James*. The Hague: Mouton.

Kappeler, Susanne. 1980. *Writing and Reading in Henry James*. New York: Columbia University Press.

McElderry, Bruce R., Jr. 1965. *Henry James*. New York: Twayne.

Macnaughton, W. R. 1974. "The First-Person Narrators of Henry James." *Studies in American Fiction* 2 (August): 145–64.

Millet, Fred B. 1950. *Reading Fiction: A Method of Analysis with Selections for Study*. New York: Harper's.

Perosa, Sergio. 1983. *Henry James and the Experimental Novel*. New York: New York University Press.

Powers, Lyall H. 1988. "James's 'Maud-Evelyn.'" In *Leon Edel and Literary Art*. Ed. Lyall H. Powers, 117–24. Ann Arbor: UMI Research Press.

Putt, S. Gorley. 1966. *Henry James: A Reader's Guide*. Ithaca, NY: Cornell University Press.

Sicker, Philip. 1980. *Love and the Quest for Identity in the Fiction of Henry James*. Princeton: Princeton University Press.

Todorov, Tzvetan. 1977. *The Poetics of Prose*. Trans. Richard Howard. Ithaca, NY: Cornell University Press.

Wagenknecht, Edward. 1984. *The Tales of Henry James*. New York: Frederick Ungar.

Wright, Walter F. 1962. *The Madness of Art: A Study of Henry James*. Lincoln: University of Nebraska Press.

A Tragedy of Error

Publication History

James's first published story appeared anonymously in the February 1864 issue of *The Continental Monthly*, an abolitionist paper founded in 1860. Its authorship, however, was not known until 1953 when Leon Edel established the attribution to James in the first volume of his James biography.

Circumstances of Composition, Sources, and Influences

Edel based his discovery on a previously unknown letter from a Mrs. George de Kay remarking that Smith van Buren had forbidden his niece to read James's tale, a fact "which brought a smile of quiet contempt to Harry's lips but anger and indignation to those of Miss Minny Temple" (*Life* 1, 215).

The discovery of James's first tale reversed the traditional belief that James was a published critic before he was a published writer of fiction (*Life* 1, 215). Still, the tale has signs of the critic writing, being, according to Putt, an "imitative literary exercise" (33). Most of the sources James is imitating are French. The love triangle and the cruel heroine, according to Delbaere-Garant, mark the tale as typically French (227–28). As Edel remarks, this tale fits Thomas Sergeant Perry's description of James as a young man at Newport writing tales in which the heroines appeared to have "read all Balzac in the cradle and to be positively dripping with lurid crimes" (*Life* 1, 216). Although Adams sees no specific source in Balzac, both Levy and Kraft view the tale as being written under what Levy calls "the great shadow" of the French master (Adams 461; Kraft 1, 120 n. 2; Levy 12). Other critics, including Edel and Martin and Ober, see traces of Mérimée as well as Balzac, Buitenhuis particularly noting the resemblance of Hortense to Mérimée's fatal Venus (CT 1, 17; Martin and Ober 13; Buitenhuis 206). Jones offers a different source for Hortense in Madame Bovary, both women being trapped, self-centered romantics who are in some ways pitiful (96). In Tintner's view, Hortense's name along with other Napoleonic names in the tale, such as Josephine, lend the story a Napoleonic aura, stemming perhaps from James's recent visit to the Galerie d'Apolon (1986, 21–22)

While noting the French setting and subject, Habegger observes that adultery was becoming a frequent subject of American domestic literature and would shortly be treated in works by Anne Crane, Louisa May Alcott, Adeline Whitney, and Elizabeth Stoddard (104). Wagenknecht also combines French and American parallels, finding the twist ending in the style of de Maupassant or the later O. Henry (206).

The tale's most specific allusions appear to be to the British tradition. Mrs. de Kay had written of the tale as "A Tragedy of Errors" (*Life* 1, 215). Her plural may be a scribal error induced by her recall of the title's source, Shakespeare's *Comedy of Errors*, an allusion noted by Tintner, Martin and Ober, and Leyburn, who considers the allusion "misleading" (Tintner 1987, 9; Leyburn 3). Melchiori points out that Shakespeare's early comedy was the first play James ever saw (9). Savarese specifies as a similarity between the works, the use of mistaken identity, although "without the benefit of twins" (434).

According to Martin and Ober, the primary source of the work is even older, namely Chaucer's *Franklin's Tale*, which also features an absent husband returning by sea and whose opening words "In Armorik" set the locale and give the name to the story's ship. But James replaces Chaucer's themes of "honesty" and "honor" with "secrecy" and "deceit" throughout, and his happy ending with a tragic one, in a manner Martin and Ober speculate James considered more realistic. Looking even farther back, Fryer compares Hortense in her garden to Eve, dangerous women both (183).

Edel, however, emphasizes the biographical context, comparing the lame husband and strong wife to James's own parents (*Life* 71–72).

Relation to Other Works

As James's first tale, "A Tragedy of Error" has most frequently been examined in the context of the other early stories. While Kraft judges it a thing apart from James's other early tales set in America, Vaid places it in the context of nine other omnisciently narrated early tales (Kraft 1). "A Tragedy of Error" Vaid judges the most restrained, although similar in its start to "The Story of a Year," where the narrator also draws attention to the beginning of "my story" (133). Harris also looks at it together with the "first" tale it replaced, finding both a "fascinating mixture of finesse and awkwardness," praising in both the strong ending that "sums up" what went before without eliminating the need for readers to draw on their imaginations (85–86). Focusing on the heroine, Delbaere-Garant argues that the sense of women as dangerously untrustworthy was deep-seated in the young James, appearing in "The Story of a Year," "A Landscape Painter," and "A Day of Days" (228). Stein looks at the women's victims, noting that the hero of "Crawford's Consistency" ends up with a limp such as the husband has here (83).

There are connections also with the later James. According to Edel, Hortense is only the first of James's "bad" heroines, anticipating such later femme fatales as Rose Armiger of *The Other House* and Kate Croy (*Life* 1,

218). Shine notes, in contrast, the limits assigned the role of the child in comparison to late James (26). Focusing on the scene where Hortense hires the boatman, Savarese links the tale with other "attempts to penetrate the true identity of others" in such works as "The Liar," *The Aspern Papers*, *The Sacred Fount*, and *The Golden Bowl* (434). Emphasizing the continuity between early and late James, Vaid points out that even in the magisterial *The Ambassadors*, James still uses the "authorial 'I'" in the first paragraph (127).

Interpretation and Criticism

Perhaps due to its status as a modern discovery, "A Tragedy of Error" has received a good amount of attention for an early work, especially one whose flaws are so readily granted by critics. Its French melodrama might have surprised early readers of James, but as Edel notes, its luridness is typical of early James (294). Indeed, Putt comments, James "never quite freed himself" from his attraction to the melodramatic (33–34).

According to Thorp, James is attempting to write a different kind of melodrama here, with a more realistic treatment of its "strong" subjects. The result, however, he judges "somewhat crude" (xiii). The inexpertness may explain why McElderry, although he remarks on the strength of the tale's irony and avoidance of sentiment, calls its melodrama "conventional." Still, he compliments James on his comfort with the "literary" situation and "foreign setting" (26). It is the European setting, to be of such importance to James, that Buitenhuis considers the chief significance of the tale. America here, Buitenhuis remarks, appears only as a "bribe" to the killer (13, 17). Martin and Ober speak of the tale as a "diverting *jeu d'esprit*" (58). But while Edel writes of James's "exuberant boyish art," evident in planning Hortense's "operatic" scheme (CT 1, 20), it would appear that James was at least striving after something more serious here.

The predominant sea imagery, first analyzed by Gale, is according to Mull one of the work's few significances (Mull 177–78 n.1). Gale notes that water imagery would also dominate James's later work and cites in particular the lover's description of how "we are all afloat on a tumultuous sea . . . struggling toward some *terra firma* of wealth or love or leisure"(CT 1, 25). Stein similarly praises the image as a "metaphor for the terror of experience" (61). Vaid, however, objects that the imagery is not significant, focusing his analysis on the tale's narration instead (132).

The narrative technique is a rather complicated one. Edel cites the many references to suppostitious third-person observers as a sign that early on James was already working toward a deliberate narrative technique (*Life* 1, 216–19). Kraft is struck, primarily, by the contrast between the "cool . . . detached" tone of the third-person view and the tale's overwrought events

(1). Delbaere-Garant points to the use of traditional direct communication of author to reader (226). So does Vaid who also notes the use of "hypothetical spectator[s]" to keep objectivity while presenting insights, an approach more typical of the later James. As Vaid observes, James calls attention to his giving up of traditional narratorial privileges, his keeping to Hortense's remarks and actions "often from an exaggerated fear of trenching on the ground of fiction." When James does tell the reader what Hortense is thinking, Vaid finds the revelations "rather rudimentary." Both the strength and the limitation of the tale is, according to Vaid, James's refraining from attempting what he was not yet competent to do, "to present the situation of the woman in all its psychological complexity" (127–31). Savarese objects to Vaid's reading, emphasizing the tale's confusion rather than its objectivity, pointing to the numerous reflectors around Hortense and the numerous misreadings of her that they generate (234–35).

Hortense's character is indeed at the center of the tale, and has generated conflicting evaluations. In Vaid's analysis, James kept from showing her character directly in order to create suspense, until the second section shows her "terrible character" in the "vivid inset scene" where she unerringly chooses the boatman, also "finely characterized," as the man to murder her husband (128–29). With rather convoluted reasoning, Shine, who also focuses on the scene with the boatman, argues that her recognition of his cruelty to his nephew at the start renders Hortense "somehow less culpable," as it shows her recognition of her own evil, and therefore a perception of the good from which she is turning. According to Shine, James wants the reader "to be moved by her plight" (26–28). Jones is, if only slightly, commenting that while she like her lover is "pitiless," her lack of pity is at least partially explained by her frustration with her marriage, her struggle with her conscience, and her enslavement to a romantic view that dooms her (96). Delbaere-Garant has little admiration for Hortense herself, judging her not only evil but also too broadly drawn. Like Shine and Vaid, however, she praises the scene with the boatman as the best part of the story, with the juxtaposition of the faces of the beautiful woman and the brutish man its "best stroke," despite the awkward interruption by a footnote (226–27).

Savarese, who points to the abundant mention of "gazing" and "faces," also focuses his analysis on the scene depicting the "recruitment" of the boatman, which he finds handled with "subtlety and suggestiveness." In his analysis, however, he grants equal time to the boatman himself, whom he argues is not just a sinister character, but a complex one. Unlike Shine, who finds him simply unthinkingly bad, Savarese argues that the boatman exaggerates his past acts of violence and has a "primitive if unexamined sense of dignity and fairness"—so that, initially willing to help Hortense when he believes her a younger woman trapped in marriage with an older man, he develops scruples when he realize hers is not the stock situation. Savarese does not argue that James wants the boatman to be a heroic character. Still, he argues, part of the story's tragedy is the corruption of his already weak character. Hortense, the agent of his corruption, in Saverese's view, seems only to be concerned with the propriety of engaging an inferior in conversation.

Stein also praises the scene as one of the tale's more effective elements. Hortense, in Stein's view, becomes the equal of the murderer in the breaking of her marriage ties. The overall impression of the tale, he argues, is one of relations overturned or broken. If the tale presents marriage itself as frightening—he takes the husband's limp as an indication of the "possibly unpleasant physical intimacy" of marriage—its ending simply intensifies its threat (61–63).

One of the signal signs of chaos in the tale, according to Stein, is the mistake over the identity of the murder victim (63). Savarese, who contends that Hortense's lover would probably believe that she had *intended* to kill him, similarly takes the final confusion as an indication of the theme of misjudgment throughout the tale (435). The messiness of the murder is, however, also the key signal of the neatness of the plot. Its twist is likely, Rimmon argues, to prove quite satisfactory to the reader (82). Indeed Norrman, who terms the conclusion a "chiastic inversion," states that Hortense's tragedy is likely to seem comic to the reader, even as he argues that it did to James, who enjoyed such reversals (142). In arguing against Edel's assertion that such trickery is indicative of a "creaky" plot because it requires one to accept that the non-lame lover drowned, Vaid suggests a twist of his own. In his view, the fact that Hortense's husband did not die does not necessarily indicate that her lover did. Thus, he maintains, the word "tragedy" in the title is "ironic" (131–32).

Vaid asserts that the "earliest work of a great writer can be an irresistible hunting ground to the critic," and the above readings indicate that he was right (126). Still, although critics have found much of interest in the tale, they have not always praised its execution. Mull, for example, finds it "fairly pat and sordid," Jones calls it a "weak melodrama," and Leyburn judges the irony "obviously and even arduously contrived" with too much melodrama and too little complexity (Mull 178 n.1; Leyburn 3; Jones 96). Others concentrate their praise on particular features. Edel and Wagenknecht both praise the characterization, while Wagenknecht also admires the use of irony despite an inappropriate subject, and Edel the use of "calculated scenes," dramatic dialogue, and the consciousness if not mastery of technique (Wagenknecht 206; *Life* 1, 217–18; 1957, 294). In Savarese's estimate the tale is "easy to undervalue" due to its "marks of apprenticeship," but, he argues, James "mercifully foreshortened" the most melodramatic and amateur parts of the tale (431). In a balanced view, Stein argues that while the tale is "not a terribly auspicious beginning," its still has a "thematic significance that transcends the imperfections of the work," keeping it from being a "total failure" (61–63). It is, indeed, despite the roughness with which they are portrayed, the intense confrontation of characters, their desperate attempts to control their fate, and their learning that such attempts only leave them more vulnerable, that make the tale's significance both in itself and as an indication of what James would later accomplish.

Works Cited

Primary Works

James, Henry. 1864. "A Tragedy of Error." *The Continental Monthly* 5 (February): 204–16.

Secondary Works

Adams, Percy G. 1961. "Young Henry James and the Lesson of his Master Balzac." *Revue de Littérature Comparée* 35 (July–September): 458–67.

Buitenhuis, Peter. 1970. *The Grasping Imagination: The American Writings of Henry James*. Toronto: University of Toronto Press.

Delbaere-Garant, Jeanne. 1970. *Henry James: The Vision of France*. Paris: Société d'Editions Les Belles Lettres.

Edel, Leon. 1956. "Prefatory Note" [to] 'A Tragedy of Error': James's First Story." *New England Quarterly* 29 (September): 291–95.

Fryer, Judith. 1976. *The Faces of Eve: Women in the Nineteenth-Century American Novel*. New York: Oxford University Press.

Gale, Robert L. 1957. "A Note on Henry James's First Story." *Modern Language Notes* 72 (February): 103–7.

Habegger, Alfred. 1989. *Henry James and the "Woman Business."* Cambridge: Cambridge University Press.

Harris, Wendell V. 1979. *British Short Fiction in the Nineteenth Century: A Literary and Bibliographic Guide*. Detroit: Wayne State University Press.

Jones, Granville H. 1975. *Henry James's Psychology of Experience: Innocence, Responsibility, and Renunciation in the Fiction of Henry James*. The Hague: Mouton.

Kraft, James. 1969. *The Early Tales of Henry James*. Carbondale: Southern Illinois University Press.

Levy, Leo B. 1957. *Versions of Melodrama: A Study of the Fiction and Drama of Henry James, 1865–1897*. Berkeley: University of California Press.

Leyburn, Ellen Douglass. 1968. *Strange Alloy: The Relation of Comedy to Tragedy in the Fiction of Henry James*. Chapel Hill: University of North Carolina Press.

McElderry, Bruce R., Jr. 1965. *Henry James*. New York: Twayne.

Martin, W. R., and Warren U. Ober. 1987. "The Provenience of Henry James's First

Tale." *Studies in Short Fiction* 24, no. 1 (Winter): 57–58.

Melchiori, Giorgio. 1965. "Locksley Hall Revisited: Tennyson and Henry James." *Review of English Literature* 6 (October): 9–25. Reprinted in Barbara Melchiori and Giorgio Melchiori, *Il Gusto di Henry James*. Turin: Guilio Einaudi editore, 1974.

Mull, Donald. 1973. *Henry James's "Sublime Economy": Money as Symbolic Center in the Fiction*. Middletown, CT: Wesleyan University Press.

Norrman, Ralf. 1982. *The Insecure World of Henry James's Fiction: Intensity and Ambiguity*. New York: St. Martin's.

Putt, S. Gorley. 1966. *Henry James: A Reader's Guide*. Ithaca, NY: Cornell University Press.

Rimmon, Shlomith. 1977. *The Concept of Ambiguity: The Example of Henry James*. Chicago: University of Chicago Press.

Savarese, John E. 1980. "Henry James's First Story: A Study of Error." *Studies in Short Fiction* 17: 431–35.

Shine, Muriel G. 1969. *The Fictional Children of Henry James*. Chapel Hill: University of North Carolina Press.

Stein, Allen F. 1984. *After the Vows Were Spoken: Marriage in American Literary Realism*. Columbus: Ohio State University Press.

Thorp, Willard, ed. 1962. *The Madonna of the Future and Other Early Tales*. New York: New American Library.

Tintner, Adeline R. 1987. *The Book World of Henry James: Appropriating the Classics*. Ann Arbor: UMI Research Press.

———. 1986. *The Museum World of Henry James*. Ann Arbor: UMI Research Press.

Vaid, Krishna B. 1964. *Technique in the Tales of Henry James*. Cambridge, MA: Harvard University Press.

Wagenknecht, Edward. 1984. *The Tales of Henry James*. New York: Frederick Ungar.

Travelling Companions

Publication History

The only appearance of "Travelling Companions" during James's lifetime was in the November and December 1870 issues of the *Atlantic Monthly*. It next appeared in 1919 as the title story of Mordell's anthology of previously uncollected James stories.

Circumstances of Composition, Sources, and Influences

In 1869 James set off on his first adult tour of Europe and, most significantly, his first trip ever to Italy. Aziz argues, on the basis of a September letter from James to his editor, James T. Fields, requesting payment, that James composed "Travelling Companions" in May and June of 1870, immediately following his return (1, xxx–xxxii). Certainly, as many critics have noted, his hero's travel route follows James's closely, as do many of his reactions, which closely resemble those in James's letters (see e.g., Nathalia Wright 219; C. Anderson 52; Smith 370; Churchill 158).

While James was away in Europe, his cousin and kindred spirit Minny Temple died at the age of twenty-five from tuberculosis, an event he describes in his autobiography as the end of his youth (*Autobiography* 544). Quentin Anderson accordingly reads the story as James's "marriage" to Minny, written under the influence both of her death and of his father's recent essay "Is Marriage Holy?," which argues for the male's subordination to the more spiritual feminine. In the tale, according to Anderson, James draws on his memory of Minny's "moral spontaneity" to sustain him in his encounter with Italy (134–37). Curtsinger also notes a resemblance, particularly in the way Miss Evans's interest in Christ reflects Minny's in her last letters to James (17). Habegger less sympathetically links character and source, objecting to the "sick saccharinity" he detects both in the tale and in James's response to Minny's death (145).

Kelley notes that, like James, Brooke approaches Italy under the influence of such writers as Stendhal and George Sand, whose *La Dernière Aldini* takes place in Venice (114; also Mordell 371). Tintner adds Goethe's *Italienische Reise* as well as the writings of Ruskin to the list of guidebooks, and notes that the Goethe or else Baroness Tautphoeus's *The Initials* may have provided the title (1987, 8; 1986, 23, 229; 1989, 158). Although he mistakenly credits Brooke instead of Charlotte for reading "Rappaccini's Daughter," Long finds the introduction of the Hawthorne tale appropriate not only for its Padua setting, but for its shared concern with a purity preserved in compromising circumstances. He likens Charlotte to another Hawthorne heroine, Hilda of *The Marble Faun*, in her freedom of movement, her "half-prayers" in a Catholic church, and an appreciation of Italy tempered by an American Protestant morality (20–21).

Relation to Other Works

Quentin Anderson finds James here and in "A Passionate Pilgrim" beginning to use the "symbols of Europe" to portray the "deeper psychology" that interested him (47). Long sees the same concern with the different perspectives of innocence and experience in this tale and "A Light Man" (21). Looking further ahead, Anderson sees Brooke confronting the same great moral issues as Merton Densher or Prince Amerigo, and Maves finds in Brooke's buying of the false Correggio an idea reversed in Amerigo's acceptance of American distortions (Anderson 193; Maves 148).

Allen finds Charlotte fitting the best "type" of the American girl—independent and innocent—which also includes Martha of "The Last of the Valerii," Gertrude in *The Europeans*, and Bessie of *An International Episode* (212 n.9). One might also draw a comparison between the serious Charlotte and Mary Garland of *Roderick Hudson*, both of whom Long sees as deriving from Hawthorne's Hilda (166). Krook observes that, like Isabel Archer, the narrator wants to see Europe before marrying. She sees Charlotte, however, as the possessor of Isabel's character, even when faced with a potentially compromising situation that fits more with *Daisy Miller* (137). Fox argues that Isabel marries badly because she lacks the knowledge of Europe represented by the "exaltation and dread" Brooke experiences on the Campagna and so must learn it through Osmond (28). Walter Anderson remarks that while James criticizes in Miss Evans her "high, thin, and nervous" voice, he praises her "frankness and freedom." By the time of his return to America in the 1900s, Anderson argues, James will see the voice and behavior of the typical American woman as related and "grave vices," an attitude evident in his Bryn Mawr address, "The Question of Our Speech," and a series of related essays in *Harper's Bazaar* (619).

Jefferson sees Charlotte not simply as the best of the early American girls, but the first "viewed as such by a discriminating observer" (73). Appropriately, then, critics have put her and Brooke with such other pairs as Winterbourne and Daisy Miller, Mme de Mauves and Longmore, and Gilbert Osmond and Isabel (Lanzinger 135–36; Wegelin 56; Jones 59). Wilt and Lucas observe, however, that Brooke is a more innocently Europeanized American than Osmond (x).

Wagenknecht labels Mr. Evans James's "first portrait of the American businessman on European holiday" (207). Berland, too, notes how he anticipates later portrayals of millionaires who bring their female relatives to Europe even though they pay little attention to it themselves (201). Edel judges him an "excellent sketch," anticipating the portrayal of Christopher Newman and Adam Verver (CT 2,10; *Life* 1, 305; also Wilt and Lucas x; Wegelin 78). Nathalia Wright considers him "an admirable type of American aristocrat," indeed, of those characters who fail to respond to Italy, the "most admirable" (220, 236). Less effusively, Lanzinger notes in his portrait a "mild caricature," while LeClair sees his character illustrating the "vulgarity" of American society as "silhouetted against the Italian background" (Lanzinger 133; LeClair 435).

In Krook's view James's enthusiasm for Italy makes the travel writing approach that of *Italian Hours* (137). Winner compares the opening scene with the characters looking at the *Last Supper* to the opening scene of *The American* with Newman at the Louvre (71–72). Rowe gives Brooke's excursion to Rome after parting from Charlotte as an example of a "detour," an attempt to escape gathering profundities, such as Isabel's grand tour, Marcher's travels after May's death, and Strether's countryside "holiday" (195–201). In contrast, the "exaltation and dread" he encounters on the Campagna Quentin Anderson links to James's use of the Campagna as a "shorthand symbol for an equivocal and complex response to Europe," in such tales as "The Solution" and "The Author of Beltraffio" as well as in *Watch and Ward*, *The Portrait of a Lady*, and *The American Scene* (150–53; also Stone 75–76).

Slabey contrasts the sincere religion of the Vicenzas with that of Serafina of "The Madonna of the Future," Camillo of "The Last of the Valerii," and Mrs. Keith of *Watch and Ward*. Slabey also places Brooke and Charlotte at the start of a long series of James characters, including Martha of "The Last of the Valerii," Adina, Rowland Mallet, Merton Densher, Strether, and Stransom, who seek refuge in a chuch "of the old persuasion" during a time of trouble (91, 98). Tintner notes that St. Peter's in particular will figure prominently again in later works, including "Longstaff's Marriage," *Roderick Hudson*, *Daisy Miller*, and *The Portrait of a Lady* (1986, 24–25, 62).

Looking at a painting of the Crucifixion, Charlotte declares it is the subject that most interests her and Brooke is "afraid" it is the painter that interests him. Putt takes the exchange as an anticipation of what would become James's emphasis on method over observation notable in his prefaces and other late critical writings (42).

Looking at the conclusion, Curtsinger notes a foreshadowing of the farewell kiss in "The Velvet Glove" in the concluding, but reconciliatory kiss here (21). The slightly coy "Reader, I married him" revelation of the happy ending that follows—"Saying just now that my stay in Florence was peculiarly colored by circumstances, I meant that I was there with my wife" (CT 2, 225)—is used again by James much later in "John Delavoy" and in "The Death of the Lion," where the narrator at the very end reveals of his fellow admirer of Paraday—"We should be closely united by this firm tie even were we not at present by another" (CT 9, 118). (See also "At Isella.")

Interpretation and Criticism

For a story spoken of as a "trifle" and a "failure" (Wilt and Lucas x; Jones 59), "Travelling Companions" has accreted a remarkable amount of criticism over the years. This is in part because of the story's place at the head of James's international tales, with Brooke the first of James's "passionate pilgrims" (see e.g., Wilt and Lucas x; Wright 220; Wegelin 56). Critics who focus on the setting have often found it more significant than the action (e.g., Edgar 16; McElderry 31). Beach pictures the tale as constructed of "alternate blocks"— plot and rhapsodic travelogue ([1918] 1954, 187–89). Kelley points out that in the plot he created to sustain his travelogue James came upon his important theme of the contrast of cultures, the "International Situation." Kelley could safely refer to the story as "neglected" (112, 114–15). The large volume of criticism since then is largely due to those who have begun to read the travelogue not for itself, but for the symbolism that ties it to the plot.

The telling of the tale itself has received little praise. While Wilt and Lucas cite it as a "splendid instance" of James's early style (xiv), Matthiessen quotes the tale's opening sentence—"The most strictly impressive picture in Italy is incontestably the Last Supper of Leonardo at Milan"—as evidence that James was "a genius not born but made." He praises, however, the use of a "framing device," staging the story's opening around the painting as a way of treating the different perspectives of the principal characters (536). Lanzinger dissents, calling the opening scene "rather static," but as Winner notes it serves to set up the relationships between the characters and the themes of the tale (Lanzinger133; Winner 71). It also establishes the technique since, as Nathalia Wright puts it, Charlotte and Brooke meet in a "series of churches" and their deepening relationship is "reflected in a series of paintings," showing a contrast, Tintner asserts, between the sacred and the profane (Wright 220–21; Tintner 1986, 23; see also Wilt and Lucas xi).

Wright finds in the story one of James's most romantic interpretations of Europe, but notes that it is offset by Brooke's tendency to analysis and his growing awareness of the misery that often exists in the midst of the romantic (220). Maves generally concurs, remarking also on the Puritan disdain for Italians as a people threaded throughout the narrative. He praises in particular the one episode that involves an imaginary work of art, the fake

Correggio, and the sister's dream of its sale, which he reads as symbolizing the decline of Europe in the face of the new American madonna, a Europe that offers art in return for money (10–17).

The religious setting is important. Beach recalls how according to James's own account as a boy he and his brothers appear to have visited churches as simply another "aesthetic adventure," an approach one initially sees reflected in Brooke (1921, 100–1). Levy discerns a different kind of distance in the way the Protestant Americans, despite the temptation to "assimilate," appear to regard the great Catholic churches as more a part of the pagan past than anything to do with their own Christianity (27–28). Still, as Slabey makes clear, Charlotte does respond to the power of the Catholic Church (96).

Quentin Anderson in his reading traces the philosophy of the senior James, marking in it a split between two basic approaches to experience, one focusing on the true life of things, the other on their form. At first Brooke tends to take life as "a portrait, a possession." Under the tutelage of Miss Evans, he moves from the true to the false, and is granted her "sacred" love at the end in place of the "profane" he requested at first (137–41; 193–94).

Martin and Ober take issue with Aziz's claim of "documentary authenticity" for the tale, querying the inaccuracy of James's statement that Tintoretto's *Crucifixion* contains "no swooning Madonna." Curtsinger supplies an explanation, indicating that Miss Evans stands in for the missing madonna. As a madonna figure, he writes, she is associated with the Hebraic (through the scene at the Jewish cemetery), the Catholic, and the "unclassical." Sicker notes that Charlotte is associated with the madonna through the episode of the false Correggio Brooke purchases (33). Curtsinger cites Sicker on James's early fascination with both Mary and Diana figures, and contends that Miss Evans also comes to play the more classical role of muse to Brooke's artist figure. The unity of Miss Evans, the muse, and the madonna is made concrete in the fake Correggio, as is the linking between earth and heaven it symbolizes (14–16, 19–20).

This union of madonna and muse is demonstrated again in the Titian, the two halves of which, Curtsinger argues, are contained in Miss Evans and this union precedes that of artist and muse with which the story concludes (21). Similarly, Lanzinger notes the story's parallel divisions between the head and the heart, the North and the South, the male and the female, and the complementary theme of marriage introduced by Raphael's "Marriage of the Virgin" and concluded with the Titian, symbolizing the union of "ideal and passionate love" (134–35).

Both Lanzinger's and Curtsinger's readings of the Titian are in sympathy with those of modern critics, Panofsky characterizing the painting as illustrating not a "dichotomy" between the "celestial" and "terrestial" love it depicts, but a "scale of values" derived from neo-Platonic humanism (112–19). James, however, or at least Brooke, reads the painting as depicting the difference between "Love as an experience" and "as a sentiment; this of the passion that fancies, the other of the passion that knows," and Miss Evans clearly bases her acceptance of Brooke on her rejection of the one for the other (CT 2, 225).

Tintner remarks on the irrelevance of contemporary scholars declaring the nude woman the representative of the higher love, the clothed of the lower, but what does matter is that James still sees this as an absolute dichotomy without any possible reconciliation (1986, 24). Maves notices the "idiosyncratic" nature of James's insistence on dichotomy here, finding evidence of potential harmony between the two in Brooke's rapturous reaction to Italy: "For the first time I really *felt* my intellect." He discerns also in Charlotte's commentary on the two Titians, the Crucifixion and the Bacchus and Ariadne, stemming from the same hand, a hint of possible "balance between the moral and the pleasurable" (14, 18). Panofsky writes that the nude in Italian art came to be associated with truth rather than immorality (112), and this connection can be sensed earlier when Charlotte gently corrects Brooke's preference for a glossy Rape of Europe by Veronese, showing the superiority of Tintoretto's Bacchus and Ariadne, which substitutes "the shining purity and symmetry of deified human flesh" for the "shimmer of drapery" in the other, and which has— though not mentioned in the text—to give it further value the offering of a wedding ring (CT 2, 207).

Churchill writes of Brooke that he experiences no "significant contact" with Italy (158). Rowe argues, however, that in his rides on the Campagna Brooke moves beyond the conventional platitudes on past civilizations to a deeper "authentic dread" (200–1). Quentin Anderson makes further connections, arguing that Brooke's acceptance of "exaltation and dread" is of a piece with the new maturity shown in his marriage, his breaking free from a complete absorption in "the steady perception of the material present" (150–51). Wilt and Lucas and Wright all see the initially romantic Brooke as being educated in the misery behind the beauty of Italy, particularly in his encounter with the bitter woman at the Milan cathedral (Wilt and Lucas xi; Wright 220). As Wright notes, his character is "highly analytical" (220), and it is by analysis that he at first proceeds. Wilt and Lucas describe the way Brooke "unconsciously weighs" Charlotte against others and "submits [her] to comparison" over and over again. (xi). Jones calls attention to Brooke's "rather puffy pride" in his first proposal (58). He has, however, made some progress as is evident in his statement that he is "afraid" he pays more attention to the painter than the subject of the Tintoretto Crucifixion (CT 2, 206).

Nevertheless, Quentin Anderson notes that James finds it necessary to kill off the father and to implicate Miss Evans in a "compromising" situation (141). Similarly, Habegger takes exception to James's weakening of Charlotte through her father's death in order to give strength to the hero, who is now allowed to be protective, and to produce a happy ending. According to

Habegger, James overdoes the reversal, rendering Charlotte uninteresting in an attempt to make her feminine (145). Less censoriously, Long also describes the final marriage as a "kind of rescue" from the dangers of Europe (21). Krook, however, sees the marriage less as a rescue than a victory over "Europe," and considers it a "refreshing change" from the renunciations typical in James (137). One might even find it a victory *through* Europe. As Wilt and Lucas point out, Italy has helped the two more than it has harmed them (xi). Or, in Jefferson's phrase, Brooke "gets the best of two worlds" (58)—Charlotte, too, one hopes.

Edgar notes that the couple refuse to bow completely to European standards, marrying in the end "because they wish and not because they must" (16). Or, as Kraft puts it, discarding Europe's, they must "accept their own truth" (43). Wegelin uses as his main schemata for analyzing the international tales such comments as James's to his mother from Italy: "We seem a people of *character*, we seem to have energy, capacity and intellectual stuff in ample measure with *culture* quite left out"—and relates the contrast between character and culture to that between observation and imagination (79; *Letters* 1, 22). The couple here are perhaps seeking to accept the best of both Europe and America, rather than rejecting one or the other, to become cultured while not losing their character, or in the case of Brooke, regaining what he may have lost.

Looking at a Giotto, Miss Evans says to Brooke, "We ought to learn from all this to be *real*" (CT 2, 210). While Kelley argues that the concluding marriage is most likely a concession to popular taste, insignificant in itself, it is actually at the heart of the story's meaning (114). Wright remarks that though Charlotte, like Brooke, responds deeply to Italian art, she is "more realistic" (220). She is also a woman of strength and dignity, as Brooke realizes, a representative of "positive, not negative, maidenhood" (CT 2, 178). Despite the weakening Habegger describes, she provides a great deal of the strength of the conclusion.

It is significant, too, that the conclusion takes place after the start of the marriage. It, too, is real. It is this effort to be real, not only as Americans facing Europe or modern people facing the past, but as male facing female, that is at the heart of this tale. James is seeking to work out how two intelligent, conscious, and conscientious people manage the transition to marriage. In so doing, he charts the transformation Wordsworth recalls of his wife from "a phantom of delight" to "a creature not too bright or good / For human nature's daily food" who remains "a Spirit still, and bright / with something of angelic light." In 1919 a critic found the love "very mild"; it might be more accurate to call it highly intellectualized or at least schematized. It is, as Marks puts it, "a workable moral resolution" (65) to a courtship that has all the weight of Victorian morality and Jamesian psychology and European history placed upon it. Amazingly enough, it is in the end sealed with a kiss.

Works Cited

Primary Works

James, Henry. 1870. "Travelling Companions." *Atlantic Monthly* 26 (November–December): 600–14, 684–97.

———. 1919. "Travelling Companions." *Travelling Companions*. Foreword by Albert Mordell. New York: Boni and Liveright.

Secondary Works

Allen, Elizabeth. 1984. *A Woman's Place in the Novels of Henry James*. New York: St. Martin's.

Anderson, Charles R. 1977. *Person, Place and Thing in Henry James's Novels*. Durham, NC: Duke University Press.

Anderson, Quentin. 1957. *The American Henry James*. New Brunswick, NJ: Rutgers University Press.

Anderson, Walter E. 1981–82. "Henry James versus American Culture." *Dalhousie Review* 61 (Winter): 618–30.

Anon. 1919. "Books and Things." *New Republic* 19 (30 July): 422.

Beach, Joseph Warren. [1918] 1954. *The Method of Henry James*. Philadelphia: Albert Saifer.

———. 1921. "Henry James." *The Cambridge History of American Literature* 3. Ed. William Peterfield Trent, et al. Cambridge: Cambridge University Press.

Berland, Alwyn. 1981. *Culture and Conduct in the Novels of Henry James*. Cambridge: Cambridge University Press.

Churchill, Kenneth. 1980. *Italy and English Literature, 1764–1930*. New York: Barnes & Noble.

Curtsinger, E. C. 1986. *The Muse of Henry James*. Mansfield, TX: Latitudes.

Edgar, Pelham. [1927] 1964. *Henry James, Man and Author*. New York: Russell & Russell.

Fox, Hugh. 1968. *Henry James, A Critical Introduction*. Conesville, IA: John Westburg.

Habegger, Alfred. 1989. *Henry James and the "Woman Business."* Cambridge: Cambridge University Press.

Jefferson, D. W. 1964. *Henry James and the Modern Reader*. New York: St. Martin's.

Jones, Granville H. 1975. *Henry James's Psychology of Experience: Innocence, Responsibility, and Renunciation in the Fiction of Henry James*. The Hague: Mouton.

Kelley, Cornelia Pulsifer. [1930] 1965. *The Early Development of Henry James*. Urbana: University of Illinois Press.

Kraft, James. 1969. *The Early Tales of Henry James*. Carbondale: Southern Illinois University Press.

Krook, Dorothea. 1986. "Isabel Archer Figures in Some Early Stories of Henry James." *Henry James Review* 7, nos. 2–3 (Winter–Spring): 131–39.

Lanzinger, Klaus. 1989. *Jason's Voyage: The Search for the Old World in American Literature: A Study of Melville, Hawthorne, Henry James, and Thomas Wolfe*. New York: Peter Lang.

LeClair, Robert Charles. 1955. *Young Henry James, 1843–1870*. New York: Bookman.

Levy, Leo B. 1957. *Versions of Melodrama: A Study of the Fiction and Drama of Henry James, 1865–1897*. Berkeley: University of California Press.

Long, Robert Emmet. 1979. *The Great Succession: Henry James and the Legacy of Hawthorne*. Pittsburgh: University of Pittsburgh Press.

McElderry, Bruce R., Jr. 1965. *Henry James*. New York: Twayne.

Marks, Patricia. 1979. "Culture and Rhetoric in Henry James's 'Poor Richard' and 'Eugene Pickering.'" *South Atlantic Bulletin* 44, no. 1: 61–72.

Martin, W. R., and Warren U. Ober. 1987. "Henry James's 'Travelling Companions': Did the Master Nod?" *Notes and Queries* 34, no. 1 (March): 46–47.

Matthiessen, F. O. 1943. "James and the Plastic Arts." *Kenyon Review* 5 (August): 533–50.

Maves, Carl. 1973. *Sensuous Pessimism: Italy in the Work of Henry James*. Bloomington: Indiana University Press.

Panofsky, Erwin. 1969. *Problems in Titian; Mostly Iconographic*. New York: New York University Press.

Putt, S. Gorley. 1966. *Henry James: A Reader's Guide*. Ithaca, NY: Cornell University Press.

Rowe, John Carlos. 1984. *The Theoretical Dimensions of Henry James*. Madison: University of Wisconsin Press.

Sicker, Philip. 1980. *Love and the Quest for Identity in the Fiction of Henry James*. Princeton: Princeton University Press.

Slabey, Robert M. 1958. "Henry James and 'The Most Impressive Convention in All History.'" *American Literature* 30 (March): 89–102.

Smith, Carl S. 1977. "James's Travels, Travel Writings and the Development of his Art." *Modern Language Quarterly* 38: 367–80.

Stone, Edward. 1964. *The Battle and the Books: Some Aspects of Henry James*. Athens: Ohio University Press.

Tintner, Adeline R. 1989. *The Pop World of Henry James: From Fairy Tales to Science Fiction*. Ann Arbor: UMI Research Press.

———. 1987. *The Book World of Henry James: Appropriating the Classics*. Ann Arbor: UMI Research Press.

————. 1986. *The Museum World of Henry James*. Ann Arbor: UMI Research Press.

Wagenknecht, Edward. 1984. *The Tales of Henry James*. New York: Frederick Ungar.

Wegelin, Christof. 1958. *The Image of Europe in Henry James*. Dallas: Southern Methodist University Press.

Wilt, Napier, and John Lucas, ed. 1965. *Americans and Europe: Selected Tales of Henry James*. Riverside Editions. Boston: Houghton Mifflin.

Winner, Viola Hopkins. 1970. *Henry James and the Visual Arts*. Charlottesville: University Press of Virginia.

Wright, Nathalia. 1965. *American Novelists in Italy, The Discoverers: Allston to James*. Philadelphia: University of Pennsylvania Press.

Foreign Language
Battilana, Marilla. 1971. *Venezia Sfondo e simbolo nella narrative di Henry James*. Le Esperienze fiflesse 2. Milan: Laboratorio delle Arti.

The Tree of Knowledge

Publication History

Unable to find a magazine publisher for "The Tree of Knowledge," James presented it first in the 1900 collection *The Soft Side*. He revised it for the New York Edition.

Circumstances of Composition, Sources, and Influences

On May 1, 1899, while staying at the Palazzo Barbaro in Venice, James noted a story told him by his hostess, Ariana Curtis, of Gordon Greenough, nephew of Horatio Greenough, the American sculptor:

> the young modern artist-son opening the eyes of his mother (his sculptor-father's *one* believer) to the misery and grotesqueness of the Father's work: he, coming back from Paris (to Florence, Rome, the wretched little *vieux jeu*—of the American and English set, etc.) to 'set her against' the father and unseal her eyes. She *has* so admired him. I must see the son, *also*, I think, as stricken in production, as too intelligent and critical to wish to do anything but what he *can't*—and the mother, between the

pair: the son *in fact* NOT consoling her pride for the ridiculousness of the father. The latter serenely and most amiably *content de lui*. G. G. *died*. (CN 182)

When, on October 5, he reminded himself of the idea, he kept the emphasis on the family relations: "the little *Gordon-Greenough-and-his-mother-and-his-father (as to the latter's sculpture, etc.) idea*" (CN 184). He recalled in his preface his reaction to this "grain of suggestion": "How can there possibly *not* be all sorts of good things in it?" (*Criticism* 2, 1240–41). As Matthiessen and Murdock have noted, James muted the tragic potential of the germ, omitting the death of the son, making the story one of comic compromise rather than tragedy (N 289). The presence of the outside spectator Peter Brench is likewise an addition, which, as Wagenknecht comments, makes the tale "more complicated" (125). Edel and Powers also cite an entry on December 27, 1892, in reference to the story. In it James writes concerning "the deluge of cultivated mediocrity" and envisions "the reaction against the overdose of education, on the part of a youth *conscious* of his mediocrity" (CN 75–76). In the final work, however, Matthiessen judges the interest in art subordinated to a concern with psychology (1).

The works of two other sculptors, as Tintner has noted, may have provided a shape to James's description of his rather "soft" fictional sculptor (1986 *Museum,* 100). In the story, Mallow's work is seen by Brench as follows:

> The Master's intention . . . even after years, remained undiscoverable to Peter Brench. The creations that so failed to reveal it stood about on pedestals and brackets, on tables and shelves, a little staring white population, heroic, idyllic, allegoric, mythic, symbolic, in which 'scale' had so strayed and lost itself that the public square and the chimney-piece seemed to have changed places, the monumental being all diminutive and the diminutive all monumental; branches, at any rate, markedly, of a family in which stature was rather oddly irrespective of function, age and sex. (CT 11, 100)

The description is somewhat reminiscent of James's question at the death in 1895 of William Wetmore Story, another American sculptor for whom he had little respect, about the fate of "that great unsettled population of statues, which his children don't love nor covet? There were hundreds of them in his studio, and they will be loose upon the world" (*Letters* 4, 24). The description also foreshadows what was increasingly to be James's reaction to the sculpture of Hendrik Anderson, whom he met on the same trip to Italy in 1899. While he then was charmed by and purchased a simple portrait bust of a young boy (still visible at Lamb House today), he later found himself expressing the same objections to Anderson's work as Brench did to Mallow's. In 1901 he found Anderson's sculpture of Lincoln a "*softer*, smaller giant" than it ought to be; more typically, in 1904 he wrote of the "*madness* (almost) in the scale on which you are working!"; in 1906 he wrote in wonder of the "colossal multiplication of divinely naked and intimately associated gentlemen and ladies, flaunting their bellies and bottoms and their other private affairs" and again objecting to Anderson's insufficient differentiation of the sexes in his work. In later years he issued stronger and stronger warnings against "MEGALOMANIA . . . the infatuated and disproportionate love and pursuit of, and attempt at, the Big, the Bigger, the Biggest, the Immensest Immensity, with all sense of proportion, application, relation and possibility madly *submerged*." Finally, while continuing to praise Anderson's idealism, he felt compelled to declare his inability to enter into such a conception of art completely removed from the practical (*Letters* 4, 188, 310, 405, 412, 612, 641–42, 681–83). Mallow's financial independence allowed him to ignore such calls as James gave Anderson to pay heed to the marketplace, and indeed Brent never seems to have declared frankly his concerns about Mallow's isolated work, but otherwise the self-absorbed artist and the dissenting friend of "The Tree of Knowledge" found themselves replayed in James's relationship with Anderson. Tintner traces the same process of disillusionment, asserting that like Mallow's wife, James's affection for Anderson remained unchanged despite his recognition of his bad art (1986 *Museum,* 44–46).

Tintner contrasts the story with one by Edith Wharton, "The Recovery," which shows a wife whose love for her husband is, unlike Mrs. Mallow's, affected by her husband's lack of talent (1986 "Wharton," 3–4).

Relation to Other Works

Geismar first pointed to the similarity between "The Tree of Knowledge" and "The Liar," in both of which "an adoring and hypocritical wife" sustains her husband in his fraudulent career (197). Segal, followed by Bishop, judges the two outsiders in the "trio" against each other, distinguishing Brench's "almost quixotic" attempts to shield Mrs. Mallow from Lyon's attempts to expose Mrs. Capadose (Segal 279–80; Bishop 55; also Ron 233–34). Segal goes on to point to a shared flaw behind their different behavior. When Lancelot returns from Paris apparently still ignorant, she remarks, Peter is "vaguely disgruntled"; yet when Lancelot tells Peter how futile it was to try to keep him from knowledge by keeping him from Paris, Peter realizes, "I think it must have been—without my quite at the time knowing it—to keep *me*!" Ron, who contends that Brench was deliberately a second-rate writer so as not to show up his friend, also appears to see little psychological superiority in his behavior over Lyon's (233–34). Fadiman, without comparing the story to "The Liar," first noticed this "twist" to the tale: that Peter's concern and ignorance, however unconsciously, stemmed at least in part from a desire to protect *himself* from knowledge, that of Mrs. Mallow's love for her husband (Fadiman 433; also Segal 280–81). Jones adds "The Diary of a Man of Fifty" to the two tales as depicting a man's belated recognition of his false estimate of the woman he loved (195–96). Austin Wright points out that Peter's discovery like that of Mrs. Hope in "The Abasement of the Northmores" is that things are really better than he had supposed (196). Jones sees Brench prior to the revelation believing himself involved with the wife in a mutual romantic recognition and renunciation similar to that of the pair in "The Path of Duty" (196). Andreas declares without much evidence that there is indeed such a relationship, that Mrs. Mallow loves Brench, but that both remain silent, victims of the "inoffensive weakness" of Morgan Mallow (37–38). Gage compares the pledge to secrecy to the promise in "The Great Condition" (42).

Truss sets up a connection with *The Turn of the Screw*, finding a parallel between Brench and the governess, who both have care of the young given the default of the "inadequate godheads"—Mallow and the uncle—and seek inadequately to protect them from threatening knowledge. He writes further that Lancelot is what Miles might have been, had he grown up (3).

Bishop suggests a likeness between Peter Brench and John Marcher, who both discover that the "controlling scenario" of their lives has been falsely based, but distinguishes between the tragedy accompanying Marcher's discovery and the "ridicule" greeting Brench's (56).

Interpretation and Criticism

Geismar considers the work a "tricky but entertaining anecdote" (197). David Garnett included it in his 1946 anthology of what he considered James's best work, although Q. D. Leavis dismissed it in her review of the anthology as a "bore" (178). Fadiman included it in his anthology, he claims, partly because it illustrates the validity of some of the anti-Jacobeans' complaints about James. It is "'snobbish' . . . 'unreal' . . . 'over-refined,'" but while "not important," it is, he concludes, "merely perfect" in its "exhaustive" treatment of its "minor" subject (432–34).

In his October notebook entry James wrote that the idea would be "practicable on the rigid Maupassant (at extremest brevity) system" (CN 184). In his preface to the New York Edition, he still recalled the effort of keeping it and the similar "The Abasement of the Northmores" short. "As on behalf of some victim of the income-tax who would minimise his 'return'—an almost heroic dissimulation of capital" was necessary to force the two, by rights *nouvelles* to "masquerade as little anecdotes" in order to get them a chance at magazine publication. But although James says the effort with "The Tree of Knowledge" was greater even than that with "The Middle Years," in this case it failed (*Criticism* 2, 1240). Edgar, paying belated credit, finds the story's interest more in its "firmness and neatness" than its subject matter, and it is probably those qualities that, like the similar "Paste," earned it a place in several schoolroom anthologies (Edgar 178; e.g., Cassill; Davis).

Two readings look at the story through its biblical parallels, with Morgan Mallow, "the Master" as Christ, and Peter as the apostle of that name. The story presents, according to Bellman, a "parody" of the Bible story with an unworthy leader and a faulty follower, an analogy that suggests, Bellman contends, James's probable cynicism at the time, which may have caused him to see himself in a "nightmare vision" as Morgan (226–28). Truss points to the story's many ironies, particularly the faulty claim of omniscience lying behind Peter's suppression of knowledge for the sake of the Master's following. Peter's attempts to keep Lancelot from tasting of the tree of knowledge are misguided, Truss writes, as such knowledge is necessary for spiritual growth, and, as the story demonstrates, cannot be controlled. Somewhat less convincingly, Truss reads the story's characters as a criticism of Christianity, rather than the other way around, as Bellman does in using the Christian symbols to understand James's subject (1–4). Tintner, in turn, sees the symbolism as coming through Milton, while Wagenknecht rejects the religious interpretation altogether (Tintner 1987, 59; Wagenknecht 249 n.8).

Davis notes that the story is "extremely Jamesian" in its complicated study of "degrees of awareness" (183). Horne notes that Mallow is the passive "pivot" for his various observers (94). The presence of the outsider Brench multiplies the possible points of view and Truss notes the significance of James's adding Brench to the family triangle of his original germ (1). Bishop, in turn, views the story not as Lancelot's but Peter's (55). Matthiessen and Murdock are perhaps the only exceptions to this view, seeing the climax as Lancelot's discovery of Peter's and his mother's knowledge (N 289). Bellman calls Peter "almost a miniature James" in his failure to be accepted as a writer (227). Putt, too, notes what he finds an uncomfortable identity with James in one description of Brench: "a man who had reached fifty, who had escaped marriage, who had lived within his means, who had been in love with Mrs. Mallow for years without breathing it, and who, last not least, had judged himself once for all" (234). Bishop sees Brench as making up for his failure with his audience by taking on the roles of critic of Mallow's work and manager of Lancelot's life (56). Thus, Brench, like Mallow, in Bellman's reading is an "interesting failure," and, according to Bishop, it is the presence of *two* failed Masters treated humorously that has kept the story in what he sees as neglect (Bellman 227; Bishop 56–57). Horne, however, sees James as leaving himself out of this artist tale. Still she praises its technically brilliant telling of an unusual but "beautiful love story" (98). Fadiman, too, gives it high marks for being true to itself: "It takes something minor and does everything possible with it" (432).

Works Cited

Primary Works

James, Henry. 1900. "The Tree of Knowledge." *The Soft Side*. London: Methuen; New York: Macmillan, 132–49.

———. 1909. "The Tree of Knowledge." *The Novels and Tales of Henry James*. New York Edition. Vol. 16, 165–90. New York: Scribner's.

Secondary Works

Andreas, Osborn. 1948. *Henry James and the Expanding Horizon: A Study of the Meaning and Basic Themes of James's Fiction*. Seattle: University of Washington Press.

Bellman, Samuel Irving. 1964. "Henry James's 'The Tree of Knowledge': A Biblical Parallel." *Studies in Short Fiction* 1 (Spring): 226–28.

Bishop, George. 1988. *When the Master Relents: the Neglected Short Fictions of Henry James*. Ann Arbor: UMI Research Press.

Cassill, R. V., ed. 1977. *The Norton Anthology of Short Fiction*. New York: Norton.

Davis, Robert Gorham, ed. [1953] 1959. *Ten Modern Masters*. New York: Harcourt.

Edgar, Pelham. [1927] 1964. *Henry James, Man and Author*. New York: Russell & Russell.

Fadiman, Clifton, ed. 1948. *The Short Stories of Henry James*. New York: Modern Library.

Gage, Richard P. 1988. *Order and Design: Henry James' Titled Story Sequences*. New York: Peter Lang.

Geismar, Maxwell. 1963. *Henry James and the Jacobites*. Boston: Houghton Mifflin.

Horne, Helen. 1960. *Basic Ideals of James's Aesthetics as Expressed in the Short Stories Concerning Artists and Writers*. Marburg: Erich Mauersberger.

Jones, Granville H. 1975. *Henry James's Psychology of Experience: Innocence, Responsibility, and Renunciation in the Fiction of Henry James*. The Hague: Mouton.

Leavis, Q. D. 1947. "Henry James: The Stories." *Scrutiny* 14 (Spring): 223–29. As reprinted in *Collected Essays*. Vol. 2: *The American Novel and Reflections of the European Novel*, ed. G. Singh, 177–84. Cambridge: Cambridge University Press.

Matthiessen, F. O. 1944. "Introduction: Henry James' Portrait of the Artist." In *Henry James: Stories of Writers and Artists*. Norfolk, CT: New Directions. Also reprinted as "Henry James's Portrait of the Artist." *Partisan Review* 11 (1944): 71–87.

Putt, S. Gorley. 1966. *Henry James: A Reader's Guide*. Ithaca, NY: Cornell University Press.

Ron, Moshe. 1985. "The Art of the Portrait according to James." *Yale French Studies* no. 69: 222–37. Reprint. "L'Art du portrait selon James." Trans. Ruth Amossy and Nadine Mandel. *Littérature* 57 (February): 93–108.

Segal, Ora. 1965. "The Liar: A Lesson in Devotion." *Review of English Studies* n.s. 16 (August): 272–81.

Tintner, Adeline R. 1987. *The Book World of Henry James: Appropriating the Classics*. Ann Arbor: UMI Research Press.

———. 1986. *The Museum World of Henry James*. Ann Arbor: UMI Research Press.

———. 1986. "Wharton and James: Some Literary Give and Take." *Edith Wharton Newsletter* 3, no. 1 (Spring): 3–5, 8.

Truss, Tom J., Jr. 1965. "Anti-Christian Myth in James's 'The Tree of Knowledge.'" *University of Mississippi Studies in English* 6: 1–4.

Wagenknecht, Edward. 1984. *The Tales of Henry James*. New York: Frederick Ungar.

Wright, Austin McGiffert. 1961. *The American Short Story in the Twenties*. Chicago: University of Chicago Press.

The Two Faces

Publication History

This story appeared originally as "The Faces" in *Harper's Bazaar*, illustrated by Albert Herter on December 15, 1900, and as "The Two Faces" in the *Cornhill Magazine* in June 1901. James also included it in the 1903 collection *The Better Sort* and in the New York Edition.

Circumstances of Composition, Sources, and Influences

James's first record for the story in a list of possible topics on May 7, 1898, refers to "The Lady R. C. (Bourget) vindictive, bad, dressing of young wife incident." According to Edel and Powers, James refers here to a visit to the French novelist Bourget that April when he met Lady Randolph Churchill, who requested a story from him for her *Anglo-Saxon Review* (CN 169). He filled that request, however, with "The Great Condition," and the main notebook entry for what became "The Two Faces" on February 16, 1899, refers again to "The notion of the Lady R. C.'s little vengeance on the bride," which seems to imply that Lady Randolph either committed the act of vengeance or told of it, not that she was simply interested in a story about it (CN 181). Indeed, Lady Randolph had been, like Mrs. Grantham, a victim of behavior similar to Lord Gwyther's. The acknowledged lover of Prince Charles Kinsky, she was traveling with her dying husband when Kinsky telegraphed of his engagement to the much younger Countess Elisabeth zur Gracht. (Compare Lord Gwyther's new wife, the "very young" daughter of the German Countess Kremnitz.) Initially distraught and hoping to stop the marriage, she later accepted it, writing a sister that they "parted the best of friends and in a truly *fin de siècle* manner." Since the two did not meet for years, there is little evidence for an actual occurrence of "bad" dressing, but it may well be that on her visit to Bourget, a former romantic interest, in Paris where Kinsky and his bride had recently returned from their honeymoon, she may have discussed with Bourget what proper *fin de siècle* revenge would be (Churchill 167–69; Martin 1, 333–38; 2, 3, 25). If so, Bourget may then have recalled the proposals in his discussions with James.

This possibility receives support from McFarlane, who posits that the story stemmed from a talk with Paul Bourget, and notes that Bourget wrote a *nouvelle Fausse Manoeuvre* on the same theme in May 1903. The works, McFarlane writes, are similarly "compact," with two major differences: in Bourget's work the bride, not the husband, makes the request of the former lover, and there is no counterpart to the new lover, Sutton. McFarlane conjectures that Bourget's version may be truer to the actual events, but judges that James's introduction of the new lover makes the narrative more complete and graceful (157). Segal argues that the relationship between observer and subject allows for a clearer judgment of the woman's act, while Tilton sees it adding a new irony to her revenge on Gwyther, which ruins her chances with Sutton (Segal 236; Tilton xi; also Booth 344 n.3).

The central idea in the notebook or "situation" is the same as in the story, although James at first envisioned starting with a confidence from Gwyther to a friend who would also serve as narrator. At the very end of his entry, however, he puts forward the possibility of a "*new*" lover as the main witness, still with a first-person narrator as confidante (CN 181). James came up with his original title in this entry and records it again on May 16 in a list of fourteen possible "anecdotes" (CN 184).

Tintner judges the allusion to the operatic air at Burbeck Wagnerian and finds the emphasis on Sutton's "total impression" reminiscent of Sargent (210).

Relation to Other Works

Putt links the tale with "Mrs. Medwin," which he considers a more successful exposé of high society's hypocrisy (293). Dyson draws a parallel between Mrs.

Grantham in her artificial behavior to the Baroness in *The Europeans*, Miriam Rooth in *The Tragic Muse*, and most particularly to Mme Merle of *The Portrait of a Lady*, who like Mrs. Grantham appears to be an "exclusively public" creature, but who possesses secret, "private" motives so strong they lead her to betray others. He proposes additional links with "A Day of Days," *The Portrait of a Lady*, and "The Bench of Desolation" in their consideration of the "vulnerability of the self stripped of its consciousness and of suffering" (118, 125). Edel includes the tale in a larger group that shows the usually renunciative James now turning to consider revenge, which also includes "The Tone of Time" and "The Special Type" (CT 11, 7–8). McElderry, however, points out that Mrs. Dundene, unlike Mrs. Grantham, renounces rather than revenges (110). One might also note the similarity to "The Path of Duty." Both stories present images of a bewildered young wife, ignorant of her husband's relationship with another woman, surrounded by a society that refuses to explain or sympathize. Tanner classes Grantham with the Jamesian villains who exploit others, including Olive Chancellor, Gilbert Osmond, and Lady Beldonald (320).

In writing that in these stories James is "casting himself as the jealous woman," Edel seems to be ignoring the mediating presence of Sutton (CT 11, 8; *Life* 4, 325). Amacher suggests a similarity between Sutton, the central consciousness here, and Lambert, the central consciousness of *The Ambassadors*, and sees the story as a variation on one of James's favorite themes: "a highly intelligent character who makes a right moral choice when the cards are down." Kozikowski concentrates on the use of an unreliable narrator in his comparison of the story to the earlier "The Liar" (358–59, 362, 367).

Interpretation and Criticism

Claude Bragdon, writing of James in 1904, found James "more alive" than most to the change in modern manners shown in Shaw's essay "Prize Ring," which noted that modern fighting with gloves produced "less blood" but stronger blows. Thus, according to Bragdon, James shows no "scene" between the two women, but rather in the "last refinement of revenge" presents "the muffled fist dealing the mortal blow" (148).

A query in the June 1953 *Explicator* prompted renewed examination. Amacher wrote that December, finding the story worthy of "serious attention" in its treatment of moral issues. According to his reading, Mrs. Grantham has the choice of returning good for evil by helping Lady Gwyther or of taking her revenge on her faithless lover through his wife and so concealing her hurt. In choosing the latter, Amacher writes, she has made the "wrong choice," causing the innocent to suffer instead of suffering herself, and thereby jeopardizing her friendship with Sutton, whom he considers the story's "true and sentient hero."

Three years later, Rupp's explication, intended to "supplement" Amacher's reading, appeared. He first notes that, contrary to Amacher, Sutton had noticed something dangerous, "something the least bit queer" in Mrs. Grantham *before* Burbeck, although he had not understood it. He next contends that one cannot accept all of Sutton's view of Lord Gwyther's behavior since he is working with imperfect knowledge. As a result, it may be Sutton, more than Gwyther, who is "testing" Mrs. Grantham. Second, while Amacher believes Gwyther simply to be making a gesture of reconciliation in his request of Mrs. Grantham, Rupp believes he "*may*" have been genuinely concerned about his new wife's clothes. Third, and most significant, he reads Miss Banker's question "What did he see in her?" as implying that Lord Gwyther had earlier in their relationship seen the "horrible" truths and so broken with her. The "horrible" truth about Mrs. Grantham, Rupp would have it, is not that she refuses to suffer, as Amacher charged, but that she is, unlike Lady Gwyther, "incapable of suffering." While this reading seems plausible, it raises the issue of why, then, Lord Gwyther would entrust his wife to such a person, and why he would then, if Miss Banker is indeed correct, blame his wife for her victimization.

The question of the motive behind what critics have, in Jamesian vocabulary, called Gwyther's "extraordinary" request is, however, key (McFarlane 157; N 285). In his notebooks James has Gwyther describe himself as "playing a very frank, bold game—of throwing myself on her magnanimity" (CN 181). But Gwyther never declares himself directly in the tale, and the addition of Sutton complicates the reading of the other characters. As Ward observes, James is interested in the "consciousness" of evil more than the evil itself and Sutton's consciousness sets the "moral tone" of the tale as written (9). It is, as Matthiessen and Murdock note, an "impression" (N 285). Much remains unrevealed: one never knows, for example, whether there is a Mr. Grantham or what might have been his fate.

Kozikowski focuses on narration, and perceiving, like Rupp, that the narration confines itself to Sutton's perception, declares it unreliable. As with Rupp, the question of reliability leads to questions of motivation. Noting that the story appeared in the New York Edition in the same volume with other examples of unreliable narration, "The Liar," *The Turn of the Screw*, *The Aspern Papers*, and *The Sacred Fount*, and citing the preface, Kozikowski claims the story "hides rather than reveals its substance." On a scale of perception, he ranks Sutton, "a questionable judge," above Mrs. Grantham and the "least perceptive" Miss Banker, but below Lord Gwyther, whom he sees as the mainspring of the story's action. Kozikowski argues that Lord Gwyther shrewdly *expects* Mrs. Grantham to play false, counting on her cruelty to provoke sympathy for his new bride among those who disapproved of his quick marriage. But because the narrative approach never makes his motives clear, Kozikowski contends that the interest shifts to Mrs. Grantham's behavior as an index to her opinion not of Gwyther, but of Sutton. He sees Grantham as generally irritated with Sutton, so much so that her revenge on Lady Gwyther, may be intended primarily to rid herself of him, a plot that, given the unrepresented private conversation between herself and Lord Gwyther, may have been hatched in collusion with her former lover. Sutton, in turn, although observing the subtle changes in her beauty Rupp and Amacher also note, is presented as blamable for concentrating more on the beauty than the "traces of dissimulation." In the end, however, due to the unreliable narration, the truth of matters remains "inferable but not fully definable" (356–65). Kozikowski's interpretation is hurt somewhat by his mistaken claim that the new bride receives general sympathy. It is also inconsistent with James's notebook entry, which depicts Grantham as "trying for" a new lover, so that at the end "it's thus *herself* she dishes" (CN 181)—although, as seen above, James's ideas for a story often evolved from notebook to publication.

In 1981 Dyson found the story still receiving "short shrift" from critics. Unlike Amacher, Dyson has Sutton recognizing Lord Gwyther's request to Mrs. Grantham as a "test of her magnanimity," which will "indirectly" answer his own doubts about her. Dyson further explains Lord Gwyther's request as stemming from sincere fear of Mrs. Grantham, made to avert her revenge by putting her "on her honor as protectress" (116).

Dyson's particular concern, however, is to put the story in the context of the conflict between public and private roles and the moral implications of social behavior as performance. As Gill remarks, the atmosphere at Mundham is that of the theatre (78). Dyson sees in the climax of the story, appropriately set at the highly ritualized, theatrical tea at Burbeck, the final working out of "triangular perception"—"It's that," as Sutton observes, "that makes the other" (CT 11, 255)—and double roles. Here Mrs. Grantham undoes herself by forgetting that while she is playing audience to her humiliation of Lady Gwyther, she is still acting a role for Sutton's approval. Seeking to demonstrate Lady Gwyther's unworthiness to join the cast, she shows her private face in public. Sutton, looking from one face to the other, sees in Lady Gwyther Mrs. Grantham's true character, her conscious cruelty. Jones speculates further, arguing that Lady Gwyther, who is beginning to understand in James's words "what has been done with her," may retaliate in a revenge of her own, but there is no real indication of this in the text, and so it remains, as Jones admits, only a possibility (94). In some sense she has already had her revenge: as Wagenknecht points out, she has cost Mrs. Grantham two suitors (131).

As a member of the audience, Miss Banker has also received some attention. Amacher types her as a *ficelle*. Bement and Taylor praise James's economical evocation of her character and question her reading of Sutton (271). Dyson reads her as a personification of the social codes of Mrs. Grantham's circle. She, like her set, "defines the person by the perfomance," and so considers Mrs. Grantham "glorious" and Lady Gwyther "lost" (120–25).

The quality rather than the morality of the revenge has been questioned by Voss, who finds it trite and too "easily" won (153). Putt also questions the mode of revenge, writing that the implication that the Burbeck set Banker symbolizes "are universally deceived by superficial trappings" is "an even nastier comment on social life" than Mrs. Grantham's individual cruelty, but finds that it "merely falsifies the story without being developed into substantial satiric purpose" (293). Gill, however, sees James here more clearly satirizing the failure of the country house to fulfill its role in providing community, by showing it instead as almost "a zone of combat" (78). Even more broadly, Wagenknecht, who praises the tale's "moral sensitivity," considers it an example of James's ability to present moral truths through the seemingly slight medium of "high society" (129).

Putt's sense that the story cannot competently carry the burden of its "purpose" may be attributed to the extreme compression Dyson notes has been a difficulty for critics. It is, according to Matthiessen and Murdock, the shortest story of James's "maturity" (N 285). James spoke in his preface as having begun with "'too little room to turn round'" but having, although it "conceal[ed] rather than exhal[ed] its intense little principle of calculation," achieved "the turn of the *whole* coach and pair in the contracted court, without the 'spill' of a single passenger or the derangement of a single parcel" (*Criticism* 2, 1190–91). Tilton agrees, arguing that through the "economy" of the involved narrator, James succeeds at showing the cruelty of his "horrible age" (xi). Dyson, who considers Putt's comment as showing "an astonishing aesthetic naïveté" because it fails to take into account the larger issue of clothes as costume and Mrs. Grantham as performer, is not otherwise far off from Putt in his reading. As Dyson comments, the "aesthetic act" of putting together clothes has become "a moral one." Thus, the "consciousness" that Mrs. Grantham, like Mme Merle, clothes herself with can either "perfect" nature or cause evil. "Unconsciousness," on the other hand, the naked self, such as seen in Lady Gwyther or Isabel, in its vulnerability to suffering can produce beauty. The story requires Sutton, who is outside the social code, to point the moral and see the beauty in Lady Gwyther's suffering face and the evil in Grantham's (123–25). As James describes it in his notebook: "infernal in expression over all the perfection of her appearance," the moral outweighs the aesthetic (CN 181). That the crowd at Burbeck ignore the moral, while focusing on the outer clothing, is indeed a damning statement.

Kozikowski concludes by reading Edith Wharton's 1903 story "The Dilettante" as a rejection of Jamesian narration and in its depiction of a jilter jilted, a reversal in particular of "The Two Faces" (a pairing repeated in Milton

Crane's anthology) that may have spurred the alleged parody portraits of "The Velvet Glove" and "The Hermit and the Wild Woman" (365–71). Certainly there is enough in the world James describes here to reject; whether or not his depiction of it is also culpable will no doubt continue to be debated.

Works Cited

Primary Works

James, Henry. 1900. "The Faces." *Harper's Bazaar* (15 December): 2084–92.

———. 1901. "The Two Faces." *Cornhill Magazine* n.s. 10 (June): 767–80.

———. 1903. "The Two Faces." *The Better Sort*. London: Methuen; New York: Scribner's, 50–67.

———. 1908. "The Two Faces." *The Novels and Tales of Henry James*. New York Edition. Vol. 12, 389–413. New York: Scribner's

Secondary Works

Amacher, R. E. 1953. "James's 'The Two Faces.'" *Explicator* 12 (December): 20.

Bement, Douglas, and Ross M. Taylor. 1943. "Henry James: Miss Banker." *The Fabric of Fiction*. New York: Harcourt, Brace, 271.

Booth, Wayne C. [1961] 1983. *The Rhetoric of Fiction*. Chicago: University of Chicago Press.

Bragdon, Claude. 1904. "The Figure in Mr. James's Carpet." *Critic* 44 (February): 146–50.

Churchill, Peregrine, and Julian Mitchell. 1974. *Jennie: Lady Randolph Churchill: A Portrait with Letters*. New York: St. Martin's.

Dyson, J. Peter. 1981. "Perfection, Beauty and Suffering in 'The Two Faces.'" *Henry James Review* 2: 116–25.

Gill, Richard. 1972. *Happy Rural Seat: The English Country House and the Literary Imagination*. New Haven: Yale University Press.

Jones, Granville H. 1975. *Henry James's Psychology of Experience: Innocence, Responsibility, and Renunciation in the Fiction of Henry James*. The Hague: Mouton.

Kozikowski, Stanley J. 1979. "Unreliable Narration in Henry James's 'The Two Faces' and Edith Wharton's 'The Dilettante.'" *Arizona Quarterly* 35: 357–72.

McElderry, Bruce R., Jr. 1965. *Henry James*. New York: Twayne.

McFarlane, I. D. 1950. "A Literary Friendship: Henry James and Paul Bourget." *Cambridge Journal* 4 (December): 144–61.

Martin, Ralph G. 1969. *Jennie: The Life of Lady Randolph Chuchill*. Vols. 1 and 2. Englewood Cliffs, NJ: Prentice-Hall.

Putt, S. Gorley. 1966. *Henry James: A Reader's Guide*. Ithaca, NY: Cornell University Press.

Rupp, Henry R. 1956. "James's *The Two Faces*." *Explicator* 14 (Fall): 30.

Segal, Ora. 1969. *The Lucid Reflector: The Observer in Henry James' Fiction*. New Haven: Yale University Press.

Tilton, Eleanor, ed. *Henry James: "The Marriages" and Other Stories*. A Signet Classic. New York: New American Library.

Tintner, Adeline R. 1986. *The Museum World of Henry James*. Ann Arbor: UMI Research Press.

Voss, Arthur. 1973. *The American Short Story: A Critical Survey*. Norman: University of Oklahoma Press.

Wagenknecht, Edward. 1984. *The Tales of Henry James*. New York: Frederick Ungar.

Ward, J. A. 1961. *The Imagination of Disaster: Evil in the Fiction of Henry James*. Lincoln: University of Nebraska Press.

The Velvet Glove

Publication History

"'The Velvet Glove'" appeared first, with an extra set of quotation marks, in March 1909 in "the blue, the *English Review*" edited by Ford Madox Ford, James having indicated to his agent that he liked "the way one's stuff is presented on that rather handsome page" (*Letters* 4, 504). He recorded payment on March 11, 1909 (CN 600). The next year the story appeared in the collection *The Finer Grain*. After James's death, Lubbock included it in his edition of the novels and stories.

Circumstances of Composition, Sources, and Influences

One of the most debated topics concerning "The Velvet Glove," for which there is no notebook entry, is its connection with Edith Wharton (N ix). In her memoir, *A Backward Glance*, Wharton writes of returning to Paris by car with James from a dinner out of town: "As we hung there, high above the moonlit lamplit city and the gleaming curves of the Seine, he suddenly 'held' his setting, as the painters say, and though I knew nothing of it till afterward, 'The Velvet Glove' took shape that night" (308–9). Bell also cites her earlier delighted response in a letter to friends stating that James "has done no nouvelle as good in years . . . [a] delightful little story—a motor story!" (135–36). James himself acknowledged his indebtedness, writing to Wharton, "The whole thing *reeks* with you—and with Cook [her chauffeur], and with *our* Paris (Cook's and yours and mine): so no wonder it's 'really good.' It would never have been written without you—and without 'her' [the car]" (*Letters* 4, 521; Powers 113).

But what neither Bell nor James discusses is the central incident of the tale. In her memoir, Wharton herself asserted that she had "often talked" with James of a possible subject for a tale, "the fact that a very beautiful young Englishwoman of great position, and unappeased literary ambitions, had once tried to beguile him into contributing an introduction to a novel she was writing—or else into reviewing the book. . . ." He demurred, and "they parted, though still friends, with evidences on her part of visible disappointment—and surprise." James, Wharton writes, had not written up the story for want of the proper setting for what he hoped would be "not a mere ironic anecdote—that was too easy—but a little episode steeped in wistfulness and poetry." Paris had given him the setting (308–9).

Citing another episode in the Wharton-James friendship, Edel, however, maintains that Wharton herself is the importunate woman who inspired James. An exchange of letters gives the basic facts. In 1906 James had been solicited by an editor of a socialist journal for an article on Wharton's most recent novel, *The Fruit of the Tree* (1906). Writing Wharton to ascertain if the request was "authentic, & not a vain imagination of the editor," James received a denial of any such entreaty from the author (Powers 73). At the same time, she indicated, according to James, that she "would be sorry to stand in the way of my writing the little article—or *a* little article—if I am moved to it." It seemed to him an "amiable" thing to do at 3,000 words, even though the request did not come directly from her. After reading the book in question, however, which was not one of Wharton's triumphs, he wrote his agent that he was "so little eager" to write about it that he would only do so given "real guaranties of proper and punctual payment." While Tintner implies that the initial request was "apparently" made at Wharton's suggestion, Edel reports Wharton's denial years later of ever having requested such a blurb (1971–72, 493; *Letters* 4, xxviii). James, at any rate, never wrote the article. According to Edel and Tintner, he wrote the story instead.

"The Velvet Glove" began life under the name "The Top of the Tree," and James kept the title for the Princess's work in the tale that Edel and Tintner argue parodies Wharton's style. Edel offers further parallels: the young lord plays the role of the "intermediary" editor; the name Berridge recalls Wharton's friend Walter Berry; and Amy Evans recalls Edith Jones (*Letters* 4,

461–63, 504; *Life* 5, 352–55). The "Princess," too, was one of James's nick-
names for Wharton, and he referred to her once as one of "the Pampered
Princesses of this world" (Funston 227; *Life* 5, 358). Even as the Princess
seeks the acceptance of Americans, Blackall notes, the American Wharton
sought the acceptance of the French aristocracy (21–25). Offering varied
explanations of James's parody of his friend and her writing, Edel has noted
in the story a certain cautiousness, "something deeply mocking and hostile,"
and even a certain "fun and games" (*Life* 354–58; *Letters* 4, xxviii). In Edel's
reading, James felt Wharton should "stand on her ground," namely "that of a
great and perceptive lady," as he did on his (*Life* 5, 359).

According to Edel, Wharton "saw the joke at once" and "swallowed" its
criticism (*Life* 5, 359). Tintner retorts that there is no evidence Wharton got
it. Her reading emphasizes the mock-heroic Olympian allusions in the tale,
which James frequently applied to Wharton. She cites, for example, James's
reference to her as "glorious and godlike—almost too insolently Olympian"
(1975, 359). In his citation of the phrase, however, Edel offers "insistently" as
the modifier for Olympian (*Life* 5, 352). Tintner also comments on the similarity behind Wharton's position in Parisian society, as someone who could
bring together the social elite and the literary, and the "social aura" of the
tale—although by this analysis perhaps one should cast Wharton as Gloriani.
Tintner, however, casts Wharton as both the heroine and "the butt of the
joke," while asserting that James was not seeking to hurt Wharton, whom he
indeed "valued . . . as a person" (1971, 483–92; 1989, 133).

Despite her belief that Wharton never saw herself in the "The Velvet
Glove," Tintner has seen various of Wharton's tales as responses to it. Tintner
first placed the tale in the middle of a literary exchange beginning with
Wharton's 1906 short story "The Hermit and the Wild Woman," which, she
argues, so mocked James's detachment from life in the service of his art that
it excuses any malice in "The Velvet Glove." Still, in Tintner's reading,
Berridge's advice to the Princess to live and leave literature is an implicit privileging of life over literature and was received as such by Wharton. In return,
a grateful Wharton, Tintner argues, portrayed in the 1909 narrative poem
"Ogrin the Hermit" a Jamesian hermit now able to recognize the value of
human love (1974, "Hermit"). More generally, Tintner views the stories of
Wharton's 1910 collection *Men and Ghosts*, particularly "The Eyes," as
responses to *The Finer Grain* (1975, 375–78). She also suggests that the evocation of the Diana and Endymion myth in this story may be James's allusion
to Wharton's tale "The Lamp of Psyche" and its treatment of the Cupid and
Psyche myth (1975, 359).

Wharton saw more of the joke, according to Funston, and returned
James's parody in the 1911 short story "Xingu" in which the eminent Osric
Dane, author of *The Wings of Death*, is the butt of the humor of the tale's less
pretentious heroine. "Xingu" concludes, however, as Funston points out,

with the two characters laughing together at the joke. In Blackall's formulation, Wharton not only got the joke but "got her own back" through her portrayal of James in *The Backward Glance*. Nevertheless, she sees the tale as a whole a "more intimate and open response" than Edel or Tintner (21–25). Indeed, one of the problems with the readings of Edel and Tintner is that both critics seem to feel obliged to use the tale to reinforce James's alleged opinion of Wharton as "a glamorous but bad novelist" (Tintner 1971–72, 492). As Curtsinger remarks, the Princess is not the equal of Wharton (163). One might find a slight revenge for Wharton—who once wondered if she would be thought pretty in Paris and who had tried and failed, twice, to attract James's attention at earlier meetings, even wearing an especially pretty hat the second time—in being portrayed as the rivetingly beautiful Princess Lointaine. It is more appropriate, however, to find her revenge, if revenge is needed, in *The House of Mirth* and *The Age of Innocence*, in having accomplished something the Princess had never done, the writing of some genuine literature.

Edel sees the allusion to Astarte, who was worshiped by men dressed as women, invoking women who wrote under men's names. Edel mentions in particular George Sand and George Eliot, whose actual name, Mary Ann Evans, he hears echoed in Amy Evans (*Life* 5, 358). James and Wharton had visited Sand's home at Nohant together in 1907, and in his letter to Wharton, backing off from his offer to "enthuse" about her in print, James spoke of Eliot. In *The Fruit of the Tree*, James found Wharton "somehow George Eliotizing a little more frankly than ever yet," although he did not really mind it, noting that Wharton did "things which are not in dear old Mary Ann's chords at all" (Bell 258–59).

Even as they have found Wharton in the Princess, critics have found James in Berridge. Fox sees both men as needing love, but getting only "literary friendship" (81–82). Edel takes the reference to Hebe's "cup of gold" as an allusion to *The Golden Bowl*, and perhaps even Wharton's criticism of it (*Life* 5, 357; also Tintner 1989, 133). Earlier, Tintner saw the title as an allusion to Feuillet's *Le Journal d'une femme*, where the heroine is called by her younger friend "mon cœur d'or et ma tour d'ivoire," noting that the phrase thereby invokes *The Ivory Tower* as well as *The Golden Bowl* (1974 "Feuillet," 224). Gage points to another such echo. Citing James's description of Berridge's "inveterate habit . . . [of] snatching . . . the ell wherever the inch peeped out," he notes that James approvingly used the same phrase in "The Art of Fiction" of the woman author "blessed with the faculty which when you give it an inch takes an ell" (278 n.8). Tintner argues for an autobiographical association in reverse, suggesting that rereading the tale for *The Finer Grain* may have inspired James's dream of the Galerie d'Apollon recalled in his autobiography, remarking that the setting at Gloriani's, with its "splendid ceiling" and the "gods and goddesses" gathered there, recalls the Galerie as well as the library of the Luxembourg Palace, with its murals by Delacroix (1986, 12–14).

The Olympian imagery in the tale has also received much attention in its own right (e.g., Gale 151). According to Tintner in readings that link Keats, Titian, and Greek bas-relief, the tale as a whole revises Keats's *Endymion* as a mock epic (1987, 87, 93; 1986, 77; 1989, 134–37). She catalogues several other allusions, casting the princess as Artemis; Berridge, the tale's "fresh red light," as a Mars who turns into an Apollo "mutilated at the wrists"; the great dramatist as a contrastingly earthbound Atlas (1986, 12–14; 1989, 134–35). The mythological in the tale, however, mixes with the modern. Tintner finds the Astarte of the Princess's book recalling the version by Sargent, while the automobile becomes Diana's "chariot of fire" (1986, 98, 164–65). Comparing James's evaluation of the old mythology in a modern world to that of Yeats, Joyce, and Eliot, Martin and Ober see a looser contrast in Berridge's mind of the "radiant" young lord with Apollo the sun god and the more firmly rooted dramatist with his "high Atlas-back." They distinguish the central Olympian imagery, however, from the "merely heroic" Wagnerian figures of the evening's entertainment, which Dyson suggests is *Tristan und Isolde*, "that apotheosis of romanticism" (Martin and Ober 342–43, 345–46; Dyson 70–71).

Edel, on the other hand, includes the Olympian imagery as part of the tale's pastoral mood, citing allusions to Claude Lorrain and Shakespeare's *The Winter's Tale* (*Life* 5, 355; also Tintner 1987, 3; 1986, 126; Melchiori 9). In Krook's view, the "anti-romantic" tale more closely resembles Shakespeare's "bitter" sonnets (343). Gage sees a different kind of disillusionment in the story, arguing that the title *The Top of the Tree* and the redness of the book, like "a rosy round apple," suggests the Garden of Eden and the fall from innocence to the "knowledge of vulgarity" (209). Berridge's initial romanticization of the aristocracy Putt judges Proustian, while Jones sees his spinning of romance as quixotic, his failure reflecting as much on his world as himself (Putt 237; Jones 233). Wegelin finds Berridge yet another type of romantic, praising his definition of dignity, with its insistence on "the consistency of your curiosity" unyielding to "false gods, stupid conventions, traditions, examples," as Emersonian in conception (151). In its changing moods, Martin and Ober find the tale "reminiscent" of Coleridge's "Dejection: An Ode" (341). Leigh Hunt's "The Glove and the Lions" shares the tale's setting among the French aristocracy, although its lions are literary. The task set by the lady here, to earn "great glory," ends with a parting glove in the face rather than a kiss, and the realization, perhaps appropriate, that "No love . . . but vanity, sets love a task like that."

The resurrection of Gloriani, Edel notes, is a "Balzacian" technique (*Life* 5, 354). Tintner also notes a general resemblance to a *Scène de la vie parisienne* of Balzac, while proposing a specific source in an early tale, "La Paix du

Ménage," about a glittering night at a ball with its own revelations (1975, 357–58; 1971, 496).

Max Beerbohm tells a story of having declined an invitation to escort James to an art exhibition in order to read "The Velvet Glove." The written story, however, he finds "not so characteristic, not so intensely Jamesian a story" as James would have written about the prior incident, with its example of "the disciple loyally—or unloyally?—preferring the Master's work to the Master," a perhaps appropriately self-centered confusion of work and personality for such a tale.

Relation to Other Works

The earliest written of the five tales in *The Finer Grain*, "The Velvet Glove" is also generally conceded to be the lightest (e.g., Wagenknecht 163). Tintner, who calls it the most "dramatic," also finds it the only "cheerful" tale, noting the contrast between the "humorously-handled" myth here and in "The Jolly Corner" (1971, 497; 1989, 137–38). In her reading, the tales of 1909–10, following the "self-scrutiny" brought on by the Prefaces, fall either into the category of "beatific" fairy tales such as "The Velvet Glove," "Crapy Cornelia," "Mora Montravers," or their kin, nightmares such as "Julia Bride," "The Jolly Corner," "The Bench of Desolation," and "A Round of Visits" (1971, 484). Martin and Ober specifically contrast Dodd's failure of the imagination with Berridge's triumph in reclaiming his imagination (345). Gage similarly contrasts Berridge's "temporary humiliation" by the Princess with the more lasting humiliation Dodd suffers at Kate's hands (262). Using the preface to *The American* with its definition of romance, Dyson contrasts "The Bench of Desolation," in which both the tale and the perspective of the protagonist are romantic, with "A Round of Visits" and also "Mora Montravers," both of which he argues are not romantic, despite the romantic perspectives of their protagonists (68).

"The Velvet Glove" provides the third appearance of the artist Gloriani, and Maves judges it "ironic and appropriate" that James uses Gloriani once again as a witness to the ill-fated infatuation of an artist with a princess (107). While in Winner's reading Gloriani is again the "acknowledged master" of *The Ambassadors*, not the more compromised artist of *Roderick Hudson*, Martin and Ober are harsher and cite from *Roderick Hudson* as evidence that he is an artist who has abandoned the muse (Winner 65; Martin and Ober 344).

Other critics continue the comparisons with *The Ambassadors*. As Blackall notes, Berridge resembles Strether in his difficulty in reading Paris; and the description of Paris here, according to Lubbock, is even "more romantic" than in the novel (22; Lubbock 5). Berridge, like Strether, Delbaere-Garant writes, lives by the imagination, and at times envies the "rich" lives of such as

Chad and Marie and the lord and Princess. Still, both Strether and Berridge are "right" in her view for turning down temptations inconsistent with their service of art (390–91, 400). Krook, earlier, compared Berridge's vision of the young Englishman to Strether's of Chad, and saw in both the ache for what might have been, remarking particularly on the similarity between Berridge's injunction to the Princess—"Only live. Only be"—with Strether's to "live fully" (see also Tintner 1989, 133; Wagenknecht 258 n.6). The concluding kiss Krook views as "the last flicker" of the youthful glamour and romance found in not only *The Ambassadors*, but *The Wings of the Dove*, and even *The Golden Bowl*, before the "un-Jamesian commonness" of "A Round of Visits," "Crapy Cornelia," and "Mora Montravers" (344–46). Nevertheless, in Stein's reading, while Strether learns at Gloriani's home to confront life, Berridge decides there to ignore it (226).

More sympathetically, Todorov notes that Berridge is like Vawdrey of "The Private Life," in his inability to excel in both life and literature (174). In Berridge's elaborate imaginings and proud curiosity, Krook finds the same ultra-Jamesian "voice" heard particularly in the narrator of *The Sacred Fount*, but also in "The Beldonald Holbein," "The Special Type," and "Mora Montravers" (330). Putt marks an added similarity with "The Beldonald Holbein" in the combination of the perspective of an artist with the exposé of smug social pride (236). Jones focuses on the comparison with *The Sacred Fount*, which also collapses the distance between the writer and the narrator, a narrator in each case who is "socially inept and self-centered, but well-meaning." Equally prone to solipsistic delusions, Berridge, in Jones's view, at least reaches outside himself and makes himself less of an exception to his fiction-making (230, 233 n.40). In Stein's view, however, Berridge is as ignorant of himself as the narrator in *The Aspern Papers* (220). Ward compares the story's theme to that of another artist tale, "The Real Thing" (165).

The Princess, in turn, is but one of the portraits of Wharton that Tintner discovers in *The Finer Grain*, her representative becoming increasingly domineering and unsympathetic in "A Round of Visits" and "Crapy Cornelia," before emerging as the "angel of desolation," Kate, in "The Bench of Desolation." At the same time, Tintner argues that in each tale the hero becomes progressively more submissive, the "artistic integrity" of Berridge giving way to the passive acceptance of Dodd (1975, 355–74; 1971, 496). Casting Amy Evans differently as the Muse, Curtsinger places her at the end of a long series of "portraits of the imagination," including the women of "The Author of Beltraffio," *The Turn of the Screw*, *In the Cage*, and *The Sacred Fount* (164, 167). Delbaere-Garant looks further back to the heroine of James's first tale, "A Tragedy of Error," also set in France. The Princess's deceit is more psychological, she notes, than Hortense's, even as her victim is more vulnerable to her charms, a change Delbaere-Garant sees reflecting James's mature experience of Paris. Thus, while M. Bernier escaped only by mistake, the escape of the later heroes becomes a tribute to their integrity (392–93).

Both Grover and Delbaere-Garant have compared Berridge to Hyacinth Robinson of *The Princess Casamassima*, Grover comparing Berridge's "taking possession" of Paris on his ride with the Princess to Hyacinth's, while with a different emphasis Delbaere-Garant compares Berridge looking at the Princess through the window of her car to Maisie and Hyacinth, who looked at life through "figurative glass-pane[s]" (Grover 105; Delbaere-Garant 401; also Tintner 1987, 87, 93; 1986, 77; 1989, 134). The aristocracy here, Quentin Anderson observes, possess the same freedom from "angularity" that Verver sees in Prince Amerigo, and that James records in *Notes of a Son and Brother* (313). More generally, Krook notes the theme of selfishness shared with "A Round of Visits" and *The Golden Bowl* (341).

Interpretation and Criticism

James, sending off the tale to his agent, found it "sufficiently pretty," although by the time Wharton wrote him her praise he was more chastened by its having been refused by two American magazines, and by some disparaging comments by friends who didn't find it "up to [his] usual mark," and so was greatly heartened by her blowing it up into "quite a brave little flame again" (*Letters* 4, 504, 521).

Contemporary reviewers of *The Finer Grain* tended to be most struck—if not surprised—by what the critic for *The North American Review* found James's "merciless" manner of writing. Arnold Bennett, for example, objecting to the excessively mannered sentences, judged "The Velvet Glove" the most grievous of the tales in the collection, "conventional and without conviction." He continued: "I should not call it subtle, but rather obvious. I should call it finicking" (265). The critic for the *Nation* saw James as coming close to a parody of the "Jacobite style." He cites the first sentence of "The Velvet Glove" as evidence of "how far the speech of print may come to vary from its natural model," with its second semicolon "flung out as a life-belt at the last desperate moment." Worse, the critic wrote, James's "uselessly finicking" sentences tended to diminish, rather than enrich, the material of the story, so that the experience of Berridge "reduces itself to bald terms." Among modern critics, Putt, too, has found the tale's prose verging on parody. While Putt objects to the laborious conclusion with what he calls "perhaps the most inanely awkward act of hand-kissing in the whole of polite literature," Hackett in 1918 opined that "home is reached in a trice, in the language of 'The Velvet Glove'" (Putt 238; Hackett 80–81). Bell, too, without aspersion, comments on what must have been the appeal to James as a "craftsman" of the device of the car ride, with its possibility of "being a stationary center in an unrolling panorama" (135). Menikoff turns the attention to the effectiveness of the tale's punctuation, showing how James uses the question mark to produce a "disruption" that shows Berridge's mental turmoil and an informality that brings the reader into close contact with it. He stresses the importance of the subjective in a story that "turns on the puncturing of Berridge's illusion about the Princess and the aristocracy" (44). In his disagreement with Putt, Jones takes a different tack, arguing that the tale is "a parody of the romantic imagination" written with "uncanny control." Its metaphorical style, he argues, is designed to highlight Berridge's inability to "recognize the similarity between his own inflated language and that which most appalls him in Amy Evans's cheap fiction" (233). Similarly, while she praises its "densely" poetic writing, Tintner defends the tale from charges of "pomposity," by arguing that it is more "a parody of snobbery" by virtue of its comically mock-heroic tone (1971–72, 484, 487, 494; 1989, 134–36).

Most recent criticism, however, has focused less on the style of the tale than on its matter, the main bone of contention being over the comparative moral stature of the two main characters. Is Berridge a great Jamesian artist or an egotistical fool? Is the Princess a foolish amateur or the literary imagination itself? McElderry early called the tale simply "a comment on literary taste" (146). However, as Horne observes, the tale has two themes, the tension between art and life, and the standards of the artist (121). Because these themes are worked out through two characters, male and female, commoner and aristocrat, they take on additional complexities.

Traditionally Berridge, the central consciousness in the tale, has been taken as James's representative. As a writer, according to Kappeler, he starts at something of a disadvantage, his "ambiguous" fame contrasting with the security of the aristocrat's social status (91). Nevertheless, while he faces temptation in the tale, he is seen by many as triumphant in the conclusion. Edgar, for example, calling the tale an "ingenious exhibition of the literary conscience in difficulties," judges that Berridge successfully keeps his conscience clean while enjoying a "sweet revenge" (175). Tintner praises Berridge's "strong resistance" to the Princess's charms, which allows him victory (1972, 485; 1989, 134; 1975, 361). Splitting his character into two parts, Stevenson explains Berridge's behavior by seeing the writer in him eventually reclaiming his proper sense of self from the man in him, who is susceptible to flattery and envy (70).

Krook emphasizes Berridge's yearning for adventure, citing his admission that if he had been an Olympian, he would not have been a writer: "He should have consented to know but the grand personal adventure on the grand personal basis." In the tale, Krook argues, he grabs at the chance of such an adventure, and when it turns out a mistake, "claims the right to wrest a last remnant" through the kiss and the speech to the Princess, "and by the dignity, the confidence and the authority with which he claims it persuades us that he has succeeded in doing at least so much." Krook, however, does not see Berridge as a pure hero, but contends that he reflects James's own fear that he had missed not only life, but also the artistic success that was to make up for that, and that even so he had perhaps been an egoist in his attempts (345–46, 351).

Edel also observes that Berridge "happens to find life more interesting than literature," but takes the main thrust of the tale's criticism as lodging against the Princess, who should have stayed on her pedestal. Showing his superior mettle, Berridge, Edel states, responds to her failure with a stolen kiss that acknowledges her straying, but then a "show of gallantry" in his declaration that "You are romance" (*Life* 5, 355–56). In Tintner's reading, however, the Princess remains permanently reduced to Amy Evans. She cites Berridge's conclusion that "She *was*, for herself   . . . Amy Evans and an asker for lifts, a conceiver of twaddle both in herself and in him . . ." (CT 12, 261). Showing his disillusionment, Berridge "puts her back in the moon, as Diana, and eliminates Amy Evans." His action is, in Tintner's view, an appropriate sign of his superiority (1971–72, 486–88; 1989, 136–37). Purdy's reading emphasizes social issues more than literary ones, seeing the central action as the "hypocritical concealment and then abrupt revelation of social difference." Here, too, the Princess is to blame, as she "cruelly encourages" Berridge (426, 429). Calling the tale "a fable about appearance and reality," Andreas also sees the Princess at fault for appearing to offer love, while really seeking something else. In herself a "work of art," she uses her "superb appearance" for the sake of "her commonplace reality," and so, Andreas concludes, "exploited herself" (49–50).

Like Krook, Todorov sees the tale beginning by praising life over literature, an approach he judges a departure for James. His reading, however, pays equal attention to the Princess. Both characters, he argues, are attempting unsuccessfully to "become what they are not." Berridge's seeming opposition of life and literature, he continues, is more justly a contrast of "romance" and writing, so that what Berridge is really affirming is not life, but "rather the role of a character in relation to that of an author," an attitude that allows him the one "romantic gesture" of kissing the Princess. What would be the better choice, Todorov asserts, James leaves unclear (173–75). Other critics also see both Berridge and the Princess as following false impressions. In Walter Wright's view, while Berridge's romanticizing of the Princess is fairly ordinary, the Princess becomes "truly romantic" not by being the Princess, but by her "pathetic illusion" that she can be Amy Evans (138–39). Sicker sees Berridge as seeking someone who truly lives his life, but discovers instead a woman who like him lives primarily in the imagination. In a conclusion that seems to take from both the responsibility for their failure, he asserts that there is no "genuine romance" open to either as there is no "real love" in their world (172). To Delbaere-Garant, the Princess, while a "female Gloriani," remains largely a symbolic character who represents Paris and thereby life. Berridge meanwhile, she argues, is not without flaws—he accepts the Princess's invitation "out of male vanity"—but still represents James. James, she asserts, although always aware, as Berridge learns to be, "of the threatening claws inside the velvet glove," recognized both life and art as necessary, one giving matter, the other meaning (384–93).

As he bids farewell to the "momentarily suppressed" Princess, Berridge proudly thinks, "It was such a state as she would have been reduced to . . . for the first time in her life; and it was he, poor John Berridge . . . who would have created the condition" (CT 12, 262). Hardly an endearing response. Thus, in her reading of the "different scenarios" through which Berridge and the Princess approach each other, Blackall contends that both are found wanting. She is an "unworthy" author, he an "unkind" man operating from the belief that women exist to be contemplated by men (22–23). Earlier, Ward acknowledged Berridge's pride, but argued that because his pride hurt no one but himself, the situation is resolved comically (165). More dismissively, Putt called Berridge "a megalomanic if fumbling snob," a poor vehicle through which to espouse one's views of art (237). The first, however, to launch a full-scale attack on Berridge was Stein, who, while agreeing with Putt's dim view of Berridge, disagreed with his interpretation of James's characterization of Berridge as unintentional "self-caricature" (226 n.1). According to Stein, the story had been neglected because Berridge figured so unconvincingly in the heroic role in which critics cast him. Berridge, Stein counters, is a "self-deluding hack" full of mistaken romanticism. Far from being a truly Jamesian artist, Stein argues, Berridge is contemptuous of his own work— "his acted clap trap . . . his printed verbiage" (CT 12, 246). His last play is too successful to be Jamesian, its title suspiciously sentimental, his view of Paris insipid. While the Princess talks only of books to him, he attributes to her a "really 'decadent' perversity" (CT 12, 252), refusing to recognize her true interest. When the truth is unavoidable, he refuses to admit he was wrong, instead giving "his romanticizing full play" in order to turn his humiliation into "a stance of high-minded renunciation." The Princess, however, Stein asserts, chose the right person to ask for a puff: "Given what Berridge inadvertently reveals of himself through the tale, there is no reason to believe that he is not on Amy Evans's intellectual and artistic level" (219–25).

Though not as harsh, Jones gives equal prominence to Berridge's egotism. He sees James bringing the reader along on Berridge's adventure so that the tale concludes in "deflation for both." Lacking confidence in his own work, as much an innocent as an egotist, hoping to escape literature for life, Berridge misinterprets the intentions of others, and so fabricates "a fable of romance" in which he figures as "the object of their desire." Thus, Jones counters Putt, the irony of the tale is that Berridge counsels the Princess to give up writing, not to protect art, but the Princess. His refusing to write the preface is "not a triumph," but simply a part of his continuing frustration in having to give up his "vision of romance." Throughout, however, Jones observes, he ironically "translates" his experiences "into the language of art," and by being "deluded and ultimately disappointed," his figure gains a certain poignance (231–33).

Dyson seeks to counter Stein's reading, contending that Berridge's "romantic propensities" are not necessarily "jejune" (76 n.10). Dyson argues that Berridge sees himself as an artist, others as "figures of mythical romance," who are thereby free of the "intellectual rigour of the artist." Seeing himself as an "analyst" of romantic action, he suddenly finds himself as an "actor within it." He is, however, mistaken, the "social contact" being "merely another literary one." Once enlightened, he does not know how to "fit the Princess as a piece of reality into the formulas of his romantic imagination." The Princess, however, whose mercenary interest in the "American millions," Dyson notes, has an easier time in that her romanticism is far simpler. Dyson observes the resultant "system of cross-interpretations." The Princess sees herself as a writer of romance, Berridge sees her as a "figure of romance"; she sees him as a writer, while he sees himself as a "new literary star." Still, Dyson argues, Berridge regains his powers of analysis before the end, and so declares "You *are* Romance" and enforces his interpretation "with *the* symbol of romance—a kiss" (70–72).

Curtsinger, however, objects to readings based on the Princess's essential vulgarity. Instead, he emphasizes the Olympian atmosphere and allusions, and sees that Amy Evans embodies the "imagination of James's writer." As the Muse, she needs a writer to be complete, as the unstructured images of her book demonstrate. "Formed for living and breathing her Romance," she is unable to "speak directly to the reader." It is up to Berridge to "do the rest," in other words, to tell the story. Curtsinger pictures James's writing the tale in a "retrospective mood" and so takes the parting of Berridge and the Princess as a "final tribute" to the Muse. Far from a humiliation or a farce, however, he characterizes it as a "tender, moving scene" that "sums a writer's whole career." While he sees Berridge left on the other side of an "abyss" at the end as a sign that the imagination is essentially "alien," he still calls the tale, with its depiction of the partnership of writer and muse, a "bright and happy" one.

In their reading, Martin and Ober also emphasize the mythic, and see the tale as satisfactorily resolving the issues it raises. Perceptive and sensitive at the start, if prone to idealizing, Berridge "indulges himself" by playing Endymion to the Princess's goddess, even as he recognizes their other roles, as artist and amateur. He makes a "pretty clean and courageous break" from her, which, however, is unsatisfactory because it diminishes her; and "her self-confidence" is also important, as she, here too, plays the role of inspiration. Thus Berridge "reinstate[s]" her "on a different basis" by his kiss. Disagreeing with Tintner's characterization of the tale as a "mock epic," they argue that Berridge instead, like such Romantic writers as Blake, has learned that he must "create his own mythos" in place of the failed Olympian one. James, they argue, signals that Berridge is now a "mature modern artist" by first following then reversing the Endymion myth, so that at the end the shepherd bestows glory on the goddess, not the other way around. Berridge, they argue, now possesses the resources for a "purposeful and dynamic life" (341–45).

With a less exalted view of Berridge, Gage emphasizes more bluntly than most Berridge's vulnerability to the sexual attractiveness of the Princess. Gage's final attitude to Berridge, however, is hard to assemble. At one point, he refers to his "scientifically calculating and dissociated self-interest." Elsewhere he refers to Berridge's "manly superiority" and the way "the male triumphs over the manipulative female" in a manner that may or may not be ironic. He contrasts their physical closeness and intellectual distance, yet he seems to emphasize Berridge's limitations—to the observer role—more than hers—to life (204–16, 245, 275–76, 294).

Wagenknecht, meanwhile, forbears from taking sides, although he notes that Berridge's rejection of the Princess's request is "equally convincing, though very differently motivated, whether we see him as a dedicated artist who will not prostitute himself by praising trash" or according to Stein's "less flattering view" (164).

Certainly there is much in Berridge that reflects James's thinking and values, even perhaps his sense that writers write because they cannot act. His imagination, too, is Jamesian in its original neglect of self as he reflects on the "disservice, in a manner, of one's having so much imagination: the mysterious values of other types kept looming larger before you than the doubtless often higher but comparatively familiar ones of your own" (CT 12, 236). He is witty, too, as he mentally parodies the Princess's style as he rides in her car. Certainly, the tale is not quite as inept as Putt paints it, and others have praised it highly. Wharton's estimate of it as "perhaps the most beautiful of his later short stories" may possibly be explained by her personal involvement, but the tale has also been highly praised both by James's contemporaries such as Hackett and modern critics such as Purdy, who speaks of it as "small but exquisite" (Wharton 308; Hackett 80; Purdy 429).

Perhaps the most unfortunate element in the story is not so much the ego that Stein lambasts, but its connection in the tale with masculinity. The sex roles at the start are highly conventional, and there is little to brag of in Berridge's bedazzlement by a combination of physical beauty and a title. Of course, in deciding how to read Berridge's praise of the Princess's beauty and disparagement of her ambitions, one ought to take into account James's own attitude. Some anecdotal evidence from James's first female secretary, Miss Mary Weld, has James, upon sighting a short-haired woman in collar and tie, adjuring his secretary: "That young girl is the epitome of everything that a woman should not look like. . . . Glory in your femininity, Miss Weld!" (Hyde 155). So it may well be that James believes that the Princess should simply content herself with being beautiful. At the same time, reading the tale, the fact that Berridge's rejection of the Princess's writing follows his disappointment at her personal rejection casts his behavior into doubt. His consequent stealing of a kiss, too, even without invoking modern standards of sexual harrassment, seems distasteful, motivated as it is by a desire to put her in her place. But if Berridge is hardly an exalted character, neither is the Princess, and the story may regain some of its lightness by the fact that these two people with their hidden agendas should encounter the person best designed to frustrate them. Berridge is willing to use his literary status to romance the Princess, the Princess to use her romantic status to get a literary favor from Berridge. Their double-cross leaves neither seriously harmed, and so if one refrains from romanticizing either, one may safely read the tale as the comedy it seems intended to be.

Works Cited

Primary Works
James, Henry. 1909. "'The Velvet Glove.'" *The English Review* 1 (March): 625–49.

———. 1910. "The Velvet Glove.'" *The Finer Grain*. New York: Scribner's; London: Methuen, 1–46.

———. 1921–23. "The Velvet Glove." *The Novels and Stories of Henry James*. Vol. 28. Ed. Percy Lubbock. London: Macmillan.

Secondary Works
Anderson, Quentin. 1957. *The American Henry James*. New Brunswick, NJ: Rutgers University Press.

Andreas, Osborn. 1948. *Henry James and the Expanding Horizon: A Study of the Meaning and Basic Themes of James's Fiction*. Seattle: University of Washington Press.

Anon. 1911. Review of *The Finer Grain*. *The North American Review* (February): 302.

Anon. 1910. Review of *The Finer Grain*. *The Nation* 91 (1 December): 522–23.

Beerbohm, Max. 1958. "An Incident." *Mainly on the Air*. New York: Knopf, 131–33.

Bell, Millicent. 1965. *Edith Wharton and Henry James: The Story of their Friendship*. New York: George Braziller.

Bennett, Arnold. 1917. "Henry James." *Books and Persons, Being Comments of a Past Epoch, 1908–1911*, 263–66. New York: George H. Doran.

Blackall, Jean Frantz. 1985. "Henry and Edith: 'The Velvet Glove' as an 'In' Joke." *Henry James Review* 7, no. 1 (Fall): 21–25.

Curtsinger, E. C., Jr. 1981. "Henry James's Farewell in 'The Velvet Glove.'" *Studies in Short Fiction* 18: 163–69.

Delbaere-Garant, Jeanne. 1970. *Henry James: The Vision of France*. Paris: Société d'Editions Les Belles Lettres.

Dyson, John Peter. 1979. "Romance Elements in Three Late Tales of Henry James": 'Mora Montravers,' 'The Velvet Glove,' and 'The Bench of Desolation.'" *English Studies in Canada* 5: 66–77.

Edgar, Pelham. [1927] 1964. *Henry James, Man and Author*. New York: Russell & Russell.

Fox, Hugh. 1968. *Henry James, A Critical Introduction*. Conesville, IA: Westburg.

Funston, Judith E. 1984. "'Xingu': Edith Wharton's Velvet Glove." *Studies in American Fiction* 12, no. 2 (Autumn): 227–34.

Gage, Richard P. 1988. *Order and Design: Henry James' Titled Story Sequences*. New York: Peter Lang.

Gale, Robert L. [1954] 1964. *The Caught Image: Figurative Language in the Fiction of Henry James*. Chapel Hill: University of North Carolina Press.

Grover, Philip. 1973. *Henry James and the French Novel: A Study in Inspiration*. London: Paul Elek.

Hackett, Francis. 1918. "Henry James." *Horizons: A Book of Criticism*, 74–82. New York: Huebsch.

Horne, Helen. 1960. *Basic Ideals of James's Aesthetics as Expressed in the Short Stories Concerning Artists and Writers*. Marburg: Erich Mauersberger.

Hyde, H. Montgomery. 1969. *Henry James at Home*. New York: Farrar, Straus.

Jones, Granville H. 1975. *Henry James's Psychology of Experience: Innocence, Responsibility, and Renunciation in the Fiction of Henry James*. The Hague: Mouton.

Kappeler, Susanne. 1980. *Writing and Reading in Henry James*. New York: Columbia University Press.

Krook, Dorothea. [1962] 1967. *The Ordeal of Consciousness in Henry James*. New York: Cambridge University Press.

Lubbock, Percy, ed. 1920. *The Letters of Henry James*. Vol. 2. New York: Scribner's.

McElderry, Bruce R., ed. 1965. *Henry James*. New York: Twayne.

Martin, W. R., and Ober, Warren U. 1983. "The Shaping Spirit in James's Last Tales." *English Studies in Canada* 9, no. 3 (September): 341–49.

Maves, Carl. 1973. *Sensuous Pessimism: Italy in the Work of Henry James*. Bloomington: Indiana University Press.

Melchiori, Giorgio. 1965. "Locksley Hall Revisited: Tennyson and Henry James." *Review of English Literature* 6 (October): 9–25. Reprinted in Barbara Melchiori and Giorgio Melchiori, *Il Gusto di Henry James*. Turin: Guilio Einaudi editore, 1974.

Menikoff, Barry. 1970. "Punctuation and Point of View in the Late Style of Henry James." *Style* 4: 29–47.

Powers, Lyall H., ed. 1990. *Henry James and Edith Wharton: Letters: 1900–1915*. New York: Scribner's.

Purdy, Strother B. 1970. "Henry James's Abysses: A Semantic Note." *English Studies* 51 (October): 424–33.

Putt, S. Gorley. 1966. *Henry James: A Reader's Guide*. Ithaca, NY: Cornell University Press.

Sicker, Philip. 1980. *Love and the Quest for Identity in the Fiction of Henry James*. Princeton: Princeton University Press.

Stein, Allen F. 1974. "The Hack's Progress: A Reading of James's 'The Velvet Glove.'" *Essays in Literature* (Western Illinois University) 1: 219–26.

Stevenson, Elizabeth. [1949] 1981. *The Crooked Corridor: A Study of Henry James*. New York: Octagon.

Tintner, Adeline R. 1989. *The Pop World of Henry James: From Fairy Tales to Science Fiction*. Ann Arbor: UMI Research Press.

———. 1987. *The Book World of Henry James: Appropriating the Classics*. Ann Arbor: UMI Research Press.

———. 1986. *The Museum World of Henry James*. Ann Arbor: UMI Research Press.

———. 1975. "The Metamorphoses of Edith Wharton in Henry James's *The Finer Grain*." *Twentieth-Century Literature* 21: 355–79.

———. 1974. "Octave Feuillet, *La Petite Comtesse*, and Henry James." *Revue de Littérature Comparée* 48: 218–32

———. 1974. "'The Hermit and the Wild Woman': Edith Wharton's 'Fictioning' of Henry James." *Journal of Modern Literature* 4 (September): 32–42.

———. 1971–72. "James's Mock Epic: 'The Velvet Glove,' Edith Wharton, and Other Late Tales." *Modern Fiction Studies* 17 (Winter): 483–99.

Todorov, Tzvetan. 1977. *The Poetics of Prose*. Trans. Richard Howard. Ithaca, NY: Cornell University Press.

Wagenknecht, Edward. 1984. *The Tales of Henry James*. New York: Frederick Ungar.

Ward, J. A. 1961. *The Imagination of Disaster: Evil in the Fiction of Henry James*. Lincoln: University of Nebraska Press.

Wegelin, Christof. 1958. *The Image of Europe in Henry James*. Dallas: Southern Methodist University Press.

Wharton, Edith. [1933] 1985. *A Backward Glance*. New York: Scribner's.

Winner, Viola Hopkins. 1963. "Gloriani and the Tides of Taste." *Nineteenth-Century Fiction* 18 (June): 65–71.

Wright, Walter F. 1962. *The Madness of Art: A Study of Henry James*. Lincoln: University of Nebraska Press.

Foreign Language
Hönnighausen, Lothar. 1967. "*The Velvet Glove*—Zur Erzähltechnik in Henry James's Spätwerk." *Germanisch-romanische Monatschrift, Neue Folge* 48 (July): 307–22.

The Visits

Publication History

"The Visits" was the last of four stories James published in the English magazine *Black and White*, where it received a handsome presentation in the issue of May 28, 1892, with illustrations by J. Finnemore on three of its four pages, including the first, where the original title—"The Visit"—is gracefully incorporated into the picture. James revised it for publication in *The Private Life*, after which he never reprinted it. It returned to print in the 1920s in Lubbock's edition of the novels and stories.

Circumstances of Composition, Sources, and Influences

In his first telling of the tale, James pictured his heroine, Louisa Chantry, suffering "abysses of pain" at having declared her love to its object, Jack Brandon (1892, 332). One possible source for her anguish is Pushkin's and then Tchaikovsky's *Eugene Onegin*. That work contains a similar country-house setting, the innocent ingenue's declaration of love, her humiliation afterward, even the gentlemanly behavior of the rather bored man she loves. A major difference is that Pushkin's Tatyana, for all her humiliated passion, does not die.

Tintner points to a similarity with another Russian work, Turgenev's story "Faust" about a sheltered young mother who reads *Faust*, falls in love, confesses her feelings, and dies of chagrin (1987, 237).

Coincidentally, the April 23 issue of *Black and White* that year also contained a consideration of the propriety of a woman's speaking first. In "Love

in Leap Year" a rich French countess, seeking to induce the poor English captain she loves to propose, asks if it is true "that English women, in sheer
despair, have instituted a custom allowing their sex to—start the affair—one
year in every four." The captain dismisses it as a "vulgar joke among vulgar
people," but her question nevertheless helps bring about their engagement,
and shows that the matter could be treated lightly.

Relation to Other Works

Barzun classes Louisa's death with the melodramatic ends of Daisy Miller,
Valentin de Bellegarde, Morgan Moreen, Neil Paraday, and Grace Mavis of "The
Patagonia." The death of each seems needless, writes Barzun, but is for James
the consequence of living in an impure world (515). Jones makes a connection
between Louisa and Laura Wing of *A London Life*, who also "commits the intolerable indiscretion of throwing herself at a man" and who is also incapable of
reconciling herself to her act (112). A further connection might be seen in their
names, the song implied in "Chantry" echoing the birdlike associations of
"Wing." Edel, who also notes the connection with *A London Life*, links the two
more generally with *The Aspern Papers* in their depiction of a woman who
"makes some overture to the man." He further sees its message that revealed
passion can kill in other of James's works, particularly in *The Other House* (CT
8, 12). Elements of Laura's situation may be found in several stories, the last
two published in the same year as "The Visits": "Longstaff's Marriage," where
the heroine dies after making her love evident to a now indifferent man; "The
Patagonia," where the heroine chooses death partly from the pain of having
her unrequited affections exposed; "Lord Beaupré," where the heroine would
rather not marry the man she loves than speak out of turn; and "Nona
Vincent," where Mrs. Alsager rejects the comparison between herself and the
play's heroine primarily on the grounds that she would never "tell her love."

Interpretation and Criticism

Compared to other James tales, this story has received little critical attention.
Vaid has kindly included it as one of James's "few excellent anecdotes" along
with "Brooksmith," "Flickerbridge," "Greville Fane," and "The Two Faces,"
and Edel judges it nearly "Maupassantesque" (Vaid 8; CT 8, 7). Despite its
graceful writing, one would be hard pressed to argue that it warrants greater
study. Indeed, although it is illogical to hold James responsible for the social
conventions that led his heroine to her death, it is the discrepancy between
her act and her response that seems the root of the problem. Because, as
Edgar puts it, the story has little "inwardness," one has little sense of Louisa's
motives (155). Levy is almost alone in judging that the "suspenseful melo-

drama . . . convinces us that a single social error can legtimately provoke trag-ic anguish and despair—and death" (89). Even in 1893, the *Athenaeum* won-dered what "all the pother was about," suspecting the narrator may have kept something back. In America, William Morton Payne, writing for the *Dial*, found the story departing from "the lines of normal human activity," being "whimsical," if not "morbid," although he actually helps James out by seeing it as the "study of an unbalanced temperament," something the story does not clearly establish, although Edel speaks of Louisa's "panic-state" and McElderry of a "psychological aberration beyond rational explanation" (Edel 228; McElderry 115). Wagenknecht, too, finds the only explanation for her behavior madness (207). Certainly, if she dies, as Tintner has it, from the "anxieties of a young girl who has been brought up in a natural farmlike house" on first seeing a formal garden, it is the only recorded instance of such a cause of death (1987, 237). As Tintner herself earlier admitted, the maze-like garden serves more as an "analogue" than an explanation of her state of mind (1986, 102–5). Nor does Andreas's Freudian reading of Louisa as the "resentful victim" of her sexual desires seem adequate (78–79).

More recently Putt has objected to the story's "sacrifice to the double stan-dards of late-Victorian sexual morality," a standard echoed perhaps in Gale's description of Louisa's "improper advances"(85). It is important to note, however, as Gale and the reviewer for the *Athenaeum* do, that it is partly Louisa's later attack on Brandon that causes her shame. Nevertheless, it is reassuring that Putt's call for "the Feminist Movement" to overturn the story's "one sided paradise" had been in general terms already answered in Rebecca West's condemnation of the treatment of women in James's earlier stories: "The young woman of that period could get through the world only by per-petually jumping through hoops held up to her by society, a method of pro-gression which was more suited to circus girls than to persons of dignity, which sometimes caused nasty falls" (54). Louisa's fall is nasty indeed.

The psychology of Louisa's death had been somewhat clearer in the maga-zine version, when seeking again to explain to her mother "she substituted, she finished," with the words "I'm dying." Choked by her incomplete confes-sion, she dies because she cannot speak of what she has done. In the book version, this becomes " 'I'm dying,' she said articulately" (CT 8, 340). In both instances, the one who could remove the impediment, the story's narrator and friend of the girl's mother, is silenced by an early vow not to speak, such as is common in James. She tells the heroine, "When I promise I perform," but seems irritatingly complacent as she undergoes "an extraordinary week . . . one of the most uncomfortable" of her life, as she watches the girl die (CT 8, 332, 337). The story ends with her statement: "The poor parents were in stu-pefaction, and I gave up half my visits and stayed with them a month. But in spite of their stupefaction I kept my vow" (CT 8, 341). The culprit behind Louisa's death may be the demands of patriarchy on a young girl, but the narrator, a woman, is also complicit. The change in the title may reflect some awareness of this. Originally, the title referred to only one visit—either the visit to the country house where the narrator meets Louisa and witnesses her unhappy encounter with Jack or her visit to Louisa's parents afterward. Making the title plural seems to emphasize the connection of the two visits, and perhaps thereby the narrator's responsibility.

In revising, James added another layer of responsibility or witness to the story's telling. In the opening frame of the original magazine version, the woman who tells the story has died, and in a discussion of her someone remarks, "What a pity no one ever took any notes of her talk!" The frame's narrator then writes of himself, "*I* had taken many notes, but I didn't mention it then," and proceeds to present the reader with the story (1892, 696). For the book version, James added an intermediary who tells the narrator of the frame about his notes, which the narrator copies down, presenting the story as a sample. The double transcription (foreshadowing the structure of *The Turn of the Screw*) seems to imply a rather promiscuous sharing of a story withheld even from the suffering parents, and one it is hard to imagine amusing a London social gathering except, perhaps, by its oddity. As Wagenknecht notes, it provides little reward for modern readers (207).

Works Cited

Primary Works
Henry James. 1892. "The Visit." *Black and White* 3 (28 May): 696–700.

———. 1893. "The Visits." *The Private Life*. London: James R. Osgood; New York: Harper, 199–232.

———. 1921–23. "The Visits." *The Novels and Stories of Henry James*. Vol 27. Ed. Percy Lubbock. London: Macmillan.

Secondary Works
Andreas, Osborn. 1948. *Henry James and the Expanding Horizon: A Study of the Meaning and Basic Themes of James's Fiction*. Seattle: University of Washington Press.

Anon. 1893. Review of *The Private Life*. *Athenaeum* 102, no. 3428 (8 July): 60–61.

Barzun, Jacques. 1943. "James the Melodramatist." *Kenyon Review* 5 (August): 508–21. Also reprinted in *The Question of Henry James*, ed. F.W. Dupee, 254–66. New York: Henry Holt, 1945.

Edgar, Pelham. [1927] 1964. *Henry James, Man and Author*. New York: Russell & Russell.

Jones, Granville H. 1975. *Henry James's Psychology of Experience: Innocence, Responsibility, and Renunciation in the Fiction of Henry James*. The Hague: Mouton.

Levy, Leo B. 1957. *Versions of Melodrama: A Study of the Fiction and Drama of Henry James, 1865–1897*. Berkeley: University of California Press.

McElderry, Bruce R., Jr. 1965. *Henry James*. New York: Twayne.

Payne, William Morton. 1893. Review of *The Private Life*. *Dial* 15 (16 October): 228.

Putt, S. Gorley. 1966. *Henry James: A Reader's Guide*. Ithaca, NY: Cornell University Press.

Tintner, Adeline R. 1987. *The Book World of Henry James: Appropriating the Classics*. Ann Arbor: UMI Research Press.

———. 1986. *The Museum World of Henry James*. Ann Arbor: UMI Research Press.

Vaid, Krishna B. 1964. *Technique in the Tales of Henry James*. Cambridge, MA: Harvard University Press.

Wagenknecht, Edward. 1984. *The Tales of Henry James*. New York: Frederick Ungar.

West, Rebecca. [pseud]. 1916. *Henry James*. London: Nisbet.

The Wheel of Time

Publication History

Accompanied by illustrations by A. B. Wenzell and George Wharton Edwards, "The Wheel of Time" appeared first in *Cosmopolitan Magazine* in the December 1892 and January 1893 issues. The next year James collected it both in *The Private Life* and in *The Wheel of Time*. It is, however, the only James story that, having provided the title to a collection, did not gain a place in the New York Edition. It next appeared instead after James's death in Lubbock's edition of the novels and stories.

Circumstances of Composition, Sources, and Influences

"The Wheel of Time" had its start on May 17, 1892, at the dinner table of Lady Lindsay, in a conversation with Lady Shrewsbury, who told of a "woman who has been very ugly in youth and been slighted and snubbed for her ugliness, and who, as very frequently—or at least sometimes—happens with plain girls, has become much better-looking, almost handsome in middle life, and later—and with this improvement in appearance, charming, at any rate, and attractive—so that the later years are, practically, her advantage, her compensation, her *revanche*." In his notebook, James passed over various possibilities of development, all symmetrical—the pretty wife was to turn plain, the handsome man was to have an ugly son—before settling on the situation in the story (CN 69–70).

Edel points out that James recorded the conversation the same day he visited Constance Fenimore Woolson, and finds in Glanvil's contemplation of the mature Fanny's love for him James's attempt to capture Fenimore's feelings for him. Glanvil thinks of Fanny, "Women were capable of these mysteries of sentiment, these intensities of fidelity. . . . She was living for others still; it was impossible for him to see anything else at last than that she was living for him" (*Life* 3, 316). It is an identification that Putt finds both "plausible" and upsetting (285).

Tintner finds an apt source for the tale in Perrault's "Riquet with the Tuft," also the basis of *A London Life*, with its clever but ugly prince and a beautiful but foolish woman, who each have the power to give their virtues to the one they love and thus achieve a happy ending. In James's tale, Fanny, rejected by the handsome Maurice, is transformed by her husband's love, but there is no happy ending (36–45).

Relation to Other Works

Edel compares the story to "The Diary of a Man of Fifty" with a twist in that its fiftyish hero hopes that the young man of the next generation will *not* abandon his young woman (*Life* 3, 315). He cites as well the ghostly "Sir Edmund Orme" as a tale in which one generation imitates the previous (CT 8, 11). Jones classes all three along with "Louisa Pallant" as tales "in which the past haunts the present" (198).

Segal places it in a group with "The Beldonald Holbein," "Flickerbridge," "The Bench of Desolation," and "The Beast in the Jungle," which shows James as "the poet of the beauty of old age" (226)

Interpretation and Criticism

The *Athenaeum* judged the tale both "pathetic" and "truly delightful . . . told naturally, without a trace of strain or affectation" (61). Later critics have been less admiring. In particular, the symmetrical plot James constructed has come under criticism (e.g., Geismar 118). Norrman refers to it as an unpleasant example of "chiastic inversion," its patterns mechanically dominating its people (148). In Matthiessen and Murdock's reading, however, James effectively

"masks" the symmetry by focusing on the character of Fanny and her relationship with Glanvil (N xiv, 124). Wagenknecht, too, finds James bypassing the
predictable by having Fanny befriend Glanvil's daughter, Vera (207). While
strict symmetry might call for revenge, Fanny forgoes it, as Edel notes, providing an additional twist to what McElderry calls a tale of "reversal" (*Life* 3, 315;
McElderry 110). There is yet another twist in that Fanny's "magnanimous
revanche," as James terms it in his notebook, leads her to the same kind of
misguided matchmaking that had nearly killed her and does kill Vera (CN 69).

Other flaws have also been noted. Edgar faults not only the long stretch of
time necessary for the story, but also the "extreme poetic licence" necessary
to believe Fanny's transformation (156). Similarly, Wagenknecht finds James
overdrawing Fanny's early lack of beauty, given the later impression he
wished her to make (208). That James shared their doubt is evident in the
notebook in how he immediately qualifies the way women are "very frequently" transformed with "at least sometimes." His concern with appearance
is also evident in his quibbling labels: "better-looking, almost handsome . . .
charming, at any rate, and attractive" (CN 69–70).

Such an attitude toward female appearance may have allowed James to
sympathize with his hero. But it is hard to come up with much sympathy for
a man who snubs a woman "out of fastidiousness, and even fatuity and folly"
(CN 69–70). Markow-Totevy finds the rationale for the tale's symmetry in
James's sense of a controlling fate that evens things out, whether people wish
it to or not (117). Jones raises the possibility that Fanny does take her
revenge by promising to encourage Maurice's match with Vera and then
silently failing to do so, a possibility he sees indicated in the tale's final
remark about Vera: "Unlike Fanny Knocker she was never to have her
revenge." Jones indicates, however, that it is equally possible that Fanny's
revenge may simply be Maurice's frustration (94). One might almost accept
the explanation out of a desire to see Fanny rebel more against Maurice's
condescension, except that it requires the suffering of Vera, and it is that fact
that makes it unlikely. Fanny quite simply does not seem the sort to make
another suffer for her own satisfaction. Even as a victim of plot alone, not
design, Vera's death—judged by Wagenknecht as too Victorian (208)—seems
simply cruel. As Andreas notes, she is the "innocent victim" of frivolity (84).
Why should she pay for her father's mistake when he is let off so gently? As
Putt argues, the combination of "diagrammatic" plot and realistic characterization makes the reader resent the tricks played on the people in the tale
(285). In a story whose moral seems to be that men are stupid and women
must pay for it, surely James could have found a better dupe than Fanny, who
is personable both as ugly duckling and grand lady. Or, barring that, he might
have allowed her to be genuinely happy in her later success, rather than still
thinking of a fatuous fool who never saw beyond her face.

Works Cited

Primary Works
James, Henry. 1892–1893. "The Wheel of Time." *Cosmopolitan* 14 (December–January): 215–28, 348–60.

———. 1893. "The Wheel of Time." *The Private Life*. London: James R. Osgood; New York: Harper.

———. 1893. "The Wheel of Time." *The Wheel of Time*. New York: Harper.

———. 1921–23. "The Wheel of Time." *The Novels and Stories of Henry James*. Vol. 27. Ed. Percy Lubbock. London: Macmillan.

Secondary Works
Andreas, Osborn. 1948. *Henry James and the Expanding Horizon: A Study of the Meaning and Basic Themes of James's Fiction*. Seattle: University of Washington Press.

Anon. 1893. Review of "The Private Life." *Athenaeum* 102, no. 3428 (8 July): 60–61.

Edgar, Pelham. [1927] 1964. *Henry James, Man and Author*. New York: Russell & Russell.

Geismar, Maxwell. 1963. *Henry James and the Jacobites*. Boston: Houghton Mifflin.

Jones, Granville H. 1975. *Henry James's Psychology of Experience: Innocence, Responsibility, and Renunciation in the Fiction of Henry James*. The Hague: Mouton.

McElderry, Bruce R., Jr. 1965. *Henry James*. New York: Twayne.

Markow-Totevy, Georges. 1969. *Henry James*. Trans. John Griffiths. London: Merlin.

Norrman, Ralf. 1982. *The Insecure World of Henry James's Fiction: Intensity and Ambiguity*. New York: St. Martin's.

Putt, S. Gorley. 1966. *Henry James: A Reader's Guide*. Ithaca, NY: Cornell University Press.

Segal, Ora. 1969. *The Lucid Reflector: The Observer in Henry James' Fiction*. New Haven: Yale University Press.

Tintner, Adeline R. 1989. *The Pop World of Henry James: From Fairy Tales to Science Fiction*. Ann Arbor: UMI Research Press.

Wagenknecht, Edward. 1984. *The Tales of Henry James*. New York: Frederick Ungar.

Index of James's Works

947

General Index

951